THE NEW
AMERICAN
COMMENTARY

An Exegetical and Theological
Exposition of Holy Scripture

THE NEW AMERICAN COMMENTARY

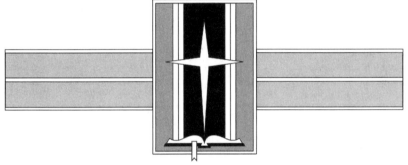

Volume
15A

ISAIAH 1-39

Gary V. Smith

PUBLISHING GROUP

Nashville, Tennessee

© Copyright 2007 • B & H Publishing Group
All rights reserved.
ISBN 978-0-8054-0115-8
Dewey Decimal Classification: 224.1
Subject Heading: BIBLE. O.T. ISAIAH
Printed in the United States of America
12 11 10 09 08 07   8 7 6 5 4 3 2 1

To

My daughter and son-in-law

Christine and Randy Brunko

Our grandchildren

Ashley, Brett, and Mitchell

"The children the LORD has given me are for signs and wonders" (Isa 8:16)

Editors' Preface

God's Word does not change. God's world, however, changes in every generation. These changes, in addition to new findings by scholars and a new variety of challenges to the gospel message, call for the church in each generation to interpret and apply God's Word for God's people. Thus, THE NEW AMERICAN COMMENTARY is introduced to bridge the twentieth and twenty-first centuries. This new series has been designed primarily to enable pastors, teachers, and students to read the Bible with clarity and proclaim it with power.

In one sense THE NEW AMERICAN COMMENTARY is not new, for it represents the continuation of a heritage rich in biblical and theological exposition. The title of this forty-volume set points to the continuity of this series with an important commentary project published at the end of the nineteenth century called AN AMERICAN COMMENTARY, edited by Alvah Hovey. The older series included, among other significant contributions, the outstanding volume on Matthew by John A. Broadus, from whom the publisher of the new series, Broadman Press, partly derives its name. The former series was authored and edited by scholars committed to the infallibility of Scripture, making it a solid foundation for the present project. In line with this heritage, all NAC authors affirm the divine inspiration, inerrancy, complete truthfulness, and full authority of the Bible. The perspective of the NAC is unapologetically confessional and rooted in the evangelical tradition.

Since a commentary is a fundamental tool for the expositor or teacher who seeks to interpret and apply Scripture in the church or classroom, the NAC focuses on communicating the theological structure and content of each biblical book. The writers seek to illuminate both the historical meaning and contemporary significance of Holy Scripture.

In its attempt to make a unique contribution to the Christian community, the NAC focuses on two concerns. First, the commentary emphasizes how each section of a book fits together so that the reader becomes aware of the theological unity of each book and of Scripture as a whole. The writers, however, remain aware of the Bible's inherently rich variety. Second, the NAC is produced with the conviction that the Bible primarily belongs to the church. We believe that scholarship and the academy provide an indispensable foundation for biblical understanding and the service of Christ, but the editors and authors of this series have attempted to communicate the findings of their research in a manner that will build up the whole body of Christ. Thus, the commentary concentrates on theological exegesis while providing practical, applicable exposition.

THE NEW AMERICAN COMMENTARY's theological focus enable the reader to see the parts as well as the whole of Scripture. The biblical books vary in content, context, literary type, and style. In addition to this rich variety, the editors and authors recognize that the doctrinal emphasis and use of the biblical books differs in various places, contexts, and cultures among God's people. These factors, as well as other concerns, have led the editors to give freedom to the writers to wrestle with the issues raised by the scholarly community surrounding each book and to determine the appropriate shape and length of the introductory materials. Moreover, each writer has developed the structure of the commentary in a way best suited for expounding the basic structure and the meaning of the biblical books for our day. Generally, discussions relating to contemporary scholarship and technical points of grammar and syntax appear in the footnotes and not in the text of the commentary. This format allows pastors and interested laypersons, scholars and teachers, and serious college and seminary students to profit from the commentary at various levels. This approach has been employed because we believe that all Christians have the privilege and responsibility to read and seek to understand the Bible for themselves.

Consistent with the desire to produce a readable, up-to-date commentary, the editors selected the New International Version as the standard translation for the commentary series. The selection was made primarily because of the NIV's faithfulness to the original languages and its beautiful and readable style. The authors, however, have been given the liberty to differ at places from the NIV as they develop their own translations from the Greek and Hebrew texts.

The NAC reflects the vision and leadership of those who provide oversight for Broadman Press, who in 1987 called for a new commentary series that would evidence a commitment to the inerrancy of Scripture and a faithfulness to the classic Christian tradition. While the commentary adopts an "American" name, it should be noted some writers represent countries outside the United States, giving the commentary an international perspective. The diverse group of writers includes scholars, teachers, and administrators from almost twenty different colleges and seminaries, as well as pastors, missionaries, and a layperson.

The editors and writers hope that THE NEW AMERICAN COMMENTARY will be helpful and instructive for pastors and teachers, scholars and students, for men and women in the churches who study and teach God's Word in various settings. We trust that for editors, authors, and readers alike, the commentary will be used to build up the church, encourage obedience, and bring renewal to God's people. Above all, we pray that the NAC will bring glory and honor to our Lord who has graciously redeemed us and faithfully revealed himself to us in his Holy Word.

SOLI DEO GLORIA
The Editors

Author's Preface

The prophet Isaiah speaks with clarity and emotions against the proud people of his day that arrogantly thought they were in full control of their world. Although King Uzziah trusted in large armies, a land full of silver and gold, and impressive walled cities with magnificent towers, the prophet Isaiah reminded him that God would humble the proud, for his ultimate plan was to glorify and exalt himself alone. Later King Ahaz proudly refused to trust God for deliverance when he was hopelessly outmatched in a war with Syria and Israel, so God reduced him to being a vassal of Assyria. These kings of Judah were no different from the proud King of Assyria who claimed that it was his hand, his wisdom, and his power that would crush the surrounding nations. Isaiah also prophesied the end of Israel's arrogance, the devastation of Moab for its pride, boasting, and haughtiness, plus the humbling of the glorious pride of Tyre. Isaiah is particularly hard on political and religious leaders who arrogantly misuse their power.

Isaiah believed the only hope for mankind was centered in trusting God, not in blindly refusing to listen to his offers of salvation. Those leaders that had a hardened heart and ears that refused to hear the voice of God would eventually suffer under the judgment of God's almighty hand. Isaiah faithfully offered many words of hope for the present situation of his listeners as well as assurances of God's eschatological plan to establish peace and a Davidic ruler on the throne of David, but even his most positive appeals caused few to turn from the stubborn path of pride. Although Hezekiah initially failed to trust God, when the Assyrians surrounded Jerusalem he eventually admitted his weakness and threw himself on the strong arms of God's mercy and trusted him.

These ancient words of admonition, rebuke, and hope still have a ring that should reverberate a warning and a hope in the ears of every present day disciple who is willing to listen to God's voice. Individually and as a community, the people of God today need to humble themselves, to fully submit to the Holy One who calls them, and faithfully trust the God who controls this world. The poor miner, the hard working farmer, the destitute unemployed factory worker, and the sick cancer patient know how to live a humble life because they have nothing and they must trust God for survival each day. God is compassionate to help many of these who trust him, but he is deeply concerned with the affluent and powerful who all too often trust in their own power. Those in positions of significant leadership in business and the state, as well as those who lead the church and its institutions must learn to trust him for everything they do. Power and leadership can mix with trust in God and trust in fellow believers, if responsibility and control are shared. Isaiah and Jesus were spiritual leaders in their communities, but neither operated from an authoritative platform that autocratically controlled or micro-managed those around them. True spiritual power and leadership is not something one can gain by political maneuvers or votes, it is a position of service graciously granted by God and gladly affirmed by those who see the hand of God and the gifts of the Spirit exhibited in a fellow traveler with leadership ability. One can only pray that the spiritual leaders of the future will have ears that hear what God communicated though the prophet Isaiah.

Writing a commentary on the prophecies of Isaiah can almost be compared to climbing Mt Everest. The challenge is more than formidable, daily patience and great endurance are required for each step of the way, and the dangers of failure are evident at every turn. So many great men of God have commented on Isaiah's messages in books and articles that it is almost impossible to read and assimilate them all. So many different opinions and interpretations of the meaning of Isaiah's words are presented that it sometimes seemed unnecessary to add one more opinion. Yet as one works step by step through the literature, it becomes very evident that some have seriously failed to understand the nature of true prophecy and others have hypothesized grand theories about the dating, authorship, and meaning of passages that stray far from the evidence presented in Isaiah's words. My prayer is that each reader of this study will be better informed about the key issues surrounding the interpretation of Isaiah's words, better equipped to make important decisions about the text, syntax, historical setting, literary context, composition, genre, meaning, and application of Isaiah's message. Although we trust in God's Spirit to teach us and lead us into all truth, it is incumbent that every reader know as much as possible about the interpretive issues surrounding each text, and humbly communicate an interpretation that is faithful to the author's original meaning.

Although at times one may feel the heavy weight of personal responsibility for each word that is written and the loneliness of the daily grind, it is very evident that the results of my inquiry into the meaning of Isaiah's messages is a collaboration of a host of fellow travelers who are earnestly searching for the best interpretation. I gladly acknowledge the contributions of former teacher and colleagues. I thank God for those who have helped shape my approach to the Hebrew text and biblical interpretation. Although I learned much from a host of past commentators, the works of H. Wildberger and W.A.M. Beuken were the most helpful in dealing with interpretive issues, even though some of their theological conclusions were unacceptable. I also owe a great debt to those who reviewed, challenged, and made suggestions that have greatly improved this study. A special word of thanks should be expressed for E. Ray Clendenen as well as the staff at Broadman and Holman who edited, refined, and prepared the manuscript for publication. Although I finished the commentary on chapters 1-39 in November of 2005, I am thankful that the publisher has allowed me to add a few references to more recent works in the final editing of this volume. Unfortunately, major commentaries like H.G.M. Williamson's ICC volume on *Isaiah 1-5*, came too late for inclusion in this work. I want to thank my wife Susan Smith and Jacob Shatzer, a student at Union University, who proofread almost everything in Isaiah 1-39. Their suggestions have made the final product more readable.

I am dedicating this volume to our daughter Christine and her family. Every believing parent entrusts each child to God even before they are born, not knowing what path that child will choose or what problems they will face as they grow and mature. One can only thank God for his grace in guiding them to marry a fellow believer, faithfully serving in a church, and raising grandchildren in a Christian home. My prayer is that God's work of grace in the heart of my children and grandchildren (like Isaiah's children in 8:18) will be "a sign and a wonder" to all those who know them. In all these things the glory goes to God.

Gary V. Smith
Union University
Jackson, TN

Abbreviations

Bible Books

Gen	Isa	Luke
Exod	Jer	John
Lev	Lam	Acts
Num	Ezek	Rom
Deut	Dan	1, 2 Cor
Josh	Hos	Gal
Judg	Joel	Eph
Ruth	Amos	Phil
1, 2 Sam	Obad	Col
1, 2 Kgs	Jonah	1, 2 Thess
1, 2 Chr	Mic	1, 2 Tim
Ezra	Nah	Titus
Neh	Hab	Phlm
Esth	Zeph	Heb
Job	Hag	Jas
Ps (pl. Pss)	Zech	1, 2 Pet
Prov	Mal	1, 2, 3 John
Eccl	Matt	Jude
Song	Mark	Rev

Commonly Used Sources

AASOR	Annual of the American Schools of Oriental Research
AB	Anchor Bible
ABD	*Anchor Bible Dictionary*
ABW	*Archaeology and the Biblical World*
AC	An American Commentary, ed. A. Hovey
AcOr	*Acta orientalia*
AEL	M. Lichtheim, Ancient Egyptian Literature
AJSL	*American Journal of Semitic Languages and Literature*
Akk	Akkadian
ALUOS	*Annual of Leeds University Oriental Society*
AnBib	Analecta Biblica
ANET	J. B. Pritchard, ed., *Ancient Near Eastern Texts*
AOAT	Alter Orient und Altes Testament
AOTS	*Archaeology and Old Testament Study,* ed. D. W. Thomas
ArOr	Archiv orientální
ATD	Das Alte Testament Deutsch
ATR	*Anglican Theological Review*
Aug	*Augustinianum*

AusBR	*Australian Biblical Review*
BA	*Biblical Archaeologist*
BAGD	W. Bauer, W. F. Arndt, F. W. Gingrich, and F. W. Danker, *Greek-English Lexicon of the New Testament*
BARev	*Biblical Archaeology Review*
BASOR	*Bulletin of the American Schools of Oriental Research*
BDB	F. Brown, S. R. Driver, and C. A. Briggs, *Hebrew and English Lexicon of the Old Testament*
BETL	Bibliotheca ephemeridum theologicarum lovaniensium
BFT	Biblical Foundations in Theology
BHS	*Biblia hebraica stuttgartensia*
Bib	*Biblica*
BKAT	Biblischer Kommentar: Altes Testament
BO	*Bibliotheca orientalis*
BRev	*Bible Review*
BSac	*Bibliotheca Sacra*
BSC	Bible Study Commentary
BT	*Bible Translator*
BurH	*Buried History*
BV	*Biblical Viewpoint*
BZ	*Biblische Zeitschrift*
BZAW	Beihefte zur ZAW
CAD	*The Assyrian Dictionary of the Oriental Institute of the University of Chicago*
CAH	*Cambridge Ancient History*
CBSC	Cambridge Bible for Schools and Colleges
CBC	Cambridge Bible Commentary
CBQ	*Catholic Biblical Quarterly*
CHAL	*Concise Hebrew and Aramic Lexicon,* ed. W. L. Holladay
CTR	*Criswell Theological Review*
DOTT	*Documents from Old Testament Times,* ed. D. W. Thomas
DSS	Dead Sea Scrolls
EBC	Expositor's Bible Commentary
Ebib	Etudes bibliques
EstBib	*Estudios biblicos*
ETL	*Ephermerides theologicae lovanienses*
Exeg	*Exegetica (Japanese)*
FB	Forschung zur Bibel
FOTL	Forms of Old Testament Literature
GKC	Gesenius' Hebrew Grammar, ed. E. Kautzsch, tr. A. E. Cowley
GTJ	*Grace Theological Journal*
HAR	Hebrew Annual Review
HAT	Handbuch zum Alten Testament

HBT	*Horizons in Biblical Theology*
HCOT	Historical Commentary on the Old Testament
HDR	Harvard Dissertations in Religion
Her	Hermeneia
HKAT	Handkommentar zum Alten Testament
HSM	Harvard Semitic Monographs
HT	Helps for Translators
HTR	*Harvard Theological Review*
HUCA	*Hebrew Union College Annual*
IB	*Interpreter's Bible*
IBC	Interpretation: A Bible Commentary for Teaching and Preaching
IBHS	B. K. Waltke and M. O'Connor, *Introduction to Biblical Hebrew Syntax*
ICC	International Critical Commentary
IDB	*Interpreter's Dictionary of the Bible,* ed. G. A. Buttrick et al.
IDBSup	IDB Supplementary Volume
IEJ	*Israel Exploration Journal*
IES	Israel Exploration Society
Int	*Interpretation*
ITC	International Theological Commentary
IOS	*Israel Oriental Society*
ISBE	*International Standard Bible Encyclopedia,* rev. ed. G. W. Bromiley
IJT	*Indian Journal of Theology*
ITC	International Theological Commentary
JANES	*Journal of Ancient Near Eastern Society*
JAOS	*Journal of the American Oriental Society*
JBL	*Journal of Biblical Literature*
JBR	*Journal of Bible and Religion*
JCS	*Journal of Cuneiform Studies*
JEA	*Journal of Egyptian Archaeology*
JETS	*Journal of the Evangelical Theological Society*
JJS	*Journal of Jewish Studies*
JNES	*Journal of Near Eastern Studies*
JNSL	*Journal of Northwest Semitic Languages*
JPOS	*Journal of Palestine Oriental Society*
JQR	*Jewish Quarterly Review*
JSJ	*Journal for the Study of Judaism in the Persian, Hellenistic, and Roman Period*
JSOR	*Journal of the Society for Oriental Research*
JSOT	*Journal for the Study of the Old Testament*
JSOTSup	JSOT—Supplement Series

JSS	*Journal of Semitic Studies*
JTS	*Journal of Theological Studies*
JTSNS	*Journal of Theological Studies, New Series*
KAT	Kommentar zum Alten Testament
KB	Koehler and W. Baumgartner, Lexicon in Veteris Testamenti libros
LCC	Library of Christian Classics
LLAVT	*Lexicon Linguae Aramaicae Veteris Testamenti*
LTQ	*Lexington Theological Quarterly*
LQ	*Lutheran Quarterly*
MT	Masoretic Text
NAC	New American Commentary
NCBC	New Century Bible Commentary
NEASB	*Near East Archaeological Society Bulletin*
NICOT	New International Commentary on the Old Testament
NJPS	*Tanakh: The Holy Scriptures: The New JPS Translation according to the Traditional Hebrew Text*
NKZ	*Neue kirchliche Zeitschrift*
NovT	*Novum Testamentum*
NTS	*New Testament Studies*
Or	*Orientalia*
OTE	*Old Testament Essays*
OTL	Old Testament Library
OTS	*Oudtestamentische Studiën*
OTWSA	*Ou-Testamentiese Werkgemeenskap in Suid-Afrika*
PaVi	*Parole di Vita*
PCB	*Peake's Commentary on the Bible*, ed. M. Black and H. H. Rowley
PEQ	*Palestine Exploration Quarterly*
POTT	*Peoples of Old Testament Times*, ed. D. J. Wiseman
RA	Revue d'assyriologie et d'archéologie orientale
RB	*Revue biblique*
ResQ	*Restoration Quarterly*
RevExp	*Review and Expositor*
RivB	*Revista biblica italiana*
RSR	Recherches de science religieuse
SANE	Sources from the Ancient Near East
SBLDS	Society of Biblical Literature Dissertation Series
SBLSCS	Society of Biblical Literature Septuagint and Cognate Studies
SBT	Studies in Biblical Theology
ScrB	*Scripture Bulletin*
SJT	Scottish Journal of Theology

SP	Samaritan Pentateuch
SR	Studies in Religion/Sciences religieuses
ST	*Studia theologica*
STJD	Studies on the Texts of the Desert of Judah
SwJT	*Southwestern Journal of Theology*
Syr	Syriac
TDOT	*Theological Dictionary of the Old Testament,*
	ed. G. J. Botterweck and H. Ringgren
Tg	Targum
TrinJ	*Trinity Journal*
TLZ	*Theologische Literaturzeitung*
TOTC	Tyndale Old Testament Commentaries
TS	*Theological Studies*
TWAT	*Theologisches Wörterbuch zum Alten Testament,*
	ed. G. J. Botterweck and H. Ringgren
TWOT	*Theological Wordbook of the Old Testament*
TynBul	*Tyndale Bulletin*
TZ	*Theologische Zeitung*
UF	*Ugarit-Forschungen*
Vg	Vulgate
VT	*Vetus Testamentum*
VTSup	Vetus Testamentum, Supplements
WBC	Word Biblical Commentaries
WEC	Wycliffe Exegetical Commentary
WTJ	*Westminster Theological Journal*
WMANT	Wissenschaftliche Monographien zum Alten und Neuen
	Testament
ZABR	*Zeitschrift für altorientalische und biblische*
	Rechtsgeschichte
ZAW	*Zeitschrift für die alttestamentliche Wissenschaft*
ZDMG	*Zeitschrift der deutschen morgenländischen Gesellschaft*
ZDPV	*Zeitschrift des deutschen Palätina-Vereing*
ZKT	*Zeitschrift für katholische Theologie*

Contents

Isaiah 1–39

--------------------------------- **INTRODUCTION** ---------------------------------

Most Bible readers are aware of those passages in Isaiah that introduce important theological themes about the Messiah that were fulfilled in the New Testament (e.g., Isa 53). Others have heard about some of the prophet's unusual experiences that stand out as pivotal events strongly impacting his life. The glorious appearance of Israel's Holy God on his throne in the Temple (6:1–8) is one such event that captures the imagination of all who read it. The wonder of the moment is enchanting, as Isaiah observed the seraphim proclaiming God's holiness and as he saw a glimpse of the glory of God sitting on a high throne. One can almost visualize the prophet bowing and humbly confessing his sins. Many have heard sermons that challenged listeners to follow the example of Isaiah and be willing to go and serve God wherever he might send them (6:8). Another well known event might be Isaiah's words of hope to Judah's king Ahaz during the Syro-Ephraimite War (734–732 BC) and his subsequent prediction that a virgin would bear a son called Immanuel (7:1–14). Equally memorable is the story of the Assyrian attack on Jerusalem during the days of Hezekiah (36:1–37:38). In response to Hezekiah's prayer God sent an angel to kill 185,000 Assyrian troops in order to deliver the city of Jerusalem. Of course, in Christian theology there are few passages as central as those about the coming "Servant of the Lord" who will establish justice on the earth (42:1–4), be a covenant and light to the nations (42:6–7; 49:6), and then suffer and die for the sins of all the world (52:12–53:12). These memorable passages only scratch the surface of Isaiah's most important messages, and in some ways they tend to draw attention away from all the other equally important ideas that the prophet communicated to his audience.

1. Contemporary Meaning and Relevance of Isaiah

Sometimes relevance is attached to a verse because readers just "intuitively" know that the prophet's words have a significant application to their life. But what someone proposes as a relevant application may not always make sense to others. Although these supposedly "natural" or "self-evident" insights sometimes are meaningful ways of applying the prophet's theology to some modern situation, it is important to think systematically about the process of discovering the relevance of God's Word so that (a) more of those verses that are not intuitively meaningful can become applicable, (b) embarrassing misapplications that are not truly based on the meaning of a biblical text can be avoided, and (c) a well thought out system of discovering the relevance of ideas in ancient biblical literature can be developed.

The first step in this process of finding contemporary relevance in an ancient text is to discover the meaning each passage had in its original setting. What did Isaiah's words mean or convey to his audience? This raises the issue of defining the meaning of the Hebrew words he employed, the grammatical forms that were used to express these ideas, the temporal setting of the audience, and the theological worldview of the audience (Why was he speaking these words to them?). Since Isaiah's message was directed to a sixth-century audience on the verge of national crisis, it only indirectly relates to people today. The key that enables the modern reader to discover an indirect relevance comes from (a) understanding the meaning of the prophet's message to his audience, (b) developing broad theological principles from these specific incidents and teachings, and (c) finding analogies between the Old Testament theological teaching and the modern world today.

Consequently, a clear understanding of the original meaning of Isaiah's words must precede any attempt to make an application. In the commentary section below, the focus will be on determining the meaning of Isaiah's messages to his original audience by following the exegetical process of interpreting the Hebrew words he spoke in light of their semantic, grammatical, and syntactic meaning in that historical setting. This should enable the modern reader to comprehend what the original audience understood when the prophet spoke. Once the first step is complete, one can formulate some theological principle from that chapter. From time to time within the commentary, theological principles are suggested in the final "Theological Implications" section of the commentary and a few questions of application are broached.

Since Assyria does not exist anymore, Isaiah's message of woe on Assyria and its proud king in 10:5–19 does not apply directly to the situation in any modern nation. Based on the authority of God's prophetic word, one cannot say that God was predicting the demise of Brazil or any other country today, because that was not what the prophet said. He specifically addressed only the fall of Assyria at that time. Nevertheless, there are timeless theological principles that are illustrated in the way God dealt with this particular proud king of Assyria. When one finds similar divine attitudes toward other proud people in Isaiah (cf.2:9–12,17,22; 3:16; 13:19; 16:5–6) and other books of Scripture, one can hypothesize that God has a timeless, consistent theological approach to dealing with leaders who proudly ignore God and pretend that they are sovereignly in control of the future. Discovering broad theological principles consistent with God's instructions in other passages helps the reader distinguish between ideas that are bound by time and those principles that broadly define God's ways throughout Scripture.

Sometimes it can be quite difficult to see how a principle might apply in contemporary situations. Could one suggest that the principles drawn from God's dealings with the proud king of Assyria might apply to arrogant presidents or prime ministers of nations today? Might that principle function today as a word of warning to governors or mayors who ignore God's role in controlling modern history, or could it even be a sober reminder for bosses in

industry and principals in schools not to take too much credit for accomplishing things that God actually does? Although the biblical text does not speak to
these situations, the principle is that pride often causes leaders to ignore God's
sovereignty and arrogantly claim authority and power over things that they do
not fully control.

Another central theological theme in the book of Isaiah is the challenge to
trust God.[1] Issues related to trusting God will repeatedly come up as theological principles that could be relevant to life today. Many people in the self-sufficient modern world, proudly independent of God's guidance, want to control
their own future rather than trust God.

For example, during King Uzziah's reign people were wealthy, safe (2:7),
and proud (3:16–17). They trusted in their own human ability to provide happiness and success (2:22) and thought that they did not need God. They were
not exalting God alone; instead, they were exalting themselves (2:11,17). Their
pride caused God to send the prophet Isaiah to warn the people of Judah not to
trust in mankind (2:22) but to trust God and glorify him. If they did not repent
and start exalting God, he would destroy their land and take away their pride.
He would demonstrate that he alone was God and was in control of their lives.
The principles that guided God's way of dealing with the wealthy who proudly
trusted themselves has not changed.

Similar theological principles are evident in a very different situation a few
years later when the weak King Ahaz was threatened with total defeat following the foreign invasion of Judah and her subsequent destruction (except
the city of Jerusalem; 7:1; 1 Kgs 16; 2 Chr 28). Isaiah approached Ahaz and
told him not to fear these armies, but to trust God for victory over his enemies
(7:4–9). Unfortunately, Ahaz refused to trust God, but instead called on the
Assyrian King Tiglath-pileser III to deliver him from those who were attacking Jerusalem (2 Kgs 16:16,20–21). Because Ahaz was unfaithful to God and
failed to trust him, God brought great judgment on the land (7:18–25). Here
again those who proudly fail to trust God are humbled, but in a unique setting
quite different from the situation that Uzziah faced.

As one traces the themes of pride and trust through the messages of this
book, one discovers the consistent theological message that (a) in all kinds of
situations God hates pride and will destroy the proud; and (b) what pleases God
is for people to trust in him for the forgiveness of sins, for security from their
enemies, for guidance in the future, and for their eternal hope. The theological
principles within Isaiah's challenge can become relevant today as we identify
our leaders' failure to trust God for guidance, and our own acts and words of
pride that take credit for things that only God can do. Of course, just finding
a relevant application is not the holy grail of all Bible study. The real sign of
relevance is the text functioning to actually bring about a transformation of a

---

[1] See section six of this introduction for an overview of the theology of Isaiah.

person's thinking and behavior. The purpose of application is only fulfilled when there is a Spirit-engendered response of repentance, trust in God, and commitment to glorify God.

2. Historical and Religious Background to Isaiah 1–39

Reading Isaiah's messages in isolation from its historical context is comparable to overhearing a person talk on the phone without knowing who is on the other end of the line and what their situation is. For example, an intelligent interpreter needs to know what events in Judah caused the prophet to condemn the leaders of Judah for trusting in Egyptian horses and chariots (31:1). Why would Isaiah condemn Hezekiah for showing all the treasures of Judah to the Babylonian king Merodach-baladan (39:1–4)? What was the point of Isaiah walking around naked for three years (20:1–4)? If one knows nothing about the setting, how is it possible to figure out what Isaiah meant in 8:12 when he said that people should not fall into the trap of becoming fearful about talk of a conspiracy? This last admonition may be understood only in connection with events surrounding the Syrian and Israelite military attack on Judah in 734 BC. In this setting people in Jerusalem were hearing all kinds of rumors about a coup, the possibility of a new king being imposed on them (7:6), and how the war progressed. Isaiah makes the persuasive exhortation that people would be far better off if they would fear God (8:13) rather than surrender to hypothetical fears. Knowing some basic facts about the background of a passage helps make sense of Isaiah's advice to his audience. If one cannot identify the political, social, and religious situation of the nation in these incidents, there is no context for interpreting what the prophet was saying.

Although some modern scholars like T. Thompson believe the Bible is a useless document for reconstructing the history of Israel,[2] there are many who think a careful use of the historical evidence in the Bible is legitimate.[3] One must remember that Ancient Near Eastern documents give a slanted version of the historical story from the author's perspective. The same thing is true of

---

[2] H. Shanks, "The Biblical Minimalist: Expunging Ancient Israel's Past," *BR* 13 (1997): 32, opposes minimalists who claim that history "must be based solely on archaeological evidence as interpreted by anthropological models." (E.g., T. L. Thompson, *The Historicity of the Patriarchal Narratives* [Berlin: de Gruyter: 1974]). P. R. Davies, "'House of David' Built on Sand," *BAR* 20 (1994): 55 and G. Ahlström, *Who Were the Israelites?* (Winona Lake: Eisenbrauns, 1988) are two other authors who question the historicity of the Bible.

[3] Three books that respond to these questions and find valid historical evidence in the Bible are W. C. Kaiser, *A History of Israel: From the Bronze Age through the Jewish Wars* (Nashville: B&H, 1998), 1–15 for an evangelical point of view; W. G. Dever, *What Did the Biblical Writers Know and When Did They Know It?* (Grand Rapids: Eerdmans, 2001) for an atheist point of view, but one who still finds history in the Bible; D. M. Howard and M. A. Grisanti, eds., *Giving the Sense: Understanding and Using Old Testament Historical Texts* (Grand Rapids: Kregal, 2003), 25–215 for an evangelical series of articles on the historical settings of specific eras in the Bible. These articles interact with those who question the historicity of the Bible.

Israelite authors. The Israelite historical authors and the prophets wrote from an Israelite point of view that understood God as the one who controlled and directed history.[4] Thus the biblical accounts primarily give a theological interpretation of the significance of events and provide only a fraction of the whole story. There is seldom a complete picture of an event because authors had limited information and had a limited amount of space to tell the story. So selectivity was required in order for the author to accomplish the purpose God designed for each message. The biblical author's purpose was not to give a completely objective and unbiased representation of all the historical evidence; in fact, no writer modern or ancient can do that, for everyone sees events through the colored lenses of his own experience. Nevertheless, in many prophetic messages there are bits and pieces of historical information that enable one to make general comments about the political and religious setting of Isaiah and his audience.

Some chapters are historically located in the reign of a certain king and can be given an exact date (e.g., the death of 185,000 Assyrians outside of Jerusalem in 701 BC in 37:36), but most are much more loosely connected to a general setting. Sometimes the only thing one knows about the setting are a few bits of information. On rare occasions, an Ancient Near Eastern document, like an account in Sennacherib's annuals, describes a campaign against some rebellious vassals and includes events somewhat parallel to Isaiah 36–37.[5] Since Isaiah was not writing a history book or trying to give a complete list of all the historical events in his life, one should not expect to find a great deal of this kind of specific corroborated information.

The prophet's purpose was focused on delivering a theological message to various audiences in Judah, so the interpreter has to search through his words for hints about the political and religious situation that are imbedded in his rhetoric. Careful observation of these factors will assist in making sense of the prophet's messages.

(1) The Time of Uzziah and Jotham

The superscription of the book of Isaiah claims that the prophet's ministry began during the time of Uzziah and Jotham (1:1). The reference to Judah's wealth and strong military power (2:7) suggest that these messages were delivered in the later part of Uzziah's reign, after he had attained considerable prosperity and military strength. This was the time when Uzziah would be tempted to become proud (2 Chr 26:6–16). Though there is little information to pinpoint the exact years within the reign of Uzziah that Isaiah spoke, one could logically hypothesize that most of these messages came between

---

[4] Anyone who has been in a car accident knows there can be multiple interpretations of events depending on one's point of view.

[5] Pritchard, *ANET*, 287–88 mentions Hezekiah by name.

750–740 BC, after the king's acts of pride. At this time Jotham was coregent and running the country because Uzziah was secluded from the public on account of his leprosy.

From a political and military point of view, Uzziah's success in the first part of his reign can be attributed to the weakness of the Assyrian kings Shalmaneser IV (783–773 BC), Asshur-dan III (773–754 BC), and Asshur-nirari V (754–746 BC). Famines, revolts, and succession problems prevented these kings from expanding Assyrian influence, though Asshur-nirari V is known to have imposed a treaty with Mati'ilu, ruler of Bit-Agusi, in the area around Arpad.[6] During these days Assyria was torn by internal strife and impacted by external pressure from the kingdom of Urartu in the north.[7] This freed Uzziah from Assyrian interference and enabled him to consolidate his control over the Philistines, Meunites, Arabs, and Ammonite areas (2 Chr 26:6–8). He was able to refortify the gates and walls of Jerusalem (2 Chr 26:9) and insure the security of the nation by training a massive army of 307,500 elite men of war. He equipped them with the best armor and fighting tools and invented various machines that would shoot arrows and throw stones from the walls of Jerusalem. In addition to all this, Uzziah opened a new seaport in Elath (2 Kgs 14:22) and promoted a strong agricultural use of the land (with new towns, wells, and defensive walls), even in the somewhat desert area in the south, called the Negev (2 Chr 26:10).[8] The biblical record provides a theological reason for Uzziah's success, for at the beginning of his rule he was willing to listen to the prophet Zechariah who instructed him in the ways of God. Thus Uzziah was viewed as one who "did what was right in the eyes of the Lord" (2 Chr 26:4–5). However, Uzziah did not destroy the popular high places where people worshiped other gods throughout the nation (2 Kgs 15:15), and Isaiah condemns the presence of idols (2:8,20), rampant social oppression (3:11–15; 5:23), and those who disrespect God by rejecting his covenant laws (5:24).

The building of Uzziah's impressive legacy was interrupted when he proudly went into the temple in Jerusalem and burned incense to God, in spite of the objections of eighty priests. In anger, Uzziah did what only the priests were supposed to do, so God struck him with leprosy (2 Chr 26:16–20). From that time on, Jotham his son ruled as coregent for about ten years until Uzziah died around 740 BC. Isaiah's messages were probably spoken in this final period of Uzziah's life, though there is no record that he ever spoke directly to this king. This kind of internal evidence suggests (though it cannot prove) that most of

---

[6] A. Kuhrt, *The Ancient Near East: c. 3000–300 BC*, II (New York: Routledge,1995), 492 this information gathered from the Sfire Treaties.

[7] Kuhrt briefly describes the difficulties faced by these three kings (Ibid., 490–93).

[8] Some evidence of this is described in L. E. Stager, "Farming in the Judean Desert during the Iron Age," *BASOR* 221 (1976), 145–58.

the material in chaps. 2–5 (some oracles lack datable evidence)[9] fits well during the time of Uzziah and Jotham.[10]

Some commentators do not accept this background evidence from the time of Uzziah because they believe 6:1–13 was Isaiah's inaugural call, which is chronologically out of order.[11] If 6:1–13 was Isaiah's inaugural calling, then all of Isaiah's messages must have come after the death of Uzziah (6:1). This alternative approach suggests that the oracles in 2–5 were given in the time of Ahaz, but most of the factors listed above do not fit the period of Ahaz. Since the background for chaps. 2–5 matches the time of Uzziah, the prophet's experience in 6:1–13 must be interpreted as a redirection of his calling to prepare him for a new, more difficult period of ministry.[12]

(2) The Time of Ahaz

The background for chaps. 7–11 and a few of the oracles against the nations in chaps. 13–23 fit the reign of Ahaz (14:28–32). The death of Uzziah in 6:1 signals this change in rulers and Isaiah's personal conversation with Ahaz about the Syro-Ephraimite War in chap. 7 verifies a date around 734–732 BC for that chapter.

Life in the ancient Near East changed dramatically when the Assyrian Tiglath-pileser III became king (745–727 BC). He took back territory in the mountainous area of Urartu to the north and east of Assyria when he defeated Sardur II. Later he defeated Babylon in 729 BC and took the name "Pulu, King of Babylon." He conducted campaigns to the western territories around 743 BC to take control of Arpad and other small states.[13] By 738 BC Tiglath-pileser III had received tribute from the western states of Hamath, Tyre, Byblos, Damascus, and the northern nation of Israel (Menahem paid tribute to him in 2 Kgs 15:19).[14] Although some earlier Assyrian kings followed a gradual pro-

---

[9] The brevity and future orientation of 2:1–5 and 4:2–6 make them difficult to date, so two options are available: (a) one could assume that they came from the same period as 2:6–4:1 (in light of the unity of the passage and common theological themes); or (b) they came from a later period and were editorially joined to these verses for theological or topical reasons. Sweeney, *Isaiah 1–39*, 95–96 suggests these verses came from another author in the Persian period because of disillusionment over the restoration of the city of Jerusalem, but this historical reconstruction is not derived from this text.

[10] J. Milgrom, "Did Isaiah Prophecy During the Reign of Uzziah?" *VT* 14 (1964): 164–82 puts 1:1–6:13 in the time of Uzziah, but the analysis of the historical data in 1:1–31 points to a time much later than Uzziah's era.

[11] J. Oswalt, *Isaiah 1–39*, NICOT (Grand Rapids: Eerdmans, 1986), 4–5, 172–73 interprets chap. 6 to be an inaugural calling, thus Isaiah's ministry started in 740 BC, the year that Uzziah died.

[12] This is discussed in the introduction to 6:1–13.

[13] S. Herrmann, *A History of Israel in Old Testament Times* (Philadelphia: Fortress, 1975), 246, identifies one opponent as Azariah of the Syrian state of Ya'udi, but W. H. Hallo, "From Qarqar to Carchemish: Assyria and Israel in the Light of New Discoveries," *Biblical Archeologist Reader II* (ed., E. F. Campbell and D. N. Freedman; Garden City: Doubleday, 1964), 169–70, identified this opponent as Azariah/Uzziah of Judah, an identification that is far from certain.

[14] *ANET*, 282–84, includes building inscriptions and excerpts from annals of Tiglath-pileser III describing his conquests. These documents refer to "Menahem of Samaria," "Rezon of Damascus," that "they overthrow their king Pekah, and I replaced him with Hoshea,"

cess of vassalage,[15] this powerful new king exerted his control over defeated areas by deporting people from a rebellious land, reducing the territory of that state, and turning the territory into an Assyrian province.

In 734–732 BC Tiglath-pileser III came west to confront an anti-Assyrian alliance by King Rezin of Damascus and King Pekah of Israel (2 Kgs 16). These two vassals of Assyria were trying to force Ahaz to join them in a coalition against Assyria. Since he refused, they attacked him in order to replace Ahaz with a ruler more sympathetic to their plans (Is 7:1–6). After Syria and Israel defeated most of Judah's forces (2 Chr 28:6–8 reports the death of 120,000 soldiers), Ahaz called on Tiglath-pileser III to help him (2 Chr 28:16). But when the Assyrian king came, he not only defeated Syria, turning it into an Assyrian province (732 BC), and took land and taxes from Israel (2 Kgs 15:29), he also made Ahaz an Assyrian vassal and required a heavy tribute from him (2 Chr 28:20–21). A successful Edomite and Philistine attack on Judah provided further evidence of Ahaz's military weakness (2 Chr 28:17–18).

When Tiglath-pileser III died in 727 BC, his son Shalmaneser V (727–722 BC) succeeded him and immediately dealt with rebellion in Babylon.[16] In 725 BC he came west and besieged Samaria for three years until it fell in 722/721 BC, the year that Sargon II came to the throne.[17] These military events did not affect Judah directly, though the Assyrian presence nearby had an indirect impact. A large influx of people from Israel migrated to Judah to escape the Assyrian onslaught, thus greatly expanding the population.[18] In addition, an Assyrian campaign in neighboring Philistia in 720 BC demonstrated that Judah was not out of the reach of the Assyrian army.

The religious situation deteriorated dramatically during Ahaz's reign in Judah. He did not do what was right in God's eyes but supported the worship of Baal (2 Chr 28:1–4). He even introduced into the courtyard of Jerusalem's temple a copy of a pagan altar he saw in Damascus (2 Kgs 16:10–16), and

---

[15] J. H. Hayes and J. M. Miller, eds., *Israelite and Judaean History* (London: SCM, 1977), 419–20, describe the common three step process of: (1) taking tribute under a treaty agreement; (2) removing rebellious leaders and replacing them with a local ruler loyal to Assyria, deporting the upper class, and reducing the territory; and, finally, (3) the removal of the rebellious ruler and replacement by an Assyrian, removal of political independence to make the area into an Assyrian province, and the deportation of natives and importation of foreigners. They note that Tiglath-pileser did not always jump immediately to step three (the Phoenician states of Tyre and Sidon stayed at step one), but often he did.

[16] J. H. Hayes and S. A. Irvine, *Isaiah the Eighth-century Prophet: His Times and His Preaching* (Nashville: Abingdon, 1987), 25, indicate that no Assyrian records have been uncovered concerning Shalmaneser V, but Josephus does report some information about this king based on what he read in Menander.

[17] *ANET*, 284 indicates that Samaria fell when Sargon was king (2 Kgs 17:1–4). K. L. Younger, "The Fall of Samaria in Light of Recent Research," *CBQ* 61 (1999): 461–82, provides a full discussion of the present evidence concerning the fall of the northern nation of Israel.

[18] M. Broshi, "The Expansion of Judah in the Reign of Hezekiah and Manasseh," *IEJ* 24 (1974): 21–26.

he probably offered sacrifices to the Assyrian gods of his conquerors.[19] He removed some of the gold and bronze from the Jerusalem temple and palace furniture and gave it to Tiglath-pileser III as tribute. Ahaz's lack of faith in God was illustrated when he failed to trust God even when military victory was promised (Isa 7:1–9). In 8:6, Isaiah concludes that the people of Judah had rejected God ("the gently flowing water of Shiloh"), and in 8:19–20 he refers to the people's pagan practices of depending on mediums and necromancy instead of following God's laws.

The death of Ahaz is mentioned in Isa 14:28 (715 BC), but since these oracles against several foreign nations are grouped topically, it is difficult to determine which ones come from the time of Ahaz and which fit into the reign of the next king, Hezekiah. The oracles against Damascus and Ephraim in 17:1–14 discuss events during the time of Ahaz, but few others fit that time. Hayes and Irvine believe the condemnation of Babylon and the lament over its king in 13:1–14:27 describe Tiglath-pileser III defeating the Babylonian king Nabushuma-ukin around 729 BC, but this hypothesis has gained little support.[20] Most of these oracles probably come from the reign of Hezekiah.

(3) The Times of Hezekiah

Two key military events took place during Hezekiah's reign. About 713–711 BC the Assyrian King Sargon II came west and defeated cities in the Philistine plain. Then the Assyrian King Sennacherib came against Judah from 703–701 BC. Sargon II spent the first few years of his reign trying to restore order in the rebellious provinces of Babylon (ruled by Marduk-apal-iddina, the Merodach-baladan of Isa 39:1),[21] Asia Minor, Media, and Urartu. Egypt's rising power also concerned the Assyrians, so around 713 BC Sargon II came to retake the rebellious city of Ashdod, which had deposed the ruler he put on the throne (Ahimiti). The people of Ashdod had installed a friendlier ruler (Yamani) and then refused to pay tribute to Assyria, hoping that Egypt would give them protection (20:1–6).[22] Egypt failed to help these people, so Ashdod fell to Assyria in 711 BC.[23] The prophet's nakedness at this time was a sign to warn Hezekiah and the leaders of Judah not to depend on the Egyptians to protect them from the Assyrians, who would eventually defeat Egypt (20:3–6).

---

[19] E. H. Merrill. *Kingdom of Priests: A History of Old Testament Israel* (Grand Rapids: Baker, 1987), 407.

[20] Hayes and Irvine, *Isaiah*, 222–23, assume that all these oracles are in chronological order, so they have to put everything before 14:28 into an early period.

[21] For further historical documentation of many of these events see Nadav Na'aman, "Historical and Chronological Notes on the Kingdoms of Israel and Judah in the Eighth Century," *VT* 36 (1986): 83–91.

[22] H. Tadmor, "the Campaigns of Sargon II of Asshur: A Chronological-Historical Study," *JCS* 12 (1958), 22–42,77–100, explains Sargon's activities on this campaign.

[23] G. L. Mattingly, "An Archaeological Analysis of Sargon's 712 Campaign Against Ashdod," *NEASB* 17 (1981): 47–64 surveys this confrontation and the archaeological evidence.

The second Assyrian incursion into Palestine was in response to king Hezekiah's refusal to pay his tribute to Sargon II (2 Kgs 18:7)[24] and to Hezekiah's
seizure of Assyrian territory in Philistia (2 Kgs 18:8).[25] Sargon was unable to
respond immediately to this act of rebellion because of trouble he was having
with Babylon in 710 BC, with king Mita in Asia Minor in 709 BC, and with
the Cimmerians in the north in 706 BC. Not long after this, Sargon II died. So
when Sennacherib came to power in 705 BC he faced widespread rebellion in
Judah, in Egypt (2 Kgs 18:21; 19:9), and by Merodach-baladan in Babylon
(39:1–8). After Sennacherib put down the Babylonian rebellion, he attacked
Sidon and then entered Palestine. Once the Assyrians had established their base
of operations in the Philistine plains, Hezekiah was required to release the Philistine king of Ekron he had imprisoned,[26] and he was probably forced to pay
his back taxes (2 Kgs 18:14–16). The Taylor Prism of Sennacherib describes
these events from the Assyrian point of view, at some point agreeing with and
at some points disagreeing with the biblical record.[27] Sennacherib refers to
his defeat of the Egyptian forces in the plain of Eltekeh, parallel to events
Isaiah records (36:6; 37:9). Although the biblical account calls the Egyptian
Tirhakah a king and a Cushite (from southern Egypt/Ethiopia) in 2 Kgs 19:9
and Isa 37:9, he was probably the coregent with his father Shebitku.[28] Having
defeated Egypt, Sennacherib turned his attention to key cities in Judah, such as
Lachish,[29] Libnah (37:8; 2 Kgs 19:8), and eventually, Jerusalem.

Hezekiah made extensive preparations in Jerusalem to withstand Sennacherib's attack. He blocked off the spring of Gihon, which was outside the eastern
city walls in the Kidron Valley, and dug a tunnel from the east side of the City
of David to the west side where it emptied out at the Pool of Siloam (2 Chr
32:3–5,30).[30] He also repaired and strengthened the city walls (22:8–11), including the "Broad Wall," whose 22-foot wide foundation was discovered by
archaeologists.[31] Hezekiah armed his soldiers well with new equipment and
did everything possible to prepare for the Assyrian onslaught. One night while

---

[24] The exact date of Hezekiah's rebellion is unknown. If it happened early, just after Hezekiah
became king (715–711 BC), surely Sargon II would have addressed this issue when he was nearby
defeating Ashdod in 711 BC. This suggests that this rebellion happened between 711 and 706 BC.

[25] The Taylor Prism of Sennacherib refers to Hezekiah throwing Padi, the king of Ekron who
was loyal to the Assyrians, into prison (*ANET*, 287).

[26] *ANET*, 288, makes this claim, but the Bible says nothing about it.

[27] *ANET*, 287–88.

[28] Merrill. *Kingdom of Priests*, 416.

[29] An Assyrian relief in the southwest palace at Nineveh depicts the Assyrian attack on Lachish
(*ANEP*, figs. 371–74). For a discussion of this relief see I. Eph'al, "The Assyrian Siege Ramp at
Lachish: Military and Lexical Aspects," *Tel Aviv* 11 (1984): 64.

[30] V. Sasson, "The Siloam Tunnel Inscription," *PEQ* 114 (182): 111–17, describes how Hezekiah's workers started from both ends of the tunnel and met in the middle. A. G. Vaughn, *Theology,
History, and Archaeology in the Chronicler's Account of Hezekiah* (Atlanta: Scholar's Press, 1999),
19–79, presents archaeological evidence that illustrates the expansion of cities and fortifications
during the time of Hezekiah.

[31] N. Avigad, "Excavations in the Jewish Quarter of the Old City of Jerusalem 1969/1970,"

the Assyrian soldiers were encamped around Jerusalem, 185,000 of them perished in the night, so Sennacherib fled back home to Nineveh (37:36–38). For political reasons, Sennacherib's Prism does not mention how this battle ended, although one is left with the false impression that the Assyrians were successful against Judah. Later Sennacherib thoroughly defeated Babylon (689 BC), but in 681 BC Sennacherib was killed in a palace plot by his sons, and Esarhaddon succeeded him (2 Kgs 19:37).

There are some uncertainties about these events. First, questions are raised about calling the Egyptian Tirhakah a "king" in 701 BC, for it appears that he did not reign as sole king until 685 BC; and second, it is hard to figure out how Hezekiah's payment of a heavy tribute in 2 Kgs 18:14–16 fits into the overall story. The studies by H. H. Rowley, B. S. Childs, and R. E. Clements survey several theories that have arisen to try to make sense of and coordinate the information in the three biblical accounts and the Assyrian accounts.[32] Some scholars hypothesize that the problem is due to the use of two contradictory literary sources in the biblical texts, while others try to resolve the enigmas embedded in these events by proposing that these chapters include improperly synthesized records of two different sieges of Jerusalem by Sennacherib. Many solutions have been proposed, but they break down into three major groups.

(1) J. Bright's solution was to find two different battles, an early one in 701 BC, when Hezekiah capitulated and was forced to pay a large sum of money, and then a second one around 688 BC, which is not mentioned in the Assyrian records but coincides with the marvelous story of divine deliverance in 2 Kgs 18:17–19:37.[33]

(2) A second group of theories prefer a literary solution which rejects the historical value of the positive theological accounts of divine deliverance in Kings and Isaiah and accepts the negative historical account of Hezekiah's surrender and payment of heavy taxes to Sennacherib (2 Kgs 18:14–16).[34] R. E. Clements views these positive narratives as a later midrashic exegetical exaggeration of Zion theology composed during the reign of Josiah.[35]

IEJ 20 (1970): 1–8, 129–40 and "Excavations in the Jewish Quarter of the Old City of Jerusalem 1969/1970," *IEJ* 22 (1972): 193–200.

[32] H. H. Rowley, "Hezekiah's Reform and Rebellion," in *Men of God: Studies in Old Testament History and Prophecy* (London: Nelson, 1963), 98–132; B. S. Childs, *Isaiah and the Assyrian Crisis* (London: SCM, 1967); R. E. Clements, *Isaiah and the Deliverance of Jerusalem* (Sheffield: JSOT, 1980).

[33] The first encounter agrees with 2 Kgs 18:14–16 and Sennacherib's account of defeating Hezekiah, while the second encounter allows for the event that fits Isaiah's glorious account of the defeat of Assyria. See J. Bright, *A History of Israel* (Philadelphia: Westminster, 1959), 264–71, 282–87.

[34] H. Wildberger, *Isaiah 28–39*, CC (Minneapolis: Fortress, 2002), 359–68, analyzes chaps. 36–37 into two independent narratives and concludes that the one story about Hezekiah's humiliation is historical. In his view, the second narrative (37:9b–35) does not fit the historical facts.

[35] Clements, *Isaiah and the Deliverance of Jerusalem*, 93, believes this addition was heavily dependent on theological implications drawn from the positive things said about the Davidic ruler in 9:2–6 and negative things said about the arrogant Assyrian in 10:5–15.

(3) A third approach fits all the details into one event (not two separate Assyrian attacks) and tries to fit everything into one consistent narrative (not two inconsistent narratives) by proposing an initial capitulation by Hezekiah when Sennacherib defeated Ekron (2 Kgs 18:14–16) and then a later divine defeat of the Assyrians at Jerusalem.[36]

No solution is without some assumptions and problems, but the first two approaches are not preferred in this commentary. If Tirhakah was a coregent in 701 BC, then some of the support for a later second invasion is removed. If Hezekiah paid the back tribute he owed when he released the king of Ekron, this removes the need for suggesting two invasions: one won by Sennacherib when Hezekiah submitted and paid his tribute, and one lost by Sennacherib when God struck down many of his troops. Although there still are many unanswered historical and literary questions about the narrative description of what happened, any wholesale rejection of a portion of the narrative does not really solve the problems,[37] but merely removes part of the problem from consideration and ignores the theological implications of having a grand theological belief that it was impossible to conquer Zion based on an erroneous narrative.

The religious situation in Jerusalem changed dramatically after Hezekiah's coronation (715 BC). The accounts of his religious reforms and trust in God vary. According to the narrative in 2 Chr 29:3–11,15–36, Hezekiah repaired the temple, consecrated priests, renewed the nation's covenant with God, removed pagan elements his father brought into the temple area, and restored worship starting in the first year of his reign (715 BC). Later, he led the people of Judah, as well as Israelites from the northern territory of Ephraim (2 Chr 30:6–11,18), in a grand celebration of the Passover and the Feast of Unleavened Bread (2 Chr 30:1,21). Sometime during these events, he destroyed many pagan places of worship in Judah and Ephraim (2 Chr 31:1; 2 Kgs 18:4). Hezekiah is pictured as a great reformer, a man of faith who encouraged his armies to trust in God for deliverance (2 Chr 32:6–8), and who did so himself when he asked God to deliver them from the Assyrians (2 Chr 32:20–21). Although Hezekiah later exhibited pride for a time (2 Chr 32:25–26), he quickly repented and was blessed by God with great riches (2 Chr 32:27–29). Some of the material in Chronicles is not mentioned in Isaiah or 2 Kings. On the other hand, the narratives in 2 Kgs 18–19 highlight Hezekiah's unique acts and prayers of faith (2 Kgs 18:5–6; 19:14–19), his courageous removal of Moses' bronze snake from the temple (2 Kgs 18:4), his humiliation and payment of a large sum of gold and silver to the Assyrian king (2 Kgs 18:14–16), and his sin of dependance on Babylon (2 Kgs 20:12–18).

---

[36] W. R. Gallagher, *Sennacherib's Campaign to Judah: New Studies*. Studies in History and Culture of the Ancient Near East, 18 (Leiden: Brill, 1999), 8, rejects the view that the biblical account has conflated two wars into one.

[37] Merrill. *Kingdom of Priests*, 412–20.

Isaiah's own representation of the spiritual situation at this time is more complex. In support of Hezekiah, Isaiah celebrates Hezekiah's final decision to trust God for the defeat of the Assyrians (37:14–20) and omits any reference to Hezekiah's humiliating payment of tribute, but by and large he does not paint a very positive picture of the spiritual condition of the people or leaders of Jerusalem in 701 BC. Instead, he condemns the revelry in Jerusalem as the people make military preparations for battle against Sennacherib (22:1–13). He condemns their "covenant with death" (28:15,18), a reference to Judah's alliance with Egypt (30:1–5; 31:1–50). He prophesies that God would bring Jerusalem low (29:1–4) but then would suddenly cause their enemies to become like dust (29:5). He portrays the people as rebellious, deceitful, unwilling to listen to the law of God (30:9), and in need of repentance (29:15). They needed to trust God, for he was the one who would shatter Assyria (30:31) and cause the Assyrians to flee (31:8–9). It is true that Hezekiah removed idolatry from Judah, and his faith in God stood in stark contrast to Ahaz (7:1–9); but in other ways Hezekiah and the leaders in Jerusalem were not much different. Both groups had a hard time listening to the prophet's word from God, both looked to foreign alliances for help, and it was equally difficult for both kings to come to that place where they could trust God for everything.

This historical and religious background serves as a backdrop for Isaiah's messages. These chapters do not give a detailed historical account of everything that happened; they are primarily theological speeches to persuade Hezekiah and the people of Judah to trust God during the Assyrian crisis when Sargon II and Sennacherib invaded the land. Some expressly mention a war on Zion, treaties with Egypt, and the demise of Assyria, so their historical background is fairly certain, though the exact date may be unknown. The setting for other chapters is more difficult to determine. If most of the surrounding chapters have a known date, it is reasonable (though not necessary) to suggest a similar date for those that are not clearly connected to known events.

3. The Life and Role of the Prophet Isaiah

The book of Isaiah was not written for the purpose of providing a biography of the prophet, so the best one can do is to sketch out a few signposts from narrative chapters that include some personal information. Isaiah's poetic oracles contain relatively little information about his personal life. They reveal much about what the prophet believed and said, but very little about his feelings, what he did, where he traveled, or how he reacted to what God was doing in Jerusalem. What was of utmost importance to Isaiah was to proclaim and then record what God was communicating to his people, not to express his own opinions or explain his own joys or struggles with God's messages of judgment or hope. Consequently, it is nearly impossible to produce anything close to a biography of the prophet, just as it would be nearly impossible to write a biography of the author of this commentary from reading what is included in the pages of this book. Since our main source of information about Isaiah comes from the writings of the prophet, we must be content to study the way his life is presented in these messages.[38] Without any secondary basis to verify information or to gain perspective on the presentation offered, it is impossible to verify or evaluate the slant given to the information. In spite of these limitations and qualifications, some general observations can be made about Isaiah's life.

(1) Overview of Isaiah's Life

The book of Isaiah begins by identifying the prophet's father as Amoz (not the prophet Amos), who might have functioned in the king's court as a scribe.[39] Jewish tradition in the Talmud (Sota 10b) suggests that Amoz was the brother of King Amaziah (the father of Uzziah: 2 Kgs 14), but there is no way of substantiating any of these suggestions.[40] This information should not be completely dismissed though, for Isaiah himself appears to have some sort of scribal responsibility during the reign of Uzziah (2 Chr 26:22)[41] and Hezekiah (2 Chr 32:32), though this role was not necessarily an inherited position. If one were writing a modern historical novel of the prophet, one might be tempted to expand on these hints to picture the young boy Isaiah sitting at his father's feet in the king's royal court as the monarch dictated a message, but such imaginative reconstructions do little to help the reader understand the real life of the prophet and should be avoided.

Isaiah's wife was called a prophetess (8:3), but there is no indication that she ever declared any prophetic messages, so this term may simply mean she was married to a prophet. The family had at least two sons, who had the symbolic names of Shear-Jashub ("a remnant will return" 7:3) and Maher-Shalal-Hash-Baz ("quick to plunder, swift to spoil" 8:3). Surely the parents would have been merciful enough to give the boys shorter nicknames. Although these family members were an important part of Isaiah's life, little is known about them. Even when Shear-Jashub enters the story on one occasion (7:3), nothing

---

[38] G. T. Shepherd, "Isaiah 1–39," *Harper's Bible Commentary*, ed. J. L. Mays (San Francisco: Harper and Row, 1988), 547, distinguishes between the modern historical biographical approach and the author's theological presentation of the prophet's life, embedded in a realistic depiction of life in the ancient world.

[39] R. T. Anderson, "Was Isaiah a Scribe?" *JBL* 59 (1960): 57–58, suggests this, based on a seal found in Jerusalem saying "Amoz the scribe." This is possible, but many people could have had the name Amoz, and the date of the seal is unknown.

[40] C. F. Keil and F. Delitzsch, *Isaiah, Commentary on the Old Testament*, VII (Grand Rapids: Eerdmans,1969), 69, question this tradition but suggest it may explain why Isaiah seems to have access to kings.

[41] This is similar to other notices of prophets who wrote about the kings of Judah. According to 1 Chr 29:29–30, Samuel, Nathan, and Gad wrote about the life of David; 2 Chr 9:29 mentions that Nathan, Iddo, and Ahijah wrote about the life of Solomon; 2 Chr 12:15 indicates that Shemiah and Iddo wrote about King Rehoboam of Judah; and 2 Chr 20:34 reports that Jehu wrote about the life of Jehoshaphat.

is known about him other than that Isaiah explained his name to Ahaz when the prophet met Ahaz at the upper pool. Isaiah was no doubt looking forward to the birth of his second son, and he announced it in bold letters on a large surface so that all could see it (8:1–3), but Isaiah never says much about him after his birth.

The first major piece of information about Isaiah's life comes at the time the prophet met with God in chap. 6. From a biographical and theological point of view, one of the first questions the interpreter must answer is: Was this Isaiah's original call or a later commissioning of the prophet for a new task? Since there is no prophetic call of Isaiah in the first chapters of his book, it is natural to conclude that chap. 6 must be his inaugural calling.[42]

Others question the notion that chap. 6 was an inaugural call and prefer to think of it as a new commissioning for a specific task. Four major arguments suggest that this was not his original call: (1) no other original calls primarily involve giving messages to harden the hearts of listeners; (2) it is fairly certain that Isaiah was functioning as a prophet during the reign of Uzziah in chaps. 2–5, so his initial call could not have happened in the year Uzziah died; (3) there is a change in Isaiah's situation after chap. 6, with much more emphasis on political affairs and a more negative response to his preaching, thus the new commission fits chronologically at this point rather than before chap. 2; and (4) the literary structure and content of this experience is more like the special commission of Micaiah ben Imlah than the initial call of Moses.[43]

Isaiah had the wonderful and awesome experience of meeting the divine King in a very close and personal way (6:1–4). He fearfully lamented his uncleanness and humbly confessed his sinfulness as he glimpsed the holy glory of God (6:5). It was probably the prophet's acute consciousness of his ministry responsibilities that kept him from being completely internally focused, for immediately after confessing his own sins, he also confessed the sins of the people of Judah. Isaiah was not self-absorbed; he was ministry-absorbed. After experiencing divine forgiveness and atonement, Isaiah quickly responded to the divine call to go and spread God's message to his people (6:6–8). Isaiah did not know the nature of the mission God designed for the one being sent, the length of the responsibility, where this person must go, the message that must be spoken, or the difficulty of the task that must be accomplished. Nevertheless, Isaiah immediately volunteered. He did not make excuses or question God's plan like Moses or Jeremiah (Exod 3:11; 4:1,10; Jer 1:6) but gladly offered to serve God. The vividness of his encounter with the holy and gloriously majestic King of

---

[42] E. J. Young, *The Book of Isaiah* (Grand Rapids: Eerdmans, 1965), 1:232, says "The fifth verse seems to support the idea that this is an inaugural call." J. N. Oswalt, *The Book of Isaiah Chapters 1–39*, NICOT (Grand Rapids: Eerdmans, 1986), 172, agrees but allows the possibility of Isaiah's preaching before this decisive experience. He sees a theological reason for the placement of chap. 6 at this point because it introduces key themes developed in chaps. 7–12.

[43] Hayes and Irvine, *Isaiah*, 108–9, also maintain that Isaiah calls people to repentance in chaps. 1–5, therefore the call to harden people does not fit those chapters.

kings made him willing to humbly submit and serve the divine King in whatever capacity God requested. Isaiah was sent to bring hardness to the hearts of the people of Judah (6:9–10). God indicated that the future was dark (6:11–12), but it was not without a small ray of hope (6:13).

This process of hardening is illustrated when the prophet Isaiah met Ahaz while the king was overseeing preparations to secure Jerusalem's water resources before the Syro-Ephraimite War in 734 BC (7:1–25). Unfortunately, 7:1–9 only discusses what Isaiah was supposed to do and say to Ahaz and does not give much insight into what the prophet and his son actually did when they met Ahaz. Assuming Isaiah followed these instructions, he would have given hope and a divine promise of deliverance to a wicked king who was hopelessly outnumbered by enemy forces. Instead of trusting God, however, Ahaz hardened his heart and refused to trust God for the victory or invite God to grant a sign (7:10–13). Therefore, Isaiah announced that the coming of the Assyrians would bring destruction on Judah (7:18–25). Since this is a narrative about Ahaz, relatively little can be learned about Isaiah himself, except that he courageously spoke what God told him to say, and his words brought hardness to Ahaz's heart.

Shortly after Isaiah's conversation with Ahaz in chap. 7, Isaiah was commanded to write the name of his next child on a large sign and have it witnessed by two men (8:1–2). His wife conceived, and nine months later they had a son who was given the name that was written on the large sign (8:3–4). Again, little is learned about Isaiah other than his obedience and that his whole family was involved with his ministry. A short time later, God challenged Isaiah and his followers not to follow the fearful worries of his fellow countrymen, but to focus on fearing God and treating him as holy (8:13).[44] Those who treat God as holy do not ignore his words, dishonor his name, or fail to trust in him. At this time of unbelief and divine judgment, Isaiah was commanded to "seal up the law among my disciples" (8:18). Each follower of God who believed Isaiah's messages was called "my disciple,"[45] but there is no way of knowing how many people this involved. Since the book of Isaiah never refers to a prophetic school of disciples (see 1 Sam 10:5–10; 2 Kgs 2:3–15),[46] it is better to think of

---

[44] H. Wildberger, *Isaiah 1—12: A Commentary*, CC (Minneapolis: Fortress, 1991), 354–55, changes the word תַּקְדִּישׁוּ, "holy," to תַּקְשִׁירוּ, "conspire," resulting in a word play with v. 12. But it makes little sense to call God a "conspirator," or to follow J. Blenkinsopp, *Isaiah 1–39*, AB (New York: Doubleday, 2000), 241, "The Lord of hosts, with him you shall conspire" based on 8:14. God is not deceptively plotting to betray anyone behind their back, but openly reveals his plans. B. S. Childs, *Isaiah*, OTL (Louisville: Westminster/John Knox, 2001), 75, rejects this emendation because it lacks textual support. God is never viewed as a conspirator in the Old Testament, and regarding God as holy emphasizes the contrast between those who do and do not fear God.

[45] לָמַד means "to learn," so a disciple is "one who learns" and follows what his teacher says.

[46] D. Jones, "The Tradition of the Oracles of Isaiah of Jerusalem," *ZAW* 67 (1955): 226–46, theorizes that there was an Isaiah school which "adapted the word of the master to contemporary situations, expanding them and adding further oracles." He believes this school was actively reworking Isaiah's word after the fall of Jerusalem.

these people simply as followers of God who accepted the truthfulness of the revelation Isaiah proclaimed. Some believe 8:16–18 describes Isaiah sealing his writings on a scroll for safe keeping, withdrawing from public ministry for a few years,[47] and then waiting for the fulfillment of God's predictions concerning the Syro-Ephraimite War. It is better to interpret this text as referring to Isaiah's active ministry of sealing God's words in the hearts of his followers, not his withdrawal into a cave to hide. His trustful waiting for God to act did not require him to cease his public ministry. His ministry was needed because many in Judah were hardening their hearts and not following God (8:19–20). Isaiah stayed strongly committed to God in spite of what was happening all around him.

Many years later when Sargon II was attacking the Philistine city of Ashdod, another personal experience of Isaiah is recorded (20:1–6). The instructions are for him to remove his sackcloth and sandals and go naked (20:2). The text does not indicate why Isaiah was mourning in sackcloth, but the command to go naked[48] was meant to symbolize what would happen to captives who would be defeated in war (20:4). War captives were usually stripped in shame.[49] Since the purpose of this command was to send a message to the people who would see Isaiah in public, Isaiah would not be disobeying the Lord if he wore a cloak in his home on cold winter evenings to keep warm. It is hard to imagine what Isaiah's kids must have thought about their father's bizarre and embarrassing behavior (cf. 2 Sam 6:20).

The text includes no explanation as to why Isaiah was to walk around naked for three years (not 36 months, but parts of three years) or what he was to say when people asked him why he was naked. We should not assume that God did not explain this behavior to the prophet for three years (an argument from silence). Since other prophetic sign acts came with divine explanations that the prophet was to declare to those who watched the sign (Jer13:12–14; 19:1–13; Ezek 5:1–17; 12:16), one expects this happened for Isaiah too. God explains Isaiah's behavior by calling him "my servant," "a sign," and "portent."

A few biographical details are also available from the era of Hezekiah. One might assume that Isaiah gave enthusiastic approval to Hezekiah's reforms—opening up of the temple, his cleansing of idolatry from its courts, the dedication of new priests, the new commitment to the covenant, and Hezekiah's great

---

[47] G. B. Gray, *A Critical and Exegetical Commentary on the Book of Isaiah 1–27*, ICC (Edinburgh: T&T Clark, 1912), 154, maintains that "Isaiah realized that a stage in his ministry was closed; that for an indefinite time to come he might speak to his people no more as he had been speaking."

[48] עָרוֹם, "naked," can mean one has no clothes on at all (Gen 2:25; 3:7; Job 1:21) or that one is almost, but not totally, naked (58:7; Job 22:6; 24:7; see Young, *Isaiah*, 2:55). An example from the culturally similar NT is John 21:7, where Peter was naked so that he could do his work, but actually all he had done was throw his outer garment off.

[49] In some ancient portrayals of captives (*ANEP*, numbers 326, 366) they are wearing some clothing, but in others they are not (numbers 333, 358, 365). See 2 Chr 28:14–15.

Passover celebration (2 Chr 29–31), but nothing is known about Isaiah's participation in any of these events. The only tidbits of information about Isaiah come when Sennacherib was threatening to destroy Jerusalem. Isaiah interacted with King Hezekiah at three points during this era. First, he had the difficult task of announcing the king's approaching death (38; 2 Kgs 20:1–11). Second, he confronted the king when Hezekiah trusted in an Egyptian alliance (30–31) and inappropriately entertained the Babylonian King Merodach-baladan (39; 2 Kgs 20:12–21). Third, after praying about Sennacherib's threats to destroy Jerusalem, Isaiah sent a positive answer of hope to Hezekiah (37:5–7,21–35; 2 Kgs 19:2,6–7,20–34). It is clear that Isaiah's announcement of Hezekiah's upcoming death in chap. 38 occurred sometime before Sennacherib's attack on Judah (38:6) and that Hezekiah's meeting with Merodach-baladan came after Hezekiah recovered from his near death experience (39:1); thus these chapters were not placed in chronological order.

In the first meeting, Isaiah announced that Hezekiah was going to die (38:1) and then a short time later (2 Kgs 20:4–6) returned to the king and proclaimed that God would give the king fifteen more years, would deliver Jerusalem, and would give the king a sign by causing the shadow of the sun to move backwards (38:4–7). Isaiah ordered someone to apply a poultice of figs to help heal Hezekiah's boil (38:21), but little is learned about the prophet during these encounters. Although one might imagine that Isaiah wept at Hezekiah's illness, this is not recorded. In a similar manner, Isaiah approached king Hezekiah after Merodach-baladan's envoy visited (39:3–4). The prophet announced God's judgment that Judah would eventually go into Babylonian exile (39:5–7) and surprisingly did not respond to Hezekiah's odd statement that, "the word of the Lord is good" (39:8). Finally, just before the Assyrian siege, Isaiah sent a letter of hope to the king after his passionate prayer for divine deliverance (37:5–7,21–35; 2 Kgs 19:6–7,20–34).

This brief survey shows that the prophet's concern was not his personal life but to lift up the words of God. He certainly was involved in some way with activities surrounding Hezekiah's reforms, but did not describe these exciting events in this scroll. The person Isaiah is known primarily through what he said, not what he did. Since he was very critical of the government policy to trust in Egypt, Babylon, and other nations during Hezekiah's reign, the prophet may have been less concerned with Hezekiah's "external" reforms and much more with the real lack of transformation in the people's thinking and beliefs. Thus Isaiah's speeches often focus on what was wrong with Judah's political policies and religious commitment to trust God. Isaiah's theological beliefs give a much deeper insight into the prophet's identity than do the few biographical points of information included in these chapters.

The scarcity of biographical references in the book of Isaiah relates directly to the purpose of the book and the genre of literature employed. As in other books that focus on recording the preaching of the prophet (Joel, Obadiah,

Micah, Nahum, Zephaniah), there are few narrative chapters that give biographical information about these prophets. In fact, many prophets seem to purposely downplay or avoid imparting information about themselves. In spite of the lack of personal information about the prophet Isaiah, there are numerous hidden references to historical events, the religious and political life of the prophet's audience, and words of comfort and judgment for specific listeners in Judah.[50] Although some find biographical information about the call of a prophet in chap. 40, the explanation of 40:1–11 in the commentary section does not interpret this section as an account of this or any other prophet's call.[51] The discussion of the experiences of the "servant of the Lord" is also not interpreted as describing the life of Isaiah.[52] Of course the absence of personal information about the prophet's situation is expected throughout the book where the literary genre points to a future fulfillment in a salvation oracle (41:8–16) or an eschatological fulfillment in an announcement of salvation (41:17–20). Interpreters should look with suspicion on biographical information about supposed prophetic figures drawn from these literary genres (40:1–11); nevertheless, there are references to wars (41:11–12) and other historical events in chaps. 40–66.

(2) The Role of the Prophet

The discussion of the role of the prophet aims to inquire into the social, religious, or political functions carried out by Isaiah. The earlier prophet Amos was originally a shepherd of sheep and denied being a professional prophet who was paid for his prophetic pronouncements (1:1; 7:14). Nathan and Gad served as court prophets, advising and guiding king David (2 Sam 12:1–15; 24:13–14). Later in the reign of Jehoshaphat, the Spirit of the Lord proclaimed God's word through Jahaziel, who functioned as a Levitical singer in the Temple (2 Chr 20:14). Of course, prophets could have several roles interchangeably, depending on their circumstances and God's instructions. Evidence from the book of Isaiah suggests that Isaiah fulfilled the role of a prophet, who announced the words of God, one who hardened the hearts of people, a wise counselor of kings, a performer of dramatic sign acts, and an author and editor.

Isaiah's role as messenger declaring the words of God shows his common heritage with all other prophets.[53] From the very beginning of his messages, Isaiah makes it clear that "the LORD has spoken" (1:2) and that his audience should "hear the word of the LORD" (1:10) because "the mouth of the LORD has spoken" (1:20). Although not every oracle contains the messenger formula

---

[50] See the Introduction to chaps. 40–55 for a fuller discussion of some of these hints about the geographical and political setting of the prophet and his audience.

[51] See the exegesis of 40:1–11 in volume two of this commentary.

[52] See the exegesis of 52:12–53:12 in volume two.

[53] J. F. Ross, "The Prophet as Yahweh's Messenger," in *Israel's Prophetic Heritage* (ed. B. W. Anderson and W. Harrelson; New York: Harper and Row, 1962), 98–107, explains the messenger speech patterns that indicate this role.

"thus says the LORD," some express the words of God using first person verbs that unveil God's thoughts (5:5–6) or include quotations that follow introductory statements like "the LORD Almighty has declared in my hearing" (5:9). The recommissioning of the prophet in 6:9 involves the sending of Isaiah to "tell this people" the message that God spoke. That is exactly what happened in 8:4 when God instructed Isaiah to go meet Ahaz and "to say to him . . . that this is what the Sovereign LORD says" (8:7). Sometimes, as in the oracle against Moab, the "burdensome message" may not contain a messenger formula (15:1–16:12), but all doubts about its source are removed in 16:13–14 when these concluding remarks refer back to 15:1–16:12 by saying that "this is the word the LORD has already spoken concerning Moab, but now the LORD says" something new.

After Isaiah's recommissioning, his role became to harden the hearts of those who would not listen to God's word (6:9–10). Most prophetic calls involved encouraging people to repent rather than to harden their hearts against God. R. E. Clements and many others maintain that God never originally told Isaiah to harden the people's hearts. Instead, these words represent a later theological reflection on what actually happened. Looking back on what transpired, Isaiah realized that a divine act of hardening explained why his prophetic words failed to persuade Ahaz and why Judah suffered so severely during the Syro-Ephraimite war.[54] Others take a more psychological view and think these words represent the prophet's bitter disappointment after the leaders and people of Judah rejected his exhortations to trust God (7:9).[55] But both these approaches severely undermine the credibility of Isaiah as an honest reporter of what he heard God say when he saw Almighty God as King on his throne. How could a true prophet dare to put his own later interpretation of these historical events in the form of a divine call in which God came to him in all his glory, when it really never happened that way at all and God never spoke the words in 6:9–10?[56]

An examination of Pharaoh's obduracy before God indicates that the Egyptian king is said to have hardened his own heart before God hardened it (Exod 7:3; 9:12; 10:12,27; 11:10).[57] Thus Isaiah's specific mission to harden people

---

[54] Clements, *Isaiah 1–39*, NCBC (Grand Rapids: Eerdmans, 1980), 71–72 and Gray, *Isaiah 1–27*, 101, have this perspective. Both still refer to this as Isaiah's call rather than a special commissioning and believe this retrospective reflection took place after the Syro-Ephraimite war.

[55] J. Love, "The Call of Isaiah," *Int* 11 (1957): 282–96, takes a psychological approach to understanding the negative tone in this command. S. Blank, *Prophetic Faith in Israel* (New York: Harper and Row, 1958), 4, is so bold as to call a literal interpretation of what God asks Isaiah to do as "bad theology," but since he understands these words as the prophet's anguish over his failures, he calls this "good psychology."

[56] O. Kaiser, *Isaiah 1—12: A Commentary*, OTL (2d ed.; Philadelphia: Westminster, 1983), 119–20, sees the error of taking a retrospective approach to 6:1–13 and believes that this explanation undermines Isaiah's credibility.

[57] C. A. Evans, *To See and Not Perceive: Isaiah 6.9–10 in Early Jewish and Christian Interpretation* (Sheffield: Sheffield Academic Press, 1989), 22–24, surveys these and other examples of obduracy.

during the era of Ahaz was not inconsistent with other Scriptures. It is also important to note that this temporary result of his prophetic preaching successfully accomplished the divine plan for this wicked king. This passage does not restrict Isaiah's message to one theme, undermine his strategy of offering repentance (28:16; 30:15; 31:6; 35:3–10), or destroy the prophet's own hope for the future (8:16–18). God does not forbid him to ask people to trust God (7:9; 12:2; 26:3; 30:15; 31:1–3; 37:10; 50:10); instead, he tells Isaiah that his messages will harden some.[58] Isaiah reports God closing the ears of some people (29:9–14), but others respond positively (Hezekiah in chaps. 36–37). Unfortunately, far too many people were stubbornly unwilling to listen to God (42:18–20; 44:18; 63:17). These passages demonstrate that God closing people's ears and the people themselves closing their own ears are not foreign to Isaiah's theology. Thus, it is appropriate to take the Lord's command to cause the people to listen but not perceive (6:9–10) as an authentic part of God's plan for certain stages of Isaiah's ministry and for certain people who were unwilling to listen to what God was saying.

One of the arenas where hardening took place was in the prophet's interaction with the wise political counselors of various kings. J. W. Whedbee's study of Isaiah's complex relationship to wisdom traditions discovered numerous common elements between wisdom thinking and the preaching of Isaiah.[59] Isaiah used parables (1:2–3: 5:1–7; 28:23–29), proverbs (3:10–11; 10:15; 29:15–16; 49:9), woe oracles (5:8–15; 10:1–5; 28:1; 29:1; 30:1; 31:1), and vocabulary that was common in wisdom literature.[60] J. Jensen's study of the use of *torah* in Isaiah also suggests a close connection to wisdom thinking.[61] Both of these studies illustrate Isaiah's contact with wisdom traditions in Israel's culture as well as his rejection of some of their conclusions. It is very difficult to conclude from Isaiah's knowledge of the literary tradition of wisdom that he had any role within the wisdom movement. Although he does offer God's wise counsel to various kings, most of his comments are critical of the king and his advisors, and it appears that his advice was not always given in the king's court (he met Ahaz by a pool of water in 7:3). The wisdom vocabulary and literary style may simply mean that the prophet was skilled at addressing those who

---

[58] Childs, *Isaiah*, 57, also carefully distinguishes between Isaiah's strategies (which were multiple and included calling people to repent) and the results of his preaching (which was hardening).

[59] J. W. Whedbee, *Isaiah and Wisdom* (Nashville: Abingdon, 1971), 13–22, opposed those who make a sharp distinction between the prophets and wise men, as W. McKane, *Prophets and Wise Men* (London: SCM, 1965) concluded. Whedbee follows in the footsteps of J. Fichtner, "Jesaja unter Weisen," *ThLZ* 74 (1949): 75–80, though Whedbee does not think Isaiah was once a professional wise man as Fichtner does.

[60] Whedbee, *Isaiah and Wisdom*, 111–43, pays special attention to the words "counsel, plans" to show a wisdom connection.

[61] J. Jensen, *The Use of tôrâ by Isaiah: His Debate with the Wisdom Tradition* (Washington, DC: Catholic Biblical Association of America, 1973), 65–121, rejects the priestly or legal meaning of "law" and argues for the meaning "wise instruction."

were giving the king bad advice, using terms that would be the most persuasive to them.

An occasional role was Isaiah's performance of sign acts. Although W. D. Stacey includes Isaiah bringing Shear-Jashub to Ahaz in Jerusalem (7:3) and the writing of the name Maher-Shalal-Hash-Baz on a large plaque (8:1–3) as dramatic acts, very little is said about these incidents, and Isaiah's actual use of these events to communicate to his audience is left largely unexplained.[62] The major sign act was Isaiah's nakedness for three years to warn the people of Judah not to put their trust in Egypt (20:1–6; see above).

The role of Isaiah in authoring this text and editing it must be implied for the most part. According to 2 Chr 26:22, Isaiah authored records during the reign of Uzziah, and 2 Chr 32:32 notes that Isaiah wrote about Hezekiah's acts of devotion in "the vision of the prophet Isaiah" (cf. Is 1:1). The book of Isaiah recounts several instances of the prophet's writing. In 8:1 he writes his future son's name for everyone to see; according to 30:8 the prophet wrote his oracle concerning the animals of the Negev on a scroll; and in 37:21–35 Isaiah wrote a message of hope to Hezekiah about God's promise to protect Jerusalem from Sennacherib. God's instruction to Isaiah to "bind up the testimony and seal up the law among my disciples" (8:16) suggests that Isaiah wrote at least some of his oracles. With such little evidence, however, any theory about the authorship of the prophecies in the book of Isaiah must be based on implications and probabilities. Since Isaiah is known to be a writer who actually penned information about the reigns of Uzziah and Hezekiah, it would not be inappropriate to suggest that he wrote out some, if not all of, his visions. In the end it is really not important to know who actually had the pen in their hand and wrote out each word (the prophet or a scribe). The important issue is that several headings indicate these words are the "visions concerning Judah and Israel that Isaiah saw" (1:1; 2:1; 13:1). If others helped in the scribal writing, it is evident throughout that the text represents itself as the oracles spoken by God through the prophet Isaiah, so he is the human author who spoke or wrote these words.

Critical scholars have questioned and some have denied Isaiah's authorship of many verses and chapters, so it is up to each interpreter to weigh the factual reasoning to judge whether various theories are convincing and based on solid evidence.[63] Everyone would agree that someone edited these oracles into their present form. Either the prophet himself or some later person organized the various sections based on a chronological, thematic, or theological plan. Since Isaiah lived many years after the prophecies concerning Uzziah (chaps. 2–5), Ahaz, (chaps. 6–12), and the 701 BC attack on Jerusalem by Sennacherib (chaps. 13–39), it would be natural to expect that the prophet had a major role in organizing these messages.

---

[62] W. D. Stacey, *Prophetic Drama in the Old Testament* (London: Epworth, 1990), includes a very wide variety of "activities" as drama.

[63] See further the section on the "Composition of Isaiah."

4. The Masoretic Text and Other Text Traditions

The primary Hebrew text of Isaiah is the Masoretic text (MT) as it is represented in *Biblica Hebraica Stuttgartensia.*[64] It is based on the Leningrad B19[A] manuscript, which dates to AD 1008–1009. Most of the Qumran Scrolls are about 1000 years older than this manuscript, but they still fit into this same general family of texts; thus, they might be called proto-Masoretic. The Masoretic form of this prophetic book contains what the Hebrew people believed was an authoritative record of what the prophet Isaiah wrote. The fully vocalized form of the texts was solidified with vowels around AD 900, but the consonantal form (without vowels) of this family of texts precedes the Dead Sea Scrolls. This family of Dead Sea texts provides a reliable witness that closely resembles the original, but there are a few problem passages where either present knowledge of Hebrew vocabulary and syntax is weak or else the text suffered through the process of scribal transmission. A few examples where the Dead Sea Scrolls seem to offer a more original reading than the later MT are dealt with in the next section. In addition, one might point to a few other examples where there appear to be irregularities in the MT:

1. In 2:6 it appears that a word has dropped out.
2. In 2:18 (and many other places) the verb does not agree with the subject (corrected in 1QIsa[a]).
3. In 9:2 the "written" text has "no, not" which is corrected in the marginal note of the "spoken" (*Qere*) version as "to him." These two words sound the same and there is only one letter difference between them.
4. In 14:4 the letters "d" and "r," which are almost identical in form in Hebrew, were confused.
5. In 16:9 there is an error of metathesis, with two letters being written in the wrong order.
6. In 25:2 the almost identical letters "d" and "r" were confused.
7. In 30:5 an extra *aleph* was inserted into a word (corrected in the *Qere*).
8. In 30:32 the letters "d" and "r" were confused.
9. The last word in 38:11 is *ḥādal*, "cease, stop," which is probably an error of metathesis. If the order of the "d" and "l" are reversed, one gets *ḥeled*, "world," which fits the context.

These problems are relatively obvious, and the solutions are not overly controversial. These are comparable to noticing the misspelling of the conjunction "and" as "amd." Although it is possible that additional old manuscripts of Isaiah will be found that will bring to light new insights that will help clarify difficult passages in Isaiah, there are only a few verses containing serious questions about what was originally written in the text. The discovery of the Dead

---

[64] *Biblica Hebraica Stuttgartensia*, eds. W. Rudolph and K. Ellinger (Stuttgart: Deutche Bibelgesellschaft, 1984).

Sea Scroll has clarified a number of passages where there were questions about the accuracy of the MT.

(1) MT and Dead Sea Scrolls

Between 1947 and the present, manuscripts containing portions of the book of Isaiah were found in caves in the general vicinity of the Dead Sea.[65] These excavations resulted in the discovery of numerous scrolls (probably 21) and many small fragments that contain only a few words or verses from Isaiah. Among the more important longer documents are these:[66]

1. 1QIsa[a], known as the "Great Isaiah Scroll," dates to around 200–150 BC. It contains all 66 chapters of Isaiah.
2. 1QIsa[b] containing 7:22–66:24 (though many chapters are only partially preserved) comes from the Herodian period.
3. 4QIsa[a] contains chaps. 1–2, 4–6, 11–13, 19–23, 33 and was copied about 35 BC.
4. 4QIsa[b] includes chaps. 1–3, 5, 9, 11–13, 17–22, 24, 26,35–37, 39–46, 48–49, 51–53, 61, 64–66 and can be dated around 35 BC.
5. 4QIsa[c] is an Herodian text that has some Paleo-Hebrew script (for the name of God) and includes chaps. 9–12, 14, 22–26, 28, 30, 33, 44–46, 48–49, 51–55, 66.

These documents must be analyzed individually for scribal characteristics because the exact words in each scroll are not completely identical. Out of the thousands of words and letters in the 1,290 verses in the book of Isaiah, E. Tov records only 234 differences between 1QIsa[b] and the Masoretic codex Leningrad B19[A], and most of these are relatively minor variations.[67]

Orthography	107
Conjunction added/omitted	29
Article added/omitted	4
Different Consonants	10
Missing letter	5
Difference in sg./pl.	14

---

[65] M. Burrows, *The Dead Sea Scrolls* (New York: Viking, 1955) has a fairly complete description of the discovery (even a picture of the Bedouin, Muhammad adh-Dhib), the strange journey of the scrolls through various hands, and the later systematic excavation of several other caves for additional written material.

[66] Lists of Qumran texts can be found in E. Ulrich, "An Index to the Isaiah Manuscripts from the Judean Desert," in *Writing and Reading the Scroll of Isaiah: Studies of an Interpretive Tradition.* Vol. 2 (ed. C. C. Broyles and C. A. Evans; Leiden: Brill, 1997), 477–80 and P. W. Flint, "The Isaiah Scrolls from the Judean Desert," in the same volume, pp. 481–89. The official publication of these texts with notes and analysis is available in the series *Discoveries in the Judean Desert* (Oxford: Clarendon, 1952–). For example the Isaiah texts from cave 4 were published by E. Ulrich et al., *Qumran Cave 4, X: The Prophets in Discoveries in the Judean Desert,* 15 (Oxford: Clarendon, 1997).

[67] E. Tov, *Textual Criticism of the Hebrew Bible* (Minneapolis: Fortress, 1992), 31–32.

Difference in pronouns	6
Different grammatical form	24
Different preposition	9
Different word	11
Omission of a word	5
Addition of a word	6
Different sequence	4

Most of these are merely alternate spellings of the same word or involve the inclusion or omission of either the conjunction "and" or the article "the" (both represented in Hebrew by a single prefixed letter). In other words, they do not have any impact on the essential meaning of Isaiah's message.[68]

1QIsa[a] has probably received the most attention because it is quite old (200–150 BC), almost covers the whole book of Isaiah, and was the first to be published (in 1950).[69] After careful examination, some found this and the other scrolls to be so similar to the MT (differing only in small details) that they concluded the scrolls added relatively little to the understanding of the original text of Isaiah.[70] Extensive detailed studies of the linguistic and scribal habits (it appears two scribes worked on 1QIsa[a])[71] were published concerning the 1QIsa[a] scroll. E. Y. Kutscher has produced long lists of examples of minor spelling variations comparing this scroll with the readings of the MT, but the vast majority of these are relatively unimportant spelling variations like the 261 variations in the writing of the full or defective *holem*.[72] These detailed examinations demonstrate that a certain lack of precision is evident in the work of those who copied 1QIsa[a], for some spellings were changed to fit the common spelling of that day and there are many errors in the text that have already been corrected by another scribe.[73] In a few places, Hebrew words have a

---

[68] Isaiah 49:5 in 1QIsa[b] has יוצרי, whereas the MT spells this word without the full *holem* as יֹצְרִי. Nevertheless, it is exactly the same pronunciation and the same meaning.

[69] M. Burrows, J. C. Trevers, W. H. Brownlee, *The Dead Sea Scroll of St Mark's Monastery, I, The Isaiah Manuscript and the Habakkuk Commentary* (New Haven: American School of Oriental Research, 1950), made this information available early, but the quality of the photographs and interpretation has expanded far beyond this initial work.

[70] H. M. Orlinsky, "Studies in the St. Mark's Isaiah Scroll," *JBL* 69 (1950): 149–66, promoted this view.

[71] It appears that a different scribe began work with column xxviii (chap. 34). R. L. Giese, "Further Evidence for the Bisection of 1QIsa[a]," *Textus* 14 (1988): 61–70.

[72] E. Y. Kutscher, *The Language and Linguistic Background of the Isaiah Scroll (1QIsa[a])* (Leiden: Brill, 1974), 128, notes that of the 424 examples of *qal* active participles,

> MT is written with a defective *holem* where the Isaiah Scroll is *plene* 256 times,
> MT is written with a defective *holem* where the Isaiah Scroll is defective 55 times,
> MT is written with a *plene holem* where the Isaiah Scroll is *plene* 108 times, and
> MT is written with a *plene holem* where the Isaiah Scroll is defective 5 times.

This illustrates the clear pattern of the Qumran scribes to add the *plene* spelling (full *holem*), probably to help people who had a limited knowledge of Hebrew to vocalize and understand the text.

[73] E. Tov, "The Textual Base of the Corrections in the Biblical Texts Found at Qumran," in *The Dead Sea Scrolls—Forty Years of Research* (ed. D. Dimant and U Rappaport; Leiden: Brill, 1992), 299–314, finds scribal corrections of the first scribe about every four lines of the text. Some of

line through them and substitute word written above the line.[74] Other common variations include the use of a longer form for the second person pronominal suffix,[75] or the lengthening of the endings on verbal forms.[76] This would be similar to the King James "forsookest" versus the modern "forsook." Sometimes the Qumran scribes substituted a more common word for a rare word that readers might not know. Often this happens without changing the meaning of what was being communicated,[77] but at other times a scribe will harmonize a shorter reading with a longer reading found in another verse. For example in 1:15 after the phrase "your hands are full of blood," 1QIsa[a] adds "your fingers with iniquity," probably copying a similar phrase from 59:3. A slightly different harmonization occurs in 37:9 where 1QIsa[a] combines readings from 2 Kgs 19:9 with the Isaiah text, probably to make them agree.[78] There are a few examples of non-duplication of words, such as "holy, holy" instead of "holy, holy, holy" in 6:3 (cf. 3:22; 26:6) or the reduplication of words that should not appear twice (a phrase in 38:19–20; the negative particle in 35:9). E. Y. Kutscher believes 1QIsa[a] has so many problems that it should not be considered an official copy of the Bible accepted in the Temple as reliable but only a personal copy for home reading and study.[79] The wording and spelling of 1QIsa[b] and 4QIsa[b] are much closer to the Masoretic tradition.

In spite of the minor spelling differences and numerous corrections that might limit a student's confidence in the quality and dependability of the Qumran scrolls, these documents provide a valuable aid in understanding textual problems in the Hebrew text of Isaiah. The readings in the scrolls should not be deemed superior just because they predate the earliest Masoretic texts by about

these "corrections" bring the scroll reading closer to the MT, and some go in the opposite direction. S. Talmon, "Aspects of Textual Transmission of the Bible in the Light of Qumran Manuscripts," in *Qumran and the History of the Biblical Text* (ed. F. M. Cross and S. Talmon; Cambridge: Harvard University, 1975), 226–63, deals with numerous conflations, changes, and corrections of the scrolls.

[74] In Isa 12:6, 1QIsa[a] has זיון בת, "daughter of Zion," but the word "daughter" has a line through it and above the line is the word יושבת, "inhabitants," which brings the Qumran text in line with the MT. Another example is in 21:1 where נוראה was added above the line so that it agrees with the MT, and a line through רחוקה suggests that it is a wrong reading, which possibly was originally based on a similar reading in 39:3.

[75] The Masoretic שְׁמְרְךָ is often spelled שמרתה, with the longer ה ending. The noun "your king" would have the longer spelling מלככה instead of the normal Masoretic spelling without the final ה. Sometimes the copyist wrote כיא instead of the more usual Masoretic כי. Many other scribal characteristics are catalogued by M. Martin, *The Scribal Characteristics of the Dead Sea Scrolls* (2 vols.; Louvain: Publications Universitaires, 1958).

[76] Tov, *Textual Criticism of the Hebrew Bible*, 110 mentions the practice of lengthening the imperfect forms of the verb.

[77] J. D. W. Watts, *Isaiah 1–33*, WBC (Waco: Word, 1985), 194, notes in Isa 13:10 that the 1QIsa[a] יאירו, "they will shine," replaces the Masoretic synonym, יהלו.

[78] Isa 37:9 begins with the verb וַיִּשְׁמַע, "and he heard," while the same clause in the middle of 2 Kgs 19:9 begins with the verb וַיָּשָׁב, "and he returned," but 1QIsa[a] includes both verbs.

[79] Kutscher, *The Language and Linguistic Background of the Isaiah Scroll (1QIsa[a])*, 78, believes the standard MT was preserved in the Temple or synagogues.

one thousand years, for not all old manuscripts are good copies of the text of Isaiah. Yet even when one has a somewhat inferior copy, as in 1QIsaᵃ, it and other better copies can provide a memory of authentic ancient textual traditions and give insights into the practices and mistakes of scribes. Once obvious mistakes and insignificant variations in spelling are discounted, even this poorer scroll gives testimony to the general accuracy of the MT.[80]

At various points in the commentary and footnotes, readings from one of the Qumran scrolls are discussed, and several are accepted as having a superior reading. Examples include:

1. In 2:18 1QIsaᵃ has a plural verb to match the plural subject "idols," and this agrees with the Old Greek. This reading is superior, and the loss of a *šureq* at the end of the verb in the Masoretic tradition (which makes it plural) could have come about as a scribal error because the first word of the next verse begins with the same letter.
2. In 11:15 the meaning of the Hebrew word *baʿyām* is unknown. It could be related to an Arabic word that means "with heat" (thus the translation "scorching"). The Old Greek has "with a strong wind," and 1QIsaᵃ has *bʿṣm*, "with a mighty wind," which makes complete sense when describing God's wind.[81]
3. In 14:5 the word *medhēbâ* is difficult to interpret, and various emendations are suggested. Early Rabbis like Kimchi read it as an Aramaic form of the word "gold," and the Latin Vulgate and the Greek recension of Symmachus have "tribute." It appears that *medhēbâ* is a mistake for *marhēbâ* because of a confusion of *d* and *r* which are written in an almost identical form in Hebrew. Since *ngś* and *rhb* have already been used in parallelism in 3:5, this makes sense and 1QIsaᵃ agrees with this reading. The root *rāhab* usually means "to be boisterous, defiant, proud," and this is fitting in the context of chaps. 13–14.
4. In 18:2 is the odd looking *qāw-qāw*, which could be translated "line line" (from "measuring line") similar to 28:10 *qaw-lāqāw*. NIV takes it to mean "gibberish, strange speech," but the oral reading of the *Qere* and 1QIsaᵃ have *qawqaw*, meaning "strength, power," which makes much more sense.
5. In 21:8 the Hebrew refers to a "lion" (*ʾāryēh*) that NASB renders "*like* a lion." This is similar to God roaring like a lion to warn his people in Amos 1:2; 3:8. lQIsaᵃ has *hrʾh*, "the seer, the watcher," which fits the context very well, but it is difficult to explain how a scribe might confuse the two words, especially to move from the very understandable "seer" to the more difficult "lion."

---

[80] Burrows, *The Dead Sea Scrolls*, 303 states that "many of differences between the St Mark's Isaiah scroll and the Masoretic text can be explained as mistakes of copying. Apart from these, there is remarkable agreement, on the whole, with the text found in the medieval manuscripts."

[81] Tov, *Textual Criticism of the Hebrew Bible*, 358, accepts this as the better text.

6. In 33:1 the Hebrew Masoretic *kanĕlōtĕkā* is an infinitive construct from *nālâ,* "he obtained, attained," which does not fit well in this sentence. 1QIsa[a] changes one letter yielding *kkltkā* from the root *kālâ,* "he ended, completed," which fits the parallelism.

Of course there are several hundred Qumran variations that are rejected as not original. Commentators and Bible translations take varying positions on Qumran readings that differ from the MT. R. E. Clements and H. Wildberger[82] accept many readings from the Dead Sea Scrolls, but every student of Isaiah must weigh the evidence carefully. Once the *plene* readings, Aramaic influences, scribal errors, and modernizations are eliminated, there are only a few cases where the Qumran texts preserve a more authentic Hebrew text than the MT. In each case one must apply good text critical methods to evaluate the alternative reading.[83]

(2) MT and the Greek Texts

Opinions differ about the value of the Old Greek text of Isaiah for understanding the message of the prophet. Voicing a negative judgment, R. R. Ottley said, "In Isaiah I find it hard to see that the LXX gives any proof at all (unless in a few isolated exceptions) of an older and superior Hebrew text; because the translators seem to have been so constantly mistaken in reading their Hebrew."[84] Later he attributes the poor quality of the Greek translation to the "illegibility of MSS . . . his knowledge of Hebrew was imperfect . . . he saw before him . . . something such as that no skilled writer of Hebrew would have written."[85] If it is true that the Greek translator or translators had an inferior Hebrew text to translate, that was written poorly, and had a weak knowledge of Hebrew, there would be little reason for anyone to put much confidence in the Greek texts. A few years later G. B. Gray challenged these conclusions because (a) even when the Greek text was not clear, the translators do not conceal the meaning before them but reveal what may be a variant of the Hebrew text; (b) even though some Greek texts do not always make sense, they leave a testimony to what the translator saw in the text; and (c) even if some Hebrew texts are difficult, everyone must deal with the difficulty, just as the Greek translators had to. He believes the chief problem with the

---

[82] R. E. Clements, *Isaiah 1–39,* 20, says, "it is certain, therefore, that throughout the entire book of Isaiah there are numerous passages where a more correct rendering or reconstruction of the original must be striven for" and later mentions "the incomparable value of the variant readings of the Heb. MSS from Qumran." Wildberger, *Isaiah 28–39,* 508–11, regards the MT as a representative of a more ancient text than 1QIsa[a] but concludes that "there are some passages for which Qa preserves the more ancient reading."

[83] E. Tov, *Textual Criticism of the Hebrew Bible,* helps introduce the topic, and pp. 287–311 specifically address these issues.

[84] R. R. Ottley, *The Book of Isaiah According to the Septuagint,* I (London: Clay and Sons, 1904), 49.

[85] Ottley, *The Book of Isaiah According to the Septuagint,* 50.

Old Greek translation was its tendency to paraphrase, but he concludes (writing long before the Qumran scrolls were discovered) that some of these cases may represent an alternative Hebrew tradition, so they are of great value.[86] J. Ziegler thought that the Isaiah translation was one of the worst in the Old Testament, as far as literalness is concerned, but the importance of Ziegler's work are his illustrations of how the Greek translators used the Koine language that is found in the papyri of that day.[87] I. L. Seeligmann observed that the Greek translators of Isaiah at times alluded to things in ways that suggest they saw some of Isaiah's prophecies being fulfilled, actualized, or updated in their own time (Isa 8:8; 10:24; 14:18–20).[88] Although he grants that there are some differences in the Greek translation that are due to transcriptional errors, many readings that do not match the Hebrew Masoretic tradition were introduced in the translation process. For example, the Hebrew song of the vineyard, which has a positive perspective, is rendered from a negative perspective in the Greek text of 27:2–4.

Hebrew	Old Greek
27:2 In that day, "Sing about a fruitful vineyard:	In that day there shall be a fair vineyard, and a desire to commence a song concerning it.
27:3 I, the LORD, watch over it; I water it continually. I guard it day and night so that no one may harm it.	I am a strong city, a city in a siege, in vain shall I water it; for it shall be taken and by day the wall shall fall.
27:4 I am not angry. If only there were briers and thorns confronting me! I would march against them in battle; I would set them all on fire.	There is no woman that has not taken hold of it; who will set me to watch stubble in the fields? Because of this enemy I have set them all on fire. her aside; therefore on this account the Lord has done all that he appointed.

The Hebrew looks forward to divine blessing, protection of the city, and the defeat of enemies, while the Old Greek refers to a fallen city. Examples like these caused Seeligmann to conclude that "the great majority of the inconsistencies here discussed must be imputed to the translator's unconstrained and carefree working method, and to the conscious preference for the introduction

---

[86] Gray, *Isaiah 1–27*, xxvii–xxix. Wildberger, *Isaiah 28–39*, 504, agrees with Gray's comment about paraphrasing, concluding that the Greek translators "did not intend to present a Greek translation that would represent the text word for word," therefore, "they do not offer us an 'accurate' rendering of the Hebrew."

[87] J. Ziegler, *Untersuchungen zur Septuaginta des Buches Isaias*, ATA XII (Münster: Aschendorffschen Verlagsbuchhandlung, 1934), 46–56.

[88] I. L. Seeligmann, *The Septuagint Version of Isaiah: A Discussion of Its Problems* (Leiden: Brill, 1948), 4, 83–86.

of variations."[89] Their hermeneutical approach to "interpreting" the text influenced their method of translation; consequently, the LXX frequently does not literally represent the Hebrew text that the translator was using.

Since the discovery of the Qumran Scrolls, it has become apparent that sometimes either 1QIsa[a], 1QIsa[b], or 4QIsa[a] and the Old Greek agree together (though they often disagree), indicating that the Old Greek translators were not always doing a poor job of translating. In a few places they were just following another text type, similar to the Qumran scrolls.[90] Nevertheless, many times the Old Greek represents a "free translation," more concerned with producing a text easily accessible to Greek readers than exactly representing what the Hebrew text says.[91] Sometimes a theological agenda caused the Old Greek translators to interpret the text rather than just translate it. For example, J. Lust illustrated the tendency to revise statements that imply it was "God who causes men to sin: Is 6,10; 8,24; 29,9–10."[92] Thus the Old Greek is not simply a translation of the Hebrew text: "It is an interpretation, but, more than this, LXX Isaiah (like all of the Septuagint documents) historically contextualizes its Hebrew *Vorlage*."[93] It also connects Isaiah's words to Hellenistic history (mentioning the Seleucids in 9:10–11), Greek rulers (Antiochus Epiphanes IV as the king in chap. 14), and recent priests (probably Onias III in 8:8).

Those interested in comparing the Hebrew and Greek translations can find numerous text-critical notes in advanced commentaries that alert the reader to important and sometimes rather insignificant differences between these texts. Although there is no attempt to systematically identify all these differences in this commentary, there are examples of the Old Greek (a) omitting whole verses or clauses (cf. 2:9b–10,22; 6:13b); (b) lengthening a reading (cf. 2:17); (c) filling in phrases to make better sense (cf. 5:9; 39:1); (d) pointing to a better reading (cf. 5:13; 13:18; 23:10); (e) reinterpreting a difficult theological passage (cf. 6:10; 28:10); (f) misunderstanding a Hebrew root (cf. 21:13; 24:16; 27:8; 38:8); and (g) interpreting in light of Greek culture in Egypt (cf. 8:1). But the best way to understand and appreciate the Old Greek translation is to investigate how it uniquely tells the story of a whole literary unit (a paragraph or chapter) as it struggles to make sense of some difficult Hebrew poetry while

---

[89] Seeligmann, *The Septuagint Version of Isaiah: A Discussion of Its Problems*, 41, does not blame these completely on the incapacity of the translators but finds "the translation breathes the spirit of the Jewish-Hellenistic milieu" (p. 44).

[90] A. van der Kooij, "The Old Greek of Isaiah in Relation to the Qumran Texts of Isaiah: Some General Observations," in *Septuagint, Scrolls and Cognate Writings* (ed. G. J. Brooke, B. Linders; Atlanta: Scholars Press, 1992), 195–213 or J. Ziegler, "Die Vorlage der Isaias–Septuagints (LXX) und die erste Isaias-Rolle von Qumran (1QIsa[a])," in *Qumran and the History of the Biblical Text* (ed. F. M. Cross and S. Talmon; Cambridge: Harvard University Press, 1975), 90–115.

[91] A. van der Kooij, "Isaiah in the Septuagint," in Broyles and Evans, *Writing and Reading the Scroll of Isaiah*, 513–529, illustrates this free method of translations by examining Isa 8:11–16.

[92] J. Lust, "The Greek Translator of Isaiah, " *Bijdragen* 40 (1979): 2–14.

[93] A. E. Porter and B. W. R. Pearson, "Isaiah Through Greek Eyes: The Septuagint of Isaiah," in Broyles and Evans, *Writing and Reading the Scroll of Isaiah*, 531–46.

giving a smooth Greek translation.[94] For example, the translation of 8:13–14 shows two different ways of looking at Isaiah's message (periphrastic material is in italics).

Hebrew	Old Greek
You shall make holy the LORD of Hosts, he shall be your fear, he shall be your dread. And he will be like a sanctuary, and like a stone of offence, and a rock of stumbling to the two houses of Israel, like a trap and a snare to the inhabitants of Jerusalem.	Sanctify the lord himself, and he shall be your fear. *And if you put your trust in him,* he shall be to you like a sanctuary and *you shall not come against him* as against a stumbling-block, neither as against the *falling* of a rock. But *the house* of Israel is a snare and the inhabitants of Jerusalem *are in a hollow.*

The Hebrew text prophetically declares what will happen in the future when God becomes a stumbling-stone that brings failure, instead of a sanctuary or rock that brings protection and security. The Old Greek quotes someone among "this people" (not God) exhorting the reader to trust and not rebel (periphrastic explanations), then it pictures the people of Israel (not God) as the ones who are already being a snare to others.[95]

A one-word illustration of this interpretive practice is found in the title of 22:1, "a burden/oracle concerning the valley of vision." This is a somewhat strange title that differs from the first verse of the surrounding chapters, for other chapters always mention a city or nation in the title. Since the following verses in chap. 22 appear to be about what will happen in Jerusalem, the Greek translator helped the reader understand the following statements by putting "Zion" in the title in v. 1. This involves exegesis and interpretation rather than literal translation.

Although in many cases the Greek rendering may not provide much assistance in "correcting" or "identifying" the original Hebrew text,[96] at times it can

---

[94] Good examples of this would be the study of Isa 23 in A. van der Kooij, *The Oracle of Tyre: The Septuagint of Isaiah XXIII as Version and Vision*, VTSup (Brill, Leiden, 1998); the study of Isa 53 in K. H. Jobes and M. Silva, *Invitation to the Septuagint* (Grand Rapids: Baker, 2000), 215–27; D. Bear, *When We All Go Home: Translation and Theology in LXX Isaiah 55–66* (JSOTSup 318, Sheffield: Sheffield Academic Press, 2001); or D. Bear, "'It's All About Us?' Nationalistic Exegesis in the Greek Isaiah (Chapters 1–12)," in *"As Those Who Are Taught:" The Interpretation of Isaiah from the LXX to the SBL*, (ed. C. M. McGinnis and P. K. Tull, Symposium 27; Atlanta: Society of Biblical Literature, 2006), 29–48.

[95] A. van der Kooij, "The Septuagint of Isaiah: Translation and Interpretation," in *The Book of Isaiah: Le Livre D'Isaïe* (ed. J. Vermeylen; Leuven: Peeters, 1989), 127–33, identifies the differences between the Hebrew and Greek of 8:11–16 but finds the Old Greek text to be coherent, but with its own separate meaning.

[96] Wildberger, *Isaiah 28–39*, 505, says that "the Masoretic text ought not to be 'corrected' on the basis of the Gk." As a general rule this is true, because of the periphrastic nature of the Greek

be helpful. Since this was the "Bible" that made sense to thousands of Jews and Christians for many years after 150 BC, it should not be ignored as irrelevant or unimportant. The frequent quotation of the Old Greek translation of verses in Isaiah in the New Testament illustrates its significance to the early church.[97]

(3) MT and the Aramaic Targum

The Aramaic Targum of Isaiah is even more periphrastic and interpretive than the Old Greek.[98] At times it appears to be more of a commentary on the meaning of Isaiah's message than a translation. An introduction and English translation of the Targum of Isaiah is available in the studies of J. F. Stenning and B. D. Chilton.[99] Stenning believes these interpretive renderings of Isaiah sought to "connect the past to the present . . . or [show] how every fresh development of religious teaching was already foreshadowed in the sacred writings."[100] The Targums demonstrate a strong tendency to alter metaphors relating to God and many other things.[101] The real value of the Targum is that it provides another early witness[102] to the theological interpretation of Isaiah's messages by early Jews. B. D. Chilton observed in the Targum a theological emphasis on (a) a dichotomy between the elect of the "house of Israel" who follow the law and the rebellious Israelites who rejected God's law and will be sent into exile; (b) the "Memra,"[103] which reveals God's will to his people and therefore characterizes God's relationship to them; (c) the "Shekinah,"[104] an

---

text, but this should not imply that it is no help at all. It must be used with care, wisely discerning the source of its reading, and the hermeneutical basis of its reading.

[97] A chapter in R. T. McLay, *The Use of the Septuagint in New Testament Research* (Grand Rapids: Eerdmans, 2003), 137–70, deals with "The Impact of the LXX on the New Testament," which includes a discussion of the quotation of Isa 7:14 in Matt 1:23; Isa 29:13 in Matt 15:9; and Isa 40:13 in 1 Cor 2:16.

[98] A. Sperber, *The Bible in Aramaic, Vol III. The Later Prophets According to Targum Jonathan* (Leiden: Brill, 1962), 3, states that in the Targum "not real translation is given but a paraphrase."

[99] J. F. Stenning, *The Targum of Isaiah. Edited with a Translation* (Oxford: Clarendon, 1949); B. D. Chilton, *The Targum of Isaiah: Introduction, Translation, Apparatus and Notes*, in The Aramaic Bible, Vol. 11 (Collegeville: Michael Glazier, 1987).

[100] Stenning, *The Targum of Isaiah*, x, believed he would gloss over older ideas and emphasize things that showed the pious character of his heroes.

[101] Hebrew "lambs" (5:17) becomes "the righteous" while "thorns and briars" (9:18) becomes "sinners and guilty." The name of "God" is often changed to "Shekinah, Glory, Word."

[102] Chilton, *The Targum of Isaiah*, xx–xxiv, suggests that the exposition of the books of Moses in Aramaic began around 485 BC when Nehemiah and Ezra were leading a revival in Jerusalem (Neh 8:1–8). Eventually these efforts concluded in the publishing of Targum available today, but that process is only partially understood today. J. A. Fitzmyer, "The Aramaic Language and the Study of the New Testament," *JBL* 99 (1980): 5–21, would compare the linguistic characteristics of this document to the Aramaic of the first and second century AD, while M. Black, *An Aramaic Approach to the Gospels and Acts* (Oxford: Clarendon, 1967), would date them closer to the fourth century AD.

[103] A complicated idea that refers to God's "word," but many times it becomes a substitute name for "God."

[104] Shekinah refers to the "dwelling of God's glorious presence" and is associated with the temple.

idea that draws attention to God's glorious presence among his people; and (d) the Messiah, an eschatological figure who will restore the nation and establish God's kingdom.[105]

Illustrations of this messianic focus[106] are evident in the interpretive comments added to the translation of numerous passages. For example, 4:2–3 is embellished to say (italicized word are interpretive):

> In that *time of the Messiah* of the LORD shall be for *joy* and for glory, and *those who perform the law* for pride and for praise to the survivors of Israel. And it shall come to pass that he who is left *will return to* Zion and he who *has performed the law will be established* in Jerusalem; he will be called holy. Every one who has been recorded for *eternal* life *will see the consolation of Jerusalem.*

The Messiah, the keeping of the law, and the reestablishment of God's rule in Jerusalem are intimately connected with the nation's hope. These interpretive additions to the text explain how the Aramaic translator understood what Isaiah meant; they are not a literal translation. But with so much interpretive information added, the Targum has a limited value in pointing to the original Hebrew text of that day.[107] One cannot reason that the presence of a phrase in the Targum means it should be added to the Hebrew text. The Targum's messianic interpretation of many passages (for example in 16:1; 43:10–12), especially its identification of the suffering servant in 52:13 as the Messiah, demonstrates that the New Testament interpretation of some of these passages was not out of the mainstream.

In places where there are question about the Hebrew text, the Targum can help confirm the reading in the MT. For example, in 8:5 the Targum refers to the people being "pleased with Rezin," which confirms that the Hebrew *mĕśôś*, "rejoice" should not be changed to *māsôs*, "melt, dissolve in fear," as some commentators suggest. On the other hand, in 11:15 the Targum supports the view that there is a scribal error where the letters *m* and *b* were confused at the end of a Hebrew word (NIV accepts this emendation). In this example, the Targum helps the interpreter make sense of a difficult passage and points to the solution to the problem. A. van der Kooij's comparison of readings in the MT, the Targum, the Old Greek, and the Vulgate of Isa 3:18–23; 25:1–6; 26:1–6; and

---

[105] A full description of various theological trends is outlined in B. D. Chilton, *The Glory of Israel: The Theology and Provenience of the Isaiah Targum* (Sheffield: JSOT, 1982).

[106] The Messiah is found in 4:2; 9:5; 10:27; 11:1,6; 14:29; 16:1,5; 28:5.

[107] Stenning, *The Targum of Isaiah*, xvii–xxi, lists numerous hypothetical errors (or purposeful variations) between the MT and what might have been the text used by the translator of the Aramaic Targum. Many of these differences may simply be due to a misreading of the Hebrew rather than a problem with the underlying Hebrew text. For example the Hebrew בְּרֶשַׁע, "with wickedness," in 9:4 was apparently misread as בְּרַעַשׁ, "in the tumult," an error of metathesis involving the last two letters, either in writing or in reading the text too quickly.

27:1 illustrates how each translation was impacted by the theological perspective of the communities they belonged to and the different times when they were translated. For example, in 25:2 the Aramaic Targum translates the Hebrew "the foreigner's stronghold is a city no more, it will never be rebuilt" into "a temple of the Gentiles will never be built in the city of Jerusalem," possibly because the Roman Emperor Hadrian was planning on building a temple to Jupiter Capitolinus in Jerusalem.[108] In all cases, the Targum must be used cautiously, but it would be foolish to ignore this valuable textual and interpretive resource.

4. Composition of Isaiah 1-39

The focus of this commentary will not be on issues of composition or the historical process of editing or redacting the book of Isaiah. Such hypothetical reconstructions are based on many dubious assumptions; therefore, primary attention will be directed toward expounding the final form of the Hebrew text. Nevertheless, it is important for students of Isaiah to be aware of the different ancient and modern methodologies scholars have employed and how those approaches impact their interpretation of Isaiah's message. This brief survey will attempt to highlight only a few of the key people and writings that have commented on the composition of the book of Isaiah. Some authors have written essays that include references to the growth of the book of Isaiah, while others have published extensive commentaries that describe in great detail their approach to understanding the composition of this prophetic message.

(1) Early Perspectives

Although Josephus (around AD 75) does not explain how Isaiah's prophecies were composed, after he describes the prophet's interaction with Hezekiah (cf. sa 38–39), he indicates that Isaiah "out of the assurance that he had never written what was false, he wrote down all his prophecies and left them behind him in books."[109] The New Testament writers frequently quote from many chapters in the book of Isaiah and often make explicit the prophecy's connection to the prophet Isaiah. The following quotes have an introduction that attributes the quoted material to him:

Isa	1:9	Rom 9:29
	6:9–10	Matt 13:14–15; John 12:40–41; Acts 28:26–27
	9:1–2	Matt 4:15–16
	10:22–23	Rom 9:27–28
	11:10	Rom 15:12
	29:13	Matt 15:8–9; Mark 7:6–7

---

[108] van der Kooij, "Interpretation of the Book of Isaiah in the Septuagint and Other Versions," in *"As Those Who Were Taught,"* 49–68.

[109] Josephus, *Antiquities*, X.ii

40:3–5	Matt 3:3; Mark 1:3; Luke 3:4–6; John 1:23
42:1–4	Matt 12:18–21
53:1	Rom 10:16
53:4	Matt 8:17
61:1–2	Luke 4:18–19
65:1–2	Rom 10:20–21

Some of the introductions to these quotations merely claim that Isaiah "said" what is quoted (Rom 10:20–21; 15:12), although Luke 3:4 refers to what "is written in the book of the words of Isaiah." These quotations indicate that people at this time viewed these words as authoritative Scripture spoken by the prophet Isaiah, but none give much insight into the process of the composition of Isaiah's large book.

In the years after the New Testament was written, the life and words of Isaiah were fertile ground for drawing historical lessons, eschatological speculations, and apologetic argumentation. The apocryphal New Testament "Ascension of Isaiah" (early second century AD) recounts that Manasseh had the prophet Isaiah sawn in two (chaps. 1–5) and provides an account of Isaiah's vision of the future (chaps. 6–11). It is evident that Isaiah did not write this story about his death, for in the midst of this document there are references to Mary and Joseph, the birth of the savior, the twelve apostles, the crucifixion and resurrection of Christ, and the corruption of the church.[110] Although there may be some historical value to statements about Isaiah's death, this document illustrates how the life of Isaiah continued as a source of inspiration for new compositions used to warn Christians about the dangers of apostasy many years after prophet's death. Documents like these provide help for the interpreter of Isaiah to distinguish between authentic and non-authentic Isaiah material.

Many early writings merely quote from the book of Isaiah to prove a point but say almost nothing about its composition. The "General Epistle of Barnabas," written after the Roman conquest of Jerusalem in AD 70, but probably before the Bar Kokhba revolt in AD 135, admonishes Gentile Christians not to be led astray by those who taught that Christians must follow the Old Testament laws. The author claims that these people misunderstand the law, for even the ancient Hebrews in Old Testament times perceived these physical requirements (circumcision, sacrifices, food laws, etc) were spiritual ways to mortify the passions of the flesh and to encourage the sanctification of the body (he even introduced some allegorical numerology). Christians must follow the way of life outlined in the *Didache*, not the way of darkness with all of its evil vices.[111]

---

[110] W. Schnemelcher, ed., *New Testament Apocrypha: Writings Related to the Apostles Apocalypses and Related Subjects* (Louisville: John Knox, 1992), 603–20.

[111] J. Quasten, *Patrology:Vol 1: The Beginnings of the Patristic Literature* (Westminster, Maryland: Newman Press, 1951), 85–91.

In making his case, this author repeatedly refers to passages in Isaiah, quoting extensive portions to prove his point.[112] There was no question about the authority, unity, or practical wisdom of Isaiah's writings. This was the general attitude toward the book of Isaiah throughout the early Church period. It does not matter if one looks at the allegorical use of Isaiah in Irenaeus's *Demonstrations of Apostolic Preaching* (AD 130–200), Origen's allegorical commentary on Isaiah 6–11 (AD 185–254), or the non-allegorical study of Isaiah by Theodoret of Cyrus (AD 393–460).[113] All were focused on explaining what the text meant and how it related to their own Christian faith. Occasionally in these writings one encounters comments which relate to the general issue of the composition of the book: (a) these are the words of God through Isaiah; (b) passages like Isaiah 7 are composed in a manner coherent with the historical background of Ahaz; or (c) there are a few structural comments that explain how certain chapters were composed to fit together.

In *Baba Bathra 15a* the Talmud expresses the opinion that "Hezekiah and his company wrote Isaiah, Proverbs, the Song of Solomon, and Ecclesiastes," but it is hard to know what they meant by the idea that they "wrote" these books. Certainly the Talmud is not claiming that Hezekiah's scribes were inspired prophets or that they wrote what the text attributes to Solomon. This idea may have originated from Prov 25:1, where it says that the "men of Hezekiah" copied or compiled the proverbs of Solomon. Of course the historical basis of this opinion is unknown, so it is difficult to judge its value. Later the great Jewish exegete Ibn Ezra (AD 1092–1167) refers to the heretical views of Moses ben Samuel Ibn Geketilla who questioned whether Isaiah wrote the second half of the book of Isaiah.[114] In spite of a few questions like these, which preceded the rise of the critical approaches in the eighteenth century, most people identified Isaiah as the writer of his prophecies, and there was little talk about the process of composition.

(2) Some Modern Scholarly Approaches

There is no need to trace every step in the history of the multiple opinions about the composition of Isaiah or to describe all the options that have been proposed. This information is available in most "Introductions" to the

---

[112] In 17 short chapters he refers to Isa 1:6–9,11–14; 3:9; 5:21; 8:14; 16:1–2; 28:16; 33:13, 16–17; 40:3,12; 42:6; 43:18–19; 45:1–2; 46:1; 49:6,17; 53:5–7; 58:4–10.

[113] B. S. Childs, *The Struggle to Understand Isaiah as Christian Scripture* (Grand Rapids: Eerdmans, 2004), 45–55 on Irenaeus, 62–74 on Origin, and 130–147 on Theodoret of Cyrus. He provides brief information about each person's life, hermeneutical approach, and a survey of their understanding of Isaiah.

[114] R. B. Dillard and T. Longman III, *An Introduction to the Old Testament* (Grand Rapids: Zondervan, 1994), 268–69, draw attention to statements made by Ibn Ezra in his commentary on Isaiah at 40:1; 42:10; 45:4–5, and 49:4. They conclude that he believed that the book of Isaiah was the product of a single author.

Old Testament and in the introductions to several Isaiah commentaries.[115] This section will take a few representative examples of several approaches to explain their rationale, methodology, and results. Every student of Isaiah should know something about the assumptions and methodology of the commentators they read so they can evaluate the strengths and weaknesses of their literary, exegetical, and theological conclusions.

SOURCE CRITICISM.   J. C. Döderlein (1789), a theology professor at Jena, reasoned that the information in Isaiah concerning the fall of Jerusalem, the return from exile, and the rise of Cyrus presume that the author of chaps. 40–66 was an exilic person living in Babylon around 550 BC.[116] A few years later (1792) B. Duhm of Göttingen proposed that there were three "Isaiah" figures who wrote portions of this book, but none of them lived in Babylon. He believed that chaps. 40–55 were written around 540 BC by a "Deutero-Isaiah" who lived in Lebanon and that chaps. 56–66 were written around 450 BC by a "Trito-Isaiah" living in Jerusalem at the time of Ezra.[117] After analyzing chaps. 1–39, Duhm found three basic documents that were well established as the building blocks for the first part of the book (chaps. 1–12, 13–23, 24–35). He identified other smaller literary units within these books (2:1–4:6; 6:1–9:6; 14:28–20:6 and chaps. 24–27), attributing a few passages (e.g., 4:2–6) to a much later period. Yet he hypothesized that the redactor who combined them probably did not finish his work until 100 BC, or possibly even in the first century AD.[118]

By the time of G. B. Gray's ICC work on Isaiah (1912), critics had already eliminated large sections of 1–39 from the prophet Isaiah (chaps. 24–27, 33–35, 36–39), and individual hopeful verses or chapters (9:1–6; 11:1–16; 12:1–6; 13–14; 19:17–25; 28:5–6; 29:17–24; 30:18–26) were attributed to an anonymous exilic or postexilic prophet or editor.[119] Gray concludes that "the Book of Isaiah is a late compilation: even the books incorporated in it and attributed to Isaiah—chaps. 2–12 and 13–23—are postexilic works."[120]

The criteria for these conclusions relate to:

1. Political and social implications: For example, since 11:1–8 implies that the dynasty of David is no longer in power, this passage must come from a much later exilic period.

---

[115] One can consult S. R. Driver, *An Introduction to the Literature of the Old Testament* (New York: World, 1956), 202–46; E. Sellin and G. Fohrer, *Introduction to the "Old Testament* (trans., D. E. Green; Nashville: Abingdon, 1968), 363–87; R. K. Harrison, *Introduction to the Old Testament* (Grand Rapids: Eerdmans, 1969), 764–800; or a commentary like Wildberger, *Isaiah 28–39*, 513–59.

[116] J. C. Döderlein, *Esaias* (Altsofi: 1789).

[117] B. Duhm, *Das Buch Jesaja* (Göttingen: Vanderhoeck and Ruprecht, 1892).

[118] Wildberger, *Isaiah 28–39*, 516, discusses Duhm's work in detail.

[119] Gray, *Isaiah 1–27*, liii–lvii, 168, 214, 223, 229, 232–33.

[120] Ibid., lvii.

2. Style and language: Chaps. 40–55 have a different style from the rest.
3. Ideas: Eschatological ideas must be late.[121]

Gray believed that as Isaiah spoke, he gathered disciples. After several years of speaking, he began to record some of his prophecies and experiences in small booklets that were preserved by his disciples. Later authors during the exile in Babylon and in the postexilic period produced additional chapters (all of 40–66) that were added to Isaiah's sermons. Finally an editor around the third century BC combined chaps. 1–39 together and some time just before 180 BC another editor added chaps. 24–27, 34–35, and 40–66 to produce the present book. Isaiah 19:18–25 was the only section added after 180 BC.[122] Throughout his treatment, Gray is cautious about his reconstruction and stated that "no synthesis of results can therefore be more than tentative" and admitted that there were many things about his theory that were uncertain.[123] This humility is to be applauded.

Other scholars, following such a broad scale sectional theory of Isaianic development, have divided the text into smaller and smaller unrelated segments that are claimed to have been added in various later stages. R. B. Y. Scott traced a complicated seven-step process in the composition of chaps. 1–39, with small insertions being added to the two basic collections over time.[124] He identifies three stages of the process that relate to the prophet Isaiah:

Stage 1: Isaiah's record of events related to Ahaz's refusal to trust God during the Syro-Ephraimite War (734 BC):

a) Judah and Jerusalem oracles (1:2–3,10–26; 3:1–17,24–26; 4:1; 5:1–13,17–24a, plus 10:1–2.
b) Insertion of two earlier oracles: 2:6–22 with 5:14–16, plus 9:8–10:4 and 5:24b–29 (and possibly 5:30; 8:19–22).
c) Isaiah's memoirs in 6:1–13; 8:1–8a,11–18 (and probably 8:8b–10).

Stage 2: Collection of oracles related to Egypt (704 BC):

a) Fragments from 28:1–4,7–13; 28:14–22.
b) Fragments from 29:15–16; 30:8–17; 31:1–3.

Stage 3: Texts connected to Sennacherib's attack on Jerusalem in 701 BC involving the expansion of the two earlier collections.

a) Added to the first collection was 10:5–16; 24–27c; 14:24–27.
c) Added to the second collection was 29:1–8; 30:27–33; 31:4–9.

---

[121] Ibid., lviii.
[122] Ibid., lvi.
[123] Ibid., lv–lix.
[124] R. B. Y. Scott, "Isaiah," *IB* (Nashville: Abingdon, 1956), 5:157–160.

The rest of the material in chaps. 1–39 was added after the death of Isaiah in four consecutive stages, with some oracles arising from sayings his disciples remembered from Isaiah's ministry and some being non-Isaianic.[125]

Such a complex compositional theory with many small 2 or 3 verse paragraphs apportioned to seven different time periods goes far beyond the evidence. All literary and conceptual continuity within chapters is largely lost, authentic prophetic authority is abandoned to unknown multiple authors and editors, and subjective reasoning ends up governing the theory. As a general rule, there is little effort to explain how or why various paragraphs were added. Such reconstructions are not particularly convincing and are not related to any known method of producing an ancient Near Eastern document. Instead, these complex scholarly reconstructions, which disagree with one another, demonstrate the futility of various aspects of this approach and the self-destructive nature of carrying things far beyond what a common sense approach would demand. J. A. Soggins views this method as "too subtle and often based on imponderable or subjective elements which limit its usefulness."[126] J. Mauchline is certainly correct in attributing many of the positive messages of hope in Isaiah to the prophet himself (rather than an exilic editor), thus paralleling the contrast between judgment and hope found in the preaching of other prophets like Hosea.[127] Besides noting the loss of the sense of a whole text, B. S. Childs states, "The frustrating part of this history of research is that the material does not lend itself readily to this kind of literary reconstruction. Many of the crucial critical questions remain unresolved."[128] Some, like Hayes and Irvine, have totally rejected this approach, stating in the introduction to their commentary on chaps. 1–39 that "Very few editorial additions were made to the Isaianic speeches."[129] Because of these weaknesses in the source critical approach, scholars developed alternative methods of studying the composition of the book of Isaiah.

COMPOSITION BY A PROPHETIC SCHOOL. In order to maintain some continuity between the oracles which Isaiah spoke and those that came from later periods, a few scholars appealed to the idea that there was a prophetic school preserving and publishing the prophet's thinking, who added more oracles to the collection that were consistent with Isaiah's theology.[130]

---

[125] A similar overly complicated presentation of the composition of 1–39 is presented by G. Fohrer, "The Origin, Composition and Tradition of Isaiah 1–39," *ALUOS* 3 (1963): 3–38 or "Entstehung, Komposition und Überlieferung von Jesaja 1–39," *BZAW* 99 (1967):113–47.

[126] J. A. Soggin, *Introduction to the Old Testament* (Philadelphia: Westminster, 1976), 258.

[127] J. Mauchline, *Isaiah 1–39* (London: SCM, 1962), 9–10.

[128] B. S. Childs, *Introduction to the Old Testament as Scripture* (Philadelphia: Fortress, 1979), 319–20. Childs recognized that this atomization of the text into hundreds of disconnected fragments destroys continuity and any attempts to gain meaning from the whole (p. 324).

[129] Hayes and Irvine, *Isaiah*, 14.

[130] S. Mowinckel, *Prophecy and Tradition: The Prophetic Books in the Light of the Study of the Growth and History of the Tradition* (Oslo: Kommisjonhos J. Dybwad, 1946), was one of the earliest to attribute the preservation of Isaiah's tradition to his disciples.

D. Jones suggested, "Later disciples—perhaps associations of cult-prophets—adapted the words of the master to contemporary situations, expanding them and adding further oracles."[131] He found evidence that this school comprised the "disciples" who received the oral teachings that were sealed in their hearts and later preserved in a scroll (8:16–18). He then hypothesized that Isaiah's disciples used his teachings repeatedly in new situations. For example, Isaiah's original teachings were "superseded by a more comprehensive application to Sion's total history as it comes down to the great finale of 586"[132] to produce the present form of chap. 1. The reference to the Day of the Lord in 2:6–22 has already occurred when God allowed Jerusalem to be destroyed. The concept of God taking away the nation's bread and water in Isa 3:1 is also interpreted, not as a prophetic warning, but as a later report by Isaiah's disciples that the prophet's preaching was fulfilled at the fall of Jerusalem in 586 BC. Jones interpreted the prophetic words about God's judgment of the proud women of Jerusalem (3:15–4:1) as a lament by Isaiah's disciples after the fall of Jerusalem.[133] In this way Isaiah's original teachings were expanded and consistently integrated with those of the prophet's disciples. J. H. Eaton expanded this approach, examining certain themes, promises (which he connects to a New Years Festival), and elements of style (like the phrase "the Holy One of Israel") to trace how the oral traditions of Isaiah were preserved for posterity.

This approach has not gained popularity for at least two reasons. First, there is little evidence of a school of disciples related to the prophet, and no evidence that any of his disciples were involved with composing what the prophet said. We cannot assume Isaiah had a prophetic school (cf. "the sons of the prophets") like the one that seems to have been attached to Elisha (1 Kgs 20:35; 2 Kgs 2:3,5,7,15; 4:1–38). The disciples mentioned in 8:16 are primarily disciples or followers of God.[134] Second, it is difficult to accept that any of Isaiah's followers would dare to add their own interpretations to the authoritative words of their master and in the process dramatically reinterpret what the prophet said. Therefore, one should not think that an organized group of disciples took Isaiah's prophecies and many years later turned these predictions into reports concerning what had already happened after God completed his judgment of Judah.

---

[131] D. Jones, "The Traditio of the Oracles of Isaiah of Jerusalem," *ZAW* 67 (1955): 226–27, is "not so much concerned with the process as a whole as . . . with two moments in particular, the moment when Isaiah handed his oracles over to his disciples and the moment when later disciples delivered them in substantially their present form." J. Becker, *Isaias- Der Prophet und sein Buch* (Stuttgart: Katolisches Bibelwerk, 1968), connects the parts of Isaiah together by reference to "the former things" and the "new thing" God would do. He hypothesizes that an Isaianic school was responsible for producing the present form of the book of Isaiah.

[132] D. Jones, "The Traditio of the Oracles of Isaiah of Jerusalem," *ZAW* 67 (1955): 239.

[133] Ibid., 242–3.

[134] Both Clements, *Isaiah 1–39*, 4, and Wildberger, *Isaiah 1–12*, 366–69, oppose the idea of a prophetic school being responsible for the book of Isaiah.

REDACTIONAL APPROACHES. Although redactional studies share some features with the source approach, they are not the same. Although there are different types of redactional approaches (only a few can be reviewed here), the basic goal is to discover how later redactors reoriented the book in a unified manner to accomplish their purpose. Those using this method of interpreting the book of Isaiah seek to discover the way in which exilic and postexilic editors influenced the content and formation of the earlier judgment and salvation oracles from the prophet.

H. Barth proposed the thesis that during the time of Josiah (around 620 BC, 70 years after the time of Isaiah) a new interpretation of Isaiah was promoted to support Josiah's reform movement. This "Assyria Redaction" added many new texts about Assyria in chaps. 2–32 to Isaiah's original writings.[135] In this new redacted material, attention was directed toward (a) the impending downfall of Assyria (which declined from 630 BC until its fall in 612 BC), (b) the salvation of Israel, and (c) God's plan to rebuild the Davidic empire (under Josiah). These themes provided hope to the people of Judah who would soon enjoy God's salvation (freedom from Assyria).

In order to understand how later redactions impacted the aim of the book, it was necessary to identify the genuine Isaiah traditions that existed before the time of Josiah. Then the interpreter could study the remaining material to understand the changes introduced by the later redaction in the time of Josiah. The original "proto-Isaiah" sayings involved numerous fragmentary sections from chaps. 2–11 (mainly 6:1–8:18) about Judah's rebellion against Assyria (written between 713–711 BC), and chaps. 28–32 (specifically 28:17–30:17) about God's continued plan for judgment (written around 701 BC). Redacted verses were added to authentic Isaiah material and inserted both in the time of Josiah and then again during the exilic period. These additions reminded the people of Israel why God judged Jerusalem and gave them some hope for the future. The exilic redaction added the oracles against the foreign nations (chaps. 13–23) and many of the hopeful passages, especially about the salvation of the nations (4:2; 11:6–8,10–16; 17:7–8; 19:18–25; 28:5–6; 31:7; 34–35). H. Wildberger's massive commentaries on Isaiah basically reject H. Barth's hypothesis of an Assyria redaction. Instead, he argues for more original material from Isaiah (the core being 2:6–11:9; 28–31), with later additions of the oracles against the nations (13–23), plus still later additions after the fall of Jerusalem (a judgment recension), and another in the postexilic period (a salvation recension).[136]

---

[135] H. Barth, *Die Jesaja-Worte in der Josiazeit: Israel und Asshur also Thema einer produktiven Neuinterpretation der Jesajaüberlieferung*, WMANT 48 (Neukirchen-Vluyn: Neukirchener, 1977), identified this new redactional material in 5:14–17,30; 6:12; 7:8b,17b,18b,20b; 8:7b,8b,9f, 23b–9:6; 10:5–19; 14:6–21,24–27; 17:12–14; 29:1–8; 30:27–33; and 32:1–9,15–20.

[136] Wildberger, *Isaiah 28–39*, 495–559, believes the prophet Isaiah wrote 304 out of the 765 verses in chaps. 1–39.

On the other hand, R. E. Clements followed many of Barth's conclusions, suggesting that the primary collection of Isaiah's authentic words were in chaps. 2–12 (especially 6:1–8:18) and 28–31. The material in chaps. 24–27 and 32–35, plus the material borrowed from 2 Kings 18–19 in Isaiah 36–39 and the oracles against the nations in 13–23, did not come from Isaiah.[137] He accepts Barth's thesis that someone later inserted an "Assyria-redaction" (he calls it the Josianic redaction) into chaps. 2–32 in the time of Josiah.[138] Although the words of Isaiah are not found in this redacted material, they do preserve the central message of the prophet. Clements disagrees with Barth's conclusion that 9:2–7 is part of the "Assyria-redaction." Instead, he assigns it to Isaiah himself.[139] He also finds later redactional work in verses added shortly after the fall of Jerusalem in 586 BC (2:18–19; 5:14–17; 6:12–13; 8:19–22; 17:7–9; 22:4–11; 32:9–14), and in postexilic additions (chaps. 24–27; 34–35 and various scattered verses) that were mostly added in the fifth century (though a few additions were made as late as the second century BC). Clements admits that it is almost impossible to pinpoint how or when various additions were made to the expanding collections of Isaiah's oracles, but he contends that it is possible to suggest a potential plan of growth (starting in the time of the prophet) based on a few reasonable assumptions.[140]

After the publication of his commentary, Clements produced several interesting articles presenting evidence for the redactional process based on the idea that "the great unnamed prophet of 40–55 . . . could have known and made allusions to the earlier prophetic collection now embedded in 1–35."[141] The use of themes like the "blindness" of the people in early (6:9–10; 29:18; 32:3; 35:5) and later chapters (42:7,17; 50:4) or concepts like God's election of Israel, he claimed, demonstrate a thematic unity created by redactors who employed earlier oracles of Isaiah. Others followed up with similar inclusive redactional themes like the "plan of God" or the "destiny of the nations."[142]

In 1977–78, J. Vermeylen produced a redactional study of Isaiah 1–35,[143] which hypothesized that older material in Isaiah was "reread, reinterpreted" (*relecture*) in line with the contemporary situation of these later redactors. He attempted to trace this process through seven stages:

---

[137] R. E. Clements, *Isaiah 1–39,* NCBC (Grand Rapids: Eerdmans, 1980), 2–3; id., "The Prophecies of Isaiah and the Fall of Jerusalem in 587 B.C.," *VT* 30 (1980): 421–36.

[138] The Josianic redaction is seen most clearly in prophecies about the destruction of Assyria in 10:24–27 and in 30:27–33.

[139] Interestingly, Clements accepts this passage as being from Isaiah but does not believe he wrote the similar passage in 11:1–5. Wildberger, *Isaiah 1–12,* 468, dates 11:1–5 to the time of Hezekiah's enthronement.

[140] Clements, *Isaiah 1–39,* 4–5.

[141] R. E. Clements, "The Unity of the Book of Isaiah," *Int* 36 (1982): 117–29.

[142] J. J. M. Roberts, "Isaiah in Old Testament Theology," *Int* 36 (1982): 130–43; G. I. Davies, "The Destiny of the Nations in the Book of Isaiah," in *The Book of Isaiah: Le Livre D'Isaïe* (ed. J. Vermeylen; Leuven: Peeters, 1989), 93–120.

[143] J. Vermeylen, *Du prophète Isaïe l'apocalyptic, Isaïa 1–35,* 2 vols. (Paris: Gabalda, 1977–78).

A. The first stage was connected to Isaiah at the time of the Syro-Ephraim-ite War and dealt with God's judgment of the nation for pride and social injustice. Isaiah's theological purpose was to announce the defeat of the nation if the people would not return to God.

B. The second stage related to changes introduced from the time of Manasseh until the exile and dealt with the theological idea that it was impossible for Sennacherib to destroy Jerusalem. Also added was a later contribution about God's establishment of a strong Davidic line (from the time of Josiah). This material maintained that Jerusalem would have a different fate from the northern nation of Israel.

C. The third through the seventh stages came from exilic (two Deutero-nomic redactions and an eschatological addition by priests) and postex-ilic times (a Torah addition, and one about the conversion of the Gen-tiles). Vermeylen did not limit these successive reinterpretations and reapplications to just a few verses here and there but believed they in-volved a total reorientation of the book's message.

Vermeylen's redactional rereading exerted a powerful influence on later crit-ics. But R. N. Whybray found that many of Vermeylen's criteria (style, vocabu-lary, catch words, linking words, discontinuity, changes in theological ideas, etc.) for assigning verses to one of the seven stages involved quite subjec-tive decisions based on numerous unproven assumptions.[144] The seven stages (some with two parts) strike one as an overly complex process, and the ability of any modern writer to identify the precise verses that should be attributed to these various stages is questionable. For example, there is little that suggests that stage four, the redaction in the fourth-century BC that stressed revenge on the ungodly, could not date to the time of Isaiah or one of Vermeylen's other stages, for there were many ungodly in each period of Israel's history. Much of his logic is suspect, some of his evidence is unconvincing, and many of his results merely present possible (not necessary) ways of understanding portions of Isaiah.

A positive aspect of the redactional approach, however, was the new focus on making theological sense of the purpose for various additions, chapters, and larger sections within the book of Isaiah. The book is no longer viewed as just a random collection of prophetic oracles, but as a work whose structure and con-tent reflect purposeful design by later redactors. Their purpose was to address the theological needs of their audiences on the basis of certain key themes. This implied a certain level of literary unity within the book and served to ex-tend the discussion to include the theological themes that draw the whole book together. M. A. Sweeney claims the "results of such research demonstrate that it is impossible to maintain that Isaiah 1–39 ever constituted a self contained

---

[144] R. N. Whybray, "Book Review: J. Vermeylen, *Du prophète Isaïe l'apocalyptic, Isaïa 1–35*," *JSS* 25 (1980): 108–111.

book."[145] Instead, modern students of Isaiah need to understand how the parts are interconnected into the message of the whole book.

Finally, H. G. M. Williamson's detailed redactional study concluded that "Deutero-Isaiah" (the unknown sixth-century author of Isa 40–55) composed and redacted the first 55 chapters in Isaiah into a unified whole.[146] Williamson attempted to demonstrate this in three ways. First, he sought to show that the style, vocabulary, and theology of Proto-Isaiah (using phrases such as "the holy one of Israel," "high and lifted up," and "blind and deaf") had a direct influence on the writing of Deutero-Isaiah. Second, Deutero-Isaiah considered himself a herald of salvation who was able to open the sealed book (8:1–18; 30:8) and offer a new message of hope. Thus his ministry and writings became connected to and intertwined with Isaiah's work. Third, Deutero-Isaiah reworked or redacted various messages in Proto-Isaiah, usually at the beginning or end of a paragraph or section. Deutero-Isaiah's redactional impact is identified in 2:2–4; 5:25–30; 8:21–22; 11:11–16; chap. 12, etc, but Williamson assigns chaps. 13–14 and 24–27 to later editors after the time of Deutero-Isaiah. Williamson's appraisal of a limited amount of evidence is carefully done, and the evidence supporting his first proposal seems solid. Nevertheless, his second point is hypothetical (the existence, time, ministry, and theology of "Deutero-Isaiah" are shrouded in mystery), and some of the evidence marshaled in his third section could frequently be explained in other ways (many could fit under his first proposal). His work is important because of the care with which he handles the evidence and his ability to interconnect numerous themes that point to some level of unity within the book of Isaiah.

RHETORICAL ARGUMENTATION.   Y. Gitay called for a fresh new approach to prophetic literature because the old critical views were exhausted and have only concluded that the prophets spoke "a short dogmatic oracle of judgment."[147] Instead, Gitay viewed Isaiah as a skilled orator, so he set about "to demonstrate the prophetic art of effective speech"[148] because he believed the "prophet's main task was to persuade" his audience.[149] Following the lead of J. Muilenburg's rhetorical method, Gitay focused on the persuasive characteristics of each message, not just the linguistic markers that tied

---

[145] M. A. Sweeney, "Revaluating Isaiah 1–39 in Recent Critical Research," *CR:BS* 4 (1996): 79–114.

[146] H. G. M. Williamson, *The Book Called Isaiah: Deutero-Isaiah's Role in Composition and Redaction* (Oxford: Clarendon, 1994).

[147] Y. Gitay, *Isaiah and His Audience: The Structure and Meaning of Isaiah 1–12* (Assen: van Gorcum, 1991), viii.

[148] Gitay is critical of the failures of other critical approaches because they ignore the nature of prophetic utterances, which are primarily a persuasive appeal to an audience (Ibid., 2).

[149] Y. Gitay, *Prophecy and Persuasion: A Study of Isaiah 40–48* (Bonn: Linguistica Biblica, 1981), 1, set about to analyze "the ways in which the prophet appealed to his audience in order to persuade them."

paragraphs together into a rhetorical unit.[150] This required him to illustrate how the prophet designed his persuasive strategies to convince his audience to accept his way of thinking. He noted the differences between the frame of reference of the prophet and his audience, and he examined the prophet's use of poetic devices, emotional and rational appeals, and the use of imagination as well as authoritative traditions to aid in the process of persuasion.[151] This analysis led to the discovery of longer unified speeches (rather than many disconnected fragments from different redactors) depicting the prophet's verbal interaction with his audience. For Gitay, persuasive prophetic speeches included both indictments and threats of punishment as well as positive visions of the future world that God has planned for his people, for both are legitimate and powerful ways to persuade people to change their thinking. His study of the prophet's rhetoric delves into invention, arrangement, and style. The first inquires into his mode of appeal—using reason, emotions, or ethics; the second factor looks for the regular arrangement of an introduction, statement of facts, a demonstration of the facts, refutation of opponents, and conclusion. In the third area he investigates the way the prophet says things (style) to catch the audience's attention.

Gitay's method is a positive way of identifying the essential unity of complex speeches, but it threatened those who followed a redactional approach, who have not welcomed his methodology.[152] His tendency to ignore form criticism and his employment of a Greco-Roman system of analysis that did not exist at the time of Isaiah is problematic.[153] But his identification of rational and emotional methods of appealing to people is helpful, and his attempt to put fragments together into a cohesive conversation between people with different theological positions makes sense. His focus on the purpose of persuading people to change their way of thinking is a welcome corrective, but his overuse of classical Greek and Latin rhetorical categories tends to force literary speeches into boxes that were foreign to the Hebrew culture at the time of Isaiah. Much can be gained from his work, if a non-classical approach to rhetorical analysis is used as one important tool to help in the interpretation process. The analysis

---

[150] J. Muilenburg, "Form Criticism and Beyond," *JBL* 88 (1969): 1–18, presents his programmatic approach, while his commentary "Isaiah 40–66" *IB* (Nashville: Abingdon, 1956), 5:381–773 illustrates his methodology.

[151] In his similar work on Isaiah 40–48, Gitay lays out his approach by proposing to use Greco-Roman categories of analysis from the classical rhetoricians, which he finds applicable to Isaiah (Gitay, *Prophecy and Persuasion: A Study of Isaiah 40–48*).

[152] M. A. Sweeney, "Book Review: YEHOSHUA GITAY, *Isaiah and his Audience*," *CBQ* 55 (1993): 542–43, notes that this approach "prevents him from raising questions concerning the possibility of redactional activity in Isaiah 1–12."

[153] Gitay, *Prophecy and Persuasion: A Study of Isaiah 40–48*, 36–41, introduces the classical theory of persuasive discourse that is heavily dependent on Aristotle's approach to the aspects of oral argumentation that will persuade people to change the way they think or act.

of the rhetorical situation and the prophet's use of rhetorical means to persuade his audience should be included in the study of the messages of Isaiah.[154]

A CANONICAL PERSPECTIVE.   B. S. Childs has challenged those who fragment the text by dissecting it into several unrelated sources and numerous redactional additions. He argues that Isaiah should be read based on the canonical form preserved through the ages. Rather than divorcing texts from their literary context and attributing fragmentary verses to different redactors, interpreters should pay attention to the early (and probably more valid) context of passages in the received form preserved in the canon. This suggests that the book of Isaiah represents a carefully thought out literary production (rather than an accidental or arbitrary collection) that has some level of literary unity (he does not argue for authorial unity).

Childs does not limit the formation of the canon to a final stamp of approval by an authoritative religious body of officials. Rather, it "involved a series of decisions deeply affecting the shape of the books. . . . The heart of the canonical process lay in transmitting and ordering the authoritative tradition in a form which was compatible to function as scripture for a generation which had not participated in the original events of revelation."[155] This approach centers on the final canonical form of the text, but Childs recognizes some texts were passed on without much editing, while others were selected or omitted, edited with additional explanations or subtractions, or rearranged. Yet none of these intermediate stages in the development of the text reflect the canonical form; only the final preserved text has canonical authority. While Childs is critical of the atomistic disunification of the text in many modern critical studies, he agrees that occasionally a multi-layered redactional history lies behind a text. He critiques complex theories that claim the ability to reconstruct complex multi-staged redactional processes over several centuries, because the basis for reconstructing is not available and because these studies divert attention from the final, unified canonical form of the text.[156] He does not view Isaiah as a series of eighth-century oracles from the prophet Isaiah that were randomly joined to a group of exilic and postexilic messages just because there happened to be a little more room on the scroll. Instead, he finds a profound editorial intertwining of Isaianic traditions with later traditions throughout the corpus, thus presenting a theological pattern that interconnects past failures and divine judgments with the future promises of divine salvation presented in the second half of the book.[157]

---

[154] In G. V. Smith, *An Introduction to the Hebrew Prophets: The Prophets as Preachers* (Nashville: Broadman and Holman, 1994), a survey of all the prophetic books, I tried to combine sociological and rhetorical studies to examine prophetic attempts to persuade their audiences.

[155] Childs, *Introduction to the Old Testament as Scripture*, 58–60, finds evidence of this canonical process in Isa 8:16–18. Isaiah's words were recognized as authoritative by people who lived outside the original historical situation.

[156] Childs, *Isaiah*, 2–4.

[157] Childs, *Introduction to the Old Testament as Scripture*, 330–32.

Childs has infused new energy to the task of developing a more theological (and less historical) study of the final form of the book of Isaiah, but redactional critics have not warmly welcomed his downplaying of their efforts. The difficulty of a canonical approach is that an attempt to define the canonical process is often just as subjective as attempts to identify the redactional process, for the text of Isaiah seldom has anything to say that might hint at the various stages in the canonical process.

(3) Signs of Compositional Design and Structure in 1–39

The book of Isaiah contains little information expressly addressing the issue of its composition. Consequently, issues of composition and structure must be largely implied from hints that are imbedded in the text. For example, most conclude that the introductory superscriptions in 1:1; 2:1; and 13:1 serve to introduce the author of the series of messages included in that literary unit. If the author wrote the book of Isaiah all at one time, there would be no need for additional superscriptions after 1:1. Such superscriptions introduce independent literary segments that were combined at some later date to form the larger book of Isaiah. That these superscriptions remain suggests that the existing literary documents probably had an independent history and had reached a stable form before they were included in the larger book of Isaiah. Thus the composition of the book of Isaiah involved (a) the recording of Isaiah's messages, (b) the collection of these messages into smaller literary units, and (c) the collection of these written units into what is now called the book of Isaiah.

At the beginning of each major section of the book, the commentary discusses the rationale for identifying a group of chapters as a structural unit, so the introductory comments here will merely summarize some of the major points in those discussions. Since the text of Isaiah never mentions the person who actually wrote down these words, edited the messages of Isaiah, or put them into the final form preserved in the present text, every student of Isaiah must make numerous assumptions about who was involved in this process. Since Isaiah was alive throughout the historical period covered in chaps. 1–39 and was a writer (2 Chr 26:22; 32:32), this commentary will assume that he was involved in the process of preserving his messages (especially the earlier ones), though it is impossible to know exactly which messages he penned or to identify what other individuals might have assisted him in this process. The focus of attention in this discussion, therefore, will not be on who composed these messages, but on the results of this editorial process.

A second problematic issue is the attempt to date the compositional activity of writing down and editing Isaiah's messages. Although one can suggest a specific message was spoken within a general timeframe (chaps. 2–5 during the later part of Uzziah's era), it is usually impossible to identify a specific date when any message was put into a written form, or when that message was combined with the prophet's other messages preserved in present literary units. This absence of datable markers makes any historical reconstruction of the editing process of limited value. One cannot assume (as some do) that all future or eschatological information came from a late period, for God repeatedly told his people about what the future held long before the time of the prophet Isaiah (Gen 12:1–3; 17:1–8; 49:1–27; Ex 3:6–22; Lev 26; Num 23–24; Deut 32:1–43; 33:1–29; 2 Sam 7:10–16). One cannot automatically pinpoint every reference to exile as a reference to the final exile of Judah in 586 BC, for the Northern tribes of Israel were exiled early in the ministry of Isaiah, and many people from Judah were taken into exile during Sennacherib's conquest (he claims he exiled 200,150 people). Although it is often possible to give a general date for the oral presentation of some messages in Isaiah (7:1–10 dates to 734–33 BC), the editing of the message would clearly be later. Emphasis is placed here on defining the literary units in 1–39, understanding the editorial plan or organization of these smaller literary units, and identifying how the parts fit together to support the overall purpose of the book.

THE STRUCTURE OF THE LITERARY UNITS. One must identify the literary units within chaps. 1–39 based on external signs (the superscription or concluding markers) and internal structural markers, then look for signs of editorial activity. The superscriptions in 1:1, 2:1, and 13:1 give objective evidence to support the claim that the final canonical form was made up of at least three smaller books, though many would find additional literary units within chaps. 13–39.

(a) 1:1–26 has all the signs of being an introduction to the book of Isaiah. It begins with a superscription and refers to the people being in rebellion against God, the desolation of the land, and Jerusalem as the sole surviving city (1:1–10). This message that the prophet spoke must be dated after 701 BC, not at the beginning of Isaiah's ministry in the time of Uzziah and Jotham (chaps. 2–5). Many themes and words are connected to similar concepts in chaps. 65–66, with both literary units closing with the thought that the wicked will burn in fire (1:26; 66:24).[158] Thus one would assume that this chapter was added late in the compositional process.

The structure of chap. 1 is clearly demarcated by the repetition of key phrases. The first section of this sermon addressed to the people and rulers is marked by the introductory "for the LORD has spoken" in 1:2, and the concluding, "for the mouth of the LORD has spoken" in 2:20. Within the first section are three smaller paragraphs clearly marked by an imperative exhortation to "hear" (1:2–9 and 1:10–17), and the imperative exhortation to "come" (1:18–20).

The text is an inclusive message that moves from past sins and divine discipline (1:2–9) to a future prediction of God's final plan to destroy his foes and restore his righteous people (1:25–26). The literary genres of a judgment

---

[158] The linguistic signs of the connection between chaps. 1 and 65–66 are described in more detail in the introductory comments on chap. 1 (see "Structure").

speech, a call to repent, and eschatological predictions all function together to challenge the audience to accept God's plan and conform their lives to his will. It is logical to assume that this chapter did not go through a long composition process if it was one of the last pieces added to the final form of the book.

(b) 2:1–12:6 is a much more complex literary unit that begins with a new superscription (2:1) and ends with a hymn (12:1–6). These introductory and concluding markers suggest that this was a self-contained unit. It records some spoken messages from the time of Uzziah and Ahaz, so it was probably put in writing shortly after 732 BC.

The structure of chaps. 2–12 is complex, but certain editorial patterns are discernable in the organization of these messages. Isaiah 2:1–4:6 is a tightly unified literary composition that begins and ends with a short description of God's future kingdom (2:1–5; 4:2–6),[159] with two long condemnations of human sinfulness and pride in between (2:6–4:1). These sermons refer to conditions in the time of Uzziah and create a logical point and counterpoint.

A 2:1–5 God's kingdom will be established
B 2:6–22 Condemnation of pride
B′ 3:1–4:1 Condemnation of pride
A′ 4:2–6 God's kingdom will be established

In a somewhat similar manner, Isaiah 9:1–11:16 begins and ends with a description of God's future messianic kingdom (9:1–7 and 11:1–16), sandwiching two condemnations of human sinfulness and pride in between (9:8–10:4 and 10:5–34). These messages seem to derive from the time of Ahaz.

A 9:1–7 The Reign of a Righteous King
B 9:8–10:4 Condemnation of the pride of Israel
B′ 10:5–33 Condemnation of the pride of Assyria
A′ 11:1–16 The Reign of a Righteous King

The remaining chapters (5:1–30; 7:1–8:18) describe how the sinfulness of the nation will result in a military attack on Jerusalem. Isaiah's pivotal new commissioning (6:1–13) was strategically placed between these events to explain that the nation's defeat could be attributed to their stubborn unwillingness to listen to God's words through Isaiah.[160]

---

[159] Sweeney, *Isaiah 1–39*, 89–90 or his *Isaiah 1–4*, 134–84, discusses the structure of these chapters. R. H. O'Connell, *Concentricity and Continuity: The Literary Structure of Isaiah* (Sheffield: Academic Press, 1994), 57–107, defines a more complex structure for chaps. 2–12. He has similar divisions of the text to those in this commentary (except he puts 2:1–5 with chap. 1), but he relates them to one another in quite different ways.

[160] A. H. Bartelt, *The Book around Immanuel: Style and Structure in Isaiah 2–12* (Winona Lake: Eisenbrauns, 1996), 18–20, briefly summarizes the present state of research on these chapters, then in the rest of the book he gives his analysis of the structure of 2–12. His results differ at numerous points from the analysis in this study.

Signs of an editor's touch are evident in the arrangement of these messages, but it is hard to identify his hand within them. A careful examination of the woe oracles in 5:8–25 reveals that it includes ideas about the holiness of God from 6:3 (introduced into 5:17,24) and repeats the theme of the humbling the proud from 2:12,17 (introduced into 5:16). These two themes seem foreign to the woe oracles in 5:8–25 and were probably inserted within this oracle in the editing process to help connect this woe oracle with the overall theological themes of chaps. 2–6. In addition, the narrative transitional statements in 9:1 appear to introduce the poetic messianic oracle in 9:2–7. Another example of editorial involvement at the written stage might be identified in the unique narrative insertion in 11:10–12. This conclusion is suggested because 11:10–12 are prose and not poetry like the rest of the chapter. Also, the introductory "in that day" clauses are not found elsewhere in the chapter; and finally, 11:10 repeats much of 11:1,12, while 11:11 summarizes 11:12,16.

Although some might hypothesize that the eschatological promises are later editorial additions, there is nothing in the text that is incompatible with an eschatological perspective. Thus, these oracles should remain as a fundamental part of the structure of this unit.[161] Although the final hymn in chap. 12 fits the earlier themes of trusting God, it is not part of any other prophetic message in chaps. 2–11 and appears to be a fitting editorial conclusion added when this unit attained written form.

(c) 13:1–23:18 concerns mainly God's condemnation of various nations. It is not clear where this unit ends (some extend it through chap. 28 and others include all of 13–39), but the lack of additional superscriptions suggests that all of chaps. 13–39 were edited together at one time, sometime after Sennacherib's attack on Jerusalem in 701 BC. One can assume that these messages were not pronounced in this order but were thematically collected to emphasize the similar ways God will deal with the nations. The common introductory title *maśśāʾ*, "utterance, burden," also marks these oracles as a group. There is little structural information to determine the criteria used to organize these chapters (they are not in a chronological order). J. A. Motyer proposed that these messages were ordered in two panels of five oracles, both beginning with statements about Babylon (13:1–14:27 and 21:1–10). The first discusses the political downfall and the second the religious demise of Babylon.

13:1–14:27	Babylon	21:1–10	Babylon
14:28–32	Philistia	22:11–12	Edom
15:1–16:14	Moab	22:13–17	Arabia
17:1–18:7	Damascus/Israel	22:1–25	Jerusalem
19:1–20:6	Egypt	23: 1–18	Tyre[162]

---

[161] Another example might be the narrative addition in 10:12.

[162] J. A. Motyer, *The Prophecy of Isaiah* (Leicester: InterVarsity, 1993), 131–32, thinks that this order puts an emphasis on Babylon.

In each series the third oracle refers to refugees looking for help (Moab in 16:1,6–7 and Arabia in 21:13–17), the fourth oracle in both groups refers to Hebrew people not trusting in God for their deliverance (17:8,10; 22:8,12–14), and the final oracles conclude with people from Egypt (to the south) and Tyre (to the north) turning to God (19:19–25; 23:18).

Someone collected these topical messages and organized them, but there are also signs of editorial work within a few of them. For example, it appears that the editor introduced this series of oracles with a general message about the eschatological Day of the Lord in 13:2–16, including a positive message of hope in the middle of the Babylon oracles (14:1–2), and added an introduction (14:3–4a) and conclusion (14:22–23) to the lament about the king of Babylon. One can assume the editor added the introductory statement in 14:28 that dates the Philistine oracle, and appended a later word from the Lord at the end of these two oracles, in 16:13–14 and 21:16–17. The oracle against Judah appears to have a later word from God appended as a conclusion to the paragraphs ending in 22:14 and 22:25. It is impossible to date any of these short additional explanations, but the prophet may have added these clarifications when these prophecies were put down in writing. There is no reason to question their authority, for several of these additions reinforce the claim that they are the words of God (14:22–23; 16:13–14; 21:16–17; 22:14,25).

(d) 24:1–27:13 has a difficult structural makeup, placing past, present, and future events side by side. In addition, the content of chaps. 24–27 includes several genres that do not naturally flow together. There is an announcement of judgment (24:1–6), hymns of praise (25:1–5; 26:1–6), a symbolic song of the vineyard (27:2–6), and a lament (26:7–27:1). It is not easy to discover how to understand these diverse perspectives as a conceptual whole. The interpretation of the themes, genres, and verb forms in the commentary below suggests that chaps. 24–25 refer to an eschatological era, except for the brief parenthetical editorial insertion of the prophet's lamenting response in 24:16b–18a. Chapters 26–27 make up a separate section within chaps. 24–27 and deal with the nation's present oppressive situation caused by Sennacherib's invasion of Judah just before 701 BC.

Chapters 24–27 are thematically connected to the messages against the foreign nations in chaps. 13–23 (especially 13:1–16), to the eschatological ideas in 2:1–5, and to the praise of God in 12:1–6. Specific theological ideas may be recalled from earlier texts: (a) the positive "song of the vineyard" in 27:2–6, which reverses the negative vineyard song in 5:1–7; (b) the establishment of God's kingdom in 2:6–21 involving the humbling of the proud (cf.25:11–13; 26:5) and the Lord reigning in Zion (cf.2:1–5; 24:23b); (c) the imagery of destruction in chaps. 24–27 closely connected to images of God's judgment of the individual nations in chaps. 13–23, and particularly some of the phrases in the eschatological introduction in 13:1–16;[163] (d) both 13:1–16 and 24:1–23 describing the destruction and desolation of the earth (13:5,9 and 24:1,3,); (e) people being in pain like a woman in labor (13:8 and 26:17–18); (f) God's coming to the earth in power (13:9 and 24:23) (g) the sun and moon being darkened (13:10 and 24:23) and the earth shaking (13:13 and 24:18–20); (h) the proud being humbled (13:11 and 25:11–12; 26:5); (i) and few people left on earth (13:12 and 24:24:6) because the people are sinful (13:11 and 24:5–6). Chaps. 24–27 are not really a summary but rather a grand finale for chaps. 13–23. This repetition of ideas unfolds a high level of theological continuity with these earlier prophecies.[164]

(e) 28:1–35:10 displays a fair bit of editorial shaping. The unity of chaps. 28–33 is signaled by a series of "woe oracles" in the first part of this section (28:1; 29:1,15; 30:1; 31:1; 33:1). The first six chapters are divided into two groups of woe oracles based on their content and structure. Each group of chapters (28–29; 30–33)[165] has three woe oracles.[166] The first group of woes (chaps. 28–29) reveals the principles underlying God's action against Judah and on behalf of Judah. The primary problem was blind political and religious leaders who made bad decisions (28:7,14). The second group of three woes (30–33)[167] explains how these principles practically apply to the political conflicts involving Judah, Egypt, and Assyria around 704–701 BC. Each of these woe oracles is shaped in a similar manner. They each have a salvation oracle right after a brief woe oracle.

1. A short salvation oracle—28:5–6; after a short woe in 28:1–4
2. A short salvation oracle—29:5–8; after a short woe in 29:1–4
3. A long salvation oracle—29:17–24; after a short woe in 29:15–16
4. A long salvation oracle—30:18–26; after a long woe in 30:1–17
5. A short salvation oracle—31:6–9; after a short woe in 31:1–5

---

[163] For additional examples, see Sweeney, *Isaiah 1–39*, 319 and D. C. Polaski, *Authorizing an End: The Isaiah Apocalypse & Intertextuality* (Leiden: Brill, 2001), 66–70; and J. Day, "A Case of Inner Scriptural Interpretation: The Dependence of Isaiah XXVI.13–XXVII.11 on Hosea XII.4–XIV.10 (Eng. 9) and Its Relevance to Some Theories for the Redaction of the 'Isaiah Apocalypse,'" *JTS* 32 (1980): 309–319.

[164] M. A. Sweeney, "Textual Citations in Isaiah 24–27," *JBL* 107 (1988): 39–52, refers to many of these as quotations, and he believes they demonstrate that the author did not write chaps. 24–27 in isolation from the rest of the book; thus, they argue for the unity of this part of the book of Isaiah.

[165] Motyer, *The Prophecy of Isaiah*, 227, also divides the woe oracles into two groups (28–29; 30–33) with three woes in each group.

[166] Oswalt, *Isaiah 1–39*, 504–505, structures the chapters into four groupings: (a) chaps. 29–30 concern the false counsel of human leaders about Judah's enemies; (b) chaps. 30–31 contain a condemnation of their desire to depend on Egypt, which is folly; (c) chaps. 32–33 give the true solution of depending on God; and (d) chaps. 34–35 contrast a desert (due to God's judgment) and paradise (due to God's blessing).

[167] W. A. M. Beuken, *Isaiah II, Volume 2: Isaiah Chapters 28–39*, HCOT (Leuvan: Peeters, 2000), 3–5, puts only the first five woes in a structural unit (28:1–31:9; 32:9–14), relegating the rest of chaps. 32–33 to a redactional expansion.

6. A long salvation oracle—33:5–24; after a short woe in 33:1 and prayer 33:2–4

By placing these two emphases together (woe and salvation) the prophet was able to show how the way of death in the lament dramatically contrasts with the alternative way of salvation that God can provide. There appear to be only a few examples where the prophet added parenthetical remarks of illustration or application when he edited these messages into their final form (ie. 29:11–12; 31:6–7).

Since the last two chapters (34–35) do not have "woe" introductions and do not explicitly discuss the Assyrian crisis, they are not as closely connected to the material in chaps. 28–33.[168] W. Brownlee suggested that chaps. 34–35 actually begin the second half of the book of Isaiah; therefore, they are not part of 28–33.[169] Instead, it seems better to interpret chaps. 34–35 as the conclusion to chaps. 28–33 or possibly the conclusion to chaps. 13–33. This is because there seems to be a literary relationship between chaps. 34 and 13. The universalistic tone in 13:1–16 and chaps. 34–35 causes these chapters to be something of an eschatological[170] introduction and conclusion to 13–35.[171] Apparently, an intentional theological plan behind the placement of these messages at the start and end of this collection. There is at least one later addition to these prophecies in 34:16–17, which refers to an earlier written "scroll of the Lord" (probably Isaiah's earlier written prophecies) that is supplemented by additional words of assurance promising the reader that God's earlier announcements will surely come to pass.

(f) 36:1–39:8 contain a narrative report of three important events in the life of Hezekiah. Either the editor of Isaiah or his source (2 Kgs 18–19 or another independent account) purposely chose to arrange these events out of chronological order, since Hezekiah's illness recounted in chaps. 38–39 actually occurred before Sennacherib's invasion in chaps. 36–37 (see 38:6). P. R. Ackroyd

---

[168] Hayes and Irvine, *Isaiah*, 13, surprisingly omit chaps. 34–35 in their commentary on Isaiah 1–39, since they do not believe Isaiah wrote these chapters.

[169] W. Brownlee, *The Meaning of the Qumran Scrolls for the Bible* (New York: Oxford University Press, 1964), 247–59, found parallel development of topics in chaps. 1–33 and 34–66, and a structural parallel to the division of Ezekiel. He believes this division of the book was signaled by the scribes leaving a space between chaps. 33 and 34 in the Qumran Isaiah scrolls. J. D. W. Watts, *Isaiah 34–66*, WBC (Waco: Word, 1987), 1–2 and Sweeney, *Isaiah 1–39*, 435 also begins the second half of the book of Isaiah at chap. 34.

[170] Delitzsch, "Isaiah," *Commentary on the Old Testament*, 66, calls chaps. 34–35 apocalyptic which give a perfect ideal of the future.

[171] Williamson, *The Book Called Isaiah*, 216–17, agrees with J. Vermeylen who found a similar structure and numerous verbal connections. Structural similarities include:

preparation for war	13:2–4	34:1
killing of the nations	13:5–9,14–16	34:2–3
cosmic upheaval	13:10–13	34:4–5a
capture of the city	13:17–19	34:5b–8
land becomes a desert	13:20	34:9–10
wild animals live there	13:21–22	34:11–15

pointed to thematic factors that partially explain why an author might want to present the material in this inverted order.[172] It made sense to place chap. 39 out of order so that the reference to the exiles going far away to Babylon in 39:6–7 could serve as a bridge to chaps. 40–55 where that is the setting. Putting chap. 39 last would assist the reader in connecting the story before chap. 39 with what follows. In addition, the present order explains how God miraculously saved both the city of Jerusalem and Hezekiah (due to his piety) and why both were granted further years of life before the future exilic period. Thus the narrative contributes to a certain idealization of Hezekiah's life and accomplishments, plus it fosters the development of a "Zion theology" that claimed it was impossible to defeat the city of Jerusalem because God dwelt there.

A primary problem with this interpretation of the editor's motivations is that there is no mention of Babylon in chaps. 40–42, so how could the reference to Babylon in chap. 39 be a link to these chapters? Sweeney objects to this hypothesis since "ch 39 contains no reference to the destruction of Jerusalem and the temple in 587 and therefore cannot be understood in relation to the later period of Babylonian exile that ch. 40–55 presuppose."[173] When H. G. M. Williamson[174] analyzed connections between chaps. 36–39 and 1–35, as well as connections between chaps. 36–39 and 40–55, he noted that there were very few themes connecting 36–39 with 40–55, but many themes linking 36–39 with 1–35.

One might suggest that the inverted order demonstrates God's amazing grace in deliverance, for God delivered a city from the grip of a stronger Assyrian army (chaps. 36–37), delivered a king who had earlier put his trust in other nations and failed to trust God (chaps. 30–31), delivered a king from certain death (chap. 38), and delivered a king who acted in distrust (39:1–4). The amazing thing is that most of this failure to trust God happened after God promised to defeat the Assyrians and performed a miraculous sign to assure the king of the truthfulness of his promises (38:5–7). God's miraculous killing of

---

[172] Ackroyd, "Isaiah 36–39: Structure and Function," and "An Interpretation of the Babylonian Exile: A Study of II Kings 20, Isaiah 38–39," in *Studies in the Religious Traditions of the Old Testament* (London: SCM, 1987), 105–20, 152–71, finds that Hezekiah's judgment and recovery "become a type of judgment in exile . . . a pointer to the possibility of such a restoration for the community." He follows hints by R. F. Melugin, *Formation of Isaiah 40–55*, BZAW 41 (Berlin: de Gruyter, 1976), 176–8 who claims that the "closest thing to a setting for chs. 40ff. is the prophecy of Isaiah to Hezekiah in ch 39 concerning the exile to Babylon."

[173] Sweeney, *Isaiah 1–39*, 480.

[174] Williamson, *The Book Called Isaiah*, 194–197 finds positive evidence of a relationship between chaps. 36–39 and 1–35 based on the work of E. W. Conrad, *Reading Isaiah* (Minneapolis: Fortress, 1991), 38–46, who postulates six connections with chap. 7 and 36–39, and the study of J. W. Groves, *Actualization and Interpretation in the Old Testament* (Atlanta: Scholar's Press, 1987). Williamson's analysis of Groves' list (pp. 198–99) of connections between chaps. 36–39 and 40–55 shows that he has found little evidence, and the evidence he cites is of questionable value, for several could just as well be connected to similar themes in Isa 1–35 instead of 40–55 (for example the condemnation of idols in 37:16–20 could just as easily be related to 2:8,20 as the polemic against idols in 44:9–20).

185,000 Assyrian troops is astonishing (37:36), but that God did this for one who had been so faithless, in spite of being richly blessed with a fifteen year extension of his life (38:5–7), is shocking.

Another reason for placing the incident with Sennacherib before the account of Hezekiah's illness may be to contrast king Sennacherib, who goes home in defeat and is killed (37:38), with king Hezekiah who almost dies, but then is delivered by God in chap. 38.[175] A second close connection between these chapters is the announcement of the defeat of the Assyrians in 37:33–37 and 38:6, which proves that God has the power to accomplish the things he plans. Third, there is a sign both in 37:30–35 and in 38:7,22 to verify God's promise to Hezekiah. Fourth, the Assyrian crisis is resolved when king Hezekiah goes to God in prayer (37:14–20) and God gives an answer of hope through his prophet Isaiah (37:22–35). In a similar manner, Hezekiah's health crisis is resolved when he prays again (38:2) and God again sends hope through Isaiah (38:4–8). Fifth, the present order allows the later chapters to modify the temptation to idealize the piety of Hezekiah based on his faith in 37:14–20,[176] by showing that he was fallible, sometimes self-centered, and in need of signs to help him trust in what God said (chap. 38).

Modern students of the book of Isaiah will never be able to identify who edited each of these 39 chapters, how the editor went about this task, and what motivated the editor to present the text in its current form, but it is evident that the work was carefully planned. Since Isaiah spoke at least many of these words, he would have a natural desire and something of a responsibility (cf. 8:16; 30:8) to see that God's words through him were accurately conveyed to future readers. Just as it would be very difficult, if not impossible, to distinguish the editorial activity in the second draft of this commentary from the first draft of this book, so it would be very difficult to give any details about the process of editing the book of Isaiah.

PURPOSE.   The prophecies within the book of Isaiah address the spiritual, social, economic, political, and personal needs of people in Judah and Jerusalem. His messages call for a consideration of Israel's current circumstances— why the nation was in trouble—and for the leaders of Judah to stop trusting in themselves or other nations. The oracles often take the rhetorical shape of pointing out the problem and warning of forthcoming dire consequences. The prophet usually suggests a possible alternative action and describes an alternative world that the audience could enjoy if they make the right choices and trust God. Isaiah believed that the present ideology that dominated Judah was misguided on issues of social justice (3:12–15), how to deal with the threat of war (7:1–12; 30:1–5), and how to please God with their worship (1:10–18). His method aimed to unmask the hopelessness of the people and the leader's false

---

[175] Blenkinsopp, *Isaiah 1–39*, 484 noticed this important connection between these chapters.

[176] It appears that Sweeney, *Isaiah 1–39*, 455–504, also idealizes the piety of Hezekiah, the exact point that chaps. 38–39 were attempting to undermine.

perception of reality (39:1–5; 31:1–3). They were all too often blind and stubborn (6:9–10; 29:9–10), needing God to open their eyes (32:3–4; 25:5).

The prophet sought to persuade his audience to transform their minds and change their behavior changed; but he also sought to harden the hearts of some unbelievers (6:9–11). The prophet's message also served political purposes when he was attempting to persuade a king or his political advisors that God had a better plan than the inappropriate political policies they were pursuing (chaps. 7–8; 28–31; 36–39). Some oracles, such as the messages of hope in 2:1–4 and 4:2–6, were designed to lift the spirits and remind God's people of his great plan to bless them and all the nations of the earth. Knowing the future can give a reason to live today in preparation to enjoy God's future kingdom and not suffer the fate of the wicked. The purpose of many of the oracles against foreign nations in chaps. 13–23 was to convince the Hebrews not to act like these nations and not to depend on or make alliances with those whom God would soon defeat. They must remove arrogance, trust God for their future, and live with the assurance that their divine, holy King will one day establish his kingdom, send forth the messianic King, and create a time of peace among his holy people.

6. Theology of Isaiah 1–39

Several factors present problems to the task of formulating a succinct theology for this book. On the one hand, the theology of any one oracle is limited to the problems addressed in that historical setting. Thus the divine revelation the prophet received about a particular situation specifically applies to the people at that time and its theological emphasis may differ from that of another chapter which arises out of a different set of circumstances. This problem could be somewhat minimized by limiting the discussion of the theological emphasis of Isaiah's message to each historical era such as the days of Uzziah (chaps. 2–5) or the period of Ahaz (chaps. 6–11). At the end of such an effort, one might discuss the development of Isaiah's theological message over the various periods of his ministry. On the other hand, it appears that chaps. 2–12 and 12–23 are literary units, so one should be able to speak of the theology of each literary unit, even if they cover two historical periods. Hypothetically, an overview which integrates the different themes within each literary unit should be able to draw together the main themes and emphases throughout these messages, ending up with a theology of the whole book.

A second difficulty relates to issues of authorship, redaction, and the date of this redactional activity. If one holds that all eschatological messages of hope were later redactional additions to the book of Isaiah, one has to face the issue that the prophet's theology was quite different from what is presented in the final form of the book. Consequently, one must decide what passages belonged to Isaiah as well as whether to deal with the theology of the prophet or the theology of the present canonical book. Those who emphasize the editorial compilation of the book over several centuries usually attempt to distinguish between various theological layers (e.g., the Josianic redaction and its theological purpose), while a more canonical approach will pay more attention to the final form of the completed manuscript. Since redactional layers and their theological purposes are elusive, that approach is based on many more subjective decisions (what texts are in a redactional level and which are not). Sometimes a theological purpose is read into the Isaiah texts from an external source (Josiah's reform in 2 Kgs 22–23). Therefore, a more canonical approach will eliminate some unnecessary assumptions and allow for a more holistic approach, making it possible to speak of the theology of the book of Isaiah.

A third tension involves the process of integrating and reducing a hundred different specific theological comments into a few broad central statements that constitute the core from which the specific messages derive their foundation. One can simply choose to abandon any pursuit of a unifying core and comment on the prophet's view of the standard systematic topics of God, man, sin, judgment, and redemption.[177] Or, in order to avoid harmonization and the charge of reductionism, one may address one of theological themes that run through many of the prophetic messages (e.g., blindness)[178] and make no attempt to construct the theology of the book. In spite of the dangers involved with a holistic approach, a more focused articulation of the theological core is worthwhile to understand both the foundation of the prophet's thinking and the central thrust of his ministry. The repeated interlinking of ideas from earlier messages within the framework of later oracles argues for a theological interdependence and a broad consistency of core convictions that do not dramatically change from oracle to oracle.[179] As J. J. M. Roberts maintains, "It should be possible, therefore, to delineate the central core of Isaianic theology, while not ignoring the different accents placed on that core in the different stages of the book."[180]

(1) Finding some Unity within the Diversity

Within the commentary itself are many discussions of the primary theological issues addressed in each message. There one will see the contrast between Isaiah's distinctive theological approach and the theology of his audience. There also are found illustrations of the diverse issues Isaiah deals with, largely unencumbered by attempts to interrelate those issues to the broader perspective

---

[177] Oswalt, *Isaiah 1–39*, 31–41, takes this option, but he also seems to find "servanthood" as a broad unifying theme throughout Isaiah's messages.

[178] R. E. Clements, "The Unity of the Book of Isaiah,' *Int* 36 (1982): 117–29.

[179] C. R. Seitz, "Isaiah 1–66: Making Sense of the Whole," in *Reading and Preaching the Book of Isaiah* (Philadelphia: Fortress, 1988), 105–26; R. J. Marshall. "The Unity of Isaiah 1–12," *LQ* 14 (1962): 21–38; M. A. Sweeney, "Toward and Understanding of the Redactional Function of Chapters 24–27 in the Book of Isaiah," *JBL* 107 (1988): 39–52.

[180] J. J. M. Roberts, "Isaiah in Old Testament Theology." *Int* 36 (1982): 131, finds many inner consistencies within the theology of Isaiah.

of Isaiah's theology. The present issue is to trace the interrelationships between ideas and to define some aspects that draw these ideas together to form a broad unified theology. The book gives frequent attention to the same broad theological perspective again and again.

A comparative analysis of Isaiah's individual messages indicates that they deal primarily with two groups of people: the Hebrew people of Judah (and sometimes Israel) and the people in other nations.[181] While chap. 1 addresses the judgment of the people in Jerusalem, 2:2–4 refers to the salvation of people from all the nations of the world. Isaiah brings words of hope to Judah and Ahaz in 7:3–10, but also news about God's plans to destroy the nations of Syria and Samaria in 7:4–9. Judah's pride is condemned in 2:6–22, an accusation of pride is lodged against Samaria in 9:9, and Assyria's pride is addressed in 10:5–15 and 37:22–29. The remnant of Judah is promised God's compassion (14:1–2), but this prophecy offers hope to the nations as well, for people from many nations will join God's people so that they too can enjoy God's compassion. The oracles against the nations announce God's judgment of Babylon, Moab, Tyre, Assyria, Philistia, Egypt and others, in addition to God's judgment of Judah (chaps. 13–23). Judah is condemned for its dependence on foreign nations like Egypt and Babylon (chaps. 30–31; 39), but God's judgment will extend to the helping nation (Egypt) as well the one helped (31:3). This consistent pattern indicates that Isaiah's theology is one that addresses God's relationship with all the nations of the earth.[182]

A second unifying trend is that God interacts with Judah and the nations of the earth in two broad ways and in two spheres of history. God seems to be as much concerned with judging Judah (chaps. 1; 3; 5–8; 10:1–4; 17; 22; 29–31; 39) as the nations (chaps. 6; 10:5–34; 13–16; 18–21; 22–23; 34; 37). However, his acts of salvation, which are available to the people of Judah and the nations, promise hope in the near future (7:3–10; 8:11–14; 27:8–27:5; 29:17–24; 31:8–9; 33:10–24; 37:6–7,21–35; 38:4–5), as well as in the future eschatological era (4:2–5; 4:2–6; 9:1–7; 11:1–16; 14:1–2; 19:18–25; 24:14–16a; 25:1–8; 30:18–26; 32:1–8,14–20; 35). These consistent patterns indicate that God's interaction with mankind encompasses all their history and all aspects (positive and negative) of their history.

In fact, God's interaction with his created world extends beyond the history of his relationships with people on the earth. As part of his eschatological plans, God intends to destroy the earth itself (24:1–6,19–20) and the heavenly powers beyond the earth (24:21–22). Then he will establish a new heaven and

---

[181] G. I. Davies, "The Destiny of the Nations in the Book of Isaiah," in *The Book of Isaiah: Le Livre D'Isaïe* (ed. J. Vermeylen; Leuven: Peeters, 1989), 93–120, looks at the importance of the nations throughout the book of Isaiah.

[182] W. J. Dumbrell, "The Purpose of the Book of Isaiah." *TB* 36 (1985): 111–28, takes a narrow approach in suggesting that the "overmastering theme" is "Yahweh's interest in and devotion to the city of Jerusalem" (p. 112).

a new earth (65:17; 66:22) and sit as king over his kingdom (2:2–4; 6:5; 24:23). These diverse factors all have God playing a pivotal role in determining what happens; thus it would be fair to say that God is at the center of all of Isaiah's theology. God's various expressions of his interrelationships (negative or positive) with people on the earth describe his methods (saving, blessing, destroying) of dealing with people. God's sovereign interaction extends to all people, for all time, and to all parts of the earth. An extremely succinct yet broad summary of all of Isaiah's theological messages would be the simple three-word statement: God controls everything. The problem with this statement is that it is too broad and too general (it might fit the theology of many books of the Old Testament); thus, it lacks the special flavor or thrust that makes Isaiah's theology unique.

(2) Trust the Holy One who Rules all the World

Isaiah's formulation of his theological message is somewhat different from what may be found in the prophetic messages of Jeremiah and Ezekiel, the wisdom texts of Job or Ecclesiastes, and the historical accounts in Joshua and Judges. The written messages in the book of Isaiah put a special flavor on the meaning of the three words: God controls everything. His unique manner of expressing God's activity is based on the historical circumstance of that day, the needs of the prophet's audience, the prophet's identity, and what God chose to say to the prophet. A brief survey of some of Isaiah's themes will give a taste of the richness and the power of his unique presentation of his core concept.

THE HOLY ONE.   The God who sovereignly controls everything is presented as the "Holy One." Although the word *qôdeš* means "to set apart," when this term is used of God it has a unique force. W. Eichrodt defines God's holiness as "a marvelous power, removed from common life . . . unapproachable because of his complete 'otherness' and perfection.[183] J. J. M. Roberts maintains that "if there is any one concept central to the whole book of Isaiah, it is the vision of Yahweh as the Holy One of Israel."[184] The impact of this distinctive image of God is evident in four ways in Isaiah's messages:

(a) Isaiah saw the splendor of the "Holy One" when he was recommissioned to serve God in a new way in 6:1–13, and this changed his life and transformed his thinking about God. The Bible refers to several people "seeing" manifestations of God that reveal various levels of his glory (Gen 16:9–13; 28:13–15; Exod 24:9–11; 34:5–10; 1 Kgs 22:19). Yet God is in reality an invisible Spirit of untold glory and majesty, so it is impossible for the human eye to behold the full manifestation of the essence of his divinity. This was a manifestation that

---

[183] W. Eichrodt, *Theology of the Old Testament* (trans. J. A. Baker; Philadelphia: Westminster, 1961), 1:271–73.

[184] J. J. M. Roberts, "Isaiah in Old Testament Theology." *Int* 36 (1982): 131, believes this emphasis derived from the prophet's vision of God in chap. 6. He notes that the adjective "holy" is used of God 17 times in chaps. 1–39 and 13 times in chaps. 40–55.

was adapted to finite mental comprehension and human observation, probably in a vision. This experience had a revolutionary impact on the prophet's understanding of God and his own role, for he had not just heard about the glory of God—he actually saw a veiled manifestation of his holiness.

Although Isaiah records only the trifold "holy, holy, holy,"[185] there is every reason to assume that the seraphs provided a continuous offering of praise that did not stop with just three declarations of God's holiness. They proclaim that God is completely, totally, absolutely, the holiest of the holy. Holiness is the essence of God's nature, and God himself is the supreme revelation of holiness. God's absolute holiness reveals how separate, different, or totally other he is in comparison to the created world. Although the word "holy" does not mean sinless,[186] God's holiness means that he is separate from everything that is sinful, utterly removed from the profane world, and glorious in majesty.[187] H. Wildberger conceives of this holiness as a "dynamic reality, not a static 'quality,'"[188] because holiness is revealed in God's actions and his will. It might be better to say that holiness is part of the inner distinctiveness of God's essence that is revealed in all his activity and that his "glory" *(kābôd)* is the outward manifestation of the brightness of his majesty and holiness.

In the presence of God's holiness, Isaiah was not struck by the profundity of his new understanding of God or the weakness of his own humanity, but by his own impurity, the uncleanness of the nation of Judah, and the marvelous glory of the King, the Lord Almighty. Isaiah confessed his sins, his guilt was removed when his sins were atoned, and he yielded his will to the sovereign plan of God for his life.

(b) One sign of the impact of Isaiah's experience was his constant reference to God's name as "the Holy One of Israel." When using this descriptive title in judgment oracles, Isaiah contrasts the sinful rebellion of the people of Judah with God's impeccability (1:4), thereby showing the failures of the Israelites and their need to repent (1:18). The people of Israel dishonored God by rejecting the instructions of a holy God who could guide them in the ways

---

[185] 1QIsaᵃ has the word קָדוֹשׁ "holy" only twice, but the various Greek translations have the word three times. For a discussion of this issue see N. Walker, "Disagion versus Trisagion: A Copyist Defended," *NTS* 7 (1961): 170–71, who prefers the double reference to holiness. A threefold declaration of God's holiness is found in Rev 4:8. The closest Old Testament parallel to this threefold repetition is in the twofold refrain "holy is he" in the kingship hymn of Ps 99:3 and 5 (though God's holiness is proclaimed again in 99:9). Although the seraphs certainly knew about the trinity, there is no way to prove that this threefold declaration of holiness is evidence to support this doctrine.

[186] A woman who had separated herself to the service of a pagan god (often as a sacred prostitute) was referred to using this root idea (קְדֵשָׁה, "holy one, sacred one") in Gen 38:21 and Hos 4:14; certainly they were not sinless.

[187] H. Ringgren, *The Prophetic Conception of the Holiness of God* (Uppsala: Lundequistska, 1948), focuses his study of this concepts only on prophetic texts, rather than surveying the whole Hebrew canon.

[188] Wildberger, *Isaiah 1–12*, 266, places these concepts in opposition, but they do not seem to be necessarily contradictory.

of righteousness (5:24). They even demanded that the prophets not confront them with the unpleasant visions and requirements of the Holy One of Israel (30:11). The prophet reveals the foolishness of depending on Egyptian horses for safety in a time of war rather than in the glorious power of the majestic Holy One who sovereignly controlled the events of history (31:1). Of course, it was not only the Israelites who insulted God; the Assyrian king Sennacherib blasphemed the Holy name of God by claiming that he was no more powerful than the gods of the nations, and by stating that he could not be trusted to deliver Jerusalem (37:23).

God's holy name also was used to support the claims of various positive promises. In the future, a remnant of the children of Israel will turn from their sinful wickedness and realize that the only secure place to put their trust is in the name of the Holy One of Israel (10:20). Then they will realize that idols are nothing compared to their creator (17:7). They will repent of their sins and rest in the salvation of the Holy One (30:15). At that point they will see his glory, and his sovereign might will carry out his will and restore the nation as he promised. Those who trust in God and have their eyes opened (29:19) will rejoice and sing about the greatness and the majestic holy God who will save them (12:6). Then God's people will walk in holiness and keep his name holy (29:23).

(c) In numerous passages, God's holiness is conceived as the basis of his just punishment of sin, which will bring judgment to the rebellious and atonement to those who turn from sin. Indeed, "The Holy God shows himself holy through his righteousness,"[189] both to forgive as well as to punish the wicked. In the presence of God's holiness, the prophet Isaiah immediately understood his own sinfulness and his need for atonement, in addition to the sinful rebelliousness of the people of Israel (6:5–7). The multifaceted implications of God's holiness are explained in the picture of God as the glorious crown of the righteous remnant, as a source of strength in the time of battle, and as a judge who sits in judgment over the wicked (28:5–6). Almighty God "will be exalted by his justice and the Holy one will show himself holy by his righteousness" (5:16) when he humbles the proud people on earth. Since God is holy, his justice directs his acts of redemption (1:27). "Justice and righteousness" will characterize the future kingdom of the Messiah (9:7), for this shoot from the stump of Jesse will make decisions based on justice (11:4; 16:5). God's justice will cause him to be compassionate and gracious to those who wait for him and trust in him for their strength (30:15,18). When God's Holy Spirit comes on mankind in that day, it will transform nature so that it will be fertile and will transform people so that justice and righteousness will blossom and bring forth a harvest of peace, quietness, and trust in God (32:16–17). Then the Lord will be exalted and treated as holy; then Zion will be full of justice and righteousness (33:5).

---

[189] Wildberger, *Isaiah 28–39*, 619.

(d) Holiness will characterize those who dwell in God's future kingdom. Since God is holy, those who wish to dwell with him eternally in his glorious kingdom must be holy. God will wash away their filth and cleanse them so that they can dwell with God in his new creation, where his glory will be revealed (4:3–5). These are the ones who have had their blind eyes opened and who will walk on the secure highway of holiness where God's redeemed people travel when they come to Zion to sing God's praises (35:8–10). Then people will dwell without fear in God's presence on his holy mountain where the knowledge of God will be complete (11:9), and they will sing his praises (25:1–8; 26:1–7). Although Isaiah attributes many characteristics and names to God, his thinking and preaching are based on his core theological conviction that the God who rules everything is the Holy One (cf. passages in Is 40–66).

ALL THE WORLD. The second aspect of Isaiah's distinctive theological message is his universal application of God's plan to "all the world." Although Isaiah's messages are primarily addressed to the people he spoke to in Jerusalem, God's sovereign plan will impact individual men and women, whole nations, and even the fertility of the land. Isaiah's mission was to describe to his listeners how the plans of the Holy God relate to everything and everyone within the created world. Since he is sovereign over this whole world and his demands for holiness impinge on the future judgment or redemption of everything in this world, God's actions have consequences for everything. God sustains a relationship with everything he created; there is nothing that exists outside of his sovereign realm of influence. Interrelationships exist on many levels.

(a) God's deals with individual people—from Maher-Shalal-Hash-Baz, the son of Isaiah, who was a sign of God's future action against Judah's enemies (8:1–4), to Shebna, the steward over the house of king Hezekiah, who was reprimanded for spending his time building his own tomb instead of focusing on the needs of the people of Jerusalem (22:15–19). God also interacts with groups, including the proud women of Jerusalem in the days of Uzziah (3:16–4:1) and the complacent women of Zion in the time of Hezekiah (32:9–14). God is especially concerned with the kings of Judah, like Ahaz who needed to trust God during the Syro-Ephraimite War (7:1–10), and Hezekiah who needed to trust God when Sennacherib attacked Judah in 701 BC (36:1–39:8). In addition, God is concerned with the pride of the Assyrian king Sennacherib (37:22–35) and Judah's alliances with the Babylonian king Merodach-baladan (39:1–8) and with Egypt (30:1–5). God will bring judgment on the unjust leaders in Judah who mistreat the poor (3:12–15) as well as the blind prophets and priests who lead people astray (28:7–8). God keeps track of every individual and each group, especially those whose names are written in his book (4:3).

(b) God seems to have special relationships with various nations. Most frequently, the prophet mentions "my/his people," referring to the special covenant relationship God has with the people of Judah (3:12,14,15). In each case,

God controls the life of these people through events that bring deliverance from enemies or judgment because of sins. From time to time, the prophet refers to God's judgment of the northern nation of Israel or Ephraim (7:1; 9:9; 17:9; 28:1), and "burdensome oracles" are spoken against Babylon, Philistia, Assyria, Moab, Egypt, and Tyre (chaps. 13–23; 30–31). The Assyrians are pictured as a rod in God's hand (10:5–6), but at other times when this nation acted contrary to God's will (10:7–15), it was necessary for God to judge it severely (10:16–19). It is clear that nations like Egypt have the ability to rebel against God or to humbly submit to him and enjoy his blessings (contrast 19:1–17 with 18–25). Nations are dealt with according to God's justice and according to his plan (14:24–27), but as Wildberger states, "Isaiah reserves rule over the whole world for Yahweh alone."[190]

(c) The natural world is impacted by God's plan for this world, because one of the key ways God blesses or judges a nation is by cursing or blessing their land. In the eschatological age, God will bless the land of Judah with rain so that it will fill the streams, the fields will produce much grain, and the sunlight will produce great fertility and healing in the land (2:2–3; 30:23–26; 32:15–20; 35:1–2,67). Other portions of the earth will suffer under the severe curse of God's wrath that will involve the devastation of the face of the earth; it will dry up with no fertility and no people (24:1–10). God's punishment of sin will impact the floodgates of heaven, the very foundations of the earth, the shaking of the earth, and the sun and moon (24:18–22). God's control is universal; no part of nature can thrive without his blessing. When Isaiah describes God's relationship with this world, he speaks of his control over absolutely everything and everyone.

TRUST THE ONE WHO RULES.   The theology of Isaiah focuses on how the Holy God carries out his rule over individuals, nations, and nature. God's relationship with people is not that of a younger brother, a slave, a lifeless idol, or an absentee landlord. It is important to understand the nature of God's relationship with his creation and how the prophet uses this to communicate persuasively to his audiences.

(a) Since God is pictured as an all-powerful King both in Isaiah's vision (6:5) and in the eschatological era (24:23; 33:17), it is not surprising that God functions in the kingly roles of Judge of the nations when he sets up his kingdom (2:4; 33:22), Judge of leaders who oppress the poor (3:12–13), and Judge of all those who are proud (2:12–17; 13:11). His judgment will apply specifically to the proud women of Jerusalem (3:16–4:1), the wicked and proud in Samaria (9:8–12), the proud Assyrian king (10:12), the proud Babylonian king (14:11–15), the proud Moabites (16:6–7), the proud people of Tyre (23:9), and the proud king Sennacherib (37: 21–35).

As king, God also functions in the role of Divine Warrior ("Lord of Hosts," 13:2–9; 34:1–8; 42:13), who defeats his enemies (people and nations); he

---

[190] Wildberger, *Isaiah 28–39*, 638.

is the Savior who is able to deliver Judah from their adversaries (7:3–10; 30:27–33; 31:8–9; 33:1; 37:6–7,36) and even deliver foreign nations from their enemies (19:20–21). When God fights, he simply commands, stretches out his hand, or rises up to fight against his enemies; therefore, it is impossible for mere men and their horses to determine who will win a battle (30:1–5; 31:1–3). At the end of this era, God will pour out his wrath on the nations, slaughter them with his sword, and take vengeance on those who reject him (34:1–10). As J. J. M. Roberts suggests, "The portrayal of Yahweh as king and the affirmation of the world-wide extent of his glory constitute a claim for the sole sovereignty of God."[191]

Although it is difficult to know exactly what metaphors were drawn from the kingly role, ancient Near Eastern kings wrote laws to regulate the behavior of their people (e.g., the Hammurabi Law Code), and God also functions as a Lawgiver who regulates civic, cultic, and ethical behavior patterns (1:10; 2:3–4; 5:24; 8:16–20) as he rules over his kingdom. These instructions apply not only to his own people (5:24) but are relevant to all the nations on earth (2:2–4).

The numerous examples of God's absolute control over all people and nations indicate that his relationship with others is that of a lord sovereignly ruling over all people on earth. But his rule is not that of a cold, tyrannical absentee landlord, nor is he just concerned about those who fear and exalt him. He cares for, redeems, and transforms sinful and obstinate people because he is compassionate and forgiving. He desires that all people will trust, praise, and glorify his name.

(b) Isaiah uniquely applies his knowledge of the way God rules over the world to support his call for repentance. God has a plan for his people and all the nations. This involves Jerusalem and the surrounding nations both in the prophet's time and also in the eschatological age.[192] Isaiah challenges the people to humble themselves before the glorious power of this holy God and trust him to rule the world with justice and authority according to his plan. Although the foundation of Isaiah's theology consistently relates to the need to trust God,[193] the prophet had to apply the principle that people need to "trust the Holy God who rules over all the world" in different ways according to the individual circumstances of his audience.

In the era of King Uzziah, people were wealthy, safe (2:7), and proud (3:16–17). They trusted in their own human ability to provide happiness and success (2:22), and they thought they did not need God. They were exalting themselves rather than God alone (2:11,17). God sent the prophet Isaiah to warn the people

---

[191] J. J. M. Roberts, "Isaiah in Old Testament Theology." *Int* 36 (1982): 132.

[192] J. J. M. Roberts, "Isaiah in Old Testament Theology." *Int* 36 (1982): 138–39.

[193] Wildberger, *Isaiah 28–39*, 642, expresses this in terms of "faith," a willingness not only to obey what God says but also to depend on God alone, both for the problems of today and hope for the future.

of Judah not to trust in mankind (2:22) but to put their trust in God and glorify him. If they did not repent and start exalting God, he would destroy their land and take away every reason for pride. He would demonstrate that he alone is God and that he is in control of their lives. These people must trust God because he alone is a holy God (the idols and mankind are nothing), because he controls their lives and in justice will punish them, and because his sovereign rule extends to all of nature (trees, towers, ships) and all mankind (2:9–22).

Similar theological principles are evident in a very different situation a few years later when the weak King Ahaz was threatened with total defeat by the neighboring nations, Syria and Israel (7:1; 1 Kgs 16; 2 Chr 28). Isaiah came to Ahaz and told him not to fear these armies, but to trust God for victory over his enemies (7:4–9). Ahaz needed to trust God the Divine Warrior to defeat his enemies (his method of ruling) and to trust in God's ability to control the destiny of his powerful enemies (his control extends to all people). Unfortunately, Ahaz refused to trust God, but instead called on the Assyrian King Tiglath-pileser III (his substitute for God) to deliver him from those who were attacking Jerusalem (2 Kgs 16:16,20–21). Because Ahaz was unfaithful to God and failed to trust him, God brought great judgment on the land (God's sovereignty over nature in 7:18–25). Here again those who proudly failed to trust God were humbled, but this all happened in a quite different setting from the period of Uzziah.

The prophetic challenge to trust God is emphasized in the hymn that closes the first literary unit of the book (12:1–6). The prophet explains how trust is based on having a relationship in which God is perceived as "my salvation" and "my strength" (God's roles legitimate the wisdom of depending on him). God did glorious things for Israel in the past and he demonstrated himself to be great in the midst of his people. Therefore, the people who heard the prophet Isaiah should rejoice and sing to express their trust and confidence in God's powerful ability to rule this world. They do not need to be afraid because they can trust in God. He has the power to overcome every threat, he functions in the world according to his royal roles, and he has jurisdiction over any problem and over all people. This hymn focuses on the basis for trust and the positive results of trusting God.

When the prophet told a later audience about the coming demise of many foreign nations (God rules over them all), he predicted that some would fall because of their arrogance (13:11). None of these nations trusted God, and none of them will last (except Egypt in 19:18–25), so the kings of Judah should not trust in armies, for they do not rule the world. God controls the armies of this world, so he should be trusted. Later, the Assyrian threat of Sennacherib was so severe that Hezekiah was faced with what seemed like total annihilation. He was condemned by the prophet Isaiah for trusting in the horses and chariots of Egypt and not looking to God for help (31:1). God should be their source of deliverance and salvation. Isaiah maintained that Egypt would not help or provide true protection (30:1–5), for its soldiers were mere men and not in control like God (31:3). Later when the Assyrian general Rabshakeh came to Jerusalem to persuade Hezekiah to give up and surrender to the Assyrians, the Assyrian general's whole approach was to undermine Hezekiah's fragile trust in God. He questioned Hezekiah's "confidence" or trust (36:4), wondered why he would "depend" on or trust God (36:7), warned the citizens of Jerusalem not to follow Hezekiah if he told them "to trust" God (36:15), and tried to undermine the people's faith in God's power, so they would not trust God (36:18–20). In spite of this, Hezekiah and Isaiah went to the temple and trusted God for the deliverance of Jerusalem (37:14–20). God answered that prayer and miraculously delivered them from the Assyrian army (37:36). Isaiah's rhetorical interaction with Hezekiah was based on the belief that an all-powerful Holy God would justly rule over the army of any human king who blasphemed the name of God.

Some of the eschatological events at the end of this age are unclear to the modern interpreter, but the patterns that explain God's holy rule over mankind are evident. God's sovereign, just rule will cause him to destroy everything in this perverse world (24:1–12; 34:1–10), but those same factors will also cause him to invite his own people who trust in him (25:9) to his glorious banquet where he will swallow up death for all time (25:6–8). Therefore, the righteous will sing of God's salvation, for he is the Rock that they trust in (26:1–4). God has the power and authority to accomplish these deeds; he is Holy so he must act in justice to remove evil. His powerful judgment will extend to the foundations of this earth to the heights of heaven (24:1–22).

Part of the good news that Isaiah brought to his audience was that God's sovereignty extends throughout history (41:21–29), that the nations and the pagan gods are nothing (40:15–23), and that he will strengthen those who are tired and weak if they will trust in him (40:31). Those who trust in idols will be put to shame (42:17); the only answer is to trust in the name of the Lord (50:10). God's revelation through the prophet was given so that everyone on earth, not just the Israelites, would know and believe that there was no God except the Lord (43:10). These persuasive speeches of hope were not only intended to convince the Hebrews at that time to trust God, but they also were designed to give relevant information about what would happen in the future. No dates are provided, but at some future time, people from the ends of the earth will be saved, bow their knee to God, trust God, and recognize him alone as God (45:22–25; 49:26). People from all nations will come and glorify God and bring others to worship him (66:18–21). Isaiah promises that those people who put their hope and trust in God will not be disappointed (49:23). Although some will not believe what God reveals about his suffering servant (53:1), he will suffer and die for the sins of all mankind. Those who seek the Lord, confess their sins, and turn to God for mercy can have their sins pardoned (55:6–7). Indeed, God is a faithful and trustworthy God who has a wonderful plan for those who will put their trust in him.

––––––––––––––––– *OUTLINE OF ISAIAH 1–39* –––––––––––––

I. God's Threatened Court Case against His People (1:1–31)
   1. Superscription (1:1)
   2. God's Accusations of Rebellion against Judah (1:2–9)
   3. God's Call for Reconciliation, Not Useless Worship (1:10–20)
   4. God's Purification of Judah's Leaders (1:21–31)
II. Depending on Human Resources or Trusting God (2:1–12:6)
   1. Exaltation of God and Humbling of the Proud (2:1–4:6)
      (1) Promises of God's Future Kingdom Produce Trust (2:1–5)
      (2) Removal of Pride and Exaltation of God (2:6–22)
      (3) Removal of Judah's Male Leaders (3:1–15)
      (4) Removal of Judah's Proud Women (3:16–4:1)
      (5) God's Glorious, Holy Kingdom (4:2–6)
   2. The Destruction of Judah (5:1–30)
      (1) A Vineyard Song of Love and Rejection (5:1–7)
      (2) Reasons for Judah's Destruction (5:8–25)
      (3) An Army's Destruction of Judah (5:26–30)
   3. A Holy King's Calling to a Calloused Audience (6:1–13)
      (1) The Vision of the Holy King (6:1–4)
      (2) The Prophet's Purification (6:5–7)
      (3) A Hardening Message for a Calloused Audience (6:8–10)
      (4) Hope in the Midst of Destruction (6:11–13)
   4. The Destruction of Judah (7:1–8:18)
      (1) Ahaz's Failure to Trust God Brings Assyria (7:1–25)
          Do not Fear; Stand Firm in your Faith (7:1–9)
          The Sign of Immanuel (7:10–17)
          Judgment of the Land (7:18–25)
      (2) Fearing God, not Military Might (8:1–22)
          The Birth of Maher-Shalal-Hash-Baz (8:1–4)
          The Coming Assyrian Flood (8:5–10)
          Fear God, not Armies (8:11–15)
          Follow God's Instructions; Other Ways Bring Darkness
          (8:16–22)
   5. The Reign of a Righteous King, the Humbling of the Proud
      (9:1–11:16)
      (1) The Reign of a Righteous King (9:1–7)
      (2) The Judgment of Proud and Sinful Israel (9:8–10:4)
          God's Wrath against Proud Israel (9:8–12)
          God's Wrath against Unrepentant Leaders (9:13–17)

God Is Destroying the Nation (9:18–21)
Lament: Judah's Oppression Will Lead to Its Demise
(10:1–4)
- (3) The Judgment of Proud Assyria (10:5–34)
  God Will Judge Assyrians for Pride (10:5–19)
  God Will Save a Remnant (10:20–27)
  Invading Assyria Will Be Cut Off (10:28–34)
- (4) The Reign of a Righteous King (11:1–16)
  The Just and Peaceful Reign of a Davidic Branch (11:1–9)
  The Gathering of the Nations to God (11:10–16)
6. A Song of Trust in God (12:1–6)
III. God's Sovereign Plan for the Nations (13:1–23:18)
  1. God's Plans for Babylon and Assyria (13:1–14:27)
    - (1) Destruction on the Day of the Lord (13:1–16)
    - (2) God Will Destroy Proud Babylon (13:17–22)
    - (3) God Will Restore Israel (14:1–2)
    - (4) A Taunt Song for the Babylonian King (14:3–23)
    - (5) God's Plan to Crush Assyria (14:24–27)
  2. God's Plans for Philistia (14:28–32)
  3. God's Plans for Proud Moab (15:1–16:14)
    - (1) A Lament for Moab (15:1–9)
    - (2) Moab Requests Help from Judah (16:1–5)
    - (3) Pride Will Cause Lamenting in Moab (16:6–12)
    - (4) Destruction in Three Years (16:13–14)
  4. God's Plans for Damascus—and Israel (17:1–18:7)
    - (1) Damascus and Israel Will Lose Their Fertility (17:1–11)
    - (2) God Will Rebuke the Raging Nations (17:12–14)
    - (3) Cush Will Honor God for Destroying Its Enemies (18:1–7)
  5. God's Plans for Egypt (19:1–20:6)
    - (1) God Will Defeat Egypt and Her Gods (19:1–15)
    - (2) God Will Save Egypt; Egyptians Will Worship God
      (19:16–25)
    - (3) Isaiah's Nakedness Symbolizes Egypt's Defeat (20:1–6)
  6. God's Plans for Babylon (21:1–10)
    - (1) The Prophet's Terrifying Vision of Babylon (21:1–4)
    - (2) Watchmen Report on the Fall of Babylon (21:5–10)
  7. God's Plans for Dumah (21:11–12)
  8. God's Plans for Arabia (21:13–17)
  9. God's Plans for Jerusalem (22:1–25)
    - (1) Jerusalem Rejoices Even Though She Faces Defeat
      (22:1–14)
    - (2) Shebna: Disgraced and Replaced (22:15–25)

I. GOD'S THREATENED COURT CASE AGAINST HIS PEOPLE
(1:1–31)
  1. Superscription (1:1)
  2. God's Accusations of Rebellion against Judah (1:2–9)
  3. God's Call for Reconciliation, Not Useless Worship (1:10–20)
  4. God's Purification of Judah's Leaders (1:21–31)

I. GOD'S THREATENED COURT CASE
AGAINST HIS PEOPLE (1:1–31)

The way a book or letter begins gives the reader a hint about its contents. Although one usually views the first paragraph of a letter as the first thing written by the author, the introduction to this commentary and the opening chapter of many other books will be written after the author finishes writing the rest of its contents. Authors do this because they do not know everything that they will write at the beginning of the process; consequently, they are not able to prepare the reader properly for what is to come in the rest of the book. Once the research is completed and the results are written, then the author can provide an informative introduction.

The evidence presented below suggests the prophet Isaiah wrote this introductory chapter very late in his lifetime, probably after he had finished writing most if not all of the book. Now he is able to reflect back on what God told him to say to the people of Jerusalem over the last years, and now he knows how they responded to God's words. At this point he can properly prepare his future readers to understand some of the key theological themes of the book and explain more about God's plan for the nation. This introduction is also a motivational attempt to convince his readers to acknowledge what God says and repent so that their sins can be forgiven (1:18–20). Why should they suffer any longer under God's discipline like those described in the pages of this book? Is it not more appealing to enjoy the day when God will bless his people and turn Jerusalem into a "City of Righteousness, the Faithful City" (1:26)?

GENRE. Some conclude that the literary background of this introductory chapter is patterned after the general characteristics of a covenant lawsuit,[1] a literary form that drew upon the vocabulary and cultural background of a

---

[1] See Hos 4 and Mic 6 for other examples of covenant lawsuits (רִיב). R. J. Marshal, "The Structure of Isaiah 1–12," *BR* 7 (1962): 19–32; H. B. Huffmon, "The Covenant Lawsuit in the Prophets," *JBL* 78 (1959): 285–95 gives the general structure of the covenant lawsuit and explains how the prophets used this structure in individual passages.

trial at court. Since this chapter has several deviations from the normal pattern of other covenant lawsuits (cf. Mic 6; Hos 4), it seems more accurate to conclude that this chapter might be compared to the negotiations that take place before a trial (similar to an arraignment), rather than a court trial itself.[2] Accusations are brought against the defendant (1:2b–9), and the defensive reasoning of the accused is refuted, similar to what one might expect at an arraignment (1:10–15). But then come unexpected exhortations on acceptable behavior (1:16–17), and one party offers to resolve the case (1:18–20), making known the consequence of both a positive or negative response (1:21–31). By using the general literary framework of a trial arraignment to structure his theological message, the prophet communicated the seriousness of Judah's sinful rebellion in a logical way that clearly demonstrated to the reader why God would judge the nation. The past evidence of the case against the accused people of Judah proved that there was a guilty party. Therefore, the people of Judah in the audience needed to confess their sins and transform their behavior if they wanted to avoid further punishment. The clear portrayal of what God would do if they do not change gave Isaiah's sermonic appeal to "reason together" (1:18) strong persuasive power. They could respond positively to God and be blessed or reject God and suffer under his destructive power along with the wicked (1:19–20).

HISTORICAL SETTING. In order to understand the reason for God's threatening arraignment, it is essential for the modern reader to know something about the historical setting of this speech. When was it given? Why was it necessary? What was the prophet trying to accomplish? The interpreter can suggest a date for this message by noticing the setting of the audience. At this time, many people were in rebellion against God and despised the Holy One of Israel, God himself (1:2–4). Not long before this sermon, the nation suffered a major military attack by some enemy (1:5–7), and only Jerusalem was spared (1:8–9). Some people in Judah were busy offering sacrifices (1:10–15) but many of their hearts were not right with God. In fact, many of these people were offering detestable sacrifices, shedding innocent blood, and not upholding justice (1:15–17). In the past Jerusalem had just rulers, but now the city was characterized by murder, robbery, bribery of judges, pagan worship, and injustice toward the poor (1:21–23,28–29).

Although the date of chap. 1 is not stated, it needs to fit somewhere shortly after a major military event when its rulers were leading the nation away from God. Four possible dates should be considered for this sermon: (a) Y. Gitay believes the book of Isaiah is arranged in chronological order, so he suggested that the battle in 1:5–9 was the Syro-Ephraimite War (734–732 BC) when Israel and Syria attacked Judah to force Judah to join their coalition against Assyria

---

[2] J. Oswalt, *The Book of Isaiah 1–39*, NICOT (Grand Rapids: Eerdmans, 1986), 85, maintains that this passage "follows not so much a legal presentation as a personal one."

(cf. Isa 7; 2 Kgs 16; 2 Chr 28).[3] This setting fits the military situation required, for the rebellious king Ahaz was ruling Judah and the nation did survive this war as a weak vassal of Assyria. It was also a time when pagan worship infiltrated Jerusalem (2 Kgs 16:1–5,10–18). Nevertheless, it is hard to determine who the earlier righteous king was (1:21) when the city had a faithful ruler, unless the author was referring all the way back to the time of David. (b) H. Wildberger and most others suggest that the historical situation was during the 701 BC attack on Judah by Sennacherib, when the whole nation of Judah was destroyed except Jerusalem (Isa 36–37; 2 Kgs 18–19; 2 Chr 32).[4] This was a time of restored worship of God at the temple (2 Chr 30–31), but since Hezekiah was a righteous king, it is hard to fit the negative comments about the evil leaders or pagan worship in the temple into this time frame. (c) C. R. Seitz suggested a date in the reign of Manasseh, a few years after the 701 BC attack by the Assyrians.[5] This view has the advantage of identifying Hezekiah's reforms as the period when righteousness characterized the city and the early reign of Manasseh (cf. 2 Kgs 21; 2 Chr 33) as the time of wickedness described in 1:4,21–23,27–29. If one hypothesizes that Isaiah's message was given when Manasseh was a co-regent with his father Hezekiah (just before Hezekiah's death), this would explain why Manasseh's name was not mentioned in 1:1. In this scenario, Isaiah was warning the nation not to reject the godly ways of Hezekiah for the worship of trees and idols that were promoted by Manasseh (1:29–30). (d) Finally, E. J. Kissane concluded that this was a prophecy about the future fall of Jerusalem in 586 BC.[6] Since Jerusalem did not escape this conquest (1:8–9) and chap. 1 seems to describe a present problem (not a future one), this suggestion seems an unlikely interpretation.

The third view satisfies the various factors outlined in the setting of chap. 1. If this dating is accepted, it naturally leads to several conclusions: (a) this was not Isaiah's first sermon; it was not composed at the beginning of his ministry but near the end; (b) Isaiah most likely added chap. 1 when his sermons were collected, edited, and put in their present form; and (c) chap. 1 serves as something of an introduction to the collection of prophecies attributed to Isaiah.

STRUCTURE.   The structural position of this chapter at the beginning of the book causes it to serve as an introduction to the rest of his messages.

---

[3] Y. Gitay, *Isaiah and His Audience: The Structure and Meaning of Isaiah 1–12*, SSN 30 (Assen: van Gorcum, 1991), 23. There is a general chronological order in Isaiah, but this will not strictly apply to every chapter. The oracles against the foreign nations (13–23) seem to be topically gathered into one place, so the interest in chronology is not the main organizing principle throughout the book.

[4] H. Wildberger, *Isaiah 1–12; A Commentary,* A Continental Commentary (Minneapolis: Fortress, 1991), 21.

[5] C. R. Seitz, *Isaiah 1–39*, Interpretation (Louisville: John Knox, 1993), 34; E. J. Young, *The Book of Isaiah*, I (Grand Rapids: Eerdmans, 1965), 33, also suggests that Isaiah's ministry continued into the initial years of Manasseh.

[6] E. J. Kissane, *The Book of Isaiah*, I (Dublin: Browne and Nolan, 1960), 9–10, takes the Hb. perfect verbs as prophetic perfects that describe what will happen.

Although this chapter is not a summary of the total content of the book,[7] it does introduce some of the main points addressed in chaps. 2–66. Commentators have noticed a strong connection between the vocabulary and themes in chap. 1 and chaps. 65–66. This verbal connection suggests that there was a purposeful attempt to tie the whole book together when chaps. 65–66 were written. L. Liebreich, R. Lack, M. A. Sweeney, D. M. Carr, and A. Tomasino identified these linguistic connections as:

	Chapter	Chapters 65–66
"Heaven and earth"	1:2	65:17; 66:1,22
People "rebelled/ transgressed"	1:2,28	66:24
Structural order of topics	1:10–20	66:1–6
"I have no pleasure/delight"	1:11	66:4
"Seek"	1:12	65:1
Sacrifices, incense, bulls, lamb	1:11,13	65:3,7; 66:3
Abomination	1:13,17	66:3; 65:4
"Hear the Word of the LORD"	1:11	66:5
The woman Zion	1:21,26	66:7–13
Killing people	1:21	66:3
"Rebels"	1:23	65:2
Blessings and curses	1:27–28	65:9–12
"Forsake"	1:4,28	65:11
Abuse of the cult	1:29–31	65:3; 66:3,17
Wicked put to "shame"	1:29	65:13; 66:5
"Gardens"	1:29	65:3; 66:17
You have "chosen"	1:29	66:4
Wicked burn in fire	1:31	66:15–16,24
"Fire not quenched"	1:31	66:24[8]

In light of these common ideas, there is enough evidence to suggest that the final publication of Isaiah's oracles was purposely designed to provide a literary connection between the first and last chapters. This design could be employed to argue for the position that the same author wrote the first and last

---

[7] G. Fohrer, "Jesaja 1 als Zusammenfassung der Verkündigung Jesajas," *ZAW* 74 (1962): 251–68, thought the five paragraphs in chap. 1 presented a cross-section of, or summary of, the five major themes in Isaiah 1–39. D. Carr, "Reaching for the Unity of Isaiah," *JSOT* 57 (1993): 71–80, argued that chaps. 1 and 65–66 do not summarize much of the content of the book (there is nothing about the Messiah in these chapters) and that a basic conflict exists between the exhortations to repent in chap. 1 and the finality of judgment (without the possibility of repentance) in 65–66.

[8] L. Liebreich, "The Compilation of the Book of Isaiah," *JQR* 47 (1956–57): 126–27; R. Lack, *La symbolique du livre d'Isaie,* AnBib 59 (Rome: Pontifical Biblical Institute, 1973), 139–41; M. A. Sweeney, *Isaiah 1–4 and the Post-exilic Understanding of the Isaianic Tradition,* BZAW 171 (Berlin: de Gruyter, 1988), 21–24; D. M. Carr, "Reading Isaiah from Beginning (Isaiah 1) to End (Isaiah 65–66): Multiple Modern Possibilities," in *New Versions of Isaiah,* JSOTSup 214 (ed. R. F. Melugin and M. A. Sweeney; Sheffield: Sheffield Academic Press, 1996), 188–218; A. Tomasino, "Isaiah 1.1–2.4 and 63–66, and the Composition of the Isaianic Corpus," *JSOT* 57 (1993): 81–98.

chapters,[9] or at least that chap. 1 was placed before 2–12 in the final edition of Isaiah to form part of an inclusio with chaps. 65–66. These connections unify and draw the messages in the book together.

Although some interpreters consider 1:1 as the title of chaps. 1–12,[10] in light of the literary connections between chaps. 1 and 65–66, it is better to understand 1:1 as the introduction to the whole book.[11] The appearance of another superscription in 2:1 suggests that a new section begins there. This second superscription serves to reintroduce Isaiah as the author of chaps. 2–12, the first major unit in the book.

The structure of chap. 1 is fairly clearly demarcated by the repetition of key phrases. The first section of this sermon is addressed to the people and rulers and is marked by the introductory "for the LORD has spoken" in 1:2, and the concluding, "for the mouth of the LORD has spoken" in 2:20. Within this section are three smaller paragraphs marked by:

1. an imperative exhortation "hear" in 1:2–9,
2. the imperative exhortation "hear" starting 1:10–17, and
3. the imperative exhortation "come" at the beginning of 1:18–20.

The second section of this sermon (1:21–31) focuses on the city of Jerusalem and its rulers with words of lamenting accusations (1:21–23) and first person statements about the consequences of the refiner's fire (1:24–26). The second section ends the chapter (1:27–31) with a clear choice for the righteous (they will be redeemed) and the wicked (they and their idols will burn with fire).

THEOLOGY. This sermon wrestles with the issue of how God will deal with his disobedient covenant people. Though they were his children through the covenant (1:2), they are now in rebellion against God (1:2–4) and do not worship him in an acceptable manner (1:10–15). God has already disciplined the people of Judah severely for their sins (1:5–9), so his people need to change course and repent of their sins (1:17–20). If they continue in rebellion, they will become the enemy of God (1:24) and he will destroy them (1:20,31). Isaiah explains that God deals with sin in two ways. He can remove the stain of sin, if people are willing to repent (1:18–19), or his refining fire can remove the sinner, so that the nation is purified and redeemed (1:25–27). In the end, God's

---

[9] This is by no means a logical necessity though, for another person could just as easily have added chap. 1 with the express purpose of tying the book together by repeating vocabulary from the last chapters in the introduction, or the author of 65–66 could have consciously referred to chap. 1 when writing the final chapters.

[10] G. B. Gray, *A Critical and Exegetical Commentary on the Book of Isaiah I–XXVII*, ICC (Edinburgh: T & T Clark, 1912), 1, concluded that the superscription was put here by a post-exilic editor, not Isaiah. Freedman (see note 12) argued against this conclusion.

[11] Seitz, *Isaiah 1–39*, 24, and Young, *Isaiah*, I, 27, understand 1:1 as a superscription for the entire book of Isaiah. Seitz considers this verse not as Isaiah's claim to authorship but the testimony of those who shaped the book.

plan will result in the establishment of a righteous and faithful nation. The question is: Will this audience respond to God's call and repent of their sins or will it stubbornly continue in its sinful ways and suffer the consequences of their choice? This is still the fundamental question that every nation and person today must answer. The prophet clearly outlines what one must do to be among the redeemed (1:27).

1. Superscription (1:1)

¹The vision concerning Judah and Jerusalem that Isaiah son of Amoz saw during the reigns of Uzziah, Jotham, Ahaz and Hezekiah, kings of Judah.

The book of Isaiah begins like most other prophetic books with an identification of (a) the nature of the material in this scroll; (b) the audience; (c) the name of the author of these words; and (d) the date of his preaching. It differs from several other prophetic superscriptions by its failure to associate Isaiah with a specific location (Mic 1:1; Nah 1:1), by omitting his former occupation (Amos 1:1 says Amos was a shepherd), and by not explicitly stating that he received "the word of the LORD" (cf. Hos 1:1; Mic 1:1; Jer 1:1). Although there is no way to determine when the superscription was added to Isaiah's messages, D. N. Freedman observed that the names of the kings in 1:1 reflect the longer orthographic spelling of the pre-exilic period, so he hypothesized a date during the reign of Hezekiah.[12] This overlaps with the initial co-regency of Manasseh, the date suggested above.

1:1 The superscription begins by announcing that the content of this book was derived from "insight, a vision" (*ḥāzôn*) by the prophet. This "visionary" qualification of the message was extremely important, for it gave divine authority to what Isaiah said and distinguished the divine truth that he spoke from the false illusions that some people followed (8:19; 30:10–11; 44:18–20). God's knowledge was marvelously transferred to the prophet in such a way that he was able to confront his audience from the divine perspective. Isaiah faithfully communicated God's message in order to transform the thinking and behavior of those who would listen (cf. Rom 12:2)[13] and to confirm the fate of the wicked people who were unwilling to listen (6:9–10). Although some prophets had elaborate visions containing images of people, places, and symbolic animals (Dan 8:1,2), the term "vision" (*ḥāzôn*) frequently refers to the general reception of a "divine revelation" of words, without any accompany-

---

[12] D. N. Freedman, "Headings in the Books of the Eighth-Century Prophets," *AUSS* 25 (1987): 9–26, argues for a relatively early date for the superscription while R. E. Clements, *Isaiah 1–39*, NCBC (Grand Rapids: Eerdmans, 1980), 29, proposes a post-exilic date for 1:1 (but does not give his reasons to justify this dating). J. Goldingay, "Isaiah I.1 and II.1," *VT* 48 (1998), 326–31, argues that 1:1 is the superscription only for chap. 1, but this seems unlikely.

[13] See G. V. Smith, *An Introduction to the Hebrew Prophets: The Prophets as Preachers* (Nashville: Broadman and Holman, 1994), 2–24, for a discussion of prophetic persuasion that was designed to transform the thinking and behavior of their listeners.

ing visual pictures (Obad 1; Nah1:1).[14] The decision to describe the content of what follows as a "vision, divine revelation" makes it unnecessary to state that these were the "words of God."

The inhabitants of "Judah and Jerusalem" were the primary audience for Isaiah's messages, though many times his messages seem specifically aimed at the kings and rulers of Judah (1:10,23; 3:1–15; 7:1–17; 30:1–5; 36–37) or some specific group of people (3:16–4:1). Sometimes the audience was a righteous king (36–37) but at other times it was a wicked king (7:1–17). Isaiah spoke to the proud and powerful during periods when people were wealthy (2:6–22; 3:16–4:1), but he also addressed the national leaders in a time of military fear and defeat (7:1–17). In some oracles he warned the wicked and at other times he encouraged the righteous. The oracles against the foreign nations (13–23) were designed to teach a Judean audience something about God's plan for these nations; they were not delivered to warn or convert the foreign nations Isaiah spoke about. Since Isaiah addressed many different groups, different kings, and people living in very different economic and political situations, it would be a mistake to imagine that he was speaking to the same audience throughout the book.

The person officially identified as the author of these words was Isaiah, though there is a great deal of speculation among scholars that later authors/ redactors wrote or edited parts of the book long after the death of Isaiah.[15] Isaiah is not described as a prophet or seer in this verse (cf. 37:2; 38:1; 39:3). His father Amoz should not to be confused with the prophet Amos. Archaeologists found the name Amoz on a seal in Jerusalem, suggesting that this person was a scribe, but there is no way to accurately date this seal or prove that it referred to Isaiah's father.[16] According to Jewish tradition, Isaiah's father was the brother of King Amaziah, making Isaiah a member of the royal Davidic family.[17] In light of Isaiah's literary skills and his recording of the history of two Israelite kings (2 Chr 26:22; 32:32), it appears that he had scribal abilities. Although nothing can be proven from this data, it fits what one would expect of Isaiah's status, background, and training.

The date of Isaiah's ministry is circumscribed by the reigns of four kings— from Uzziah through Hezekiah.[18] During these years, Judah was prosperous and powerful in the time of Uzziah (2 Kgs 15:1–7; 2 Chr 26:1–23), weak and

---

[14] חָזוֹן, "vision," is the noun form found 35 times in the Hb. text, with 12 occurring in Daniel and only two in Isaiah. The root verbal idea means "see, perceive, experience" in non-religious contexts. Its nominal form carries the idea of "divine insight/revelation." For a complete study of this root see H. R. Fuhs, *Sehen und Schauen: Die Wurzel ḥzh im Alten Orient und im Alten Testament* (Würzburg: Echter, 1978).

[15] See "Composition of Isaiah 1–39: Some Modern Scholarly Approaches" in the Introduction for a discussion of these issues.

[16] D. Diringer, *Le Iscrizioni Antico-Ebraiche Palestinesi* (Florence, 1934), 234–35.

[17] Babylonian Talmud, *Megilla* 10b; *Sota 10b; Lev Rab 6:6;* and Rashi.

[18] See "Historical and Religious Background of Isaiah 1–39" in the Introduction.

under Assyrian control for much of the reign of Ahaz (2 Kgs 16; 2 Chr 28), and then free again in the days of Hezekiah (2 Kgs 18–19; 2 Chr 29–32). This period covers the time from about 746 to 686 BC. Since Manasseh, Hezekiah's evil son, was co-regent with him for the last few years of his life, some of Isaiah's writings may reflect the beginning of Manasseh's reign (2 Kgs 21; 2 Chr 33). In the "Historical Setting" section above it was suggested that chap. 1 (including this superscription) was written near the end of Isaiah's life when Manasseh had rejected his father's religious reforms and was leading the nation into rebellion against God by worshiping other gods.

Superscriptions are important resources that help readers orient their interpretation to a time period and a specific kind of literary production. The reader's attitude toward this text would be totally different if the superscription said this was a lament, a song, or a gospel. A vision to Abram before the revelation of the law would be handled differently than a revelation to Daniel in the exilic period. Interpreters would treat a word from an Assyrian king different from an inspired vision from God. This superscription informs the reader that the words contained in this vision require attention so that one will interpret each passage according to its historical setting, as well as its literary character. A message from a divine source should also circumscribe the audience's theology and have an impact on their behavior. No one should read this revelation from God dispassionately, for it cannot be read without accountability.

2. God's Accusations of Rebellion against Judah (1:2–9)

> [2]Hear, O heavens! Listen, O earth!
> For the LORD has spoken:
> "I reared children and brought them up,
> but they have rebelled against me.
> [3]The ox knows his master,
> the donkey his owner's manger,
> but Israel does not know,
> my people do not understand."

> [4]Ah, sinful nation,
> a people loaded with guilt,
> a brood of evildoers,
> children given to corruption!
> They have forsaken the LORD;
> they have spurned the Holy One of Israel
> and turned their backs on him.

> [5]Why should you be beaten anymore?
> Why do you persist in rebellion?
> Your whole head is injured,
> your whole heart afflicted.

⁶From the sole of your foot to the top of your head
    there is no soundness —
only wounds and welts
    and open sores,
not cleansed or bandaged
    or soothed with oil.

⁷Your country is desolate,
    your cities burned with fire;
your fields are being stripped by foreigners
    right before you,
    laid waste as when overthrown by strangers.
⁸The Daughter of Zion is left
    like a shelter in a vineyard,
like a hut in a field of melons,
    like a city under siege.
⁹Unless the LORD Almighty
    had left us some survivors,
we would have become like Sodom,
    we would have been like Gomorrah.

Isaiah's actual sermon begins in v. 2. He does not overtly announce a "legal case" (*rîb*) against his audience like in Hos 4:1 or Mic 6:1, but the call for witnesses in 1:2 is reminiscent of similar calls for the heaven and earth to witness what God is doing (Deut 30:19; 31:28; 32:1; Ps 50:4). The structure of a legal court case is only vaguely followed, so this may be a more personal warning of an impending case, more like an arraignment. Isaiah gave the audience insight into what charges God would bring and what the consequences would be if the people did not repent. If Isaiah could persuade his audience to change immediately, there would be no need for an official covenant lawsuit and the nation would avoid any further divine judgment.

This first paragraph is made up of two parts:

God charges his sons with rebellion	1:2–3
An appeal to heaven and earth	2a
A charge of rebellion	2b
A comparative metaphor	3
Questions about the foolishness of more suffering	1:4–9
A lament over sinfulness	4
Questions about Judah's condition	5–6
Lamenting total destruction	7–9

1:2 The prophet begins by announcing God's appeal,[19] "hear, pay attention" (*šimʿû*), to the heavens and earth, which draws on theological themes in

---

[19] The imperative verb שִׁמְעוּ is used as an exhortation. GKC § 109a provides a review of the possible syntactical uses of the imperative.

the covenant traditions from Deuteronomy. The heavens and earth served as a witness to the blessings and curses that God gave to Israel. The personified heaven and earth knew what marvelous privileges God offered to his people. The continual reception of these blessings or God's curse of judgment was directly related to the people's love or rebellion against God (Deut 30:15–20; 31:28). There was no way for the people to claim ignorance about what God desired, or for them to change the theological terms of God's relationship with them. The truth was known and firmly established. Thus the heaven and earth served as a silent witness to the facts of past covenant history, but at this point they were not yet called on to testify in a lawsuit about Israel's sinfulness.[20] God is the speaker, and he brings the charges against Israel.

The accusation explains the charges based on the people's surprising response to God's gracious action (this paragraph also ends with a recognition of God's grace in 1:9). God faithfully and tenderly cared for his adopted "sons/children" (cf. Hos 11:1–2), a reference to the nurturing of Israel (Exod 4:22) in its early days (notice he avoids the father imagery for God[21]). These metaphors starkly contrast the divine care, blessing, and "raising up, exaltation" (*rwm*, also in 23:4) of Judah with their willful opposition to God and rebellious refusal to submit to his authority.[22]

1:3   In light of everything God did, this rebellious attitude was inexcusable. With proverbial skill, Isaiah claims that even dumb animals like the ox and donkey know (*yādaʿ*) better than to behave like this. Isaiah used farm animals that the listeners could identify with to make this logical point from common experience more persuasive. The comparison probably drew a smile on people's faces, because almost everyone in his audience could tell stories about being unable to handle a stubborn ox, or how stupid their idiot donkey was.[23] Yet everyone also knew that these dumb animals were smart enough to realize that they needed to come home at night if they wanted to eat. Although these animals were sometimes unwilling to submit to authority (just like Israel), they maintained their relationship with their owner. In contrast, the dumber Israelites who were "my people" (*ʿammî*) did not seem to "know" (*yādaʿ*) that they needed to maintain their covenant relationship with God. Unfortunately, there still are some religious people around who make unwise sinful decisions that

---

[20] Gitay, *Isaiah and his Audience*, 22–23, believes that this is a trial and that the heaven and earth are the judges of the case. This reads far too much into this reference to the heaven and the earth; surely God is always seen as the judge of his people.

[21] Wildberger, *Isaiah 1–12*, 13, inappropriately inserts the father-son relationship here, but God is not compared to a father in this verse (see Hos 11:1–4 for that imagery).

[22] פָּשַׁע, "rebelled," in political life is a willful act of defiance against a ruler's will, a revolt against authority (1 Kgs 12:19; 2 Kgs 1:1). It charges the people with rebellion against God's rule over their lives, a defiant refusal to follow his will.

[23] The difficulty of controlling the ox and ass was proverbial in Israelite experience (Prov 7:22; 15:17; 26:3). See E. Nielsen, "Ass and Ox in the Old Testament," *Studia Orientalia Ioanni Pedersen* (ed. F. Hvidberg; Copenhagen: Munksgaard, 1953), 263–74.

make the average donkey look like a genius. This analogy about the failures of God's chosen people should cause "church people" today to ask the question: Have we ever acted like the rebellious people Isaiah is talking about (1:2–4)?

1:4–9 Having made this accusation, Isaiah breaks out with a brief lament: Some limit the lament to the "woe oracle" (*hôy*) in v. 4,[24] but it seems best to view the prophet as lamenting all the way from v. 4 through v. 9. Laments and woe oracles often contain questions that ask why something bad is happening (Amos 5:18,20; 6:2; Hab 1:2–3; Ps 13:1–2) and usually have a section describing the terrible trouble the person or nation is enduring (5:9–10; 28:7–8; 29:1–4). In this lament, Isaiah grieves because of the bruised condition of the punished nation of Judah. He identifies with his audience's condition in order to show them that he cares (an emotional appeal) and that there is a way out of their difficulty.

1:4 The woe oracle laments the spiritual cause of Judah's problems. Total depravity is emphasized in this cry of despair. The flurry of negative descriptors concentrates on the fact that the people are sinful, guilty, evildoers, corrupt, and that they have forsaken, spurned, and turned their backs on God. They are called a sinful "nation" (*goy*), a term usually used to define pagan nations, rather than the "people" (*'am*) of God. There is no doubt about why these difficult days have fallen on Judah. The prophet points to the seriousness of the situation by saying the people are "loaded/burdened" with guilt (as opposed to just a few sins) and have "forsaken/divorced" and "spurned/scorned" (as opposed to having just a minor difference with) the Holy One of Israel.[25] This unfathomable rejection of the almighty, glorious, holy, and just covenant partner who loved them was tantamount to a rejection of his covenant love, a repudiation of his importance in their daily lives, and a denial of his divine character. These terms for sin do not indicate what the people replaced God with after they rejected him, but in other passages in the Old Testament these terms are sometimes connected to serving other gods (cf. 1:21–31; Deut 31:20; 32:19).[26]

1:5–6 Isaiah laments this situation and asks the question any friend or parent would ask: Why are you doing such foolish things that cause you to get

---

[24] See C. Westermann, *Basic Forms of Prophetic Speech* (Philadelphia: Westminster, 1967), 190–94, and E. Gerstenberger, " The Woe Oracles of the Prophets," *JBL* 81 (1962): 249–63, for a discussion of the lamenting woe oracle. J. Blenkinsopp, *Isaiah 1–39*, AB (New York: Doubleday, 2001), 182, identifies only v. 4 as a lament, while Clements, *Isaiah 1–39*, 31, claims that the woe "serves as a meaningful expression of rebuke." This interpretation seems to remove the sadness and grief aspect of the lament. S. Niditch, "The Composition of Isaiah 1," *Biblica* 61 (1980): 516–17, demonstrates how the woe oracle in 1:4–9 fits the same pattern as the woe oracles in Isa 5:11–13, 18–24, Amos 6:1–8, and Hab 2:15–17.

[25] Since chap. 1 was written long after chap. 6 (they are not in chronological order), the idea of the Holy One of Israel comes from Isaiah's earlier experience of seeing the glory of God in Isa 6.

[26] עָזַב, "forsake/divorce," and נָאַץ, "spurn/scorn," are often used in the context of serving other gods (Deut 30:20; Judg 2:12; 10:6,10; 1 Sam 12:10; Jer 2:13; Ezek 14:5). Blenkinsopp, *Isaiah 1–39*, 179, makes this observation concerning the phrase "turned their backs," which is used in Ezek 14:5 in the context of idolatry.

into so much trouble? The implication is, if you will address the root cause of your problems, the terrible consequences you are suffering will end. Judah is pictured as a person who was brutally beaten over her whole body (1:6). She is covered from head to toe with open bleeding wounds and ugly bruises that have not had any medical treatment.

1:7–9 This is a symbolic representation of a nation that was almost completely defeated in a war.[27] This refers to the Assyrian attack by Sennacherib in 701 BC when he captured and desolated all the major cities of Judah except Jerusalem.[28] In this case, the foreigners and strangers mentioned in 1:7 would refer to the Assyrian army that devastated the land. The Daughter of Zion was the only city left, and she was in a weakened state all by herself, like a lonely little temporary hut out in the field. The Daughter of Zion is a theological reference to the inhabitants of the glorious city of Jerusalem (a political term) who lived on the sacred mountain where God dwelt in his holy temple. Ironically, Zion looked more like the devastated cities of Sodom and Gomorrah (1:9; Gen 19) than the majestic city of the great King (Ps 48:1–2)—a shocking comparison that purposefully raised painful comparative issues (the wickedness of both nations) that most Israelites would not want to recognize. The only difference between these cities that Isaiah mentions is that God graciously intervened and allowed a few survivors in Zion, while he totally destroyed Sodom (except Lot and his family). The distinction between Sodom and Jerusalem is not in the behavior of the people, but in the marvelous grace of God in miraculously delivering them from the Assyrian army (Isa 36–37).

3. God's Call for Reconciliation, Not Useless Worship (1:10–20)

> [10]**Hear the word of the LORD,**
> **you rulers of Sodom;**
> **listen to the law of our God,**
> **you people of Gomorrah!**
> [11]**"The multitude of your sacrifices —**
> **what are they to me?" says the LORD.**

---

[27] J. H. Hayes and S. A. Irvine, *Isaiah, the Eighth-Century Prophet: His Times and His Preaching* (Nashville: Abingdon, 1987), 73, think this language describes the earthquake in Uzziah's reign about 760 BC, but this interpretation seems unlikely. The metaphors are from the military siege of a city.

[28] *ANET*, 287–88, refers to this battle where Sennacherib attacked 46 strong cities and countless villages. He claims to have taken 200,150 people captive, but admits that Jerusalem held out against him. The biblical account in Isa 36–37 is not identical to the Assyrian record. J. A. Emerton, "The Historical Background of Isaiah 1:4–9," *Eretz-Israel* 24 (1993): 34–40, connects these verses with Sennacherib's attack. This is a much better option than J. D. W. Watts, *Isaiah 1–33*, WBC (Waco: Word, 1985), 20, who states that in light of "the description of Israel's problems given in vv 4–7b, the period under discussion must come during one of Assyria's incursions into the land before the fall of Samaria in 721 B.C."

"I have more than enough of burnt offerings,
  of rams and the fat of fattened animals;
I have no pleasure
  in the blood of bulls and lambs and goats.
¹²When you come to appear before me,
  who has asked this of you,
  this trampling of my courts?
¹³Stop bringing meaningless offerings!
  Your incense is detestable to me.
New Moons, Sabbaths and convocations —
  I cannot bear your evil assemblies.
¹⁴Your New Moon festivals and your appointed feasts
  my soul hates.
They have become a burden to me;
  I am weary of bearing them.
¹⁵When you spread out your hands in prayer,
  I will hide my eyes from you;
even if you offer many prayers,
  I will not listen.
Your hands are full of blood;
¹⁶wash and make yourselves clean.
  Take your evil deeds
  out of my sight!
Stop doing wrong,
¹⁷learn to do right!
Seek justice,
  encourage the oppressed.
Defend the cause of the fatherless,
  plead the case of the widow.

¹⁸"Come now, let us reason together,"
  says the LORD.
"Though your sins are like scarlet,
  they shall be as white as snow;
though they are red as crimson,
  they shall be like wool.
¹⁹ If you are willing and obedient,
  you will eat the best from the land;
²⁰but if you resist and rebel,
  you will be devoured by the sword."
  For the mouth of the LORD has spoken.

The reference to Sodom and Gomorrah in 1:10 creates a natural connection with 1:9, but in these verses the theme changes dramatically to focus on the temple worship of the people in Judah. It is unclear why temple worship is addressed at this point, but the covenant lawsuit in Mic 6:6–7 also discusses the people's unacceptable worship. In Micah, someone in his audience tried to defend himself against Micah's accusations by proclaiming that the people sacrificed often and did everything God asked of them. This assertion is then followed in 6:8 with God's statement of what he actually required of them, thus demonstrating that God was not pleased with just a multitude of sacrifices. It is possible that Isaiah's audience also objected to Isaiah's accusations, claiming that God should not punish them since they were bringing him sacrifices. If someone in Isaiah's audience made such a claim, Isaiah's response in 1:10–15 would be a fitting answer.[29]

The structural organization of this paragraph falls into three interrelated topics:

1. What does not please God   1:10–15
2. What does please God   1:16–17
3. How to resolve these differences with God   1:18–20

This critique of Judah's worship is unique in its form,[30] but some phrases resemble other prophetic condemnations of unacceptable worship (Hos 6:4–6; Amos 4:4–5; 5:21–25; Mic 6:6–8; Jer 7:1–12,21–22). This was not a rejection of the sacrificial system of worship,[31] but of the inadequacy of repetitious religious acts without appropriate confessions of sin, rejection of evil, and a commitment to live according to God's revealed standards of holiness and justice. If Manasseh was starting to introduce foreign worship into temple services around this time, that would explain why these religious acts were so detestable.[32]

1:10 The transition from 1:9 to 1:10 is eased by the common reference to Sodom and Gomorrah in both verses, but the flow of thought is interrupted by a new imperative exhortation[33] to "hear" (*šimʿû*), by a new "word of the LORD"[34] (similar to 1:2), and by the identification of a more specific audience (the rul-

---

[29] Oswalt, *Isaiah 1–39*, 95, also suggests that Isaiah may be responding to a comment by someone in his audience.

[30] Wildberger, *Isaiah 1–12*, 37, connects these verses to "the realm of wisdom teaching" based on similar criticisms in wisdom texts (Prov 4:1; 7:24; Job 33:31; Ps 49:2), Westermann, *Basic Forms of Prophetic Speech*, 203–205, compares these verses to the prophetic judgment speech and calls them "the prophetic torah," while Blenkinsopp, *Isaiah 1–39*, 184, calls this a "sarcastic imitation of a priestly *tora*."

[31] J. P. Hyatt, "The Prophetic Criticism of Israelite Worship," in *Interpreting the Prophetic Traditions* (New York: KTAV, 1969), 208, or R. E. Clements, *Prophecy and Tradition*, SBT (Naperville: Allenson, 1965), 86–102, discuss earlier critical interpretations that view these verses as a rejection of cultic worship. Now most reject that older critical interpretation.

[32] Although Isaiah does not specifically mention pagan worship of Baal in 1:10–14, several terms and comparisons imply that he is not just talking about approved Hebrew ritual. When he calls their worship something "detestable, an abomination" (תּוֹעֵבָה) he is probably not referring to Hebrew ritual.

[33] The imperative verb שִׁמְעוּ is used as an exhortation (GKC § 109a), paralleling 1:2, thus it linguistically marks the beginning of the next paragraph.

[34] It is unnecessary to connect the reference to the word and "teachings, law" (*tôrâ*) to wisdom circles as suggested in J. Jensen, *The Use of tôrâ by Isaiah: His Debate with the Wisdom Tradition* (Washington D.C. : Catholic Biblical Association, 1973).

ers). These factors indicate the beginning of a new paragraph. The comparison moves from a physical comparison of differences in 1:9 (Sodom did not survive, but by God's grace Jerusalem did) to an astonishing comparison of similarities between the rulers of both nations in 1:10.[35] But how are the rulers and the people of Jerusalem like the terribly sinful rulers of Sodom? The answer is found in the two kinds of sins addressed: oppression of the weak and unacceptable worship. Ezekiel 16:49–52 mentions that the people of Sodom did not help the poor and needy (1:15–17 applies this problem to Jerusalem), while Jer 23:13–14 and Isa 1:10–14 describe their harlotry with idols and detestable sacrifices. Second Kings 21:2–5,9,16 reports that Manasseh followed the detestable practices of the Canaanites, built pagan altars in the temple courts, shed innocent blood, and did more evil than any earlier inhabitants in the land (including Sodom). The prophet's strong words from God did not have a modern "enlightened" pluralistic view that focused on the toleration of all religious practices. God views some acts as unacceptable abominations.

1:11–15 In defense of Isaiah's audience, one might claim that a major difference between the people of Sodom and Jerusalem was that the Hebrews offered sacrifices to Israel's God. Nevertheless, God's evaluation of his people's temple worship was entirely negative. God was not pleased with the large numbers of sacrifices that the rulers and people brought (1:11; see also 1 Sam 15:22). These were "your sacrifices," not God's. God was not "pleased" (*ḥāpāṣtî*) with what they were offering, though sacrifices were supposed to be "an aroma pleasing to God" (Lev 1:9,13,17). In God's mind there was a big difference between appearing before him at the temple and destructive "trampling"[36] of his courts (1:12). Trampling does not simply refer to many people walking around in the temple; it describes an act of disrespect and the destruction of something (see 5:5). God does not want "false, deceptive" sacrifices (better than NIV's "meaningless" in 1:13),[37] "detestable, abominable" incense, or "evil" assemblies. Many commentators believe God was simply unhappy with a ritualistic religion that had no true heart relationship with God,[38] but

---

[35] This comparison with Sodom and Gomorrah is not uncommon when talking about God overthrowing a nation (Deut 29:22; Jer 49:18; Amos 4:11; Zeph 2:7) or when comparing the evil condition of Jerusalem with Sodom (Jer 23:14; Rom 9:29; Rev 11:8).

[36] רָמַס, "to trample," is almost always (the exception is Nah 3:14) used in a negative sense of destroying (Isa 16:4; 26:6; 28:3; 63:3). Other roots meaning "tread" also refer to destruction (5:5; 28:18; 51:23).

[37] J. F. A. Sawyer, "שָׁוְא *šāw᾿* deceit," *TLOT*, III (ed. E. Jenni and C. Westermann; Peabody: Hendrickson, 1997), 1310–12, holds that the primary meaning is "deceit, wickedness, falseness" and concludes that "the usually accepted attenuated meaning of 'nothingness' or adv. 'in naught, in vain'. . . is somewhat problematic."

[38] J. A. Motyer, *Isaiah*, TOTC (Downers Grove: InterVarsity, 1999), 45, refers to these as "people long on religion and short on morality." W. C. Brueggemann, *Isaiah 1–39*, WBComp (Louisville: Westminster John Knox, 1998), 17, claims "Yahweh rejects them because Israel's gestures of worship are no longer vehicles for a serious relationship. . . . Yahweh will no longer participate in a charade of receiving gifts from people who are not sincere."

these sacrifices were "false," "abominations," and "detestable," terms normally
saved for pagan sacrifices like those instituted by Manasseh (2 Kgs 21:2,11).
Wildberger correctly says, "it is really a heathen 'abomination' which Israel
has appropriated for its own use."[39] Not only did Isaiah oppose meaningless
Hebrew ritual, he also opposed the repetitious pagan ritual that had infiltrated
and polluted Hebrew worship.

In strong emotional terms God reveals that his very essence, his soul (*napšî*),
hates their appointed feasts and he cannot bear to put up with them any longer (1:14). This statement represents the conclusion God has come to; he will
"hide his eyes . . . will not listen" (1:15) because their hands[40] were full of
blood (cf. 1:21; 2 Kgs 21:16) from murderous acts of violence.[41] The people
must repent or God will refuse to listen to any of their prayers. This principle
applies to all worshipers. Everyone who wishes to worship God should ask the
question: "Is my worship acceptable to God, or has sin kept God from accepting my praise and prayers (1:10–15; 59:1–2)?"

1:16–17   This paragraph ends with a series of nine imperative exhortations
that show what pleases God. The prophet is persuasively and forcefully calling
on his listeners to change the way they live. Seven of these are positive things
one should do; two (16b) call for the audience to stop doing something they
were already doing. It might appear that there is an abrupt shift to a discussion
of social ethics in v. 16 because the prophet does not appear to connect any of
these phrases to temple sacrifices. Nevertheless, in 52 out of 73 cases, "wash"
(*raḥăṣû*) refers to cultic cleansing and the *hithpaʿel* reflexive[42] "make yourself
clean" (*hizzakkû*) usually refers to what people do as part of their cultic responsibility,[43] not to what God does (a passive verb would be required). Therefore,
God is encouraging an internal change of the heart that is revealed in the symbolic outward action of washing. Contextually, to "take your evil deeds from
my sight"[44] instructs the people to remove the pagan detestable worship from

---

[39] Wildberger, *Isaiah 1–12*, 44, properly understands the term "detestable, abomination"
(תּוֹעֵבָה), though he does not make a connection between it and the false religion introduced by
Manasseh.

[40] 1QIsaᵃ adds at the end of this verse "your fingers (are full of) iniquity," possibly drawing on
59:3, thus most reject it as not part of the original reading of 1:15 (see O. Kaiser, *Isaiah 1–12*, OTL
(Philadelphia: Westminster, 1983), 25. This reading gives a nice parallel line to "your hands are
full of blood," but it is not found in 4QIsaᶠ.

[41] Oswalt, *Isaiah 1–39*, 98, argues that this fits better with 1:16–17, rather than the view that it
refers to the blood of sacrifices. Since there is nothing wrong with offering the blood of sacrifices,
that interpretation seems unlikely.

[42] A. M. Honeyman, "Isaiah 1:18, *hizzakku*," *VT* 1 (1951): 63–65, suggests the verb should
be read as a *niphal* "be cleansed" like some versions translate it. Oswalt, *Isaiah 1–39*, 93, follows
this translation, but if this word is referring to man's responsibility in worship, the reflexive idea
is more appropriate.

[43] Oswalt, *Isaiah 1–39*, 98 claims that "the prophet's point is to stress the responsibility the
people do have. Of course, apart from God's free grace in forgiveness, repentance and changing
the course of one's life are valueless."

[44] מַעַלְלֵיכֶם, "your deeds," can refer to acts of pagan worship (Judg 2:19; Ps 106:28–29,39; Jer

before God's presence in the temple. The most natural flow of thought from vv. 10–15 to vv. 16–17 would be to interpret the cleansing of v. 16 as part of the solution to the problem of improper worship in vv. 10–15.

The implications of a changed life are not limited to following proper practices at worship. Acceptable behavior extends to all areas of life and particularly how leaders treat the weak and vulnerable in society (1:17). Such behavior requires that everyone in a position of authority should learn the principles of justice from the laws of God (Exod 20–23) and learn how to put those principles into practice. Shedding the innocent blood of the weak is unacceptable (1:15; 2 Kgs 21:16). Instead, God is pleased when rulers act justly and defend the widow and orphan from the unscrupulous ways of their oppressors (Deut 10:18; 24:17).[45] In 66:3–4 the prophet makes the same point; proper worship and judicial ethics go hand in hand for those who desire to please God.

1:18 Although the situation may appear to be hopeless, Isaiah refers to the possibility of settling the conflict between God and Judah before this problem causes a complete separation between these covenant partners (1:18–20). Isaiah quotes another word from God ("says the LORD" in 1:18) that (a) informs the audience of an opportunity to resolve the accusations against Judah and to request God's forgiveness of sins (1:18), and (b) explains the implications of either accepting or rejecting God's ways (1:19–20). This invitation has a persuasive quality to it because it is not demeaning, demanding, or closed to Judah's positive response. The door is open for resolution and restoration.

The verb root *ykh*, which is in a cohortative form,[46] encourages or requests action. The term sometimes is rendered "enter a lawsuit" or "let us test each other,"[47] but the basic meaning of the term is "to determine what is right."[48] The imperative "come" requests a meeting of the parties "to determine what is right" in order to restore the relationship between God and his people. The spirit with which God desires to enter this discussion is not to argue whether Judah has sinned, nor to re-evaluate the legitimacy of people's worship, nor to reassess whether justice was provided for the widow or orphan. "Though

---

25:5–6; 35:15; 44:22; Mic 3:4) as well as acts of oppression (Ps 28:4; Jer 7:5; 21:12)

[45] F. C. Fensham, "Widow, Orphan, and the Poor in Ancient Near Eastern Legal and Wisdom Literature," *JNES* 21 (1962): 129–39, shows that these values were present throughout the ancient Near East. T. L. Leclerc, *Yahweh is Exalted in Justice: Solidarity and Conflict in Isaiah* (Minneapolis: Fortress, 2001), 34–39, reviews the different ways Fensham, Hammershamb, Patterson, Machinist, and Hanson emphasize this call for justice as a common ancient Near Eastern social value or a divine imperative.

[46] See GKC § 108b for the idea of encouragement in the cohortative verb. Wildberger, *Isaiah 1–12*, 53, takes a forensic meaning where God and Judah would have a time to reprove one another. This overstates Judah's role in a lawsuit with God. Sinful Judah is not an equal partner; God is the judge.

[47] Watts, *Isaiah 1–33*, 13, thinks this is a court case, but this is not an appropriate translation, for it is not man's place to test God's perception, his laws, or his decisions.

[48] Thus G. Liedke, "יכח *ykh* hi. to determine what is right," *TLOT*, 542–44, though Blenkinsopp, *Isaiah 1–39*, 185, suggests the meaning "to settle out of court."

your sins are like scarlet" assumes that Judah's sinfulness is an irrefutable fact; there is nothing to argue about. Instead, God offers grace through forgiveness to restore the relationship if Judah is willing to change. God does not have an agenda to end the relationship with punishment.

The nature of what is proposed in the second half of 1:18 is controversial, based on how one interprets the second half of each conditional sentence. Some take these words as questions: "shall they be as white as snow?" or "can they (then) pass for white like snow?"[49] These commentators reject the common "they shall be as white as snow" because it appears to be an unconditional promise with no need for repentance. An alternative is to opt for a subjunctive or modal use of the verb ("they may/can become as white as snow"[50]) or a jussive translation ("they must become as white as snow"[51]) because these translations recognize the conditional nature of God's forgiveness. It appears that the modal "may/can" is the better way of understanding these conditional clauses.[52]

The metaphor of sins as an indelible scarlet/red/crimson sign of guilt from a bloodstain (cf. 1:15; 63:1–3) is contrasted with the unstained pure white color of snow and wool that symbolizes forgiveness of sins (cf. Ps 51:7, "Wash me and I will be whiter than snow."). Verse 18 does not explain how that transformation was possible through atonement;[53] all it suggests is that God can bring about this change. The imagery employed conveys the idea that through atonement God removed the sins and their stain; he did not just cover them up or hide them (Ps 103:12; Mic 7:20–21).[54]

1:19–20 A resolution and restoration of fellowship between God and his people is dependent on God's ability to remove the stain of their sins (1:18) and the people's willingness to turn from sin and rebellion against God to faith and obedience to God. Verse 19 deals with the human choice to submit and follow God, while v. 20 addresses the choice of selfish rebellion against God's will. There are no other choices, for people must either serve God or reject God.

---

[49] Wildberger, *Isaiah 1–12*, 53 and 56, depends on Duhm who states that "God never offers the forgiveness of sins in such a polite manner," and that such a translation would contradict the rest of God's charges in chap. 1.

[50] Gray, *Isaiah 1–27*, 26–29, has a general discussion of numerous alternative translations, including Marti's ironic interpretation that sarcastically offers repentance. According to this approach Isaiah is mocking the people's view that a few sacrifices will remove their sins. Oswalt, *Isaiah 1–39,* 100–101, rejects Marti's view.

[51] J. Goldingay, "If Your Sins Are Like Scarlet . . . (Isaiah 1:18)," *StudTh* 35 (1981): 137–44, defends this translation because it has the advantage of offering mercy dependent on repentance.

[52] J. T. Willis, "On the Interpretation of Isaiah 1:18," *JSOT* 25 (1983): 35–54, reviews the arguments for and against six different ways of translating 1:18.

[53] The Israelites were familiar with temple worship, the shedding of the blood of a lamb, the principles of salvation revealed in the Levitical sacrifices (Lev 1–5), and the symbolic meaning of events on the annual Day of Atonement (Lev 16–17).

[54] In the OT forgiveness was complete and the relationship between God and the sinner was restored. The sin was put on Christ's account to be paid for when he died on the cross.

The consequences of the people's choice will consist of divine blessing ("you will eat," *ʾākal* in the active voice) or divine cursing (lit. "you will be eaten/devoured," *ʾākal* in the passive). This covenantal way of thinking clearly laid out the future and "determined what was right." In the New Testament Jesus is just as clear and uncompromising when he says that people will either serve God or their own desires (Matt 6:24). People have to choose, and their choices will determine their eternal fate.

4. God's Purification of Judah's Leaders (1:21–31)

21 See how the faithful city
    has become a harlot!
  She once was full of justice;
    righteousness used to dwell in her —
    but now murderers!
22 Your silver has become dross,
    your choice wine is diluted with water.
23 Your rulers are rebels,
    companions of thieves;
  they all love bribes
    and chase after gifts.
  They do not defend the cause of the fatherless;
    the widow's case does not come before them.
24 Therefore the Lord, the LORD Almighty,
    the Mighty One of Israel, declares:
  "Ah, I will get relief from my foes
    and avenge myself on my enemies.
25 I will turn my hand against you;
    I will thoroughly purge away your dross
    and remove all your impurities.
26 I will restore your judges as in days of old,
    your counselors as at the beginning.
  Afterward you will be called
    the City of Righteousness,
    the Faithful City."

27 Zion will be redeemed with justice,
    her penitent ones with righteousness.
28 But rebels and sinners will both be broken,
    and those who forsake the LORD will perish.

29 "You will be ashamed because of the sacred oaks
    in which you have delighted;
  you will be disgraced because of the gardens
    that you have chosen.
30 You will be like an oak with fading leaves,
    like a garden without water.

31 The mighty man will become tinder
   and his work a spark;
  both will burn together,
   with no one to quench the fire."

The second section of this sermon addresses the moral changes (negative ones) that characterized Jerusalem at that time and God's refining discipline that affected the future of Jerusalem (based on the principles given in 1:19–20). There is a strong contrast in these verses between past faithful leaders (like Hezekiah) who were willing and obedient to God (1:21a,c), and the present evil leader (likely Manasseh), who was resisting and rebelling against God (1:21b,d, 22–23). Parallel to the comparison in 1:19–20, the evil leaders and the nation will be purified through fire (1:24–25,28,29–31) but the righteous will be restored (1:26,27). The repeated use of vocabulary from 1:2–20[55] suggests that the concluding comments in this paragraph are an integral complement to the first half of the chapter. The purpose of this additional information is to convince the hearers that they need to choose obedience (1:19) if they want to avoid the purifying fire of God's wrath (1:29–31).

The structure of the paragraph is:

The purification of Jerusalem	1:21–26
Their sins	21–23
Their purification	24–26
The fate of the righteous and the wicked	1:27–31
Redemption for the righteous	27
Destruction for the wicked	28–31

The beginning and the end of the first subparagraph in 1:21–26 are marked with references to the "City of Righteousness" and the "Faithful City," which link these verses as a cohesive unit. The contrasting fate of the righteous and the wicked in 1:27–31 continues the theme of 1:19–20, thus ending each major paragraph (1:2–20; 1:21–31) with a similar conclusion that presents the hearers with a choice they need to make. The choice to replace the wickedness of the past with righteousness in the present requires an act of the will and the redeeming power of God (1:26).

1:21–26 These verses are divided into a series of accusations of sinfulness against the rulers of Jerusalem (1:21–23) and God's consequent determination to purify the city (1:24–26). This judgment speech traces the history of Jerusalem through four theological steps: (a) it was formerly a city that acted in a way that was faithful to God (1:21a,c); (b) it is now unfaithful (1:21b,d, 22–23); (c)

---

[55] M. A. Sweeney, *Isaiah 1–39*, XVI, FOTL (Grand Rapids: Eerdmans, 1996), 66 and 68, points to the repetition of words like "plead for the orphan and widow" in 1:17,23 or "justice" in 1:17,21.

God will soon purge the evil city with his refining fire (1:24–25); and (d) the
city will once again be faithful (1:26).

The prophet begins by lamenting the sinful degeneration of Jerusalem
(1:21–23), expressing his sorrow in a manner parallel to his lament over the
sinfulness of the people in the first paragraph (1:4–9). A terribly sad and dis-
couraging thing has happened.[56] As one might expect in a eulogy, the prophet
begins by fondly remembering the time when the city was characterized by
faithfulness to God (the era of Hezekiah). The lament moves from praising the
past to lamenting the present—one characterized by prostitution and murder.
Murder does not seem to be a metaphor in this context, so the problem of shedding innocent blood in the era of Manasseh may be in view (2 Kgs 21:16).
There is no reason to understand harlotry as a metaphor of anything other than
the worship of idols (this practice was common during Manasseh's reign), as
1:29–30 suggests.[57] Although at one time the city was firmly established and
faithful (from the root 'āman), being "full of"[58] or completely ruled by the
principles of justice (mišpāṭ) and relationships of righteousness (ṣedeq), later
the people stopped following the principle of justice in their relationships (they
murdered others). My, how the holy have fallen!

How could beautiful and valuable silver degenerate completely into worthless waste metal (v. 22)? How could expensive sparkling wine turn into cheap,
watered-down booze? Both products suffered a deterioration of quality because large dosages of impurities diluted them. This is what had happened
in Jerusalem (v. 23). One of the central impurities was the leaders' love for
money. This led them to steal and accept bribes in court, and it encouraged
those looking for favors to give them gifts and to oppress the poor widows and
orphans (cf. v. 16).

God, "therefore" (lākēn), was determined to purify the city (vv. 24–26). The
emphasis is on God himself and his acts. He is the sovereign Lord and master;
he is Yahweh of the heavenly armies, the Divine Warrior; and he is the All-
Powerful One. The titles of God are stacked up to emphasize that God is able
to do whatever he plans to do. God's purposes at this time are threefold: (a) to
satisfy his holiness (v. 24b), (b) to remove impurity (v. 25), and (c) to restore

---

[56] Brueggemann, *Isaiah 1–39,* 21, emphasizes the astonishment of Isaiah's grief over the
city's sins.

[57] Clements, *Isaiah 1–39,* 35, thinks this section originated from unfaithfulness in the time of
Ahaz. His reasons demonstrate why the time of Hezekiah's reform around 701 BC does not fit the
situation for chap. 1. It makes more sense to relate the whole chapter to the early years of Manasseh, rather than connect vv. 2–20 to Hezekiah and then vv. 21–31 to 30 years earlier in the time of
Ahaz. The chapter is far too unified to draw it from such diverse eras. Gray, *Isaiah 1–27,* 33 and
39, does not view this prostitution as the worship of other gods, but does believe 1:29–30 refers
to pagan worship. Leclerc, *Yahweh is Exalted in Justice,* 41, reinterprets harlotry as "abandoning
the demands for justice," thus rejecting any reference to idolatry in chap. 1. Interestingly, he never
discusses the sacred oaks and gardens in 1:29.

[58] מְלֵאֲתִי, "full of," looks like a first person singular, but it is a feminine singular construct
noun; cf. GKC § 90l, 95h.

his city of righteousness (v. 26). The holiness of God is offended when people sin, so the offensive matter must be removed before a relationship with God can be established. This removal involves the satisfaction (or "comforting," *nāḥam*) of God's holy sorrow and anger, plus the implementation of divine justice (better than "avenge," *nāqam*) on his enemies; that is, on his own people in Jerusalem. This will involve both God's determination[59] to "turn against" (v. 25) his enemies to remove their sins (compared to a purifying process),[60] and God's "turning toward"[61] (v. 26) others to restore them. The future means of purification that will reverse the process of deterioration in v. 22 is not fully explained, but the transformation will be complete. "I will thoroughly purge your dross" in v. 25 leaves out the Hebrew reference to the metaphorical use of "lye," a strong chemical that could expose the pure metal.[62] The results of God's miraculous work of grace will be a restored "City of Righteousness" as at the first (possibly a return to the era of a new Davidic king)[63] and leaders that value righteous relationships. This promise is an encouragement to anyone who suffers through life with sinful and selfish leaders who do not care about justice or God. A day will soon come when God will transform this world, remove all sin, replace all evil leaders, and rule his kingdom in righteousness and justice. This passage is also a warning to every leader. You will be held accountable for how you lead the people God has called you to serve.

1:27–31   The final verses draw the audience to the point of decision about the choices they must make.[64] Their choices will have eternal consequences, for they will either enjoy God's wonderful redemption (1:27) or suffer disgrace and destruction from God (1:28–31). Now there should be no false hopes based on sacrificial offerings, political privilege in government, or a person's national origin. Zion's future is totally dependent on God's grace and their repentance.

God has a wonderful plan for his people. He does not desire to judge or destroy anyone (Ezek 18:32). His will is that Zion, his holy place of dwelling, would be filled with repentant and redeemed people (1:27). W. Brueggemann refers to these as "those who repent in justice and righteousness"[65] by acting

---

[59] The cohortative verbs "I will turn away," "I will remove" (1:25) and "I will restore" (1:26) express strong resolve or determination to do something (GKC § 108a). This gives greater persuasive assurance that God will do these things.

[60] Malachi 3:2–3 portrays the Messenger of the covenant purifying his people, especially the Levites, when he comes to his temple at the end of time.

[61] 1:25 and 1:26 begin with the same word, וְאָשִׁיבָה, "and I will turn," but the two different audiences will be treated very differently.

[62] The NIV substitutes the word "thoroughly" to represent the kind of complete effect lye has on metal.

[63] Wildberger, *Isaiah 1–12*, 71, and Oswalt, *Isaiah 1–39*, 107, suggest a return to the era of David (and Solomon), but the last part of Solomon's reign was one of unfaithfulness to God.

[64] There is no justification for the conclusion of Clements, *Isaiah 1–39*, 36, that this was written about the reform of Jerusalem's government after the fall of Jerusalem in 587 BC and just before Nehemiah's return.

[65] Brueggemann, *Isaiah 1–39*, 23, believes the majority of the people will not choose this path.

justly toward the widows and orphans. J. A. Motyer views God's plan as his redemptive act in which he "does not overlook but satisfies the claims of his holy precepts . . . his righteous claims have been met."[66] The best interpretation may be to take the phrases "with justice" and "with righteousness" in light of the usage of these terms in Isaiah 55–66 (chap. 1 was added at the end of Isaiah's ministry). In these passages "justice" and "righteousness" connote God's vindication and salvation.[67] This interpretation focuses attention on God as redeemer[68] and the only source of hope for salvation. This provides a stark contrast with the unrepentant people who put their hope in idols of wood (1:29–31).

A very different future awaits those who forsake God (1:28). The rebellious sinners (as in 1:2,4) will perish (the opposite of salvation). The reason given in 1:29 (NIV misses the introductory "because," *kî*) is their choice (also in 65:12; 66:3) to worship idols of wood (*'êlîm*) rather than commit their lives to the redeeming power of God (*'ēl*—a word play). The lush gardens and sacred groves were an integral part of the Canaanite fertility religion (27:9; 57:5; 65:3; 66:17; Jer 17:2; Ezek 6:13) that Manasseh promoted (2 Kgs 21; 2 Chr 33).[69] The substitution of worship of the creation for worship of the Creator was hopeless. The plants in these gardens represent life and fertility that the god Baal could provide worshipers at these sanctuaries. But the gods Baal and Asherah will disappoint these people because plants and trees wither, dry up, and die when they have no water (1:30). The failure to sustain life demonstrates the powerlessness of these gods; they are nothing. Those who trust and delight in these gods will feel disgrace and shame because they foolishly chose to worship false gods (1:29).[70] In the end, they will realize that they were deceived and put their trust in something that has no power to nourish or protect them. Their humiliation will be bitter, for God revealed the truth to them long ago, but they rejected it. "The mighty one" (1:31) is an ambiguous term that primarily refers to the great cultic oak tree, but metaphorically it also pictures the worshipers of these trees.[71] Their substance and their works of worship will not look like

---

[66] J. A. Motyer, *The Prophecy of Isaiah* (Leicester: InterVarsity, 1993), 51.

[67] Blenkinsopp, *Isaiah 1–39*, 187, bases this viewpoint on passages like 51:6,8; 56:1; 59:9,16–17; 61:10–11; 63:1.

[68] The passive verb implies that they "will be redeemed" by someone else. Isaiah sees God as the Redeemer גֹּאֵל (41:14; 43:14; 44:6,24; 47:4; 48:17; 49:7,26; 54:5,8; 59:20; 60:16; 63:16) and he is the one who redeems: פָּדָה (29:22; 35:10; 50:2), גָּאַל (43:1; 44:22–23; 48:20; 50:2; 51:11; 52:3,9; 63:16).

[69] These common themes suggest that the last chapters of Isaiah were also addressing the situation when Manasseh was promoting the pagan Baal religion in Judah.

[70] The Hebrew MT and 1QIsa[a] have "They will be ashamed," יֵבֹשׁוּ, but NIV follows the Aramaic Targum "You will be ashamed," תֵּבֹשׁוּ, which smoothes things out and gives both 1:29a and b second person plural verbs.

[71] K. Nielsen, *There is Hope for a Tree* (Sheffield: *JSOT*, 1989), 209, and M Tsevat, "Isaiah I 31," *VT* 19 (1969): 261–63, give an extensive review of a variety of interpretations of these verses by various different commentators.

solid oak wood, but like loose fibers, like the worthless fuzz of chaff. These products ignite easily, burn quickly, and create an intense fire that is impossible to extinguish (cf. 66:14–15,24).

THEOLOGICAL IMPLICATIONS. Isaiah's message has theological significance for two audiences. First, there was the original audience that heard this sermon, and second, there is the audience that reads this chapter as an introduction to the long scroll. Although the message of chap. 1 does not change in its content, the context of the chapter and the audiences do change. Thus, the first audience that heard this sermon did not perceive that this message would eventually serve as an introduction to an extensive collection of Isaiah's writings.

Isaiah's theological perspective demarcates people into two groups: the rebellious people who forsake God and the redeemed people who trust God. Isaiah's goal was to open the eyes and hearts of both audiences to (a) God's view of the sinful people of Judah; (b) God's offer of grace; and (c) the seriousness of God's judgment on those who do not worship him. This evangelistic message should cause all his listeners to review the true nature of their relationship to God. Is there a spirit of rebellion, or does justice and faithfulness characterize the values of God's people? Is their heart attitude and practice of worship acceptable to God, or is worship time just the repetition of a series of deceptive rituals? Is there a need to request God's forgiveness for any sin (1:18–20)? There is a serious and inevitable consequence for choosing not to follow God, for one day God will take vengeance on his enemies (1:21–31).

Questions about true faithfulness to God require a penetrating and brutally honest examination of the heart. It is likely that many of the Hebrews who originally heard Isaiah thought that everything was fine between themselves and God, just like the "average person" in most churches today. Nevertheless, God's penetrating standards of justice and righteousness all too often uncover a veneer of piety and religious intentions hiding a life of selfishness, rebellion, and unwillingness to trust God. Isaiah challenged these people to carefully choose the path they wanted to follow and to know where that path would lead them. There are two ways to live and two destinations after death; all paths do not lead to God. They must reject the worldview of acceptable religious and social behavior promoted by Manasseh and return to God and his just ways as Hezekiah did.

The later audiences that read this chapter in Isaiah's scroll (and readers today) looked back on these words that address the problems of another generation and saw this message introducing a theological agenda for the prophet's messages. One learns what the prophet thought about God, about the sinfulness of the people, and about God's purification of his people. Isaiah's perspective guides one to look at the following chapters in a certain theological way. If Isaiah's positive message of hope in chap. 40 were to replace chap. 1 as the introduction to this book, that would definitely alter how one approached the book. When editing the text, it was determined that the scroll should not begin by offering unmitigated comfort and hope (40:1–11); instead it should present the possibility of "eating the best of the land—if you are willing and listen" (1:19) or "the sword will devour you—if you refuse and rebel" (1:20). This chapter presents choices: (a) being God's children or rebelling against God (1:2–3); (b) continuing to receive God's punishment through more wars or having the wars stop (1:5–9); (c) offering prayers and sacrifices that please God or having God hide his face and reject useless ritual (1:11–15); (d) making efforts to remove the stain and guilt of sin or allowing that stain to bring a curse (1:18–20); (e) acting like faithful and righteous people or behaving like harlots and murderers (1:21); and (f) accepting God's redemption or being burnt up with fire in disgrace (1:27–31). These alternatives prepare the reader for the following narratives because Uzziah, Ahaz, Hezekiah, and the people of Judah had to make these same choices. What worldview would they follow? Would people trust God and exalt his righteousness or would they exalt themselves? These choices face everyone who is attentive to the message of this book.

II. DEPENDING ON HUMAN RESOURCES OR TRUSTING GOD
    (2:1–12:6)
    1. Exaltation of God and Humbling of the Proud (2:1–4:6)
        (1) Promises of God's Future Kingdom Produce Trust (2:1–5)
        (2) Removal of Pride and Exaltation of God (2:6–22)
        (3) Removal of Judah's Male Leaders (3:1–15)
        (4) Removal of Judah's Proud Women (3:16–4:1)
        (5) God's Glorious, Holy Kingdom (4:2–6)
    2. The Destruction of Judah (5:1–30)
        (1) A Vineyard Song of Love and Rejection (5:1–7)
        (2) Reasons for Judah's Destruction (5:8–25)
        (3) An Army's Destruction of Judah (5:26–30)
    3. A Holy King's Calling to a Calloused Audience (6:1–13)
        (1) The Vision of the Holy King (6:1–4)
        (2) The Prophet's Purification (6:5–7)
        (3) A Hardening Message for a Calloused Audience (6:8–10)
        (4) Hope in the Midst of Destruction (6:11–13)
    4. The Destruction of Judah (7:1–8:18)
        (1) Ahaz's Failure to Trust God Brings Assyria (7:1–25)
            Do not Fear; Stand Firm in your Faith (7:1–9)
            The Sign of Immanuel (7:10–17)
            Judgment of the Land (7:18–25)
        (2) Fearing God, not Military Might (8:1–22)
            The Birth of Maher-Shalal-Hash-Baz (8:1–4)
            The Coming Assyrian Flood (8:5–10)
            Fear God, not Armies (8:11–15)
            Follow God's Instructions; Other Ways Bring Darkness
            (8:16–22)
    5. The Reign of a Righteous King, the Humbling of the Proud
        (9:1–11:16)
        (1) The Reign of a Righteous King (9:1–7)
        (2) The Judgment of Proud and Sinful Israel (9:8–10:4)
            God's Wrath against Proud Israel (9:8–12)
            God's Wrath against Unrepentant Leaders (9:13–17)
            God Is Destroying the Nation (9:18–21)
            Lament: Judah's Oppression Will Lead to Its Demise
            (10:1–4)
        (3) The Judgment of Proud Assyria (10:5–34)
            God Will Judge Assyrians for Pride (10:5–19)

II. DEPENDING ON HUMAN RESOURCES OR TRUSTING GOD (2:1–12:6)

Trusting God completely, not only in theory but also in practice, remains a key challenge for every believer—trusting him for provision, safety, health, children, business, church, the political situation of the nation, and all those minor issues that one faces every day. Kings and common citizens alike must humble themselves, realizing that God alone can supply all their needs in this world and the next. People do not need to manipulate business or political events so that they will come out right or to misrepresent the truth to insure a proper conclusion to an embarrassing problem. God can resolve all the so-called problems of life and his plans are not subject to the manipulation of mankind. Sometimes it may seem far easier for people to trust in something tangible, like money, another person, an army, alliances with other nations, the votes of friends, or their own wisdom. It is often hard to let go and completely let God be in control. Nevertheless, without faith and trust in God, it is impossible to please him (Heb 12:6).

In the time of Judah's King Uzziah (ch 2–5), prosperity, power, and pride made it difficult for people to trust God. When everything was going well, there was a sense that they really did not need God because they were doing very well on their own. Later, during the reign of King Ahaz when the nation was relatively weak (ch 7–12), forging political alliances seemed like a more reliable method of managing the nation's vulnerability to attack than trusting in God. The stories, sermons, messages of hope, laments, and songs of Isaiah 2–12 cry out to ask every listener the penetrating question: "Are you truly trusting in God, or is your trust in something or someone else?"

The actual date when Isaiah's sermons in 2–12 were written down on a scroll is unknown, but three factors suggest this happened sometime after the Syro-Ephraimite War in 734–32 BC: (a) The references to God as the Holy God/Holy One (even in 5:16,19,24) supports the idea that this message was edited and written down some time after Isaiah's vision of the Holy One on a throne in the Temple in 6:1–7. Isaiah's powerful encounter with God's glory impacted the prophet's life in a dramatic way, influencing his way of talking about God. (b) The structure of chaps. 2–12 seems to be organized as a unit (see the discussion on structure below), indicating that 2–5 was put together with

6–12 in mind; thus the final written organization of this material occurred some time after the Syro-Ephraimite War. (c) A few verses (e.g., 5:15–16) interrupt the flow of thought by quoting earlier and later verses (2:9,11,17; 6:3), thus providing additional evidence of Isaiah's hand in editing his earlier sermons in order to provide theological unity and continuity to the whole.[1] Since little can be discovered about the exact date when each message was spoken and even less information is available about the process of editing Isaiah's messages into the canonical form of chaps. 2–12, it is best to avoid undue speculation unsupported by linguistic evidence. The best one can hope to do is to attempt to identify information about the setting of the audience (political, social, or religious conditions) from the internal content of Isaiah's messages.

STRUCTURE.   The structure of any larger literary document should show what chapters go together and how they are related to one another. The larger literary context will provide clues about the historical setting of a group of related oracles, as well as contextual evidence for interpreting the meaning of words and themes within that literary unit. In addition, the literary context offers valuable assistance in understanding the progressive revelation of theo-logical concepts within and beyond that unit.[2]

The first major section covers prophecies announced in the prosperous days of Judah's King Uzziah (2:1–5:30) and at the time of the Syro-Ephraimite War (734–732 BC) during the tumultuous reign of King Ahaz (7:1–12:6). The unit begins with another superscription in 2:1 (shortly after 1:1), suggesting that 1:1–31 was added as an introduction at a later time.[3] Thus the material after 2:1 probably represents the earliest of Isaiah's writings. The next superscription is found in 13:1 where a new major literary section begins with Isaiah's oracle concerning Babylon and several other nations. The concluding song of trust and thanksgiving in 12:1–6 also signals the end of this first major unit. Isaiah 6 plays a pivotal role at the center[4] of these two sections (2–5 and 7–12). It does not exclusively fit in either section, for it has connections with both. The first half of chap. 6 dates to the end of Uzziah's reign and deals with the theme of

---

[1] For an explanation of the linguistic evidence that the later literary context provides to clarify the meaning, consult the exegesis of 5:15–16 or 7:14 as well as the later chapters these passages are connected to.

[2] A theological concept may be introduced in one chapter but its meaning may only be margin-ally explained. Its full meaning can only be understood by discovering how this same concept was progressively explained in later passages. In these cases it is best not to read later, clearer informa-tion back into earlier texts. In order to be faithful to the meaning of each passage, one must simply admit that the prophet only had a limited or a somewhat fuzzy idea initially, but later understood the idea more clearly when God explained things more fully. The fact that the prophet recorded the earlier idea without changing it to conform to the information he later received through further progressive revelation is a testimony to the faithfulness of the documents.

[3] There is a discussion of this idea in the Introduction to chap. 1 or in the exegesis of 2:1.

[4] L. J. Liebreich, "The Position of Chapter Six in the Book of Isaiah," *HUCA* 25 (1954): 37–40 and his "Compilation of the Book of Isaiah," *JQR* 47 (1956): 126–27 both treat chap. 6 as both a conclusion to 2–5 and an introduction to 7–12.

the exaltation of Judah's glorious and holy God (consistent with 2:10–11,17; 5:15–16). The second half of chap. 6 mentions the people's unwillingness to listen to God, the military destruction of the land, and the holy seed that will remain. These are important themes in chaps. 7–12.[5]

The structure of 2–12 is complex, although certain patterns are discernable. Isaiah 2:1–4:6 is a tightly unified literary composition that begins and ends with a short description of God's future kingdom (2:1–5; 4:2–6),[6] with two long condemnations of human sinfulness and pride in between (2:6–4:1).

> A 2:1–5   God's kingdom will be established
>   B 2:6–22   Condemnation of pride
>   B′ 3:1–4:1   Condemnation of pride
> A′ 4:2–6   God's kingdom will be established

In a somewhat similar manner, the structure of Isaiah 9:1–11:16 begins and ends with a description of God's future messianic kingdom (9:1–7 and 11:1–16), with two condemnations of human sinfulness and pride in between (9:8–10:34).

> A 9:1–7   The Reign of a Righteous King
>   B 9:8–10:4   Condemnation of the pride of Israel
>   B′ 10:5–34   Condemnation of the pride of Assyria
> A′ 11:1–16   The Reign of a Righteous King

The remaining chapters (5:1–30; 7:1–8:18) describe how the sinfulness of the nation results in a military attack on Jerusalem. Isaiah's pivotal new commissioning (6:1–13), strategically placed in between these events, explains that the nation's defeat could be attributed to their stubborn unwillingness to listen to God's words through Isaiah. These structural matters will be further addressed at the beginning of each major sub-section of this unit, but the broader design of the whole structure of chaps. 2–12 can be diagrammed as:

> A 2:1– 4:6   God will be exalted, the proud humbled
>   B 5:1–30   Destruction of Judah
>   C 6: 1–13   The Holy King's Calling of Isaiah
>   B′ 7:1–8:18   Destruction of Judah
> A′ 9:1–11:16   A Righteous King will be exalted, the proud humbled

---

[5] A. H. Bartelt, *The Book around Immanuel: Style and Structure in Isaiah 2–12* (Winona Lake: Eisenbrauns, 1996), 18–20, briefly summarizes the present state of research on these chapters, then in the rest of the book he gives his analysis of the structure of 2–12. His results differ at numerous points from the analysis in this study.

[6] M. A. Sweeney, *Isaiah 1–39, with an Introduction to Prophetic Literature,* FOTL 16 (Grand Rapids: Eerdmans, 1996), 89–90, or his *Isaiah 1–4 and the Post Exilic Understanding of the Isaianic Tradition,* BZAW 171 (Berlin: Walter de Gruyter, 1988), 134–84, have a discussion of the structure of these chapters. R. H. O'Connell, *Concentricity and Continuity: The Literary Structure of Isaiah* (Sheffield: Academic Press, 1994), 57–107, defines a more complex structure for chaps. 2–12. He has similar divisions of the text (except he puts 2:1–5 with chap. 1) to those in this commentary, but he interrelates them to one another in quite different ways.

The compositional organization of these messages implies a conscious effort by the writer to put the prophet's early prophecies during the reign of Uzziah in a group at the beginning of the unit (chaps. 2–5) and the later prophecies in the days of Ahaz as a group in the second half of the unit (chaps. 7–11).[7] A balance was achieved between positive words of hope (2:1–5; 4:2–6; 9:1–7; 11:1–9) and passages that have many accusations and threats of impending punishment (chaps. 5–8). The repetition of themes within the unit exposes the central theological concerns of the prophet.

THEOLOGY. The structural parallelism between these messages highlights key emphases about (a) the approaching destruction of Judah due to its sins; (b) God's future establishment of justice in his kingdom and the coming rule of a Messianic king; and (c) a broad emphasis on God's holiness and sovereign control over this world. These themes portray two very different worldviews in conflict. Great tension exists between God's ideal kingdom that he will establish and the present sinful kingdom of mankind. By placing these two worldviews next to one another, the author has created a contrast between the peace that will exist among the nations when God's kingdom is established and the present evil world where proud and powerful men struggled against each other in politics, unjustly oppressed the weak, and killed one another in wars. In the earthly realm kings and nations exalted themselves, while in God's kingdom the nations will be humbled and God alone will be exalted. The powerful theological message of chaps. 2–12 juxtaposes numerous themes that illustrate the tension between the ideals of the kingdom of God and the human kingdoms that vied for power during the time of Isaiah.

God's kingdom	Man's Kingdom
2:1–4 People come to hear God's law	5:24; 10:1–2 People reject God's law
2:4 End of war	5:28; 7:1; 10:6 Wars between nations
2:18–20 People reject gold and idols	2:7–8 Land full of gold and idols
2:11,17; 5:16; 12:4 God alone exalted	2:7–16 People and possessions exalted
2:11,17; 5:15; 10:12 People humbled	2:11,17; 3:16; 5:15; 9:8; 10:12 People proud
7:9; 8:17; 10:20; 12:2 Trusting God	2:22; 7:12; 10:13 Trusting man
4:2–3 Zion will be holy and cleansed	3:9; 5:8–24; 6:5; 8:6,19 Zion sinful

---

[7] W. A. M. Beuken, "The Emergence of the Shoot of Jesse: An Eschatological or a Now Event?" *CTJ* 39 (2004): 88–108, recognized the negative and positive counterpoint themes in chaps. 10–11 and compared them to a similar contrast in chaps. 2–4, but he did not expand his analysis to make a comparison between chaps. 2–4 and all of 9–11 as illustrated above.

6:3; 8:13 God is holy	6:5,9–10 Man is not holy
9:1–2; 10:17 God is light	8:22–9:1 Earth is in darkness
9:3; 12:3,6 Joy	5:8–24; 8:22; 10:1,5 Woe and gloom
9:6–7; 11:4–5 Just and righteous king	7:12; 9:14–17; 10:12 Wicked kings
11:3; 8:13; 12:2 Fear of God	5:12; 7:2; 8:12 No fear of God; fear of man
11:9; 12:4–5 Will know the Lord	5:19; 6:9 Do not know God

These factors put in bold opposition the lifestyle, worldview, and theological convictions of the people who live according to God's kingdom and the ungodly selfish ways people were living in the time of Uzziah and Ahaz. In order to persuade the prophet's audience to reject their sinful ways, Isaiah's messages highlight the negative consequences of trusting in the wrong things. By contrasting these results with the positive consequences of trusting God, the prophet created a logical argument that persuades the listeners to humble themselves before a holy and all-powerful God (2:5,22). Isaiah's personal testimony of humbling himself in 6:1–8 sets a powerful example for the people in his audience, but as the Lord prophesied (6:9–10), Isaiah's words frequently brought greater hardness of heart and only increased the audience's unwillingness to listen. As a result of the people's pride and refusal to exalt God alone, the nation was eventually overcome by fear, depressed with the hopelessness of war, and destined to miss the joy of experiencing the blessings of God's reign.

Any earthly kingdom today that follows the path of Uzziah or Ahaz and refuses to trust God will undoubtedly end up in a somewhat similar situation. Thus, the central principles embedded in Isaiah's admonitions and warning can function as criteria by which any nation can evaluate its own spiritual condition to see if it is acting in conformity with the ideals of the kingdom of God. Every generation has the opportunity to bow humbly before the glorious revelation of God just as the prophet Isaiah did (6:1–8) or they can arrogantly refuse to interpret reality as God sees it, thereby closing their eyes and ears so that they do not humbly respond by repenting of sin, glorifying God, or serving as his faithful messengers (6:1–10).

1. Exaltation of God and Humbling of the Proud (2:1–4:6)

HISTORICAL SETTING. The internal evidence suggests that some sections of this message were proclaimed during the time of Uzziah[8] (other parts

---

[8] J. Milgrom, "Did Isaiah Prophecy During the Reign of Uzziah?" *VT* 14 (1964): 164–82, puts 1:1–6:13 in the time of Uzziah, but the analysis of the historical data in 1:1–31 points to a time much later than Uzziah's era.

lack datable evidence).[9] 2 Chronicles 26 briefly describes a few of the highlights of Uzziah's fifty-two year reign as king, his military conquests, his large army (consistent with 2:7), and his great pride (2:9; 2 Chr 26:16–21). This was a time when high towers were built (2:15; 2 Chr 26:8), the nation had a significant interest in ships and seaports (2:16; 2 Kgs 14:21), and the king knew what it meant to be proud and then humbled by God (2:9; 2 Chr 26:16). Because of the military superiority of Uzziah's army over the surrounding nations, Judah enjoyed a period of great economic prosperity (consistent with 2:7; 3:16–23; 5:8–12,21–24).[10] Although Uzziah was known as one who did some things that were right in the sight of God, he did allow the people of Judah to continue to offer sacrifices on the high places (2:8,20; 2 Kgs 15:3–4) and did not bring about a national spiritual revival. His reign ended in disgrace, for after King Uzziah inappropriately offered a sacrifice at the temple, God struck him with leprosy (2 Kgs 15:16–21).

THEOLOGY. Isaiah 2:1–4:6 is unified by two short salvation oracles about God's future kingdom at the beginning and end of the section (2:1–5; 4:2–6). One theological purpose of this sermon was to critique the great kingdom Uzziah had proudly built. The imperative verbs in 2:5,22 call for change and suggest that the prophet hoped his words might transform the thinking of the audience so that they would not be so proud and self-absorbed. The kind of change needed is explained by placing the evils of Uzziah's earthly reign in stark contrast with the glorious principles that govern the future kingdom of God (2:1–5). The prophet argues that the audience should trust God and walk in his ways (2:5) so that they can be among those who will eventually enjoy the ideal kingdom where God reigns supreme and everyone reverently lives in his presence in an era of peace and prosperity (2:1–5). To clarify this choice and encourage a positive response to his message, Isaiah explained the devastating things that God was planning to bring on his proud people (2:6–22) and what he would do to their riches (3:16–24). This sermon's theological goal was to focus people's attention on the necessity of exalting God and walking in his ways (2:5), rather than exalting themselves (2:22). Trusting in possessions, a social position, political power, or human accomplishments has never

---

[9] The shortness and future orientation of 2:1–5 and 4:2–6 make them difficult to date, so two options are available: (a) one could assume that they came from the same period as 2:6–4:1 (in light of the unity of the passage and common theological themes) or (b) one could assume they came from a later period and were editorially joined to these verses for theological or topical reasons. Sweeney, *Isaiah 1–39*, 95–96, suggests these verse came from another author in the Persian period because of disillusionment over the restoration of the city of Jerusalem, but this historical reconstruction is not derived from this text in Isaiah.

[10] R. Davidson, "The Interpretation of Isaiah II 6ff," *VT* 16 (1966): 1–7, and J. D. W. Watts, *Isaiah 1–33*, WBC 24 (Waco: Word, 1985), 34, believe the "House of Israel" in chap. 2 indicates that this is about the Northern nation of Israel, not Judah. Davidson dates this passage to the Syro-Ephraimite War (743–742 BC), while Watts prefers a date in the time of Uzziah /Jotham. Isa 2–5 fits the prosperous era of Uzziah, not the difficult time of military weakness that plagued the kingdom of Ahaz.

impressed God. He is looking for humble people who will boldly devote their lives to exalting the Lord alone (2:11,17).

(1) Promises of God's Future Kingdom Produce Trust (2:1–5)

[1]This is what Isaiah son of Amoz saw concerning Judah and Jerusalem:

[2]In the last days

> **the mountain of the LORD's temple will be established**
> **as chief among the mountains;**
> **it will be raised above the hills,**
> **and all nations will stream to it.**

[3]Many peoples will come and say,

> **"Come, let us go up to the mountain of the LORD,**
> **to the house of the God of Jacob.**
> **He will teach us his ways,**
> **so that we may walk in his paths."**
> **The law will go out from Zion,**
> **the word of the LORD from Jerusalem.**
> **[4]He will judge between the nations**
> **and will settle disputes for many peoples.**
> **They will beat their swords into plowshares**
> **and their spears into pruning hooks.**
> **Nation will not take up sword against nation,**
> **nor will they train for war anymore.**

> **[5] Come, O house of Jacob,**
> **let us walk in the light of the LORD.**

STRUCTURE.   What is the logical order of Isaiah's message? How does he move from premise to conclusion so that his listeners will be moved to change their worldview? Before the answer to that question can be outlined, three controversial structural factors must be addressed: (a) Does 2:1–5 provide the conclusion to chap. 1, or the introduction to 2:1–4:6? (b) Does 2:5 go with 2:1–4, or with 2:6–22? And (c) how is 2:2–5 related to the almost identical passage in Micah 4:1–4?

P. R. Ackroyd[11] and G. Fohrer[12] argue that 2:1 is a later intrusive addition, 2:2–5 does not introduce the material in the rest of chap. 2, and 2:2–5 functions better as a positive climax to the negative message in 1:1–31 (similar to the positive climaxes at the end of Micah's negative messages). These arguments

---

[11] P. R. Ackroyd, "Note on Isaiah 2:1," *ZAW* 75 (1963): 320–21, or his "Isaiah 1–12: Presentation of a Prophet," in *Studies in the Religious Tradition of the Old Testament* (London: SCM, 1987), 92–93, supports this interpretation. He is followed by A. J. Tomasino, "Isaiah1. 1–2. 4 and 63–66, and the Composition of the Isaianic Corpus," *JSOT* 57 (1993): 81–98.

[12] G. Fohrer, "Jesaja 1 als Zusammenfassung der Verkündigung Jesajas," *ZAW* 74 (1962): 251–68, takes 2:1 as a secondary insertion.

are not particularly convincing because (a) no one can prove when 2:1 was written or that it was a later intrusive addition; (b) there is no independent evidence that Isaiah followed Micah's structuring of his messages; in fact, several of Isaiah's negative messages in this unit were not followed by a positive conclusion (see 3:1–15; 5:1–7,8–30); and (c) the structural connection between the kingdom themes in 2:1–5 (at the beginning of this section) and the kingdom themes in 4:2–6 (at the end of this section) argues for an inclusion of 2:1–5 into the present unit, not in 1:1–2:5.

The second problem centers on where to divide the text—before or after 2:5? Sweeney[13] has summarized three arguments for excluding 2:5 from 2:1–5: (a) 2:5 is not syntactically connected to 2:4; (b) 2:6 is syntactically connected to 2:5 by *kî*, "for"; and (c) the imperative verbs in 2:5 differ from the imperfect verbs in 2:4. The interpretation of 2:5, which is explained in the exegetical comments below, interprets the *kî* in 2:6 as "Truly/Surely" (*kî* also introduces 3:1 in the same way), thus removing the syntactical connection with 2:5 that Sweeney hypothesizes.[14] Furthermore, it makes more sense to see the imperative call for action in 2:5 as a concluding application to 2:1–4 (similar to the conclusion of 2:22 at the end of 2:6–21) rather than as an application at the very beginning of a new paragraph.

The third issue centers around who originally spoke 2:2–4. (a) Wildberger believes Isaiah was the original author and Micah quoted him in 4:1–4; (b) E. Cannawurf thinks Isaiah copied Micah; (c) G. von Rad proposes that Isaiah and Micah adapted an earlier liturgical oracle; (d) J. Gray finds a connection with earlier Zion songs; and (e) J. Blenkinsopp and Sweeney contend that this piece was editorially added much later during a post-exilic time of euphoria.[15] There are no clear answers to this question, so it would be unwise to base any interpretive arguments on any one of these solutions.[16] Since Zion songs share similar theological ideas (though uniquely expressed),[17] it is likely that both

---

[13] Sweeney, *Isaiah 1–4*, 136, also sees a similarity between the imperatives in 2:3 and 2:5.

[14] כִּי can mean (a) that; (b) when, if; (c) since, because; or (d) yea, certainly, surely as BDB, 471–475 suggests. H. Wildberger, *Isaiah 1–12: A Commentary*, CC (Minneapolis: Fortress, 1991), 97, concludes that the "let us" in 2:5 is a call for the people to act appropriately in the future, but the "you" in 2:6 refers to God's past action, so there is not an easy flow of meaning from 2:5 to 2:6. Bartelt, *The Book around Immanuel*, 189–91, 231, justifies putting 2:5 with 2:5–22 because he believes the calls for action in 5 and 22 form an inclusio.

[15] Wildberger, *Isaiah 1–12*, 85–87; E. Cannawurf, "The Authenticity of Micah IV 1–4," *VT* 13 (1963): 26–33; J. Gray, "The Kingship of God in the Prophets and Psalms," *VT* 11 (1961): 1–29; G. von Rad, "The City on the Hill," in *The Problem of the Hexateuch and Other Essays* (New York: McGraw-Hill, 1966), 232–42; J. Blenkinsopp, *Isaiah 1–39* (New York: Doubleday, 2000), 190–91; Sweeney, "Micah's Debate with Isaiah," *JSOT* 93 (2001): 111–124.

[16] J. J. M. Roberts, "Isaiah 2 and the Prophet's Message to the North," *JQR* 75 (1984): 290–308, suggests that vv. 2–22 make a unit, but 2:2–4 has an eschatological emphasis that is different from 2:6–22. It is also very unlikely that Isaiah was addressing the Israelites in the northern tribes.

[17] Sweeney, *Isaiah 1–4*, 165–68 points out that the nations come to Jerusalem for battle and God destroys their weapons in the Psalms, but that is not what is happening in Isa 2:1–5. J. T. Willis, "Isaiah 2:2–5 and the Psalms of Zion," VTSup, LXX. 1 (1997): 295–316, finds a close con-

prophets were drawing on past traditions known to their audiences (regardless of who first uttered these words). If this is the case, Isaiah would be reminding people in Jerusalem of the great future plans God has for Zion, in order to contrast it with what will actually happen to them because they were not exalting God.

The content of 2:1–5 is organized around:

An introductory superscription	2:1
An eschatological salvation oracle	2:2–4
A concluding call for action	2:5

The prophet's description of the exaltation of Zion and peace among the nations would have persuasive power because some in the audience would want to enjoy the glorious kingdom of God. They would want to dwell in Zion when it is exalted, when God teaches his people his ways, and when peace and prosperity exist on earth.[18] The conclusion calls the listeners to make a decision to commit themselves to walk in God's ways.

2:1   This new section begins with another superscription, indicating who received these words from God. Isaiah's name is inserted in the slot where one would expect the author's name to occur (cf. 1:1; 13:1). He is identified as the son of Amoz, confirming that these messages belong to the same Isaiah that was introduced in 1:1. The superscription claims that these words did not arise from his own imagination; these were words he "saw, perceived through divine revelation" (ḥāzâ).[19] The meaning of this word is evident in Lam 2:9 and Ezek 7:26, for both texts associate this concept with the special "insight" that prophets received from God's supernatural revelation of his will.[20] The claim gave special meaning and power to the words of the prophet, for his spoken and written words carried the authority of God's power, guidance that could lead to life, the wisdom to make wise choices, and results that were absolutely sure.

The only thing that is missing, when this superscription is compared to the one in 1:1, is the date of this message. In the "historical setting" section above, evidence was presented that suggests that chap. 2 comes from the time of Uzziah, although there is little internal evidence to supply a date for 2:1–5. The audience was primarily those people who lived in Judah and Jerusalem.

---

nection between songs of Zion in Psalms and this passage.

[18] J. Magonet, "Isaiah 2:1–4:6: Some Poetic Structures and Tactics," ACEBT 3 (1982): 71–81, notes within the chiastic arrangement of 2:1–4:6 an upward movement toward Zion at the beginning (2:1–5) and a movement out of Zion towards the end (3:1–4:1).

[19] The verb חָזָה, "he saw, perceived," is the same root for חֲזוֹן in 1:1. Both terms take on a technical significance when referring to prophecy and do not refer to what people see (רָאָה) with their natural eyes, but what the prophet perceives through divine insight.

[20] A. Jepsen, "חָזָה chāzāh," TDOT, IV, 280–90, believes חָזָה is an Aramaic loanword (used about 45 times in recovered Aramaic texts and in various verbal and nominal forms about 129 times in Hb.), but the same root is found in other Semitic languages. 1 Sam 9:9 indicates that in earlier days "prophets" were called "seers" (from the root רָאָה), and Gad was called a prophet and a seer (from the root חָזָה). The goal of both was to declare the words that they "saw" from God.

Under normal circumstances there would be no need to add another superscription so soon after 1:1. Its inclusion here must indicate that the material in
chaps. 2–12 originally circulated independently from chap. 1 (chap. 1 dates
from a much later period).[21] Some of the themes here parallel 66:18–21 at the
end of the book. The emphasis on God's plans to redeem the nations in 11:12;
14:1–2; 19:20–25; 45:20–23; 49:22–26; 60:1–9 demonstrates that this is a central theme in his writings.[22]

2:2–4   The purpose for describing God's future kingdom was to present
a vision of what God will ultimately do in Zion, so that the audience can
choose either to be a part of God's plan (2:5) or to reject it. Isaiah described
what will take place "in the last days," a phrase filled with eschatological
significance in this context.[23] This new era will inaugurate a series of new
relationships between (a) God and his dwelling place in Zion, (b) God and
the people who come to hear him teach, and (c) God and various warring
nations. God will transform the present world by his presence, his teaching,
and his just judgment.[24]

The new Zion will have great prominence as the "highest, chief" (rô'š)
mountain in order to symbolize the new importance given to the dwelling place
of God (2:2; Ezek 40:2).[25] The geographical setting of the historical city of
Jerusalem is located on a lower mountain than the Mount of Olives to the east,
which might imply something of an inferior status in the eyes of some ancient
people. In the ancient Near Eastern world temples were usually built on the
highest place available, so they would be closer to heaven. This new exaltation of God's dwelling place will symbolically demonstrate to the nations the
superior glory and greatness of God. Although the city of Jerusalem was an
important political place with a great deal of gold and military strength during

---

[21] The discussion of this issue above (pp. 70 and 121–22) disagrees with J. Goldingay, "Isaiah I
1 and II 1,"*VT* 48 (1998): 326–32, who thinks that the "vision" of Isaiah in 1:1 refers only to chap.
1 and that the superscription in 2:1 is a colophon marking the conclusion to 1:1–2:5.

[22] G. I. Davies, "The Destiny of the Nations in the Book of Isaiah," in *The Book of Isaiah:
Le Livre D'Isaïe* (ed. J. Vermeylen; Leuven: University Press, 1989), 93–125, traces this theme
through the book of Isaiah.

[23] The phrase "in the last days" (בְּאַחֲרִית הַיָּמִים) cannot be associated with the millennium or
with the church age in Isaiah's thinking, because such concepts were not known to the prophet. He
is simply talking about the last events in human history, when the kingdom of God would begin.
New Testament readers must be careful not to read later NT information back into earlier texts and
make them say things that God did not reveal to the prophets. G. W. Buchanan, "Eschatology and
the 'End of Days,'" *VT* 11 (1961): 392–405, discusses the various ways this phrase is used.

[24] Somewhat similar prophecies are found in Hos 2:16–23; Amos 9:11–15; Isa 4:2–6; 9:1–7;
11:1–9; 19:18–25; 60–61.

[25] The phrase אֶל בֵּית יהוה, "unto the house of God," was omitted in 1QIsaᵃ due to haplogra-
phy and is not the original text. In the Ancient Near Eastern world the gods lived on top of high
mountains and altars were put on high hills. The physical elevations and spiritual significance go
together. Where else would a great God place his temple? נָכוֹן יִהְיֶה is a *niphal* participle followed
by an imperfect verb. The imperfect verb indicates that the participle should be understood in the
future sense of "will be established." GKC § 116r.

the reign of Uzziah (2:7), at that time the glories of God's dwelling place were not valued as highly as the accomplishments of mankind (2:6–22).[26] In the future that situation will change when the majestic glory of God comes to dwell on his throne, removes every false source of trust and pride, and God alone is exalted (2:11,17).

Surprisingly, Isaiah does not focus on Judah's response to God's glorious presence in Zion,[27] but on the nations coming to hear God's words (2:2b–3; see also 19:19–25). God's plans for mankind always included his desire to reach the whole world, not just the small nation of Judah (45:22–23; 49:26; 60:3). This text even ignores the role the chosen people of Judah would play in God's plan to reach the nations (Gen 12:1–3). Instead Isaiah describes an endless stream of people from all over the world who will encourage others to join them as they go up (see also 14:1–2; 56:6–7; 60:1–14; 66:18–21).[28] What will be the attraction that will draw the nations? Why will there be this mass migration to Zion? What will motivate these foreigners to stream[29] to Jerusalem? It is the opportunity to attend the best and latest seminar that anyone can imagine! The God of Israel will be the main speaker and he will teach[30] those who accept his ways and follow his truth. Isaiah does not reveal the detailed contents of what God will say, but part of his instruction will be to explain his "law, instruction" (tôrâ).[31] This Hebrew root points to God's will for mankind (Exod 18:16; Ps 105:45) and should not be given a legalistic definition of "law."[32] God's "in-

---

[26] Uzziah's desecration of the temple is another sign of not treating God or his temple as holy (2 Chr 26:16–21).

[27] J. Oswalt, *Isaiah 1–39*, NICOT (Grand Rapids: Eerdmans, 1986), 114–115, contends "the focus is upon Israel's glorious destiny as a lighthouse to the nations for truth and peace," but this text offers no emphasis on Judah or her role of bringing other nations. God is the attraction, not Israel. Israel's role is discussed in chaps. 40–66.

[28] The Hb. cohortative verb נַעֲלֶה, "let us go up," in 2:3 is used to exhort others to join those who were already traveling to Zion (GKC § 108a). In Ps 46:8; 122:4 this terminology describes people on a pilgrimage to Jerusalem.

[29] The JPS translation has "and the nations shall gaze on it with joy," based on the interpretation of נָהֲרוּ as "be radiant, gaze upon." J. J. M. Roberts, "Double Intendre in First Isaiah," *CBQ* 54 (1992): 39–48, follows a similar translation ("all the nations shall be radiant over it") based on his comparison of 2:2 with Jer 31:12; 51:44 because the ideological context of these passages is similar. Nevertheless, the idea that many nations will "come" and "go up" to Jerusalem fits better with the idea of people "streaming" to Zion.

[30] The result clause "so that he may teach us" has a *hiphil* imperfect verb וְיֹרֵנוּ that expresses a subjunctive idea of possible action. See GKC § 107q. This phrase indicates that the people know why they are going to Zion. They have the clear purpose of learning what God says.

[31] תּוֹרָה refers to God's "instruction" that he will teach. J. Jensen, *The Use of tôrâ by Isaiah* (Washington: Catholic Biblical Association, 1973), considers this word a reflection of wisdom terminology and its worldview. He dates the laws in Deuteronomy and Leviticus to a later period than Isaiah. There seems to be very little evidence that points to a wisdom context in these verses, but there are numerous references to the nation's legal and wisdom traditions within Isaiah. In this case Isaiah refers to a future proclamation of God's will, not to the past revelation of the statutes and commandments that is found in Deuteronomy.

[32] G. Liedke, C. Petersen, "תּוֹרָה tôrâ instruction," *TLOT*, III, 1415–22, find תּוֹרָה used 220 times in the Hebrew scriptures. In wisdom literature this root refers to the oral "instructions" of the

struction" will involve a practical explanation of how people can live in a way that is pleasing to God. The foreign nations' eager desire to follow God's ways stood in stark contrast to the negative picture of the spiritual life of the people of Jerusalem in Uzziah's time (2:6–4:1). After hearing these wonderful things, it is possible that some Hebrews in Isaiah's audience would have felt marginalized and would have experienced a little jealousy, because the other nations were receiving more attention than they were.[33]

One consequence of the coming of the nations is that the nations will trust God and submit to his just decisions (2:4). As king and ultimate judge of the universe, God will help these nations settle their differences and will remove the reasons for war. There will be no need for swords to kill people, so a marvelous reign of peace will begin. This was quite the opposite of Uzziah's impressive efforts to prepare for and carry out several wars against neighboring states (2 Chr 26:6–15). All war preparations can end when people focus on God, who is the true source of their security.

2:5 Isaiah ends this brief look at the ideal Zion of the future with a call for his audience to transform their thinking, to reorient their worldview, and to change their behavior based on their knowledge of what God will do in the future (2:5). Judah and its leaders can go their merry way and continue to be self-absorbed, or they can choose to glorify God and follow his instructions. Using the same Hebrew grammatical structure found in 2:3 (imperative plus cohortative), Isaiah exhorts his own people in Jerusalem to follow the example of the foreign nations of the future. In this exhortation the "light of the LORD" in 2:5 is parallel to the teaching of God in 2:3.[34] The people's response to this choice will determine whether Isaiah's audience will enjoy the kingdom God has prepared for those who follow him, or miss out on this great privilege. That same choice is required of all people since the time of Isaiah. People in every generation must choose to come to God, learn of his ways, and enjoy his kingdom, or they can proudly focus on their own accomplishments, close their

---

parents (Prov 4:4,11; 5:13; 6:20; 7:2), so when God is the speaker it refers to his "instructions" on how to live and think. The Scriptures condemn the priests who do not teach God's "instructions" (Hos 4:6; Mal 2:6), which was an important part of their role (Deut 33:10). The godly prophets condemned other prophets who "taught" lies or who did not "instruct" people with God's words (Isa 9:14; Jer 6:19; 8:8). Jeremiah predicted a time in the future when God would write his "instructions" on the hearts of his people (Jer 31:33).

[33] F. Delitzsch, *Isaiah*, Commentary on the Old Testament VII (trans J. Martin; Grand Rapids: Eerdmans, 1969), 117. Although this idea about jealousy is read in from the New Testament and is not explicitly found in 2:1–5, Delitzsch suggests that the close relationship that develops between God and the nations was meant to provoke Judah to jealousy (cf. Rom 11:13–14), causing the Hebrews to realize that they will miss out on God's great plans for Zion if they do not pay attention to what God says. Israel is included in Isaiah's discussion of God's new kingdom in 4:2–6.

[34] In contrast to this approach, J. Goldingay, *Isaiah* NIBC (Peabody: Hendrickson, 2001), 44, interprets the image of light as a metaphor of God's deliverance, provisions, or his face. He concludes that walking by God's light "suggests living by Yahweh's blessings." It is better to follow H. G. M. Williamson, *The Book Called Isaiah: Deutero-Isaiah's Role in Composition and Redaction* (Oxford: Clarendon Press, 1994), 145, who identifies the "light" as "God's self-revelation."

ears and eyes to what God says, and suffer a humiliation similar to what Isaiah prophesies (2:6–22).

(2) Removal of Pride and Exaltation of God (2:6–22)

⁶ You have abandoned your people,
  the house of Jacob.
 They are full of superstitions from the East;
  they practice divination like the Philistines
  and clasp hands with pagans.
⁷ Their land is full of silver and gold;
  there is no end to their treasures.
 Their land is full of horses;
  there is no end to their chariots.
⁸ Their land is full of idols;
  they bow down to the work of their hands,
  to what their fingers have made.
⁹ So man will be brought low
  and mankind humbled—
  do not forgive them.

¹⁰ Go into the rocks,
  hide in the ground
 from dread of the LORD
  and the splendor of his majesty!
¹¹ The eyes of the arrogant man will be humbled
  and the pride of men brought low;
 the LORD alone will be exalted in that day.

¹² The LORD Almighty has a day in store
  for all the proud and lofty,
  for all that is exalted
  (and they will be humbled),
¹³ for all the cedars of Lebanon, tall and lofty,
  and all the oaks of Bashan,
¹⁴ for all the towering mountains
  and all the high hills,
¹⁵ for every lofty tower
  and every fortified wall,
¹⁶ for every trading ship
  and every stately vessel.
¹⁷ The arrogance of man will be brought low
  and the pride of men humbled;
 the LORD alone will be exalted in that day,
¹⁸ and the idols will totally disappear.

¹⁹ Men will flee to caves in the rocks
  and to holes in the ground
 from dread of the LORD

and the splendor of his majesty,
    when he rises to shake the earth.
²⁰ In that day men will throw away
    to the rodents and bats
  their idols of silver and idols of gold,
    which they made to worship.
²¹ They will flee to caverns in the rocks
    and to the overhanging crags
  from dread of the LORD
    and the splendor of his majesty,
    when he rises to shake the earth.

²² Stop trusting in man,
    who has but a breath in his nostrils.
  Of what account is he?

STRUCTURE.   The Hebrew text of 2:6–22 is frequently emended in commentaries because many scholars consider it very corrupt.[35] Since there is no objective method of identifying what words are corrupt and why some words were added, it is always better for the interpreter to deal with the text as it is, rather than some hypothetical subjective reconstruction. The repeated clauses within each paragraph suggest the following structure:

> A. 2:6–11 The present humbling of Judah
>   2:6b "is full of"
>   2:7a "is full of . . . there is no end"
>   2:7b "is full of . . . there is no end"
>   2:8a "is full of"
>   2:9 "man was brought low and mankind humbled"[36]
>   2:10 "Go . . . hide (imperatives) in the ground from the dread of
>   the LORD"
>   2:11 "the arrogant man will be humbled and the pride of men
>   brought low"
> B. 2:12–22 Future humbling of the proud and exaltation of God
>   2:12 "for all . . . for all"
>   "they will be humbled"
>   2:13 "for all . . . all"

---

[35] For example, Blenkinsopp, *Isaiah 1–39*, 194–95, believes 2:8b,18,20 were added in the late Babylonian or early Persian period. Questions are also raised about 2:9b and 2:22, plus the refrains in 2:10,19,20. G. B. Gray, *The Book of Isaiah: A Critical and Exegetical Commentary on the Book of Isaiah 1–27* (Edinburgh: T & T Clark, 1912), 48–49, treated similar concerns and concluded that the Old Greek had a better reading than the Hb. in 2:6 and that 2:21–22 were later additions to this text. This helped him explain differences in the text preserved in the various Qumran Scrolls, the Old Greek, and the MT. B. S. Childs, *Isaiah*, OTL (Louisville: Westminster John Knox, 2001), 31, concludes, "I question in this case whether a reconstruction of an original prophetic oracle is either possible or fruitful."

[36] NIV has "man will be brought low," a questionable translation of this verb.

2:14 "for all . . . all"

2:15 "for every . . . every"

2:16 "for every . . . every"

2:17 "the arrogance of man will be brought low and the pride of men humbled"

2:18–21 "Men will flee . . . in the ground from the dread of the LORD"

2:22 "Stop (imperative) trusting in man[37]

These two subparagraphs are internally unified by repeated phrases and are closely interlinked together by common refrains in 2:9,11,12,17 ("man was/will be humbled") and 2:10,19,21 ("the dread of the LORD") that emphasize the main points of this message. The imperatival exhortation at the end of the first paragraph contains the application "go" (2:10–11), which corresponds to the imperative exhortation "stop" (2:22) at the end of 2:12–22 (this is similar to the application clause using the imperative "come" (2:5) at the end of 2:1–5. There is a development within the two paragraphs from the past or present situation in Jerusalem in 2:6–9 to a more future and universal outlook on the Day of the Lord in 2:12–21. But both interventions by God lead to the common human response of trying to hide in the rocks because people dread the splendor of God. In both situations, the pride of man will be humbled (2:9,11–12,17,22). M. Barré found a chiastic relationship within 12–17,[38] but a fuller comparison of 2:9–11 and 2:17–22 suggests that 2:17 is not the end of the second paragraph.

A bold and dramatic discontinuity arises between 2:1–5 and 2:6–22. Although God comes to earth in both sections, in 2:2 Jerusalem is exalted by God's presence, but in 2:14–15 the high mountains, walls, and towers of this world are devastated. Foreigners come to worship God in 2:2–3, but they are the source of false beliefs and idols in 2:6 and 2:8. In 2:4 people give up war, while in 2:7 Uzziah multiplied horses and chariots to fight wars. These contrasts may partially explain why Judah's role is not emphasized in the establishment of God's kingdom in 2:1–5. The message encourages a Hebrew audience to change whom they honor; thus, the text implies that if the Hebrew people in

---

[37] Williamson, "The Formation of Isaiah 2.6–22," in *Biblical and Near Eastern Studies: Studies in Honor of K. J. Cathcart*, JSOTSup 375 (ed. C. McCarthy and J. F. Healey; Sheffield: Sheffield Academic Press, 2004), 57–67, divides this material into two paragraphs, 6–9 and 10–19, believing that 20–22 are later additions.

[38] M. L. Barré, "A Rhetorical-Critical Study of Isaiah 2:12–17," *CBQ* 65 (2003): 522–34 found the chiasm to include:

a) a day in 2:12

    b) against things of wood (using construct plural nouns plus a geographical name) in 2:13

        c) against things of earth or stone (using absolute plural nouns plus a modifier) in 2:14

        c) against things of earth or stone (using absolute plural nouns plus a modifier) in 2:15

    b) against things of wood (using a plural construct noun plus a geographical name in 2:16

a) a day in 2:17

Isaiah's audience remain unwilling to humble themselves and exalt God alone, they will not participate in the events in 2:1–5.

2:6–11 The topic of this new paragraph moves from the acceptance of the nations that will come to learn God's way in Jerusalem in the future (2:2–5), to the rejection of the people who presently make up the house of Jacob,[39] the audience Isaiah was speaking to during the prosperous reign of Uzziah. Just when Isaiah had his audience remembering all the good things God would do at the end of time (2:2–5), he surprised them in this new paragraph with the terrible news that God would humble them. No doubt his audience listened approvingly to the grand ideals of 2:2–5, thinking that they would be in Zion enjoying God's presence when the nations finally would submit to his rule. But God had a different plan for Isaiah's audience because the "house of Jacob" (2:5) was not walking in God's ways. "Surely" (kî, omitted in NIV)[40] God had "abandoned" (nāṭaštâ) them (2:6a)[41] in the sense of not paying any attention to them, or leaving them alone to depend on their own resources.[42] This implies a removal of God's direction and protection because of their sinfulness (2 Kgs 21:14; Jer 12:7). The natural response of any Hebrew listener would be: How could this be possible? Why would God do this?

Isaiah 2:6b–8 includes several charges to justify God's action[43] and to explain why Judah will not participate in the positive events in 2:2–5. Four reasons are provided:

The assimilation of pagan religious practices	2:6b
A focus/dependence on wealth	2:7a
Relying on the security of a large army	2:7b
The worship of idols	2:8

---

[39] Although "house of Jacob" is used in Amos 3:13; 9:8 and Hosea 6:8; 7:2,5,7; 10:11 to refer to the Northern nation of Israel, and the evil religious influences in Isaiah 2:6 and 8 could fit the situation in Israel during the Syro-Ephraimite War (as Davidson, "Interpretation of Isaiah II 6ff," 1–7, suggests), still, the wealth and riches of the audience in 2:7 do not fit that period in Israel. Consequently, it is best to conclude that the audience in 2:6–22 is the same as the Jerusalem audience in chap. 3.

[40] G. M. Tucker, "The Book of Isaiah 1–39," *The New Interpreter's Bible,* Vol VI (Nashville: Abingdon, 2001), 72, translates כִּי, "surely," as an asservative. He sees 2:6a as a prayer of complaint to God.

[41] This same idea is found later, in Jer 7:29; 12:7; 15:6; 23:33.

[42] BDB, 643–44. The root נָטַשׁ can refer to a field that is fallow and left alone (Exod 23:11) or an injured warrior that is left alone on the battle field with no one to help (Amos 5:2). The root is sometimes parallel to עָזַב, "to forsake, abandon, leave" (1 Kgs 8:57; Jer 12:7; Ps 27:9). When one abandons someone they are left to their own fate (Ezek 29:5; 31:12; 32:4). J. Lundbom, "נָטַשׁ nāṭaš; נְטִישָׁה nĕṭîšâ" *TDOT,* IX, 407–10, suggests that within the covenant context, abandonment has serious consequences, for it implies a major rift in the relationship between God and his covenant people and a consequent withdrawal of grace and favor. Abandonment removes God's hand of protection and allows Israel's enemies to defeat them (Judg 6:13). This is why some prayed that God would not abandon them (1 Kgs 8:57; Ps 27:9).

[43] J. Goldingay, *Isaiah,* 44, does not consider these accusations as reasons that justify God's action, but the consequences or the results of God's abandonment (because they are mentioned after God's abandonment as in Ps 94 or Rom 1).

2:6b The text of 2:6b contains three statements. The first statement is short and seems incomplete because it has no Hebrew word parallel to "practice divination" in the second line. The NIV and most other translations (NASB, HCSB) supply a parallel term like "superstitions, divination,"[44] assuming a scribal error in which a word dropped out of the original text. This charge indicates that Judah openly accepted forbidden foreign religious ideas (cf. Deut 18:9–14) from the area to their east and to their west (just the opposite of the nations who will come to worship God in the future in 2:3). This acceptance of other religious practices could be due to Uzziah's conquest of several Philistine cites to the west and the Arabs and Ammonites to the east (2 Chr 26:6–8). The last line of 2:6 refers to the obscure practice of "clapping, slapping, or grasping" (*yaśpîqû*) hands with the children of foreigners, which some interpret either as a gesture used in making alliances, sealing a commercial agreement (Prov 6:1), or some kind of foreign religious worship practice.[45] Although the custom may have some religious significance in the context of this verse, the nature of this practice is now unclear. The fundamental point is that foreign thinking and behavior was influencing the worldview of Hebrew people. In contrast to what was happening, the Hebrew law forbade the use of divination and magic (Lev 19:26; Deut 18:9–14) and argued against developing close relationships with pagans (Deut 4:9–20; 7:1–6,25–26).

2:7 The second and third charges point to the people's excessive dependence on (being "full of" [*wattimmālē'*] and having "no end of" ['ēn qēṣe']— both repeated) wealth (2:7a) and military might (2:7b). Wealth, a large army, and political stability characterized Uzziah's long reign. When a nation has a large army as Uzziah did (2 Chr 26:11–15), there is the temptation to think that it is not necessary to depend on God for military security. When a nation is rich, it may seem unnecessary to trust God for food and other daily needs, but this is a false source of security. The early instructions in the Pentateuch warned future kings to avoid both the danger of multiplying horses and accumulating great wealth (Deut 17:16–17) so that they would always have to depend on God. The Psalmist confessed, "some trust in chariots and some in horses, but we trust in the name of the LORD our God" (Ps 33:17; cf. 76:6–7; 147:10). Later Isaiah will warn King Hezekiah not to trust in the horses and chariots of Egypt, but to trust in God (31:1–3). Isaiah's audience and people today need to see God as the provider of every good gift (including wealth and security) so that people do not depend on the gift, but on the Giver. The positive economic and military success of any nation throughout history never was and

---

[44] The Hb. has מִקֶּדֶם, "from the east," and most translations assume that the similarly spelled מִקְסָם, "divination," was dropped out because of a scribal error. A literal translation is "They are full from the east," which seems to be missing an object that explains what they are full of.

[45] Oswalt, *Isaiah 1–39*, 122, thinks this may refer to alliances with foreigners, which implies a tacit recognition of their gods, while J. A. Motyer, *The Prophecy of Isaiah* (Leicester: InterVarsity, 1993), 56, suggests that it could imply religious worship with foreigners.

never will be achieved just through human efforts or man's great abilities; God decides the status and future of every ruler and nation (Dan 2:21; 4:35–37).

2:8 The final accusation pinpoints the problem that the land of Judah was full of idols—false gods that the people worshiped. The word for idols means "nothing, worthless,"[46] a fitting attribution for objects of worship formed by human hands. Later sermons emphasize again and again the stupidity of worshiping pieces of wood (41:6–7,28–29; 44:9–20: 45:16–20; 46:1–7). The irony is cutting.[47] The people of Judah have a glorious God (2:2–5) who has chosen them as his special people and desires to bless them with everything they would ever need, but they prefer to worship "worthless" pieces of wood and stone that can do "nothing." People in every era of human history have varying degrees of difficulty with living in complete trust of God for all their needs. It is not hard to begin to develop a level of trust in a good paying job, a healthy pension fund, and the military might of nuclear bombs. All too often people begin to trust in what they can provide for themselves, rather than relying on God's provision.

2:9 Finally, the prophet describes the consequence of the nation's actions (plus what some think is a final brief prayer in the last line). Isaiah presents a broad principle that applies specifically to his audience. Proud humans are humbled. The prime example of a human being who "was humbled" (*wayyišaḥ* is usually not a future tense as NIV)[48] was Uzziah the king of Judah. In pride he improperly offered a sacrifice in the temple (2 Chr 26:16–21). Isaiah 2:9 refers to a past punishment for improper pride and dependence on wealth, armies, and idols, though it is stated as a fact, not overtly as a punishment. W. Brueggemann observes the irony of how the people who were "full" in 2:6–8 become "empty" of well-being and security when they were humbled.[49] Later verses in this paragraph amplifies this process and explain what happens when the people of Judah are humbled in the future (2:12–21). At this point, the

---

[46] אֱלִילִים ("nothing, worthless") is close to the spelling of אֱלֹהִים, "God," but the term "God" relates to the idea of "strength, power," so the contrast with "nothing" is powerful and pointed.

[47] Gitay, *Isaiah and his Audience: The Structure and Meaning of Isaiah 1–12* (Assen: Van Gorcum, 1991), 52, believes the basis for the prophet's rhetorical argument is an "appeal to the absurd" in which he ridicules anyone who would be so foolish as to trust in idols, which are nothing.

[48] The imperfect verbs with consecutive *vav* in 2:7–9 are translated in the NIV in present tense in 2:7–8 to describe the present situation in the time of Uzziah (since they are stative verbs) and as a future in 2:9 (to be consistent with 2:11,17). But וַיִּשַּׁח אָדָם, "and mankind was humbled," refers to a past event. Wildberger, *Isaiah 1–12*, 98, and O. Kaiser, *Isaiah 1–12: A Commentary,* OTL (Philadelphia: Westminster, 1983), 57, translate them all as past tense verbs and have them refer back to an earlier era (Wildberger refers to past events in the time of Jeroboam II and Uzziah). J. H. Hayes and S. A. Irvine, *Isaiah, the Eighth-Century Prophet* (Nashville: Abingdon, 1987), 96–87, think 2:9 refers to the past earthquake in the time of Amos when the nation was humbled. A catastrophe based on the earthquake (cf. Amos 1:1) will happen in the future (2:10,19,21), but it seems highly unlikely that people would risk hiding in a cave during an earthquake.

[49] Brueggemann, *Isaiah 1–39*, WBC (Louisville: Westminster John Knox, 1998), 29, explains this as another case of gaining the whole world in their power and success but losing their own soul in the process.

prophet merely sets forth the essential concept consistent with the theological perspective taught elsewhere in Scripture: people should humble themselves before God and avoid pride (Ps 18:28; 35:13; 38:6; 75:8) because God honors the humble and judges the proud (Prov 15:33; 18:12; 22:4; 29:23). This principle applies to every nation and every leader that exhibits pride, not just to the people of Judah at the time of King Uzziah.

The final line in 2:9 has several textual, interpretive, and theological problems. The NIV "do not forgive them" translates this clause as if it was a fragment of a prayer that was abruptly appended at the end of this sub-paragraph. The fact that this phrase and 2:10 are missing from 1QIsa[a] might suggest that the problematic phrase should be dropped, but it is present in 4QIsa[a], 4QIsa[b], and the Old Greek translation. But to interpret this as a prayer is problematic because it (a) is unusually short (there are no others like this in Isaiah); (b) is unexpected at this point in the paragraph (it might fit better at the end of the chapter); (c) does not match the content or genre of other parallel verses (2:11,12,17; 5:15); and (d) seems to run contrary to the positive exhortation in 2:5 and 22—they suggest that the prophet wanted the people to repent, assuming that there was still hope for God's forgiveness. One might suggest that this clause is a brief expression of the prophet's own alignment with God's view of this sinful people. Such an interpretation maintains that Isaiah did not plead for mercy or assume divine forgiveness (contrast Amos 7:1–6) but recognized the true implications of these evil actions—they require punishment, not forgiveness.[50]

An alternative approach that seems more consistent with the surrounding statement about humbling the proud would not understand these words as an abrupt prayer by Isaiah, but a simple concluding statement that "you (God) should not lift up/exalt them."[51] In light of what was said about the sinfulness of these people, it is logical to reach the conclusion that the sinful person should not be exalted. This interpretation avoids the difficulty of having a one-line, fragmentary prayer and removes the theological idea that Isaiah did not want God to forgive these people. It also fits the contextual emphasis that God has humbled the proud and will not lift them up again. Isaiah indicates that there is no hope for restoration or an eventual healing for proud people like Uzziah. People can avoid this fate only (a) by not trusting in mankind and all their earthly achievements (2:7–8,13–16,22), and (b) by exalting God alone (2:11,12,17).

---

[50] Oswalt, *Isaiah 1–39*, 124, finds the prophet "in deep despair over his people's condition. He seems to be afraid that God might relent and, in violation of his own justice, forget their heinous sins." On the other hand, Watts, *Isaiah 1–33*, 35, translates this phrase וְאַל תִּשָּׂא לָהֶם as "Do not lift up for them," which he interprets to mean that these people will not be allowed to go up to Jerusalem in the pilgrimage with the other nations (2:2–3), but this draws an interpretation from outside the immediate context of 2:6–9.

[51] נָשָׂא can mean (a) lift up; (b) bear, carry; (c) take away, forgive (BDB, 669–72). This same root is used in 2:12,13,14 to mean "lifted up, exalt, lofty," not "forgiven."

2:10–11   The prophet moves from the accusations of 2:6–8 to an ironic futile exhortation to his audience in 2:10–11 (other portions in this section have exhortations at the end of the paragraphs in 2:5,22). All the proud can do is to try to hide because God will soon come to humble the proud and exalt himself. The prophet emphasizes again and again that the proud will be humbled and God alone will be exalted (2:11,12,17). This theme is central to the core theology of the book of Isaiah. God's plan was to show his glory through the revelation of his majestic splendor by ruling creation through his sovereign acts of grace and judgment. This divine plan was enacted to humble the proud people who tried to build the tower of Babel (Gen 11) and will result in the demise of the proud leaders and arrogant nations that claim God's sovereignty for themselves (cf. 10:4–34; 13–14; 16:6). Although the leaders of Judah are not specified in 2:6–22 (in chap. 3 these leaders are addressed), it seems that the proud people in Judah mentioned in 2:6–22 would surely include the wealthy and powerful leaders of the nation, rather than poor people who had no political power or financial standing in the community. The revelation of God's holiness and glory will put people in their rightful humble place, yet repeatedly people have asserted their wills and failed to bow before his glorious presence. Throughout history, leaders are eventually forced to chose one of two options: (a) they arrogantly trust themselves, or (b) they humble themselves and trustingly follow the Almighty God who sovereignly controls the universe.

Two things will happen in the future: (a) the splendor of God's majesty will be revealed; and (b) the dread of God's presence will cause people to hide (2:10). The "splendor of his majesty" (*mēhadar gĕʾônô*) is an attempt to describe the visible appearance of the glorious presence of God in its exalted fullness. This revelation of God's glory in many ways exceeds human comprehension. Isaiah's experience of seeing the holy exalted glory of the King in Isaiah 6 is as close as a human can get to visualizing the "splendor of his majesty." When such an event happens, people are immediately aware of God's holiness and power, and they immediately sense their sinfulness and unworthiness in his presence. Two responses are possible when God reveals his glory: (a) unrepentant people may attempt to hide from God (Gen 3; Ps 139:11; Isa 2:21), or (b) humble people will confess their sins, repent, and commit themselves to serving God (6:6–8). There is no way to escape from God (cf. Ps 139:1–16; Amos 9:2–4) or circumvent his sovereign holy rule of the earth, so every person in the past, present, and future must choose how they will respond to God, because one day everyone will meet him face to face.

Isaiah's imperative exhortation sarcastically[52] encourages his audience to hide on the day that God meets the proud, the arrogant, the lifted up ones, and the high people of Jerusalem. Since there is no possible way for people

---

[52] The imperatives בֹּוא, "go, enter," and הִטָּמֵן, "hide" are used in a sarcastic way (IBHS § 34. 4) or as an "ironical challenge" (GKC § 110a, cf. Amos 4:4), for no one can successfully hide from God, as Jonah found out (Jonah 1–2; Amos 9:1–4).

to actually hide from God, this must be an ironic picture of people foolishly running into graves cut from the rocks or holes dug in the ground—hardly safe places to hide if one is fearful of death. In spite of their resistance to and avoidance of God, the people of Judah will be humbled and God will be exalted (2:11). That will be a day of divine judgment on the proud; that will be the day that God reveals his power and glory as he intervenes in Judah's history. God makes no apology for that day, nor is there any attempt by the prophet to make God's actions more humane or "politically correct." God will totally devastate the proud. They will finally meet the real holy God that they attempted to define out of existence by reconstructing his ways after the desires of their own imagination.

2:12–22 This new paragraph begins by describing God's vicious attack on everything that could possibly be considered an exalted object that a person might trust. The concept of the Day of the Lord (2:12)[53] included God's judgment of the wicked and his salvation of his own people, so this application of the Day of the Lord theology against his own people was an unusual twist (Amos 5:18–20 is similar). The basic principle is that everything that was exalted will be reduced to nothing. The majestic cedars of Lebanon, the oaks of Bashan, the tall mountains, city towers and walls,[54] and even the great luxury trading ships[55] on the sea will be eliminated. Although Oswalt claims "There is thus every reason to see the passage as figurative,"[56] it seems like Uzziah and the people of Judah might have literally taken pride in their fortified cities, tall towers, large ships, and their beautiful trees. The prophet said that God will remove all the things that made Uzziah's kingdom so great. This list of specific objects could be representative of a host of other similar objects that exhibit strength, beauty, independence, self-sufficiency. God is against any objects that enabled people to believe they can control their own destiny. These verses communicate God's declaration of holy war "against" (*'al*) not just a few things, but also "all/every" (*kōl*) thing that might possibly replace God.

The issue of the humbling of the proud and the exalting of God at the beginning of the paragraph (2:12)[57] is repeated in 2:17 to persuade the prophet's

---

[53] There is a vast amount of literature on the Day of the Lord, including D. Stuart, "The Sovereign Day of Conquest," *BASOR* 221 (1976): 159–64; M. Weiss, "The Origin of the 'Day of the Lord'—Reconsidered," *HUCA* 37 (1966): 29–60; Y. Hoffmann, "The Day of the Lord as a Concept and a Term in the Prophetic Literature," *ZAW* 93 (1981): 37–50.

[54] Towers and walls are not intrinsically wrong. Some of these in Jerusalem were built by Asa, who honored God and was blessed by God (2 Chron 14:6–7).

[55] The NIV obscures the literal Hb. "Tarshish ship" (תַּרְשִׁישׁ) in 2:16 and focuses on the Phoenician use of these boats to haul trade across the Mediterranean Sea and beyond.

[56] Oswalt, *Isaiah 1–39*, 126, rejects an allegorical approach but views all of these things as representative of the spiritual condition of the nation.

[57] The final word וְשָׁפֵל, "he shall be humbled," does not match all the other descriptions of the exalted objects in this verse, but explains what will happen to the proud. 1QIsaᵃ and the Targum generally agree with this text, but the Old Greek translation has a longer text that reads, "against everyone that is high and lifted up and they shall be humbled." Although RSV follows this longer reading, the

audience of this central truth. The prophet stays focused on his main message and he repeats the dominant theme to reemphasize the truthfulness of God's claim. God alone will be exalted! God's exaltation will determine everything that happens because the world was created to bring him glory.

2:18–22 Having stated the main point in 2:12–17, the prophet addresses what will happen to the people who continue to depend on the idols that fill the land (cf. 2:8,18,20). The structure of these verses is intertwined with three repeated themes picked up from the end of the first paragraph in 2:10:

    2:18 removal of idols
        2:19a hide in the rocks
                2:19b from the dread of the Lord
    2:20 removal of idols
        2:21a hide in the rocks
                2:21b from the dread of the Lord
    2:22 stop esteeming people

The idols are not listed with the other lofty parts of nature or the impressive human creations in 2:13–16 because there is nothing exalted about these idols of "nothingness." They will disappear[58] and be abandoned (2:18,20) because people will finally understand that they are nothing when they experience first-hand the majestic power of God's glory. Picking up themes from 2:10, the text describes the people as hiding in fear and shame (2:19) and throwing away their useless idols to unclean bats and rodents[59] (2:20). God knows that the rebellious people who worship idols will eventually realize the truth when they see the majesty and terror of God.[60]

2:22 A final word of application is added (an exhortation parallel to 2:5,10–11) to admonish the audience concerning what they should do now.[61] Interestingly the prophet's aim is not merely to stop idol worship[62] but to

---

[58] The verb יַחֲלֹף, "pass away," is surprisingly a singular verb with a plural subject "idols" (an ironic plural of majesty). This would be normal if it were referring to Judah's one true God, but usually in a reference to idol gods one would expect to have a plural verb after "idols." 1QIsa[a] and the Old Greek have the plural form of the verb because "idols" is plural. The plural ending may well be the original Hb. form.

[59] The two words לַהְפֹּר פֵּרוֹת should be one word as in 1QIsa[a] לחפרפרים, "to the moles."

[60] NIV refers to God rising "to shake the earth" at the end of 2:21, and this could refer to some earthquake. An alternative translation might be, "when he rises to strike terror on the land." Hayes and Irvine, *Isaiah,* 83, see this as a sign of the earthquake in Uzziah's reign while Blenkinsopp, *Isaiah 1–39,* 196, concludes that it refers to a life-threatening storm. If the people had recently suffered from the major earthquake during the reign of Uzziah that would make this text come alive to the audience.

[61] 2:22 is missing from the Old Greek translation and is considered a late addition to the text by Wildberger, *Isaiah 1–12,* 102, but it is firmly established in the Hb. text. In light of the imperative application in 2:5 and 2:10–11, one would expect another imperative application in 2:22.

[62] Oswalt, *Isaiah 1–39,* 128, makes this wise observation.

shorter text is preferred. Since all these texts have "and he shall be humbled," this phrase should not be dropped from the verse as suggested in Wildberger, *Isaiah 1–12,* 98,101,115.

address the sinful hearts of people. People make themselves gods by giving themselves center stage and glorifying their importance. They tend to measure everything by how it is related to or how it affects them—not how it affects God. They are important, their pleasure and desires are paramount, and every-thing is judged by their self-created standards. This needs to stop.[63]

If anything is to change in Judah, there must be an accurate appraisal of the status of mankind. People are actually very transitory, like a breath of air. They come to and depart from the earth in a relatively short time, and the contribu-tion of each individual is relatively unimportant when one looks at things from the perspective of eternity (cf. Eccl 1:1–11). If the people in Isaiah's audience would quit regarding themselves so highly, there would be a potential oppor-tunity to remove pride and adopt God's view of humanity. This admonition is applicable to people in every culture and every time period, for all people tend to be self-centered rather than God centered. If people do not transform their view of themselves and God, some day God will humble them himself (cf. 3:1–4:1).

THEOLOGICAL IMPLICATIONS.   This sermon provides two unmis-takable theological choices to any reader/listener. One can follow the path of proud leaders like Uzziah, or a person can "stop trusting in man" now and exalt God alone. The theological choice is clear and presented as two opposite alter-natives with two opposite consequences: life with God in his glorious kingdom (2:1–5), or frightful humiliation and destruction (2:6–22). There is no middle ground for people to hide.

Is Isaiah making a broad theological principle that people should cut down all tall trees, disrespect important leaders, and avoid building tall buildings (the Trade Centers of 9/11) and big ships? This is unlikely. There is nothing intrinsically wrong with any of these tall/important objects, nor is it evil to put a person in a position of leadership and then honor that person for a job well done. What is important is people's attitude toward these objects or people. When people trust in armies, money, people, or idols instead of God, the glo-rification of God on earth is diminished. God will not allow other things or people to be raised up above himself for long. If people become proud of their accomplishments and do not put their confidence in God, if they end up trust-ing their leaders more than God; God will eventually destroy everything they have depended on. There is nothing more important than exalting and glorify-ing God; there is nothing more devastating than glorifying yourself or putting something else higher than God.

Both the exaltation of God and the humbling of the proud will happen on the Day of the Lord. No one ever wants to be among the proud on that day of accountability. Instead, people naturally want to be among those from all over

---

[63] חִדְלוּ, "stop," is an imperative command requiring a change in action, but there is no Hb. word representing the word "trusting" in the NIV. The literal "stop yourself from man" could just as easily be translated "stop glorifying man" or even "stop following after man."

the world who will enjoy the privilege of living in the paradise of God's kingdom. It will be a great day of peace, reconciliation, and inspiration (2:2–4). The recompense that each person will receive will be based on decisions made long before that final day arrives. Thus, all listeners who hear Isaiah's words must choose whom they will serve and glorify. Will it be God—or man?

(3) Removal of Judah's Male Leaders (3:1–15)

¹See now, the Lord,
  the Lord Almighty,
 is about to take from Jerusalem and Judah
  both supply and support:
 all supplies of food and all supplies of water,
²the hero and warrior,
 the judge and prophet,
  the soothsayer and elder,
³the captain of fifty and man of rank,
  the counselor, skilled craftsman and clever enchanter.

⁴I will make boys their officials;
  mere children will govern them.
⁵People will oppress each other —
  man against man, neighbor against neighbor.
 The young will rise up against the old,
  the base against the honorable.

⁶A man will seize one of his brothers
  at his father's home, and say,
 "You have a cloak, you be our leader;
  take charge of this heap of ruins!"
⁷But in that day he will cry out,
 "I have no remedy.
 I have no food or clothing in my house;
  do not make me the leader of the people."

⁸Jerusalem staggers,
  Judah is falling;
 their words and deeds are against the Lord,
  defying his glorious presence.
⁹The look on their faces testifies against them;
  they parade their sin like Sodom;
  they do not hide it.
 Woe to them!
  They have brought disaster upon themselves.

¹⁰ Tell the righteous it will be well with them,
  for they will enjoy the fruit of their deeds.
¹¹ Woe to the wicked! Disaster is upon them!
 They will be paid back for what their hands have done.

12 Youths oppress my people,
   women rule over them.
O my people, your guides lead you astray;
   they turn you from the path.
13 The LORD takes his place in court;

   he rises to judge the people.
14 The LORD enters into judgment
   against the elders and leaders of his people:
"It is you who have ruined my vineyard;
   the plunder from the poor is in your houses.
15 What do you mean by crushing my people
   and grinding the faces of the poor?"
      declares the Lord, the LORD Almighty.

This section relates closely to 2:1–22, for this message addresses the people of "Jerusalem and Judah" (2:1) about the questionable character of the leaders of the nation; that is, those who were apt to be proud and who tended to trust in human accomplishments. Chapter 2 emphasized the demise of mankind in general, but chap. 3 considers the specific removal of the leaders of Judah. All these sections are unified by a common discussion of what God will do on his special "day" (*yôm*) (2:11,12,17, 20; 3:7,18; 4:1,2), but this new message comes at these issues from a slightly different angle than 2:6–22. It does not repeatedly focus on the "humbling of the proud," the exaltation of "God alone," or the rejection of idolatry as in 2:6–22. Instead, it illustrates the hopelessness of trusting in the specific accomplishments of the human leaders in Judah at that time, a natural progression that is an application of the general exhortation not to put your trust in mankind in 2:22. These earthly leaders will not last, for God will remove those who were "defying his glorious presence" (3:8). People should not trust in human leaders to solve their difficulties (2:22; 3:7) because they do not have the power to bring about any real, lasting solutions.

HISTORICAL SETTING.   R. E. Clements thinks this passage refers to the incompetent leaders who let the nation become an Assyrian vassal during the Syro-Ephraimite War (734–732 BC),[64] while Childs prefers a time after the fall of Jerusalem (587 BC).[65] Although the date of this message is not exactly signaled in the text, its structural and thematic integration into the larger unit in 2:1–4:6 implies that it comes from the time of Uzziah, just like 2:6–22. The political setting precedes a major decline in military and economic status (3:1–5,8–9); there were still many wealthy women in Jerusalem (3:16). The era of Uzziah was a time of wealth and pride in Jerusalem that fits the cultural

---

[64] R. E. Clements, *Isaiah 1–39*, NCBC (Grand Rapids: Eerdmans, 1980), 47. Wildberger, *Isaiah 1–39*, 128, also believes Isaiah is referring to this period.

[65] Childs, *Isaiah*, 32, sees a connection to 2 Kgs 25:3. Sweeney, *Isaiah 1–39*, 109, suggests that it may refer to the consequence of Sennacherib's conquest of Judah in 701 BC, but this seems unlikely, since in 701 BC Jerusalem escaped the removal of its leaders (Isa 36–37).

setting of chap. 3. Dating this event during Uzziah's reign also could suggest that the judgment predicted in chap. 3 was fulfilled a few years later during the Syro-Ephraimite War.

STRUCTURE. The section begins with *kî*, "surely/truly" ("See now" in NIV), similar to the beginning of the last section in 2:6 (*kî* also begins the paragraph in 3:8). This message ends in 3:15 with the concluding, "declares the Lord, the LORD Almighty,"[66] similar to the paragraph ending at 1:20. The message is structured in three steps:

God will remove Judah's leaders	3:1–7
The leadership vacuum	1–3
Anarchy will reign	4–7
God will judge the leaders who oppress others	3:8–11
Sin will bring their fall	8–9
Fate of the righteous and wicked	10–11
God will take incompetent leaders to court	3:12–15
Judgment for oppression	12–14
Why do you crush my people?	15

This judgment speech reverses the usual order of accusations followed by punishments, for 3:1–7 functions as an announcement of punishment, while 3:8–11 provides the reasons that God will judge the nations. These two paragraphs are followed by a final announcement that God will remove the oppressive leaders of the nation (3:12–15).

3:1–3 The first half of the first paragraph (3:1–3) describes the leadership vacuum that will arise in Judah. God is the one who will cause this major social upheaval (3:1); this will not be some event out of the control of "the Lord, the LORD Almighty."[67] He is totally sovereign, but the text does not immediately reveal what method God will use to "remove" (*mēsîr*)[68] the ungodly leaders (3:24–26 and 5:25–30 indicate a war will accomplish this task). The loss of food and the removal of key leaders (including military officials) imply a military siege and captivity. "Supply and support" (3:1) are the masculine and feminine forms of the same word[69] and together they emphasize that God would remove

---

[66] The Old Greek translation omits this phrase, but since Isaiah uses similar phrases to conclude other paragraphs (1:20; 17:3; 31:9), it should be considered an authentic clause that concludes this authoritative message from God. Maybe the Greek translators thought it was redundant because 3:16 repeats the same idea.

[67] The NIV translation "Almighty" is unusual. צְבָאוֹת refers to the "host, army" of God, a title stressing God's sovereignty and military superiority over all forces.

[68] The verbal idea is expressed using a participle (מֵסִיר), which expresses something that is current, immanent, or future. Frequently it is immanent when it follows הִנֵּה, as in this case.

[69] Clements, *Isaiah 1–39*, 47, argues that מַשְׁעֵן וּמַשְׁעֵנָה, "supply and support," are metaphorical terms to describe the political and military leaders of Judah. He then eliminates the reference to "bread and water" at the end of the verse as late editorial glosses that link this situation to a famine at the time of a military siege. However, it seems natural that Isaiah would be thinking of a military

everything that supports life and social order. Specifically, this included food and water, and a host of key military (hero, warrior, captain of fifty[70]), political (judge, elder, man of rank,[71] and counselor), religious (prophet, soothsayer, enchanter),[72] and economic (skilled craftsman or possibly conjurer[73]) leaders. These people had a role and status in society that gave order and security to the common people. The average citizen relied on them and took the advice of these leaders. It is a little surprising that the king and the priests are not mentioned in this list of people God would remove from power. Any argument from silence is precarious, but it could be that the king was not an active leader at that time and that the corruption was not found in the lives of the priests. These circumstances would fit 2 Chronicles 26:16–21, where it is reported that Uzziah was separated from society for several years because of his leprosy, and that a group of at least eighty priests faithfully served God.

3:4–7   The removal of all the key leaders would have devastating implications for any social group, particularly if it were on a national scale and after a war. Isaiah predicted that God would replace these leaders with "children" (*ta'ălulîm* in 3:4). This could be understood literally or it could be a metaphorical[74] way of saying that the new leaders would be people who act like immature, unwise, mischievous, strong willed, and "inexperienced children."[75] In a sense God seems to be saying, "If you want to trust in incompetent leaders then I will give you some really bad ones." This would lead to anarchy and the oppression of those who would naturally get along together (3:5). The reversal of the natural social order will cause the young no longer to respect their elders, but to scorn them. Those having no redeeming qualities will oppose the honorable. Real competent and godly leaders will be very rare and the social

---

siege (in light of the loss of military leaders in the next verse) as 3:24–26 makes so clear. Since armies usually cut off a city's source of food and water during a siege, there is nothing objectionable about this phrase.

[70] חֲמִשִּׁים, "fifty," refers to the number of men the leader would be in charge of in his unit. The Israelite army was organized into groups of 10, 50, 100, and 1000 men (2 Sam 18:1; 2 Kgs 1:9).

[71] This is "the one whose face is lifted up" (וּנְשׂוּא פָנִים), a descriptive term that refers to a highly respected and proud person (2 Kgs 5:1; Job 22:8).

[72] Soothsaying and enchanting were forbidden in Deut 18:9–14 and 1 Sam 28:9. Their presence here suggests that these certain types of forbidden religious practices were carried on in Jerusalem (cf. 8:19), which is consistent with 2:2,8.

[73] There is uncertainty surrounding this person, not only because a skilled craftsman is not usually a leader in society, but because the author usually lists more than one person in a class (in vv. 2–3). The rare term חֲרָשִׁים is used only here. Wildberger, *Isaiah 1–12*, 124, suggests this person is a sorcerer or conjurer, based on the Aramaic חַרְשָׁא, "sorcery."

[74] K. P. Darr, *Isaiah's Vision and the Family of God* (Louisville: Westminster, 1994), 49, takes a metaphorical approach because she believes Isaiah was calling the current leaders "children" in 3:4,12.

[75] Oswalt, *Isaiah 1–39*, 129, prefers "tyrant" rather than "children" as the translation of תַּאֲלוּלִים but in light of the parallelism with "boys" in the line above, it appears that Isaiah is referring to people who demand to have their own evil way, a characteristic of many children. נְעָרִים, "boys," carries the essential idea of people who are "inexperienced" (Tucker, "Isaiah 1–39," *NIB*, vi, 77).

situation will be so bad (things will be in a state of "ruin," *wĕhammakšēlâ*) that no one will want to serve in a position of leadership (3:6–7). In a deliberate mockery of the situation, Isaiah predicted that the only qualification for a leader will be: Do you own a coat?[76] Even with these minimal ridiculous qualifications people will strenuously resist positions of leadership, making the claim "I do not own a coat" in order to avoid leadership responsibility. No one will have any answers to alleviate or heal[77] the situation, and consequently, the least qualified will end up as leaders. This can even happen today, for when godly people fail to step into positions of leadership, then people with poor leadership or questionable moral qualifications get appointed or elected to positions of responsibility.

3:8–11 The second paragraph also begins with *kî*, "surely/truly" (omitted in NIV) to emphasize that these things will indeed happen. Here Isaiah offered a justification for God's action so that the audience would understand why God acted the way he did. In essence, Isaiah claimed that the people of Judah were bringing this disaster on themselves because all God would do is to justly reward the people for their own deeds. Jerusalem "will fall" (prophetic perfect,[78] not "is falling" as in NIV) because the deeds and words of the people directly defied God. This syntactical construction with an infinitive construct expresses the motivations of the people's heart:[79] they did this "in order to defy his glorious presence." This shockingly defiant behavior was boldly done right before God's glorious and holy eyes. These evil people in Judah did not even try to hide their sinful deeds but openly paraded their sins in public like the people did in Sodom (3:9b; cf. Gen 19–20). God could plainly observe this open rebellion because it was clearly written all over their faces (3:9a; in legal terminology, they testify against themselves)[80] and evident in their words (3:8b), so there was no doubt about their guilt. The prophet lamented and the Lord expressed his grief with words of woe in 9b and 11. This was a terrible situation. How could they bring such a terrible disaster on themselves?

Verses 10–11 contrast the fate of the righteous and the wicked. Although these verses have a theological slant similar to wisdom literature (Prov 12:14; 16:20), it is more likely that Isaiah is thinking of God's covenantal blessing on the righteous and his cursing of the wicked,[81] not a wisdom maxim about God

---

[76] The NIV properly implies "and say" in 3:6 (though it is not in the Hb.) because someone seems to be directly addressing someone else—referring to "you." Kaiser, *Isaiah 1–12*, 72, says, "No one will even allow himself to be forced to take office under pressure from his clan . . . in order to evade the thankless task."

[77] לֹא אֶהְיֶה חֹבֵשׁ, "I am not a healer, doctor," is a better translation than NIV's "I have no remedy."

[78] GKC §106n. The prophetic perfect use of כָּשְׁלָה, "will stumble," and נָפַל, "will fall," views an act as completed as it is viewed from the perspective of a future time.

[79] The infinitive construct לַמְרוֹת is often used to express purpose or aim (GKC § 114f-g).

[80] הַכָּרַת פְּנֵיהֶם at the beginning of 3:9 literally means "the cut/expression of their faces," referring to their appearance.

[81] This connection with wisdom literature has led some to see this verse as a later addition and

prospering the wise and judging the fool. The theological principle is: you will reap what you sow (cf. Gal 6:7). The righteous will have good times and enjoy their rewards, while the wicked will receive[82] the disasters that they so richly deserve. Isaiah does not deal with the dilemma of the suffering of the righteous that Job and Ecclesiastes address; he is simply supporting the point that the wicked leaders justly deserve a covenantal punishment for all their evil deeds. One could hypothesize that 3:10 functions as a word of encouragement to the righteous remnant in Isaiah's audience, but it is more likely that the phrase serves as simply a rhetorical strategy to remind the wicked that divine justice will require full accountability; all people will be "paid back"[83] evil for evil and rewarded good for good. The justice of God is still a significant motivation for people to act responsibly today, for whatever people sow will come back to them when God allows them to reap the rewards of their labors (Gal 6:7).

3:12–15   In light of the evidence presented so far (the charges of sinfulness), God threatened that he might have to take these unacceptable leaders to court (3:13–14).[84] The judgment will fall specifically on the leaders of Judah who (a) oppress others; (b) lead people astray; (c) plunder the poor; and (d) crush God's people. These social sins included misusing their power and status to take unlawful advantage of weaker people. These practices show that the leaders of Judah were irresponsible, selfish, mean, and knew very little about servant leadership. The Lord brought his case against the elders and leaders who were entrusted with the tasks of maintaining true justice in God's land. They were supposed to lead God's chosen people[85] to follow God's instructions; they were supposed to care for his precious vineyard (cf. 5:1–7). Part of their responsibility was to defend the poor and helpless

---

to change "say" (אִמְרוּ) to "blessed" (אַשְׁרֵי) (Blenkinsopp, *Isaiah 1–39*, 198), which is accepted in the NEB. W. Holladay, "Isaiah III 10–11: An Archaic Wisdom Passage," *VT* 18 (1968): 481–87, wisely argues that the language is old (not from a late date) and that the verb should not be changed to "blessed, happy."

[82] The Hebrew Masoretic texts has יֵעָשֶׂה, "it will be done," while 1QIsaᵃ has יָשׁוּב, "it will return." Both make good sense, but Wildberger, *Isaiah 1–12*, 126, prefers the Qumran reading while Oswalt, *Isaiah 1–39*, 134, prefers the Masoretic text. The Masoretic is the more difficult reading and probably the original.

[83] גְּמוּל is a noun meaning "dealings, benefit, recompense." In the NIV the verb form of this root is translated "bought" in the last line of 3:9, while the noun form in 3:11 is translated "will pay back" as if it were a verb. Literally 3:11 says, "for the dealings of his hands will be done unto him." Although the NIV translation does not pervert the overall meaning of the text in these two verses, there is an unfortunate inconsistency in the translation of the same root and an inappropriate paraphrasing of a noun as a verb clause.

[84] Hayes and Irvine, *Isaiah*, 91 properly interpret this "contending" (רִיב) as pre-trial statements before the trial actually goes to court.

[85] 3:12 refers to "my people" (עַמִּי) twice and 3:15 has it once, plus the end of 3:14 mentions "his people" (עַמּוֹ), so it is surprising to see "peoples, nations" (עַמִּים) at the end of 3:13. The Old Greek, Syriac, and Vulgate have "his people" in 3:13 (the Targum has "peoples"). One could hypothesize a scribal error here or view the prophet connecting the judgment of "my people" with the judgment of other "peoples" as well.

(1:17), people who for economic or social reasons could not defend themselves against powerful landlords and skillful lawyers. Instead they allowed
young boys to rise to the throne and permitted women (maybe the queen
mother or women in the harem)[86] to rule over the people (3:12). The youths
(young boys) and women could be interpreted literally or one could view
this as a sarcastic remark comparing the inept male leaders to young boys or
women.[87] These advisors led the people astray and "confused"[88] (better than
NIV "turn") them so that they did not follow God's path for life (3:12). The
situation was so impossible that God saw little reason for hope. If they would
not change, then he must intervene against these leaders (3:13–14) to remove
them from office.

The final question in 3:15 reveals the Lord's astonishment at such behavior. How can someone do this to "my people,"[89] the ones that God cared
for so much? Do these leaders not have a conscience? Do they not realize
that these poor people are valuable in God's eyes? By "ruining, burning"[90]
the vineyard (3:14) that belonged to God and by inhumanely "grinding the
faces of the poor" in the dirt, they demonstrated their utter callous rejection
of their God-given duty as leaders and their total disrespect for the value
of human life. God could not support these leaders who "crush" (*tĕdakkᵓu*)
others and he would not allow them to continue in their present leadership
positions.

Today God still has high standards for people in positions of leadership in
government, business, the family, religious institutions, and the church (Matt
24:45–51; 2 Tim 4:1–2; Jam 3:1). Deeds that involve the misuse of authority
in business or the church are always despicable in God's eyes. God loves and
cares about all people, especially those who are believers, "his own people."
Without just and godly leaders, political and religious organizations will be
doomed to disaster and divine judgment. Let all leaders beware; God knows
your deeds! There will be a day of accountability.

---

[86] The text of 3:12 is problematic because the various translations have "plunderers/extractors"
(Old Greek; Vulgate, Targum) instead of "children/youths," and "creditors/usurers" from the root
meaning "to lend for usury" (נֹשֶׁא) instead of "women" (נָשִׁים). Wildberger, *Isaiah 1–12*, 137, prefers "tyrants" and "extortionists," partially based on his interpretation of 3:4.

[87] B. G. Webb, *The Message of Isaiah*, BST (Downer's Grove: Inter-Varsity, 1996), 49, views
the reference to youths and women as a means of describing the weakness of these male leaders.

[88] בִּלְּעוּ usually means "to swallow, destroy," but in some verses the context does not fit this
interpretation. Thus one can hypothesize another root using the same letters meaning "confuse,
confound" (parallel to "lead astray" in the line above), which is used in 9:15; 19:3; 28:7 and Ps
55:10. NASB and NRSV use "confuse" in this verse.

[89] The *Kethib* does not begin 3:15 with a question, but most translations follow the *Qere*, which
has מַה לָּכֶם, "Why do you . . . ?/ What do you mean?"

[90] The root בָּעַר means to "burn," which fittingly describes the way to ruin a vineyard, but
burning was also the chief way of destroying a city. F. C. Fensham, "The Root *bᶜr* in Ugaritic and
in Isaiah in the Meaning 'to Pillage,'" *JNSL* 9 (1981): 67–69, proposes a legitimate meaning, but
in the context of vineyard imagery, "burning" makes better sense.

(4) Removal of Judah's Proud Women (3:16–4:1)

¹⁶ The LORD says,
　　"The women of Zion are haughty,
　walking along with outstretched necks,
　　flirting with their eyes,
　tripping along with mincing steps,
　　with ornaments jingling on their ankles.
¹⁷ Therefore the Lord will bring sores on the heads of the women of Zion;
　　the LORD will make their scalps bald."

¹⁸ In that day the Lord will snatch away their finery: the bangles and head-bands and crescent necklaces, ¹⁹ the earrings and bracelets and veils, ²⁰ the head-dresses and ankle chains and sashes, the perfume bottles and charms, ²¹ the signet rings and nose rings, ²² the fine robes and the capes and cloaks, the purses ²³ and mirrors, and the linen garments and tiaras and shawls.

²⁴ Instead of fragrance there will be a stench;
　　instead of a sash, a rope;
　instead of well-dressed hair, baldness;
　　instead of fine clothing, sackcloth;
　　instead of beauty, branding.
²⁵ Your men will fall by the sword,
　　your warriors in battle.
²⁶ The gates of Zion will lament and mourn;
　　destitute, she will sit on the ground.
¹ In that day seven women
　　will take hold of one man
　and say, "We will eat our own food
　　and provide our own clothes;
　only let us be called by your name.
　　Take away our disgrace!"

In addition to the male leaders in government, the military, the economy, and religion (3:2), God condemned the pride of the wealthy women of Jerusalem. This is a judgment on the upper class ladies, probably including the ruling women in 3:12. Since the time of Uzziah was a period of independence and prosperity, the wives of many government officials,[91] businessmen, and military leaders gained the financial resources to spend excessively on themselves so that they could dress lavishly. The exact description of the behavior and attire of these beautiful women is somewhat problematic because several Hebrew terms in 3:16–24 only occur in this passage in the Bible. In these cases comparable roots in Hebrew or other languages can help identify these items of clothing or adornment, but not all interpreters agree on the identity of the objects described.

---

[91] Blenkinsopp, *Isaiah 1–39*, 201, suggests that these were women from the royal court, but it would be difficult to limit this group just to the wives of politicians.

This section can be divided into three sub-paragraphs:

God will judge the proud wealthy women	3:16–17
God will remove all objects of pride	3:18–24
The women will be humiliated	3:25–4:1

3:16–17 This new oracle is quite harsh, controversial, and rather satirical; a speech that would be considered politically incorrect by many today. In order to carify the true source of these provocative statements, Isaiah begins with the announcement that this is another authoritative word from God (3:16a). God's perspective on the women of Zion is contained in the accusation (3:16) and punishment (3:17) of a judgment speech. The essential problem that brings God's judgment is "because" (*ya'an kî*, 3:16, omitted by NIV) the women "are haughty" (*gābhû*), self-engrossed, or proud. Their looks, jewelry, makeup, and demeanor all called attention to themselves as very special and important people. Thus, there was a good reason for God's action. He earlier stated his opposition against all pride (cf. 2:9–22), so now the prophet applies this principle to the situation of these rich women in Jerusalem. Isaiah noticed these elite women in Zion; that is, in the temple area in Jerusalem, the very place where God should be glorified and exalted. This was the last place these wealthy women should be lifting themselves up as spectacles to behold.

The haughty attitude was evident from the women's pompous demeanor (the stretched out neck put their nose in the air) and flirtatious glances as well as their provocative manner of walking with short hops or steps[92] that jingled the jewelry on their ankles (3:16). This high society look drew attention to these women and communicated their importance. The way they carried their heads breathed sophistication as they flirtatiously looked from side to side and down their noses at the lower class. These exhibitionists, who boldly strutted in their finest attire, displayed a proud heart that God hates. On account of this (3:17), God was determined to remove everything that made these women beautiful and in the end leave them humiliated, shamed, and repulsive. Although this verse does not explain how this will be accomplished, Clements concludes that this humiliation will be due to the rape and savagery that accompanies defeat in war (based on 3:24–26).[93] Instead of looking like stately beauty queens fresh from the beauty parlor, these humiliated women will soon be displaying ugly scabs, unsightly baldness, and uncovered foreheads.[94] This is the abrupt and dramatic reversal that God will bring on those who were so proud of themselves.

---

[92] טָפֹף, "quick little steps," is derived from טַף, "children," and probably refers to their manner of walking with small steps.

[93] Clements, *Isaiah 1–39*, 51–52, thinks this refers to abuse during wars in the time of Ahaz, which makes good sense, but the text itself provides no hint concerning the exact historical date of the fulfillment of this prophecy.

[94] פַּת does not mean female "private parts" as Blenkinsopp, *Isaiah 1–39*, 200–201, suggests, but "forehead," based on the Akkadian *pūtu*.

3:18–24   The devastating impact of God's hatred of pride is seen in the catalogue of things God will "take away" from these beautiful women (God also "took away" things in 3:1).[95] The extensive list includes the latest fashions and accoutrements that the proud women would wear. The beauty and glory (*tip'eret*) provided by beads, necklaces, earrings, bracelets, rings, anklets, veils, headdresses, crowns, robes, capes, purses, and mirrors will be gone. Although it is impossible to know what each of these articles looked like[96] the main point is obvious: God will mercilessly and totally remove every last thing that these women use to make themselves look important.

Although the humiliation of the women was already described in the previous subparagraph, by repeating this judgment again in a slightly different form in v. 24, the prophet makes it abundantly clear that this judgment will devastate the proud women of Jerusalem. The prophet must do everything possible to cause the listeners to turn from their pride and avoid the terrible fate that potentially awaits them. If they do not humble themselves, their world of luxury will dramatically end. "Instead" (*tahat* used 5 times in v. 24) of having everything attractive and beautiful, these women will wear the marks of captivity and utter shame. Their fragrant perfume,[97] derived from the balsam tree, will not radiate from their skin like it used to, "instead" anyone close to them will smell the stench of decaying flesh from festering wounds. "Instead" of fine white linen clothes, they will wear sackcloth. The enemy soldiers will replace their beautiful makeup with an ugly and painful brand.[98] The humiliation will be so horrible and extreme that it will be almost unimaginable. Yet, this is the length that God will go to in order to remove pride from the heart of mankind. These graphic warnings should cause every listener to double check their attitudes and reexamine the ways they present themselves to others. Pride has no place in the life of God's people. This sermon demonstrates that it is far more important to worry about how one looks in God's eyes, for God's eye penetrates to discern what is in a person's heart (cf. 1 Sam 16:7).

3:25–4:1   The final verses of this paragraph move from the physical removal of outward signs of status and pride to the personal shame of not even having a husband. The coming war will result in the death of many brave sons

---

[95] יָסוּר, "remove, take away," in 3:18 has the same root as the participle מֵסִיר, "remove, take away," in 3:1.

[96] Wildberger, *Isaiah 1–12*, 152, suggests that the "headbands and crescent necklaces" were in the shape of the sun and moon because these terms are derivative from the nouns "sun" and "moon."

[97] It appears that בֹּשֶׂם, "fragrant perfume," is connected to בְּלֶשֶׂם, the "balsam" tree from which it was derived.

[98] The text is unclear at the end of v. 24. In the initial examples in 3:24, the two words compared come after "instead of" (תַּחַת) in Hb., but in this case only "beauty" comes afterwards. One could hypothesize that a word dropped out by a scribal error. 1QIsaᵃ adds בֹשֶׁת, "shame," at the end of the line, which makes good sense ("instead of beauty, shame" as in NRSV). Others suggest that כִּי at the beginning of the verse is from כְּוִיָּה, "brand" (Exod 21:25). This yields "branding instead of beauty" as in NASB, which is similar to NIV.

and husbands who will be soldiers[99] in the coming war (3:25). Their death will deprive the women of Zion of their source of income, their social status, their security, and the opportunity to have children. Then the personified gates of Zion, like destitute women, will mourn and lament concerning their helpless situation (3:26). This crying will be caused both by their losses and by their hopeless future. This contrasts with the personified gates that rejoice and "lift up their heads" at the entrance of "the King of Glory" in Ps 24:7–9.

So many men will die in this war that seven women will pursue one man to try to convince him to be their husband. Under normal circumstances, a husband must pursue a woman and promise to provide for the physical needs of his wife (Exod 21:10), but in this case the women will be so desperate for a husband that they will "strongly grab hold"[100] of him. Surprisingly, they will gladly offer to share him with several other women and not require him to provide financially for any of their physical needs. They will do anything they can to avoid the shame and disgrace of not having a husband and children.

THEOLOGICAL IMPLICATIONS.   This passage provides a clear understanding of one of God's ways of dealing with pride. He hates, even loathes, pride and arrogance in his people. He will eventually remove those things that cause or encourage an attitude of pride. This passage challenges people to test their own heart to see if that tattoo, that new pair of shoes, that new job, that new house, or the purchase of that new car was motivated by pride or if it will result in a prideful attitude. Although pride differs from self-esteem, the concern for my rights, my opinions, my way, and my honor is a sign of a sick self-centered society that fails to give complete honor and glory to God. Focusing on accumulating what some might call the "necessary luxuries of life" might result in honor or respect from a few people, but these things usually do not impress God or exalt him. Rationalizations like "everyone has these things" will not suffice in God's eyes, if a person's possessions produce a proud spirit. God looks at the heart (cf. 1 Sam 16:7), not the clothes one wears or the jewelry one has on. Certainly God does not believe that a person's true beauty or value depends on wearing the most expensive makeup and jewelry. This sermon asks the listeners to evaluate the central theological motivations and highest priorities that guide their lives. If people (male or female) do not exalt God, but exalt themselves, how can they expect to be treated any differently than the women of Zion?

(5) God's Glorious Holy Kingdom (4:2–6)

²In that day the Branch of the LORD will be beautiful and glorious, and the fruit of the land will be the pride and glory of the survivors in Israel. ³Those who

---

[99] מְתַיִךְ means "your men, husbands," but in a military context it refers to "men of war, soldiers."

[100] וְהֶחֱזִיקוּ is "take hold" in NIV. The root emphasizes the idea of "seizing, having strong hold on something, prevailing over."

are left in Zion, who remain in Jerusalem, will be called holy, all who are recorded among the living in Jerusalem. [4]The Lord will wash away the filth of the women of Zion; he will cleanse the bloodstains from Jerusalem by a spirit of judgment and a spirit of fire. [5]Then the LORD will create over all of Mount Zion and over those who assemble there a cloud of smoke by day and a glow of flaming fire by night; over all the glory will be a canopy. [6]It will be a shelter and shade from the heat of the day, and a refuge and hiding place from the storm and rain.

The immediate future will be terrible for Judah if the nation does not stop trusting mankind and start exalting God alone. In spite of the severity of the warning in 2:6–4:1, Isaiah wanted to make it clear that the nation's present pride will not defeat God's ultimate plan to establish his glorious kingdom in the future. The long unit, 2:1–4:6, comes to a close in 4:2–6 with the prophet returning to the same positive themes that opened this unit in 2:1–5.[101] Both messages of hope describe what will happen "in that/the last days" when God gathers his special people to Zion. But there are profound differences between these two salvation oracles, in spite of their general similarities. This message focuses on the purification of a holy remnant of Hebrew people in Jerusalem, not on the coming of the Gentile nations to hear the laws of God expounded (as in 2:1–5).

The salvation oracle in 4:2–6 is thematically related to its immediate preceding literary context by interlinking vocabulary like the reference to the return of "beauty" to Jerusalem (3:18 and 4:2), the transformation of evil "pride" into "glory" (2:19b,21b; 4:2b),[102] and the removal of the filth of the "women/daughters of Zion" (3:16; 4:4). These interconnected themes of the removal of human glory and the triumph of divine glory demonstrate that God's judgment has the ultimate purpose of purifying his people, not destroying them. The structure of this future hope is developed in three steps:

The future glory that will beautify Zion	4:2
God's cleansing of his holy people in Zion	4:3–4
God's glory will protect Zion	4:5–6.

4:2 The history of the interpretation of the "branch/sprout (*ṣemaḥ*) of the LORD" has followed two distinct paths.[103] One views this phrase as a messianic title of the promised Davidic ruler, the other interprets it as a sign of God's blessing on nature and considers the sprouting "branch" to be parallel to the "fruit of the land." Three questions need to be asked to decide which interpretation fits best in this context: (a) Are there earlier passages before the time of

---

[101] Magonet, "Isaiah 2:1–4:6," 71–85, also finds a unity designed into the purposeful editorial arrangement of the positive statements at the beginning (2:1–5) and end (4:2–6) of this section.

[102] "Beauty" (תִּפְאֶרֶת) in 4:2 and ""pride, glory" (גָּאוֹן) in 4:2.

[103] S. Amsler, "צמח *ṣmḥ* to sprout," *TLOT*, 3, 1086, connects צמח to the vocabulary of plant life and translates the verb "to sprout, cause to grow, bloom" and the noun "sprout." He recognizes a specialized royal Davidic usage of the term to represent the expectations of a future king (2 Sam 23:1–7; Ps 132:17; Jer 23:5), though he does not classify 4:2 in this category.

Isaiah that give a messianic meaning to the verb *ṣāmaḥ*, "spring forth," a word that is from the same root as the noun "branch?" (b) Does Isaiah or other later authors use this term (or related terms) to refer to the Messiah, thus providing a later biblical commentary on what the biblical authors thought "branch" means? And (c) does the messianic meaning "Branch of the LORD" or the agricultural meaning "fruit of the land" fit the context in Isaiah 4:2–6 better?

EARLY TRADITIONS. Although it is difficult to date the written form of any biblical text, the oral traditions about David's last words in 2 Sam 23:5 recall him asking, "Will he [God] not bring to fruition [make it spring forth] my salvation?" And the Psalmist in 132:17 proclaims "Here I will make a horn grow [spring forth] for David, and set a lamp for mine anointed one." Based on the context in each of these passages it appears that both connect the idea of "springing forth" to the coming of the Messiah from the line of David. Second Samuel 23:5b expected salvation to "spring forth" in the context of God making an "everlasting covenant" with David, a covenant that promised a son to reign on the throne of David forever (23:5a; 2 Sam 7:1–16). In Psalms 132:17 it is the "horn of David" (*qeren lĕdāwid*), "my anointed One" (*limšîḥî*), whom "I will make spring forth, grow" (*'aṣmîaḥ*) so this also points to the promised future messianic king (cf. Ezek 29:21). If Isaiah knew these songs, and there is no reason to think he was not aware of them,[104] one can conclude that a messianic interpretation of the root *ṣemaḥ* was well known before the time of Isaiah. The use of the word *ṣemaḥ* in a Phoenician document from Cyprus (third century BC) to refer to the legitimate heir to the throne demonstrates from a secular source that the term can refer to a royal heir. Although this occurrence does not determine how Isaiah used this word, it shows that this imagery was an appropriate term to represent the appearance of a new king in the ancient Near Eastern world.

LATER INTERPRETATIONS. The earliest commentary on the concept of the messianic Branch is found in Isaiah 11:1,10 where Isaiah uses a different Hebrew term but says of the Messiah, "a shoot (*ḥōṭer*) will come up from the stump of Jesse; from his roots a Branch (*nēṣer*) will bear fruit."[105] Later Jeremiah refers to the "Righteous Branch" from David (23:5; 33:15) and Zechariah (3:8; 6:12) uses the term "Branch" with a messianic connotation. When the verbal form of *ṣāmaḥ* is used, it is normally connected to a noun (hair, herbs, trouble, truth, health, vine, east wind, horn, tree) so that it is clear what is "springing forth/growing." The nominal form of "branch" (*ṣemaḥ*) is used seven times of literal plant growth or a "shoot from the ground" (61:11; Gen 19:25), but the phrase "Branch of the LORD" or "righteous Branch" never refers to the literal growth of plants elsewhere in the Old Testament. The Aramaic

---

[104] L. C. Allen, *Psalms 101–150*, WBC (Waco: Word, 1983), 206–208, surveys opinions on the date of Psalm 132. Some connect its origin to David bringing the ark to Jerusalem or a Zion festival. Most give it a pre-exilic date due to various archaic linguistic features.

[105] Isaiah 14:19 refers to the rejected Babylonian king as a rejected "branch" (נֵצֶר).

Targum translates Isaiah 4:2 as "Messiah of the Lord," showing that early Jewish interpreters thought this was a messianic reference.[106]

CONTEXT. The main argument against a messianic interpretation of 4:2 is the parallelism between "branch of the LORD" in 4:2a with "fruit of the land" in 4:2b. Clements states that Isaiah was simply indicating that the survivors in Jerusalem would live in a very fertile land that will yield plentiful crops.[107] To avoid this interpretation, E. J. Young considered "fruit of the land" as an indication of the earthly origin of the Messiah, while "branch of the LORD" refers to his divine nature,[108] but this seems almost an allegorical approach. K. Nielsen attributes both of these phrases to a kingly figure because the adjectives "beautiful" and "glorious" describe the positive characteristics of a person, not a plant.[109] Nielsen's interpretation means 4:2 has two references to the Messiah, while removing all mention of the fertility of the land. Although this approach is within the range of hypothetical possibilities, these last two alternatives seem to stretch the figurative use of the language far beyond what would naturally be expected. A better solution is to conclude that the two clauses in 4:2 refer to two parallel acts of God that will transform Zion. God will (a) cause his messianic Branch to spring forth, and also (b) bring marvelous fertility to the produce of the field. This interpretation shows how God will reverse the situation in 2:6–4:1. He will (a) replace the proud leaders of his people and give them a new leader, the Branch of the Lord, and (b) replace the ruin, devastation, and shame of the destroyed land with lush crops that will have great fertility. This fits the context of what God will do in parallel Old Testament messianic passages that describe the coming of God's glorious kingdom. Ezekiel also presents both aspects (the Messiah and fertility), parallel to Isaiah's vision of the future. Ezek 34:20–31 refers to God's glorious kingdom as a place where "my shepherd, my servant David" will tend God's sheep (Ezek 34:23; cf. 36:29–30) and "the trees of the field will yield their fruit and the ground will yield its crops" (Ezek 34:27; cf. 37:24–25), but the fruit or vegetation is never called the "vegetation, branch of the Lord."

---

[106] J. G. Baldwin, "Ṣemaḥ as a Technical Term in the Prophets," *VT* 14 (1964): 93–97, supports a messianic interpretation based on how later authors (Jeremiah and Zechariah) use this terminology. Although later usage is significant, contemporary descriptions within Isaiah and earlier Davidic texts are far more important. J. J. M. Roberts, "The Meaning of 'ה צמח' in Isaiah 4:2," *JQR* 28 (2000): 20–27, discusses the issues related to the translation "branch, vegetation." W. H. Rose, *Zemah and Zerubbabel: Messianic Expectations in the Early Postexilic Period*, JSOTSup 304 (Sheffield: Sheffield Academic Press, 2000), 91–107, surveys various approaches to understanding this root.

[107] Clements, *Isaiah 1–39*, 54, considers this verse a late addition in the Persian period that is consistent with 10:20–23; 37:30.

[108] E. J. Young, *The Book of Isaiah*, (Grand Rapids: Eerdmans, 1965–72), I:173–78; but it is not very clear why the term "sprout of the LORD" refers to the divinity of the Messiah.

[109] K. Nielsen, *There is Hope for a Tree* (Sheffield: JSOT, 1989), 184–87, thinks that "beautiful," "glorious," "pride," and "glory" are not fitting adjectives for plants.

Returning now to the main thrust of 4:2–6, one finds Isaiah communicating wonderful promises about what will happen when God finally establishes his kingdom. This picture sharply contrasts with what will happen to the proud (2:6–4:1), so this brief reference to the hopeful themes of 2:1–5 was another reminder to the audience of the choices they could make. There was an advantage to exalting God rather than themselves.

The prophet begins by creating a picture of Zion's future glory and beauty (4:2). The Branch is God's eternal Davidic ruler of the people. He will sprout forth like a new growth and be "beautiful" and "glorious." These are positive metaphors describing the very best qualities of attractiveness and honor ("glory, splendor" is also attributed to God in 2:19,21; 4:5). These are qualities totally missing from the inferior leaders of Jerusalem in 3:1–15 and the proud women in 3:16–4:1. Zion's future inhabitants will also see a wonderful transformation of nature (cf. 60:13; 61:11; Ezek 34:25–27; Hos 3:21–22; Amos 9:13–14). The arrogant human attempts to display "beauty" in the past will be gone (3:18) and a new understanding of the beauty of God's blessings on the land will arise. False concepts of human "pride" in 2:6–22 and 3:16 will be removed and the "glory/ beauty" (a word play on *tip'eret* in 3:18) of God's created order and his holy people will be evident (4:2b).

4:3–4 God's cleansing of those left in Zion will transform them into a holy people, a select group whose names are securely recorded in God's books. This miraculous change will take place in the future when "it will be/come about" (omitted by NIV). This is an additional sign that Isaiah is referring to the things that will happen "in that day" (4:2). The "survivors" are those "who remain" (the definite participle *hānniš'ār*) but they are not identified specifically by race, age, sex, nationality, or status. They will include people like the sinful women of Zion (4:4), who will be marvelously cleansed of their filth. Their definitive traits are holiness and having their names written down. The text says that they "will be called holy" (lit. "holy will be said to him").[110] This is not a characteristic that these people will gain through pious acts on their part, but the results of the purifying acts of God. At this point there is no clarification about how these sinners will be cleansed, but later chapters will address this issue (cf. 53:1–12). The term "holy" (*qādôš*) is a reminder of God's original plan in Exodus 19:6 to establish Israel as his "treasured possession" and "holy nation." Holiness implies being set apart from others (and from sin) and set apart to God alone. The holiness of these people will make them fit to dwell in God's kingdom and their holiness presents a contrast with the pride and sinfulness of the present generation that lived in Zion (2:6–4:1). The connection between being holy and having one's name recorded in God's book is not stated, but a connection is implied, for both appear to identify the new status of the inhabitants of Zion. The registry of names, which preserves

---

[110] קָדוֹשׁ יֵאָמֶר לוֹ. Later the city of Jerusalem is called a "holy city" because all uncleanness will be removed (52:1) and because the Lord will redeem them (62:12).

the identity of the holy ones, may refer to God's book of life (Exod 32:32–33; Ps 69:28; Dan 12:1; Mal 3:16).[111] Having one's name in this book provides assurance of being one of God's children.

Verse 4 gives some information about how the people of Zion will become holy. This transformation takes place "when[112] (omitted by NIV) God washes away" sin, using a slightly different metaphor than the purification through smelting metaphor in 1:25. God himself will "wash away" (*rāḥaṣ*) and "cleanse, rinse" (*yādîaḥ* is from sacrificial terminology), meaning that he will purify and remove the stain of sin from his people. Their sinfulness is graphically compared to repulsive "filth, human excrement, vomit" (36:12).[113] This is how God views the sins described in 2:6–4:1 and how he views all sin since then. Another means of purification is by a "spirit of judgment and a spirit of fire." Gray believes this phrase refers to the "spirit of Yahweh" that will come in judgment, while Clements prefers "a hot, searing wind."[114] Based on other references to burning and judgment (1:31; 28:6; 30:27–28; 66:15–16), Isaiah seems to be describing God's purification of Zion by destroying the remaining sinful people in Jerusalem.

4:5–6 After Zion is purified, God will create something new in Zion. The use of "create" (*bārā*)[115] suggests that this activity is parallel to Isaiah's later elaborations on God's special act of re-creating the new heaven and the new earth (65:17; 66:22) at some point in the eschatological era. One of the primary new factors in that kingdom will be the glorious presence of God himself. The cloud by day and the fire by night symbolize his presence in Zion. Isaiah draws these images from the Exodus tradition, where God's presence was known through the cloud and fire that led the Israelites out of Egypt and eventually dwelt in the tabernacle and temple (Exod 13:21–22; 14:19,24; 40:34; Deut 1:33; 31:15; 1 Kgs 8:10–11). The divine presence demonstrates God's acceptance and nearness to his holy people. The surprising difference is that God's presence will not be limited to a temple building; it will be like a canopy over the whole of Zion (cf. 60:1–2; 62:2; Ezek 39:25–29), because all of Zion and its people will be holy. The canopy (4:5 *sukkâ*) is sometimes associated with weddings in Hebrew culture (Ps 19:6; Joel 2:16), but its function here seems to point to the divine protection of all the holy people in Zion. God's glory is

---

[111] One should not connect these ideas to Nehemiah's transfer of people to Jerusalem and his registry of names (Neh 11–12) as in Blenkinsopp, *Isaiah 1–39*, 204. S. M. Paul, "Heavenly Tablets and the Book of Life," *JANES* 5 (1973): 345–53, discusses how this theme was dealt with in ancient Near Eastern, OT, and later Jewish and Christian writings.

[112] אִם often means "if," but in this context "when, since" is more appropriate.

[113] צֹאָה describes the most putrid filth imaginable and can be used for vomit or the content of the bowels. God's perspective on the "beauty, glory" of the women in 3:16–4:1 perceived their best as worse than filthy rags.

[114] Gray, *Isaiah 1–27*, 80; Clements, *Isaiah 1–39*, 54. Oswalt, *Isaiah 1–39*, 148, refers to this as "the process of burning and judgment," taking "spirit" as an abstract concept.

[115] בָּרָא, "create," is a divine activity of making something new, either by transforming something that already exists (Ps 51:10) or by bringing into existence something new (Gen 1:26).

imaginatively pictured as a shelter or refuge from the harshness of the weather. These symbols represent any danger that might threaten the people of God. God is there to care for and to protect his people.

THEOLOGICAL IMPLICATIONS. These promises were made to the Hebrew people of Jerusalem to help them choose between exalting themselves or exalting God. God will cleanse people of their sins, establish the new heavens and the new earth (cf. Rev 21), and rule his holy kingdom as he dwells among his people. This will be a glorious day when the messianic Branch will be exalted, and the productivity of the earth will be transformed. What is certain is what God will do. What is uncertain is what the people will do. Will they choose to accept God's purification so that they can be holy and dwell in God's presence, or will they arrogantly continue in their sinful ways?

The most significant questions to ask about 4:2–6 are not centered on whether this prophecy will be fulfilled in the millennial age or if one should take an amillennial interpretation. The question of when, where, or exactly how these promises will be fulfilled (in the eschatological future or during the church age) is not directly addressed in this passage. The major dilemma is, Who believes that God hates sinful human pride and who believes that only those who are holy will enjoy God's future kingdom with him? None of these other minor theological issues will matter to those who exalt themselves in rebellion against God, for they will be destroyed in fire. None of these side issues will really matter that much for those who are holy either, for they will be enjoying a wonderful life in the presence of the glory of God. The primary lesson people must remember is that those who exalt and glorify God in their present life will have many opportunities to exalt him in the future.

God is at the center of all eschatological promises. God will wash away sin and make it possible for people to be holy. God is the one who writes people's names in his book (4:3–4). God will create a new world order over Mt. Zion, and his glorious presence there will bring protection for his people. He will make the messianic Branch beautiful and he will increase the productivity of the earth. God is the one people can trust and he is the one to exalt. The future of this world is completely dependent on God.

Every listener who hears the words of the prophet must decide where they would like to spend eternity. One thing is abundantly clear: there will be no place in God's kingdom for proud men and women who attempt to exalt themselves.

2. Destruction of Judah (5:1–30)

STRUCTURE. The announcement of a song introduces a new literary section in 5:1. The beginning of the next new section is demarcated by the announcement of the death of Uzziah in 6:1 and the introduction of a biographical narrative account about Isaiah's new call to serve God. In spite of these fairly clear markers that limit this section to 5:1–30, commentators have struggled to discover the extent, order, and setting of the woe oracles within 5:8–30.

The appearance of common phrases in the woe oracles in 5:8–23 and 10:1–14 and the presence of the refrain that God's "hand is still stretched out" in 5:25–30 and 9:8–10:4 have caused some commentators to search for a literary connection between these two passages.[116] Because of these similarities between the two sections the hypothesis developed that they belonged to one literary document that got divided when an editor put Isaiah's messages into writing. This approach suggests that the narrative of Isaiah's personal memoirs in 6:1–9:7 were inserted in the middle of this material by an editor in the days of Josiah, thus causing a dislocation of the second half (9:8–10:14) of what was once a cohesive unit.[117] This reconstruction can be diagramed as:

> Woe Oracles 5:8–23
> Outstretched Hand 5:24–30
>   (Intrusive Isaiah Memoirs 6:1–9:7)
> Outstretched Hand 9:8–21
> Woe Oracles 10:1–14

This outline of the material looks balanced (in a chiastic structure) and appears to flow together quite naturally, if the intrusive Isaiah memoirs are removed. But the actual process scholars hypothesize to arrive at this explanation is overly complicated and filled with unsubstantiated conclusions concerning how and when verses were added, modified, and changed in order (Vermeylen has three stages of redaction: in the time of Josiah, the exile, and after the exile).[118] These explanations are not based on highly convincing evidence so some scholars have raised questions about the validity of this broad hypothetical reconstruction of the growth of these texts.

C. E. L'Heureux recognizes that there are literary similarities between chaps. 5 and 9–10, but he found no reason why someone could not intentionally arrange these chapters in their present order from the start (instead of claiming that someone inserted Isaiah's Memoirs in the middle at some date hundreds of years later).[119] W. P. Brown went further by rejecting the prevailing assumption that the "outstretched hand" passages in 5:25–30 and 9:8–21 were parts

---

[116] Sweeney, *Isaiah 1–39*, 114–131, provides a full discussion of the key issues of this theory and provides bibliographical references that investigate various interpretations on these issues.

[117] Clements, *Isaiah 1–39*, 55–56, gives a brief reconstruction of this hypothetical process, while C. E. L'Heureux, "The Redactional History of Isaiah 5. 1–10. 4," in *In the Shelter of Elyon: Essays on Ancient Palestinian Life and Literature in Honor of G. W. Alstrom*, eds W. B. Barrich and S. J. Spenser (Sheffield: JSOT, 1984), 99–119, presents an analysis of J. Vermeylen *Du prophéte Isaïe à l'apocalyptique: Isaïe I–XXXV, miroir d'un demi-millénaire d'expérience religieuse en Israël*, I (Paris:Gabalda, 1977), 160–249, and then critiques it with his own proposals.

[118] J. Vermeylen, "L'unité du livre d'Isaïe," in *The Book of Isaiah: Le Livre D'Isaïe*, 11–53.

[119] C. E. L'Heureux, "The Redactional History of Isaiah 5. 1–10. 4," 115–116, also allows for a redactor in the time of Josiah as another possibility. This is similar to G. T. Shepherd, "The Anti-Assyrian Redaction and the Canonical Context of Isaiah 1–39," *JBL* 104 (1985): 193–216, who

of one original unit,[120] thus he partially removed the need for the complex reconstructions of chaps. 5–10. His analysis of 5:25 demonstrates that it was not written following the pattern of the refrains in 9:8–10:4 but was intimately tied to its own surrounding context in chap. 5. R. H. O'Connell's asymmetrical concentric chiasmic arrangement of 4:2–11:16 works off of different criteria and methodological procedures (using rhetorical criticism) to demonstrate a unique way of understanding the unified coherent structure of the final form of this long section.[121] His approach connected the woe and outstretched hand passages but did not focus on issues of authorship or redaction (though he doubts chaps. 5 and 9–10 were ever one contiguous entity).

It would take an enormous amount of space and detailed information to describe and fully critique each of these contributions point by point.[122] The exegetical comments and structural organization in each of the following chapters will draw from observations in these studies by finding some similar connections between the parts of chaps. 5–10, but will reject other observations. The analysis in this commentary is based on the evidence that chap. 6 is a central pivotal chapter from an historical (the change from the time of Uzziah to Ahaz), literary (it connects both with what precedes and what follows), and ministry calling (the new calling in 6:1–13 influences Isaiah's later message). Thus chap. 6 (and what follows) was not part of a later insertion that divided the woe oracles in 5:8–23 and 10:1–14, but was central to understanding the changes in Isaiah's prophetic messages and the structure of the

---

divides the text slightly differently and sees these changes as part of an anti-Assyrian campaign during the time of Josiah.

[120] The approach of W. P. Brown, "The So-Called Refrain in Isaiah 5:25–30 and 9:7–10:4," *CBQ* 52 (1990): 432–43, demonstrates that the common phrases were used in different ways in the two passages, thus they were not part of one continuous document.

[121] O'Connell, *Concentricity and Continuity*, 81–107, especially 95. He depends heavily on the covenant lawsuit genre throughout the book. This rhetorical analysis looks for repeated pattern of words and phrases to identify "tiers" (larger blocks) in a concentric chiastic order.

[122] For example: (a) The "outstretched hand" theme is restated twice in one verse in 5:25 but is limited to only one verse, so it does not function as a repeated refrain as in 9:7–12; 9:13–17; 10:1–4 where it is mentioned only once in each section. (b) The "woe oracle" in 10:4–11 (against Assyria) is not comparable to the woes in 5:18, 20, 21, or 22, plus chap. 5 relates to individual woes rather than an international woe oracle as in 10:5. Thus 10:5 would never fit into the series of woes in chap. 5. (c) This whole approach does not integrate chap. 11 into its structure, but makes it a later addition. (d) This theory inappropriately groups 5:1–30, which comes from the time of Uzziah, with texts from the time of the Syro-Ephraimite War (chaps. 7–10), thus its historical context within chaps. 2–5 is ignored. And (e) chap. 5 and 9:8–21 are seen as a unit because they both refer to Israel, yet 5:3 and 14 specifically mention Jerusalem. Childs, *Isaiah*, 42–44, concludes that this approach is untenable because (a) it rests on the theory of an accidental interpolation and dislocation of verses; (b) newer theories that give an explanation for some changes (the Assur Redaction at the time of Josiah) have difficulty tracing the history of how this redactional reinterpretation happened; (c) these readings replace the present witness to Isaiah's thoughts with a "critically reconstructed redactional scheme that runs roughshod over the canonical shape of the biblical text itself"; and (d) reliance on formal stylistic linguistic markers and sociological theories at the expense of the theology of the book distract from the intention of the book, rather than clarify it.

whole unit. No direct literary connection (being part of the same document) is required between sermons that happen to use similar phrases (chaps. 5 and 9–10) if they were spoken years apart under different historical and theological conditions. An author may choose to repeat phrases in unrelated sermons to emphasize a point or to remind the reader of what was said in the earlier passage.[123] This rhetorical structuring by repeatedly using similar terms and phrases influenced the design of chaps. 2–12 (not just 5–10), but the repetition of and the location of the woe and outstretched hand oracles do not seem to be the primary keys (though they are important repetitive markers) to discovering the overall structure of this literary unit. The structural markers suggest the following organization:

> God will be Exalted and the Proud will be Humbled (2:1–4:6)
>> An Enemy will Destroy Judah (5:1–30)
>>> A Holy King's Calling to a Calloused Audience (6:1–13)
>> Assyria will Destroy Judah (7:1–8:18)
> A Righteous King will Rule and the Proud will be Humbled (8:19–11:16)

This approach puts chap. 6 in a pivotal position, with the general prediction of Judah's destruction by an unknown enemy coming before it (chap. 5) and the specific description of Assyrian destruction (chaps. 7–8) after Ahaz's unbelief and collaboration with the Assyrians. The absence of the regular pattern of woe and "therefore" clauses in 10:1–14 (following the pattern of 5:8–25), and the absence of a series of "outstretched hand" oracles in 5:25–30 (comparable to 9:8–10:4) suggests that these two messages are not part of one consistent document. It is also evident that the specific historical circumstances of the Syro-Ephraimite War did not exist when chap. 5 was written in the time of Uzziah, but later in chaps. 7; 8; and 9 this war between Syria, Israel and Judah became part of a new justification for condemning Israel. The correlation of Israel's pride in 9:8–10:4 with Assyria's pride in 10:5–19 draws attention to a parallel structure of God's condemnation of pride in 2:6–4:1. The overall unit also begins and ends with parallel passages that exalt God/the Messiah's rule (2:1–5; 4:2–6 and 9:1–7; 11:1–16) and predict the humbling of the proud. Thus the woe and outstretched hand oracles in 9:8–10:4 should be related to 2:6–4:1, not to 5:8–30.

God's Future Kingdom Produces Trust	2:1–5
The Exaltation of God, not the Proud	2:6–22
The Removal of Judah's Male Leaders	3:1–15
The Removal of Judah's Proud Women	3:16–4:1
God's Glorious Holy Kingdom	4:2–6

---

[123] Many teachers or preachers deal with the same themes (Christmas, Easter, New Year, funerals) on repeated occasions. Their words often are related to things said years earlier, but the new setting in a different church will give a unique slant to what is said. So the prophet could repeat similar themes years later without the later message having any direct literary connection with what was said at an earlier time.

The Reign of a Righteous King	8:19–9:7
The Judgment of Proud and Sinful Israel	9:8–10:4
The Judgment of Proud Assyria	10:5–34
The Reign of the Righteous King	11:1–16

These outlines show that the content as well as genre must be taken into consideration and that one genre (i.e. the woe oracle) can function in two different ways within the structure of a longer unit.

Watts and Blenkinsopp[124] view the two oracles in chap. 5 as oracles addressed against the Northern nation of Israel (similar to 9:8–10:4) because (a) both use a woe oracle and the outstretched hand ideas; (b) 9:8 is clearly against the Northern nation of Israel; (c) 5:8–30 has many contacts with phrases in the northern prophet Amos; and (d) the opening up of Sheol may refer to the opening up of the earth at the time of the earthquake in Israel (Amos 1:1).[125] Nevertheless, Childs and Wildberger are certainly correct in concluding that chap. 5 was addressed to Judah (cf. 5:3,7, about problems in both nations). Isaiah could speak to the people of Judah about God's condemnation of foreign nations, as in chaps. 13–23, without going to those locations and addressing those foreign nations directly. Thus Isaiah's knowledge of Amos and the earthquake does not determine where he preached his messages or who his audience was. Although the prophet could critique the sins of Israel (9:8–10), there is no evidence that he ever actually preached in the northern nation of Israel. The woes in 5:8–23 concern the destruction of Judah and closely relate to Isaiah's later messages about the destruction of Judah in chaps. 7–8. The "outstretched hand" oracles in 9:8–10:4 are securely tied to the later historical context of the Syro-Ephraimite War, which is not the same setting as 5:1–30. The prophet's condemnation of pride and social sins in 9:8–10:15 creates a literary parallel with the earlier section that condemns pride and social sins in 2:1–4:6.

The structure of the material in chap. 5 is divided into three paragraphs:

The vineyard song of love	5:1–7
Woe oracles against Judah	5:8–25
The military defeat of Judah	5:26–30

The general statement about the future military defeat of Judah by an unknown enemy in 5:26–30 contrasts with the specific statements found later in chaps. 7–8 where Assyria is known as the aggressor who will defeat Israel and Judah. Several literary connections between the extended parable in 5:1–7 and the

---

[124] Watts, *Isaiah 1–33*, 56, 60, and Blenkinsopp, *Isaiah 1–39*, 218.

[125] The common phrases in Isaiah and Amos include (a) quaking of the land in 5:25 and Amos 1:1; 8:8; (b) dead bodies in 5:25 and Amos 6:11; 8:3; (c) God will not return his anger in 5:25 and Amos 1:3,6,9,11,13; (d) drunkenness in 5:11,22 and Amos 6:6; and (e) oppression of the poor in 5:8,23 and Amos 2:6–8; 4:1; 5:10–12.

woes in 5:8–24 suggest that this material fits together in its present context as a larger unit.[126]

HISTORICAL SETTING.   Isaiah 5 describes a period when God prospered his vineyard, but the vineyard produced the worthless fruit of bloodshed and oppression (5:2,4,7). The prosperity of the wealthy is pictured in their many homes (5:8), their luxurious banquets (5:11–12), and their oppression through bribery (5:23). The coming military conflict (5:26–30) suggests that the prophet spoke a few years before a major military battle. These circumstances point to a time during the prosperous years of Uzziah and Jeroboam II, some years before the Syro-Ephraimite War in 734–732 BC. The audience Isaiah confronted in these oracles is primarily the wealthy and powerful upper class in Judah. These "rulers of Jerusalem"[127] who are confronted in 5:3,8–24 are parallel to the audience addressed in chap. 3.

(1) A Vineyard Song of Love and Rejection (5:1–7)

> [1] I will sing for the one I love
>   a song about his vineyard:
> My loved one had a vineyard
>   on a fertile hillside.
> [2] He dug it up and cleared it of stones
>   and planted it with the choicest vines.
> He built a watchtower in it
>   and cut out a winepress as well.
> Then he looked for a crop of good grapes,
>   but it yielded only bad fruit.
>
> [3] "Now you dwellers in Jerusalem
> and men of Judah,
>   judge between me and my vineyard.
> [4] What more could have been done for my vineyard
>   than I have done for it?
> When I looked for good grapes,
>   why did it yield only bad?
> [5] Now I will tell you
>   what I am going to do to my vineyard:
> I will take away its hedge,
>   and it will be destroyed;
> I will break down its wall,
>   and it will be trampled.
> [6] I will make it a wasteland,

---

[126] See the list of these connections in the introductory material to 5:8–25 below.

[127] יוֹשֵׁב, "the one who sits, is enthroned" (5:3), implying a ruler, rather than simply "the one who dwells," which points to the general "inhabitants" of Jerusalem. M. L. Chaney, "Whose Sour Grapes? The Addresses of Isaiah 5:1–7 in the Light of Political Economy," *Semeia* 87 (1999): 105–22, argues this interpretation most forcefully. He claims these rulers were ruining the nation by their economic policies, consistent with the accusations in 3:12–15 and 5:8–10.

neither pruned nor cultivated,
and briers and thorns will grow there.
I will command the clouds
not to rain on it."

⁷ The vineyard of the LORD Almighty
is the house of Israel,
and the men of Judah
are the garden of his delight.
And he looked for justice, but saw bloodshed;
for righteousness, but heard cries of distress.

GENRE.   The song is filled with agricultural images about a vineyard, but commentators have differed concerning whether this is an allegory or a parable, and whether this is a love song, a judicial song, or a polemic against a fertility cult.[128] Since all the images of the vineyard in the song do not have parallel allegorical interpretations, the paragraph should be treated as an extended parable, not an allegory.[129] The function of this song reminds the reader of the function of Nathan's parable about the poor man who had only one lamb and the rich man who had many (2 Sam 12:1–10). Both stories aim to trap the unsuspecting listeners who do not expect the final shocking application of the story (5:7; 2 Sam 12:7). The song presents evidence against the vineyard and requests a judgment, but this does not appear to be any kind of lawsuit at court.[130]

STRUCTURE.   The design of the paragraph is organized with:

An introduction	5:1a
The care of the vineyard	5:1b–2
The request for a decision	5:3–4 ("now")[131]
The decision to destroy the vineyard	5:5–6 ("now")
The identification of the vineyard	5:7 (*kî*, "truly")

---

[128] J. T. Willis, "The Genre of Isaiah 5:1–7," *JBL* 96 (1977): 337–62, reviews 12 different options, including, for example: W. C. Graham, "Notes on the Interpretation of Isaiah 5:1–12," *AJSL* 45 (1928/29): 167–69, who offers a Baal fertility interpretation, and G. Yee, "A Form-Critical Study of Isaiah 5:1–7 as a Song and a Judicial Parable," *CBQ* 43 (1981): 30–40, which draws on comparisons with the lawsuit genre of Deut 32.

[129] Sweeney, *Isaiah 1–39*, 126, rejects the parable approach because he believes a parable must convey a moral or maxim, and this story does not have one. It seems like there is a clear moral to this story even if it is not stated succinctly at the end of the parable. But having or not having a moral does not make something a parable. It is also not necessary to conclude that Isaiah borrowed this didactic story from the Wisdom School, since anyone could make up or tell parables. Cf. J. W. Whedbee, *Isaiah and Wisdom* (Nashville: Abingdon, 1971), 43–51,who sees a strong wisdom connection.

[130] Watts, *Isaiah 1–33*, 54, claims, "The setting is that of a court of justice dealing with family matters," but in this case the punishment (5:5–6) has already taken place; it was not decided in this parable by a judge.

[131] וְעַתָּה, "and now," marks the beginning of new parts of the paragraphs in 5:3,5.

This is not an oracle against the northern kingdom of Israel, but as vv. 3 and 7 indicate, Isaiah addresses the rulers of Judah and Jerusalem about the failure of the leaders to care for his people.[132]

5:1a   The people mentioned in this extended parable are initially and purposely disguised so that the audience does not recognize the singer's ploy until the end of the song. The "me" who sings this song must be the prophet,[133] but the identity of the "beloved" person who owns the vineyard is kept secret. The use of "for my beloved" plus "my beloved"[134] in v. 1 communicates the expectation of a love song similar to the Song of Solomon (not just a song about a friend).[135] Since there is no verb in the Hebrew text for " I love," to represent the NIV "I will sing for the one I love," this phrase should be simply translated, "sing for my beloved." The second phrase in the NIV, "a song about his vineyard" hides the difficult "a song of my beloved concerning his vineyard." Was this a song written by the beloved one that the prophet is quoting, or is this a song to his beloved? 5:1b–2 appears to be about the beloved, but the first person singular verbs in 5:3–6 indicate that the beloved is now speaking about his vineyard. One way of looking at this issue is to suggest that the original song is only in 5:1b–2; in 5:3–6 someone interrupts the song with some questions.

5:1b–2   The existence of "vineyard" imagery in the context of a lover/ bride in Song of Solomon (2:15; 4:16; 8:11) might have initially encouraged the listeners to have a male-female interpretation of the symbolism, though similar terminology in 3:14 makes one aware that Isaiah could use the word "vineyard" as a symbol of God's people. Although the modern reader knows how the parable ends and understands that a female interpretation of the vineyard is wrong, one needs to realize that Isaiah was probably trying to hide the full import of his words from his listeners at this point. He wanted them to agree with his anger at the vineyard (the symbol for his lover) before they perceived the full application of his final condemnation in 5:7. If Isaiah wanted to surprise his audience at the end of the song, there is good reason to believe he would purposely conceal the exact identity of the vineyard at the beginning of the song,

The lover's devotion to the vineyard is highlighted in 5:2. He plowed the ground, removed stones[136] (used to make the tower and walls of 5:5), planted

---

[132] Watts, *Isaiah 1–33*, 56, believes Isaiah is addressing people in Judah about the immanent demise of the northern kingdom.

[133] אָשִׁירָה, "let me sing," is a cohortative, which expresses a wish or requests permission. See GKC § 108c.

[134] "My beloved" is found twice in 5:1, "to my beloved" (לִידִידִי) and "my beloved" (דּוֹדִי).

[135] J. A. Emerton, "The Translation of Isaiah 5. 1," *The Scriptures and the Scroll: Studies in Honor of A. S. van der Woude on the Occasion of his 65th Birthday* (ed. F. G. Martinez, A Hilhorst, C. J. Labushchagne; Leiden: Brill, 1992), 18–30, recognizes that a sexual connotation in the two words for "beloved" in texts like Jer 11:15; Ps 45:1; and the Song of Solomon, but prefers the translation "friend." Thus he translates the text with "a song about a friend," viewing this as an objective genitive.

[136] The *pi'el* of סָקַל refers to the removal of stones (privative usage; GKC § 52h) rather than

the best variety of plants available, and prepared for the harvest by building a wine press. The tower gave him a place to live as he protected the vineyard from predators during the harvest season. At the end of the verse, the song turns into a complaint because, after a long time of "hopeful waiting"[137] for the vines to mature, he found only sour rotten fruit.

5:3–4 Suddenly (*wĕʿattâ*, "and now"), the one who owns the vineyard interrupts the song with questions that invite the listeners in Jerusalem to decide who was at fault. These "rulers/inhabitants of Jerusalem," whose action frequently determined the future of the nation, were now asked to declare their judgment. With this invitation the author begins to set the trap so that the audience will end up condemning themselves, for they were the ones ruining the fruit of the nation. He asks the audience two questions: (a) If the owner of the vineyard was responsible and worked hard, did he not have every reason to expect good grapes instead of the sour rotten ones? (b) What has the owner not done,[138] that should have been done? Who was at fault? Although the response of the listeners is not recorded, it is obvious that these rulers of Jerusalem would have agreed that the vineyard owner was not at fault for he worked very hard in the vineyard.

5:5–6 So what should happen? Suddenly (*wĕʿattâ*, "and now") the owner of the vineyard resolves[139] to take a course of action, but first he presents his plan of action to his audience for the purpose of gaining interaction and approval. The owner decides not merely to abandon the vineyard for a better plot of land, he attacks it[140] by removing what protected it from animals who might walk through it (no thorn hedges or stone walls will remain), by no longer cultivating or caring for the plants (no hoeing or pruning), and by cursing the field to prevent rain from falling on it (cf. Lev 26:19; Deut 28:23–24; Amos 4:7–8).[141] Although this might appear to be a severe over reaction by the disappointed lover, it was totally appropriate, since there was no hope of ever getting anything of any value to grow in this vineyard.

"stoning" by throwing stones (BDB, 709), just like "dusting" refers to the removal of dust, not throwing dust.

[137] וַיְקַו, "and he waited," from the root קָוָה carries the idea of "hopeful waiting." For the unusual form see GKC § 75bb. This verb is used later in 5:4 "I looked" and in 5:7 "he looked for."

[138] The NIV has "than I have done for it" in 5:4, but the text literally says, "that I have not done for it," לֹא עָשִׂיתִי בּוֹ.

[139] In אוֹדִיעָה, "I will tell," the cohortative expresses the speaker's strong resolve or fixed determination to a new course of action. See GKC § 108b or IBHS § 34. 5. 1 for this use of the cohortative form.

[140] הָסֵר, "I will take away," and פָּרֹץ, "I will break down," in the NIV (5:5) are actually Hb. infinitive absolutes that are substitutes for a finite verb (GKC § 113y). GKC § 113ee suggests that the infinitive absolute can replace a finite imperfect verb to give an emphatic promise, thus " I will take away" seems appropriate. Infinitive absolutes also function as imperatives (GKC § 113bb) so one could easily see this as a command to destroy the vineyard. See also J. Huesman, "Finite Uses of the Infinitive Absolute," *Bib* 37 (1956): 271–95, for additional examples.

[141] The NIV has "not to rain on it" in the last line of 5:6. The use of מִן, "from," before the infinitive construct (מֵהַמְטִיר) conveys the idea of "restraining from, refusing, withholding," so the text is lit. "withholding rain from raining upon it." See GKC § 119x.

5:7 The decisive conclusion is introduced with *kî*, "surely/truly" (omitted in NIV, translated "for" in NASB), to emphasize the prophet's confidence. The vineyard is finally identified as a symbol of Israel and Judah, referring to all the covenant people. God, the beloved one, "expected, hoped" (as he "waited in hope" in 5:2) the life of his wonderful vines would produce the fruit of justice and righteousness, but in reality his chosen people (specifically the wealthy oppressive leaders) produced only bloodshed and a distressing cry from the weak.[142] The prophet's application was shocking and devastatingly clear. God's grace would end and his curse would fall on these oppressive leaders because their lives did not demonstrate the basic godly characteristics of justice and righteousness.

These are some of the same criteria God has used down through the centuries and still uses today to evaluate the behavior of people in positions of leadership—especially religious people in positions of authority. Jesus agreed with this concept when he said, "by their fruit you will recognize them" (Matt 7:16), and "every tree that does not bear good fruit is cut down and thrown into the fire" (Matt 7:19). The evidence is pretty clear: Jesus is just as hard on the oppressive leaders who treat people unjustly as Isaiah was.

THEOLOGICAL IMPLICATIONS. Songs sometimes contain a great deal of theology packed into a few lyrical phrases. This song reminded the listener that God was the lover who had poured out his love for his special vineyard. Each person in his vineyard was specially created, planted, and continually cared for by God's grace. People deserved no credit for their election or their privileged status; it happened totally by grace. Once God chooses an individual or a people, he tenderly cares for and protects his own. As this happens he patiently waits for his people to produce good fruit in their lives. In his sovereign oversight of his people God observes what happens in society and he knows what kind of fruit his chosen vines produce. He views all fruit as either rotten or good according to his standards (not ours—Matt 7:15–23). God's protection and care may be withdrawn from those who are unrighteous or who fail to produce godly fruit (cf. John 15:1–7). God is especially severe on privileged people who mistreat others through injustice.

The specific contextually limited questions of the prophets Nathan and Isaiah direct an application primarily to political and religious leaders who have the ability to either abuse or support those who are vulnerable. The basic theological principle could be more broadly extended to evaluate the fruit produced by each person, all leaders, every church, or any nation. This extended applicability is evident when Jesus uses a somewhat similar parable of the vineyard in Mark 12:1–9 to condemn those who were supposed to take care of God's vineyard.[143] The prophet's words ask the piercing questions: Will God joyfully

---

[142] These contrasts are word plays using similar sounds. For example, *mišpāṭ*, "justice," sounds like *miśpāḥ*, "bloodshed," and *ṣĕdāqâ*, "righteousness," sounds like *ṣĕʾāqâ*, "cry out."

[143] C. A. Evans, "How Septuagintal is Isa 5:1–7 in Mark 12:1–9?" *NT* 45 (2003): 105–110,

accept your fruit or destroy the vine that produces such rotten fruit? Jesus' parable asks the question: How do people who are workers in God's vineyard treat God's vineyard and his Son? People who are true to God produce good fruit, walk in the ways of justice, and honor God's Son.

(2) Reason for God's Destruction of Judah (5:8–25)

8 Woe to you who add house to house
  and join field to field
till no space is left
  and you live alone in the land.

9 The Lord Almighty has declared in my hearing:

"Surely the great houses will become desolate,
  the fine mansions left without occupants.
10 A ten-acre vineyard will produce only a bath of wine,
  a homer of seed only an ephah of grain."

11 Woe to those who rise early in the morning
  to run after their drinks,
who stay up late at night
  till they are inflamed with wine.
12 They have harps and lyres at their banquets,
  tambourines and flutes and wine,
but they have no regard for the deeds of the Lord,
  no respect for the work of his hands.
13 Therefore my people will go into exile
  for lack of understanding;
their men of rank will die of hunger
  and their masses will be parched with thirst.
14 Therefore the grave enlarges its appetite
  and opens its mouth without limit;
into it will descend their nobles and masses
  with all their brawlers and revelers.
15 So man will be brought low
  and mankind humbled,
  the eyes of the arrogant humbled.
16 But the Lord Almighty will be exalted by his justice,
  and the holy God will show himself holy by his righteousness.
17 Then sheep will graze as in their own pasture;
  lambs will feed among the ruins of the rich.

18 Woe to those who draw sin along with cords of deceit,
  and wickedness as with cart ropes,
19 to those who say, "Let God hurry,

---

found a connection between these two passages in that both refer to what the owner planted, hewed out, and built, though Jesus focuses on the violent tenants who killed the owner's servants and son, which is not specifically addressed in Isaiah's parable.

> let him hasten his work
> so we may see it.
> Let it approach,
> let the plan of the Holy One of Israel come,
> so we may know it."

[20] Woe to those who call evil good
and good evil,
who put darkness for light
and light for darkness,
who put bitter for sweet
and sweet for bitter.

[21] Woe to those who are wise in their own eyes
and clever in their own sight.

[22] Woe to those who are heroes at drinking wine
and champions at mixing drinks,
[23] who acquit the guilty for a bribe,
but deny justice to the innocent.
[24] Therefore, as tongues of fire lick up straw
and as dry grass sinks down in the flames,
so their roots will decay
and their flowers blow away like dust;
for they have rejected the law of the LORD Almighty
and spurned the word of the Holy One of Israel.
[25] Therefore the LORD's anger burns against his people;
his hand is raised and he strikes them down.
The mountains shake,
and the dead bodies are like refuse in the streets.

Yet for all this, his anger is not turned away,
his hand is still upraised.

The woe oracles in this paragraph give a detailed justification of God's accusation against his people, who produced the sour rotten grapes of bloodshed and cries of distress (5:7). Undoubtedly, some who heard Isaiah's stinging conclusion to the song of the vineyard would have questioned his statements about injustice in Judah. In these lamenting woe oracles the prophet expressed his sorrow as he identified with the cries of distress from the oppressed people in God's vineyard (5:7). This new paragraph repeats words and themes from 5:1–7: (a) the vineyard in 5:1,3,4, and 7 is brought up again in 5:10 (wine is also mentioned in 5:11 and 22); (b) social injustice is discussed in 5:7 and 5:23, plus divine justice in 5:17; (c) agricultural ruin appears in 5:5–6 and in 5:9–10,17; and (d) the verbal roots "know" (*yādaʿ*) and "do" (*ʿāśâ*) appear in 5:2 ("do" twice), 5:4 ("do" three time), 5:5 ("know" and "do"), 5:10 ("do" twice), 5:12 ("do"), 5:13 ("know"), and 5:19 ("do" and "know").[144] These linguistic

---

[144] See C. E. L'Heureux, "The Redactional History of Isaiah 5. 1–10. 4," 117, for a few other less obvious connections.

connections indicate that these two paragraphs comprise one united sermon,[145] probably with a common audience who recognized the literary connections.

STRUCTURE. Using a system of counting syllables, stresses, and words, A. H. Bartelt found two well-balanced panels (8–17 and 18–25) with three balanced stanzas each (a woe in 8–12,18–23, "therefore" clauses in 13–14,24, and a refrain in 15–17,25).[146] This structural analysis is weakened by the presence of two "therefore" clauses in both 13–14 and in 24–25, and the absence of a refrain after v. 25; therefore, his structural proposal is inadequate. B. W. Anderson presents a more helpful outline of the irregular pattern of "woe" and "therefore" classes in an orderly structure around the central exaltation of God.[147]

5:8–12 Two woe oracles
   5:13–14 Two "therefore" sayings
      5:15–16(17) Coda: Yahweh's Exaltation in Righteousness
   5:18–23 Four woe oracles
5:24–25 Two "therefore" sayings

The often-questioned double "therefore" clauses are left intact by this structural scheme, and the final paragraph following the woes begins after 5:25 not before. This approach to the arrangement of these woes demonstrates that the exaltation of God and the humbling of man in 5:15–16 are central to understanding the purpose of these woes. Consequently, 5:15–16 should not be viewed as peripheral insignificant additions by a late exilic redactor.[148] But the content of 5:15–16 is somewhat unusual in this context because it quotes theological concerns also mentioned in chaps. 2 and 6. Thus it appears that 5:15–16 was likely added in the middle of this list of woes at the time when Isaiah composed these written oracles. The evidence for this conclusion is (a) 5:15–16 seems to interrupt the natural flow of punishment from 5:14 to 17; (b) the wording of 5:15–16a is derived from the tradition in 2:9,12,17 that is not found elsewhere in these woes; (c) the emphasis on God showing his holiness implies Isaiah has already seen the holiness of God in chap. 6 (which happened

---

[145] J. Goldingay, *Isaiah*, 53, views the six woes and two "therefore" clauses as interpreting what the prophet meant in the parable of the bad grapes in 5:1–7.

[146] A. H. Bartelt, "Isaiah 5 and 9: In- and Interdependence?" *Fortunate the Eyes that See: Essays in Honor of D. N. Freedman*, ed. A. B. Beck, A. H. Bartelt, P. A. Raabe, C. A. Franke (Grand Rapids: Eerdmans, 1995), 157–163.

[147] B. W. Anderson, " 'God with Us'– In Judgment and in Mercy: The Editorial Structure of Isaiah 5–10 (11)," in *Canon, Theology, and Old Testament Interpretation: Essays in Honor of B. S. Childs*, ed. G. Tucker, D. Petersen, R. Wilson (Philadelphia: Fortress, 1988), 230–45. Cf. R. B. Chisholm, "Structure, Style, and the Prophetic Message: An Analysis of Isaiah 5:8–30," *BSac* 143 (1986): 46–60, for a different chiastic structure to 5:8–30 that is based on the alternating accusations and announcements of punishment into three segments (5:8–10; 5:11–17; 5:18–30).

[148] Clements, *Isaiah 1–39*, 61, explains 5:14–17 as later redactional additions after the fall of Jerusalem in 587 BC, while Wildberger, *Isaiah 1–12*, 194–95, 205, considers 5:15–16 as later additions.

some years later when Uzziah died); (d) 5:15–16 has general doxological state-ments[149] about the humbling of mankind and God's holiness, while the sur-rounding verses pinpoint specific sins of people; and maybe most important, (e) the perfect verb in 5:13–14,17 refers to future punishments, while the *vav* with imperfect verbs in 5:15–16 probably refer to past events[150] (NIV hides this problem by translating the verbs in 5:15–16 as futures). No one knows the thought process of Isaiah that caused him to insert these clauses in the middle of these woes at the written stage, but the clauses (a) tend to unify 5:8–30 into the overall theological emphasis of chaps. 2–6; (b) verify to the reader from a later perspective that the punishments mentioned in this passage did happen; and (c) explain from a broader perspective what God accomplished through these judgments (God exalted himself and humbled mankind).

A similar late editorial addition is found in 5:25a-b by M. Korpel,[151] be-cause these phrases also place the punishment in the past (rather than the fu-ture). This conclusion seems unnecessary in 5:25 because in this verse Isaiah described the earthquake during the lifetime of Uzziah as a past event when God began to punish his people. This event was mentioned in order to warn the listeners that God was going to strike again. The social and religious situa-tion of the second group of woe oracles in 5:18–25 seems to fit the prosperous period of Uzziah before the Syro-Ephraimite War in 734–732 BC but after the earthquake (Amos 1:1; ca. 765–760 BC).

GENRE. The woe oracle[152] derives from the social context of lament-ing the death of someone at a funeral (1 Kgs 13:30; Jer 22:18), or mourning the approaching death of someone (Ps 6; Jer 11:18–23). Weeping, shaving the hair, wearing sackcloth, and the presence of some professional mourners could accompany a woeful lament.[153] The pervasive reality of death in this passage is confirmed by references to the mansions that have no occupants (5:9), the descent of nobles into the grave (5:14), the decaying roots (5:24), and the dead bodies (5:25). This genre implies that Isaiah wept as he com-municated the words in this chapter. Why? Isaiah lamented because he loved the people of Judah and did not want to see this beloved nation destroyed. He also knew that a lament could sometimes attract more attention and serve as a more effective tool of communicating God's Word than an uncompromising

---

[149] B. W. Anderson, "God with Us," 235, refers to these as doxologies. Amos also uses doxolo-gies in the middle of oracles in 5:8–9 and 9:5–6.

[150] For example, אָדָם וַיִּשְׁח, "mankind was humbled," at the beginning of 15 contrast with the prophetic perfect verbs in v. 14 that refer to the nation's future judgment.

[151] M. C. A. Korpel, "Structural Analysis as a Tool for Redation Criticism: The Example of Isaiah 5 and 10:1–6," *JSOT* 69 (1996): 64, suggests this because a series of future punishments are interrupted with past verbs (perfects and *vav* with imperfect) in 5:25.

[152] They normally begin with הוֹי, "woe," plus a participle that identifies who is being ad-dressed.

[153] W. Janzen, *Mourning Cry and Woe Oracle*, BZAW 125 (Berlin: de Gruyter, 1972), or G. V. Smith, *Amos* (Fearn: Christian Focus, 1998), 206–207, for additional background on laments and woe oracles.

lecture of condemnation. In a lament the speaker sides with the sorrows of the audience and demonstrates an emotional attachment with the listener. After all, what kind of doctor do people want to listen to if they have cancer and are about to die: a heartless, cold, blaming one or one who might shed a tear and cry with them? Isaiah's pastoral heart is breaking as he reveals this bad news to the people he loves.

5:8–14   The first two woes in 5:8–12 and the accompanying two "therefore" (*lākēn*) clauses in 5:13–14 make up the first half of the prophet's mournful lament. This section includes:

A woe against the wealthy	5:8
God's oath: wealth will disappear	5:9–10
A woe against drunkards	5:11–12
Therefore, exile and death will come	5:13–14

Those who will die are the wealthy people who have accumulated vast tracts of land. They live peacefully all alone in their elite mansions and have the ideal life of grand luxury. Isaiah does not accuse them of illegally stealing property, since these are woe oracles, not judgment speeches, therefore it is inappropriate at this point to get into the details as to how these people gained such riches.[154] Isaiah wants his audience to see that he is sorry to hear that the good life in the nation will soon end. Later in 5:23 Isaiah will condemn the way the wealthy illegally took land from the poor people of Judah (cf. 1 Kgs 21; Amos 2:6; 5:10–13; Mic 2:1–4,9) and did not return it at the end of seven years to its rightful owner (Lev 25). At this point he is just weeping for the nation and for these people who will soon suffer great loss.

5:9–10   Isaiah mourns God's curse on these people's land. The verb describing God's action in the NIV is the verb "declared" (NASB has "sworn")—absent in the Hebrew (the Old Greek has "was heard"), but it seems like some verb is needed in order to understand what God did "in my hearing" (cf. 22:14 for a comparable phrase with the verb included). The quotation begins like an oath ("surely")[155] against their beautiful large homes (5:9) and against the fertility of their crops (5:10). It is very sad; these historic mansions will soon be desolate, "without occupants" in them. There is a sense of justice: if they take other people's homes away from them, God will take their home away from them. Even their large fields of grain and immense vineyards will produce only a fraction of what would normally be expected,[156] just like the parable implied

---

[154] Wildberger, *Isaiah 1–12*, 198, calls this a reproach while Sweeney, *Isaiah 1–39*, 124, finds a "judicial pattern of an indictment followed by an announcement of judgment." Most commentaries cannot resist the temptation to deal with the cause of these riches, a topic not raised in this verse. Brueggemann, *Isaiah 1–39*, 51–52, properly focuses on the lamenting quality of this message.

[155] GKC § 149e discusses the use of אִם־לֹא in oaths to express the absolute certainty of God's action. When God gives an oath, the predicted outcome will happen as he said.

[156] Watts, *Isaiah 1–33*, 60, believes Isaiah is referring to the amount of land ten oxen can plough in one day. That piece of land will only produce one bath of wine—about 5 ½ gallons.

in 5:6. Wildberger suggests that the cursed land in 5:10 will give back only one-tenth of what was sown, a consequence he relates to the covenant curses in Deut 26:20; 28:38. There is no hint as to why these curses have fallen on the grapes and grain, though it is obvious from 5:1–7. At this point Isaiah is only concerned about making a tearful identification with the loss these people will suffer.[157] Possibly his tears will bring them to the point where they will begin to re-examine their lives and repent.

5:11–12   The second woe laments the people who spend too much time (when they first get up and until the late evening hours) drinking wine. This woe must refer to wealthy people who can afford the leisure time and have the resources to be able to pursue[158] such pleasurable activities (instead of pursuing God and his righteousness). The evening drinking should probably be associated with lavish parties where people would be entertained by wonderful music (5:12a, cf. Amos 6:4–6),[159] but soon this will all end. Sadly, this intoxicating behavior has dulled their observation of what God was doing in their world (5:12b). What God did was not considered significant, and these divine acts were not understood as part of God's providential rule of the earth. They did not regard the economic and political changes that had already happened within their nation and on the international scene as designed and directed by God's plan for his people. They lacked spiritual perception, for they viewed political events as just the outworking of politicians, not as the hand of God. As Oswalt states, "When the passion for pleasure has become uppermost in a person's life, passion for God and his truth and his ways are squeezed out."[160] Certainly the focus on pleasure and leisure activities in our day has the potential of doing the same thing.

5:13–14   Suddenly, Isaiah leaves his list of woe oracles and gives two predictions that begin with "therefore" (*lākēn*) to introduce the results of the audience's actions. 5:13–14 makes it clear that when people pursue the possession of more and more property, they will end up losing it. Sadly, they

---

Gray, *Isaiah 1–27*, 91, claims that the ten acres is ten times as much as one pair of oxen can plough. The Hb. refers literally to "a ten yoke vineyard," which probably means the amount that ten oxen could plough in a vineyard. On those figures a pair of slow moving oxen can plough about one acre a day.

[157] Oswalt, *Isaiah 1–39*, 159, views this as the self-defeating result of covetousness, but that is never mentioned in this text.

[158] Roberts, "Double Entendre," 39–54, finds a wordplay between the idea of "pursuing" (רדף) beer and "pursuing/burning" (דלק) after wine, giving the translation "so that wine hotly chases them," which is slightly different from the translation of E. J. Kissane, *The Book of Isaiah* (Dublin: Browne and Nolan, 1960), 1:58, "that they may pursue wine."

[159] T. C. Mitchell, "Music of the Old Testament Reconsidered," *PEQ* 124 (1992): 124–43, and J. Braun, *Music in Ancient Israel/Palestine: Archaeological, Written, and Comparative Sources* (Grand Rapids: Eerdmans, 2002), provide information about the various musical instruments mentioned in the Bible.

[160] Oswalt, *Isaiah 1–39*, 160, compares this to 1:3 where Israel is said to be worse than dumb animals.

will go into exile and may not even understand[161] why this happened, or that it was part of God's plan (5:12). They totally ignored God, his revealed instructions in the law, and his powerful providential hand shaping history. If they could not perceive their own spiritual problems, then there would be no way for them to learn from their errors and change their behavior. Isaiah considers this blindness a perennial spiritual problem of the people of Judah throughout the book. Years later they did not understand the plan of God when Sennacherib attacked the city (22:11), so they gained confidence in a false perception of reality (28:15) and acted like dumb dogs that know nothing (56:9–12).

The last two lines of 5:13 show nice parallelism in the NIV, but the verb "will die" is a reconstruction of the Hebrew to try to make sense of the verse. The line literally reads, "his glory/honorable one, men of hunger/famine," which does not make much sense. Since the word "dying of" (*mētē*) is spelled almost the same as "men of" (*mĕtē*)[162] and the Old Greek and Targum translations have "die," it seems that the best solution is to accept the reading "dying of," which provides a good parallel to the next line. The prophet is saying that the rich people who now have more than enough to eat and drink at their banquets will have nothing in the future. The punishment fits the crime.

When this happens, Sheol (not just the "grave" as in NIV), the place of the dead spirits, will develop an enormous appetite (5:14). The irony is that the insatiable appetite of Sheol will consume those who have a great appetite for wine and food in 5:11–12. The world of the afterlife will open its doors wide for thousands of people (especially the upper class nobles) and swallow them all (5:14). Isaiah's imagery seems to personify death as a hungry monster, but he could be playing off the well-known ancient myth that pictured death as a monster swallowing its helpless victims.[163]

5:15–17 At the center of this message (5:8–30) the fundamental principle that explains God's actions is reiterated (quoted and imported from the revelation in 2:9 [cf. 2:11,17] to help unify this message with chaps. 2–6).[164] Using

---

[161] דַּעַת, "understanding, knowledge," can refer to their perception of God's hand and purposes in this world, which they do not comprehend. Their lack of knowledge is not just due to ignorance, but is also due to their lack of a meaningful relationship with God. 5:19 also addresses this fundamental problem of not understanding God or his purposes.

[162] When one realizes that the Hb. text originally did not have vowels, it is easy to see how different words could get confused. In this case both words would be spelled מתי. The oral tradition helps to preserve accurately the proper vocalization of words, but in a few cases, like this one, confusion developed over the proper pronunciation of a word.

[163] See J. C. L. Gibson, *Canaanite Myths and Legends*, 2nd ed. (Edinburgh: T & T Clark, 1978), 68–69, for all the gory details. The illustrative use of a mythical story does not mean that Isaiah believed the myth any more than the use of an illustration in a sermon from the Wizard of Oz means that one believes in the reality of that story or its theological way of looking at life.

[164] Chisholm, "Structure, Style, and the Prophetic Message," 52, believes "the central place of verses 15–16 in the structure of this particular announcement highlights their thematic centrality in the passage."

the past tense (not future as in NIV),[165] Isaiah describes what God has done. The divine plan on earth was designed to bring people to the place where their lives and actions would exalt God alone (2:11–22; 5:16). Because God's sinful people were not glorifying him, it was necessary to humble the proud (5:15) by removing those things that made them so arrogant. This principle was, is, and will always be an important factor in understanding God's work on earth. A second central principle governing the divine plan is that God will be exalted because he acts with justice and righteousness to demonstrate his holiness (5:16).[166] This holy character of God is not just an abstract concept that defines God's nature or being; it was something Isaiah himself personally experienced in chap. 6. God's holiness describes his glorious divinity and the justice with which he rules the world and deals with mankind. Although he allows even his own people to suffer terribly because of their sins, his ultimate goal is to use every providential act to cause his holiness to infiltrate all of creation. This happens both through God's acts of dire judgment and through his grace. Ultimately God, who will always be holy, will finally be seen as holy. In the end the world will all be holy too (4:3–4); then God will be glorified. Every person and nation must ask, Is it better to experience God's holy judgment, or join those righteous people who glorify his holy name?

With this brief doxological confession about God, Isaiah interrupted the flow of his original oral presentation of this punishment section (5:14,17) with these parenthetical comments. Some years later when Isaiah wrote his scroll, God had already fulfilled his plan to humble these sinful and proud people, so it seemed appropriate to assure the reader of the scroll that the punishment described in these woe oracles accomplished God's central theological goal: the humbling of man and the exaltation of God.

After this brief interlude, this sub-section ends in 5:17 by reflecting on the results of God's holy judgment of Judah. The status quo will be so transformed that lambs will graze on the grass in the ruined cities, while young rams[167] will

---

[165] The imperfect verb with *vav* consecutive אָדָם וַיִּשַּׁח means "man was humbled." It presents a contrast with the verbal action of the perfect verbs in preceding verses. R. W. L. Moberly, "Whose Justice? Which Righteousness? The Interpretation of Isaiah V 16," *VT* 51 (2001): 55–68, footnote 2, seems to prefer to emend the *vav* on these two verbs to a simple *vav* (making the verb a future tense) rather than the *vav* consecutive that is found in the MT. Certainly the *vav* consecutive would be the harder reading and indicates this verse's connection with 2:9, so it should not be emended.

[166] Moberly, "Whose Justice?" 55–68, questions whose justice and righteousness is being described because the Hb. does not have the pronoun "his" on either noun (NIV adds "his," meaning God's justice). Almost all commentators conclude that this verse describes God's justice and righteousness, though Moberly connects this verse to the human practice of justice in 5:7 (which is parallel to God's justice). W. Brueggemann, *Isaiah 1–39*, 53, also connects this justice in 5:16 to the "human practice of justice," partially based on 5:7.

[167] The Hb. word גָּרִים means "strangers, aliens," but this does not provide a good parallel to the "lambs" in the first line. Thus NIV and most commentators suggest a slight copying error of גְּדִים, "little rams," which provides a good parallel with lambs.

eat grass where the rich[168] used to dine in luxury. Although the exact text is
somewhat unclear there is no doubt that the prophet is describing the desolate
conditions of Judah after God destroys it.

5:18–25 The pattern of woes and two "therefore" clauses is now repeated,
similar to 5:8–14.

Woe for deceit and mocking God	5:18–19
Woe for confusing right and wrong	5:20
Woe for the wise and clever	5:21
Woe for injustices	5:22–23
Therefore, God's anger will come	5:24–25

These four short woe oracles focus on the lamentable tragedy of false beliefs
and the people's cynical refusal to listen to God. Their mocking of God, reversal of godly values, and self-deception about reality are especially sad because
these perversions have made it almost impossible to help them. In the light of
these conditions, the anger of God and the destruction of his hand (5:25) are
justified. God will punish this nation.

5:18–19 The first woe laments those who purposely attach themselves
to sin through "useless deceitful falsehoods."[169] The picture is of an animal
pulling a cart with ropes.[170] Unfortunately, Isaiah's audience did not reject
this wagon of wickedness as an unworthy or useless burden, but laboriously
pulled it along because of a powerful deceitful connection (the strong cords) to
the people. This perverted attachment to false beliefs led the people of Judah
to make preposterous claims about God's work in this world (5:19); a seeming confirmation of Isaiah's point in 5:12b. Young calls these people "practical
atheists, who would not believe unless they could see."[171] Mocking God with
sarcastic bravado they challenge God to do something now so that they can
see that he is real.[172] Instead of being convicted and repenting of their sins,
they brazenly taunt the Holy One of Israel to act according to his plans "in
order that" (*lĕmaʿan* shows the purpose of their challenge) they can actually
verify with their eyes that he exists. Although Isaiah has just told them what
God's plans for Judah were in the earlier woe oracles, they stubbornly claim
that they must see it before they will ever believe it. The people of Judah are

---

[168] מֵחִים, "fat," is related to "fat sheep" by Wildberger, *Isaiah 1–12*, 189. Watts, *Isaiah 1–33*,
58, pictures strangers eating the wasted bodies of fatlings. NIV interprets the "fat" to refer to the
wealthy people of Judah. All of these are attempts to make some sense out of a difficult text.

[169] שָׁוְא means "nothing, empty, a falsehood, deceit."

[170] Numerous emendations are proposed in commentaries to improve the understanding of this
verse. Clements, *Isaiah 1–39*, 65, suggested "like sheep on a tether" instead of "cords of deceit"
and "like a heifer on a rope" instead of "with a cart rope," but it is better to stick as closely to the
Hb. text as possible even if it is difficult to understand the metaphorical comparisons.

[171] Young, *Isaiah*, I:218, sees the depravity of their thinking and the sarcasm of their challenge
to God.

[172] יְמַהֵר, "let him hasten," and חִישָׁה, "let him speed" (and two later verbs in the verse) are jussives that express a wish (GKC § 109b). NIV supplies "God" in 5:19a to clarify what is implied.

in a lamentable moral and theological state of denial and defiance. Their taunts are blasphemous. These people are consciously rejecting the ability of the Almighty God to do anything, thereby essentially denying his relevance to their lives. This is how they reason: If there is no all-powerful God controlling this world and if there is no holy God who sets absolute standards of just behavior, then there is no need for us to change our ways.

5:20 The second woe laments the consequent deterioration of morality among those who reject God. Without the divine standards of God, a good thing can be reinterpreted as something evil, while an immoral act (killing someone with cancer) can be twisted into something that actually appears to be good (a merciful termination of their pain). Without an absolute standard of divine justice, false human reasoning and uncontrolled passion can rationalize and justify almost any act, particularly if the primary criteria is "Will it benefit me?" When sweet and bitter, light and darkness, and good and evil are relative values based on wishes, whims, and selfish ends, righteousness and justice do not exist. Much of the crime and immorality that afflicts modern society goes right back to similar personal and societal redefinitions of right and wrong. People in any generation can senselessly and defiantly reject the idea that they are doing wrong because they have no moral anchor. But human defiance and ignorance cannot lessen the authority or reduce the practical relevance of God's just instructions about moral human behavior.

5:21 The third woe mourns the cause of the moral reversals in the previous woe. People do not do what is right because they believe that they are the judges of their own actions. They make up their own moral standards, instead of allowing God or his divine law to guide them. No one else can tell them what to do because they in their arrogant shrewdness and wisdom know what is best. A certain prideful egotism allows them to think that they are wise enough to handle any situation and clever enough to get out of any trouble. A humble dependence on the wisdom of others or God is rejected because they want the freedom to be in control. They do not realize that true wisdom is given by God and comes from fearing him (Prov 1:7; 3:7; 9:10).

5:22–23 The fourth woe addressed the issues of drinking and social oppression once again, the problems lamented in the second woe in 5:11–12. Isaiah sarcastically points to these people as "heroes, military champions" (*gibbôrîm*), but the skill that has made these people "famous" is their ability to mix and drink wine, not their valor and bravery in war. The text does not make a direct link between their heavy drinking and their social oppression, but one could imply that there is a logical connection.

The oppression of the poor involved taking homes and fields in 5:12. This was wrong because the land belonged to God (Lev 25:23) and he gave it to various tribes and families. The rich and powerful stole what God gave to others

as their eternal inheritance (Exod 19:5; Deut 32:9).[173] Injustice in the courts
(5:23) was another way the powerful were able to oppress the poor, enslave
them, and take their land. The root *ṣdq*, "justice," is used three times in 5:23.
These people pay off judges and witnesses so that the guilty people are "declared just," but "justice" for the "just, innocent" person is denied. This is a
sorrowful state of affairs and this behavior is totally opposite the just and holy
character of God (5:16).

5:24–25   Like the first list of woes and two "therefore" (*lākēn*) clauses
in 5:8–14, the second list of woes is followed by two "therefore" (*lākēn* and
ʿal kēn) clauses in 5:24–25.[174] The first result in 5:24 gives (a) comparative
images describing the destruction of plant life and (b) some reason why this
destruction will happen. The prophet pictures those being punished as "straw,
stubble," "dry grass," "roots," and a "flower." All of these parts of a plant are
important to preserving the life of a plant, but all of these can wither and dry
up, thus causing the plant to die. If this dried up flower is set on fire, it will
quickly be devoured by the flames.[175] If decay starts to destroy the roots of a
plant, a strong wind will dry up and blow off the petals of a beautiful flower.
All plants are fragile and vulnerable to the forces of nature to either provide life
or death. Likewise, the people of Judah are like helpless plants dependent on
what God might bring into their lives. As stubble is helpless before the flames
of a windblown fire, so the people of Judah will be consumed by God's anger
on their day of judgment.

Why is this severe judgment coming? God's holy response to all of the
lamented activities listed in these woe oracles is based on what the people
already know from the revealed will of God in the law (*tôrâ*). When "they
reject, repudiate" (*māʾasû*) what the Almighty God outlines as just and righteous behavior, "they spurn, despise" (*niʾēṣû*) the precious words of the Holy
One. Isaiah uses strong words to describe their utter refusal to follow God's
guidance. Although the people may have looked at their deeds as insignificant
or as merely a slight difference of interpretation, God saw them as a direct af-
front to his will, character, and authority. These were willful acts that show no
respect for God's instructions. The people defiantly refused to submit to his

---

[173] See C. J. H. Wright, *An Eye for an Eye: The Place of Old Testament Ethics Today* (Downers Grove: InterVarsity Press, 1983), 46–62, or his *God's People in God's Land: Family, land, and
Property in the Old Testament* (Grand Rapids: Eerdmans, 1990), 3–43 and 119–141, for a discussion of God's plan for the land.

[174] Tucker, *Isaiah 1–39,* 97, makes 25–30 a unit, thus disconnecting it from 24, while Blenkinsopp, *Isaiah 1–39,* 215–18, connects 5:25 with the "outstretched hand" clauses in 9:7–20. The
parallel structure of woe oracles and the two "therefore" clauses in 5:8–17 argue for keeping the
same basic pattern in 5:18–25.

[175] כֶּאֱכֹל, "devour, eat," in the first line of 24 is an infinitive construct, having the preposition
"as, like" (כְּ) preceding it. The normal order is for the subject of the infinitive construct to come
right after the verb form and then the object after the subject (GKC §115h), but common sense
dictates in this case that order is reversed (GKC §115k).

requirements. This kind of human response will eventually bring the fire of God's judgment.

The second "therefore" clause in 5:25 reemphasizes the reality of God's wrath in order to give a persuasive punch to 5:24 and to motivate the listeners to accept the inevitability of God's destruction—if there is no change. Repeatedly, both at the beginning and end of this verse, Isaiah reminds his listeners of the burning anger of God and his powerful outstretched hand of judgment. Although it may seem unnecessary, or an editorial blunder, to mention God's anger twice, the initial reference appears to be pointing to God's past act of anger in the great earthquake that killed thousands of people, a likely reference to the earthquake that happened during the time of Amos around 765–760 BC (Amos 1:1; 2:13; 6:11; 8:8; 9:1).[176] The second reference to God's burning anger at the end of the verse emphasizes that in spite of all God did in the past to punish them, his holy anger will not stop (comparable to phrases used in Amos 1:3),[177] for his powerful hand will continue to execute divine justice against sin in the future. In these clauses God's almighty hand accomplishes on earth the satisfaction of God's burning anger by justly delivering recompense for sinful rebellion against God (cf. Amos 8:3 for similar dead bodies). Certainly God's character has not changed since the days of Amos and Isaiah, and his hatred of sins has not diminished. Every person who despises what God reveals in Scripture should stop and pay attention to God's just ways of dealing with sin. It is a fearful thing to be caught by the outstretched hands of an angry Almighty God.

(3) An Army's Destruction of Judah (5:26–30)

> [26] He lifts up a banner for the distant nations,
>   he whistles for those at the ends of the earth.
>   Here they come,
>   swiftly and speedily!
> [27] Not one of them grows tired or stumbles,
>   not one slumbers or sleeps;
>   not a belt is loosened at the waist,
>   not a sandal thong is broken.
> [28] Their arrows are sharp,
>   all their bows are strung;
>   their horses' hoofs seem like flint,
>   their chariot wheels like a whirlwind.
> [29] Their roar is like that of the lion,
>   they roar like young lions;
>   they growl as they seize their prey
>   and carry it off with no one to rescue.
> [30] In that day they will roar over it
>   like the roaring of the sea.

---

[176] G. V. Smith, *Amos*, 48, 129, 282, 344, 360.

[177] לֹא־שֵׁב אַפּוֹ in 5:25 is similar to לֹא אֲשִׁיבֶנּוּ in Amos 1:3.

**And if one looks at the land,
he will see darkness and distress;
even the light will be darkened by the clouds.**

The conclusion of this message describes in poetic images how God is going to bring about the destruction predicted in the song (5:5–6) and in the woes (5:13–17,24–25). This paragraph illustrates how God will lay waste the land and it demonstrates the inevitability of defeat at the hands of an overwhelming military force that is on the march. Its persuasive force is found in the fearful images of a gigantic and fast moving war machine that is unstoppable. The implications are: either quit despising the Holy One of Israel or the nation will face this destructive army. It is their choice. The general unnamed enemy army from a distant land in 5:26–30 contrasts with the specific identification of the Assyrian army at a later date in chaps. 7–8. Thus the oral presentatioin of this paragraph should be dated in the time of Uzziah (like the rest of chaps. 2–5).

5:26 This attack will not simply be the work of one of Judah's traditional enemies (one of the small nations around it), for it is pictured as an invasion by a mysterious nation that will travel a great distance to reach Judah. There is a fearful, unknown quality to something that is totally foreign. If the people of Judah do not know what to expect from an enemy or what kind of troops they have, it is difficult to make the proper preparations to defend the nation. The swiftness of its movement means that it will come unexpectedly fast and without much warning. These factors are enough to strike terror into most people, but the most fearful aspect of this ensuing war will be that God is the one who will orchestrate this plan and sovereignly rule over everything that happens. He will choose the enemy nation; he will call that nation to arms[178] by whistling for this mysterious enemy (cf. 7:18 where God's whistling will bring the Assyrians); and he will lift up a "banner, signal" (*nēs*) in a prominent place (cf. 13:2; 31:9) so that troops can gather together. God himself will direct and facilitate their path to Jerusalem. The protector and savior of Judah will now oversee the destruction of his vineyard.

5:27–28 Naturally, the people in Isaiah's audience would be wondering who this nation was. In the following verses Isaiah does not provide a name, but instead increases the audience's fear when he describes the well-oiled military machine that is on its way. This army is strong and it has many determined troops (they do not need to sleep and never tire), it has the very best equipment (belt, sandals, arrows, and bows[179]), and good support from chariots drawn by

---

[178] נֵס, "signal flag," was put on a pole on a high place so that people could gather around it. It was then carried out in front of the army as it marched. In this case God is responsible for raising up standards for the army that will come to Judah. Later, in 11:10–12, God lifts up a standard when he restores the remnant that was scattered among the nations.

[179] The "treading of the bow" refers to putting a foot on one end of it in order to bend it so that the string can be attached to the other end. J. A. Emerton, "Treading the Bow," *VT* 53 (2003): 465–86.

tough[180] horses. This represents a disciplined army that is ready to win, for the foot soldiers, archers, and charioteers are all prepared to fight.

5:29–30   The paragraph ends with a description of the conclusion of the battle using the imagery of lions capturing their prey. This is fitting because kings sometimes compared themselves to lions (e.g., the lion of Judah) and Amos compares God to a roaring lion (Amos 1:2; 3:8). Like a roaring lion[181] pouncing on its prey (comparable to the yell of troops when they charge), they will howl as they seize their prey (Judah) and then carry it off to a safe place where there is no possibility for escape. These lions will snarl with a loud growl (like the thundering of the ocean) to announce the greatness of their deeds (5:30).

What will the land of Judah look like after this devastating defeat? There will be darkness, distress, gloom, clouds of smoke shading the light; that is all the people will see. This is where the people's sinful behavior and defiance of God is leading them. Is this what they want to happen to their nation? In this chapter Isaiah offers no positive options, but the implications of each accusation is that sin is causing these results. Thus a rejection of their sinful ways and a listening to God's instructions (5:24) might provide an avenue of hope for God to have compassion on them.

THEOLOGICAL IMPLICATIONS.   These woes assure the reader that God will judge sin severely. The lament conveys the truth that God is terribly saddened when his people reject him or his revealed instructions. Nevertheless, in the end he will hold all people accountable for their actions, especially his own privileged people. This message maintains the justice of a Holy God even as God cries over the rebelliousness of his children. In spite of his deep desire to care for his people, his holiness will be exalted only through the execution of his justice (5:16). People can pretend God does not exist or question whether he actually controls what goes on in this world (5:19a), but their unbelief will not change or nullify the fact that God has a plan for the righteous and the wicked (5:19b). All sinful and proudly independent people who scorn God's standards will have to face the anger of God's wrath (5:25). God's methods of punishment will vary over time, but he rules the world according to key principles that people must heed (5:12,17). Everything happens according to God's plan (14:24–26) and no one is able to alter his will or prevent him from accomplishing his plans (14:27).

The prophet's role, and each reader's responsibility, is to warn others of God's impending holy judgment and to persuade the ungodly to change their ways. Like Isaiah, preachers, teachers, and parents need to weep over the evil that pervades this world. It is especially sad when friends, neighbors, fellow

---

[180] כַּצַּר probably should be pointed כְּצוֹר, "like hard rock, flint," as in 1QIsa[a].

[181] An extensive study of lions is found in B. A. Strawn, *What is Stronger than a Lion? Leonine Imagery and Metaphor in the Hebrew Bible and the Ancient Near East* (Göttingen: Vandenhoeck and Ruprecht, 2005).

workers, children, and fellow church members do not classify their evil deeds as sins against God. People need to communicate their deep sadness, explain the just demands of God, encourage people to humble themselves, and warn of irresistible judgment for those who do not glorify God. There is no hope for those who ignore, scorn, or reject God (5:12,17,24). One day an Almighty Lion will roar over them (5:29).

3. A Holy King's Calling to a Calloused Audience (6:1–13)

Chapter 6 records a pivotal turning point in Judah's history and marks the beginning of a new era in Isaiah's preaching. The death of Uzziah (6:1) ends a period of relative strength and prosperity in Judah, when Assyria was weak. The wicked king Ahaz will now rule Judah (7:1), war and weakness will characterize this king's reign, and Assyria will become the dominant international power on earth. Chapter 6 also serves a literary function as the conclusion to chaps. 2–5 and the introduction to chaps. 7–11.[182] Many questions about the nature and significance of God's unusual meeting with Isaiah are still partially unanswered, but its formative impact on the thinking of the prophet is evident throughout his writings. The experience of having a glimpse of the majesty of God's glory dramatically impacted his theology and caused him to understand God's purpose for his life in a new way.

GENRE. One of the first questions the interpreter must answer whether this is Isaiah's original call or an important revised commissioning of the prophet for a new task due to changes in the historical setting. Since there is no prophetic call of Isaiah in the first chapters of his book, it would be natural for the reader to conclude that chap. 6 is a record of his inaugural calling.[183] This would mean that chap. 6 is out of chronological order and placed here for a theological or literary reason devised when Isaiah edited these messages in the written form that exists today. Those who take this approach imply that in chaps. 6–12 Isaiah was concerned that people understand his unique role and prophetic authority to harden the people's hearts during the reign of Ahaz. Thus his prophetic call is strategically placed here to support and justify what happened during these difficult circumstances. But if the prophetic call in chap. 6 actually happened before the messages in chap. 1, one would expect that this same evidence would be found in chaps. 1–5, not just in 6–12.

Others question the notion that chap. 6 was an inaugural call and prefer to think of it as a recommissioning for a specific historical task. They suggest

---

[182] L. Liebreich, "The Position of Chapter Six," 37–40, understands the pivotal nature of 6:1–13 as the center of chaps. 2–12.

[183] Young, *Isaiah*, I:232, says, "The fifth verse seems to support the idea that this is an inaugural call." While Oswalt, *Isaiah 1–39*, 172, agrees, he does allow the possibility of Isaiah's preaching before this decisive experience. He finds a theological reason for the placement of 6 at this point because it introduces key themes developed in 7–12.

that (a) no other original calls primarily involve giving messages to harden the hearts of listeners; (b) it is clear that Isaiah was functioning as an inspired prophet of God during the reign of Uzziah in 2–5 (before 6:1–13 happened), so this could not be his initial call; (c) there is a change in Isaiah's messages after chap. 6 (not in chap. 1 or 2) with additional emphasis on political affairs and the refusal to follow God's instructions (7:1–12), thus the new commission chronologically fits here rather than before chap. 1; and (d) the structure and content of this experience is more like the special recommissioning of Micaiah ben Imlah, rather than Jeremiah's initial call.[184]

W. Zimmerli's form critical analysis of call narratives divides them into two groups. In the first group Moses (Exod 3), Gideon (Judges 6), and Jeremiah (Jer 1) have a divine vision, a divine sending, a series of excuses by the person being called, a divine sign and promise, and then a divine commissioning to give the word of God. In contrast the second group, including Micaiah ben Imlah (I Kgs 22) and Isaiah were prophets before they received a new message, experienced some sort of theophany of the divine council, and were told about the task of hardening the listeners.[185] This second type of commissioning does not fit into the pattern of other prophetic inaugural callings, thus it seems best to understand Isaiah 6 as God's special recommissioning for a new task because the nation would be facing a new political situation and be led by a new unbelieving king.[186]

THEOLOGY.   A second and more difficult question arises over the Lord's command for Isaiah to harden the hearts of his audience. Most prophetic calls involve encouraging people to repent and not harden their hearts against God. Clements and many others maintain that God never originally told Isaiah to harden the people's heart. Instead these words are a later retrospective theological reflection on what happened when Ahaz rejected Isaiah's message. Looking back on what happened, Isaiah realized that the divine act of hardening explained why his prophetic words failed to persuade Ahaz and why Judah suffered so severely during the Syro-Ephraimite War.[187] Others take a more

---

[184] Hayes and Irvine, *Isaiah*, 108–109, maintain that Isaiah calls people to repentance in 1–5, therefore the call to harden people does not fit 1–5.

[185] W. Zimmerli, *A Commentary on the Book of Ezekiel, Chapters 1–24*, Hermeneia (Philadelphia: Fortress, 1979), 97–100, recognizes some differences between 1 Kgs 22 and Isa 6 but believes these two passages follow a different pattern than the other call narratives. G. Y. Glazov, *The Bridling of the Tongue and the Opening of the Mouth in Biblical Prophecy* (Sheffield: Sheffield Academic Press, 2001) rejected Zimmerli's distinction between these two kind of call narratives, but Glazov's evidence does not fundamentally undermine Zimmerli's essential observation.

[186] C. R. Seitz, *Isaiah 1–39*, Interpretation (Louisville: Westminster John Knox, 1993), 53, rejects the view that this is a call narrative and sees it as a "specific commission to make hearts fat—a commission that is carried out in the events of 734–732 B.C." Blenkinsopp, *Isaiah 1–39*, 223, says "that it functions in a more limited way as Isaiah's commissioning for a specific political mission in connection with the threat of a Syrian-Samarian invasion." He sees it introducing "Isaiah's Memoirs" (*Denkschrift*) in chaps. 6–8, but he does not connect 6 it to themes in chaps. 2–5.

[187] Clements, *Isaiah 1–39*, 71–72, and Gray, *Isaiah 1–27*, 101, have this perspective. Both

psychological view and think these words represent the prophet's bitter disappointment after the leaders and people of Judah rejected his exhortations to trust God (7:9).[188] But both of these approaches severely undermine the credibility of Isaiah as an honest reporter of what happened when he saw Almighty God as King on his throne. How could a true prophet dare to put his own later reinterpretation of these historical events in the form of a divine call, suggesting that God came to him in all his glory, forgave his sins, and then told him to do something like this, when it really never happened that way at all and God never really spoke the words in 6:9–10?[189]

An examination of the hardening of Pharaoh indicates that the Egyptian king hardened his own heart and then later God hardened his heart (Exod 7:3; 9:12; 10:12,27; 11:10). Some years later God sent evil spirits on the sinful people of Shechem (Judg 9:23) and on the disobedient Saul (I Sam 16:4; 18:10; 19:9), thus giving them over to their sinful ways and assuring their self-destruction.[190] Micaiah ben Imlah's encounter with God (1 Kgs 22:19–23) states that God directed the hardening of the wicked and presumptuous King Ahab through the use of a deceptive spirit. Thus Isaiah's specific mission to harden people during the era of Ahaz is not an unheard of directive or something inconsistent with other Scriptures. This command does not restrict Isaiah's message to only one theme, or undermine his strategy of offering repentance (28:16; 30:15; 31:6; 35:3–10), or destroy the prophet's own hope for the future (8:16–18). God does not forbid him to ask people to trust God (7:9; 12:2; 26:3; 30:15; 31:1–3; 37:10; 50:10), he just tells Isaiah that his messages will end up having the result of hardening some.[191] The following chapters illustrate that from time to time Isaiah saw God closing the ears of some people (29:9–14), but allowing others to respond positively (Hezekiah in 36–37). Unfortunately, far too many people were stubbornly unwilling to listen to God (42:18–20; 44:18; 63:17). These later passages demonstrate that both the idea of God closing people's ears and the concept that people themselves closing their own ears are not foreign to the theology of Isaiah, or for that matter, the thinking of Jesus.[192] It

---

refer to this as Isaiah's call rather than a special commissioning and believe this retrospective reflection took place after the Syro-Ephraimite War.

[188] J. Love, "The Call of Isaiah," *Int* 11 (1957): 282–96, takes a psychological approach to understanding the negative tone of in this command. S. Blank, *Prophetic Faith in Israel* (New York: Harper and Row, 1958), 4, is so bold as to call a literal interpretation of what God asks Isaiah to do "bad theology," but since he understands these words as the prophet's anguish over his failures, he calls this "good psychology."

[189] Kaiser, *Isaiah 1–12*, 119–20, understands the error of taking a retrospective approach to 6:1–13 and believes that this explanation undermines Isaiah's credibility.

[190] C. A. Evans, *To See and Not Perceive: Isaiah 6. 9–10 in Early Jewish and Christian Interpretation* (Sheffield: Sheffield Academic Press, 1989), 22–24, surveys these and other examples of obduracy.

[191] Childs, *Isaiah*, 57, carefully distinguishes between Isaiah's strategies (which were multiple and included calling people to repent) and the results of his preaching (which was hardening).

[192] K. Snodgrass, "A Hermeneutic of Hearing Informed by the Parables with Special Refer-

appears that Isaiah's messages will confirm the hardened hearts of those who are already refusing to listen to God. Thus, it is appropriate to take the Lord's command to cause the people to listen but not perceive (6:9–10) as an authentic part of God's plan for certain stages of Isaiah's ministry and for certain people who were unwilling to listen to what God was saying.

STRUCTURE.   The structure of this chapter is divided by a series of spoken announcements, dialogues, and questions as God, Isaiah, and the seraphim interact together. It begins with the prophet "seeing" the Lord (6:1–7), and once the prophet is cleansed he "hears" the Lord speaking to him (6:8–13). The narrative includes:

A vision of the Holy King	6:1–4
The prophet's Purification	6:5–7
A Hardening Message for a Calloused Audience	6:8–10
Hope in the midst of Destruction	6:11–13

The narrative contrasts what Isaiah "saw" (6:1,5) and "heard" (6:8) with what the audience will not be able to "see and hear" (6:9,10). It juxtaposes God's "glory" (*kābôd*) filling the land (6:3) with the "dull/hardened" (the verb *kābad*) ears of the people leaving the land (6:11–12). Only the holy seed that is purified by God (4:3–4) can dwell in the presence of a holy God (6:3,13).

(1) A Vision of the Holy King (6:1–4)

[1]In the year that King Uzziah died, I saw the Lord seated on a throne, high and exalted, and the train of his robe filled the temple. [2]Above him were seraphs, each with six wings: With two wings they covered their faces, with two they covered their feet, and with two they were flying. [3]And they were calling to one another:

> **"Holy, holy, holy is the LORD Almighty;**
> **the whole earth is full of his glory."**

[4] At the sound of their voices the doorposts and thresholds shook and the temple was filled with smoke.

6:1   The vision appeared to Isaiah in the year Uzziah died (dated by commentators as early as 742 and as late as 735 BC). The text assumes that Uzziah has already died when the vision was received,[193] since the prophet does not say it was the fifty-second year of Uzziah's reign. The end of this king's life

---

ence to Mark 4," *BBR* 14 (2004): 59–79, explains that Jesus' use of the deeper insights of parables enabled him to bring greater hearing to some, but hardness to others just like Isaiah, who is quoted in Mk 4:12.

[193] Wildberger, *Isaiah 1–12*, 259, believes the vision may have come before or after the death of Uzziah and advises that one should not make an inner connection between the death and the vision. But if this were the case, why did Isaiah even mention the date? It seems more likely that a monumental change took place after the death of Uzziah; therefore, God redirected the prophet and prepared him to face an obstinate King Ahaz. Hayes and Irvine, *Isaiah*, 111, think the death of Uzziah triggered this event.

marked a turning point in Judah's history (2 Kgs 15:1–7; 2 Chr 26) and a new phase in Isaiah's ministry.

The claim that Isaiah saw the Lord (6:1)[194] does not contradict statements that it is impossible to see God (Gen 32:30; Exod 19:21; 33:20; Judg 13:22). The Bible refers to several people "seeing" manifestations of God (Gen 16:9–13; 28:13–15; Exod 24:9–11; 34:5–10; 1 Kgs 22:19) that reveal various levels of his glory. Yet God is in reality an invisible Spirit of untold glory and majesty, so it is impossible for the human eye to behold the full manifestation of the essence of his divinity. This was a limited manifestation that was adapted to finite mental comprehension and human observation, probably in a vision. Isaiah's report says nothing about God's face or nose; instead Isaiah describes where God was, what was happening around him, and what was being said. Wildberger believes that what he "saw"[195] was a heavenly visionary revelation rather than a theophany in the earthly temple in Jerusalem.[196] The verbal similarities to Micaiah ben Imlah's experience argue for a limited vision of heavenly reality (1 Kgs 22:19–20).

Isaiah gives the briefest account of the marvelous scene before him: (a) a glorious divine king was sitting on a throne that was highly elevated; (b) the hem of his robes filled the heavenly palace-temple; (c) winged seraphs were praising God; and (d) the building was shaking and filling with smoke. The description leaves more unsaid than said, but the mystery of the divine majesty in the vision was probably so otherworldly that it was difficult to find adequate words to describe God's glory in human terms.[197] This description of God reaffirms the point made in 2:11,17 that God is "high and lifted up," that he should be exalted, and that man should humble himself before God.

The central feature of this revelation was the appearance of God sitting as a king on a highly elevated "royal throne" (*kissēh* 6:1). Not surprising, a description of God's own appearance is missing; he is simply compared to a great king (6:5). The earthly king of an empire was the most powerful ruling authority in the world, so it is natural that God would reveal himself as the great sovereign king over the whole earth. Kingship is a concept that synthesizes in human

---

[194] Beuken, "The Manifestation of Yahweh and the Commission of Isaiah: Isaiah 6 Read against the Background of Isaiah 1," *CTJ* 39 (2004): 72–87, shows how several repeated themes unify the chapter, and he contrasts Isaiah's (chap. 6) and the people's (chap. 1) response to God.

[195] Although some prophets refer to the divine words of revelation as what they "saw, perceived" using the root חָזָה or חָזוֹן (Amos 1:1; Isa 1:1;2:1), on this occasion Isaiah used וָאֶרְאָה to represent his act of seeing the mysterious hidden glory of God and all that was going on around the throne of God.

[196] Wildberger, *Isaiah 1–12*, 260–63, defends a heavenly vision while Seitz, *Isaiah 1–39*, 54, proposes that this was "probably not a pure vision but takes place within the temple itself, even as it explodes the limitations of the sacred space."

[197] Ezekiel also seems to have trouble explaining what he saw when God revealed himself to the prophet by the river Kebar in Ezek 1. D. I. Block, *The Book of Ezekiel 1–24,* NICOT (Grand Rapids: Eerdmans, 1997), 89–103, demonstrates that Ezekiel had an even more difficult time explaining what he saw of the glory of God.

terms God's many functions. God's roles as creator, protector, savior, lawgiver, warrior in chief, and judge were perceived as comparable to the roles of earthly kings (Ps 24; 47; 95–99), so kingship terminology provided an appropriate metaphor to summarize God's various relationships to mankind.[198] The fact that other ancient Near Eastern religions referred to their gods as kings of a part of nature or a territory shows that this was a common way of talking about a divine power.

The throne sat at the top of a series of steps ("high and lifted up," *rām wĕniśśāʾ*) and the enormous size of the edge of his royal garment[199] testifies to the exalted importance of this divine king. A similar tradition in Ps 104:1 does not mention his robe but testifies that God is "clothed with splendor and majesty" (cf. Ps 93:1). The picture Isaiah paints strikes awe and terror into one's heart; a person gets the idea that the observer has come a little too close to the majesty of the glory and has seen something that is beyond the human sphere of experience and understanding. This is the throne room of the palace-temple of the King, the inner sanctum dedicated to the dwelling of God. The prophet is not just relating what might be seen in the holy of holies in the earthly temple at Jerusalem, this is a vision that unveils the windows of heaven.[200]

6:2 This heavenly royal dwelling place was far different from Uzziah's or Ahaz's palace and the attendants around the throne were different from anything Isaiah saw in the Jerusalem palace of the king. Although Micaiah ben Imlah saw "all the hosts of heaven standing around him" (1 Kgs 22:19), Isaiah calls some of those hosts "seraphs" (*śĕrāpîm*, lit. "burning ones") who were either "standing"(*ʿōmdîm*, omitted in NIV) higher than God or flying above the throne. The seraphs are not identical to the two lifeless gold cherubim on the ark of the covenant (Exod 24:17–22; 1 Sam 4:4; 1 Kgs 8:6–7), for the beings Isaiah saw were very much alive and actively worshiping God.[201] It is possible

---

[198] See G. V. Smith, "The Concept of God/the gods as King in the Ancient Near East and the Bible," *Trinity Journal* 3 (1982):18–38, for a detailed comparison of ancient Near Eastern and biblical references to God/the gods as king. God is called king 47 times in the OT, but other imagery (shepherd in Ezek 34 or throne in Ps 103:19) also communicates this understanding of God. M. Z. Brettler, *God is King: Understanding an Israelite Metaphor* (Sheffield: Sheffield Academic Press, 1989), has chapters on royal appellations, qualities, and trappings of God and ANE kings.

[199] שׁוּל in BDB, 1002, is defined as the "skirt, train" and represents the lower edges of a garment, but this is probably the best word Isaiah could imagine to describe the indescribable surrounding presence of God that was filling the temple. L. Eslinger, "The Infinite in a Finite Organical Perception (Isaiah vi 1–5)," *VT* 45 (1995): 145–73, does not believe this term refers to God's clothing.

[200] R. Knierim, "The Vocation of Isaiah," *VT* 18 (1968): 51, concluded that these events took place in the earthly temple because the train could not fill the heavenly temple, and the altar and threshold belonged to the earthly temple. None of these reasons are particularly convincing, for who knows the size of the heavenly temple or the extent of God's garments? Who can say that God's temple in heaven does not have a threshold? Was not the earthly model patterned after the heavenly temple (Exod 25:9,40; 1 Chr 28:11–19)?

[201] Wildberger, *Isaiah 1–12*, 263, rejects the view of Origen that there were only two seraphs, the Logos and the Holy Spirit.

that the seraphs have some connection to the cherubim in Ezekiel's two visions of the glory of God (Ezek 1; 10).[202] The seraphs in Isaiah, like the cherubim in Ezekiel's experience, seem to have hands, faces, feet, and wings. Particularly significant is Ezekiel's description of these living creatures being "like burning coals of fire or like torches" (Ezek 1:13). But in contrast to Isaiah's seraphs, each living creature in Ezek 1:5–14 had four faces and was located under the throne of God, in order to move it from place to place. Thus these mysterious creatures in Isaiah are probably not cherubim simply functioning in different roles. The term "seraph" can refer to serpents (Num 21:8; Deut 8:15: Isa 14:29; 30:6), so K. R Joines maintains that these beings were something like the Egyptian winged cobra or uraeus that guarded the throne of the king of Egypt.[203] It may be possible that there is some outward connection in color, movement, or looks to the cobra, but these seraphs were not guarding God's throne and their appearance (with hands, six wings, and speaking) suggests that they were not creatures like Egyptian snakes. Maybe these were fiery angelic beings, like the hosts of heaven surrounding the throne in Dan 7:10.

What is most important is the actions of the seraphs: what they did with their wings and what they said. With two sets of wings they were covering[204] their own faces and feet, not from shame or guilt, nor because of their inability to look at God. Their humble posture was likely motivated by the natural tendency to bow in worship before the holy glory of God.[205] The most important thing about the seraphs was not their looks, their wings, or their flying. They are known for their simple yet profound antiphonal declarations of the holiness of God (6:3). In heaven God alone was exalted (contrast 2:11,17; 5:16).

6:3 Although Isaiah records only one triple declaration of "holy, holy, holy,"[206] there is every reason to assume that these beings provided a continuous

---

[202] D. I. Block, *Ezekiel 1–24*, 93–98 and 318–25, discusses the distinctive characteristic of the cherubim.

[203] K. R. Joines, "Winged Serpents in Isaiah's Inaugural Vision," *JBL* 86 (1967): 410–15, interprets these as serpent symbols of sovereignty borrowed from Egyptian iconography. P. Provencal, "Regarding the Noun שָׂרָף in the Hebrew Bible," *JSOT* 29 (2005): 371–78, sees the שָׂרָף in 6:2,6 as mythical beings, but elsewhere this term refers to the cobra.

[204] The verb יְכַסֶּה is an imperfect Hb. verb of repeated or continuous action (GKC § 107f) in present time, thus "were covering" (parallel to "were flying") would be better than NIV "covered."

[205] Oswalt, *Isaiah 1–39,* 179, suggests that, "even the most perfect of creatures dare not gaze into the face of the Creator." Clements, *Isaiah 1–39,* 74, considers the reference to covering his feet as a euphemism for covering the sexual part of the body, but it is doubtful that these heavenly beings have sexual characteristics.

[206] 1QIsaᵃ has the word קָדוֹשׁ, "holy," only twice, but the various Greek translations have the word three times. For a discussion of this issue see N. Walker, "Disagion versus Trisagion: A Copyist Defended," *NTS* 7 (1961): 170–71, who prefers the double reference to holiness. Rev 4:8 uses the threefold declaration of God's holiness. The closest OT parallel to this threefold repetition is found in the twofold refrain "holy is he" in the kingship hymn of Ps 99:3 and 5 (though God's holiness is proclaimed again in 99:9). Although the seraphs certainly knew about the Trinity, there is no way to prove that this threefold declaration of holiness is evidence to support this doctrine.

offering of praise that did not stop with just three declarations of God's holiness. The repetition of a word is a way of expressing a superlative idea in the Hebrew language (2 Kgs 25:15 "gold gold").[207] Thus the seraphs claim that God is completely, totally, absolutely, the holiest of the holy. Holiness is the essence of God's nature and God himself is the supreme revelation of holiness. God's absolute holiness reveals how separate, different, or totally other he is in comparison to all other aspects of the created world. Although the word does not mean sinless,[208] God's holiness means that he is separate from everything that is sinful, utterly removed from the profane world, and glorious in majesty.[209] Wildberger conceives of this holiness as a "dynamic reality, not a static 'quality,'"[210] because holiness is revealed in God's actions and his will. It might be better to say that holiness is part of the inner distinctiveness of God that is revealed in all his activity and that his "glory" is the outward manifestation of the brightness of his majesty and holiness. Thus some Hebrew songs praise God's holiness (Pss 96–99) while others magnify the glory of God (Ps 24:8; 29:3; 97:6). In the New Testament the Apostle John interprets this event as Isaiah seeing the glory of Jesus (John 12:41) because he believed that Jesus and God are one.

But what do the seraphs mean when they say, "the whole earth is full of his glory?" How can the seraphs claim that the sinful and rebellious world where Isaiah was ministering is full of God's glory? Watts alleviates some of the tension when he translates the phrase "the fullness of all the earth (is) his glory," while Wildberger proposes, "His glory shouts out, that which (always) fills the earth."[211] These commentators suggest that the seraphs are referring to the heavenly planets and stars that declare God's glory every night (Ps 8:1,9; 19:1,3; 97:6). R. Knierim claims God's glory is revealed not only in nature but also in his judgment of sin.[212] In contrast to these interpretations Ps 72:19 looks to a future time and offers the prayer, "may the whole earth be filled with his glory." F. Delitzsch uses the information from this cross-reference to

---

[207] GKC §133k discusses the expression of the superlative by repeating the word more than once. This is similar to saying, "It was a big, big, big crowd," which means that it was a very big crowd.

[208] A woman who had separated herself to the service of a pagan god (often as a sacred prostitute) was referred to using this root idea (קְדֵשָׁה) "holy one, sacred one" in Gen 38:21and Hos 4:14, and certainly they were not sinless.

[209] H. Ringgren, *The Prophetic Conception of the Holiness of God* (Uppsala: Lundequistska, 1948), focuses his study of this concept only on prophetic texts, rather than surveying the whole Hebrew canon.

[210] Wildberger, *Isaiah 1–12*, 266, opposes these concepts, but these do not seem to be necessarily contradictory.

[211] Watts, *Isaiah 1–33*, 76. Wildberger, *Isaiah 1–12*, 267, uses Ps 19:1–4 to support his interpretation and says that his glory "can be seen in all the richness of its manifestations throughout the earth. . . . the living and nonliving cosmos, which speaks of the majesty of Yahweh."

[212] R. Knierim, "Vocation of Isaiah," 55–56, calls this a doxology of judgment, but it appears that the Seraphim are simply praising and magnifying God.

conclude that: "The design of all the work of God is that His holiness should become universally manifest . . . that His glory should become the fullness of the whole earth."[213] Since there is no verb in the seraphs' short statements of praise, one needs to be supplied by the translator. NIV and most translations supply "is" but it might be better to assume "will be" based on the Psalms parallel passage. Thus the seraphs are prophetically praising God for what he will do when his holy eschatological kingdom is established and he dwells with his people on earth (cf. 2:2–4; 4:2–6). Then the whole earth will be filled with his glory.

6:4 Finally, the prophet observed that the seraphs' thunderous words of praise were causing the foundations of the doorway (either the threshold or the door pivots) to shake and the room "was being filled"[214] with smoke. The smoke or cloud (Exod 19:16–18; 1 Kgs 8:10–11) is traditionally associated with God's appearance and serves the function of concealing the awesome majesty of God from human eyes. Each of these experiences stresses the infinite distance between the world of man and the realm of God. Even reading about Isaiah's experience strikes wonder and awe into a person's heart; Isaiah is actually standing in the very presence of God Almighty.

(2) The Prophet's Purification (6:5–7)

[5]"**Woe to me!**" **I cried. "I am ruined! For I am a man of unclean lips, and I live among a people of unclean lips, and my eyes have seen the King, the LORD Almighty."**
[6]**Then one of the seraphs flew to me with a live coal in his hand, which he had taken with tongs from the altar.** [7] **With it he touched my mouth and said, "See, this has touched your lips; your guilt is taken away and your sin atoned for."**

6:5 Seeing all this, Isaiah immediately was aware of his own unworthiness (6:5) and the need for atonement (6:6–7). In the presence of God's holiness Isaiah was not struck by his humanity or mortality, but by (a) his own impurity; (b) the uncleanness of the nation of Judah; and (c) the sight of the King, the Lord Almighty. Isaiah could not join the seraphs in praising God until his lips were purified. He cried out, "woe is me" (*'ōy lî*) because he was in the presence of a holy God. Since Isaiah mentions his lips, Wildberger suggests that the second clause (NIV "I am ruined") should be translated "I must be silent."[215] This makes some sense since he has unclean lips, but is not the best

---

[213] Delitzsch, *Isaiah*, 192, recognizes that Isaiah was in a world that was moving toward the goal that would eventually come to the earth as a reality. Kaiser, *Isaiah 1–12*, 127, follows this same approach. Isaiah refers to what will happen at the consummation of the age.

[214] The *niphal* imperfect verb יִמָּלֵא describes continual or incipient action (GKC §107f). These imperfect verbs give the impression that Isaiah is describing the action as it was happening, rather than giving a summary of what had already happened (the NIV "was filled" takes the verb as completed action).

[215] Wildberger, *Isaiah 1–12*, 248–49, draws this meaning from the root דָּמָה, "to be silent," rather than דָּמָה, "to destroy, ruin" (though on 268 he allows the translation "I am lost"). Watts,

choice. Isaiah is not silent in the following verses; he openly confesses his sin and recognizes that the consequences of his sinfulness will be his own destruction. Although "uncleanness" (*tĕmē'*) is often used of ritual unworthiness to come into the presence of God, the later atonement of Isaiah (6:7) removes his guilt and sin, not just his ritual uncleanness. Thus the lips seem to represent the expressions of a sinful heart that is not pure. Psalm 15 provides a detailed list of prerequisites before a person can enter God's presence to worship. Among those requirements is that one must "speak the truth from his heart" (Ps 15:2).

More surprising is Isaiah's reference to the fact that he was living among unclean people in Judah. One might expect Isaiah to recognize his own sinfulness, but Isaiah's pastoral heart cannot separate his own condition from the state of the people he loves. Like parents facing the threat of death, who are just as concerned about saving their children as they are about saving themselves, Isaiah is not totally self-absorbed; he is ministry-absorbed.

The reason for Isaiah's recognition of guilt is simple: he has seen the King, the Lord Almighty (lit. "the LORD of hosts"). The necessary first step before any true confession of sin is having an understanding of the glory and holiness of the Almighty God who rules the heavens and the earth. The transforming power of this vision was not because Isaiah for the first time understood that God was holy, or that he now finally understood that God was an almighty king who ruled the world. These were traditional conceptions of God that were known from earlier covenantal, Levitical, and hymnic texts. The shocking, life changing aspect of this vision was that Isaiah himself experienced a vivid and powerful personal meeting with God that allowed him to have a firsthand glimpse of the supernatural realm. Cultural imagery and religious platitudes about God were suddenly overpowered by the reality of the overwhelming experience of his awesome presence.

6:6–7 Once Isaiah confessed his sinfulness and his need for deliverance ("I am ruined"), God reached out through the instrumentality of a seraph to bring atonement. This was an act of God's grace; Isaiah did nothing to accomplish his atonement. Isaiah offered no sacrifices, did not promise to be a missionary to gain it, and had no power to save himself from certain ruin. To help Isaiah understand that God was removing his guilt, a seraph took a coal from an altar and touched Isaiah's unclean lips. Gray thinks this live coal came from the altar of burnt sacrifices, while Wildberger prefers a coal taken from the altar of incense because it was inside the temple.[216] It is more likely to view these as coals from under the throne of God, the same coals that Ezekiel saw in his second vision (Ezek 10:2). These were not magical coals (neither are people baptized in magical water), rather they figuratively represent the miraculous accomplishment of God's gracious purification and forgiveness.

Isaiah 1–33, 74–75, chooses "I was silent." Blenkinsopp, *Isaiah, 1–39*, 223, is correct in criticizing Wildberger's translation because the perfect verb usually is not translated "must."

[216] Gray, *Isaiah 1–27*, 108, and Wildberger, *Isaiah 1–12*, 269.

When the seraph symbolically touched Isaiah's lips, it announced that God "removed" (*sār*) Isaiah's guilt (an active verb) and that his sin "was atoned" (*tĕkuppār*) by God (a passive verb). God did not want Isaiah to misunderstand what was happening, so a clear explanation was provided to interpret the symbolic action. The removal of guilt indicates that the consequent punishment will not be exacted from Isaiah. This guilt can no longer keep Isaiah from God's presence. The atonement means that God's wrath and the sin that motivated it were satisfied and taken away, making renewed fellowship possible. Sin no longer separated God and Isaiah (cf. 59:1–2). Isaiah's experience illustrates how any believer can identify sin (have a clear vision of the holiness of God), how everyone should respond when sin is recognized (admit it), and how God deals with confessed sin (he removes it). People who presume upon God's mercy because of their supposed goodness will fail to receive his forgiveness, but those who perceive the holiness of God will quickly acknowledge their great guilt and experience his atoning love.

(3) A Hardening Message for a Calloused Audience (6:8–10)

8Then I heard the voice of the Lord saying, "Whom shall I send? And who will go for us?"
And I said, "Here am I. Send me!"
9He said, "Go and tell this people:

> **"'Be ever hearing, but never understanding;**
> **be ever seeing, but never perceiving.'**
> **10Make the heart of this people calloused;**
> **make their ears dull**
> **and close their eyes.**
> **Otherwise they might see with their eyes,**
> **hear with their ears,**
> **understand with their hearts,**
> **and turn and be healed."**

6:8 The imagery explaining Isaiah's commissioning sounds like other passages where the divine heavenly council of God meets together. Micaiah ben Imlah also "saw the LORD sitting on a throne with the hosts of heaven standing around him" (1 Kgs 22:19). God asked who would go, and a spirit came forward and volunteered to deceive and harden Ahab's heart (similar to Isa 6:8–10). Ps 89:6–7; Job 1–2; Zech 1:8–17, and 3:1–10 provide other examples of God talking with angelic beings around his throne. At one point Eliphaz challenged Job by asking if he listened in when the divine council was meeting (Job 15:8). The prophet Jeremiah contrasts himself with the false prophets by asking if any of them received their revelation by listening in on what was happening at a divine council meeting (Jer 23:18,22). In God's question, "Who will go for us?" (6:8), the "us" may represent the members of the divine council, though some see "us" as similar to the royal "we," a plural of majesty,[217] or a hint of the Trinity.[218]

Isaiah did not know the nature of the mission God had designed for his emissary, the length of the responsibility, where this person must go, the content of the message, or the difficulty of the task that must be accomplished. Nevertheless, Isaiah immediately volunteered to go. He did not make excuses like Moses or Jeremiah (Exod 3:11; 4:1,10; Jer 1:6) but gladly volunteered to serve God. From this example one might propose the theological principle that the clarity and reality of a person's vision of the holiness and glory of the majestic King of Kings is directly related to the clarity of a person's sense of call and their willingness to humbly submit and serve God in whatever capacity he desires.

6:9–10   God's charge is that the prophet is to dull the ears and eyes of his audience, those people who have unclean lips (6:5) who are called "this people" (*lāʿām hazzeh*) in 6:9.[219] The syntactical construction of the two imperatives ("hear" and "see") plus the two infinitive absolutes ("hearing" and "seeing") stress the continuation of an activity;[220] thus the people should constantly listen to God's words (including challenges to trust God as in 7:9), even though many will never really comprehend or apply them enough to change their lives. This sounds similar to God's warning to Ezekiel that his audience was rebellious, stubborn, as hard headed as flint, and would not be willing to listen (or obey) to the prophet (Ezek 2:1–3:9). Similarly, God warns Isaiah that there will be no positive results in the hearts of many who will listen to what Isaiah says. Instead of bringing conviction, humility, and confession of sins, Isaiah's divine messages will have the primary effect of hardening people or confirming their hardened unwillingness to respond positively to God. Hearing God's word from Isaiah will make their hearts calloused (lit. "fat" *hašmēn*, 6:10), their ears dull (lit. "heavy" *hakbēd*), and their eyes closed to the truth. Why will this happen? It seems that these people have repeatedly chosen to refuse to follow God; therefore, God has decided that this is the appropriate time to punish these hardened people. For most of them it is past the time of repentance; the time of judgment is at hand. Now is not the time for them to see, understand, and be healed—that opportunity was offered but is now passed. Now judgment will happen.

---

[217] Brueggemann, *Isaiah 1–39*, 60, thinks this first person plural pronoun was the royal plural of government, while Oswalt, *Isaiah 1–39*, 185, prefers a plural of majesty (GKC §124g).

[218] Young, *Isaiah*, I:254, believes this passage suggests that there is a plurality of persons here and foreshadows the doctrine of the Trinity more fully revealed in the New Testament.

[219] Hayes and Irvine, *Isaiah*, 112, think "to this people" (לְעָם הַזֶּה) refers to Ahaz's subjects who prefer an anti-Assyrian policy and have given up on the Davidic house, but Isaiah is concerned with theological willingness to listen to God, not their political party.

[220] See GKC §113r on the use of the infinitive absolute to express the duration of an activity of "hearing" (שָׁמוֹעַ) and "seeing" (רָאוֹ).

Those who think of God as one who offers only grace and mercy may have trouble accepting this image of God. It might appear that this plan contradicts the usual prophetic task of calling people to repentance.[221] A. Davies believes it is rather unethical and unfair that "God is judging Israel for their failure to do something that he himself had made impossible."[222] But this is not the case; God is judging them for their sin. The people had many opportunities to repent in the past when repentance was possible,[223] so God is not unjust in punishing them at this point. It is also inappropriate to claim that God's commands are merely ironic or later reflections back on Isaiah's failed ministry to Ahaz.[224] The interpreter should also not be tempted to solve this dilemma by accepting the translation of the Old Greek (in it the people harden their own hearts), since this is a clear theological modification of a difficult Hebrew text.[225] The Qumran manuscript 1QIsa^a makes more drastic revisions of 6:9–10, transforming the mood of the message by revising it into an encouragement for the people to "Keep on listening, because you may understand. . . . Let them understand in their heart and return and be healed."[226] These changes were attempts to remove the difficulty of God hardening the hearts of the people of Judah, but this is exactly what God did.

The last half of 6:10 is even stronger and clearer in expressing God's plan to punish the nation rather than heal it. The prophet is exhorted with three imperatives to "make fat" (hašmēn) their hearts, "make heavy" (hăkbēd) their ears, and "make closed" (hāša') their eyes. God laments this hardness of hear and unresponsiveness, but this is the path that the nation has chosen.[227] Isaiah's preaching will not prohibit the few repentant people from responding positively (Hezekiah), but for the vast majority it will only lead to further hardening

---

[221] R. P. Carroll, *When Prophecy Failed: Reactions and Responses to Failure in the Old Testament Prophetic Tradition* (London: SCM, 1979), 134.

[222] A. Davies, *Double Standards in Isaiah: Re-evaluating Prophetic Ethics & Divine Justice* (Leiden: Brill, 2000), 143–144, states that, "Yahweh is certainly to blame for a considerable proportion of the misery and misfortune that befalls his people."

[223] If one were to compare this to a parent punishing a disobedient child, one would say that once the stubborn child is over the knee and the hand is swinging, it is too late to offer repentance to avoid punishment. If the child refuses to repent or admit his guilt, it is not unfair or unethical to bring punishment at some point.

[224] Clements, *Isaiah 1–39*, 76–77, takes this position because "the prophets undoubtedly did, very passionately and sincerely, want the people to hear and to understand."

[225] The Old Greek says, "for the heart of this people exalted itself and they heard with heavy ears and they shut their eyes" and does not see this as an act of God, or the purpose of Isaiah's preaching. Evans, *To See and not Perceive*, 61–63, discusses the different perspectives of the various translations of this difficult Hb. text.

[226] Evans, *To See and not Perceive*, 53–56, depends on the work of W. Brownlee, *The Meaning of the Qumran Scrolls for the Bible* (New York: Oxford University Press, 1964), 186–87.

[227] Clements, "Patterns in the Prophetic Canon: Healing the Blind and Lame," in *Canon, Theology, and Old Testament Interpretations: Essays in Honor of B. S. Childs* (ed. G. M. Tucker, D. L. Peterson, R. L. Wilson; Philadelphia: Fortress, 1988), 189–200, traces the themes of seeing and hearing, blindness and deafness from 6:9–10 into other passages (29:9–10,18; 35:5; 42:16–19; 43:8; 44:18).

and opposition to God's ways. At some point these hardened people who refuse
to hear God's words will pass the time of repentance. Eventually God will give
them over to destruction. What is abundantly clear is that God has already
decided to judge his people now. There is no opportunity to reverse the plan of
God once it is set in place. Although this passage does not talk about what the
people did to deserve this severe treatment by God, 2 Kgs 16, 2 Chr 28, and Isa
2–5 give ample evidence of the people's refusal to follow God. Now the fearful
justice of God is about to establish divine justice on earth. Indeed, it is a fearful
thing for any person to be under God's wrath with no hope on judgment day.
Why would anyone choose such a hopeless predicament if they were given the
opportunity to avoid the wrath of God?

(4) Hope in the Midst of Destruction (6:11–13)

¹¹ Then I said, "For how long, O Lord?"
And he answered:

"Until the cities lie ruined
   and without inhabitant,
until the houses are left deserted
   and the fields ruined and ravaged,
¹² until the LORD has sent everyone far away
   and the land is utterly forsaken.
¹³ And though a tenth remains in the land,
   it will again be laid waste.
But as the terebinth and oak
   leave stumps when they are cut down,
   so the holy seed will be the stump in the land."

6:11–12 Isaiah fully understood the severity and finality of God's plan.
He did not object to what God would do, but agonized over what he would
have to do. As the prophet faced his unpleasant future responsibility, he knew
it would be difficult and he wondered how long this hardening process would
take. N. Habel takes the prophet's question "How long?" (*'ad mātay*) as an
objection to what God had asked Isaiah to do, but there is no direct refusal,
no excuse, and no alternative offered.[228] It is better to see this question about
"how long" as Isaiah's cry of dismay and lamentation (cf. similar terminology in other laments in Ps 74:10; 79:5) over the hopeless situation that lies
ahead.[229] Perhaps Isaiah is also wondering if there is any possibility of hope
at some point after God's judgment. This commission is not exactly what Isaiah had wanted to happen to himself or to God's people in Judah, yet from

---

[228] N. Habel, "The Form and Significance of the Call Narratives," *ZAW* 77 (1965): 312,
finds this question about "how long" to be similar to other objections by Moses, Gideon, and
Jeremiah.

[229] S. Blank, "Traces of Prophetic Agony in Isaiah," *HUCA* 27 (1956): 81–83, correctly sees
the agony in Isaiah's cry.

earlier prophecies he knew about God's intention to destroy Judah because of its pride (2:6–4:1), oppression, disrespect for God's deeds, and mockery of God's plans (5:1–30) .

God's answer is twofold. First, he indicates that this hardening responsibility will continue until the land is destroyed (6:11b) and the people are exiled (6:12). The description of the military disaster is painted as a total ruination and abandonment of cities, homes, and fields (cf. 5:26–30; 7:18–25). Using some hyperbole, he says that there will be no inhabitants left in the land; instead, God himself will send them to another land. God does not soften the description of what will happen or blame it on some cruel and vicious pagan army (5:27–30); he himself will send the people out of their land. This is exactly what the covenant curses promised (Deut 28:21,63).

6:13 The concluding verse is often read as a message of hope in the midst of destruction because it refers to a tenth being left and it mentions a holy seed. Because the Old Greek translation does not have the last line about the holy seed, because the Qumran text has a different reading, and because this phrase inserts a positive hope in the midst of a message of doom, Clements considers these hopeful ideas as late post-exilic additions to the text and not part of Isaiah's commissioning.[230] Making this statement more consistent with the negative tone of the passage, G. K. Beale interpreted this verse as a judgment against Judah's idolatry because (a) elsewhere the oak tree is associated with idolatry (1:29–31), (b) the Qumran text has "high place,"[231] and (c) *maṣṣebet* is viewed as a "cultic pillar" instead of a "stump."[232] In light of all this textual and interpretive confusion, the first thing that any interpreter must humbly confess is that the problems are numerous and difficult, without many obvious answers. Admittedly, the textual evidence of various versions points in different directions, but these changes are only a witness to the translators' and scribes' attempts to struggle with the obscurity of the ideas and difficulty of the theological imagery.

---

[230] Clements, *Isaiah 1–39*, 72, 78; but K. Nielsen, *There is Hope for a Tree*, 148, dates this passage to shortly after the fall of Samaria in 721 BC. Blenkinsopp, *Isaiah 1–39*, 226, and Williamson, *The Book Called Isaiah*, 32–35, believe the "holy seed" idea comes from Ezra 9:2 and that it refers to the community that returned from exile. There are two main ways of interpreting the Qumran reading: (a) J. Sawyer, "The Qumran Reading of Isaiah 6:13," *ASTI* 3 (1964): 111–13, translates "How can the holy seed be its stump?" which means, how can the holy seed (people of Qumran) be its stump (the wicked religious leaders in Jerusalem). (b) W. H. Brownlee, "The Text of Isaiah VI 13 in Light of DSIᵃ," *VT* 1 (1951): 296–98, translates the text "(so there shall be) among them the holy seed, its stalk." In both these approaches the main idea of having a holy seed preserved (in Qumran) is included.

[231] This substitutes בָּמוֹת, "high place," for בָּם, "in them."

[232] G. K. Beale, "Isaiah VI 9–13: A Retributive Taunt Against Idolatry," *VT* 41 (1991): 257–78, finds the theme of not seeing and being blinded by idolatry in other Isaiah texts (Isa 42:16–20; 43:8–12; 44:8–20). J. A. Emerton, "The Translation and Interpretation of Isaiah VI. 13," in *Interpreting the Hebrew Bible: Essays in Honor of E. I. Rosenthal* (Cambridge: Cambridge University Press, 1982), 85–118, gives an extensive summary of proposed interpretations of this verse.

It is best to prefer the Masoretic reading (not Qumran or the Old Greek) and conclude that a message of hope is included, though it is a very small ray of hope. It appears that less than a tenth (presumably of people) will survive in the land, for after the forest is cut (the destruction of the land) it will be burned[233] again (6:12–13a). This situation is compared to what happens when trees (the oak and terebinth) are cut down (6:13 b) and only a stump is left in the ground, then the remaining brush is burned. Since the holy seed comes from a stump,[234] this must represent life that still remains in the tree that was cut down. This is mostly a discussion of hopelessness, for the positive promise is only a very small source of hope.[235] The "holy seed" (*zera' qôdeš*) is not specifically identified, but 4:3 does talk about the holy ones in Jerusalem at the end of time.

Hayes and Irvine argue that 6:12–13 uses the analogy of cutting down trees to refer to the destruction of Israel and to the fact that "the stump from which new life will grow is the house of David, the holy seed."[236] But similar pictures of desolation by an enemy also apply to Judah (5:29–30; 7:17–25; 8:6–9) during the coming Syro-Ephraimite War (not just Israel). The text does not refer to the stump as a "dynastic stela," so it is impossible to identify the stump specifically with the dynasty of David. Seitz claims Isaiah refers to "graded judgments" one after the other in this passage, as in the repeated "outstretched hand" texts in 9:7–10:4, and in the historical records where Assyria gradually conquered more and more territory. First they took tribute from Israel (2 Kgs 15:29), next totally defeated Israel (2 Kgs 17), then took tribute from Judah (2 Kgs 16), and finally attacked Judah and took captives (2 Kgs 18–19).[237] If 6:11–13a refers to that gradual and repeated process, then the stump in 13b could be the few that will be left of Judah and the holy seed might refer to the "holy ones" left in Jerusalem in 4:3. J. A. Motyer goes even further out on a limb to connect the holy seed from the stump in 6:13 to the shoot from the stump of Jesse (the Messiah) that is described in 11:1.[238]

THEOLOGICAL IMPLICATIONS.   God is revealed in a marvelous and mysterious way in this passage. His holiness and glory are awesome and beyond human comprehension, yet the veiled perception that is available is clear enough to require each person's response. He is holy, thus all who are in his

---

[233] The Hb. בָּעַר, "burn, destroy," describes how the land will be "laid waste" (NIV).

[234] NIV adds at the end of 6:13 "in the land," which is not in the Hb. text.

[235] If someone told you that your house was destroyed by fire, but that one picture was preserved, it would not sound like a great message of hope. Relative to the great destruction of Judah, this was a very small ray of hope. There is no indication that Isaiah responded to this announcement with any joy.

[236] Hayes and Irvine, *Isaiah*, 113, suggest that the word chosen for stump may represent a memorial stone or a dynastic stela, indicating that the Davidic dynasty will continue.

[237] Seitz, *Isaiah 1–39*, 58–59, believes the remnant theology was an important part of Isaiah's theological message throughout the book.

[238] Motyer, *The Prophecy of Isaiah*, 80, also thinks that the holy seed could have included the remnant mentioned in 4:3; 41:8; 43:5; 45:25; 53:10; 59:21; 65:9,23; 66:22.

presence must be holy, that is, must have their sins forgiven. He is the king of the universe who rules over the hosts of heaven and the people on earth, so he must be honored and served. Those who reject God's holy ways and refuse to serve the king must eventually confess their sins (6:5) or be hardened to sin so that judgment can be accomplished.

From this passage one can conclude that the servants of the Holy King may be called upon to (a) worship God and praise him with the heavenly hosts; (b) repent of daily sins in order to enter the presence of a holy God; (c) serve the king; (d) speak the message God gives regardless of its popularity or severity; (e) cause some to harden themselves for destruction; or (f) give a ray of hope in times of disaster and hopelessness. Although some of Isaiah's responsibilities might not seem very inviting, personal preferences and fear fade into the background when a person has had the privilege of seeing the glory of the Holy King.

The doctrine of hardening people's hearts is a controversial perspective that initially seems almost inappropriate for a preacher or for God. Yet Rom 1:18–32 speaks of a similar situation in which people knew the truth of God's revelation but refused to follow it. As a result "their thinking became futile and their foolish hearts were darkened" (Rom 1:21). Consequently "God gave them over in the sinful desires of their hearts . . . to a depraved mind" (1:24,28). These sinners deserve death and will experience the wrath of God, with no hope of healing because they purposely reject what they knew to be the will of God. Thus hardening comes at the end of God's dealing with rebellious sinners and just before their judgment. God starts out graciously revealing his will and offering repentance, but if people repeatedly reject God, eventually the day of hardening and judgment will come. At times it may be hard for the believer to follow God, but life will be far harder for those who harden their hearts and refuse to listen to God's voice.

In the parable of the sower Jesus repeatedly encourages those with ears to hear to respond positively, yet the parable makes it clear that sometimes the Word of God falls on the soil of hard hearts and it will not sprout or produce fruit (Mk 4). In these cases the parables that Jesus taught only furthered the hardness of the audience and confirmed their rejection of God. His warning to all who are exposed to God's Word is that they should be careful what they hear and accept because more of what you accept will be given (Mk 4:23–25). The path of hardening usually leads to more hardening, so it is wise not to start down that path.

4. The Destruction of Judah (7:1–8:18)

HISTORICAL SETTING.   This long section is set in the reign of Judah's King Ahaz, the son of Jotham and grandson of Uzziah (7:1). The events described in chaps. 7–8 recall circumstances surrounding the Syro-Ephraimite

War (734–732 BC) when the Israelite king Pekah and the Syrian king Rezin attacked Judah. These kings wanted to force Ahaz to join their coalition against the mighty Tiglath-pileser III of Assyria, or to replace Ahaz with a more co-operative ruler if Ahaz would not join them (Tabeel in 7:6).[239] Second Kings 16:1–4 and 2 Chronicles 28:1–4 describe Ahaz as a wicked king who did not follow David's godly ways but led the people of Judah to worship Baal and even sacrificed his own son to a pagan god. Therefore, as punishment for these sins, God brought the Syrians and Israelites against Judah (2 Chr 28:5,9). In this war the Syro-Ephraimite armies killed over 120,000 soldiers from Judah, took around 200,000 people captive, and plundered the land (2 Chr 28:6–8). Nevertheless, the city of Jerusalem was not conquered. Since Ahaz saw no way to win this war, he sent gold and silver from the royal palace and the temple (2 Kgs 16:8–9) to the Assyrian king Tiglath-pileser III and offered to be his vassal if the Assyrians would rescue him from these enemies. The Assyrians came and after attacking Syria, destroyed Damascus (2 Kgs 16:9). Then the Assyrian king made Israel and Judah his vassals. It appears that Isaiah first spoke to Ahaz early in this war when preparations were being made to protect Jerusalem's water resources (7:3), before the king appealed to the Assyrians for help. Isaiah offered Ahaz God's protection for Judah, if the king would put his trust in God. Ahaz "piously" refused to trust God (7:12) and consequently God promised that the Assyrians would actually become Judah's conqueror (Isa 7:17).

If the events in chap. 8 are sequential, they took place more than nine months later in the following year, since Isaiah's wife became pregnant and a new child was born (8:1–4). The reference to the coming of the Assyrian army (8:7) implies that Ahaz had already asked for help from Tiglath-pileser III, since they are now approaching Palestine and will soon flood into Judah as well (8:8).

Although it is common to include chaps. 7–8 as part of Isaiah's memoirs that cover 6:1–9:7,[240] this understanding is not overly convincing when chap. 7 is examined. It describes what Isaiah did in the third person and is not a first person autobiographical account that one would expect in a prophet's memoirs.[241] These two chapters are connected to 5:1–30 because both sections discuss the fall of Judah. For example, 5:26 and 7:18 refer to God whistling for an enemy to come, 5:5–6,10 and 7:23–25 describe the destroyed vineyard of Judah, and 5:16 and 8:13 emphasize the need for the people to treat God as holy. These

---

[239] R. Tomes, "The Reason fo the Syro-Ephraimite War," *JSOT* 59 (1993): 55–71, raises problems with the traditional understanding of this war, but his alternative explanation of local problems is not especially convincing.

[240] Kaiser, *Isaiah 1–12*, 114–117, traces these memoirs (*Denkschrift*) from 6:1–8:18 or 6:1–9:7. These are Isaiah's own account of his life experiences during these difficult days, but some maintain that they come from later redactors (Sweeney, *Isaiah 1–39*, 118, 149–59).

[241] Consult the discussion of this point in H. G. M. Williamson, "The Messianic Texts in Isaiah 1–39," in *King and Messiah in Israel and the Ancient Near East: Proceedings of the Oxford Old testament Seminar* (ed. J. Day; Sheffield: Sheffield Academic Press, 1998), 244–46, or S. A. Irvine, "The Isaianic *Denkschrift:* Reconsidering an Old Hypothesis," *ZAW* 104 (1992): 216–31.

sections contrast the plans of God that people do not respect (5:12,19) with the plans of the people that will fail (8:10). Plus there is a contrast between the enemy army that will not stumble (5:27) and the people of Judah who will stumble (8:14–15). The main differences between these two presentations of the fall of Judah is that 5:1–30 emphasizes Judah's social and religious decay as the main reason for judgment and gives very general information about an unidentified enemy army. In contrast, 7:1–8:18 provides much more specific information about the known enemies who have already attacked Judah (Syria, Israel, and Assyria) and connects the judgment to a specific instance when the king and the people did not trust God or believe his words.

(1) Ahaz's Failure to Trust God Brings Assyria (7:1–25)

INTERPRETING THE IMMANUEL PROPHECY. The interpretation of the Immanuel prophecy in 7:14 has produced an enormous number of books and articles that have proposed quite different interpretations of the sign Isaiah gave to Ahaz. These theories differ in (a) the identification of the woman; (b) the identification of Immanuel; (c) the time when the sign would be fulfilled; (d) the interpretation of curds and honey; (e) the understanding of the time implied for the child to reject the wrong and choose the good; (f) the evaluation of 7:14–17 as positive, negative, or of dual significance; and (g) the use or non-use of 9:1–7 and 11:1–10 as commentaries that explain and expand on the ideas in 7:14–17. A brief review of some of the main proposals will highlight the strengths and weaknesses of each approach.

    a.   *Unknown woman or women who will have sons.* W. McKane believes that 7:14–17 contain both promises of salvation (14,16) as well as threats of judgment (15,17).[242] The "young woman" of 7:14 refers to any woman or all the women who were pregnant at that time. "Emmanuel" will be the name that these women will give to their children because they believe God will deliver Judah from its attackers. Gray has a similar interpretation of 7:14 but does not consider 7:17 as positive as McKane does, but both interpret the "curds and honey" as positive indications of blessing.[243]

Few hold this view because there is no indication that many godly women called their sons "Emmanuel" during the devastating events surrounding the

---

[242] W. McKane, "The Interpretation of Isaiah VII 14–25," *VT* 17 (1976): 208–219, eventually gave up on interpreting 7:15 and concluded that it was a later addition to the text.

[243] Gray, *Isaiah 1–27*, 129–30,137, considers 7:17 a later addition but admits to some difficulty with this positive interpretation. It is also hard to follow his view that a woman will call her child "God is with us" when in reality the removal of Judah's enemies does not take place for at least 2 to 3 years after the birth of the child. This forces him to "*infer* [his italics] that the presence of God with Judah at the time when the child is born will be manifested in the withdrawal just at that time of the Syro-Ephraimitish army." Of course, everything argues against the view that this war ended exactly at the time this child was born.

Syro-Ephramite War and later Assyrian vassalage. The singular noun "young woman" (7:14) and "the lad" (7:15) suggest that the speaker had one woman and one child in mind, though it does not have to be someone standing in the room at the time.[244] It is also unlikely that the splitting of the nations (Judah and Israel), the curds and honey, and the coming of Assyria in 7:16–17 are positive trends. This approach tends to downplay the terrible negative results of Ahaz's refusal to trust God and ignores the fact that "curds and honey" are negative signs in 7:22.

> b.   *A wife of the prophet will bear Maher-shalal-hash-baz.* This hypothesis
> has many more followers because it connects the maiden and child who
> are signs in 7:14 with the prophetess and child in 8:1–4, thus giving the
> prophecy almost immediate relevance to Ahaz and the people of Judah.
> The early Jewish commentators Rashi and Ibn Ezra believed this was
> the best interpretation and many contemporary scholars also connect
> these two births because of common phraseology like "before the boy
> knows" in 7:16 and 8:4, and the birth of a son in 7:14 and 8:3–4.[245] Thus
> the Immanuel sign contains the positive side of God's message because
> it predicts the defeat of Judah's enemies, while the Maher-shalal-hash-
> baz sign depicts the negative side, for it describes God's plan to defeat
> Judah's two enemies and then Judah itself.[246] This approach often finds
> both a negative and a positive side to the signs God gave (7:14–17; 8:1–
> 4) and avoids any direct connection between these promises and the son
> spoken of in 9:1–7.

Nevertheless, other scholars find this view difficult to accept. (a) Isaiah direct-ly connects himself to the other two sons who are signs (7:3; 8:3). Why would he not mention that this would be his own son? (b) How could Isaiah consider his own wife a "maiden, virgin" since she was already married and had one child (it is pure imagination to suggest his first wife died and that this was a new wife)?[247] (c) The "house of David" is being addressed in 7:13–14 so the sign should relate to it, not to Isaiah. (d) The time factors in 7:16 state that the child "knows to choose good and reject evil" (from 12–20 years) but in 8:4 that child "knows how to say 'my father'" (about 2 years), making it highly unlikely

---

[244] GKC §126 indicates the article can refer to a specific class of people like "the righteous," but this does not seem to fit this context.

[245] H. M. Wolf, "A Solution to the Immanuel Prophecy in Isaiah 7:14–8:22," *JBL* 91 (1972): 449–56, proposes that Isaiah married a new bride and the birth of a son in 8:1–4 fulfilled 7:14.

[246] J. T. Willis, "The Meaning of Isaiah 7:14 and Its Application in Matthew 1:23," *RestQ* 21 (1978): 1–17, finds a similar structure in the two passages in chaps. 7 and 8, as well as signs that are related in meaning (7:15–16; 8:3–4), but for him the sign is primarily the birth of the child in 7:14. He concludes that there are two different sons in chaps. 7 and 8, not the same person.

[247] N. K. Gottwald, "Immanuel as the Prophet's Son," *VT* 8 (1958): 36, and Wolf, "A Solution to the Immanuel Prophecy," argue that Isaiah marries a new wife in 8:1–4, suggesting his first wife died. But this is special pleading; the idea is nowhere in the text.

that these two boys are the same person.[248] (e) The later description of Judah as "your land, O Immanuel" fits a royal figure rather than the prophet's son.

   c. *A wife of Ahaz bears Hezekiah.* This popular solution is based on the fact that Isaiah is talking about the future of the royal Davidic dynasty in this oracle (7:2,6,13,17). Isaiah's emphasis on the need to "believe, make firm" (*'āman*) in 7:9 is reminiscent of the Davidic dynastic promises in 2 Sam 7:16 about "establishing, making firm" (*'āman*) the dynasty of those Davidic kings that are faithful to God.[249] In addition, the dynastic promise to David that "the Lord is with you" (2 Sam 7:3) fits the promise of Immanuel "God is with us" (7:14). The "maiden, virgin" would then be a definite young woman in the king's harem, probably Abijah, the mother of Hezekiah (2 Kgs 18:2). The designation of the righteous King Hezekiah as "Immanuel" fits the statement that "God was with him" in 2 Kgs 18:3. Thus the sign (7:14) and its following implications (7:15–17) include both a threat of the end of Ahaz's rule as well as a promise of hope in the future because of the new son Hezekiah.

The main criticism of this solution is that Hezekiah was already born when Isaiah spoke to Ahaz in chap. 7; in fact, most conclude that he was already about nine years old (2 Kgs 16:2; 18:2).[250] It must be admitted that the chronology is not well understood in this period because of some conflicting information; nevertheless, this is an almost insurmountable problem for this interpretation. Consequently, J. H. Walton concludes that this young woman was another woman in the harem and that Immanuel should not be identified with Hezekiah.[251] Yet, it would also seem highly unlikely that the wicked idolatrous King Ahaz would allow one of his wives to name their child "God is with us" at the same time he was refusing to trust God (7:9). This would be highly ironic.

   d. *The birth of Jesus.* The fourth theory is best known from the New Testament identification of Jesus as the one who was born of the virgin Mary in Matthew 1:18–24. This interpretation views the "young girl" as a

---

[248] J. H. Walton, "Isa 7:14: What's in a Name?" *JETS* 30 (1987): 296, rightly notes that the differences in the time factors demonstrate that Immanuel and Maher-Shalal-Hash-Baz cannot be one person, but P. D. Wegner, *An Examination of Kingship and Messianic Expectation in Isaiah 1–35* (Lewistown: Mellon, 1992), 129, hypothesizes that the two boys could possibly be the same if you assume "knowing how to choose right and reject wrong" merely means the elementary ability to distinguish pleasant from harmful things, or good and bad food—an interpretation that seems inappropriate.

[249] J. J. Scullion, "An Approach to the Understanding of Isaiah 7:10–17," *JBL* 87 (1968): 288–289, shows that the setting involves the issue of the continuation of the Davidic line, and Wildberger, *Isaiah 1–12*, 290, supports this Davidic interpretation.

[250] F. L. Moriarty, "The Immanuel Prophecies," *CBQ* 19 (1957): 226–233, concludes that since 701 BC was the 14th year of Hezekiah (2 Kgs 18:13) and Hezekiah was 25 when he began to reign (2 Kgs 18:2), he was born before 740 BC, well before the events in chap. 7 (734 BC–32 BC).

[251] Walton, "Isa 7:14: What's in a Name?" 296, thinks it was a well-known woman in the harem who was pregnant.

virgin and connects "Immanuel" with the messianic ideal described in more detail in 9:1–7 and 11:1–9.[252] Since Ahaz rejects God's offer of a sign, E. E. Hindson claims that the sign was not primarily directed to Ahaz, yet the time factors in 7:15–17 did apply as a sign to him and the rest of the house of David.[253]

The main critique of this Messianic approach is that it appears to read back into the Isaiah passage a meaning that is difficult to develop from the words in 7:14. It almost seems that this interpretive conclusion is controlled by theological beliefs derived from the New Testament rather than exegetical evidence in Isaiah 7. It proposes an interpretation that will be fulfilled 700 years after the time of Ahaz, thus many feel that it has little practical relevance to Ahaz's situation.

e. *Two fulfillments: both a local birth and the future birth of the Messiah.* These interpreters believe there is a need for the prophecy to have meaning for Ahaz, but they cannot deny the authoritative interpretation of the New Testament. Thus, they conclude that the first fulfillment was either Isaiah's son or Ahaz's son, and that Christ is a later complete fulfillment of Isaiah's prophecy.[254] J. T. Willis categorizes these two-fold fulfillment theories according to how they explain the second fulfillment by using the hermeneutical technique of (a) allegory; (b) accommodation; (c) analogy; (d) a primary and secondary meaning; (e) typology; (f) midrash; (g) pesher; or (h) sensus plenior.[255]

This two-fold approach provides an easy way out of a difficult problem because it enables the reader to maintain contemporary relevance for Ahaz as well as the New Testament perspective on the fulfillment of these verses. Yet most of these double fulfillment approaches (except the analogy view) have the fundamental hermeneutical weakness that they suggest two different meanings for 7:14. It seems fundamentally illegitimate to claim that God inspired Isaiah to say things that meant one thing (the meaning he was aware of), and then suggest that these words also mean something different from what Isaiah understood

---

[252] Motyer, *The Prophecy of Isaiah,* 84–87, believes the additional information in 9:1–7 provides a divine identification of who this son will be.

[253] E. E. Hindson, *Isaiah's Immanuel* (Philadelphia: Presbyterian and Reformed, 1978), argues this approach.

[254] W. C. Kaiser, "The Promise of Isaiah 7:14 and the Single Meaning Hermeneutic," *EJ* 6 (1988): 55–70, argues against a double fulfillment approach because the goal of exegesis is to interpret the meaning of the original author. He favors the view that Hezekiah was the "Immanuel" of Isaiah 7 (in spite of the chronological problem) but that a later expansion of the original meaning by "generic extension" allowed the prophecy to apply to later events. This interpretation appears to be very close to finding a double fulfillment, although the "generic extension" meaning may not be understood as the meaning of the original prophecy, thus avoiding the idea of having two meanings. The second extended meaning was added later.

[255] Willis, "Meaning of Isaiah 7:14," 14–17, believes all of these are acceptable theories for one who believes in the inspiration of Scripture.

them to mean (the New Testament meaning). It seems that if a two-fold meaning is proposed, then that two-fold understanding of a verse must be supported from the exegesis of that verse in Isaiah. Otherwise one would be attributing a meaning to a verse (the second meaning) that was not revealed to the prophet and there would be no legitimate authoritative basis for the second meaning. It would be more legitimate to hypothesize that the New Testament authors under divine authority found a "new significance" to the words in an older text through progressive revelation, but in that case the older text would not be prophesying the "new significance" (the birth of Jesus) that the New Testament supplies through a progressive revelation. The New Testament would be adding a "new significance" in the light of later information and new spiritual insights, so that meaning should not be attributed to the Old Testament passage.

In the process of examining the meaning to the words and phrases in the exegesis of 7:10–17 it will become clear which of these approaches makes the most sense. In that context two key hermeneutical issues will be addressed: (a) the issue of interpreting passages based solely on their immediate historical and literary context (7:1–25); and (b) the importance of interpreting this text within its broader literary context (including later revelation after this event in chap. 9), which the prophet knew at the time he put chaps. 6–12 into a written form. Although God may introduce some ideas without a full explanation (7:14), more evidence from later progressive revelations (9:1–7) may clarify what was meant in the earlier passage. In such cases one must honestly admit a limited level of understanding in the first revelation, with greater understanding once the second expanded and clarified revelation was received.

Do Not Fear, Stand Firm in Your Faith (7:1–9)

¹**When Ahaz son of Jotham, the son of Uzziah, was king of Judah, King Rezin of Aram and Pekah son of Remaliah king of Israel marched up to fight against Jerusalem, but they could not overpower it.**

²**Now the house of David was told, "Aram has allied itself with Ephraim"; so the hearts of Ahaz and his people were shaken, as the trees of the forest are shaken by the wind.**

³**Then the LORD said to Isaiah, "Go out, you and your son Shear-Jashub, to meet Ahaz at the end of the aqueduct of the Upper Pool, on the road to the Washerman's Field.** ⁴ **Say to him, 'Be careful, keep calm and don't be afraid. Do not lose heart because of these two smoldering stubs of firewood — because of the fierce anger of Rezin and Aram and of the son of Remaliah.** ⁵ **Aram, Ephraim and Remaliah's son have plotted your ruin, saying,** ⁶ **"Let us invade Judah; let us tear it apart and divide it among ourselves, and make the son of Tabeel king over it."** ⁷ **Yet this is what the Sovereign LORD says:**

" **'It will not take place,**
    it will not happen,
⁸ **for the head of Aram is Damascus,**
    and the head of Damascus is only Rezin.

> Within sixty-five years
>   Ephraim will be too shattered to be a people.
> ⁹ The head of Ephraim is Samaria,
>   and the head of Samaria is only Remaliah's son.
> If you do not stand firm in your faith,
>   you will not stand at all.' "

The new narrative is marked by the end of God's conversation with Isaiah in first person dialogue (6:8–13) and the beginning of a military conflict during the reign of Judah's new king Ahaz (7:1). The paragraph contains:

An introduction to the conflict setting	7:1–2
God's assurance: do not fear	7:3–6
God's challenge: have faith; they will not stand	7:7–9.

7:1–2 The narrative begins by reporting the participants in the Syro-Ephraimite War (734–732 BC), when Syria (Aram) and Israel (Ephraim) joined forces to attack Judah. Based on information in 2 Kgs 15:37, it appears that the initial stages of this political conflict began during Jotham's reign (Ahaz's father). When the young, twenty-year-old Ahaz became king, he continued the policies of non-cooperation with Syria and Israel, so a military conflict was initiated in order to replace Ahaz (7:6). Since Rezin, king of Syria is mentioned first, he probably was the leader who successfully pushed for Israel's assistance and tried to force Judah to join him in opposing Assyria. The Assyrian annals report that the Assyrian army was involved in a campaign of taking control of territory in Philistia in the south and around Tyre and Hamath in the north in the summer of 734 BC,[256] so it was very clear to most of the remaining nations along the Mediterranean Sea that they needed to band together before the next year, or they would each be defeated, one by one, by the much stronger Assyrian army. In 7:1 the narrator summarizes the first segment of this war, then he goes back in 7:2–9 to provide details of what happened in the first few months before the initial attack. The overview simply states that Judah was attacked, but the enemy armies did not overcome the city of Jerusalem immediately.

Supplemental information about these early stages of the war in 2 Chr 28 indicate that God gave Ahaz into the hand of Syria (indicating Syrian leadership in this plan), thereby allowing them to defeat Judah's army in battle and take prisoners (2 Chr 28:5). Israel's army also inflicted heavy casualties on Judah, killing 120,000 troops, the king's son, and the person who was second in command to the king (2 Chr 28:6–8). Nevertheless, the two armies of Syria and Israel were never able[257] to defeat the city of Jerusalem.

---

[256] D. J. Wiseman, "Two Historical Inscriptions from Nimrud," *Iraq* 13 (1951): 21–26, describes the campaign of Tiglath-pileser III against Gaza in 734 BC.

[257] Hb. לֹא יָכֹל, "he was not able," with the singular subject contrasts with the plural subject "they were not able" in 2 Kgs 16:5 (and the Old Greek and 1QIsaᵃ in Isa 7:1), but the singular is the harder reading and it may be pointing to the fact that Rezin could not conquer Jerusalem.

This crisis was a direct threat to the house of David, to "Ahaz and his people" in the royal court. The reference "to the house of David" (*lĕbēt dāwid*) is not a common way of referring to the king in Isaiah (used also in 7:13,17), so special attention is being drawn in this chapter to the problem of the continuation of the Davidic dynasty. A question is raised by these events: Will the promise of a king to sit on the throne of David (2 Sam 7) now be interrupted because of this war, or will the king trust God and continue the Davidic line of rule in Jerusalem? The talk about war became very real one day when a messenger came and told the royal court that Aram (Syria), who was allied[258] with the northern nation of Israel, was invading Judah. Naturally, this caused fear among the leaders of Judah, for they knew that many people would die in the coming war and Judah would be far outnumbered by the two armies coming against them. There would be internal political pressure to join the anti-Assyrian coalition rather than fight it and the leaders of "the house of David" probably would lose power and might lose their lives if they did not win this war. The imagery of shaking like a leaf illustrates the level of fear and panic that pervaded Judah's leaders. It seemed that they were doomed, so their courage was severely undermined.

7:3–6   The solution to Judah's fear was provided by an oracle of salvation that God gave to the prophet Isaiah. The text only reveals what God told Isaiah to do and say. It does not describe what actually happened when Isaiah met the king by this pool of water. The king appears to be occupied with securing one of the city's water supplies in preparation for a long siege. The reader assumes that Isaiah did what God told him to do sometime before the conflict began. There is also no description of Ahaz's immediate response to the good news Isaiah provided the king.

God instructed Isaiah and his son Shear-Jashub to go to the end of the aqueduct that draws water from an upper pool. Likely, this pool was on the northern, higher side of the city, rather than a pool that was south of the Gihon spring in the lower Kidron valley, south of the city of David.[259] On the north side of the city there is relatively flat ground for the officers of the Assyrian army to set up a large encampment for thousands of troops and to prepare their attack on Jerusalem (the Kidron Valley has little room). Although Shear-Jashub was instructed to go with Isaiah, God never addresses the significance of his being there. Thus he appears to play a very minor role in the narrative. His name means "a remnant will return," which probably complemented Isaiah's positive

---

[258] נָחָה meaning "to lead, guide" (BDB, 634–35) does not fit well in this context. The Greek, Syriac, and Targum translations all refer to "making an alliance," which fits the Akkadian root *nāḫu*, "enter into a treaty agreement" (Wildberger, *Isaiah 1–12*, 283). Others draw their interpretation of this verb from נוח, "to rest, settle," implying that Syria now rests in or occupies Israel and is ready to attack Judah (Watts, *Isaiah 1–33*, 86—textual note 2a).

[259] M. Burrows, "The conduit of the Upper Pool," *ZAW* 70 (1958): 221–27, and Watts, *Isaiah 1–33*, 91, 282–84, prefer a location at the Gihon spring since an aqueduct ran from it to a lower pool, but a large army would not likely attack Jerusalem from the bottom of the Kidron Valley.

message of hope.[260] Since the story never reveals how Shear-Jashub's name was employed in this conversation, the most appropriate thing for the interpreter to do is to admit that no one knows how his presence actually assisted in communicating God's message to Ahaz.[261]

The two related messages Isaiah spoke to Ahaz were clear promises of salvation. The first encouragement begins with four imperatives that admonish Ahaz to "be careful, keep calm, don't be afraid, do not lose heart."[262] The four-fold repetition of words of assurance to calm Ahaz's fear indicates that the king needed a lot of encouragement and that God made it very clear to Ahaz that his enemies would not be victorious. Isaiah would try to persuade Ahaz not to act with a normal response of fear, but to rest in God's promises, even though he was a wicked king and did not deserve God's grace. These were words of assurance to calm his fears,[263] but they also challenged Ahaz to respond appropriately by accepting God's knowledge of the future and by trusting in God's deliverance from the two enemy armies that were about to attack Judah. Ahaz needed to "watch himself, guard his ways" (*hiššāmēr*) lest he jump to the wrong conclusion or foolishly make a premature decision. Obviously there was some panic in Jerusalem, so the king probably had advisors suggesting a multitude of possible options. Some were likely promoting a move to join the coalition against Assyria in order to avoid being attacked by Syria and Israel, while others were encouraging him to call on the Assyrians to rescue them. He needed to "be calm" (*hašqēṭ*) and think through the consequences of each choice of action. The greatest danger was to be controlled by fear and discour-

---

[260] Oswalt, *Isaiah 1–39*, 200, places these events after Ahaz has suffered defeat at the hands of Syria and Israel. Thus the boy's name is a message that Judah will have a remnant left. It seems better to understand this whole conversation and the subsequent call for Ahaz to trust God as happening before Judah was attacked, based on v. 2 and the preparations being made in v. 3 (7:1 is a summary of what happened).

[261] His name שְׁאָר יָשׁוּב could mean that (a) only a remnant of the enemy troops (Syria and Israel) will return home, i.e., they will be severely defeated by the Assyrians; (b) a remnant of people in Judah will turn to God, i.e., they will repent; (c) a remnant of Judah's troops will return, i.e., Judah will not be totally defeated but some troops will return victoriously from the battle; or possibly (d) a remnant of the house of David would survive. It seems that his name must have a positive meaning in this context. It would be hermeneutically inappropriate to use this idea in 10:21–22 to justify an interpretation of this passage. Among the many articles on the child's name, G. Hasel, "Linguistic Considerations Regarding the Translation of Shear-Jashub: A Reassessment," *AUSS* 9 (1971): 36–46, evaluates various proposed understandings of the name.

[262] GKC §110a,c suggests that imperatives (הִשָּׁמֵר וְהַשְׁקֵט, "be careful, keep calm") can be used to give an admonition, exhortation, or to "express a distinct assurance." These negative exhortations with the jussive (GKC § 109c-e) express a warning that something should not happen.

[263] These words of encouragement should not be understood as a command to be passive and do nothing as in Exod 14:14, as Kaiser, *Isaiah 1–12*, 141–2, suggests, but as encouragement toward active faith of trusting God and not turning to other nations for help, not trying the patience of God. G. C. I. Wong, "Faith in the Present Form of Isaiah VII 1–17," *VT* 51 (2001): 535–47, connects this call for faith with chaps. 1–5 and suggests that Isaiah was calling Ahaz to faith by demonstrating a concern for justice and righteous acts of kindness, but these chapters come from the time of Uzziah and issues of justice never directly enter the discussion in chap. 7.

agement, so Isaiah exhorts him to "not be afraid" and "not lose heart." The admonition to "not fear" (*ʾal tîrāʾ*) is used elsewhere in war oracles (Deut 20:3; Jer 51:46) while the exhortation "be still and see the salvation of the Lord" was what the Israelites needed to do when they were trapped beside the Reed Sea (Exod 14:14). These exhortations called Ahaz not to look at this war through the perspective of human eyes but from God's perspective. The justification for adopting this astonishing response of confidence in the face of such a severe danger was the divine promise that these two kings were mere smoldering sticks (a metaphor for the angry kings) that cannot do much damage to Ahaz. They wanted to overthrow Ahaz ("your ruin" NIV; lit. "evil," *rāʿâ*, in 7:5) and replace him with Tabeel, but God promised that this plan would not succeed. The quotation of their plans in 7:6 indicates that the enemies were about to begin the war. They were determined to "go up" (*naʿăleh*) to attack Jerusalem, to confidently carry out their goal of spreading terror,[264] in order to break into the city and carry out their own plans.[265]

Surprisingly, Isaiah does not condemn Ahaz for worshiping other gods or any of the other things mentioned in 2 Kgs 16:1–4, nor does he interpret this war as a punishment from God as in 2 Chr 28:5. Isaiah focused on God's instructions for him to guide and direct Ahaz to the place where he could trust God with his kingdom. If he would act out of fear of defeat by stronger military forces, Ahaz would not be trusting in what God promised. If Ahaz would summon needless help from other nations to protect himself from Syria and Israel, then he would not be trusting in God's strength to deliver him. Ahaz needed to believe in God's faithfulness to the house of David and his promise to the king on that throne (2 Sam 7). He had to decide: Is God sovereign enough to protect his people and his plans for the Davidic dynasty, or will God allow these two small states to enact their plans to usurp the Davidic ruler on the throne by installing the imposter Tabeel? No one knows who this man was or where he was from.[266] He may be an associate of Rezin from Syria or a Hebrew from Judah who supported the idea of joining a coalition against Assyria.

---

[264] קוץ is translated "tear it apart" in the NIV based on the Arabic root *qāṣa*, but Wildberger, *Isaiah 1–12*, 284, rejects this suggestion proposed by S. Speier and prefers to stay with the meaning "to bring terror."

[265] The four cohortative verbs "Let us invade Judah; let us tear it apart, let us divide it up, and let us make a king" in 7:6 probably should be taken as expressions of the "firm resolve" of these kings (rather than mutual encouragement as in NIV). Thus it should read "We will invade Judah . . .". IBHS § 34. 5. 1 or GKC § 108b, which refers to a fixed determination for the cohortative.

[266] A. Dearman, "The Son of Tabeel (Isaiah 7. 6)," *Prophets and Paradigms: Essays in Honor of G. M. Tucker* (ed. S. B. Reid; Sheffield: Sheffield Academic Press, 1996), 33–47, traces various suggestions commentators have hypothesized (another name for Rezin, a son of Uzziah by an Aramean princess from the tribe of Tab'el, a nobleman from an influencial Judean family that supported Ahaz's enemies, the Phoenician Tubail who paid tribute to Tiglath-pileser III [from the Iran Stele]). Dearman prefers to identify him with the Phoenician Ithba'al and concludes that the name is a polemical distortion of his real name and now means "good for nothing."

7:7–9 The second part of God's message for Ahaz contains a promise of victory and a challenge to believe God. The "it" which will not take place in 7:7 is usually related to the "evil" plan in v. 5 (translated "ruin" in NIV), but the parallel structures of 7:7–9 suggest that the prophet is predicting

> it will not stand (implying Syria will fall—7:7b)
> > even though the head of Damascus is Rezin (7:8a),
> it will be shattered (implying Ephraim will fall—7:8b)
> > even though the head of Samaria is Remaliah's son (7:9a).

Thus the oracle in 7:7 would be better translated, "It (meaning Syria) will not stand." It will not exist "even though"[267] (7:8) Damascus is the head or most important city of Aram (Syria) and powerful Rezin is the head or most important person (the king) of Damascus. Instead, the plan of God will be accomplished (14:24; 46:10; Prov 19:21). This reading implies that these so called important people who rule as kings of other nations are not that important or significant in God's eyes. Who is Rezin? What power does he have? The indication that the nation of Israel/Ephraim will not exist in 65 years parallels 7:7, yet it provides little immediate assurance to Ahaz (he will not be alive in 65 years). This date should not be seen as an attempt to date when Israel would actually go into exile. That date was 721 BC, only 13 years after 734 BC.[268] Although one cannot put exact dates on when the last Israelites were taken from Palestine, Ezra 4:2 and 2 Kgs 17:24–33 probably refers to Israelites being exiled and foreigners imported into the land about 65 years later during the time of Esarhaddon (ca. 670 BC).

Since neither Syria nor Israel will last, the leaders in the Davidic court (the verbs are plural) must "stand firm," or they too "will not stand" (they will end up like Rezin and Syria). The verb that means 'believe, stand firm"[269] occurs twice in 7:9b.[270] The first instance relates to the need for the Davidic house to stand firm in its faith in God, while the second refers to Judah's political survival. Isaiah's wording of this challenge suggests that Ahaz's response will affect the continuation of God's Davidic promise (2 Sam 7:16) that "your house and your throne will endure (*ʾāman*, "stand firm") forever before me, your throne will be established forever."[271] Thus

---

[267] כִּי is used concessively to mean "though, even though." See GKC §160. NIV interprets this word causally: "for, because."

[268] Gray, *Isaiah 1–27*, 119, and Blenkinsopp, *Isaiah 1–39*, 229, believe the 65 years date was added by a later editor in the time of Esarhaddon to refer to his exile of Hebrews (Ezra 4:2) around 670 BC. They do not think it fits the context and that the dating is too exact.

[269] אָמַן, "stand firm," can depict the solid commitment needed for acts of faith that rely on God's promises as well as God's solid commitment to fulfill his promises for those who trust him.

[270] G. W. Menzies, "To What Does Faith Lead? The Two-stranded Textual Tradition of Isaiah 7. 9b," *JSOT* 80 (1998): 111–28, tries to justify the Old Greek rendition, "If you do not believe, then neither will you understand," based on 6:9–10 and 43:10. But Ahaz's "understanding" is not the problem; rather, it is his ability to put his faith in God to deliver him.

[271] H. G. M. Williamson, *Variations on a Theme: King, Messiah, and Servant of the Lord*

the stakes are not limited merely to Ahaz's selfish desires or fears. Rather his faith will affect one of the key theological foundations of the nation, its divinely approved Davidic future. Isaiah's persuasive call to faith is strengthened by reminding Ahaz about what will be lost if he does not turn from his wicked ways and trust God. At this point Ahaz's intentions are unknown. Will he trust God or follow some other plan? The risks of simply trusting God are tremendous because Judah's armies could not match the power of the combined armies of Syria and Israel. Does trusting God mean that a person is totally passive and does nothing? Does God want people to (a) do the best they can; (b) trust and do the best they can; or (c) just trust and do nothing?

THE SIGN OF IMMANUEL (7:10–17)

[10]Again the LORD spoke to Ahaz, [11]"Ask the LORD your God for a sign, whether in the deepest depths or in the highest heights."
[12]But Ahaz said, "I will not ask; I will not put the LORD to the test."
[13]Then Isaiah said, "Hear now, you house of David! Is it not enough to try the patience of men? Will you try the patience of my God also? [14]Therefore the Lord himself will give you a sign: The virgin will be with child and will give birth to a son, and will call him Immanuel. [15]He will eat curds and honey when he knows enough to reject the wrong and choose the right. [16]But before the boy knows enough to reject the wrong and choose the right, the land of the two kings you dread will be laid waste. [17]The LORD will bring on you and on your people and on the house of your father a time unlike any since Ephraim broke away from Judah — he will bring the king of Assyria."

This paragraph is structured with three parts:

The rejection of a sign	7:10–13
The Immanuel sign	7:14–15
The destruction of Judah	7:16–17

7:10–13   The time lapse from the first messages of assurance (7:1–9) and this second message is unknown, but the interconnectedness of the material requires a relatively short period of time.[272] God offered to provide Ahaz a sign in nature to prove to the king that he was powerful enough to handle Ahaz's enemies. Although some signs are miraculous (the turning back of the sundial in Isa 38:7–8 or Gideon's fleece in Judg 6:36–40), a sign is merely a symbolic

---

(Carlisle, UK: Paternoster, 1998), 107–9, maintains that this act of faith (or rebellion) will have implications on the continuation of the Davidic dynasty.

[272] Hayes and Irvine, *Isaiah*, 130–31, find a level of literary unity between 1–9 and 10–17 ("terrify" in 7:6 and 16), but they put 7:10–17 in the king's palace at a different time. Wildberger, *Isaiah 1–12*, 287, rejects this approach because the sign in 7:1–12 has meaning only in light of the challenge and promise in 7:4–9; therefore, he believes both conversations took place at the same time and place. J. T. Willis, "The Meaning of Isaiah 7:14," 4, note 5, thinks that the second meeting with Ahaz was sometime later, after Ahaz decided to ask the Assyrians to deliver him.

representation of something else and does not have to be miraculous.[273] Circumcision was a memorial sign of the covenant (Gen 17) and a group of twelve stones from the middle of the Jordan in Joshua's day were a memorial sign to remind future generations of God's great deeds on the day the people crossed the Jordan (Josh 4:1–7). A prophetic sign concerning the future was given to Moses when God met him in the burning bush (Exod 3:12). This sign functioned to assure Moses that God would fulfill his promise to bring the Israelites out of Egypt and meet them again at Mt Sinai. The nature of God's offer to move heaven and earth for Ahaz suggests a miraculous event (maybe even the rising of the dead from Sheol), but if Ahaz had asked for God to have a rainbow appear, this would probably not be considered very miraculous. This sign was to offer assurance and confirmation to Ahaz that God is real, powerful, and will act on his behalf. Thus the first sign in 7:11 was not prophetic like the later sign of Immanuel in 7:14.

Ahaz rejected God's offer of a sign based on the biblical injunction that prohibits putting God to the test (Deut 6:16). Although most interpreters tend to deride Ahaz's false piety, there is a real faith issue to struggle with in this offer. Should the king only act when God proves something to him through some "miraculous" fleece (hardly a position of unbridled faith), or should the king step out in faith and reject the quest for a fleece because it borders on manipulating God? The obvious answer is to walk by faith without a sign (Matt 16:4; Mk 8:12; Lk 11:29), but in this case it is not a question of whether Ahaz should ask for a sign, for God is offering a sign. Ahaz's rejection of God and what God might have to tell him is an indication of little faith in God. He is not really interested in trusting God, for he probably has already developed his own plan to put his trust in Assyria to deliver him from Syria and Israel.

Isaiah's response is one of condemnation for the "House of David," the royal court that was led by Ahaz (7:13,17). Their response frustrated the patience of Isaiah and God. When patience runs out and one is wearied by useless excuses and indecision, usually something negative will happen next. Control of the situation is usually removed from the person causing the frustration and someone else sets a new direction. It this case God seems to give up on the present Davidic dynasty run by Ahaz and looks forward to another solution to the problem in 7:14–17.

7:14–15 Isaiah describes God's future plans "for you" (plural *lākem*), the Davidic dynasty. This involves a sign of a child in 7:14–15 and a prediction of the end of Ahaz's control of Judah in 7:16–17. Isaiah shows how Ahaz's negative response to God's positive promise of 7:4,9 will impact the Davidic dynasty, which would rather trust Assyria than God (Ahaz failed to believe and stand firm as required in 7:9). The name of the promised new son is Immanuel

---

[273] J. Walton, "Isa 7:14: What's in a Name?" 293–295, does not believe the Immanuel sign was necessarily miraculous because he thinks that the name of the child "Immanuel" is the sign (parallel to the sign factor in the son in 7:3 and 8:3 (in 8:18 the children are called signs).

(*'immānû 'ēl*) "God is with us." The name of this son suggests a general hope for an heir who will be a godly Davidic ruler to replace Ahaz at some point in the future, but the name Immanuel is not applied to any specific situation until a later message (8:8,10; 9:1–7). The child's age and moral abilities are mentioned in 7:15–16, but otherwise his importance is largely ignored in the following verses. Thus the contextual surrounding of 7:14 does not give very much information that would help the reader understand exactly who this mysterious son will be.

The identity of the woman having the child is unknown. The author uses the term *'almâ*, "young woman," a root that does not specifically address the issue of virginity in young women, or "young men" (1 Sam 17:56; 22:20), or as an abstract concept "youth" (Job 20:11; 33:25; Ps 89:45; Isa 54:4). G. J. Wenham's study of *bětûlâ* suggests that a parallel Hebrew term also primarily means "young woman," not "virgin,"[274] so youthfulness (which implies virginity) is the focus of both terms. The definite article on "the young woman" could signify that a definite and specific woman was in mind, but Hebrew can even use the article for a definite unidentified person.[275] The enigmatic nature of this sign, the avoidance of naming this woman, and the absence of modifiers like "your wife, your young woman, this young woman" argues against this being either Ahaz's or Isaiah's wife. Suggestions that identify this as a new wife of Isaiah or Ahaz are just guesses that try to pinpoint a specific woman based on interpreting the definite article "the/this," yet the text refuses to identify her. All one knows is that she is young, will become pregnant,[276] and will name her child Immanuel, "God is with us." In light of these facts it appears that his name is the significant part of this sign, not the unknown young woman becoming pregnant. Isaiah does not say what this child will do or why his mother will call him Immanuel, but God's earlier repeated promises to "be with" the dynastic line of David (2 Sam 7:9; 1 Kgs 1:37; 11:38; Ps 89:22,25) caused Wildberger to conclude that this son would be a king in the line of David.[277]

---

[274] G. J. Wenham, "*bětûlāh* "A Girl of Marriageable Age," *VT* 22 (1972): 326–47, looks at Akkadian, Ugaritic, and Hb. usage of this term. The modifying clause "who has never known a man" in Gen 24:16; Lev 21:1–3; Judg 21:12 suggests that the word itself did not carry the meaning of virgin, plus Joel 1:8 probably uses בְּתוּלָה of a married woman.

[275] GKC §126 classifies the uses of the article ה as (a) demonstrative force meaning "this," (b) to identify a specific person or thing meaning "the," (c) to denote things that are unique like "the" high priest, (d) as a vocative meaning "O Joshua," (e) to indicate a well known class of people or things like "the enemy," (f) to express an abstract idea like "the blindness," (g) to denote a single person or thing that is unknown but present in the mind of the speaker (usually translated in English as indefinite). This last usage certainly could apply in 7:14 to the young woman.

[276] הָרָה is probably a feminine adjective. It is interpreted by Wildberger, *Isaiah 1–12*, 286, as a feminine singular participle, which is used as the verb in this clause (GKC §116f,m) with its temporal aspect determined from context (GKC § 116d, n-p). Wildberger prefers a present tense interpretation, though after הִנֵּה, "behold," in 7:14, the participle often has a future significance.

[277] Wildberger, *Isaiah 1–12*, 311–312, concludes that this refers to Ahaz's son Hezekiah, but Hezekiah was already nine years old at this time.

If so, this will be a godly king who will bring God's blessing on the nation, so he is primarily a sign of hope to the godly people in Judah. Indirectly, this new king is also a threat to replace the wicked and unbelieving Davidic administration of Ahaz because Ahaz refused to act in faith (7:9).[278]

In 7:15 Isaiah informs Ahaz about this child's diet and moral behavior. Although eating curds and honey can have a positive sense of much good food (Gen 18:8; Deut 32:13–14; Judg 5:25; Joel 3:18), Isaiah uses these terms to describe a return to a nomadic lifestyle, rather than a settled farming context. In light of the negative use of this same terminology in 7:21–22, it is better to interpret curds and honey in 7:15 as a sign that this son will live in a time of deprivation (Judah was dependant on a strong agricultural economy). The reason for this negative setting is not explained immediately, but the later reference to a similar situation in 7:21–22 suggests that it will be the result of a military conquest of Judah, specifically the invasion of the Assyrians (7:17b). Instead of focusing on the reason for the nation's devastated condition (Ahaz's lack of trust in God in 7:9), 7:15 emphasizes the moral development of the young son. This son will live in a difficult era (very different from the luxury of Ahaz) "in order that/so that"[279] (not "when" as in NIV) he will make good and just decisions (in contrast to the evil decisions of the dynasty of Ahaz) and reject evil choices.[280] This implies that this godly son will reject Ahaz's wicked and faithless life and rule the nation following the ideal of justice. This information about the child Immanuel in 7:14–15 provides hope for the future of the Davidic dynasty but no hope for Ahaz.

7:16–17	These verses are full of difficulties and confusing information. Most translations (including NIV) interpret 7:16 as a promise that the wicked king Ahaz will be delivered because the territory of the Syrian and Israelite kings will be destroyed. Thus 7:16 reaffirms and expands the promises in 7:4,7–9. This interpretation seems like an inappropriate positive promise for King Ahaz, who did not believe God, and there are several textual and interpretive difficulties:[281] (a) the "land, ground" is singular and the two kings of Syria and Israel ruled two different lands so it is hard to view this "ground" as a reference to their two countries; (b) the text does not use *ʾereṣ*, the usual term for "country, land" but *ʾădāmâ*, "ground, soil, tilled earth," so the term probably

---

[278] H. G. M. Williamson, "The Messianic Texts," 238–270, holds that Immanuel "represents a radical discontinuity with the present heirs of the Davidic family, who have collectively failed to live up to the hopes which might be reasonably be expected of them."

[279] The ל plus infinitive construct does not introduce a temporal clause but a purpose or result clause (GKC §114f). To be temporal the infinitive would need to have ב, "when," before it.

[280] מָאוֹס, "reject," and וּבָהוֹר, "choose," are infinitive absolutes that function as the object of the verb (GKC §113d,f) to describe the attendant circumstances of the main verb. Thus "the lad will know about choosing and refusing."

[281] G. Rice, "The Interpretation of Isaiah 7:15–17," *JBL* 96 (1977): 363–69, and W. McKane, "Interpretation of Isaiah VII 14–25," 208–19, regarded 7:16 as a secondary addition. In contrast, Wildberger, *Isaiah 1–12*, 287–88, believes 7:15 is a foreign element that was added later.

does not refer to these two "countries;" (c) the relative clause at the end of 7:16 is awkward (lit. "the ground, which you tore apart, because of their two kings, will be forsaken") with most translations paraphrasing or omitting portions (many omit *mippnē*, "because," in the phrase "because of their two kings"); (d) there is no contrasting connector at the beginning of 7:17 (the Old Greek added "but" to solve this problem) to show a transition from a positive statement in 16 to a negative prophecy in 17, so one must wonder and question if a contrast was ever intended to exist between vv. 16 and 17; (e) it is not clear why Isaiah would refer to "the young man" in 7:16 with a different term than "son" or "Immanuel" (7:14) if he was referring to the same person (or was he pointing to someone different?); (f) if 7:16 refers to the fall of the two kings why did Isaiah need to give a third version of this same prophecy in 8:1–4 (7:2–9 was the first), or does it refer to something else?; and (g) it is odd that 7:16 repeats half of v. 15 (about eating curds and honey).

The solutions to these complicated problems are not obvious, but the problems should not be ignored as if they do not exist. One could suggest that it would be more proper to have the "ground, soil" (singular *ʾădāmâ*) refer to the soil of Judah, rather than the two "countries" (usually described by using the word *ʾereṣ*) of the two foreign kings. In addition, in light of the negative perception of Ahaz throughout this section, one could make Ahaz the subject of "you will be abandoned on the ground" (the verb could be a third feminine referring to the land as subject or second masculine singular referring to Ahaz). The relative clause would support this conclusion because one might expect God to abandon evil Ahaz if "the ground, which you tore apart (this root is used in 7:5) because of (*mippnē*) their two kings" means that Judah was torn apart by war because of the king's lack of faith (7:9). With this translation 7:16 does not repeat the news in 8:1–4 and naturally fits in with the negative tone of 7:17 (both refer to the judgment of Ahaz) so there is no need for a contrasting conjunction between 16 and 17. This interpretation of 7:16 predicts that God would abandon Ahaz before "the young lad" (possibly Shear-Jashub from 7:3, since he does not refer to this "young lad" as a "son" or "Immanuel")[282] becomes an adult who knows how to choose good and reject evil. This date (probably less than twenty years based on Num 14:29; Deut 1:39) shows that Ahaz's days were numbered. If one accepts this understanding of 7:16, it could be translated: "For before the young boy (Shear-Jashub) knows how to refuse evil and choose good (within 15 years), you (Ahaz) will be abandoned on the soil (in Judah), which you tore up because of these two kings (Rezin and Pekah)."

---

[282] Isaiah could to be referring to Immanuel in 7:16, but it is very odd that he refers to this person with the word הַנַּעַר, "the young lad," instead of making it explicit by using בֵּן, "son" or עִמָּנוּ אֵל, "Immanuel," from 7:14. Since the "son" was not yet born and a "young man," it is possible that the young man in 7:16 was Shear-Jashub who was with Isaiah (7:3). If this is the case, the repetition of "eating curds and honey" would be explained by the need to draw an analogy between the two boys (Immanuel in 14 and Shear-Jashub in 16).

Consistent with this conclusion, 7:17 extends this judgment to the whole Davidic dynasty in power. It compares the severity of what will happen in the future to the terrible division of the Northern and Southern kingdoms after the death of Solomon (1 Kgs 12) and identifies the king of Assyria as the instrument God will use to deliver this severe judgment on the nation of Judah.

The limited amount of information about the virgin and Immanuel can be interpreted from two or three perspectives: (a) the context of 7:1–17 alone; (b) the broader literary context found in chaps. 2–12; and (c) in light of the complete revelation in Scripture. As God progressively revealed truth, greater clarity about the future became known. The original meaning of the prophecy in 7:1–17 must coincide with the level of specificity provided in its own context and should not be based on unknown information that was revealed at some point much later. Since 7:1–17 lacks many of the strong messianic signals found in other passages (cf. 9:1–7), it must first be interpreted solely on the general knowledge provided in these verses.

This passage reveals that a Davidic dynastic replacement for Ahaz would come at some point after a time of defeat by the Assyrians and that "Immanuel" would be a godly ruler who would make just choices. The possibility remains that this new ruler could be the Messiah or some other godly, righteous king, but this text alone does not give clear irrefutable evidence that points exclusively to a messianic ruler (Gen 12:1–3 refers to the "seed," but also is not specific). Thus, this incipient messianic text needs greater clarification concerning the significance of this son named Immanuel. The word Immanuel occurs again in 8:8 and 10. In addition, 9:1–7 refers to a coming son who will be a future Davidic messianic ruler who will reign forever. These later passages serve as commentaries that clarify the identity of Immanuel through progressive revelation. Thus what was not completely clear in chap. 7 becomes very clear to Isaiah by chap. 9. Later prophetic and New Testament texts further the interpreter's insight into these themes by progressively uncovering more and more information about the person and work of the Messiah.

JUDGMENT OF THE LAND (7:18–25)

[18]In that day the Lord will whistle for flies from the distant streams of Egypt and for bees from the land of Assyria. [19]They will all come and settle in the steep ravines and in the crevices in the rocks, on all the thornbushes and at all the water holes. [20]In that day the Lord will use a razor hired from beyond the River — the king of Assyria — to shave your head and the hair of your legs, and to take off your beards also. [21]In that day, a man will keep alive a young cow and two goats. [22]And because of the abundance of the milk they give, he will have curds to eat. All who remain in the land will eat curds and honey. [23]In that day, in every place where there were a thousand vines worth a thousand silver shekels, there will be only briers and thorns. [24]Men will go there with bow and arrow, for the land will be covered with briers and thorns. [25]As for all the hills once cultivated by the hoe, you

**will no longer go there for fear of the briers and thorns; they will become places
where cattle are turned loose and where sheep run.**

These oracles are connected to 7:1–17 by common themes in 7:15 and
22 ("will eat curds and honey"), in addition to a reference to the Assyrian in
7:17 and 18. This section shares much in common with the description of the
destruction of Judah in chap. 5. The four "in that day" oracles in 7:18–25 give
more specific information about the devastation of Judah than what is found
in 5:26–30, but now the name of the enemy army is known. These oracles
predict that:

Assyria and Egypt will infiltrate the land	7:18–19
Assyria will shave the land	7:20
People will eat nomadic food	7:21–22
Agriculture will end	7:23–25

In Isaiah's earlier description of the destruction of Judah in 5:26–30, the prophet focused on the overwhelming strength of an unknown attacking army, but
here Isaiah underscores the damage the known enemy (Assyria) will do to
the land (the military defeat of Judah is assumed). The first two "in that day"
oracles describe what God will do to the people and land of Judah, while the
last two oracles indicate the impact God's action will have on the people still
living in the land.

7:18–19 At some undefined point in the future God will call a large number of foreigners into the land. This gathering is compared to God "whistling"
(*yišrôq* cf. 5:26) for swarms of flies and bees, a metaphor that pictures a large
swarm of enemy troops occupying the land. It is not clear why Isaiah chose
these exact symbols (cf. 18:1),[283] since these insects are not primary national
symbols for either Egypt or Assyria. Possibly he was just interested in emphasizing the overwhelming picture of millions of swarming insects that make life
unbearable. Although Egypt was weak and not an immediate threat to Judah at
that point, years later (609–605 BC) the Egyptians did defeat Josiah and ruled
the nation for a short time (2 Chr 35:20–36:4).[284]

7:20 The second oracle pictures a hired barber (the Assyrians) humiliating their Hebrew captives by shaving all their hair off.[285] It is unclear if this
imagery should be understood literally describing the treatment of war prisoners, or if the imagery reflects a general metaphor of the shaving of the land.
In either case God will use these foreigners (they lived on the other side of

---

[283] Deut 1:44 also compares Israel's enemies to a swarm of bees.

[284] Less likely is the suggestion by Hayes and Irvine, *Isaiah*, 139, that Isaiah may be referring
to Piye (730–716 BC), an Ethiopian ruler over Egypt who fought the Assyrians in Judah around
720 BC.

[285] Several commentators interpret "the hair of their legs" as a euphemism for genital hair.
The Ammonites, who suspected David of treachery, humiliated the group of men David sent to the
funeral of the Ammonite king by shaving their hair off (2 Sam 10:1–5).

the Euphrates River) to accomplish his will against his own sinful people (cf. 10:5–6,15), though Ahaz thought he was hiring the Assyrians to deliver him from Syria and Israel.

7:21–25 The third and fourth oracles focus on the devastation of the land and how the few remaining people will survive. 7:21–22 is not a positive salvation oracle, even though v. 22 refers to an abundance of nomadic food.[286] Notice that the man in 7:21 has only one calf and two goats, which make a very small herd. The indication that everyone left in the land must live on nomadic food suggests that grain farming and cities will not exist at that time. Oracle four (7:23–25) is consistent with this interpretation for it also pictures the people as hunters and gatherers instead of farmers using the hoe. The land will no longer have nice cultivated fields (cf. 5:5–6) or expensive vineyards, but it will have plenty of thorns and briers (exactly like God's vineyard in 5:6) and "trampled" ground (*mirmas*: NIV has "run"). Isaiah seems to identify the destruction of God's vineyard in 5:1–7 with the destruction God will bring through the Assyrians in 7:18–25.

THEOLOGICAL IMPLICATIONS. God's message to Ahaz teaches that people need not fear their enemies if God has promised salvation. They need to be careful and calm, standing firm in their faith in God because failure to trust God will lead to their own demise (7:3). This incident in the life of Ahaz also warns the reader not to test the patience of God by repeatedly refusing his assistance or ruling out the possibility that he can do miraculous things (7:10–12). God's punishment for acting without faith is personal devastation, national disgrace, the interruption of the Davidic promise, and suffering under God's curse on the land (7:18–25). In spite of all the negative theological implications of Ahaz's action, God did not totally give up on his plans for the Davidic dynasty. Out of the midst of suffering, another ruler unlike Ahaz will arise. Immanuel will choose the good and reject the evil. This unknown son, the child of a young woman, is a future Davidic figure of hope. Isaiah may have had messianic concepts in the back of his mind at the time, but these are not extensively identified or developed in these verses. Nevertheless, the understanding of the implications of Immanuel's role is expanded when this son is viewed in the light of God's progressive revelation about a Davidic son in 9:1–7. Certainly when Isaiah reflected back on these words from a later perspective, he could more clearly identify Immanuel with the righteous son who would rule over the house of David (9:1–7). What is amazing is how faithful Isaiah was to the original limited amount of information he knew in Isaiah 7. Rather than loading up the revelation of chap. 7 with new information learned in Isaiah 9, Isaiah faithfully recorded the general prophecy of Immanuel with all its ambiguities and unanswered questions. Each reader must follow the same pattern and avoid reading into

---

[286] Gray, *Isaiah 1–27*, 139, and W. McKane, "Interpretation of Isaiah VII 14–25," 216, view this abundance of food as a positive prophecy.

Isaiah 7 things that were later revealed in chap. 9. The goal of interpreting Isaiah 7 is to understand what God's message meant to people at that time in that setting.

In light of an expanded understanding of Isaiah 7 (aided by 9:1–7), it is not surprising that the New Testament writers saw Jesus as the Messiah (Matt 1:23). In light of the expanded explanation of this son as the Messiah in 9:1–7, there is no need to suggest that 7:14–15 should be understood as double fulfillment or typology. Isaiah 7:14–15 is a general prophecy about a future just ruler with whom God would dwell. This ruler was not Ahaz's son or Isaiah's son, but an unknown future king specifically identified in 9:1–7 in clear messianic terms. Isaiah 7:16–25 and 8:8–10 connect themes from the Immanuel prophecy to demonstrate that the unbelieving Ahaz and his dynasty will suffer, so the overall prophecy in chap. 7 had both present (chaps. 7–8) and future significance (9:1–7).[287]

(2) Fearing God, not Military Might (8:1–18)

LITERARY SETTING.   Chapters 7–8 deal with the broad theme of the destruction of Judah more specifically than the general descriptions of destruction in chap. 5. Verbal affinities with the destruction themes in chap. 5 include (a) the enemy will not stumble in 5:27 but Judah will in 8:14–15; (b) the people of Judah will be famished and thirsty in 5:13 and 8:21; (c) the people reject God and his word in 5:24 and 8:6,12–13,19; (d) the result of rejection will be darkness in 5:30 and 8:22; (e) God will show himself holy in 5:16 and 8:13; (f) the people do not fear God in 5:12,19,25 and 8:13; (g) Judah will suffer destruction in 5:6,13,25 and 8:8; and (h) both chapters talk about plans (5:19; 8:10).

Chapter 8 begins a new message (separate from chap. 7), though it is closely related to chap. 7, because both mention a child who will be a sign of God's plans for the future and both talk about the consequences of the Syro-Ephraimite War. Verbal affinities strengthen this connection between chaps. 7 and 8: (a) the repetition of "before he knows" in 7:16 and 8:4; (b) references to Immanuel in 7:14 and 8:8,10; (c) the people being in fear in 7:2,4; 8:12; (d) a woman

---

[287] Kaiser, "Promise of Isaiah 7:14," 55–70, correctly considers this prophecy a "generic prediction" with a single meaning, but then surprisingly suggests that Hezekiah was the near fulfillment of Isaiah 7 (a conclusion that raises tension with his "generic" and his single meaning approach). Childs, *Isaiah*, 66–69, believes 7:14 is "mysterious, even vague, and indeterminate" and must be interpreted in light of the clarifications found in chaps. 8 and 9. He concludes that "there are many clear indications that it was understood messianically by the tradents of the Isaianic tradition, and shaped in such a way so as to both clarify and expand the messianic hope." Seitz, *Isaiah 1–39*, 74, maintains: "Whatever one may think of the Immanuel child in chapter 7–8 (prophet's son; royal figure; symbol; Hezekiah), one's reading of the Immanuel passage is now affected by the larger context, specifically the royal oracle in 9:2–7. . . . The child would be called 'God with us' and 'he is named Wonderful Counselor, Mighty God.' . . . It is virtually impossible to read the Immanuel passage in the light of 9:2–7 and not catch the clear connections."

becomes pregnant and has a son in 7:14 and 8:3; and (e) a common setting involving Damascus, Samaria, and the king of Assyria (7:1,7–9,16–17; 8:4–7).

Having finished his conversation with Ahaz in chap. 7, Isaiah now addresses the people on the street concerning their military situation through his birth announcement in 8:1–4 (they were not there when Isaiah gave a sign to Ahaz) and by offering information about God's plan for the nations (8:5–10). Then Isaiah turns to encourage his followers by contrasting what God has told them to believe with what other people in Judah believe (8:11–22). Since Ahaz has already hardened his heart, Isaiah's rhetorical strategy changes to warning the population of Judah (and especially his own followers) to fear God and follow his instructions, rather than listening to political analysts who speak about conspiracies (8:12). Religious leaders who prognosticate on political events based on pagan cultic practices should be avoided (8:19–20); instead, people should look to what God has said. This chapter implies that Ahaz has already called on the Assyrians to rescue him from the attacks by Syria and Israel.

STRUCTURE. The end of this literary unit is not clearly defined and a break could be placed after 8:15, 8:18 or 8:22. Sweeney argues that this unit ends at 8:15 because 8:1–15 use a first person autobiographical style structured around three introductory "the LORD spoke/said to me" oracles (8:1,5,11). 8:16 begins with an imperative exhortation that breaks the pattern of 8:1–15 and the content of 8:16–18 is connected to 8:19–22 ("when men tell you," that is, the disciples of 8:16).[288] Yet the oracle in 8:9–10 contains a series of imperatives, and 8:11–22 is concerned with whether Isaiah and his followers are going to trust God and his teachings, so Sweeney's structural division is not totally convincing. Thus it seems best to extend this unit through 8:22. In spite of the diversity of topics and audiences within these oracles, unbelief is consistently cited as the reason for Judah's destruction.

The unit can be divided into several paragraphs based on the topics discussed, the introductory clause "the LORD spoke to me," and the internal consistency within each paragraph. These paragraphs discuss:

The birth of Maher-shalal-hash-baz	8:1–4
The coming Assyrian flood	8:5–10
Fear God, not human armies	8:11–15
Following God's instructions	8:16–22.

THE BIRTH OF MAHER-SHALAL-HASH-BAZ (8:1–4)

[1]The LORD said to me, "Take a large scroll and write on it with an ordinary pen: Maher-shalal-hash-baz. [2]And I will call in Uriah the priest and Zechariah son of Jeberekiah as reliable witnesses for me."

---

[288] Sweeney, *Isaiah 1–39*, 166–67,176–77, makes 8:16–9:6 a unit, but the royal oracle about a son to rule on the throne of David in 9:1–7 seems to be a separate unit. Although he puts 8:16–18 with the following material, he claims 8:16–18 was originally the conclusion to the Isaiah Memoirs.

³Then I went to the prophetess, and she conceived and gave birth to a son. And the LORD said to me, "Name him Maher-Shalal-Hash-Baz. ⁴Before the boy knows how to say 'My father' or 'My mother,' the wealth of Damascus and the plunder of Samaria will be carried off by the king of Assyria."

This brief text describes a prophetic sign act and is divided into two parts:

Witnesses see Isaiah's writing   8:1–2
The birth and naming of the son   8:3–4

8:1–2 The Lord instructs Isaiah to write a message on a large writing surface (not a "scroll" as in NIV), presumably so that many people can plainly see it. In 3:23 this large surface is a "mirror,"[289] but here it must refer to a polished surface of stone or metal that will clearly reveal the message that Isaiah will write. He is to write the words "to/concerning[290] Mahal-shalal-hash-baz" with an "ordinary pen,"[291] and have his writing witnessed by two people.[292] The two witnesses, as required by Hebrew law (Deut 17:6; 19:15), include Uriah, one of Ahaz's trusted priests (2 Kgs 16:10), and Zechariah, the father of Ahaz's wife Abijah (2 Kgs18:2). These men were probably not supporters of Isaiah. Rather they are most likely hostile witnesses that even Isaiah's enemies would believe. These men could testify to the people in Judah exactly what Isaiah wrote and when he wrote it. The text does not say if Isaiah explained what these words meant to his witnesses. In fact, at this point there is no reason to believe that Isaiah knew that this would be the name of a new son. The text does not indicate what was to be done with this large tablet over the next several months. Apparently God wanted Isaiah to be able to return to these witnesses, after the child was born and given this name, and ask them to count back the days and witness that Isaiah wrote this approximately nine months earlier.

---

[289] גִּלָּיוֹן is from the root גָּלָה, "to reveal," so "mirror" (3:28) is a fitting translation for a metal object that reveals how you look. The Aramaic Targum translates this as a "tablet," while the Old Greek speaks of "papyrus," which was the common material used to write a message in Egypt.

[290] The Hb. לְ may show possession (GKC §119u) or just mean that this message is about the person named.

[291] Literally, the Hb. reads "stylus of man," which might mean a "common script" (Gray, *Isaiah 1–27*, 143) so that it can be easily read (see Hab 2:2). F. Talmage, "חרט אנושׁ in Isaiah 8:1," *HTR* 60 (1967): 465–68, uses the Akkadian root *enēšu*, "to be weak," to conclude that this was a weak or soft pen, while Wildberger, *Isaiah 1–12*, 330,332, has the unlikely suggestion of a "disaster stylus," meaning that it gives a disastrous message.

[292] וְאָעִידָה, lit. "and I will cause to witness" or "I will call" (NIV), suggests that God called these witnesses, but the Old Greek has "appoint" and the Targum "I appointed witnesses." Wildberger, *Isaiah 1–12*, 332, suggest the minor change of making the verb a consecutive imperfect and reads "and I appointed," or one could follow 1QIsaᵃ and have an imperative "call." This latter approach would result in the translation of 8:2 "Call for me (for God) two witnesses . . ." Kaiser, *Isaiah 1–12*, 179, keeps the first person, but translates the verb "I took as witnesses," but an imperfect more frequently refers to things that will happen in the future. H. Wolf, " A Solution to the Immanuel Prophecy in Isaiah 7:14–8:22," *JBL* 91 (1972): 450–56, suggests the witnesses are there because this is Isaiah's marriage ceremony to his new wife, but this reads into the text far more than what is present.

8:3–4 The second half of this paragraph describes the conception, birth, and naming of Isaiah's son. It is possible that the "prophetess" simply refers to the prophet's wife, though there are no other examples of this in Scripture. It is possible that Isaiah's wife had a prophetic gift,[293] but this gift is not affirmed elsewhere. After conceiving and giving birth to this child, God told Isaiah to name this son Maher-Shalal-Hash-Baz, which signifies that both the spoils (*šālal*) of Samaria (the capitol of Israel) and Damascus (the capitol of Syria) will be plundered by the king of Assyria (8:4). Literally, the Hebrew name contains two parallel imperative verbs ("quick; swift") plus two parallel words for booty ("spoil; plunder"), thus it says the same thing twice. It could be translated "hurry spoil, be swift plunder,"[294] two cryptic exhortations that expect the defeat of some nation in the near future. The interpretation of this name in 8:4 fits this translation and explains who will be plundered (Samaria and Damascus) and who will defeat these nations (Assyria). No exact date is given for the fulfillment of this prophecy, but the general period of about one year is implied by comparing this phrase to the time it will take Isaiah's child to say "my father" or "my mother." This prophecy was fulfilled in less than two years, in 732 BC, when Damascus and Samaria were defeated by Assyria. Of course, this prophecy of judgment on Judah's enemies was welcome news to the people in Jerusalem. God's deliverance of Judah from her attackers should have given Isaiah's audience a reason to trust God because he is sovereign over the nations and will fulfill his promises (7:4–9).

THE COMING ASSYRIAN FLOOD (8:5–10)

[5]The Lord spoke to me again:

[6]"Because this people has rejected
    the gently flowing waters of Shiloah
and rejoices over Rezin
    and the son of Remaliah,
[7]therefore the Lord is about to bring against them
    the mighty floodwaters of the River —
    the king of Assyria with all his pomp.
It will overflow all its channels,
    run over all its banks
[8]and sweep on into Judah, swirling over it,
    passing through it and reaching up to the neck.
Its outspread wings will cover the breadth of your land,
    O Immanuel!"

---

[293] Tucker, *Isaiah 1–39*, 117, believes she was a prophetess because women were not identified by the vocation of their husband. This conclusion is not always the case, for queens were identified by the role of their husbands.

[294] The use of the imperatives מַהֵר, "hurry," and חָשׁ, "swift," is not very apparent, but one could see them as exhortations or as a threat (GKC §110a or c).

⁹**Raise the war cry, you nations, and be shattered!**
   Listen, all you distant lands.
 Prepare for battle, and be shattered!
 Prepare for battle, and be shattered!
¹⁰**Devise your strategy, but it will be thwarted;**
   propose your plan, but it will not stand,
 for God is with us.

There is no way of knowing when God declared this oracle to the prophet, but if it came relatively soon after 8:1–4 (similar to the expanded explanation after the sign in chap. 7), then it would have served as a fuller adumbration of the implications of the cryptic name of Isaiah's son. Once the audience knew that Samaria and Damascus were destined for destruction, joy must have filled people's hearts. They probably concluded that they had made the right choice to trust the Assyrian king to deliver them and assumed that now they would live in peace (many probably did not hear Isaiah's earlier message of destruction to Ahaz in 7:17–25). This oracle undercuts the people's joy about deliverance from the attacks of Syria and Israel. Since Judah did not trust God for deliverance (they rejected him) and had already called on Assyria, God could not honor them. This paragraph contains two related messages:

Assyria will sweep through Judah like a flood   8:5–8
God will defeat the plans of the nations   8:9–10

8:5–8 When God spoke to Isaiah again about these matters (8:5), he gave a typical judgment speech, which includes an accusation (8:6; "because," *ya'an kî*) and punishment (8:7–8; "therefore," *lākēn*). The accusation explains two sides of the same coin. On the one hand the people of Judah have rejected God, who is metaphorically compared to the gentle flowing waters of Shiloah (coming from the Gihon spring in the Kidron Valley) and at the same time the people rejoice in Rezin the king of Damascus.

The interpretation of 8:6 is complicated because "this people" is not conclusively identified and because it seems unlikely that the people of Judah would rejoice over Rezin, who was attacking them. Watts and Motyer solve this dilemma by proposing that "this people" refers to rejoicing by the people in the northern nation of Israel who joined Rezin's anti-Assyrian coalition.[295] In contrast, Hayes and Irvine believe that Isaiah was referring to a group of people in Judah who wanted to join the anti-Assyrian coalition and follow Rezin (they disagreed with Ahaz's policies).[296] Several commentators prefer to

---

[295] Watts, *Isaiah 1–33*, 117, and Motyer, *The Prophecy of Isaiah*, 91, make good sense of this oracle with this change, but there is no basis for identifying "this people" as the northern nation of Israel. Isa 6:9 identifies "this people" as the people of Judah.

[296] Hayes and Irvine, *Isaiah*, 146–149, hypothesize an anti-Davidic party that opposed Ahaz. Thus they do not need to emend the verb "rejoice" to some other verb. Oswalt, *Isaiah*, 224, thinks the people rejoice over Rezin's withdrawal from Jerusalem.

emend the verb "rejoice" to "melt,"[297] thus the people of Judah were "melting with fear" because they were being attacked by Rezin. All these options ignore Isaiah's announcement in 8:1–4 that Rezin will be defeated. In light of this fact, it is natural that the people of Judah should rejoice at his defeat because their Syrian enemy will soon be gone. They think they were correct in siding with Assyria rather than Rezin; they think that they chose wisely when they trusted in Assyria rather than God (7:9).

The punishment clauses in 8:7–8 (following "therefore," *lākēn*) demonstrate that the people of Judah totally misconceived what was happening. They will not have peace because they sided with Assyria and rejected God. Instead, God will destroy Judah and their proud king with a great flood of Assyrians. Using the metaphor of the river Euphrates overflowing its banks (in contrast to a gentle stream in 8:6) and stretching its floodwaters out like wings to every low-lying valley in Judah, Isaiah depicts a nation almost totally destroyed, with the flood waters reaching up to the neck.[298]

This judgment oracle ends with a surprising reference to " Immanuel," presumably making a reference to Isa 7:14. If Isaiah understood Immanuel as a generic prediction of a future Davidic king who would rule the nation justly, then this could be a prophetic cry to this Immanuel, asking him to take note of what will happen to his land and people and to do something to intervene. "Immanuel" would be a brief exclamation of grief or a prayer asking, "God be with us" during this Assyria flood.[299]

8:9–10 The appeal to Immanuel for protection seems to cause the prophet to remember what God promised about his plans for his people in Zion. Imitating thoughts in earlier Zion songs (cf. Pss 2; 46; 48; 76), Isaiah assures his audience that God does not intend to destroy his people completely. Nations and armies may come and fight; they may develop great strategies to defeat God's people, but God will shatter them. This salvation oracle ironically challenges the nations using imperatives[300] because God will not let any of their plans

---

[297] Childs, *Isaiah*, 69–70, supports changing מָשׂוֹשׂ, "rejoice," to מָסוֹס, "melt, dissolve in fear" (see Isa 10:18), but this would require several other syntactical changes in the verse. Sweeney, "On *ûměśôś* in Isaiah 8:6," in *Among the Prophets: Language, Image and Structure in the Prophetic Writings* (ed. P. R. Davies and D. J. A. Clines; Sheffield: JSOT, 1993), 42–54, has shown that the present Hb. reading מָשׂוֹשׂ, "rejoice," is supported by the reading of the 1QIsaᵃ, the Targum, the Old Greek, and the Peshita, though he reads the DSS as a *hiphil* form of the verb. He takes the use of the same verb in 66:10b as dependent on 8:6 and a verification of the text of 8:6.

[298] Wildberger, *Isaiah 1–12,* 347, suggests that the wings that stretch out over the land are God's protective wings (cf. Ruth 2:12; Ps 17:8; 36:8), but there is no indication that 8:8b has suddenly dropped its analogy of the destructive Assyrian army and introduced a picture of God offering salvation to his people.

[299] G. C. I. Wong, "Is 'God With Us' in Isaiah VIII 8?" *VT* 49 (1999): 426–32, rejects the view that the flood reaching only to the neck provides some assurance of hope to Jerusalem, and he rejects the view that "O Immanuel" is a prayer. He views it as an expression of grief because of the severity of the Assyrian threat.

[300] GKC §110a refers to commands that are not to be taken literally but as ironic challenges. Thus, the imperatives רֹעוּ, "raise a war cry," הַאֲזִינוּ, "listen," and הִתְאַזְּרוּ, "prepare," in 8:9–10 are

stand (any more than Rezin's wicked plans in 7:7), for God will be with his people to accomplish his own plans. Whatever God plans will happen (14:24), and no one can frustrate his plans (14:25–27; Prov 21:30–31). This type of promise assured the person of faith that God's cares, even in times of great trials and defeat, but it also warned the naive not to trust in human armies or even the best political strategies their leaders could devise.

FEAR GOD, NOT ARMIES (8:11–15)

[11]The LORD spoke to me with his strong hand upon me, warning me not to follow the way of this people. He said:

[12]"Do not call conspiracy
    everything that these people call conspiracy;
  do not fear what they fear,
    and do not dread it.
[13]The LORD Almighty is the one you are to regard as holy,
    he is the one you are to fear,
    he is the one you are to dread,
[14]and he will be a sanctuary;
    but for both houses of Israel he will be
  a stone that causes men to stumble
    and a rock that makes them fall.
  And for the people of Jerusalem he will be
    a trap and a snare.
[15]Many of them will stumble;
    they will fall and be broken,
    they will be snared and captured."

The third oracle emphatically confronted[301] Isaiah and his followers with hard choices they had to make as they lived in a political and religious atmosphere that frequently did not honor God. It is organized into three parts:

God speaks to the prophet	8:11
Fear God, not what people fear	8:12–13
God can be a sanctuary	8:14–15

8:11 It appears that God "instructed, admonished" (from the root *yāṣar*) the prophet about the popular conception of reality that existed in Judah at that time. Isaiah and his followers must "turn aside" (*sûr*) from this path and

---

not commands for nations to come and prepare to fight, but more of an ironic call to battle, which becomes a threat of defeat if anyone should dare to fight against God's plans.

[301] It came "like a strong hand" (כְּחֶזְקַת הַיָּד) or literally "like the strong grasping of the hand," which apparently does not refer so much to the level of inspiration he felt, but the importance of obeying (he was under deep conviction) what God said. This "hand" refers to the power of the Spirit's influence over the one receiving the message (cf. Ezek 3:14; Jer 15:17). This does not refer to a psychological experience of a trance, but points to the extraordinary theological power of God's presence.

must not succumb to the social, religious, or political pressure to conform to the beliefs or behavior patterns of the people in Judah ("this people," *hā'ām hazzeh*).[302] God knew that Isaiah and his followers were a minority who held unpopular political views about the Syro-Ephraimite War, about God's prophetic promises for the future, and about where to go for hope in the dark days that would follow.

8:12–13 The righteous must stand firm; they cannot fear what other people say or do.[303] Although others will talk about a "conspiracy" (*qešer*),[304] Isaiah and his followers were not to get caught up in this talk and fear mongering. The nature of the conspiracy is not explained but several options are available. (a) In 7:4 God warned Ahaz not to fear the conspiratorial alliance of Rezin and Pekah against Judah; (b) Ahaz's agreement with Assyria might be seen as a conspiracy; (c) some could have accused Isaiah and his disciples of planning a conspiracy because of their opposition to Ahaz's plans; (d) rumors could arise about an internal coup to depose Ahaz (with Tabeel in 7:6); or (e) some might view God as having a conspiracy to destroy his people.[305] Since God warns them not to agree with "everything" others present as a conspiracy, it appears that the people of Judah were talking about several conspiracies. The exhortation does not deny that there will be some conspiracies, it merely warns against being paralyzed by fear concerning all the rumors that will arise in the coming days.

Using the same Hebrew root from 8:12 ("fear, dread," *yārē'*) God challenges Isaiah and his followers to focus on fearing God and treating him as holy (8:13).[306] To set God apart as holy requires one to perceive him as the high and exalted king praised by the seraphim in Isa 6. He is totally different from man

---

[302] This phrase usually carries a negative connotation, as in 8:6 where "this people" reject God.

[303] The commands in 8:12 (קֶשֶׁר לֹא־תֹאמְרוּן) express strong prohibitions (GKC §107o) that could be translated, "you must not say conspiracy." This and the following imperatives, "you must not fear; you must not dread," should not be translated as mild prohibitions.

[304] C. A. Evans, "An Interpretation of Isa 8:11–15 Unemended," *ZAW* 97 (1985): 112–13, does not emend "conspiracy" or "treat as holy." He believes Isaiah is telling his followers not to look at Isaiah's objections to Judah's treaty with Assyria as a conspiracy; God views any trust in a foreign nation as rebellion against him.

[305] God would not need to warn Isaiah about option a, c, d, or e because Isaiah had already received a divine word that the alliance would not succeed, so Tabeel was not a real threat. Surely there is no danger of Isaiah believing that he and his followers are mounting a conspiracy or that God has a conspiracy. This unspecified conspiracy must refer to rumors that could potentially cause the righteous to lose faith in God.

[306] Wildberger, *Isaiah 1–12*, 354–355, changes the word "holy" (תַּקְדִּישׁוּ) to "conspire" (תִּקְשִׁירוּ) so that one has a word play with v. 12, but it makes little sense to call God a "conspirator," or to follow Blenkinsopp, *Isaiah 1–39*, 241, "The Lord of hosts, with him you shall conspire" based on 8:14. God is not deceptively plotting to betray anyone behind their back, but openly reveals his plans. Childs, *Isaiah*, 75, rejects these emendations because they lack textual support. God is not a conspirator in the OT. Regarding God as holy emphasizes the contrast between those who do and do not fear God.

in his essence, glorious presence, magnificent power, and character. Those who treat God as holy do not ignore his words, dishonor his name, or fail to trust in him. They bow in awe, give him due reverence, and in faith obey what he says. People do not honor God as the holy king of this universe when they do not trust his promises, but instead allow themselves to be guided by the common fears of unbelievers. Those who follow God must do things differently than others within society (cf. 2 Cor 6:17) because they perceive God as holy and themselves as his holy people (Lev 19:2).

8:14–15   The results of treating or not treating God as holy are starkly contrasted in order to help the listeners decide what action they should take. If Isaiah and his followers fear God, then he will be a sanctuary,[307] a place of solid strength and refuge (4:4–5; Ps 27:5; Ezek 11:16), a blessing, and a comfort for those who were struggling with all the political changes going on at that time. But for those in Judah and Israel who did not fear God, he would become a rock to stumble over, like a snare or trap. Here Isaiah plays with neutral images that can be pictured as positive or negative. On the one hand God can be praised because he is a solid rock and refuge (Pss 18:2–3,31–32,46; 19:14; 62:7; 89:26) who rescues people entrapped in the snares of evil people (Pss 64:5–7; 91:3; 124:7; 140:4–5; 141:9), but for other people that role is reversed if they do not fear God. The rock will lead to ruin instead of refuge, and the people will be destroyed instead of being delivered from these traps. God warns that many will fall into these traps by unbelief because of their ungodly worldview (8:15).[308] This is a strong warning to Isaiah and his followers about the serious consequences of failure to treat God as holy.

FOLLOW GOD'S INSTRUCTIONS; OTHER WAYS BRING DARKNESS (8:16–22)

> [16]Bind up the testimony
>   and seal up the law among my disciples.
> [17]I will wait for the LORD,
>   who is hiding his face from the house of Jacob.
>   I will put my trust in him.

[18]Here am I, and the children the LORD has given me. We are signs and symbols in Israel from the LORD Almighty, who dwells on Mount Zion.

[19]When men tell you to consult mediums and spiritists, who whisper and mutter, should not a people inquire of their God? Why consult the dead on behalf of the living? [20]To the law and to the testimony! If they do not speak according to this word, they have no light of dawn. [21]Distressed and hungry, they will roam through

---

[307] In 8:14 many commentators (e.g., Blenkinsopp, *Isaiah 1–39*, 241) also change "holy place, sanctuary" (מִקְדָּשׁ) to "conspiracy" (מַקְשִׁיר) following the change they would make in 8:13. Another reason for this change is that God is pictured in the rest of v. 14 in negative images, so Watts, *Isaiah 1–33*, 119, feels the positive image of "sanctuary" does not fit the rest of the verse.

[308] Isaiah uses similar imagery in 28:16, where trust is the key to determining whether the "stone" (אֶבֶן) will have a positive or negative effect. This idea is picked up in the NT in Lk 20:18, Rom 9:33, and 1 Pet 2:8 with a similar emphasis on trusting in God/Christ.

the land; when they are famished, they will become enraged and, looking upward, will curse their king and their God. ²²Then they will look toward the earth and see only distress and darkness and fearful gloom, and they will be thrust into utter darkness.

The conclusion to this chapter contains two diverse elements:

Isaiah's commitment to trust God	8:16–18
God's words are the only source of light . . .	8:19–20
. . . Darkness falls on those who curse God	8:21–22

Clements connects the setting directly to 8:1–4 because the word "testimony" (*tĕʿûdâ*) in 8:16 uses the same root found in 8:2, when Isaiah calls reliable witnesses to testify about the name Maher-Shalal-Hash-Baz. Clements also suggests that the disciples in 8:16 are the two witnesses in 8:2,[309] but there is no indication that the high priest and father-in-law of Ahaz were Isaiah's disciples.

Some believe 8:16–18 describes Isaiah sealing his writings, withdrawing from public ministry for a few years,[310] and then waiting for the fulfillment of God's predictions concerning the Syro-Ephraimite War. But this text refers to Isaiah's active ministry of sealing God's words in the hearts of his followers, not going into hiding. His trustful waiting did not require him to cease his public ministry. It is better to understand this concluding paragraph as Isaiah's report about the hardening of the people. The hardening predicted in 6:9–10 has come, therefore it was important for the prophet to strengthen the resolve and solid biblical foundation of his disciples. In contrast to this negative trend in society, Isaiah and his followers have to make a firm commitment to remain faithful to God. Isaiah has witnessed with divine words and signs so that the people of Judah could see and hear (7:10–17; 8:1–4), but the reality was that they did not understand God as holy, fear him, or follow his words. Instead, the royal Davidic dynasty refused to trust God and instead depended on Assyria. The nation refused to accept God's promise to deliver them from Syria and Israel; they rejected God and rejoiced in their own political alliance to eliminate the threat of Syria and Israel (7:4–9; 8:6). They continued to fear conspiracies rather than God (8:12–13). Isaiah's preaching from God was rejected; therefore, all he could do was to preserve the words of God in the hearts of his disciples (8:16), wait for God to act according to his promises (8:17), and meanwhile encourage more people to reject all sources of "light" other than God's word (8:19–22).

8:16–18 This paragraph begins with two exhortations.[311] The binding and sealing could be interpreted literally as God instructing Isaiah and his

---

[309] Clements, *Isaiah 1–39*, 100, believes that a later editor separated these verses from 8:1–4 and in the process extended the "testimony" to mean all of Isaiah's Memoirs in 6:1–8:15.

[310] Gray, *Isaiah 1–27*, 154, maintains that "Isaiah realized that a stage of his ministry was closed; that for an indefinite time to come he might speak to his people no more."

[311] Oswalt, *Isaiah 1–39*, 230, understands צוֹר and חֲתוֹם as infinitive absolutes. GKC §113bb

followers to bind up a scroll and put a seal on it so that no one could open it or change what was written there (cf. Isa 29:11; 30:8; 1 Kgs 21:8; Dan 12:4,6).[312] But since Isaiah is the speaker in the rest of 8:17–18, it makes more sense to interpret this metaphorically as Isaiah asking God to bind the revelations that God has given him in the hearts of his followers. Since the "testimony" refers to what someone has spoken, "law, instruction" (tôrâ) is probably to be understood in a similar way; although a case could be made that these two terms cover the oral prophetic word though Isaiah and written words of God (the first five books of the Bible). This verse does not comment on whether the words to be bound were in a written or oral form. The followers of God who were willing to listen to God's instructions through Isaiah are called "my disciples"[313] but there is no way of knowing how many people this involved. Since the book of Isaiah never refers to a prophetic school of disciples (cf. 1 Sam 10:5–10; 2 Kgs 2:3–15),[314] it is better to regard these people simply as followers of God who accepted the truthfulness of the revelation Isaiah proclaimed.

Isaiah cannot force people to believe; in fact, God told him that most would refuse to listen to what he said (6:9–10). All Isaiah can do is to trust God and wait. Behind the concept of "trust" and "wait" are the basic ideas of "hope, confidently trust."[315] Isaiah is not depressed by Judah's hardened rejection of God, nor does he question what God is doing. He understands that God is not pleased with his people's sinful rejection of God's Word and that God cannot shine down his favor on those who do not trust him. God has not rejected Isaiah, but he has turned his face from his rebellious people. The choice is always there: either fear and trust God and have him "lift up his countenance upon you" so that you receive his blessing (Num 6:24–27), or reject God and have him hide his favor so that you reap the penalty (cf. Ps 104:29; 143:7). Isaiah recommitted himself to God and his plan in spite of the rebelliousness of the rest of the people in Judah.

---

includes examples of the use of the infinitive absolute as an imperative in the example of the Sabbath command, " keep the Sabbath holy." Here an infinitive absolute would be used to express an imperative idea. BDB, 864 indicates that this form (חַתּוֹם) is actually an imperative since the infinitive absolute would be vocalized slightly differently (חָתֹם).

[312] Williamson, *The Book Called Isaiah*, 98–99, rejects the metaphorical interpretation and believes Isaiah literally tied up and sealed a scroll at this time.

[313] לְמַד means "to learn," so a disciple is "one who learns" and follows what his teacher says.

[314] D. Jones, "The Traditio of the Oracles of Isaiah of Jerusalem," *ZAW* 67 (1955): 226–46, theorizes that there was an Isaiah school that "adapted the word of the master to contemporary situations, expanding them and adding further oracles." He believes this school was actively reworking Isaiah's words after the fall of Jerusalem and publishing them.

[315] In 7:9 Isaiah used תַּאֲמִינוּ, "you shall believe, stand firm," to define "trust," while here he uses וְחִכִּיתִי, "I will confidently wait," and וְקִוֵּיתִי, "I will hope/trust confidently." Both of these latter terms express confidence and full assurance that God will be with him and that all these prophecies will be fulfilled.

This commitment is personal and involves himself and his children (8:18). Isaiah perceived himself and his children as "signs" (*'ōtôt*) and "symbols" (*môptîm*) that were given by God. Although Isaiah, Shear-Jashub, and Maher-Shalal-Hash-Baz were never called signs earlier in the narrative, Isaiah can now look back and perceive that each of them symbolized a message sent from God. Perhaps Isaiah saw his name ("God saves") as a sign just like the names of his children, or that his preaching or his recommissioning in chap. 6 represented a sign to people.

8:19   Now Isaiah turns from talking about himself and his family to address his followers ("unto you," *'ălēkem*, is plural) with words of warning about the dangers involved with some of the false religious practices of his day. The first section (8:19–20) contrasts the wrong way to inquire about the future with the right way to find out about God's will and his future plans. Isaiah's followers need to be aware that some will reject what God has said through words and signs; instead, they may say[316] that the only way to find out about the future is to consult the pagan spirit world. It is not clear whether Isaiah is talking about inquiring (*dāraš*) of one skilled in necromancy or if this term refers to inquiring directly with the "spirits of the dead."[317] The term "spiritists" is ambiguous in the same manner. It may refer to the "spirits" themselves or to the person who contacts the spirits. The description of their communication as "whisper and mutter" could be an accurate portrayal of the shadowy world of the spirits, but these negative descriptions also are meant to ridicule this pagan source of information. Although Isaiah does not discuss where the Israelites received this information from (cf. 2:6–8) or who encouraged the inquiry, 2 Chr 28 and 2 Kgs 16 give ample evidence of Ahaz's promotion of Baalism, worship of Syrian gods, and the closing of the Jerusalem temple. Even today in our scientific age, some people who are turned off by traditional religious ritual are turning to psychics, eastern religions, witchcraft, and séances to learn about the future.

To counteract these pagan practices Isaiah (a) asks two cryptic questions about the validity of these other worldly resources; (b) offers an alternative source of divine knowledge; and (c) provides a criterion people should use to judge the validity of any claims to supernatural knowledge. The two questions ask: Should people not "inquire" (*dāraš* is the same verb used in the first half of the verse)[318] of their own God? Why would anyone want to talk to a dead

---

[316] NIV has "When some men tell you," assuming it will happen. Watts, *Isaiah 1–33*, 125, turns the phrase into a conditional "If they say to you," while Blenkinsopp, *Isaiah 1–39*, 243, makes the phrase emphatic with "they will surely say to you." Each of these is equally defensible since כִּי can introduce a temporal or conditional clause, or can function as an emphatic asseverative. If this is a conditional hypothetical sentence, then the imperfect verb will be a subjunctive, "If they should say to you." (GKC §107x).

[317] The term אוֹב, "the pit," can refer to (a) the pit where one could call up dead spirits (I Sam 28:7–8); (b) the spirits of the dead (Isa 29:4); or (c) the necromancer who called up the spirits of the dead (Deut 18:11; 1 Sam 28:3,9). See *TDOT*, 1:132–133.

[318] The subjunctive translation of the imperfect verb is appropriate in questions (GKC §107t).

person's spirit about the living? It is illogical for God's covenant people ('am) to seek advice from anyone other than their own covenant God. He knows them, loves them, protects them, and guides them, so why would they go else-where? It also does not make much sense to go to the dead to find out about the living. The spirit of a dead person does not become a divine being with super-natural knowledge about the future.[319] Earlier traditions repeatedly condemn any attempts to contact the dead (Lev 19:31; 20:6,27; Deut 18:10–11). To do so may cause the people to drink blood, defile themselves, worship other gods, and give up their status as the holy people of God.

8:20 Isaiah quickly interrupts this objectionable train of thought with a cryptic "to the law and to the testimony," which is not even a complete sen-tence. He is attesting that a better alternative is available in the true words of God contained in the testimonies and laws (oral and written instructions) God gave the nation. These are all one needs and the only source of true revelation about God's will; they are a test that people can use to judge all prophetic statements. Blenkinsopp interprets this phrase as an oath[320] confirming that those who use the word of the spirits will be ineffective, but is seems better to view this as a conditional clause that sets up the following criteria. If anyone might[321] not speak according to "this word" (the law and the testimony), one can be sure that there is (better than "they have" in NIV) therein no true access to the divine light (lit. "the dawn," šāhar).[322] God's past revelation is the only valid guide to judge any new wisdom about the future. Anything that contra-dicts what God has said or leads one in a direction inconsistent with the clear teachings in the nation's traditions is untrustworthy and misleading. The light of God's truth is not in it.

8:21–22 This paragraph ends with a brief description of what will hap-pen to the people of Judah who reject God's revelation and rely on the spirits

---

The introductory הֲלוֹא is used to indicate something is absolutely true (GKC §150e). Thus this sentence could be rhetorically rendered as a question, "Should not a people inquire of their God?" (meaning, obviously they should), or as a statement, "Surely people should inquire of their God!"

[319] Isa 14:10 and Ps 88:3–7 picture the departed spirits as weak, forsaken, and in a dark place, while Eccl 9:5 suggests that the dead do not know anything and Isa 38:18 portrays them as cut off from God. E. F. Sutcliffe, *The Old Testament and the Future Life* (London: Burns Oates and Washbourne, 1947), reviews Egyptian, Babylonian, OT, and Intertestamental views of life after death (including the resurrection of the dead).

[320] P. Sheehan, "Some Textual Problems in Isaiah," *CBQ* 22 (1960): 47–55, and Blenkinsopp, *Isaiah 1–39*, 243, believe אִם־לֹא introduces an oath and translate it "surely" (GKC §149). The alternative approach ("if . . . not") is based on "this word" referring to the law and the testimony (the near antecedent) rather than the words of the spirits at the beginning of v. 19.

[321] The imperfect יֹאמְרוּ in a conditional sentence will frequently be in a subjunctive mood (GKC §107x).

[322] The imagery of dawn and light as representatives of divine truth and hope make a fitting contrast to the darkness and gloom that will come to Judah (8:21–21). One should not give up this natural contrast for alternative proposals like Sweeney, *Isaiah 1–39*, 184, who takes שַׁחַר, "dawn," to mean "efficacy" (depending on Isa 47:10–12), Watts, *Isaiah 1–33*, 125, who reads "the power to overcome disaster," or Kaiser, *Isaiah 1–12*, 199, who suggests "magic."

of the dead. They (lit. "he, one") will end up walking around looking hungry, distressed at their misfortune, and angry about this hopeless situation. Their dire situation will lead to total disillusionment and rejection of the political maneuvers of the king (Ahaz) and any religious help from the gods (better than NIV "God"). The phrase "looking upward" (*lĕmā'lâ*) actually comes at the end of the verse and could hypothetically mean that they will now finally turn to look up to God, yet there is nothing in what follows in 8:22 to suggest that these individuals have repented and turned to God. Blenkinsopp suggests the possibility of connecting these final two words in 8:21 with the initial words of 8:22.[323] Thus, when people look upward or across the land, all they will see will be distress, darkness, and gloom. Being banished to "utter darkness" in some context could imply going to their grave, but here it primarily indicates God's intention not to deliver these unbelievers from their just punishment of gloom and darkness. This parallels the darkness due to war described at the end of the previous prophecy about the destruction of Judah (cf. 5:30).

THEOLOGICAL IMPLICATIONS. This message stresses the sovereignty of God in the history of Judah and the other nations involved in the Syro-Ephraimite War. God knows events ahead of time and his plan was to bring about the destruction of Syria and Israel by using the king of Assyria (8:1–4). None of these nations can ever hope to implement their imaginative human strategies if they continue to oppose God's plans (8:9–10). This is true of past political situations involving Judah, as well as present political situations around the globe today. It is foolish to deny God's involvement in politics or to oppose the plan of God.

As in chap. 5, Isaiah again reminds his audience of the terrible consequences of rejecting God and trusting in military power or apparent military victories (8:6). If people do not treat God as holy and fear him (8:13), then they will end up fearing man and his power (8:12). Thus God, who wants to protect his people, will end up being a snare that will bring about their demise. The nation's only hope lies in fearing and trusting God and his divine revelation (8:16–17); any other source of hope or information is useless and deceptive (8:19). If people reject God and his Word, then there is no other source of light. Life without God leads to destruction, painful distress, and darkness (8:21–22).

These negative experiences teach a positive lesson. People need to pay attention to God's revealed will and follow it, as Isaiah and his followers did. This obedience leads to a faithful relationship of respect and awe before the presence of a holy God, as well as hopeful waiting for God to act and confident assurance in his plan (8:17). Temptations to follow the false messages of proud political leaders, secular materialistic philosophies, and misguided religious

---

[323] Blenkinsopp, *Isaiah 1–39*, 243, considers אֶרֶץ to mean "underworld," thus creating a contrast between heaven above and the world of the dead below, but this unusual meaning of אֶרֶץ is unnecessary, for the usual translation "earth" makes good sense.

leaders will be less attractive when people put them under the scrutiny of divine truth (8:20).

5. The Reign of a Righteous King, the Humbling of the Proud (9:1–11:16)

STRUCTURE.   This new section matches the general structure of the earlier material in 2:1–4:6.

God's Future Kingdom Produces Trust	2:1–5
The Removal of Pride and Exaltation of God	2:6–22
The Removal of Judah's Male Leaders	3:1–15
The Removal of Judah's Proud Women	3:16–4:1
God's Glorious Holy Kingdom	4:2–6
The Reign of a Righteous King	9:1–7
The Judgment of Proud and Sinful Israel	9:8–10:4
The Judgment of Proud Assyria	10:5–34
The Reign of a Righteous King	11:1–16

Both of these sections begin (2:1–5; 9:1–7) and end (4:2–6; 11:1–16) with promises of hope based on the eschatological promise of God's rule over his people and all the nations. These new oracles of salvation in Isaiah 9 and 11 are not just repetitions of the earlier promises in chaps. 2 and 4; instead, they are more focused on a Davidic king and the nature of his reign. Both of these parallel sections include similar messages of condemnation for pride and oppression (2:6–4:1; 9:8–10:34) in between these messages of hope. Although some connect the woes and outstretched hand oracles in 9:8–10:14 with the woes and outstretched hand oracles in 5:8–30,[324] it is very unlikely that these two sections originally stood as one unit that was divided by the insertion of the Isaiah Memoirs in 6:1–9:7. Instead, chap. 5 is closely related to the discussion of the destruction of Judah in 7–8, while 9:8–10:34 is related to the discussion of God's opposition to pride and oppression in 2:6–4:1. This new material on pride and oppression (9:8–10:34) does not deal with problems of pride in Judah; rather, the new examples of pride and oppression are focused on the behavior of the nations that troubled weak Ahaz, the northern nation of Israel, and the foreign nation of Assyria. Both are condemned because they did not recognize the sovereign control God has over all the nations of the earth.

HISTORICAL SETTING.   There is some disagreement over the dating of parts of chaps. 9–11. What is clear is that there are several paragraphs that reflect the historical events surrounding the Syro-Ephraimite War. Israel and Syria have acted proudly by attacking Judah, so now their foes (the Assyrians) are being strengthened against them (9:8–11) and have already taken some of their land (8:23). Thus Israel has not completely fallen, but very soon it will (10:3–4). The

---

[324] See the discussion of these issues in the Introduction to 5:1–30.

Assyrian army is arriving or is about to arrive on the scene (10:28–32). It has exerted its muscles against Samaria but has not yet completed its work against Judah (10:11–12). In the near future God will judge Assyria (10:33–34).

In spite of this general historical picture, there is widespread disagreement over dating the paragraph dealing with the route the Assyrian army traveled in 10:28–32. Some suggest that this represents (a) the Assyrian invasion by Tiglath-pileser III around 734 BC; (b) the attack on Jerusalem by Sennacherib in 701 BC when Hezekiah revolted; (c) Sargon's conquests in the Philistine plain between 712–711 BC; or (d) Sargon's earlier invasion in 720 BC.[325] Since Sennacherib approached Jerusalem from the south, the 701 attack is automatically eliminated as a possibility. A secondary key factor in dating this chapter is the status of the key cities in 10:9: Calnah and Arpad fell in 738 BC, Hamath in 729 BC, Carchemish in 742 and 717 BC, and Samaria in 722 BC. The interpreter must decide if these cities and the march of the army are prophecies of future events or descriptions of present or past events.[326]

Although it is not required that all of 9:1–11:16 come from the time of the Syro-Ephraimite War, such a time frame may offer the best approach to the historical data in this section. Some prophetic speeches (11:1–9) have few historical hints in them, so it is impossible to identify their original setting.

PURPOSE.   In this section, Isaiah attempted to convince his listeners that God can be trusted and that his promises for a glorious kingdom for his people will be fulfilled (even though he knows that most will be hardened according to 6:9–10). Judah must not follow the mistaken pattern of sinful pride and oppression like Israel and Assyria lest they suffer the same fate. Instead, they should trust God in spite of their oppressors, for the good news is that God will soon remove their enemies Israel and Assyria. Eventually, their Messiah will reign forever over the all nations and God will establish a period of justice and peace.

(1) The Reign of a Righteous King (9:1–7)

1Nevertheless, there will be no more gloom for those who were in distress. In the past he humbled the land of Zebulun and the land of Naphtali, but in the future he will honor Galilee of the Gentiles, by the way of the sea, along the Jordan —

2The people walking in darkness
have seen a great light;
on those living in the land of the shadow of death
a light has dawned.

---

[325] S. A. Irvine, *Isaiah, Ahaz, and the Assyrian Crisis* (Atlanta: Scholars Press, 1990), 274–79, considers this event as the invasion of Tiglath-pileser III during the Syro-Ephraimite War; Wildberger, *Isaiah 1–12*, 450–455 (with an excellent map of the route on page 454), thinks this was Sargon II who campaigned against Philistia in 712–711 BC; Kaiser, *Isaiah 1–12*, 238–48, points to Sennacherib's route in 701 BC, while Sweeney, *Isaiah 1–39*, 206, supports the date of 720 BC. D. Christensen, "The March of Conquest in Isaiah X 27c–34," *VT* 26 (1976): 395–99, has the unlikely suggestion that this is the march of God against Jerusalem.

[326] This issue is decided below in the historical introduction to 10:28–32.

³You have enlarged the nation
     and increased their joy;
they rejoice before you
     as people rejoice at the harvest,
as men rejoice
     when dividing the plunder.
⁴For as in the day of Midian's defeat,
     you have shattered
the yoke that burdens them,
     the bar across their shoulders,
     the rod of their oppressor.
⁵Every warrior's boot used in battle
     and every garment rolled in blood
will be destined for burning,
     will be fuel for the fire.
⁶For to us a child is born,
     to us a son is given,
     and the government will be on his shoulders.
And he will be called
     Wonderful Counselor, Mighty God,
     Everlasting Father, Prince of Peace.
⁷Of the increase of his government and peace
     there will be no end.
He will reign on David's throne
     and over his kingdom,
establishing and upholding it
     with justice and righteousness
     from that time on and forever.
The zeal of the LORD Almighty
     will accomplish this.

The first paragraph in this section introduces a future righteous Davidic king who will bring a period of light and peace to God's people. This figure is not directly or explicitly contrasted to King Ahaz, but the light, joy, and peace of his era sharply contrasts with the war, distress, and darkness of Ahaz's reign in 7:1–8:22. There is also an interesting connection between the Davidic son called Immanuel, who will choose what is right (7:14–15), and the Davidic son called Wonderful Counselor, Mighty God, Everlasting Father, and Prince of Peace, who will rule the nation with justice (9:6–7). This new progressive revelation about an important future son gave Isaiah new insight into his earlier prophecy, clarifying both the identity and the role of this son.

The peace and justice that the future Davidic ruler will establish is also contrasted with the sinful pride and oppression that led to the downfall of both Israel and Assyria (9:8–10:34). 9:1–7 is also thematically connected to the final matching prophecy of hope in 11:1–16, for both envision a glorious future time of peace when a righteous Davidic ruler will reign forever.

GENRE. J. Lindblom and A. S. Herbert consider 9:2–7 to be a thanksgiving hymn.[327] The hymn addresses God in the second person (9:3–4) and gives three reasons why people should be joyful (9:4–6). Nevertheless, the poem lacks a call to praise God, never uses the word thanksgiving, and centers on future positive changes rather than focusing on what God has already done.[328] A. Alt and G. von Rad thought that a better way of classifying this oracle would be to compare it to accession oracles used when a nation installs a new king (using Egyptian coronation texts as a model).[329] Some connect this ceremony to the coronation of Hezekiah, which may reflect God's adoption of this righteous king as his son (cf. 2 Sam 7:14; Ps 2:6–12).[330] Nevertheless, if this was the case, one would expect God to speak directly to the king in a coronation oracle (cf. Ps 2:7) and one would expect to find some reference to the king being God's son in an adoption statement. Any attempt to draw Egyptian parallels is suspect, for in contrast to Israelite rulers, the Egyptians often considered their kings as divine beings. Also, Isaiah only refers to four titles, not the five names that are common in Egyptian coronations. Finally, there is no clear evidence that would suggest that the Israelites patterned their monarchy after an Egyptian model.[331] Because of these problems, Wildberger views 9:5a as an announcement of the birth of a royal child.[332] In other birth announcement passages (Gen 16:9–12; 17:19; Judg 13:2–5; Isa 7:13–15; 8:1–4) a difficult situation is described, the birth is announced, the name is declared, and an explanation of the name or the role of the child is explained. This is similar to the construction of 9:1–7 and fits the joyous occasion of a special royal birth. The

---

[327] J. Lindblom, *A Study on the Immanuel Section in Isaiah, Isa 7,1–9,6* (Lund: Gleerup, 1958), 34–36. A. S. Herbert, *Isaiah 1–39* (Cambridge: Cambridge University Press, 1973), 74, thinks the hymn applied to the enthronement of Hezekiah, Josiah, and then later to the Messiah.

[328] Kaiser, *Isaiah 1–12*, 207, finds no praise of God in v. 1, but an emphasis on God's future salvation (not thanks for past deeds), so it is not like other thanksgiving hymns and has some aspects of the salvation oracle.

[329] A. Alt, "Jesaja 8,23–9,6. Befreiungsnacht und Krönungstag," *Kleine Schriften zur Geschichte des Volkes Israel*, Vol II, 3rd (Munich: Beck, 1964): 206–25, thought 9:5 is an announcement of a new king by a royal herald, while G. von Rad, "Royal Ritual in Judah," *The Problem of the Hexateuch and Other Essays* (New York: McGraw-Hill, 1966), 222–31, compares Israelite coronations with Egyptian practices, specifically the practice of giving five royal names. H. Frankfort, *Kingship and the Gods* (Chicago: University of Chicago, 1978), 46–47, lists examples of titles given to Egyptian kings.

[330] While many hypothesize a connection to the coronation of Hezekiah, H. Barth, *Die Jesaja-Worte in der Josiazeit*, WMANT 48 (Neukirchen-Vluyn: Neukirchener, 1977), 176–77, argues that it refers to the coronation of Josiah, while Hayes and Irvine, *Isaiah*, 175–84, surprisingly suggest that this spirit-led king refers to Ahaz. This is most unlikely, for he was a very wicked king.

[331] R. A. Carlson, "The Anti-Assyrian character of the Oracle in Is. IX 1–6," *VT* 24 (1974): 130–35, also rejects the Egyptian background to chap. 9.

[332] Wildberger, *Isaiah 1–12*, 398–400, relates the first half of 5 to a birth, but then associates the names in 5b with an act of enthronement.

close proximity and verbal similarities between this birth announcement and the earlier announcement of another Davidic ruler called Immanuel in 7:14–15 suggests there is a close connection between the sons in these two passages.

The narrative introduction in 9:1 [Hb. 8:23] does not fit with the poetic parallelism that dominates the rest of 9:2–7. This suggests that 9:1 was not part of the original poem but was added later as an introduction or transition sentence to introduce the poem by the author, probably when this oracle was placed in its present written form. Four reasons support this conclusion: (a) In the announcement of a royal birth there would be no need to include the geographical information in 9:1, so 9:1 would only need to be included if one were telling about the event at a later time. (b) 9:1 unnecessarily repeats the basic contrast between light and darkness that is already found in 9:2. (c) 9:1 serves as a transition that connects the darkness theme in 8:21–22 with what follow in 9:2–7. (d) 9:1 is narrative and not part of the poem in 9:2–7.

STRUCTURE.   The development of this royal birth announcement is divided into three sub-paragraphs:

Light will come to those living in darkness	9:1–2
God will defeat the nation's oppressor	9:3–5
A son will justly rule the Davidic kingdom	9:6–7.

9:1–2   The introduction in 9:1 is the last verse in chap. 8 in the Hebrew Masoretic tradition, not the first verse of this new chapter. Some commentators include all of this verse with the preceding paragraph, since it continues the narrative form of 8:19–22, while others make a paragraph division after 9:1a.[333] The positive tone predicting the end of gloom shows that this verse makes the transition to a new paragraph that gives the nation hope. The translation of 9:1 is complicated by (a) the unclear temporal contrast between events "in the past" and "in the future;" (b) the difficulty of translating the two perfect Hebrew verbs ("humble" and "honor"); (c) the possibility of textual emendation;[334] and (d) uncertainty about what "the way of the Sea, along the Jordan" means.

This transitional verse appears to move the reader from the darkness and distress of 8:22 to look forward to the light and hope of the new era in 9:2–7. Although the "first, former, past" time period (kĕʿēt hārišôn) is not defined specifically, it contrasts with an unspecified "future, later" time (wĕhāʾaḥărôn, probably the time of this new king in 9:5–6). In contrast, H. Eshal believes that "the former" refers to a former king, Ben-Hadad of Syria (855 BC), while "the later" refers to Tiglath-Pileser III of Assyria (747–732 BC), but this approach

---

[333] Oswalt, *Isaiah 1–39*, 240, and Gray, *Isaiah 1–27*, 161, follow the Hebrew tradition and divide these paragraphs after 9:1 [Hb. 8:23], while Kaiser, *Isaiah 1–12*, 202–203, divides this material in the middle of 9:1.

[334] Williamson, *Variations on a Theme*, 32, prefers to replace הַגּוֹי, "the nation," with הַגִּילָה, "rejoice," because it gives a better parallel with "joy" in the next line.

should be rejected.[335] Since there is no verb in the first clause, this further complicates the translation. Thus the verbs "there will be" no gloom and those who "were" in distress are supplied based on the context of the paragraph. The verb "he humbled, made insignificant" (*hēqal*) is the normal translation for a perfect verb, particularly after the introductory clue "in the past time." This rendition exerts pressure to translate the second perfect verb in a similar manner as "was honored" (*hikbîd*). But the prepositional phrase "in the future days" contextually requires "will be honored," implying the use of a prophetic perfect.[336]

The geographic location of the tribes of Zebulun and Naphtali indicates that the author is referring to the northern part of Galilee, the area of Israel first humbled by foreign military invasions, and the region most influenced by foreign cultures and religions. Although unspecified in this verse, Isaiah may refer to gloom caused by recent invasions by the Assyrians under Tiglath-pileser III (he conquered this area in the Syro-Ephraimite War). This is the same general area as Galilee of the Gentiles, a negative title that shows how pervasive non-Hebrew people and cultures were in this area. The last two geographical terms are not as clear. "By the way of the Sea" is sometimes connected to the Assyrian province established along the Mediterranean Sea near the seaport of Dor, but it seems more likely that this phrase refers to the northern area around the Sea of Galilee. "Along the Jordan" (NIV) refers to the Transjordan area east of the Jordan River. In summary, this verse surprisingly predicts that the least likely area of Israel, the far northern section that was the most militarily oppressed and most influenced by pagans, will in some way be honored by God when he sends a new "light" in the future.

In 9:2 the actual poetic royal birth announcement begins. The verse contrasts those who "are walking" (a participle) in darkness with those who "will see" (not "have seen" as in NIV)[337] a light of hope in the future. At this point the light is not identified, but it was certainly a sign of hope and deliverance from the darkness that pervaded the land. This light was a sign that God had not completely given up on his people. A new day of hope and light will eventually arrive. Elsewhere God is the light (Ps 27:1) or God's words are a light (Ps 119:105; Isa 8:20). Later in 60:1–3 God's glorious coming to his kingdom is pictured as a light. The following verses explain what this light will be.

---

[335] H. Eshal, "Isaiah VIII 23: An Historical-Geographical Analogy," *VT* 40 (1990): 104–9. However, J. A. Emerton, "Some Linguistic and Historical Problems in Isaiah VIII 23," *JSS* 14 (1969): 151–75, has shown the weakness of this approach.

[336] See GKC §106n for a perfect verb referring to future events. Blenkinsopp, *Isaiah 1–39*, 245–246, translates the second verb הִכְבִּיד, "oppressed," since the root כבד can mean "to be heavy" or "to honor, glorify." He argues that since both verbs are perfects referring to past completed action and there was no "honor, glory" in the nation's recent history, it only makes sense for this verb to refer to "oppression" of a heavy hand by a more powerful nation. His reference to the "former" and "latter" enemies allows this interpretation, but עֵת refers to a former "time" not a former enemy. J. A. Emerton, "Some Linguistic and Historical Problems," 151–75, has a lengthy discussion of the technical problems of translating this verse.

[337] This should be interpreted as another prophetic perfect verb. GKC §106n.

9:3–5   Consistent with the metaphor of light is the mood of joy and rejoicing in 9:3. The second clause in the first line in the written Hebrew Masoretic
text has a negative (*lō'*, "no, not"), which is interpreted in the oral Hebrew
tradition as a preposition with a suffix (*lô*, "to him/them").[338] Since a negative
particle would contradict the positive message of the rest of the verse, it makes
more sense to follow this oral tradition and translate the second clause, as "you
will increase/give great joy to them." This is parallel to the positive prediction
that "they (plural) will rejoice before you," referring to God's people not a
singular nation.

Two illustrations of wild celebrative joy are used to compare the people's
future happiness. The people will rejoice and jump for joy like people do when
they see an unusually massive harvest (possibly referring to the joy at the Feast
of Weeks; Deut 16:9–12) or when they observe the hoards of goods brought
home by the troops after an enemy nation is plundered.

Using God's great victory over Midian (see Judg 6–7) as a comparison,
Isaiah predicts that God "will shatter/break"[339] (*haḥittôtā*) the oppressive
yoke of their enemy. The yoke, bar, and rod (used of Assyria's oppression in
10:24–27) were instruments used to dominate people and force them to work
physically, or they could be used as metaphors to describe a heavy burden
put on people through increased taxation or domineering rule. The burning
of the boots and the bloody clothes of enemy soldiers in 9:5 signify a victory
in holy war where spoils were dedicated to God and military equipment was
set on fire (cf. Josh 11:6,9; Ezek 39:9).[340] Although this may usher in a time
of peace without war (as in 2:4),[341] the focus of this promise is simply on the
utter defeat of the enemy. There is no prediction concerning when in the future
this will happen.

9:6–7   This positive oracle comes to a climactic end by announcing the
birth of a son who would reign forever as a righteous Davidic ruler (one very
different from Ahaz). The prophet's message provides information about his
(a) birth; (b) role in government; (c) names; (d) reign of peace; and (e) just
eternal rule on the throne of David. It also offers strong assurances that God
will accomplish all these things.

---

[338] לֹא, "not," in the written text (*Kethib*) is changed to לוֹ, "to him/it," in the spoken (*Qere*)
reading. Gray, *Isaiah 1–27*, 175, combines the two words to form הֲגִילָה, "jubilation, rejoicing,"
to give a good parallel with the second part of the line, but this is not the simplest option for correcting this problem.

[339] This should be interpreted as another prophetic perfect verb. GKC §106n.

[340] The attempt by M. B. Crook, "A Suggested Occasion for Isaiah 9. 2–7 and 11. 1–9," *JBL*
68 (1949): 213–24, to connect the burning of boots and clothes to the usurping of the throne from
Athaliah and the coronation of Jehoash (2 Kgs 11) is pure speculation. M. E. W. Thompson, "Isaiah's Ideal King," *JSOT* 24 (1982): 79–88, is more accurate when he suggests that this is not a
description of any king's past coronation but a picture of Israel's ideals for the perfect king, similar
to expressions about kingship in the royal Psalms (Pss 93–99).

[341] Oswalt, *Isaiah 1–39*, 243–44, emphasizes peace and the end of war in his exposition, but
this reading goes beyond the content of this verse.

The initial announcement that a child "will be born" (*yullad* prophetic per-fect verb) is further explained in the parallel phrase, God "will give a son to us," that is, to the people of Judah. The second line emphasizes that this is a work of God's gracious giving, not just a coincidence. No date of birth in the future is hinted at, and the only comparable son promised by God in earlier oracles was Immanuel in 7:14–15. An identification marker that links these two sons is that they both will be righteous Davidic rulers.[342] But the two sons do not have identical names. Concerning this Davidic ruler, "he [presumably God] will call his name"[343] (not passive, "he will be called" as in NIV) titles that represent his character and roles.[344] The eight words that follow could be eight names, but since Immanu-el, Shear-Jashub, and many other Hebrew names comprise two words (Isaiah means "God saves), it seems natural to divide these eight words into four titles.[345]

a) "Wonderful Counselor" combines the idea of doing something "wonder-ful, extraordinary, miraculous" (*pele³*) with the skill of "giving wise advice, making plans, counsel."[346] This suggests that this son's life will somehow ex-hibit "miraculous acts of God"[347] employed in the sphere of wise planning or decision-making. Since God is the source of all miraculous events and his plans are the wisest counsel to follow, God will work in and through this son to demonstrate his extraordinary wisdom to plan wonderful miraculous things. These unspecified wonderful plans will be the subject of later revelation.

---

[342] W. Harrelson, "Non-Royal Motiffs in Royal Eschatology," *Israel's Prophetic Heritage: Essays in Honor of J. Muilenburg* (ed. B. W. Anderson and W. Harrelson; New York: Harper and Row, 1962), 151, believes Isaiah purposely did not call the Davidic ruler a "king" because the title was so disgraced by the beliefs and behavior of Ahaz.

[343] See GKC §111w for the use of the *vav* plus imperfect consecutive to continue a prophetic perfect, thus justifying the future tense in "he will call his name."

[344] J. Goldingay, "The Compound Name in Isaiah 9:5(6)," *CBQ* 61 (1999): 239–44, believes these four names are not the names of the child who will reign on the throne of David, but the names of God who supports and who will enable the Davidic ruler to succeed (he cannot imagine that these divine titles could be used of an earthly Davidic king). However, that is exactly the point: this is not a "regular, normal" Davidic king, but a divine king. Verse 5 refers to a son, describes how the government will be upon "his shoulders," and then tells what "his names" will be—all referring to the son, not God.

[345] P. Wegner, "A Re-examination of Isaiah IX, 1–6," *VT* 42 (1992): 103–112, follows the pattern of the four-word name of Maher-Shalal-Hash-Baz and finds only two names: "wonderful planner (is) the mighty God" and "the Father of eternity (is) a prince of peace." Although this configuration is hypothetically possible, it seems unlikely. Maher-Shalal-Hash-Baz is an irregular name in Hb., and it really says the same two words twice (because one name referred to the plunder of Israel and the other to the plunder of Syria).

[346] יוֹעֵץ can mean "to plan" in Isa 14:27; 23:9; "to give advice" in 1 Kgs 1:12; Jer 38:15; "to counsel" in 1 Kgs 12:8–9. This new ruler will replace the bad counselors God will remove (3:3). Isa 1:26 also predicts good counselors in the time of the nation's restoration. This name implies that this son will have unusual wisdom, the ability to take that wisdom and create a marvelous plan, and then the authority to apply that wisdom to Judah's situation to bring about the predicted plan.

[347] See *TDOT*, XI, 533–48, for an extensive study of the verbal and noun forms from this root. J. Conrad claims that this word deals with the accomplishment of "certain goals impossible for humans to attain by their own devices" (535), generally referring to a mighty act of God.

R. A. Carlson noticed that if one connects the first word of the first name *pele'* and the first word of the last name *śar* (a connection that few readers would naturally put together) one gets a word (*pele'śar*) almost identical to the second name of the Assyrian king Tiglath-pileser III, thus he thinks this future Jewish king is being presented as one greater than their Assyrian overlord who was trusted to save Ahaz from Pekah and Rezin in the Syro-Ephraimite War.[348] Although Carlson hypothesized this and other Akkadian connections to make this message an anti-Assyrian oracle, these connections are not particularly strong and draw attention away from the prophet's fundamental purpose of focusing his audience's attention on their future Davidic messianic king.

b) The second dual name "Mighty God" (*'ēl gibbôr*) includes a divine name similar to the name Ezekiel (God will be my strength). If one supplies a verb, the name might mean, "God is mighty" or "God is a mighty warrior," similar to Deut 10:17; Ps 24:8; 89:14. By itself, this name does not automatically mean that this son is a divine person, because many names include the name of God in them. But the later use of this same name to describe God himself in 10:21 demands that this son be identified with God in a very close manner. No other person ever has God's name and God is never called Moses, Abram, David, or Jeremiah, so there must be something very special about this son that causes him to have God's name.[349]

c) The third name is one word in Hebrew, combining two ideas in one concept. It is possible to translate it as an adjective and noun "Everlasting Father" (*'ăbî'ad*), as a sentence "my father [is] eternal," or as a genitive phrase "father of eternity." "Father" is a relatively rare way of describing God in the Hebrew Bible (Deut 32:6; Jer 3:4,19; Isa 63:16; 64:7; Mal 2:10) and a rarer way of describing a king (1 Sam 24:12), though the Israelites are frequently called God's sons (Exod 4:22–23). This tendency may be a conscious attempt to avoid pagan images of the gods giving birth to people. Since fathers were the heads of tribes who wisely led the people, it is a fitting title for a ruler if one wants to avoid some of the negative connotations of kingship. "Everlasting" is a title that does not apply to any human ruler, except that the Davidic promise speaks of one who will rule on the throne of David forever (2 Sam 7:16). Since 9:7 refers to a person ruling forever on the throne of David, the "everlasting father" in 6 must be the same ruler.

d) The last pair, "Prince of Peace" (*śar šālôm*), is less controversial because every king wanted to bring peace and prosperity to his subjects. Peace implies an end of war and is reminiscent of the ideal peace described in the kingdom

---

[348] R. A. Carlson, "Anti-Assyrian Character of Is. IX 1–6," *VT* 24 (1974): 130–35.

[349] W. Holladay, *Isaiah: Scroll of a Prophetic Heritage* (Grand Rapids: Eerdmans, 1978), 107, says the "second name can be nothing other than a title for God. . . . Isaiah is referring to *God* here in 9:6 by this title, and any attempt to water down the meaning of the phrase to apply it to a human king (such as the translation in the *New English Bible*, 'in battle God-like') is simply inadmissible."

of God in 2:4. It is also comparable to the promise in the Davidic covenant that God's people will not be oppressed again and that they will have rest from their enemies (2 Sam 7:10–11). No specific examples or illustrations of this peace are included (as in 2:4). In 11:6–9 this ideal is discussed in more detail.

9:7   Four things are known about the government this ruler will establish. First, when this new son rules, he will limitlessly expand[350] his influence and create peace without end (cf. Ps 2:8). This promise implies that no one will be able to successfully oppose his authority or undermine the positive effects of his government. Such strong statements imply that Isaiah is talking about the final eschatological ruler. Second, this ruler will reign on the throne of David and reestablish his kingdom. This pledge certifies beyond the shadow of a doubt that the text refers to the ultimate fulfillment of the Davidic covenant through a "messianic" figure. Third, his method of ruling will be based on the principles of justice and righteousness. This fact is consistent with the emphasis on justice in 11:4–5 (and 7:15) and contrasts with the behavior of Ahaz, Judah's present king. Fourth, this Davidic ruler will reign forever as explained in the Davidic covenant (2 Sam 7:16). These descriptive parameters, titles, time frame, and interlinking references to the Davidic promises rule out any attempt to identify this son with Ahaz, Hezekiah, or Josiah.

Finally, Isaiah offers a rhetorical assurance to his listeners concerning the fulfillment of this promise. Simply stated, God Almighty himself will do it. With unassailable zeal, determination, and passion God will concentrate his efforts to accomplish this marvelous deed. Isaiah's listeners can be absolutely sure that an omnipotent, soverign God will stand behind the fulfillment of this wonderful plan.

THEOLOGICAL IMPLICATIONS.   This message of hope functions as a reassurance that God's previous promises to the Davidic dynasty will be fulfilled in spite of all the terrible, dark circumstances the nation faced in the time of Ahaz. Light, joy, the end of war, and a new, righteous, Davidic ruler empowered by God himself will replace the gloom that surrounded the nation in the middle of the Syro-Ephraimite War. This hope was an encouragement to Isaiah and his faithful followers to continue speaking about the things of God, even if most people would not listen or understand (6:10–11). God's promise to bring peace and justice to this world through the Messiah is also an encouraging message that people can share today, because the political situation in modern times is sometimes about as dark and hopeless as in the days of Isaiah. This good news offers another opportunity for rebellious people to turn from trusting in political alliances, mediums, and the spirits of the dead because God is their only true source of hope. Neither Ahaz nor any modern

---

[350] The first word in 9:7 is problematic because the second letter in the middle of the word is written as if it is a final letter (לְמַרְבֵּה) "of/to the increase," which suggests that there should be two words (רבה and לם) "for them" and "great." Essentially, both readings convey a similar meaning.

political figure can ever hope to bring about an era of perfect peace and justice. Only God's wonderful plans will bring about these ideals, not the plans of Ahaz (8:10) or any other fast talking politician. God's promises will only be accomplished through his chosen messianic ruler, so placing trust in any other solution is folly.

(2) The Judgment of Proud and Sinful Israel (9:8–10:4)

AUDIENCE AND PURPOSE.   Following the pattern established in 2:1– 4:6, the prophet now delivers a powerful oracle of judgment that describes God's anger over the pride and oppression found in the northern nation of Israel.[351] One should not imagine that Isaiah traveled north to this war-torn land in the middle of the Syro-Ephraimite conflict to deliver these oracles. Instead, Isaiah speaks to the Hebrew people in Judah about the consequences of Israel's sin. Although initially it might appear that a prophecy of judgment on Israel is by definition a prophecy of hope for Judah, Isaiah's main goal was to challenge the theology of the people of Judah so that they would change their ways and not follow the terrible example of Israel. Two primary rhetorical purposes guide the structure and goals of these oracles. These messages reaffirm earlier prophecies and warn of future judgments. Isaiah makes it clear to the people of Judah that (a) God's punishment for Israel is not yet complete; she will be destroyed as God predicted earlier; and (b) since God will destroy Israel because of pride and oppression (9:8–21), God's earlier prophecies to destroy Judah for its pride and oppression will also come true (2:6–4:1). Judah is being given an opportunity to learn from the terrible mistakes of Israel and apply those lessons to evaluate the logic of Isaiah's prediction of Judah's demise. Why would God's anger not destroy Judah, if it will destroy Israel? His anger is not turned back and his hand is still outstretched (9:12,17,21; 10:4).

In the prophet's climax to this series of oracles, Isaiah turns from his accusations against Israel in 9:8–21 to directly address his audience in Judah in 10:1–4.[352] Evidence of this change includes (a) the use of "you" in 10:3, referring to his audience; (b) the change from accusations in 9:8–21 to a woeful lament in 10:1; (c) the change from past judgments in 9:8–21 to future punishments in 10:3–4; (d) the lack of reference to any northern tribe, city, or ruler in 10:1–4 (in contrast to 9:8–21); and (e) the change of topic from defeat in war to oppression of the poor.

These oracles reaffirm God's promise to destroy Judah's enemies, found in 7:4–9. There is no need to fear the armies of Israel and Syria who were attacking Judah, for God's "anger is not turned away and his hand is still

---

[351] Note the references to Jacob, Israel, Ephraim, and Samaria in 9:8–9 and then Ephraim and Manasseh in 9:21.

[352] Seitz, *Isaiah 1–39*, 91, found 10:1–4 to be directed against the remnant of Judah.

outstretched" against Israel. God will destroy Israel. Therefore, the people of
Judah should trust in God for deliverance in the Syro-Ephraimite War. Their
deliverance will not come from Assyria. Certainly, they do not want to suffer
the same destiny as Israel.

HISTORICAL SETTING.   The date of these oracles is hinted at by references to several historical events. Unfortunately, it is impossible to exactly date
some of the events described in this chapter. The general time period is during
the Syro-Ephraimite War (734–732 BC) before Israel has fallen (9:8). Israel
has suffered an attack (9:10) by the same foe (Assyria) that attacked Rezin king
of Syria (9:11), and soon the land will be scorched (9:19). These factors all indicate Isaiah gave this message sometime near the end of the Syro-Ephraimite
War, after the messages in chaps. 7 and 8.

STRUCTURE.   These oracles are sometimes reconstructed to be a continuation of the "outstretched arm" oracles in 5:25. This hypothesis suggests
that a later redactor inserted the "Isaiah Memoirs" (6:1–9:6) in the middle of
what was otherwise a unified message. Thus the woe oracles in 5:8–24 originally included the woe in 10:1–4 (the seventh woe) and the refrain at the end
of 5:25 was connected to identical refrains in 9:8–21.[353] This commentary is
not based on that theory, for it is not viewed as the best interpretation of the
structural organization of this material.[354] Though there are some interlinking
connections between common genres and themes in these two passages, all
oracles using a woe oracle or mentioning God's anger should not automatically
be interpreted as part of one literary piece.[355] The content and historical background of these oracles was different: 5:25–30 was against Judah in the time
of Uzziah, warning of a general attack, while 9:8–21 is about Israel who has
already been attacked in the Syro-Ephraimite War. These differences prevent
them from being one cohesive unit.

The structure of this sermon is easily discerned from the repeated refrains in
9:12,17,21 and 10:4. Each oracle is made up of an accusation, a description of
past judgment, and a refrain. The four oracles in this message include:

God's wrath against proud Israel	9:8–12
God's wrath against unrepentant leaders	9:13–17
God's destruction of the nation	9:18–21
Lament: Judah's oppression will lead to its demise	10:1–4

---

[353] This theory is discussed and rejected under "Some Modern Scholarly Approaches: Source
Criticism" in the Introduction.

[354] The theory that there is a connection between 5:8–31 and 9:8–10:4 is explained in more
detail in the Introduction to 5:1–30.

[355] A. H. Bartelt, "Isaiah 5 and 9: In- and Interdependence?" 157–174, considers 5:8–25 and
9:7–10:4 as independent poems that are interdependent, but it might be wiser to refer to them as
having similar phrases, for it is hard to prove that there is a literary interdependence. A preacher
can preach two sermons on Easter that use similar terms, but the second sermon may have no literary interdependence on the first; that is, it was not consulted or copied.

GOD'S WRATH AGAINST PROUD ISRAEL (9:8–12)

⁸**The Lord has sent a message against Jacob;**
   it will fall on Israel.
⁹**All the people will know it —**
   Ephraim and the inhabitants of Samaria —
who say with pride
   and arrogance of heart,
¹⁰**"The bricks have fallen down,**
   but we will rebuild with dressed stone;
the fig trees have been felled,
   but we will replace them with cedars."
¹¹**But the LORD has strengthened Rezin's foes against them**
   and has spurred their enemies on.
¹²**Arameans from the east and Philistines from the west**
   have devoured Israel with open mouth.

Yet for all this, his anger is not turned away,
   his hand is still upraised.

This oracle is divided into four parts:

Introduction	9:8
Accusation of pride	9:9–10
Punishment	9:11–12a
Refrain	9:12b

9:8–10 The introduction simply announces a message from God concerning or against (not "to") the northern nation of Israel. The Hebrew verbs in 9:8 are both perfects, thus both should be translated in the past tense as completed action (NIV has one in the future tense).[356] This means that at some earlier time, God revealed his will to the people of Israel (possibly referring to the preaching of Amos, Hosea, or Isaiah himself) and now the will of God expressed in those earlier prophecies "has fallen" (*nāpal*) on them, for it is now being fulfilled. Isaiah wanted his Judean audience to understand the theological principle that God does what he says he will do, that his warnings through the prophets come true. This implies that if they have already begun to come true for Israel, then it will not be long before they will also come true for Judah, the people in his audience.

All the people of Israel "knew" (*weyādǝ'û*; not "will know" as in NIV) about God's warnings (9:9), for these challenging words were not hidden from anyone. Thus, the entire nation carried a responsibility to respond appropriately to what God said. But, instead of humbling themselves, repenting of sin, and seeking God's gracious deliverance from destruction, the people of Israel proudly[357] and defiantly proclaimed that they would never let a few negative

---

[356] The perfect form refers to completed action, GKC §106b.

[357] וּבְגֹדֶל לֵבָב is lit. "and with a big/great heart," a fitting description of the proud.

events discourage them (9:10). Isaiah quotes their boastful chant, "You can't defeat us!" Even though there was an initial blow that caused some mud brick walls and their sycamore roof timbers to fall,[358] the people were determined to rebuild things better than they were at the first. Notice that there is no request for God's help after this event; instead, the people of Israel believed that they could fix everything themselves. Hayes and Irvine think the fallen bricks refer to the damage caused by the strong earthquake that Amos predicted in the time of Uzziah around thirty years earlier (Amos 1:1; 8:8; Zech 14:4),[359] but that happened too many years ago to have relevance to Isaiah's audience at this time. Clements suggests that the prophet was describing some initial destruction caused when Assyria first destroyed cities in Israel around 733 BC.[360] This arrogant response demonstrates how stubborn and overconfident the people of Israel were. They thought they could determine their own destiny.

9:11–12 Since the people remained in their sinful pride and did not ask for God's help, God raised up, strengthened, and encouraged an adversary against Rezin king of Syria (Israel's ally in the Syro-Ephraimite War against Judah). The foe that God raised up was the Assyrian king Tiglath-pileser III (2 Kgs 15:29). This demonstrated God's sovereign control over all the nations of the earth, even the pagan ones. Although this verse does not describe the whole series of events in this war, 2 Kgs 16:7–9 provides the additional fact that Tiglath-pileser III was invited to enter this war by Judah's King Ahaz because Ahaz refused to trust in God to deliver him (Isa 7:1–12). In addition, Israel suffered further defeat when troops from Philistia attacked, though the date of this military conquest is unknown (for similar attacks see Amos 1:3–8; 2 Kgs 16:6; 2 Chr 28:18).

This oracle ends with a refrain that characterizes this whole unit. The refrain has three parts: (a) even though God has already brought all these judgments to pass; (b) his anger has not stopped; and (c) his sovereign hand is still outstretched and ready to punish more. Although it would have been wise to turn to God as soon as the first punishment came (Exod 7–11; Amos 4:6–11), the people did not repent. Consequently God will continue to exert more and more pressure to convince his people in Israel to turn to him, rather than to rely on themselves. The continued work of God's wrath parallels Amos's repeated reminder to the Israelites that because of three sins and even four, God will not turn back his wrath against any sinful nation (Amos 1:3,6,9,11,13). Either punishment for sin must be exacted before God's wrath is satisfied and removed (Deut 13:17; Josh 7:26) or else one must seek to atone for these sins (Exod

---

[358] שִׁקְמִים refers to the tall straight sycamore tree of Israel, not a gnarly fig tree (NIV), which was not of much use for building homes. The cedar wood from Lebanon was more expensive but even stronger, bigger, and longer.

[359] Hayes and Irvine, *Isaiah*, 185, also find evidence of this earthquake in Amos 9:1.

[360] Both Clements, *Isaiah 1–39*, 67, and Sweeney, *Isaiah 1–39*, 193, believe that this damage was caused by a recent military conflict.

32:12,20, 31–32; Lev 4–5). The image of the "outstretched hand" (*yādô nĕṭ ûyâ*) of God is a symbol of power ready to act, either for good, as in the exodus (Exod 15:12; Deut 4:34; 5:15; 7:19), or for punishment of sin (Jer 21:5; Ezek 6:14; Zeph 2:13). God's outstretched hand demonstrates his power to carry out his plans for all the nations of the earth (Isa 14:26–27). In this case God's outstretched hand still has plans to enact more punishment against Israel.

GOD'S WRATH AGAINST UNREPENTANT LEADERS (9:13–17)

¹³**But the people have not returned to him who struck them,**
  nor have they sought the LORD Almighty.
¹⁴**So the LORD will cut off from Israel both head and tail,**
  both palm branch and reed in a single day;
¹⁵**the elders and prominent men are the head,**
  the prophets who teach lies are the tail.
¹⁶**Those who guide this people mislead them,**
  and those who are guided are led astray.
¹⁷**Therefore the Lord will take no pleasure in the young men,**
  nor will he pity the fatherless and widows,
for everyone is ungodly and wicked,
  every mouth speaks vileness.

Yet for all this, his anger is not turned away,
his hand is still upraised.

The second oracle explains part of the reason the nation of Israel continued to suffer under God's wrath. The oracle can be outlined:

What the people did	9:13
God's punishment	9:14–17a
Refrain	9:17b

9:13   God's first acts of judgment did not result in the transformation or "repentance" (*lō' šāb*) of his people Israel. The purpose of God's initial disciplinary punishment was to restore his people, but the people stubbornly refused to turn to him (cf. Amos 4:6–11). The people's central fault was failure to seek God. This seeking is not a searching for something that is lost and cannot be found (Lev 10:16) or the process of investigating to see if something is true (Deut 17:4). Seeking God is a purposeful looking for assistance from the Almighty (31:1). It requires people to admit they need help and causes them to rely on someone stronger than themselves. It involves a heart's desire[361] for God, a willingness to ask for guidance, and by implication includes a commitment to "turn, repent" and follow God's answer.

---

[361] Frequently דָּרַשׁ, "seek," is modified with phrases like "with all his heart" to emphasize the seriousness of the soul's commitment to the task (2 Chr 12:14; 19:3; 30:19; Ps 119:2,10). 1 Chr 28:9 indicates that those who seek God will find him.

9:14–17 Since the first act of discipline did not bring about a humble confession of sins, a second punishment was necessary. God has already "cut off" (*wayyakrēt*, not "will cut off" as NIV)[362] both small and great, the symbolic head and tail (cf. the imagery in Deut 28:13; Isa 19:15). Specifically, the head is interpreted as the leaders of the nation (elders, men of high status) and the tail refers to the prophets (9:15). Those who suffered included the weak and insignificant young men, fatherless, and widows (9:17a). Three points are emphasized: (a) both important and unimportant people—that is, everyone—will suffer; (b) religious and political leaders who have deceived people are responsible for this suffering; and (c) the sin is so great that God will not even pity the helpless, for wickedness characterizes everyone. The primary sin of the leaders is that of leading people astray by offering misleading guidance and even outright lies (3:12; 28:7; 32:5–7; Amos 2:4; Mic 2:11; 3:5–8; Jer 23:13,23). This failure of leadership resulted in the acceptance of wicked behavior and foolish vile talk by the average citizen. These people repeatedly failed to please God,[363] and the pleasure and joy God desired to have with his holy people was missing (9:17a; see Zeph 3:17). Therefore God's anger still existed, and more judgment would come to Israel from his powerful hand (9:17b).

GOD'S DESTRUCTION OF THE NATION (9:18–21)

[18]Surely wickedness burns like a fire;
  it consumes briers and thorns,
 it sets the forest thickets ablaze,
  so that it rolls upward in a column of smoke.
[19]By the wrath of the LORD Almighty
  the land will be scorched
 and the people will be fuel for the fire;
  no one will spare his brother.
[20] On the right they will devour,
  but still be hungry;
 on the left they will eat,
  but not be satisfied.
 Each will feed on the flesh of his own offspring:
[21] Manasseh will feed on Ephraim, and Ephraim on Manasseh;
  together they will turn against Judah.

---

[362] The *vav* with imperfect verb וַיִּכְרֵת is frequently translated as a past (if after a perfect verb—as in 9:13), often showing the logical consequences "so . . ." (GKC §111a,I).

[363] 1QIsaᵃ has "to spare," which creates a good parallel with "to pity" in the next line. Wildberger, *Isaiah 1–12*, 219, 221, accepts this as a better reading. This involves replacing יִשְׂמַח, "he will delight, rejoice," with יַחְמוֹל, "he will spare," but these words are so different that a scribe is not likely to make such an error. The Masoretic tradition is the harder reading, while the Qumran could be seen as an attempt to improve or clarify a hard text. The imperfect verb "he will take no pleasure" could be interpreted as continual or repeated action in past time (GKC § 107b,e), meaning "he did not continually/repeatedly take pleasure."

**Yet for all this, his anger is not turned away,
his hand is still upraised.**

The third oracle in this series closes the negative illustrative examples drawn from Israel's recent history. It brings the events in Israel up to the present time, for the Israelites had already attacked Judah (9:21). The implied question for Isaiah's audience in Judah is: Do the people of Judah want to follow in the footsteps of the people of Israel and have similar divine punishment fall on their nation? Isaiah paints a picture in three parts:

Fiery destruction of Israel	9:18–19
Internal self-destruction	9:20–21a
Refrain	9:21b

9:18–19 Two fires are burning in Israel. One is a fire caused by the sinful wickedness of the people (9:18), while the other is the fire of God's wrath against the land (9:19). Burning is a fitting metaphor to describe the destructive nature of sin. The burning of dried up thorns and briers would be quick and intense. Isaiah has already defined the wicked people as briers and thorns in his vineyard parable in 5:6 and has pictured the land as being full of thorns and briers in 7:23–25, but neither of those passages spoke of sin as a burning flame destroying the thorns and briers. The burning power of sin has now caused massive destruction (not "will scorch" as in NIV) and a "rising, majestic, proud" smoke cloud for all to see.[364] Another cause for burning was the fury of God's wrath against their sin (9:19). These evil events in Israel were not outside God's sovereign control or his ability to administer justice. God was involved with the initial destruction of parts of the land; it was not caused just by a political accident or bad luck. But in the future (the last phrase uses an imperfect verb) things will get even worse, for people will turn against one another and have no mercy on each other. The meaning of this prediction is interpreted in 9:20–21a.

9:20–21 The internal disintegration of society is pictured as a period of cannibalism and tribal conflict. This future situation in 9:20b is justified in 9:20a by pointing to inhumane ways people have treated one another.[365] This cannibalism probably should not be interpreted literally, but possibly as a metaphor for past political assassinations in Israel (cf. 2 Kgs 15), as well as the

---

[364] גֵּאוּת is used in Isaiah to mean "proud" (28:1–3; a related term גַּאֲוָה is used in 9:9), suggesting that Isaiah has purposely chosen this word to portray the people's attitude toward their sin. Instead of hiding it, they proudly display it (cf. 3:8–9). Their sin has found them out and is very evident to God.

[365] NIV translates all these verbs as future, which is what one might expect after the future prediction at the end of 9:19. Nevertheless, one must take seriously the two *vav* plus imperfect verb forms (often noting past events) at the beginning of the verse and note the change to the simple imperfect (often noting future events) at the end of the verse. By leveling these all out as future verbs, the NIV has missed the fact that Isaiah is drawing on past behavior (20a) to legitimate his prediction about what will happen in the future (20b).

inhumane treatment of the weak by the strong (cf. Mic 3:1–4; Hos 4:2; 6:8–9; 7:1–2,7; 8:4). But in the future (20b) things will get even worse, for the common people will show no respect or care for anyone, not even for their own children. The theological acceptance of certain sins as normative or acceptable in dire situations will only lead to an escalation of wickedness due to the selfish and depraved state of the people controlled by the power of sin.

9:21a describes the disintegration of the national unity of Israel. No verbs connect the ideas in the first half of 9:21, so it is most natural to translate these verbless noun clauses with the present tense.[366] Not only are the main northern tribes unable to get along together, but they also have turned to attack their blood relatives in Judah. This conflict, called the Syro-Ephraimite War, began because Ahaz refused to join the anti-Assyrian coalition supported by Syria and Israel (7:1–4). Consequently, God's anger has not yet finished its purposes and his hand is still stretched out to bring more judgment on the northern nation of Israel.

Up to this point, Isaiah's audience in Judah would have agreed with everything Isaiah has said. The northern nation of Israel was proud, violent, wicked, and about to fall apart. Judah agreed with the Lord's judgment of the nations and especially God's conclusion that they deserve punishment for attacking Judah. Like the prophet Amos in Amos 1:3–2:3, Isaiah convinces his audience of the sinfulness of others first, so that he can apply the theological principles of those situations to similar problems that existed in his present audience.[367]

LAMENT: JUDAH'S OPPRESSION WILL LEAD TO ITS DEMISE (10:1–4)

¹Woe to those who make unjust laws,
  to those who issue oppressive decrees,
²to deprive the poor of their rights
  and withhold justice from the oppressed of my people,
 making widows their prey
  and robbing the fatherless.
³What will you do on the day of reckoning,
  when disaster comes from afar?
 To whom will you run for help?
  Where will you leave your riches?
⁴Nothing will remain but to cringe among the captives
  or fall among the slain.

 Yet for all this, his anger is not turned away,
  his hand is still upraised.

---

[366] GKC §140–142 views noun clauses as describing the present state of affairs, with the "to be" verb supplied in English, though the surrounding contextual presence of perfect or imperfect verbs may argue for another tense.

[367] Smith, *Amos*, 52, 102, 131, explains how Amos used the first part of his War Oracle to establish several theological principles, so that he could apply them to Israel in the last oracle. This is similar to Nathan's trapping of David through the use of a parable that illustrated David's behavior (2 Sam 12:1–7).

Suddenly, the pattern of the preceding oracles is temporarily broken and a new approach interrupts the prophet's presentation of his message. A change is evident because now the prophet (a) cries out in lamentation in a woe oracle, (b) condemns leaders for oppression against the poor, and (c) asks questions about what "you," his audience, will do. These factors indicate that Isaiah is coming to his conclusion and is directly addressing the leaders in Judah in 10:1–4.[368] Following a pattern used in earlier woe oracles in 5:8–25, Isaiah tries to persuade his stubborn audience not to follow the path of Israel, for if they do, God's wrath will fall on them as well. The oracle can be outlined in three parts:

Condemnation of the courts	10:1–2
Warning of judgment	10:3–4a
Refrain	10:4b

10:1–2 A woe oracle is designed to communicate a person's sorrow over the death of an individual/nation or an approaching judgment that is close at hand (Amos 6:1–8). The oracle could be accompanied with weeping, the donning of sackcloth, and all the other behaviors that express deep grief over the expected death of someone (Jer 22:18; 34:5). Isaiah probably thought he would have a better chance of convincing his audience to change their behavior if he sympathized with his audience over the tragic consequences of Judah's sins. Isaiah's lament should not be seen an expression true, heartfelt sorrow over Judah's inevitable demise if she does not change.

The cause of Isaiah's lament is connected to the leaders' oppressive treatment of the poor. Unjust laws[369] and injustice in the courts enable the powerful to steal money and property and deny the rights of fellow Hebrews, thus making it possible for the wealthy to enrich themselves even more. This oppression indicates that legal injustices were committed in both the legislative (10:1) and judicial (10:2) branches of the royal administration under Ahaz. These accusations show an arbitrary slanting of justice for the selfish financial gain of a few. The leaders made evil and oppressive laws, thus legitimating their removal of equal rights and fair processing of matters of law and justice. Instead of mercifully caring for the helpless widows and orphans, these leaders purposely[370] treated the possessions of others like the spoils of war. These were heartless acts of selfishness, just as evil as the deeds of the leaders of Israel.

10:3–4 Instead of immediately condemning his audience, Isaiah asked a question, similar to the invitation to reason together in 1:18 (cf. 2:22; 5:3–4).

---

[368] Seitz, *Isaiah 1–39*, 91, and Childs, *Isaiah*, 86, are among those commentators who interpret 10:1–4 as an address to leaders in Judah.

[369] Literally the Hb. laments הַחֹקְקִים חִקְקֵי־אָוֶן, "those who decree decrees of iniquity," using a participle and a noun from the same root.

[370] The Hb. infinitive construct verb לְהַטּוֹת in 10:2 express the purpose of their action (GKC §114f). They did these things for the purpose of "depriving, withholding, making, and robbing." This suggests that their behavior was an intentional plan, not just something that happened.

The question is, "What will you do?" It gives his listeners the opportunity to respond with sorrow, repentance, and a determination to make things right. He framed the question around their accountability on the "day of reckoning," assuming that day will come. The superior power that will bring this day of reckoning on them is not identified by name. Two simple questions are presented: "Where will you turn for help? What will you do with all your riches?" If Ahaz has already called on Assyria for help to relieve him from the attack of Syria and Israel, Isaiah seems to be saying that the military power of Assyria will not deliver the leaders of Judah from the disaster that will come when they have to give an account to God for their unjust treatment of the weak in Judah. Assyria may temporarily deliver Judah in this war, but who will save these sinful people on the day of God's reckoning?

Isaiah answers his own questions with a sorrowful conclusion (10:4). There will be no one to turn to, no nation, no leader, and not even God. There will be "nothing, no options" (biltî). They will be brutally treated like all the other prisoners and killed like all the others who will be slaughtered in war. Why? The anger of God that destroyed Israel is the same power that will move the outstretched hand of God to destroy Judah (10:4b). God will play no favorites.

(3) The Judgment of Proud Assyria (10:5–34)

AUDIENCE AND PURPOSE.   Having introduced a woe oracle against Judah in 10:1–4, Isaiah continues with a woe oracle against Assyria in 10:5–11. Although this juxtaposition produces continuity with 10:1–4 in the written text, it is unlikely that these two woe oracles were connected so closely when they were orally presented in Judah. The purpose of this new sermon is hinted at in 10:24–27. In those verses Isaiah directly addresses his audience in Zion ("my people" 10:24) using second person pronouns. The news that God will destroy Assyria (10:5–19) was probably heard with mixed feelings. On the one hand, Judah needed Assyria to defend it against Israel and Syria in the Syro-Ephraimite War, so many people in Isaiah's audience wanted a strong Assyrian nation. On the other hand, the Assyrian taxation and oppressive control of Judah that came after the war was not welcome. So the destruction of Assyria was a sign of deliverance from a "friend" who had turned out to be an enemy. Assyria's destruction is an amazing indication of divine grace to his undeserving people who chose to trust Assyria instead of God.

This passage gives a broader understanding of God's plans for Judah. (a) God's just anger against Judah will be satisfied through the Assyrians (10:6). (b) Eventually, God will remove the Assyrian yoke by destroying them (10:25–27). (c) After Israel's destruction there will, in time, be a remnant that will trust God and be restored (10:20–23). The theological implications are (a) God is in control; (b) God always destroys the proud; (c) Judah should trust God, not Assyria; and (d) God has great plans for his righteous remnant in the future.

This message has interlinking connections with earlier messages: (a) the unidentified enemy in 5:26–30 and the Assyrians' desolation of Judah in 7:17–25 is the rod in God's hand that executes his anger on Judah in 10:5–6; (b) God's condemnation of Assyria's pride in 10:12 and his opposition to pride in 2:9–17; 3:16; 5:15 and 9:9; (c) the burning of thorns and briers in 9:18 appears again in 10:17; (d) the return of the remnant is found in both 8:3–4 and 10:20–23; and (e) there is an encouragement not to fear in 8:13 and 10:24. Although each of these motifs must be interpreted within the present context in chap. 10, the earlier development of each theme has provided some pre-understanding of what that concept entails. The use of these motifs may be a virtual repetition of earlier messages and not involve any reapplication or development (the central issue of a proud heart in 10:12), or they may be expanded in a different direction by introducing new ideas not employed earlier (the people who are proud and the evidence of pride changes from 9:9–10).

HISTORICAL SETTING.   The date of this message is placed sometime before the destruction of Assyria (10:16–19,33–34) and after its attack on Samaria (10:11). Assyria is either about to arrive (10:11) or is just arriving at Jerusalem (10:28–32), so this message probably comes almost at the end of the Syro-Ephraimite War. Two factors cause some to date this sermon much later, to the time of Sargon or Sennacherib. First, many assume that 10:9 is referring to the past destruction of Calnah and Arpad (in 738 BC), Hamath (729 BC), Carchemish (742 BC), Damascus (733 BC), and Samaria (732 BC) based on the Assyrian king's plans in 10:7. Since there are no verbs in 10:9, one must imply either a past, present, or future verb. If one takes the comparison between the Assyrians' future hope to deal with Jerusalem and the Assyrian's past work at Samaria in 10:11 (there are verbs in this verse) as a clue to the pattern implied in 10:9, then the translation would be: "Will not (the future defeat of) Calno be like (the past defeat of) Carchemesh, will not (the future defeat of) Hamath be like (the past defeat of) Arphad?" This future/past comparison (in 10:11) vividly reveals Assyria's pride about its future purposes to overpower more nations. This interpretation would put this verse towards the end of the Syro-Ephraimite War, around 732 BC.

The second factor that may indicate the date of this message is the march of the Assyrian army in 10:28–32. Some suggest this describes the Assyrian invasion by Tiglath-pileser III around 734–32 BC, or the attack on Jerusalem by Sennacherib in 701 BC when Hezekiah revolted, or Sargon's conquests in the Philistine plain between 712–711 BC, or Sargon's earlier invasion in 720 BC.[371] Since Sennacherib approached Jerusalem from the south, the 701 attack is eliminated as a possibility. Because the army's route described here

---

[371] See footnote 325 above.

cannot be firmly identified with any past Assyrian advances, Childs considers this a vision of what will happen in the future.[372] But others maintain that the identification of such a specific route and the unusualness of the march on Jerusalem argue for a literal description of an approaching army. It is probably best to admit that it is impossible to determine the date of this Assyrian march since there are no biblical or Assyrian records to verify which king took this route. Other information in the context must be used to suggest an appropriate time.

The fact that there is no report of fighting on this march, nor a battle at Jerusalem, implies that the Assyrians were not at war against Judah (this eliminates the Sargon and Sennacherib attacks). This situation fits the Syro-Ephraimite War, when Tiglath-pileser III rescued Ahaz from the attack of Syria and Israel (ca. 732 BC) and then made Ahaz his servant. Although it is not required that all of 9:1–11:16 come from the time of the Syro-Ephraimite War, this date is consistent with other historical data in this section.

STRUCTURE.   The organizational arrangement of 10:5–34 is centered around God's challenge to Judah in 10:20–27. The unit is divided into three paragraphs:

God will judge Assyrians for pride	10:5–19
God will save a remnant	10:20–27
Invading Assyrians will be cut off	10:28–34

GOD WILL JUDGE ASSYRIA FOR ITS PRIDE (10:5–19)

⁵"Woe to the Assyrian, the rod of my anger,
  in whose hand is the club of my wrath!
⁶I send him against a godless nation,
  I dispatch him against a people who anger me,
to seize loot and snatch plunder,
  and to trample them down like mud in the streets.
⁷But this is not what he intends,
  this is not what he has in mind;
his purpose is to destroy,
  to put an end to many nations.
⁸'Are not my commanders all kings?' he says.
⁹'Has not Calno fared like Carchemish?
  Is not Hamath like Arpad,
    and Samaria like Damascus?
¹⁰As my hand seized the kingdoms of the idols,
  kingdoms whose images excelled those of Jerusalem and Samaria—
¹¹shall I not deal with Jerusalem and her images
    as I dealt with Samaria and her idols?'"

¹²When the Lord has finished all his work against Mount Zion and Jerusalem, he will say, "I will punish the king of Assyria for the willful pride of his heart and the haughty look in his eyes. ¹³For he says:

---

[372] Childs, *Isaiah*, 96, concludes that this is "a prophetic oracle, not an historical report."

"'By the strength of my hand I have done this,
  and by my wisdom, because I have understanding.
I removed the boundaries of nations,
  I plundered their treasures;
  like a mighty one I subdued their kings.
¹⁴As one reaches into a nest,
  so my hand reached for the wealth of the nations;
as men gather abandoned eggs,
  so I gathered all the countries;
not one flapped a wing,
  or opened its mouth to chirp.'"

¹⁵Does the ax raise itself above him who swings it,
  or the saw boast against him who uses it?
As if a rod were to wield him who lifts it up,
  or a club brandish him who is not wood!
¹⁶Therefore, the Lord, the Lord Almighty,
  will send a wasting disease upon his sturdy warriors;
under his pomp a fire will be kindled
  like a blazing flame.
¹⁷The Light of Israel will become a fire,
  their Holy One a flame;
in a single day it will burn and consume
  his thorns and his briers.
¹⁸The splendor of his forests and fertile fields
  it will completely destroy,
  as when a sick man wastes away.
¹⁹And the remaining trees of his forests will be so few
  that a child could write them down.

It seems somewhat incongruous that Isaiah would lament the fall of Assyria in this woe oracle. He should be happy that God would judge Assyria and save Jerusalem. It is clear that Isaiah's woe is not addressing an Assyrian audience directly, so the purpose of a woe directed to a third party is significantly different from one declared directly to the people who will die. Consequently, the lament over the fall of Assyria functions as good news of assurance to Isaiah's audience in Judah. This helps support the prophet's call for the people of Zion not to be afraid of the Assyrians (10:24) and to wait patiently for God to act against Assyria (10:25–26). Secondarily, this oracle demonstrates the foolishness of Ahaz's dependence on Assyria for protection. The Assyrians will come against Judah (hardly the help Ahaz wanted) and will soon be destroyed (hardly a dependable ally).

The first paragraph is made up of three parts:

Assyria did not follow God's plan	10:5–11
Assyria's pride denies God's power	10:12–15
God's judgment of Assyria	10:16–19

10:5–6 It is often difficult to identify the hand of God in history because he frequently uses human instruments to accomplish his will. It is also difficult for the human instruments chosen by God to distinguish between their own desires and God's will. Consequently, it is easy to deny God's involvement in events or to pervert his plans because of human desires or emotions. The prophet's divine perspective enables him to clarify God's role in using Assyria and to point out Assyria's perversion of God's plan. Initially the Assyrians are pictured as instruments used by God to accomplish his will. God is sovereign and he employs many nations to accomplish his plans on earth. But the Assyrians can only act according to God's directions. This perspective has two implications for the people of Judah: (a) it encourages them because Assyria's power is limited by parameters set by God; and (b) it creates fear because the parameters of Assyrian destruction are motivated by God's wrath. The Assyrian role of being a "rod, club" (*šēbeṭ*) in God's hand[373] sounds threatening, though the "rod, club" can symbolize the beneficent or punitive power of a king who holds a scepter (14:6; Jer 48:17; Ps 110:2; Amos 1:5,8), the rod of a teacher that disciplines a student (Prov 13:24; 22:15; 26:3), or the miraculous power of God (Moses' rod in Exod 4:2–4; 7:9–20; 17:9). The negative context suggests this rod delivers punishment (cf. Job 9:34; 21:9) based on God's indignation and wrath. God will send the Assyrian army as his rod against the "godless nation" (*ḥānēp* in 10:6) Judah because he is "furious, angry"[374] with his people. Israel was described as "godless" in 9:17 and God has already said he was "furious" (9:19) with them, but now this pejorative title "godless nation" refers to Judah.

Although 2 Kgs 16:7–9 indicates that faithless Ahaz called on the Assyrians to deliver him in the Syro-Ephraimite War, Isaiah now reveals that God will intervene and "send him"[375] against Judah, thus Judah's supposed protector will become their destroyer. The consequence of falling into the hands of an angry God is military defeat, becoming an object of plunder (cf. 8:1), and being trampled on like mud in the street (10:6b, see 5:5;). These consequences represent the total humiliation of the sinful nation of Judah.

10:7 This poem contrasts the Assyrian perspective on their role as a conqueror of nations with God's original intention in 10:5–6. The Assyrians had their own ideas about what they would do. Their mind's desire caused them to think in sinful ways that were beyond and contrary to God's purposes. Their

---

[373] The Hb. text has בְּיָדָם, "in their hand," in the second half of 10:5, but H. D. Hummel, "Enclitic Mem in Early Northwest Semitic, Especially Hebrew," *JBL* 76 (1957): 94, has suggested that the final *mem* could be an enclitic *mem* rather than the pronominal suffix "their," thus giving the translation "in the hand," which makes more sense. Another possible interpretation is, "the club of my anger is in their hand."

[374] עֶבְרָתִי describes the fierceness of God's anger, so "infuriate me" would be a better translation than "anger me" in the NIV of 10:6.

[375] אֲשַׁלְּחֶנּוּ is lit. "I will send him" with *nun energicum* before the suffix (GKC §58i-j).

purpose (lit. it was "in their heart") was to "destroy, annihilate"[376] people, not just to defeat an enemy.

10:8–9   To solidify the audience's acceptance of God's just punishment of Assyria, Isaiah quotes what the Assyrian king proudly said in 10:8–11 (similar to the quotation of Sennacherib's proud words in Isa 36–37). The Assyrian king asks two rhetorical questions (10:8–9) and makes two arrogant claims (10:10–11). The first question compares the strength of the Assyrian military commanders with the power of the kings who rule over small city-states in the countries around Palestine. The question expects a yes answer; in fact it is more of a statement than a question to be debated.[377] Certainly some Assyrian generals were as powerful as, if not more powerful than, the kings of small city-states, so there is some truth to these claims (10:8).[378] Everyone knew that the Assyrian commanders had defeated the kings of several of these small city-states. The second question lists a series of cities north of Judah, but the nature of the comparative question is unclear. The noun clauses have no verbs, thus translations often supply present tense verbs ("Is not Hamath like Arphad?") or past tense verbs ("Was Hamath not like Arphad?").[379] Both approaches assume that these cities were already conquered. A problem raised by this assumption is that if all these cities in 10:9 were already conquered, the date of this oracle would have to be about 15 years later, in the time of Sargon II, not during the Syro-Ephraimite War.[380] Motyer solves this problem by suggesting that the king is proudly looking to what he will do in the future, not describing past historical conquests.[381] Yet Carchemish and Arphad had fallen to Tiglath-pileser III in campaigns from 742–738 BC and Damascus had fallen in the Syro-Ephraimite War, so it would not be out place for the king to brag about what he has already done in this military expedition. Because of these historical factors and the nature of the explicit comparison between Jerusalem (a future event) and Samaria (a past event) in 10:10–11, it seems appropriate to accept a variation of Motyer's approach. It appears that the Assyrian king Tiglath-pileser III is bragging by saying, "Will not Calno (a future conquest) be

---

[376] לְהַשְׁמִיד, the *hiphil* infinitive construct, expresses the purpose or aim (GKC §114f). The word is often used in the context of the complete annihilation of people in Holy War (Deut 4:3,26; 6:15; 7:23–24).

[377] Questions beginning with הֲלֹא ask an obvious rhetorical question (GKC §150e). Thus the question "Do you not know?" is equivalent to "Surely you do know." Thus the question form should not be taken as an inquiry about something that the Assyrian king wants to know. He is actually making an arrogant claim that has some basis in facts.

[378] P. Machinist, "Assyria and its Images in First Isaiah," *JAOS* 103 (1983): 734–35, suggests that this arrogant claim is partially a word play based on the fact that the Hb. word שַׂר, *śar*, "prince, official" is a cognate word with the Akkadian *šarru*, "king."

[379] Blenkinsopp, *Isaiah 1–39*, 251, prefers the past tense verbs, while NIV chose present.

[380] Sweeney, *Isaiah 1–39*, 206–207, dates the fall of Carchemish to Sargon II in 717 BC and the fall of Arphad to Sargon II in 720 BC.

[381] Motyer, *The Prophecy of Isaiah*, 114, interprets this as "an impressionistic expression of inexorable advance" in the future, not past events.

like Carchemish (a past conquest)"—similar to the comparisons of 10:10–11. This is more consistent with the historical data, provides the king's arguments with a rational basis of past experience, and demonstrates his presumptuous pride about what he will do in the near future.

10:10–11 The proud king tries to demonstrate his superiority over all the idols and gods in the ancient Near East. He again argues on the basis of past experience defeating various cities and destroying the idols that were supposed to defend the people who lived in those cities. Here the Assyrian king refers to cities that believed their pagan gods (like Baal, Hadad, or Marduk) would protect them. In the Assyrian victory over these cities, the idols proved to be worthless. The logical case the Assyrian king makes is fairly persuasive. If he has conquered the cities and gods of much larger places than Jerusalem (10:10b), will he not in the future be able to conquer the city of Jerusalem and her worthless idols (10:11a)—just as he has already attacked and defeated Samaria and its gods (10:11b)? In one sense Tiglath-pileser III is right, the pagan idols that were so prevalent in Israel (2 Kgs 17:7–17) and in Jerusalem during the time of Ahaz (2 Chr 28) would not protect these cities. As Motyer comments, "It is not failure at arms etc. that rendered them helpless before Assyria; it was spiritual falsity and, in the case of Samaria and Jerusalem, apostasy."[382] Of course, the Assyrian king was totally ignorant of the fact that Judah's true God was not a worthless idol.

10:12–15 This paragraph presents additional evidence in the form of another quotation (10:13–14) to prove that the Assyrian king deserves God's punishment. Although some of the listeners may have wondered about God's power to thwart the Assyrians' mistreatment of Jerusalem, Isaiah assures them that God will hold Tiglath-pileser III accountable for his willful rebellion against the divine role God gave the Assyrians (10:5). The structure of the second half of this woe oracle is similar to the first—both have quotations and both end with questions (see 10:8–11)—but this time it is God's rhetorical question (not that of the Assyrian king). God's evidence against the Assyrian king begins with an unexpected prose interpretation of Assyrian motives in 10:12.

10:12 The presence of 10:12 in the middle of these accusations against Assyria is problematic because (a) it begins like a new narrative, "and it will come to pass," as if it is introducing a new topic; (b) it is written in prose, rather than the poetry that characterizes the rest of this passage; (c) it prematurely announces God's future judgment, instead of including it with 10:16–19; and (d) it interprets the words of 10:8–11 as "pride" in order to integrate this section with one of his central themes in 2–12 (cf. 2:11,17; 3:18; 9:9; 13:19; 28:1). These factors suggest that the author added these interpretive words to

---

[382] Motyer, *The Prophecy of Isaiah,* 114. Although it is hard to know what Tiglath-pileser III knew about the worship of Yahweh, Rabshakeh's presentation of Sennacherib's demands repeatedly refer to Yahweh—though he mistakenly thought that Hezekiah had destroyed the altars and idols of Yahweh in his reforms (36:7).

his original prophecy when he put this material in written form,[383] probably for the express purpose of contrasting God's words in 10:12 with the Assyrian king's words in 10:8–11,13–14 and of connecting this oracle with a key theological theme in chaps. 2–12—God will humble the proud (2:9,11,12,17; 3:16; 5:15–16; 9:9).

God's future plan will allow the Assyrians to finish[384] the work he assigned them at Jerusalem (10:12a), even though they are very arrogant and acted inappropriately in violent ways (10:7). Lest anyone in Isaiah's audience get the wrong idea about what will happen (cf. Hab 1:12–13), God's intention is not to bless Assyria. Instead, God will punish[385] the exalted heart and proud look of this king. The audience in Judah need not fear the Assyrians; they need to trust God and refrain from prideful actions themselves.

10:13–14 The second quotation of the Assyrian king focuses on the king's pride in his own abilities and power, consistent with the pattern already stated in 10:11. The king is proudly claiming for himself sovereignty over the world, thus putting himself in God's place. In first person speech in v. 13 the king admires his own strength, wisdom, and might. He praises himself by recounting what he has done in 13a and what he will accomplishment in 13b.[386] The removal of boundaries relates to the Assyrian practice of deporting people, annexing provinces into other countries, and turning independent countries into provinces of Assyria. In the last line of 13 the king claims to be like a "mighty one,"[387] a not so subtle attempt to claim God's divine name (see 1:24; 9:6; 10:21; 49:26; 60:16).

The task of plundering whatever the Assyrian king wanted is illustrated and compared to taking eggs from a hen that has left the nest. His pride is evident both in the ease with which he took what he wanted and his total humiliation of the people he plundered. Essentially, the king brags that he has superior power over everyone else and can do whatever he wants. Presenting himself as almighty, he believes that no one can stop him. Isaiah and his audience would naturally lament this attitude of pride in this Assyrian king that they had trusted

---

[383] Wildberger, *Isaiah 1–12*, 424, dates this verse much later, connecting 10:12 to the reconstruction of the temple in the time of Haggai (520 BC; see Zech 4:9). He thinks the reference to the king of Assyria is a code name for the great king of Persia, but this interpretation should be rejected.

[384] יְבַצַּע is a *piel* imperfect verb, so "he will finish" is the most natural translation when referring to what God will do when certain preconditions are met.

[385] אֶפְקֹד, "I will punish," introduces a quotation of God's intentions. "He will say" in the NIV is added to clarify that this is a quotation of God, but the Hb. text does not contain these words.

[386] NIV translates the imperfects with *vav* conjunctive as past completed action "I removed . . . I plundered . . . I subdued," but this translation would require a *vav* consecutive formation. שׁוֹשֵׂתִי, "I will plunder," is probably a *piel* form of שָׁסָה, with the ס and שׁ being variations of the same sound (GKC §6k).

[387] The Hb. word כְּאַבִּיר means "like a mighty one" and can refer to God (Gen 49:24), angels (Ps 78:25), people (Ps 68:31), or animals (Jer 50:11), so it is possible (but not the best choice here) to translate this comparison "like a bull" as in Blenkinsopp, *Isaiah 1–39*, 252.

to save them, for that king had already and would continue to cause much human suffering for the people of Judah (2 Chr 28:16,20–21).

10:15   In the conclusion to this paragraph God asks a series of rhetorical questions that expose the lie that the king of Assyria was proudly expounding. The questions inquire about the real power of the Assyrian king. The king is compared to an ax, a saw, and a rod (10:5), three common tools that can do nothing unless a person picks them up and swings them. The questions inquire about how an ax can "glorify"[388] itself, how a saw can boast about itself, or how a rod accomplishes its intended tasks by itself? These are just lifeless, inert objects of wood, stone, and metal that have no ability to do anything unless a skillful person picks them up and uses them properly. The power to accomplish something comes not from the ax, saw, and rod; it comes from the person using them. The illustration pointedly makes the analogy that Assyria (the rod in 10:5) has nothing to brag about because it can do nothing unless God allows it to accomplish his purpose (10:6). The implication for Isaiah's audience is that they should trust God, the one who is the real power behind the nations, rather than fear or trust the Assyrians.

10:16–19   The conclusion of the woe oracle describes God's punishment against Assyria for its pride. God Almighty, the true lord of the nations, is the sovereign power who rules the nations of this world. First, he "sent" (*šālaḥ*) Assyria as his rod of punishment (10:6) and now he will "send" (*šālaḥ*) judgment on the Assyrians (10:16). God is also the "Light of Israel" (2:5; 60:1; Ps 27:1; Mic 7:8), the Holy One, and a destructive "fire" (*'ēš*, cf. 3:14; Exod 24:17; Deut 4:24; 9:3) that will devastate the powerful nation of Assyria. The theological emphasis on God should cause the audience to accept his sovereign lordship because he is the one who will burn up the enemy, completely decimate the proud, and quickly demonstrate his flaming power.

Clements maintains these verses are a prediction of the defeat of the Assyrian army of sturdy warriors (NIV in 10:16) because he takes the briers, thorns, and forest trees as symbols of army personnel (cf. 17:4–6).[389] The military interpretation of the imagery in 10:16–19 is unlikely, for in other passages the forest fire imagery is not used of an army (5:26–30). In 10:16 the wasting will come to one who is fat—who has "pomp, glory" (*kĕbōdô*)—terms that K. Nielsen properly associates in this context with the proud Assyrian king.[390] If 10:16 refers to the king, the burning of forests in 10:17–19 (see also 10:33–34;

---

[388] יִתְפָּאֵר in the reflexive stem of the *hithpael* means to "glorify oneself, boast about oneself," which matches "boast" in the next line and is more appropriate than the NIV "raise itself."

[389] Clements, *Isaiah 1–39*, 114, believes this passage comes from a Josianic Redaction, which was describing the destruction of Sennacherib's troops in 701 BC. Hayes and Irvine, *Isaiah*, 200–201, date the material to the time of the Syro-Ephraimite War but interpret the imagery as a reference to the destruction of the Assyrian army.

[390] Nielsen, *There is Hope for a Tree*, 191–93, connects the fatness and forest life to fertility religion imagery. The fall of the Assyrian king who thought of himself as a god is then depicted as the removal of fertility.

17:6) describes the destruction of the nation of Assyria, just like the burning of forests and briers described the destruction of the nation of Israel in 9:18. So little will be left that even a child who can only count to five or ten can number what is left of that great forest (10:19).[391]

GOD WILL SAVE A REMNANT (10:20–27)

[20]In that day the remnant of Israel,
  the survivors of the house of Jacob,
will no longer rely on him
  who struck them down
but will truly rely on the Lord,
  the Holy One of Israel.
[21]A remnant will return, a remnant of Jacob
  will return to the Mighty God.
[22]Though your people, O Israel, be like the sand by the sea,
  only a remnant will return.
Destruction has been decreed,
  overwhelming and righteous.
[23]The Lord, the Lord Almighty, will carry out
  the destruction decreed upon the whole land.

[24]Therefore, this is what the Lord, the Lord Almighty, says:

"O my people who live in Zion,
  do not be afraid of the Assyrians,
who beat you with a rod
  and lift up a club against you, as Egypt did.
[25]Very soon my anger against you will end
  and my wrath will be directed to their destruction."

[26]The Lord Almighty will lash them with a whip,
  as when he struck down Midian at the rock of Oreb;
and he will raise his staff over the waters,
  as he did in Egypt.
[27]In that day their burden will be lifted from your shoulders,
  their yoke from your neck;
the yoke will be broken
  because you have grown so fat.

The prophecy abruptly drops the discussion of the destruction of Assyria in order to introduce God's gracious plan to save a remnant of his own people. It is impossible to say exactly when Isaiah originally spoke these words during the Syro-Ephraimite conflict, but the topic naturally fits the discussion of the small "remaining trees," the "remnant[392] of the Assyrians" in 10:19. This

---

[391] Darr, *Isaiah's Vision*, 48, thinks this is implying very young children that can only count to 3, but the text makes no comment on the age of the child or how far it can count.

[392] The word "remnant" (שְׁאָר) is used in both vv. 19 and 20, thus linking these two paragraphs together.

salvation oracle predicts a day when Israelites will trust God, rather than rely on the Assyrian king to save them (10:20–21). The message was spoken when God was still angry with his people and when the Assyrian yoke was still heavy upon the nation (10:25,27). The audience was in Jerusalem, not the northern nation of Israel.[393]

These verses are arranged into two subparagraphs:

A Remnant of Judah will be preserved	10:20–23
The remnant will trust God	20–21
Many will die	22–23
Do not fear Assyria; God will destroy it	10:24–27
Do not fear Assyria	24–25
God will destroy Assyria	26–27

In these two subparagraphs God speaks about the fate of Isaiah's audience "my people" ('ammî in 10:24). At times he directly addresses his people using second person "you" pronouns (10:24–27). He promises the return of the remnant "in that day" (12:20–23), an undefined time sometime in the future (10:24–27). The audience is explicitly encouraged not to fear Assyria who is oppressing them (10:24) and implicitly exhorted to return to God and trust him (10:20–21).

10:20 The hope of God's people awaits "that day," sometime in the near future after God brings destruction on the whole land (10:23), not in a distant eschatological period. The remnant concept has both a negative and a positive side to it. The idea is derogatory because many people will die and only a small remnant will remain, but it is positive because at least some will survive God's judgment. The remnant[394] is defined as those people who "escape" (pĕlēyṭāt) in 10:20 (4:2; 6:13, NIV has "survivors") and as those who turn and rely on God in 10:21. These descriptors differentiate between a person who foolishly "leans"[395] on someone who turns out to be an enemy (2 Chr 28:19–21) and those who will one day wisely lean on God out of a righteous and sincere heart. The truthfulness of the nation's faith will be demonstrated by their action of choosing to trust the Holy One of Israel rather than the Assyrians. This is directly the opposite of what happened in 9:13, where the people of Israel refused to turn to God.

10:21 The announcement that the "remnant will return" (šĕʾār yāšûb) reminds one of the name of Isaiah's son in 7:3 (Shear-Jashub).[396] This prom-

---

[393] Watts, *Isaiah 1–33*, 153, believes 10:20–23 is about Israel's oppressor (10:20) Rezin and 10:24–27 is about Judah's oppressor Assyria, but it makes more sense to see these as two salvation oracles concerning Judah.

[394] G. Hasel, *The Remnant* (Berrien Springs: Andrews University Press, 1980), 96–98, shows that the remnant motif (שְׁאָר) is frequently found in Assyrian texts.

[395] The root שָׁעַן is found only in the *niphal* reflexive and means to "lean oneself, support oneself" upon something else for stability, thus it expresses trust and dependence.

[396] One should not read this later positive use of the phrase back into 7:3, for almost any phrase

ise in 10:21 assures the listeners in Judah that no one should have any doubts about God's glorious promise that a remnant will return. This event will happen and Jacob will return to the Mighty God. The title "Mighty God"[397] (identical to the name in 9:5) emphasizes God's strength and ability to accomplish what he plans.

10:22–23 Unfortunately, only a small fraction of God's people will return to the land. The original promise to Abram of innumerable descendents like the sands of the sea (Gen 22:17; 32:12) will not be fulfilled at this time, because the same Mighty God that will save them must first carry out his righteous decrees of punishment against those who trust in Assyria. This does not mean that God will never keep his promises to Abraham; it only means that these promises are not an absolute guarantee of blessing for people who fail to trust God.[398] Others will suffer under the great destruction that God will execute against the sinful people in Judah.

10:24–25 Knowing that a remnant will return (10:20–23), Isaiah encourages the people of Judah "not to fear" (*'al tîrā'*) the Assyrians. Three reasons support this admonition and infuse these words with persuasive power: (a) soon God will end his wrath against Judah (10:25a); (b) God will attack Assyria (10:25b–26); and (c) God will remove the yoke of the Assyrians from Judah (10:27).

Initially in 10:24, the prophet assures his audience that this promise of salvation is authorized and empowered by the same Almighty God of the preceding verses. This means that there is no reason to question the truthfulness or the fulfillment of this promise. His plea is for the people of Zion not to fear—identical to his admonition to Ahaz in 7:4–9. The audience is still "my people;" they live in Zion, God's glorious dwelling place; and they are under the covenant protection of their God. The Assyrians oppressed Judah like the Egyptians did before the exodus (Exod 1–14), even though the Hebrew people at the time of Ahaz were not slaves in another country. In both circumstances the Hebrew people were controlled by a stronger nation, forced to work or pay heavy taxes to another nation, and felt the burden of an oppressive rod over them (10:5). The implication is, if God can deliver Israel from Egypt in the past, he certainly can deliver them from Assyria now.

A radical change will come in the near future (10:25–26), though it is impossible to quantify the number of months or years intended. It appears that the

---

can be used in a negative or positive sense, depending on the context.

[397] אֵל גִּבּוֹר "El Gibbor" is the same name given to the messianic figure in 9:5, though there is no indication that the prophet is referring to the "Davidic son" at this time.

[398] Paul also understood that not all Israelites were of Israel and that God would save a remnant out of those he judged (Rom 9:27–28). J. P. Heil, "From Remnant to Seed of Hope for Israel: Romans 9:27–29," *CBQ* 64 (2002): 703–20, suggests that Rom 9:27 is based on Isa 10:22a and Hos 2:1a. He interprets כִּי־אִם at the beginning of 10:22 not as a concessive (NIV "though") but as a statement of assurance ("for if") that introduces something that is expected to happen. Wildberger, *Isaiah 1–12*, 437, argues that the destruction in 10:22–23 will fall on Judah.

deliverance is imminent, but there is no knowledge of an immediate defeat of Assyria around 732 BC. O. Kaiser believes this was fulfilled when God miraculously destroyed 185,000 Assyrian troops when Sennacherib attacked Jerusalem in 701 BC (37:35)[399] rather than the fall of Assyria over 100 years later in 612 BC. Since God's just punishment of Judah's sins will soon be complete, in the near future God will direct his wrath against the Assyrians. The last line of 10:25 omits the verb in the clause, thus the "will be directed" in NIV is supplied to make sense out of the phrase. This solution is proposed because the verse creates a contrast between what God does against "you" and "their destruction," meaning the Assyrians. This solution is somewhat problematic for two reasons: (a) Poetic lines often restate the same idea twice, though this is not required. (b) Usually when a word is left out of the second line the parallel word from the first line is supplied, not some other word. An alternative way of looking at the second line would be to supply the verb from the first line. This would give the meaning:

"Very soon my anger against you will end,
   my wrath   (will end)[400] their destructive action."

The first line would be promising "you," the remnant of v. 24, hope because God's wrath will be satisfied with the punishment the nation has already received. The second line would parallel the end of God's anger with the end of Assyria's destructive activity against Judah. Since Assyria is the rod in God's hand that justly punished Judah (10:5), the end of God's wrath should mark the end of Assyrian aggression.

10:26–27 When God ends his destructive activity against Judah, he will turn his attention against the Assyrians as 10:12,16–19 predict. He will whip them, exactly like Assyria whipped Judah with the rod. To strengthen his point Isaiah draws on two historical examples of Almighty God defeating Israel's enemies. He encourages his audience to put their faith in God because he miraculously helped a small force of Israelites under Gideon to destroy thousands (Judg 7:25; cf. Isa 9:4) and he demonstrated his strong power by defeating the great Egyptian army in the Red Sea (Exod 14–15). God is known from these past acts as a worker of salvation for his weak and helpless people. He has proven in the past that he has the power to defeat all their enemies, so there is no doubt about his ability to accomplish his plans for the future.

This will result in Judah being freed from the yoke of Assyrian domination (10:27) and taxation. The last phrase "because you have grown so fat" seems out of place, so the RSV translates it "he has gone from Rimmon" and connects

---

[399] Kaiser, *Isaiah 1–12*, 244, believes this sermon was based on information from 26:20; 28:15–18; 29:17; and 30:18, but it seems more appropriate to see those chapters influenced by Isaiah's earlier words in chap. 10.

[400] This would mean that וְכָלָה, "he/it will complete, end, finish," would be implied in the second line of v. 25.

this name of a city to the list of cities in 10:28–32, but Wildberger prefers "he went up from Samaria."[401] Three factors guide one to a clearer understanding of this difficult clause: (a) "fatness" was earlier associated with the Assyrians who will waste away and become lean in 10:16a,18b; (b) there is no Hebrew verb in the final clause so "you have grown" is a periphrastic addition not found in the text; and (c) Assyrian fatness gained through its heavy yoke on Judah is part of the reason for God's judgment. Thus, "The yoke will be broken because of fatness" simply means that wealthy Assyrians who have become fat will not get any fatter by their heavy taxation of Judah, in fact their oppressive taxation will cause their downfall.

INVADING ASSYRIANS WILL BE CUT OFF (10:28–34)

28They enter Aiath;
  they pass through Migron;
  they store supplies at Micmash.
29They go over the pass, and say,
  "We will camp overnight at Geba."
 Ramah trembles;
  Gibeah of Saul flees.
30Cry out, O Daughter of Gallim!
  Listen, O Laishah!
  Poor Anathoth!
31Madmenah is in flight;
  the people of Gebim take cover.
32This day they will halt at Nob;
  they will shake their fist
  at the mount of the Daughter of Zion,
  at the hill of Jerusalem.

33See, the Lord, the Lord Almighty,
  will lop off the boughs with great power.
 The lofty trees will be felled,
  the tall ones will be brought low.
34He will cut down the forest thickets with an ax;
  Lebanon will fall before the Mighty One.

The date of the military invasion of Judah described in this paragraph is unspecified. Some suggest this account describes the Assyrian invasion by Tiglath-pileser III around 734 BC, or the attack on Jerusalem by Sennacherib in 701 BC when Hezekiah revolted, or Sargon's conquests in the Philistine plain between 712–711 BC, or Sargon's earlier invasion in 720 BC.[402] In the introduction to 10:5–34[403] it was determined that it is simply impossible to

---

[401] Wildberger, *Isaiah 1–12*, 446–447, makes this proposal because שׁמן, "fat," is written somewhat similar to שׁמרון, "Samaria."
[402] See footnote 325 above.
[403] Page 252.

determine the date of this invasion since there are no biblical or Assyrian records to verify which king took this route. Childs is probably right in concluding that this is a prophetic oracle of what will happen some day in the future, rather than a historical record of what did happen.[404] This paragraph is divided into two parts:

The path of the invading army	10:28–32
God's destruction of the forest	10:33–34

10:28–32   The path of cities moves from north to south along the road from Bethel, arriving at Jerusalem in 10:32. The route is unusual in that the invaders leave the main road to avoid several strong cities in the area. The people in these cities[405] run in panic as the army advances, and then the enemy taunts Jerusalem with fists in the air. No war is mentioned, only threats.

10:33–34   Suddenly, the Almighty God of Judah intervenes by destroying majestic trees, humbling the lofty, and cutting down a forest with an ax. Although the meaning of the symbolic forest or trees is not explained explicitly, these themes pick up the idea of God humbling the proud and lofty from 2:11–17 (including trees), of the ax swung by God to cut down a tree in 10:15, and the destruction of the trees, thorns, and briers that represent Assyria in 10:17–18.[406] God's sovereignty over Assyria is demonstrated when the Mighty One humbles the proud king of Assyria and his army.[407] This final prophetic look into the future provides one more basis to bolster Isaiah's argument that the people of Judah should not fear Assyria. Although political reality looked bleak and Assyria seemed unstoppable, God is almighty and his power is unlimited, so he is able to strike down all who exalt themselves in pride. God has always been the power that determined the outcome of wars, not the generals or kings.

THEOLOGICAL IMPLICATIONS.   The center of this message focuses on the contrasting themes of pride and trust—the danger of pride in past accomplishment, in a sense of complete self-sufficiency, or boasting about what "I will do." God hates those who pretend to be able to control the future or arrogantly boast about how easy it is to destroy others. The people who claim to be in control are actually setting themselves up to lose control to God. The

---

[404] Childs, *Isaiah*, 96, believes the purpose of this account is to show that an "unstoppable, invincible, and utterly terrifying enemy" will attack Judah.

[405] Aiath is probably Ai, close to Bethel.

[406] Kaiser, *Isaiah 1–12*, 251, believes these verses originally described God's falling on the city of Jerusalem to destroy the proud people in it, while Sweeney, *Isaiah 1–39*, 201, maintains the emergency of the Davidic monarch as a shoot from a tree in 11:1–9 as a result of the fall of Assyria.

[407] G. C. I. Wong, "Deliverance or Destruction? Isaiah X 33–34 in the Final Form of Isaiah X–XI," *VT* 53 (2003): 544–52, interprets the destruction of the trees and forest as a metaphor for the destruction of Jerusalem (cf. vv. 5–6 and 25, which mention God's punishment of his people), but this would run counter to the message of assurance and hope just provided in 10:20–27.

people who do not recognize the power of God will soon experience the devastating effect of his almighty ax destroying them. Those who think they can plan the future to their advantage will soon find that God's plans supercede their hopes and dreams. Every person and nation must realize that its real power comes from God and that God uses each nation for his own purposes. To misuse power by violently abusing others will only stir up the divine wrath of God. God hates violence and pride.

The prophet's message also addresses the fears and hopeless feelings of the oppressed. The abused can be assured that God is well aware of their oppressors and will justly deal with them in his own time and way. Those under the yoke of a ruthless superior need to fear God, not man's power, for God will eventually humble every oppressor. Those who are weak need to remember God's past acts of salvation (Gideon's victory and God's deliverance at the exodus) and put their trust in the Almighty Holy God who is a source of light to his own people, but a fire of destruction to his enemies.

Sometimes righteous people do not know why they suffer, but at other times God clearly reveals that people are being punished for their sins (as in Isaiah 10). In such cases, it is always wise for the sinners to return to God and rely on him. Trusting in other men or nations will only lead to disappointment. The only true source of hope is to lean on Almighty God and fear only him.

(4) The Reign of a Righteous King (11:1–16)

THEOLOGY.   This new hopeful section returns to the theme of God's kingdom provisions and the messianic hope for the world, corresponding to the initial discussion of this theme in 9:1–7. Although the audience may presently suffer under adverse conditions as a consequence of Ahaz's sins and Assyria's oppression (11:16), they should trust God because of what he will do in the future. He will not abandon his people, but will cause the remnant to return (10:20–27; 11:10–12), deliver them from oppression, re-establish them as his holy people in Zion (cf. 4:2–6), and inaugurate an era of peace between the nations (2:1–5). This future glorious kingdom and its just ruler (9:1–7; 11:1–9) are set in contrast to the Assyrian kingdom and its arrogant ruler in 10:5–14. A Davidic king who rules with justice and gathers people from the far reaches of the world will replace the proud Assyrian tyrant who destroys and scatters many nations. The wisdom, strength, and Spirit of the LORD will empower this new king (11:1–4); he will not arrogantly depend on his own wisdom and strength as did the haughty king of Assyria. God's people will no longer be weak and under a foreign yoke (10:10–11,24–27), but will be powerful and free of domination (11:10–16).

Common theological themes play an important part in linking chaps. 10 and 11. For example, the remnant's return to the land in 11:10–14 is consistent with the remnant's return to God in 10:20–23. In both 10:26 and 11:15–16, the prophet recalls God's mighty deliverance of his people from Egypt at the Red Sea in order to arouse faith in the listeners. Throughout these chapters hope comes from trusting and fearing God (as in 7:3–9, 8:12–13,17; 9:13; 10:20–24), not from relying on some strong foreign power. Though there is little historical information that would help date this message, these themes would be an appropriate message of hope (similar to 9:1–7) during the difficult time of Ahaz when everything seemed hopelessly lost. The future orientation of this chapter means that there are almost no hints concerning the actual date when this message was spoken.[408]

The text describes a new ruler from Jesse's Davidic line (11:1) who fears the Lord (11:2–3), practices justice (11:4–5), establishes peace (11:6–9), slays the wicked (11:4), restores the oppressed people of Judah and Israel (11:10–16), and causes the earth to be full of the knowledge of the Lord (11:9). This figure calls to mind another kingly figure who will rule justly (Ps 72:1–2,7), establish a time of peace and prosperity (72:3,7,16), deliver the oppressed (72:2,4,12–14), and cause the earth to be full of the glory of the Lord (72:19).[409] This king in Ps 72 will rule the whole earth, from sea to sea, forever. He appears to be the same messianic figure mentioned in Ps 2, the one in the Davidic covenant in 2 Sam 7:11–16, and the one ruling justly on the throne of David in Isa 9:1–7. It seems totally inappropriate to identify this new king with Ahaz or Hezekiah.[410]

GENRE.   These messages begin with an announcement of the coming of a royal savior in 11:1–5 (not a birth announcement as in 9:1–7), a vision of a peaceful kingdom in 11:6–9, and a salvation oracle concerning the restoration of Israel in 11:10–16. The common theme of hope and divine deliverance from the evils of corrupt national and international relationships infiltrates the whole section. Although 11:10–11 fits the themes of the second half of the chapter, its narrative form is surprising in the middle of the poetic oracles all around it.

The idyllic description of a paradise-like condition in 11:6–9 presents numerous hermeneutical problems for interpreters. Hosea already has introduced the theme of God's covenant with the animals (Hos 2:18) and one of the covenant blessings looked forward to a time when there would be peace with the

---

[408] Wildberger, *Isaiah 1–12,* 469, hypothesizes that this message reflects Isaiah's disappointment in Hezekiah when he turned to Egypt for help. Thus Isaiah realized that Hezekiah was not that ideal Davidic king he was looking for, so in chap. 11 he envisions another hope for the nation. This, along with Sweeney's, *Isaiah 1–39,* 204, attempt to connect the "little boy will lead them" in 11:6 with Josiah, should be rejected as guesses that have little evidence to support them.

[409] Although these pictures of this new king may seem somewhat fantastic, some of the "Assyrian apocalyptic prophecies" also foresee times of great peace, prosperity, justice, joy, and the end of oppression. See W. W. Hallo, "Akkadian Apocalypses," *IEJ* (1966): 231–242, or A. K. Grayson, "Akkadian Prophecies," *JCS* (1964): 7–30.

[410] Hayes and Irvine, *Isaiah,* 213, think the author is presenting his great expectation of Ahaz after the end of the Syro-Ephraimite War, while Watts, *Isaiah 1–33,* 174, believes "the context calls for a near fulfillment. . . . This was fulfilled: Hezekiah (and a century later, Josiah) was to occupy the throne." Oswalt, "God's Determination to Redeem His People," *RE* 88 (1991): 153–65, argues strongly for connecting this figure to the messianic figure in 9:1–7.

animals (Lev 26:6), but none of these are as explicit or as detailed as the peaceful relationship between the animals and mankind in 11:6–9. Some regard this as a later insertion based on similar motifs in 65:25, but J. van Ruitan has shown that it makes more sense to see 65:25 as dependent on the traditions in 11:6–9.[411] It was not uncommon in the ancient Near East (and still today) to expect that the rise of a new political leader will produce an idyllic time of peace[412] and a return to Eden-like conditions (51:3). One might interpret these animals metaphorically (Ezek 22:27 calls Judah's officials wolves and Ezek 34:6 calls the people sheep) though later prophets also seem to understand the ideal that God will restore the paradise of Eden once again at the end of time (cf. Ezek 34:25; 36:35). One should not be concerned with trying to explain the biology of how lions can survive by eating straw or how it is possible for there to be such dramatic changes in the animal behavior of vicious wild beasts. The prophet draws a picture of how God will transform the world. The picture communicates the beauty of his revolutionary transformational power, no matter how one interprets the scene (literally or metaphorically).

STRUCTURE.   The hopeful promises of a Davidic shoot out of a stump in 11:1 is not directly connected to the fallen trees of Assyria in 1:33–34.[413] The section includes two main paragraphs:

The just and peaceful reign of a Davidic Branch	11:1–9
The Davidic ruler	1–5
The idyllic kingdom	6–9
The Gathering of the nations to God	11:10–16
Reclaiming the remnant	10–12
Relations between the nations	13–14
God will bring the nations	15–16

Through the repetition of the same words, the emphasis of the first paragraph is directed toward how the "Spirit" will give "knowledge/wisdom" in order to

---

[411] J. T. van Ruiten, "The Intertextual Relationship between Isaiah 65. 25 and Isaiah 11. 6–9," in *The Scriptures and the Scrolls: Fs A. S. van der Woude*, ed. F. G. Martinez, et al., VTSupp 49 (1992): 31–42, examines the evidence and develops argument to show that the shorter discussion in 65:25 was based on the whole context of 11:6–9. Blenkinsopp, *Isaiah 1–39*, 265, also holds 11:6–9 as the source of 65:25.

[412] The Egyptian "prophecy" of Nefer-Rohu (*ANET*, 444–446) and similar Mesopotamian "prophecies" (*ANET*, 606–607) expect ideal days ahead when the new king begins his rule. There is some question about whether these were actually prophecies about the future; instead, they appear to be political propaganda to support the coronation of a new king.

[413] Kaiser, *Isaiah 1–12*, 251,254, takes 10:33–34 as a description of God's destruction of Judah in 586 BC and 11:1 as God's development of eschatological hope (the shoot) out of the fallen trees of Judah in 10:33–34. Beuken, "Emergence of the Shoot of Jesse," 88–108, found syntactical continuity in the verbs within chaps. 10 and 11, so he interpreted 10:5–11:16 as one unit made up of two diptychs (one negative and one positive) in the same temporal era. However, this ignores the change of genre in 11:1–9 that points to a new literary unit. The eschatological focus of chap. 11 also separates it from the Assyrian crisis that dominates chap. 10.

establish "righteousness and justice." The second half of the chapter focuses on the gathering of the remnant of both Gentile and Hebrew peoples from the distant corners of the earth (11:10–16). This paragraph is introduced by two "in that day" clauses (11:10–11) that were probably added when Isaiah put this material into written form. This conclusion seems evident because (a) 11:10–11 is prose and not poetry like the rest of the chapter; (b) the introductory "in that day" clauses are not found elsewhere in the chapter; and (c) 11:10 repeats much of 11:1,12, while 11:11 summarizes 11:12,16.

THE JUST AND PEACEFUL REIGN OF A DAVIDIC BRANCH (11:1–9)

[1]**A shoot will come up from the stump of Jesse;**
   from his roots a Branch will bear fruit.
[2]**The Spirit of the Lord will rest on him—**
   the Spirit of wisdom and of understanding,
   the Spirit of counsel and of power,
   the Spirit of knowledge and of the fear of the Lord—
[3]**and he will delight in the fear of the Lord.**

He will not judge by what he sees with his eyes,
   or decide by what he hears with his ears;
[4]**but with righteousness he will judge the needy,**
   with justice he will give decisions for the poor of the earth.
He will strike the earth with the rod of his mouth;
   with the breath of his lips he will slay the wicked.
[5]**Righteousness will be his belt**
   and faithfulness the sash around his waist.

[6]**The wolf will live with the lamb,**
   the leopard will lie down with the goat,
   the calf and the lion and the yearling together;
   and a little child will lead them.
[7]**The cow will feed with the bear,**
   their young will lie down together,
   and the lion will eat straw like the ox.
[8]**The infant will play near the hole of the cobra,**
   and the young child put his hand into the viper's nest.
[9]**They will neither harm nor destroy**
   on all my holy mountain,
   for the earth will be full of the knowledge of the Lord
   as the waters cover the sea.

11:1 The contrast between the lofty/proud trees of Assyria and the lowly "slip, stump"[414] of Jesse confirms that God is in the business of demonstrating

---

[414] N. Stokholm and S. R. Willesen, "*geza*ʿ," *Scandinavian Journal of Old Testament* 18 (2004): 147–56, views גֵּזַע as coming from the Semitic root meaning "to cut, saw, lop off," so this noun would refer to what was cut off: a "slip, cutting." This would be a cutting from a branch that would be stuck in water to root and later planted. K. E. Pomykala, *The Davidic Dynasty Tradition*

his glory by raising up people of humble means. This has always been God's methodology. The unimpressive green "shoot" (*ḥōṭer*) that will sprout from the stump of Jesse is a person from the Davidic royal line of Jesse,[415] apparently the same Davidic son mentioned in 9:6–7. Although 4:2, 9:6 and 11:1 employ different Hebrew terms to refer to this messianic figure, the writer seems to be making a conscious connection between the "Branch of the LORD" in 4:2, the Davidic ruler in 9:7, and the shoot that will come from the stump of Jesse in 11:1.[416] This twig/branch/shoot, which is the sign of life within the stump, will bear fruit—it will not die out or be cut off. The "shoot" (*ḥōṭer*) is a symbol of hope and a clear contrast to the hopelessness of Ahaz's policies, which nearly destroyed the nation and its Davidic line of rulers (the stump).

11:2 This Davidic individual will experience God's abundant blessing on his life. Israelite history causes one to expect that God would give his chosen kings a special measure of his spirit so that the king will follow God's ways (1 Sam 10:6,10; 11:6; 19:9; 20:23). As the Spirit of God rested on his servant David in the past (1 Sam 16:1–13; 2 Sam 23:2), so the divine Spirit will dwell or "rest" (*nāḥâ*) on this new Davidic Branch, enabling God to use him in a special way.[417] Three pairs of explanations define the Spirit's impact on the character and abilities of this person. First, the Spirit's influence will affect the mental abilities of wisdom and understanding as well as the moral ability to make right choices in judicial decisions (11:3; 1 Kgs 3:12,28). Although the focus is on the internal capacity to perceive the relationships between factors and consequences, this gifting was aimed at the practical enabling of this future leader to rule with God's wisdom (11:3–5), not just to create an extremely smart person. Wildberger contrasts these two characteristics by relating wisdom to handling problems of daily living, while understanding is the ability "to see beyond the details of a particular situation, make an appropriate assessment, and come to conclusions about necessary decisions."[418] This new ruler

---

in Early Judaism: Its History and Significance (Atlanta: Scholar's Press, 1995), 171–216, explains how the Qumran community connected the branch of David with the "slip" of Jesse, giving a messianic meaning to both.

[415] Essarhaddon, the Assyrian king about seventy years later, was called a "precious branch of Baltil, an enduring shoot" according to *Die Inschriften Asarhaddons, Konigs von Assyrien* (ed. R. Borger; Graz: Im Selbstverlags des Herausgebers, 1956), § 20, so the use of this imagery for a king is well known.

[416] In 4:2 צֶמַח, "growth, sprout, branch" is found, but in 11:1 חֹטֶר and נֵצֶר, "shoot" and "twig, branch," are used because they describe the growth coming from the roots of a tree. The stump imagery was used earlier in 6:13.

[417] The Spirit of God (רוּחַ יהוה) gives special abilities to this person, just like he filled Bezalel and gave him "skill, ability and knowledge in all crafts" (Exod 31:3–5). The Spirit came upon Gideon and Samson to give them the courage to fight (Judg 6:34; 14:6), and he dwelt in Moses, Joshua, and the seventy elders of Israel to give them the authority and ability to lead the nation (Num 11:17; 27:18). Later Isaiah connects the coming of the Spirit with the transformation of nature, revival and just behavior, and a time of peace (32:15–18; 44:1–5). The so-called "Servant Songs" also indicate that God will pour out his Spirit on God's special servant (42:1; 61:1–2).

[418] Wildberger, *Isaiah 1–12*, 472, believes these were given to enable to rule and judge justly.

will not make the foolish mistakes of Ahaz who acted based on what made sense from a shortsighted, human, political perspective.

Second, the Spirit of God will equip leaders with gifts related to the practical accomplishment of tasks. Because God will guide him, this person will give counsel ("wonderful counsel" in 9:6), devise amazing plans, and have the power to carry them out. This equipping does not relate to military planning alone (cf. 36:5), but would certainly include it (see 11:14–16). His action stands in contrast to Ahaz (2 Chr 28; Isa 7:1–13) and the Assyrian king (10:5–14), who made arrogant and unwise plans with the main purpose of surviving militarily rather than honoring God by trusting in his power (cf. 7:1–25).

Third, God will grant this person experiential knowledge of God that will be characterized by a fear of God.[419] These two factors, knowledge and fear, point to an intimate relationship between this ruler and God.

Through the work of the Spirit and his close contact with God, this new leader will allow God to speak through his words and reveal himself through his actions. These are characteristics of an ideal charismatic royal leader who trusts God. These are the kind of spiritual leadership qualities that believers should use as a model when they are looking for godly leadership even today.

11:3–5   These gifts of the Spirit will enable the new Davidic ruler to govern very differently from Ahaz. Kings were ultimately responsible for establishing justice in each nation and the establishment of a just society was an ideal of ancient Near Eastern kings.[420] Godly kings like David, Jehoshaphat, and Josiah did what was just in their judgments (2 Sam 8:15; 2 Chr 19:5–7; Jer 22:15–16), and the expectations for the future included a strong emphasis on an ideal era of justice (Ps 72:1–4). When a king "enjoys, delights in"[421] his close relationship with God, he has a source of moral direction derived from a divine perspective on judicial affairs. This will cause him to make decisions as God judges, not based on the outward appearance of the person (that one can see) or on false claims (that one may hear). Decisions will be based on the true nature of the heart (1 Sam 16:7). Status, money, or political influence

---

[419] Childs, *Isaiah,* 103, says, "The knowledge (*da'at*) of God is the essence of the right relationship of a creature to the creator (Hos 2:22[20]; 4:1). It is based on love and devotion."

[420] The prologue to the Lipit Ishtar Laws indicates that the gods made Lipit Ishtar king "in order to establish justice in the land" (*ANET,* 159), while Danel in the Keret Epic from Ugarit speaks of his role of "Judging the cause of the widow, adjudicating the case of the fatherless" (*ANET,* 151). F. C. Fensham, "Widow, Orphan, and the Poor in the Ancient Near Eastern Legal and Wisdom Literature," *JNES* 21 (1962): 129–39, has an overview of the literature that discusses this ideal.

[421] The root רִיחַ means "to smell an odor" (Gen 8:21; Lev 26:31), but it metaphorically expresses the idea of the "delight, pleasure" one has in smelling a good odor (Am 5:21). This verb is a *hiphil* infinitive construct, which often introduces a circumstantial clause when it is preceded by a preposition (causal, purpose, result, means, temporal), or in a looser connection to express attendant circumstances (GKC §114 f,o). If the latter approach is taken here (since there is no preposition before the infinitive construct), one might read the first clause, "by his delighting in the fear of the LORD, he will . . ." making the first clause subordinate to the main verb in the second line.

will not derail this new Davidic ruler's perspective on justice, for idle boasts, excuses, deceptive lies, and false information by the guilty will not prevent the truth from being known. This is the kind of justice and righteousness already attributed to the eternal reign of the one who will sit on the throne of David in 9:7. This justice will be available to all (Lev 24:15; Deut 19:20), especially for the needy and poor, who frequently were cheated by the upper class (1:17,23). This would contrast greatly with the oppression of the poor and robbing of the fatherless that existed in the reign of Ahaz (10:1–2).

This reign of justice will require the condemnation of wickedness, the imposition of penalties on the wicked, and the removal of God's enemies (11:4b). The means of judgment will be the mouth of the Davidic ruler (the "rod/scepter of his mouth" and the "breath of his lips"), meaning royal decrees. Although the phrasing is peculiar, since lips do not literally slay people, it is clear that the authority of the word of this ruler is fully identified with the execution of his will. No one can resist his power and no injustice will remain in his kingdom. The aim is not to present a negative view of uncontrolled slaughter of wicked people, but to emphasize that everything will be guided by principles of justice, upright behavior, and consistent faithfulness (11:5). The righteous character of the Messiah will enable him to do the right thing in all circumstances while his faithfulness will ensure his consistent dependability. He will display perfectly the character of God because the divine Spirit's gifts will hang like clothes (a belt or sash) around him (cf. 59:17–20; Eph 6:10–18).

11:6–9 The future kingdom is described as something similar to a paradise with peace and security, even the removal of the original curse on the relationship between man and the animals (Gen 3:14–19). Natural enemies in the animal kingdom will live together,[422] feed together, and play together,[423] but the strong or poisonous beasts will not harm anyone. Fear and danger will disappear and they will be replaced with harmony and peaceful relationships. Formerly dangerous animals (like the wolf, lion, or cobra) will not even harm the most vulnerable children. This fundamental change in the nature of animals omits mention of the change in the nature of mankind, but the emphasis on righteousness and the end of evil requires a radical change in man's behavior too. This rather idyllic picture points to a future kingdom when there will be no evil, conflict, or death on God's holy mountain (cf. 2:2–5; 4:2–6; 65:25). The text does not fully explain what has brought about this transformation of the enmity between creatures; it just states that it will exist. One could certainly

---

[422] Both in v. 6 and 7 the verb יִרְבָּץ, "to stretch out, lie down," is used to describe how these animals live and relax together.

[423] The first two phrases and the last phrase have a verb in 11:6, but the third phrase, "the calf, the lion, and the yearling together," has no verb. S. Talmon, "DSIa as a Witness to Ancient Exegesis," in *Qumran and the History of the Biblical Text*, ed. F. M. Cross and S. Talmon (Cambridge: Harvard University, 1975), 123–24, follows the reading יִמְרוּ, "they will grow fat," in 1QIsaᵃ (instead of the Masoretic מְרִיא, "fatling") but most reject this as a correction since this root is never used as a verb elsewhere in the Hebrew Bible (though it is found in Ugaritic).

assume that the coming of the Spirit-filled ruler of righteousness from the line of David will have something to do with this new world order. This will be the kingdom where God will live on Mount Zion and will teach all the people who come there (2:1–2). All the people there will be holy (4:3–4; 11:9). This will be the time when "the earth will be full of the knowledge of the LORD" (11:9). This is the time that the seraphim looked forward to in their song of praise in 6:3. It will be a glorious kingdom that will make everyone forget about "the magical kingdoms" that people build on this earth.

THE GATHERING OF THE NATIONS TO GOD (11:10–16)

[10]In that day the Root of Jesse will stand as a banner for the peoples; the nations will rally to him, and his place of rest will be glorious. [11]In that day the Lord will reach out his hand a second time to reclaim the remnant that is left of his people from Assyria, from Lower Egypt, from Upper Egypt, from Cush, from Elam, from Babylonia, from Hamath and from the islands of the sea.

[12]He will raise a banner for the nations
    and gather the exiles of Israel;
he will assemble the scattered people of Judah
    from the four quarters of the earth.
[13]Ephraim's jealousy will vanish,
    and Judah's enemies will be cut off;
Ephraim will not be jealous of Judah,
    nor Judah hostile toward Ephraim.
[14]They will swoop down on the slopes of Philistia to the west;
    together they will plunder the people to the east.
They will lay hands on Edom and Moab,
    and the Ammonites will be subject to them.
[15]The Lord will dry up
    the gulf of the Egyptian sea;
with a scorching wind he will sweep his hand
    over the Euphrates River.
He will break it up into seven streams
    so that men can cross over in sandals.
[16]There will be a highway for the remnant of his people
    that is left from Assyria,
as there was for Israel
    when they came up from Egypt.

This part of the message is introduced by a parenthetical remak (11:10–11), and the whole is organized around three issues:

Reclaiming the remnant	11:10–12
Relations between nations	11:13–14
God will bring the nations	11:15–16

11:10–11 The second paragraph connects the gathering of many people "in that day" to the Davidic ruler in Zion. Using themes from 2:2–5, 4:2–6, and 11:1, the prophet reminds his audience that God has planned their future, so their hope has not disappeared. The salvation oracle in 2:2–3 predicted a day when the nations will come to Jerusalem to receive God's instruction, though a Davidic Messiah is not mentioned. This chapter provides additional information indicating that the "root of Jesse" (from 11:1)[424] plays a central role in the process of gathering people from the nations.[425] This Davidic king "will be standing,"[426] he will not be defeated like Ahaz (see 7:7–9). He will serve as a banner[427] to rally around, so the nations "will seek, consult" (*yidrōšû*) him (reversing 9:13; 45:14–15), implying a level of trust and dependence on his advice (cf. 2:3–4). Their trust will not bring disappointment, for he will provide a glorious place of rest. Elsewhere God promises his people a blessed place of rest[428] (Deut 3:20; 12:9; Josh 1:13; 2 Sam 7:11; Ps 95:11; 132:14) and great glory (4:2,5; 60:1–3). This presents a context very different from what the nation was presently experiencing during the Syro-Ephraimite War.

The second "in that day" statement (11:11) refers to God's second act of grace, drawing on idea expressed in the poetic material in 11:12,16. The verb "will reach out" (NIV) simply means "will add, increase, do" (*yôsîp*) in the Hebrew text, but many translators have smoothed out the sense.[429] God's purpose

---

[424] שֶׁרֶשׁ יִשַׁי, "root of Jesse," uses a different word than חֹטֶר מִגֵּזַע יִשַׁי, "shoot from the stump of Jesse," but the two phrases seem to mean the same thing.

[425] Young, *Isaiah,* I:393, believes the nations are Gentile nations, while Clements, *Isaiah 1–39,* 125–26, considers the whole section as a restoration of the Jews scattered in the exile. Childs, *Isaiah,* 105–106, thinks the root of Jesse is a representative of the remnant of Israel, while Blenkinsopp, *Isaiah 1–39,* 267, rejects this communal approach.

[426] The participle עֹמֵד, "standing," has no tense, but the "in that day" clause at the beginning of verse implies that this action should be placed in a future time period, so "will be standing" is an appropriate translation.

[427] לְ in a few instances shows a comparison and means, "like, as" (BDB, 512). In 5:26 God raised another banner/flag to the nations, but there it was a call to war against Judah. Here a person is the signal/flag for the nations to follow. There is less evidence to support the view of Clements, *Isaiah 1–39,* 125, who follows Barth in interpreting the "banner" collectively of a group of Jews who resettled in the land at an early date and thus signaled to others that is was safe to return. It also seems inappropriate to suggest that lifting Jesus up on the cross was a signal that would draw the nations.

[428] This theme is dealt with extensively by G. von Rad, "There Remains Still a Place of Rest for the People of God," in *The Problem of the Hexateuch and Other Essays,* (New York: McGraw-Hill, 1966), 94–102, and W. C. Kaiser, "The Promise Theme and the Theology of Rest," *BSac* 130 (1973): 135–50.

[429] The Old Greek translation has "the Lord will stretch forth his hand again." Many just add a verb (NIV adds "reach"), while Wildberger, *Isaiah 1–12,* 486–87, emends the reading to get שְׂאֵת, "will raise high," instead of שֵׁנִית, "second." A more literal translation is "the LORD will add his hand a second time," which gives the sense that "God will act once again in power" to accomplish his will. H. G. M. Williamson, "Isaiah XI 11–16 and the Redaction of Isaiah I–II," *Congress Volume: Paris 1992,* VTSup (Leiden: Brill, 1995): 343–57, finds identical terminology (hand, raising the hand [see 49:22], nations from afar) in 5:25–26 and 11:11–12, which both end major sections of 1–12, with the first using these ideas to point to the fall of Judah and the second pointing to the restoration.

will be "to reclaim"[430] the remnant, an idea parallel to the idea of paying a price to redeem a person from slavery (cf. Exod 15:16). This second divine act draws a comparison with God's initial redemption of his people from Egyptian bondage.[431] The idea expressed is similar to the concept of paying a ransom (*kāpar*) to gain freedom from slavery (as in 43:3) or the idea of God redeeming (*gā'al*) his people (as in Ps 74:2).

The people being "purchased" (the root *qānâ*) are probably the same ones identified as the remnant that will return to God in 10:20–23. This passage focuses on the nations from which the people will return. Since it is a prophetic statement, one should not assume that these people are exiles in each of these nations, though the Assyrians did exile many from Israel and Judah during this time period.[432] These nations represent places all over the world where Jewish people might live and work: in the south (Egypt and Cush), the north (Assyria and Hamath), the east (Elam and Babylon), and the west (islands of the sea). The Lord's restorative work will be complete so that none of his people will be left behind involuntarily in some distant nation.

11:12 Here the text returns to the poetic form of communication after the brief parenthetic prose transition in 11:10–11. It is unclear whether the subject of the sentence is God ("he"), who will raise up a signal (the subject of 11:11), or whether the Davidic king (the subject of 11:10) is the one who will raise up the signal.[433] Since they work together as one in the rest of the chapter, the distinction is not of material significance. God will assemble three groups of people: (a) the nations; (b) the dispersed[434] Israelites; and (c) the scattered people of Judah. People from all over the world will return—there is no mention of any supposed "lost tribes of Israel" in Isaiah's teachings. God knows where all his people are and he will bring them all back.

11:13–14 Once everyone is back in the peaceful land with a new Davidic king, the people will give up their feelings of inferiority, jealousy, superiority,

---

[430] The *qal* infinitive construct לִקְנוֹת comes from קָנָה and means "to purchase, acquire" something, usually by paying money. This text does not define what will be paid to secure the people's release from captivity in other nations. In Gen 14:19,22 and Deut 32:6 קָנָה seems to have the meaning of "create," thus this purchase creates a new entity, the people of God in their land.

[431] Wildberger, *Isaiah 1–12*, 491, believes this refers to a second return from exile and thus dates 11:11 to the time of Ezra and Nehemiah, years after the first return under Sheshbazzar (Ezra 1) in 538 BC. In his view this prophecy is promising the completion of the return, yet history indicates that many Jews never returned to Jerusalem at this time.

[432] Some find no connection between 9:1–7 and chap. 11 while others see 11:10–16 as a very negative example of Jewish nationalism gone awry (not consistent with Isaiah's theology) because they are especially offended by the vicious attacks on Judah's enemies in 11:13–14). Childs, *Isaiah,* 105, rejects such interpretations and warns about creating a "canon within a canon," by accepting certain verses and rejecting others.

[433] It seems best to make 11:12 consistent with 11:10, so that in both cases God is raising up the Davidic ruler as a signal.

[434] "Dispersed of" and "scattered of" are two *niphal* passive plural participles (one masculine נִדְחֵי, "banished, exiled," and the second feminine נְפֻצוֹת, "dispersed, scattered") that function as construct nouns expressing the genitive idea in a construct relationship (GKC §116g-i).

and acts of war. These conflicting interests and hostilities go back to the time of Saul and David when the northern tribes made Ishbosheth, Saul's fourth son, king of Israel, while Judah made David their king (2 Sam 2:8–11). These conflicts resulted in the division of the nation into Israel and Judah after the death of Solomon (1 Kgs 12). Later Israel and Judah fought several wars against one another (2 Kgs 14:11–14; 16:5–9). But in this new era there will be a reversal of present hostilities between the nations during the Syro-Ephraimite War (7:1–6; 9:21). The verse does not proclaim the unification of the people into one nation, just a period of reconciliation between nations and an end of war (cf. 2:4).

Not only will internal conflict between brother nations end, but Judah and Israel will work together to defeat all their enemies, just as in the time of David. This idea is not contradictory to the idea of peace expressed in 11:6–9, but a prerequisite for peace, for 11:4b also refers to the Davidic ruler slaying the wicked when he initally sets up his kingdom. These conquests also assure the listener that all the land God promised to their forefathers will be part of this new community. Isaiah does not promise a return to a small province or a partial restoration of a few tribal territories; he proclaims reestablishing the glorious theological ideal of a new Davidic kingdom comparable to or greater than the one that existed in the past. Finally, because of these battles, the people in the surrounding nations "will listen to/obey them" (*mišma'tām*—better than NIV "will be subject"), suggesting an era of peace and harmony, not a time of oppressive forced subjugation of foreigners.

11:15–16 The message of hope ends with a description of God's mighty acts that will make the return of the remnant possible. Using exodus imagery to remind the audience of God's great power, the prophet predicts another event parallel to God's "defeat, annihilation" (NIV has "dry up")[435] of the Red Sea and "the river" (*hānāhār*, probably the Nile).[436] The total annihilation of these obstacles creates an appropriate parallel to his "smiting of it" (*wĕhikkāhû*, NIV has "break up") in the next line. These acts represent the complete defeat of any natural or human force that might try to stand in the way of God's plans. As in the original event, God used a strong east wind (Exod 14:21) that he "blew with his breath" (Exod 15:8,10) so that his people could walk across in sandals on dry ground (cf. Exod 14:21–22). This is parallel to the "mighty[437]

---

[435] The Hb. הֶחֱרִים from חרם, "to devote, ban, annihilate," comes from the practice of dedicating a city to God through destruction, so the imagery does not quite fit what one does to the sea. NIV follows those who emend the text (see Wildberger, *Isaiah 1–12,* 486–88) to הֶחֱרִיב, "to dry up" (only a change of one letter), based on the Targum's translation "he will dry up."

[436] Since "the river" (הַנָּהָר) is undefined, it could refer to the Euphrates based on a return from Assyria in 11:16 (as NIV) or the Nile based on the context of Egypt in 11:15a. Both usages are found elsewhere in Scripture ("river" refers to the Nile 19:5). The Nile Delta matches the idea of dividing a great river into "seven streams" at the end of this verse.

[437] The meaning of the Hb. word בַּעְיָם is unknown, though it may be related to an Arabic word that means "with heat" (thus the translation "scorching"). The Old Greek has "with a strong wind"

(NIV scorching) wind" he will use in the future. The prophet communicated to his audience that God's power to save is unlimited. They can depend on him to deliver them in the future; there is no reason to give up on God even if things looked very bleak in the days of Ahaz. The people of Judah can trust God's promises.

God's promise of deliverance is not some vague hope that applies only to an eschatological future people; it has implications for those listening to Isaiah during the time of Ahaz. Judah could see how the violent Assyrian Empire was sweeping through the land, devastating Israel and taking advantage of Judah during the Syro-Ephraimite War. This military defeat and subsequent captivity might have seemed like a contradiction to Isaiah's lofty dreams in chap. 11, but God revealed that a remnant from among the exiles in Assyria would return, just like people returned from Egypt (10:23–26; 11:16). God would prepare a highway and lead them home, just like he guided the Israelites out of Egypt and through the wilderness.

THEOLOGICAL IMPLICATIONS. The theological message in chap. 11 provides additional progressive revelation on the earlier themes in 2:1–5; 4:2–6; 9:1–7; and 10:20–27. Some ideas are repeated, others are new, and some connections are made between independent ideas. At this point, Isaiah and his audience understand the character of the Branch from the root of Jesse (11:1) better than they did 4:2 or 9:1–7. His names revealed something about him (9:6) but the seven gifts of the Spirit (11:2) clarify his intimate connection to God through the Spirit. Although 2:3–4 introduced the idea of a time without war, 11:6–9 demonstrates that this era of peace will encompass all creation—even the animals. The coming of the nations (2:2–3) and the return of the remnant from Assyria (10:20–27) are clarified and connected to the raising up of this new Davidic ruler who will be a signal to all people.

In analyzing and comparing these future promises, it is evident that God is the one who will accomplish all these things for his people. It is his kingdom and he will rule it (2:2–4; 4:5–6). Initially, the Davidic sprout is pictured in unusual ways as a child on the throne of David (9:1,6), but later he will rule as a powerful king. Since people in this kingdom will be cleansed of their sins and holy (4:3–4) and desirous of learning divine truth from God at Zion (2:2–4), many earthly duties of a king will not apply in this new setting. Consequently, the Davidic Messiah is not even mentioned in 2:1–5, only hinted at in 4:2–6, and never called a king in any of these salvation oracles. His glorious names are highlighted in 9:6, while 9:7 focuses on the peace and justice of his kingdom. 11:1–3 lists his Spirit-filled qualities and 11:6–9 illustrates the peace of his kingdom. Most of the typical kingly characteristic (defeating enemies, giving justice to the needy, bringing captured people home, making laws, etc.) relate only to his role at the initial establishment of his kingdom.

---

but 1QIsaᵃ has בעצם, "with a mighty," which makes complete sense (HCSB has "mighty").

The distinctions between what will happen in God's future kingdom and what was happening during the time of Isaiah force the interpreter to assess carefully the hope presented in these chapters. Some portions address the concerns of an audience that needed to know how its present situation could be transformed and a new kingdom established. These prophecies of hope show how the old world will pass away and a new one will be established. These words were intended to give the audience confidence in God's eternal plan for his people and this world. Other parts of this message of hope address life in the future kingdom that God will establish (2:2–4; 4:2–5; 9:6–9), promising that one day the ideal will become reality. Both aspects of the nation's hope contribute to their faith in God in a time of deep distress that offered no peace. These promises can motivate any believer in periods of depression or times of oppression under the forces of ungodliness. Present problems must be evaluated in light of God's eternal promises. God will be victorious; the Messiah will reign over all the earth! Nothing will stop him from establishing his kingdom.

6. A Song of Trust in God (12:1–6)

¹In that day you will say:

"I will praise you, O Lord.
  Although you were angry with me,
your anger has turned away
  and you have comforted me.
²Surely God is my salvation;
  I will trust and not be afraid.
The Lord, the Lord, is my strength and my song;
  he has become my salvation."
³With joy you will draw water
  from the wells of salvation.

⁴In that day you will say:

"Give thanks to the Lord, call on his name;
  make known among the nations what he has done,
  and proclaim that his name is exalted.
⁵Sing to the Lord, for he has done glorious things;
  let this be known to all the world.
⁶Shout aloud and sing for joy, people of Zion,
  for great is the Holy One of Israel among you."

THEOLOGY.   The conclusion to the first major unit of the Book of Isaiah (2–12) does not summarize the preceding chapters, but looks forward to what will happen when the nation experiences the fulfillment of these prophecies. It is filled with thanksgiving to God for the marvelous things he will do for his people when he establishes his kingdom. The introductory, "In that day you will say," connects this hymn with a similar introductory "in that day" in 11:10–11. The salvation for which people here thank God is most naturally

related to the salvation promised in 11:1–16. As Israel experienced God's salvation in the past and thanked him for his deliverance at the time of the exodus (Exod 14:13–14,29–31; 15:1–18),[438] so future generations will praise God
when they experience his salvation (12:1–6). The two subparagraphs in 12:1–6
begin by announcing what people will say (12:1,4) and both end with a similar
note of joy (12:3,6). While the first part of the hymn looks back at a time when
God was angry with the sinful people (12:1), the second half (12:4–5) points
forward in anticipation of chaps. 13–23 to proclaim what God will do among
the nations. A dramatic theological change triggers this shift in perspective.
Between the two extremes stands the person who trusts God and experiences
his salvation

This theological ordering of themes highlights what the audience must do
to bring about a reversal of their past and present difficult situations. They
will not be able to defeat the Assyrians and they have nothing to brag about
to the nations of the earth right now. God is the one who defeats one nation
and saves another. Fearing God and trusting him is what makes the difference (12:2). This trust is based on God's personal deeds of salvation for
his people (e.g., the exodus). Experiencing God's great salvation will give
people a new attitude. They will tell everyone about their joy, sing about
their holy God, and praise his exalted name (12:4–6). These are the attitudes
that every person who trusts God as "my salvation" should exhibit every day
of his or her life.

GENRE. The structure of this short hymn resembles a song[439] of
thanksgiving, including characteristic phrases like "I will praise/thank you"
(12:1) and exhortations to "sing, shout, proclaim, and give thanks" (12:4–6).
The first three verses emphasize thanksgiving (cf. 40:9–11; 52:9–10; Pss
66; 67), while the second half follows the style of imperatival hymns of
praise (cf. Ps 100:1–4) with an exhortation to praise (12:4–6a) followed by
a reason for praise (12:6b).[440] This kind of hymn would give confidence and
hope to the audience because it exudes a spirit of salvation, joy, thanksgiving, and victorious shouting. It would kindle an attitude of trust because
there was no longer any question or doubt about what God will do. They
affirm, "He is my salvation and strength; my joy is to praise him and sing
about his greatness."

The hymn is closely related to the theological claims of other hymns of
praise and shows some linguistic connection to the song the Israelites sang
after crossing the Red Sea in Exodus 15.

---

[438] W. A. M. Beuken, "The Prophet Leads the Readers into Praise: Isaiah 25:1–10 in Connection with Isaiah 24:14–23," *Studies in Isaiah 24–27: The Isaiah Workshop- De Jesaja Werkplaats*
(ed. H. J. Bosman and H. van Grol; Leiden: Brill, 2000), 144–50, and Williamson, *The Book
Called Isaiah*, 118–25, find the influence of chap. 12 in chap. 25 and in 40–66.

[439] There are other songs in 5:1; 25:9; 26:1; 27:2.

[440] C. Westermann, *Praise and lament in the Psalms* (Atlanta: John Knox, 1981), 131–132,
describes the twofold (praise and reason for praise) structure of these hymns.

12:1a ≈ Ps 118:21	"I will give you thanks"
12:1b ≈ Isa 9:12,17,21	"his anger is not turned away"
12:2 ≈ Exod 15:2 and Ps 118:14	"The Lord is my strength and my song; he has become my salvation."
12:4 ≈ Ps 105:1	"Give thanks to the Lord, call on his name; make known among the nations what he has done."
12:5 ≈ Ps 9:11	"Sing praises to the LORD . . . proclaim among the nations what he has done."
or Exod 15:21	"Sing to the LORD, for he is highly exalted."

Exodus 15 and Ps 118 appear to have had an impact on Isa 12. The reversal in Isa 12:1b of God's anger that is expressed in 9:12,17,21 connects this hymn to the context of the preceding chapters,[441] while the witness to the nations in 12:4–6 seems connected to the return of the nations in 11:10,12.[442] These connecting themes suggest that the hymn was originally written as a conclusion to chaps. 2–11 (chaps. 13–27 also end with a hymn in 27). Once the Davidic ruler arrives to lead Israel and the nations to Zion and establish his kingdom of justice and peace (11:1–16), the people will have good reason to thank and praise God (12:1–6).

STRUCTURE. The hymn is divided into two paragraphs, each marked by the introductory "in that day you will say" (12:1,4). Sweeney found a sense of structure was created by the use of second person masculine singular as the subject of the verbs in 12:1–2 and second person plural masculine subjects in 12:3–5 (12:6 is second feminine singular). These common trends draw those paragraphs together,[443] but thematic and the rhetorical repetition of the same introductory clause in 12:1 and 4 argue against using these subject pronouns as the primary criteria to structure this hymn. The prophet quotes what individuals will say in 1–2 and then describes how this will impact the joy of the group in 12:3. He then goes back to quoting the encouraging words the people will say to others in 4–6 as they joyfully sing praise to God. The text can be outlined into two parts:

---

[441] This connection argues for 12:1–6 being an integral part of 2–12. Although several ideas, words, and phrases in these verses are reused later in the book, these linguistic connections do not prove that they were added at a later time by a later redactor (H. Williamson, *The Book Called Isaiah,* 118–23). Blenkinsopp, *Isaiah 1–39,* 268, rejects Williamson's hypothesis since chaps. 40–54 have no interest in the reunification of Israel and Judah. This hymn of praise to God serves as a fitting conclusion to chap. 11. It appropriately draws attention to God as savior using exodus terminology, the need to trust God, and the opportunity of declaring this good news to all the nations on the earth (they are not all-powerful, as 10:5–13 would have one believe).

[442] Exodus themes in 11:15–16 reappear in 12:2,5, while the exaltation and praise of God in 12:4–5 reminds the reader of 2:11–17.

[443] Sweeney, *Isaiah 1–39,* 198, outlines the hymn (12:1–2,3–6) based on the use of the pronouns.

I will trust the God of my salvation   12:1–3
Make his name known to others   12:4–6

12:1–3 The introductory "in that day" points to the future use of this hymn when God saves his people. Then individuals will stand up and openly declare the glory of God through words of praise. Praise is essentially a thankful confession that gives honor to God. This word of praise will recognize that God can be angry because of sin (11:1; 9:12,17,21), but he is willing to take away his anger and give comfort when sins are confessed and forgiven (cf. 6:5–7). The NIV translates "you have turned away" as if the verb was a perfect, but the Hebrew jussive verbs in the hymn represent the person as one who is humbly recognizing his unworthiness and asking God, "let your anger turn away that you may have compassion on me."[444] It is appropriate in praise to admit that whatever was received from God was undeserved, completely dependent on God's loving grace. Chapters 2–11 repeatedly demonstrate that the people's sinfulness deserved God's wrath.

A second basis for praise and thanksgiving is God's salvation, a theological theme explicitly repeated at the beginning and end of 12:2. The initial "behold" (*hinnēh*) expresses the wonder of this new experience: "look, can you believe this?!" Attention is directed solely to God who is the epitome of salvation. God's salvation is not an abstract philosophical concept; it has a relational dimension that is personal, for the LORD[445] is "my salvation" (*yĕšû'ātî*). This statement does not merely say that God is generally involved in delivering his people in salvation history. This verbless noun clause identifies God with salvation, using this term to represent his state of being rather than a progression of events that he carries out.[446] Although God will save his people from total destruction and does act as the savior of his people, Isaiah is describing the character of God that circumscribes his course of action. One should not read into this statement a New Testament perspective about God saving people from their sins through Christ's death on the cross, or even the theological idea of substitutionary atonement from Isa 53. The praise simply claims that God is a source of salvation that delivers people from anything that might destroy them. The one praising God is making a personal statement of participation in God's salvific character that leads to the commitment of trust. Having made that decision, the person can face the future depending on God rather than fearing what might happen because of some strong enemy. This person will not fear man or nations like Ahaz (7:4,9; 8:12–13); he will reverence God so highly that he will

---

[444] יָשֹׁב, "let it turn away," and וּתְנַחֲמֵנִי, "and may you have compassion," are jussive forms that entreat God to act (GKC §109b).

[445] LORD is repeated twice with two different spellings of Yahweh (יהוה and יה). The shorter form is used in Exod 15:2 and Ps 118:14; the second was added to emphasize the point.

[446] אֵל יְשׁוּעָתִי literally says "God my salvation," with the verb "is" implied. GKC §140e says, "Noun clauses with a substantive as predicate, represent something *fixed, a state* or in short *a being* so and so."

stake his life on the strength of God's ability to save. This faithful trust is not a doubting or hesitant following but a bold attachment to a strong resource that is unfailing. Such trust will quickly lead to joyous singing (12:2b). By drawing the expression of these ideas from Exod 15:2, the picture of confidence, complete trust, utter peace, joy in a commitment, and total dependence on God is given a contextual frame of reference. As God was the salvation of the Israelites at the exodus (Exod 14:13–14; 15:1–18) so God will become the salvation of future generations. Although this song does not delve into the basis of God's salvific action, Scripture tells us God was motivated by his choice of this people, his love for them, and his faithfulness to his promises (Deut 7:6–9).

Having quoted in 12:1–2 what an individual will say, the first section ends with a prediction about the community's joy over the salvation they have experienced (12:3). Although some think the text refers to a literal ceremony where water was drawn and poured out to God (a day of fasting and confession of sins as in 1 Sam 7:6; a drink offering as in 2 Sam 23:15–17; or as at the Feast of Tabernacles[447]), it is better to view God as the metaphorical source or "well of salvation" (cf. 55:1; Ps 36:10; Jer 2:13; John 4:10–14), which the people will gladly rely on.

12:4–6 The second half of the hymn follows the pattern of the imperatival hymn of praise, with a series of calls for the people to praise God (12:4–6a) followed by a reason the people should give God praise (12:6b). The imperatives ("give thanks, call, make known, proclaim, sing") function as imperatival exhortations[448] that encourage the community of believers to respond to God's great salvation. Through praise directed to God, his name is exalted in community praise and other nations are reminded[449] of the greatness of God. This sounds like a practical formula for worship and evangelism. The focus is always on glorifying and exalting God, the method is to use singing and retelling of the story, the content focuses on God's great deeds and exalted name, and the results spread the good news of God to others. This response reminds one of the repeated emphases on the importance of the nations knowing about God and coming to worship him (2:2–4; 11:10–12; 19:19–25; 45:22–25; 60:1–9; 66:19–21). These songs will exalt God alone, as 2:11,17 predict. God's people will no longer be those who are "ever hearing but never understanding" (6:9) or never responding to God's grace.

The song ends with an exhortation to the people of Zion[450] to celebrate their joy just like the children of Israel and Miriam did at the time of the exodus

---

[447] Hundreds of years later in the Talmud, *Sukkah* 4:9–10, there is a reference to this passage in connection with the Feast of Tabernacles.

[448] GKC §110a refers to admonitions. The following imperatives should not be interpreted as giving the consequence of the first conditional imperative (GKC § 110f) because these imperatives are not connected with a *vav* conjunctive.

[449] NIV translates הַזְכִּירוּ as "proclaim," but a more literal rendition would be "cause to remember."

[450] צַהֲלִי וָרֹנִּי, "shout, sing," are second feminine singular imperative verbs addressing Zion as

(Exod 15:20–21). Zion, of course, is the place of the temple, the place where the name of the Holy One of Israel dwells. The reason for joyful singing and praise does not lie in material wealth, absence of fears, or the return to Zion. Praise relates primarily to God's greatness, his holiness (12:6b), and his great deeds (12:5b). Praise is also given because God is "in your midst" (*bĕqirbēk*). He will personally be present with his people in his glory, the stain of sin will be removed, his people will be holy, and the knowledge of the Lord will fill the earth (2:1–4; 4:2–6; 6:3; 11:9).

THEOLOGICAL IMPLICATIONS. This short hymn of praise looks to a future day and anticipates what it will be like. Salvation will come from God. He is man's only source of hope. A new day very different from the era of Ahaz will arrive at some point in the distant future. Although the date is unknown, God promises to bring that future time of joy and thanksgiving when his anger and punishment are past (12:1). At some point people will experience God's compassion instead of his anger (cf. 10:20–27). This song of praise does not focus on the date, the chronology of events, the reason God's anger ends, or how God's strength brings salvation. When the people experience salvation, they will be so completely overwhelmed by God compassion that they will completely trust in him. All they will be interested in is singing and praising God. All these other factors will be secondary, summarized simply by "he has done great things" (12:5). The focus of attention will be on God, just like Isaiah's focus was on God when he saw his glory in 6:1–4. The people's overflowing joy and natural exuberance will exalt God's name and tell others about him. Just as Isaiah wanted to go tell others about God (6:8), so these people will want to make known the exalted name of God among the nations.[451] In this picture, worship and evangelism are connected at the hip, inextricably joined as two sides of the same coin. Evangelism is joyfully shouting about the exalted glory of God and retelling his wonderful deeds. Worship is joyfully shouting about the exalted glory of God and retelling his wonderful deeds. For worship to become evangelism it has to be done outside of the four walls of a church, where non-believers can hear God's praise.

---

a unit. Nations and cities were usually considered to be feminine in Hebrew and in English ("give Chicago her due," or "her amber waves of grain" referring to America).

[451] The next unit demonstrates both God's destruction of many proud and violent nations as well as his compassionate salvation of those peoples that trust in him.

III. GOD'S SOVEREIGN PLAN FOR THE NATIONS (13:1–23:18)
    1. God's Plans for Babylon and Assyria (13:1–14:27)
        (1) Destruction on the Day of the Lord (13:1–16)
        (2) God Will Destroy Proud Babylon (13:17–22)
        (3) God Will Restore Israel (14:1–2)
        (4) A Taunt Song for the Babylonian King (14:3–23)
        (5) God's Plan to Crush Assyria (14:24–27)
    2. God's Plans for Philistia (14:28–32)
    3. God's Plans for Proud Moab (15:1–16:14)
        (1) A Lament for Moab (15:1–9)
        (2) Moab Requests Help from Judah (16:1–5)
        (3) Pride Will Cause Lamenting in Moab (16:6–12)
        (4) Destruction in Three Years (16:13–14)
    4. God's Plans for Damascus—and Israel (17:1–18:7)
        (1) Damascus and Israel Will Lose Their Fertility (17:1–11)
        (2) God Will Rebuke the Raging Nations (17:12–14)
        (3) Cush Will Honor God for Destroying Its Enemies (18:1–7)
    5. God's Plans for Egypt (19:1–20:6)
        (1) God Will Defeat Egypt and Her Gods (19:1–15)
        (2) God Will Save Egypt; Egyptians Will Worship God (19:16–25)
        (3) Isaiah's Nakedness Symbolizes Egypt's Defeat (20:1–6)
    6. God's Plans for Babylon (21:1–10)
        (1) The Prophet's Terrifying Vision of Babylon (21:1–4)
        (2) Watchmen Report on the Fall of Babylon (21:5–10)
    7. God's Plans for Dumah (21:11–12)
    8. God's Plans for Arabia (21:13–17)
    9. God's Plans for Jerusalem (22:1–25)
        (1) Jerusalem Rejoices Even Though She Faces Defeat (22:1–14)
        (2) Shebna: Disgraced and Replaced (22:15–25)
    10. God's Plans for Tyre (23:1–18)
        (1) Lament over Proud Tyre (23:1–14)
        (2) Restoration after Seventy Years (23:15–18)

III. GOD'S SOVEREIGN PLAN FOR THE
NATIONS (13:1–23:18)

A new section begins in 13:1 with the announcement that Isaiah the son of Amoz (cf. 1:1; 2:1) saw[1] a "burdensome divine revelation" concerning Babylon. A similar formulary introduction begin each new message with the standard "an oracle concerning . . ." These parallel introductions end at 23:1, then a new series of related but independent oracles are grouped together in 24:1–27:13. The oracles in chaps. 13–23 focus on the destruction of several nations (mostly foreign nations), and thus chaps. 13–23 are set apart from 2–12. Chapters 13–23 pick up some of the themes in chaps. 2–12; for example, many people in these nations are proud (13:19; 14:11; 16:6; 23:9), just like the people of Judah (2:11–12,17; 3:16), Israel (9:8), and the Assyrian king (10:5–14). Earlier prophecies affirmed that God will judge some of these nations (11:14) and that a godly remnant of people will come from these nations (11:11). Consistent with these earlier announcements, the nations in chaps. 13–23 will suffer various levels of divine judgment, though a remnant from many of these nations will turn from their old ways and worship God with his people (14:1–2; 17:7–8; 18:7; 19:18–25; 23:18; cf. 2:1–5).

GENRE. As one reads chaps. 13–23, it appears that the prophet employs a new genre of literature that impacts all these messages. The prophet prefixed the same title to each of the ten main "utterances, oracles" in chaps. 13–23, and a common topic pervades throughout these messages. The introductory title *maśśāʾ* communicates that each oracle is a "burden, something carried," a term that has the negative connotations of bearing something heavy.[2] H. S. Gehman and R. B. Y. Scott focused on the threatening meaning of the term, but it is not clear if this word means that these were heavy messages for the audience to hear or if these oracles were a burdensome word for the prophet to deliver.[3] H. Wildberger takes a more neutral approach to defining this term by interpreting the noun *maśśāʾ* as an idiomatic abbreviation for "raising one's voice."[4]

---

[1] חָזָה, "to see, have insight, perceive," is used to refer to special knowledge received from God, not what one observes in nature with the natural eye, learns through good or bad experiences, or picks up from talking with a friend. It would go far beyond the evidence to suggest that this seeing "may indicate a scene witnessed in the Divine Council" (J. D. W. Watts, *Isaiah 1–33*, WBC [Waco: Word, 1985], 190).

[2] מַשָּׂא is a noun that comes from the verbal root נָשָׂא. The verb means, "to carry, lift up," though its extended use includes such diverse concepts as the idea of forgiveness (lifting up, or bearing sin) or pride (lifting up the head). L. Koehler and W. Baumgartner, *Hebrew and Aramaic Lexicon of the Old Testament* (Leiden: Brill, 1953) find two different possible roots for this word, one meaning "burden," the other "utterance."

[3] H. S. Gehman, "The 'Burden' of the Prophets," *JQR* 31 (1940–41): 107–21, and R. B. Y. Scott, "The meaning of *maśśāʾ* as an Oracle Title," *JBL* 67 (1948): v–vi, emphasized the negative connotations of a "burden." Another important study is by P. A. H. Boer, "An Inquiry into the Meaning of the Term מַשָּׂא," *OTS* 5 (1948): 197–214.

[4] H. Wildberger, *Isaiah 1–12; A Commentary,* A Continental Commentary (Minneapolis: For-

Thus when a prophet raises his voice to give the word of God, he delivers an "utterance, oracle, verdict," which may or may not have negative implications (cf. Zech 12:1). These different approaches cause one to raise these questions: Does the repeated use of the title *maśśā'* at the beginning of these oracles signal a specific genre of literature? Does it help define that genre? Or does this term just refer to the reception of a divine revelation, without providing a key to identifying the genre of these chapters?

M. Floyd and R. Weis claim that *maśśā'* signals the use of a distinct genre of literature.[5] They claim that this genre includes three basic elements: (a) an assertion that God is involved in a particular situation; (b) a clarification of the status of earlier prophecies; and (c) new directives that instruct people how to respond to what God is doing. Although these three factors can be identified in some messages in Isa 13–23,[6] they are not consistently found in all ten examples in these chapters. Therefore, the conclusions of Floyd and Weis about this genre of literature remain suspect.

Since many foreign nations are condemned, one might think that it would be better to compare these "utterances, oracles" in chaps. 13–23 to "oracles against foreign nations" that are found in other prophetic books (cf. Jer 46–51; Ezek 25–32; Amos 1–2). The difficulties with this suggestion are that there is a wide variety of different ways to structure oracles against foreign nations, and oracles against Israel and Judah (17:1–14; 22:1–14) were included within chaps. 13–23. J. H. Hayes believes that oracles against foreign nations originally developed out of the army's preparations for war. Before a military battle a prophet would pronounce a curse on the enemy (Num 22–24) or announce the defeat of the enemy (1 Kgs 20:28–29), thus assuring God's people of victory in the war.[7] This may explain the origin of some oracles against foreign nations in the early history of the nation, but such an explanation does not fit the oracles included in chaps. 13–23, for there is no indication that Judah is about to go to war and defeat these nations.[8] Judah was not promised victory over Cush or Egypt; in fact, both of these nations will end up joining Judah in the worship of God (18:7; 19:18–25). Thus, one must carefully distinguish between the predictions that these nations will suffer military defeat and the actual historical relationship between Judah and these nations.

---

tress, 1991), 11–12, chose to translate this term "verdict," though the choice of this terminology is not meant to imply that these oracles are the "verdict" of a court case.

[5] M. H. Floyd, "The מַשָּׂא (*maśśā'*) as a Type of Prophetic Book," *JBL* 121 (2002): 401–22, builds his case primarily on the work of R. Weis, *A Definition of the Genre Maśśā' in the Hebrew Bible* (Ph.D. dissertation, Claremont Graduate University, 1986).

[6] The first and third criteria are too general, for these characteristics are true of almost every genre in the Hebrew Bible. The second criterion is missing from several chapters.

[7] J. H. Hayes, "The Usage of the Oracles against Nations in Ancient Israel," *JBL* 87 (1968): 81–92, finds a condemnation of the enemy, a promise of victory, and a declaration of divine recognition as three elements in many of these oracles.

[8] There is also no evidence that Jeroboam II was planning to go to war against the nations Amos condemned in chaps. 1–2.

When one looks in detail at the internal arrangement of the content of these oracles, it is evident that they are not consistently structured in an identical pattern.[9] It seems that it is not possible to talk about a consistent genre of "oracles against foreign nations" in Isaiah 13–23 as a distinct literary phenomenon with a unique structure and purpose. Different oracles in chaps. 13–23 served different purposes,[10] but all are related to the way God will direct the affairs of the nations in that part of the world. From a genre perspective, it will be more productive to focus on the diverse genres within each message, such as the lament, woe oracle, judgment speech, and even the salvation oracle.

HISTORICAL SETTING.   The prophet left most of the messages in this section undated. One would assume that these oracles were edited together at some later time in the prophet's ministry because of their common themes. J. H. Hayes and S. A. Irvine attempt to find a chronological factor in the arrangement of these oracles, but it is difficult to assign an exact date to many of these oracles.[11] From time to time a few historical events are noted (see 20:1–6), but it is difficult to know if these dated events have any impact on what oracles come before and after these historical notices. The death of Ahaz is recorded in 14:28, so it is clear when Isaiah received the short Philistine oracle. Unfortunately, this date only provides information that is specifically related to the date of the Philistine oracle. The burden concerning Damascus and Ephraim (17:1–7) is naturally related to past events during the Syro-Ephraimite War (734–732 BC), but it was spoken at some unknown date many years after that war. Isaiah 20:1–6 is connected to Sargon's attack on Ashdod and the defeat of Egypt around 713–711 BC, but chap. 17 was composed some time after the events it mentions in order to serve as a negative illustration to the people in Judah. Even in these few dated examples one can conclude that these oracles were not historically arranged, for Ahaz did not die (14:28) before the Syro-Ephraimite War (17:1–7). In addition, the first oracle in 13:17–14:27 was most likely one of the later oracles (shortly before 701 BC), not the very first one given by the prophet. One can propose a hypothetical date for most of these messages

---

[9] J. B. Geyer, "Mythology and Culture in the Oracles Against the Nations," *VT* 36 (1986): 129–145, carried out a form critical analysis of this genre in an appendix (pp. 142–44) and found five common elements in these oracles: (a) superscription; (b) destruction; (c) lamentation; (d) flight; and (e) Yahweh. Yahweh is referenced in nearly every kind of oracle, destruction is a common theme in many oracles except salvation oracles, and the superscriptions were not a part of the oral presentation, so it appears that Geyer has not identified a unique structure for these oracles.

[10] P. R. Raabe, "Why Oracles against Nations?" in *Fortunate the Eyes that See: Essays in Honor of D. N. Freedman* (ed. A. B. Beck, A. M. Bartelt, P. A. Raabe, C. A. Franke; Grand Rapids: Eerdmans, 1995), 236–57, outlines the various purposes for the oracles against the nations as (a) to humble the proud and destroy the wicked; (b) to proclaim salvation for Judah; (c) to admonish Judah against alliances with certain nations to convince the people to trust God; and (d) to honor the name of God and show the impotence of pagan gods.

[11] J. H. Hayes and S. A. Irvine, *Isaiah, the Eighth-Century Prophet: His Times and His Preaching* (Nashville: Abingdon, 1987), 221–223, tried to put these chapters in chronological order, though they find no common theme that draws these chapters together.

based on the scant historical information that is available within each oracle, but the lack of unambiguous historical data means that interpreters frequently disagree on the historical background for these prophecies.[12] A closer analysis of the historical hints within these prophetic messages will suggest that several, though not all of these "burdensome utterances," date around 704–701 BC when the Assyrians were in the process of defeating Judah.

STRUCTURE. Similar introductory phrases using the word *maśśāʾ* ("utterance, burden") begin messages in 13:1 concerning Babylon (and Assyria), in 14:28 concerning the Philistines, in 15:1 concerning Moab, in 17:1 concerning Damascus (and Israel), in 19:1 concerning Egypt, in 21:1 concerning the Desert by the Sea, in 21:11 concerning Dumah (Edom), in 21:13 concerning Arabia, in 22:1 concerning the Valley of Visions (Jerusalem), and in 23:1 concerning Tyre. These common titles draw these oracles together as a unit. The organization of this large group of chapters is partially dependent on how one evaluates the independence of the message to each nation. R. E. Clements hypothesizes a separate oracle for Cush (18:1–7),[13] but since there is no introductory identification of this as a separate *maśśāʾ*, it appears that the author of the text was signaling to the reader that this prophecy should be included within 17:1–18:7. M. A. Sweeney included the oracle about Philistia (14:28–32) as part of the Babylon oracle,[14] and B. S. Childs made one unit out of the three short oracles about Babylon, Dumah, and Arabia (21:1–17).[15] However, each of these was identified as a separate *maśśāʾ*, so this commentary will treat each message that begins with *maśśāʾ* as an independent oracle.

Comparing the organization of Isaiah's oracles against the nations with similar oracles in other prophetic books might be helpful, but Amos's pairing of oracles and his geographical framework[16] was not followed in Isaiah. The organizational construction of Ezekiel's oracles against foreign nations in chaps. 25–32 around a central message of hope in 28:24–26[17] is another pattern that

---

[12] The late dating proposed by O. Kaiser, *Isaiah 13–39*, OTL (Philadelphia: Westminster, 1974), 2–5, places chaps. 13–14 at the fall of Babylon in 539 BC, the Philistine prophecy in 14:28–32 around 333 BC, the Egypt oracle in 19:1–25 at 217 B. C, and the Tyre message around 332 BC when Alexander the Great defeated that city. This approach to dating these oracles is not convincing and is not accepted in most commentaries.

[13] R. E. Clements, *Isaiah 1–39*, NCBC (Grand Rapids: Eerdmans, 1980), 163–66, seems to deal with the Cush prophecy as an independent oracle separate from chap. 17 or the Egypt oracle in 19.

[14] M. A. Sweeney, *Isaiah 1–39*, XVI, FOTL (Grand Rapids: Eerdmans, 1996), 229, claims that the Philistia oracle is a "summary-appraisal" drawn from the preceding material, thus it is not a separate oracle even though it has the word *maśśāʾ* in its introduction.

[15] B. S. Childs, *Isaiah*, OTL (Louisville: Westminster John Knox, 2001), 148, says, "These three have been brought together to form a larger unit."

[16] G. V. Smith, *Amos* (Fearn, Scotland: Christian Focus, 1998), 64–65, describes the pairing based on repeated themes and the structure of each oracle.

[17] D. I. Block, *The Book of Ezekiel: Chapters 25–48* (Grand Rapids: Eerdmans, 1998), 4–5, found 97 verses before this message of hope and 97 verses after it.

was not employed in Isaiah.[18] Isaiah has several hopeful statements, but some occur in the middle of an oracle (14:1–2; 16:5), while others appear at the end of oracles (18:7; 19:18–25; 23:17–18), but none function like a centerpiece similar to Ezek 28:24–26. The only geographic observations one can make is that Isaiah's messages began with a description of the pride of two major eastern powers (Babylon and Assyria in 13–14) and ended with the pride of a major western power (Tyre in 23).[19]

J. A. Motyer proposes that these oracles were ordered in two panels of five oracles, both beginning with statements about Babylon (13:1–14:27 and 21:1–10). The first discusses the political downfall and the second the religious demise of Babylon.

13:1–14:27	Babylon	21:1–10	Babylon
14:28–32	Philistia	22:11–12	Edom
15:1–16:14	Moab	22:13–17	Arabia
17:1–18:7	Damascus/Israel	22:1–25	Jerusalem
19:1–20:6	Egypt	23: 1–18	Tyre[20]

In each series the third oracle refers to refugees looking for help (Moab in 16:1,6–7 and Arabia in 21:13–17), the fourth oracle in both groups refers to Hebrew people not trusting in God for their deliverance (17:8,10; 22:8,12–14), and the final oracles conclude with people from Egypt (to the south) and Tyre (to the north) turning to God (19:19–25; 23:18). This is an attractive way of identifying some degree of order in the midst of a series of oracles that appear to be unrelated to one another.

Finally, one will discover that not all commentaries limit this structural unit to chaps. 13–23. J. Blenkinsopp extends this cohesive unit from chap. 13 through chap. 27 (rather than 13–23) and proposes that the concluding oracle against "the city" (24:10,12), which he identified as Babylon, balances the initial Babylon oracle in chaps. 13–14.[21] On the other hand, R. H. O'Connell lengthens this section to include chaps. 13–39 (rather than 13–23) and proposes that the initial Babylon oracle in chaps. 13–14 is balanced by the final

---

[18] J. Goldingay, *Isaiah* NIBC (Peabody: Hendrickson, 2001), 92, attempts a similar construction around the central prophecy about the fate of many nations in 17:12–14. He places around this central oracle the northern nations (13:1–14:27), Judah's neighbors (14:28–17:11), the southern nations (18:1–20:6), and the northern nations (21–23). But Arabia (21:13–17) is not really in the north and this approach does not explain why Israel and Judah are included.

[19] J. Oswalt, *Isaiah 1–39*, NICOT (Grand Rapids: Eerdmans, 1986), 298–300, says that these oracles have "no geographical order" but later he recognizes the first and last messages represent the east (Babylon) and west (Tyre).

[20] J. A. Motyer, *The Prophecy of Isaiah* (Leicester: InterVarsity, 1993), 131–32, thinks that this order puts an emphasis on Babylon.

[21] J. Blenkinsopp, *Isaiah 1–39* (New York: Doubleday, 2000), 271–72, finds a contrast in chaps. 24–27 between God's destruction of the city of Babylon and his restoration of the city of Jerusalem.

reference to Babylon in 39:1–8.[22] Although there are some interlinking textual connections between the introductions and the conclusions in both of these proposals, it is easy to overplay the significance of these interlinking factors and interpret them as structural markers. Repetition is a legitimate key that helps identify the structure of a passage, but some later repetition is designed simply to remind the reader of what was said earlier without pointing to any structural design. These linguistic connections will be explored further when chaps. 24–27 and 39 are interpreted in order to discover the significance of these repeated themes.

AUDIENCE AND PURPOSE. There is no evidence that Isaiah traveled to all these different nations to deliver messages in each of these foreign countries. Isaiah's primary audience was the people of Judah in Jerusalem. The prophet communicated God's plans for these nations to the people of Judah because Judah had a political relationship with them. The announcement that God would defeat Israel, Assyria, Syria, and Philistia should have encouraged many politicians in Jerusalem, but the eventual defeat of these nations also meant that it would be foolish for the king of Judah to make alliances with or depend on any of these nations. Although some interpreters believe these oracles express an inappropriate joy and nationalistic fervor at the downfall of other nations,[23] others interpret them as positive announcements of salvation for Judah because her enemies will be defeated.[24] Y. Hoffman realized that not all oracles against neighboring nations were promising salvation for Israel; some were intended to warn Israelite kings against false policies of entering into political alliances with its neighbors (30:1–5).[25] Each oracle has to be evaluated for its own function in order to discover the persuasive purpose for each message to the people of Judah.[26]

THEOLOGY. These prophecies about the punishment of various nations are actually oracles about God's sovereign power over all the nations of the earth. The conclusion to the first oracle (14:24–27) indicates that the reason for the fall of Babylon and Assyria was not just to remove the pride of these powerful nations (13:19; 14:11–14), but they also demonstrate that (a) God was the sovereign power that rules over that nation; (b) God has a plan for every nation

---

[22] R. H. O'Connell, *Concentricity and Continuity: The Literary Structure of Isaiah* (Sheffield: Sheffield Academic Press, 1994), 124–27, found several correlations between chaps. 13 and 39.

[23] R. H. Pfeiffer, *Introduction to the Old Testament* (New York: Harper and Row, 1941), 443, says these oracles "reflect on the whole, not the moral indignation of the great pre-exilic prophets, but rather the nationalism of the false prophets and the late Jews chafing for centuries under alien rule."

[24] C. Westermann, *Basic Forms of Prophetic Speech* (Philadelphia: Westminster, 1967), 205, maintains that these speeches "imply salvation for Israel." S. Erlandsson, *The Burden of Babylon: A Study of Isaiah 13:2–14:23* (Lund: Gleerup, 1970), 66, says that they "generally function as salvation oracles for the prophet's people."

[25] Y. Hoffman, "From Oracle to Prophecy: The Growth, Crystallization and Disintegration of a Biblical Gattung," *JNWSL* 10 (1982): 75–81, focuses on their political purpose.

[26] See note 10 above.

on earth; (c) God will crush those who oppose him; (d) God will bring salvation to his oppressed people; and (e) many people from these foreign nations will eventually come and worship the God of Judah. It is best to view all these theological themes working together rather than prioritizing one. C. R. Seitz (who quotes G. Hamborg) concludes that "the oracles against foreign nations are not primarily oracles of salvation for Israel; rather, they make clear that God's sovereignty over human pride and arrogance reaches to every nation on earth."[27] Although God can use any nation for his purposes (10:5; 14:24), no nation can proudly claim to do anything without God. Through these messages God is announcing "the imposition of YHWH's rule in the world."[28] Isaiah's vision of God's worldwide activity demonstrates that he is not just interested in what will happen to his chosen people; he is also actively involved with all people in every nation in order to incorporate some of them into his eternal kingdom (2:1–5; 14:1–2; 19:19–25). God is the Lord and Savior of Israel, but he is also the universal Lord and Savior of all people on earth.

The rule of God is associated with his plans to raise up and defeat nations (14:24–25; 22:11; 23:8–9), demonstrating that God is more powerful than any earthly king, army, or pagan god. These plans fulfill God's purposes for each nation (14:24; 19:12,17), showing that God is moving history toward the goal of humbling the proud and establishing his righteous kingdom where he will be exalted. Some of the people in these nations will "turn their eyes to the Holy One of Israel" (17:7) and ultimately come to Zion to worship God (14:1–2; 18:7; 19:19–25; 23:18). God's plans often run counter to the violent and prideful plans of the kings of these great nations, so judgment is mixed with compassion to defeat the wicked and save those who repent and trust God.

If Isaiah's theological treatise could convince Judah and her kings to believe that God rules the world, this would be a major accomplishment toward a radical transformation of their political ambitions and theological orientation. Then they would be able to confidently trust God as they faced the political challenges of their day and declared his glorious deeds to others. These chapters teach the principle that believers should not be motivated by fear to compromise their beliefs about the sovereignty of God. They should confidently serve God regardless of their situation, knowing that his plans are being fulfilled. Even though some arrogant individuals (the king of Babylon in 14:4–23) or nations (Moab in chaps. 15–16) may selfishly try to play God and bring great suffering

---

[27] C. R. Seitz, *Isaiah 1–39*, Interpretation (Louisville: Westminster John Knox, 1993), 122, understands God's dealing with arrogant Assyria as paradigmatic of what God will do with all the nations. He agrees with G. R. Hamborg, "Reasons for the Oracles against Foreign Nations of the Prophet Isaiah," *VT* 31 (1981): 145–59.

[28] Sweeney, *Isaiah 1–39*, 214, later claims that "the establishment of Persian rule over these nations constitutes the establishment of YHWH's rule," but this seems too simplistic. Every time a nation was defeated, God directed it according to his purposes (10:5; 14:24), so it is inappropriate to identify God's rule too closely with the Persians. In fact, the kingdom of God in 2:1–5; 4:2–6; 9:1–7; 11:1–9 seems quite different from Persian rule.

on others, those proud people must either face the justice of God's wrath or humble themselves and accept his mercy.

1. God's Plans for Babylon and Assyria (13:1–14:27)

HISTORICAL SETTING. The title of the first message introduces an "oracle" (*maśśāʾ*) that appears to be about the nation or city of Babylon. Commentators have related the defeat of Babylon and the death of its king to several different eras of Babylonian history: (a) Hayes and Irvine believe that these chapters predict the war when the Assyrian king Tiglath-pileser III defeated the Babylonian king Nabu-shuma-ukin around 729 BC. The mention of the Medes in 13:17 refers to fierce Median soldiers who were an important element in the Assyrian army when it attacked Babylon.[29] (b) J. D. W. Watts concluded that these prophecies come from around 720 BC when Merodach-baladan controlled Babylon (he is the king in 14:4–22). Watts believes that this prophecy was fulfilled when Sargon II took control of Babylon around 710 BC. Based on 21:2 where Elam and the Medes attack Babylon, Watts concludes that these nations were allies in Assyria's conquest of Babylon in 710 BC.[30] (c) Clements surprisingly maintains that in 13:1–16 Babylon was commissioned to destroy Judah and Assyria. Then in the rest of the oracle (13:17–22), Cyrus the king of the Medes and Persians will defeat Babylon, long after the death of Isaiah.[31] (d) In another similar odd twist, E. Kissane finds God's judgment of Judah in 13:1–16 and his destruction of "Assyria" in 13:17–22 (the name "Assyria" was supposedly changed to "Babylon" by a later editor).[32] There is strong evidence that the Medes and Assyrians were enemies, so a Median attack on Assyria makes sense. (e) S. Erlandsson follows much of Kissane's logic but attributes all of chaps. 13–14 (except 13:19–22) to the fall of Assyria.[33] (f) J. Oswalt believes that chaps. 13–14 refer to the fall of Babylon, but he concludes that the early Babylonian period "is being used in the symbolic way" to refer to Mesopotamia's glory and pride and that the Medes symbolically "represent fierce, implacable destruction"[34] for Babylon.

The suggestion that the condemned nation of Babylon was employed by God to destroy other nations does not fit the pattern of any other oracles in Isa

---

[29] Hayes and Irvine, *Isaiah,* 222–223.

[30] Watts, *Isaiah 1–33,* 188 and 198, dates the Babylon prophecies in chap. 21 to the time of Sennacherib.

[31] Clements, *Isaiah 1–39,* 132–33, interprets 13:2–5 as the Babylonian revolt of Merodach-baladan against Assyria.

[32] E. J. Kissane, *The Book of Isaiah* (Dublin: Browne and Nolan, 1960), 146–47, points to other places where he believes "Assyria" was changed to Babylon by later editors (Mic 4:10; 2 Chr 33:16; Isa 23:13), but many would disagree with these examples.

[33] Erlandsson, *The Burden of Babylon,* 109–114. He provides an extensive record of the relationships between Persia (Elam), the Medes, Assyria, and Babylon on pages 86–92.

[34] Oswalt, *Isaiah 1–39,* 300–301, frequently takes a more symbolic approach to these kinds of issues.

13–23[35] (the nation mentioned is always being punished), so this approach should be rejected. Since Isaiah elsewhere openly condemns Assyria and predicts its destruction (10:5–34; 14:24–28; 37:21–35), there is no reason for the prophet to use a symbolic name here[36] or for him to substitute the name "Babylon" when he really meant Assyria.[37] Therefore, it may be best to date this prophecy sometime shortly before 701 BC, when Judah was tempted to depend on the Babylonians (39:1–7) to defeat the Assyrians. At that time, Assyria was about to crush Hezekiah at Jerusalem and Babylon was a rising empire on the eastern horizon that had the potential of being able to help Hezekiah escape from Assyria's iron grip. If this is the context for the message of chaps. 13–14, the prophet is exposing the foolishness of Hezekiah's trust in Babylon and arguing against this political alliance. The prophet affirms the approaching defeat of Babylon (13:19; 14:22; 21:1–10) and later affirms the fall of Assyria (14:25).

THEOLOGY. God said in 10:12,16–19,33–34 that he would destroy the great forest Assyria, which Ahaz trusted, but now in chaps. 13–14 he announces the defeat of Babylon, the nation that Hezekiah was tempted to trust and make an alliance with (39:1–8). God's warnings in chaps. 13–14 demonstrate that it makes no sense to put one's faith in any earthly kingdom or king (and especially not Babylon), for God will determine the destiny of each nation.

The prophet begins by laying a theological foundation for God's involvement with military battles in 13:1–16. The defeat of the mighty kingdoms of this earth will be an act of God, accomplished by God's army on the "Day of the LORD" for that nation (13:2–5). Although human troops may fight, the spiritual reality is that God and his heavenly forces will come to determine the outcome of every battle and bring punishment on his enemies (13:9,13). Those who proudly and arrogantly pretend to control the world (13:11) or claim to be above God (14:12–14) will end up dead (14:9–11). The execution of God's plan on the Day of the Lord was just as determined as God's immediate plan to destroy the Assyrian army that was surrounding Jerusalem (14:24–25). Everything that happens fits together to accomplish God's purposes on earth; there is no one or no nation that can prevent God's plan from being accomplished (14:26–27).

In light of these assertions, the rhetorical aim of this passage seems to argue the theological point that it is senseless for Hezekiah to fight against

---

[35] Assyria was God's instrument of destruction in 10:5 and the Medes do God's bidding in 13:17, but the oracles in chaps. 13–23 consistently predict God's judgment on the nations listed.

[36] Though later authors may choose to see Babylon as a symbol of an evil empire (Rev 17:1–6), this has no influence on how Isaiah understood or used the name Babylon. People today may mistakenly view Babylon and Assyria as parallel or nearly identical nations in the ancient world, but they were mortal enemies for centuries. Isaiah and his audience certainly knew that Assyria was the enemy that was attacking Jerusalem and that Babylon was an ally that might help them oppose the Assyrians.

[37] These commentators do not interpret the fall of Babylon in 21:1–10 as the fall of Assyria.

God's plan by trusting a proud nation like Babylon, for God has already condemned Babylon to destruction. A second reason that it makes no sense to trust in Babylon is that God has already announced his plan to have compassion on Israel, return their captives to the land, and cause many foreigners to worship Israel's God (14:1–3; cf. 2:2–3; 10:20–27; 11:10–16). A third argument against trusting Babylon is that God's people do not need the protection of Babylon to survive an Assyrian attack, for God himself will destroy Assyria (14:24–27). If the people of Judah would believe that this is the certain conclusion to God's plan and that no one can change the plans that God has determined (14:27), the nation of Judah should be willing to trust God Almighty with its present problems. It has always been true that what people believe about God will determine their practical walk, just as their practical walk will reveal what they really believe about God. The extent of each person's trust in God is evident in the decisions they make and the things they do.

A major theological theme that epitomizes man's rebellion against God is pride. The people of Judah were proud in the time of Uzziah (2:6–21) and the wealthy women walked around proudly strutting their stuff (3:16–4:1). The nation of Israel was haughty (9:8–9), and the Assyrian king arrogantly bragged about what he was going to do to conquer the world (10:5–14). In a similar manner, this message declares that God will destroy those who are proud (13:11) and any proud king who tries to play God (14:12–14). The Israelites listening to Isaiah needed to learn from these negative examples so that they would not overstep their rightful place and become proud. They do not determine the future, God does. They do not have the power to defeat their enemies, God does. They have no reason to exalt themselves in pride; God is the one who should be exalted. People need to humble themselves before the mighty power of God and simply put their trust in him.

STRUCTURE.   The structure of this section can be outlined into several paragraphs:

Destruction on the Day of the Lord	13:1–16
God Will Destroy Proud Babylon	13:17–22
God Will Restore Israel	14:1–2
A Taunt for the Babylonian King	14:3–23
God's Plan for Assyria	14:24–28

The Day of the Lord theme in 13:1–16 introduces the chapters against the nation, just like the positive and negative aspects of the Day of the Lord in chap. 2 introduced the earlier literary unit in chaps. 2–12.[38] The Day of the Lord will also be the theme of chap. 24, which introduces chaps. 24–27.

---

[38] A. J. Everson, "Serving Notice on Babylon: The Canonical Function of Isaiah 13–14," *Word and World* 19 (1999): 133–40, recognizes the connection between chaps. 2 and 13.

(1) Destruction on the Day of the Lord (13:1–16)

¹An oracle concerning Babylon that Isaiah son of Amoz saw:
²Raise a banner on a bare hilltop,
　　shout to them;
beckon to them
　　to enter the gates of the nobles.
³I have commanded my holy ones;
　　I have summoned my warriors to carry out my wrath—
　　those who rejoice in my triumph.

⁴Listen, a noise on the mountains,
　　like that of a great multitude!
Listen, an uproar among the kingdoms,
　　like nations massing together!
The Lord Almighty is mustering
　　an army for war.
⁵They come from faraway lands,
　　from the ends of the heavens—
the Lord and the weapons of his wrath—
　　to destroy the whole country.

⁶Wail, for the day of the Lord is near;
　　it will come like destruction from the Almighty.
⁷Because of this, all hands will go limp,
　　every man's heart will melt.
⁸Terror will seize them,
　　pain and anguish will grip them;
　　they will writhe like a woman in labor.
They will look aghast at each other,
　　their faces aflame.

⁹See, the day of the Lord is coming
　　—a cruel day, with wrath and fierce anger—
to make the land desolate
　　and destroy the sinners within it.
¹⁰The stars of heaven and their constellations
　　will not show their light.
The rising sun will be darkened
　　and the moon will not give its light.
¹¹I will punish the world for its evil,
　　the wicked for their sins.
I will put an end to the arrogance of the haughty
　　and will humble the pride of the ruthless.
¹²I will make man scarcer than pure gold,
　　more rare than the gold of Ophir.
¹³Therefore I will make the heavens tremble;
　　and the earth will shake from its place
at the wrath of the Lord Almighty,
　　in the day of his burning anger.

14Like a hunted gazelle,
    like sheep without a shepherd,
each will return to his own people,
    each will flee to his native land.
15Whoever is captured will be thrust through;
    all who are caught will fall by the sword.
16Their infants will be dashed to pieces before their eyes;
    their houses will be looted and their wives ravished.

The first paragraph concludes that God will defeat his enemies on every occurrence of the Day of the Lord. When God wipes out a nation for its sin, the Day of the Lord happens for that group of people. Amos 5:20–21 predicts the coming Day of the Lord for the nation of Israel, which happened when it was defeated in 721 BC. Zephaniah 1:14–18 describes the Day of the Lord for Judah, which eventually took place when the Babylonians destroyed the city of Jerusalem in 587/586 BC. At the end of human history the final Day of the Lord will take place when God defeats all his enemies, sets up his glorious kingdom, and reigns over this world as King.

At the end of this chapter Isaiah specifically relates the Day of the Lord to the destruction of Babylon (13:17–22). These oracles about the Day of the Lord became a valuable source of Babylon traditions and later biblical writers freely employed them in literal (Jer 50–51) and symbolic ways (Rev 16–18).[39] This paragraph can be divided into two subparagraphs:

Preparation for Battle	13:1–5
Superscription	1
Solders summoned	2–3
Soldiers arrive	4–5
The Battle on the Day of the Lord	13:6–16
People will wail	6–8
Destruction of heaven and earth	9–13
People will be hunted and killed	14–16

13:1–5 The text itself marks the beginning of each new sub-paragraph with some grammatical marker: (a) A new superscription in 13:1 introduces this message and marks it off from the sermons that precede it in chaps. 2–12.

---

[39] H. Wildberger, *Isaiah 13–27: A Commentary*, CC (Minneapolis: Fortress, 1997), 17, finds a connection with Zeph 3, while Blenkinsopp, *Isaiah 1–39*, 277–78, maintains that Jer 50–51 "provided the author of Isa 13 with his raw material." It is difficult to determine who borrowed from whom, but Jeremiah and Zephaniah served in the time of Josiah, years after Isaiah's ministry ended. K. W. Allen, "The Rebuilding and Destruction of Babylon," *BibSac* 133 (1976): 19–27, takes a dispensational approach and connects the defeat of Babylon to what will happen in the second half of the final "week" of the tribulation and connects these events to Matt 24 and Rev 16. This reads into the prophecy of Isaiah material that was only revealed much later. Although Isaiah's prophecy may have influenced NT authors, their information was unknown to Isaiah and cannot be used to interpret his oracle.

(b) 13:2–5 begins with a second person imperatival exhortation for God's warriors to "raise a banner . . . shout." In these verses God calls his troops together to prepare for battle.

13:1 This is not a song (5:1–7), a woe oracle (5:5–25), or a salvation oracle (2:1–5); it is a *maśśā'* ("utterance, oracle") about the foreign nation of Babylon. This general title does not identify this message as a separate literary genre (see above under GENRE) but simply indicates that the prophet Isaiah son of Amoz received new insights ("he saw," *ḥāzâ*) from God. The extended introduction of "Isaiah son of Amoz" (just like 1:1 and 2:1) signals that this superscription begins a group of sermons that probably existed as a separate unit at one time, which explains the need to restate who the author was. Although other chapters within the series (chaps. 13–23) do not mention Isaiah as the author, the superscription at the head of a section implies a similar source for the material that follows.[40] This superscription was added when these messages were put in a written form and were not part of what the prophet spoke when he initially delivered these words orally. This is a quite significant point, for it means that the audience in Judah probably did not know that this message was about Babylon until 13:17. Consequently, in order for a reader today to hear the same message Isaiah spoke to his audience, one needs to hear the prophet's messages on the Day of the Lord in 13:2–16 as an introduction to all the oracles in chaps. 13–23. It refers to God's great battle against the forces of evil on earth. The emphasis on Babylon only begins in 13:17.[41]

13:2–3 The message abruptly begins with a command for warriors to gather for battle, but initially it is unclear who is giving the command and who is being sent out to "raise the banner."[42] Later it becomes clear that God is mustering an army for war (v. 4). The ones who go to proclaim this message are never identified, but one could imagine the prophet and his followers or angelic messengers (cf. Zech 1:11–13; 6:1–8), but maybe these instructions are primarily included for the rhetorical effect of showing the urgency of the need. The people assemble when a banner is raised on a prominent and spacious hill where everyone can see the banner and gather together (cf. 5:26; 11:10–12; Jer 51:27). A very visible banner will identify where people are to gather and the nature of the cause. The shouting and waving of the hands give additional encouragement for people to come. The NIV translation states that the purpose is for these warriors "to enter the gates of the nobles,"[43] which frequently is inter-

---

[40] Single authored books have the author identified on the title page and introduction but do not identify the author as the author of every chapter (the book of Amos). On the other hand, books that have multiple authors, like the book of the twelve Minor Prophets, usually have the authors identified at the beginning of each new section.

[41] Long ago, J. P. Peters, "Notes on Isaiah," *JBL* 38 (1919): 77–93, understood 13:1–16 as an oracle about the Day of the Lord, with the destruction of Babylon at the end in 13:17–22.

[42] In light of the military context and the urgency of the situation the imperative verb שְׂאוּ, "lift up, raise," should probably be taken as a command (GKC §111a).

[43] נְדִיבִים, "nobles," is translated "free willing ones" by Wildberger, *Isaiah 13–27,* 19 (based on

preted as the noble gates of Babylon.[44] This interpretation should be rejected for two reasons: (a) this part of the sermon is about the Day of the Lord and there are no references to Babylon up to this point; (b) if this text is describing the military summons for men to fight, it is too early to mention specific military tactics like entering the gates to conquer the city. At this point in the story, the troops are just gathering together to form an army. Motyer's suggestion that these warriors come to the city gates to enroll for service is a more fitting alternative while Watts believes these are just the gates of the camp.[45]

In 13:3, God himself explains why his warriors were called. God identifies those he has summoned as "my holy ones, my warriors, those who rejoice in my triumph." Clements believes these are Babylonian troops,[46] like the Assyrians who were the rod of God's judgment in 10:5, but it makes more sense to interpret these warriors as God's holy troops in his heavenly army[47] who have dedicated themselves for holy war (cf. Josh 3:5; Deut 23:9–14). These are "my warriors" (*gibbôray*) who are ready to fight for God; they are "those rejoicing/exulting in my majesty/exaltation."[48] If religious people who claim to be fighting God's battles today do not give all glory and honor to God, there is good reason to question exactly who they are really trying to exalt.

13:4–5   The response to God's call is overwhelming. NIV adds the verb "listen," but the Hebrew text has no verb here. Verse 4 merely describes the great noise created by many people who are gathering[49] together as God's army. The place where they meet is not identified; the people and nations that come are not named. The impression is that people from the far ends of the earth will be willing to serve as instruments of God's wrath in order to bring destruction on his enemies. The group also comprises those who are coming "from the ends of the heavens,"[50] an idea that suggests that these may be the

---

Judg 5:2,9), and he thinks it refers to those who are freely willing to be available to fight for God.

[44] Hayes and Irvine, *Isaiah,* 224, and many others take this approach, but the verb וַיָּבֹא is not an infinitive construct verb (as in 13:5b) that would express the purpose for gathering troops. A "noble" refers to a person of rank based on criteria established by each society (age, wealth, wisdom, status).

[45] Motyer, *The Prophecy of Isaiah,* 137, interprets this analogy based on the practice of people signing up for military service at the city gate under the leadership of a local nobleman. Watts, *Isaiah 1–33,* 196, suggests that the nobles are the volunteers who come to fight.

[46] Clements, *Isaiah 1–39,* 133.

[47] Goldingay, *Isaiah,* 98, concludes that these are "Yahweh's heavenly army."

[48] NIV's "in my triumph" misses the main thrust of גַּאֲוָתִי, which means "majesty, pride, exalt," describing those who "rejoice in God's majesty." Seitz, *Isaiah 1–39,* 133, views the Babylonians as proud (13:11,19) and connects "exalting, proud ones" (13:3) with the Babylonians. So he believes God is calling the Babylonians to fight for him. This does not seem like the best option.

[49] בָּאִים, "coming," is a participle, which usually shows durative or progressive action (GKC §116c), so the text is describing how "they are coming," not "they have come" (NIV), which suggests the process was completed.

[50] The phrase מִקְצֵה הַשָּׁמָיִם, "from the ends of the heavens," argues for the position that the hosts of the Lord included heavenly beings. J. B. Geyer, "Twisting Tiamat's Tail: A Mythological Interpretation of Isaiah XIII 5 and 8," *VT* 37 (1987): 164–79, also interprets these forces as the

same warriors seen by Elisha, the heavenly hosts who fight for God (2 Kgs 6:16–17), not just human troops. The impression the audience would get from this revelation is that God is going to war with a massive destructive force that is unstoppable. This means that victory is sure.

13:6–16 This new paragraph begins with another imperative call (like in 13:2) for everyone who will experience the Day of the Lord to "wail, shout" (*hêlîlû*). This initial description of the Day of the Lord is generic and introductory to all the following messages against specific nations. Years earlier, Amos had predicted that the Day of the Lord[51] for Israel would bring darkness and gloom, implying the defeat of the nation of Israel (Amos 5:18–20).[52] Amos's prophecy was fulfilled in 721 BC when the Assyrian king Sargon II destroyed Samaria and exiled the survivors (2 Kgs 17). In the time of Isaiah, the Day of the Lord is related to the final day when God will humble the proud and he alone will be exalted (2:6–22), as well as his final day of vengeance on the nations (34:1–17 and 63:1–6). In some cases an historical nation is employed by God to conquer his enemies but in other texts God seems to act directly in the fullness of his power. Some passages about the Day of the Lord refer to the historical destruction of nations in the near future (Israel and Judah), while others appear to refer to events in an eschatological era (13:1–16; 24:1–23) when God will defeat all his enemies and set up his holy kingdom.

13:6–8 Since the Day of the Lord is near there is some urgency about the announcement of the prophet. This coming day is when God will personally intervene in the affairs of mankind in an extraordinary way to bring about his will. In these verses the forces that will fight and those who will be defeated are left largely unidentified because the prophet wanted to emphasize that this

---

"heavenly host of Yahweh." In 13:5 he rejects the translation "to destroy" for לְחַבֵּל and prefers "to twist," which he connects to the mythical story of the Enuma Elish where Marduk twists Tiamat's tail when he defeats her. This obscure connection is not preferred, for the usual translation "destroy" makes perfectly good sense.

[51] The origin of the Day of the Lord concept is unknown, but concepts within this tradition suggest that it may have arisen from several sources. (a) C. van Leeuwen, "The Prophecy of the YOM YHWH in Amos 5:18–20," *OTS* 19 (1974): 119, considers H. Gressmann's proposal that the idea came from a common ancient Near Eastern myth about a catastrophic end of the world in which the sun, stars, and earth were destroyed. Van Leeuwen rejects this conclusion because not all Day of the Lord passages deal with the end of the world. (b) S. Mowinckel, *He that Cometh* (Oxford: Blackwell, 1959), 125, drew Day of the Lord concepts from the worship at the autumn New Year's Festival when God was enthroned as king. The Day of the Lord was seen as the future time when God would destroy all his enemies. One of the weaknesses of this approach is that there is no evidence that Judah ever had a New Year's Festival in which God was enthroned as king. (c) The view of G. von Rad, "The Origin of the Concept of the Day of Yahweh," *JSS* 4 (1959): 97–108, that this idea was connected to God's holy war against his enemies makes more sense, yet Amos makes no reference to war in 5:18–20. (d) M. Weiss, "The Origin of the Day of Yahweh Reconsidered," *HUCA* 37 (1966): 517–25, saw the idea developing out of theophany traditions about God appearing in power. A combination of these last two ideas seems to fit most Day of the Lord passages.

[52] G. V. Smith, *Amos*, 237–248, for a discussion of the Day of the Lord in Amos 5:18–20.

"destruction" (*šōd*) will affect everyone on the earth and because the primary cause will be the Almighty Destroyer (*šadday*), God himself.[53]

The author introduces this topic by calling people to "howl, wail" (*hēylîlu*) in astonishment and anguish because what is about to happen will be almost unimaginably horrible. What follows in 13:7–8 is not a lament, but a description of people's reaction to the destruction on the Day of the Lord. Because of this (*ʿal kēn*), people will experience excruciating pain and utter helplessness comparable to what a woman experiences when giving birth to a child (cf. 21:3; 37:3). The people who go through this horrible experience will have falling hands,[54] melting hearts, terror, anguish, writhing in pain, astonishment, and "faces aflame."[55] People will be completely helpless, dismayed, numb, in shock, and deathly afraid. Unfortunately, no one will be able to help them when God decrees their final destruction. The terror of this day should motivate every person who hears the words of the prophet to not be among those who will experience the wrath of God's anger on the Day of the Lord.

13:9–13   The next subparagraph is linguistically marked with the introductory "behold, see"[56] (*hinnēh*) and another announcement that the Day of the Lord is coming. That day will reveal what it means to experience the fullness of the wrath of God. The aim[57] of God's holy anger will be focused on the extermination of evil sinners and the desolation of the places where they may live on the earth. The cosmic significance of this catastrophe (13:10) will shut out the light from the sun, moon, and stars (cf. Amos 5:18,20; Jer 4:23; Joel 2:10). This phenomenon is not explained in detail, but the imagery is identical to the eschatological imagery of complete destruction on the final Day of the Lord (cf. 24:1–23). Amos 5:18–20 applies similar consequences of gloom and darkness to an intermediate historical "day" when God came in power to destroy the nation of Israel in 721 BC. Indeed, when a nation and its cities are destroyed and burned, the lights go out for those people when the smoke from the burning city blocks out the sun. That day is the end of the world for them.

---

[53] There is a word play in the phrase כְּשֹׁד מִשַּׁדַּי that could be interpreted "like destruction from the Almighty Destroyer." This statement does not contradict the idea that God acts in compassion and grace. God is a God of great love, but those who oppose him, hate him, and exalt themselves will suffer a day of great judgment because they have rejected his love, have not trusted him, and have not glorified him as God. Oswalt, *Isaiah 1–39*, 305, suggests that "the cause of it all is the confrontation between the supremacy of God and that thirst for supremacy which is lodged in the human heart."

[54] The falling, limp hands are a sign that there is no fight left, their courage is gone (2 Sam 4:1; Job 4:3; Jer 6:24; 50:43; Ezek 7:17; 21:12), and a "melting heart" (Josh 2:11; 5:1; Isa 19:1; Ezek 21:12) points in the same direction. Courage and strength for battle will not exist.

[55] It is not clear if the red face (פְּנֵי לְהָבִים) is from anger, embarrassment, or fright. In Nah 2:10 [2:11 in Hb.] when things go bad faces will go pale because Nineveh is destroyed.

[56] הִנֵּה is used to introduce a new paragraph in 10:33; 13:9,17; 17:1; 19:1; 22:17; 24:1.

[57] The infinitive construct לְשׂוּם, "in order to make," expresses the purpose or aim of God's action (GKC §114f).

The sinners (13:9) that will suffer under the wrath of God are the arrogant and proud (13:11). They will be humbled and God will put an end to those high-minded leaders who lift themselves up and ruthlessly act like tyrants in their pride. This reminds one of God's judgment of the proud in 2:11–12, of Israel's pride in 9:8, and the haughty arrogance of the Assyrian king in 10:12. God alone should be exalted; people who exalt themselves are evil and must be humbled. In this process millions of sinful people will die[58] and the population of the earth will almost be completely wiped out. People will be as rare as "pure gold."[59] The heavens and the earth itself will totter and shake (13:13; 24:19–20). These descriptions portray the enormous power of God and the hopelessness of surviving his onslaught. Isaiah 24, which begins the next major section of Isaiah, presents a somewhat similar picture of the destruction of the earth and mankind on the Day of the Lord. It will be a fearful day when this sinful earth comes face to face with the wrath of a holy God. In righteous indignation God will destroy these sinners.

13:14–16 This paragraph ends with images of scattered and confused people being hunted like wild animals and without a leader.[60] Like frightened animals, people will run, and when necessary they will turn against one another just to stay alive. Their destiny is compared to the fate of wild game; they will be captured and killed (13:14). No one will be left alive; every man, woman, and child will die. Even the small innocent children will be mercilessly and savagely killed while their parents helplessly watch. Their wives will be raped;[61] anarchy and inhumanity will reign. There will be no safe place where one can hide, not even in a person's own home (13:16). These verses picture the horrors of war and the inhuman suffering of those who are defeated in battle. Oswalt maintains one should not assume "that God is happy about this turn of events,"[62] but this is the immoral pit that sin will eventually lead this violent world to wallow in.

The picture is more horrible than what anyone can imagine or describe. The earth will be in disarray as the dependable forces of nature will disintegrate and people will turn to a savage form of debased animal existence. Government, respect, civility, kindness, and hope will totally disappear. The vile evil of sin

---

[58] The verb יַשְׁמִיד conveys the idea that God will "annihilate, exterminate, destroy" these sinners.

[59] The gold from Ophir was highly prized, but rare, since it came from a distant land (either in Africa or southern Arabia).

[60] The participle מְקַבֵּץ refers to "one who gathers, collects, assembles," so the translation "shepherd" is appropriate when speaking of one who gathers sheep together.

[61] The Masoretes suggested reading the less offensive שָׁכַב, "to lie with," in the *Qere* (which is also found in 1QIsaᵃ) instead of the *Kethib* שָׁגַל, "rape" (cf. Deut 28:30), which is an offensive word describing sexual relations that violate a person. Isaiah purposely chose the harsher, more offensive term to depict the horror of that day.

[62] Oswalt, *Isaiah 1–39*, 307, appears to see this as the natural results of human pride that pits one person against another.

and its horrible consequences will be in full view, but God will finally eradicate it all from the face of the earth.

(2) God Will Destroy Proud Babylon (13:17–22)

> ¹⁷See, I will stir up against them the Medes,
> who do not care for silver
> and have no delight in gold.
> ¹⁸Their bows will strike down the young men;
> they will have no mercy on infants
> nor will they look with compassion on children.
> ¹⁹Babylon, the jewel of kingdoms,
> the glory of the Babylonians' pride,
> will be overthrown by God
> like Sodom and Gomorrah.
> ²⁰She will never be inhabited
> or lived in through all generations;
> no Arab will pitch his tent there,
> no shepherd will rest his flocks there.
> ²¹But desert creatures will lie there,
> jackals will fill her houses;
> there the owls will dwell,
> and there the wild goats will leap about.
> ²²Hyenas will howl in her strongholds,
> jackals in her luxurious palaces.
> Her time is at hand,
> and her days will not be prolonged.

13:17–18 Having described the horrors of God's judgment on the Day of the Lord, the prophet now turns to apply the principle that God will destroy proud sinners on the Day of the Lord (13:6–16) to the present situation in the nation of Babylon (13:17–22). The introductory "behold, see" (*hinnî*) in 13:17 marks the beginning of this new paragraph. This paragraph does not describe the final fate of Babylon on the Day of the Lord (13:2–16). Instead, the author confirms that the same principles that will direct God's action on the final Day of the Lord will direct his control of history when Babylon's Day of the Lord arrives.

The reference to the Medes as the nation that God will use to defeat the Babylonians is parallel to God's use of Assyria as his rod of punishment in 10:5 or God's sending Nebuchadnezzar to defeat Judah in Jer 25:1,9. In each case God was the one directing the course of history through the use of strong armies. These examples provide parallels to how God controls history even today and how he will bring about his will through historical events in every era.

God's activity will be to "stir up, arouse"[63] (45:13; Ezra 1:1; Jer 50:9; 51:1,11 use this terminology) the Medes to action against Babylon (13:19). The Median army is described as a group of soldiers who are determined to win and who will not be susceptible to bribery (silver and gold). They will ferociously destroy their enemies, without having "motherly compassion" (from the root *rāḥam*) on anyone, not even on infants or young children (13:18). The NIV's "the bows will strike down the young men" is a possible translation of 13:18, but it is not the best option.[64] The verb used here means to "dash to pieces," (*rāṭaš*), which is not the usual way of describing what an arrow does to a person. Wildberger provides a better solution by translating the clause "the bows of the young men will be dashed to pieces," thus the attack will leave the army of Babylon defenseless without its archers. The consequence of this is that the Medes will be unstoppable.[65]

13:19–22 The enemy the Medes will attack is the great kingdom of Babylon. Babylon is pictured as one of the most precious or elegant (*ṣĕbî*) kingdoms,[66] a glorious accomplishment of a "proud" (*gĕʾôn*) people. These are the kind of arrogant people that God hates (cf. 2:12,17; 5:15; 9:8; 10:12; 13:11), so God will overthrow them. The comparison with the annihilation of the people of Sodom and Gomorrah (cf. Gen 18–19; Deut 29:22; Amos 4:11) is explained in 13:20–22. As he did Sodom, God will overthrow Babylon; like Sodom, Babylon will never be rebuilt. Sensing a curse on this place, even shepherds and wandering nomads will avoid the area. Only strange, exotic, wild animals[67] will haunt the ruins of these wealthy palaces (13:20–21a). Finally, the prophet indicates that this will happen to Babylon in the near future, not some distant period centuries later.

Isaiah's prediction of the defeat of Babylon has caused considerable discussion about the fulfillment of this prophecy. First, it should be established that when prophets gave predictions, they usually did not know the date of the fulfillment of their prophecies. The main point of this prophecy is that God sovereignly controls the events of history and consequently will bring about the destruction of the proud Babylonians. There is no indication that the prophet knew who would be ruling Babylon at the time this would be fulfilled.

---

[63] מֵעִיר is a *hiphil* participle form of עוּר, which means "to awaken to action, arouse from sleep or inaction, stir up excitement" (BDB, 734–356).

[64] NASB has a similar translation: "And *their* bows will mow down the young men," but רָטַשׁ never has the meaning "strike, mow down." E. J. Young, *The Book of Isaiah*, (Grand Rapids: Eerdmans, 1965-72), I:426, appeals to an Akkadian text to suggest that the bows did not literally dash men to pieces, but because men were hit by arrows the men were dashed to pieces.

[65] Wildberger, *Isaiah 13–27*, 9. This involves reading the active *piel* תְּרַטַּשְׁנָה with one vowel change, thus making it a passive *pual* form. This is also the reading of the Old Greek translation.

[66] Although NIV uses the translation "the jewel of kingdoms" to capture the idea of a precious thing, that translation unnecessarily concretizes the general idea of being beautiful and precious into a specific example of one precious thing.

[67] J. B. Geyer, "Desolation and Cosmos," *VT* 49 (1999): 49–64, interprets these animals not as wild beasts, but as mythical creatures or demons.

Although the exact date of fulfillment was unknown to the prophet, he knew it would happen relatively soon (13:22).

The best option is to suggest that Isaiah delivered this prophecy a short time before 701 BC, when Babylon was tempting Hezekiah to rebel and form an alliance with Babylon. If that is the setting, Isaiah would be announcing the demise of the Babylonian kingdom, thus implying that it was useless for Hezekiah to trust Merodach-baladan (39:1–6). It is impossible to determine if the prophet foresaw the coming fall of Babylon in 689 BC when the Assyrian king Sennacherib defeated Babylon, tore down its walls, flooded the area, depopulated the city, and made the city into a meadow[68] or if he was predicting the final end of the political power of Babylon when Cyrus, king of the Medes and Persians, defeated the city in 539 BC (cf. Dan 5). Isaiah was more concerned with assuring his audience that there was no doubt about the fulfillment of this event; he was not concerned with predicting an exact date for these events or trying to specify who would be ruling when this prophecy was fulfilled.

(3) God Will Restore Israel (14:1–2)

> [1]The LORD will have compassion on Jacob;
>   once again he will choose Israel
>   and will settle them in their own land.
> Aliens will join them
>   and unite with the house of Jacob.
> [2]Nations will take them
>   and bring them to their own place.
> And the house of Israel will possess the nations
>   as menservants and maidservants in the LORD's land.
> They will make captives of their captors
>   and rule over their oppressors.

There is no way to determine if the prophet originally spoke 14:1–2 in conjunction with the Babylon oracles here in chaps. 13–14, but is it likely that these verses were editorially placed here at the time when the author put these oracles in their present written order. No direct evidence of Hebrew exiles in Babylon occurs in 14:1–2[69] or in 13:17–22, though many people from the

---

[68] Erlandsson, *The Burden of Babylon,* 91, for Sennacherib's detailed description of the destruction of Babylon. The weakness of this choice is that it is odd to find 13:17 referring to the Medes as the conquerors of Babylon (rather than the Assyrians). This may simply be due to our limited knowledge of Median history in this period. Another possible solution to this problem would be to suggest that the prophet saw the final demise of Babylon in telescopic view (referring to 539 BC when Medo-Persia defeated Babylon), but that he was not given enough information to distinguish all the various individual conquests and conquerors. He did know that at some point the Medes would be involved in the process of destroying Babylon.

[69] G. M. Tucker, "The Book of Isaiah 1–39," *The New Interpreter's Bible,* Vol VI (Nashville: Abingdon, 2001), 157, assumes this was written in the exilic period after Judah had already gone into exile in Babylon. He believes 14:1 assumes the conditions in chaps. 40–55 and that 14:2

northern nation of Israel were exiled by Assyria during the lifetime of Isaiah (before and at 721 BC). If this promise is associated with events around 701 BC, then this promise might refer to the 200,150[70] Hebrews exiled by Sennacherib. Clements believes the prophet referred to the people who returned to Judah after the Babylonian captivity in 539 BC.[71] It is always dangerous to read into a prophecy the later fulfillment, for the prophets usually had little information about when their prophecies would be fulfilled. All that is required for people to understand this prophecy is for some Israelites to be in exile. This salvation oracle indicates that God's people will experience a different future than Babylon, though a direct grammatical connection between Israel's hope and Babylon's demise is not clearly stated. The *kî* (omitted in NIV) at the beginning of 14:1 does not provide a causal connection to suggest that the judgment of Babylon will occur "because" of God's compassion on Israel.[72] It would be better to interpret this *kî* either as a contrast with Babylon's fate ("but") or as having a temporal significance ("when" as in NASB).

Israel will not deserve God's salvation and will not meet any predefined conditions to earn God's grace. God will be compassionate to his people just like he was before (Exod 34:6; Deut 4:31). He will pour out his love, a love that is comparable to the deep emotional feeling that a mother has for her child (contrast 13:18).[73] God will again choose Israel to be his people, just like he originally elected Israel to be his holy people (Deut 4:37; 7:6–7). This does not mean that Israel was not God's chosen people for a period of time, but that God did not always deal with them in compassion because of their sin. Later, he will choose to give compassionate love to his people in a manner reminiscent of his love when he originally chose them. God also will give them rest[74] and peace in their own land (Deut 3:20; 12:9).

---

assumes the conditions in chaps. 56–66. These conclusions ignore the captivity of thousands of Hebrews when Sennacherib attacked the nation.

[70] Sennacherib claimed that he destroyed 46 strong cities in Judah and took 200,150 Hebrews captive (*ANET*, 288).

[71] Clements, *Isaiah 1–39*, 138, maintains that this refers to "the restoration of Israel after the overthrow of Babylon."

[72] Oswalt, *Isaiah 1–39*, 312, accepts "because" though Sweeney, *Isaiah 1–39*, 224, interprets it as a contrasting "but." Wildberger takes 14:1–2 as an addendum (based on כִּי) to chap. 13. While Childs, Isaiah, 123, and others find these verses to be an editorial addition by Second Isaiah because these themes are also discussed in chaps. 40–66. But is it possible to objectively prove this? Why could one not hypothesize that chaps. 40–66 pick up themes from 1–39? E. J. Kissane, *Isaiah*, I, 157, saw a connection with themes in Isaiah 1–5 and concluded that this was the source of Second Isaiah teaching. Blenkinsopp, *Isaiah 1–39*, 282, agrees, stating that Williamson's (*The Book Called Isaiah: Deutero-Isaiah's Role in Composition and Redaction* [Oxford: Clarendon Press, 1994], 165–67) attempt to claim that these verses were written by Second Isaiah "is going beyond the evidence."

[73] רִחַם, "motherly love," is related to רֶחֶם, "mother's womb," and describes her selfless devotion and love for a child who is unable to respond with love, yet desperately needs her care.

[74] NIV translates וְהִנִּיחָם as "and will settle them," but the essence of this root is God's gift of rest and peace, not just the ability to settle in a certain place. "Rest" (נוּחַ) is a broader concept that

It appears that three groups of foreigners will have close social relationships with the Israelites at that time. First, the "alien residents" (*gēr* in 14:1b) will join themselves with God's people (cf. 2:2–4; 11:10–16; Exod 12:38) and become one with them. This implies that these foreigners will convert and become part of God's people (like Rahab or Ruth). Second, some unidentified nations will assist the Israelites in the process of returning to their land. Israel will inherit servants from this group, though their nationality and spiritual condition is unknown. Third, there is a final group of unidentified foreigners who previously took the Israelites captive (possibly some Egyptians, Assyrians, or Babylonians; cf. 19:19–25). These former oppressors will now be under the authority of God and his people. Although it may be tempting to interpret these promises as a description of the Israelites' return from Babylonian captivity with the aid of the Persian king Cyrus, a reading of Haggai, Zechariah, Ezra, and Nehemiah demonstrates that this prophecy in Isaiah is talking about something far more wonderful than what happened in the post-exilic era. This prophecy should be connected to God's grand eschatological transformation of the hearts of mankind (2:1–5; 11:10–16; 19:18–25), not a minor post-exilic fulfillment that failed to demonstrate the characteristics of welcoming foreigners into the community of Israel (Ezra 9–10; Neh 9:1–2; 10:28–30; 13:23–27). God wants his people to include foreigners in his kingdom, even those who had previously been their enemies. Later prophecies will expand on these eschatological hopes (45:14–17; 49:22–23; 60:1–8; 61:5–7; 66:20).

These promises about foreigners being servants should not be misunderstood as a sign of revenge or a form of oppressive Jewish nationalism. The text describes a reversal of roles for Israel, not an evil oppressive enslavement of innocent foreign people. Although the Messiah is not mentioned in this context, God's judgment and rule over the nations in 14:1–2 is consistent with the earlier vision of his rule over the nations (9:1–7; 11:1–16).[75]

(4) A Taunt Song for the Babylonian King (14:3–23)

[3]On the day the LORD gives you relief from suffering and turmoil and cruel bondage, [4]you will take up this taunt against the king of Babylon:

> How the oppressor has come to an end!
> How his fury has ended!
> [5]The LORD has broken the rod of the wicked,
> the scepter of the rulers,
> [6]which in anger struck down peoples
> with unceasing blows,
> and in fury subdued nations
> with relentless aggression.

---

has theological implications of divine blessing without war, not just putting down roots.

[75] Wildberger, *Isaiah 13–27*, 37, maintains that "Although the theme 'establishment of divine rule' is not explicitly mentioned, it is implicitly still the most important point" of this chapter.

[7]All the lands are at rest and at peace;
    they break into singing.
[8]Even the pine trees and the cedars of Lebanon
    exult over you and say,
 "Now that you have been laid low,
    no woodsman comes to cut us down."
[9]The grave below is all astir
    to meet you at your coming;
it rouses the spirits of the departed to greet you—
    all those who were leaders in the world;
it makes them rise from their thrones—
    all those who were kings over the nations.
[10]They will all respond,
    they will say to you,
"You also have become weak, as we are;
    you have become like us."
[11]All your pomp has been brought down to the grave,
    along with the noise of your harps;
maggots are spread out beneath you
    and worms cover you.

[12]How you have fallen from heaven,
    O morning star, son of the dawn!
You have been cast down to the earth,
    you who once laid low the nations!
[13]You said in your heart,
    "I will ascend to heaven;
I will raise my throne
    above the stars of God;
I will sit enthroned on the mount of assembly,
    on the utmost heights of the sacred mountain.
[14]I will ascend above the tops of the clouds;
    I will make myself like the Most High."
[15]But you are brought down to the grave,
    to the depths of the pit.

[16]Those who see you stare at you,
    they ponder your fate:
"Is this the man who shook the earth
    and made kingdoms tremble,
[17]the man who made the world a desert,
    who overthrew its cities
    and would not let his captives go home?"

[18]All the kings of the nations lie in state,
    each in his own tomb.
[19]But you are cast out of your tomb
    like a rejected branch;
you are covered with the slain,

with those pierced by the sword,
those who descend to the stones of the pit.
Like a corpse trampled underfoot,
20you will not join them in burial,
for you have destroyed your land
and killed your people.

The offspring of the wicked
will never be mentioned again.
21Prepare a place to slaughter his sons
for the sins of their forefathers;
they are not to rise to inherit the land
and cover the earth with their cities.

22"I will rise up against them,"
declares the LORD Almighty.
"I will cut off from Babylon her name and survivors,
her offspring and descendants,"
declares the LORD.

23"I will turn her into a place for owls
and into swampland;
I will sweep her with the broom of destruction,"
declares the LORD Almighty.

GENRE. The introduction to this poem identifies it as a *māšāl*, a general Hebrew term that describes a proverb, parable, wisdom saying, or poem. The *qinâ* meter and the discussion of death signals that this is a dirge or lament because a Babylonian king will die. But a lament by a Hebrew prophet for a Babylonian king seems unusual. Why would a Hebrew lament his death? Oswalt interprets this poem to be an example of the prophet turning the lament on its head so that the "song for the dead is a song of joy, not grief."[76] Clements finds the poem "heavily ironic and satirical in its expression, and it is designed to express rejoicing."[77] This ironic reading means the funeral lament is an abrasive taunt. But what king is the prophet taunting? Certainly this poem was not spoken in the city of Babylon as a taunt in the presence of any Babylonian king or his supporters. The prophet was speaking to people in Jerusalem. The idea that this is a taunt is one possible interpretation, but that approach may not adequately take into consideration what the prophet was attempting to communicate to his audience in Judah. If he wanted his audience in Judah to rejoice, why use a lament about death? Why would he not use a salvation oracle? Where in this poem is the call for the Israelites to rejoice? A hymn of thanksgiving and praise would express this attitude more fully.

---

[76] Oswalt, *Isaiah 1–39*, 316, concludes that "the singer welcomes death as a blessing," that is, the death of this terrible king.

[77] Clements, *Isaiah 1–39*, 140, believes the poem is "aimed at celebrating the passing of a hostile and hated world-dominion."

A look at the political relationship between Babylon and Israel may help explain what the prophet was trying to communicate. Isaiah 39:1–8 indicates that the Babylon king Merodach-baladan approached Hezekiah in order to develop an alliance between Babylon and Judah so that together they could resist the Assyrian king Sennacherib. God did not approve of this alliance because it meant that Hezekiah was not completely trusting in God. Therefore, it is understandable why God would want to remove this false basis for hope and destroy the Babylonian king. The death of this pivotal Babylonian ally would be a terrible blow to Judah, and many in Judah would naturally lament his passing. His death would undermine their coordinated plan to rebel against Assyria and dash their hopes of maintaining their freedom from Assyrian domination. If this accurately reconstructs the setting, then Isaiah's lament would have initially gained a sympathetic ear from those in his audience who were trusting in this Babylonian king. The content of the lament shockingly presents this king in a light that is not very complementary, demonstrating that the leaders of Judah should not trust him. His rule will soon end (14:5), he will join other dead kings in Sheol (14:9–15), and he and his sons will end up slaughtered and disgraced (14:16–21). The purpose of this prophetic lament was to convince the leaders in Judah that the approaching death of this king made it senseless for his audience to trust this hopeless king. Thus it is not so much a taunt of the king but a sober lament. Many will weep, for God is going to end the life of the Babylonian king that Judah was trusting.

HISTORICAL SETTING. The hypothetical setting for this lament depends on which king is described and whether the lament refers to a Babylonian king or to an Assyrian king who has declared himself king over the province of Babylon. Hayes and Irvine identify the subject as the Assyrian king Tiglath-pileser III who claimed the title king of Babylon, while Clements prefers either the proud and powerful Nebuchadnezzar or the last king of Babylon, Nabonidus.[78] Watts thinks the lament refers to Merodach-baladan, Sweeney defends the view that Sargon II fits best, and Oswalt says this is merely a symbolic representation of every bygone tyrant, rather than a specific king.[79] This commentary places all of chaps. 13–14 in the context of the political events in 39:1–8 because that was the time during the life of Isaiah when Babylon became an important person in Israelite politics (just

---

[78] Hayes and Irvine, *Isaiah,* 227–31, quote passages where Tiglath-pileser III claims to be king of Babylon, plus some of his proud boasts of being "the great king, the mighty king, king of the universe." Clements, *Isaiah 1–39,* 149. finds Nebuchadnezzar "the most plausible candidate," but then goes on to say that Nabonidus is "even more probable."

[79] Watts, *Isaiah 1–33,* 188; Sweeney, *Isaiah 1–39,* 232–33, and K. L. Younger, "Recent Study on Sargon II, King of Assyria," in *Mesopotamia and the Bible* (ed. M. W. Chavalas and K. L. Younger, Grand Rapids: Baker, 2002), 288–329, believes the lament refers to Sargon II because his body was abandoned on the battlefield (14:18–20); Oswalt, *Isaiah 1–39,* 314, 325, takes a symbolic approach partially because 14:22–23 interpret the figure in the song as a reference to Babylon as a whole, not to an individual.

before 701 BC). Merodach-baladan's reign ended and the city of Babylon was decimated in 689 BC. Merodach-baladan was a king that the Hebrews should not have trusted. His name was not mentioned in this lament because it was God's purpose to cut off his name so that it would not be mentioned again (14:20b–22). This Babylonian king, who appears to give hope to Judah (with analogies to the messianic figure in 9:1–7), is unmasked in this lament. He will not be their savior; instead, the scepter will be taken from this one (14:5) who attempts to be like God. His death will bring great sorrow, his kingdom will be cut off, and his name will disappear. Certainly it would be wiser to trust in God's plans (14:24–27) than the scheming plots of this proud Babylonian king.

STRUCTURE. The lament proper extends from 14:4b to 21, with an introduction in 14:3–4a and a conclusion in 14:22–23. R. H. O'Connell extended the lament to include 14:4b–23 and organized it into a seven-tiered concentric structure with 14:12–14 as the central axis. He believes the purpose of the poem is to prove the justice of overthrowing the king that tried to usurp God's high station.[80] The subtleties he uses for this complex concentric structure are not very obvious or convincing. It is better to interpret this lament as telling a story about the king's entrance into Sheol. The movement of the story has the following structure:

Introduction to the lament	14:3–4a
Death of this oppressive king	14:4b–8
King's spirit enters into Sheol	14:9–11
King's fall from heaven	14:12–14
King's humiliation	14:15–21
God's judgment of Babylon	14:22–23

The lament is constructed around an introductory "how"[81] in 14:4b,12 and "but, nevertheless" in 14:15.[82] Each paragraph includes quotations of what different people will say about this king (14:8b,10–11,13–14,16,22–23). The poem ends with the assuring declaration that this will be the work of God (14:22–23). The structure shows that although this king will attempt to "ascend into heaven" to be like God (in the center of the poem), his ultimate destiny is that he will be "laid low" (14:7), "brought down to the grave" (14:11,15), and in shame the king will even be "cast out of [his] tomb" (14:19).

[80] R. H. O'Connell, "Isaiah XIV 4B–23: Ironic Reversal Through Concentric Structure and Mythic Allusions," *VT* 38 (1988): 407–418, believes the seven arrogant acts in 14:13–14 are reversed in the rest of the poem, but the parallelism between each aspect within his chiastic structure is sometimes quite weak.

[81] אֵיךְ, "how," is often used in laments or in lamentable situations (cf. 2 Sam 1:19; Jer 9:18; 48:39; 51:41; Isa 20:6; Mic 2:4).

[82] W. L. Holladay, "Text, Structure, and Irony in the Poem on the Fall of the Tyrant, Isaiah 14," *CBQ* 61 (1999): 633–45, and Kaiser, *Isaiah 13–39*, 29, divide the paragraph after v. 15 and put 16–21 together, ignoring the "nevertheless" at the beginning of v. 15.

14:3–4a   The beginning of this new unit is clearly marked with the introductory "and it shall happen" (*wĕhāyâ*, which is omitted in NIV). The conclusion of this short narrative introduction in v. 4a is signaled by "you will take up this taunt against the king of Babylon." This is a prose editorial introduction to the lament that orients the Hebrew audience to the future time when this lament will make more sense to them. At the time, this lament was not consistent with the thinking of the leaders of Judah who wanted to trust this Babylonian king for help against Assyria in 703–701 BC. Since Merodach-baladan was very much alive and ready to fight the Assyrians, this lament did not fit reality as the people of Judah understood it. Later, when God delivers his people from suffering and turmoil (probably referring to the end of suffering because of the death of Sennacherib's troops in 37:36) and the Babylonian king does not help them, they will realize what a terrible mistake they made to trust the Babylonians. So Isaiah takes up a lament "concerning" (*ʿal*) the demise of the king of Babylon to convince them of the major mistake they are making in trusting the Babylonians; this is not actually "a taunt against the king of Babylon" (NIV). Later, they will discover that they never needed this Babylonian king at all, for God will deliver them, similar to their earlier deliverance from Egyptian bondage. Then they will have relief (lit. "rest"; cf. Deut 3:20; Josh 1:13,15; 21:44) from bondage and hardship (cf. Exod 1:14; 2:23; 5:9,11) because of God's grace. God repeatedly acts in similar ways on behalf of his people to fulfill his promises, so it is lamentable when some still trust in human religious leaders or powerful politicians instead of God.

14:4b–8   The lament begins by announcing the restful "end"[83] (implying the death) of one who is styled as a repressive ruler. This is not the kind of person one should ever make an alliance with or depend on. He comes with a resume of past experiences that are not at all complimentary. The NIV translation of the last line, "How his fury has ended," is problematic, but if the Hebrew letters *dālet* and *rēš* were confused in the word translated "fury" (a common mistake in Hebrew because the letters are almost identical), then one could translate the line "his boasting will end."[84] These sins provide a justification for ending the life of this king. It was God's consistent commit-

---

[83] שָׁבַת, "to rest, cease," by extension implies the end of what is now happening. "Resting" is what the dead do, so the choice of this word is appropriate. His "resting" in death and defeat contrast with the "rest" of God's people in 14:1.

[84] The word מַדְהֵבָה is difficult to interpret and various emendations are suggested. Early Rabbis like Kimchi read it as an Aramaic form of the word "gold" and the Latin Vulgate and Symmachus have "tribute." Erlandsson, *The Burden of Babylon*, 29–31, accepts this translation. Wildberger, *Isaiah 13–27*, 43, has an extensive note on various attempts to solve this problem. It is often thought that מַדְהֵבָה is a mistake for מַרְהֵבָה because of a confusion of ד and ר. Since נגש and רהב have already been used in parallelism in 3:5, this makes sense and 1QIsaᵃ agrees with this reading. The root רָהַב usually means "to be boisterous, defiant, proud," which is fitting in the context of chaps. 13–14. Wildberger, *Isaiah 13–27*, 43, views this person as a "tyrant," which appears to be better than Oswalt, *Isaiah 1–39*, 314, who prefers the translation "fury."

ment down through the ages to break the scepter of wicked rulers (14:5)[85] who arrogantly ruled nations by repeatedly mistreating their subjects (14:6). The Israelite audience, who was tempted to trust this Babylonian king, needed to understand that this king was not a righteous person God could support. God will not let this kind of oppressive, angry, arrogant, and endlessly[86] aggressive king continue in power (13:6), so why would Israel want to depend on such an obnoxious ruler?

Verses 7–8 explain the consequence of the king's death. Although Judah may lament the passing of this king, the rest of the world will finally be able to have some peace. The people in the lands where he aggressively ruled can rejoice, instead of suffering under his oppressive hand.[87] Both man and nature (the whole world) can shout with jubilation (*rinnâ*, "singing") because this terrible king has already been "laid low" (*šākbtā*, funeral terminology). He will no longer be able to ravage foreign countries by indiscriminately decimating fine forests by cutting down their great trees.[88] The cutting of trees could support military operations (building bridges or siege engines) and help to construct grand palaces back home, or a spiteful king might just cut down prized trees to humiliate a people and destroy the valuable property of an enemy nation.

14:9–11   The second stanza laments the king's entrance into Sheol, the place of the dead spirits. Clements believes that in this section "the poem now moves into its most triumphant satirical theme by picturing the abject humiliation of the tyrannical king."[89] The picture that is painted is that of spirits[90]

---

[85] In 9:4 [Hb. 9:3] and 10:24 God also promises to remove the "rod" (מַטֶּה) and "scepter" (שֵׁבֶט) from the hand of the oppressor. These are symbols of the power of this repressive king in 14:5. In 9:6–7 and 11:4 the hand of the true Messiah of Israel will rule his people with righteousness, not with oppression.

[86] The phrase בְּלִי חָשָׂךְ, "without refrain, restraint, sparing," emphasizes a repeated pattern of unacceptable behavior that showed no mercy or consideration for the suffering of others.

[87] The prefect verbs in vv. 7–8 could be translated in present tense because they describe the state of the earth after the death of this king (GKC §106g). Although these events will happen at some point in the future, from the perspective within those events (after the death of this king) it is appropriate to talk of the present state of circumstances that will exist at that time.

[88] One approach is to take this literally, for ancient kings did brag about how they cut down forests to build their palaces. But K. Nielsen, *There is Hope for a Tree* (Sheffield: *JSOT*, 1989), 162–63, offers a metaphorical interpretation in which the trees represent vassals of the great king. Very unlikely is the idea that this is a remnant of an old fertility cult in which the tree represented a god, thus the cutting of the trees refers to the killing of the god.

[89] Clements, *Isaiah 1–39*, 142 has this satirical approach, but the mocking of the Babylonian king was not to humiliate the Babylonian king, for he probably never heard this speech. Its purpose was to show the prophet's Israelite audience the utter foolishness of trusting such a weak and powerless king. To do this Isaiah does mock this impotent king.

[90] The word רְפָאִים can refer to ancient strong men on earth (Gen 14:5; Deut 3:11), but here they are the spirits of the dead who were formerly strong men on earth. It seems that the idea could be applied to the spirits of dead people beyond just kings (26:14; Ps 88:10; Prov 2:18). M. L. Brown, "רְפָאִים" DOTTE, 3, 1173–1180 discusses the use of this word in Ugaritic literature and the Bible, summarizing various theories about its meaning and whether the root is related to (a) heal; (b) weak; (c) sleep; or (d) lord.

aroused from their coffins and excited to meet the famous Babylonian king who has just died. These leaders from all over the world (probably the very ones killed by this Babylonian king) rise to sit on their thrones in honor of this great one. The dead kings[91] immediately respond that "even you,"[92] the great Babylonian king, are now weak and no different from the other kings who have died. His glory and the splendor of his court have disappeared, majesty and pride have evaporated, and vulgar maggots and thousands of worms eat away at his decomposing corpse. The message to Isaiah's audience is clear; this great Babylonian king cannot save Judah from Assyria. He is just like everyone else; even the dead know that this king will not reign forever. The obvious question that this scene in Sheol raises is: Should the people of Judah put their trust in such a weak king? The implied answer is obvious. No, he has no power; they should repent and trust Almighty God.

14:12–14 At the center of this poem is a description of this king's prideful attempt to take God's place in heaven. D. E. Gowan has surveyed several attempts to find mythical allusions in "O morning star, son of heaven" and other phrases.[93] M. Pope suggests that the original myth was about a lesser god, Helel, son of Shachar,[94] who tried to dethrone the Canaanites' high god El who lived on a high mountain in the north.[95] Another comparison is with the god Athtar who tried to replace Baal as king.[96] One can also identify some

---

[91] Wildberger, *Isaiah 13–27,* 62 follows עָנָה root IV in Koehler-Baumgartner and translates the word "sing, strike up a song," while NIV has the more traditional reading "answer," which is parallel to "say" in the next line of 14:10.

[92] גַּם־אַתָּה, "even you," emphasizes that after death all are the same, even the greatest on earth are powerless. Oswalt, *Isaiah 1–39,* 318 states that the kings in the underworld will realize that he "is no different from they. Although his glory made him seem almost immortal, he too must bow to corruption and decay."

[93] D. E. Gowan, *When Man Becomes God: Humanism and Hubris in the Old Testament* (Pittsburgh: Pickwith, 1975), and J. W. McKay, "Helel and the Dawn Goddess: A Reexamination of the Myth of Isaiah XIV 12–15," *VT* 20 (1970): 451–64, review and critique the inadequacies of theories that connecet "Helel" to the moon god, the sun god Nergal, the planet Jupiter (the royal star representing Marduk), or Venus the morning star. Gowan is attracted to P. Grelot's connection of Helel with the Greek Phaethon, but he does not see a connection between Phaethon and the Ugaritic Athtar. J. C. Poirier, "An Illuminating Parallel of Isaiah XVI 12," *VT* 49 (1999): 371–89, also connects this story with the Greek myth of Phaethon based on a third century Alexandrian inscription of the poet Callimachus, *Epigram,* 56, who speaks of Hesperus as fallen. Many of these reconstructions are quite speculative, assuming the influence of Greek mythology on the ANE mythology and on Judah (which is doubtful).

[94] הֵילֵל means "shining one," while שַׁחַר means "dawn." The shining one in the morning probably refers to the morning star Venus that was a symbol of a god in the ancient Near Eastern world. The Latin Vulgate gives the translation Lucifer, "light bearer, morning light." The Early Church Fathers Tertullian and Gregory the Great connected the fall of Satan from heaven like lightning in Luke 10:18 with Isa 14:12, thus developing the unfounded view that 14:12 describes the fall of Satan.

[95] M. H. Pope, *El in the Ugaritic Texts,* VTSupp (Leiden, Brill, 1955), 27–32, 61–63.

[96] *ANET,* 129–42. P. C. Craigie, "Helel, Athtar and Phaethon (Jes 14:12–15)," *ZAW* 85 (1973): 223–25. Although Athtar may represent the morning star, he voluntarily left Baal's throne because he did not fit it, so a comparison with this text is weak. Wildberger, *Isaiah 13–27,* 64–65, mounts a strong case against identifying Helel, Athtar, and the Greek god Phaethon.

comparisons with "Ishtar's Descent into the Underworld" or "Inanna's Descent into the Underworld,"[97] though R. van Leeuwen found an intriguing parallel in the Gilgamesh Epic.[98] Although none of these texts provide an exact parallel to 14:12–14, if the prophet's audience had some knowledge of these mythical stories (many had worshiped Baal during the reign of Ahaz) this would have enabled the prophet to get his point across very effectively by showing how this Babylonian king acted in a similar manner.[99] Even today, speakers refer to ideas from a non-biblical story (*The Wizard of Oz*, a movie like *Gone with the Wind*, or a joke) to illustrate a point by making analogical remarks without quoting from it directly or committing themselves to the truthfulness of the story.[100]

14:12   The introductory "How" (*'êk*) in 14:12 (repeating 14:4b) marks the beginning of this new paragraph, reminding the audience that this is a lament for a dead person who has fallen (cf. the lament for Saul in 2 Sam 1:19). The lament mourns the humiliation of one who formerly enjoyed a high position. Being cast down to earth implies a loss of power, status, self-determination, and influence. The "morning star" (lit. "shining one," *hêlēl*) probably refers to Venus, which is the "son of the dawn," the morning star that was sometimes used to represent a divinity in ancient Near Eastern religion. This analogy indicates how high this Babylonian king had raised himself up and how far he would fall. Similarly, religious and political leaders today who claim for themselves undue power and authority will need to resist the temptation to think that they control everything (setting themselves up as gods), lest God cause them to suffer the same humiliating fate.

14:13–14   Why did this morning star fall? An attitude of selfish pride led to an attempt to usurp someone else's authority. The "I will"[101] clauses trace his arrogant actions: (a) He moved from his proper place to putting his throne

---

[97] *ANET*, 52–57, 106–109. Ishtar, the queen of heaven, was associated with Venus. She went to the underworld (Sheol), was mourned, and was eventually rescued by Ea.

[98] R. van Leeuwen, "Isa 14:12, *hôlēš 'al gwym* and Gilgamesh XI,6," *JBL* 99 (1980): 173–84, found the phrases "Thou art not strange at all, even as I art thou" (cf. 14:10), and "[Yet] thou liest indolent on thy back" is compared to "you who once laid low the nations" (14:12), which van Leeuwen translates "you lie indolent on your back."

[99] Goldingay, *Isaiah*, 103, concludes that "Babylonian and Canaanite stories spoke of gods who tried to take over the power of the highest god, and the poem here turns such stories into a parable of what the Babylonian king is doing." B. L. Keowen, *A History of the Interpretation of Isaiah 14:12–15* (Ph.D. dissertation, Southern Baptist Theological Seminary, Louisville, KY, 1979) provides a useful survey of various approaches to this problematic text.

[100] J. Oswalt, "The Myth of the Dragon and Old Testament Faith," *EvQ* 49 (1977): 163–72, discusses legitimate ways the biblical authors used ancient Near Eastern ideas and literature to argue against pagan beliefs. Just like one today might refer to evolution to confront one of its false assumptions, so the biblical authors often referred to religious beliefs in their day to cause their audience to question or reject an untenable theological position. Motyer, *The Prophecy of Isaiah*, 144, finds "Behind Isaiah's reference to a *morning star . . .* lies a Canaanite mythology of a 'revolt in heaven' genre. . . . The Old Testament uses such allusions without attributing reality to the dramatis personae (*cf.* on 51:9ff.)."

[101] Four "I will" verbs, beginning with "I will ascend" (אֶעֱלֶה), dominate 14:13–14.

above other heavenly beings ("the stars of El"). (b) He enthroned himself in the meeting of the divine assembly on a sacred mountain in the north. (c) He ascended above the clouds. (d) He made himself like the Most High God. Several of these concepts run parallel to stories in myths in ancient Near Eastern religions where one god fought with another god in order to gain greater power and sit on his throne. Some myths had the pantheon of gods assemble at meetings on the northern mountain of Zaphon. The intention of this arrogant morning star was to ascend over the clouds to become equal or higher than the highest deity Elyon.[102] The behavior of the king of Babylon was parallel to what the morning star tried to do, though the poem does not reveal exactly what this king did. In essence he tried to rule the world by supplanting God.

14:15–21 The beginning of the previous paragraph about the morning star indicates that pride led to failure and the arrogant one was eventually cast down to earth in shame (14:12). This new paragraph begins with *ʾak* similar to 14:4b and 14:12,[103] but it applies this same fate to "you," meaning the king of Babylon, because the king will end up in the same place as the morning star (14:15). Instead of replacing God in the heights of the sacred mountain in the north, the king of Babylon will go to Sheol, even to the remotest depths of the pit of Sheol. Elsewhere the "pit"[104] is a synonym for Sheol (Ezek 26:20; 32:18–24), but here it seems to be a particularly distant place in Sheol, the furthest place one can get from the heights of heaven.[105]

In light of the king's great accomplishments and pride, the people on earth (or the kings in Sheol)[106] will be astonished at how far this great king has fallen (14:16). He will be utterly humiliated and shamed by what will happen. Once he had the power to cause any nation to tremble in fear and could change the course of history for any city he might attack. He was a ruthless tyrant who could turn a defeated city into a desert place without inhabitants and he could treat people unmercifully (14:17). But now in Sheol he has absolutely no power to do anything at all.

A second sign of his humiliation is related to his disgraceful burial (14:18–19). His shameful treatment of others will come back to haunt him. Instead

---

[102] For more information on Canaanite religions see M. Pope, *El in the Ugaritic Texts*; W. F. Albright, *Yahweh and the Gods of Canaan* (Garden City: Doubleday, 1969); and W. R. Smith, *The Religion of the Semites* (New York: Meridian, 1956).

[103] אַךְ, "but, nevertheless," plus a return to second person singular verbs mark the beginning of this new paragraph. Now the topic is the king, not the morning star.

[104] בּוֹר can refer to a "cistern" (Jer 2:13), a deep hole that could function as a "prison" (Gen 37:20–29; 40:15; 41:14; Jer 38:6–13), or the "place of the dead" (Ps 88:4,6; 143:7).

[105] For a fuller treatment of Sheol and the pit see N. J. Tromp, *Primitive Conceptions of Death and the Nether World in the Old Testament,* BibOr 21 (Rome: Pontifical Biblical Institute, 1969) or E. F. Sutcliffe, *The Old Testament and the Future Life* (London: Burns, Oates, & Washbourne, 1947).

[106] Holladay, "Text, Structure, and Irony," 633–45, maintains that the kings in Sheol are the ones seeing this defeated king, but Wildberger, *Isaiah 13–27*, 68–69, rejects that view as repetitious of 14:9–11 and because vv. 16–19 describe people coming across corpses on a battle field.

of having an impressive burial chamber or an elaborate gold-filled tomb dedicated in his honor like most kings, this king will have no glory at all after his death.[107] He will have a dishonorable burial; there will be no royal tomb because he will be considered a "rejected, loathed" (*nit'āb*) branch.[108] This picture contrasts with the messianic shoot or sprout in 11:1; he is full of the Spirit and will rule the nations in justice.

The imagery in 14:19 is not that clear.[109] The idea of being "cast out of your tomb" does not coincide very well with the rest of the verse. Wildberger suggests that "the OT normally speaks of the corpse being 'cast forth' in situations in which no one is able to bury someone who has died or else no one wishes to do so (cf. 1 Kgs 13:24f; Isa 34:3)."[110] Thus the whole verse seems to picture the Babylonian king as one among many who were slain in battle and left unburied by a victorious enemy. This great "shoot, branch" (a symbol of a king as in 11:1) will be loathed as his body rots among the dead bodies of fellow soldiers who died trying to defend the king. The state of the "trampled corpse" (*kĕpeger mûbās*) is unknown, but if a body was trampled underfoot by men or horses, this treatment would do grave injury to the corpse, desecrating and humiliating the dead. This kind of desecration of a dead body was especially shocking in the ancient Near Eastern world where honoring the dead was very important. To go unburied and be left on a battle field for the dogs and vultures to eat was the greatest fear of every soldier (Ezek 39:4, 17–20). Leaving people unburied was the ultimate way to disgrace their memory (Jer 22:19; 36:30). The spirits of those slain (including this proud king) will descend to the "stones of the pit," an enigmatic phrase that probably does not refer to the practice of burying people by piling stones over them (Josh 8:29; 2 Sam 18:17). Stones always go down to the very bottom of any hole, so if one goes down to the stones, that person is as low as one can get in the pit of Sheol.[111]

The Babylonian king's final humiliation will involve being rejected by his people and family (14:20–21). Even if enemies might defeat a king in battle or shame a king at his death, usually his own people would rise up to defend his honor and support him. He would be considered a military hero who valiantly and sacrificially gave his life for his people. At the very least, the king's own family would tell stories of his great character and honor his memory with

---

[107] The text points out the honoring of other kings and the dishonor for the king of Babylon by the constrast phrase "but you yourself" (וְאַתָּה) at the beginning of v. 19.

[108] The word נֵצֶר, "sprout, branch," is an appropriate term for a king, but Wildberger, *Isaiah 13–27*, 42 and 46, prefers נֵפֶל, "miscarriage," which fits the Targum.

[109] The interpretation that suggests that these verses are talking about the king not being released from prison (G. B. Gray, *The Book of Isaiah: A Critical and Exegetical Commentary on the Book of Isaiah 1-27* [Edinburgh: T & T Clark, 1912], 258) misses the focus on death in this paragraph.

[110] Wildberger, *Isaiah 13–27*, 70, connects this verse to events in a battle scene.

[111] Oswalt, *Isaiah 1–39*, 324, believes this simply refers to the grave, not Sheol, but the story appears to represent the spirit of the king in Sheol and the body unburied on the battle field.

monuments and parades. But this evil king will never receive even the slight-est recognition from anyone, not even from his own offspring.[112] This will happen because it will become very clear to everyone that the king's selfish actions caused the destruction of his own nation and the deaths of thousands of his own people. Instead of blaming their destruction on their vile enemies, his own people will realize that the Babylonian king killed thousands of them by his foolish actions. Although leaders may be able to fool their followers for a time, eventually people can see through the rhetoric and realize that some leaders in the past and today are more interested in their own power than anything else. They really do not care if they destroy a nation, a company, a seminary, or a church; all they want to do is to further their own cause and create a name for themselves.

Consequently, the king's ideal of being buried in the family tomb with his ancestors and children will not happen (14:20a). Instead, this king's name and the name of his children will not be mentioned ever again. No one will want to remember the tremendous shame he brought on the nation, so every attempt will be made to remove his name.[113] One way of wiping out a name is to kill all the children of the king, so that none of them will ever restore the family name to power (14:21; see 2 Kgs 10:17). The urgency of the situation is in the demand that "they must not rise and must not inherit the land."[114] The people themselves will conclude that it is best to exterminate this family line so that none of the king's heirs will come back at a later time and try to make a legitimate claim to authority. A second reason why the children will be killed is because of the sins of their father. This indicates that evil and pride were characteristic of several Babylonian kings in this family. A third justification for this action is that the people did not want another king to follow the same pattern by going on the offensive again and trying to conquer all the cities on the earth (14:21b). It appears that the people just wanted to live in peace and were not interested in empire building by planting powerful Babylonian cities over the whole inhabited world.

14:22–23   The lament ends with a conclusion somewhat similar to 13:17–22. These verses focus on what God says ("declares the Lord" occurs three times)[115] and what he will do. Ultimately, Babylon's enemies cannot control the future and what the people in Babylon do to their king's family will not determine what happens in Babylon. God will rise up to act in order to control

---

[112] Holladay, "Text, Structure, and Irony," 633–45, maintains that the "offspring of the wicked" refers to the king himself, not the king's children.

[113] In Egypt, kings would send men to chisel out the names of earlier kings from stone monu-ments, thus erasing their memory from history.

[114] The imperfect verb יָקֻמוּ is probably used in the subjunctive mood, indicating what ought or must not happen (GKC §107w). In this sentence בַּל is the emphatic negative (GKC §152t).

[115] נְאֻם־יהוה (declares the Lord) is not found elsewhere in this poem, suggesting that these verses were added (probably during the written stage) as a conclusion at the same time the intro-duction (14:3–4a) was prefixed at the beginning.

the future. With strong statements of determination, God declares his sure plan. His decision is that "I will" destroy Babylon's great reputation and her people, not just her evil king. This will leave the city empty, a flooded swamp to be inhabited by wild animals. There is no need to take Babylon as a "code word" for any other imperialistic nation in history,[116] since in 689 BC. Sennacherib completely destroyed the city of Babylon by burning and leveling its houses, walls, and temple, then he finished the job by flooding the city with water.[117] Of course when he spoke it, the prophet Isaiah had no idea when this prophecy would actually be fulfilled; he just knew that someday God would accomplish his plans for Babylon.

(5) God's Plan to Crush Assyria (14:24–27)

[24]The LORD Almighty has sworn,
"Surely, as I have planned, so it will be,
     and as I have purposed, so it will stand.
[25]I will crush the Assyrian in my land;
     on my mountains I will trample him down.
His yoke will be taken from my people,
     and his burden removed from their shoulders."

[26]This is the plan determined for the whole world;
     this is the hand stretched out over all nations.
[27]For the LORD Almighty has purposed, and who can thwart him?
     His hand is stretched out, and who can turn it back?

The author added an appendix about Assyria at the end of the Babylon oracle, probably because the destiny of Assyria was integrally connected to what would happen to Babylon. A second and even more important factor is that the alliance between Babylon and Judah in 39:1–8 was against Assyria.[118] After encouraging Judah not to trust Babylon in their war against Assyria in 13:1–14:22, Isaiah now offers a promise that God, not the coalition of Judah and Babylon, will defeat Assyria "in my own land" (14:25),[119] that is, in the land of Judah. If this prophecy came just a few years before 701 BC (notice the fulfillment in 37:36–37), this promise of salvation would demonstrate the uselessness of Judah's alliances with Babylon and Egypt. There was no need to do anything but trust God's plan; his purposes will be accomplished in spite of

---

[116] Wildberger, *Isaiah 13–27,* 73, takes the "code word" approach. This confuses the exegetical meaning of the message to the original audience (who would have thought of Babylon) with an application of the principle in the text for later listeners.

[117] D. D. Lukenbill, *The Annals of Sennacherib* (Chicago: University of Chicago, 1924), 78–79, gives Sennacherib's description of the 689 BC conquest, which included flooding the city.

[118] Wildberger, *Isaiah 13–27,* 82, says that "the downfall of Assyria 'on my mountain.' This could refer to nothing other than Sennacherib's invasion of Judah."

[119] This statement excludes the possibility that this prophecy had anything to do with the final fall of Assyria in the time of Josiah in 612 BC, as some suggest (Clements, *Isaiah 1–39,* 147). Assyria was not defeated in "my land" in the time of Josiah.

Assyria's attack. In light of these historical circumstances it seems inappropriate to take this Assyria oracle as a general oath against all the nations, or to apply it to Babylon.[120] Assyria is the focus of 14:24–25, while 14:26–27 expands
God's plans to all the nations of the earth. These later generalizations about all
nations should not be allowed to annul the specific address about Assyria in
14:24–25. The structure of this short paragraph is:

God's plan to crush Assyria	14:24–28
God's plan for Assyria	24–25
God's plan for all nations	26–27

There are some similarities between the content of this oracle and God's
earlier prophecy about the defeat of the proud Assyrians in 10:5–34 (especially
10:27 and 14:25b) and also Isaiah's earlier warnings about God's "outstretched
hand" against various nations (cf. 14:26b,27b with 5:25; 9:12–10:4; 13:2).
However, these common elements do not require an appeal to wisdom sources
instead of Isaiah himself.[121] Childs found similarities between 14:24–27 and
the reflective "summary appraisals" at the end of other oracles (17:14; 28:29),
but none of the other examples include an oath against a different nation, so the
comparison is not complete.[122] 14:24–27 is not a summary of the preceding
material; only 14:26–27 gives what might be called a theological appraisal of
God's broad plans for all the nations.

14:24–25 This is a record of the oath that God swore. When an earthly oath
was taken, the consequences it describes were unchangeable and irreversible.
When God swears to something, the listener can be fully assured that it will
happen. God's holiness guarantees the execution of his plans, for he stakes his
holy reputation on his promises (cf. similar holy oaths in Amos 4:2; 6:8; 8:7).
This oath assures the prophet's audience of the truthfulness of what God has
proclaimed. These verses confirm the consistency, reliability, and faithfulness
of God's words. As Oswalt maintains, Isaiah "insists that it is the God of Israel
alone who guides history in a purposive and ultimately beneficial way."[123]

The oath begins with an emphatic "surely" (*'im lō*) to help remove doubt.[124]
The claim is made that there is a direct connection between God's plans and

---

[120] Sweeney, *Isaiah 1–39*, 229, takes these verses as a summary appraisal, but that conclusion
does not automatically destroy their intended reference to Assyria.

[121] V. O. Eareckson, "The Originality of Isaiah XIV 27," *VT* 20 (1970): 490–91, suggests that
v. 27 was a later expansion because some of the terminology is also found in wisdom literature.
Since these terms are also common in the prophetic writings of Isaiah, there is no need to look
elsewhere. The idea that 14:24–27 originally belongs after 10:5–19 (or 10:34) is based on the idea
that all common material must be grouped together, but if the Babylon oracle relates to events just
before 701 BC, when Assyria was about to attack Jerusalem, then it seems natural to talk about the
defeat of Assyria in the context of discussing Babylon.

[122] B. S. Childs, *Isaiah and the Assyrian Crisis* (London: SCM, 1967), 128–30.

[123] Oswalt, *Isaiah 1–39*, 328, thinks Isaiah was countering a question that many people in Judah were raising in light of all the military trouble that Judah was facing.

[124] אִם־לֹא begins several oaths to emphasize the certainty of the statement (GKC §149b-e).

purposes and what actually will happen. The things that God has planned refer to his thoughts, intentions, and deliberations—what he imagines or devises.[125] These plans were directly related to what God had purposed, a term that describes the goal of God's wise counsel, advice, plan.[126] Both words point to the divine activity of decision making about what will happen in the future. They indicate that God thoughtfully takes into consideration the various factors involved in a situation and wisely decides what the plan for future events will be in order to accomplish his purposes on earth. There is no statement in this text that every event was planned (though it is not denied), only that when God does make a plan, it happens according to God's predetermined design. This contrasts with man's inability to carry out his plans (8:10; cf. 46:10; Ps 33:9–11; Prov 19:21). Although the specific term for God's "plan" ('ēṣâ) is not often repeated (cf. 19:12,17; 23:8–9; 25:1; 28:29), all of Isaiah's predictions of future events can be included within the scope of God's thoughts about what will happen. Many people and nations do not know God's plans (Mic 4:12), so knowledge of God's purposes is vitally important for believers because they give insight into the thoughts that make up God's plans. Isaiah was sharing the good and the bad news about the future events that God had planned for the world so that his audience could choose to follow God and experience God's grace.

God's thoughts about Assyria developed into a plan to shatter the Assyrian forces and trample them down "in my land" and "on my mountain" (14:25). Although the prophet gives no insight as to when or how this would eventually happen, the miraculous killing of 185,000 Assyrian troops in 701 BC at Jerusalem (37:36–37) seems to fulfill this prediction. The Assyrian yoke that God removed was the burden of foreign domination and heavy taxation that usually came after the Assyrians took control of a nation.

14:26–27 The final two verses extrapolate the principles in 14:24–25 and apply them to God's plans for the whole world. This does not mean that Assyria was a symbol of all the other nations. The comparison suggests that God makes sovereign plans not only for specific events related to the future of Assyria, but also for every nation on earth. Thus 14:26–27 serves as a fitting conclusion to 13:1–14:25 and as an introduction to the rest of God's plans in 15:1–23:18. In these verses the prophet relates God's plans to use his powerful outstretched hand (14:26b,27b, cf. 5:25; 9:12,17,20; 10:4), which will carry out his designs for the nations. There is no other way for things to happen in this world, no

---

[125] God says "I planned" (דָּמִיתִי) and "I purposed" (יָעַצְתִּי), which directly contrasts with the Assyrian king's claim that he is the one who plans and has purposes in 10:7. It is prideful for that king to claim that he accomplished anything (10:12), for in reality it was God who did it all (10:15).

[126] Watts, *Isaiah 1–33*, 215–16, thinks of God's "strategy" (יָעַץ) as his plan for the world, while Wildberger, *Isaiah 13–27*, 82–83, centers the meaning of יָעַץ around making specific "decisions" in history rather than God's predestined plan for the future.

second choices, no alternative plans but God's plans. No one can resist the hand of God, and no one can turn God's hand away from doing his will.

THEOLOGICAL IMPLICATIONS.   The first prophecy about God's dealings with foreign nations sets a pattern that helps one understand the will and ways of God. His plans are already set, and he will carry them out according to his wise design to fulfill his purposes. This prophecy explains four events that God has already planned.

1.   On every Day of the Lord and especially on the final Day of the Lord, God will muster his armies, shake the heavens and the earth, and destroy the arrogant sinners on earth (13:1–16).

2.   In compassion, God will restore his chosen people to their land and any others who choose to join them. Then he will remove all threats from other nations (14:1–2).

3.   A proud Babylonian king will die (14:4–21), and the Medes will be involved in destroying the glorious city of Babylon (13:17–22; 14:22–23).

4.   God will crush the Assyrian army at Jerusalem (14:24–25).

The prophet did not know the order and dating of these plans when he spoke these words, he did not specifically identify the people involved in each event (only broadly as Babylon or Assyria), and he did not fully explain the interlocking connections between the events.

It is somewhat dangerous to extrapolate theological principles from these specific events (the fall of Babylon or Assyria) and apply them as guidelines for understanding how God will deal with other nations at other times, or in modern times. Since the rebellion of nations differ, the circumstance surrounding each situation is not the same, and God's purposes for each nation will vary. No one except a divinely inspired prophet can predict what God will do to other nations in the future. Nevertheless, these verses are consistent with other prophecies in three ways. First, in numerous messages God consistently plans to bring destruction on proud people who do not trust God (2:6–21; 3:16–4:1; 9:8; 10:5–15). They will be humbled and the glorious things that these people were so proud of will be removed. Second, God desires to be compassionate to those who trust him, and he will eventually gather Hebrews and many other people from various nations to Jerusalem to enjoy his kingdom (2:1–5; 4:2–6; 9:1–7: 11:1–16; 14:1–2). Third, God has the future planned for each nation, and there is no doubt that every historical event will work out to fulfill his purposes (14:24–27).

The prophet's primary purpose for describing these events was not just to give the Hebrew people some factual information about God's mysterious plans for the future. If these messages came just before Sennacherib's attack on Jerusalem in 701 BC, information about these four events had the theological purpose of persuading those living in Jerusalem (specifically the king and other leaders) not to depend on foreign kings or nations (the Babylonians in

39:1–8) and not to fear the mighty power of Assyria when it attacked Jerusalem (chaps. 36–37). These nations are not trustworthy, dependable, or very powerful, for God will crush both nations. Based on these promises, the people of Judah must trust God to defeat their enemies. He will not reject his own chosen people, but in compassion he will work on their behalf. The theology of chaps. 13–14 revolves around trusting God even in life and death situations. The prophet's words challenged the people of Judah, as well as any other readers, to answer these questions:

1. Can God sovereignly control what happens with his powerful out stretched hand (14:26–27)?
2. Will his plans actually be fulfilled (14:24)?
3. Does his wise design actually cover all the nations (14:1–2,26)?
4. Can His sovereign power be trusted completely (14:27)?

No one can avoid the issue of trust; people either believe what God has said he will do, or in pride they make their own "better" plans. When arrogant people (especially those who profess to be believers) reject God's plans and try to raise themselves up as the ruler of their lives, they are actually attempting to take God's place and exalt themselves higher than God. Their fate is clear; the wrath of God, humiliation, and the maggots of the grave await them.

2. God's Plan for Philistia (14:28–32)

28This oracle came in the year King Ahaz died:

29Do not rejoice, all you Philistines,
    that the rod that struck you is broken;
  from the root of that snake will spring up a viper,
    its fruit will be a darting, venomous serpent.
30The poorest of the poor will find pasture,
    and the needy will lie down in safety.
  But your root I will destroy by famine;
    it will slay your survivors.

31Wail, O gate! Howl, O city!
    Melt away, all you Philistines!
  A cloud of smoke comes from the north,
    and there is not a straggler in its ranks.
32What answer shall be given
    to the envoys of that nation?
  "The LORD has established Zion,
    and in her his afflicted people will find refuge."

This *maśśāʾ* ("oracle") advises a Hebrew audience in Judah (probably the king and his court) about a Philistine plan to resist the Assyrians ("the rod that struck you").[127] Isaiah's purpose was to convince the new king Hezekiah not to join the Philistines in revolting against Assyria, but to trust God and his promises (14:32). Second Chronicles 29–31 discusses the religious reforms Hezekiah instituted in his first year (the same period as this message), but there is no discussion of his political situation at that time. This paragraph includes:

An introduction	14:28
A warning not to rejoice and a rationale	14:29–30
An encouragement to lament and a rationale	14:31
A call to trust God	14:32

Although a coalition with Philistia might make some military sense because of Assyria's military threat, Isaiah argues that the nation of Judah will only find peace and protection from Assyrian affliction if it depends on God.

14:28 This oracle is dated in the year that Judah's King Ahaz died, the year that Hezekiah began to reign.[128] Hayes and Irvine correlate this oracle not only with the death of Ahaz but also with the death of "the rod that struck you," referring to the Assyrian king Tiglath-pileser III (c. 727 BC).[129] This dating of Ahaz's death is based on the chronological evidence provided in 2 Kgs 18:1,9–10. On the other hand, it is possible to date the death of Ahaz and this oracle to 715 BC, because the beginning of Hezekiah's reign was fourteen years before Hezekiah was attacked in 701 BC (based on 2 Kgs 18:13). There is no easy solution to this problem of dating this prophecy, and commentators can be found who support either historical context.[130] Nevertheless, it seems much more appropriate to conclude that Tiglath-pileser III was the earlier "rod" and "snake" who attacked Philistia and that Sargon II was the "venomous serpent" who would rise up after him (14:29). Ahaz did not attack Philistia, so he is not the snake; instead, Judah was attacked by Philistia (2 Chr 28:18). In addition, it seems incongruous to suggest that Hezekiah would be a flying venomous serpent (the one who followed the snake) against Philistia. Therefore, it is best to associate this oracle with events around 715 BC.

14:29–30 The death of the great Assyrian king Tiglath-pileser III brought some hope of relief from further Assyrian aggression. Isaiah's mild negative

---

[127] Wildberger, *Isaiah 13–27*, 95, believes this refers to the plan for Judah and Philistia to oppose Assyria. It is possible that the prophet was actually speaking in the king's court and also addressed some Philistine ambassadors ("all you Philistines" in 14:31; "envoys" in 14:32) who were in Jerusalem to present a plan for Judah to join an alliance against Assyria, though the second person "you" could be used just for rhetorical effect.

[128] This parallels a similar introduction that marked the date of a prophecy at the time of the death of Uzziah in 6:1.

[129] Hayes and Irvine, *Isaiah*, 236, believe the Philistines are rejoicing and trying to get Judah to join in a rebellion against the new Assyrian king Sargon II.

[130] Kissane, *Isaiah*, 170, thinks the kingdom of Judah is the rod (David was the first to defeat them) and that the kingdom of the Messiah is the flying serpent.

prohibition[131] exhorts the Philistines not to rejoice over the death of this adversary who used the "rod" (cf. 10:5; 14:5) to oppress them. Tiglath-pileser III was the "root"[132] or kingly source of the next generation of rulers. The mixed metaphors in 14:29 also describe the past Assyrian king as a "snake" (nāḥāš) who would be replaced by a poisonous viper, and his son (or fruit) would be a more dangerous "flying serpent."[133] The rationale for not rejoicing is that things will get even worse when the new king comes to rule and imposes his will over the ancient Near East (probably a prophecy about Sargon II).

Commentators frequently interpret 14:30 as contrasting statements of positive words about Judah in v. 30a (based on statements in 14:32) and negative words about Philistia in vv. 30b–31.[134] But there is little that might hint that the prophet has suddenly inserted two phrases about Judah at the beginning of v. 30. One must question the positive interpretation of 14:30a. Reference to the poor and needy in the Bible usually describe those who are under oppression, thus in light of the coming of an oppressive rod against Philistia in 14:29, it appears that the prophet is describing the Philistine people whom the Assyrian kings impoverished through war and heavy taxation. Although one could hypothetically interpret this imagery as a picture of the people safely feeding in a pasture and associate it with God's positive promises to pasture his sheep in their land in a safe environment (Jer 23:3–4; 30:10; 32:37; Ezek 34:23–25), the Hebrew verb meaning "to pasture, feed, lead"[135] is used of bad kings and has the negative connotation of evil "ruling, devouring" (Mic 5:6, cf. Ezek 34) of people. Therefore, the translation "they [the evil kings of 14:29] will devour the poorest of the poor" refers to what will happen to the poor people left after the fall of Philistia. The wealthy and powerful Philistines will not exist any longer (they will be exiled), and only the oppressed and downtrodden will live there. Even those few poor people left to represent the lineage ("root") of the Philistines will die of famine and the sword (14:30b).

14:31 The poem returns to an imperative exhortation (like 14:29), but this time there is a call to wail and howl, clearly a sign of lamentation for the destroyed Philistine cities and their people. The rationale for weeping is the ominous sign of cities burning just north of Philistia. By watching the rising

---

[131] אַל plus the jussive יִשְׂמְחִי gives a mild prohibition or warning (GKC §109c), "you should not rejoice."

[132] מִשֹּׁרֶשׁ, "from a root," is similar to the phrase in 11:1 that says the Messiah would come "from the root of Jesse." The root refers to the father or lineage of a family.

[133] שָׂרָף מְעוֹפֵף, "flying burning ones," uses the same root "burning" that was used for the "seraphim" in 6:2, though there is no indication this passage refers to the seraphim.

[134] Oswalt, *Isaiah 1–39,* 332–33, says, "Presumably, in light of v. 32, it is the poor of Judah who are intended, in contrast to the mighty ones of Philistia." Motyer, *The Prophecy of Isaiah,* 147–48, thinks the rod in 29 was David, so a comment about Judah in v. 30a makes more contextual sense, yet both of these approaches are questionable.

[135] רָעָה means "to feed, eat, pasture" when referring to sheep, but good kings "shepherd, guide, rule" their people like sheep. The evil "rule" of a bad king destroys the flock and the sheep feed on it (Ezek 34).

smoke in the distance, the Philistines will be able to observe the strong Assyrian army (there are no stragglers in it) conquer and burn city after city as they approach Philistia. This verse communicates the hopelessness of sure defeat as an unstoppable Assyrian military machine draws near.

14:32 In light of this certain future for Philistia, Isaiah asks his audience in Judah a rhetorical question. What should the leaders of Judah say to the envoys from the "nation" (*gôy* refers to Philistia) who want Judah to join their coalition against Assyria? Does it make any sense to join them in light of the approaching defeat of Philistia? The prophet points to a better way. The king and people of Judah know that God has promised that he will "establish" (*yissad*) his kingdom in Zion (2:1–5; 4:2–6; 9:1–7; 2 Sam 7; Ps 46:6–10; 48:5–8; 74:2–10), so it only makes sense to take refuge in God and his sure promises. Why would anyone think that it is wise to trust a coalition with weak Philistia, instead of trusting God? Weak and insecure people can only find "refuge" (*yehĕsû*) in Zion, the place where God dwells. Isaiah does not promise immediate victory over Judah's Assyrian enemies; he only maintains that God is the only secure place of protection in times of trouble (cf. Ps 14:6; 27:5; 46:1–2; 61:3–4; 62:8).

THEOLOGICAL IMPLICATIONS.   Every generation of leaders is called to acts of faith, to choose a path of utter dependence on God rather than alternatives that initially look more defensible. People are challenged not to do what may seem the most reasonable thing from a human perspective, but to do what God instructs them to do. Instead of relying on alliances, money, status, the political influence of others, or any other human support system, they must simply trust in God's promises to motivate and empower them when things look dark and hopeless. The circumstance may be a health crisis, the loss of a job, or an International political crisis, but the answer is always the same: trust in God for refuge. Most of the time people know what God would want them to do. The really difficult question is: Are they willing to follow God's direction? There is no indication in the prophet's thinking that there is a way to straddle the fence and partially trust God in order to hedge your bets; it is either man's way or God's way.

3. God's Plan for Proud Moab (15:1–16:14)

HISTORICAL SETTING.   The Moabites were the descendents of Lot's oldest daughter (see Gen 19:31–37) who settled in the territory east of the Dead Sea (Deut 2:9,18). The close relationship between Judah and this country is illustrated when Naomi and Elimelech lived in Moab (Ruth 1) and the Moabite woman Ruth married Boaz in Judah (Ruth 2–4).[136] Because both countries claimed some of the same territory in the Transjordan (Ruben and Gad settled

---

[136] A. van Zyl, *The Moabites* (Leiden: Brill, 1960) gives a detailed history of Moab based on biblical and ancient Near Eastern documents.

there according to Num 32:1–5), there were several military conflicts between Judah/Israel and Moab (Judg 3:12–30; 11:22–26; 2 Sam 8:2; 2 Kgs 3:4–27). Hayes and Irvine propose a date for this prophecy around 727 BC when Shalmaneser V became king of Assyria (Hos 10:14–15). At this time, Moab was a part of an anti-Assyrian coalition, so in this message the prophet is encouraging Hezekiah not to allow Moabites to take refuge in Judah.[137] Watts believes Moab was attacked by desert tribes (not Assyria) and dates the oracle to 718 BC. Kissane suggests that Isaiah repeated this prophecy in 723 and 718 BC before Sargon's attacks in 720 and 715 BC, while Oswalt leans toward the 715–711 BC time frame.[138] In the end, it is probably necessary to admit that this oracle is not specifically dated to any known event. It simply refers to the future destruction of Moab in three years (16:14). It makes sense to place it sometime during the reign of Hezekiah when the Assyrians were trying to gain control of all the countries in and around Judah, but it is impossible to provide an exact date or setting for this prophecy.

GENRE. The oracle about Moab includes a lament that begins in 15:1 and is picked up again in 16:7. Both sections contain news of the coming ruin of several Moabite cities, many people, and fertile fields, plus there are several references to the people wailing (15:1,3,5,8; 16:7,9,11). These two laments are not about a defeat that happened in the past; they lament the awful devastation that will happen in three years (16:13). The weeping, mourning, shaving of the beard, and wearing of sackcloth are typically connected with behavior at funerals when someone has died or the announcement that someone is about to die.

There is no widely accepted way of dealing with the literary form of 16:1–5. Motyer finds a request for asylum by Moab in 16:1–4a, then a divine answer of Messianic assurance to Moab in 16:4b–5, but in the end Moab's pride will lead to wailing because Moab will refuse the offer in 16:4b–5.[139] B. C. Jones gives a thoroughly ironic interpretation to the lament based on the presence of irony in chaps. 15–16, other ironic laments over foreign nations in the Old Testament, other mocking songs about Moab (Num 21:27–30; Jer 48; Zeph 2:8–11), and his analysis of lament vocabulary in the poem.[140] O. Kaiser follows the same

---

[137] Hayes and Irvine, *Isaiah,* 238–40.

[138] Kissane, *Isaiah,* I, 176–77, does not think the prophet quoted an earlier prophecy as W. Rudolph suggested (he dated the original back the defeat of Moab by Jeroboam II in the time of Amos) but hypothesizes that this warning could have been given as early as 738 BC. Oswalt, *Isaiah 1–39,* 335, thinks that the three-year time period applies from the beginning of Moab's revolt until its final conquest by Sargon.

[139] Motyer, *The Prophecy of Isaiah,* 152, makes 14:4b–5 a salvation oracle. He views Moab's pride as keeping the nation from responding positively to this hope (16:6).

[140] B. C. Jones, *Howling over Moab: Irony and Rhetoric in Isaiah 15–16* (Atlanta: Scholars Press, 1996), 6, 50–161, traces the ironic interpretation of the Moab oracle back to Luther (*Luthers' Works* [ed. J. Pelikan et al.; Saint Louis: Concordia, 1969], 146–53) in AD 1532. A van Zyl (*The Moabites,* 1960) championed the view that this was an ironic mocking song full of sarcasm.

general approach but limited the mocking taunt to only 16:6–12.[141] In contrast to these approaches, the exegetical discussion below suggests that God and his messenger Isaiah truly lamented the destruction of the neighboring people of Moab. Sweeney also concluded that these laments represent the prophet's true empathy for Moab, which supports his proposal that Moab should request assistance from Judah (16:1–5).[142] The Moabites knew about the way of protection through trust in God (16:4b–5), but sadly the Moabites did not accept it.

STRUCTURE.   An understanding of the natural progression of thought in this message is aided by the presence of laments beginning in 15:1b and 16:7. The brief introduction (15:1a) and the narrative prose ending containing another word from the Lord (16:13–14) were not part of the prophet's oral message, but were added when this message was put into a written form. Within the paragraphs are internal rhetorical markers like "therefore, so" (15:4b,7; 16:7,9,11) and "surely" (which is frequently omitted in NIV in 15:1,5–6,8–9; 16:8), plus changes in the subject of the verb (second masculine plural imperatives in 16:1, second feminine singular in 16:3, and first person plural in 16:6) that signal changes in the flow of thought. Vocabulary centered around weeping and destruction are common in the two laments, while 16:1–5 mentions the possibility of the Moabites coming to Zion to the tent of David for protection. The geographic location of the cities of Moab in the northern sector (15:2–4) and the southern half of the nation (15:5–7) also aid in grouping verses together. The oracle includes:

A lament over the ruin of Moab	15:1–9
A Moabite request for shelter in Judah	16:1–5
A lament: pride will cause the devastation of Moab	16:6–12
An announcement: Moab's end within three years	16:13–14

THEOLOGY.   When reading these laments one is captivated by the depth of the sorrow, wailing, weeping, and lamenting over the complete destruction of the cities of Moab. But this emotional outburst seems almost surreal and too empathetic for some to accept as genuine. This is probably because people today would only weep about the death of those they love, so it seems rather unlikely that Isaiah would lament over the destruction of one of Judah's neighbors, the Moabites. Consequently, some interpreters have concluded that Isaiah is actually mocking the Moabites,[143] giving a more sinister and revengeful rhetorical response to the "bad luck" of others. Nevertheless, there is reason to think that God and Isaiah were deeply grieved about the death of these Moabites. Since

---

[141] Kaiser, *Isaiah 13–39*, 73, interprets 16:6–12 as Judah replying to Moab's request with a mocking taunt.

[142] Sweney, *Isaiah 1–39*, 246, rejects the view that this lament was a sarcastic proposal, so it should not be given an ironic meaning. Isaiah was attempting to get the Moabites to act on his proposal in 16:1–4. Tucker, "Isaiah 1–39," 167, also accepts these as heartfelt laments.

[143] Hayes and Irvine, *Isaiah*, 242–45, find cutting irony in this lament rather than true sympathy.

there was a way for the Moabites to gain refuge from their enemies (16:4b–5), it was very sad to see them reject the opportunity. The prophet is reflecting God's sorrowful attitude, so that the people of Judah would also lament and recognize both the hopelessness of following Moab's path and the foolishness of depending on the Moabites for help. Isaiah's audience must learn that pride will lead a nation to ruin (16:6–7), but God will lead his people to a time of justice without oppression through a faithful ruler from the house of David (16:4b–5).

(1) A Lament for Moab (15:1–9)

¹An oracle concerning Moab:

> Ar in Moab is ruined,
>   destroyed in a night!
> Kir in Moab is ruined,
>   destroyed in a night!
> ²Dibon goes up to its temple,
>   to its high places to weep;
>   Moab wails over Nebo and Medeba.
> Every head is shaved
>   and every beard cut off.
> ³In the streets they wear sackcloth;
>   on the roofs and in the public squares
> they all wail,
>   prostrate with weeping.
> ⁴Heshbon and Elealeh cry out,
>   their voices are heard all the way to Jahaz.
> Therefore the armed men of Moab cry out,
>   and their hearts are faint.
>
> ⁵My heart cries out over Moab;
>   her fugitives flee as far as Zoar,
>   as far as Eglath Shelishiyah.
> They go up the way to Luhith,
>   weeping as they go;
> on the road to Horonaim
>   they lament their destruction.
> ⁶The waters of Nimrim are dried up
>   and the grass is withered;
> the vegetation is gone
>   and nothing green is left.
> ⁷So the wealth they have acquired and stored up
>   they carry away over the Ravine of the Poplars.
> ⁸Their outcry echoes along the border of Moab;
>   their wailing reaches as far as Eglaim,
>   their lamentation as far as Beer Elim.
> ⁹Dimon's waters are full of blood,
>   but I will bring still more upon Dimon—

a lion upon the fugitives of Moab
and upon those who remain in the land.

The lament in 15:1b–9 is divided into three sub-paragraphs:

Laments over the ruined northern Moabite cities   15:1b–4
Laments over fugitives who flee south   15:5–7
The inevitability of Moab's dire situation   15:8–9

The first part of the lament ends with a "therefore" (ʿal kēn) clause in 15:4b, the second unit ends with a "therefore" (lākēn) clause in 15:7, and the final section includes two verses beginning with "surely" (kî, missing in the NIV).

15:1–4 This prophecy begins with the typical superscription indicating that this is a burdensome oracle about another nations. No historical data from Israelite or Moabite history is included in this superscription (cf. 14:28), so the date of this oracle is unknown.

The first part of the lament (15:1b–4) attempts to convince[144] the audience that an attack will bring the devastation of key places in Moab. This will be a surprising event because of the swift ("in a night") fall of the capital of Moab. The conquest will be a cause for great weeping because of the severity of the enemy's action against Moab (it is "ruined," šuddad). One day a strong city will exist and the next day it will disappear. Ar and Kir both mean city, but Ar almost sounds like the border district of Moab mentioned in Deut 2:9,18,29. Kir is usually identified with the capital of Moab, which was in the district of Ar. The focus moves from the destruction of a city to the distraught behavior of the Moabites in v. 2.

The people of Moab will go to their "temple" (lit. "house," bayit) and high places to weep and pray for divine intervention (15:2). They will also shave their hair[145] and beards to show their grief (Jer 47:5; Amos 8:10; Mic 1:16). The intensity of the people's distress will be evident because everyone will walk around the streets of the cities of Moab dressed in sackcloth and wailing in agony (15:3). The people in all the main cities of Moab north of the Arnon River (Dibon, Nebo, Medaba, Hesbon, Elealeh)[146] will cry out for help in an-

---

[144] Each line in 15:1 (after this introductory clause) begins with כִּי, "surely," to emphasize that this is true. The problem was not just that an army came to attack these cites; "surely, without a doubt," they will thoroughly complete the job by totally devastating these cities.

[145] E. Easterly, "Is Mesha's qrḥḥ Mentioned in Isaiah XV 2?" VT 41 (1991): 215–19, suggests the word "baldness" (קָרְחָה) is the name of a city, but Jer 48:37 seems to confirm that the original text was similar to the Masoretic Text, not Easterly's reconstructed text based on the Old Greek.

[146] The location of some of these cities is known. For example, Nebo (15:2) is close to Mount Nebo where Moses died (Deut 34:1). It and the cities of Heshbon and Elealah (15:4; Num 32:3,37–38; Josh 13:15–19) were cities of Reuben, while Dibon (15:2; Num 32:3,34) was a city of Gad until the Moabites took control of it. Jahaz (15:4) is mentioned in Josh 13:18; 21:36 as a city of Reuben. The waters of Nimrim (15:6) probably refer to a spring at the city by that name (Num 32:3,36; Josh 13:27), and Zoar (15:5) was south of the Dead Sea (Gen 13:10; Deut 34:3). Jer 48 also mentions Lihith, Horonaim, and Nimrim. Some of these names have been associated with certain places, but most cannot be firmly identified with a specific abandoned site until greater

guish. This first section ends with "therefore" (*'al kēn*, in 15:4b), announcing that even the soldiers in the army will be in shock over this disaster. Everyone will be totally demoralized and in a hopeless frame of mind.

15:5–7 The second part of the lament describes the refugees escaping to the southern borders of Moab. Verse 5 begins with the prophet expressing his own heartfelt (*libbî*, "my heart") lamentation over what is happening in Moab, particularly for the innocent fugitives who were trying to escape the horrors of war. He pictures them lamenting as they trudge in a long line down the road (15:5), passing dried up streams and withered fields (15:6). This means that they are entering a desert area and they will have no water to drink or food to eat. This section ends with a "therefore" clause (*'al kēn* in 15:7), describing the refugees carrying all their worldly possessions to an oasis, the "Ravine of Poplars." Things seem to be completely hopeless. The reference to Zoar indicates that the refugees who are fleeing[147] are now at the southern border of Moab and ready to escape either to Edom or into Judah.

15:8–9 The final part of the lament summarizes this debacle and emphasizes the truthfulness of these predictions. By beginning both verses with "surely, truly" (*kî*, omitted in NIV; "for" in NASB), the text claims that these horrific prophecies will "surely" come true. The wailing of the people is so loud that their lamenting voices are heard in the cities along the borders of Moab. The blood of the dead will fill the stream at Dimon,[148] and even more death will arrive because the foe, pictured as a lion, will attack anyone who remains in the land. Amos 3:8 pictures God as a roaring lion, but here Isaiah uses the lion as a symbol of a fierce enemy army (see 5:29; Jer 50:17).[149]

(2) Moab Requests Help from Judah (16:1–5)

[1]Send lambs as tribute
  to the ruler of the land,
from Sela, across the desert,
  to the mount of the Daughter of Zion.

---

archeological work is completed in Jordan. Scribal mistakes may also hinder progress; for example נַחַל הָעֲרָבִים, "Ravine of Poplars," could refer to the Arabah, or even to Iye-abarim in Num 21:11 if the ב and ר were reversed (Oswalt, *Isaiah 1–39*, 335).

[147] This line in 15:5 does not have a Hb. word for "flee"; it was added by the NIV translators to make a complete thought. In such cases, the "to be" verb is usually added, which would give "her fugitives are as far as Zoar." Both approaches show where they ended up.

[148] דִּימוֹן, "Dimon," may be a misspelling of דִּיבֹן, "Dibon," the city mentioned in 15:2. This would make a nice inclusio with 15:2 and the misspelling could be a purposeful play on דָּם, "blood," in 15:9. The Qumran 1QIsaᵃ and the Old Greek have readings that agree with the spelling "Dibon," though "Dimon" is clearly the harder reading. Jones, *Howling over Moab*, 191–95, discusses the textual problem and the possible connection of this place with *Khirbet ed-Dimna*, which is about two miles northwest of er-Rabba.

[149] Young, *Isaiah,* I:460, thinks this refers to literal lions (as in 2 Kgs 17:25), while F. Delitzsch, *Isaiah*, Commentary on the Old Testament VII (trans J. Martin; Grand Rapids: Eerdmans, 1969), 329, suggests that Isaiah was referring to the lion of Judah (Gen 49:9).

²Like fluttering birds
   pushed from the nest,
so are the women of Moab
   at the fords of the Arnon.

³"Give us counsel,
   render a decision.
Make your shadow like night—
   at high noon.
Hide the fugitives,
   do not betray the refugees.
⁴Let the Moabite fugitives stay with you;
   be their shelter from the destroyer."

The oppressor will come to an end,
   and destruction will cease;
   the aggressor will vanish from the land.
⁵In love a throne will be established;
   in faithfulness a man will sit on it—
   one from the house of David—
one who in judging seeks justice
   and speeds the cause of righteousness.

16:1 At this point, someone (possibly an advisor to the king) interrupts the lament and exhorts the Moabites to send a tribute or a gift.[150] Since no Hebrew preposition precedes "ruler," it is not clear if the lamb is to come "from the ruler of the land [the Moabite king]"[151] or if it is to be sent "to the ruler of the land [the Israelite king]." The parallelism in the second half of the verse argues for the latter approach (as in NIV). This act of sending a gift must be interpreted as an attempt to remedy the problem that the refugees in Moab were facing in the dry desert of Moab. The refugees were at the southern tip of Moab and some have already crossed over into Edom (Sela is modern Petra), but if they want to cross over to Judah for protection they need to send lambs to Zion (cf. 2 Kgs 3:4). Sending a lamb could be interpreted as a gift, a tribute to show loyalty, or an act of submission in order to gain favor from the ruler of Judah. At this point, the exact nature of the assistance requested by the Moabites is not stated (military aid, food, taking care of refugees).

---

[150] שִׁלְחוּ, "send," is a second masculine imperative used to exhort or admonish (GKC §110a). Could this be Isaiah exhorting the Moabites? The term כַּר ("lamb") is found in the Hebrew Bible in the singular only in this passage (possibly a collective use), elsewhere it is always a plural form. Clements, *Isaiah 1–39*, 153, takes the verb as a perfect and makes the ruler the subject of the verb, thus he translates the beginning of 16:1 as "the rulers of the land have sent lambs." There is little in the grammar that would support this interpretation.

[151] Wildberger, *Isaiah 13–27*, 105, translates this as "a ram of the sovereign," indicating that the animal came from the flock of the Moabite king. Either interpretation can make sense.

16:2–4a The imperative verbs do not continue in v. 2, but reappear in vv. 3–4; consequently, some put v. 2 after 15:9 (both describe the refugees) or delete it altogether.[152] Sweeney correctly interprets 16:2 as a description of the situation of the poor distraught Moabites who need help;[153] thus it gives the rationale for requesting asylum in Judah. "It will happen" (*wĕāyâ*, omitted by NIV) that the young Moabite women at the southern border of Moab (at the River Arnon), who are in danger of being violently abused by enemy soldiers, will be helpless and hysterical, like confused fluttering birds chased from the nest.

Verses 3–4a appear to be Isaiah quoting what the Moabite envoy will or should ask the ruler of Judah when they come to ask permission to enter the territory of Judah.[154] The one giving the advice suggests that the Moabites should request an opinion, decision, counsel, or advice from some ruler (probably the king of Judah). Moab is now made up of refugees, outcasts, and sojourners who need help. Would[155] Judah allow these refugees to sojourn in peace under the shadow of Judah's protection and "not betray" (*'al tĕgallî*) them by giving them over to Moab's enemies? Like a shady place protected from the sun during the noonday heat, Judah can be a "refuge" (*sēter*) for these Moabites from the one who wants to "devastate" (*šôdēd* is also in 15:1) their land.

16:4b–5 Judah's answer to Moab's request is a word of assurance and hope. Verses 4b–5 are not a continuation of the Moabites request in vv. 3–4a.[156] In this answer from Judah the prophet promises two things.[157] The first promise relates to the one oppressing Moab and the second relates to the coming of a just Davidic king in Judah. Many take the introductory *kî* that starts 16:4b as a temporal marker, "when" (RSV) or "for" (NASB; NIV omits the word), but if the prophet wanted to give as strong statement of assurance,

---

[152] Wildberger, *Isaiah 13–27,* 119, deletes it as a later gloss, feeling that it does not fit after 15:9 (Kissane accepts this approach), but this theory implies that the later editor was totally incompetent.

[153] Sweeney, *Isaiah 1–39,* 240. Oswalt, *Isaiah 1–39,* 342 views v. 2 as the beginning of the Moabite's request and the rationale for their request.

[154] הָבִיאוּ, "bring, give," and עֲשִׂי, "make, render," are vocalized like second masculine plural imperatives, like the imperative in 16:1. The *Qere* reading, הָבִיאִי, is second feminine singular, meaning that someone else is addressing "you," that is, Judah. The second feminine form is preferable since it is used in the other verbs in 16:3 and pronominal suffixes ("with you") in 16:4.

[155] יָגוּרוּ must be either a modal imperfect that expresses a willed action (similar to the subjunctive) or a jussive form (GKC §107n or 109b). Both are used to request, wish, advise, or express an obligation. This means, lit., "May my Moabite refugees sojourn among you."

[156] Hayes and Irvine, *Isaiah,* 243, believe 16:3–5 contain the Moabite request, with v. 4b stipulating the length of time the refugees will need protection, and v. 5 being a flattering compliment to Hezekiah, Judah's king. Oswalt, *Isaiah 1–39,* 343, also says "the prophet here puts words in the Moabite messenger's mouth," but Childs, *Isaiah,* 132, properly attributes "vv. 4b–5 to the voice of the prophet."

[157] This interpretation disagrees with Kaiser, *Isaiah 13–39,* 71, who contends that 16:5 "cannot meaningfully be interpreted as a promise to the Moabites."

"surely, truly" would express that most forcibly.[158] The promise is that the ruthless oppressor who violently tramples the land of Moab will definitely stop what he is doing and leave the land, though no specific date is set for the fulfillment of this prediction (16:4b). There is also no question that a faithful Davidic king will establish himself on Judah's throne and rule with faithfulness, truth, justice, and righteousness (16:5). Sweeney concludes that this means that Davidic "rule will be established over Moab as a result of this petition," but this reads into the text more than it actually says.[159] Instead, Isaiah describes how God's steadfast lovingkindness and grace will enthrone a ruler in Judah who is completely different from the oppressive king who will trample the land of Moab. Using terminology similar to what is found in 9:1–6, this king will follow the ideals of being faithful and truthful in all he does—righteous in his judgments and actions. There is no direct encouragement for the Moabites to trust in this figure, and there is no demand that they submit to his rule.[160] Yet the very existence of this ruler is a source of hope, and the positive character of his rule creates the possibility for the Moabites to look to him in their time of crisis.[161]

The Judean audience that was listening to the prophet's words to Moab would immediately be aware of the hope Isaiah has expressed for their nation. They too had to make some choices. Those in Judah could choose to resist the oppressive foreign kings and be attacked like Moab, they could submit to these destructive monarchs and hope for survival, or they could look for hope in God's righteous and faithful ruler from the house of David. No call is made for anyone to choose one path or the other, but the future will require the people of Judah to choose whom they will serve. The implications of this message to the Moabites have an impact on all who hear the prophet's words, for everyone must decide how to survive in this oppressive world. No one wants to end up in a situation like the fleeing Moabites, so it is wise to pay close attention to the alternative the prophet offers.

(3) Pride Will Cause Lamenting in Moab (16:6–12)

⁶We have heard of Moab's pride—
  her overweening pride and conceit,
her pride and her insolence—
  but her boasts are empty.

---

[158]GKC §159ee refers to כִּי as an expression that was intended to give "absolute certainty" to the expected results.

[159] Sweeney, *Isaiah 1–39*, 244, implies this interpretation, but the text does not express how the new Davidic king will relate to the Moabites, mentions no covenant between Judah and Moab, and does not promise Moab that this Davidic king will defeat Moab's violent oppressor.

[160] Young, *Isaiah*, I:464, interprets these as demands that Moab should treat Judah with kindness and come to Judah in repentance, but these commands are not explicitly made.

[161] If one is drowning and someone mentions that there is a boat to his left, it is not necessary to tell the drowning person to grab onto the boat.

⁷Therefore the Moabites wail,
   they wail together for Moab.
Lament and grieve
   for the men of KirHareseth.
⁸The fields of Heshbon wither,
   the vines of Sibmah also.
The rulers of the nations
   have trampled down the choicest vines,
which once reached Jazer
   and spread toward the desert.
Their shoots spread out
   and went as far as the sea.
⁹So I weep, as Jazer weeps,
   for the vines of Sibmah.
O Heshbon, O Elealeh,
   I drench you with tears!
The shouts of joy over your ripened fruit
   and over your harvests have been stilled.
¹⁰Joy and gladness are taken away from the orchards;
   no one sings or shouts in the vineyards;
no one treads out wine at the presses,
   for I have put an end to the shouting.
¹¹My heart laments for Moab like a harp,
   my inmost being for Kir Hareseth.
¹²When Moab appears at her high place,
   she only wears herself out;
when she goes to her shrine to pray,
   it is to no avail.

Although the meaning of these individual verses is relatively easy to understand, their function in the chapter is more problematic. In relationship to 16:7–12, the pride of Moab in 16:6 provides a rationale for the lament over Moab and a justification for its destruction in 16:7–12. The primary difficulty is in following the flow of thought from the previous paragraph. One option is to view all of 16:3–5 as a Moabite request for help and 16:6–12 as Judah's sarcastic rejection of that request because of Moab's pride.[162] In contrast to this interpretation, it is better to view the prophet's personal laments as real (15:5; 16:9) rather than sarcastic; therefore 16:6–12 is not a sarcastic response to the request in the first half of the chapter. The future choice of Moab is left unstated, just as the future choice of Isaiah's audience in Judah is unknown. This conclusion means that Isaiah is now returning to repeat some of the themes of his original lament in 15:1–9 in order to strengthen his

---

[162] Hayes and Irvine, *Isaiah,* 244–45, think 16:6–12 is Isaiah's sarcastic lament that rejects the Moabite flattering request for help in 16:3–6. Oswalt, *Isaiah 1–39,* 340 and 345, rejects this sarcastic approach and finds the prophet reflecting on proud Moab's destruction. Motyer, *The Prophecy of Isaiah,* 153, believes Moab rejected Judah's offer and now will be punished (16:6–12).

argument for trusting in the ruler of Judah so that they can avoid the suffering he describes in these verses.

It does not appear that the prophet is lamenting Moab's refusal to choose to find refuge in the house of David (16:4–5). The text never explicitly reveals how Moab responded to the offer in 16:4b–5 because at this point the invitation was still open for them to respond. Thus both 15:1–9 and 16:6–12 function as comparable reasons for Moab (and by implications the prophet's audience in Judah) to lament and stop making false boasts about their present status. The laments predict what will happen (desolation of Moab) and tell why it will happen (pride); thus they legitimate the choice of depending on the Messiah of Judah. There is only one hope (16:5); the Moabite sacrifices and prayers at the high places will not help (16:12).

The structure of 16:6–12 is:

Moab is proud	16:6
Moab will wail, its field ruined	16:7–8
Prophet laments; there is no joy in Moab	16:9–10
Prophet weeps; Moab's prayer is useless	16:11–12

16:6 The subject of the verb is a first person plural ("we") and the topic is the pride of Moab, so a new paragraph begins in 16:6. The people of Judah must be the subject ("we") of the verb. We (the people of Judah) know about the pride, conceit, arrogance, haughtiness, and empty boasts of the Moabites. What the Moabites boasted about is left unstated in 16:6. If 16:7–12 can be used as a hint about the nation's pride, one might conclude that Moab was proud of its great cities and choice fertile vineyards.

16:7–8 Verse 7 begins with "therefore" (*lākēn*), pointing to a conclusion that can be reached about the consequence of Moab's arrogance. Wailing and howling (15:2,3,8) will happen; grieving and lamenting will fill the land of Moab. The phrase "men (*'anšēy*) of Kir Hareseth" in the NIV follows the rendition of this verse in the Old Greek and in Jer 48:31, but the Hebrew text reads "raisin cakes (*'ăšîš*) of Kir Hareseth."[163] These delicacies from compressed dried grapes were eaten at feasts (2 Sam 6:19; Hos 3:1; Song 2:5), but once the vineyards of Moab are destroyed, they will no longer be available. "Surely, truly" (*kî*, omitted in 16:8 in NIV) the loss of vineyards will extend across the nation of Moab, for unnamed foreign rulers will trample down the choice vines throughout the land.

16:9–10 Following a similar structure as vv. 7–8, v. 9a begins with "therefore" (*'al kēn*) and is followed in v. 9b by "surely" (*kî*, omitted in NIV) to emphasize that these events will definitely occur. In these verses the prophet expresses his own personal grief, as he did earlier in 15:5. He does not laugh at or mock the Moabites; he does not rejoice over their troubles. He identifies with

---

[163] Oswalt, *Isaiah 1–39*, 344, and Wildberger, *Isaiah 13–27*, 111, keep "raisin cakes," while the Aramaic Targum has "mankind," which appears to be a simplification of a difficult text.

the terrible emotional traumatic weeping[164] of the Moabites in Jazar, Sibmah, Heshbon, the Dead Sea, and Elealeh (see 15:4). After years of caring for and cultivating these grape plants, there will be no joy in harvesting the vineyards, at the wine press, or in the orchards—everything will be destroyed. This is a terrible tragedy that brings no joy or jubilation to the prophet or God. God does not want to see people punished; he does not take pleasure in the destruction of the wicked or their land (Ezek 18:23).

16:11–12   The lament ends with a final "therefore" in 16:11 (ʿal kēn, omitted in NIV). When the prophet points to "my bowels" (mēʿay, not "my heart" as in NIV) and "inmost being" (qirbî) aching like a moaning harp, he is describing a deep anguish that causes the passions of his inner being to upset the physical condition of his body. This intense agitation of soul and body was not a superficial response that was gone in a few seconds. One of the reasons for this response is that the Moabites will foolishly look for hope in the wrong place. Even though they have knowledge of the true God and his future messianic ruler, they will continue to go to their traditional pagan high places of worship and put great effort into sacrificing and praying, but nothing will help.[165] This hopeless feeling should cause the listeners in Judah to think back to the one ray of hope that was presented earlier in the chapter (16:5). If Judah wants to experience a different outcome, they will need to follow a different path than Moab.

(4) Destruction in Three Years (16:13–14)

[13]This is the word the LORD has already spoken concerning Moab. [14]But now the LORD says: "Within three years, as a servant bound by contract would count them, Moab's splendor and all her many people will be despised, and her survivors will be very few and feeble."

16:13–14   Suddenly, two narrative verses appear, beginning with an announcement of a new word from God that was different from what God spoke in the past in 15:1–16:12. These verses do not seem to be part of the poetic lament in the rest of the chapter. It appears that they were received from God at another date,[166] three years before this prophecy was fulfilled. The time period between these two messages is unknown, but it is probably a relatively short

---

[164] "I drench you" follows 1QIsaᵃ, which spells this word correctly, with the ʾ after the ו. אֲרַוֶּיַךְ in the Masoretic text is a misspelling because it reverses the order of these two letters. 1QIsaᵃ also misspells the word with אֲרָזִיךְ, "your cedar wood," though it got the letter ʾ in the right place in the word.

[165] The last phrase וְלֹא יוּכָל, "it is to no avail," literally means "it will not be able/possible." No subject is identified, so it could mean that Moab will not be able to stop the destruction, its god Chemosh will not be able to do anything, or that the prayer will not be able to make a difference in what will happen.

[166] Oswalt, Isaiah 1–39, 348, recognizes that "formerly" (מֵאָז) could refer to something from long ago in the past or just a short time ago.

time. These two prophecies about Moab were brought together in the editing of Isaiah's oracles because they relate to the same country.

This prophecy contrasts Moab's present glory and large population (cf. Babylon's glory in 13:19) with her future despised position with a small remnant of just a few feeble people. Moab will be transformed from its position of pride and honor to utter humiliation within three years. The time period before this final conquest is compared to the time a servant is bound to a master. This implies that the three years until the final conquest will involve hard labor of forced service to another nation. Nevertheless, the nation of Moab does have some time to choose what it will do before the final judgment of God falls on them.

THEOLOGICAL IMPLICATIONS. The prophecy concerning Moab makes several significant theological points that have much broader applications. First, God controls what is happening to all the people on earth and he understands why they wail and suffer pain and ruin. God sovereignly knows what is happening in each nation and is aware of the plight of all people, in all the cities of Moab, and even the frightful status of the refugees who will try to escape danger. Second, God's message and his relationship with people is one of identification with the pain of the sufferer (15:5; 16:9). His heart cries out for them and he agonizes at man's terrible destiny. This identification with those who suffer does not cause him to hide future painful events; instead, he sides with the oppressed and warns them ahead of time about the real destruction that an oppressor may bring on a nation (16:4b). He does not pretend that everything will be fine for the proud, but he does not favor oppressive nations either. Third, God warns people about the future and then confronts them with their errors (particularly pride) for two reasons: (a) so that they will have some comprehension of why they will suffer (16:6), and (b) so that they will have an opportunity to choose a different path. God provides information about a solid resource of righteous and faithful hope for those who wish to choose that way (16:5). He warns people about false hopes that will not help people avoid judgment (16:12).

All this is an illustration to the people of God (in Judah and today) that God is concerned about people in every nation on the earth. He cares deeply, like a father cares for his son. He wants everyone on earth to come to a clear knowledge of the truth, even people in far away foreign nations. He is not just interested in the "chosen nation," but cares about all people in this world. He holds all people and all nations responsible for their choices—particularly their pride. If this is the accountability criteria that pagan nations are judged by, how much more severe will be the expectations on those who experience the grace of God in a clearer and more powerful way. God hates all pride, but pride in the heart of anyone who claims to be one of his children is inexcusable. Their ruin will surely be worse than the suffering of Moab.

4. God's Plans for Damascus—and Israel (17:1–18:7)

Although it might appear initially that chap. 17 is an independent oracle distinct from God's message about Cush in 18:1–7, Sweeney provides four reasons that these two chapters belong together. (a) There is no introductory announcement of a new *maśśāʾ* oracle in 18:1, so the next unit must not begin until 19:1. (b) These chapters are unified by a common use of agricultural imagery of harvest and the gleaning of the fields (17:4–6,10–11,13; 18:3–6). (c) Each oracle in chaps. 13–23 describes how God is involved in human affairs, but in this case that explanation is not found until 18:3–6. (d) Cush is an example of one of the "nations of the earth" (17:12; 18:3), but it is one that recognizes God's sovereignty (17:7; 18:7) and is not among the "roaring" nations that God will rebuke (17:12–14).[167]

HISTORICAL SETTING. This oracle describes the fall of Damascus and the fortified cities of Ephraim (the northern nation of Israel) The events in the oracle belong to the period of the Syro-Ephraimite War (734–32 BC) when Ahaz asked the Assyrian king Tiglath-pileser III to rescue him from an attack by Syria and Israel (7:1–11:16; cf. 2 Chr 28). The pagan religious practices described in 17:7–8 fit this period when Ahaz promoted the worship of Baal (cf. 2 Kgs 16).

A new paragraph begins at 17:12 that refers to many nations coming against God's people. This was the time when an enemy nation (Assyria) did try to "loot" Isaiah's audience in Judah ("us" in 17:14). These soldiers were defeated one evening and found dead in the morning (17:14; 37:36). Wildberger proposes to connect 17:12–14 to Sennacherib's attack on Jerusalem in 701 BC.[168] If this is the event the prophet was referring to, one can say that the prophecy occurred sometime before that event, but a more specific date is not possible. Since the oracle seems to be related to two different events, one has two choices in hypothesizing a setting. (a) The interpreter can date this prophecy within a few years of 701 BC and view the prophet as quoting an earlier prophecy about the Syro-Ephraimite War as an historical illustration teaching principles that were still valid in 701 BC. (b) One can place this prophecy during the Syro-Ephraimite War and understand 17:12–14 as a warning to Ahaz that he should not trust Assyria, because eventually God will destroy that nation sometime in the future. The first option fits best in this context.

The date for the oracle about Cush in 18:1–7 needs to reflect a period when Judah and Cush were sending envoys back and forth, probably to discuss a political alliance. Three suggestions are worth consideration. (a) Sweeney

---

[167] Sweeney, *Isaiah 1–39*, 254, presents good reasons for the interpreter not to understand 18:1–7 as a separate condemnation, but to include it with chap. 17. Childs, *Isaiah*, 135, in his analysis, found Sweeney's arguments to be persuasive.

[168] Wildberger, *Isaiah 13–27*, 197. On the other hand, Childs, *Isaiah*, 138, believes the language is so different from the description of those events in chaps. 36–37 that it must fit an earlier period.

believes this oracle describes Israel's King Hoshea attempting to form an alliance with King So of Egypt in 724 BC (2 Kgs 17:4).[169] (b) Oswalt suggests a date around 715 BC when a Nubian or Cushite dynasty ruled Egypt and Shabaka was king.[170] In this setting the envoys were trying to arrange a coalition between various states in Palestine and Egypt to oppose Sargon II.[171] (c) Wildberger believes the sending of envoys best fits Hezekiah's attempt to enlist support from Egypt (cf. 30:1–5; 31:1–3) against Sennacherib a few years before 701 BC.[172] This last setting would fit both 17:12–14 and 18:1–7. A problem for each of the above dates is that they all assume that the envoys from Cush arrived in Jerusalem to make an alliance against Assyria. But there is no explicit statement that these envoys were talking about an alliance in 18:1–7; therefore, the basis for suggesting these dates rests on a major unproven assumption about the setting.

GENRE. This oracle departs from the literary patterns of the preceding messages. There are no laments, but a series of "in that day" announcements of judgment (without a rationale describing the people's sin in 17:1–6). The first two announcements of judgment (17:1–3,4–6) and the final paragraph (17:12–14) function as messages of hope for the people of Judah because they predict the fall of Judah's enemies. These should have encouraged the kings of Judah, to believe God and trust in him (cf. 7:3–9). The last two sections, beginning with "alas, woe" (17:12; 18:1), do not introduce typical lamenting woe oracles (cf. 5:8–25). Instead, the term "alas, woe" (hôy) simply serves as an exclamation to draw attention to an astonishing new point the prophet is presenting.

STRUCTURE. The division of this unit into paragraphs is not difficult to discern due to the use of the introductory phrase "in that day" (17:4,7,9) and "alas, woe" (17:12; 18:1). The messenger formula "declares the LORD" (17:3b,6b) also helps mark the end of subparagraphs. It is more problematic to know how to group the subparagraphs and identify the audience the prophet addressed. The material is structured into three main paragraphs:

God's judgment on the fertility of Damascus and Ephraim   17:1–11
God rebukes the raging nations   17:12–14
Cush will honor God for destroying its enemies   18:1–7.

All these messages were spoken to an audience in Judah (a) to encourage them to trust God and not to make alliances in a time of war; (b) to warn the

---

[169] Sweeney, *Isaiah 1–39*, 261, connects these verses to an alliance by Israel, while most others look for alliances Judah was making, since the gifts are brought to Mount Zion in 18:7.

[170] K. A. Kitchen, *The Third Intermediate Period in Egypt (1100 to 650 B.C.)* (Warminster: Aris and Phillips, 1973), 369. This dynasty began in 728 BC when Pianchi defeated the Libyans and took control of Egypt as far north as Memphis. When Shabaka came to power in 716 BC, he consolidated power over all Egypt.

[171] Oswalt, *Isaiah 1–39*, 360, and Watts, *Isaiah 1–33*, 245, favor this period.

[172] Wildberger, *Isaiah 13–27*, 212, and Childs, *Isaiah*, 138, point to similar attempts at alliances in 14:28–32; 31:1–3; 39:1–8.

leaders not to fear their enemies, for God will destroy them; and (c) to cause the people of Judah to realize that one day tall and strange-looking people from foreign nations will come and worship the great God of Judah. If all this will happen, why would the people of Judah not trust this God in their present circumstances?

(1) Damascus and Israel Will Lose Their Fertility (17:1–11)

¹An oracle concerning Damascus:

"See, Damascus will no longer be a city
    but will become a heap of ruins.
²The cities of Aroer will be deserted
    and left to flocks, which will lie down,
    with no one to make them afraid.
³The fortified city will disappear from Ephraim,
    and royal power from Damascus;
the remnant of Aram will be
    like the glory of the Israelites,"
        declares the Lord Almighty.

⁴"In that day the glory of Jacob will fade;
    the fat of his body will waste away.
⁵It will be as when a reaper gathers the standing grain
    and harvests the grain with his arm—
as when a man gleans heads of grain
    in the Valley of Rephaim.
⁶Yet some gleanings will remain,
    as when an olive tree is beaten,
leaving two or three olives on the topmost branches,
    four or five on the fruitful boughs,"
        declares the Lord, the God of Israel.

⁷In that day men will look to their Maker
    and turn their eyes to the Holy One of Israel.
⁸They will not look to the altars,
    the work of their hands,
and they will have no regard for the Asherah poles
    and the incense altars their fingers have made.

⁹In that day their strong cities, which they left because of the Israelites, will be like places abandoned to thickets and undergrowth. And all will be desolation.

10You have forgotten God your Savior;
    you have not remembered the Rock, your fortress.
Therefore, though you set out the finest plants
    and plant imported vines,
¹¹though on the day you set them out, you make them grow,
    and on the morning when you plant them, you bring them to bud,

yet the harvest will be as nothing
in the day of disease and incurable pain.

This paragraph contains four subparagraphs, with 17:4,7,9 introducing "in that day" sayings about what will happen in Damascus and Israel. These short messages do not directly address circumstances in the city of Jerusalem during the Syro-Ephraimite war, but focus instead on the fate of Judah's two enemies (Syria and Israel). God's past desolation of these nations provided hope for Isaiah's audience in Judah during the time of Sennacherib's attack (701 B. C), but they also stand as a warning that Judah should not follow the same path as these nations for it will lead to destruction. The paragraph is structured in four segments:

Key cities of Syria and Israel will disappear	17:1–3
Israel will be gleaned with few gleanings left	17:4–6
People will reject idols and turn to God	17:7–8
Judah warned not to follow Israel's path	17:9–11

17:1–3 The prophet first deals with the destruction of Syria, especially the key cities of Damascus and Aroer (plus Israel in 17:3), because Rezin, the king of Syria, attempted to force Israel and Judah to join in a coalition against Assyria (7:1–2; 8:6; 2 Chr 28:5). Ahaz, king of Judah, resisted joining this coalition (7:1–6; 2 Kgs 18:5–6), and Isaiah promised that God would not allow these nations to destroy Judah (7:8–9). All Ahaz had to do was not to fear and trust God for his deliverance from these military forces (7:4,9). Isaiah 17:1–3 provides additional assurance that Damascus (and Israel) will not stand, so Isaiah's audience could be calm and believe God's promises (7:4).

The two powerful cities of Damascus and Aroer (Deut 2:36 or Josh 13:25) will go no longer exist.[173] After the destruction of the walls, palaces, fortresses, and towers of these strong cities, all that will be left will be one huge pile of stones. The place will be unfit for human habitation, so it will return to being a place for shepherds to stay with their flocks (cf. 5:17; 13:20–22). The shepherd and flocks will not have to fear that someone will try to chase them away because no one will be living in these cities. This foreshadows the conquest of Damascus and portions of Israel by Tiglath-pileser III around 732 BC. In 17:3 the destiny of the royal power of Rezin (the king of Syria) is connected to the fate of the fortified cities of Israel, its coalition partner. Rezin's authority will evaporate with only a small remnant of people left. The implication is that Ahaz should not fear these nations (cf. 7:4), but he should instead trust God.

---

[173] מוּסָר is a participle, thus a time frame is not clearly provided. Participles can be translated as past tense (Blenkinsopp, *Isaiah 1–39,* 304) to indicate that Damascus had already been defeated, as present tense to show that it is happening right now, or (frequently with הִנֵּה, "behold") to represent a future action (GKC §116n-p). Since הִנֵּה begins this oracle, a future orientation is reflected here.

The last part of 17:3 has produced a great deal of confusion, and several have suggested emendations[174] to help make sense of what the Hebrew text says. Clements simply states that this clause "scarcely makes good sense, and must be the result of some corruption."[175] Motyer finds a message of hope (cf. 18:7) by interpreting this clause as a promise that both Aram and Israel will have a glorious remnant left after their judgment.[176] The question is: How will the remnant of Aram (Syria) be like the glory of Israel? If Israel will be defeated in this war and have no glory, then the prophet means that the glory of Syria will also disappear.[177] This seems consistent with 17:4, which picks up the discussion of the fading "glory of Jacob." Both nations will have no strong cities, no gold, no glorious palaces, no prosperous economy, and no powerful armies (cf. 2:7–17; 10:16). Thus these nations will be humbled with nothing to be proud of (cf. 2:11–12). This reminds the reader that people should exalt only in the glory and majesty of Almighty God (as in 2:11–12,17) and stop regarding man-made objects, cities, armies, or special people as something glorious (2:22).

17:4–6 The first of the three "in that day" oracles refers to that day when Israel will be destroyed. The focus is directed to the "fading, lowering" (*yid-dal*) of the glory (*kĕbôd*) of Israel.[178] The days of fat and plenty in the past will be replaced by a period when people and their riches will waste away. The nation's glorious state is compared to what is left after the harvest of grain (17:5) and olives (17:6). Although harvesters were careful to gather the entire crop when they cut the grain and collected the bundles of grain together on their arms, a few stalks of grain sometimes remained (cf. Deut 24:19–20). Of course, there would be even fewer stalks of grain left after the gleaners picked up 99 percent of what the reapers left.[179] What was left after the reapers and gleaners is comparable to what will be left of Israel. This illustration demonstrates that there will be a dramatic decrease in Israel's size and glory.

The second illustration comes from the practice of harvesting olives (17:6). To collect the olives, people would put a cloth under the olive tree and then beat the branches until all but a few of the high or unripe olives had fallen to the ground (leaving a few as Deut 24:20 requires). The few pieces of remaining

---

[174] The Old Greek says, "the remnant of Syria will perish." Watts, *Isaiah 1–33,* 235, translates the clauses, "Aram is a remnant, like the 'glory' (which) the Israelites have become."

[175] Clements, *Isaiah 1–39,* 158, ends up following the reading of the Old Greek text "and the remnant of Syria will perish," deletes the verb "will be," and reads the final phrase as "together with the children of Israel."

[176] Motyer, *The Prophecy of Isaiah,* 157, interprets this as another example of God's mercy and grace.

[177] Oswalt, *Isaiah 1–39,* 350, says, "While Syria will not be totally destroyed, it will, like Israel, be left as just a shadow of itself. Its glory will be like Israel's."

[178] They were raising up their own glory, but they were supposed to be exalting/raising up the glory of God (2:11–22); therefore, God will lower their glory and humble them.

[179] The Valley of Rephaim was a short distance southwest of the city of Jerusalem and would be well known to Isaiah's audience in Jerusalem.

fruit are comparable to the small number of remaining Israelites after the nation's destruction. These results are sobering to think about but there is no lamenting for Israel, because the Israelites were attacking Judah, Isaiah's audience. These results should demonstrate to Isaiah's audience that Judah should not join the coalition against Assyria, for it is doomed to failure. This prophecy also assures Isaiah's audience that Israel and Syria will not defeat Judah in the Syro-Ephraimite War.

17:7–8 The next "in that day" oracle does not refer to the final Day of the Lord; it points to the near destruction of Syria and Israel, though neither nation is mentioned (but notice 17:9). Isaiah steps back to draw some broad principles about "mankind" (*hāʾādām*) and their relationship to "their Creator/Maker" (*ʿōśēhû*) on the Day of Judgment. Isaiah understands that there will be a change in people's behavior. There was at that time a tendency to "look at, pay careful attention to" (*yišʿeh*) altars where people sacrificed, their carved images of gods, Asherah[180] fertility poles from the Baal cult, or incense altars molded out of mud with their fingers (17:10). But on the day of judgment people will "look at, pay careful attention to" (*yišʿeh*) their creator, the Holy One of Israel (17:7). This picks up some of the previously mentioned contrasts between the Holy God of Israel and idols (2:6–22).[181] These two verses argue that it is foolish to center devotion on man-made religious objects or rituals. They cannot give life or protect one on the day of God's judgment. God is the creator of man and the universe; people cannot create a real God. The only real God is holy, the all-powerful Creator who is worthy of every person's attention and exaltation.

This indictment of Israel's sins would probably be heard in Judah during the time of the wicked King Ahaz as an attack on the pagan Baal worship that Ahaz encouraged throughout the land of Judah (2 Kgs 16:1–4; 2 Chr 28:1–4,22–25). Although this message does not contain a call to repentance to Isaiah's listeners, the broad statement about turning to God from pagan idols allowed the prophet to use this comparison as a challenge to the pagan worship going on in Judah.

17:9–11 The statements included in the third "in that day" segment lack unity in their literary style and do not have a consistent topic throughout;[182] there are also several textual problems. Consequently, the standard transla-

---

[180] Asherah was a female fertility goddess who was a consort of the high god El. She was a mother of the gods and the goddess of the sea. It is possible that some pagan Israelites thought of Asherah as God's wife. These wooden poles have all rotted so there is no record of what was carved on them (2 Kgs 23:4–6). See J. C. de Moor, "Asherah," *TDOT*, I, 438–40, for further background.

[181] Clements, *Isaiah 1–39*, 159, derives this condemnation of idols and pagan alters from Josiah's reform movement or a post-exilic redactor, while Kaiser, *Isaiah 13–39*, 84, thinks this describes the eschatological repentance of Israel from a post-exilic redactor.

[182] Verse 9 is a narrative text, while vv. 10–11 are poetic. Verse 9 refers to the destruction of cities (using third plural verbs), while vv. 10–11 refer to plants and "you" (second feminine singular), forgetting God.

tions vary considerably. The RSV translation follows the Old Greek in 17:9 and refers to the deserted Hivite and Amorite[183] cities that the Israelites destroyed when they first took the land under the leadership of Joshua (Gen 15:21; Josh 9:1,7). With this reading, Isaiah is comparing God's future desolation of Israelite cities with Israel's earlier desolation of Canaanite cities. This is actually close to what the Hebrew text says without emending it with the Old Greek. But the Hebrew text does not mention the Hivites or Amorites; it simply states that some strong cities will be like the forsaken places that the Canaanites abandoned when the Israelites invaded the land. These populated and strong cities will be like a desolate wooded area at the top of a hill. This pictures an old castle fortress at the top of a hill[184] with walls dilapidated and trees growing among the ruins,[185] reiterating a point already made in 17:1–3.

A second concern is the lack of continuity between 17:9 and 17:10–11. Why reiterate in 17:9 a point already made in 17:1–3, and why change to a direct address ("you") in 17:10–11? If the "you" (second feminine singular) in 17:10–11 refers to Isaiah's audience in Jerusalem, as Watts and Wildberger[186] suggest (rather than Israel or Damascus as in 17:1–6), there is a logical explanation for the change to "you" in 17:10–11.[187] Isaiah is now making application to his audience in Judah, so the text draws a parallel between events in Damascus and Israel (17:1–3) and what will happen in Judah (17:9). The *kî* ("because") at the beginning of 17:10 (omitted by NIV) then introduces the reason why these strong cities will be desolate.

Isaiah says that the people of Jerusalem have forgotten that God is "your Savior" (*'iśēk*), "[your] Rock" (*ṣûr*), and "your Fortress" (*mā'uzzēk*); that is why judgment will come. These three analogies call to mind God's past acts of salvation for his people, his rock solid dependability, and his protection of them like a place of refuge. The Psalms celebrate God as "my rock, my salvation, my refuge" who defeats my enemies (Ps 18:46; 31:2–3; 71:3), "my salvation" who guides me into all truth (Ps 25:5), "my salvation" who is trustworthy and praiseworthy (Ps 18:2; 65:5; 89:27; 95:1), and the one who forgives sins (Ps 79:9). The people of Judah are no better than the Israelites (Isa 17:8) who failed to pay attention to their Creator.

---

[183] הַחֹרֶשׁ, "the woods," is connected to הַחִוִּי, "the Hivite," but the words are not spelled the same, while הָאָמִיר, "the summit," is much closer to the spelling of הָאֱמֹרִי, "the Amorite."

[184] הָאָמִיר refers to something at "the top, summit" rather than "undergrowth" as in NIV.

[185] Oswalt, *Isaiah 1–39*, 353, connects these to places of pagan worship rather than "strong cities." This gives greater continuity with 17:10–11, but there is no evidence that the Israelites had abandoned these high places during this period. Ahaz was a strong supporter of Baalism (2 Kgs 16:1–5).

[186] Watts, *Isaiah 1–33*, 241–42. Wildberger, *Isaiah 13–27*, 161 and 181, thinks vv. 10–11 were originally addressed to Jerusalem, but the redactor thought they referred to the Northern Kingdom.

[187] שָׁכַחַתְּ, "you have forgotten," is second feminine singular, referring to Judah.

Instead, what happened in Judah is pictured as a person (17:11) (a) planting various plants, including foreign ones; (b) caring for the plants; but (c) at
harvest time having nothing but grief and incurable pain. H. Ewald was the first
person to connect these verses to the Greek Adonis religious cult by interpreting the "foreign, imported" thing (NIV "imported vines") as a foreign god,
rather than an imported foreign plant.[188] This act was then connected to other
condemnations of pagan worship in gardens (1:29; 65:3; 66:17). Because these
plants and gods of fertility will soon die and become nothing, they are of no
help in time of need (17:11).

Two other approaches are more attractive: (a) this could be a literal description of God's curse on the produce of the land of Judah, comparable to the
covenant curses in Deut 27–28; or (b) the prophet could be playing with the
same images used in the parable of the vineyard in 5:1–7. With these last two
approaches the results are the same; failure and hopelessness awaits those who
forget God. Long ago God warned his people to remember who he was and
what he has done for them in the past, because he remembers and will judge
people according to what they have done for him.[189] The application that Oswalt makes fits what the prophet says: "If God has touched my life, yet my life
is not different, then I have not perceived the implications of that touch, and it
is in fact void of significance (1 Cor 11:24–29; Gal 3:1–5)."[190]

(2) God Will Rebuke the Raging Nations (17:12–14)

> [12]Oh, the raging of many nations—
>   they rage like the raging sea!
>   Oh, the uproar of the peoples—
>   they roar like the roaring of great waters!
> [13]Although the peoples roar like the roar of surging waters,
>   when he rebukes them they flee far away,
>   driven before the wind like chaff on the hills,
>   like tumbleweed before a gale.
> [14]In the evening, sudden terror!
>   Before the morning, they are gone!
>   This is the portion of those who loot us,
>   the lot of those who plunder us.

---

[188] H. Ewald, *Die Propheten des Alten Bundes*, I (1867), 364, knew that the Greeks planted
little gardens in vases, bowls, or small boxes. The plants reminded the people of the fertility that
the gods produced, which was followed by the death of the plant (Plato, *Phaedrus*, 276). A similar
kind of mythical fertility cycle represented other fertility religions: the Baal and Mot struggle at
Ugarit, the Osiris myths in Egypt, and the Tammuz cult in Babylon. Wildberger, *Isaiah 13–27*,
182–83, thinks a connection with the Baal religion is more likely than the Greek Adonis cult.

[189] B. S. Childs, *Memory and Tradition in Israel* (Naperville: Allenson, 1962). In an era when
few people had access to written texts of Scripture, drawing on memory was the only way people
had access to what God commanded in the covenant documents. Encouragements to remember are
emphasized in Deut 5:15; 6:12; 7:18; 8:2,11,18; 9:7,27; 15:15; 16:2,3; 24:9,17,18,22; 32:7.

[190] Oswalt, *Isaiah 1–39*, 353, believes the significance of God's acts on their behalf was lost
because the people did not trust God.

The abrupt break in the flow of thought in 17:12 is signaled by (a) the exclamation *hôy* ("alas, woe, oh"), (b) a change of topic from Damascus, Israel, and Judah to many roaring nations, and (c) a reference to a fulfillment many years later (probably 701 BC). Nevertheless, this new paragraph still does relate to Judah (the "us' in the phrase "those who plunder us") and appears be a commentary on the "incurable pain" (17:11) that will cause the harvest "to be as nothing" for the people of Judah. Although the initial *hôy* can introduce a woe oracle that laments a nation's death, there is no lamenting here. Instead, 17:13–14 offer hope to Isaiah's audience because those who will plunder Judah will disappear when God rebukes (*gāyar*) them. Thus the prophet is calling on the people of Judah to trust God for protection in their military conflicts, for the nations (probably Assyria) will attack them and then later God will defeat the nations.

In 17:12 some nation is being attacked by a great hoard of people that make an enraged roaring[191] sound like thunder, like a raging sea (Jer 6:23; 50:42). Earlier in 8:7–8 Isaiah spoke of a nation (Assyria) as a flood that would overflow Judah, and in 5:29–30 he compares the coming of enemy troops (Assyria) with the sound of lions. Here he focuses on the terrible frightening sound of their bloodthirsty screams as they go on the attack.

But suddenly vv. 13b–14 paint a very different picture, for he (presumably God) will rebuke these forces and then this multinational military force will turn into useless chaff or rootless tumbleweed.[192] The enemy forces will melt away; having no substance or worth, they will be completely dispersed as if blown by the wind. The terror in the evening that will cause their dispersal in the morning (17:14) is left unexplained, but this prophecy fits the night when an angel struck dead 185,000 Assyrian troops who were attempting to plunder Jerusalem in 701 BC (37:36–37). In the morning the Assyrian king Sennacherib and the few troops left alive quickly departed and headed back to Nineveh. This paragraph presents a dramatic contrast with the preceding verses about the utter destruction of everything in Judah because the nation forgot God (17:9–11). Although defeat will come for Damascus and Israel (17:3–11), after Judah is initially attacked (17:9) God will miraculously demonstrate his protection of his people and the city of Jerusalem by defeating the roaring nation of Assyria. In this message Isaiah's audience heard both the frightful expectation of a terrible war and the wonderful hope of divine deliverance at

---

[191] יֶהֱמָיוּן, "they will thunder, rage," is third masculine plural with a *nun paragogic* at the end (GKC § 47m). "They will roar" in 12 b and 13a have the same *nun peragogic* at the end.

[192] Kaiser, *Isaiah 13–39*, 88, interprets this rebuke as God's conquest of the sea and chaos, an idea developed in comparison with Baal's defeat of the sea god Yam, an idea hinted at in Pss 46, 48, and 76. For an evangelical treatment of this theme, see J. Oswalt, "The Myth of the Dragon and Old Testament Faith," *EvQ* 49 (1977): 163–72, who finds the OT drawing on some of these widespread ideas, though rejecting the theology of those myths. In this case it seems that the prophet is just using common poetic imagery of war, so there is no need to suggest that he is borrowing from ancient mythology.

some point in the battle. Now they must respond by trusting God's promise to
deliver them from their enemy.

(3) Cush Will Honor God for Destroying Its Enemies (18:1–7)

> [1]Woe to the land of whirring wings
>   along the rivers of Cush,
> [2]which sends envoys by sea
>   in papyrus boats over the water.
>
> Go, swift messengers,
> to a people tall and smooth-skinned,
>   to a people feared far and wide,
> an aggressive nation of strange speech,
>   whose land is divided by rivers.
>
> [3]All you people of the world,
>   you who live on the earth,
> when a banner is raised on the mountains,
>   you will see it,
> and when a trumpet sounds,
>   you will hear it.
> [4]This is what the LORD says to me:
>   "I will remain quiet and will look on from my dwelling place,
> like shimmering heat in the sunshine,
>   like a cloud of dew in the heat of harvest."
> [5]For, before the harvest, when the blossom is gone
>   and the flower becomes a ripening grape,
> he will cut off the shoots with pruning knives,
>   and cut down and take away the spreading branches.
> [6]They will all be left to the mountain birds of prey
>   and to the wild animals;
> the birds will feed on them all summer,
> the wild animals all winter.
>
> [7]At that time gifts will be brought to the LORD Almighty
>
> from a people tall and smooth-skinned,
>   from a people feared far and wide,
> an aggressive nation of strange speech,
>   whose land is divided by rivers—

the gifts will be brought to Mount Zion, the place of the Name of the LORD Almighty.

The last paragraph of this section begins with another exclamation *hôy*
("alas, woe, oh") parallel to the previous paragraph (17:12).[193] This exclama-

---

[193] Seitz, *Isaiah 1–39,* 143, puts 18:1–20:6 together as a unit and connects them all to the Assyrian attack on Philistia in 711 BC based on the historical data supplied in 20:1–2. He interprets the downfall of the coastlands in 20:6 as a reference back to Cush in chap. 18. A Niccacci, "Isa-

tion relates to Cush, which is frequently associated with people living in the south of Egypt in the general area of Nubia, Sudan, or Ethiopia. As early as 732 BC the Nubian Pi'ankhi began to take control of the northern delta area of Egypt to solidify the power of a new dynasty from Cush. When his successor Shabaka came to power around 716 BC, he took control of Upper Egypt and had contacts with Judah and Philistia when the Assyrians attacked Palestine in 713–11 and 703–701 BC.[194] This message and 17:12–14 probably came shortly before one of these Assyrian invasions.

There are three major ways that commentators have interpreted the message in 18:1–6. This diversity is caused by uncertainties. (a) Who were the tall messengers in 18:2? (b) Where were the messengers sent? (c) What did the message of God to these messengers mean in 18:4–6? (d) How should one understand the gifts that the people will bring to Mt Zion in 18:7?

Three main approaches to these problems are proposed. (a) The tall and smooth messengers come from God's divine council to warn all the nations of God's impending judgment from Babylon, after which the "bird of prey" (Cyrus) will bring judgment on Babylon, and many nations will bring gifts to Zion.[195] (b) The tall and smooth messengers are from Cush, but Judah will send them to Assyria to try to arrange peaceful conditions between Assyria and Cush so that Assyria would not interfere when Shabaka tried to take over Lower Egypt. The gifts in 18:7 would be Jerusalem's reward for their loyalty to Assyria.[196] (c) The messengers are sent to Cush to announce God's plan to destroy an unnamed nation (possibly Egypt in light of 20:1–6, or more likely Assyria in light of 17:12–14), so Cush should honor God along with the other nations (cf. 2:1–4). The analysis of the text below will provide the most support for the third interpretation. Of course any interpretation has to keep in mind that whatever is said in this message is primarily for the benefit of influencing Isaiah's audience in Judah, not these foreign nations.

---

iah XVIII–XX from an Egyptological Perspective," *VT* 48 (1998): 214–38, connects chap. 18 to events around 720 BC, chap. 19 to unrest during the reign of Piankhi just after 720 BC, and chap. 20 to 712 BC, but his identification of several verses with specific events in these periods is highly speculative.

[194] Kissane, *Isaiah,* 195, connects the events in chap. 18 with Sargon's attack on Philistia in 711 B. C, the same events described in 20:1–6. Wildberger, *Isaiah 13–27,* 212–216, makes stronger arguments for dating this to 701 BC.

[195] Seitz, *Isaiah 1–39,* 145–49, has an ingenious approach based on material from the second half of Isaiah, but it is very unlikely that Isaiah's audience would make all these symbolic connections, especially if this oracle was delivered before those messages. W. Janzen, *Mourning Cry and Woe Oracle,* BZAW (Berlin: de Grutyer, 1972), 60–62, considers them divine messengers.

[196] Watts, *Isaiah 1–33,* 245–46, finds historical evidence of a peaceful relationship between Egypt and Assyria in 712 BC when Egypt extradited to Assyria Iamani the king of Ashdod who had fled to Egypt for protection. W. Janzen, *Mourning Cry,* 60–62, believes the messengers were going to Assyria. Although these verses relate to Assyria, the tall and smooth messengers are from Cush and go to Cush, not Assyria.

The paragraph can be divided into three subparagraphs:

Instructions for messengers of Cush   18:1–3
God's message for Cush   18:4–6
Cush will honor God in Jerusalem   18:7

18:1–3 A second exclamation of "woe, alas" (*hôy*) signals the beginning
of this new paragraph concerning envoys from Cush. The parallelism of this
woe oracle with the preceding one in 17:12 suggests that the prophecy about
Cush may be related to the prophecy about the defeat of Assyria in 17:12–14.
The description of Cush as a land of "whirling, buzzing wings" probably refers
to the tsetse fly or the winged beetle.[197] These messengers have traveled in
papyrus boats[198] over long distances to arrive in Jerusalem, but the text never
reveals the message they delivered to the leaders in Jerusalem. Consequently,
no one knows what this meeting was about. The text is totally silent about the
political relationship (past, present, or future) between Judah and Cush, so it
is somewhat dangerous to read into the text political intrigue and plots that
are never mentioned, but what other reason would cause the Cushites to visit
Jerusalem?

This prophetic oracle describes how the Cushite messengers[199] are commanded to go and deliver (18:2) an important message.[200] The message was not
delivered to the Assyrians[201] but to the people of Cush (the "tall and smooth-
skinned" people[202]) who were feared because of their recent conquest of Upper Egypt and their strength to conquer.[203] All the nations on earth, including

---

[197] M. Lubetski, "Beetlemania of Bygone Times." *JSOT* 91 (2000): 3–26, argues that this word
refers to the winged beetle because it was a well-known symbol of Egypt. The Old Greek and Targum refer to "boats, ships" because there is an Aramaic word צְלָצַל that means "ship."

[198] גֹּמֶא, "papyrus," is a Egyptian loan word, coming from *qm'*. The "vessels of papyrus" were
not ships but more like small rafts made by binding papyrus reeds together.

[199] Since nothing new is added to suggest that these people are divine messengers, the most
natural reading implies that the הַשֹּׁלֵחַ, "the one sent," by sea (v. 2) is a collective reference to the
messengers being sent (v. 3).

[200] Motyer, *The Prophecy of Isaiah*, 162, believes v. 2b is the message the envoys were given in
Egypt, which they would speak to foreign courts. Verse 3 is Isaiah's message to them and the rest
of the world. This approach is problematic because there is no message in v. 2; instead, messengers
are commanded to "go . . . to a tall people," the people in Cush.

[201] Hayes and Irvine, *Isaiah*, 254–55, believe the messengers were not Ethiopian ambassadors,
but Isaiah sent messengers to Assyria to complain (18:3) that the Ethiopians were involved in
intrigue.

[202] מֹרָט is a *pual* participle with the two מ's assimilated from מְמֹרָט. It refers to not having
hair, being bald, or having hair plucked out; thus they have "smooth skin."

[203] קַו־קָו could be translated "line line" (from "measuring line") similar to 28:10 קַו לָקָו, "line
by line, rule by rule." NIV takes it to mean "strange speech," but the oral reading of the *Qere* and
1QIsaᵃ have קוֹקוֹ meaning "strength, power," which makes more sense. Blenkinsopp, *Isaiah 1–39*,
310, thinks that Isaiah is being sarcastic and does not really believe that the Cushites are strong and
fearful, so he is rejecting any political negotiations between Judah and Cush. This reads too much
into the text. On the other hand, Goldingay, *Isaiah*, 116, states that these Cushite messengers were
sent "to a people feared far and wide" in 18:2, that is, to the Assyrians.

Isaiah's audience in Jerusalem, are called to pay attention because something important will happen when a banner is raised and a trumpet blown (18:3). This will be a sign that God is at work. It sounds like war (11:10; 13:2; Jer 51:27) but Isaiah does not yet say who will declare war against whom. Apparently the words of the Lord in 18:4–6 are meant to explain these coming events.

18:4–6 In these verses God reveals to Isaiah what will happen. First, God explains his presence (18:4) and his role (18:5), then he describes what will happen to his enemies (18:6). These factors are discussed using agricultural metaphors (similar to the judgment in 17:11), but the specific enemy is not identified by name. If this woe oracle is read as being against the same nation mentioned in 17:12–14, it is probably about the roaring enemy that will be cut off in one night, meaning the Assyrians, the dominant power in the ancient Near East at that time.

Gray thinks God assumes a position of "unconcerned inactivity, but observation free from anxiety" in 18:4,[204] but any understanding of these metaphors about God must be based on the comparative analogy of the heat and dew in the second half of the verse. God is fearlessly (calm is the absence of fear in 7:4) watching over what is happening "in" (not "from" as in NIV) his heavenly dwelling place. Wildberger warns that this description of God "is certainly no sign of weakness or a lack of interest in the affairs of the world, but expresses Yahweh's indisputable superiority."[205] But how is his watching like "simmering heat," and how is a "cloud of dew" a sign of sovereignty? The heat at harvest time is intense, overpowering, and will not let one out of its oppressive grip, while the cloud of moisture and humidity smothers the land with dew. These analogies do not describe God as distant and uninvolved, but intensely present everywhere (like the heat and humidity) as he sovereignly watches over what is happening.

At just the right moment (18:5) when it is time (like the most appropriate time to harvest a crop) God will act and cut off and remove his enemies (like a vine dresser prunes his vines of unwanted sucker branches). The branches, leaves, and fruit that were cut off will be left to the birds and wild animals to consume, a picture that fits not only the imagery of plants, but also the leaving of dead soldiers on the battlefield for the wild animals to eat (18:6; cf. Jer 7:33; Ezek 39:17–20). This message of God's destruction of his enemy (probably the Assyrians) would be a positive message to both the people of Cush and Judah.

18:7 In the conclusion, the oracle turns away from the talk of war to address the topic of worship. Once God has defeated his enemies, people from Cush (those tall people with smooth skin, as in 18:2) will bring gifts to God

---

[204] Gray, *Isaiah 1–27,* 313. Clements, *Isaiah 1–39,*165, interprets this to mean that God will not favor Assyria or Ethiopia; therefore, Hezekiah should not join either in a coalition.

[205] Wildberger, *Isaiah 13–27,* 220.

in Mount Zion,[206] a sign of their loyalty and desire to honor God for destroy-ing their enemy. This is consistent with the idea that nations will stream to Zion (2:1–5), that the nations will gather (including Cush) and the remnant of his people when the "root from Jesse will stand as a banner for the peoples" (11:10–11), and that the news that nations will come to Jerusalem (14:1–3). Later, Isaiah prophesies that people from Cush and the tall Sabeans will bring products from Egypt to Zion, bow down, and confess that there is no other God except Israel's God (cf. 45:14; 55:3–5; 49:7; 60:4–11). This is another word of encouragement and hope to Isaiah's audience, for one day many nations will recognize the power and authority of God (cf. 2:1–5; 19:18–25).

THEOLOGICAL IMPLICATIONS. These two chapters function both as warnings and encouragements to Isaiah's audience in Judah. His audience needs to realize that the northern nation of Israel will be devastated because it did not carefully pay attention to the Holy One of Israel, her Maker. Instead Is-rael paid attention to man-made gods and religious ritual at her temples (17:7–8). Consequently, Israel will be punished and her fortified cities destroyed (17:3). The central point that Isaiah makes in 17:9–11 is that Judah is actually not much better than Israel, because she has also forgotten God, her Savior, her Rock, and her Refuge. Thus a similar destiny is coming (17:9) if the people of Judah do not change. Therefore, by implication Judah needs to return to God and trust in her Savior. Imbedded in this warning are two theological principles that apply to every nation. First, people should not allow their attention to be sidetracked to focus on human accomplishments, religious ritual, or man-made theological idols, for that will bring God's judgment. Second, people should pay attention to God their Creator, remember that he is holy, is able to save them, and can protect them in times of trouble. No one today should repeat the mistakes of Israel and Judah, unless they want to suffer the same fate.

Three words of encouragement are provided in order to motivate the audi-ence in Judah to dare to trust God in their difficult military situation. (a) Earlier prophecies indicated that God would defeat Judah's enemies in the Syro-Ephra-imite War (17:1–6), but Ahaz refused to trust God. Judah should not make this same mistake but should put her trust in God for deliverance (7:4–9). (b) God will defeat many roaring nations (Assyria) in one night and leave their bodies for the birds to eat (17:14; 18:5–6; cf. 37:36); therefore, the people of Judah should trust God and not fear Assyria. (c) In the end, many foreign people will come to worship God in Jerusalem; therefore, Judah should realize what a great God they worship and honor their holy God in Mount Zion. The evidence is clear: God can deliver individuals and nations from those who oppose them,

---

[206] The text does not clearly say who will bring the gift because the "from" in the NIV is not in the Hb., but the reference to a "people" in the next line implies the gifts were brought by them. Later in the verse מֵעַם, "from a people," is used in the phrase "from a people feared." The NIV expands its reading of the last clause by adding, "the gifts will be brought" (missing in Hb.) to help make sense of the phrase "to the place of the Name of the LORD of Hosts—Mount Zion."

but there is no promise to take away all times of persecution or oppression. Believers need to trust him and honor him, because he is God and he sovereignly controls the destiny of every nation and every person on earth.

5. God's Plans for Egypt (19:1–20:6)

The next message announces a new "oracle/burden" (19:1), indicating that this message about Egypt was considered separate from the material about Cush in 18:1–7. The material within these chapters describes both the initial ruin of Egypt as well as God's miraculous deliverance of Egypt in the future (19:16–25). The last portion of this unit contains Isaiah's sign-act that warns the people of Judah not to trust in Egypt (20:1–6). This lesson comes from the experience of the people of Ashdod who suffered after the Assyrian king Sargon II attacked Philistia in 711 BC. Although it is tempting to interpret these chapters in light of Isaiah's warning against alliances with Egypt in chaps. 30–31, those chapters relate to different events just before 701 BC when Sennacherib attacked Jerusalem. There may indeed be some verbal parallels between these two chapters (20:3; 30:2) but they are not the same event. Therefore, since the prophet spoke chaps. 30–31 around ten years after chaps. 19–20, the situation that arose out of these later events should not be read into the present context.

HISTORICAL SETTING.   The historical setting in Egypt depicts a time of civil war (19:2) followed by the rule of a "cruel master" who is a "fierce king" (19:4). These events could be related to Sargon's attack on the Philistine city of Ashdod in 714–711 BC (20:1) and the subsequent shaming of Egypt (20:3–4), but the interpreter does not know if the events in chap. 20 provide the background for chap. 19 too. Several possible settings are hypothesized. Sweeney connects 19:1–15 to the revolt of Israel against the Assyrians in 724–721 BC when Israel appealed to Egypt for help (2 Kgs 14:4; Hos 7:11; 12:1) because at that time there was internal division within Egypt and because the fulfillment of the prophecy fits the Assyrian defeat of Egypt at Raphia in 720 BC.[207] Isaiah 20:1–6 is related to a later date when Sargon attacked the Philistine city of Ashdod around 711 BC. Watts points to a date around 716–12 BC when the Ethiopian Shabaka forcibly gained control over Egypt (he is the "fierce king"). Wildberger looks to the same era, but believes this passage refers to the unrest in Egypt caused by the Egyptian ruler Osorkan IV. In his view the Assyrian king Sargon is the "fierce king" in 19:4.[208] Any of these interpretations could

---

[207] Sweeney, *Isaiah 1–39*, 270–75, proposes this as the background for the oracle because at this time more than one dynasty was vying for control of Egypt. He places 19:16–25 in the reign of Manasseh when the Assyrian king Esarhaddon defeated Egypt, and believes 20:1–6 is describing the Philistine revolt in 713–711 BC. Nevertheless, he oddly maintains that this chapter was written in the time of Josiah shortly after 627 BC.

[208] Wildberger, *Isaiah 13–27*, 238–39, suggests that Sargon is the one making a foreign takeover, while Watts, *Isaiah 1–33*, 253 treats the Ethiopian Shabaka as a foreigner within upper Egypt. Attempts to place this in the Persian period of Artaxerxes III (343 BC) or the Greek period of

fit most of the data; but unfortunately, Isaiah does not name the kings he refers to, so the exact setting is unknown. The text describes four different kings who were trying to control Egypt around 720–711 BC, the Ethiopian Shabaka finally asserting his harsh rule to gain control over the nation.

STRUCTURE.   The structure of 19:1–20:6 is clearly marked. In 19:1–15 a poetic description of three signs predicts the collapse of Egypt because the Egyptian gods were impotent. "Declares the Lord, the LORD Almighty" in 19:4 marks the end of the first subparagraph, while *'ak* ("surely," omitted in NIV) at the beginning of 19:11 introduces the last subparagraph. A prose narrative in 19:16–25 explains what will happen in Egypt "in that day" (see vv. 16,18,19,23,24), focusing mainly on the conversion of the Egyptians and their worship of Israel's God. The final narrative segment (20:1–6) records Isaiah's sign-act of walking around naked to illustrate the foolishness of relying on some other nation instead of relying on God. These chapters can be outlined as follows:

God will defeat Egypt and her gods	19:1–15
Civil war	1–4
Economic disaster	5–10
Poor leadership	11–15
God will save Egypt; they will worship God	19:16–25
Egypt's trials	16–17
God's deliverance, Egypt's revival	18–22
Egypt and Assyria will Worship God	23–25
Isaiah's nakedness symbolizes Egypt's defeat	20:1–6

These prophecies addressed people in Judah in order to motivate the Hebrew leaders not to rely on Egypt as the Philistines did. It makes no sense to look to Egypt for help because Egypt's actions demonstrate that it will not defend other nations against the Assyrians (20:1–6), the nation of Egypt is headed for disaster and ruin (19:1–15), and eventually both Egypt and Assyria will come to the place where they will worship the God of Judah (19:16–25). This was an important lesson for the leaders of Judah to learn because later they will be tempted to trust in Egypt when the Assyrians attack Judah (cf. chaps. 30–31). This is a lesson that modern nations need to pay attention to as well because alliances do not assure success; God alone controls all nations, and he alone brings victory in war.

(1) God Will Defeat Egypt and Her Gods (19:1–15)

[1]An oracle concerning Egypt:

> See, the LORD rides on a swift cloud
> and is coming to Egypt.

Antiochus III (160 BC) make no sense in this context (Kaiser, *Isaiah 13–39*, 99–100).

The idols of Egypt tremble before him,
  and the hearts of the Egyptians melt within them.

²"I will stir up Egyptian against Egyptian—
  brother will fight against brother,
  neighbor against neighbor,
  city against city,
  kingdom against kingdom.
³The Egyptians will lose heart,
  and I will bring their plans to nothing;
 they will consult the idols and the spirits of the dead,
  the mediums and the spiritists.
⁴I will hand the Egyptians over
  to the power of a cruel master,
 and a fierce king will rule over them,"
  declares the Lord, the LORD Almighty.

⁵The waters of the river will dry up,
  and the riverbed will be parched and dry.
⁶The canals will stink;
  the streams of Egypt will dwindle and dry up.
 The reeds and rushes will wither,
⁷   also the plants along the Nile,
  at the mouth of the river.
 Every sown field along the Nile
  will become parched, will blow away and be no more.
⁸The fishermen will groan and lament,
  all who cast hooks into the Nile;
 those who throw nets on the water
  will pine away.
⁹Those who work with combed flax will despair,
  the weavers of fine linen will lose hope.
¹⁰The workers in cloth will be dejected,
  and all the wage earners will be sick at heart.

¹¹The officials of Zoan are nothing but fools;
  the wise counselors of Pharaoh give senseless advice.
 How can you say to Pharaoh,
  "I am one of the wise men,
  a disciple of the ancient kings"?

¹²Where are your wise men now?
  Let them show you and make known
 what the LORD Almighty
  has planned against Egypt.
¹³The officials of Zoan have become fools,
  the leaders of Memphis are deceived;
 the cornerstones of her peoples
  have led Egypt astray.

> [14] **The Lord has poured into them**
>   **a spirit of dizziness;**
>   **they make Egypt stagger in all that she does,**
>   **as a drunkard staggers around in his vomit.**
> [15] **There is nothing Egypt can do—**
>   **head or tail, palm branch or reed.**

19:1–4 The first subparagraph includes the superscription identifying this section as a *maśśā'* ("oracle") about Egypt (v. 1a), God's confrontation of the gods of Egypt (v. 1b), and God's decimation of Egypt through civil war (vv. 2–4).

The superscription follows the standard pattern and divides the discussion of Cush in 18:1–7 from these messages about Egypt in chaps. 19–20. The oracle itself begins with an exclamation, "See, Behold," to draw attention to the sudden appearance of God in Egypt riding on a swift cloud (cf. Ps 18:10; 68:33; 104:3).[209] This symbolism means that God can move quickly though the heavens to execute his will by granting salvation or judgment. He does not stand immobile like the Egyptian gods and his movement is not limited to one country, for he is able to swiftly move to control any nation under the clouds.

The idols of Egypt, which amount to nothing,[210] will shake and quiver in fear at the presence of a real and powerful divine Being, while the Egyptian people will be astonished, disoriented, and without any strength in the midst of God's presence.[211] Although the main purpose of this chapter is not to attack Egypt's gods, God's sovereign control over politics, the economy, and his ability to confound the wise men demonstrates his superiority, which the Egyptians eventually recognize (19:18–25).

The political situation will deteriorate into civil war, bringing one Egyptian against another. God's act of stirring up this trouble (19:3) does not refer to the Assyrian attack of Sargon, but the period when four different dynasties struggled to take control of the nation a few years before 711 BC. This violence and hopeless fighting will get so bad that the spirits of the Egyptian people "will be empty" (*nābqâ*, NIV "lose heart" in 19:3). Their dreams of greatness, their political plans to control the world, and their hopes for a basic life of security and peace will disappear because God will "swallow"[212] them up in his plans and confound them. As in 8:10 and 30:1, man's plans and strategies will not stand when God intervenes because he has already determined his own plans for the whole world (cf. 14:24–27). The Egyptians will learn that what God

---

[209] In Ugaritic literature Baal, the god of the storm and rain, was also called the one who rides the clouds.

[210] אֱלִילִים, "idols," literally means "nothing," a fitting evaluation of the power and reality of the Egyptian idols.

[211] בְּקִרְבּוֹ, "in the midst of it," could mean that the heart melts within them, but "in his midst" is an even better translation. This creates a better parallel with "before him" in the line above.

[212] אֲבַלֵּעַ means either "I will swallow up, engulf, devour" or "I will confound, confuse, destroy."

plans happens! The Egyptians will search for help and answers from Egyptian idols, speak to the dead, and inquire of fortunetellers, but nothing will help. Instead of gaining a false hope, God will "stop"[213] the Egyptians through the power (lit. "hand") of a harsh overlord.[214] The text does not identify this strong king, but the Ethiopian Shabaka did impose his will over Egypt around 715 BC to end a period of civil war in Egypt. If Isaiah's audience in Judah was considering some sort of alliance with Egypt or thinking that Egypt might strengthen their hand in dealing with the Assyrians, Isaiah's news of God's devastating plans for Egypt demonstrates that Egyptian assistance would not help Judah.

19:5–10 The second paragraph focuses on a drought that will dry up the Nile and ruin the Egyptian economy. God's role in accomplishing this is not emphasized; instead, the attention is on the devastating effect this drought will have on everyone in the nation. Most of Egypt is a desert except a few fields along the Nile and the broad fertile delta area near the mouth of the Nile. Egyptian life depends on the yearly flooding of the Nile to provide fresh soil for the fields and water to grow the crops. If the "waters of the sea" (NIV has "waters of the river") refers to the sea created by the flooding Nile River, then one can comprehend how devastating this dry period will be. If there will be no flowing water, the irrigation canals in the Nile delta will stink[215] because of the stagnant water and dead fish. Plant life, water reeds, and crops that depend on irrigation in the lush Delta area will dry up, be parched by the hot sun, and cease to exist (19:6–7).[216] Of course if there is no flowing water the fish will soon die, leaving nothing for the fishermen to catch with their nets or hooks (19:8). This will cause even more economic disaster and hunger. Finally, in 19:9–10 the author shows how this drought will affect the industry of making clothes. The farmers who raise the flax and the weavers[217] that comb the fine

---

[213] וְסַכַּרְתִּי, "and I will stop," refers to stopping of water in Gen 8:2 and stopping liars from speaking in Isa 63:12 (the only other two places the root is used). NIV "I will hand over" in 19:4 is rather periphrastic.

[214] אֲדֹנִים, "lord," is a plural form, not because there were many overlords over Egypt. The plural is probably a plural of majesty meaning a "great overlord" (GKC § 124i).

[215] וְהֶאֶזְנִיחוּ, "and they will stink," is spelled with an extra א that is not found in 1QIsaᵃ. GKC § 19m, 53g, refers to this as an *aleph prostheticum* that was added to aid in the pronunciation of the word.

[216] The "Prophecy of Nefu-rohu" (*ANET*, 445) refers to a similar situation when a new king will come to power in Egypt to rescue it from bad times. The disaster that will hit Egypt is described as: "The rivers of Egypt are empty, (so that) the water is crossed on foot."

[217] שְׁתֹתֶיהָ is problematic and could be derived from שָׁת, "pillar," so one gets "her pillars," or from שָׁתָה, "drink," so one can translate it "her drunks," or from שְׁתִי, "weaver," yielding "her weavers." Weaving fits the context of 19:9. I. Eitan, "An Egyptian Loan Word in Is 19," *JQR* 15 (1924/1925): 419–22, found several Egyptian loan words in the Bible (possibly coming through the Coptic language of Egypt), including *štit*, "weaver," which is similar to the Hb. שְׁתִיהָ, "her weaver" (19:10), and the Akkadian *šatu*, "weave." The verse ends with the noun חֹרִי, "linen," but one would expect a verb in the second line parallel to וּבֹשׁ, "and they will be ashamed." 1QIsaᵃ has the verbal form חוֹרוּ, "they will be white, pale" (a minimal change of י to ו), which is followed in NASB, NIV, HCSB, though Watts, *Isaiah 1–33*, 251, rejects it because the Masoretic texts makes

linen into cloth will despair because of this drought. With no water, there will be no flax, no clothes, no work, no income, and no way to make a living. This economic disaster will impact those who earn an hourly wage because there will be no work for them to do; everyone will be despondent and grieving. This natural disaster pictures the breakdown of Egyptian society (19:2–4); nature, the economy, politics, and the gods are in irrational disorder. The land has no *maat*, "order," and the people have no hope. The prophet does not weep over Egypt; he merely exposes the weakness of Egypt.

19:11–15 This paragraph ridicules and rebukes the leaders of Egypt, particularly the wise men and the king who guide the political direction of the nation. These are the leaders of the nation who could provide some hope for the people. The repetition of words like "wise" draws attention to the duties of the princes, the king, the king's counselors, leaders, and officials. The leaders claim, "I am one of the wise men" (19:11), "but" (*'ak*, missing from the beginning of 19:11 in NIV) in contrast to what one would think, these men are really fools and provide senseless advice from the capital (Zoan or Tanis), so how can they brag about their wisdom (19:10–11)? With a taunt in his voice, the prophet asks these wise sages to reveal God's plan for Egypt in the future (19:12). These people were supposed to provide the foundation (they are the "cornerstone," *pinnat*) for interpreting reality for the rest of society, but they did not have any insight into the plans of God. Because their idols and mediums are nothing (19:3), their deceptive ways will become known as they lead their people astray (19:13). Such is the nature of every man's limited perspective. Without access to God's wisdom and plan, people are left confused and misguided. Fearing God and depending on his wisdom is where every wise person must start (Prov 1:7).

How has this stupidity overcome Egypt? Using imagery of drunkenness (19:14), the prophet pictures God as "mixing, brewing" (*māsāk*; NIV "poured") a confusing and distorting concoction that makes the Egyptian wise men disoriented in their spirits. They stagger about not knowing what direction to go; like shameful drunks, they will fall down in their own vomit. In this state there is nothing anyone can do to help them.[218]

This passage presents an astonishingly harsh picture about what will become of the renowned kingdom of Egypt and her leaders. There is no weeping about Egypt's fall and no explicit advice to Isaiah's audience in Judah, so it is difficult to know what specific point Isaiah was trying to impress on his listeners in Jerusalem. Since Judah was weak and threatened by Assyria, she was tempted to rely on Egypt for help on several occasions. This may be

---

sense as it is. S. Talmon, "DSIa as a Witness to Ancient Exegesis of the Book of Isaiah," in *Qumran and the History of the Biblical Text* (ed. F. M. Cross and S. Talmon; Cambridge: Harvard University, 1975), 122–123, argues in favor of the reading in the scroll.

[218] "Head or tail, palm branch or reed" might be using the same imagery as 9:14–15 where the elder and prominent men were the head and the prophet was the tail.

another situation where some in Jerusalem were thinking about asking Egypt for assistance. By proclaiming this prophecy about the future of Egypt's demise, Isaiah did not need to say anything more because its application was obvious. The royal court officials in Judah would know that Egypt could not provide any solid help for them because Egypt itself was about to fall apart. In addition, the audience learned that the only hope for Judah was for them to be informed about God's plan for each nation. God's wisdom is not deceptive and his plans are always fulfilled, so every nation has the choice to either walk in the light of God's wisdom or to follow the foolish ideas that appear to be wise in man's eyes.

(2) God Will Save Egypt; Egyptians Will Worship God (19:16–25)

[16]**In that day the Egyptians will be like women. They will shudder with fear at the uplifted hand that the LORD Almighty raises against them.** [17]**And the land of Judah will bring terror to the Egyptians; everyone to whom Judah is mentioned will be terrified, because of what the LORD Almighty is planning against them.**

[18]**In that day five cities in Egypt will speak the language of Canaan and swear allegiance to the LORD Almighty. One of them will be called the City of Destruction.**

[19]**In that day there will be an altar to the LORD in the heart of Egypt, and a monument to the LORD at its border.** [20]**It will be a sign and witness to the LORD Almighty in the land of Egypt. When they cry out to the LORD because of their oppressors, he will send them a savior and defender, and he will rescue them.** [21]**So the LORD will make himself known to the Egyptians, and in that day they will acknowledge the LORD. They will worship with sacrifices and grain offerings; they will make vows to the LORD and keep them.** [22]**The LORD will strike Egypt with a plague; he will strike them and heal them. They will turn to the LORD, and he will respond to their pleas and heal them.**

[23]**In that day there will be a highway from Egypt to Assyria. The Assyrians will go to Egypt and the Egyptians to Assyria. The Egyptians and Assyrians will worship together.** [24]**In that day Israel will be the third, along with Egypt and Assyria, a blessing on the earth.** [25]**The LORD Almighty will bless them, saying, "Blessed be Egypt my people, Assyria my handiwork, and Israel my inheritance."**

The second half of this chapter contains a series of narrative eschatological promises (19:18–25) about what will happen sometime after Egypt's judgment (19:16–17). The paragraph contains five short "in that day" statements (19:16,18,19,23,24) that outline what God will do against (19:16–17) and for Egypt—including how the Egyptians will positively respond when God delivers them from danger (19:18–25). Some date these salvation promises to the post-exilic period because they believe the five cities in 19:18 refer to the cities where Jews lived after the destruction of Jerusalem in 586 BC (Jer 44:1).[219]

---

[219] Kaiser, *Isaiah 13–39*, 107–110, hypothesizes that this prophecy was written after these Jewish settlements were already established in Egypt. He connects the altar in 19:19 with a temple built at Leontopolis by the high priest Onias IV around 170 BC and relates the "highway" to a peace treaty between the Ptolomies and Seleucids at Apamea in 118 BC. But Leontopolis was not

This argument is weak because the people in Jeremiah 44 did not "swear allegiance to the LORD" as 19:18 requires. History teaches that this great event has not taken place yet, unless one interprets the expansion of the early church into Egypt in the Byzantine era as its fulfillment. This prophecy seems to be pointing to an eschatological event when Jews and Muslims throughout the Middle East will join God's people in worshiping Yahweh as one community of believers. This will finally solve the Middle East crisis and bring real lasting peace among these nations.

19:16–17 The first "in that day" promise goes beyond anything mentioned in 19:1–15, though it continues the theme of Egypt's judgment in 19:1–15. Now the Egyptian's are compared to fearful shuddering women[220] (cf. Jer 51:30; Nah 3:13) rather than strong, valiant, and fearless soldiers. The reason for their fear is the "uplifted"[221] hand of God that was about to punish Egypt (cf. the use of God's hand in 5:25; 9:12,17,21). As the Egyptians stand against God, they will finally realize that they are defenseless and helpless before him. The mighty hand of God is about to strike. The statement that the "land of Judah" will terrify the Egyptians is not a reference to a large army from Judah attacking Egypt.[222] Apparently, the "soil/land of Judah" is a circumlocution for the place where God lives; it is God and his plans that will cause Egypt to be terrified (cf. 19:12). Watts stated, "The news that Yahweh, of Passover fame, has plans for Egypt is reason enough for fear,"[223] but his interpretation seems to add an exodus connection that the text does not explicitly make at this point. When one observes the uplifted hand of God, it is a strong hint about his plans.

Egypt's fear of God also involves a recognition of their own inability to control their future. Learning to fear God has a positive side to it, because it brings the person who fears God to the place where they recognize the power and glory of Almighty God. Pride and self-sufficiency are removed and a humble attitude of submission arises. Thus the threatened punishment of God is not just designed for the purpose of fulfilling the demands of his justice. God's plan is to use his discipline to teach men and nations to fear him as God.

"in the heart/center of Egypt" (19:19) and the Seleucids were not Assyrians.

[220] A. Niccacci, "Isaiah XVIII–XX," 214–37, compares this imagery with a line in the Pi'ankhy Stela (lines 157–58), "you came and ravaged Lower Egypt by reducing the bulls to women." Earlier (line 72) the stela refers to "mighty kings, bull routing bull," so the imagery of Isaiah is very fitting.

[221] תְּנוּפַת (from נוּף) means "to move, swing, shake, wave" (BDB, 631–32). In 11:15 God shook his hand over a river and divided it into seven parts; in 10:15 one raised up his hand and shook his rod to hit someone; in 30:31–32 God will swing his scepter and shatter Assyria.

[222] Hayes and Irvine, *Isaiah*, 263–64, suggest that Judah supplied troops for Sargon II when he defeated Egypt in 720 BC and consequently Egypt was fearful of Judah.

[223] Watts, *Isaiah 1–33*, 255, and Kaiser, *Isaiah 13–39*, 106, find references to exodus events, but it is unlikely that any Egyptians would have any fearful memories of events that took place over 700 years earlier.

19:18 The second "in that day" message announces the beginning of a deeper relationship between God and Egypt, which was part of God's marvelous and surprising plan. Initially things will start slow with people from only five Egyptian cities speaking Hebrew and swearing loyalty to God. These cities are often identified as Memphis (Noph), Migdol, Tahpanhes, Pathros (from Jer 44:1), and the "City of Destruction/Sun"[224] where Jewish people lived after the fall of Jerusalem (cf. Jer 43–44). The existence of a Jewish temple at Elephantine in southern Egypt in the fifth century BC and at Leontopolis around 170 BC[225] is sometimes seen as a fulfillment of these prophecies,[226] but these are misdirected solutions. Isaiah is talking about converts among the Egyptians, not Jews living in Egypt.[227]

Signs that the Egyptians have had a true change of heart are evident because the Egyptians will speak Hebrew, the language of the Old Testament, and they will make oaths of allegiance to the Lord. Like all language groups, the Egyptians were proud of their language, so the move to speak Hebrew would only develop from a deep heart's desire to read and study the Scriptures and to participate in worshiping God. The fact that five cities (particularly Heliopolis, where the sun god Re was worshiped) worship God demonstrates that a large number of Egyptians radically changed and turned to God. Such promises should encourage missionary agencies to send missionaries to Egypt, for they know for certain that many people in Egypt will eventually fear God.

19:19–22 The next "in that day" prophecy describes why the Egyptians will turn to Israel's God and how they will worship him. The building of an altar in the heart of Egypt is surprising because one might expect the Egyptians to go to Jerusalem to worship God (Deut 12). In contrast to this expectation, God allows an Egyptian cultural expression of their relationship to God through their own altar and pillar (this *maṣṣēbâ* is probably a memorial stone). Verse 21 indicates that these objects are a sign and witness of the faith of these people; their existence is an important testimony of their commitment to God and to their unity with those who worshiped in Jerusalem. Many years earlier, the two and one half tribes that lived on the east of the Jordan built an altar as a sign of their faithfulness to God and their unity with the tribes on the western side of the Jordan River (Josh 22), and now here is another example of this

---

[224] "City of Destruction" is an odd name for an Egyptian city, especially when the prophet is referring to people who will be followers of God and he is giving a positive promise of salvation. A number of Hb. MSS, the Aramaic Targum, and 1QIsaᵃ have a slightly different reading: הֶחֶרֶס, "the sun," instead of הַהֶרֶס, "the destruction." The Targum has "Beth-Shemesh," which means "house of the sun," pointing in the same direction. Heliopolis ("city of the sun") was a well-known city, but in other texts it is called אֹן, "On" (Gen 41:50; Ezek 30:17).

[225] Josephus, *Antiquities*, XIII, 65.

[226] Kaiser, *Isaiah 13–39*, 107–109, mentions Alexandria where thousands of Jews lived during the Greek period.

[227] Kissane, *Isaiah*, 210, rightly concludes, "the whole passage deals with Egypt's conversion to the true God, so it is difficult to fit this verse into the context if it deals with *Jewish* colonies."

idea. Frequently, great men of God built altars and pillars[228] to commemorate great events in their lives (Gen 12:7,8; 28:18; Josh 4:8–9).

The reason for this dramatic conversion of Egyptians is God's miraculous salvation of the Egyptians from an unidentified oppressor (19:20b). The event the memorial stone pillar commemorates may be their salvation from this enemy. When these oppressors attack Egypt, the Egyptians will cry out in prayer to Israel's God, seeking his mercy (as the Israelites did when they were oppressed by the Egyptians in Exod 5:8,15; 8:8; 14:10,15). God will send them a "savior" (*mâšîaʿ*) who will fight and deliver them.[229] There is no way to determine if this savior will be a man or a heavenly being, nor is it possible to know when or how this deliverance will happen. The important thing is that God will deliver them.

The results of these events will be a new experiential understanding of who God is (19:21) because God will make himself known to them at this time in a special way. This terminology about "knowing God" is repeatedly used in the plague story in Exod 7–12, but this time the hearts of Egyptians will be transformed and they will acknowledge him as their God. In gratitude to God, they will sacrifice, make vows of commitment, and worship[230] the Lord. These will not be idle words spoken as a ritual or to impress others. Whatever they promise will come from the heart, and they will follow through on their commitments.

The final verse of this paragraph presents some confusion when it mentions God striking the Egyptians and then healing them (19:22). Three interpretations are proposed. (a) This could just be a repetitious summary statement of what was already said in 19:20 about God delivering the people of Egypt from an oppressor. (b) This could be a second striking of Egypt to bring more Egyptians (beyond the five cities) to faith in God. (c) Motyer views this as "providential discipline" because God chastens those he loves (Prov 3:12). Since there seems to be some chronological order to what will happen in these verses, the last two options should be favored.

The "striking" (Exod 7:17) of Egypt with a "plague" (Exod 8:2; 12:13; cf. "afflicted, plagued" in Josh 24:5) is consistent with God's earlier attempt to cause the Egyptians to know that he is God. Now he openly reveals his power again and calls the Egyptians to be a part of his people. This time, instead of hardening their hearts and suffering further destruction, the Egyptians will turn

---

[228] The pillar (מַצֵּבָה) is usually associated with pagan worship on the high places (Deut 16:22; 1 Kgs 14:23; 2 Kgs 17:10; 18:4; 23:14), but men of God used a pillar to simply mark an important spot—usually a place where God appeared to them. Pillars were also used to designate a border (Gen 34:45).

[229] Hayes and Irvine, *Isaiah*, 265, think all this was fulfilled in Isaiah's day, so they identify the Assyrian king Sargon II as the person who saved the Egyptians from the Ethiopian king Shabaka. Few accept this interpretation.

[230] וְעָבְדוּ literally means "and they will serve," but in Hebrew thinking this is the nature of true worship (Exod 3:12; 4:23).

to God and truly repent and he will heal them. God's "healing" (*rāpô'*) can refer to a general restoration or deliverance from any number of problems. Later, the prophet Ezekiel will reveal more about God's plans for the punishment of Egypt and their eventual recognition of Israel's God (Ezek 29–32).[231]

19:23–25 The last "in that day" prediction describes the religious and political unity that will eventually characterize the relationships between Egypt, Israel, and Assyria. Earlier (11:10–16), Isaiah predicted the return of the remnant of Israel from the four corners of the world and on a highway from Assyria and Egypt. God also foresaw a time when people from all nations would stream to Jerusalem to worship God and learn from him (2:2–4), but this prophecy presents a surprising new status for the foreign nations of Egypt and Assyria.

To adequately understand the radical nature of this prophecy, one has to remember that Egypt and Assyria were strong international political empires while Judah was a small insignificant state. All these nations were far more interested in defending their borders than building bridges of peace and highways of communication. Relationships were defined by the stronger nations defeating and forcing the weaker nations to submit and pay heavy taxes. The highway for travel between these nations does not primarily reflect the advanced development of trading relationship; it symbolizes a close spiritual bond between peoples who are in constant contact. Walls keep people out and ensure that they will be kept separate; roads connect people and allow them to interact.

The reason for their unification is also surprising. These mortal enemies will be worshiping[232] the same God together, and that will be the God of Israel. Although 19:18–22 tells how God will bring Egypt to himself, the reader is quite unprepared to hear that Assyria will also be worshiping God. Equally shocking is the suggestion that God will now view Israel, Assyria, and Egypt as his special people. Previously, Israel alone was "my people, my inheritance, and my handiwork," but now God will pour out his blessing on the whole earth—not just one nation. At this time God will not put Israel in some special status; God will accept all of these people as important members of his one holy family. These nations will no longer be at war, fighting for superiority over one another. They will be at peace under God's rule. This image must describe eschatological events when God establishes his kingdom.

Although no words are directed to Isaiah's audience in Jerusalem in this paragraph about Egypt, they were hearing astonishing news about a miraculous

---

[231] Block, *Ezekiel 25–48*, NICOT (Grand Rapids: Eerdmans, 1998), 128–234. Ezekiel 29:6; 30:8,19,25; and 32:15 refer to the Egyptians knowing that "I am Yahweh," while 29:13–14 mentions the gathering and restoration of Egypt after punishment.

[232] The Old Greek has "the Egyptians will serve the Assyrians," which reads the Hb. עָבְדוּ in the sense of "work" rather than in the theological sense of the "service of worship." A. Niccacci, "Isaiah XVIII–XX," 214–37, prefers "serve" rather than "worship," but that idea hardly fits the overall context of the next few verses.

transformation in both Egypt and Assyria. What impact should these words have on them? What does God expect of them? Judah is not commanded to do anything special or to refrain from one activity or another. Instead, the people in Isaiah's audience simply learned about God's amazing future plans for their neighbors. If the Israelites now know what will happen in the future, that should influence the way they treat people and it should impact the decisions they make. They must trust God's plans and not try to manipulate their situation through their own power or cleverness. God is not confused or surprised by Judah or Egypt's situation; he was using them in his own way to bring about his ultimate solution. In the end, everyone will be worshiping the Almighty God together.

Knowing how the radical Muslims control much of Egypt, Iraq, and Iran today, this prophecy still seems an amazing promise of the miraculous transforming power of God's presence and grace. The prayer of every believer should be that the people in their own nation would respond as the Egyptian's will and consequently join the many nations that will worship at God's throne some day in the future.

(3) Isaiah's Nakedness Symbolizes Egypt's Defeat (20:1–6)

[1]In the year that the supreme commander, sent by Sargon king of Assyria, came to Ashdod and attacked and captured it— [2]at that time the LORD spoke through Isaiah son of Amoz. He said to him, "Take off the sackcloth from your body and the sandals from your feet." And he did so, going around stripped and barefoot.

[3]Then the LORD said, "Just as my servant Isaiah has gone stripped and barefoot for three years, as a sign and portent against Egypt and Cush, [4]so the king of Assyria will lead away stripped and barefoot the Egyptian captives and Cushite exiles, young and old, with buttocks bared—to Egypt's shame. [5]Those who trusted in Cush and boasted in Egypt will be afraid and put to shame. [6]In that day the people who live on this coast will say, 'See what has happened to those we relied on, those we fled to for help and deliverance from the king of Assyria! How then can we escape?'"

The final paragraph in this Egyptian section describes a prophetic sign-act completed by Isaiah when an Assyrian military commander under Sargon II attacked the Philistine city of Ashdod in 712–711 BC. Some years before this event (714 BC), opposition to Assyrian rule was rising in Ashdod, so Sargon replaced Ashdod's King Azuri with a friendlier leader, Ahimiti. The people of Ashdod did not like this new ruler, so they replaced Ahimiti with the anti-Assyrian leader Yamani.[233] Sargon did not appreciate this act of rebellion, so just before Assyria captured Ashdod in 711 BC Yamani fled to Egypt to escape the

---

[233] See *ANET*, 286, for Sargon's account of these events. H. Tadmor, "The Campaigns of Sargon II of Asshur: A Chronological-Historical Study," *JCS* 12 (1958): 22–42, 77–100, explains and interprets Sargon's activities including this campaign against Ashdod. See Younger, "Recent Study on Sargon II," 288–329, for a discussion of all of Sargon's campaigns. The 712–711 BC campaign against Ashdod is discussed on pp. 313–18.

wrath of the Assyrians. But when the Assyrian army threatened the Egyptians, they handed Yamani over to Assyria. This was about the same time that Hezekiah decided not to pay tribute to the Assyrians and Shabaka the Ethiopian solidified his rule over Egypt. With this context as a backdrop, Isaiah's symbolic acts can be seen as a warning to the people of Judah so that they would not make the same mistake of trusting Egypt. His message to King Hezekiah and the leaders of Judah was: Do not follow the example of Ashdod and make alliances with Egypt or trust in Egyptian assistance.

The story follows the typical structure of a prophetic sign act[234] as follows:

A command to act in a symbolic manner	20:1–2a
A report about the accomplishment of the sign act	20:2b
An interpretation of the sign act	20:3–6.

20:1–2 The date the "supreme commander" (cf. 2 Kgs 18:17) of Sargon's army captured Ashdod was 711 BC. This date appears to be the year (v. 2 "at that time")[235] that God directed the prophet to perform a sign act of going naked for three years to warn his audience in Judah. Isaiah's radical actions symbolically point out that the Assyrian defeat of Ashdod has serious implications for Judah. Ashdod's reliance on the Egyptians for protection from Assyria should serve as a lesson for Judah's future military policy (vv. 5–6).

There is some disagreement concerning whether Isaiah's three years of walking around naked took place before or after Ashdod was conquered. Childs follows the common interpretation that views v. 2 as an "awkward parenthesis" about what happened years earlier than v. 1, so he maintains that Isaiah walked naked for three years before the fall of Ashdod.[236] Some interpret the prophet's admonition in vv. 5–6 as a warning addressed to the people of Ashdod that they should not trust Egypt. This view is made possible when "at that time" in v. 3 is stretched to mean "in that general time period," but the interpreter must pay attention to what the antecedent of "that" is. Clearly "that time" in v. 2 was the time mentioned in v. 1. Wildberger is more forthright with the evidence, so he concludes that the later redactor who added v. 1 was wrong about his dating of God's command in v. 1.[237] His solution to the problem is unacceptable, but his identification of a serious problem with the traditional interpretation is one that

---

[234] For a detailed study of the general nature and purpose of prophetic sign acts, see E. R. Fraser, "Symbolic Acts of the Prophets," *Studia Biblica et Theologica* 4 (1974): 45–53, or K. Friebel, *Jeremiah and Ezekiel's Sign acts: Their Meaning and Function as Nonverbal Communication* (Ph. D. dissertation, University of Wisconsin, Madison, 1989).

[235] One could argue whether the command to function as a sign came (a) when Sargon "was sending" (infinitive construct) the supreme commander of the army (an earlier date), (b) or when the city of Ashdod was captured (a later date).

[236] Childs, *Isaiah*, 145 realizes that his view has difficulty with 20:3, which reapplies the sign act of Egypt. Following Seitz, *Isaiah 1–39*, 144–45, he interprets the "coastlands" in v. 6 as the distant nations (41:5; 42:4) rather than the Philistines.

[237] Wildberger, *Isaiah 13–27*, 287 believes Isaiah's function as a sign ended when Ashdod fell; therefore, he identifies the problem in the dating in v. 1 (rather than v. 2).

should not be avoided.[238] Verse 2 seems to require that Isaiah's sign act began in the year of Ashdod's conquest, which would not prevent him from beginning his sign act a few months before Ashdod fell. This timing would allow his audience in Judah to interpret his nakedness in light of what was happening with the people of Egypt who did not rescue Ashdod. The connection of this sign act with the fall of Ashdod would teach Isaiah's audience in Judah not to trust Egypt as the people of Ashdod did, for if they do they will also end up going naked into captivity just like the Egyptians and the people of Ashdod.

The instructions to Isaiah are for him to remove his sackcloth and sandals and go naked (v. 2). Literally the Lord says, "go, open your sackcloth," but when a man uncovers something (his nakedness) and opens[239] it up to sight he is taking off his clothes. Sackcloth is usually associated with mourning the death of a loved one (Gen 37:34; 2 Sam 21:10; 2 Kgs 6:30), mourning and repenting of sin (Dan 9:3; Jonah 3:5–8), or lamenting a devastation that is about to happen (37:1–2; Esth 4:1–4; Jer 4:8). The text does not indicate why Isaiah was already mourning in sackcloth (though it may have been to mourn for the soon-to-be-defeated people of Ashdod and Egypt who would go into captivity), but the command to go naked[240] was meant to symbolize what will happen to captives who will be defeated in war (v. 4). Based on pictures of war captives, they were often completely naked to bring greater shame on them.[241] Since the purpose of this command was to send a message to the people who would see Isaiah in public, Isaiah followed God's command. God did not say that he had to be naked 24 hours every day or even every day of the week, so he would not be viewed as disobeying the Lord if he wore a cloak in his home on a cold winter evenings to keep warm or if he was clothed when he worshiped God in the temple on the Passover. He was not an exhibitionist who randomly flashed people to gain attention. He was trying to send God's message to certain leaders in a very graphic way, so he probably chose appropriate times to go naked to influence them.

The text includes no initial explanation as to why Isaiah was to go naked for three years (not 36 months, but parts of three years) or what he was to say when people asked him why he was naked. One cannot say that God did not offer an explanation of this behavior to the prophet for three years (an argument

---

[238] A second problem with the traditional reconstruction of these events is that Isaiah's nakedness is somehow related to what will happen in Ashdod, yet the oracle relates his nakedness to Egypt. This is sometimes explained as a reapplication of the original meaning by a later editor.

[239] An example of this: פָּתַח, "open, take off, loosen," military armor is set opposite the idea חֲגֹר, "put on," armor in 1 Kgs 20:11.

[240] עָרוֹם, "naked," can mean one has no clothes on at all (Gen 2:25; 3:7; Job 1:21), but it can also be used in situations where one is almost but not totally naked (58:7; Job 22:6; 24:7; Young, *Isaiah*, II:55). A clear NT example is John 21:7 where Peter was naked so that he could do his work, but actually all he had done was throw off his outer garment.

[241] In the pictures of captives in *ANEP*, numbers 326 and 366 have some clothing on, but the captives in numbers 333, 358, and 365 are wearing no clothing. See 2 Chr 28:14–15.

from silence). All that can be said is that the text does not tell the reader what explanation God gave to Isaiah when he first started to act as a sign. Since other prophetic sign acts came with explanations from God that the prophet was to declare to those who watched them (Jer 13:12–14; 19:1–13; Ezek 5:1–17; 12:16), one expects this happened in Isaiah's case as well. What the story reveals is that Isaiah did what he was told (v. 2b).

20:3–6 The interpretation of the sign act comes at the end of this literary report, but this literary position does not require one to assume that God's explanation was not provided until the end of the three years period of nakedness.[242] Verses 3–4 tend to explain what the sign was all about, while vv. 5–6 make some applications based on the explanation in vv. 3–4. It may be that Isaiah knew what the sign meant from the beginning (vv. 3–4) but the important application to Judah in vv. 5–6 was added at the end of the three-year period. As a result, Hezekiah and his officials allowed God's plans for Egypt to influence their foreign policies toward Assyria and Egypt.

God explains Isaiah's behavior by calling him "my servant" and "a sign, and portent." Isaiah should be compared to earlier prophets who were God's servants: Moses (Josh 1:1–2,7,13-15), Elijah (1 Kgs 18:36; 2 Kgs 9:7), Jonah (2 Kgs 14:25), and others (Amos 3:7). Servants do the will of their master and all these did what God asked them to do. As a sign and portent, Isaiah symbolized something that did or would happen. A sign act can communicate a difficult message that some people might otherwise ignore, but the sign can teach the central point of the message in an interesting, attention getting, shocking, or somewhat mysterious way.

At the end of v. 3 the audience learns that this sign relates to what will happen to the Ethiopian dynasty run by Shabaka and the Egyptian people (at least it was not the people of Judah). Isaiah's sign (his nakedness) depicts the Egyptians who will be taken into captivity by the Assyrians—naked and without sandals (v. 4). No date is set, but this prophetic announcement implies that Assyria will defeat Egypt and shamefully treat[243] both the young and the old.

The lesson to be drawn from these events (vv. 5–6) are (a) anyone who trusts and puts their hope in Egypt or Cush will suffer a similar shame; and (b) with Egypt defeated, those who were disappointed in Egypt's help in the past (Ashdod) should realize they cannot depend on Egypt in the future. Since v. 5 seems very repetitive of v. 4 (both talk about shame), it must be making

---

[242] Delitzsch, *Isaiah*, 373, argues that the perfect verb הָלַךְ, "walk, go," is an expression of "what has already commenced, and is still continuing," thus he does not put vv. 3–6 at the end of the three years. An imperfect verb would have expressed this idea better, but it was not used here. הָלוֹךְ is an infinitive absolute form used adverbially to express the manner the person performed the action (GKC §113i).

[243] וַחֲשׂוּפַי שֵׁת is an awkward phrase because the ending on the first word is not the construct ending (ַ) that one would expect in this situation ("uncovering of the buttock"). GKC § 87g treats this as a construct form and compares it to the Syriac construct state that has this ending. Similar problematic forms exist in Judg 5:15 and Jer 22:14.

a comparison with someone else's shame rather than Egypt's. It makes more sense to have the subject of v. 5 ("they") refer to Isaiah's audience in Judah rather the people of Ashdod, for the people of Ashdod are not the topic of vv. 2–5. They are never mentioned specifically, but the "people of this coast" in v. 6 refer in a general way to the testimony of the Philistines. They would say that their past experience proves the truthfulness of what Isaiah has said about trusting in Egypt. In light of Egypt's earlier betrayal of them and Egypt's approaching demise, the people of Judah know that no one can rely on Egypt. Consequently, the practical lesson that Hezekiah and his advisors needed to understand from this event was that they should not trust in Egypt for political assistance in fighting the Assyrians.

THEOLOGICAL IMPLICATIONS. Egypt was an important political power to the south of Judah, Assyria was taking more and more control of the area, and Hezekiah was trying to gain independence for Judah from Assyria. Any divine message about what God was planning for one of these three main players was extremely important. The people of Judah and their leaders needed to know how to survive in this situation. What did God want them to do? These paragraphs about Egypt (19:1–20:6) address three theological issues that were applied to the people of Judah.

The first thing they learn is that God's sovereign plan is to destroy Egypt (19:1–17). God will come to Egypt bringing a period of civil war, destroying Egypt's great hopes, and causing the people to seek their useless gods for answers. Their gods will have no answers and their wise men will have no wisdom. The Egyptians will suffer under a harsh ruler, see their economy ruined because of a drought, and have God confuse their king and political leaders. The theological and political implications are clear: (a) God controls the economy and political vitality of this foreign nation; (b) Egypt will not be a strong nation for Judah to depend on in this political climate; (c) God will humble Egypt and defeat her gods. Although it is always tempting to look up to or depend on strong nations or people around us, victory and power rest only in the hands of those that God blesses.

The second theological truth is even more surprising. At some point in the future after Egypt's defeat, God will graciously reveal himself by delivering Egypt from oppression. God will be the savior of the Egyptians. In response many Egyptians will worship God and erect a pillar to celebrate the memory of what God did for them. In the end, many people from both Egypt and Assyria will become part of the people of God. God plans to bring an end to all the conflict between these nations. Eventually, all these nations will come to worship him. God's plan is the only hope for this world; he is the only one who can bring peace between the nations.

The third message is to not trust in Egypt now. The Egyptians did not help the people of Ashdod when they trusted in them in 711 BC and they will not help Judah, for soon the Assyrians will overpower the Egyptians. The primary lesson throughout is that God is in control of all the nations on earth—including Egypt, Judah, Ashdod, and Assyria. Though the people of Judah might take some comfort in the promises that God will judge these nations (14:24–27; 19:1–17), the ultimate solution to their problems will happen only when God unites these nations as one people under his rule. The only secure hope for the people of God in every age is for them to trust God in the midst of the turbulent political situations that bring fear and war.

6. God's Plans for Babylon (21:1–10)

HISTORICAL SETTING. This new oracle is a prophetic vision of the fall of Babylon, with some similarities to 13:17–22.[244] Since Babylon was defeated several times, commentators connect the setting of this prophecy to different events. Early Jewish commentators (Rashi, Ibn Ezra), the conservative exegete F. Delitzsch, and modern critics like Clements point to the 539 BC destruction of Babylon because the feasting in 21:5 fits Belshazzar's feast in Dan 5 and the attacking Medes and Elamites correlates with Cyrus's conquest of Babylon (21:2). From this perspective the fall of Babylon in 21:9 is a point of rejoicing for the Hebrews.[245] Sweeney raises three serious objections to this analysis. (a) Elam ceased to exist after 646 BC so it would not be mentioned as an independent country if the date of this conquest was in 539 BC.[246] (b) Cyrus the Persian never defeated Babylon, but just walked in almost completely unopposed. (c) It would be a little bit odd for an Israelite prophet in the exilic period to weep over the fall of their great enemy Babylon.[247]

Hayes and Irvine point to Sargon II's recovery of Babylon in 710 BC while S. Erlandsson prefers Sennacherib's recovery of Babylon in 702 BC as the backdrop for this prophecy. However, neither of these events involved a complete conquest of the city of Babylon.[248] It seems best to interpret Merodach-baladan's coalition with Hezekiah in 39:1–8 as the background to this prophecy (as well as the prophecy in 13:17–22) because (a) Merodach-baladan was from the desert area just off the marshy lowland (so "desert of the sea" in 21:1 makes sense); (b) Babylon was an ally of Judah at this time, so its defeat would

---

[244] Kissane, *The Book of Isaiah*, 1:218–220, proposes that 21:1–5 is about the fall of Jerusalem in 586 BC, which explains the prophet's strong emotional reaction in these verses, and the second half of the chapter is about the fall of Babylon in 540–538 BC. However, there is nothing in 21:1–5 to solidly link it to the fall of Jerusalem.

[245] Delitzsch, "Isaiah," 376–380, or Clements, *Isaiah 1–39*, 176–77. Slightly different is A. A. Macintosh, *Isaiah xxi: A Palimpsest* (Cambridge: Cambridge University, 1980), who thinks that this originally referred to an Assyrian campaign against Babylon, but later was written over and revised (a palimpsest) to fit it into the later Persian defeat of Babylon in 539 BC.

[246] This argument is less decisive because Elamites were still identified as an ethnic, linguistic, or cultural group in Cyrus' army many years after the nation ceased to exist.

[247] Sweeney, *Isaiah 1–39*, 279, thinks these difficulties rule out the 539 BC date, and his assessment of the evidence makes good sense.

[248] Hayes and Irvine, *Isaiah*, 272–74, and Erlandsson, *The Burden of Babylon*, 81–92.

explain the sorrowful pain Isaiah expressed in 21:3–4,10; and (c) the Medes and Elamites in 21:2, who were allies of Babylon, were fighting against the Assyrian king Sennacherib to save Babylon. Thus Isaiah is prophesying the future conquest (689 BC) of Babylon (the only time Babylon was truly destroyed) and by implication warning Hezekiah and the people of Judah not to count on this Babylonian ally for support. Babylon will fall and be destroyed. The implication is plain: Hezekiah needs to trust God, not an alliance with Babylon.

STRUCTURE.   Based on the design suggested at the beginning of the Oracles about the Nations,[249] chap. 21 returns to a discussion of the destiny of Babylon as the second series of oracles begins.

13:1–14:27	Babylon	21:1–10	Babylon
14:28–32	Philistia	22:11–12	Edom
15:1–16:14	Moab	22:13–17	Arabia
17:1–18:7	Damascus/Israel	22:1–25	Jerusalem
19:1–20:6	Egypt	23: 1–18	Tyre

The oracles in the second grouping have thematic connections to the first series, but they are not mirror images of the earlier ones. A cursory reading of 13:17–14:23 and 21:1–10 demonstrates that Babylon will be destroyed in both oracles, but the content of 21:1–19 is very different from chaps. 13–14. The lament for the proud king of Babylon in Sheol (14:4–23) is completely missing in chap. 21, though 21:3–4 does include a brief lament over the fall of Babylon.

The message of this vision is divided into two paragraphs, but it is difficult to know what to do with v. 5. The new "messenger formula" announcing a word from God in 21:6 suggests that it begins the second paragraph. On the other hand, the preponderance of imperatives in 21:5–6 draws them together. An advantage to dividing the paragraph before v. 5 is that both paragraphs would then end with the prophet's reaction to bad news (21:3–4, 10). Verses 1–4 would have an introduction (1a), the vision (1b–2), and the prophet's distressing reaction (3–4), which is similar to the report by the watchman (8–9) and the prophet's distressed reaction (10) in the second paragraph. If this arrangement is accepted, the two paragraphs are:

The prophet's terrifying vision of Babylon	21:1–4
Watchmen report on the fall of Babylon	21:5–10.

(1) The Prophet's Terrifying Vision of Babylon (21:1–4)

¹An oracle concerning the Desert by the Sea:

Like whirlwinds sweeping through the southland,
an invader comes from the desert,
from a land of terror.

---

[249] See Motyer, *The Prophecy of Isaiah*, 131–32..

²A dire vision has been shown to me:
  The traitor betrays, the looter takes loot.
Elam, attack! Media, lay siege!
  I will bring to an end all the groaning she caused.

³At this my body is racked with pain,
  pangs seize me, like those of a woman in labor;
I am staggered by what I hear,
  I am bewildered by what I see.
⁴My heart falters,
  fear makes me tremble;
the twilight I longed for
  has become a horror to me.

21:1–2   This message begins like all the other *maśśāʾ* "oracles," but instead of introducing a well known country like Egypt or Moab, this oracle is about the enigmatic sounding "Desert by/of the Sea."[250] Since southern Babylon was sometimes referred to in Assyrian sources as *māt tāmti(m)* ("sea land") because of the swampy marshes between the Tigress and Euphrates rivers, and since Merodach-baladan II came from that area, this vision relates to Merodach-baladan's territory.

Isaiah 21:2 describes this as a "harsh, difficult (*qāšâ*) vision" (presumably from God) about an invading army attacking and looting some unidentified place—presumably the area of the "Desert by the Sea." The army will quickly sweep through the southland (the southern marsh area of Babylon) like a strong destructive storm (cf. 5:26–29). The enemy is not named but comes from a terrible or feared land.[251] The description of the invading enemy uses the same root twice; once the participle functions as a noun and then as a verb.[252] Thus the invaders' activity is described as the "betrayer who betrays" (used of Assyria in 33:1)[253] and the "looter who loots" in a war that involves Elam and Media. This probably relates to the Assyrian attack on Babylon around 689 BC.[254] Babylon's neighbors are being encouraged to attack the Assyrian invading forces (21:2) to divert their attention from Babylon. The final part of the vision quotes someone promising to end Babylon's groaning/suffering.[255]

---

[250] The textual evidence for this phrase is very mixed with the Old Greek having "vision of the desert," which omits "sea," while 1QIsaᵃ has "words of the sea," which assumes דבר, "word," instead of מדבר, "desert." The Aramaic Targum paraphrase has "Armies that come out of the desert like water from the sea." Wildberger, *Isaiah 13–27*, 301–302, has a discussion of various attempts to make sense of this reading—some by emending what the text says.

[251] נוֹרָאָה is a feminine singular *niphal* participle from the root ירא, "he feared," thus a "feared land."

[252] For the use of the participle as a verb and noun, see GKC §116f-g.

[253] Tucker, "Isaiah 1–39," 186, believes the "betrayer" and "looter" refer to Babylon.

[254] A. A. Macintosh, *Isaiah XXI: A Palimpsest* (Cambridge: Cambridge University: 1980) 5–15, seems to suggest that the date of the defeat of Babylon can be both the early (710,701,689 B. C) and later date (540 BC).

[255] NIV's "the groaning she caused" is a questionable interpretation of "her groaning" (אַנְחָתָה).

Hayes and Irvine believe God is announcing the end of Babylon's groaning, that is, the groaning of the Mesopotamian people who suffered under the Babylonian rule of some evil kings.[256] Merodach-baladan and Mushezib-Marduk (692–689 BC) rebelled against Assyria repeatedly, so this defeat is pictured as one that will end the common people's suffering under repeated Assyrian counterattacks. Of course, the news of the approaching defeat of Babylon was not good news to the political aspirations of Hezekiah or Judah.

21:3–4 The strong emotional reaction (in first person pronouns) to this news appears to be the response of Isaiah.[257] "Therefore/On account of this" (*'al kēn*), anguish and severe pains (like a woman in labor) dismayed the prophet. He seems to be describing physical signs of cramps that brought him to his knees and a psychological astonishment that knocked the wind out of him. His heart stopped briefly and a horrendous thought brought great fear over him (21:4). He was hoping to enjoy a good night's rest, but now God has turned this vision into a nightmare. Why would a prophet from Judah respond so strongly and emotionally? He probably was not so much incapacitated because he felt sorry for the people of Babylon; he was struck by the consequences this defeat would have for Judah, who was now Babylon's ally (39:1–8). The defeat of Babylon meant that Judah would probably have to face Assyria by itself, with little hope to defend itself against Assyria. Isaiah dreaded the thought of what might happen next. Although this theological news from God exposes the truth about the future political status of Babylon, God's sovereign plans are not always what people want to hear and are not always easy to accept.

(2) Watchmen Report on the Fall of Babylon (21:5–10)

[5]They set the tables,
    they spread the rugs,
    they eat, they drink!
Get up, you officers,
    oil the shields!

[6]This is what the Lord says to me:

"Go, post a lookout
    and have him report what he sees.
[7]When he sees chariots
    with teams of horses,
riders on donkeys
    or riders on camels,

---

[256] Hayes and Irvine, *Isaiah*, 275, quote from Sargon's campaign: "The people of Sippar, Nippur, Babylon, Borsippa, who were imprisoned therein through no fault of their own—I broke their bonds and caused them to see the light."

[257] Watts, *Isaiah 1–33*, 273, thinks this is the response of Shebna, a high officer in Hezekiah's government, but R. B. Y. Scott, "Isaiah XXI 1–10: The Inside of a Prophet's Mind," *VT* 2 (1952): 278–82, properly views this as the subjective experience of Isaiah.

let him be alert,
   fully alert."

⁸And the lookout shouted,

"Day after day, my lord, I stand on the watchtower;
   every night I stay at my post.
⁹Look, here comes a man in a chariot
   with a team of horses.
And he gives back the answer:
   'Babylon has fallen, has fallen!
All the images of its gods
   lie shattered on the ground!'"

¹⁰O my people, crushed on the threshing floor,
   I tell you what I have heard
from the LORD Almighty,
   from the God of Israel.

21:5 This section does not continue the first person comments of despair found in 21:3–4. The four infinitive absolutes are not used in conjunction with another verb to show emphasis, adverbially to show the manner of action, or to express continuous action—the three most common uses of the infinitive absolute. Because of the imperatives at the end of v. 5, these infinitives fit a context where one would use a "hurried or excited style" where there is no preceding verb before the infinitive absolute.[258] The mention of setting/arranging the tables, spreading out the rugs or cushions,[259] and eating and drinking, recreates a scene of people eating a meal. There is no condemnation of this meal, no suggestion that this was a sign of careless ease, and no indication that this meal involved debauchery. Either during or after the meal, a command is given to the princes attending the meal to get up and oil their shields. Getting up can be a call to battle (Jer 6:4,5; 49:14), and oiling a shield may be a preparation for war.[260] It is not clear if these verses are describing a meal and preparations for war by the Babylonians or, more likely, by the enemies of Babylon.

Many think this meal describes Belshazzar's carefree banquet in Babylon on the night the Persians defeated the city (Dan 5), but the context relates much earlier to events when Merodach-baladan was ruling Babylon. Motyer suggests that this is Hezekiah's banquet when he accepted Merodach-baladan's ambassadors (39:1–8), but there is no indication in the text about when or where this

---

[258] GKC §113aa-ff describes situations where the infinitive absolute begins a new paragraph.

[259] צָפֹה הַצָּפִית looks like it could come from the root that means "to watch, look," thus "the watchmen are watching" makes sense and is consistent with the Aramaic Targum's interpretation. A second possibility is the Syriac idea of "to lay, overlay," so this is a tablecloth that is laid over the tables or rugs that are laid out beside the tables.

[260] The purpose of oiling a skin shield is unclear. Was it to make the leather more pliable so that it would not break if a stone hit it, or was this merely a dedicatory act seeking God's blessing?

meal happened.[261] Far more important is the word of the Lord (21:6–9) that came to Isaiah.

21:6–7 In what appears to be the continuation of Isaiah's vision, God instructs him to post a watchman to observe the invasion of an enemy force that will attack some city (21:9 indicates that Babylon was attacked). The watchman's responsibility was to watch and listen for any sign of movement on the horizon, so that he could give people plenty of time to secure the city and prepare to defend its walls. Typically one might see a farmer bringing goods to market on the road or a caravan of merchants coming to trade with people in the village. But if the watchman detected chariots, pairs of horsemen, and camels and donkeys carrying baggage, he had to be very alert to notice them immediately and to distinguish them from the regular traffic on the road. He would not want to sound a false alarm, but he dare not sleep while an enemy was quietly approaching.

21:8–9 Suddenly the instructions about the watchman are interrupted by a report from the watchman. It appears that he either sees a lion, describes the enemy as a lion, or cries out a warning like a lion (according to the Masoretic text). More understandable is the Qumran reading "seer, watcher,"[262] which fits in with the context better (21:6). Initially, the watchman defends his reputation by declaring his faithful execution of his responsibilities. Day after day, night after night, he faithfully fulfilled his role, staying alert on his post (21:8).

Then all of a sudden the watchman notices a military procession of chariots and horses, but it appears that these are troops coming from a battle at Babylon. Although it is not clear who is speaking to whom, someone (maybe a man in the chariot) tells the watchman that Babylon has fallen and her idols, which represent her gods, were broken in pieces. The watchman is then able to relay the news that the power of Babylon has ended and her gods are impotent. This is a factual statement of what has historically happened and a theological statement about the power of idols, but it is unaccompanied by words of joy or sorrow. This astonishing news about Babylon's defeat would have had major political significance for the subsequent balance of power in the ancient Near East.

This may be a vision about what will happen when the Assyrians attack Babylon in 689 BC, although since so little historical information is provided, it is impossible to specify an exact date for the fulfillment of this prophecy. The significance of the future fall of Babylon for the people of Judah was abun-

---

[261] Motyer, *The Prophecy of Isaiah*, 175, presents this as a possible setting for this chapter, but there is no way to verify this suggestion. One must simply conclude that the setting is unknown and is not important to understanding the basic message from God.

[262] The Hb. refers to a "lion" (אַרְיֵה), which NASB renders "like a lion." This is similar to God's roaring like a lion to warn his people in Amos 1:2; 3:8. 1QIsaᵃ has הראה, "the seer, watcher," which fits the context very well (21:6), but it is difficult to explain how a scribe might confuse the two words, especially to move from the very understandable "seer, watcher" to the more difficult "lion." It might make sense to call Isaiah a seer, but there is no indication that the watchman who was sent out had or needed to have a prophetic gift to accomplish his task.

dantly clear. Should Hezekiah be considering an alliance with the Babylonian king Merodach-baladan to oppose the Assyrian army? If the king of Judah was sure that Babylon would soon be defeated, then it would not be wise to rely on that nationas a partner or to create a coalition with Babylon against a common enemy. Isaiah's audience now knows that Babylon's attempt to undermine Assyrian power will not succeed.

21:10 The report of the watchman ends in 21:9 and the prophecy returns to first person verbs of regret similar to 21:3–4. Isaiah addresses his audience in Judah ("O my people," NIV) about their future status.[263] He actually views the people of Judah as "my crushed/threshed ones" (*mĕdušātî*), "sons of the threshing floor" (*ben gārnî*)—images that arise from the practice of having animals walk on a threshing floor to separate the grain from the stalks. The Hebrew terms ("my threshed ones" and "sons of the threshing floor") imply that this is what the future holds for God's people. These figures of speech refer to the people of Judah as those who will be trampled like stalks of grain (41:15; Mic 4:12–13). The one doing the threshing of Judah is not identified anywhere in this paragraph, but if Babylon has already fallen, the most logical conclusion would be that Assyria will be the oppressor.

The paragraph ends with a word of assurance that everything that Isaiah has said[264] was based on what he heard God say. Isaiah did not make up this strange visionary sequence of events. He was trying to be faithful to his task of revealing what the Almighty God of Israel said, so the audience needs to hear these words as truth. It would make no sense to follow some preplanned political agenda of making an alliance with Babylon, if Judah's king knows that it is destined to fail.

THEOLOGICAL IMPLICATIONS. This prophecy proclaims God's sovereign plan for Babylon. It will fall and the pagan idols of Babylon cannot stop this from happening. The gods of Babylon are powerless because God Almighty has determined the destiny of Babylon. In the light of this fact, the leaders of Judah must decide how they will respond to this news. Isaiah's reaction of shock and trembling suggests that Judah also needs to tremble because of this news. They were depending on Babylon to help them undermine the power of Assyria (39:1–8), but if Judah follows this path, they will soon find out that Babylon will give them no help at all. Instead Babylon will be defeated (21:9) and the people of Judah will be oppressed (21:10). The prophet's message is simply this: do not put your trust in Babylon or any other political power. The implication is: all nations need to trust in God, the one who controls the future of every nation. God knows the future because he has planned it, therefore

---

[263] R. B. Y. Scott, "Isaiah xxi 1–10: Inside a Prophet's Mind," *VT* 2 (1952): 278–82, thinks Isaiah is speaking to the Babylonians in 21:10, but it would be odd for God or Isaiah to call the Babylonians "my people" in this context.

[264] NIV "I tell you" translates a perfect verb (הִגַּדְתִּי) as a present, but in this context it is more natural to translate the verb, "I have told you."

people should not depend on the useless abilities of other nations (cf. similar themes in Isa 46–47).

7. God's Plans for Dumah (21:11–12)

11An oracle concerning Dumah:

> **Someone calls to me from Seir,**
> **"Watchman, what is left of the night?**
> **Watchman, what is left of the night?"**
> **12The watchman replies,**
> **"Morning is coming, but also the night.**
> **If you would ask, then ask;**
> **and come back yet again."**

21:11 This oracle is quite mysterious. Watts believes that Dumah is not a place name, so he translates the title of this section "silence."[265] Since Dumah is parallel to Seir, a mountain range in Edom, the Old Greek took Dumah as a reference to Idumea (an area of Edom).[266] The name Dumah was given to one of Ishmael's sons (Gen 25:13–15), as was Kedar and Tema (mentioned 21:13–14), so the name is most likely to be associated with an oasis in the northern part of the Arabian Desert, northeast of Edom. This was an important site on the trade route from Mesopotamia to Edom, and traders coming there would bring news about what was happening in Babylon (21:1–10). Oswalt dates all three oracles in chap. 21 to the same time period and suggests either a date somewhere before 700 BC, during the reign of Sargon or Sennacherib (which fits 21:1–10), or a much later date when the Babylonian king Nabonidus was conquering various tribes in the Arabian Desert (550–540 BC).[267] Because so little information is provided about the setting of these events, it is impossible to date this oracle with any precision.[268]

The surface meaning of v. 11 is not problematic. Someone from the Edomite mountains of Seir asks a watchman, What time it is? How much longer will it be dark? When will the light appear? But this is probably not a literal question about the end of physical darkness but about the end of political darkness. Wildberger comments that night "is used to convey the image of oppression and lack of free-

---

[265] Wattts, *Isaiah 1–33*, 275.

[266] If a copyist accidentally dropped the א before דּוּמָה as Blenkinsopp, *Isaiah 1–39*, 329 suggests then one would get a word very close to אֱדוֹם, "Edom."

[267] Oswalt, *Isaiah 1–39*, 398, thinks these words were directed to Isaiah's contemporaries around 700 B. C but also believes they had a larger application to later events as well. Wildberger, *Isaiah 13–27*, 331–334, provides a detailed documentation of references to Dumah in ancient documents from the time of Tiglath-pileser III to Nabonidus, plus a map of the cities mentioned in this and the next oracle.

[268] Macintosh, *Isaiah XXI: A Palimpsest*, 79, fails to see any strong anti-Edomite sentiment in this oracle; therefore, he concludes that it must be dated before the fall of Jerusalem when the Edomites mistreated the people of Judah (Obad 10–14; Ezek 35–36).

dom, in this case, no doubt, when one is under foreign rule"[269] caused by some undefined enemy that has taken away freedom from the land. Since the people in Dumah were on the trade route closer to Assyria and Babylon, they would likely hear the news first. The question comes "unto me" (*ʾēlay*) suggesting that the "watchman" (*šōmēr*) or guard is the prophet himself, but when the answers was given the watchman does not say "I said" as one might expect if the speaker was the prophet.[270] Maybe the prophet was seeing all this action in some sort of visionary experience. The question that was asked of the watchman was one that the audience of Isaiah in Jerusalem would want answered as well. When will all this war and oppression end and when will this nightmare be over?

21:12   The watchman's answer suggests that hope (morning) was coming, but after that more trouble (night) will follow. Thus a momentary glimmer of better days is in sight, but this time of relief will only be temporary.[271] The final clause invites the inquirer to seek[272] more information later, implying that maybe more news will be available then.

THEOLOGICAL IMPLICATIONS.   It is difficult to surmise the theological impact of this message to the people in Judah. These verses say nothing about God and do not mention Judah. If one knew more about the setting, the message would make more sense. It is best to be humble and admit that although the message was significant to its original hearers, its theological implications are largely a mystery today. About all that can be derived from these words is that people can pray and ask for information about the future and receive divine information about what will happen. If this prophecy came during the time when the Assyrian kings were oppressing Judah and Babylon (21:9–10), this news would give the people of Judah a general assurance that better days are ahead, but also warn them that these good times would be followed by more dark days. It is possible that Isaiah's audience might conclude from these words that they must not expect that their alliance with Babylon will quickly solve all their problems with Assyria. The previous oracle tells why: Babylon will fall (21:9).

8. God's Plans for Arabia (21:13–17)

> [13]An oracle concerning Arabia:
>   You caravans of Dedanites,
>   who camp in the thickets of Arabia,

---

[269] Wildberger, *Isaiah 13–27*, 337–38, interprets this message as a warning to the people of Judah not to have false hopes about the future. Things still look quite dark, so do not get impatient.

[270] Clements, *Isaiah 1–39*, 180, thinks the prophet is the watchman. One might also try to connect the "watchman" in 21:6 or 8 with the "guard" in 21:11, but two different Hb. words are used.

[271] Macintosh, *Isaiah XXI: A Palimpsest,* 136, believes the oracle warns the Edomites not to join in the anti-Assyrian conspiracy, but this seems unlikely.

[272] The verb forms בְּעָיוּ and תִּבְעָיוּן are both from בָּעָה, which normally drops the ה and does not replace it with a ʾ when a vocalic ending is added (GKC § 75h). When a word is in pause or before a final ן, the ʾ will sometimes be found before the vocalic ending (GKC § 75u).

¹⁴**bring water for the thirsty;**
  you who live in Tema,
    bring food for the fugitives.
¹⁵**They flee from the sword,**
    from the drawn sword,
  from the bent bow
    and from the heat of battle.

¹⁶**This is what the Lord says to me: "Within one year, as a servant bound by contract would count it, all the pomp of Kedar will come to an end. ¹⁷The survivors of the bowmen, the warriors of Kedar, will be few." The LORD, the God of Israel, has spoken.**

This is a short oracle about people who live in the Arabian desert,[273] not far from Dumah and Edom. It is difficult to date the time when the prophecy was spoken to the prophet, and he had no idea exactly when it would be fulfilled. It refers to a future time when fugitives will flee for their lives. The reference to the escaping fugitives from the region of Kedar may point to a future date when Sennacherib conquered this area of Arabia around 691–689 BC—the same conflict implied in 21:1–10 about Babylon's defeat. The introduction of a new word from God in narrative form marks 21:16–17 as a separate paragraph similar to 16:13–15.

This brief oracle is structured into two brief subparagraphs:

The Needs of the Fugitives	16:13–15
God's Word: Kedar Will End	16:16–17

21:13–15. These verses refer to "caravans of Dedanites" out in the desert who asked the people from Tema to bring food and water to refugees fleeing from a war. The enemy who attacked them and forced them to flee is not identified (possibly it was Assyria). Dedan and Tema are places that are grouped together with the kings of Arabia (Jer 25:23–24; Ezek 27:20–21). Dedan and Tema are about 100 miles apart in northeast Arabia with Kedar to the north of them. The location of the Dedanite caravan in this oracle is unknown, but it seems to be on the road somewhere between Tema and Dedan.

When word comes from the refugees that they need food and water, one assumes that they have traveled or lived in the desert for some time. Those traveling on the trade routes by camel were informed of the plight of the refugees and fugitives who asked for assistance.[274] It is unclear why the caravans of Dedanites were camping out in the open among the scrub bush in the desert,[275]

---

[273] Wildberger, *Isaiah 13–27*, 339, prefers the translation "in the desert" rather than "concerning Arabia" (the Old Greek has "in the evening"). Although any of these are hypothetical possibilities, since earlier titles give the name of a place, Arabia is the best choice.

[274] הֵתָיוּ, "come, bring," is an imperative of exhortation (GKC § 110a). Twice v. 14 talks about the people "meeting" (לִפְרֹאת and קִדְּמוּ) the needy fugitives (missing in NIV).

[275] יַעַר usually means "forest," but in the desert area it must mean "bush" or "thicket" (NIV).

rather than at an oasis, though if war was breaking out in the area, it is possible that the caravan did not take the main trade route to avoid trouble.

21:16–17. God spoke to the prophet about this desperate situation so that Isaiah's audience would understand the significance of what was happening in Arabia. Following almost the exact pattern already introduced in 16:13–14,[276] God indicates that within one year the political power over the region of Kedar will end, its glory will disappear, and the warriors left to defend it will be few. Like the other nations that grew proud of their glorious accomplishments (13:11,19; 16:6) and trusted in their warriors and archers, Kedar will succumb under the attack of a greater military force. It is possible that the fleeing Dedanites are the first signs of this military process; later, people from the Kedar region will be forced out of their territory.[277] A quite different approach might suggest that the people of Kedar, who will be pushed from their land, will suffer judgment because they were the one who attacked those from Dedan.[278]

THEOLOGICAL IMPLICATIONS. This brief paragraph informs Isaiah's audience in Jerusalem that the whole Middle East, cities, nations, and even the obscure desert tribes will be in an uproar, probably because of Assyria's expansion of its power into the remotest parts of the world. This is just another demonstration of God's sovereign plan for every nation and tribe—even those that have little significance for the immediate welfare of Judah. God would allow a major power (probably Assyria) to overthrow nations far and wide (Babylon, Dumah, Kedar, etc.), so Judah must not fall into the trap of thinking that it will somehow escape.

9. God's Plans for Jerusalem (22:1–25)

HISTORICAL SETTING. In light of the reference to the "defenses of Judah" (22:8), "the city of David" (22:9), "the buildings of Jerusalem" (22:10), the "Old Pool" (22:11), and Hezekiah's government officials Shebna (22:15) and Eliakim (22:20), this chapter about the "Valley of Visions" (22:1,5) must relate to God's plan for Judah and Jerusalem. In this vision the prophet sees people being captured and imprisoned (22:2–3), the walls of the city being battered, and Jerusalem's defenses being worthless (22:5–8).

Commentators have associated this attack on Jerusalem with (a) Sargon's invasion of Philistia in 712–711 BC; (b) Sennacherib's siege of Jerusalem in

---

[276] Both 16:13–14 and 21:16–17 have (a) a messenger formula; (b) a time frame; (c) a comparison with the time a servant is bound by contract; (d) the removal of the glory of a nation; and (e) an announcement that few will be left.

[277] Goldingay, *Isaiah*, 126, suggests that these fugitives are the remnant left from Kedar.

[278] Tucker, "Isaiah 1–39," 189, proposes this as a possibility, but recognizes that this is impossible to prove from the text. The text does not tell why the Kedar region will have fewer and fewer people.

701 BC;[279] and (c) the Babylonian conquest of the city in 587/586 BC.[280] It
is very unlikely that this prophecy fits 711 BC because there is no information
that Jerusalem was attacked then (22:2). The references to restoring breaches
in city walls (22:9–10) and directing water to the Lower Pool through a tunnel
(probably Hezekiah's tunnel, 22:9–11) demonstrate that preparation for the
Assyrian siege were already complete (2 Chr 32:1–5) and that this message
came during the Assyrian siege in 701 BC[281] (not after it was over). The joy
and revelry demonstrate a sense of confidence (or overconfidence) in what the
city of Jerusalem did to prepare itself for this attack (22:2,13). In stark contrast
to this attitude, the prophet lamented (22:4,12) because the people were not
putting their trust in God who planned all of these events (22:11). The period
of Hezekiah was the time when Shebna and Eliakim worked within the king's
court (36:3), though in a couple of different official positions because of Shebna's unwise behavior (22:15–25).

STRUCTURE.   This material is unified by its repeated reference to "that
day" (22:5,8,12,20,25) when Judah's enemies attacked Jerusalem. The prophecy is clearly divided into two messages:

Jerusalem Rejoices Even Though She Faces Defeat   22:1–14
Shebna: Disgraced and Replaced   22:15–25

This division between the paragraphs is marked by (a) the concluding, "says
the Lord, the LORD Almighty" at the end of 22:14 and the introductory "this is
what the Lord, the LORD Almighty says" at the beginning of 22:15; (b) there
is a change in topic to address the individual Shebna in 22:15–25; and (c) a
parallel concluding final revelation was appended at the end of both paragraphs
(vv. 14 and 25).

---

[279] Oswalt, *Isaiah 1–39*, 407–408, prefers 711 BC because in 701 BC (a) Hezekiah did trust
God in the end; (b) this chapter does not refer to a siege of Jerusalem, which is necessary if it
were referring to 701; (c) the flight of officials fits 586 BC (2 Kgs 24:10–17) since Hezekiah did
not flee in 701; (d) Eliakim, not Shebna was steward in 701 BC, so 22:15–25 fits a date earlier
than 701 BC. In response one could say (a) this chapter does not comment on Hezekiah, but the
people (second plural verbs in 22:11) not looking to God; (b) "battering down walls" in 22:5 and
"horsemen at the city gate" in 22:7 does sound like a siege of the city; (c) 22:3 does not say the
king fled; (d) the timing of the replacement of Shebna in 22:15–25 is not exactly known (was it in
701 just before the war or sometime during the war in 701), so it is hard to use that information
to date this message.

[280] Hayes and Irvine, *Isaiah*, 277–79, prefer 711 BC but Sargon's annals mention no attack on
Jerusalem at this time. Clements, *Isaiah 1–39*, 182, connects vv. 5–11 to the fall of Jerusalem in
586 BC (because of God's deliverance, Jerusalem never fell in 701 BC—see 37:36). He takes the
mention of Elam in 22:6 as a reference to Babylonians fighting against Jerusalem. Isaiah spoke
the rest of the chapter (22:1–4,12–14) after God delivered Jerusalem from Sennacherib in 701 BC.
Young, *Isaiah*, II:88, interprets the whole chapter as prophetic of 586 BC while Seitz, *Isaiah 1–39*,
159–62, connects these events to 701 BC.

[281] Sweeney, *Isaiah 1–39*, 295–96, makes a strong case for placing this message during the
Assyrian siege of Jerusalem. Some people were already taken captive (22:3) and he finds no indication of an Assyrian withdrawal, so it must be before that took place.

The final paragraph is rather unique, dealing with a judgment on an individual person (22:15–22) within a series of oracles against various nations. Childs justifies this paragraph based on the parallelism "between the impending fall of unfaithful Jerusalem in v. 14 and the collapse of the house of David symbolized by Eliakim (v. 25)."[282] Hayes and Irvine explain the inclusion of the Shebna prophecy by identifying Shebna as (a) the person in charge of the administration of Judah (Hezekiah was sick at this time); (b) the leader of Judah's revolt against the Assyrian king Sargon; and (c) the official who caused the people to trust in their human defenses (22:8b–11).[283] This reconstruction of events is rather speculative and beyond anyone's ability to verify. A third way to justify the Shebna oracle is to view it as an illustration (in the specific behavior of one person) of the general problem that was widespread in Judah.[284] In a similar manner, the life of the arrogant king of Babylon is a concrete illustration of the general sin of glorious Babylon (14:4–21). In Judah, the people foolishly did not understand the stupidity of rejoicing before their war with Assyria was over (22:1–2,13), the arrogant leaders did not yet conclude that they should trust God rather than trust in military preparations (vv. 8a–11), and the self-centered Shebna did not realize that he should be more concerned with the responsibilities of his office instead of building a monumental tomb for himself (vv. 15–19).

(1) Jerusalem Rejoices Even Though She Faces Defeat (22:1–14)

[1]**An oracle concerning the Valley of Vision:**

What troubles you now,
    that you have all gone up on the roofs,
[2]**O town full of commotion,**
    O city of tumult and revelry?
Your slain were not killed by the sword,
    nor did they die in battle.
[3]**All your leaders have fled together;**
    they have been captured without using the bow.
All you who were caught were taken prisoner together,
    having fled while the enemy was still far away.
[4]**Therefore I said, "Turn away from me;**
    let me weep bitterly.
Do not try to console me
    over the destruction of my people."

---

[282] Childs, *Isaiah*, 159, cf. 162. Childs understands in both cases that people have responded to God's grace in the wrong way, so the kingdom of Judah and its officials will come to an end some day in the future.

[283] Hayes and Irvine, *Isaiah*, 277–84, believe all of chap. 22 was the result of Shebna's leadership and his abuse of power.

[284] Oswalt, *Isaiah 1–39*, 405 and 416, views Shebna as a specific particularization of Judah's sinfulness in an influential person in leadership.

⁵The Lord, the LORD Almighty, has a day
　　of tumult and trampling and terror
　　in the Valley of Vision,
　a day of battering down walls
　　and of crying out to the mountains.
⁶Elam takes up the quiver,
　　with her charioteers and horses;
　　Kir uncovers the shield.
⁷Your choicest valleys are full of chariots,
　　and horsemen are posted at the city gates;
⁸the defenses of Judah are stripped away.

And you looked in that day
　　to the weapons in the Palace of the Forest;
⁹you saw that the City of David
　　had many breaches in its defenses;
you stored up water
　　in the Lower Pool.
¹⁰You counted the buildings in Jerusalem
　　and tore down houses to strengthen the wall.
¹¹You built a reservoir between the two walls
　　for the water of the Old Pool,
but you did not look to the One who made it,
　　or have regard for the One who planned it long ago.

¹²The Lord, the LORD Almighty,
　　called you on that day
to weep and to wail,
　　to tear out your hair and put on sackcloth.
¹³But see, there is joy and revelry,
　　slaughtering of cattle and killing of sheep,
　　eating of meat and drinking of wine!
"Let us eat and drink," you say,
　　"for tomorrow we die!"

¹⁴The LORD Almighty has revealed this in my hearing: "Till your dying day this sin will not be atoned for," says the Lord, the LORD Almighty.

This prophetic oracle about God's plans for Jerusalem is divided into several subparagraphs that communicate the prophet's disappointment in the attitude of the people of Jerusalem toward the Assyrian threat against Jerusalem.

People foolishly rejoice	22:1–4
The attack on Jerusalem	22:5–8a
False trust in human preparations	22:8b–11
Call to trust God	22:12–13
Divine judgment, not atonement	22:14

The prophet persuasively attacks his audience's inappropriate reactions of joy (22:1–2,13) with questions (22:1b), evidence that reveals the inappropriateness of their response (22:2b–3,5–8a), and his own example of weeping (22:4). He contrasts the human behavior that "you" did (22:8b–11a,13) with what "you" did not do (22:11b–12). He concludes that further judgment will come (22:14), if they do not learn from their past mistakes.

22:1–4 The prophet begins this sermon like all the others in this large grouping (vv. 13–23). The superscription in 22:1a entitles this as another *maśśāʾ* ("oracle") from God. Instead of identifying a specific nation as in earlier messages, the title refers to a valley (mentioned in 22:5), usually translated the "Valley of Vision." Since there is no valley by this name around Jerusalem, some interpret the word "vision" as a figurative title for either the Kidron, Hinnom, or Tyropoean Valley that surrounds Jerusalem.[285] The context in 22:5 does not clarify why a certain place around Jerusalem was called a "valley of vision," so the phrase may be referring to a valley seen in the vision. Isaiah seems to be connecting what was now happening in the valleys around Jerusalem with the fulfillment of other prophetic visions—like the vision of judgment on Jerusalem in chap. 29 (cf. 29:11).[286] The unique factor about this oracle is that it is about the people of Judah, not some foreign nation. Through this message Isaiah's audience came to realize that Judah would be treated the same as the other nations, if it failed to follow God's plans. God's justice does not play favorites with any nation; he will continue to hold all people accountable for their actions, especially his own people who have greater accountability.

Although Kissane interprets 22:1–4 as a prophetic vision of what will happen in the future (the people will mourn),[287] the connection between vv. 1–4 and vv. 12–13 argues that the prophet was concerned over the people's present rejoicing during a military encounter with some enemy. The people act like they are the victors, but the prophet interpreted these events quite differently. The prophet begins with a question that asks for an explanation to justify the behavior of his audience (22:1b). Literally, the text says "What's with you?"[288] He does not ask what their troubles are (NIV), implying something has gone wrong. He asks them why they are making so much joyful noise on

---

[285] Hayes and Irvine, *Isaiah*, 279, suggest this word חִזָּיוֹן comes from the Arabic *ḥāzâ*, meaning "calamity" (Job 34:32), which would make more sense. If "vision" is kept, they suggest that it be read as a sarcastic term describing the false vision of the leaders of Judah who were rejoicing. G. R. Driver, "Isaiah 1–39: Textual and Linguistic Problems," *JSS* 13 (1968): 36–57, earlier suggested the reading "valley of calamity."

[286] Like 22:1–3,12–13 the joyous festivals in 29:1–2 are contrasted with mourning; like 22:5–7 the enemy will be all around Jerusalem in 29:5–8; like 22:11b the people are not in tune with God's plans in 29:15. The blindness, unrepentant behavior, and ignorance of God's prophetic vision (29:10–12) are evident in the behavior of the people in chap. 22.

[287] Kissane, *Isaiah*, 232, does not equate or connect 22:1–3 (mourning after some defeat) with vv. 12–13 (people rejoicing over their treaty with Egypt).

[288] מַה־לָּךְ, "what to you?" could be paraphrased "what are you doing; what do you mean; what's with you?"

the roofs of their homes. The shouts, uproar, and jubilation[289] must be due to some news that they interpreted very positively. Isaiah's question indicates that he does not understand why this news should cause everyone to be so happy. Some hypothesize that the good news was that (a) Judah has successfully finished all its war preparation; (b) Assyria was lifting its grip on Jerusalem and withdrawing its army to address the Egyptian threat (37:9–10); (c) Hezekiah has decided to pay Sennacherib a large amount of gold and thus appease Sennacherib's anger (2 Kgs 18:14–16); or (d) the complete withdrawal of Assyrian troops after God killed 185,000 of them in one night (37:36–37). This last option, though often accepted as the context for this rejoicing[290] does not fit the situation because in 22:7 enemy horsemen were still at Jerusalem's gates and enemy chariots were still filling her valleys. In 22:13 some people were feasting because tomorrow they might die. This implies that the threat of a major battle was very immanent; therefore, this rejoicing was probably due to the successful completion of war preparations, not a temporary end of hostilities.

Isaiah's perception of the situation was radically different from his audience (22:2b–4). He was aware that many people had died (but not during a battle), some leaders of the nation fled to escape being defeated, and many people from other cities were taken captive, so he was mourning the terrible state of the nation. Isaiah focused on the nation's losses over the last several months rather than any potential "good news" about their ability to withstand an Assyrian attack. Although other biblical accounts of this war say little about these negative aspects of Judah's war with Assyria, the text of the Prism of Sennacherib[291] indicates that the Assyrians took 46 strong cities of Judah and countless unwalled villages, 200,150 people as captives plus cattle, and that some elite troops deserted Hezekiah. Although it is impossible to verify most of Sennacherib's claims, Isaiah knew that Sennacherib captured many people and devastated many cities in Judah.

Isaiah's response was to turn away from the popular joyful interpretation of these events to weep bitterly[292] (22:4). This was a time to lament and repent for all of Judah, not a time to rejoice because a few of the people in Jerusalem were

---

[289] עָלִיז, "jubilation, exaltation," is used in the positive sense in 13:3; 23:7; 24:8; 32:13, often in contrast to mourning.

[290] Wildberger, *Isaiah 13–27*, 358, believes this is the best reason to explain the peoples' joy, but this option does not fit the overall picture of what was happening.

[291] *ANET*, 287–88, gives an account from the biased perspective of the Assyrians, but that does not mean that it has none of the facts correct. This text never mentions the loss of 185,000 troops at Jerusalem, so it is clear that the author was twisting some of the facts to make the Assyrians look good.

[292] אֲמָרֵר בַּבֶּכִי—this *piel* form of the verb could be interpreted as expressing a real factitive result of the military action, so the stative verb could be translated, "I am bitter with weeping," or the *piel* could be a declarative-estimative sense to declare that he was in the psychological state of bitterness—"I pronounce bitterness with weeping." Waltke and O'Connor, IBHS, 397–403, discuss the different meanings of piel forms.

still safe. Isaiah sympathizes and identifies with the nation's loss and is sick to his stomach over the inappropriate response of those rejoicing in Jerusalem.

22:5–8a The prophet compares what was happening in Judah to events expected on the Day of the Lord. The prophet remembers the tumultuous panic and yelling, the terrifying confusion in Jerusalem as people and troops attempted to stop the Assyrian attack on the city. This kind of activity was expected on the Day of the Lord (13:6–8), and Isaiah realized that God's sending of Assyria against Jerusalem ("the Valley of Vision," i.e., the valley the vision was about) was comparable to an intermediate Day of the Lord for Judah (10:6; 29:7). The NIV translation has Isaiah remembering the troops "battering down walls" of the city[293] with battering rams (22:5). This translation is based on a questionable etymology and is not parallel to the last line in v. 5. An alternate approach based on comparable roots in other Semitic languages yields the more likely translation of "shout with a shout," an idea more parallel to "crying out" in the last line.[294] These are the brutal and savage sounds of war. People on the mountains surrounding Jerusalem will hear innocent people and troops crying out for help[295] (possibly to God on Mount Zion) as they face death at the merciless hands of vengeful enemy soldiers who are about to stab them with swords.

In 22:6 Isaiah specifically mentions the fighting by bowmen, charioteers, horsemen, and infantrymen from Elam and Kir. Little is known about the history of Kir, but Elam was an ally of Babylon in its fight for independence from Assyria. Clements used this information to conclude that Isaiah was actually describing Nebuchadnezzar's use of foreign mercenaries when he attacked Jerusalem in 587 BC.[296] Wildberger hypothesizes that small contingents of specially trained mercenaries from these two nations[297] were captured when Assyria defeated Babylon (Elam was fighting with Babylon) and that these troops were then integrated into the Assyrian army.

This paragraph ends with a description of the siege of Judah (22:7–8a). The nation was not free of all foreign influence, implying that the Assyrian troops have not yet withdrawn to Nineveh (37:36–38). The fruitful valleys of Judah

---

[293] מְקַרְקַר קִר is difficult to translate. In rabbinic Hb., קִרְקֵר means "tear down," so commentators have guessed that this phrase has something to do with "tearing down a wall."

[294] In Arabic and Aramaic this root means "bellow, screech," and in Ugaritic *qr* means "to make a sound." See Driver, "Textual and Linguistic Problems," 47–48.

[295] שׁוּעַ, "cry out," is not the cry of a soldier attacking, but the cry of the one being attacked who needs someone to come and rescue him (Job 30:24).

[296] Clements, *Isaiah 1–39*, 182–85. Oswalt, *Isaiah 1–39*, 406–8, finds a two-layer approach in chap. 22, which combines issues from Judah's war with Sargon in 711 BC with utterances referring to the destruction of Jerusalem in 586 BC. The opinion of Seitz, *Isaiah 1–39*, 159, and Childs, *Isaiah*, 159, is that there is little evidence of influence from the later 587 BC conquest by Babylon on the material in chap. 22.

[297] Wildberger, *Isaiah 13–27*, 197–98, 364–5, gives examples of Tiglath-pileser III of Assyria using troops from various states within his empire, of Manasseh supplying troops for Esarhaddon, and Ashurbanipal employing troops from 22 states in this military conquests.

that produced the grain that fed the nation were full of the chariots of their enemies. They controlled the key towns that protected the hill country of Judah, so Judah was defenseless. The literal translation of 8a ("he/it uncovered the support/protection of Judah") is sometimes connected to God removing his protection over Jerusalem,[298] but in this context the prophet was referring to the Assyrian conquest of the major cities in the valleys leading up to Jerusalem. With these key defensive cities now destroyed, Jerusalem had no protection from the invading Assyrians.

22:8b–11   The prophet now explains why Jerusalem was in such a difficult situation and what went wrong "in that day." Before this Assyrian war ever moved to the capital city of Jerusalem (the Assyrians were busy defeating Lachish), the people of Jerusalem began to trust in their own strength and military preparation (vv. 8b–11b), rather than trusting completely in God (vv. 11b, cf. 30:1–5; 31:1–3). These verses became an indictment of the people's foolish ways and justify Isaiah's weeping in 22:12. Isaiah's critique analyzed what the people trusted in by examining the focus of their eyes. They were "looking at, paying attention to" (*wattabbēṭ*) (a) having many weapons (v. 8b; see 2 Chr 32:5b) stored in the Palace of the Forest, a 150 by 75 foot building with four rows of cedar pillars that Solomon built near the Temple (1 Kgs 7:2; 10:17,21); (b) repairing the breaches in the walls of the city, plus building a second wall (22:9, see 2 Chr 32:5a);[299] (c) digging a tunnel to carry water from the Gihon Spring that was outside the wall on the east side of the City of David to a new pool inside the wall on the west side of the City of David (22:9b, see 2 Chr 32:3–4); (d) destroying homes to strengthen the walls of Jerusalem (22:10); and (e) building a reservoir to hold more water (22:11a). Although all of these things seem to be normal activities for a city threatened by a military siege, it is apparent that the leaders of Jerusalem were not trusting God; they were doing everything humanly possible to defend themselves. They did not just repair the walls; they went the second mile and even tore down houses to build new walls. They did not just expand the existing old pool to increase their water supply; they dug a tunnel over 1700 feet long through solid rock in order to insure that they would have a steady supply of water from the Gihon Spring. Everything points to a self-sufficient philosophy that Isaiah condemns. They were "looking to, paying attention to" (the root *nābaṭ*) themselves for protection (22:8b) instead of "looking to, paying attention to" (the root *nābaṭ*) God for his deliverance from their enemies (22:11b). They could "see, perceive" (the root *rā'â*) the importance of the breaches in the walls (22:9a) but did not "see, perceive" (the root *rā'â*) the importance of the plans of God (22:11b). Just as earlier gen-

---

[298] Childs, *Isaiah*, 160, views this as a stark contrast to God's statement that he would protect Jerusalem in 37:33–35.

[299] N. Avigad, "Excavations in the Jewish Quarter of the Old City of Jerusalem," *IEQ* 20 (1970), 129–40, and 22 (1972), 193–200, describes the excavation of some of the fortifications Hezekiah built to protect people on the western hill.

erations in the time of Uzziah failed to pay attention to what God was doing as he guided history (cf. 5:12), the present generation was failing to perceive the hand of God directing events in their day.

Why should the people of Jerusalem look to God? They were fully prepared to withstand a long Assyrian attack on their own. Isaiah maintained that they should have "looked to" (*hibbaṭṭem*) or trusted in God instead of their own efforts, because God "made it" (*ʿôśeyha*) and he "planned it" (*yôṣrāh*) long ago (22:11b). These two themes pay a key role in Isaiah's theological understanding of God's relationship to mankind. God was "the One who made, created" (*ʿāśâ*) the world as a whole at the beginning of history (see Gen 1–2), and he is "the One who formed, shaped" (*yāṣar*) a plan concerning how he would rule the world he created. This means that God created things for the purpose of accomplishing the goals embedded in his plan. Later, in 43:7, Isaiah indicates that the ultimate purpose for God's creation of the world was to bring glory to his name. God did not just create the heavens and the earth without any plan; his plan also involved the creation of a people to be his own (44:24). As Creator he controls what he created, like a potter controls his clay, bringing blessings on some and curses on others (45:7,9; Deut 27–28). God's direction of history through blessings and curses was not an impersonal affair, for God was constantly involved with the people on the earth (especially his own people) in order to accomplish his plan to bring about glory to his name. In light of these facts it would be foolish for God's people not to recognize God's creative power, his plan to glorify himself, and his control of history to fulfill that plan. Surely his own people should trust the God who made them and controls their future. The war and killing in Judah (the Assyrian attack) were not a surprise to God or Isaiah (cf. 10:5–15); they were part of God's plan made long ago[300] to destroy Assyria in God's land (14:24–27). Yet Isaiah's audience in Jerusalem seemed to ignore God, his power to save them, and his purpose in history. Political decisions were based more on finding allies (Egypt in 30:1–5 or Babylon in 39:1–8) or making very good preparations for war (22:8b–11a), rather than looking to God for wisdom and deliverance.

22:12–14 God's summons on that Day of Judgment was for his people to lament and wail, to cry out to God for mercy and divine intervention (29:1–3). This was what the prophet was doing in 22:4, and what he and others did at other crisis points (15:2–3,5,8; 16:9). Lamentation was the process of sorrowfully and humbly recognizing one's complete inability to handle the events of life. The one mourning saw defeat or death as inevitable, if God did not intervene.

---

[300] מֵרָחוֹק means "from afar, from a distance" when it relates to issues of space between two places. Isaiah is not saying that God is a long distance away from his people; God is very much involved with what was happening at Jerusalem. When this word is related to time as in this context, it refers to a "far, distant" time period (see 25:1; 37:26) when God put his plan together. BDB, 935.

Weeping and sorrow would naturally lead the person who was mourning to cry out to God for help (Jer 3:21–4:4; Joel 1:13–14; 2:12–17).

But the people of Judah reacted in an entirely different way when they faced the trials of life and the approaching threat of death (22:13–14). They deluded themselves into thinking that their preparations for war would save them. Consequently they rejoiced over their accomplishments and held a jubilant feast of cattle, sheep, and wine. Elsewhere Isaiah condemns such behavior (5:11–13; 28:1; 29:9), but it was especially unacceptable at this point in time. Their attitude was: "No problems, be happy. Enjoy life today, it may be your last party." This was an unbelievable attitude. Since they were under siege, they needed to preserve the limited supply of food available, for soon all the food in the city would be gone because of the Assyrian blockade. This behavior made no sense at all, for at the same time that they were rejoicing over their excellent preparation, they were resigned to defeat tomorrow. Just when they should be committing themselves to sacrifice for one another to win the battle, just when they should be seeking God's help to defeat their enemies, they were telling one another that there was no hope and death was certain. Indeed the people were blind (cf. 6:9–10) and were in a deep sleep that had taken away their spiritual sight (29:9–12).

The prophet ends this message in 22:14 with a very harsh word of judgment revealed from the Lord.[301] Its distinctive tone, narrative style, and the introduction of a new word from God suggest that this announcement was received separate from 22:1–13. It is impossible to date this later revelation (or the similar addition in 22:25) with any precision (maybe it came just a week later), but this revelation assured Isaiah and his audience in Jerusalem that God took their sins very seriously. This description of his message was meant to enhance its authority and its timeliness for this situation. If the people of Jerusalem would not recognize their sinfulness and seek atonement, there was absolutely no hope for them. All their preparations would come to nothing but death if the people refuse to trust in God. In spite of the dire tone of this concluding warning, the door was still open to receive forgiveness from God, if the people would choose to look to God for forgiveness of their sins.

(2) Shebna: Disgraced and Replaced (22:15–25)

15This is what the Lord, the Lord Almighty, says:

"Go, say to this steward,
     to Shebna, who is in charge of the palace:
16What are you doing here and who gave you permission
     to cut out a grave for yourself here,
hewing your grave on the height
     and chiseling your resting place in the rock?

---

[301] Wildberger, *Isaiah 13–27*, 375, considers this as a modified oath formula similar to 5:9; 14:24. Although this passage is without the word "swear an oath," this statement of God is similar to other oaths.

¹⁷"Beware, the LORD is about to take firm hold of you
    and hurl you away, O you mighty man.
¹⁸He will roll you up tightly like a ball
    and throw you into a large country.
There you will die
    and there your splendid chariots will remain—
    you disgrace to your master's house!
¹⁹I will depose you from your office,
    and you will be ousted from your position.

²⁰"In that day I will summon my servant, Eliakim son of Hilkiah. ²¹I will clothe him with your robe and fasten your sash around him and hand your authority over to him. He will be a father to those who live in Jerusalem and to the house of Judah. ²²I will place on his shoulder the key to the house of David; what he opens no one can shut, and what he shuts no one can open. ²³I will drive him like a peg into a firm place; he will be a seat of honor for the house of his father. ²⁴All the glory of his family will hang on him: its offspring and offshoots—all its lesser vessels, from the bowls to all the jars.

²⁵"In that day," declares the LORD Almighty, "the peg driven into the firm place will give way; it will be sheared off and will fall, and the load hanging on it will be cut down." The LORD has spoken.

The message to Shebna illustrates (he is one representative example) how the faulty worldview of the people of Jerusalem resulted in one man's theological confusion. Because Shebna was a secretary/scribe and Eliakim was the steward of the king's house when Sennacherib finally attacked Judah in 36:3, some believe that the Shebna who was the steward of the king's house in 22:15 was a different man.[302] Although there is limited knowledge about the historical or political dynamics within the king's court at this time, it is possible to hypothesize that Shebna was the king's steward while preparations were made for Sennacherib's attack (chap. 22), but that he was demoted to secretary shortly before the attack actually took place as Isaiah predicted in vv. 15–19. Eliakim became the king's new steward during Sennacherib's attack, as 36:3 confirms. Isaiah never says exactly why Hezekiah would change Shebna's responsibility, though Isaiah's criticism here may have influenced the king. The change in roles for these men from chap. 22 to 36 argues for placing chap. 22 chronologically before chap. 36.

The paragraph is divided into three sub units:

Shebna's removal from office	22:15–19
Eliakim will replace Shebna	22:20–24
Eliakim will be cut off	22:25

---

[302] Seitz, *Isaiah 1–39,* 160, says, "the Shebna of 22 cannot be the same Shebna, the secretary who appears with Eliakim and Joah in chapters 36–37." See J. Willis, "Historical Issues in Isaiah 22, 15–25," *Bib* 74 (1993): 60–70, for another opinion.

The interpretations of this paragraph in commentaries reveal a considerable amount of speculation both about the person attacked (Was it really Shebna or someone else?) and the reason for Isaiah's condemnation of Shebna (Was it for political, sociological, or theological reasons?).[303]

22:15–19 The paragraph begins with an announcement that God has spoken, indicating the beginning of a new authoritative divine message. God instructs the prophet to speak to Shebna, who is identified as the steward in charge of the king's house. The role of the steward (*sōkēn*, meaning "to care for") is not that clear. He may have filled the role of chief administrator or prime minister who carried out the will of the king, in which case he was second in command under the king.[304] If this is so, Shebna was intimately involved in the preparations to make Jerusalem ready for Sennacherib's attack (see 22:1–14). The reference to him as "this steward" has negative connotations (cf. "this people" in 7:4).

The prophet's question to Shebna is almost identical to the question in 22:1b: "What's with you here?" plus, "Whom do you have here?" (a slightly different tone than "who gave you permission [here]" as in NIV). The use of "here" (*pōh*) three times in v. 16 indicates that the prophet went to an area where there were tombs to deliver this message. These two questions express surprise and confusion about the tomb that Shebna was digging. Things did not make sense. Why was Shebna carving out a tomb at this time in this prominent place? This implies that it was a place for more important people and that Shebna did not have people in his family who were that famous. Since Shebna's name is not followed by the name of his father, many conclude that he was a commoner or foreigner, thus he was not worthy of having such a large tomb in such an important place.[305] In addition, if one dates 22:15–19 to the same time period as 22:1–14, it would be very inappropriate for Shebna to be working on his tomb instead of focusing on preparing Jerusalem to defend itself against Sennacherib. This may explain why King Hezekiah demoted Shebna.

Although the exact location of this tomb is not provided, Shebna was "chiseling" his grave out of the rock high up on the cliff (22:16). Across the Kidron from Jerusalem in the modern village of Silwan are many tombs cut out of the rock, including one attributed to Solomon's wife. N. Avigad published an

---

[303] Clements, *Isaiah 1–39*, 187–88, suggests that this was not originally about Shebna (his name was added later), though he rejects Vermeylen's suggestion that this paragraph was about the royal steward at the time of Josiah. Clements says the purpose of the oracle was to magnify the importance of the Davidic Dynasty. Hayes and Irvine, *Isaiah*, 284, believe Shebna was condemned for leading the nation to revolt against Assyria, since he was in charge at this time while Hezekiah was sick. Sweeney, *Isaiah 1–39*, 297, believes the modern problems in understanding this paragraph were caused by a "confusion or distortion of historical facts" by later redactors.

[304] Ugaritic *skn* (C. Gordon, *Ugaritic Textbook* (Rome: Pontifical Biblical Institute, 1965), no. 1754, refers to the chief officer under the king. See C. Gordon, *Ugaritic Textbook* (Rome: Pontifical Biblical Institute, 1965, for a study of the various officials within the government.

[305] Blenkinsopp, *Isaiah 1–39*, 338, says that these are normally an indication of status and honor, so their absence may indicate a lack of status.

inscription on a large tomb that some have identified as Shebna's tomb. An inscription on it says, "who was over the house/palace," but the name of this person is missing.[306]

God's judgment of Shebna in 22:17–18 seems very severe, indicating that the sin was great. NIV reverses the order of the verbs giving "taking hold of" and then "hurling," but this reverses the Hebrew order in order to make the passage sound more logical. The Hebrew order must make some sense as it is, but the problem is that one does not take hold of something after he has already hurled it away from himself. Therefore, a better translation of the first verb is "lay you low, overwhelm you" rather than "hurl."[307] By using two forms of the same root to emphasize the nature of each of these actions, the prophet emphasizes that God will "totally overwhelm you." [308] Similarly, "sieze you with seizing" communicates that he will be "tightly seizing you," meaning he will take complete control of this "mighty man" (*gāber*, intended sarcastically) Shebna. Once he is under God's control, God will wrap him up like a ball (a symbol of his bondage) and he will end up in a distant country, implying that Shebna will be exiled somewhere. Instead of proudly riding around Jerusalem in a fancy palace chariot and eventually being buried in a grand tomb, Shebna will die in exile and be a source of great shame on the king's house (which he was supposed to be serving). Oswalt rightly comments that "the quest for our own glory is most likely to disgrace us."[309] This prophecy (*yehersekā*, lit. "he will cast you down") signals that God no longer accepted Shebna as steward (22:19). It appears that before long Hezekiah also removed him from his government position (36:3).

Isaiah's accusations against Shebna are brief, but it appears that Shebna was a very proud man who was more concerned with providing for himself than serving the king. One wonders if some of the misperceptions of reality by the people in 22:1–14 were also due to some failures on Shebna's part. Shebna's responsibility was to prepare the city for Sennacherib's siege, not to build a

---

[306] This inscription was discovered by Clermont-Ganneau in 1870 and was moved to the British Museum in London. N. Avigad, "The Epitaph of a Royal Steward from Siloam Village," *IEJ* 3 (1953), 137–52, reads the full inscription to say, "This is [the grave of . . .]ihu, who was in charge of the palace. There is no silver or gold here, only [his bones], and the bones of his slave girl are with him. Cursed be the man who opens this." The name is missing, but this could be the grave of "Shebanayahu."

[307] Job 41:9 uses this verb טוּל to describe what happens when one faces the power of Leviathan. Because of his power one is "laid low, overwhelmed."

[308] מְטַלְטֶלְךָ טַלְטֵלָה has a *pilpel* participle plus a noun "overwhelming you with overwhelming," though this does not match the following parallel formulas that end with infinitive absolutes. Wildberger, *Isaiah 13–27*, 380, suggests that this is an infinitive absolute like the others. The final ה on the noun is moved to the next word (הַגָּבֶר), making it a vocative, "oh man," which makes good sense, restores the parallelism between the three infinitive absolutes, and does not change the basic meaning of what was being communicated. The article could also take the place of a demonstrative giving "this mighty man" " (GKC § 126b).

[309] Oswalt, *Isaiah 1–39*, 421, finds that Shebna's action, which was supposed to bring great honor to himself, actually brought shame to the king and to himself.

beautiful large tomb. This great man brought shame on himself, and he lost his high position of responsibility in the government because he did not look to God (22:11). His focus was always on himself. His life stands as an example of the accountability God requires of his servants in positions of leadership.

22:20–24 In contrast to Shebna, a new steward will arise who will be "my servant" (*'abdî*). He will not just be interested in self-promotion or building mortuary monuments for future generations to admire. On some future day God will replace Shebna with Eliakim—he will have the royal clothes[310] and the authoritative seal that gives him the power to transact government business. He will function as a father who truly cares for his children and will sacrifice his wishes for the good of his children, the people of Jerusalem. These characteristics of a good leader stand in sharp contrast with Shebna's self-serving behavior, which ended up disqualifying him for a position of leadership

Isaiah was not usurping the king's authority and installing Eliakim as prime minister at this time (or acting as a king in place of Hezekiah), he was prophesying what would happen at some future date. The responsibilities and power given to Eliakim were great. He would have the keys of the kingdom[311] that to controlled who gets into the palace to see the king and who does not. His control over who advised the king gave him tremendous power in determining what decisions were made. These decisions would even have an impact on the future of the Davidic dynasty in Jerusalem.[312]

Eliakim came to his office (22:23–24) with God's approval and God's promise to make him a firmly secure peg that would provide a solid foundation for the government of the nation. Using the imagery of a tent stake driven into solid ground or a strongly rooted hanger driven into the wall of a house, God promises that Eliakim will be a solid support for all who depend on him. Since Eliakim served in Jerusalem during the siege by Sennacherib (36:3,11), this promise is extremely significant, for it implies that Eliakim's period of rule over the king's house will not be destroyed by Sennacherib's attack. His appointment will have a positive effect on the nation and his behavior will bring great honor to his reputation. This contrasts with the shame that Shebna brought on the king's house because of his inappropriate action (22:18). The honor he will bring to his "father's house" could refer to his blood relatives or to the king's house.

---

[310] כתנת refers to a "linen robe." Similar robes were worn by priests (Exod 28:4) or by common people for special events. אבנטך refers to "your sash" or decorative cloth worn over the garment that probably had a symbol or title on it to identify the important office he held.

[311] Wildberger, *Isaiah 13–27*, 402, notes that similar terminology about the "keys of the kingdom" was used in the NT in Matt 16:19 when Jesus was speaking to Peter. In addition, Rev 3:7 indicates that Jesus is the one who has the authority to open and shut, implying that he has these keys.

[312] It is best to reject the interpretation of Hayes and Irvine, *Isaiah*, 286–87, who interpret "my servant" as a sarcastic title, find the prophet chiding Eliakim in 22:23–24 for looking after his father's house rather than the king's house, and view the "seat of honor" as a euphemism for the toilet.

Some interpret 22:24 as a conditional warning to Eliakim that he should not practice nepotism by bringing family members into government[313] and v. 25 as an announcement of punishment for nepotism. But 22:25 starts a new negative word from God that should not be grammatically joined to 22:24 to form a protasis and apodosis. Rather 22:24 indicates that the "glory of his father's house" will depend on him, demonstrating his importance and dependability. The prophet lists the various objects that depend on this peg (Eliakim), using the imagery of vessels, bowls, and jars. One can interpret these symbols as referring to Eliakim's relatives (NIV) depending on him, but that is a very subjective interpretation of bowls, jars, and vessels. It seems more likely that Isaiah is simply saying everything and everyone will depend on him. If the bowls and jars are symbolic of "everything," the other symbols ("offspring and offshoots") should be symbolic of "everyone."

22:25 The paragraph ends with a final additional narrative word from God similar to the narrative addition that concludes 22:1–14. God announces in a separate oracle that Eliakim,[314] the peg that God will drive into a firm place (22:23), will fail "on that day." No reason is given to explain why this peg will fall to the ground, but with the glory or burden of the king's house resting on him, one could assume that the weight got too heavy or that someone destroyed Eliakim. This indicates that Jerusalem will be properly cared for during the immediate future, but that at some later date Eliakim's leadership will fail and all those who depended on him will be cut off. The prophet provides few hints about the fulfillment of this prophecy. This prediction may apply literally to Eliakim or it may refer more broadly to the children of Eliakim in future generations.

THEOLOGICAL IMPLICATIONS. The inclusion of an oracle against Judah demonstrates that sinful behavior is also present among God's people; it is not just a character flaw of people in foreign nations. The people of Judah who know about God can be just as blind and stubborn as any other group of people. Believers can deceive themselves and place their trust in human efforts instead of looking to God for help (22:8–11). They can become overconfident and rejoice over how well they have protected themselves and forget that God is the only source of real protection. Even important spiritual and political leaders (like Shebna) can become infatuated with their own importance and fail to serve God or his people. This is a clear warning to business, church, educational, and political leaders. God knows whom you are really serving. Do not follow the path of Shebna.

The clarity of Isaiah's perception of the situation should parallel the accuracy of the insight of the believer that observes reality through God's eyes.

---

[313] Gray, *Isaiah 1–27*, 381, believes it is improbable that the perfect verb וְתָלוּ in 22:24 would serve as a conditional form. Kissane, *Isaiah*, 243, does translate the initial verb in 22:24 as "should they hang," making it conditional.

[314] Sweeney, *Isaiah 1–39*, 294, suggests that this refers to the cutting off of Shebna (22:19), but this seems to be a most unlikely interpretation because these verses are on Eliakim, not Shebna.

The person of faith who serves God can recognize when others use selfish pride and human efforts to manipulate circumstances to their own advantage. Godly people should also be able to honestly evaluate their own motives and be willing to admit selfishness when it is discovered. The people of God should refuse to be deluded by powerful rulers who are arrogant and selfish; believers know that the power of God will determine what happens to Jerusalem and in every country in the world today and that God cannot bless leaders that honor themselves instead of God. Those who follow the footsteps of Isaiah lament the failure of God's people to root out selfish ambition. They should prayerfully try to convince those who have gone astray that the way that seems right to them (the way that furthers their glory) may actually lead to their destruction.

Leaders who fail to lead people to depend on God will not last; instead, God will raise up true servants (22:20) who care for others, like a father cares for his children (22:21). God will firmly establish them and give them great opportunities for service and influence (22:22). Nevertheless, people are not the basis for a secure future in any organization; God is the only truly dependable resource for hope.

10. God's Plans for Tyre (23:1–18)

This oracle completes this series of ten messages from God. Oswalt finds these oracles (chaps. 13–23) covering the nations of the earth from east (Babylon in chaps. 13–14) to west (Tyre in chap. 23).[315] The series of *maśśā'* oracles begins by pinpointing the defeat of the great political power Babylon, and they end by describing the fall of the great economic power of Tyre. These nations are not just symbolic representative cities; they are real nations at the time of Isaiah that God will judge for their sins.[316] God's destruction of all these nations, including the great sea power Tyre, clearly demonstrates God's sovereign power over every people on land and sea. Looking at these messages from another perspective, Motyer interprets the Tyre oracle at the end of the second group of five oracles as a parallel to the Egypt oracles at the end of the first group of five oracles. Both of these messages conclude with a surprising turning of people in foreign nations to worship God (19:18–25; 23:18).[317]

As with the previous nations, Isaiah integrates the work of God with the nation of Tyre (a) into the synthetic "plan" God has for all nations (14:24,26,27; 16:3; 19:12,17; 23:9; 25:10); (b) by consistently working to "humble the proud" and haughty (2:9,11,12,17; 5:15; 10:12; 23:9); (c) through the power

---

[315] Oswalt, *Isaiah 1–39*, 427, notes similarities between the Babylon oracles in chaps. 13–14 and Tyre in chap. 23. He thinks both were used to develop ideas about the great city in Rev 18.

[316] Oswalt, *Isaiah 1–39*, 427, concludes that these nations are symbolic or representative.

[317] Motyer, *The Prophecy of Isaiah*, 132–33, finds three parallel developments, the last one involving chaps. 24–27, but this final set of parallel features is not a very strong parallel that is anchored in identical repeated vocabulary. The ideas in 23:18 are actually closer to those in 18:7.

of his "outstretched arm" (5:25; 9:12,17,21; 10:4; 14:26–27; 23:11); which (d) will shake ("cause to tremble") the nations (13:13; 14:16; 23:11). Therefore it is time to "wail" (13:6; 14:31; 15:1–2; 16:7; 23:1,14) because God's hand of judgment is about to fall on Tyre.

R. Lessing considers this a satirical lament because of (a) the textual context; (b) 18 verbal markers; and (c) the presence of contradictions, disparity, and anomalies.[318] In taking this approach, he is following the general interpretative methodology of F. W. Dobbs-Allsopp, who found many satirical city-laments in ancient Near Eastern literature and the Bible. He determined that chap. 23 had eight of the nine typical characteristics of this genre.[319] R. Lessing finds satirical laments over Babylon in chaps. 13–14 and over Moab in chaps. 15–16, so having one in chap. 23 fits the context of the way the prophet deals with other nations. He takes all nine imperatives as satirical and finds disparity in the idea that the prophet called Judah to lament for Tyre, a nation that was hardly a friend of Judah. Although one cannot deny that there is some irony in weeping for Tyre, nevertheless, if Judah was depending on Tyre to help resist the power of Assyria, this prediction of the loss of Tyre would be a blow to those who opposed Assyria and a legitimate reason to lament.

In spite of the frequent call for others to wail ("the ships of Tarshish" in 14:1,14), Isaiah still speaks to a Hebrew audience in Judah about God's sovereign control over all the nations of the earth. The Hebrews not only observed the mighty power of God's outstretched arm against other nations; they also learned from these examples why God would judge each nation. As God's people faced the reality of military action against Judah, it became clear that it made no sense to look to any of these nations for security through alliances. Since God will soon destroy all of these nations, Judah's only hope was to trust in the power of Almighty God. This basic theological commitment to trust God for everything in life is held up again and again as the only hope for mankind. Life, liberty, security, and prosperity are dependent on the gracious plan of a sovereign God, not on any arrogant attempts to manipulate circumstances through human wisdom, military might, or political alliances. God has revealed this truth to his prophets and history proves that it is so; therefore, each generation and each nation must choose how it will respond. The proud and self-reliant will be humbled; the humble people who trust God will walk in the security of his plan.

---

[318] R. Lessing, "Satire in Isaiah's Tyre Oracle," *JSOT* 28 (2003): 89–112, depends on D. C. Muecke, *The Compass of Irony* (London: Methuen, 1969), 19–20, to define satire as (a) a "double-layered or two-storied phenomenon," (b) with opposition between these two levels, and (c) a touch of innocence.

[319] F. W. Dobbs-Allsopp, *Weep, O Daughter of Zion: A Study of the City-Lament Genre in the Hebrew Bible* (Rome: Pontifical Biblical Institute, 1993), 158, also connects the book of Lamentations to this genre.

HISTORICAL SETTING.   Commentators suggest four possible dates for the historical circumstances surrounding this lament concerning the devastation that will come on the Phoenician cities of Tyre and Sidon. (a) The mention of the Assyrian conquest of Babylon in 23:13 led S. Erlandsson to conclude that this prophecy was fulfilled shortly after Sennacherib defeated Babylon (703 BC). Sennacherib mentions that in his third year that he overcame "Luli king of Sidon" (this refers to King Elulaeus) and put Tyre under siege for five years.[320] (b) Wildberger, who does not believe 23:1–14 was written by Isaiah, concludes that this lament came after the defeat of Tyre and Sidon, and therefore he relates these events to the Assyrian king Esarhaddon's claim that, "As to Sidon, which lies in the midst of the sea, I leveled it" (674 BC) and "I conquered Tyre, which is located in the midst of the sea, I took away from its king Baal, who had trusted in *tarqu* the king of KUR*kusi*" (Tirhakah king of Cush/Egypt).[321] (c) O. Kaiser argues that the conquest of Sidon by Artaxerxes III Ochus in 343 BC best fits the historical circumstances. (d) J. Lindbloom associates these events with Alexander the Great who defeated Tyre around 332 BC.[322]

The most natural way of understanding this lament is that it was given in anticipation of the fall of Tyre and Sidon during the time of Isaiah. Since the Phoenician people will flee to Cyprus and Babylon was recently defeated (23:13 happened in 703 BC), this prophecy could be placed a short time before Sennacherib's attack on Jerusalem in 701 BC. If God had planned the defeat of all the nations around Judah (including Babylon, Egypt, and Tyre), where can the people of Judah go for help? There is only one answer.

STRUCTURE.   The paragraphs are marked by the repetition of similar calls for the ships of Tarshish to wail (23:1,14) and a series of exhortations to different groups of people (23:1,2,4,6,10,13,14). The first paragraph could be divided into six subunits based on each new imperative exhortation (like Sweeney). Alternately, the repeated references to Tarshish wailing because the harbor of Tyre is destroyed (23:1,6,10,14) could be taken as structural markers identifying three subparagraphs (like Kissane). It seems best to group some of these smaller units into a couple of main paragraphs.[323]

---

[320] Erlandsson, *The Burden of Babylon*, 99–101, thinks the 70 years of decline in 23:15 refers to the life span of the ruling king and should be connected to the period of 700–630 BC when Assyria impeded the growth of Tyre. After the death of Ashurbanipal around 630 BC, Assyria lost most of its power to control its vast empire.

[321] *ANET*, 291, or Wildberger, *Isaiah 13–27*, 418, for translations of these texts. Wildberger also notes that the time of Esarhaddon explains why Egypt will weep and that time frame fits a period when the Assyrians controlled Cyprus, thus justifying the claim that he controlled the islands of the sea (23:2,6,11–12). Clements, *Isaiah 1–39*, 192, also rejects Isaianic authorship and dates these events to the time of Essarhaddon's attack on Sidon.

[322] Kaiser, *Isaiah 13–39*, 162; J Lindbloom, "Der Ausspruch uber Tyrus in Jes. 23," *ASTI* 4 (1965): 217–21.

[323] Sweeney, *Isaiah 1–39*, 306–307, identifies a command and a reason in each paragraph. Kissane, *Isaiah*, 251–52, finds three paragraphs of eight, seven, eight poetic units. Watts, *Isaiah 1–33*,

(1) Lament over Proud Tyre (23:1–14)

[1]An oracle concerning Tyre:

Wail, O ships of Tarshish!
  For Tyre is destroyed
  and left without house or harbor.
From the land of Cyprus
  word has come to them.

[2]Be silent, you people of the island
  and you merchants of Sidon,
  whom the seafarers have enriched.
[3]On the great waters
  came the grain of the Shihor;
the harvest of the Nile was the revenue of Tyre,
  and she became the marketplace of the nations.

[4]Be ashamed, O Sidon, and you, O fortress of the sea,
  for the sea has spoken:
"I have neither been in labor nor given birth;
  I have neither reared sons nor brought up daughters."
[5]When word comes to Egypt,
  they will be in anguish at the report from Tyre.

[6]Cross over to Tarshish;
  wail, you people of the island.
[7]Is this your city of revelry,
  the old, old city,
whose feet have taken her
  to settle in far-off lands?
[8]Who planned this against Tyre,
  the bestower of crowns,
whose merchants are princes,
  whose traders are renowned in the earth?

303, prefers a more theological arrangement of 23:1–7 and 23:8–14.

⁹The LORD Almighty planned it,
   to bring low the pride of all glory
   and to humble all who are renowned on the earth.

¹⁰Till your land as along the Nile,
   O Daughter of Tarshish,
   for you no longer have a harbor.
¹¹The LORD has stretched out his hand over the sea
   and made its kingdoms tremble.
He has given an order concerning Phoenicia
   that her fortresses be destroyed.
¹²He said, "No more of your reveling,
   O Virgin Daughter of Sidon, now crushed!

"Up, cross over to Cyprus;
   even there you will find no rest."
¹³Look at the land of the Babylonians,
   this people that is now of no account!
The Assyrians have made it
   a place for desert creatures;
they raised up their siege towers,
   they stripped its fortresses bare
   and turned it into a ruin.

¹⁴Wail, you ships of Tarshish;
   your fortress is destroyed!

23:1–7 The first sub-paragraph focuses on the call for people around the Mediterranean Sea to lament because of the approaching fall of Tyre and Sidon. The lament shares some similarities with the one over Moab in 15:1–16:14, though that one described the people of Moab lamenting rather than announcing the need to lament (with imperatives) as in chap. 23. These differences suggest that chaps. 15–16 were given while Moab's day of disaster was in progress, while chap. 23 announces the need to lament because of what would soon happen to Tyre and Sidon.

23:1 The message begins with the traditional superscription, declaring that this is another "oracle, burden" from God about Tyre. "Tyre" (*ṣōr*) means "rock" because one part of the city was built on a large rock in the Mediterranean Sea that created an island. In this case Tyre represents the Phoenician people, with Tyre and Sidon being two of the main commercial centers for business and shipping. The later portrayal of the wealth and security of Tyre in Ezek 26–28 should not be read back into the situation of Tyre in this text, but those chapters give the modern reader a fuller understanding of the wealth and stature of this great nation.[324] The city of Tyre included both a village on the shores of the Mediterranean Sea as well as a city on an island about five

---

[324] Block, *Ezekiel 25–48*, 28–128, has a thorough discussion of Ezekiel's description of Tyre and his lament over the fall of the city.

hundred yards off the coast. This commercial city had an outstanding harbor and boats brought goods from as far away as Tarshish in Spain.

The lament begins with an imperative exhortation for the sailors coming to Tyre in large ships from Tarshish to wail. These sailors from Tyre will probably hear the news about the fall of Tyre when they stop to deliver goods at Cyprus or some other nearby port. The second half of the verse is difficult to translate for it literally says, "for it is destroyed without a house without an entrance from the land of Kittim, it will be revealed to them." NIV smoothes out this cryptic message by identifying "Tyre" as what was destroyed and the "entrance" as the harbor.[325] This will be terrible news to the sailors when they learn that their homes, families, and secure city no longer exist. They will naturally wail in agony about what has happened.

23:2–3 The second imperative calls for the rich merchants in Sidon and the coastal islands of Phoenicia to "mourn" (better than "be silent").[326] The Dead Sea Scroll text of Isaiah has "your messengers" (NASB; HCSB)[327] pass over the sea in the second half of v. 2, but the Hebrew Masoretic text makes good sense as it is (followed by NIV). The verse calls on the merchants and sailors to mourn. They are the ones who "fill you" (*milʾûk*); that is, they fill Tyre and Sidon with all the wealth that it has (a similar statement is found in Ezek 27:25). These cities were wealthy because Phoenician ships were paid richly to carry Egyptian grain to markets in many foreign nations. Isaiah is prophesying that the coming destruction will soon bring all this prosperity to an end.

23:4–7 This brief exhortation calls the Phoenician people to express shame and embarrassment because they will lose all their honor and glory. Both "the sea" and the "fortress of the sea" are mentioned before the quotation in the second half of the verse, but it is unclear if these are two different entities or (as is more likely) if the "fortress of the sea" simply refers to the island city of Tyre, which subsequently speaks.[328] The words quoted reflect the embarrassing state

---

[325] מִבּוֹא, "without entrance," is the preposition "from, without" plus the infinitive construct of "enter, come, go," so it could mean "from coming, entering," but מִן can have the meaning "without" as in "without a bow" in 22:3 (GKC §119w). The question still remains, does this refer to the entrance to their house or the entrance (harbor) to the island?

[326] דֹמּוּ could come from דמם, "to be silent," but another root of דמם means "to mourn," which provides a better parallel to "wail" in v. 1. M. Dahood, "Textual Problems in Isaiah," *CBQ* 22 (1960): 400, who relies on Ugaritic, supports "mourn," but long ago (1886) Delitzsch, *Isaiah*, connected this word to Akkadian *damāmu*, "grieve, mourn."

[327] The 1QIsaᵃ reading מַלְאָכַיִךְ, "your messengers," is widely accepted as a better parallel for "your merchants" in the preceding line, but this is deceptive. The three subjects, all participles, are "those who dwell, the inhabitants" (יֹשֵׁב), "those who travel, local merchants" (סֹחֵר), and "those who cross over [the sea], foreign merchants" (עֹבֵר). It is inappropriate to make the last word in this verse a subject. The three subjects are those who should wail, and it is also they who "fill, enrich" the city of Tyre.

[328] A. van der Kooij, *The Oracle of Tyre: The Septuagint of Isaiah XXIII as Version and Vision*, VTSupp (Brill, Leiden, 1998), 23, takes this approach. Oswalt, *Isaiah 1–39*, 430–31, thinks this is the Canaanite god "yam" (the sea), the "mighty one" of the sea who speaks these words, but this is unlikely for this is not a poem about Phoenician religion. Another approach might be to take

of a childless woman (cf. 54:1,4,6; 1 Sam 1:1–8). The destruction of the Phoenician cities (the sons and daughters of the main cities) means that the mother
cities will no longer give birth to new cities, no longer nurture these colonies,
and will have no descendent cities still alive. This terrible news about the total
decimation of Phoenicia will also severely affect Tyre's trading partners. The
Egyptians will be in anguish (23:5) because their wealth was heavily depended
on the Phoenician ships that transported their products to markets throughout
the Mediterranean.

The paragraph ends in 23:6–7 with another imperative exhortation very
similar to the exhortation to wail in 23:1. It calls for wailing and for people to
go far away for protection from this disaster. But how will these wailing people
from the defeated cities of Tyre and Sidon be able to pass over and escape to
Tarshish? Although many will want to escape, it will be impossible. Thus this
imperative ironically brings to people's mind the hopelessness of Tyre's situation.[329] It will be hard to fathom the enormous changes in life at Tyre. Once
this city was full of riches and excitement, the wild carousing life of sailors
and merchants, and all the exuberant nightlife that goes with that. This was the
nation that had everything going for it. It colonized various cities to protect
and establish its trading operations far away from home. But now what has
happened to that very old city? This devastating defeat will transform it into
something totally different from what it was in the past.

23:8 In the second part of the prophet's lament, Isaiah raises a rhetorical
question to get his Hebrew audience to think about their own situation and to
teach them a valuable lesson from history (v. 8). What will happen in Tyre is
not totally unrelated to what will happen in Judah. Although politicians, rulers, and people looking back on it will have theories as to what went wrong
at Tyre, Isaiah challenges the people in Jerusalem to give the real reason Tyre
and Sidon will change from an exciting and prosperous commercial center that
influenced all the Mediterranean nations to a place of no importance. Was this
just a freak accident that is unexplainable, was its defeat due to poor leadership by the king of Tyre, or was the fall of Tyre based on the wise strategy of a
cunning Assyrian king? How could a powerful nation that had crowned many
kings of small city-states suddenly have this happen to it? How could merchants be treated one day like a prince or famous person and then suddenly be
gone? What happened to these proud, wealthy, and powerful people? Someone
is responsible for bringing about the dramatic defeat of a nation that for years
seemed to have unlimited wealth, power, friends, and trading partners.

23:9 Isaiah's answer to this question is that the Almighty sovereign God
of the nations has planned these things this way. From the beginning of Isa-

---

"the fortress of the sea" as the object the sea was speaking to, though the expected preposition ל,
"to," is missing.

[329] Wildberger, *Isaiah 13–27*, 427, takes this and the imperative in 23:12 as ironic (see the
discussion of this usage in GKC §110a, though this passage is not specifically treated).

iah's prophetic preaching (2:9,11–12,17; 5:15–16) he has emphasized that God's theological plan is "to profane, defile" (*lĕhallēl*[330]) the pride of mankind that brings glory to people. God alone is to be glorified and set apart as holy; so all exaltation of mankind, which takes away from the glory of God's majesty, will be defiled and be made putrid. Isaiah takes this known plan of God and explains how it will apply to those renowned people (lit. the "glorified ones, honored ones," *nikbaddê*) who think they are so great. They will be brought low and completely humiliated (lit. "to be esteemed lightly," *lĕhāqēl*). This fundamental principle governs how God will deal with the arrogance (13:11) of Babylon's proud king (14:12–15), the haughty Moabites (16:6), the people of Tyre (23:9), and all people on the earth (2:9–17) on the Day of the Lord. The future defeat of Tyre was a vivid lesson of what could happen to Jerusalem in the near future. The principle is that anyone, past or present, who trusts in their own human abilities and attempts to control their destiny independent of God's sovereign grace and direction is doomed to failure. If rich and poor people do not humble themselves before God, God will humble them in due time. The implication of this threat for the people of Judah is that if they follow the pride and self-sufficiency of Tyre and do not look to God (22:8–13), they too will be humbled.

23:10–12 The text of v. 10 is difficult to understand, and the translations of the Hebrew do not agree. Two textual problems are complicated by the cryptic nature of this exhortation. The literal translation, "pass over your land like the Nile," contains the unusual image of people flooding over the land like the Nile River flooded the delta of Egypt. But what does this mean? Is this an odd way of saying that their needs to be a massive movement of people from the merchant city of Tarshish back to farming in the countryside? The Old Greek and 1QIsa[a] read "work your land,"[331] which the NIV follows, suggesting that the people of Tarshish will need to depend on what they can raise in their farms to make a living because there will be no way for merchants to make a living by selling goods brought from Tyre. A second puzzle is the reference to there being no "girdle, waistband," or the variant "harbor" (NIV).[332] Motyer viewed the loss of the girdle as a removal of Tyre's control over Tarshish, but Gray appropriately interprets the removal of a girdle as a sign that someone is defenseless.[333] This fits 23:11, which claims that all the nations (including Tarshish) are defenseless before the powerful outstretched hand of God (cf. 5:25;

---

[330] לְחַלֵּל is a piel infinitive construct that shows purpose. See GKC §114f.

[331] This was caused by confusion between עבר, "pass over," and עבד, "serve," because the letters ר and ד are almost identical in Hb..

[332] מֵזַח is a "girdle, waistband" but with a reversal of the last two letters and a vowel change one gets מָחֹז, "harbor," which better fits the context of ships, though girdle might have a metaphorical meaning here.

[333] Motyer, *The Prophecy of Isaiah*, 191–92, thinks מָחֹז means "ship building" not "anchorage," thus he keeps the idea of "girdle, control." Gray, *Isaiah 1–27*, 39,1 uses Job 12:21 to show that the removal of the girdle leaves one vulnerable to attack and defeat.

9:12,17,21: 10:4). He controls what happens on the sea, not the people of Tyre, and his powerful command will lead to the desolation of the great fortress of Tyre. Lamentably, Sidon also will have no reason for revelry, because Sidon will suffer like an abused virgin who is violated and oppressed (23:12). There is no hope of relief, not even in the friendlier context of Cyprus, since being exiled from the homeland does not bring true peace. Later history indicates that Luli king of Sidon did escape to Cyprus to flee from the attack of Sennacherib,[334] but this was not any real escape, for Assyrian control extended beyond the shores of the Phoenician coast. Isaiah uses God's plan, his outstretched hand, and his words to convince his audience in Jerusalem that God will sovereignly work to remove the glory of Tyre and humble its people.

23:13 If one or two people might still doubt the power of God's hand or his ability to fulfill his plan, Isaiah offers one final proof that what God says actually happens. Some of God's past predictions about Babylon have already come true by this time, so it would be foolish for anyone to question what God says. Shortly before 702 BC and the giving of this message, Sennacherib put down a revolt by Merodoch-baladan by attacking the cities of Babylon, tearing down its fortresses, making it a place for wild animals, and turning the land into ruins. Now that great country is nothing. If God can do this to Babylon, why can he not do the same to Tyre or any other nation (even Judah)?

23:14 The paragraph ends with the same exhortation that was at the beginning of the paragraph. The sailors on the ships of Tarshish should wail because God will destroy Tyre, that great fortress in the sea! There is no hope for it.

(2) Restoration after Seventy Years (23:15–18)

15At that time Tyre will be forgotten for seventy years, the span of a king's life. But at the end of these seventy years, it will happen to Tyre as in the song of the prostitute:

> **16**"Take up a harp, walk through the city,
>   O prostitute forgotten;
>   play the harp well, sing many a song,
>   so that you will be remembered."

17At the end of seventy years, the LORD will deal with Tyre. She will return to her hire as a prostitute and will ply her trade with all the kingdoms on the face of the earth. **18**Yet her profit and her earnings will be set apart for the LORD; they will not be stored up or hoarded. Her profits will go to those who live before the LORD, for abundant food and fine clothes.

23:15–16 After predicting the fall of Tyre, the prophet surprisingly speaks about the future revival of Tyre after seventy years, similar to the positive words at the end of the Egypt oracle in 19:18–25 (at the end of the first se-

---

[334] *ANET*, 288. Later, during the reign of the Assyrian king Esarhaddon, ships from Tyre were not allowed to trade with the cities on the island of Cyprus (see *ANET*, 533–34).

ries of five nations). Just as the Egyptians and Assyrians will one day worship God (19:21), so the people of Tyre will one day present holy gifts to the Lord (23:18). The implication of this prophecy for the prophet's audience in Judah is that the people of Judah need to trust God, for several of these foreign nations will eventually see the error of their ways and come to trust God.

Once Tyre is destroyed, it will be in decline for about seventy years (23:15). Instead of being a major player in international trade, it will be forgotten.[335] The seventy years specifies the average life of a king—or a man—in Ps 90:10. This time frame is much longer than the earlier "one to three years of a hired worker" in 16:14 and 21:16. It is impossible to say when this seventy-year period began or ended, but if the Assyrians humbled the Phoenicians around 702 BC then the seventy years would extend to around 630 BC, the time when the Assyrian empire collapsed after the death of Ashurbanipal.[336] Since Tyre will be insignificant during this seventy-year period, the text does not give any details concerning what will happen there. Instead it moves immediately to the period after the seventy years by quoting the "Song of the Prostitute"—probably a song that Isaiah's audience had heard before.

The song seems to deride or mock a haggard prostitute who is forgotten and no longer popular. Instead of men knocking on her door to visit her, she must take to the streets to play beautiful music and sing suggestive songs that will attract some business. The hope is that she will be remembered instead of forgotten, just like Tyre will want to be remembered after her period of decline. Tyre is not called a harlot here; her period of decline is only compared to the life of a forgotten harlot.

23:17–18 The final few verses describe how God will treat Tyre at the end of the seventy years. Now Tyre is compared to a harlot, but this symbolizes a return to being an important player in international trade. Because God will look with favor on Tyre, she will once again actively return to prominence and not be a forgotten merchant. Some of the money[337] Tyre earns from international trade will be set apart as holy to God. Instead of hording tons of gold in their vaults for their own pleasures, they will generously give it to the temple of God to be used to support temple personnel who dwell in God's presence. This suggests a dramatic change of priorities and a heart transformation that desires to glorify God. Although history provides no information about the fulfillment of this prophecy,[338] the spirit of this prophecy is consistent with the

---

[335] וְנִשְׁכַּחַתְּ is a *niphal* perfect third feminine singular with *vav* consecutive with an unusual ה ending (GKC §44f), which was an old feminine form.

[336] Motyer, *The Prophecy of Isaiah,* 193, makes this suggestion, though there is little evidence to indicate a turning of people in Tyre to God after 630 BC.

[337] אֶתְנַנָּה, "her wages," as a prostitute (as in Mic 1:7).

[338] Shortly after the end of the seventy years (630 BC), the Israelite king Josiah rebuilt the temple (621 BC). There is no clear statement that Tyre helped (2 Kgs 22; 2 Chr 34), though timber was bought from Phoenicia, and it is possible that Josiah depended on masons from Tyre, just as Solomon had done (1 Kgs 5).

idea in 2:1–4 that all nations will come to Zion to see God, as well as the later indications that in the eschatological era many nations will bring their wealth to Zion to offer it to God (cf. 45:14–25; 60:1–14).

THEOLOGICAL IMPLICATIONS.   The lament over Tyre demonstrates that God has power over the greatest financial nations of the earth. International trade may make one rich, but without God's blessing there is no way that money or human connections can bring real security. When God turns against a nation, all that people can do is wail and lament their great loss.

The one who knows God (the people of Judah and believers today) understand why these things happen. God has a plan (23:8) for every nation, and the central goal of that plan is that all people should honor and glorify Almighty God. When nations refuse to do that, God's plan is to stretch out his powerful hand and humble them (23:9,11). He did that with Babylon by bringing the Assyrians against them (23:13), so it should not surprise anyone if he will do something similar to the Phoenicians. The lesson for Judah and for everyone who hears God's plans for Tyre is clear. Everyone has a choice of becoming proud of their greatness and accomplishments and consequently depending on their own great financial strength for security, or of humbly giving all glory to God and using their wealth to support his work (23:18).

IV. TRUSTING NOW IN GOD, WHO WILL REIGN OVER ALL
    (24:1–27:13)
   1. God's Final Curse on an Evil World (24:1–23)
     (1) God's Curse Brings Destruction (24:1–3)
     (2) The Reason for God's Curse (24:4–13)
     (3) Joy and Sorrow over God's Destruction (24:14–16a)
     (4) After Destruction, God Will Reign (24:16b–23)
   2. Eschatological Words of Praise to God (25:1–12)
     (1) A Song of Thanksgiving (25:1–5)
     (2) God's Joyous Feast (25:6–8)
     (3) A Song of Praise for God's Deliverance (25:9–12)
   3. Judah's Trust in God for Deliverance (26:1–27:1)
     (1) A Song of Trust in God (26:1–6)
     (2) A Lament while Waiting for Salvation (26:7–19)
     (3) God Will Destroy the Enemy (26:20–27:1)
   4. God's Assurance of Salvation (27:2–13)
     (1) God's Song of Care for His Vineyard (27:2–6)
     (2) An Explanation of God's Ways (27:7–11)
     (3) Gathering to Worship (27:12–13)

IV. TRUSTING NOW IN GOD, WHO WILL REIGN OVER ALL (24:1–27:13)

The messages in this new section were not given the title "oracles, burdens," like the *maśśāʾ* oracles in chaps. 13–23, and they do not discuss the destiny of a series of individual nations. The prophet's messages now are more universal in perspective (especially in chaps. 24–25), dealing with events happening throughout heaven and earth. This section begins with a clear eschatological perspective explaining how God will judge the whole world and set up his glorious kingdom for his people (24:1–3,19–23). These prophecies reveal how God will finally deal with the rebellious nations in chaps. 13–23 so that he can bring an end to the pride and violent sinfulness that has polluted the earth. God will destroy the wicked and establish peace on the earth, and then the holy people who remain will worship God alone and sing songs to exalt him.

These words were important to Isaiah's audience because God's fulfillment of his promise to destroy the earth with his curse (24:6) and establish his reign in Zion for those who trust him (24:23; 25:9; 26:1–6) could begin to happen at any time. Therefore the people in Jerusalem who were looking for deliverance from their enemies (26:7–27:1) could and should trust God now (26:1–5), so that they can survive the discipline of God's present judgment on them (26:16–20) and later participate in the joy of God's kingdom when it finally arrives (27:2–6,12–13). These promises have a similar importance to believers in every era of history, for no matter what the problems may be that people face, everyone who trusts God knows that after God's final judgment of this earth, he will establish his glorious kingdom.

The prophet discusses these theological themes only in chaps. 24–27, for a new literary unit (chaps. 28–35) is marked by the appearance of a series of "woe oracles" (28:1; 29:1; 30:1; 31:1; 33:1). The new sermons in the next unit do not focus on the final judgment of the world. They reinforce the teachings that God will humble the proud and powerful (28:1–2; as in 25:11) and that Judah needs to trust God (28:16, as in 26:3–4) and not rely on other nations (30:1–5; 31:1–5, as in 20:1–6). God will deliver the Hebrews from their enemies (30:30–31; 31:8; as in 26:20–27:1); consequently, God will be exalted as he reigns in Zion (32:1; 33:5,10,21–22, as in 24:23).

Chapters 24–27 are thematically connected to the messages against the foreign nations in chaps. 13–23 (especially 13:1–16), to the eschatological ideas in 2:1–5, and to the praise of God in 12:1–6. Specific theological ideas are recalled from earlier texts: (a) The positive "song of the vineyard" in 27:2–6 reverses the negative vineyard song in 5:1–7. (b) The establishment of God's kingdom in 2:6–21 will involve the humbling of the proud (cf. 25:11–13; 26:5) and the Lord reigning in Zion (cf. 24:23b). (c) The imagery of destruction in chaps. 24–27 is closely connected to images of God's judgment of the individual nations in chaps. 13–23, and particularly some of the phrases in the eschatological introduction in 13:1–16.[1] (d) Both 13:1–16 and 24:1–23 describe the destruction and desolation of the earth (13:5,9 and 24:1,3,). (e) People will be in pain like a woman in labor (13:8 and 26:17–18). (f) God will come to the earth in power (13:9 and 24:23). (g) The sun and moon will be darkened (13:10 and 24:23) and the earth will shake (13:13 and 24:18–20). (h) The proud will be humbled (13:11 and 25:11–12; 26:5). And (i) few people will be left on earth (13:12 and 24:24:6) because the people are sinful (13:11 and 24:5–6). Chapters 24–27 are not so much a summary but the grand finale for 13–23. This repetition of ideas unfolds a high level of theological continuity with Isaiah's earlier prophecies,[2] but the meanings of these phrases in 24–27 are not

---

[1] M. A. Sweeney, *Isaiah 1–39, with an Introduction to Prophetic Literature*, FOTL 16 (Grand Rapids: Eerdmans, 1996), 319; see D. C. Polaski, *Authorizing an End: The Isaiah Apocalypse & Intertextuality* (Leiden: Brill, 2001), 66–70, or J. Day, "A Case of Inner Scriptural Interpretation: The Dependence of Isaiah XXVI.13–XXVII.11 on Hosea XII.4–XIV.10 (Eng.9) and Its Relevance to Some Theories for the Redaction of the 'Isaiah Apocalypse,'" *JTS* 32 (1980): 309–319, for additional examples.

[2] Sweeney, "Textual Citations in Isaiah 24–27: Toward an Understanding of the Redactional Function of chapters 24–27 in the book of Isaiah," *JBL* 107 (1988): 39–52, refers to many of these as quotations, and he believes that they demonstrate that the author did not write chaps. 24–27 in isola-

limited to their meaning in earlier paragraphs. Though earlier reference may provide a background from which to draw meaning, the interpreter needs to evaluate carefully the new contexts in chaps. 24–27 to find out if new meanings have developed to clarify God's eschatological work.

GENRE.   Since the time of B. Duhm many have viewed chaps. 24–27 as belonging to the apocalyptic genre of literature.[3] God's judgment of the world, the establishment of his rule from Zion, his defeat of the mythological Leviathan, the reaction of the sun and moon, the interpretation of earlier prophecies, and claims of pseudonymous authorship have led some to consider 24–27 as apocalyptic. W. Rudolph and J. Lindblom examined this thesis and concluded that these chapters describe an eschatological judgment within history, but they did not find many features of later full blown apocalyptic texts.[4] Consequently, most studies now appropriately interpret chaps. 24–27 as eschatology (or at best a sort of proto-apocalyptic).[5]

A second approach to this unit suggests that chaps. 24–27 follow the pattern of the "Divine Warrior Hymn," parallel to similar ancient Near Eastern mythical hymns. These hymns included (a) a threat of destruction; (b) a divine war; (c) victory; and (d) a feast to celebrate the victory.[6] P. Hanson found evidence of the Divine Warrior Hymn in Exod 15, Isa 9, 11, 24–27, 34–35, Zech 9–14, and 17 different Psalms, but his analysis of this hymn type usually does not include the "threat of destruction," plus he adds two additional factors (processional, manifestation of God's reign) as key parts of this hymn.[7] Although no one doubts that some of these themes exist in chaps. 24–27, this hymnic pattern is not consistently followed throughout 24–27 (it even includes two laments), therefore it does not seem to offer an adequate unified explanation for the order and contents of all the paragraphs in chaps. 24–27.

---

tion from the rest of the book, thus they argue for a unified view for this part of the book of Isaiah.

[3] B. Duhm, *Das Buch Jesaia*. HKAT (Göttingen: Vandenhoeck & Ruprecht, 1892), 172–94; consequently, this section has frequently carried the name "Isaiah's little apocalypse."

[4] W. Rudolph, *Jesaja 24–27*, BWANT (Stuttgart: Kohlhammer, 1933), and J. Lindblom, *Die Jesaja-Apokalypse, Jes 24–27* (Lund: Gleerup, 1938). These chapters have no pronounced dualistic thinking, no pessimistic view of the world, no angelic interpreters or guides, and no periodization of history. See D. B. Sandy and M. G. Abegg, "Apocalyptic," *Cracking Old Testament Codes* (ed. D. B. Sandy and R. L. Giese; Nashville: Broadman and Holman, 1995), 177–196, for a list of contrasting characteristic between prophecy and apocalyptic.

[5] J. N. Oswalt, "Recent Studies in Old Testament Eschatology and Apocalyptic," *JETS* 24 (1981): 289–302, for an evaluation of both apocalyptic and non-apocalyptic approaches to chaps. 24–27. Sweeney, *Isaiah 1–39*, 313–314, states that, "these chapters can hardly be characterized as apocalyptic in the fullest sense, although they may represent an early stage in the development of apocalyptic." P. Hanson, *The Dawn of Apocalyptic: The Historical and Sociological Roots of Jewish Apocalyptic Eschatology* (Philadelphia: Fortress, 1979), prefers to call 24–27 "proto-apocalyptic" because it is more pessimistic than regular eschatology.

[6] W. R. Millar, *Isaiah 24–27 and the Origin of Apocalyptic* (Missoula: Scholars Press, 1976), 65–71, compares these themes to similar themes in the Baal Epic. He also found these themes in Ps 132 and several chapters in Isaiah 40–52.

[7] Hanson, *The Dawn of Apocalyptic*, 300–314.

A third perspective simply focuses on the hymns in chaps. 24–27 (without tying to connect them to the "Divine Warrior Hymn" pattern) and concludes that this unit was a liturgy or cantata used at a great celebration of victory over one of Judah's enemies.[8] There is no doubt that songs of joy and praise are found in these chapters (25:1–5; 26:1–6; 27:2–6) but there is no evidence that the negative and positive sections were sung antiphonally by two prophetic choirs to produce a cantata at some military victory celebration in Jerusalem. The military imagery of battle or the taking of spoil from the enemy does not dominate the discussion in chaps. 24–27.[9]

Finally, Sweeney believes a disputation arose between a rejoicing group of people (24:14–16a) and the more somber outlook of the prophet (24:16b–18a). The exegetical discussion of these verses below suggests that this is not a conflict in which the prophet disagrees with the idea of those who were praising God; he simply cannot praise God now because the people presently on the earth must go through much suffering and death before that final day of great rejoicing can arrive.[10]

In the light of these factors, it seems best for the interpreter to evaluate the contribution of each genre of literature as it appears within each chapter, rather than focusing on the genre of the whole unit. The interpreter must analyze the contribution that each smaller literary segment makes to the understanding of the structure and the theological message of the whole. Announcements of judgment, hymns of praise, laments, and oracles of salvation play a key role in explaining God's rule of the earth now and in the future. The role that each genre of literature plays in communicating God's message of hope for Judah is addressed in the introduction of each paragraph below.

HISTORICAL SETTING. The date when the prophet received these prophecies is not explicitly connected to the reign of any Israelite king, and the time when these prophecies will be fulfilled is only hinted at by the nebulous "in that day" phrase (24:21; 25:9; 26:1; 27:1,2,12,13). Hayes and Irvine date this material to Judah's revolt against Sargon in 705 BC when the people of Judah destroyed the Assyrian citadel in Jerusalem ("the city" in 24:10; 25:2; 26:5; 27:10) and celebrated their independence from Assyria with songs of praise (possibly at the autumn New Year Festival).[11] This interpretation rests on

---

[8] J. Lindblom, *Die Jesaja-Apokalypse,* was following the ideas of G. Hylmo. J. H. Hayes and S. A. Irvine, *Isaiah, the Eighth-Century Prophet* (Nashville: Abingdon, 1987), 297, interpret these as hymns of celebration after the overthrow of the Assyrian army.

[9] J. B. Geyer, "Desolation and Cosmos," *VT* 49 (1999): 49–64, does not find a war context in chap. 24, rather the undoing of nature because of a breach in the cosmic covenant. He tries to make connections with mythological themes in 24–27, but since these themes were available in Hebrew texts (Sweeney, "Textual Citations in Isaiah 24–27," 39–52), there is no need to look elsewhere.

[10] Sweeney, *Isaiah 1–39,* 311–13, and J. Loete, " A Premature Hymn of Praise (Isaiah 24:14–16a)," *Studies in Isaiah 24–27: The Isaiah Workshop-De Jesaja Werkplaats* (ed. H. J. Bosman and H. van Grol; Leiden: Brill, 2000), 226–38, both find a disputation speech here.

[11] Hayes and Irvine, *Isaiah,* 295–99, finds specific evidence of the revolt in 24:14–16; the move to expand Hezekiah's territory in 26:15; the religious reform of Hezekiah in 27:9; the destruction

a series of hypothetical historical events and minimizes both the universality of God's punishment of the forces of evil in heaven and earth as well as the radically transformed nature of the kingdom of God that he will establish in the future. These chapters (24–25) look forward to a much greater worldwide fulfillment (both negatively and positively) than what happened during Hezekiah's reign.

The identification of the "city" in 24:10; 25:2; 26:5; 27:10 as the Moabite city in 25:10 led O. Eissfeldt to place these chapters in the third century BC, while W. Rudolph proposed that this passage celebrated Alexander the Great's destruction of the city of Babylon in 331 BC.[12] Hanson and Millar suggested that this story about a destroyed city was an exilic poem describing how Jerusalem fell in 586 BC,[13] but H. Wildberger and J. Oswalt interpret "the city" purely as a symbol rather than a reference to a specific city.[14]

It seems best to conclude that the identification of the "city" is unknown and that it is not the main key to understanding the historical situation surrounding these prophecies. In 24:1–16a, 18b–23 the prophecies describe God's final punishment of the world, and 25:1–12 records the joy of the righteous who glorify God after his glorious eternal kingdom is established, thus some of these chapters are not about events during Isaiah's lifetime. Instead, several messages provide a vision of how God will set up his reign in Zion in the distant future (24:23).

On the other hand, most of chap. 26 refers to present or near future events in the life of the prophet, not to the eschatological activities in chaps. 24–25. First, the faithful are instructed to sing (26:1–6) about how God cares for the righteous. The imperative exhortations[15] challenge the people to open the gates (26:2) and trust in God (26:4) because he will humble those who are high and mighty. This indicates that the author is trying to persuade his listeners to trust God based on who God is and what he will do for them (26:1–3,5–6), not what he has already done. It appears that the audience the prophet is addressing is facing an immediate problem, so they need to trust God for help in the midst of this oppression. This interpretation of 26:1–6 fits in with the purpose of 26:7–10. These verses aim to develop confidence in God so that those who are righteous in Judah will be willing to wait/trust in his deliverance.

---

of the bronze serpent in 27:1; and the death of Sargon in 26:14. Some of these interpretations are quite suspect.

[12] O. Eissfeldt, *The Old Testament: An Introduction* (New York: Harper, 1965), 326; Rudolph, *Jesaja 24–27*, 61–64. Lindblom, *Die Jesaja-Apokalypse*, 72–84, prefers to relates these events to Xerxes' attack on Babylon in 485 BC, and J. Blenkinsopp, *Isaiah 1–39* (New York: Doubleday, 2000), 348, opts for the defeat of Babylon by Cyrus in 539 BC.

[13] Hanson, *Dawn of Apocalyptic*, 314, and W. R. Millar, *Isaiah 24–27*, 20.

[14] H. Wildberger, *Isaiah 13–27: A Commentary*, CC (Minneapolis: Fortress, 1997), 462, J. Oswalt, *Isaiah 1–39*, NICOT (Grand Rapids: Eerdmans, 1986), 441, and G. M. Tucker, "The Book of Isaiah 1–39," *The New Interpreter's Bible,* Vol VI (Nashville: Abingdon, 2001), 212, all believe this city symbolized all cities or the world of mankind.

[15] בִּטְחוּ in 26:4 is an imperative of admonition that makes a request to an audience to act (GKC § 110a).

The specific oppressive historical context is hinted at in the lament in 26:7–18.[16] The petition in 26:16–18 describes a nation in distress because God was disciplining it. The people are in great pain (like the pain of childbirth) with no salvation in sight. They are waiting for God to act (26:8) and hoping that God's zeal for his people will soon bring deliverance (26:11). What they need to do right now is wait until God's wrath has passed (26:20) and then they will see God's great deliverance when he defeats their enemy (26:21–27:1).

Although the evidence of a specific historical event is limited, the interpreter can use various hints to suggest what the prophet was describing. D. Johnson placed the setting of chap. 26 after the fall of Jerusalem and just before the fall of Babylon in 539 BC. The nation had experienced the wrath of God through the Babylonian defeat and needed to trust God and wait in exile until God destroyed the wicked nation of Babylon.[17] Then they would see his salvation and their restoration to the land. This makes much more sense than placing chap. 26 in an eschatological setting, but the immediate canonical context of chaps. 13–23 and 29–39 suggests a more likely date. The primary example of divine discipline was the attack on Jerusalem by the Assyrian king Sennacherib in 701 BC, in which God used another nation to compel Judah to trust him. Judah was exhorted not to trust in Egypt (30:1–5; 31:1–3; 36:6) or rely on the devious propaganda of the Assyrians (36:4–20), but were to rely on God for salvation (30:15; 37:14–20). Sennacherib's defeat of the main cities of Judah, except for Jerusalem, qualifies as a day of great distress and rebuke for the nation. During Sennacherib's attack on Judah, Hezekiah used exactly the same words that Isaiah used to describe the historical situation: the metaphor of Jerusalem being in pain like the pain of a woman giving birth (37:3; cf. 26:17–18). This linguistic interlinking provides an important key to finding the historical setting of chaps. 24–27.

In the light of the total context of chaps. 24–27, it appears the prophet is using an eschatological analogy of God's destruction of all of his enemies (chaps. 24–25) to motivate the people of Judah (chaps. 26–27). In the future God's people will trust God and see his salvation when he destroys all his enemies (25:9), therefore the prophet exhorts his audience in Jerusalem to trust God to deliver his people from the Assyrians now in 701 BC.

STRUCTURE AND PURPOSE. The content of chaps. 24–27 includes several genres of literature. There is an announcement of judgment (24:1–6), hymns of praise (25:1–5; 26:1–6), a symbolic song of the vineyard (27:2–6), and a lament (26:7–27:1), so it is not easy to discover how to put these diverse perspectives together in one unified conceptual whole. Because of this diffi-

---

[16] Consult the exegesis of this section below, plus the "Historical Setting" section in the introduction to chap. 26.

[17] Johnson, *From Chaos to Restoration: An Integrative Reading of Isaiah 24–27* (Sheffield: JSOT Press, 1988), 69–70. Hayes and Irvine, *Isaiah*, 313, propose that the present crisis for Judah was the invasion of Sargon around 711 BC.

culty recent redactional studies have concluded that there were three different layers of material that reveal little unity.[18] On the other hand C. R. Seitz assumes the unity of 24–27 and works to uncover how the interrelated threads tie the pieces together.[19]

A central problem that needs to be solved is the temporal perspective of these texts. Do these paragraphs refer to God's past dealings, present work on earth, or some future events within his plans? Or is there a combination of past and present events along with future prophecies? Hayes and Irvine believe chaps. 24–27 describe a past event (the fall of the Assyrian citadel in Jerusalem around 704 BC) that was celebrated with singing in a special festival, while Millar thinks that most of chaps. 24–27 came after the fall of Jerusalem in 586 BC (the destroyed city), though some parts look forward to God's future deliverance of the nation after the exile.[20]

In light of the catastrophic destruction of the world and the victorious establishment of God's reign on earth in chaps. 24–25, it seems wiser to conclude that the cataclysmic events in theses two chapters did not happen in Isaiah's day. Therefore it is best to take the participle preceded by *hinnēh* in 24:1 as a reference to a future event[21] and the perfect verb in 24:2 as a prophetic perfect verbs referring to future events. This approach is consistent with the future imperfect verb "will be completely laid waste" in 24:3. The joy expressed in 24:14 is a future imperfect "they will raise their voices" (not the present "raise" in NIV). In contrast to this temporal perspective is the prophet's contrastive statement (24:16b) "but I said" (*vav* with imperfect verb), which refers to the prophet's present response to this rejoicing. This interpretation of the themes and verb forms results in assigning all of chaps. 24–25 to an eschatological era, except the prophet's brief parenthetical lamenting response in 24:16b–18a. These eschatological prophecies about what God will do some time in the distant future had the rhetorical function of giving hope to the prophet and his audience in Jerusalem as they faced the "treachery . . . terror and pit" that the prophet was lamenting (24:16b–18a). If God can destroy the evil forces on the world through his power at the end of time, certainly the people of Judah can trust him to take care of them during the difficult days they were enduring because of the Assyrian attack on Judah.

---

[18] Wildberger found an original section in 24:1–6,14–20; 26:7–21, an eschatological section in 24:21–23; 25:6–8; 9–10; city songs in 25:1–5 and 26:1–6; plus a series of one-or-two-verse later additions scattered here and there (*Isaiah 13–27*, 459).

[19] C. R. Seitz, *Isaiah 1–39*, Interpretation (Louisville: Westminster John Knox, 1993), 172–79, or B. S. Childs, *Isaiah*, OTL (Louisville: Westminster John Knox, 2001), 171–74. Although this commentary may not agree with the entire conclusion in these two studies or even their way of identifying unity, at least they can assist in the process of developing a more holistic perspective on chaps. 24–27.

[20] Hayes and Irvine, *Isaiah*, 296–97, say "Internal evidence in chaps. 24–27 indicates that some of the events had already taken place or were in progress"—for example the Assyrian citadel was already destroyed. Millar, *Isaiah 24–27*, 20 and 108, heavily depends on the arguments of W. March.

[21] GKC §116p discusses the use of *hinnēh* with the participle.

Chapters 26–27 make up a separate section within 24–27, with a major emphasis on the nation's present oppressive situation caused by Sennacherib's invasion of Judah just before 701 BC. The lament in 26:7–18 describes the audience as under the rule of other rulers (26:13), in distress like a woman giving birth (26:16–18), and waiting and yearning for God to intervene (26:8–9). The answer to this lament exhorts the people to wait a little while until God's anger passes, because soon God will judge their enemies (26:20–27:1). Some in the nation were being driven from their homes (27:8) and there was a need to remove pagan idols from the nation (27:9). In spite of all these present problems, in the future God will gather his people to Jerusalem to worship him (27:12–13). The hymn in 26:1–6 promises hope for those who will trust God, which legitimates the call to wait in hope for God to act (26:8). The "song of the vineyard" also legitimates that hope, for "in days to come Jacob will take root" (27:6), after the enemies of God are defeated (27:1). At the present time Isaiah's audience must accept their punishment and trust their lives to God's sovereign plan. He will not fail them or fail any of his people in the distant future.

THEOLOGY. The goal of God's future acts is his plan to reign over the earth from Zion (2:1–4; 24:23). This is where God's historical plan for the earth is headed once God has destroyed all his enemies and has purified the defiled earth of those who reject his ways (24:5). His curse on the earth will demonstrate his unlimited sovereign power to shake, break, and humiliate everything in heaven and earth (24:18b–23a). This unveiling of the future makes it certain that he will win the victory in the end. Nothing and no one will prevent Almighty God from establishing his eternal reign. The implications of this fundamental message are clear to all. Every audience that hears Isaiah's words must decide whether they want to stand in opposition to God and be punished, or to stand with him and enter his glorious kingdom.

The shouts of praise, hymns of joy (24:14–16a; 25:1–4), and the banquet feast (25:6–8) represent a theological opportunity for people to exalt God, acclaim his majesty, and thank God for his faithfulness and intervention on their behalf. At some point many people will trust their lives to God's care and recognize that he is the source of their salvation (25:9), that he is the one who has defeated their proud enemies (25:10b–12). Their fate and joy is contrasted with the future punishment of the proud and exalted people who now defile the earth (24:5; 26:5–6). There is no hope for them when the wrath of God's curse falls on the earth.

Although the future seems secure and God's treatment of people is already decided, the people in Judah who were hearing this message faced a theological dilemma because they did not now see God's all powerful hand of judgment on their Assyrian oppressors and were not able to rejoice in peace at the present time. God was not yet reigning in power from Zion. Instead they faced suffering from treachery, terror, and the pit (24:16b–18a); they were in distress and under God's discipline (26:16). In this context the prophet calls for his audience to make a theological commitment to honor God and trust him for today and the future (26:3–5,8) and this is what this message calls every reader to do. If God has the future under control, certainly he is able to accomplish his will in spite of the present terrible circumstances his people may face. The prophet's message about God's final theological and political victory over the forces of evil is a powerfully persuasive argument that should motivate every believer to trust God with the major and minor problems they face each day because God is truly in control of this world. His plan is set; his victory is sure.

1. God's Final Curse on an Evil World (24:1–23)

This chapter continues the announcements of divine judgment on sinful humanity and the places where they live, consistent with the preceding prophecies in chaps. 13–23. Similar images of destruction, death, and ruin were used to describe the demise of individual cities and nations, but now one finds a climactic curse on all humanity and the whole earth[22] (24:1–13, 18b–23). This destruction of wickedness will bring relief to the oppressed, and the righteous will exalt God's name because of his wondrous deeds (24:14–16a), but these events will not happen immediately. Instead, God's people must now endure a lamentable situation (24:16b–18a) and wait for that future day when God will reign as king from Zion (24:23). Nevertheless, the outcome of life's struggle is set and is absolutely sure; God will be victorious. The structural outline of this message is:

God's Final Curse on the earth	24:1–13
The curse brings destruction	1–3
The reasons for God's curse	4–13
Joy and Sorrow over God's destruction	24:14–18a
Future joy and praise of God	14–16a
The prophet's present sorrow	16b–18a
After destruction, God will reign	24:18b–23

(1) God's Curse Brings Destruction (24:1–3)

¹**See, the LORD is going to lay waste the earth**
and devastate it;
  he will ruin its face
    and scatter its inhabitants—
²**it will be the same**

---

[22] E. J. Kissane, *The Book of Isaiah* (Dublin: Browne and Nolan, 1960), I:271, interprets אֶרֶץ as referring to the "land" of Judah based on a similar description of the desolation of Jerusalem in Jer 4:23–24. Although the word does frequently refer to the "land" of Israel, the context of chap. 24 argues for the broader interpretation of "earth."

> for priest as for people,
> for master as for servant,
> for mistress as for maid,
> for seller as for buyer,
> for borrower as for lender,
> for debtor as for creditor.
> ³The earth will be completely laid waste
> and totally plundered.
> The LORD has spoken this word.

24:1 This new literary section is introduced with "see, behold" (*hinnēh*) to draw attention to what the prophet is saying, then it ends with the messenger formula "the LORD has spoken this word" (24:3) to draw attention to what God has said. The use of the root *bqq*, "lay waste, empty," at the beginning of v. 1 and in v. 3 draws this short paragraph together as a unit. This announcement of judgment at the beginning of the paragraph is somewhat parallel to the conclusion at the end of this chapter in 24:18b–23 (forming an inclusio and thus enhancing the overall continuity), although the final verses of this chapter expand God's judgment to include forces in the heavens. God's decisive action to destroy evil from the earth will enable God to establish a new era where he reigns supreme over the world from Zion. God's punishment in 24:1–23a explains what God will do with the evil powers in heaven and earth so that he can fully establish his reign (24:23b).

God is pictured as "emptying"[23] the land, leaving it void, or making it a waste place. People will be scattered[24] from where they now live and only a few people will be left on the earth (in comparison to its population before God's great judgment). This divine attack on mankind will include a terrible catastrophic "distorting, twisting" (*'iwwâ*) of the surface of the earth (1b), parallel to the violent shaking and breaking mentioned in 24:19–20. At this point the prophet is simply describing the shocking and astonishing acts of God against the earth; in the next paragraph he will focus on why God will do this to the earth.

24:2 This divine punishment will affect everyone without respect to a person's social, economic, religious, national, or political status. By putting the favored or higher status people (priest, master) in the same lot with the lower status people (servant, maid) the orator indicates that everyone, no matter who they are or what their occupation is, will feel the painful effect of God's powerful hand when he curses the earth. God will not play favorites on the basis of sex, race, nationality, hemisphere where one lives, or religious affiliation; everyone on the earth will suffer under the effects of his curse.

---

[23] בָּקַק describes the emptying of the land (see Jer 51:2) or the emptiness of the spirit of the Egyptians (19:3), not the "ravaging" of the land (Wildberger, *Isaiah 13–27*, 475).

[24] פּוּץ, "scatter," is parallel to God's judgment of the people at the Tower of Babel in Gen 11:8. The covenant curse on Israel in Lev 26:33 also foretold the day when the disobedient nation would be scattered and the land would become desolate.

24:3 The last verse of this short paragraph emphasizes the decisiveness of the divine activity by combining an infinitive absolute with a finite verb (*hibbôq tibbôq*, "it will surely be emptied") to show that there is absolute certainty[25] (rather than "completeness" as in NIV) about God's plan to lay waste the earth. The text makes it absolutely certain that God will do this by (a) repeating the idea that the earth will be laid waste from 24:1, (b) using the emphatic form of the verbs, and (c) emphasizing that God decisively said this would happen. After these exclamations, no one should have any doubt about what God's plan is or whether God's promises will be fulfilled. The big question that people will be asking at this point is Why will these things happen?

(2) The Reason for God's Curse (24:4–13)

> [4]The earth dries up and withers,
> the world languishes and withers,
> the exalted of the earth languish.
> [5]The earth is defiled by its people;
> they have disobeyed the laws,
> violated the statutes
> and broken the everlasting covenant.
> [6]Therefore a curse consumes the earth;
> its people must bear their guilt.
> Therefore earth's inhabitants are burned up,
> and very few are left.
> [7]The new wine dries up and the vine withers;
> all the merrymakers groan.
> [8]The gaiety of the tambourines is stilled,
> the noise of the revelers has stopped,
> the joyful harp is silent.
> [9]No longer do they drink wine with a song;
> the beer is bitter to its drinkers.
> [10]The ruined city lies desolate;
> the entrance to every house is barred.
> [11]In the streets they cry out for wine;
> all joy turns to gloom,
> all gaiety is banished from the earth.
> [12]The city is left in ruins,
> its gate is battered to pieces.
> [13]So will it be on the earth
> and among the nations,
> as when an olive tree is beaten,
> or as when gleanings are left after the grape harvest.

---

[25] GKC §113n indicates that the infinitive absolute followed by the finite verb strengthens "either the certainty (especially in cases of threats) or the forcibleness or completeness of an occurrence." Since some righteous people will remain on the earth (27:12–13) when God sets up his kingdom after the judgment of the earth, it seems improper to push the "completeness" of God's destruction of mankind.

These verses fall into two groups: (a) vv. 4–6 teach that sin will bring God's curse on mankind (ending with two "therefore," *ʿal kēn*, statements in v. 6); and (b) vv. 7–13 explain how this curse will remove all joy and bring utter devastation. Both sections deal with the withering of plants as well as the loss of human life. Both subsections end by noting that few people will be left on the earth. The first section focuses on why God will do this; the second emphasizes the results of God's curse.

24:4 The land, its vegetation, and its people will dry up, wither, and waste away to nothing.[26] Five fairly synonymous words (two of them were used twice) for loss of fertility and life are employed, one after the other, to draw attention to this point (24:4). The imagery chosen to convey these ideas pictures a situation where there is a lack of water, suggesting a God directed drought rather than a military cause for death. The special reference to the ruin of the "exalted people of the earth"[27] reminds one of the common theme of God's goal of "humbling the proud" in earlier passages (2:9,11–12,16; 5:15–16; 10:12; 13:11; 16:6; 23:9) as well as later in this section (25:11–12; 26:5). As 2:9–17 proclaims, on the Day of the Lord only God will be exalted; everything else will be destroyed and humbled.

24:5 The prophet legitimates God's judgment by giving five reasons that explain why God will remove fertility and life. (a) The first explanation for this drought is that God finds the earth defiled. Evil people have polluted or desecrated the land by their action, so it is impossible for the land to produce fruit and support life. J. D. W. Watts summarizes this factor by pointing out that "a moral breakdown lies at the core of the problems."[28] This parallels the situation at the time of the great flood when the violence of mankind so polluted the land that God destroyed both land and people (Gen 6:11). Elsewhere the verb *ḥnp*, "pollute, defile" (24:5), is used in contexts where the shedding of blood (Num 35:33) or the worship of pagan gods (Jer 3:9) defiles the land, but in this context the second and third reasons are broadly stated as, (b) people have disobeyed instructions (*tôrôt*) and (c) statutes. These two terms frequently summarize God's covenant requirements in the Pentateuch, so it is possible to conclude that this accusation was made against the Hebrew people who received the "laws and statutes" from God at Mount Sinai.[29] In addition the fourth reason, (d) the breaking of the "eternal covenant," sounds like a reference to a specific biblical covenant. D. Johnson concludes these three factors (laws, statutes, and covenant) demonstrate that the condemnation was for

---

[26] There is a word play of assonance using similar sounds in 24:4, *ʾābelâ nābelâ*.

[27] מְרוֹם could mean "heights, mountain tops" or point to "heaven" (24:18,21), if עַם, "people," were not in the text (cf. NRSV), but Wildberger, *Isaiah 13–27*, 478, rightly rejects the Old Greek's omission of "people" and concludes that this must refer to the "exalted people."

[28] J. D. W. Watts, *Isaiah 1–33*, WBC 24 (Waco: Word, 1985), 317, refers to a lack of obedience to laws, no maintenance of common morality, and an unwillingness to keep contractual agreements.

[29] Kissane, *Isaiah*, 272, believes these refer to the Mosaic covenant, and Johnson, *From Chaos to Restoration*, 27, agrees.

breaking the Mosaic covenant (it has "eternal" factors in Judg 2:1; Ps 111:5,9; and Exod 31:16). In favor of this option is the fact that the Noahic covenant was not one that people could break[30] while the Mosaic one was conditional and could be broken. Seitz disagrees with this conclusion because these three factors (laws, statutes, and covenant) refer to the sins of people throughout the world, not just the Hebrew people. Since the context of 24:1–23 involves the whole world, Seitz connects the breaking of the "eternal covenant" with Noah's everlasting covenant (Gen 9:16) that impacted all mankind.[31] But how could people break God's eternal unbreakable covenant with mankind? That sounds like an oxymoron. Oswalt attempts to solve this dilemma by suggesting that the word "law" was used in a way similar to Paul's use in Rom 1–3, that is, "it is the fundamental principles of human behavior that are as accessible and incumbent, as the elementary principles of physics."[32] Not one of these solutions by itself is totally convincing, so Wildberger proposes that the writer joined ideas from the covenant with Noah that affects the whole world (it was eternal, world wide, and involved the windows of heaven—see 24:18) with ideas from the Mosaic covenant (it was breakable by man, and included laws and statutes) and its curses. Thus the prophet spoke in terms his Hebrew audience would understand but expanded their meaning to demonstrate the worldwide implications of God's covenants with all mankind and all the earth.[33] This approach recognizes an influence from two covenant traditions (Noah and Moses), does not try to read foreign information into either tradition, and assigns a certain level of exegetical freedom to the prophet's integration of both traditions in this context.

24:6 The final reason for God's curse on the earth is that the people must bear the consequences of their own guilt for sin. This statement is based on the view that God is righteous and holds people accountable for their behavior. Sinful behavior is cursed and righteous behavior is not cursed. This was a theological truth the Hebrews understood from the covenant (cf. Lev 26–27), but it was also a basic principle that applies to child rearing, all ancient Near Eastern legal codes, and even pagan religions that direct people to appease the wrath

---

[30] Johnson, *From Chaos to Restoration*, 27–29, believes God is judging the nations for pride, not for breaking a covenant, so this passages refers to Judah's sins. He maintains that idolatry was the means of polluting the land (Jer 3:2,9).

[31] Seitz, *Isaiah 1–39*, 180–81, points to Noah's covenant being called an "everlasting covenant" (Gen 9:16) and notes that both situations refer to God's curse on the whole earth, both have the "windows of heaven opened" (25:18; Gen 7:11), and both leave the earth with few inhabitants.

[32] Oswalt, *Isaiah 1–39*, 446, maintains that this as a broader reference to the "implicit covenant between the Creator and creatures, in which the Creator promises abundant life in return for the creature's living according to the norms laid down at creation."

[33] Wildberger, *Isaiah 13–27*, 479–80. R. Chisholm, "The 'Everlasting Covenant ' and the 'City of Chaos': Intentional Ambiguity and Irony in Isaiah 24," *CTJ* 6 (1993): 237–53, thinks both Mosaic and Noahic covenants are in the background. He asserts that the Noah's covenant had both divine promises (9:8–17) and well as mandates (9:1–7), but Gen 9 never presents the mandates as conditions of the covenant.

of their gods to remove their punishment. When people fail to be responsible and rebel against God, there is a price to pay and shame to suffer. God does not arbitrarily deal out punishment; there is a good reason why the people on the earth must suffer punishment. They became guilty because they sinned; therefore, it is appropriate that they bear the consequences of their choices. Apparently, few people will be inclined to confess their sins and receive forgiveness at this time.

The paragraph ends in 24:6 by describing two additional results (beyond the drought in 24:5), each beginning with "therefore" (*'al kēn*): (a) a curse will consume the earth; and (b) few people will remain on the earth. The prophet's Hebrew audience would immediately understand the idea of God's curses (Deut 27–28).[34] When God makes an "oath"[35] to bless or curse people, it surely happens. This oath results in the "consuming, eating up" (*'ākal*) of the earth because the people remain in sin and refuse the path of repentance. The prophet emphasizes the destruction of vegetation (24:4) and a decrease in population (24:6b). The NIV understands that the people are "burned," which would explain how they are consumed, but this root (*hārâ*) usually refers to the "burning anger" of God or some person. Although God does use his fire to "burn" (*bā'ar*) and destroy the wicked in other texts (9:18; 10: 16–17; cf. Rev 18:8–10,16–19), those texts use a different root. Since God is not the subject here, this word probably means "disappear,"[36] which explains why so few people remain. This will be an era of catastrophic events that will bring death to millions—no, probably even to billions of people.

24:7–13   The beginning of this portion resembles 24:4–6, an announcement of withering and death because of a severe drought. This doom will bring a quick end to drinking parties, celebration, and times of human joy. Instead, there will be groaning, no music, silence, and gloom. The joy of life will stop

---

[34] Polaski, *Authorizing the End*, 103, illustrates how the response of God fits the covenant curses in Deuteronomy: (a) people scattered (Deut 28:36, 63–64; Isa 24:1); (b) lending relations confused (Deut 28:44; Isa 24:2); (c) drought (Deut 28:22–24; Isa 24:4,7); (d) few people (Deut 28:62; Isa 24:6,13); (e) wine gone (Deut 28:39,51; Isa 24:7,9,11); (f) cities destroyed (Deut 28:52; Isa 24:10,12); (g) houses empty (Deut 28:24; Isa 24:16); (h) oppression and treachery (Deut 28:24; Isa 24:16); and (i) destruction from heaven (Deut 28:12; Isa 24:17). The lack of exact quotations from Deuteronomy indicates that the prophet was not quoting directly from these texts but drawing from the principles expounded there. The oracles against the nations (chaps. 13–23) demonstrate that many of these same curses will fall on foreign nations, even though they are not part of the covenant. M. Biddle, "The City of Chaos and the New Jerusalem: Isaiah 24–27 in Context," *PRS* 22 (1995): 7–8, emphasizes some of the parallels between the punishments in chaps. 13–23 and 24–27.

[35] אָלָה, an "oath," is something that one swears will happen. When it involves negative consequences the oath promises to bring a curse on the offending party.

[36] 1QIsaᵃ has חורו, "to be pale, white," but G. R. Driver, "Notes on Isaiah," *Von Ugarit nach Qumran* BZAW (Berlin: Topelmann, 1958): 44, connects this root to an Arabic word meaning "weak," while L. Koehler and W. Baumgartner, *Lexicon in veteris testamenti libros* (Leiden: Brill, 1951–3), חרר II, propose "reduce, remove, take away," giving the sense "the inhabitants of the earth will disappear."

(24:8); wine will bring about a bitter experience rather than a "happy hour" (24:9; cf. a similar situation in 16:8–10). Verses 10 and 12 indicate how this future disaster will impact life in the cities of the world (7–9 deals with its effect on agriculture). Some imagine a return to utter chaos in the cities, but the translation "chaos" could mislead one to think this verse refers to the end of human order governed by laws of respect and civil government. Instead this Hebrew word primarily means that something is "void, empty, uninhabited."[37] This is not an indictment against the evils of city life or some evil world system (the Assyrians or Babylonian culture); it merely reports that the desolation will be so severe that few people will be left in the cities of the world. Since most people live in cities, it would be natural for them to suffer the most when God's curse falls on the earth. The text does not explain if some city people will move to the country to find food (thus the cities will be empty) or if these city dwellers will be killed in war or an earthquake. The desolation of the cities and the destruction of their gates (24:12) could be seen as the results of military conquests, a plague, or some other cause.

24:13 The paragraph concludes by reflecting on the inevitable ("surely, so it will be") puacity of population remaining in the various nations on the earth. Like 17:6 this verse compares those people left with the gleanings remaining on a vine after the grapes are already harvested, or the olives left on a tree after the majority of the fruit is harvested. No numbers or percentages were given, but the common Israelite who heard this message knew that the prophet was talking about a very small number. God's final harvest will decimate the population of the world.

(3) Joy and Sorrow over God's Destruction (24:14–18a)

> [14]They raise their voices, they shout for joy;
>   from the west they acclaim the LORD's majesty.
> [15]Therefore in the east give glory to the LORD;
>   exalt the name of the LORD, the God of Israel,
>   in the islands of the sea.
> [16]From the ends of the earth we hear singing:
>   "Glory to the Righteous One."
>
> But I said, "I waste away, I waste away!
>   Woe to me!
> The treacherous betray!
>   With treachery the treacherous betray!"
> [17]Terror and pit and snare await you,
>   O people of the earth.
> [18]Whoever flees at the sound of terror
>   will fall into a pit;

---

[37] תֹּהוּ is paired with words like delusion, nothing, void (Isa 40:23; 41:29). In Gen 1:2 it indicates that the watery mass was "empty, void" without land, trees, animals, or people (45:18).

> **whoever climbs out of the pit**
> **will be caught in a snare.**

Initially the text describes a time of joy, but then suddenly the mood changes to lamenting. Interpreters have understood the relationship between the two subparagraphs in this section in several ways: (a) Most believe the two views (rejoicing in 14–16a, lamenting in 16b–18a) are in conflict, with the prophet rejecting the inappropriate rejoicing of his audience. Isaiah laments in pain over the massive destruction of life that will occur in the future and does not believe there is any reason to rejoice or offer hope to his audience.[38] (b) Slightly different is B. Child's perspective, which considers the rejoicing as legitimate, being similar to the joy expressed in 12:1–6 or 42:10–12. He proposes that the timing of the rejoicing is wrong for the prophet, since victory has not been accomplished and severe divine judgment is now approaching.[39] Complicating the matter, the people who are rejoicing are simply identified as "they" in 24:14, so it is hard to know who was singing God's praise. "They" could be the righteous remnant left after the harvest (in 24:13) at the end of time when God judges the earth or "they" could be the righteous people in Isaiah's present audience.[40] If Isaiah was proclaiming this message shortly before the Assyrian siege of Judah in 701 BC, his Israelite audience might interpret this prophecy about the destruction of God's enemies in 24:1–13 as a message of hope. Yet when one reads Isaiah 28–39 there is little indication that people listened to or believed Isaiah until Sennacherib's troops actually surrounded the city of Jerusalem. Thus it makes more sense to interpret the "they" who are rejoicing as the eschatological righteous remnant that will survive God's judgment on the earth (not Isaiah's audience).

Why then does the prophet respond with lamentation (24:16b–18a, similar to 21:4) instead of thanksgiving? Isaiah probably believed that rejoicing would be appropriate when God was finally victorious over the forces that were aligned against him, but thus far Isaiah and Judah have not seen God's hand of victory over their enemies, the Assyrians, so it is impossible for them to rejoice right now. If the "I" who laments in 24:16b–18a and the "we" who lament in 26:7–18 represent the actual historical situation of the nation at the

---

[38] Wildberger, *Isaiah 13–27*, 494–95, views these people as the "Diaspora of Judaism" spread through the furtherest edges of the earth, though not everyone would identify these as Jewish people (Sweeney, *Isaiah 1–39*, 328).

[39] Childs, *Isaiah*, 180, focuses on the premature rejoicing, since judgment still awaits the earth. Thus the contrasting views of the people and prophet in 21:2–4 are not exactly parallel to the situation here. W. A. M. Beuken, "The Prophet Leads the Readers into Praise," in *Studies in Isaiah 24–27*, 121–56, finds no condemnation of this praise, instead "and I said" in 16b is to introduce his quotation of 21:2, which simply remind the worshipers that God's judgment is approaching (p. 130).

[40] Tucker, "Isaiah 1–39," 212, follows R. E. Clements, *Isaiah 1–39*, NCBC (Grand Rapids: Eerdmans, 1980), 203, in interpreting these as "doxologies of judgment" by the condemned, drawing on the analogy that Achan (Josh 7) was required to give glory to God.

time this oracle was delivered by Isaiah, then Isaiah's grief would represent his application of these promises to his present situation. The principles that God will destroy mankind and will leave only a few remaining does not bode well for the untrusting people of Judah who are enduring the Assyrian siege of Jerusalem. At this point the prophet wonders if the majority of the people of Judah will be among the remnant that will be left to praise God. He has already prophesied that Judah is trusting too much in its man-made fortifications and is not trusting in God (21:8–11), therefore he cannot rejoice now (cf. 21:1–4,12–13) for it appears that Judah will be on the losing end of God's judgment. He does not condemn or reject rejoicing at the appropriate time, but now is not the time. His heart is heavy for the lost sheep of Israel.

24:14–16a The text includes the personal pronoun "they"[41] for emphasis and as a contrast with what "I" say in 16b (the prophet's perspective). "They" must refer to the remnant of people who will survive God's harvest when he judges the earth in 24:13. When "they" observe what God does to those who defile the earth, they will rejoice and lift up their voices in a chorus of praise and exultation to give glory to God. Those who sing will come from the west (lit. "from the sea"),[42] from the east, from the coastlands, and from the far ends of the earth. This indicates a worldwide multi-lingual chorus from all nations. These people will witness the awesome power of God at the end of history and respond in praise and adoration. There is no reason to believe that these will only be exiled Hebrew people living in distant lands around the Middle East, for repeatedly Isaiah speaks of a much larger remnant from all nations praising God (2:2–5; 11:10–16; 14:1–3; 18:7; 19:18–25; 23:18; 66:18–21). When people see God's power in action, many will believe and bow in worship. Their praise will include: (a) magnifying the majestic supremacy (*gāʾôn* in 24:14) of God; (b) giving glory or honor (*kabbĕdû* in 24:15) to God; (c) exalting God's name; and (d) proclaiming "majesty to the Righteous One" (24:16). This worship focuses completely on God. It is a response to his revelation of his majestic supremacy over man through his powerful acts of judgment. God's reputation as God is acknowledged and his character as "the Righteous One" (*laṣaddîq*) is justified by his destruction of the evil people on the earth. There will be no question about who is God or what he is like. God's majesty, glory, and righteousness will be on full display for all to see. Praise naturally flows from those who know God and observe what he has done.

This response functioned as an encouragement for people in Isaiah's audience and every reader since that time to trust God, for he is all-powerful, righteous, and glorious. He will win the victory over evil in the end, so he is a God that people can depend on for the trials of each day. As those in Jerusalem faced the Assyrians, they could trust God for victory over the proud forces that

---

[41] הֵמָּה is a third masculine plural subject pronoun that is unnecessary grammatically but added to emphasize the subject of the verb (GKC §135a).

[42] מִיָּם, "from the sea," refers to the Mediterranean Sea, which was west of Judah.

claimed to control the world, for their mocking reproaches of the name of the living God will soon bring God's wrath (36:14–20).

24:16b–18a The second half of this paragraph is a parenthetical glimpse at the prophet's reaction to God's future deeds. The text moves abruptly from words of praise to cries of lament by the prophet. "But I said" (*wā'ōmar*) contrasts the future joy of people from around the world with the prophet's sorrow over Judah's present dire circumstances. He does not reject or condemn the joy of the nations that praise God; he merely recognizes that God has not yet defeated the forces of evil in the world, thus the armed forces of Judah will have to face the vastly superior military power of the Assyrians surrounding Jerusalem. His sorrow was motivated by what was going to happen to Jerusalem, if they did not trust God.

The second half of the exclamation "I waste away, Woe is me!" is certain, but the first phrase is uncertain. It must be another expression of shock and utter terror.[43] Based on the contextual meaning of the parallel poetic line in 17:4 (and the use of the same noun in 10:16) the idea has something to do with a loss of glory, fertility, fullness, or health.[44] This is opposite the fullness of God's majesty. Thus a translation parallel to "woe is me!" would be an expression that the prophet is totally powerless and incapable of vitality. He admits that he is nothing and has no power in comparison to God's glorious strength. The prophet can only unmask the hopelessness of the people of Judah in their present context of terror and devastation (24:16b–18a). This despondency does not mean that the prophet has no hope in God; it means that without God's gracious intervention the people of Judah have no strength. The prophet's sorrow represents the response that every person should have when they face problems that overwhelm them. There is no salvation in trusting in human strength for deliverance. There is no salvation apart from God.

Isaiah characterizes his setting as one full of great treachery,[45] "panic, pit, and pitfall."[46] Isaiah clearly visualized the terror, bloodshed, and death that

---

[43] Blenkinsopp, *Isaiah 1–39*, 352–56, relates רָזִי to the Aramaic word "secret" (Dan 2:18–19,27–30; 4:6) based on the Targum and several other translations, so this phrase is translated "I have my secret," but this approach does not fit the parallelism.

[44] רָזִי־לִי is repeated twice in parallelism with אוֹי־לִי, "woe to me." These verbless clauses are interjections of pain, loss of strength, and hopelessness. רָזִי has to do with being waste, desolate, unproductive, and powerless. Clements, *Isaiah 1–39*, 204, has "I pine away." J. Niehaus, "*rāz-pěšar* in Isaiah XXIV," *VT* (31 (1991): 376–78, follows the Old Greek, Targum, and Peshitta to translate this word "my secret." He compares this to Daniel's interpretation of the handwriting on the wall in 5:25–28, meaning that the interpretation of the secret is found in 24:18, just like the interpretation of Daniel's secret was found in 5:26–28. This approach seems an unlikely interpretation of this difficult passage.

[45] Assonance is created by using the same word twice along with a preposition that has the same three consonants—b, g, d: *bōgdim bāgād beged bôgdim bāgādû*, lit. "those who are treacherous are treacherous, and with the treacherous they are treacherous." Isaiah used similar vocabulary in 21:2 and 33:1.

[46] Johnson, *From Chaos to Restoration*, 41, picks up the assonance in 24:17 *pahad wāpahat wāpāh* with this translation. Jer 48:43–44 later used these same images to describe his situation,

would happen when the Assyrians attacked the city of Jerusalem. It frightened him and he realized that there is no human way to escape (24:18a).[47] The speech by Rabshakeh in chap. 36 illustrates the treachery and deceptiveness of the Assyrians as well as their past pattern of killing thousands of people in order to assert their control over rebellious nations. If the Hebrew could escape from one threat (the pit), surely some other (the snare) would catch them. The prophet clearly realizes how hopeless Judah is without God, so he laments.

(4) After Destruction, God Will Reign (24:18b–23)

**The floodgates of the heavens are opened,
the foundations of the earth shake.**
**¹⁹The earth is broken up,
the earth is split asunder,
the earth is thoroughly shaken.**
**²⁰The earth reels like a drunkard,
it sways like a hut in the wind;
so heavy upon it is the guilt of its rebellion
that it falls—never to rise again.**

**²¹In that day the LORD will punish
the powers in the heavens above
and the kings on the earth below.**
**²²They will be herded together
like prisoners bound in a dungeon;
they will be shut up in prison
and be punished after many days.**
**²³The moon will be abashed, the sun ashamed;
for the LORD Almighty will reign
on Mount Zion and in Jerusalem,
and before its elders, gloriously.**

The paragraph after Isaiah's parenthetical lament returns to the themes of 24:1–3 to describe God's judgment of the heavens and the earth:

God's devastating punishment of the earth	24:18b–20[48]
God will destroy all powers in heaven and earth	24:21–23a
God will establish his reign over the world	24:23b

---

probably based on a common proverbial saying that both prophets knew. Williamson, *The Book Called Isaiah: Deutero-Isaiah's Role in Composition and Redaction* (Oxford: Clarendon Press, 1994), 252, thinks Isaiah copied Jeremiah, but the flow of dependence is nearly impossible to prove one way or the other.

[47] Compare different images used by Amos to communicate the same idea—that it was impossible to escape God's judgment (5:19; 9:2–4).

[48] Sweeney, *Isaiah 1–39*, 329, puts 24:16b–20 all in one paragraph, which contains the prophetic response in a disputation speech (Johnson, *From Chaos to Restoration*, 41–42 follows this same division), but Wildberger, *Isaiah 13–27*, 500, correctly finds a "completely different line of thought" beginning in 24:18b.

The "surely" (*kî*; NIV omits it) in 24:18b introduces this new paragraph and the "in that day" (*bayyôm hahû'*) clause in 24:21 marks the beginning of the second part of this paragraph. The first person prophetic lamentation is missing from these verses (which were in 24:16–18a); instead the message is directed back to a discussion of God's judgment. Once evil is finally defeated, then God will reign over all (24:23b).

24:18b–20 The final punishment of the earth (not the attack on Jerusalem) will involve a major disruption of the normal patterns of nature. Enormous floods will occur once again as the "windows of heaven" (cf. Gen 7:11; 8:2) are opened. Extremely strong earthquakes will shake the land plates from their moorings.[49] It will seem like the earth is collapsing, falling apart, and splitting in two (cf. Rev 6:12–15). There will be no stable, safe place to hide, for the earth will convulse like an unstable drunk that cannot walk, or like a small hut struck by a major windstorm. The sinful rebellion of the people on the earth will be so great that nothing can preserve them. The earth will collapse; this old world will never rise again.[50] The prophet is saying that the world as it is known today will come to a final end.

24:21–22 The defiled natural, inanimate world will feel the brunt of God's wrath, but so will all living creatures, especially those powers in heaven and earth that oppose God. Once these are defeated "in that day," God's final and victorious reign will be fully established. The purpose of God's final visitation will be to bring low the powers on earth (24:21b,22) and in the heavens (24:21a,23a), leaving God himself as the reigning king (24:23b).

Verse 21 indicates that God is the one who will assert his authority over the "hosts, armies, powers" (*ṣĕbā'*) of heaven and the kings on earth (consistent with chaps. 13–23). The heavenly hosts could refer to the stars and planets (40:26; 45:12; Ps 33:6), but it seems more likely that this is a reference to enemy angelic beings (2 Kgs 22:19; Job 1:6; Dan 4:32; 8:10; 10:13), not inanimate objects.[51] The parallelism between the two halves of this verse invites the comparison between the defeat of the powerful evil rulers on earth (21b) and the powerful rulers in heaven (21a). Once these are defeated God alone will rule the world.

---

[49] The finite verb with the infinitive construct enables the author to emphasize the verbal idea to show the absolute certainty of these results (GKC §113n). רָעָה הִתְרֹעֲעָה is lit. "breaking, it will break" or "it will surely break." This pattern is used 3 times in each line of 24:19 and once in the first line of 24:20.

[50] Isaiah may be using images from Amos 5:1–2. Amos employed similar words to describe the fall of the northern nation of Israel about fifty years earlier.

[51] Deuteronomy 32:8 connects nations with certain angelic beings as does Dan 10:13. G. B. Gray, *The Book of Isaiah: A Critical and Exegetical Commentary on the Book of Isaiah 1-27* (Edinburgh: T & T Clark, 1912),422–23, concludes this refers to angelic beings. Johnson, *From Chaos to Restoration*, 55, argues that the heavenly powers were pagan gods. The apocryphal book of 1 Enoch speaks of these issues in much more detail but it was written 600 years after the period of Isaiah, so it cannot be used to decide what this passage means.

These evil forces are pictured as prisoners locked up in a pit or dungeon. The term *bôr*, "pit, hole, dungeon," is associated with Sheol, the place where the spirits of the dead go (it was the abode of the king of Babylon in 14:15; cf. Rev 20:1–5). The final temporal clause refers to a punishment after many days,[52] which could be interpreted in two ways: (a) the judgment of the powers "in that day" will not come immediately but will be carried out "after many days," [53] or (b) the powers of heaven and earth will be judged by God in some sort of final judgment after they are imprisoned for many days. The contextual placement of this phrase after the powers are already imprisoned (at the end of 22) instead of before they are imprisoned (at the beginning of 21) argues that God has planned a final judgment after these powers are initially imprisoned in Sheol (cf. Rev 20). Although one needs to be careful not to read later New Testament revelation into Old Testament texts, these words do uncover significant bits of information that are progressively developed in a much fuller way in later texts.

24:23 This verse should not be considered a continuation of the defeat of all earthly and heavenly powers in vv. 21–22,[54] but a separate thought describing what will happen after the powers in heaven and earth are defeated. The "white, the white one" refers to the moon while the "hot, the hot one" refers to the sun (also in 30:26).[55] In 13:10 these heavenly bodies and the stars are darkened because of God's destruction, but 24:23 is probably not referring to any punishment of these heavenly sources of light. It describes the same eschatological events as 60:19–20. When the glory of God appears (60:1), the light from the sun and moon will be irrelevant because it will pale in comparison to the glorious everlasting light from God. Thus the physical powers that God ordained to rule over the day and night will lose their role. The white light of the moon will be so weak that the moon will be put to shame. Even the bright burning hot sun's light will be an embarrassment when compared to the God's glory.[56] Although this text focuses on the "glorious" (*kābôd*) nature of the reigning king (rather than his light), the Hebrews knew from their tradition that God's glorious appearance was always associated with a bright light (Exod 3:1–6; 19:16,18; Deut 5:24–26; Ezek 1). This contrasting comparison between God and the sun only increases the mystery and majesty of the glory of God when it appears in its full radiance.

---

[52] וּמֵרֹב יָמִים, "after many days," with the מִן preposition.

[53] Johnson, *From Chaos to Restoration*, 56, holds this view. It emphasizes that the audience needs to trust God now and patiently wait for God's timing of judgment.

[54] Sweeney, *Isaiah 1–39*, 330, says, "the moon and sun, major deities in the pagan religions of the ancient Near East, will become ashamed because YHWH will rule"; he views this as a continuation of 21–22. Watts, *Isaiah 1–33*, 327, makes a major division after 24:22 and puts v. 23 with the following unit, 24:23–25:8.

[55] The descriptors הַלְּבָנָה, "the white one," and הַחַמָּה, "the hot one," rather than sun and moon, indicate that the writer is talking about the light from these heavenly bodies.

[56] O. Kaiser, *Isaiah 13–39*, OTL (Philadelphia: Westminster, 1974), 195, agrees with this interpretation and point to parallel passages like Zech 14:7 and Rev 21:23; 22:5.

This glorious revelation of God will accompany his establishment of himself as king of the universe in Zion before the elders of Israel.[57] Isaiah had seen something of the glory of the Lord of Hosts reigning as a king on a throne in a vision some years earlier (6:1,5) and that emphasis continues throughout his writings (32:1; 33:17,22; 41:21; 43:15; 44:6; 52:7). This was also a consistent theme of many of Israel's hymns (Ps 29:10; 44:4; 47; 48:2; 93, 95–99).[58] There is no indication that this is a coronation of God as king at this point as Gray suggests,[59] it is rather the establishment of God's rule over his people. This implies that the full implementation of "divine rule" over all creation will characterize the essence of these eschatological events.

THEOLOGICAL IMPLICATIONS. This section outlines the plans of God that will be fulfilled at the end of this age. God will destroy the evil forces that have defiled the heavens and the earth, devastate what these rebellious powers have built, and allow his curse to fulfill its consequences on polluted nature and sinful mankind. The power of God to destroy will be fully visible as he scatters, ruins, desolates, and consumes all that is exalted and powerful in heaven and earth. Those who rebel against God, violate his statutes, and break his covenants will pay for their guilt at an enormous cost. Billions will die, and everything that they have made will be ruined. Joy and happiness will end, so gloom and bitterness will increase. The very foundations of the earth will be shaken and the angelic beings will be held accountable for their actions. God will rule what happens in heaven and earth, so all other powers will lose their authority and ability to control portions of the earth. Sin and sinners will eventually be expunged out of existence, freeing the world of their deadly influence. Thus the forces that brought sin into the world in the Garden of Eden will finally be removed so that they will no longer defile what God made. God will be victorious over the power of sin. The Revelation to John in the New Testament also mentions great earthquakes, the sun and moon being darkened, the stars falling into the earth, and mountains and islands moving (Rev 6:12–15; 9:1–2). Peter also refers to the angels being put in dungeons until the final judgment (2 Pet 2:4; Rev 20:1–6), but the most important factors are the removal of the curse of sin on the earth and the establishment of God's reign as king forever (24:23; Rev 20–21).

The revelation of the glorious power of God will cause many throughout the world to shout for joy and sing God's praise (24:14–16a). People will rejoice to see the majesty and glory of God in action as he righteously deals with sinners. God will finally get the praise that he deserves as people exalt his name and

---

[57] T. M. Willis, "Yahweh's Elders (Isa 24:23): Senior Officials of the Divine Court," *ZAW* 103 (1991): 375–85, prefers to think of these elders as members of the Divine Council.

[58] G. V. Smith, "The concept of God/the gods as King in the Ancient Near East and the Bible," *TrinJ* 3 (1982): 18–38, and M. Z. Brettler, *God is King: Understanding an Israelite Metaphor* (Sheffield; JSOT, 1989), discuss the biblical role God has as king.

[59] Gray, *Isaiah 1–27*, 428, takes 24:23 in conjunction with the banquet in 25:6–8 to reconstruct a coronation of God as king.

recognize his divine power. Although there is no indication where this praise in Isaiah will happen, Rev 4–5 and 19:1–8 describe the chorus of praise to God in heaven by millions of people and angels at the end of time.

Nevertheless, as Isaiah reminds the reader (24:16b–18a), the world is not yet at that time in history, for sin is still powerful and the enemies of God are still at work. Today, people groan like the prophet because the agony of the curse is still very real in this world. People still die; oppression and treachery are more common than righteousness; terror and death occur every day. Like the prophet, believers still lament over the woes and the devastation created by sin. But there are reasons to be encouraged, for the people of God know that the ultimate and final victory will come to those who worship God, the King. One day some time in the not too distant future, God will reign in power over the heaven and earth. There is no doubt about that; therefore, believers can confidently trust him for today and each tomorrow.

2. Eschatological Words of Praise to God (25:1–12)

The second part of this eschatological scenario in chaps. 24–25 involves a celebration in which God and his people rejoice over his establishment of his victorious reign over the world. This victory celebration involves:

Singing God's praise	25:1–5
Enjoying God's bountiful feast	25:6–8
Expressing trust in God	25:9–12

The literary genres change from announcements of judgment in 24:1–13 to a song of thanksgiving in 25:1–5. This song is characterized by first person words of praise to "you" (that is God) and a celebration of what "you" have already done. Beginning with 25:6–8, proclamations like "I will honor you" are replaced by a description of what God will do for those people from Israel and the nations who trust him. God will supply abundant food for his people at a festive banquet and will announce that he has removed the consequences of the curse on mankind (25:7–8). The concluding messenger formula, "the LORD has spoken," marks the end to this paragraph. The final paragraph (25:9–12), introduced by "in that day," records further words of trust in God as the only source of salvation (25:9–10a) because he will humble all his powerful and prideful enemies (25:10b–12).

Differences in the interpretation of these verses hinge on three questions. (a) Do interpreters find a chronological ordering of events in 25:1–12 or merely a topical discussion of one event? (b) How do commentators understand the purpose of the banquet in 25:6–8 (coronation of God as king, sacrifices, or reinstitution of the covenant)? (c) How does one explain the judgment of Moab in 25:10b–12? At this point it is important to answer the first question. The other issues are addressed in the exegesis of those paragraphs.

It seems natural to suggest that the song of thanksgiving in 25:1–5 functions as the response of God's people for the victory he will win over his
enemies and for the establishment of his reign as king over heaven and earth
(24:1–23). Similarly, the final paragraph of trust and confidence (25:9–12)
could be a response to the announcements made at the banquet in 25:6–8. In
contrast, Sweeney historicizes these events and relates them to celebrations
for victories over Israel's present enemies.[60] Those who take a liturgical interpretation of chaps. 24–27, believe the thanksgiving song was sung at the
banquet in 25:6–8. But both of these approaches are questionable: How could
Moab still rebel against God (25:10b–12) after God has already defeated his
enemies (24:1–23) and eliminated death and sorrow (25:7–8). Consequently,
it is best not to view 25:1–12 as a chronological series of events that take
place after 24:23, but as reflections of activities and responses surrounding
one central event (the establishment of God's kingship).[61] Thus the defeat of
Moab probably took place at the same time as the defeat of God's enemies
in chap. 24; it is not some later revolt after God has already established his
perfect kingdom.[62]

(1) A Song of Thanksgiving (25:1–5)

¹O LORD, you are my God;
 I will exalt you and praise your name,
 for in perfect faithfulness
  you have done marvelous things,
  things planned long ago.
²You have made the city a heap of rubble,
  the fortified town a ruin,
 the foreigners' stronghold a city no more;
  it will never be rebuilt.
³Therefore strong peoples will honor you;
  cities of ruthless nations will revere you.
⁴You have been a refuge for the poor,
 a refuge for the needy in his distress,

---

[60] Sweeney, *Isaiah 1–39*, 333–37, explains 25:1–5 as thanksgiving for God's defeat of Babylon (24:10; 25:2) and his protection of the poor Israelites in exile, while the fall of Moab refers
to Babylon's later conquest of that land. This approach relativizes God's defeat of death and his
establishment of his kingship into a temporal restoration of the nation rather than a literal final
eschatological defeat of all forces that oppose God.

[61] Polaski, *Authorizing an End*, 161–64, put 24:21–23 at the same time as chap. 25, thus eliminating a sequential ordering of events.

[62] Childs, *Isaiah*, 183–85, interprets Moab "as a representative symbol of ontological resistance to God's purposes for creation," for "the universal restoration of God's creation does not
remove all tension between good and evil." Thus he concludes Moab is able to choose to reject
inclusion in the kingdom of God, even at this time. But this perspective runs counter to the claim
that God will destroy all enemy powers on heaven and earth (24:21–22), limits God's kingship to
only parts of the world (exclusive of Moab), and denies the reality of God's complete elimination
of all sorrow and death.

a shelter from the storm
and a shade from the heat.
For the breath of the ruthless
is like a storm driving against a wall
⁵and like the heat of the desert.
You silence the uproar of foreigners;
as heat is reduced by the shadow of a cloud,
so the song of the ruthless is stilled.

This song of thanksgiving includes:

Thanksgiving to God	25:1a
Reasons why people are thankful	25:1b–5
God was faithful to his plan	1b
God defeated their enemies	2–3
God gave refuge to the weak	4–5

25:1a The new paragraph begins with a direct address to God, identifying the singer's relationship with Yahweh. This is a confessional acknowledgement of devotion and commitment, similar to other statements of loyalty in the Psalms (31:14; 40:5; 86:2; 118:28; 140:6). This confession expresses a personal choice to identify with the name and deeds of God. Claiming that the Lord is "my God" (*'ĕlōhay*) is also a statement of commitment to a personal relationship with God. The relationship is one in which the singers exalts and thanks[63] God, openly expressing appreciation for his grace and faithfulness. These statements represent a faith relationship of worshipers who humbly proclaim the glory of the one they exalt.

25:1b–3 The singer provides two reasons (introduced by *kî*, "because," in 1b and 2) for praising and thanking God and one consequence ("therefore," *'al kēn*, in v. 3). The first reason for praise relates to God's faithfulness in accomplishing marvelous deeds,[64] a term usually reserved for miraculous divine acts of salvation. These are clear manifestations of God's wondrous power on behalf of his people. This term serves as a fitting description of God's salvation of his people from the sin and evil in this world in 24:1–22. In that eschatological era the people will look back at God's revelation of his plans and realize that God planned these eschatological events many years earlier. The worshipers will also thank God because God faithfully followed the plan he made long ago (*mērāḥōq*). His faithfulness bespeaks his sovereign power and his dedication

---

[63] יָדָה means to "thank, praise" the name (שֵׁם, "name," is a substitute expression representing God and his reputation). NIV chose the translation "praise" because it is more parallel to "exalt," but "thank" would be more appropriate to connect this statement with the reasons for thanksgiving in the following verses.

[64] פֶּלֶא is a name for the coming Messiah in 9:5, but here it refers to salvific acts of deliverance like God's miraculous plagues and his deliverance of Israel from Egypt through the Red Sea (Exod 15:11; Ps 77:11–20; 78:12–16). The prophet Jeremiah believed God would restore the nation from exile because "nothing is too hard (miraculous) for you" (Jer 32:16).

to do what he plans. These plans are permanently set—there is no changing them. These words of thanks serve as words of assurance to those hearing the prophet speak in Judah. Although Judah was being attacked by Assyria, the people could rest assured that what God has said about the future will happen exactly as predicted. Believers today can have that same confidence. Nothing is outside the plan or power of God; no evil power or circumstances will interfere with God's accomplishment of his will for his people.

The second reason for thanksgiving (25:2) provides more specific details about God's miraculous deeds. People will thank God "because" (*kî*; omitted in NIV) he has defeated a "city" (*'îr*), even a "fortified town, a fortress" (*běṣûrâ*), and has made it into a ruin or pile of rubble. The identification of the "city" in 24:10; 25:2; 26:5; 27:10 as a Moabite city in 25:10 led Eissfeldt to identify this city as one of the chief Moabite cities, while Rudolph proposed that this passage celebrated the destruction of the city of Babylon.[65] Hanson and Millar suggested that this exilic poem describing how Jerusalem fell in 586 BC,[66] but Wildberger and O. Kaiser saw "the city" as a symbol rather than a reference to a specific historical city.[67] This last option makes the most sense since the name of the city was purposely omitted (cf. 24:10). Its demise is certain and complete; it will never exist again (similar to 24:20b). The defeat of this city confirms the defeat of those "proud"[68] forces that oppose God in chap. 24.

As a result of God's action (25:3 begins with "therefore," *'al kēn*), an un-identified "strong people" (*'am 'āz*) and the cities of ruthless nations will praise and glorify God. At first it is somewhat surprising to find these foreign people praising God; nevertheless, this text proves that God can and will radically transform formerly ungodly, oppressive, and proud people throughout the world. People from these former powerful nations will see the power of God displayed when he destroys the world; consequently, some of them will respond with submission to God and praise. Isaiah 2:1–5; 14:1–2 and 19:18–25 (cf. also 60:1–21; 66:19–21) indicate that people from many nations will stream to Zion. This also implies the transformation of many people who previously did not depend on God. Finally, when all human strength and pride is removed, many will turn from their old ways and glorify God.

---

[65] Eissfeldt, *The Old Testament: An Introduction*, 326; Rudolph, *Jesaja 24–27*, 61–64. Lindblom, *Die Jesaja-Apokalypse*, 72–84, prefers to relate these events to Xerxes attack on Babylon in 485 BC, and Blenkinsopp, *Isaiah 1–39*, 348, opts for the defeat of Babylon by Cyrus in 539 BC.

[66] Hanson, *Dawn of Apocalyptic*, 314, and Millar, *Isaiah 24–27*, 20. It would seem odd that Hebrews would be thanking God for the fall of Jerusalem or that they would say that Jerusalem would never be built again. Other prophetic promises would directly contradict this notion (cf. Ezek 40–48).

[67] Wildberger, *Isaiah 13–27*, 462, and Kaiser, *Isaiah 13–39*, 173–77.

[68] J. A. Emerton, "A Textual Problem in Isaiah 25:2," *ZAW* 89 (1977): 64–73, discusses a variety of textual problems in this verse. The one change that is minimal, yet significant, is to hypothesize that זָרִים, "strangers," is a result of the common confusion between the almost identical letters ר and ד, thus he proposes the reading זֵדִים, "proud, arrogant, impudent," which fits the context well and is consistent with 25:11 and 2:6–21. Isaiah 13:11 has a similar transcription error.

25:4–5 An additional reason for thanking God is "because" (*kî*; omitted in NIV) of his protection of the oppressed, the poor, and the needy. In the time of their persecution and weakness, God mercifully will become a "refuge, stronghold" (*māʿôz*) of protection for those who could not protect themselves. This concept is illustrated with two analogies. God will be like a "shelter" (*maḥseh*) that protects a person from the heat of the penetrating summer sun or the pounding rain, hail, and lightning in a cloudburst (cf. 28:2; 30:30). Both natural situations can be life threatening, for the unrelenting scorching heat will kill just as surely as lightning or a flooding stream. These two metaphors were employed to describe the behavior of the ruthless people who opposed the people of God. If the "spirit, breath, roaring"[69] of these ruthless people was as powerful as a flood of water pushing against a wall or as oppressive as the heat in summer, then the prophet is describing the unbearable pressure of unrelenting forces that suffocate life. In contrast, God is seen as one who subdues the "proud, arrogant"[70] (NIV keeps "foreigners"), just like the shade of a cloud subdues the heat. Thus God's protection nullifies the opportunity for the ruthless to sing their victory songs. Instead God's people will sing a new song of praise, which celebrates God's past salvation of his people from oppression during the final eschatological events. Although many have suffered and died during this period, in the end God will be victorious over his proud enemies (24:1–22). Many people, even many former ruthless people, will end up glorifying God because of his miraculous deeds.

If chaps. 24–25 were spoken just before Sennacherib's attack on Jerusalem, as suggested by the laments in 24:16b–18a and 26:7–19, it would not be hard to understand how this song would be an inspiration to those in Jerusalem. Although this prophecy did not promise them deliverance from Assyrian oppression or victory in their present battle, it reminded them that everything happens according to God's plan, that their God can do miraculous wonders to save his people, that God is a refuge in times of trouble, and that ultimately God will win the victory over all ruthless peoples. If this was true, Isaiah's audience could also trust God in the midst of their present trial.

(2) God's Joyous Feast (25:6–8)

> **⁶On this mountain the LORD Almighty will prepare**
>   **a feast of rich food for all peoples,**
> **a banquet of aged wine—**
>   **the best of meats and the finest of wines.**
> **⁷On this mountain he will destroy**
>   **the shroud that enfolds all peoples,**
> **the sheet that covers all nations;**

---

[69] רוּחַ can refer to the "spirit, mind" of a person, "life, being," or the "breath, wind." Some think it refers to the "angry snorting" of the ruthless (Wildberger, *Isaiah 13–27*, 516) or the "mind of the ruthless" (Kaiser, *Isaiah 13–39*, 197).

[70] זָרִים, "strangers," is a result of the common confusion between the almost identical letters ר and ד, thus the reading זֵדִים, "proud, arrogant, impudent," fits the context here and in 25:2.

> [8]he will swallow up death forever.
> The Sovereign LORD will wipe away the tears
>   from all faces;
> he will remove the disgrace of his people
>   from all the earth.
>   The LORD has spoken.

The scene changes from singing praise to feasting at a banquet God will prepare for his people in Zion. There is little agreement about the background and purpose for this banquet. The reference to "this mountain" (*bāhār hazzeh*) suggests that the banquet is closely connected to events in 24:23 when God reigns as king from Mount Zion. Little background is provided, but some commentators suggest that the context involves people from the nations making a pilgrimage to Zion (2:2–3; 60:1–22) to present their gifts to God (18:7; 60:1–22) and celebrate God's kingship a banquet of coronation.[71] This practice is also compared to the mythological enthronement of Baal at a feast of the gods on Mt Zaphon, or the coronation feast for the Babylonian god Marduk, but it seems unlikely that the prophet Isaiah would apply these pagan customs to God's kingship.[72] God has always been king; he will not initially be crowned as king at a coronation ceremony at the end of time. A cursory reading of these verses reveals that there is no actual reference to a pilgrimage, bringing gifts to God, offering sacrifice, or the crowning of a king in 25:6–8. Since these components are not present, it would be inappropriate to relate this passage to a coronation ceremony. Since God has always been a reigning king, a coronation service at this late date would not be fitting.

25:6 The banquet is a joyous celebration of God's rule by people from around the world. This gathering is not just the twelve tribes or a small remnant of Hebrews; it will include Hebrews and Gentiles from every tribe and nation on the face of the globe (cf. 2:2–3; 14:1–2; 19:18–25; 45:20–25; 49:22; 60:1–22; 66:18–21). Since there is no indication about the length of this banquet feast, some suggest that this feast serves as a metaphor for God's continual provision of the best meat and finest aged wine the earth can produce.[73] This wonderful feast is very similar to what the Psalmist envisions when God finally rules the earth in Ps 22:25–31. This picture of blessing, fruitfulness, and

---

[71] Gray, *Isaiah 1–27*, 428, found a parallel in 1 Sam 11:15 where Saul was made king in Gilgal, and the people sacrificed to God and rejoiced greatly (see also 1 Kgs 1:9,25). Oswalt, *Isaiah 1–39*, 463, explains this as an inaugural banquet when a king is crowned and subjects from around the world will gather at Jerusalem (2:2–3; 4:5; 11:9). Clements, *Isaiah 1–39*, 208, finds a pilgrimage and ceremony echoing Exod 24:9–11, but no coronation.

[72] Millar, *Isaiah 24–27*, 71–102, traces the comparisons between the Baal Epic and the reaffirmation of God's kingship in Isa 24–27. Polaski, *Authorizing the End*, 171, notes the weaknesses of this approach and rejects it.

[73] God's future feast for his people is developed in Matt 8:11 as a feast in heaven and in Rev 19:9 as a wedding feast of the Lamb. There is assonance between the similar sounding שְׁמָרִים, "aged wine," and שְׁמָנִים, "fatness."

prosperity presents a stark contrast with the desolation, withering, death, ruin, and curse on the earth in chap. 24.

25:7–8 The second thing that will happen "on this mountain" will be even more spectacular. In addition to the blessings of food for all peoples in the kingdom, God will do three additional things: (a) swallow up, destroy death, which covers all people; (b) wipe away all tears; and (c) remove disgrace. Since the verb "swallow up, destroy" (*billaʿ*) describes both the action in 25:6 and 25:7a, one should assume that the sheet or shroud of mourning that covers[74] all people in v. 6 is explained in v. 7 in the statement about swallowing up death. If the prophet says that the shroud people wore to mourn the death of their loved ones is taken away (2 Sam 15:30), one can say that there will be no need for it because death will not happen. This theological doctrine should not be relegated exclusively to late post-exilic texts like Daniel 12:2, nor minimized as a metaphorical way of saying that God will vanquish his enemies so that death in warfare will end.[75] No, the complete removal of death will be central to the establishment of God's sovereign reign, for death is the punishment the enemies of God justly deserve because of sin. Once the enemies of God in heaven and earth are vanquished, no one will deserve to die. The mystery of God's action is not fully revealed in this text, but the end of death must also imply the end of sin and the removal of sinful people from the earth. There is no hint here of resurrection from the dead for those who died in the past, though later 26:19 will touch on this subject. The means of removing the curse of sin and the power of death is also missing from consideration in this series of divine promises.[76] The focus is not on how God will do these miraculous things; Isaiah is completely enthralled with just communicating the fact that this will happen. When God rules over his kingdom, death will have no power over people in this new world.

As if that were not enough, God also promises the removal of all tears. This includes tears shed when people die, but certainly also tears of oppression, sickness, pain, disappointment, loneliness, rejection, military defeat, financial trouble, and other kinds of loss. All these experiences will be obsolete in God's kingdom. Finally, God's removal of the reproach of "his people" (*ʿammî* 25:8b) should not be interpreted as a specific reference to removing Israel's reproach of the exile,[77] for at this point all people (*ʿam*, "people," is used in 25:3,6,7,8)

---

[74] פְּנֵי־הַלּוֹט הַלּוֹט is lit. "the face of the covering that covers," with the second הַלּוֹט being an active participle. A similar Hb. construction is used in the second half of the verse in "the covering that covers."

[75] Clements, *Isaiah 1–39*, 208, argues that certain elevated theological doctrines were not understood until the intertestamental period, while Polaski, *Authorizing an End*, 175, understands this as this referring to the end of death in warfare.

[76] The substitutionary death of Christ on the cross to pay the penalty for the sins of the world and to defeat the power of death is more fully discussed in Rom 6:14; 1 Cor 15:12–57; Rev 1:17–18; 21:4 and other texts. There is no need to hypothesize that this was an anti Baal polemic by the prophet as Blenkinsopp, *Isaiah 1–39*, 359, proposes.

[77] D. Johnson, *From Chaos to Restoration*, 64, limits "my people" to Judah.

in God's kingdom are his people. When people are reproached they are objects of derision, mockery, shame, and humiliation by others. These evil actions will not be experienced any longer. If the enemies of God are defeated, there will no longer be people to give a reproach, and there will be no sinful people who will deserve to be reproached. This paragraph ends (25:8b) with the affirmation that God has declared that this is what will happen; thus, one can know that all these statements are true.

(3) A Song of Praise for God's Deliverance (25:9–12)

⁹In that day they will say,
"Surely this is our God;
　　we trusted in him, and he saved us.
　This is the LORD, we trusted in him;
　　let us rejoice and be glad in his salvation."

¹⁰The hand of the LORD will rest on this mountain;
　　but Moab will be trampled under him
　　as straw is trampled down in the manure.
¹¹They will spread out their hands in it,
　　as a swimmer spreads out his hands to swim.
　God will bring down their pride
　　despite the cleverness of their hands.
¹²He will bring down your high fortified walls
　　and lay them low;
　he will bring them down to the ground,
　　to the very dust.

25:9 The final paragraph is marked off by the introductory "in that day," which also marks the next paragraph (26:1). This paragraph contains a response of trust in God, somewhat similar to the song of thanksgiving in 25:1–5. The song has two parts, a declaration of trust in 25:9, and a reason for trust in 25:10–12 (beginning with *kî*, "because"). The people gathering on "this mountain" (*bāhār hazzeh* in 25:10b; cf. 24:23; 25:6) from all over the earth to celebrate God's rule will sing of their trust in God.[78] The song itself begins with statements about God who rules in Zion (similar to 25:1), but this time the community sings about their relationship to "our God" (*'ĕlōhēnû*). The repetition of the statement that "this is our God" excludes all other explanations for their salvation. He is the one who accomplished it, not any human leader or political process. His saving acts are a part of the wondrous deeds (in 25:1) he graciously performed for those who exalt him as their God. All credit and glory is directed to God. The community's relationship to God has two aspects: (a) they chose to place their trust in God in the past; and (b) now they rejoice because of what God has done. The term used to describe their "trust"

---

[78] 1QIsaᵃ has "you will say," while the Old Greek has "they will say" (followed by NIV), but the Hb. וְאָמַר, "and one will say," is quite acceptable as a collective expression of the whole.

(from *qāwâ*) represents a "hopeful act of waiting" before the establishment of God's kingdom. Oswalt says that, "It is the kind of confident expectation that is willing to put the times in God's hands and to believe in spite of the long interval."[79] Those who trust in this way know that God is sovereign, that he has a plan, that the plan will be accomplished, and that there is a good reason for God's timing of events. As recipients of such grace, his people joyously respond with gladness over the salvation God provides (25:9b).

25:10–12   The reason why the people can sing this song and rejoice in God's salvation is "because" (*kî*; omitted in NIV) they see God's power doing two things when he sets up his kingdom: (a) his hand continually rests on mount Zion; this is a sign of his guiding and protecting power over his people (cf. 11:2); and (b) his foot tramples down proud nations like Moab (as explained in 24:1–22). The mention of a specific nation is unusual in chaps. 24–27, but it is not a sign of a strong Jewish hatred for the Moabites, or due to the political destruction of the Moabites at this time in Isaiah's life.[80] Instead Moab serves as a fitting symbol of those who are excluded from God's people for two reasons. First, Deut 23:1–8 instructed the Israelites long ago to exclude the Moabites from the assembly of the Lord. Second, the Moabites were known for their excessive pride (16:6), so their humiliation and the destruction of their sources of pride illustrates what God will do to all those who do not trust him. This does not describe a rebellion that breaks out after God has established his kingdom on Zion.

The imagery of the defeat of Moab is shocking. The people are pictured as being trampled under foot like straw is trampled in the water[81] in a manure pit (equivalent to being thrown into the sewage pond at the town treatment plant). Obviously, anyone would try to escape such a despicable death by swimming out of the pit as fast as possible (25:11a). In this illustration none of these swimming efforts will help this poor soul who is trampled down like straw; instead that person will quickly sink to the bottom of the pit. This imagery should not be applied literally to Moab or any other nation. It is merely a picture of someone helplessly dying in the most disgusting circumstances imaginable. This imagery communicates that it will be impossible to escape God's judgment.

The imagery will be realized by God humbling the pride of all arrogant people who oppose him (25:11b).[82] As a result, high and secure walls that

---

[79] Oswalt, *Isaiah 1–39*, 466, concludes that the one who confidently waits must not be dependent on instant gratification.

[80] Clements, *Isaiah 1–39*, 210, interprets this as a sign of intense feelings against the Moabites, while Sweeney, *Isaiah 1–39*, 337, thinks that this notice acknowledges the downfall of Moab in the sixth century BC.

[81] בְּמוֹ is an orthographic variant of בְּמוֹ, "in it," in the Masoretic Hebrew text, but it is spelled בְּמֵי, "in the water," in 1QIsaᵃ and the oral *Qere*, which makes better sense.

[82] The NIV phrase "despite the cleverness of their hands" is difficult to interpret. The preposition עִם usually means "with," so this phrase could refer to God humbling their pride along with

men built to protect themselves and control their destiny will be brought down, humbled, cast down to the dust (25:12). This is a picture of military defeat aimed at the humiliation of all who formerly opposed God. Since God will do these things to defeat his enemies when he sets up his kingdom (24:1–22), the people who gather together to celebrate, worship, and feast with God will sing about how their wonderful salvation (25:10) differs from the humiliating destruction of the other nations of the earth (25:11–12).

THEOLOGICAL IMPLICATIONS.   All people of God love to praise God. They exalt and honor him because they have a personal relationship with him and therefore all believers can call him "our God." God's people glorify his name because of his faithfulness, his marvelous deeds, his plans, his defeat of the ruthless, his protection of the weak, his conquering of the threat of death and sorrow, his humbling of the proud, and his salvation. His victories should be celebrated with singing and feastings each day, just as they will be celebrated in the future.

One of the greatest victories will be God's elimination of death (25:7–8). The text declares what God will do but does not explain exactly how God will abolish death. Although the prophet does not spell out the theological implications, one could logically argue that sin no longer existed after the destruction of the defiled earth and the imprisonment of all sinful powers in heaven and earth in chap. 24. Once the curse of sin has brought its destructive power on all sinners, it would be logical to conclude that there would be no need for death because sin no longer exists. Isaiah does not provide this logical explanation, he merely states what God will do. Later New Testament writers grapple with these thoughts and understand God bringing the believers from death to life because through grace sin no longer exercises mastery over them (Rom 6:13–14). This was possible because Jesus gained victory over death when he rose from the dead (1 Cor 15:12–28). Nevertheless, the full fulfillment of the prophet's prediction will not be realized until God establishes his kingdom and reigns as king over this world at the end of time (Rev 21:1–4).

Since God is so great and powerful, it is natural for his people to respond in confident trust. When they need refuge from the ruthless, guidance, or protection, God is a sure and a dependable source of hope. This recounting of what people will say after God's eschatological victory serves as a motivation for Isaiah's audience (and all of those who read his words) to reject the way of pride and to wait confidently for God to display his salvation. Then they can sing God's praise with others at his great banquet at the end of time. People may not understand why they suffer so much oppression today or why God waits so long to establish his kingdom, but all believers know that God has a

---

their efforts or skillful things made with their hands. Another completely different option would be take the phrase as a description of what God will do "with his hands" (יָדָיו ... עִם) to humble Moab, like the NEB "with the stroke of his hand." This takes all the actions in 11b–12 as being the acts of God against his enemy.

perfect plan that he will accomplish. It is a known fact that one group of people will feast and rejoice with God and that another group will be humbled and destroyed. That is because some people chose to exhibit pride and ruthlessness while others will demonstrate trust in God. What is not known is when "that day" finally will arrive and who will be at the table rejoicing and praising God. Every nation and every individual will be responsible for the choice they make and their choice will affect their eternal destiny.

3. Judah's Trust in God for Deliverance (26:1–27:1)

HISTORICAL SETTING. The prophetic messages now move from their focus on future eschatological events when God rules the world from Mount Zion (24:23) to the present situation of the people of Judah. Childs maintains that this section is "a highly theological presentation directed to the faithful, who . . . still experience the full weight of divine and human judgment."[83] But is this simply a return to discuss the oppression of God's people just before God's eschatological judgment in chap. 24 as Childs suggests? Arguing in favor of that position would be (a) the phrase "in that day" in 26:1 and 27:1 could refer to final eschatological events as it does in 24:21 and 25:9; and (b) the meaning of common phrases used in chaps. 24–25 could point to the meaning they have when these words and phrases are used in chap. 26.[84] However, "in that day" in prophetic texts can refer both to distant and near future events. The immediate context of the lament in 26:7–18 must be the primary determinative factor that identifies what "day" the prophet refers to. In addition, the meaning of previously used words and phrases always depend on their present context for meaning. Past usage is significant, particularly when they are repeated within a single literary unit, but an author may purposely choose to alter, contrast, or develop the meaning of a term or idea in an analogous way but not in the exact same way that they were used in earlier verses. Thus "the city" in 24:10–13 is ruined and desolate with no joy, but this is purposely contrasted with the image of "the strong city" of God in 26:1. These are not the same places; consequently, while the earlier meaning has an impact by creating a contrast, the immediate context of 26:1 determines its later meaning.

Two factors suggest that most of chap. 26 refers to present or near future events in the life of the prophet, not to the eschatological activities in chaps. 24–25. First, the faithful are instructed to sing (26:1–6) about how God cares

---

[83] Childs, *Isaiah*, 189, follows Seitz. *Isaiah 1–39*, 193 and 195, in finding a temporal shift here, with chaps. 16–18 giving details about what will happen just before the judgment of God in chap. 24. Polaski, *Authorizing an End*, 219, calls chap. 26 a retelling of chaps. 24–25 that emphasizes the different treatment of the righteous and wicked.

[84] References to the "strong city" in 26:2 (probably Jerusalem) and the "lofty city" that is laid low in 26:5 probably refer to the cities mentioned in chaps. 24–25; "the nations" or "people of the world" in chap. 26 relate to those mentioned in 24–25.

for the righteous. The imperative exhortations[85] challenge the people to open the gates (26:2) and trust in God (26:4) because he will humble those who are high and mighty. This indicates that the audience is not in Zion after God has become king, but are still facing opposition here and now. The author is trying to persuade his listeners to trust God based on who God is and what he will do (26:1–3,5–6), not what he has already done. In the hymns the author reuses the future testimony of God's people in 25:9 ("we trusted in him and he saved us") in a new way to exhort his own audience to follow the example of future worshipers. He is confident that the same results will happen now, if people will only put their trust in their Eternal Rock (26:4). 25:9 refers to what has already happened at the end of time, while 26:1–6 describes what will happen if people will trust God now. It appears that the people are facing an immediate problem, so they need to trust God for help. This interpretation of 26:1–6 fits in with the purpose of 26:7–10. These verses aim to develop confidence in God so that those who are righteous in Judah will be willing to wait for and trust in his deliverance in the near future (deliverance has not already happened).

The specific context of 26:1–6 is hinted at in the lament in 26:7–18. The petition in 26:16–18 describes a nation in distress as a result of God's discipline. The people are in great pain (like the pain of childbirth) with no salvation in sight. They continue to for God to act (26:8) and hope to see God's zeal for his people soon (26:11). What they need to do is wait until God's wrath is past (26:20) and then they will see God's deliverance when he defeats their enemy (26:21–27:1).

Although the evidence of a specific historical event is limited, the interpreter can use various hints to decide what the prophet was describing. First, it is important to notice that there is no indication in the eschatological events in chaps. 24–25 that God will discipline his people by having them attacked before the final establishment of his kingdom.[86] Consequently, D. Johnson placed the setting of chap. 26 after the fall of Jerusalem and just before the fall of Babylon in 539 BC. The nation had experienced the wrath of God through the Babylonian defeat and needed to trust God and wait in exile until God destroyed the wicked nation of Babylon.[87] Then they would experience his salvation and be restored to the land. This makes more sense than placing chap. 26 in an eschatological setting, but the canonical context of chaps. 13–23 and 29–39 suggest a more likely date. The primary example of divine discipline at the hand of another nation, forcing Judah to trust God, was the attack on Jerusalem by the Assyrian king Sennacherib in 701 BC. Judah was exhorted not to trust in Egypt (30:1–5; 31:1–3; 36:6) or to rely on the devious propaganda of the Assyrians (36:4–20),

---

[85] בִּטְחוּ in 26:4 is an imperative of admonition that asks an audience to act (GKC § 110a).

[86] Isaiah 25:4 does mention that God is a refuge for the needy in a time of distress, but this is very different from saying that God in his wrath will discipline his people for a time.

[87] Johnson, *From Chaos to Restoration*, 69–70. Hayes and Irvine, *Isaiah*, 313, propose that the present crisis for Judah was the invasion of Sargon around 711 BC.

but were to rely on God for salvation (30:15; 37:14–20). Sennacherib's defeat of the main cities of Judah, except for Jerusalem, qualifies as a day of distress and rebuke for the nation (37:3). One key to connecting these events with this lament is the way both describe the oppressive situation. When Sennacherib attacked Jerusalem, Hezekiah compared their distress to experiencing the pain of labor but not having the strength to deliver the child (37:3), exactly the same metaphor used to describe the historical situation in 26:17–18.

In the context of chaps. 24–27, the prophet uses an eschatological analogy of God's destruction of all of his enemies (chaps. 24–25) to convince the people of Judah to place their faith in God now (chaps. 26–27). In the future God's people will trust God and experience his salvation when he destroys all his enemies (25:9), therefore the prophet exhorts his audience in Jerusalem to trust God to do the same thing now in the midst of their present Assyrian distress.

O. Ploger has attempted to describe the situation more specifically by identifying a conflict within the post-exilic community of Judaism in chap. 26 (as well as in Zech 12–14 and Joel) between the "righteous," who are totally dedicated to God and await his eschatological coming (24:14–16a), and their opponents "the godless" Jews, who have broken the covenant, are pessimistic about the future, and are not interested in eschatology. This second group is then identified with those disinterested in eschatological issues in the book of Chronicles. These people comprise the ruling class and governing priests.[88] P. Hanson also finds a conflict in the Jewish community, though he focuses more on 24:14–18 and chaps. 55–66. Hanson locates the dispute between the disenfranchised Levitical-prophetic group of eschatological "visionaries" who followed the program of "Third Isaiah" and their opponents the "realists" who were Zadokite priests. The Zadokites were in control of the priesthood and followed Ezekiel's vision of the future (Ezek 40–48).[89] Although there is no doubt that different groups with different theological opinions existed in Judah, in the text of Isaiah these are simply defined as the righteous Jews and Gentiles who trust God and the proud and ruthless who do not. There is no indication of an internal conflict between Hebrew Levites in Jerusalem over their eschatological hopes,[90] thus these attempts specifically to identify conflicting groups do not appropriately define the situation in 26:1–27:1.

---

[88] O. Ploger, *Theocracy and eschatology* (Richmond: John Knox, 1968), 54–78. R. Albertz, *A History of the Israelite Religion in the Old Testament Period* (Louisville: Westminster/John Knox, 1994), 495–597, located these apocalyptic ideas with a lower class group within Judaism that saw their only hope in the assurance of salvation through eschatological events.

[89] Hanson, *The Dawn of Apocalyptic*, 46–100, 228–69. P. Redditt, "Once Again, the City in Isaiah 24–27," *HAR* 10 (1987): 330, also finds a conflict between the ruling priestly theocracy that the Persians controlled and an anti-city peasant group that opposed those in power and were awaiting the day when God would rule in a pure Jerusalem.

[90] Johnson, *From Chaos to Restoration,* 75, rightly rejects these approaches because the language of Isaiah shows a distinction between the godless enemy and the righteous Hebrews, not a division within the Jewish community.

STRUCTURE AND GENRE. The chapter is unified by its focus on the "righteous" people who enter the gates of God's strong city (26:2), whose paths are level and smooth (26:7,7), and whose righteous ways are contrary to the ways of the wicked (26:9,10). An increase in imperative (26:2,4,20,20,20,20), modal (26:9); and jussives (26:11,11) verbs that express willed action indicate that the whole chapter was designed to convince people to trust God for deliverance from their present situation.

Sweeney treats the whole chapter as one complaint song with four distinctive subsections (praise, affirmation of confidence, petition, exhortation), though the final exhortation containing God's answer (better described as an oracle of salvation) is not a common part of most laments in the book of Psalms (though it is not uncommon in Jeremiah's laments).[91] These categories can be helpful in understanding this lament, but it is best to divide the chapter into three larger paragraphs:

A community song of trust	26:1–6[92]
A community lament	26:7–18
A salvation oracle	26:19–27:1

Each section expresses the need to trust and have confidence in God's ability to save his people and defeat their enemies. Each section exhorts the audience to act in faith because they know what God can do for them. Their enemy is the wicked people who do not glorify God in 26:11, and the metaphorical Leviathan in 27:1. God is pictured as the source of salvation, the ruler over the nations, an eternal Rock, the one who has enlarged and disciplined the nation, and the one who will defeat their enemies. These diverse themes enable the prophet to express his own sympathetic pain over the nation's problems as well as provide initial (26:1–6) and final (26:19–27:1) exhortations of hope based on his understanding of God's character and the way he plans to deal with the righteous and the wicked.

(1) A Song of Trust in God (26:1–6)

[1]In that day this song will be sung in the land of Judah:
We have a strong city;
God makes salvation
its walls and ramparts.

---

[91] Sweeney, *Isaiah 1–39*, 338–40. Gray, *Isaiah 1–27*, 434–38, defines 26:1–19 as the larger unit, separating the exhortations in 26:20–27:1 out as a separate section. In the prophetic literature (Jer 11:21–23; 12:5–6; 15:19–21) several laments are followed by God's answer, which may be positive or negative.

[92] Wildberger, *Isaiah 13–27*, 544, calls this a hymn, a song of praise and Oswalt, *Isaiah 1–39*, 470, states that it is "typical of a classical hymn of praise." Johnson, *From Chaos to Restoration*, 68, correctly notes the futuristic slant of the song where the central call to praise is replaced by a call to trust (26:3–4), thus changing its focus and purpose.

²Open the gates
    that the righteous nation may enter,
    the nation that keeps faith.
³You will keep in perfect peace
    him whose mind is steadfast,
    because he trusts in you.
⁴Trust in the LORD forever,
    for the LORD, the LORD, is the Rock eternal.
⁵He humbles those who dwell on high,
    he lays the lofty city low;
  he levels it to the ground
    and casts it down to the dust.
⁶Feet trample it down—
    the feet of the oppressed,
    the footsteps of the poor.

26:1a The chapter begins with an introduction to a song that people will sing in Judah. The time ("that day") for this song is sometime after God humbles the proud (26:5) and creates a strong city for his people (26:2). The following lament suggests that the people will have to wait "for a little while" before God will punish the people of the earth for their sins (26:20–21). This means that the people will not have to wait until the eschatological age to see God's discipline on them end and experience his deliverance from their distress (26:16). The singing of this song "in the land of Judah" argues that it applies to Hebrews, not to "all the peoples of the earth" at the end of time (24:14–16a; 25:6–8).

26:1b–2 Since the people still need to trust God (26:4) and are awaiting the time when God will humble the lofty (26:5), the song begins with a confident statement about what the righteous firmly believe will happen, not about what has already happened (the later would fit an eschatological situation). The initial verbless clause (lit. "city of strength to us") is a typical Hebrew way to expresses possession ("we have a strong city"), but the tense of the supplied verb depends on the context. Since the verb *yāšît*, "he will set up, establish," in the next phrase is imperfect, it is most natural to translate the supplied verb as a future in order to match the tense of the parallel line. Thus "we will have a strong city, he will establish salvation, (as) walls and ramparts," is a confident statement of faith in God, who will replace man made physical defenses with his own presence. Continuing the city metaphor, the song exhorts[93] a righteous nation (not plural "nations" as in 25:6–8), meaning Hebrews who are right with God, to enter into God's protective care through the open gates of the city of God. These righteous people are further defined as "the ones who remain faithful." The patterns of righteousness and faithfulness are not presented as qualifications for entrance into this city but as characteristics of behavior now exhibited by the people of God.

---

[93] פִּתְחוּ, "open," is an imperative of admonition that makes a request for someone to act (GKC §110a).

26:3–4 These verses follow the organizational pattern already established in 1b–2. First, the song expresses a statement of confidence in God (26:3, like v. 1b) and then the audience is exhorted to act in trust based on that confidence (26:4, like v. 2). The song confidently states that certain people will have perfect peace.[94] Two factors characterize these people. The NIV translation indicates that they have a "frame of mind, perspective, constitution" (*yēṣer*) that is "steadfast" (*sāmak*), which implies an undeviating commitment to a purpose, conviction, or person. The root meaning of the translation "steadfast" is "to support" but the Hebrew passive participle carries the idea of "leaning on, depending on, resting on" something.[95] So in 36:6 the idea that the people "are depending" (*bāṭaḥtā*) on Egypt is metaphorically signified as the people "leaning" (*yissāmēk*) on the staff of Egypt. Thus the prophet confidently confesses that the people who have a "dependent perspective" (as opposed to a proud self-confident demeanor) will have complete peace because they trust in God. Humble dependence engenders a peaceful trust in God's abundant strength.

If this is so, the exhortation to trust God makes sense, for God is like a solid rock that is eternally stable and unmovable (26:4, cf. 17:10). If the audience wants to find peace that will truly last forever, Yahweh, the God of Israel, is a stable and reliable source to depend on. The threefold repetition of the name Yahweh ("LORD") in v. 4 emphasizes which God they should rely on (contrast this with 27:9).

26:5–6 The songwriter repeats his expression of confidence in God's deeds on behalf of his people. This sense of assurance is heightened by (a) an initial *kî* that expresses confidence that "surely" (omitted in NIV) this will happen; (b) four words that describe God's act of humbling[96] or laying low the proud; and (c) the humiliation of the high and lofty to the ground, to the dust, or someplace low. The audience can be assured that God will do these things; therefore, they can trust him.

One would expect another imperative verb in 26:6 to introduce a final exhortation (following the pattern in vv. 2 and 4). If the verb "trample" (*tirmĕsennâ*) is understood as a jussive form, then there would be a final exhortation to "let feet trample it (the lofty city) down."[97] If the verb is a simple imperfect, then v.

---

[94] שָׁלוֹם שָׁלוֹם repeats the word "peace" to express the superlative idea of "complete peace" in Hb. (GKC §133i–l).

[95] סָמַךְ has the idea of (a) "leaning or resting" hands on a sacrificial lamb (Lev 1:4; 3:2,8,13); (b) God "supporting, sustaining" someone who needs help (Gen 27:37; Ps 3:5; 37:17,24; Isa 59:16); and (c) people "relying, trusting" God for support (26:3; 48:2; Ps 71:6; 2 Chr 32:8).

[96] The second line appears to have a dittography (the same word written twice). The unusual יַשְׁפִּילֶנָּה יַשְׁפִּילָה is reflected in the Targum but one of the duplicate forms is missing in the Old Greek and 1QIsa^a. A possible solution to this problem that would justify the MT would be to connect the first verb with the preceding phrase about the lofty city and then connect the second word with the ground, which is in the phrase after the verb (cf. NRSV; NIV).

[97] The jussive form תִּרְמְסֶנָּה is identical to the imperfect in this verb, so only context can guide the interpretation. The jussive expresses a wish, request, desire or encouragement (GKC §109a–b).

6 would describe the results of God's destruction of the lofty city—the people
will be so powerless that the poor and oppressed can walk all over them ("trample them down"). This does not celebrate the strength of the poor and weak, for
they will not humble the proud, it only demonstrates how low the lofty will lie
on the land. Surely the powerless can trust a God who is this strong!

(2) A Lament while Waiting for Salvation (26:7–18)

> [7]The path of the righeu is level;
>   O upright One, you make the way of the righteous smooth.
> [8]Yes, LORD, walking in the way of your laws,
>   we wait for you;
> your name and renown
>   are the desire of our hearts.
> [9]My soul yearns for you in the night;
>   in the morning my spirit longs for you.
> When your judgments come upon the earth,
>   the people of the world learn righteousness.
> [10]Though grace is shown to the wicked,
>   they do not learn righteousness;
> even in a land of uprightness they go on doing evil
>   and regard not the majesty of the LORD.
> [11]O LORD, your hand is lifted high,
>   but they do not see it.
> Let them see your zeal for your people and be put to shame;
>   let the fire reserved for your enemies consume them.
>
> [12]LORD, you establish peace for us;
>   all that we have accomplished you have done for us.
> [13]O LORD, our God, other lords besides you have ruled over us,
>   but your name alone do we honor.
> [14]They are now dead, they live no more;
>   those departed spirits do not rise.
> You punished them and brought them to ruin;
>   you wiped out all memory of them.
> [15]You have enlarged the nation, O LORD;
>   you have enlarged the nation.
> You have gained glory for yourself;
>   you have extended all the borders of the land.
>
> [16]LORD, they came to you in their distress;
>   when you disciplined them,
>   they could barely whisper a prayer.
> [17]As a woman with child and about to give birth
>   writhes and cries out in her pain,
>   so were we in your presence, O LORD.
> [18]We were with child, we writhed in pain,
>   but we gave birth to wind.

We have not brought salvation to the earth;
we have not given birth to people of the world.

Although one may consider the change from a song of trust (26:1–6) to the present lament as an abrupt mood swing, in actuality the statements of confidence in God's ways at the beginning of the lament (26:7) create a natural transition from the statements of confidence in the song of trust (26:1b,3,5). Since these verses do not exactly follow the pattern of most laments in Psalms, some prefer simply to call this a prayer.[98] Nevertheless, if one is willing to allow some freedom of expression based on the circumstances being lamented and the creativity of the individual lamenting, then this paragraph falls within the general structure of what one would expect in a lament.[99] The paragraph structure includes:

An affirmation of confidence in God	26:7–10
A petition requesting God's action	26:11–15
A lament	26:16–18
(God's answer	26:19–27:1)[100]

The lamenter is confident in God's ability to punish the wicked, even though he does not see God acting yet (26:9,11). He realizes that God is disciplining the nation in his anger (26:16) but he asks God to act zealously on behalf of his people and bring peace (26:11). In light of the canonical context of this chapter, located between chaps. 13–23 and 28–39, and in light of the similar terminology to describe Hezekiah's situation of being under siege (26:17 and 37:3), it is possible to connect this lament to the setting where Sennacherib was attacking Jerusalem.

This lament serves as a good example to all believers, for it contains a healthy acceptance of present pain, a firm faith that God is teaching people the ways of righteousness through it, a recognition that God is the only source of real peace, and a strong yearning to have deliverance from this severe trial. The placement of the lamenter's confidence in God first (26:7–10) communicates a trust that puts God's chastening (26:16–18) in its proper context. The grieving people are not without hope, though this trial (the attack of Sennacherib) is very severe and painful.

---

[98] Kissane, *Isaiah*, 282, calls it a prayer of the people in acute distress, Watts, *Isaiah 1–33*, 340, classifies it as a pilgrims song, and Oswalt, *Isaiah 1–39*, 477, does not think the form matches the regular form of the lament.

[99] C. Westermann, *Praise and Lament in the Psalms* (Atlanta: John Knox, 1981), 52, indicates that the main part of a lament are the (a) introductory address to God; (b) lament; (c) confession of trust; and (d) vow of praise. He also indicates (p. 61–63) that where the final vow of praise is missing, some laments insert an oracle of salvation to answer the request of the lament. This fits the pattern of 26:7–27:1 in this lament, though the order is different.

[100] God's answer can be the conclusion to the lament, but it will be dealt with in the next paragraph.

A special characteristic of 26:7–10 is the repetition of key terms to gain a greater rhetorical force on specific ideas.

7a		path	righteous	is level/straight
7b	upright/straight	way	righteous	
8	your judgments	desire	our hearts (lit. "soul")	
9		yearns	my soul	
		longs	my spirit	your judgments
9b	learn		righteousness	
10a	do not learn		righteousness[101]	

26:7–10 The lament begins with an affirmation of faith in God and his ways. The lamenter may be quoting or referring to known wisdom traditions that reflect on the path of the righteous (cf. ideas in Ps 1; 27:11; Prov 3:6; 4:18). According to both covenant and wisdom beliefs, God blesses and guides the righteous by putting them on straight, direct, and level paths. Ideally the road of life for the godly will not be dangerous, crooked, hard to traverse, or filled with rocks and ruts. But the actual path of the righteous often deviates from the ideal because people repeatedly fail to live pure and righteous lives and because they live among people in this world who are wicked and oppressive.

The NIV takes the second reference to "level, upright" as a vocative address to God, "the Upright One,"[102] which is possible, but the parallelism with "level, upright" in the first line argues against this translation. The prophet is simply confessing his belief that God will make the path of the righteous level. Even God's "judgments" (the negative experiences of punishment, not "laws" as in NIV)[103] that he puts people through are aimed at molding them and making the road they walk more upright and level (26:8a). This "level path" is not something that people can hope to achieve through power, money, or the manipulation of circumstances; it is something that God prepares for believers though his divine intervention. The imperfect Hebrew verb "you make/will make smooth" (*tipallēm*) suggests that this is something the lamenter confidently believes God is doing or will accomplish in the near future.

The present situation of Isaiah's audience (and most people today) includes plenty of bumps and uphill climbs, in addition to the smooth and level paths. Nevertheless, the lamenting community should confess that "we are confidently waiting" with faith in God,[104] even though the present circumstances may

---

[101] W. H. Irwin, "Syntax and Style in Isaiah 26," *CBQ* 41 (1979): 240–61, also finds chiastic structures, e.g., in the wording of 26:9b–10a with "grace will be shown" at the center of the chiasm.

[102] יָשָׁר, "straight, upright, level."

[103] Although מִשְׁפָּט can refer to God's laws, the overall context, particularly of 26:9–11, indicates that he is talking about experiences of God's judgment where the people can see the hand of God at work establishing righteousness.

[104] 1QIsaᵃ, Old Greek, and Targum omit the object pronoun "you" in the phrase, giving "we

not be ideal (26:8a). God is the key to the future and the only hope for establishing a transformed level life. The righteous community believes that in due time God will accomplish his purposes and fulfill his promises to bring into existence that time when the way of the righteous will be smooth. In a sense, this prayer is an admission of personal inability to control the future and the need to totally depend on God.

26:8b–9a Therefore, their priority, longing, and deep desire (repeated three time in 8b–9a) was to see the name and reputation of God magnified. This desire exhibited itself in a focus on God's glory rather than their own personal peace and happiness. They knew that their future was tied to God, so if he is glorified, they will be just fine. This constant longing within me (early[105] and at night) indicates that a serious problem exists and that those lamenting desperately need God to address their situation.

26:9b–10 The problem is that God has not yet judged the wicked. The lamenter begins by making a general statement of truth in 9b, amplifying the earlier statement about the "way of your judgments" in v. 8a. That truth is: when[106] God disciplines people with a time of judgment, people "learn, should learn"[107] what is right and what is wrong. This recognizes that there is a pedagogical purpose in God's acts of judgment. They are educational just like the discipline of a parent, but sometimes people do not turn to God in repentance (Amos 4:6–12), so nothing is actually learned.

Of course there is no possibility to learn from God's judgments when[108] God patiently and mercifully withholds the execution of his judgment on the wicked (26:10). The wicked may live among righteous people and know what is right and wrong, but they twist the truth or manipulate life[109] to their advantage in order to get away with their oppressive behavior. As long as the wicked

---

wait/hope," which suggests the reading קִוִּינוּ instead of the Hebrew Masoretic קִוִּינוּךָ, "we hope in you." J. de Waard, *A Handbook on Isaiah: Textual Criticism and the Translator*, I (Winona Lake: Eisenbrauns, 1997), 111, argues that the Masoretic Hebrew text is more original

[105] בְּקִרְבִּי does not mean "in the morning" but "in my midst, within me," so Blenkinsopp, *Isaiah 1–39*, 366, translates the clause "my spirit within me seeks you eagerly." The verb contains the idea of "seeking early" (implying early in the morning) thus providing the contrast with late at night.

[106] כִּי often means "because" to introduce a subordinate clause or "surely" to emphasize the truth of an independent clause, but in this case the temporal marker "when" seems most appropriate, particularly with כַּאֲשֶׁר immediately after it.

[107] It is hard to know if the prophet is stating a general proverbial truth that people "do learn" through punishments (which is not always true), or if he is indicating that the purpose of judgments is that people "should learn" about righteousness. The perfect verb לָמְדוּ can have a subjunctive meaning. It refers to actions in the past as possible, rather than as accomplished (GKC §106p). Thus, this word refers to what should have happened.

[108] There is no introductory particle (as in v. 9b) indicating that this is a conditional or temporal clause. The contrasting parallelism between 9b and 10a suggests that the temporal "when" in 9b is implied at the beginning of 10a.

[109] The verb עֻוֵּל means to sin by twisting the truth or by twisting behaviors so that they are not consistent with what is right.

do not see the majestic and glorious supremacy (*gēʾût*) of God in action against their sinful ways, there is no regard for God or righteousness. At this point in the lament it is still unclear what evil people the lament refers to, but the desire to see God act in power against evil is a common yearning for all believers as they experience the trials in life. All believers confidently know that when God acts, things will get better, thus they earnestly pray.

26:11–15   The lamenter now requests that God stop waiting and act on behalf of the community that is suffering. It is time for him to punish their enemies. The community makes a vocative direct address to God ("O LORD") at the beginning of vv. 11, 12, 13 and in the middle of v. 15. After a relatively brief call for God to act (11–12a), the rest of the paragraph provides a rational as to why God should act.

26:11–12a   The lamenter saw God as powerful and active in history, with his sovereign hand raised against evil nations and intervening on behalf of Israel. The person lamenting was probably thinking about examples of the exodus from Egypt, the conquest of the Canaanites, and other events throughout Israel's history. But the problem was that the wicked in the prophet's time either did not know about what God had done in the past or refused to recognize God as the real power controlling history. Therefore four requests[110] are made: (a) let them see the zeal of God; (b) let them be ashamed; (c) let fire consume them (26:11); and (d) establish peace for us (26:12a). Zeal (*qinʾâ*) is an excited emotional fervor that motivates uncompromising decisive action to defend one person and oppose another. The request is for God to act zealously on behalf of his people so that their enemies will be forced to see the hand of God in their demise. This action will turn their pride into shameful defeat, when God consumes this enemy. The lamenter's desire was that God would put in place[111] a time of peace for his people by defeating their enemies. This was the promise when God establishes his messianic kingdom (2:1–5; 9:6–7); it was their confident hope in the preceding song of trust (26:3). A similar confident faith in the power of God is needed today as believers intercede for those who are suffering persecution at the hands of the ruthless enemies of God.

26:12b–15   Although Wildberger[112] and many others interpret 12–15 as confident statements about what God will do for his people, it is more appropriate (since the statements of confidence were already given in 26:7–10) to classify these verses as the reasons for the requests in 11b–12a.[113]

---

[110] These verbs could be understood as jussives or modal imperfects that express a desire or wish (GCK §107n, 109b).

[111] 1QIsaᵃ has "will judge" from שָׁפַט instead of the Hb. שָׁפַת, "set up, establish." This is another request (thus a modal imperfect) rather than a confident statement of what God will do.

[112] Wildberger, *Isaiah 13–27*, 563, maintain that the lamenter is basing his confidence on what God did for the people in the past.

[113] Sweeney, *Isaiah 1–39*, 338–40, interpret these verses as the basis for God's action on behalf of the one praying.

Verse 12b begins with "because" (*kî*; omitted in NIV) to present the first rationale for God's zealous action. God should act because all that has ever been accomplished by his people was always and only the sovereign work of God.[114] This is a humble admission that the people have always been dependent on God's providential intervention on their behalf. This point is illustrated by contrasting (a) past examples when foreign lords ruled the land—who are now long forgotten, with (b) the fact that the people "will remember" (NIV "honored") only God's name (26:13, cf. Hos 13:4).[115] The lamenter is claiming that the people never forgot, never gave up on God, and will always cause his name to be remembered in Judah. In spite of all their past oppressors and in spite of periods of idolatry, they will always trust only Yahweh as their God. This could be called an optimistic revisionist view of past and future Israelite history, but the main point is that the community now is loyally committed only to God, therefore past failures are interpreted as temporary failures.

"Consequently, truly" (*lākēn*; omitted in NIV in the middle of 26:14) God zealously intervened to punish all those foreign rulers, so they would not live and their departed spirits (*rĕpāʾîm*) would not rise again to oppress the land. God has wiped out any memory of them (26:14). This is significant in the present context, for as God acted in the past, so he needs to act again in Jerusalem. As a result of the defeat of these past enemies, God multiplied the people of Judah, expanded the borders of Judah, and gained great glory for himself (26:15). If God has gone to all this trouble in the past, surely he would not abandon his people now. Now is the time for God to act on behalf of his people by removing another foreign nation that is oppressing Judah.

The past rulers are not identified and the present period of expanded borders is not tied to any Judean king. Gray hypothesizes that the text may refer to the time when David and Solomon expanded the United Kingdom of Israel,[116] but it would prove little to say that Judah was faithful hundreds of years ago. To be a significant claim of loyalty the author must maintain that people were loyal in the recent past. The period of expanded borders and religious loyalty to God in Isaiah's lifetime was during the reign of Hezekiah (2 Kgs 18:1–14; 2 Chr 30–32).

---

[114] Johnson, *From Chaos to Restoration*, 76, proposes to translate 12b, "since you have also requited our misdeeds," based on the Targum, which refers to "our transgression." However, there is no confession of sins in this lament.

[115] J. Day, "The Dependence of Isaiah 26:13–27:11 on Hosea 13:4–14:10 and its Relevance to some Theories of the Redaction of the 'Isaiah Apocalypse.'" *Writing and Reading the Scroll of Isaiah: Studies of an Interpretive Tradition*, VTSup (ed. C. C. Broyles and C. A. Evans; Leiden: Brill, 1997), 357–68, believes the author of Isaiah was influenced by the discussion of similar themes in Hosea 13:4–14:10. One problem with relating this verse to Hos 13:4 is that in Hosea these words were spoken by God about the people's relationship to God at the time of the exodus, rather than being a confession by the people of their loyalty to God in the time of Isaiah. Although some words may be similar, the two passages are significantly different.

[116] Gray, *Isaiah 1–27*, 444.

26:16–18 This paragraph ends with a lament over the people's present distressful situation (26:16), comparing it to the agony of woman giving birth to a child (26:17–18). The text of v. 16 is very difficult to understand and the NIV somewhat periphrastic. The chief problems are (a) one would expect first person "we came to you" in v. 16, which would be more personal than "they" and more consistent with the first plural usage in vv. 17–18;[117] (b) in Isaiah the verb *pāqad* ("they came" in NIV) frequently refers to God's negative visitation or punishment of others (1:4; 2:15; 4:14; 8:13; 10:3,12; 24:21, 22; 26:14) but "O LORD, they punished you" makes little sense; (c) *laḥaš*, "whisper, mutter, exorcism," suggests a magical incantation, which seems inappropriate for people in Judah, but the word may be an alternate spelling of "affliction" (*laḥaṣ*), which gives a better parallel for "in distress" in the first line; and (d) the verb *ṣûq* could mean either "pour out" or "press upon." The central issues resolve themselves into two very different interpretations of what this verse says. Either the prophet is positively describing how "we" (emended from the Hebrew "they"), the righteous people of God, are seeking God during a time of painful distress (16–18a), but are not yet delivered (18b); or the prophet is lamenting the failure of the unfaithful people of Judah ("they" as in the Hebrew) to seek God in their time of distress, for they have been unable to save themselves. Is the problem that God has not paid attention to them or is the problem more with the people not truly pouring out their hearts in complete confession and trust in God?

The following tentative solution is based on the position that the present Hebrew text should be kept without emendation, unless it is absolutely necessary. Thus the verbs in 26:16 should not be changed to first person plural "we"[118] to agree with 26:17–18. The verbal root *pāqad* is best related to the concept of "inspecting, or having oversight," thus God's "visitation" of his people involved his seeking them out, examining, evaluating, and consequently punishing them if they failed to meet his standards. The word is also used in cases where a person fails to find something upon inspection, thus conveying the general idea of something "missing, not found" (Num 31:49; Judg 21:3; 1 Sam 20:6,18, 25; 25:7,15; 2 Sam 2:30; 1 Kgs 20:39; 34:16; Jer 3:16).[119] This yields, "O LORD, they missed/

---

[117] Wildberger, *Isaiah 13–27*, 555, believes one should follow two Hb. MSS and the Old Greek to read "we sought you," while J. A. Emerton, "Notes on two verses in Isaiah (26.16 and 66.17)," *Prophecy: Essays in Honor of Georg Fohrer* (ed. J. A. Emerton. BZAW; Berlin: W. de Gruyter, 1980), 12–25, follows the Hb. with "they entreated thee." D. M. Fouts, "A Suggestion for Isaiah XXVI 16," *VT* 41 (1991): 472–74, proposes several emendations to solve these problems, making the verbs first person plural: "we paid attention," "we poured out," and "your discipline on us." Such emendations may solve a host of problems, but who can be sure that any of these changes have any validity?

[118] Two Hb. MSS in Kennicott have פְּקַדְנוּךָ, "we visited you," while the Old Greek has "I remembered you," but the Masoretic text is by far the more difficult reading, and these other texts appear to be attempts to make the translation easier.

[119] W. Schottroff, "פקד *pqd* to visit," *TLOT*, 2 (Peabody: Hendrickson, 1997), 1018–1031. On 1021 he discusses the meaning "miss, not find." F. Delitzsch, *Isaiah*, Commentary on the Old

did not find you" in 24:16a, which may provide another reason why the prophet lamented before God. He is confessing that the people of Judah failed to trust God during their time of distress (they trusted Egypt in 31:1–5). The first line tells what the people did not do, while the second describes what they did do. "They poured out magical incantations (making no emendations of the Hebrew) when you disciplined them."[120] This is somewhat similar to their earlier pattern of evil behavior during the Syro-Ephraimite War in 8:19 when they relied on mediums, spiritists, and contacted the dead instead of trusting God.

26:17–18 compares Judah's present state to a woman in labor pains. The serious distress of her situation creates writhing cries of pain. The last line of 17 indicates that this happened "because of you, O LORD,"[121] meaning that it was God's sovereign choice to allow the events of history to bring this kind of severe pain on the nation. Elsewhere, the pain of childbirth is used to illustrate the hopeless severe suffering on the final Day of the Lord (13:8), the military battle involving the destruction of Babylon (21:3), the suffering from Sennacherib's devastating attack on Judah (37:3), or the lack of labor pains in the future when there will be many new births (66:6–9).[122] The close verbal overlap between this statement and Hezekiah's speech in 37:3 suggests a likely historical context for chaps. 24–27.[123] The people are finally admitting that all the efforts that "we did" (cf. 22:8–11; 30:1–5) were of no avail. They are humbly confessing that they could not save themselves and that their efforts have produced nothing but more pain.

Instead of giving birth to a healthy child, it was "like giving birth to the wind" (meaning the bloated pregnant woman just had a bad case of gas). There was no salvation or deliverance from their writhing agony, no benefit for all the labor pain, no new life to bring joy after the pain—nothing.[124] This writh-

---

Testament VII, trans. J. Martin (Grand Rapids: Eerdmans, 1969), 449, also favored this solution, as does B. Doyle, *The Apocalypse of Isaiah Metaphorically Speaking: Study of the Use, Function and Significance of Metaphors in Isaiah 24–27* (Leuven: Peeters, 2000), 307, who follows the suggestion of Gese.

[120] "Discipline" in the second line is parallel to "distress" in the first line, so it would be redundant to change the spelling of *laḥaš*, "incantation, whisper," to the alternate spelling of "affliction" (*laḥaṣ*) since it already has a parallel thought in the second line.

[121] מִפָּנֶיךָ is translated "in your presence" in NIV but that phrase is normally derived from לְפָנֶיךָ.

[122] Sweeney, "Textual Citation in Isaiah 24–27," 39–52, looks at other passages that relate to the imagery of child birth (especially 13:6; 26:17–18, and 66:7–9) but strangely does not even include 37:3 in his list. On the other hand, J. Day, "The Dependence of Isaiah," 357–68, connects the woman in child birth pain in 26:17–18 with Hos 13:13. However, the Hosea passage focuses on the unwise child who refuses to be born rather than the mother, plus the verbal connections between the passages are minimal. In spite of this, Hosea's text may have had an influence on Isaiah—on the thought level rather than the direct literary level.

[123] Using a different perspective, Seitz, *Isaiah 1–39*, understands 26:16–21 as returning the prophecy back to the final desolation of the earth in chap. 24. But chap. 24 does not have the resurrection of the dead like 26:19, or any commands to hide until God's wrath is over as in 26:20.

[124] רוּחַ means "spirit, wind," but wind is also a symbol of nothingness since it has no substance.

ing pain is an image of hopeless military defeat sent as a discipline from God (37:3). No new era of peace was inaugurated (no child was born) because they were still suffering from the Assyrian attack. This was a lamentable situation where God allowed the wicked to discipline his people and had not yet taught the wicked to learn righteousness through his punishment (26:10). At this point everything seemed dark and hopeless. The one positive result is that the people finally realized that "we" are not the true source of salvation.

(3) God Will Destroy the Enemy (26:19–27:1)

¹⁹But your dead will live;
   their bodies will rise.
You who dwell in the dust,
   wake up and shout for joy.
Your dew is like the dew of the morning;
   the earth will give birth to her dead.

²⁰Go, my people, enter your rooms
   and shut the doors behind you;
hide yourselves for a little while
   until his wrath has passed by.
²¹See, the LORD is coming out of his dwelling
   to punish the people of the earth for their sins.
The earth will disclose the blood shed upon her;
   she will conceal her slain no longer.

¹In that day,

   the LORD will punish with his sword,
      his fierce, great and powerful sword,
   Leviathan the gliding serpent,
      Leviathan the coiling serpent;
   he will slay the monster of the sea.

This final paragraph contains God's salvation oracle of hope, a positive response that does appear after a few laments in the Hebrew canon (cf. Jer 11:20–23; 15:19–21). God graciously answers this lament by saying that, at some point in the future, he will reverse the problem of pain, death, and lack of new life (26:17–18). This reversal is expressed in terms of bringing the dead back to life in 26:19, waiting a little while until God's punishment is over in 26:20, and the defeat of God's enemies, symbolized as the serpent Leviathan in 27:1.

The concept of the resurrection of the dead in 26:19 is metaphorically compared in the next phrases to waking up from sleep and having the dew provide enough moisture to revive plant life. The implications and meaning of this idea are much debated for three reasons. First, since the clearest reference to the resurrection of dead individuals is dated to the post-exilic Persian era (Dan 12:1–

2), the origin of this idea is frequently viewed as a late theological development within Israelite thinking and thus not present in Isaiah 26:19. This evolutionary approach to the development of Israelite religion is undermined by many ancient Near Eastern texts that describe widespread knowledge of Egyptian beliefs in individual life after death as well as the Canaanite Baal mythology about Baal's resurrection after being killed by Mot, the god of death.[125] Although the Israelite prophets rejected Baalism and did not model their beliefs in life after death on the pagan Egyptian religions, many Israelites worshiped Baal and were familiar with the teaching that he would come back to life at the beginning of the fertile wet season. Thus one cannot base an interpretation of 26:19 on the views of other religions or on the view that the idea of resurrection was unknown in Israel until the time of Daniel. The fact that Elijah and Elisha brought to life two different dead boys (1 Kgs 17:17–24; 2 Kgs 4:18–37) and that a dead man was brought back to life after his body touched the bones of Elisha's bones (2 Kgs 13:20–21) indicates that individual resurrection from the dead was known long before the days of Isaiah.

Second, some view the idea of the resurrection of the dead as simply a metaphor for the restoration of the nation after the exile. At that time God will give them new life, thus this passage refers to the restoration of the nation, not individual resurrection of the dead.[126] This passage is often compared to Ezekiel's vision of the metaphorical revivification of dry bones (37:1–14, see also Hos 6:1–3) and Isaiah's own metaphorical description of God's punishment as "death" (5:13–14) and barrenness (54:1–2) while restoration was pictured as "rising form the dust" (52:1–2) or bearing children (66:7–9). The psalmist offers another metaphorical idea related to resurrection, using the imagery of being brought back to life from Sheol as a picture of being delivered from troubles (Ps 16:10–11; 18:5–6; 49:14–15). These examples indicate that a metaphorical understanding of the revival of the nation from exile is legitimate in some instances, but that does not mean the interpretation must always be metaphorical or national. In the context around this verse there is no explicit mention of the restoration of the nation from exile, so there is no clue that it should be understood metaphorically or nationally in this context. There is no reference in this section to leaving Babylon, going though the desert, returning to the land, the restoration of Davidic rule, rebuilding ruined cities or any of the other themes so commonly associated with the restoration of the nation in other passages.

---

[125] For Egyptian ideas about life after death, see H. Frankford, *Ancient Egyptian Religion: An Interpretation* (New York: Colombia University Press, 1948), 100–23. Most of the focus was on the king's life after death, but later this privilege was democratized to include all Egyptians. For Canaanite ideas, see the discussion in K. Spronk, *Beatific Afterlife in Ancient Israel and in the Ancient Near East*, AOAT 219 (Neukirchen-Vluyn: Neukirchener, 1985).

[126] Wildberger, *Isaiah 13–27*, 567–568, and Johnson, *From Chaos to Restoration*, 80, are two examples of this approach.

Third, the national interpretation is sometimes derived from the preceding context of the lament in 26:7–18 where the prophet was speaking about "the strong city" (26:2), "the righteous nation" (26:2), "the righteous" (26:7), "the people of the world" (26:9), "the wicked" (26:10), "your people" and "your enemies"(26:11), and "the nation" (26:15), All of these are groups of people, thus, it is argued, God's answer should logically address his restoration of the nation from its distress. This is the strongest evidence that this idea refers to national restoration, but the force of this argument is weakened because the focus in these verses is on the "righteous individuals," "your people," or "your enemies," terms that morally define people, rather than politically defined nations.[127] The prophet even recognizes within his own people that there are some individuals who are righteous (26:7) and some who are not (26:16).

Thus the ideas in 26:19–27:1 are not the common set of images employed by Isaiah to describe the restoration of the nation after God's punishment. Instead these verses offer three solutions to Judah's present problems faced when Sennacherib attacked Jerusalem in 701 BC. Isaiah's audience can be assured that (a) "your dead will live" (v. 19); (b) you will need to hide for a while until the heat of God's wrath passes (v. 20); and (c) God will defeat his enemy Leviathan (36:21–27:1). Since 37:3 identifies the historical period when the people were laboring in the pain of child birth with the Assyrian attack by Sennacherib on Judah in 701 BC, the idea of hiding for a while until God's judgment passes (26:20) is quite understandable and applicable to Isaiah's audience. It also makes good sense to describe metaphorically God's defeat of the Assyrians under Sennacherib as his defeat of the serpent Leviathan in 27:1. Bringing the dead back to life is more difficult to explain from this immediate context. R. Martin-Achard thinks the allusion to resurrection here refers to giving life to the faithful Jews who were martyrs during this war against Assyria,[128] but a better possibility might be to connect this promise to the near death experience of King Hezekiah.[129] As a result of Hezekiah's pride, God became angry with him (2 Chr 32:25). The king became sick and soon was at the point of death (38:1). Isaiah announced God's judgment, "you will die, you will not live" (38:1). In deep anguish of soul Hezekiah humbled himself and God caused this dead man "to live" (38:16). Isaiah's promise in 26:19 would then be a theological expression of God's ability to bring an individual condemned to death (Hezekiah) back to new life (not to bring national restoration), a promise that

---

[127] G. Hasel, "Resurrection in the Theology of the Old Testament Apocalyptic," *ZAW* 92 (1980): 267–76, emphasizes this distinction.

[128] R. Martin-Achard, *From Death to Life: A Study of the Development of the Doctrine of Resurrection in the Old Testament*, trans. J. P. Smith (Edinburgh: Oliver and Boyd, 1960), 131–35. M. G. Kline, "Death, Leviathan, and the Martyrs: Isaiah 24:1–27:1," in *A Tribute to Gleason Archer* (ed. W. C. Kaiser and R. P. Youngblood; Chicago: Moody, 1986), 229–49, also takes the idea of the earth disclosing her blood in 26:21b as the revelation of the martyrs who were killed.

[129] In Hezekiah's song he described his experience as going through the gates of death (38:10), and after the was healed he shouted and praised God (38:18–19; cf. 26:19)

later would have direct application to Hezekiah's situation, if he would trust God. There is no indication that Isaiah was speaking directly to Hezekiah in 26:19–27:1, but the three issues dealt with in these verses answer three vital questions that everyone was asking in 703–701 BC: (a) Will the king die or live? (b) Will Judah be able to survive this Assyrian attack? (c) Will God defeat Judah's enemies?

26:19 The change from anguish, pain, and failure under divine discipline (26:16–18) to the hope of new life is dramatic and shocking. God's gracious answer is not a word about Judah's army having a military victory over her enemy Assyria. This promise that "your dead" will live is also different from the promise to remove the curse of death in the eschatological era (25:8). This new promise would most naturally apply to the distressful situation (being attacked by Assyria) of God's people in 26:7–18, but the only "dead ones" mentioned in that context are the dead rulers who "will live no more" (26:13–14). Since the dead who will live are identified as "your dead" and "a corpse"[130] in 26:19, the dead must refer to Israelites. If 26:20 is an exhortation to "my people" then "your" dead must refer to Hebrews. This promise is not applied more specifically to any person or limited to events at a specific time frame, though the present troubles described in 26:7–18 suggests a present rather than eschatological time of fulfillment. Since 26:19–27:1 are so far removed from earlier eschatological hopes in 25:1–12, there is no way of tying these miraculous events to the joyous gathering of God's people in Zion to praise him and celebrate at his banquet at the end of time. This prophecy makes a claim that the prophet's audience must either accept in faith, or reject as impossible.

Isaiah was claiming that God has the power to restore life to the dead. There is no indication when this will happen, how this will happen, or who will rise. God is simply making the claim to lamenters in Jerusalem. So one could imply that God will accomplish this great miraculous deed through some appropriate situation that will be significant in the lives of people in his audience. The focus is on the transformation from death, from being a corpse in the dust to being alive, awake, shouting, and joyful. The comparison of the positive experience of birth and joy (19c) contrasts with the negative inability to give birth and the great anguish in the preceding verse (26:18). This resurrection of the dead is compared to the power of the morning dew to give life to plants (cf. 18:4; Hos 14:5–6). Although in 26:14 the dead do not live and the departed spirits do not arise to be reborn, now God declares just the opposite will happen to "your dead." These are not promises of national restoration but a commitment to bring someone who was considered dead back to life.

Although the general promise of the verse is not directed explicitly to the dying King Hezekiah, the truth that it expresses must have given Hezekiah the faith to believe that God could bring life to a condemned man who was

---

[130] P. C. Schmitz, "The Grammar of Isaiah 26:19a-c," *JBL* 122 (2003): 145–49, considers וּנְבֵלָתִי a gentilic "as corpses" rather than a noun with a first person suffix "my corpse."

destined for death (38:1–22). Thus he prayed for mercy and God gave him life, even though he was as good as dead.

26:20 The second promise also relates to the prophet's audience and its suffering (26:7–18). The prophet exhorts them (a) to go and hide; (b) to stay hidden for a short time; and (c) to wait for God's wrath to pass. This last point indicates that God's discipline (26:16) was interpreted as God's punishment for sins. No specific sins are listed, but in the following chapters Judah is condemned for trusting in Egypt during the Assyrian attack (30:1–5; 31:1–9) and therefore God was specifically angry with Hezekiah (2 Chr 32:25) the king in charge of national policy. As a result of God's death sentence on Hezekiah, he confessed his pride (2 Chr 32:26) and God promised to deliver him from the king of Assyria (38:6).

Israel may have hoped that this prophecy would yet be fulfilled during Sennacherib's attack on Jerusalem, but God does not indicate that there would be immediate relief from Assyria. The people will suffer under God's wrath a little while longer (see 10:25) until God chooses to destroy the Assyrian army (37:36). The only relief possible is for them to run and hide behind closed doors to escape from the Assyrians, the instruments of God's wrath. If the prophet spoke to an audience in Jerusalem, the prophet implied that if the people hide behind the walls and gates of the city, they will find some protection.[131] Once again the general promise is not explicitly applied, but those in the audience could choose to believe and act appropriately, or ignore these words from God. Those of faith would see God justly judging his people for sins, but also knew that a marvelous change would take place once God's punishment was endured.

26:21–27:1 A change in the situation was immanent: God was about to act.[132] In language reminiscent of a personal theophany by God himself (Judg 5;4; Ps 68:8; Mic 1:3), God will leave his dwelling place in the temple and exact judgment on the guilty. In this case the punishment falls on the sins of the "people of the earth," specifically for shedding much blood. (26:21). The earth will no longer hide the blood of those slain by the sword but the full extent of this iniquity will be revealed. The judgment of "the people of the earth" could hypothetically be interpreted as a final eschatological judgment, but two factors suggest that it may apply to the Assyrian army, which included soldiers from many conquered nations. First, this promise sounds like an answer to prayer. Earlier, Judah had asked God to cause the people of the earth to learn righteousness by consuming Judah's enemies (26:9–11), that is the Assyrians. Second, the sin of slaying frequently refers to killing in war (27:7–8), thus

---

[131] It is pointless to compare this instruction to Noah hiding in the ark to protect himself from God's wrath on the earth (Gen 6–8) or the Israelites hiding in their homes at the Passover to protect themselves from the angel of death (Exod 12; see Johnson, *From Chaos to Restoration*, 81–83). In those examples God was angry with others; in this example he is angry with his own people who are hiding.

[132] אָצָי, "is coming/going," is a participle used verbally to express what is about to happen, especially when preceded by הִנֵּה as in this verse (GKC §116p).

Hayes and Irvine suggest, "God will hold the Assyrians accountable for the violence they have carried out across the face of the earth."[133]

This act is also metaphorically pictured as the punishment[134] or the slaying of Leviathan with a sword (27:1). The monster Leviathan (Job 3:8; 41:1–32; Ps 74:14; 104:26) appears to be a wild sea serpent much like the monster Rahab, which often symbolizes Egypt (Job 26:12; Ps 87:4; 89:10; Isa 30:7; 51:9).[135] This will be a mighty battle between the "fierce, great, and powerful sword" of God battling the gliding, coiling, and great monster. Although the Israelites and the prophet Isaiah were well aware of ancient mythological beliefs concerning monsters that battle one another (Baal and Mot; Marduk and Tiamat), the imagery in this passage is demythologized and functions as a symbolic metaphor[136] of a strong nation. Since Isaiah does not identify that political power, one can assume that his audience would have automatically connected it with the evil enemy of Judah at the time (Assyria). God assures his listeners that he has the power to conquer every foe, no matter how strong or fierce.

This marvelous promise confronts the audience with the challenge of believing God. Are his promises true? Will the king and the people of Judah trust God to deliver them from the mighty Assyrian army that was aiming its military might at Jerusalem at that time?

THEOLOGICAL IMPLICATIONS. The Hebrew audience was in dire trouble because it was enduring the discipline of God's wrath against it (26:16,20). This message does not focus on condemning the audience for past sins, but sympathetically cries out for divine mercy in the midst of great pain and distress (26:17–18). The basis for this cry for divine help lies in four confident statements in the initial hymn (26:1–6): (a) God is a person's real source of salvation and protection (26:1); (b) only God can provide complete peace (26:4); (c) God is an eternal rock of stability that people can trust in (26:5), and (d) God will humble the proud that oppress the humble (26:6). In the context of distress these theological statements provide hope and a solid persuasive basis for faith and trust in God (26:3–5). The hymn's declarations were not designed to provide an abstract theological treatise of Israelite faith; they construct a solid basis for action in the lives of those who heard it. Since God acts in certain ways, people are exhorted to respond with acts of confident trust in spite the present distress that they face. These theological statements merely describe the practical relationships God has with mankind (salvation, peace,

---

[133] Hays and Irvine, *Isaiah*, 315, see him referring to the killing by Sargon II rather than Sennacherib.

[134] פָּקַד the repetition of "punish" in 26:21 and 27:1 identifies the one act with the other and argues against making 27:1 part of the following paragraph.

[135] Ezek 29:3 and 32:2 also connect a monster with the Egyptian Pharaoh.

[136] E. M. McGuire "Yahweh and the Leviathan: An Exegesis of Isaiah 27:1," *RQ* 13 (1970): 165–79. M. G. Kline, "Death, Leviathan, and the Martyrs: Isaiah 24:1–27:1," in *A Tribute to Gleason Archer*, 229–49, takes Leviathan to be a reference to the final judgment of Satan himself (Rev 12:9; 20:2), but this approach was only understood at a later time through further progressive revelation.

protection), therefore a righteous person who trusts God is one who lives consistently within the framework of the relationships God has established. These basic principles are still applicable to nations today, so they provide practical guidance that should not be ignored.

Because of sin a nation's relationship with God is sometimes temporarily destroyed and the discipline of divine wrath is required to restore justice, peace, and salvation (26:16,20). In the midst of divine discipline nations and individuals can (a) confidently look to God in hope, waiting for him to smooth out one's path (26:7–8a); (b) maintain a strong desire to see the name of God glorified (26:8b–9a); (c) request for God to discipline the wicked and zealously intervene on behalf of his own people (26:9b–11); (d) recognize God's sovereignty, admit past failures, and realize that God acts to bring himself glory (26:12–15); and (e) confess past sins and lament the agony of divine discipline (26:16–18). This is a practical theology of suffering that honestly faces the causes for discipline, the consequences of being disciplined, and the hope that God provides to overcome divine discipline. No one should forget the way back to God.

God's answer to this prayerful lament (26:19–27:1) provides assurances that God holds in his hand the power to bring death or life from the dead (26:19), that his discipline lasts only for a short time (26:20), and that he will one day act on behalf of his people to destroy their enemies (26:21–27:1). God is the answer; his sovereign power will reign in the end. His is determined to judge sin but his overall plan is to use judgment to bring glory to himself in the end. These events and promises should encourage the righteous to put their complete trust in God, even when they experience his discipline.

4. God's Assurance of Salvation (27:2–13)

The final section of chaps. 26–27 is unified by the agricultural imagery that flows throughout it. The vineyard is cared for (27:3), it takes root, blossoms, and has fruit (27:6). Later negative imagery describes a fierce wind blowing, the fruit stripped from the tree, and the barren branches burned in the fire (27:7–11). The final positive paragraph (27:12–13) refers to the agricultural processes of gathering and threshing. The unified message of 27:2–13 can be divided into three paragraphs:

A song of hope for Israel, God's vineyard	27:2–6[137]
An explanation of God's judgment on his people	27:7–11
A promise: God will return to his holy mountain	27:12–13

---

[137] Wildberger, *Isaiah 13–27*, 583, limits this song to 27:2–5 (not 27:2–6) because there are no agricultural images in 27:6. But threshing and gathering in 27:6 are agricultural metaphors, plus Johnson, *From Chaos to Restoration*, 85–86, properly criticizes such a division and argues for the break after v. 6 because (a) the subject matter changes from grace (2–6) to punishment (7–11); (b) 27:2–6 is future, v. 7 is past; (c) the question in v. 7 marks it off as a new unit; and (d) the ending of this song is comparable to 5:7.

(1) God's Song of Care for His Vineyard (27:2–6)

²In that day—

"Sing about a fruitful vineyard:
³I, the LORD, watch over it;
  I water it continually.
I guard it day and night
  so that no one may harm it.
⁴I am not angry.
If only there were briers and thorns confronting me!
  I would march against them in battle;
  I would set them all on fire.
⁵Or else let them come to me for refuge;
  let them make peace with me,
  yes, let them make peace with me."

⁶In days to come Jacob will take root,
  Israel will bud and blossom
  and fill all the world with fruit.

This positive song of hope for God's vineyard stands in sharp contrast to the earlier song about God's destruction of his vineyard in 5:1–7. In 5:5–6 God was angry with the vineyard, but in the future God will harbor no anger against it (27:4). Briers and thorns destroy the vineyard in 5:6, but God will destroy any briars and thorns that might appear in 27:4. God stops the rain on the bad vines in 5:6 but freely waters the vineyard in 27:3. The fruit from the first vines was sour (5:7), while the blossoms and grapes in this second vineyard produce good fruit for all to eat (27:6). The vineyard in both cases represents the whole house of Israel (Judah and Ephraim), not just the northern kingdom of Israel as Sweeney suggests.[138] The song should be interpreted as a celebration of God's future goodness to his people and therefore it would probably be inappropriate to historicize it into a commentary on a specific set of political events.[139]

The song in 27:2–6 is somewhat similar to the song in 26:1–6. Like 26:1–6, this hymn focuses on what God will do for his people—the ones who trust him. Both hymns offer peace to those who rely on God (26:3–4; 27:5). But in the second hymn God is no longer angry (27:4), therefore this new hymn is one that the people will sing in the future when Israel will blossom in the land (27:6). It presents a unified parable describing God's care for his vineyard

---

[138] Sweeney, *Isaiah 1–39*, 350–51, maintains that the "fortified city" in 27:10 was the city of Bethel, connects the false worship in 27:9 to Israelite idolatry, and derives some of the vocabulary from the earlier oracle against Israel in 17:1–11.

[139] Wildberger, *Isaiah 13–27*, 584, believes "the author was focusing on the antagonism between the Jews and Samaritans in the postexilic era, recalling what is said in Hag. 2:10–14; Ezra 4:23; Neh 1:3; 2:3." He takes v. 5 as an invitation to the Samaritans to return to worship at Jerusalem and forsake their worship at Gerizim. This reconstruction is extremely subjective, for there is nothing in the text to indicate that this refers to the Samaritans.

without a series of imperative exhortations for the present audience to trust God (26:1–6). Nevertheless, this hymn has the motivational purpose of arousing faith because it presents to the audience a series of promises about what God will do for his people in the future. It assumes the restoration of the people in 27:12–13.

27:2–3 In both vineyard songs God is the primary actor who sovereignly works to determine the future of his vineyard. In both situations God meticulously cares for his vines (5:2; 27:2) and someone sings[140] about God's pleasant vineyard. First person statements by God, declaring what "I" do for the vineyard, characterize v. 3. His acts include watching over and repeatedly watering the vineyard; two signs of devotion, attention, care, and sovereignty over it. Every attempt is made to make the vineyard fruitful. Defensive measures of constant surveillance ("day and night") guarantee that no wild beasts will visit it[141] and trample down the vines (5:7b). All these ideas build confidence in God's love and care for his people.

In contrast to the first song, there is no report at the end of this section about the kind of fruit produced by the vineyard (5:2b; 27:2a assumes it is good fruit) and no invitation for the audience to advise the Lord (the vine dresser) about what to do with the vineyard as in 5:3–4. There will be no destruction of the vineyard this time; instead God himself sings about his devotion to his vineyard.

27:4–5 Since God moved with punishment against the earlier vineyard to destroy it (5:5–6), the next stanza assures the audience that when this prophecy is fulfilled the emotions of anger[142] or wrath against God's vineyard will not exist any longer. This contrasts with past statements that his anger still burns and his hand is still stretched out against his evil people and their leaders (5:25; 9:12,17,21; 10:4). Instead God's anger is directed against "briers and thorns" that might try to overtake the vineyard. The interpreter is faced with several difficulties in interpreting this section. (a) Should one see God wishing for thorns and briers as some translations suggest? (b) What do the thorns and briers refer to? (c) How should one interpret the masculine and feminine suffixes in vv. 4–5? The hypothetical question and response in 27:4 ("if only there were, . . . then I would" in NIV) expresses a hypothetical desire that could be translated "O that I had thorns and briers," but this seems like an incongruous wish in this context.[143] NIV periphrastically adds "if" at the beginning and "confronting

---

[140] עֲנוּ is a *piel* imperative from עָנָה, which exhorts the audience to "sing."

[141] פֶּן יִפְקֹד, "lest anyone should visit/punish," is a modal use of the imperfect representing a potential danger that might harm the vines (GKC §107q).

[142] The Hb. חֵמָה, "anger," was apparently read as הֹמָה, "wall," by the Old Greek translators. This is understandable since there were no vowels in the text when the Old Greek text was made and it is natural to expect there to be walls associated with vineyards. The Hebrew Masoretic tradition is clearly superior in this example.

[143] מִי־יִתְּנֵנִי asks lit. "who will give me," but this became an idiomatic expression of desire, something like "O that one would give me" (see Num 11:4; GKC §151a–b for the desiderative

me" at the end of this line, thus turned it into a hypothetical situation that is not a wish. If the interrogative *mî*, "who," is translated literally[144] and not turned into a statement of desire then the question asks, "Who will give me (show me) briers and thorns?" With this translation God is rhetorically claiming that his vineyard has no thorns. To strengthen his claim to the purity of his vineyard and his desire to protect it, the song assures the audience that God would assuredly[145] burn any thorns.

Who are the thorns and briers? In 5:6 the thorns take over the vineyard when God punishes the land, thus they could symbolize the wicked people of Judah or even foreigners who rule over the land. Since no specific enemies are identified one should avoid historicizing the song by making these thorns and briers a specific group. They represent anyone who would oppose God's work among his people.[146]

The final problem is the use of feminine singular pronouns "her" in 27:4 ("them" in NIV) and the third masculine singular subjects of the verbs in 27:5 ("let them come" in NIV). The feminine pronouns "it" in 27:3 refers to the feminine noun "vineyard." The continued use of the same feminine pronoun in 27:4 implies that God will "march against the vineyard ("it") in battle" to destroy it (similar to 5:5–6), not just against the "briers and thorns ("them" as in NIV). 27:5 proposes an alternative to the possibility of war in v. 4, introducing this contrast with ao "unless, except, rather, or else." The alternative is that the enemy of God (the briers and thorns, two masculine nouns) "would be strengthened in my protection." In that case "it" (the enemy, made up of thorns or briers) would make peace with God.[147]

The essence of this verse is that God is not angry, there presently are no enemies (thorns and briers), and God is willing to destroy or make peace with the enemies of his people. If there ever were some enemies of his people, they would either be eliminated or would soon see the wisdom of establishing a peaceful relationship with God. All of this is a reason for joy and hope because of God's love and sovereign care for his vineyard.

27:6 The song ends with a direct application to his audience, similar to 5:7. In the coming period[148] his people (Judah and Israel) will be like a well

---

usage).

[144] In Job 31:31 this construction is properly translated (not as a desiderative) in NIV as, "Who has not had his fill of Job's meat?" or in NASB as, "Who can find one who has not been satisfied with his meat?"

[145] The cohortative form of אֶפְשְׂעָה expresses strong resolve or fixed determination ("I will march") to do what is stated (GKC §108b).

[146] Wildberger, *Isaiah 13–27*, 584, points to the Samaritans as those who oppose what Haggai and Nehemiah were doing in Jerusalem, while Sweeney, *Isaiah 1–39*, 35–51, thinks the song is referring to Israelite exiles from the northern nation of Israel.

[147] It seems best to treat the three verbs in 27:5 not as jussives (as in NIV) but as modal imperfects describing a possibility or potential that could arise if these enemies make the right choice (GKC §107m,r). Thus לִי שָׁלוֹם יַעֲשֶׂה means "he would make peace to me."

[148] The first word in 27:6 is הַבָּאִים, "the coming ones," which could refer to the people in 27:5,

rooted plant that produces many buds and blossoms (cf. Hos 14:6). The result will be that the fruit of God's people will have a positive impact on the whole world. Since this "fruit" is not explained as material, political, or a spiritual positive impact, one should not read into it a specific interpretation when the image is so general. The fruitfulness of the land is the topic in 4:2, and 2:2–3; 11:10–12 and 14:1–2 refer to people from all the world coming to Jerusalem. These passages may all be referring to similar characteristics.

The intention of the song was to provide hope for the future, in spite of the nation's present suffering (26:7–18). That hope is based on God's sovereign care for his people, not on Israel's worth or righteous deeds. These promises were an encouragement for the prophet's audience to trust God because eventually he will fulfill this promise and his vineyard will bless all the nations of the earth.

(2) An Explanation of God's Ways (27:7–11)

> ⁷Has [the LORD] struck her
>> as he struck down those who struck her?
> Has she been killed
>> as those were killed who killed her?
> ⁸By warfare and exile you contend with her—
>> with his fierce blast he drives her out,
>> as on a day the east wind blows.
> ⁹By this, then, will Jacob's guilt be atoned for,
>> and this will be the full fruitage of the removal of his sin:
> When he makes all the altar stones
>> to be like chalk stones crushed to pieces,
> no Asherah poles
>> or incense altars
>> will be left standing.
> ¹⁰The fortified city stands desolate,
>> an abandoned settlement, forsaken like the desert;
> there the calves graze,
>> there they lie down;
>> they strip its branches bare.
> ¹¹When its twigs are dry, they are broken off
>> and women come and make fires with them.
> For this is a people without understanding;
>> so their Maker has no compassion on them,
>> and their Creator shows them no favor.

The interpretation of this paragraph is complicated by the prophet's failure to identify who is striking whom in 27:7, what fortified city will be desolate in 27:10, and who will receive no compassion in 27:11b. The reference to Jacob's guilt and

---

but it is more likely that this is a shorthand way of saying "in the coming days" (cf. Eccles 2:16; Jer 7:32).

the removal of pagan idols supports the position that vv. 8–9 are primarily about Israelites (though not just the northern nation of Ephraim).[149] Sweeney sees a negative situation turning positive in both 8–9 (for Jacob) and in 10–13 (for the city Bethel, or Jerusalem)[150] but it difficult to see how God could have no compassion on Jerusalem (11b) and then have compassion on Jerusalem (12–13).

The solution to this problem is hinted at in 27:7 where two groups are struck and killed, one more severely than the other. 27:8–9 discusses the group less severely struck, Israel, whose sins will be forgiven, while 27:10–11 treats the group more severely struck, Israel's enemy, who will receive God's compassion. God's ways of dealing with people are clearly defined, based on his gracious atonement or his wrath. Thus the present "fortified city" in 27:10 will be treated comparable to the enemies of God in the eschatological era (cf. 24:10–12; 25:2,12).

A specific setting must be implied from various hints in the message. There is little to suggest that these verses provide an explanation of God's past historical dealings as the NIV translation suggests. Instead it explains what God will do. Knowledge of the reason for God's actions should cause the audience to understand why some in Israel will die, why there is a need to atone for their sins and remove all idolatry from the land, and what God will do to their enemies. The need for atonement and the removal of idolatry is reminiscent of Hezekiah's reform movement and attempts to remove the idolatry from the high places throughout the land (2 Kgs 18:4). The ordering of events in this paragraph suggests that the prophet gave it in a period of oppression by an enemy from the east (27:7–8; cf. 26:7–20) and that the people needed to turn form the worship of pagan idols as Hezekiah suggested (27:9). Their enemy ("the fortified city") will eventually be desolate and rejected by God (27:10–11) and God will restore the people to Jerusalem (27:12–13). In light of these promises the audience should be motivated to act so that the second part of God's plan for them (27:9) and their enemies (27:10–13) can be implemented.

27:7   The first line of this verse contains three different grammatical forms of the root *nākâ*, "smite, strike," while the second half of the verse has three different grammatical forms of the root *hārag*, "kill." Within this complex series the people struck, the striker, and those who struck her are not identified. NIV suggests that the question asks:[151] "Has (God) struck her (Israel) as he

---

[149] Johnson, *From Chaos to Restoration*, 88–93, has an extensive discussion demonstrating why he believes this is about the northern nation of Israel. He depends on the work of the French scholar J. Vermeylen and some verbal connections between chaps. 27 and 17, plus Hosea.

[150] Sweeney, *Isaiah 1–39*, 347–51, at one point identifies the city as Bethel, which Josiah destroyed (2 Kgs 23:15–20) because of its pagan idols, but in another section of his explanations he identifies the city as Jerusalem, based on the mention of the city in 27:13. Polaski, *Authorizing an End*, 297, argues that 27:10–11 does not refer to Israel.

[151] The initial ה followed by a *dagesh* in the following letter usually signifies an article, but the infinitive construct verb is actually preceded by the interrogative particle. The *dagesh* is added when the first letter of the word has a *šĕwâ* under it (GKC §100,l)

(God) struck down those (Israel's enemy) who struck her (Israel)?"[152] This is interpreted as a positive message of hope that God does not treat his people as severely as others (cf. 27:8–9 and 10–11 to see this contrast). If one views the prophet as prophetically asking about God's future action, then one could translate v. 7 to say, "Will he (God) strike him (Israel) as his (the enemy) strikers are striking him (Israel)."[153] The question asks if God will make Israel's punishment as severe as their enemies. This prophecy was an attempt to explain God's future plans of judgment and grace toward Israel.

The answer to this question is no. God will not strike down Israel in the same way he will strike down their enemies (cf. 10:5–27 for a similar contrast). Although both will be punished and people in both countries will die, God sees a different final outcome for Israel (27:8–9) and the fortified city (27:10–11, their enemy).

27:8–9   The situation for Israel will involve three steps. First God will bring punishment (27:8), as v. 7 implies and 26:7–19 confirms, then the people must remove their pagan idols (27:9b), and finally God will atone for their sins (27:9a). In translating the first word in v. 8 "by warfare" the NIV follows the reading of the Old Greek translation. The Targum connects this word to a "measure" (a third of an ephah) and saw God gradually measuring out his punishment measure by measure. This obscure word functions as a parallel companion to God's "sending" Israel away, thus the same Arabic root "shoo, drive" [154] makes better sense. God will punish many people in the nation by sending against them his fierce heat of a blasting east wind off the desert (possibly a metaphor for the Assyrians). By these acts of discipline God will contend for the heart and soul of his people in order to get them to turn back to himself.

Verse 9 explains why Israel's discipline will be very different from her enemy's punishment. Although God's people will suffer, through these experiences their sins will be atoned and the guilt of their sin will be removed. This does not mean that suffering brings atonement of sin, but that the process of suffering brings a person to the place where sins are recognized and confessed so that God can forgive them. One of the chief sins that needed atonement was the worship of pagan gods at pagan altars. When the people finally realize that these gods are nothing, the "full fruit" or consequences will be that they will smash these altars and idols. This external act will signify a change in their heart devotion and this is a sign that forgiveness will be possible.

---

[152] An alternative understanding proposed by Hayes and Irvine, *Isaiah*, 317, is, "Like the smiting of the one (Assyria) who smote him (Israel) has he (God) smote him (Assyria)."

[153] In this translation the participle "his strikers," מַכֵּהוּ, functions as the subject of the infinitive construct verb form (GKC §115e).

[154] סַאסְּאָה can refers to a "measuring" of grain. Most now follow G. R. Driver, "Some Hebrew Verbs, Nouns, and Pronouns," *JTS* 30 (1929): 371–2, who connected this word with the Arabic "shoo," which is used in urging animals or people to move. To parallel the next verb he also suggests that the final ה be ה with the *mappik* to represent the feminine suffix "her," which fits the understanding of most ancient translations.

The prophet foresees a time when the people will take the altars at high places (cf. Lev 26:30; 2 Chr 14:4; Isa 17:8) and smash the stones into chalk. No wooden pole that represents the goddess Asherah and no fancy incense altars will be left standing at these pagan cult sites. This prophecy would have served as an encouragement for people to follow the instructions of Hezekiah (and later Josiah) to institute religious reforms that purified the land of pagan places of worship (2 Kgs 18:4; 23:14–15; 2 Chr 31:1; 34:3–6). This prophecy demonstrated that God's punishment of his people would be a temporal discipline and not the same as his plans for their enemies.

27:10–11 In contrast to the positive future, "surely" (*kî*; omitted in NIV) this city, which is a symbol of the enemies of God's people, will some day be abandoned, deserted by all people, and will look like a forsaken desert. Desolation and ruin will be everywhere; only cattle will graze there among the bushes (cf. 13:19–22). Even the dead branches of former trees will be burned up in the fire; there will be nothing left. Religious, commercial, political, human, and animal life will no longer exist in this place.

Why will this city suffer so much more severely than Israel (27:7)? 27:11b reveals a contrast with 27:9. In one circumstance people will come to know who God really is, be forgiven of sins, and abandon all worship of false gods (27:9), but the people in the fortified city will never come to fully discern how their sinfulness will affect their relationship to God. Therefore, their Creator will have no compassion on them.[155] Later in the book of Isaiah this theme of the stupidity of idolatry is addressed again and again in order to persuade the prophet's audience to understand God and reject pagan worship (44:9–20; 47:10–11). The audience of the prophet needs to understand the ways God works. They need a theological understanding concerning why God sends the discipline of punishment. They need to be motivated to repent of their sins and reject idols. Then they will find that God will forgive their sins, have mercy on them, and defeat their enemies.

(3) Gathering to Worship (27:12–13)

¹²In that day the LORD will thresh from the flowing Euphrates to the Wadi of Egypt, and you, O Israelites, will be gathered up one by one. ¹³And in that day a great trumpet will sound. Those who were perishing in Assyria and those who were exiled in Egypt will come and worship the LORD on the holy mountain in Jerusalem.

The final paragraph is reminiscent of similar paragraphs about the gathering of people back to Jerusalem to worship God. In 2:2–3; 11:10; 14:1b–2 and 19:19–25 the Gentiles are gathered to worship God when God sets up his

---

[155] God is a God of love, but eventually his longsuffering patience will end and compassion will not be available. Withheld compassion means that God will not stop the impending judgment on sinful people (Isa 9:16; 13:18; Jer 15:1)

kingdom, while 10:20–22; 11:11–16 and 14:1a address the issues of the gathering of Israelites. The harvest imagery in 27:12 does not mention what will happen to unbelievers, thus this is not a description of how God will divide the loyal Israelites from the apostates Israelites and the wicked Gentiles.[156] God's gathering of his people involves two phases: (a) gathering of Israelites from within the borders of Israel (27:12)–from the Euphrates to the River of Egypt (Gen 15:18; 2 Kgs 24:7); and (b) gathering perishing people that were living outside the borders of Israel (27:13a)–in Assyria and Egypt. Everyone will be gathered; none will be excluded or left behind. Since Israelites at home are gathered in 27:12, one could naturally assume that exiled Israelites in Assyria and Egypt are gathered in 27:13. Nevertheless, 27:13 never describes these people as Israelites. Instead they are the "perishing, lost" and "outcasts" living in other lands. Thus the interpreter who identifies these people exclusively as Israelites is moving beyond the evidence found in v. 13. It is just as likely that Isaiah envisioned both "perishing, lost" Israelites and Gentiles coming to Jerusalem in v. 13.[157]

The role of the great trumpet in v. 13 is not clearly explained. In other passages it was sounded to signal or call people (a) to battle (Judg 6:34); (b) to the temple for worship (Lev 25:9; Joel 2:1,15); (c) to announce the beginning of a feast or new moon celebration (Lev 23:23–25; 25:9); (d) to announce the coronation of a new king (1 Kgs 1:39; 2 Kgs 9:13); or (e) to signal the beginning of God's final battle against evil (Zech 9:14). In each example, the trumpet announces the beginning of some special event. Like the banner or trumpet blast in 11:11–12 and 18:3, this great trumpet in 27:13 will be employed to signal the beginning of a unique new opportunity to worship God at Jerusalem. The holy mountain where the glory of God dwells will be the center where people will gather. Nothing is said about the specific nature of this worship experience but certainly it will be a time of praise to God.

THEOLOGICAL IMPLICATIONS. This prophecy describes how God can make something beautiful and productive (the vineyard in 27:2–6) out of something that was quite hopeless (the vineyard in 5:1–7). The credit goes to God who cares and protects his vineyard, but the choice to produce good or sour grapes was the choice of the vines, the people of Israel. This second song reminds the reader that God has the ability to transform people into beautiful blossoming plants in spite of their former rebellion. He does not give up on

---

[156] Clements, *Isaiah 1–39*, 223, interprets this beating of the grain as an analogy of how God will divide between the God-fearing and the unbelievers (it is implied that they will be removed), but the imagery of this verse does not involve the separation of the wheat from the chaff.

[157] K. D. Jenner, "The Big Shophar (Isaiah 27:13)," *Studies in Isaiah 24–27*, 157–82, concludes that this passage is referring to the gathering of Israelites from Israel and all over the world, that it does not refer to a return of exiles, that Assyria instead of Babylon is the reigning power, and that Isaiah's conception of these events is consistent with Jeremiah and Ezekiel. J. A. Motyer, *The Prophecy of Isaiah* (Leicester: InterVarsity, 1993), 225, concludes that both Jews and Gentiles will be gathered for this event.

rebellious people but loves them and by his grace gathers them to worship together at his temple (27:12–13). His wonderful grace is still available to those
who remain in rebellion against him.

In between the time of rejection of God and gathering to worship him are
three periods that people usually go through. There are the dark days of separation from God when God actually disciplines the wayward (5:4–7; 27:7–8). The
good news is that every rebellious sinner is able to confess their sins and turn
from false idols (self, money, reputation, sports, etc) and have their sins forgiven (27:9). For these people punishment is a temporary punishment, but for
others who do not know God or who will not submit to him, God has no mercy
(27:10–11). Their punishment will be much more severe. Thus the prophet
delivers the good news of hope (27:2–6), throws out the invitation to reject the
past and turn to God for cleansing (27:8–9), and warns of the dire consequence
for those who refuse to develop a personal relationship with God (27:10–11).
Can the choice be any plainer and the consequence more dramatic?

―――――― **V. NOT TRUSTING IN ENEMIES, WHO WILL** ――――――
BE DEFEATED (28:1–35:10)

These chapters share several common characteristics with the oracles against the nations in chaps. 13–23 and the eschatological prophecies in chaps. 24–27. Since there is no new superscription announcing that these are prophecies by "Isaiah the son of Amoz" in 28:1 (as in 1:1; 2:1; 13:1), it appears that chaps. 28–35[1] were joined together with the preceding chapters at a very early stage; therefore, they should be considered a subunit within the long literary unit that began in 13:1. All these chapters deal with God's rule over the nations, including his judgment of the oppressors and his salvation of the righteous in Zion. In all three sections (chaps. 13–23; 24–27; 28–35) there is a mixture of prophecies that relate to the historical circumstances of Assyrian aggression against Isaiah's audience in Jerusalem, as well as promises about God's eschatological salvation of his people when he will destroy all the wicked at the end of time. In these chapters the prophet is attempting to persuade his audience in the beseiged city of Jerusalem not to foolishly put their trust in other nations or their own defensive fortifications. Instead, they need to trust in God's sovereign ability to save them and God's plan to establish his righteous kingdom.

HISTORICAL SETTING. There are numerous indications that these prophecies speak to the situation in Judah when the Assyrians were invading the land, thus they should be placed somewhere around 705–701 BC.[2] These prophecies refer to the scourge that beats down Judah (28:18) and a siege of Jerusalem (29:2–3) when hordes of people will attack it (29:7). God also promises to defeat their enemy by shattering Assyria (29:5; 30:31). He will shield Zion from defeat (31:5) by causing Assyria to fall by a sword not wielded by a man (31:8–9, fulfilled in 37:36). At the time, some people in Jerusalem were quite complacent (32:9) and its leaders were trying to gain additional security by making political treaties with Egypt (30:1–5; 31:1–3). But none of this human effort will save Jerusalem, for the land will mourn in agony and their treaties will be broken (33:7–9). God is their only hope, so they should repent of their sins and trust him (28:17; 30:15; 31:1–3,6)

The date when the prophet spoke the messages in chaps. 34–35 about eschatological events is unknown, for these sermons are devoid of the historical hints present in chaps. 28–33. The prophet could have spoken these messages at several points in his ministry and then placed them here in his scroll for topical

---

[1] G. M. Tucker, "The Book of Isaiah 1–39," *The New Interpreter's Bible,* Vol VI (Nashville: Abingdon, 2001), 230, 273, limits this unit to chaps. 28–33, putting chaps. 34–35 as a separate segment of the book because those chapters do not have "the style and substance" of the following or preceding chapters. He does not believe Isaiah wrote chaps. 34–35 and dates them to a time after the Hebrews returned from the Babylonian exile. Using a similar approach, O. Kaiser, *Isaiah 13–39,* 234–35, 242, attributes chaps. 28–32 to Isaiah when the Assyrians were attacking Judah around 701 BC, but separates out chaps. 33 and 34–35 and dates them to an exilic (34–35) or Hellenistic (33) period. W. A. M. Beuken, *Isaiah II, Vol 2: Isaiah Chapters 28–39,* HCOT (Leuven: Peeters, 2000), 2, concludes that these "events took place between 705 and 701 BC" while Judah was facing the invading Assyrians.

[2] This fits the internal evidence in the text much better than J. D. W. Watts, *Isaiah 1–33,* WBC 24 (Waco: Word, 1985), 352, who places chaps. 28–33 in the reign of Josiah and Jehoiakim (640–605 BC) and chaps. 34–35 in the reign of Jehoiakim and Zedekiah (605–586 B.C). He believes chaps. 30–31 come before the fall of Assyria (from 650–620 BC), but this reconstruction puts these events long after the lifetime of Isaiah, ignores the canonical context of the Assyrian attack on Jerusalem in chaps. 36–39, which provided an appropriate setting for these chapters, and fails to explain why Babylon was never mentioned in chaps. 28–33.

reasons. The theological themes surrounding God's destruction of the nations (34:1–3) and his upholding of Zion (34:8) are fitting promises that would have engendered trust in God during a crisis era, so they match the contextual and thematic emphasis in chaps. 28–33. The encouragement to strengthen the weak and not fear because God will come with vengeances to save them (35:3–4) supplies a fitting message of hope to a desparate people in a period shortly before God saved Jerusalem from some enemy. Their canonical placement at this point in the scroll, between chaps. 30–33 and 36–39, which are both securely dated to 705–701 BC, might suggest a similar date for chaps. 34–35, but no one can prove when these messages were spoken or written.

GENRE.   Although these chapters contain a wisdom parable (28:23–29), judgment speeches (28:7–13; 28:13–22), and salvation oracles (29:17–24; 30:18–33), a series of six woe oracles dominate this section of the book. The woe oracles come from the social context of lamenting the death of someone at a funeral (1 Kgs 13:30; Jer 22:18), or mourning the approaching death of some person or nation (Ps 6; Jer 11:18–23; Amos 5:1–17). Weeping, shaving the hair, wearing sackcloth, and the presence of some professional mourners could accompany a woeful lament.[3] This form of literature implies that Isaiah was probably weeping when he spoke the words in these chapters. Why? Isaiah mourned because he loved the people of Judah and did not want to see this beloved nation destroyed. He also knew that a lament could sometimes attract more attention and serve as a more effective persuasive tool of communicating God's Word than a hard-nosed lecture of condemnation. In a lamentation the speaker sides with the sorrows of the audience and demonstrates an emotional attachment with the listener. After all, what kind of prophet do most people want to listen to: a heartless, cold, blaming one, or one who might shed a tear and cry with them when things are tough? Isaiah's pastoral heart is breaking as he reveals this bad news to the people he loves. Maybe his broken heart would soften their rebellion as they realize the serious consequence of their sins. Some years later Jesus wept over the city of Jerusalem because he wanted to gather these people to himself as a hen gathers her chicks, but they also refused (Mat 23:37).

These lamenting woe oracles are unusually constructed to give a twist to what the prophet wanted to communicate. Traditionally, the person lamented is named, the reason for lamenting is stated (often including some accusations), and God's judgment is summarized. The woe oracles in these chapters are unusual in that most have a salvation oracle right after a brief woe oracle.

1.   A short salvation oracle in 28:5–6; after a short woe in 28:1–4
2.   A short salvation oracle in 29:5–8; after a short woe in 29:1–4

---

[3] W. Janzen, *Mourning Cry and Woe Oracle*, BZAW 125 (Berlin: de Gruyter, 1972), and G. V. Smith, *Amos* (Fearn, Scotland: Christian Focus, 1998), 206–207, contain additional background on laments and woe oracles.

3. A long salvation oracle in 29:17–24; after a short woe in 29:15–16
4. A long salvation oracle in 30:18–26; after a long woe in 30:1–17
5. A short salvation oracle in 31:6–9; after a short woe in 31:1–5
6. A long salvation oracle in 33:5–24; after a short woe in 33:1 and prayer in 33:2–4

By placing these two emphases together (woe and salvation) the prophet was able to show how the way of death in the lament dramatically contrasts with the alternative way of salvation that God can provide. The pattern in the first three examples is similar. Each woe deals with sinfulness within God's blind people, but the salvation oracles offer hope based on what God will do to defeat their enemies and save a righteous remnant. In these examples the motivation to change is equally spread between the fear of death and the hope for salvation. The pattern of woe oracles in chaps. 30–32 suggests that the prophet is lamenting a serious mistake that the nation has made (trusting in Egypt) that will lead to the death of many in Judah. In these texts the salvation oracles include a call to repent and trust God, thus making explicit the need to change their perspective of reality (30:15; 31:6). The final woe is unique. After the final one-verse woe about the defeat of their enemies (33:1), there is a prayer for help from God (33:2–4), followed by a long salvation oracle. With this unusual mixture of oracles, the prophet hoped that the people would realize their sinfulness, walk righteously, and trust God their king (33:22). The interpretation and emphasis on the lamentation of the woe is directly influenced by the subject of the lament (Israel, Judah, Assyria) and the message of salvation that follows.

STRUCTURE.   The unity of chaps. 28–33 is signaled by the repeated use of "woe oracles" throughout (28:1; 29:1,15; 30:1; 31:1; 33:1). These chapters are divided into two groups based on their content and structure. Each group (chaps. 28–29; 30–33)[4] has three woe oracles.[5] The first group of woes (chaps. 28–29) reveals the principles underlying God's action against Judah and on behalf of Judah. The primary problem is blind political and religious leaders who make bad decisions (28:7,14), do not pay attention to the word of God (28:9–13), do not honor God in their hearts (29:13), deny the sovereignty of God (29:15–16), and lack wisdom (28:23–29). Initially God will seal up his truth from these wicked people and punish them (29:9–11), but later he will defeat their enemies (29:5–7), open their eyes and ears (29:18), give them understanding (29:24), and cause their children to stand in awe of God (29:17–23).

---

[4] J. A. Motyer, *The Prophecy of Isaiah* (Leicester: InterVarsity, 1993), 227, also divides the woe oracles into two groups (28–29; 30–35) with three woes in each group.

[5] J. N. Oswalt, *Isaiah 1–39*, NICOT (Grand Rapids: Eerdmans, 1986), 504–505, structures the chapters into four groupings: (a) chaps. 29–30 are about the false counsel of human leaders about Judah's enemies; (b) 30–31 contain a condemnation of Judah's desire to depend on Egypt, which is folly; (c) 32–33 give the true solution of depending on God; and (d) 34–35 contrast a desert (due to God's judgment) and paradise (due to God's blessing).

The second group of three woes (chaps. 30–33)[6] explains how these principles practically apply to the political conflicts involving Judah, Egypt, and Assyria in 705–701 BC. Judah's political alliance with Egypt was a mistake that illustrates a lack of wisdom and the bad decisions of their leaders (30:1–5; 31:1–3). This treaty illustrates how they did not honor God (30:1; 31:1), but instead rejected God's instruction (30:9–11). Consequently, God's judgment will make Egypt's military assistance utterly worthless (30:7; 31:3), and God will rise up against his wicked people (30:2). Eventually God will defeat Assyria (31:31; 32:8) and deliver Jerusalem (31:7). He will open his people's eyes (30:20; 31:6; 32:3) and cause them to reject idols (30:22; 31:7). Then the people will not make foolish and unwise decisions (32:4–8; 33:8), complacency will disappear (32:9–14), righteousness and security will exist (32:15–20; 33:5–6,15–16), and the people will praise God their king from their hearts (30:29; 33:10,20–22) and trust him (30:15).

Since the last two chapters (34–35) do not have "woe" introductions and do not explicitly discuss the Assyrian crisis, they are not as closely interconnected to the material in chaps. 28–33.[7] W. Brownlee suggested that chaps. 34–35 actually begin the second half of the book of Isaiah; therefore, they are not part of 28–33.[8] Chapters 34–35 are so different from the earlier woe oracles that some think that they were written by a later prophet (often called Deutero-Isaiah, the author of chaps. 40–55) because (a) the bitter hostility toward Edom arose long after the days of Isaiah when the Edomites abused the people of Jerusalem after the city was destroyed in 586 BC (cf. Obad 10–14; Ezek 35–36; Lam 4:21–22); and (b) the thoughts and phrases in chap. 35 are similar to ideas expressed in Isaiah 40–55.[9] This theory is suspect, for chap. 34 is actually about God's

---

[6] Beuken, *Isaiah II*, 3–5, puts only the first five woes in a structural unit (28–31:9; 32:9–14), relegating the rest of chaps. 32–33 to a redactional expansion.

[7] J. H. Hayes and S. A. Irvine, *Isaiah, the Eighth-Century Prophet* (Nashville: Abingdon, 1987), 13, surprisingly omit chaps. 34–35 in their commentary on Isaiah 1–39, since they do not believe Isaiah wrote these chapters.

[8] W. Brownlee, *The Meaning of the Qumran Scrolls for the Bible* (New York: Oxford University Press, 1964), 247–59, found parallel development of topics in chaps. 1–33 and 34–66, found this structure parallel to the division of Ezekiel, and believes this division of the book was signaled by the scribes leaving a space between chaps. 33 and 34 in the Qumran Isaiah scrolls. J. D. W. Watts, *Isaiah 34–66*, WBC (Waco: Word, 1987), 1–2, and M. A. Sweeney, *Isaiah 1–39, with an Introduction to Prophetic Literature,* FOTL 16 (Grand Rapids: Eerdmans, 1996), 435, also begins the second half of the book of Isaiah at chap. 34.

[9] R. B. Y. Scott, "The Relation of Isaiah, Chapter 35 to Deutero-Isaiah," *AJSL* 52 (1935): 178–91, found common themes: (a) the desert rejoices in 35:1 is also in 42:11; 51:3; 52:9; (b) the steppe blooms in 35:1–2 is also in 41:19; (c) Lebanon as a symbol of majesty in 35:2 is also in 40:16; (d) the revelation of the glory of the Lord in 35:2 is also in 40:5; (e) vengeance and retribution in 35:4 is also in 40:10; 49:25–26; (f) water in the desert in 35:6–7 is also in 41:18; 43:19–20; 44:3, etc. However, he admits that many words in chap. 35 are not used in 40–55, and the parallels are on the idea level and sometimes not a repetition of vocabulary. M. Pope, "Isaiah 34 in Relation to Isaiah 35,40–66," *JBL* 71 (1952): 235–43, reached a similar conclusion about chap. 34 (i.e., Deutero-Isaiah wrote it). H. Wildberger, *Isaiah 28–39: A Commentary*, CC (Minneapolis: Fortress, 2002), 348–49, examined Scott's evidence and found that many of the themes he mentions were

judgment of all the nations on earth (Edom is just a symbol here), so it would be improper to try to connect this message to Edom's oppression of Judah after the fall of Jerusalem in 586 BC.

A more fruitful avenue of inquiry about literary interdependence is the relationship between chaps. 34 and 13, for the universalistic tone in 13:1–16 and chaps. 34–35 cause these chapters to be something of an eschatological[10] introduction and conclusion to 13–35.[11] These similarities suggest that there was an intentional theological purpose behind the placement of these messages together at the start and end of this collection.

In addition, one can find numerous common themes and the repetition of vocabulary that indicate a relationship between chaps. 34–35 and 28–33, which draws them together. A brief listing of examples could be organized under two themes:

(a) God will come to renew the earth and fill people with joy:
  – Lebanon as a symbol of fertility—29:17; 33:9 and 35:2 (2:13; 10:34)
  – Eyes of blind will see—29:18; 30:20; 32:3 and 35:5
  – Rejoicing in God—29:19; 30:29 and 35:1–2,10
  – Abundant water and fertility—30:23,25; 32:2,20 and 35:6–7
  – God will come/ be seen—28:21; 30:30; 31:6; 33:10,22 and 35:2,4

(b) God's judgment on mankind and the earth:
  – God's wrath—30:27 and 34:2
  – Slaughter will be like a sacrifice—29:2 and 34:6–7
  – Measuring line and plumb line—28:17 and 34:11
  – Day of great slaughter—30:25; 31:8 and 34:2,6
  – No travelers on roads—33:8 and 34:10
  – Streams of sulfur and fire—30:33 and 34:9

Although the emphasis is unique in each chapter, the vocabulary and theology of chaps. 28–33 and 34–35 have much in common. This is consistent with the interpretation that chaps. 34–35 serve as an eschatological conclusion for chaps. 13–33 (34–35 are not a summary). Chapters 28–33 describe God's pres-

---

not identical (thus showing no direct connection) and that many of the key themes in chaps. 40–55 are absent from chap. 35; therefore, he concludes that 35 was not written by Deutero-Isaiah.

[10] F. Delitzsch, *Isaiah*, Commentary on the Old Testament VII, Trans J. Martin (Grand Rapids: Eerdmans, 1969), 66, calls chaps. 34–35 apocalyptic that gives a perfect ideal of the future.

[11] H. G. M. Williamson, *The Book Called Isaiah: Deutero-Isaiah's Role in Composition and Redaction* (Oxford: Clarendon Press, 1994), 216–17, agrees with J. Vermeylen who found a similar structure and numerous verbal connections. Structural similarities include:

preparation for war	13:2–4	34:1
killing of the nations	13:5–9,14–16	34:2–3
cosmic upheaval	13:10–13	34:4–5a
capture of the city	13:17–19	34:5b–8
land becomes a desert	13:20	34:9–10
wild animals live there	13:21–22	34:11–15

ent work in Judah in ways that are parallel to his future acts of judgment and salvation in chaps. 34–35.

1. Trusting Blind Leaders or Trusting God (28:1–29:24)

The first two chapters within 28–35 deal with the spiritual problems that Judah faced because blind political and religious leaders guided the nation. Three woe oracles (28:1–4; 29:1–4; 29:15–16) introduce the three main sections within this unit. The first woe against the leaders of Ephraim (28:1–4) is a rhetorical illustration from the experience of the northern nation of Israel that serves as a warning to the leaders in Judah (28:7) who were following the same path as the blind and drunken leaders of Ephraim. The purpose of this message was to persuade the leaders of Judah to trust God so that their nation would not suffer the same fate as Israel (28:14–22). The second woe predicts the future siege of Jerusalem, because the people are blind, drunk, and have no wisdom (29:1–14). In the third woe the people deny the sovereign power of God (29:15–16), but Isaiah illustrates God's sovereign power by showing how he will transform nature and open the eyes of the blind. In the future God's people will revere him and accept his instruction (29:17–24). These diverse paragraphs are unified around the need for the blind, drunk, scoffing, and unwise leaders to open their eyes, humble themselves, trust God, and learn from his wisdom.

HISTORICAL SETTING. Wildberger dates 28:1–13 during the reign of King Hoshea just before the fall of Samaria in 721 BC, 28:14–29:16 to a time shortly before Sennacherib's siege of Jerusalem in 701 BC, and 29:17–24 much later to the fifth century BC.[12] In contrast, Sweeney believes the present form of chap. 28 goes back to the time when Hezekiah was preparing to defend himself against an Assyrian invasion; thus, it presupposes the fall of Samaria.[13] If the message is viewed as a unit, a date around 705–701 BC seems to fit the various hints about the situation of the audience, particularly if the "covenant with death" (28:15,18) is interpreted as Judah's treaty with Egypt. This dating fits well with the interpretation that the coming siege in the second woe (29:2,7) was Assyria's attack on Jerusalem.

(1) First Woe: God's Instruction to Proud Leaders (28:1–29)

STRUCTURE. There are several messages associated with the first woe. They can be structured into the following paragraphs.

---

[12] Wildberger, *Isaiah 28–39*, 7–8,19,70–71,108–10, hypothesizes that a redactor pulled these divergent pieces together. He draws this message from three completely different eras, eliminating any attempt to understand this material as a unified message to a single audience. The text then reflects what different people have gone through in different eras of Israelite history rather than a cohesive prophetic vision of what will happen and what a single group of people need to do to avoid God's punishment around 705–701 BC.

[13] Sweeney, *Isaiah 1–39*, 367, finds a later Josianic and fifth century redaction of all of Isaiah. He dates chap. 29 to a period after the fall of Jerusalem (p. 381), but it seems wiser to relate the attack on Jerusalem in all these chapters to the siege of Sennacherib.

The paragraphs are held together by comparisons ("so also" in 28:7) between the drunkards of Ephraim (28:1) and the drunkards of Judah (28:7). The second paragraph refers to the resting place (28:12) where the people can take "refuge," but they rejected the "refuge" God provides. The third paragraph explains how their covenant with death was their attempt to make a lie their "refuge" (28:15), although God gave them a trustworthy cornerstone that was a sure "refuge" (28:16). Consequently, their refuge will be swept away (28:17). The final paragraph describes a farmer who accepts God's instruction (28:26,29) instead of rejecting the instructions of God (28:11–13, 16–19) like the people of Ephraim and Judah. Throughout these paragraphs there is a common threat of "a driving flood" (28:2), an "overwhelming scourge" (28:15), "water that will overflow your hiding place" (28:17), and an "overwhelming scourge" (28:18), which refer to "the destruction decreed against the whole land" (28:22). This threat is the Assyrian army of Sennacherib.

WOE TO THE FADING WREATH OF EPHRAIM 28:1–6)

¹**Woe to that wreath, the pride of Ephraim's drunkards,**
    to the fading flower, his glorious beauty,
set on the head of a fertile valley—
    to that city, the pride of those laid low by wine!
²**See, the Lord has one who is powerful and strong.**
    Like a hailstorm and a destructive wind,
like a driving rain and a flooding downpour,
    he will throw it forcefully to the ground.
³**That wreath, the pride of Ephraim's drunkards,**
    will be trampled underfoot.
⁴**That fading flower, his glorious beauty,**
    set on the head of a fertile valley,
will be like a fig ripe before harvest—
    as soon as someone sees it and takes it in his hand,
    he swallows it.

⁵**In that day the LORD Almighty**
    will be a glorious crown,
a beautiful wreath
    for the remnant of his people.
⁶**He will be a spirit of justice**
    to him who sits in judgment,
a source of strength
    to those who turn back the battle at the gate.

The initial paragraph includes two distinctive literary genres that are interlinked to one another because a common theme is carried throughout the paragraph.

A woe oracle	28:1–4
Pride in glorious Samaria	1
God will remove pride	2–4
A salvation oracle	28:5–6
God will be glorious for his people	5
God's justice will gain the victory	6

The woe and salvation oracles are closely integrated by the repeated use of vocabulary concerning the crown or wreath and the glorious or fading flower.[14] By connecting these two diverse literary messages together the prophet effectively contrasted the lamentable tendency for people to trust in the supposed glorious crown of Ephraim (28:1, the city of Samaria) instead of the real glorious crown—the Lord (28:5–6).

28:1 The woe begins in a somewhat typical manner (its style can be compared and contrasted with the series of woes in 5:8–25), announcing the prophet's lamentation concerning a group of people living in the northern nation of Ephraim. The weeping tone is carried throughout vv. 1–4 as the prophet laments the "fading flower" that will be flooded, trampled, and swallowed up (28:1,4). The prophet's audience in Judah would easily accept these negative comments about Judah's neighbors to the north (the nation of Israel). They would agree that the fall of Samaria in 721 BC was positive proof of the consequences of the sinful behavior of the people of Samaria. The audience's agreement with the theology of vv. 1–4 would strengthen the force of these ideas when the prophet later applied some of the same principles to the people of Judah in 28:7–22.[15]

The people in Israel are metaphorically described as a "proud garland of drunkards,"[16] a "fading flower," and a "glorious beauty." Usually crowns were worn by kings (2 Sam 12:30), the high priest (Zech 6:11,14), people at a wedding (Ezek 16:12), or an honored person (Job 19:9), so it is surprising to hear

---

[14] עֲטֶרֶת is translated "wreath" in 28:1a,3a in NIV, but "crown" in 28:5; צְבִי, "glorious," is found in 28:1 and in 28:5; תִּפְאָרָה, "beauty," is in 28:1,5. J. C. Exum, "'Whom Will He Teach Knowledge?' A Literary Approach to Isaiah 28," *Art and Meaning: Rhetoric in Biblical Literature* (ed. D. J. A. Clines, D. M. Gunn, A. Hauser; Sheffield: JSOT Press, 1982): 108–39, provides an excellent discussion of the use of repeated words in this chapter.

[15] G. Smith, *Amos*, 52–134, explains how Amos used a similar technique to get his audience to agree with key theological principles illustrated in God's judgment of six foreign nations and Judah. Then the prophet applied these same principles to Israel his audience. This is similar to Nathan's trapping of David by asking him to judge the rich man who had taken the one sheep of the poor man (2 Sam 12:1–5).

[16] גֵּאוּת refers to the idea of "pride, being haughty," thus identifying the unworthiness of the crown, which ironically was worn by an undeserving person.

that drunkards wore the "wreath, crown" (*yăṭeret*) of flowers. The prophet may well have drawn this analogy from his own personal experience of seeing a drunk in his stupor,[17] proudly boasting of some great accomplishment and arrogantly putting on his head a crown of flowers to represent his importance.[18] In this verse these inebriated people were not just common drunks; the prophet was making a reference to the leaders of Samaria (comparable to 5:11–12,22), who acted in the past the same way that the leaders of Judah are now acting (see 28:7). Oswalt suggests that they were at some sort of party, but the description of this event is not that precise.[19] Usually in Isaiah, it is the rich and powerful that are accused of pride (13:9; 23:9), not the poor oppressed common people or the drunks.

The lamenting prophet also interprets the capital city of Samaria as a beautiful crown,[20] probably because this capital city was a most important place on the crown of a hill overlooking a fertile valley. But this city was actually a fading crown that now, at the time Isaiah was speaking, had no real glory at all (it was destroyed in 721 BC). This mixture of positive features of "glorious beauty" and the negative feature of "fading flower" suggests that the ones being described were behaving like proud and drunken people who thought they were glorious, but who were actually quite the opposite. Because of the past destruction of the nation of Israel in 721 BC, everyone in Isaiah's audience knew that this great crown became a wreath of dried up flowers (a sign of death). Their glory lasted but for a moment.[21]

The last line of 28:1 in the NIV ("to that city, the pride of those laid low by wine") is periphrastic.[22] Literally, it simply says "of those who are overcome with wine," referring to the drunkards who were the inhabitants of the city of Samaria. Although the phrase may seem unnecessary, it connects the identification of the drunkards at the beginning of the verse with the drunken city of Samaria at the end of the verse.

28:2–4 The rest of the lament describes the destruction of the glorious wreath of Samaria. Two strong forces will reduce this city to nothing. God is the prime mover who determines the flow of historical events, though he frequently works through the secondary cause of an unidentified strong (*ḥāzāq*) and powerful one (*'ammiṣ*) (probably referring to the Assyrian king or army).[23]

---

[17] Isaiah also condemns the people who drink too much wine in 5:11,22; 19:14; 22:13; 24:9.

[18] B. A. Asen, "The Garlands of Ephraim: Isaiah 28:1–6 and the *marzēaḥ*," *JSOT* 71 (1996): 73–87, believes Isaiah is referring to a funeral banquet (similar to Amos 6:1–7), but this seems unlikely since there is no mention of eating in this passage and there is no knowledge of people wearing a wreath at these events.

[19] Oswalt, *Isaiah 1–39*, 506.

[20] Its walls might look similar to a crown on top of a hill. In 7:9 Samaria is the "head" or capital.

[21] צִיץ נֹבֵל refers to a "shriveled/fading flower" that has withered and died. Isaiah uses similar analogies of the grass withering (24:4; 40:6–7) to describe the short life of something.

[22] 1QIsaᵃ does have גֵּיא, "pride of," but it is better to stick with the Masoretic גֵּיא, "valley of."

[23] Beuken, *Isaiah II*, 26, observed that these two roots are often found in a military context

The strong nation that threw[24] this wreath (Samaria) to the ground is meta-phorically compared to a hailstorm, a destructive storm, and a great flooding rain. The audience could easily connect the Assyrian defeat of Samaria in 721 BC with this descriptive metaphor, for the prophet had already employed imag-ery of Assyria as a mighty flood that would overflow its channels in 8:7; 17:12; and 25:4. Later, Isaiah will use similar imagery to promise the people of Judah that God will protect them from the heat, wind, and storm that represent Assyr-ia's destructive power (32:2; 37:36–37).

If v. 2 describes the attack on Samaria, vv. 3–4 picture the consequenc-es of that attack. The defeat is pictured using the analogy of someone being "trampled" (*tērāmasnâ*) and consequently destroyed. Possibly he had in mind the comparison between what happens when people trample on tender flower blooms and what will happen when soldiers trample on the proud people of Sa-maria, that formerly glorious wreath. The reference to Samaria being quickly swallowed up, like fresh ripe fruit that is snatched from the tree and eaten, suggests nothing about the length of the seige of Samaria (about three years in 2 Kgs 17:5), but that the Assyrian conquerors quickly consumed everything of value in the city of Samaria once the city fell.[25]

28:5–6   The mood suddenly and dramatically changes in this salvation oracle about events sometime "in that day," a temporal marker that refers to the time when prophecies will be fulfilled—often, but not always, with escha-tological significance (cf. 2:11,12,20; 4:2; 19:19,23; 24:21; 25:9). The prophet maintains his focus on the wreath or crown concept (28:1,3,4) to develop his thoughts about the good things God will do in the future. Now instead of the proud drunken rulers or the city of Samaria being the wreath, God the king is connected to it in three ways. First, he is the true glorious crown or beautiful diadem (*šĕpîrat*). He is not the crown of the whole nation, but only the glori-ous wreath of the remnant of people that honor him. They will glory in God rather than Samaria. They will honor him as their beautiful leader who is wor-thy of the crown, rather than the proud drunken leaders in Samaria. Second, God their just king, will bring a spirit of justice (cf. 1:26; 11:1) that will pro-vide spiritual guidance to the political and judicial leaders who address legal

---

(Josh 1:6,9,18; 10:25; Isa 35:3; Amos 3:14; 1 Chr 22:13; 28:20) and concludes that this is a refer-ence to the Assyrians.

[24] Two questions are raised: (a) Is "his hand" that acted, the hand of God or the hand of As-syria? Since God used Assyria as his instrument (10:5) either interpretation is possible and both would be true. (b) How should the verbs be translated? הֵנִיחַ is a perfect verb, which is best taken in this context as describing past completed action, rather than a prophetic perfect of future action as NIV interprets it (GKC §106a for past, 106m-n for future). If one interprets this as a speech given many years after God used Assyria to defeat Samaria in 721 BC, it is not something that God "will" do.

[25] There are always a few figs on a tree that ripen early ("its first fruits," בְּכוּרָהּ) before one can harvest the majority of the fruit. Once a person finds one piece of fruit that is ripe at the beginning of the harvest season, it is tempting to grab it and quickly eat the fig to enjoy the wonderful taste.

matters (28:6a). Third, as king he will be a source of "strength, valor"[26] for those who fight military battles. Although these promises of divine empowerment address only two areas of leadership (judicial and military), they illustrate the principle that the transformed remnant will have a new relationship with God that will revitalize many areas of life. Although some find messianic implications in 28:5–6, drawn from 11:1–4 (the "spirit of justice"), the text focuses more on what God will do, with no specification that a messianic king will accomplish this.[27]

The prophet's audience in Judah could learn several basic theological principles from this woe and salvation oracle. They would know that (a) God hates pride and incompetent leaders; (b) he punishes and removes proud and incompetent leaders; (c) people should glorify God (not any earthly place or political institution); and (d) God is a nation's true source of strength and his justice provides true hope. One day the remnant will glorify him and enjoy the implementation of justice when God establishes his kingdom. The people in Judah and those who read his words today would probably agree with all these theological points and would conclude that God dealt properly with the arrogant leaders of Samaria. Now that the prophet has explained his theology, he is ready to address the analogy between the past situation in Samaria and present life in Jerusalem. His goal will be to persuade his audience in Judah (and later people who read his prophecies) not to follow the path of the leaders of Samaria.

THE FAILURE OF PRIESTS AND PROPHETS IN JUDAH (28:7–13)

> [7]And these also stagger from wine
> and reel from beer:
> Priests and prophets stagger from beer
> and are befuddled with wine;
> they reel from beer,
> they stagger when seeing visions,
> they stumble when rendering decisions.
> [8]All the tables are covered with vomit
> and there is not a spot without filth.
>
> [9]"Who is it he is trying to teach?
> To whom is he explaining his message?
> To children weaned from their milk,
> to those just taken from the breast?
> [10]For it is:
> Do and do, do and do,

---

[26] The word גְּבוּרָה is often related to the characteristics of a "valiant, mighty" warrior (3:2; 5:22), which is fitting in this context about war, but its meaning can extend to broader ideas such as being excellent or of "noble character" (Ruth 3:11).

[27] The Targum interpretively inserts מְשִׁיחָא, "the Messiah," in this verse, but it is not in the Hb..

> rule on rule, rule on rule;
> a little here, a little there."

[11]Very well then, with foreign lips and strange tongues
>   God will speak to this people,
[12]to whom he said,
>   "This is the resting place, let the weary rest";
>   and, "This is the place of repose"—
>   but they would not listen.
[13]So then, the word of the LORD to them will become:
>   Do and do, do and do,
>   rule on rule, rule on rule;
>   a little here, a little there—
> so that they will go and fall backward,
>   be injured and snared and captured.

Some interpreters believe the prophet is still talking about problems in Samaria because "and these also" at the beginning of 28:7 is seen as a continuation of the preceding paragraph.[28] But "and these also" (*wĕgam ʾēlleʾ*) can just as easily be used to compare a group in Israel to another group in Judah. If the drunkenness that caused the leaders to make wrong decisions (28:7) and reject the instructions of God (28:12) is connected to the foolish decision to make a "covenant with death" with Egypt (28:15), then this paragraph is directed at leaders in Judah (28:14). This part of the message is made up of two subparagraphs:

Judah's drunken prophets and priests teach babble	28:7–10
Prophets and priests are drunks	7–8
They teach senseless babble	9–10
God teaches through babble of strange language	28:11–13
God will speak through foreign lips	11
The people reject God's plan to give rest	12
They will hear babble as they are defeated	13

28:7–8   Initially a connection is made between this new group and the people mentioned in 28:1–4. The priests and prophets were the leaders that were responsible for leading the nation in God's ways, but these spiritual leaders were leading them away from God. According to the law (Lev 10:8–10) the priests were not supposed to drink wine, though the prophet Hosea found that worship at the high places was heavily influenced by pagan ritual and they were full of debauchery encouraged by drunkenness (Hos 4:10–14; cf. 1 Sam 2:12–22). Those who propose that this refers to drinking at a funeral banquet

---

[28] Oswalt, *Isaiah 1–39*, 509 realizes the evidence is unclear, but prefers to see 28:1–13 as a unit. Since the salvation oracle in 28:5–6 breaks the connection with 28:1–4, it is better to view 7–13 as an application to Isaiah's audience in Jerusalem.

(*marzēaḥ*) go far beyond the evidence in the text.[29] Both the priests and prophets in Judah allowed wine (mentioned five times in this verse) to control their behavior and thinking. The results were the physical confusion of a staggering walk and mental confusion[30] that led people astray[31] (3:12–15; 5:11–12) into errors through their prophecies. The wine caused the priests to make bad decisions or give inappropriate spiritual advice. Hayes and Irvine conclude that this refers to bad military advice, while K. van der Toorn suggests they used necromancy,[32] but the text does not define the specific area of negative influence beyond suggesting that their drunkenness impacted their "vision/seeing" (*rōʾeh*) and "judgment, decision" (*pĕlîlîyyâ*). These two terms could be interpreted very broadly to refer to everything they saw and decided, but they probably should be interpreted more narrowly to mean false prophetic visions and poor legal decisions on Levitical and moral issues. These people somehow maintained their roles as prophets and priests within Judean society, but God rejected them. The putrid and disgusting aftermath of this drunken confusion is compared to a table[33] completely covered with their vomit (*qîʾ*) and filth (*ṣôʾâ*). This is hardly a table where anyone would want to dine, and these are hardly the kind of leaders that anyone would want to follow. Although the source of misguided spiritual information may be different today, many who claim to be spiritual leaders are just as confused and the food on their table looks and smells just as putrid. Nevertheless, some people are so blind that they do not realize that the nutritional value of the "spiritual food" they are fed is not much better than vomit.

28:9–10 Isaiah now attacks these spiritual leaders by demonstrating their incompetence, the childish nature of their teaching, and the severe consequences of following them. Since the subject "he" is not identified in the question in v. 9a and is not even expressed with a separate word in Hebrew, commentators have proposed three different approaches to identify who is speaking: (a) the question was spoken by the drunken priests and prophets who mock and

---

[29] J. J. Jackson, "Style in Isaiah 28 and a Drinking Bout of the Gods (RS 24.258)," in *Rhetorical Criticism. Essays in Honor of J. Muilenburg* (ed. J. J. Jackson and M. Kessler; Pittsburg: Pickwick, 1974), 85–98, and B. Halpern, "'The Excremental Vision': The Doomed Priests of Doom in Isaiah 28," *HAR* 10 (1986): 109–21, discuss this feast and connect it to the background of Isa 28.

[30] נִבְלְעוּ, "are befuddled," in NIV refers to the "confusion, disorientation" caused by being "swallowed up" (the literal meaning of בָּלַע) by wine.

[31] תָּעוּ in the first line refers to the physical confusion that leads to "staggering," but the use of this term in relationship to seeing visions does not refer to physical but to mental confusion or staggering. Coming from this same era, Mic 3:5–7 presents evidence confirming the irresponsibility of the prophets who prophesied for money in Jerusalem.

[32] Hayes and Irvine, *Isaiah*, 324, refer to advice regarding plans to revolt against Assyria, and K. van der Toorn, "Echoes of Judean Necromancy in Isaiah 28,7–22," *ZAW* 100 (1988): 199–217, points to magic cults, but neither view can be conclusively drawn from the text. Wildberger, *Isaiah 28–39*, 22, points to their unjust legal decisions at court.

[33] Wildberger, *Isaiah 28–39*, 21, suggests that these tables were temple furniture, but the place or use of these tables is unknown. Tables with vomit all over them is a metaphor that is not to be taken literally; it draws a mental picture of something very repulsive.

belittle the pedantic teaching "he" (Isaiah) is giving, so they compare Isaiah's prophecy to the babbling of infants;[34] (b) Isaiah sarcastically quotes the unintelligible words of the false prophets drawn from pagan religious practices or necromancy;[35] or (c) the Lord is contrasting his past speaking in 9–10 with his future speaking in 11–13.[36] When looking at these options, there is no doubt that the Lord will correct the message in 28:10 with his new message in 28:11–13, but it is not clear who asked the question in v. 9, or whose message is negatively characterized in v. 10. Since there is no introductory clause like "the priests say to me" (cf. the "you say" introduction of a boastful quotation in 28:15), the interpreter does not have any linguistic clue to suggest that a new person is now speaking. Therefore, there is little that hints that v. 10 is a quotation of what the drunken leaders were saying to mock Isaiah (option "a"). It would be totally inappropriate and out of character for Isaiah to stylize God's plain instructions to his people in the derogatory terms of v. 10 (option "c"), and there is little to point to the solution that these are the words of the dead (option "b"). Instead, it appears that Isaiah is belittling the quality of the instruction given by the drunken prophets and priests in v. 7. The literal question in 28:9, "Who is teaching knowledge?" is asking whether the authoritative speakers (the priests and prophets) have true worthwhile knowledge to share with the people of Judah. Why would any audience want to be instructed by a useless message from drunken prophets or priests? It is just senseless gibberish. In the last part of v. 9, Isaiah answers this inquiry by suggesting that their message is most appropriate for infants who are still drinking from their mother's breasts (from one to three years old). To justify this conclusion, Isaiah mocks their ineffective message in v. 10 by trying to replicate their gibberish.

The message in v. 10 is made up of a series of monosyllables repeated several times. The meanings of these words are somewhat mysterious. (a) They could be the stuttering words of a drunk, which makes about as much sense as the babbling of an infant.[37] (b) These words could be referring to letters of the

---

[34] Beuken, *Isaiah II*, 32–33, believes the adversaries of Isaiah are denouncing what "he" (Isaiah) says. Isaiah quotes his enemies' claims in this disputation.

[35] K. van der Toorn, "Echoes of Judean Necromancy in Isaiah 28,7–22," *ZAW* 10 (1988): 199–217, connects the strange words in vv. 10 and 13 with (a) the covenant with Death and Sheol who are deities of the underworld; (b) words from ghosts in 29:4; and (c) the necromancy in 8:19. These words are Isaiah's satirical mocking of such senseless sources of knowledge. This hypothesis seems unlikely.

[36] Examples of those who hold position (a): E. J. Young, *The Book of Isaiah*, (Grand Rapids: Eerdmans, 1965–72), II:274, and R. E. Clements, *Isaiah 1–39*, NCBC (Grand Rapids: Eerdmans, 1980), 227–228, believe the false prophets are mocking Isaiah's infantile teaching. For option (b): Sweeney, *Isaiah 1–39*, 632–33. And for approach (c): Exum, "Whom Will He Teach Knowledge?" 108–39, and A. van Selm, "Isaiah 28:9–13: An Attempt to Give a New Interpretation," *ZAW* 85 (1973): 332–39 believe God is speaking.

[37] B. S. Childs, *Isaiah*, OTL (Louisville: Westminster John Knox, 2001), 207, believes the words are childish gibberish—though his interpretation suggests that the priests are claiming that Isaiah speaks childish gibberish, an interpretation that does not agree with the conclusion above.

alphabet,[38] which a teacher might drill into the heads of students by repeating them again and again, thus showing the simplistic and pedantic nature of this repetitive and boring message.[39] (c) Those who see these words as a mocking summary of Isaiah's message view *ṣaw* as an abbreviated form of "commandment," "filth," or "vanity"[40] and take *qaw* to mean "plumb line" or " rule." Chapter 18 vv. 2 and 7 have already used *qaw qaw* as a means of describing speech that is unintelligible, so that influences the sense here.[41]

Since this commentary takes these strange repeated words in v. 10 as Isaiah's derogatory description of the speaking of the ungodly prophets and priests (28:9), the first option fits best with the recurrence of these words in v. 13. Isaiah is saying that their babbling nonsensical repetition of words sounds like the gibberish of babies. The words should just be transliterated in the English text and given no meaning, demonstrating it as meaningless chatter.

28:11–13 Now the Lord addresses the leaders and people of Judah to show what he will do.[42] He will speak to them a divine message similar to the supposed divine message the false priests and prophets were speaking in 28:10. But this time the divine message will come from a stammering lip and a strange tongue, a threat that implies that he will speak to them through the babbling speech of foreign conquerors (cf. Deut 28:49; Jer 5:15). God's speech will be mediated through the Assyrian's stammering tongues (33:19; 36:11).

God had originally promised his people that the land of Israel would be a place of "rest" (*měnûhâ* 28:12; cf. Deut 12:9–10; 25:19; 1 Kgs 5:8; 8:56) where they could be secure from danger and war. This theological promise was secured by the presence of God himself, who rested in Zion in his holy dwelling place among his people (cf. 32:18; Deut 12:9; Ps 95:11; 132:8–14). Because of this "Zion theology," a perspective of Jerusalem's invincibility developed.[43] God granted peace to his people and his people were encouraged

---

[38] צַו could represent a teacher asking students to write the letter צ, and קַו asks them to write ק, according to W. H. Hallo, "Isaiah 28:9–13 and the Ugaritic Abecedaries," *JBL* 77 (1958): 324–38. The Old Greek translation has "take for yourself tribulation upon tribulation, hope upon hope," which suggests that they read צַו as צָר, "trouble." Watts, *Isaiah 1–33*, 363, also says these words recall a "bumbling schoolmaster, repeating letters of the alphabet."

[39] Wildberger, *Isaiah 28–39*, 16, interprets these words as a rejection of Isaiah's message.

[40] צַו in Hos 5:11 is thought to be (a) a shortened form of "commandment," מִצְוָה; (b) F. Andersen and D. N. Freedman, *Hosea*, AB (Garden City: Doubleday, 1980), 409–10, suggest that צַו in Hos 5:11 is an abbreviated form of צֹאָה, "filth, excrement," which was the interpretation given in the Vulgate; (c) A. A. Macintosh, *Hosea*, ICC (Edingurgh: T & T Clark, 1997), 204–205, suggests the meaning "empty, vanity," from Arabic *ṣww*.

[41] Motyer, *The Prophecy of Isaiah*, 232, takes this interpretation of these strange words, though he interprets this to be a critic's mocking view of Isaiah's teaching.

[42] NIV "very well then" is not a bad translation of כִּי, *kî*, "surely/assuredly," which NIV so frequently omits in translating other passages of Isaiah.

[43] This is surveyed in J. H. Hayes, "The Tradition of Zion's Inviolability," *JBL* 82 (1963): 419–25, or C. R. Seitz, *Isaiah 1–39*, Interpretation (Louisville: Westminster John Knox, 1993), 205–208, who discusses how chaps. 28–39 affected the people's views of God's protection of Zion, especially in light of the contrasting ways Ahaz and Hezekiah responded to the Assyrians.

to give the weary rest[44] from their troubles. Of course, this covenant blessing was based on the people's love for God and their willingness to follow the covenant stipulations. God was gracious, kind, and willing to bless, but at this time the people were rebellious and would not listen to or obey God (Lev 26:21; Ps 81:12; Ezek 3:7). As a result of their sinfulness, God would now need to temporarily remove the protection of these promises and allow them to be attacked.

Consequently, Isaiah announces (28:13) that God will speak to them a new message. Verse 13 repeats the words of v. 10, but now the words have a different meaning. They still are gibberish that makes no sense, but A. van Selm has connected these phrases to the strange, obscure, and incomprehensible language of the Assyrians (cf. 33:19), which the people would not be able to understand. After comparing these words to Akkadian, van Selm suggests that:[45]

the first phrase means: "Go out! Let him go out!"
the second phrase means: "Wait! Let him wait!"
the third phrase means: "Servant, listen!"

The Israelites probably would not understand the message of these words; all they might perceive was that someone was speaking the incomprehensible Akkadian language. It will make about as much sense as the gibberish of the unfaithful prophets and priests, but its meaning will be quite different. The prophet's explanation at the end of v. 13 spells out the implication of these words. The results[46] will be that they will go out, stumble, be broken in pieces, and imprisoned (cf. 8:15), exactly what happened to countless Hebrews when the Assyrians invaded Judah. There is no sign that Zion will have rest or be saved by God. The incompetent leaders of the nation spew out senseless drivel rather than listening to the word of God, so God will remove them and demonstrate that their pious pronouncements are false. These warnings to the spiritual and political leaders of past years illustrate the accountability God demands of all who would aspire to lead his people. This applies especially to those in positions of spiritual leadership (comparable to the priests and prophets) in churches, seminaries, and denominational leadership. Incompetence and pride lead to bad decisions and a garbled message, for those who do not truly listen to God are doomed to fail God and his people.

GOD'S CORNERSTONE REJECTED BY JUDAH'S LEADERS (28:14–22)

**¹⁴Therefore hear the word of the LORD, you scoffers
who rule this people in Jerusalem.**

---

[44] הָנִיחוּ is an imperative form that encourages the audience to "cause to rest."

[45] A. van Selm, "Isaiah 28:9–13," 332–39, explains *ṣi* as an imperative Akkadian verb meaning "go," *qi* as an imperative verb meaning "wait," and *šeme* as an imperative verb meaning "hear, listen."

[46] לְמַעַן, "so that," introduces a final or result clause (IBHS 38.3a-b).

¹⁵You boast, "We have entered into a covenant with death,
    with the grave we have made an agreement.
When an overwhelming scourge sweeps by,
    it cannot touch us,
for we have made a lie our refuge
    and falsehood our hiding place."

¹⁶So this is what the Sovereign LORD says:

"See, I lay a stone in Zion,
    a tested stone,
a precious cornerstone for a sure foundation;
    the one who trusts will never be dismayed.
¹⁷I will make justice the measuring line
    and righteousness the plumb line;
hail will sweep away your refuge, the lie,
    and water will overflow your hiding place.
¹⁸Your covenant with death will be annulled;
    your agreement with the grave will not stand.
When the overwhelming scourge sweeps by,
    you will be beaten down by it.
¹⁹As often as it comes it will carry you away;
    morning after morning, by day and by night,
    it will sweep through."

The understanding of this message
    will bring sheer terror.
²⁰The bed is too short to stretch out on,
    the blanket too narrow to wrap around you.
²¹The LORD will rise up as he did at Mount Perazim,
    he will rouse himself as in the Valley of Gibeon—
to do his work, his strange work,
    and perform his task, his alien task.
²²Now stop your mocking,
    or your chains will become heavier;
the Lord, the LORD Almighty, has told me
    of the destruction decreed against the whole land.

Many of the people in the prophet's audience probably had trouble accepting these dire words of judgment and some readers today will deny that these words have any application to them. In order to persuade his audience to change its theological understanding of what God will do to his people, the prophet strengthens his argument by delivering a second judgment oracle to the scoffing leaders of Jerusalem. This paragraph is held together by repeated references to:

(a) mocking, scoffing[47]	28:14 and 22
(b) the covenant with death	28:15 and 18
(c) lies	28:15 and 17
(d) refuge	28:15 and 17
(e) hiding place	28:15 and 17
(f) overwhelming scourge	28:15 and 18

Those who were given the opportunity to find rest and security in God (28:12) are now placing their trust in someone other than God (28:15). God's secure foundation (28:16) offers hope to those in Zion, but it was rejected for a political solution (the "covenant with death" made with Egypt) that would end up destroying the nation. In this judgment speech Isaiah claims that:

The leader made a false hope their refuge	28:14–15
They reject God's secure hope, so they will fail	28:16–19a
God's strange work will bring terror	28:19b–22

The theological principle Isaiah promotes is that if people trust God for security, they will have nothing to fear, but if they refuse to trust God and depend on man's strength, political treaties, or human attempts to fix things, God will purposely work against them (his "strange work" in 28:21) to get them to change their thinking and trust him.

28:14–15 "Therefore, hear the word of the LORD" introduces a new paragraph. The "therefore" (*lākēn*) indicates that these words are a response to the people's unwillingness to listen to the word of God in the previous paragraph (28:12). They now have another chance to listen, to understand, and to stop mocking before God's "strange work" (*zār maʿaśēhû* in 28:21) of judging his own people begins.

The audience the prophet was speaking to included the rulers of Jerusalem who behaved scornfully and arrogantly (28:14–15).[48] The book of Proverbs portrays this kind of person as one who is not wise (Prov 29:8), refuses correction (Prov 13:1), rejects repentance (Prov 14:9), and is arrogant (Prov 21:24). Oswalt suggests, "he mocks the right way. He is not merely misled, he delights to mislead others,"[49] The proud self-confidence of these people is evident in the quotation of what they speak, but this is the prophet's negative characterization of what they say, not an exact quote. Their perverted perspective leads them to

---

[47] The noun לָצוֹן, "scoffer," at the beginning of the paragraph is matched by the verb לִיץ, "to scoff," in the last verse of the paragraph. Beuken, *Isaiah II*, 43, finds a chiastic structure in vv. 15–18 with 16b at the center. The repetition is incomplete and the chiasm should include v. 19a, so it is hard to find a genuine chiastic structure.

[48] C. Barth, "לִיץ," *TDOT*, VII, 547–552, explains that this root describes an unwise, presumptuously arrogant person who swaggers about. He disassociates it with speech and connects it to scornful or arrogant behavior, though it appears that there are several ways of expressing this attitude.

[49] Oswalt, *Isaiah 1–39*, 516, concludes that this person is just the opposite of the wise man.

scornfully reject what God has provided for them because they were placing their hope in what the prophet ironically calls their deceptive "covenant with death" (*bĕrît ʾet māwet*). What they thought would bring life and hope in their military crisis, the prophet interpreted as a source of death. Their "vision"[50] (NIV "agreement") with Sheol is more difficult to understand, but it must be Isaiah's way of mocking their alliance with Egypt. They were probably presenting this as something God revealed to them, but the prophet saw it as a vision that would assure that they would soon be in Sheol, the place of the dead. E. J. Kissane goes so far as to suggest that the people "entered into a pact with the gods of the underworld," while J. Day suggests a connection with the worship of Molech,[51] but there is no reason to think that this is anything other than a political arrangement with another country (probably Egypt, based on 30:1–5; 31:1–5). The rulers of Judah believed the message of this vision provided protection from Sheol; but in reality this "covenant with death" only hurried their arrival. The rulers in Jerusalem gained this false hope because they believed their political treaty with Egypt would give them refuge from the invading Assyrians, that "overwhelming flooding scourge" (picking up the flood imagery in 8:7–8; 28:2).[52] In contrast to his audience, Isaiah claimed that Egypt would not be a source of "our refuge" (*maḥĕsēnu*), a "hiding place" that would keep the Assyrians from coming to their land. In other contexts, people trust in God using the imagery of taking "refuge" (Ruth 2:12; Ps 13:6; 46:1; 61:4; 62:7) or finding a dependable "hiding place" (Ps 17:8; 27:5; 31:20–21; 32:7; 91:1). Isaiah understood this vision of their future as political suicide, a lie (*kāzāb*), a false perception of reality (28:15), and an idea that had no legitimate basis. This reminds one of the proverb that warns people to be careful, for they may discover

---

[50] The translation "agreement" in NIV is questionable since this word is a participle that comes from חֹזֶה, "seer, vision." Because of the parallelism with "covenant" people have suggested this word means "agreement" (the Old Greek translation of this word is "covenant"), but this would be the only place where this word would have this meaning. The literal translation, "we have had a vision concerning Sheol" must be seen as the prophet's attempt to express the reverse of what the audience understood. The audience would not call their covenant, a "covenant with death" or a "vision concerning Sheol," but the prophet used these terms to ridicule their alliance with Egypt.

[51] E. J. Kissane, *The Book of Isaiah* (Dublin: Browne and Nolan, 1960), I:306–307. This might be the Egyptian god Osiris or the Canaanite god Mot. In the time of Ahaz some consulted the dead during an earlier Assyrian crisis (8:19). J. Day, *Molech: A God of Human Sacrifice in the Old Testament* (Cambridge: Cambridge University Press, 1989), 62–64, suggests that this was a covenant with Molech (cf. Lev 18:21; 2 Kgs 17:17; Isa 57:9), but J. Blenkinsopp, "Judah's Covenant with Death (Isaiah XXVIII 14–22)," *VT* 50 (2000): 472–83, wisely rejects this option since nothing in the context hints of Molech or child sacrifice. Instead, he proposes a connection with a covenant with Mot (the god of death) who can defeat Hadad, the storm god who was the enemy of Mot and an Assyrian god of war. Beuken, *Isaiah II*, 45, suggests that this may have something to do with speaking to the dead (necromancy; see 8:19; 29:4).

[52] שׁוֹט שׁוֹטֵף is a noun plus a participle. The *Qere* and 1QIsaᵃ have שׁוֹט, parallel with the reading in 28:18, which is the more common spelling of "scourge, whip." This combination emphasizes that the "scourging scourge" will be severe, even greater than the flooding scourge of Assyria that attacked Judah in the days of Ahaz (8:7).

a way that seems right to them, but that way will actually lead to their death (Prov 14:12). But why was it wrong to make a political treaty with Egypt?

28:16–19a The introductory "therefore, thus says the LORD" signals the opening of God's response to this problem of trusting Egypt. God reminds the audience that he has already provided them security (28:16), and their treaty will bring death and terror (28:17–19a).

Now the audience learns why it was wrong to trust in treaties with Egypt. The first reason it was wrong (28:16) is "surely, assuredly" (*kî*; omitted in NIV) God has already provided the nation with a solid basis for security, so it is an act of distrust to reject God's protection. To explain this concept, Isaiah uses the analogy of constructing a building (cf. 1 Kgs 5:31). The building that God constructs will stand in times of trials (the Assyrian conflict) because it is built[53] on a solid foundation; therefore, there is no need to be afraid or dismayed because of some enemy. The foundation stone of this building could function as a symbol of (a) the cornerstone of the temple building; (b) the law of God; (c) the faithful people who were the pillars of the community; (d) Jerusalem, God's chosen dwelling place; or (e) the Davidic monarch (like Hezekiah);[54] but the best option is (f) to understand God and his promises as the secure foundation of the nation.[55] The Hebrew text has several grammatical difficulties because the first word "behold, I" (*hinnî*) has a first person singular suffix, which does not match the third person subject of the perfect verb, "he founded, established" (*yissad*). Although the Hebrew Masoretic text indicates that God "has established"[56] in Zion this stone, two Qumran manuscripts solve the grammatical problem by making the verb a participle, thus they read, "surely I am establishing/will establish,"[57] with the first person suffix as the subject of the verb.[58] This is the preferred reading.

---

[53] The phrase יֹסֵד הִנְנִי is translated "See, I lay" in NIV. Beuken, *Isaiah II,* 12, 49, translates this perfect verb as past tense, "Behold, I myself have laid in Zion for a foundation stone," and believes that Israel's history is based on the foundation of God's "kingship as he resides in the temple." Wildberger, *Isaiah 28–39,* 40, observes that this verbal concept is parallel to the prophetic perfect verb "I will make justice" in v. 17; therefore, a past understanding of the verb is questionable.

[54] See O. Kaiser, *Isaiah 13–39,* 253, for these and several other identifications of this stone down through the centuries. Beuken, *Isaiah II,* 49, believes this stone foundation refers to "YHWH's election of Zion as his abode."

[55] The Aramaic Targum interpreted "stone" and wrote "a king, a strong king" possibly thinking in terms of the Messiah. Peter saw the analogy between this stone in Isaiah and Jesus (one of God's promises) and encouraged his readers to trust in him (1 Pet 2:4–6). The Old Greek reads "he who believes in him" in v. 16b, which could refer to trusting in God the Rock, or the Messiah.

[56] יָסַד is a *piel* perfect, which represents completed action.

[57] 1QIsaᵃ has this form as a *qal* active participle יֹוסֵד, while 1QIsaᵇ has מִיסֵד, a *piel* participle. With הִנְנִי, "behold," these participles could be translated "is establishing" or "will establish." This reading is to be preferred because participles referring to the future frequently follow הִנְנִי. J. J. M. Roberts, "Yahweh's Foundation in Zion (Isa 28:16)," *JBL* 106 (1987): 27–45, finds no parallels to the Masoretic Hebrew construction, so he argues for following the Qumran texts. The Old Greek has "behold, I will establish."

[58] GKC §116p-q, 147b describes the suffix functioning as the subject of a participle.

This stone is far more dependable and trustworthy than Egypt because it is a "tested stone, a precious cornerstone, a sure foundation." These appositional characteristics all describe one stone, not three stones. These three images remind the reader that God and his promises function as a sanctuary for believers and as a stumbling stone for unbelievers (as in 8:14; 30:29). This is a "tested" (*bôḥan*) stone that has proven its worth as a safe and solid piece of rock (not a stone for testing other stones),[59] one that could function as a valuable cornerstone of a wall. Because it had all the right characteristics, it would serve as a "sure foundation"[60] for a building. Isaiah was saying that God and his promises provide the nation what it needs to stand firm in these circumstances. The nation did not need to rely on this covenant with Egypt that would lead to death. The people must trust God and believe his promises so that they can rest securely in the peace of his protection (2:2–5; 26:3–4). If they do trust God (cf. 7:9), they will not be overcome with fear and anxiety.[61] God has done his part in establishing the firm foundation, now the people must do their part and place their faith in God and his promises. Then they will live and be blessed by God. This is not calling for blind faith in the unknown, which is rather foolish, but a challenge for the audience to make a willful act of dependence based on what is already known about God's past deeds and what he has already promised about the future.

28:17 As God builds his house made up of his people, he will use the measuring lines or plumb lines of justice and righteousness (cf. Amos 7:7–9) to make sure that the building will stand firm on this secure stone foundation. God can build a sure house that will stand the storms of life because he builds using the right foundations and the right building tools. Since the leaders did not allow justice and righteousness to characterize their nation, the building they constructed would not stand (as in 7:7). The nation's deceptive refuge in their treaty alliance with Egypt would not provide a solid foundation for the nation's future. Picking up earlier storm imagery from the time of Ahaz (8:8; 17:12; 28:2; 30:28), the prophet finds hail and an overflowing flood (images of Assyrian destructive power) destroying the deceptive lie (from 28:15b) that Egypt will be a safe hiding place or refuge (from 28:15b).

---

[59] T. O Lambdin, "Egyptian Loan Words in the Old Testament," *JAOS* 73 (1953): 145–56, explains this as an Egyptian loan word and gives it the Egyptian meaning "sure, safe" rather than "tested," but the two ideals seem closely related (if a stone passed the test, it would be safe to use). It seems most Hebrews would have identified this root with a Hb. root meaning "tested," rather than with an Egyptian meaning. Beuken, *Isaiah II*, 15, believes this imagery is built on the metaphor of a foundation stone that was tested to determine if it was strong enough to hold the weight of the rest of the wall.

[60] The text has מוּסָד מוּסָד, repeating the same root twice, which Wildberger, *Isaiah 28–39*, 31, concludes is a case of dittography. However, the *hophal* participle (GKC §71) מוּסָד could be an adjective, thus giving the meaning "a founded foundation." Exum, "Whom will he Teach Knowledge?" 108–39, keeps both forms of the root as authentic.

[61] יָחִישׁ means "he will have haste, excitement, anxiety," just the opposite of peace. Cf. 7:2 where Ahaz and the people of Judah were having great anxiety and were shaking like a leaf in the wind because they feared Assyria and did not trust God.

28:18–19a The great deceptive national hope, that "covenant of death" (from 28:15a), will bring no help because Egypt will not save Judah when the Assyrians come. Instead, the flooding scourge will violently sweep through the land, carrying people away with it in the process. They will be trampled (28:18b), just like the people of Israel were trampled (28:3), because they made the same mistake of trusting in alliances with foreign nations, rather than trusting God. The Assyrians will be an irresistible power that will come against them with unrelenting force. Day after day they will suffer, time and time again as each city falls, this enemy (Assyria) will carry people away into exile.[62]

28:19b–22 The paragraph ends with:

A warning of terror	28:19b
A proverb of failed expectations	28:20
Warning to stop, for destruction is coming	28:21–22

Isaiah hoped these final arguments would persuade the audience to change their ways and trust God. The warning in 28:19b contrasts (a) the false message of the drunken spiritual leaders, who speak gibberish and think that everything will go fine because of this covenant of death with Egypt (28:9–10,14–15), with (b) the message of Isaiah, which indicates that Egypt will not help them resist Assyrian aggression. When the people experience the terror of these fateful events in the near future they will finally understand what Isaiah was talking about in these warnings. Then the people of Judah will realize that they trusted the wrong people. Unfortunately, their understanding of God's message through the prophet will come too late, if they wait that long to wake up. It is better to listen now, rather than experience the disappointment of trusting Egypt rather than God.

The enigmatic, proverbial sounding imagery in 28:20 supports this perspective by claiming that what people think will be adequate (a bed with blankets) will not be adequate to do the job. They will be short sheeted by the false hopes of Egyptian protection. What appears to be a good deal will turn out to be no protection at all. There is no need to identify this bed with a bed of maggots in Sheol (cf. 14:11; 57:2; Ps 139:8).[63]

What will actually happen (28:21) is that "Surely [*kî*; omitted in NIV] God will arise" and accomplish a strange work among them. God's past supportive work allowed David to defeat his enemies and chase the Philistines from Gibeon to Gezer (2 Sam 5:17–25; 1 Chr 14:16). In the past God burst forth as a flood of waters against the Philistines and helped David establish Jerusalem as his capital, but now his strange, paradoxical, providential power will do just the opposite, and an overflowing flood will come against his people in Jerusalem.

---

[62] Sennacherib claimed to take over 200,000 captives from Judah in 701 BC. Watts, *Isaiah 1–33*, 370, thinks this refers to the three conquests by Nebuchadnezzar.

[63] B. Halpern, "Excremental Vision," 109–21, draws these allusions from a mortuary context, which fits in with the idea of a "covenant with death."

His power is unlimited to save those who trust him, but that same powerful passion for justice and righteousness will destroy those who reject him.

Consequently, the prophet pleads with his audience to stop proudly scoffing (28:22 is picking up a theme from 28:14) at God's warnings, for if they do not change their ways, God will make their suffering even worse.[64] His audience must take this warning seriously, because the prophet knows all this will happen—it was not something he just imagined. God Almighty, who controls the armies of heaven and earth, was the source of this message of destruction against "the whole land" (cf. 10:23).[65] Now his audience needs to act upon these warnings.

PARABLE OF THE FARMER: ACCEPT GOD'S WISDOM (28:23–29)

[23]Listen and hear my voice;
   pay attention and hear what I say.
[24]When a farmer plows for planting, does he plow continually?
   Does he keep on breaking up and harrowing the soil?
[25]When he has leveled the surface,
   does he not sow caraway and scatter cummin?
Does he not plant wheat in its place,
   barley in its plot,
   and spelt in its field?
[26]His God instructs him
   and teaches him the right way.

[27]Caraway is not threshed with a sledge,
   nor is a cartwheel rolled over cummin;
caraway is beaten out with a rod,
   and cummin with a stick.
[28]Grain must be ground to make bread;
   so one does not go on threshing it forever.
Though he drives the wheels of his threshing cart over it,
   his horses do not grind it.
[29]All this also comes from the LORD Almighty,
   wonderful in counsel and magnificent in wisdom.

The final portion of this section (28:1–29) introduces a story or a parable (not an allegory or disputation)[66] about a farmer. Since no other version of

---

[64] יַחְזִקוּ מוֹסְרֵיכֶם (lit. "they will strengthen your chains") refers to the increasing of pain and suffering on the prisoners from Judah, and in this context it could be understood literally or as a symbol of Assyria tightening its grip around Judah.

[65] Wildberger, *Isaiah 28–39*, 45, takes כָּל־אָרֶץ to mean "all the earth" in an eschatological sense and therefore attributes this verse to a later editor, but Beuken *Isaiah II*, 60, rejects this approach because this verse is parallel to 7:24 and 10:23; therefore, "against the whole land" would be more appropriate in this context.

[66] Sweeney, *Isaiah 1–39*, 364, calls this an allegory; Clements, *Isaiah 1–39*, 232, and J. Goldingay, *Isaiah* NIBC (Peabody: Hendrickson, 2001), 157, describe it as a parable; G. Fohrer, *Das Buch Jesaja*, II (Zürich: Zwingli Verlag, 1967), 66–67, calls it a disputation. J. W. Whedbee, *Isaiah and*

this text exists, it is impossible to demonstrate whether this was an original composition or if the prophet adapted ideas from an existing story. The idea of God/the gods giving farmers wisdom about the process of farming is not an uncommon theme in ancient Near Eastern literature,[67] so the audience would have understood this story without any trouble.

Commentaries have difficulty determining the significance of this parable in the context of this chapter. The analysis below concludes that this parable is not (a) an analogy offering an argument against Baalism; (b) a prophetic defense against opponents who claim that the prophet keeps changing his message; (c) a warning of coming suffering; or (d) an argument against a rigid view of cause and effect.[68] Childs rightly perceives that this wisdom analogy did not rise out of any effort for Isaiah to defend himself.[69] The farmer's activity should not be allegorically applied to God's activity of judging and saving. The farmer's work is just an easily understood example that illustrates the two conclusions found in 28:26 and 29. These conclusions, which essentially say the same thing, capture the central lesson that God teaches people how to live (28:26) and gives people wonderful counsel (28:29). The application is: if God gives the farmer wise instruction, then the audience should take seriously God's counsel for them. What was God's wise counsel? In the first part of chap. 28 God teaches them about "the right way" (*mišpāṭ*). The prophet admonishes his audience not to follow the path of the northern nation of Israel (28:1–4), not to listen to the gibberish of the drunken prophets and priests (28:7–13), not to depend on their political alliances, their covenant of death with Egypt (28:14–22), but to trust in God as their only secure foundation (28:16). They must stop doing what they are now doing (28:22) and listen to what God is saying (28:23). The wise farmer hears God's instruction and is successful because he follows God's wise counsel. Should not the spiritual and political leaders of Judah do the same?

The story of the farmer is structured into two parallel parts related to the work of the farmer, with a conclusion at the end of each sub-paragraph.

The farmer's work at planting	28:24–26
Plowing and planting	24–25
Conclusion: God instructs him	26

Wisdom (Nashville: Abingdon, 1971), 51–68, deals with aspects of wisdom influence in the parable.

[67] S. N. Kramer, *History Begins at Sumer* (London: Thames and Hudson, 1958), 105–108, 137, gives examples where the god Ninurta is a farmer and another where Enlil teaches his son Enten to be a farmer. In Egypt the gods Isis and Osiris taught people how to farm.

[68] Wildberger, *Isaiah 28–39*, 53–55, summarizes and critiques these approaches and concludes that this passage arises from a disputation between Isaiah and his audience.

[69] Childs, *Isaiah*, 210–11, rightly focuses on the message in the theological statements in 28:26 and 29. These conclusions support the prophet's view of God's work in v. 21.

The farmer's work at harvest	28:27–29
Threshing different grains	27–28
Conclusion: God instructs him	29

28:23 The story of the farmer is preceded by an introductory call to attention. It has four imperative exhortations[70] that emphatically invite the audience to listen to what is said in order to learn an important truth. They should not continue to be unwilling to listen (28:12b) to what God has to say to them. God is instructing them in "the right way" (*mišpaṭ*) to live, for God's evaluation of their lives will be based on his "justice" 28:17, *mišpaṭ*). The imperatives grab people's attention and imply that vital information is about to be proclaimed. This introduction marks the beginning of a new paragraph in a manner similar to what is found at the beginning of paragraphs in wisdom and prophetic texts.[71]

28:24–26 The illustration asks two questions about the plowing and planting activities of the farmer in vv. 24 and 25, then it concludes with a theological explanation of why the farmer does what he does in v. 26. The first question asks if the farmer spends all his time plowing and preparing his field for planting. The obvious answer is no. The second question asks if he does not also spend time sowing his seeds, each in its proper place? The obvious answer is yes.

Only a few passages contain detailed information about these kinds of agricultural activities in ancient Israel. A pair of oxen (1 Kgs 19:19) were often used to pull iron tipped plows (1 Sam 13:20) to break up the soil. The plowed field would then be harrowed to smooth out the rough surface and prepare it for planting. The farmer would then plant various crops (wheat, barley, cumin, or dill spice[72]) in appropriate plots based on soil type and moisture.

The theological conclusion that explains all this activity is that God taught the farmer how to do these things the right way so that he would have a good crop (28:26). The central principle is simple and straightforward, without any allegorical interpretation that makes Isaiah or God the farmer who is plowing, smoothing out the soil, or planting various crops. All the prophet is emphasizing is that God teaches people "the right way" (*mišpāṭ*) to do things. Although this term often carries the judicial meaning of "judgment, justice," here it is used in a non-judicial context to refer to the proper way of doing things in life. This should raise the analogous question in the mind of the listener: What has God's word through the prophet been teaching his people to do in the right way? The answer to that question is found in 28:1–22.

---

[70] Both וְשִׁמְעוּ and הַאֲזִינוּ are imperatives that function as exhortations (GKC §110b). The use of four imperatives in this verse draws attention to the seriousness and importance of listening to what is being said.

[71] For wisdom cf. Job 33:1,34; 34:2; Prov 3:1; 4:1; 7:24. For prophecy cf. Isa 1:2,10; 7:13; 28:14; 32:9,13; 37:17; Amos 3:1,13; 4:1; 5:1.

[72] Beuken, *Isaiah II*, 64, claims that the term קֶצַח, which is sometimes translated "dill," is the name for "black cummin."

28:27–29   The second half of the parable describes the different ways a farmer threshes different seed (28:27–28) and then ends with a theological conclusion (28:29). The illustrations of harvesting are statements rather than questions. Each line describes the unique way each kind of seed must be treated in order not to crush it and render it useless. In one case you simply hit the plant with a stick and the grain falls off, but in another case one would drive a threshing sledge over it to thresh[73] the grain. Once again the interpreter should avoid the temptation to allegorize by comparing these activities to Assyria's plan to thresh Judah with rods.

These insights into threshing grain are given merely to illustrate the theological principle (28:29) that the farmer knows how to do all these things because of God's wonderful counsel and wisdom. The two conclusions in vv. 26 and 29 simply communicate to the audience that God teaches people wisdom so that they can do the right thing. Now the prophet's audience must listen to what God has said about Israel's mistakes, the false instructions of the prophets and priests, and the deceptive covenant with death in 28:1–22. If they will listen to God's wisdom and respond the right way, they can avoid the disasters that Isaiah has predicted in 28:7–22.

THEOLOGICAL IMPLICATIONS.   No one has trouble accepting the idea that God should stand against drunken ministers and proud political leaders in other nations (28:1–3); they deserve to be judged (28:3–4). It is more difficult to accept the idea that the religious and political leaders in his "chosen nation" are just as drunk and incompetent and that these leaders deserve God's punishment (28:7–13). The criteria for God's judgment of all leaders are (a) their pride (28:1,3); (b) the quality of their instruction to others (28:9–10); (c) their dependence on lies and human political alliances instead of God (28:15); (d) the measurements of their actions based on the values of justice and righteousness (28:17); and (e) their rejection or acceptance of the wisdom of God's instruction (28:26,29). Since God is all-powerful (28:2), everyone should be glorifying him (28:5), for he is that sure foundation that can be trusted (28:16). He acts in justice (28:16–17) and will do "a strange work" against his own people (28:21) if they do not follow his wisdom (28:26,29).

It is always easy to be critical of the faults of others (a politician, a parent, a pastor, or a neighbor), but it is difficult to deal with the truth that many of these same characteristics would be found in God's chosen people (and not just in God's people in the Old Testament). Pride reflects an attitude that something other than God should be glorified, that human alliances are more powerful than the sure foundation of Almighty God, and that a person does not have to follow the path of justice or accept God's wisdom. The acceptance of these lies can deceive anyone, but God will unveil these ideas as falsehoods when he

---

[73] אָדוֹשׁ appears to be an infinitive absolute from דּוּשׁ with an unusual prosthetic א at the beginning. Normally this is written דּוּשׁ. 1QIsaᵃ has הדשׁ, which is probably a *niphal* infinitive absolute (GKC §113w, footnote 3).

judges those blind people who scoff and refuse to trust God. The apostle Paul saw the need for the people in his day to learn this lesson (Rom 9:33; 10:11). If only God's people today will listen to God's wisdom and trust him as their sure foundation, he will expose the inner pride, shameful deeds, deceitful lies of modern preachers, and the false places of refuge in the modern religious culture of our day. It is better to see the light today than have God reveal it when it is too late.

(2) Second Woe, to the Oppressed of Jerusalem (29:1–14)

The second woe expands on the idea that God will judge Judah (28:17–22). This new lament draws attention to the dire consequence of Judah's unwillingness to trust God. An enemy nation (29:7–8) and God (29:2–3) will siege the city, but then suddenly God will destroy Jerusalem's enemies (29:5). Although Assyria is not mentioned, the surprising crushing of Jerusalem's enemies "in an instant" (29:5) was fulfilled a short time later when God struck down 185,000 Assyrian troops in one night (37:36).

JERUSALEM BESIEGED, THEN RELIEVED (29:1–8)

> ¹Woe to you, Ariel, Ariel,
>   the city where David settled!
> Add year to year
>   and let your cycle of festivals go on.
> ²Yet I will besiege Ariel;
>   she will mourn and lament,
>   she will be to me like an altar hearth.
> ³I will encamp against you all around;
>   I will encircle you with towers
>   and set up my siege works against you.
> ⁴Brought low, you will speak from the ground;
>   your speech will mumble out of the dust.
> Your voice will come ghostlike from the earth;
>   out of the dust your speech will whisper.
>
> ⁵But your many enemies will become like fine dust,
>   the ruthless hordes like blown chaff.
> Suddenly, in an instant,
> ⁶the LORD Almighty will come
> with thunder and earthquake and great noise,
>   with windstorm and tempest and flames of a devouring fire.
> ⁷Then the hordes of all the nations that fight against Ariel,
>   that attack her and her fortress and besiege her,
> will be as it is with a dream,
>   with a vision in the night—
> ⁸as when a hungry man dreams that he is eating,
>   but he awakens, and his hunger remains;

> as when a thirsty man dreams that he is drinking,
> but he awakens faint, with his thirst unquenched.
> So will it be with the hordes of all the nations
> that fight against Mount Zion.

This woe includes two somewhat parallel paragraphs (29:1–8; 29:9–14), each beginning with negative words of judgment, but both include God's astonishing divine work that will surprise his people.

Jerusalem besieged, but its enemies disappear	29:1–8
The siege will humble the City of David	1–4
The horde of the nations will vanish	5–8

This first paragraph is held together by references to Ariel, the city of David, mourning (29:1), being besieged (29:2), and being attacked by hordes of foreigners (29:7). There are several references to the "hordes" (*hămôn* in 29:5,7,8) that will surround Zion and the repetition of the phrase "and it will be" (29:2a,2b,4b,5a,5b,7a,8a) connects these verses with each other. Although Clements attributes these verses to the redaction of Isaiah during the time of Josiah, 80 years after the fulfillment of these events, one should not reject these words as true prophetic announcements before 701 BC.[74] God will do astonishing things against his people (29:1–3), but also against their enemies (29:5–7).

29:1a The superscription to the message identifies this as another lamenting woe. The weeping is for Ariel, which is identified as the city where King David encamped to establish it as his capital (2 Sam 5). This means that this woe is directly addressed to Mount Zion (29:8), or Jerusalem.[75] Though the title "Ariel" could mean "lion" (2 Sam 23:20) or "lion of God," most believe in this context the prophet is using the meaning "altar-hearth" (29:2b; Ezek 43:15,16),[76] the place where sacrifices were burned within the temple complex. Since people worshiped God there, this was a place that God would be very zealous to protect. A lamenting woe against Zion's altar, God's holy dwelling place where he was worshiped, probably did not make much sense to the people in Jerusalem. Why would God allow his sacred temple to be attacked? Initially, 29:1–4 appear, to undermine the "Zion theology" that God would never allow Jerusalem to be destroyed.

---

[74] Clements, *Isaiah 1–39*, 235, believes "the aim of this redaction was to interpret the failure of Sennacherib to take Jerusalem in 701 B.C.," however, there is no proof given to deny this prophecy to Isaiah, and there is no statement that implies or requires one to date this material in the time of Josiah. There is no reason why this could not be a real prophecy given before these events happened.

[75] The direct address "to Ariel" is unusual but parallel to the direct address to Assyria in 10:5. Usually a more indirect approach is taken by proclaiming, "Woe to those who go to great depths to hide" (29:15).

[76] The Aramaic Targum has "altar of God."

29:1b–4 The beginning of this and the next paragraph are marked by introductory imperative verbs ("add" in 29:1b and "be stunned" in 29:9).[77] The prophet sarcastically encourages the people to continue to sacrifice and conduct their feasts year after year. (Does this mean the siege is still a year away?) In spite of this apparent attempt to please God with their Levitical ceremonies (29:2; cf. 29:13), God will bring distress, mourning, and lamenting to his people, causing the city to become like an altar hearth (a place of burning where God's just wrath is satisfied). The reason for this lamentable news is because God will encamp against Zion, instead of dwelling in Zion to protect it (like David in 29:1). Although the people will see an army with siege works surrounding the city (probably a reference to Sennacherib's later attack in 701 BC), the spiritual reality is that God is the real power fighting against them. He is directing an enemy nation (the Assyrians) to encircle the city and besiege Jerusalem. This imagery was designed to undermine the people's false confidence in Zion's great theological traditions that idealized it as an absolutely secure and undefeatable place because God dwelt there in the temple (Ps 46; 48). By indicating that Jerusalem will become a place of slaughter and burning, God indicates that he is not obligated to protect a sinful place where blind people do not pay attention to his revelation or truly worship him (29:9–13).

The result will be devastating, for "after you are humbled"[78] (cf. 2:9,11,17; 5:15; 10:33) the people of Judah will speak humbly from the dust on the ground (29:4). In defeat their voices will be transformed to sound like the mutterings of ghosts or the weird chirping[79] of the dead (cf. 8:19). This analogy contrasts the loud and confident military bragging that existed in Jerusalem (28:14–15) with the future humble whispering of the people as they face defeat.

29:5–8 A change of topic begins in v. 5 with the mention of a "multitude, horde" (also in vv. 7 and 8)[80] of strangers[81] (NIV "enemies") from all nations who will fight against Zion (29:8). The large horde of troops that will threaten to attack Jerusalem (29:5,7) will be "like fine dust" (*kĕābāq daq*) and blown chaff (*kĕmôṣ*). This could potentially refer to the vast strength of this enemy (as many as the dust of the earth),[82] but chaff generally has the connotation of uselessness

---

[77] סָף (from the verb יָסַף), "add, increase, do," in 29:1b, and הִתְמַהְמְהוּ, "be amazed, astonished," in 2:9. These are ironic or sarcastic imperatives (GKC §110a; see also Amos 4:4).

[78] וְשָׁפַלְתְּ functions adverbially describing the manner in which something happens (GKC §120a,g), making the first verb in the sentence subordinate to the main idea ("you will speak"). The idea of humbling the proud repeats key ideas in 2:6–22.

[79] תְּצַפְצֵף relates to the sound birds make, some kind of "chirp" (10:4), the same dreadful moaning sound that King Hezekiah made when God humbled him and announced that he would soon die (38:14).

[80] הָמוֹן refers to a large group of people, the vast army of an enemy nation.

[81] 1QIsaᵃ has זֵדָיִךְ, "your insolent ones," rather than זָרָיִךְ, "your strangers," a simple confusion of ר and ד in Hb. Wildberger, *Isaiah 28–39*, 66, follows the reading of the Dead Sea Scrolls, while Oswalt, *Isaiah 1–39*, 525, keeps the Hebrew Masoretic reading.

[82] Kaiser, *Isaiah 13–39*, 268, takes this approach based on 1:7; 17:12; 40:15, but none of these passages really provides much support for this interpretation.

and in this context describes what is left of defeated nations (cf. 17:13; 41:15) that have no weight or power, no value, and no control over themselves. The final clause in v. 5 refers to the speed at which this change will happen, though "suddenly, in an instant" (*lĕpetaʿ*) could refer either to the sudden defeat of the enemy in 5a, or to the sudden appearance of God in v. 6.[83] Maybe the visitation of God (29:6) in the theophany power of a thunderstorm, earthquake, and fire[84] happened at the same time, or this is the same event as God defeating the enemy that attacked Jerusalem (29:7a). God's sovereign power over his people and all the nations will be dramatically seen through this event. God's deliverance of his people will be an astonishing reversal of the people's hopeless situation.

This event "will be like" (vv. 7b,8a,8b) an unreal experience for the hordes of enemy troops surrounding Jerusalem.[85] Three comparisons are given: (a) this will seem like a terrible nightmare, but suddenly when one wakes up, everything has changed; (b) it will be like a hungry man who dreams he ate, but it never happened; and (c) it will be like a thirsty person who dreams he had something to drink, but he never did. These are illustrations of how unreal the change will be for the Assyrians when God dramatically intervenes and prevents Assyria from defeating Jerusalem.[86] It will be astonishing and almost unbelievable for the Assyrians, who could just about taste and touch the riches of Jerusalem. Suddenly, they will come up empty handed and 185,000 of their troops dead (37:36–37). Certainly this was a marvelous promise of miraculous divine intervention to save Jerusalem and defeat Assyria. Having heard this promise, Isaiah's audience should now be willing to put their trust in God as they face the Assyrians in the coming days. Unfortunately, God has not chosen to always deliver his people so miraculously in the midst of their trials (Nebuchadnezzar destroyed Jerusalem in 586 BC); even today some of God's people are called on to lay down their lives for what they believe.

THE BLINDNESS OF PROPHETS AND PEOPLE (29:9–14)

⁹Be stunned and amazed,
blind yourselves and be sightless;

---

[83] Beuken, *Isaiah II*, 85, connects this clause to 29:6. Note that this brief sentence starts with וְהָיָה, "and it will be" (omitted in NIV), similar to the beginning of vv. 5a and 7a.

[84] A theophany reveals something of the awesome glory of God in visible form. When God appears people see fire, wind, and cloud (Ezek 1:4), thunder, roaring, shaking, and fire (1 Kgs 19:11; Ps 18:14; 83:16; Deut 5:22). One could view this coming of God as a negative visitation against Jerusalem (תִּפָּקֵד, "you will be visited/punished"), but that would fit better with 29:4. Verses 5–8 discuss God's judgment of Judah's enemies, so this is a negative visitation/intervention against the enemies ("it will be visited," a third feminine singular verb referring to the enemy army).

[85] Kaiser, *Isaiah 13–39*, 268, believes this attack and sudden intervention by God seemed like a dream to the people of Jerusalem.

[86] J. C. Exum, "Of Broken Pots, Fluttering Birds, and Visions in the Night: Extended Simile and Poetic Technique in Isaiah," *CBQ* 43 (1981): 346, concludes that the attack on Jerusalem (29:7) was like a bad dream for them and God's attack on the Assyrians (29:8) was like a bad dream for them.

be drunk, but not from wine,
    stagger, but not from beer.
[10]The LORD has brought over you a deep sleep:
    He has sealed your eyes (the prophets);
    he has covered your heads (the seers).

[11]For you this whole vision is nothing but words sealed in a scroll. And if you give the scroll to someone who can read, and say to him, "Read this, please," he will answer, "I can't; it is sealed." [12]Or if you give the scroll to someone who cannot read, and say, "Read this, please," he will answer, "I don't know how to read."

[13]The Lord says:

"These people come near to me with their mouth
    and honor me with their lips,
    but their hearts are far from me.
  Their worship of me
    is made up only of rules taught by men.
[14]Therefore once more I will astound these people
    with wonder upon wonder;
  the wisdom of the wise will perish,
    the intelligence of the intelligent will vanish."

This part of the woe oracle can be broken down into three parts.

The prophets and people are blind	29:9–14
The people are blind	9–10
God's word is sealed	11–12
Worship and wisdom will not help	13–14

This is the second paragraph of this woe oracle. It centers around the theme of blindness and an inability to understand God's instructions (vv. 9–12), to worship God (v. 13), or to act with intelligence (v. 14). In spite of the failure of the people of Jerusalem, God will perform a miraculous wonder on their behalf (v. 14), which is probably a reference to what he will do to their enemies (v. 5).

Although one would think that God's great promises of grace would engender responses of trust and praise in Jerusalem, the people of Judah acted like they were blind and deaf because they did not respond positively to God's promises. Consequently, God hardened their hearts and increased their blindness even deeper so that they would reap their just rewards. These themes show that this paragraph is connected to the historical and theological issues discussed in chap. 28 (blindness and drunkenness in 28:1,3,7 and 29:9; the inability to explain God's message in 28:9 and 29:11). By repeating these ideas, Isaiah emphasizes the nature and the depth of the problem of sin in Judah.

29:9–10 Beginning with another imperative verb (like the first paragraph in 29:1b), the prophet ironically calls his audience to "astonish yourselves," "blind yourselves,"[87] and be drunk. The two pairs of imperative verbs point to two parallel acts, though the syntax of this kind of construction implies that the second imperative in the pair describes the consequence of the first imperative verb.[88] This approach would yield the translation, "astonish yourself and consequently you will be amazed; blind yourself and consequently you will be blind." This shows how the choices people make will naturally pervert (though not because of wine) their understanding of God and his will for them. Those who do not want to understand God's way naturally create a slanted view of reality that prevents them from understanding correctly.

Once the people of Judah have chosen their own evil path (30:9), God will harden them by pouring out on them a "deep sleep" (*tārdēmâ*) so that they will be spiritually blind (cf. 6:9–10). They are fully responsible for their choices, but God will give them over to their own sinful desires (as in Rom 1:18–27). The reference to prophets and seers is unclear. Possibly, Isaiah is suggesting that the reason the people will be blind is because God will seal his truth from them by blinding the eyes of their prophets and seers who will no longer receive divine revelations from God (28:7; 30:10; Mic 3:5–7; Jer 23:9–40). This is a spiritual state that every person and every nation should avoid, for there is the danger that this free choice to rebel against God's revelation will inevitably lead to disastrous consequences without any choices in the future. There is always a connection between the harvest one reaps and the seeds that one plants (Gal 6:7–8).

29:11–12   The brief narrative illustration in these verses explains the people's inability to understand the meaning of what God says. It is unclear if this is an illustration the prophet used when he originally spoke this message or an illustration he added when he edited these texts. It should not be understood as a later reference to the people's refusal to read Isaiah's written prophecies in a literal scroll.[89] It is simply an illustration that makes a point that Isaiah's divine vision of the future (in these verses or in earlier messages) was not understood. Why is this so? The answer is simple. God's words to the prophet are "like" a closed ("sealed," *ḥatûm*) book that no one can read—for the readers were blind (29:9). The emphasis in the illustration should not be put on people's lack of education or inability to sound out Hebrew letters,[90] but on their inability to

---

[87] The verbs הִשְׁתַּעַשְׁעוּ and הִתְמַהְמְהוּ are *hithpa'el* reflexive forms, not passives as the NIV suggests in its translation.

[88] GKC §110f indicates the first imperative sets the "condition, while the second declares the consequence which the fulfillment of the condition will involve."

[89] Wildberger, *Isaiah 28–39*, 84, and many others commentators view 29:11–12 as a late post-exilic addition to Isaiah that was added when all of Isaiah's prophecies were collected together in a scroll. This whole approach fails to understand that this is merely an illustration (which is also missed in the NIV translation), for the prophet's vision is "like the words of [כְּדִבְרֵי] a sealed scroll."

[90] NIV "I don't know how to read" is lit. "I do not know/understand a scroll" (לֹא יָדַעְתִּי סֵפֶר).

read prophecies with understanding and appreciation. Oswalt concludes that these scribes had "the technical ability to understand God's word, but they lack the spiritual insight which would enable them to see the plain meaning."[91] Beuken interprets the two readers in 29:11–12 as being disinterested and not wanting to read what God has said in the prophetic scroll,[92] but the problem goes much deeper to the blindness of their hearts. The truth of God's word is sealed from their minds.

29:13–14 This woe ends with another divine explanation ("the Lord says") of why[93] these blind people are unwilling to listen to God (29:13) and what God will do about this ("therefore," *lākēn*, in 29:14). They are blind "because" (*ya'an kî*; omitted in NIV) "this people" (usually a negative title replacing "my people") come near to God during their temple worship with flowery words of external praise, but the real status of their heart's trust and love of God was very different. Childs calls this a "form of false piety . . . perfunctory and superficial. Judah is only going through the motions."[94] Worship was supposed to be a time of heart-felt praise and joy to be in God's presence (Ps 63:1–4; 71:22–24; 99:1–6), for God is pleased with a broken and contrite heart (57:15; Ps 34:18; 51:17). Such love and fear will naturally lead to a close trusting relationship with God. This was not what God saw in the people in Jerusalem. "Their fear, reverence"[95] of God actually was quite illusionary, for their outward signs of reverence only amounted to keeping a few commandments that the priests taught them and saying a few rote prayers (bow here, repeat this blessing there). This suggests that Hezekiah's reform movement did not bring real reformation in the hearts of many of the people in Judah.

Consequently (*lākēn* in 29:14), God will act again to cause a marvelous, astonishing, and wonderful thing to happen.[96] Although one would think that God would judge his people because of their stubborn sinfulness, God acts in a totally unexpected way on behalf of his people, right in the midst of their blindness and the punishing siege. The miraculous wonder is not identified in v. 14, but God may simply be referring back to his earlier promise to destroy the enemies that will surround Jerusalem when he comes in power (29:5–7).

---

[91] Oswalt, *Isaiah 1–39*, 532, believes that in some ways the modern church is in a similar situation.

[92] Beuken, *Isaiah II*, 96, takes both of the responses in vv. 11 and 12 as examples of indifference that demonstrate that these people do not want to know what God said.

[93] יַעַן כִּי means "because" (omitted in NIV). D. E. Gowan, "The Use of *ya'an* in Biblical Hebrew," *VT* 18 (1973): 49–83, demonstrates its common use in accusations to describe the reason God will judge someone.

[94] Childs, *Isaiah*, 218–29, views this as the "routine of following religious customs," a danger that every believer faces if he is not careful.

[95] יִרְאָתָם, "their fear," is not identical to NIV "worship," though the two ideas overlap because worship is an important way to demonstrate reverence for God.

[96] לְהַפְלִיא is an infinitive construct verb from פָּלָא, "he did wonders, miracles, astonishing things." This same root is used three times in this phrase—"I am going to do a wonder with this people, a miracle and a wonder."

This marvelous act of divine grace will confound the king's wise advisors who guided the king to make an alliance with Egypt in order to save Judah from Assyria (chaps. 30–31). They act contrary to the wise instructions of God. There will be no wisdom found in all the shrewd political scheming of the so-called "intelligentsia." In every era, God's ways are marvelous and totally beyond natural human reasoning, yet they are plainly explained for all to understand in his revelation. If people would only listen to what God says and trust him, the disastrous results of blindness could be avoided.

THEOLOGICAL IMPLICATIONS. This prophecy provides a brief glimpse at the astonishing ways of God. First, this message teaches the principle that no nation or place is too sacred that it cannot be destroyed, especially if it becomes defiled and its people reject God. God himself and a large enemy army attacked the holy city of Zion, that sacred place where God dwelt in his temple. Why would God bring this humiliation on Jerusalem or any other sacred place where he is worshiped? God would come against these people because (a) they had spiritually blinded themselves; (b) they did not understand God's words; and (c) they worshiped God hypocritically.

Second, people can become so deeply ingrained in their sinful thought patterns and actions that God will give them over to their sinful ways and harden their misunderstanding (cf. Rom 1). Sin can capture a person's mind and soul so tightly that a person acts like a senseless drunk who cannot see the truth right before his eyes.

Third—this truth is even more astonishing than the first two—God may choose to miraculously and powerfully intervene in history and marvelously deliver people who do not deserve his grace. Knowing this about God should produce trust and thanksgiving in the hearts of all people, for human wisdom cannot fathom his ways and certainly sinful people do not deserve his grace. All people can do is listen to his voice, stand in awe of his power, and follow in faith.

The problems that existed in Isaiah's day still persisted in the time of Jesus and continue until the present day. Far too many religious people only give God lip service and not their hearts (Mark 7:6–7). Though the humble heart has always been able to hear God's voice in the words of his prophets, his truth is often hidden from the wise and proud people of this world (Matt 11:25; 1 Cor 1:18–25). The eyes of faith on the attentive person open the door to the possibility of understanding God, but the blind person who will not attend to God is hopelessly destined to self-destruction.

(3) Third Woe: A Reversal for the Rebellious (29:15–24)

> [15]Woe to those who go to great depths
>   to hide their plans from the LORD,
>   who do their work in darkness and think,
>   "Who sees us? Who will know?"

[16]You turn things upside down,
>as if the potter were thought to be like the clay!
>Shall what is formed say to him who formed it,
>>"He did not make me"?
>Can the pot say of the potter,
>>"He knows nothing"?

[17]In a very short time, will not Lebanon be turned into a fertile field
>and the fertile field seem like a forest?
[18]In that day the deaf will hear the words of the scroll,
>and out of gloom and darkness
>the eyes of the blind will see.
[19]Once more the humble will rejoice in the LORD;
>the needy will rejoice in the Holy One of Israel.
[20]The ruthless will vanish,
>the mockers will disappear,
>and all who have an eye for evil will be cut down—
[21]those who with a word make a man out to be guilty,
>who ensnare the defender in court
>and with false testimony deprive the innocent of justice.

[22]Therefore this is what the LORD, who redeemed Abraham, says to the house of Jacob:

>"No longer will Jacob be ashamed;
>>no longer will their faces grow pale.
[23]When they see among them their children,
>>the work of my hands,
>they will keep my name holy;
>>they will acknowledge the holiness of the Holy One of Jacob,
>>and will stand in awe of the God of Israel.
[24]Those who are wayward in spirit will gain understanding;
>>those who complain will accept instruction."

The new "woe" in v. 15 introduces a new speech in the middle of this chapter.[97] The date of this woe oracle must be implied from various hints made in the prophecy: (a) in the future the ruthless people who are now a problem will be gone (29:20); (b) at the present time, someone is making inappropriate plans that they are trying to hide from God (29:15); (c) the idea that the deaf will hear and the blind will see (29:18–19) connects this woe to the time of the deaf and blind in the preceding woe oracle (29:9–10); and (d) a series of similar terms are used in both the anti-Assyrian oracles in 10:5–34 and 29:15–24.[98] J.

---

[97] Some do not see this as a major literary break. Sweeney, *Isaiah 1–39*, 374, does not treat 29:15–24 as a separate woe oracle, while Clements, *Isaiah 1–39,* 237–40, treats vv. 9–10, 13–14, and 15–16 as three short independent sayings that go together, so the bigger break comes in v. 17 with the announcement of the coming kingdom of God.

[98] W. A. M. Beuken, "Isa 29,15–24: Perversion Reverted," in *The Scriptures and the Scrolls: Studies in Honor of A. S. van der Woude on the occasion of his 65th Birthday* (ed. F. C. Martinez, A. Hilhorst, C. J. Labuschagne; Leiden: Brill, 1992), 54, finds six verbal connections between

Blenkinsopp fits these pieces together by viewing this passage as an attack on
the secret plans of Hezekiah's wise politicians who were making an alliance
with Egypt (30:1–2) in order to withstand the invading Assyrian army.[99] The
prophet rejects the plans of those who do not consult God, do not treat the poor
with justice, do not fear God, and do not trust in his promised deliverance from
the ruthless Assyrians.

The structure of the paragraph is designed around the initial "woe" in v. 15,
the question in v. 17, and the "therefore" clause in v. 22.[100]

A lamenting woe	29:15–16
Transformation of the land, the deaf, the blind	29:17–21
Spiritual revival of the wise who do not honor God	29:22–24

Everything is presently turned upside down with people thinking that they
can hide something from God (v. 15) and with the clay questioning and critiqu-
ing the potter (v. 16). God's plan upsets this mixed-up world. The problem of
disrespect for God (v. 15–16) is resolved when the blind begin to see (v. 18)
and when rebellious people revere God and accept his instruction (22–24).

29:15–16   In this woe the prophet laments the making of secret plans that
the wise men try to hide from God. That is, these royal counselors make their
plans in the dark without consulting God, the master planner who has devised
plans for all the nations on the earth (14:24–27) and gives wonderfully wise
counsel (28:29). These wise planners must be the advisors of King Hezekiah
who concluded that a political alliance with Egypt could save them from the
Assyrian invasion by Sennacherib (30:1–2). God has already revealed his plans
that (a) he will crush Assyria in his own land (14:29); (b) he has decided to turn
the hordes that were besieging Jerusalem into fine dust (29:5–6); and (c) he
would eventually bring the Assyrians into his worshiping community (19:23–
25). Therefore, the human planning by the wise men in Judah was worthless.
The prophet Isaiah laments the political plans of the leaders because they ignore
what God has promised in his plans. Instead, they did the opposite of what God
wanted (they were to trust God) and hid their secret plans from God. Their depravity separated them from God. They were apparently thinking[101] that God
would not see or notice what they were doing (cf. Job 22:12–14; Ps 64:5–6;
94:7; Ezek 8:12). They apparently did not realize that it is completely impossible to hide from God (Ps 139:7–12). Childs bluntly claims, "Their stupidity

---

10:5–34 and 29:15–24 that support his idea that this prophecy is against Assyria. E.g., it appears
that 29:17 will reverse 10:34, while both have the phrase "in a little while."

[99] J. Blenkinsopp, *Isaiah 1–39* (New York: Doubleday, 2000), 408; but Wildberger, *Isaiah
28–39*, 96, 108, dates only 29:15–16 to the time of Hezekiah. He finds a strong eschatological
emphasis in vv. 17–24 and disconnects it with the rest of the chapter. Instead, he finds a connection
between 29:17 and 32:15; between 29:17 and 32:15; and between 29:17 and 35:2; 41:19; 51:3.

[100] Each subparagraph has a כִּי clause in the middle of the paragraph (vv. 16b,20,23).

[101] וַיֹּאמְרוּ, "and they said," probably refers to what "they thought" in their minds.

lies in thinking that their plans were unnoticed by God."[102] All the descriptions of their devious actions point to an attempt to manipulate their political situation to their advantage, even though they had heard from the prophet Isaiah that it was unnecessary.

The next verse explains how God views their action. The first word in 29:16 is a noun, "your perversity,"[103] which should be translated as an exclamation. NIV expresses this exclamation in the verbal clause "you turn things upside down!" Their perverse, upside-down way of thinking is illustrated in their confused way of viewing the relationship between the potter and the clay. Should the potter be thought of in the same way as the clay?[104] The answer to this rhetorical question is obvious, yet some people in Judah hold them to be equals. Should the object made out of clay deny the work or wisdom of the one who formed it? The point is that since God formed man out of clay (Gen 2:7; Job 10:9; 33:6), it makes no sense for clay people to deny that they were created creatures, or to say that God did not know what he is doing when he put his wise plans together. Certainly Isaiah's audience would have to agree with this logical example, though they might not think they were acting in a perverse way. Would politicians dare to suggest that they are as smart as God or that God does not know what he is doing (29:15)? God is the magnificent Creator, who in his infinite wisdom put the human body together and gave man a soul (Gen 2:7). He gave men their wisdom, he providentially controls what he created, and he is the foundation of all moral order. The other depraved kind of thinking is the height of arrogance, and it demonstrates that these men lacked true wisdom.

29:17–21 The prophet's message counters the fears that drive the king's advisors to make their secret plans with Egypt. There is no need to fear the Assyrians, for God has promised that in a short time the present situation will be dramatically reversed. Though the definition of a "short time" (*mĕ'aṭ mizʿār*) is not provided, the term is used elsewhere in regard to the approaching demise of the Assyrians (10:25 and 26:20), so the repetition of that unique idea should have reminded the audience of those prophecies.[105] The initial phrase in v. 17 is a question that implies a positive answer,[106] so it provides assurance to the listener that God will act soon.

---

[102] Childs, *Isaiah*, 219, believes this is a polemic against the political leaders of Judah.

[103] הַפְכְּכֶם—the noun means "overturn, pervert" and the suffix כֶם means "your." GKC §147c classifies this as an exclamation that lacks a verb owing to the excitement of the speaker. Beuken, *Isaiah II*, 102, rejects the Qumran reading הֹפֵךְ מֹכֶם and interprets this as an exclamation, translating it like the NIV. An exclamation, "Oh, your perversity!" might be even better.

[104] אִם introduces a question (GKC §150f), and the *niph'al* passive imperfect verb, "should be thought of," in a question should be translated as a subjunctive.

[105] Beuken, *Isaiah II*, 118, lists six similarities between 10:5–25 and 29:15–24 and concludes that this would have informed his audience that he was talking about Assyria.

[106] Questions that begin with הֲלֹא, "is it not," imply the positive idea, "surely it is" (GKC §150e).

At some future day that God chooses (probably eschatological) he will "transform, turn back" (*šāb* is an active verb, not a passive as in NIV) nature by making Lebanon a garden (cf. 32:15), transforming Carmel so that it "will be regarded, thought of"[107] in a totally new way. Other prophecies refer to the destruction of the tall trees of Lebanon (10:33–34; 33:9),[108] but at some later point God will bless that land with great fertility. God will also transform the spiritually deaf people, who would not listen to his word (6:9–10; 28:12; 29:9–12; 30:9), into those who will listen and obey God (32:3; 35:5). Then the blind will see what God is doing and not be in hopeless darkness (29:18), reversing the condition described in 29:9. Then they will be wise and not need to hide anything from God.

Verses 19–21 predict a spiritual renewal that will impact the social relationships between the strong and the weak. This spiritual transformation pictures the humble and needy rejoicing and praising God. These pious people who trust God will be overjoyed to experience the salvation their Holy God provides (29:19). Holiness will not be a forgotten concept and God's holiness will be honored. Therefore, people's behavior will change and the oppression of the strong tyrants and scoffers will end. Wicked judges and false witnesses, who accuse the innocent at court, will cease to exist (29:20–21). Justice will reign supreme in the courts. This will be a new day, for the old moral standards in Judah will no longer be followed. People will rejoice in what God has done to spiritually transform the moral behavior of the nation and this will bring about a dramatic change from conditions in Isaiah's day.

29:22–24 The logical consequences of God's transformation of Judah is the creation of a new people of Israel. Since the Genesis story never refers to the patriarch Abraham being "redeemed" (*pādâ*), some (a) assume that this "redeeming" refers to God calling him from Ur (as Israel was called and redeemed from Egypt); or (b) generalize the meaning of "redeemed" into God "cared" for Abraham throughout his lifetime.[109] But if the patriarch Jacob can serve as a symbol to refer to the Israelite people in the second line, why is it not possible for the name Abraham to have the same basic symbolic meaning

---

[107] The use of the exact same passive verb יֵחָשֵׁב ("regard, think") in vv. 16 and 17 may imply that when this change takes place there will also be a reversal in the way people "regard, think" about the one who formed them.

[108] In 10:17–18, 33–34; 37:24 the destruction of Assyria is compared to the destruction of the trees of Lebanon. This passage could be seen as a reference to God's transformation of nature, rather than the Assyrians. Beuken, *Isaiah II*, 119, takes Lebanon "as a symbol for those who oppose YHWH in their arrogance . . . who have raised themselves up in their pride against YHWH."

[109] The Hb. text is difficult and literally reads, "the LORD says to the house of Jacob who redeemed Abraham," which seems an impossible idea. Blenkinsopp, *Isaiah 1–39*, 410, prefers the idea that God delivered Abram from Ur or from the idols of Ur (*Apocalypse of Abraham*, chap. 8), while Childs, *Isaiah*, 220, considers this "a loose paraphrase for God's constant concern for Abraham."

in this line?[110] Then the idea of redeeming his people (the seed of Abraham) makes complete sense.

The result of God's transformation of his people will be (a) the people will never be shamefully defeated by their enemies after refusing to trust God (29:22b); (b) their children will live holy lives dedicated to God (thereby acknowledging God's holiness); and (c) people will sanctify God's name by glorifying him, and will show reverence toward God (29:23, cf. 8:13). These changes will happen because the sinful people who were leading people astray[111] and complaining about God's treatment of Judah will gain a new understanding of who God is. Consequently, they will learn/accept his teachings and gain wisdom from God (29:24). This divine transformation will be complete, changing nature (the fields will be fertile, 29:17), social relationships (oppression will end, 29:20), and people's relationship to God (people will rejoice in the Lord, 29:19). These changes demonstrate the practical significance of having a vibrant theological and personal relationship with God. God is the potter whose plans determine what will happen to the clay. As clay, people can choose to trust the Holy Potter and follow his instructions or reject God's plans. Those who humbly submit to God and accept his wisdom will one day enjoy the pleasures of a transformed world that God has planned for them.

THEOLOGICAL IMPLICATIONS.   There are two ways to face a difficult situation like the Assyrian attack on Jerusalem. On the one hand, people can develop their own hidden agenda, pretend that God does not know what is happening, and plan to do things that are contrary to God's promises (29:15–16). This is a lamentable approach, for it assumes that God does not know what is best and that people do not need to fit into God's plans. These kinds of people arrogantly act like God does not know anything and behave like they are not required to follow God's instructions. They rule their own lives and attempt to take on the role of God; so God's desires become irrelevant and his ways are ignored. It is sad, but far too many religious people arrogantly follow this approach even today. People in positions of power in government, the church, the denomination, or in business are especially prone to be deceived into thinking that they are in control and that they know best. They may talk piously but their actions clearly demonstrate they have no regard for God and no respect for other believers who have received some direction about the will of God. God knows the people who act this way, and most Christians can spot their arrogance very quickly too.

On the other hand, some people humbly accept the principle that God is in charge of this world and that they cannot fix the evils of this world through

---

[110] Childs, *Isaiah*, 220, believes the mention of both Abraham and Jacob "serves to emphasize the unity of the one people of God," showing that even the drunkards of Ephraim in 28:1 will be restored.

[111] עֹתֵי is a *qal* active participle (masculine plural construct) from תָּעָה, which means "to lead astray" (3:12; 9:15; 28:7), and it probably has a durative sense here.

their own efforts. They believe they can trust God to transform the desolation of this world into fertility, to change the darkness that comes from blindness into light, and to end the unjust oppression of others (29:17–21). These people have hope and their different view of life is seen in the way they rejoice in God, the way they treat God as holy, and the reverent way they stand before him (29:19,23). No shame faces these people, for they allow God to transform their thinking and they accept his divine plans for their lives (29:22,24). This requires complete trust in God and great personal humility. People in every generation have to choose the path they will follow.

2. Disgrace from Trusting Egypt; Redemption of Zion (30:1–33:24)

This group of three oracles (chaps. 30–33) explains how the principles identified in 28:1–29:24 directly apply to the political conflicts involving Judah, Egypt, and Assyria around 704–701 BC.[112] Judah's political alliance with Egypt was a mistake that illustrates a lack of wisdom, trust, and good decision-making by Judah's leaders (30:1–5; 31:1–3). The leaders of Judah did not honor God (30:1; 31:1), but rejected God's instruction (30:9–11). Consequently, God's judgment will make Egypt's help utterly worthless (30:7; 31:3) and God will rise up against his own wicked people (30:2). The leaders of Judah need to trust God, for he will defeat Assyria (31:31; 32:8) and deliver Jerusalem (31:7). At some point in the future God will open his people's eyes (30:20; 31:6; 32:3) and cause them to reject idols (30:22; 31:7). Then the people will not make foolish and unwise decisions (32:4–8; 33:8), complacency will disappear (32:9–14), righteousness and security will exist (32:15–20; 33:5–6,15–16), people will praise their king from their hearts (30:29; 33:10,20–22), and trust God (30:15).

In this section, Isaiah has three woe oracles in chaps. 30, 31, and 33, but chap. 32 does not begin with a "woe"—it is a continuation of the second woe. Each woe oracle begins with a formal woe and each offers hope for the future when God transforms this world and implements his plans. In 32:1–8 Isaiah reminds the audience that when God transforms the world and opens the eyes of the blind (32:3), a righteous king will reign on the earth, probably an echo of an earlier messianic prophecy in 9:1–7.

---

[112] For a broad overview of the setting, genre, and structure of chaps. 28–35, see pages 467–73 above. Although most commentaries connect these events to 701 BC (eg. Young, *Isaiah*, II:335, or Goldingay, *Isaiah*, 165), Wildberger, *Isaiah 28–39*, 123, prefers to date these events along with chaps. 18–20 to 713–711 BC when Assyria put down the rebellion of Ashdod. Watts, *Isaiah 1–33*, 395, prefers a date in the reign of Josiah, while Hayes and Irvine, *Isaiah*, 337, connect chap. 30 to Hoshea's (the king of Israel) attempts to survive an Assyrian attack around 726–721 BC (1 Kgs 17:1–4). J. K. Hoffmeier, "Egypt's Role in the Events of 701 B.C. in Jerusalem," in *Jerusalem in Bible and Archaeology: The First Temple Period* (ed. A. G. Vaughn and A. E. Killebrew; Leiden: Brill, 2003), 219–34, also follows this approach.

(1) First Woe, to Those Who Trust Egypt (30:1–33)

The first woe is structured into three paragraphs:

Woe, do not trust worthless Egypt	30:1–17
God's future grace will transform Judah	30:18–26
God's plan to destroy Assyria	30:27–33

These messages are very different and their unity is not obvious because some paragraphs lament the nation's disobedience (30:1–17) and others paradoxically promise hope because of God's grace (30:18–26). These two rather contradictory themes come together in the historical circumstances of the Assyrian attack on Jerusalem around 701 BC. God condemns the people of Judah for not trusting him and instead leaning on Egypt, but he also promises in his grace to defeat the Assyrians (30:31). Such contradictory acts of God are possible because God is gracious and will lead his people to repent and rest in him for salvation (30:15). Then he will eventually transform their sinful world (30:23–26).

The story traces the lives of those who were initially condemned for not listening to God's plan (30:1,9) because they have rejected the message of God (30:12). These stubborn people will hear God speak to them again in the future when he will help them in their time of severe trouble (30:21). Then they will respond to him, for they will also see his majestic arm (30:30) defeat Assyria (30:31). The leaders who reject God's plan prefer to depend on the horses of Egypt (30:1–2,16), which is a deceitful hope (30:12) that will result in great shame (30:3,5). Although God is angry with his people and will punish them (30:1–14), his wrath will destroy Assyria (30:27–33) and then the people will weep no more (30:19). These promises (30:23–26) are legitimated by the transforming power of God. If God can and will do these things in the future, the people of Judah should be persuaded to repent and rest in his grace now (30:15,18), for he is worthy of their trust in the midst of this Assyrian crisis.

This woe oracle picks up numerous themes that were introduced in earlier chapters: (a) the flood as an image of punishment in 30:30 was used earlier in 8:7; 17:12–13; 28:2,17; (b) the rejection of the prophet's words in 30:9–12 is also found in 1:10; 5:24; 28:9–10; and (c) the need to rest in God in 30:15 is picking up a theme that was important in 11:10; 14:3; 28:12; 32:17.[113]

WOE AGAINST TRUSTING WORTHLESS EGYPT (30:1–17)

> [1]"Woe to the obstinate children,"
> declares the LORD,

---

[113] Motyer, *The Prophecy of Isaiah*, 244, deals with these and other common themes (false security, hope, the Assyrian threat, and God's wrath).

"to those who carry out plans that are not mine,
  forming an alliance, but not by my Spirit,
  heaping sin upon sin;
²who go down to Egypt
  without consulting me;
who look for help to Pharaoh's protection,
  to Egypt's shade for refuge.
³But Pharaoh's protection will be to your shame,
  Egypt's shade will bring you disgrace.
⁴Though they have officials in Zoan
  and their envoys have arrived in Hanes,
⁵everyone will be put to shame
  because of a people useless to them,
who bring neither help nor advantage,
  but only shame and disgrace."

⁶An oracle concerning the animals of the Negev:

Through a land of hardship and distress,
  of lions and lionesses,
  of adders and darting snakes,
the envoys carry their riches on donkeys' backs,
  their treasures on the humps of camels,
to that unprofitable nation,
⁷to Egypt, whose help is utterly useless.
Therefore I call her
  Rahab the Do-Nothing.

⁸Go now, write it on a tablet for them,
  inscribe it on a scroll,
that for the days to come
  it may be an everlasting witness.
⁹These are rebellious people, deceitful children,
  children unwilling to listen to the LORD's instruction.
¹⁰They say to the seers,
  "See no more visions!"
and to the prophets,
  "Give us no more visions of what is right!
Tell us pleasant things,
  prophesy illusions.
¹¹Leave this way,
  get off this path,
and stop confronting us
  with the Holy One of Israel!"

¹²Therefore, this is what the Holy One of Israel says:

"Because you have rejected this message,
  relied on oppression
  and depended on deceit,

¹³this sin will become for you
    like a high wall, cracked and bulging,
    that collapses suddenly, in an instant.
¹⁴It will break in pieces like pottery,
    shattered so mercilessly
that among its pieces not a fragment will be found
    for taking coals from a hearth
    or scooping water out of a cistern."

¹⁵This is what the Sovereign LORD, the Holy One of Israel, says:

"In repentance and rest is your salvation,
    in quietness and trust is your strength,
    but you would have none of it.
¹⁶You said, 'No, we will flee on horses.'
    Therefore you will flee!
You said, 'We will ride off on swift horses.'
    Therefore your pursuers will be swift!
¹⁷A thousand will flee
    at the threat of one;
at the threat of five
    you will all flee away,
till you are left
    like a flagstaff on a mountaintop,
    like a banner on a hill."

The first subparagraph of the first woe oracle includes:

A woe oracle against Judah for trusting Egypt	30:1–7
Woe, going to Egypt is not God's plan	1–2
Shame will come from Egypt	3–5
Sending an envoy to Egypt is useless	6–7
Rejecting God's word will result in defeat	30:8–17
Rejection of critical words from God	8–11
Rejection will result in collapse	12–14
Rejecting repentance, for fleeing horses	15–17[114]

These paragraphs are held together by the repeated description of the people of Judah as obstinate and rebellious (30:1,9), their unwillingness to follow God's plan/word/vision (30:1,10,12), the deceitful decision of depending on Egyptian military might (30:2–3,16), and even word plays ("obstinate" in 30:1 and "leave" in 30:11).[115]

---

[114] Oswalt, *Isaiah 1–39*, 556–57, ends this paragraph after 30:18, taking the "therefore" clause that begins 30:18 as the conclusion to this paragraph. The poetic form of v. 18 also argues that it should be included with vv. 1–18, not the narrative style that follows in vv. 19–26. Nevertheless, the positive tone of v. 18 argues that it fits in the next paragraph.

[115] W. A. M. Beuken, "Isaiah 30: A Prophetic Oracle," in *Writing and Reading the Scroll of Isaiah: Studies in Interpretive Tradition*, VTSupp (ed. C. C. Broyles and C. A. Evans; Leiden: Brill,

It is surprising that Isaiah does not specifically condemn King Hezekiah for this unfaithful political dependence on Egypt. He speaks against the "scoffers who rule this people in Jerusalem" and make a covenant with Egypt (28:14), the wise men who counsel the king (29:14), those who hide their plans from God (29:15), and those obstinate ones who make plans without consulting God (30:1), but no specific mention is made of the king.[116] This raises the question: Is Isaiah addressing the politicians in order to condemn what the nation's leaders are doing, or is he primarily addressing the public in order to castigate the dominant position that won the palace political arguments? Since Hezekiah allowed envoys to go to Egypt, he carries responsibility, yet the prophet's failure to condemn Hezekiah (in contrast to Ahaz in chap. 7 and Hezekiah in chap. 39) may indicate that he was not the driving force or a strong proponent of this policy. Later Hezekiah supports another alternative and trusts God rather than Assyria (chaps. 36–37).

30:1–2 The prophet announces God's lamenting woe over the rebellious attitude that caused his covenant children to act independently and contrary to his plans. Children should be obedient and act in ways consistent with their covenant instructions, but God's children demonstrated their disrespect for him "by making a plan"[117] that had no connection to God's will. They already had an alliance with God and needed to follow God's plan, but at this time they broke their covenant agreement and attempted to make another alliance with Egypt. When they poured out a libation offering[118] to confirm their treaty with Egypt, they never stopped to see if this is the will of God's Spirit. They did not pay attention to the warning from past experiences where obstinate acts of rebellion against their covenant agreement, taken without consulting God, brought failure (8:19; Josh 9:14; 1 Chr 10:14).[119] This independent action resulted[120] in "adding/heaping"[121] sin on top of sin (cf. Amos 4:4). In contrast

---

1997), 369–97, identifies a word play between סוֹרְרִים, the noun "obstinate" and סוּרוּ, the verb "leave," for those who leave God's ways are stubborn or obstinate.

[116] Seitz, *Isaiah 1–39*, 215–20, also struggles with the significance of no reference to King Hezekiah.

[117] The infinitive construct לַעֲשׂוֹת, "to make," functions not as a participle (as NIV "those who carry out"), but to describe the manner of rebellion. Thus the clause has an adverbial function: "by making a plan" (GKC §114f,o).

[118] The second infinitive construct in the phrase "forming an alliance" in NIV is לִנְסֹךְ מַסֵּכָה, lit. "by pouring out a drink offering," interpreting this as the root נָסַךְ, "he poured out." Oswalt, *Isaiah 1–39*, 545, derives this word from סָכַךְ and translates "weave a web."

[119] Going down to Egypt was not inherently wrong if it was part of the plan of God. In Gen 46:1–4 it was God's plan for Jacob to go down to Egypt where Joseph could supply his family with food.

[120] לְמַעַן can express the purpose of an action (NASB "in order to"), which would be a rather sarcastic accusation (Oswalt, *Isaiah 1–39*, 542), or to express results "so that" ("and therefore" in Wildberger, *Isaiah 28–39*, 119).

[121] The word סְפוֹת appears to be an infinitive construct from יָסַף, "he added," though the form appears to follow the paradigm of a ל"ה verb, suggesting the existence of the root סָפָה (GKC §69h, note 1).

to this approach, Oswalt suggests that "the whole basis of the life of faith is summed up in Jesus' words in the garden of Gethsemane, 'Not my will, but thine be done' (Mark 14:36)."[122]

The nature of this plan is clarified in v. 2, for these sons went to Egypt to find refuge and protection in the armies of Pharaoh without asking God for advice on the matter. Three sources of divine wisdom were available for these officials, if they would have bothered to ask. First, they could look to past revelation to see if God supported making political alliances with other nations. A few years earlier when the northern nation of Israel was in political trouble, Hosea condemned their leaders for trying to make alliances with Assyria and Egypt (Hos 5:13; 7:8,11; 8:10; 9:3; 12:1), and Isaiah himself warned Ahaz about the terrible consequences of trusting in Assyria during the Syro-Ehraimite War (7:1–8:15). A second resource would be to go to a priest and have him inquire of God through the Urim and Thummim as the nation did on earlier occasions when it went to war (Num 27:21; Judg 1:1; 20:23). A third source of information would be a prophetic word from God. All of these were rejected (30:9–11) or ignored, so instead of going to God in order to[123] find "refuge" (*mā'ôz*; cf. Ps 27:1; 28:8; 37:40; 90:1) or "shelter" (*ṣēl*; cf. Ruth 2:12; Ps 17:8; 57:1; 91:1), they trusted in Egypt for protection (30:2b).

30:3–5 The prophet describes how worthless this plan was and warns the leaders of Judah that it would bring great embarrassment to the nation. The prophet confronts and condemns this senseless choice because trusting in Egypt for refuge or shelter will only bring greater shame (used three times in vv. 3–5) and disgrace. All their plans will go awry and Judah will be humiliated instead of helped. Though[124] some Hebrew officials[125] were already in the delta city of Zoan (probably Tanis), which was the capital of the Nubian/Ethiopian Pharaoh Shabako, others "will arrive"[126] (not "have arrived" as in NIV) in Hanes (only mentioned here in the Old Testament).[127] Judah's shame[128] is connected to the Egypt's uselessness, who gave no help and provided no profit

---

[122] Oswalt, *Isaiah 1–39*, 545.

[123] The two infinitive constructs לַחְסוֹת, "in order to seek shelter," and לָעוֹז, "in order to take refuge," are used to show the purpose for this action (GKC §114f).

[124] כִּי should probably be translated "though" in a concessive sense (GKC §160b) or conditionally "if" when with a perfect verb (GKC §159aa).

[125] Although it is possible to view "his princes" to be Egyptians, since Pharaoh and Egypt are the antecedents in 29:3 (as Beuken, *Isaiah II*, 134, 154, maintains), Wildberger, *Isaiah 28–39*, 127, argues that "its princes" refers to princes from Judah, for the Egyptian princes were already in Egypt and did not have to arrive in Hanes.

[126] יַגִּיעוּ, "they will arrive, are arriving," is a *hiphil* imperfect from נגע, which describes incomplete action.

[127] Wildberger, *Isaiah 28–39*, 127, thinks Hanes is Herakleopolis, a Nile delta city, though others suggest that Hanes was south of the delta.

[128] The *Kethib* הבאיש ("he made stink") is likely a mistaken scribal writing of הביש ("he put to shame"), which is what is read in the *Qere* form of the text. 1QIsaᵃ had trouble with this odd word and ended up with באש, "with fire."

or advantage to Judah. This crutch will not assist in the defense of Judah in dire times (cf. 36:6; 2 Kgs 19:9), for they will not be willing to stand up to the Assyrians to defend Judah. Isaiah's warning was absolutely clear. Their action opposed God's will of God and would lead to utter failure.

30:6–7 This brief burdensome oracle (*maśśāʾ*) reminds one of the long series of similar burdensome messages in chaps. 13–23, but in this context a discussion of the dangerous animals in the southern desert between Judah and Egypt serves as a warning to the envoys that were traveling from Judah to Egypt. The connection between vv. 1–5 and 6–7 is that both describe people going to Egypt to form a useless alliance that will not help Judah.[129] This diplomatic effort is doomed because (a) the road to Egypt is dangerous with lions[130] and snakes (30:6a; see Num 21:4–9); (b) it will be very expensive for Judah to bribe Egypt to defend it from Assyria (30:6b); (c) Egypt cannot/will not help[131] Judah and will be a worthless ally (30:6c–7a); and (d) God declares Egypt will do nothing (30:7b). This final clause uses the name Rahab (51:9; Job 9:13; 26:12; Ps 87:4; 89:11), the great sea monster from ancient Near Eastern legends, as a symbol for Egypt.[132] The final cryptic clause, "Rahab the Do-Nothing" (NIV), interprets "Do-Nothing" as a sarcastic name for this supposedly powerful monster. Beuken prefers to interpret this as Rahab "who sits still," meaning that Egypt will not come to assist Judah in her conflict with Assyria.[133] Another possible translation is Rahab the dead one.[134] All these warnings argue for a policy that does not depend on Egypt. It makes no sense to trust in a political policy that is sure to fail. It is futile to follow a plan that God opposes.

---

[129] Childs, *Isaiah*, 224, notes the connecting devices "therefore" connecting vv. 11 and 12, "be gracious" in 18 and 19, plus "Holy One of Israel" in 11,12,15.

[130] "Lions and lionesses" in NIV skips over the Hb. word מֵהֶם, "from them," which Oswalt, *Isaiah 1–39*, 542, and Wildberger, *Isaiah 28–39*, 131, emend to נֹגֵ, "growling," which gives a parallel to "flying/darting snakes." The other option is to leave the text as it is and translate it, "lions and lioness (are) from there/belong there," which is the option taken by Beuken, *Isaiah II*, 135.

[131] NIV "to that unprofitable nation" translates עַל־עַם לֹא יוֹעִילוּ "unto a nation that cannot/will not help." The imperfect verb can be understood in a modal sense ("can"—as in GKC §10m,r) or as an indicative ("will"—as in GKC §107i).

[132] J. N. Oswalt, "The Myth of the Dragon and the Old Testament Faith," *EvQ* 49 (1977): 163–72, discusses the use of ideas within the popular culture as illustrations that helped the listeners understand the point being made, even though the biblical writer did not believe the story was true. Similarly, one can use an event in an untrue popular movie or an idea out of Cinderella to illustrate a point today.

[133] Beuken, *Isaiah II*, 156 points to Egypt's inertia; she will just sit back and do nothing to help Judah.

[134] The text is problematic, for in the clause רַהַב הֵם שָׁבֶת the function of הֵם, "they," is unclear. W. H. Irwin, *Isaiah 28–33, Translation with Philological Notes* (Rome: Biblical Institute, 1977), 77, suggests that it is a shortened form of הָמוֹן, "roaring." The root שָׁבֶת could come from "sit" (from יָשַׁב) or "cease" (from שָׁבַת). Literally, the text could be saying, "Rahab, they (are) sitting," which means the Egyptians (symbolized as Rahab) are sitting down and doing nothing to help Judah. An alternative that is more attractive is the Egyptians (symbolized as Rahab) have ceased, implying that Egypt as a military power is dead.

30:8–11 The second part of this paragraph is marked by an imperative command for the prophet to write a message on a tablet and in a scroll (cf. 8:1,16 or Deut 31:16–29) to provide both public and private documentation[135] of what God says about future events. If Isaiah would write down what God said before the event, people would know that God's words are true if the actual events matched the predictions. Isaiah's credibility as a messenger of God is certain and his prophecies will be confirmed. The length and content of the message is unknown, though based on the analogy in 8:1–4 one would assume that the message was relatively short and concerned events related to the Assyrian attack on Judah. Hayes and Irvine think the message was the name given to Rahab at the end of 30:7, Oswalt favors the idea that major portions of chaps. 28–32 were on this scroll, while Childs thinks the message contained the following prophecy of judgment in 30:9–16.[136] A public tablet by necessity would need a short message, but the scroll could be much longer and detailed, so a combination of the approaches above would satisfy both the need for widespread knowledge (on the public tablet) and detailed verifiable information (on the scroll).

In 30:9–11 God warns the prophet that his audience is "obstinate" (cf. 30:1). They are stubborn because they "rebel" (*měrî*; cf. 1:19–20) by refusing to listen (cf. Ezek 3:7); they purposely choose not to follow the instructions of God in past revelation (in the *tôrâ* and from the mouth of the prophet). This attitude of rebellion characterized the nation during the wilderness journey (Num 17:25; 27:14; the rebellious son in Deut 21:18–20) until Isaiah's time and beyond (Ezek 3). They also practiced "deceitfulness, unfaithfulness" (*kĕḥāšîm*) implying that they were untruthful and inconsistent in their relationship to God (matching 29:12; 59:13).

To legitimate this charge the prophet quotes what his audience is thinking, though they would probably never be so bold as to actually say this (30:10–11, as in 29:15). They reject, even prohibit,[137] those who declare God's will about what is right and wrong from announcing their visions. Instead they desire to hear "pleasant things" and "illusions,"[138] even though they may not be true. There is irony in the prophet's characterization of their wishes, but what it all boils down to is that these people are in effect demanding to be deceived by

---

[135] לָעַד, "forever," is redundant because it is followed by the same word. But if one vowel is changed to give the reading לְעֵד, the text reads "as a witness," and the redundancy is removed.

[136] Hayes and Irvine, *Isaiah*, 340, conclude that the message predicts that Egypt (Rahab) would sit and not act to defend Judah; Oswalt, *Isaiah 1–39*, 551, argues that "a rather complete record would be needed so that future readers could understand the meaning of the witness." Childs, *Isaiah*, 226, claims that "the antecedent thus relates in a more general way to the following prophecies of impending judgment."

[137] The negative prohibition is syntactically expressed as a strong prohibition לֹא תִרְאוּ, "you shall not see visions" (GKC §107o; 109c).

[138] חֲלָקוֹת refers to a "smooth, slippery" stone in a river (57:6), or the slippery words of a person's mouth (Ps 12:3; Prov 5:3). מַהֲתַלּוֹת comes from the root תָּלַל, which conveys the idea of "deceive, mock" (1 Kgs 18:27).

false assurances. This desire to optimistically believe that the love and grace of God will somehow make everything work out well in the end is still a false hope that many church attendees rely on today, even though their daily walk demonstrates that they have little interest in following the instructions in God's Word. Although positive messages of hope are much more encouraging and enjoyable to hear, the truth should always be valued above a deceptive lie that lulls one to sleep. These people rejected God's "path" (*derek*) and do not want the true prophets to talk about the "Holy One of Israel" (30:11). The Holy God requires righteous behavior, holy living, obedience to his instructions, and trust in his deliverance, but Isaiah's audience just did not want to be reminded of these things. In many ways things are not much better than in the days of Isaiah. People still want to follow their own plans, not God's.

30:12–14 The beginning of the next unit of thought is marked by the introductory "therefore" (*lākēn*) and the announcement of a new word from the Holy God Judah did not want to hear from. Verse 12 repeats the reason for God's judgment, while vv. 13–14 describe the consequences of the people's sins. The people's rejection of "this message/word"[139] from God (as stated in 30:10–11) reflects a choice to not accept the wisdom of God's instructions concerning making a covenant with Egypt. Instead they chose to "trust, rely" (*bāṭaḥ*) on human methods of dealing with their problems. The NIV translation indicates the people depend on "oppression" and "deceit," though it is difficult to know what oppression the leaders of Judah were depending on.[140] Possibly they were oppressing people in the process of building up the defenses of Jerusalem by forcing them to work or confiscating the stones from their homes in order to build the walls higher (22:9–11). Irwin puts the two words together to indicate that they trust in a "perverse tyrant," suggesting the foolishness of trusting in the Egyptian king. Wildberger proposes a more appealing translation, "crooked," instead of "oppression," based on a slight textual change,[141] thus creating two related foundations ("crookedness and deceit") that guided Judah's political behavior.

The punishment in vv. 13–14 begins with "therefore" (*lākēn*; omitted in NIV) to describe the consequences of Judah's choices in v. 12. Their false trust in Egypt will result in catastrophic events (their punishment) comparable to a wall falling over (30:13) and a piece of pottery breaking (30:14). The analogy pictures a wall with a breach or large crack that is about to cause the wall to fall

---

[139] הַזֶּה הַדָּבָר, "this message," must refer to the words the prophet actually spoke, not the abbreviated words on the tablet in 30:8.

[140] Beuken, *Isaiah II*, 165, interprets "oppression" in the sense of "an unethical attitude and practice . . . as well as an unjustly acquired good in itself," but this does not create a very convincing parallel to "deceit." Oswalt, *Isaiah 1–39*, 553, believes the author is talking about a bad style of political leadership that has "relied on the politics of coercion and deception."

[141] Irwin, *Isaiah 28–33*, 84. Wildberger, *Isaiah 28–39*, 148–49, reverses the first two letters, changing עֹשֶׁק, "harassment, extortion," to עִקֵּשׁ, "twisted, perverted"—a simple scribal error of metathesis.

over[142] because it is bulging out. Although the wall may stand for a while, after the crack gets big enough, suddenly the wall will collapse. Its collapsed status is compared to a piece of pottery that is smashed into a thousand small useless pieces. Usually when a pot breaks there are some small chunks of pottery that survive, and they can be used for picking up hot coals from a fire or for scooping up water to drink, but in this case the smashing of the pottery (a symbol of Judah) will leave no useful pieces. Childs finds these metaphors "portraying irreversible destruction without hope of minor repairs."[143] The point of the analogy is Judah's destruction will happen suddenly with little warning when its protection is removed, and its destruction will totally destroy everything of value.

30:15–17   A second introduction, indicating that this is indeed a message from "the Sovereign LORD, the Holy One" (cf. 30:11,12), implicitly challenges the audience to recognize God as Lord and Holy, and then respond appropriately. What God wants the people to do (30:15a) is dramatically contrasted with what the people want to do (30:15b–16a). The results of trusting God or choosing another way also are contrasted (30:15b,16b–7).

God's plan for dealing with the Assyrian crisis is for the people of Judah to "turn and rest," but the idea of "turning, repenting" (běšûbâ)[144] could be interpreted in several ways. One could interpret this as turning from making an alliance with Egypt—a turning to trust in God. "Resting" (nahat) could be interpreted as "sitting still" and not opposing Assyria. Since the nation had already sinned by going to Egypt for help (30:1–4) and by rejecting God's instructions (30:9–12), it is more appropriate for the prophet to call the leaders to "repent" (19:22; 31:6) of their rebellious ways by turning from their present path of self-destruction. Instead of worrying about the Assyria attack or resting in Egyptian military assistance, the people of Jerusalem need to "be calm" (cf. Ahaz's requirement in 7:3–4), and to "rest" securely by trusting (7:9; 28:16) in God's promises of deliverance. Fearing an enemy is the opposite of being calm. The nation needs to rest by putting its confidence in God, for he is the only reliable source of heroic strength or military power that is dependable. God's promise of salvation and divine strength was intended to arouse calmness and trust in the hearts of the prophet's audience, but first the people needed to repent of their ways and humbly submit to God's plan for the deliverance of Jerusalem.

In some ways it is very surprising that the people of Judah refused to trust in God's marvelous promises of salvation when they were in such a hopeless situation. The prophet indicates that the primary stumbling block was that they

---

[142] The participle נֹפֵל must refer to something that "is about to fall" (GKC §116d).

[143] Childs, *Isaiah*, 226, believes these words picture the humiliating defeat of Judah.

[144] Hayes and Irvine, *Isaiah*, 341, think בְּשׁוּבָה is a noun that comes from the root יָשַׁב, which means "he sat," because sitting and resting are more parallel ideas. This is interpreted to mean that it was God's will for Judah to quietly submit to Assyria and accept the status quo as an Assyrian vassal. This agrees with M. Dahood, "Some Ambiguous Texts in Isaiah (30:15; 52:2; 33:2; 40:5; 45:1)," *CBQ* 20 (1958): 41–49. The view that this word comes from שׁוּב, which means "he repented, turned" is a more acceptable root for the noun "returning, repenting."

were not willing[145] to trust God with their lives (30:15c). Putting it bluntly, they said "no" to God. Instead of having a calm trust in God's strength, they chose to put their trust in horses (30:16), a symbol of military might. The NIV translation, "we will flee" (30:16), is literal, but it does not clarify the word play that is evident in the two quotations of Isaiah's audience. In the first quotation the people of Jerusalem were not saying that they wanted to escape from Jerusalem on horseback in order to avoid the onslaught of the Assyrian army. They wanted to "ride swiftly" (a word play on "fleeing"[146]) to Egypt before the battle started because they wanted to get help through an Egyptian alliance. This act of distrust in God will end up backfiring and will turn into a negative "fleeing" from their enemy, the Assyrians. The second quote of the audience expresses a similar intention using a similar reversal. They plan to ride off on swift horses to Egypt to get help, but the Assyrians will pursue them on swifter horses. These two quotations demonstrate that their hasty human efforts to make alliances (the opposite of being calm and trusting God in 30:16) and their speedy action to strengthen their defenses will not deliver Judah from the Assyrians. God is their only real source of strength and salvation (30:16). The facts of the situation are clearly laid out and the right choice is obvious, but the rebellious will of mankind frequently chooses to reject God's way.

Since the nation did not trust God, his earlier blessing (Lev 26:8; Deut 32:30) will turn into a curse; thus, instead of one from Judah threatening one thousand, the reverse will happen (30:17; cf. Amos 5:2–3). This is a sign of a great military defeat for Judah, for all that will be left of Judah will be a measly flagpole or banner on a hill. This parallels the situation described in 1:8 where Jerusalem was pictured as "a shelter in a vineyard" all alone with the rest of the nation defeated. This warning prophetically pictures the defeat of Judah's military, the loss of almost all its territory except one small hill. This fits the situation in 701 BC when the Assyrians defeated all the fortified towns in Judah except the city of Jerusalem (chaps. 36–37). Isaiah's sermon sets a challenge that many believers will face sometime in their lifetime: Should they calmly trust God's strength and deliverance in a time of difficulty against insurmountable odds, or should they do everything humanly possible to bring victory though their own (along with others') strength? God's way offers life; any other choice will bring failure and death.

GOD'S FUTURE GRACE TRANSFORMING JUDAH (30:18–26)

> **18Yet the LORD longs to be gracious to you;**
> **he rises to show you compassion.**

---

[145] לֹא אֲבִיתֶם means "you were not willing" (NIV "you would have none of it"), which indicates this was a choice they did not make during this time of crisis.

[146] Beuken, "Isaiah 30: A Prophetic Oracle," 376, suggests a word play. The root נוס has the primary meaning of "flee, escape," but it also refers to "swift movement," which characterizes the person who is trying to flee.

> For the LORD is a God of justice.
> Blessed are all who wait for him!

¹⁹O people of Zion, who live in Jerusalem, you will weep no more. How gracious he will be when you cry for help! As soon as he hears, he will answer you. ²⁰Although the Lord gives you the bread of adversity and the water of affliction, your teachers will be hidden no more; with your own eyes you will see them. ²¹Whether you turn to the right or to the left, your ears will hear a voice behind you, saying, "This is the way; walk in it." ²²Then you will defile your idols overlaid with silver and your images covered with gold; you will throw them away like a menstrual cloth and say to them, "Away with you!"

²³He will also send you rain for the seed you sow in the ground, and the food that comes from the land will be rich and plentiful. In that day your cattle will graze in broad meadows. ²⁴The oxen and donkeys that work the soil will eat fodder and mash, spread out with fork and shovel. ²⁵In the day of great slaughter, when the towers fall, streams of water will flow on every high mountain and every lofty hill. ²⁶The moon will shine like the sun, and the sunlight will be seven times brighter, like the light of seven full days, when the LORD binds up the bruises of his people and heals the wounds he inflicted.

The tone of this salvation oracle stands in stark contrast to the hopelessness of the situation of Judah when the Assyrians were attacking it. The near-term period of affliction for Judah (30:1–17,20) will bring great pain and destruction to Judah (30:19), but amazingly this military disaster will not end God's plans for his people. This disaster for Judah would have called into question the people's strong belief that God would protect Jerusalem, his holy city. Their "Zion theology," which was centered on God's special relationship with his temple in Jerusalem, might have seemed like a false hope at first, but in these verses God describes his desire to bless his people in order to establish a righteous kingdom on earth. But the problem was God would not pour out these marvelous blessings on a stubborn and rebellious people that would not trust him or listen to his instructions. Thus his blessing would come at some point in the future. God will not totally give up on his people but will even now begin to inaugurate his wonderfully gracious plan to compassionately and justly deal with those who will choose to wait on him (30:18) and listen to his words. God will help them, open their eyes to the truth, send them rain and prosperity, and dwell in their midst (30:19–26). These promises are true and will be fulfilled, so the people of Judah should trust God and follow him. He is trustworthy and all-powerful; he has not completely abandoned his chosen people. If his rebellious people will not be persuaded to repent because of God's punishment, maybe their desire to enjoy the wonderful blessings of God will motivate some to be willing to trust God now, so that they can enjoy God's kingdom plans for the future.

The prophet's rehearsal of God's future promises is recorded in narrative form (except 30:18). This change from poetry to a narrative account is surprising, but narrative promises of hope are found elsewhere (19:16–25; 23:15–18). It is not necessary to postulate that this positive message was proclaimed long after the judgment of 30:1–17 or to hypothesize that a completely different political situation served as the background for these words of compassion.[147] One should not assume that the early prophets knew nothing about the eschatological events God had planned for his people. In other sermons, Isaiah illustrates how rebellion against God will bring destruction and then contrasts that outcome with the hope of God's salvation for those that trust and exalt God (cf. 2:1–5 with 2:6–22; 7:1–11 with 7:12–25; 19:1–15 with 19:16–25). Another point that draws this paragraph into the mainstream of the surrounding chapters is the idea that God (or the prophets) will be their teacher and they will have their blind eyes opened (30:20). This is very consistent with the theological emphasis of the surrounding chapters (6:9–10; 28:23–29; 29:11–12,18,24; 30:8).[148]

The audience is a group of people who are weeping about the terrible situation in Jerusalem (30:19a). The contrasts found in this chapter dramatically illustrate how people's choices are related to the different ways God responds to human action. Nevertheless, in spite of many bad choices and the people's failure to trust God on many occasions, their future is not hopeless or unknown. Although the people of Judah are now rebellious and blind to the truth, ultimately God will overpower their sinful ways and graciously transform their blind eyes through the power of his grace. All glory and honor belongs to God, for the only hope mankind has is for God to transform their depraved and unrepentant will.

The structure of this paragraph includes the announcement that:

God will have compassion on helpless Zion	30:18–19
God will give understanding of his ways	30:20–22
God will give agricultural prosperity and healing	30:23–26

30:18–19 The paragraph begins with two parallel "therefore" clauses (*lākēn*; "yet" in NIV, and then omitted in the second line), indicating that the sinful rebellion of the people will eventually require God to intervene in a different way. Consequently, because of the nation's sinfulness, God will "wait"[149] for a time until it is appropriate for him to be gracious. It is more common to read of the need for mankind to wait for God to respond (8:17; 64:3; Ps 33:20), but in this situation the people will have to wait an unknown period of time before they will actually experience the fulfillment of these divine promises.

---

[147] Wildberger, *Isaiah 28–39*, 170–71, and Tucker, "Isaiah 1–39," 255, believe the theology of 30:18–26 is inconsistent with Isaiah's thoughts and attributes this message to some unknown teacher in the post-exilic era.

[148] Seitz, *Isaiah 1–39*, 219–220, draws attention to this as a central aspect of chaps. 28–30.

[149] יְחַכֶּה means to "wait" in all usages (8:17; 64:4 [v. 3 in Hb.]; Zeph 3:8; Ps 106:13), not "longs" as in NIV.

Clements maintains that this contextual description is a "reflection of the political situation in the post-exilic, Persian, period,"[150] but that is completely
foreign to the setting of 30:1–5. The sinful people are rebellious in the time of
Hezekiah (30:1–5), not in a frame of mind to receive God's blessings or in a
spiritual condition to understand God's compassion. God plans to bring Assyrian judgment on Judah because the leaders trust in Egyptian horses, but there
is no doubt that eventually the time will come when "he arises[151] to show you
compassion" and bring salvation. God is known for his grace and compassion
(14:1; 49:10,13, 14–15; 54:7,8,10; 55:7; see Exod 34:6; Jonah 4:2), for he desires to bless and protect his people, but he must act in justice (the right way)
for he is also a God of "justice" (*mišpāṭ*, 1:27; 3:14; 28:17). Thus justice is
not unrelated to God's acts of salvation (32:15–16; 33:5–6). In spite of the circumstances that prevent God from saving his people immediately, those who
wait for God will be blessed (30:18b). Patiently waiting for God to act in grace
requires one to trust in God's power and his promises to save. The essence of
faith is to hope for what is not seen (Heb 11:1).

Although Jerusalem's terrible situation (30:19a) of defeat by the Assyrians
would naturally cause one to weep[152] in hopelessness and want to go to Egypt
for military deliverance, blessings only come to those who expectantly wait for
God to bring salvation. God promises that someday weeping will end (30:19;
25:8), for "he will surely be gracious"[153] when he hears the sound of the cries
of his people. God heard the prayers and crying of his people in the past when
they were suffering in bondage in Egypt (Exod 2:23–25; 3:7), and he will hear
their call for help in the future. When people finally see the hopelessness of
trusting in their own efforts and finally look to God for a solution to their problems, he will answer them (30:19b). This is the hard lesson that every person
must learn. Worrying and fretting will not help, and getting angry with God
will not resolve the situation. The human inability to solve serious problems
often leads to weeping, but humble people who trust in God will one day experience his grace in abundance. Scripture does not promise a life without trouble
or testing, but the person who faithfully waits for God to act is described as
one who will experience blessed happiness (64:3; see Ps 33:19–21; Hab 2:3–4;
Zeph 3:8–20; Dan 12:12).

---

[150] Clements, *Isaiah 1–39*, 249–50, puts this section after the fall of Jerusalem, but how can
this setting fit 30:1–5 or the defeat of the horsemen in 30:16–17, and in what sense could one say
that the promises of a fertile land in 30:23–26 was fulfilled after the exile? The images about the
sun and moon as well as divine healing point to an eschatological era.

[151] When God "will arise, arises," יָרוּם, he moves to action (26:11; Ps 18:47; 46:11: 99:2),
indicating that the waiting time is over. This root not only means "arise" but also to "exult, lift up,"
indicating that when God moves into action to reveal his power in history, he raises himself above
all other powers and in the process exalts his power and glory.

[152] בְּכוֹ is an infinitive absolute with the final ה missing (see GKC §75n). It functions as an
adverb (GKC §113h) to describe the manner of life of those who dwell in Jerusalem.

[153] The choice of an infinitive absolute plus a finite verb (חָנוֹן יָחְנְךָ) strengthens the verbal idea
to emphasize the certainty that this action will happen (GKC §113n).

30:20–22 The text emphasizes that God "gives" (*nātan*) his people different experiences (also in v. 23; cf. Eccl 3:1–12), including times of adversity or punishment for sin. In Isaiah's situation he did not intervene immediately when the Assyrians invaded: instead, he allowed the Assyrian attack on Judah to defeat 46 walled cities and take 200,150 people captive. But in the future[154] some "teachers/a Teacher" will instruct the people in the way that they should walk.[155] NIV takes these as teachers (probably prophets) who will guide the people in God's ways, but Oswalt argues that the singular verb points to a divine Teacher, God himself,[156] who will instruct his people. God will no longer hide himself in the sense of seeming distant or of a failure to act on their behalf (45:15; 59:1–2; Ps 27:8–9; 4:23–24; 102:1–2). His presence will be seen, for he will be active among them, instructing in the way they should walk. This pictures God, the teacher, giving moral instruction to his people with his own voice (cf. 2:2–4; Ps 25:8–14) so that they will stay out of trouble. The Lord will gently teach his disciples in "the way" (*haderek*) of God, instructing them in the disciplines of godliness so they will not turn in any other moral directions (right or left). This reminds one of God's original instructions for his people to follow his instructions (Deut 5:32–33; 17:19–20; Josh 1:7–8; 23:6–7).

God's presence and his teaching will result in the total rejection of idols (30:22) covered with a thin layer of gold or silver to make them look important.[157] Once the people's eyes are opened and they hear God's instructions, the people will see the foolishness of trusting in lifeless images that can do nothing. The people became defiled (*timmē'tem* Lev 15:31; 20:3; 2 Kgs 23:16; Jer 7:30) by these idols, but in the future their defilement or desecration of these statues of wood will show an utter disrespect for the gods these idols represent (cf. 2:20; 13:17; 31:7; 44:15–17). They will no longer reverence or treat these idols as holy, but will reject them and throw them out,[158] as if they

---

[154] The *vav* on וְלֹא is probably adversative, "but," showing the contrast between the two halves of the verse.

[155] Kaiser, *Isaiah 13–39*, 301, connects this to later persecution of the Jews in the Intertestamental period (165 BC) when the Greek ruler Antiochus Epiphanes IV defiled the temple with a pagan altar. Kaiser connects the teacher with the leader of an eschatological group of faithful people who followed Jason the high priest. There is no need to look for a setting outside the Assyrian crisis in the time of Isaiah.

[156] Oswalt, *Isaiah 1–39*, 560, proposes a connection with the teaching instructions in Deuteronomy. W. A. M. Beuken, "What Does the Vision Hold: Teachers or One Teacher? Punning Repetition in Isa 30:20," *Heythrop Journal* 36 (1995): 451–66, argues that the first example should be plural and refers to their "teachers" (the prophets), while the second creates a pun by referring to God as their Teacher. Blenkinsopp, *Isaiah 1–39*, 421, hypothesizes that the "Teacher" is perhaps identical to the "Servant" in chaps. 42 and following.

[157] Hezekiah's spiritual reforms involved a return to the true worship of God and the elimination of the idols favored by his father Ahaz (2 Kgs 16:1–4; 18:4).

[158] The Hb. word תִּזְרֵם means "you will scatter them," an idea that may be explained by recalling that the nation ground the golden calf at Sinai into powder and "scattered" it on the water (Exod 32:20). By grinding the gold into powder and scattering it, one demonstrates a destructive power over the image, proving that it is powerless, assuring that its scattered remains will never be used

were getting rid of an object that was repulsive.[159] As Oswalt suggests, "bless-ings can be received only after the abandonment of one's own efforts and a complete commitment to God."[160]

30:23–26 The second thing God will "give" (*nātan*, NIV "send") is the blessing of rain and fertile crops in the land, the ideals of an agricultural so-ciety. The curse on creation will end, for God will bountifully pour out his covenant blessings on the nation (cf. Deut 8:6–14; 11:13–17; 28:12). This theological theme was a common part of Israel's eschatological expectations "in that day" (cf. 32:20; Ezek 34:26–27; Hos 2:21–22; Joel 2:22–24; Amos 9:13). Beuken rightly cautions that any attempt to limit these themes to some later "Deuteronom(ist)ic interpolation is a little rash . . . [for] an explicit call for obedience to the commandments, which in Deuteronomy would constitute a prior condition to the granting of fertility, is absent."[161] In the future the nor-mal everyday parts of agricultural life will exist in an ideal setting of great fer-tility. A person will once again be able to observe cows grazing freely in large pastures, work animals plowing, and others eating harvested crops.[162] Verse 25 returns to the theme of abundant water (cf. 23a), picturing it flowing freely in the mountains of Judah at the time that God blesses his people, slaughters their enemies (34:2), and destroys everything exalted (towers in 2:12–15). These conditions were just the opposite of the present state of affairs when Judah was being attacked and desolated by the Assyrians. This wonderful picture assured Isaiah's audience that God was not finished with his people, even though things looked very hopeless at the time.

The final verse promises a slaughter of God's eschatological enemies and then the blessing of an extremely bright light from the sun and moon, de-scribed in hyperbolic language. This idea seems to almost be in conflict with the eschatological picture in 24:23 where the moon and sun are ashamed of their puny light when the glorious light of God is revealed on earth (cf. 4:5; 60:1,19–20; Joel 2:31). Also problematic is the consideration that an extreme-ly hot sun would usually be expected to have the negative effect of destroy-ing life on earth (49:10). If this were the intention, the author would be con-

---

again for a similar purpose, and showing that it is worthless (its gold is not valued).

[159] NIV translates דָּוָה as "menstrual cloth," an association based on Lev 15:33; 20:18, though elsewhere the word means "sickness" (Lev 12:2; Deut 7:15; 28:60; Lam 1:3). This provided a eu-phemistic way of referring to menstruation without actually saying the word, similar to the modern use of "period," which skirts the issue with a euphemism.

[160] Oswalt, *Isaiah 1–39*, 562, explains that this is true because God does not want people to get the wrong idea and think that the idols were the source of their blessings. Therefore, the idols must go first.

[161] Beuken, *Isaiah II*, 173, looks at these concepts as early apocalyptic themes.

[162] The last part of v. 24 is difficult to understand. It refers to cattle feed that was "stirred, win-nowed" with a pitchfork or shovel, but the exact meaning of בְּלִיל חָמִיץ is obscure. BDB, 330, defines חָמִיץ as "seasoned with salt," while L. Koehler, "בְּלִיל חָמִיץ Jes 30,24," *ZAW* 40 (1922): 15–17, suggests "sour sorrel," a plant that is still eaten by Bedouins, either raw or cooked. When better food was available for people, this plant would be given to animals.

trasting God's destruction of his enemies through burning heat (he acts with "consuming fire" in 30:27,30) and his healing of his people in the second half of the verse. Alternatively, the bright sun could be a picture of the optimum brightness of the sun needed to produce unparallelled fertility in nature, matching the unparallelled amount of water in v. 25.[163] All these blessings will be God's way of "healing" (*rāpā'*) the wounds he inflicted on his people in their time of judgment.

GOD'S PLAN TO DESTROY ASSYRIA (30:27–33)

[27]See, the Name of the LORD comes from afar,
   with burning anger and dense clouds of smoke;
his lips are full of wrath,
   and his tongue is a consuming fire.
[28]His breath is like a rushing torrent,
   rising up to the neck.
He shakes the nations in the sieve of destruction;
   he places in the jaws of the peoples
   a bit that leads them astray.
[29]And you will sing
   as on the night you celebrate a holy festival;
your hearts will rejoice
   as when people go up with flutes
to the mountain of the LORD,
   to the Rock of Israel.
[30]The LORD will cause men to hear his majestic voice
   and will make them see his arm coming down
with raging anger and consuming fire,
   with cloudburst, thunderstorm and hail.
[31]The voice of the LORD will shatter Assyria;
   with his scepter he will strike them down.
[32]Every stroke the LORD lays on them
   with his punishing rod
will be to the music of tambourines and harps,
   as he fights them in battle with the blows of his arm.
[33]Topheth has long been prepared;
   it has been made ready for the king.
Its fire pit has been made deep and wide,
   with an abundance of fire and wood;
the breath of the LORD,
   like a stream of burning sulfur,
   sets it ablaze.

The final paragraph returns to address Judah's present military problem with the Assyrian army (30:31). It announces God's promise to come in all his

---

[163] This is the interpretation taken in the apocryphal *Book of Jubilees* 1:29; 19:25 and the *Ethiopic Enoch* 91:16.

theophanic power[164] to destroy the Assyrians with fire, his voice, his scepter, and his rod. If God can defeat Judah's future enemies and bring great blessings on his people (30:18–26), then the people of Judah should trust him to come in wrath to defeat their present Assyrian enemy (30:27–33). There is no need to depend upon the Egyptians if God will consume the Assyrians in his wrath.

The reference to an Israelite celebration in v. 29 causes some to speculate that this refers to a celebration on the joyous Feast of Tabernacles or possibly at Passover,[165] but the information is so minimal that it is impossible to come to any secure conclusions. It seems more likely that this is a special celebration of a victory in war, rather than one of the annual festivals. This paragraph fits the same time period as 30:1–17, though it is impossible to know how many months or years before God's miraculous defeat of the Assyrian army at Jerusalem in 701 BC that the prophet spoke these words.

This paragraph is structured around the three things the Lord promises he will do (30:27a,30a,32a).

God's theophany presence brings joy	30:27–29
God's victory over the Assyrians	30:30–31
God's burning pit for Assyria	30:32–33

30:27–29 The oracle announces an astonishing ("behold, look, see," *hinnēh*) theophany of judgment highlighted by the glorious appearance of God in a cloud and fire.[166] This display of God's power in anthropomorphic imagery of his anger, lips, and tongue and the portrayal of a fire or a rushing stream create a frightening picture of God's presence. God's coming is often interpreted geographically to imply that he is coming from the wings of a storm (Judg 5:4), from the Sinai desert (cf. Hab 3:3), from heaven (26:21; Mic 1:3), or from Zion to Tophet (30:33). If the idea is viewed theologically, God's coming can simply refer to his movement to act on behalf of his people, rather than being far away, inactive, or hidden (30:20). His fiery and wrathful appearance may seem offensive to some who only want to think about God's compassion.

Once God's people observe the victory his glorious presence will bring, they will respond with singing and celebration (30:29) because God will save them by punishing their enemy. This theophany of God mixes traditional literal images of observable reality (God does appear in the midst of smoke and fire on Mount Sinai in Exod 19) with the emotional vocabulary that compares

---

[164] Beuken, "Isaiah 30: A Prophetic Oracle," 385, illustrates the regular grammatical patterns in the structure of 30:27–33. In vv. 27–29 there are four comparisons, two related to God's anger (vv. 27–28) and two related to Judah's joy (v. 29). The second (vv. 30–31) and third (vv. 32–33) parts of the paragraph both end with a כִּי clause (both omitted in NIV) in vv. 31 and 33.

[165] Wildberger, *Isaiah 28–39*, 199–200, discusses the possibility of connecting this festival with the New Year Festival (Rosh Hashanah), Hezekiah's Passover celebration (2 Chr 30), or the Feast of Tabernacles.

[166] Other somewhat similar theophany appearances are recorded in Ps 18:7–15; Nah 1:3–8; and Hab 3:3–15.

God's revelation to burning anger, words of wrath from his lips, and a power-ful torrent of roaring or flooding water from his mouth (cf. 8:8; 28:2,15,17 where Assyria was pictured as a mass of water). The results[167] of God's ac-tion against the nations are imaginatively compared to putting a deceptive bridle in the mouth of a horse (30:28b). Watts notes that in "17:2 and 29:7 the plural was used to describe military actions involving Assyria. Its army was composed of different ethnic units."[168] This would cause one to conclude that God was leading Assyria on a path that will result in its own destruction (cf. 1 Kgs 22:22–24). Assyria was called to serve God's purpose (10:5), but its pride will lead to its fall (cf. 10:5–15; 37:22–29). The meaning of the imagery of shaking "in a sieve" (bĕnāpat) is less apparent, and the meaning of this Hebrew root is far from certain. Three alternative options are available: (a) the Arabic root jafun, "yoke," creates a much better parallel with "bit, bridle" in the last line;[169] (b) in connection with the hand, the root nph could describe God's waving (or shaking) his hand to cause dread (10:32; 19:16), waving to give directions (13:2), or waving his hand to destroy (11:15); and (c) the "shaking" motion might refer to putting the nation in God's sieve to separate the good from the bad (cf. Amos 9:9). Each one makes tolerable sense, for in the first case God would be yoking the nation with a worthless yoke (parallel to the deceitful bridle), in the second God would be waving to the nations a worthless signal, and in the third the deceptive sieve separates nothing so all the nations are destroyed. In the sieve of historical events, the Assyrians think they will have victory at Jerusalem, but God is leading them there so that he can destroy them at Jerusalem.

The response of the people of Judah will include singing, celebration, and rejoicing similar to the joyous celebration on one of their holy feast days (30:29). A second comparison likens this joy to the celebration when pilgrims come marching into Jerusalem singing and dancing to the sound of musical instruments because they are entering the presence of God, the Rock and sure foundation of Israel (8:14; 17:10; 26:4; 2 Sam 23:3). This celebration does not refer to Passover or the Feast of Tabernacles; it is a celebration of God's mili-tary victory over the Assyrian army (30:31).

30:30–31 The second act of the theophany of God is to openly cause people to hear his voice and see his powerful arm of wrath at work. The im-agery of fire, lightning, thunder, and hail make it abundantly clear that God is present and at work. "Without a doubt, surely" (kî; omitted in NIV in 30:31)

---

[167] NIV's "He shakes the nations" is translated as a statement of fact rather than as a result clause "so that the nations shake," which is a more appropriate understanding of the *hiphil* infini-tive construct לַהֲנָפָה.

[168] Watts, *Isaiah 1–33*, 405, believes through these actions "God's intervention will rein in Assyria's power."

[169] H. L. Ginsberg, "An Obscure Hebrew Word," *JQR* 22 (1931–31): 143–45, translates the phrase "to yoke the nations in a yoke of error."

the commands of God's voice will completely terrify[170] the mighty and proud army of Assyria; his rod will smite it. Earlier, Assyria was the rod God used to smite his people (10:5,15,24); now the sovereign God of all nations will turn his rod against Assyria to punish it and glorify himself (10:12). The imagery does not spell out exactly how he will defeat the troops, just that God will give the powerful decree that will empower his arm to accomplish his will. Later, after God miraculously sent his angel to strike 185,000 Assyrian troops dead, the remaining forces immediately fled in terror back to Nineveh.

30:32–33   The conclusion of God's work with Assyria involves punishment and the burning of the booty left by the enemy. God is pictured as a warrior, fighting not with sword or spear, but with his sovereign arm passing over the enemy to defeat them. Drawing on a typical war scene to communicate the message in terms that the people could understand, the prophet depicts every stroke of God's staff of "punishment"[171] that will strike to the beat of musical instruments as he fights in battle. The divine warrior does not struggle to overcome the Assyrian enemy, as if he were in mortal combat with an equal. Instead, God decrees with his voice (30:30,31), passes his staff over the condemned (30:30,32), and accomplishes his will. Although the defeat of the enemy is not stated in this verse, it is assumed. Instead attention is directed toward Tophet, the place for burning garbage in the Bin Hinnom valley on the south side of Jerusalem. This was also the place where the dead bodies of the enemy could be cremated. Cremation was only practiced for the worst criminals (Lev 20:14; 21:9; Josh 7:25) or in times of war when thousands die (Amos 6:9–10). In light of the thousands that God will kill (37:36 refers to 185,000), a large and deep pit would be needed and a great pile of wood would have to be set in place in order to burn all the dead bodies and their belongings. Then God will set the wood on fire and destroy them. The historical account of the defeat of the Assyrians outside Jerusalem in chaps. 36–37 makes no mention of how the bodies of the 185,000 Assyrian soldiers were actually disposed of following the event. At this point the prophet attempts to create in his audience a belief in God's almighty power so that they will trust him. He assures them that God will do all this to demonstrate his power over the Assyrians (37:21–29). Knowing all these promises about what God intended to do, it would seem that Isaiah's audience in Jerusalem would be willing to trust God to protect them from Assyria, rather than make an alliance with the Egyptians. Because people

---

[170] The word יֵחַת refers to "being terrorized, stricken with terror" (7:8; 8:9; 20:5; 31:9) because of God's voice (30:30), not "crushed" as in NIV.

[171] The Masoretic מוּסָדָה means "foundation" in most situations, though "appointed" in a few cases (Hab 1:12). Most commentaries and translations suggest there was a scribal confusion between ד and ר, thus preferring to read מוּסָרָה, "punishment," though either "appointed staff" or "staff of punishment" makes sense. Wildberger, *Isaiah 28–39*, 202, finds cultic imagery in the "waving, wave offering," תְּנוּפָה, which is then dedicated to God on the altar and burnt as a burnt offering (30:33). He believes this would mimic the practice of offering human sacrifices to the god Moloch in this valley (2 Kgs 23:10; Jer 19:6).

today now know what God actually did to miraculously fulfill this prophecy, they are even more obligated to trust God in the difficult times of their lives. Proof of God's power and grace is known; there is no doubt about it.

THEOLOGICAL IMPLICATIONS. The leaders and people of Judah were struggling with a life-changing decision that would determine their future welfare. Facing a large Assyrian army that had already defeated the many cities in Judah, there seemed to be little hope for the city of Jerusalem. They had at least four choices: (a) The people could submit to the Assyrians and suffer the consequences of death and severe punishment for rebellion. This would mean heavy taxation, death for soldiers, the raping of women, and foreign domination. (b) They could resist as long as possible, meaning that some would probably die of starvation, while others would perish in the many battles that would follow in the coming months. Possibly the Assyrians would give up and leave the city undefeated. (c) They could seek the help of a strong neighbor like Egypt who might protect them from the Assyrians. Finally, (d) they could trust God to miraculously deliver them. Since choices (a) and (b) would involve severe suffering, some loss of life, and no freedom, the real serious options boil down to the choice of relying on manipulating the balances of power through human alliances or trusting in God's plan of deliverance. These two alternatives have faced believers through the centuries as they live in a hostile world that despises them. The question is: Can people control their own circumstances and fulfill their own plans, or should they humble themselves and trustingly submit to God's plans? When one faces sure death, this is usually not an easy or automatic decision.

How can a prophet, or any believer for that matter, minister to people who struggle with the idea of following God's plan under these kinds of circumstances? First, the messenger of God must persuasively explain God's plans and warn people of the consequences of refusing to listen to God. Knowing God's message makes people responsible for each choice. The people of Judah knew God's plans and they were aware that no human alliance or manipulation of their circumstances would solve their problem (30:1–5). The message of God clarifies what it means not to follow God's path and reveals the consequences—Egypt will not protect them from Assyria. All human efforts would be a useless waste of effort and money (30:6–7), for following man's rational plans would cause them to act in rebellion against God. Judah's alternative plan would be a refusal to listen to what God has said (30:9–10); it was a sure road to defeat (30:12–14). This is parallel to what happens when anyone resists the will of God.

But trust in God in such dire circumstances is a risk that is not easy to accept. It puts everything on the line for what often appears to be a nebulous hope that God will act. What does one have to do to truly trust God? Isaiah indicates the people need to (a) repent of their present rebellious acts; (b) rest securely in God's salvation; (c) be calm rather than fearful; (d) rely on God's heroic strength; and (e) stop trusting in human power (30:15–16). But how can people be calm and trusting in the midst of a nearly impossible situation that threatens death? Faith is engendered when one remembers that (a) God acts in compassion and justice; (b) he will answer all who cry out to him for help; (c) he will teach people how to act rightly; (d) he will bless and heal; and (e) in his wrath he will defeat their enemies (30:18–33). When one actually "sees" the power and glory of God, as revealed in this theophany and his action, one is no longer blind, for then one has personally experienced a glorious sure foundation that makes acting in faith justifiable (28:16). Faith is not blind acceptance of something totally unknown; it is a confident relational walk based on spiritual knowledge that directs the will to act in reliance on the character and promises of someone who sovereignly controls this world.

(2) Second Woe, to Those Who Trust Egypt (31:1–32:20)

The second woe oracle also attempts to persuade an audience in Jerusalem shortly before 701 BC not to trust in Egypt. There is no specific condemnation of Hezekiah in these verses,[172] though as king he certainly carries some responsibility for failing to counter the pro-Egyptian leanings of his advisors. The prophet laments over these rebellious choices, for past (cf. 20:1–6) and present events support the conclusion that Egypt will not come forward to save Judah. It appears that this woe oracle came after the woe in chap. 30,[173] after the Egyptian army came north to defend Judah (37:9), and after the Assyrians have turned back the Egyptians at Eltekeh.[174]

The structural pattern of joining woe oracles with messages of salvation in previous woe oracles is used again in this series of messages.

Woe against reliance on Egypt rather than God	31:1–9
God's exalting of a righteous king	32:1–8
Mourning from complacency; life from the Spirit	32:9–20

The prophet describes his circumstances as a time when the leaders of Judah foolishly depended on Egypt for deliverance from Assyria (31:1–2). Such dependence was hopeless, so the proud women of Zion should lament about the terrible situation of Jerusalem (32:9–14) and put their trust in God's promise to

---

[172] Seitz, *Isaiah 1–39*, 224–25, makes much of the absence of any condemnation of the king of Judah; instead the focus is on a group of people (the plural verbs in 31:6), a pro-Egyptian group of political advisors who support a treaty with Egypt.

[173] This is the position of Wildberger, *Isaiah 28–39*, 208–209, but Kaiser, *Isaiah 13–39*, 312, places this chapter before 30:6 and does not assume that the Egyptians have already been defeated at Eltekeh. Clements, *Isaiah 1–39*, 256–57, connect 30:4–9 with an Assyrian redaction in the time of Josiah when Esarhaddon was a strong Assyrian king.

[174] *ANET*, 287–88, gives Sennacherib's own discussion of this battle against the Egyptian forces in the plains around Eltekeh and Timnah. Though there is no way to determine how accurately the Assyrian account is, its record of the defeat of Egyptian forces is consistent with the biblical data.

transform society through his justice and the work of his Spirit in the hearts of his people (32:15–20). The prophet persuasively encourages[175] his audience to admit that they cannot protect themselves from other oppressive nations (meaning Assyria) and cannot bring about an ideal era of righteousness and peace on earth through their own efforts. Judah must end its complacency and look to the Holy One of Israel for help, trust in his wisdom, and realize that only God is able to change their situation. They must realize that depending upon Egypt is by implication a denial of God's authority to sovereignly control history.

WOE AGAINST RELIANCE ON EGYPT RATHER THAN GOD (31:1–9)

> [1]Woe to those who go down to Egypt for help,
>   who rely on horses,
> who trust in the multitude of their chariots
>   and in the great strength of their horsemen,
> but do not look to the Holy One of Israel,
>   or seek help from the LORD.
> [2]Yet he too is wise and can bring disaster;
>   he does not take back his words.
> He will rise up against the house of the wicked,
>   against those who help evildoers.
> [3]But the Egyptians are men and not God;
>   their horses are flesh and not spirit.
> When the LORD stretches out his hand,
>   he who helps will stumble,
>   he who is helped will fall;
>   both will perish together.

> [4]This is what the LORD says to me:

> "As a lion growls,
>   a great lion over his prey—
> and though a whole band of shepherds
>   is called together against him,
> he is not frightened by their shouts
>   or disturbed by their clamor—
> so the LORD Almighty will come down
>   to do battle on Mount Zion and on its heights.
> [5]Like birds hovering overhead,
>   the LORD Almighty will shield Jerusalem;
> he will shield it and deliver it,
>   he will 'pass over' it and will rescue it."

> [6]Return to him you have so greatly revolted against, O Israelites. [7]For in that day every one of you will reject the idols of silver and gold your sinful hands have made.

---

[175] Sweeney, *Isaiah 1–39*, 402–403, rightly understands that this is a persuasive speech that was intended to convince an audience not to do certain things.

> [8]"Assyria will fall by a sword that is not of man;
>   a sword, not of mortals, will devour them.
> They will flee before the sword
>   and their young men will be put to forced labor.
> [9]Their stronghold will fall because of terror;
>   at sight of the battle standard their commanders will panic,"
> declares the LORD,
>   whose fire is in Zion,
>   whose furnace is in Jerusalem.

This woe oracle (31:1–3) is tightly organized around issues related to Judah's foolish trust in Egyptian military horsepower. Their false hope in Egypt will only bring disaster on Judah, so their only real hope is to trust in God's promise to protect Jerusalem (31:4–5). Therefore, they need to return to God (31:6–7), for he has promised to destroy the Assyrian army (31:8–9). One would think that Isaiah's audience would respond positively, seeing the error in their ways because Egypt was already in a marginalized status. The structure of this message is divided into four paragraphs.

Woe: trusting Egypt will not work	30:1–3
A promise of God's protection	30:4–5
A call to return to God	30:6–7
Assyria will fall	30:8–9

The insertion of a parenthetical narrative in 31:6–7 about repentance and the rejection of idols on the Day of the Lord interrupt the natural flow of thought in the poetic style of vv. 1–5 through vv. 8–9. It appears that Isaiah probably added these remarks (quoting ideas from 2:20; 30:22) to his original speech when he put this message in written form. Isaiah sought to draw out an application to his readers, but the thoughts in these verses do not suggest that some unknown post-exilic editor added them.[176]

31:1–3 The initial woe oracle directs the audience to lament because some representatives from Judah traveled to Egypt to make a military alliance with the Pharaoh. They and their government supporters in Jerusalem wanted the Egyptian horses (cavalry and chariots) to protect them from the Assyrian invaders who had destroyed parts of Judah. Since horses were much faster than the infantry and could disrupt a charge of ground troops, they became a valuable tool to intimidate and defeat an enemy. They could speedily inflict damage and then escape to safer ground. By making this alliance with Egypt, the princes of Judah were in essence relying on horses to save them, rather than God. This passage does not teach that nations should not have armies or good military machinery; it simply argues against the false assumption that

---

[176] Clements, *Isaiah 1–39*, 256, concludes that a later redactor added these verses in post-exilic times, but the concepts in this verse were present in Isaiah's thinking or preaching as far back as the time of Uzziah (2:6–22).

bigger armies and better armaments determine who wins a war. The soldiers with the longest spears, the most horses, or technologically superior rifles do not determine who will be victorious, it is God who determines and directs the course of history.

The grammar of the verbs in vv. 1b–2 changes from the present participles in v. 1a ("those who go down") to a series of imperfects with *vav* consecutives and perfect verbs, indicating that the action happened in past time.[177] This suggests that in 1:1b–2 the prophet explains the reason these officials went down to Egypt. Verse 1b should be translated "they trusted" in the Egyptian cavalry "because" (*kî*) the Egyptians had many horses, in chariots "because" (*kî*) they were very strong. Their action discounted the fact that God was strong and all-powerful and contradicted instructions against foreign alliances (Deut 17:16; Ps 20:7; 33:17; Prov 21:31). The tragedy of this action was magnified by making this decision without even "looking to, relying on" (*šāʿu*) the Holy One of Israel (contrast 10:20; 17:7; 30:12) or "seeking" (*dārāšu* 1:17; 8:19; 9:12; 11:10) God's wisdom on this matter. The prophet points to the complete removal of God from the decision-making process. Judah did not even have enough respect for God to rely on his wisdom, for one usually only looks to or depends upon one that is trustworthy.[178] In past years when the nation went to war a priest or a prophet would seek wisdom from God in order to discover if it was the will of God to fight a battle (1 Sam 23:2,4,9–12; 2 Sam 5:19,23; 1 Kgs 22:5–8). Past experience demonstrated the serious consequences of not looking to God when making military decisions. Because the people failed to seek God's wisdom when the Israelites made a covenant with the Gibeonites (Josh 9:14) and Saul failed to look to God at key points in his life (1 Chr 10:13–14), God would not prosper their ways. However, God did bless Jehoshaphat (2 Chr 17:4; 20:6–12) because he inquired to find out the Lord's will.

In 31:2a God's response to these acts is tied to his wisdom, his control of history, and his faithfulness to his word. The wise men who counseled the king with the best of human wisdom may have considered themselves very intelligent and astute in devising a policy of alliance with Egypt, but God gives much wiser counsel (28:29). His wisdom can make the wisdom of men seem like foolish advice (cf. 19:11–14; 29:14). The political leaders thought they had made a "covenant with death" (28:14–15) to escape the scourge of the Assyrians, but their foolish alliance with Egypt was a sinful act that was not part of God's plan (30:1–2). The result was that God "brought" (past tense)[179]

---

[177] The imperfect with *vav* is often found after a perfect verb in a temporal or logical sequence (GKC §111a) that has the potential of being translated in any tense (GKC §111n,r,w), with past being most frequent, present occurring with stative verbs, and the future tense when following an imperfect. The perfect verbs in vv. 1b–2 also support interpreting this section as past time.

[178] Isaiah 17:7–8 indicates that in the future the nation will look to God and reject idols.

[179] NIV has a subjunctive, "can bring," that refers to future possibilities, but the imperfect with the *vav* וַיָּבֵא, "and he brought," fits with the perfect verbs that follow. All of them seem to refer to past events.

about some disaster, possibly the Assyrians' defeat of the Egyptians, as God announced in 30:1–7. His words are true and he does what he says he will do. He said he would destroy the house of the wicked (probably referring to Judah),[180] as well as those who help (meaning the Egyptians) the wicked people of Judah (31:2b). These perfect verbs indicate that God has already punished Egypt, so certainly the Hebrews in Jerusalem should not be so foolish as to think Egypt will ever be able to help them in the future. They need to turn to God now before it is too late (31:6).

31:3 The reason for the failure of the Egyptians is lamentably simple. The men are mere men, and the horses are simply horses. This is not a philosophical thesis to highlight the difference between the material and spiritual world, but a practical argument that demonstrates divine superiority. The Holy God who is an almighty unseen spirit power will decide the destiny of Egypt and Judah, not some mortal army or a sinful alliance. This was true for Ahaz (7:1–11) and all the nations of the world (chaps. 13–23), so why would it not be true in this case? God's powerful hand controls the destiny of the nation that wanted help (Judah) as well as the one that made a feeble attempt to help (Egypt). Help, protection, and deliverance come from God. Falling, stumbling, and perishing happen when one relies on the strength of mankind. This warning should persuade Isaiah's audience and every reader today to trust in God, not in human wisdom, brute strength, or political alliances.

31:4–5 There is considerable disagreement about how to interpret these two verses. The problem arises because the analogy of God as a lion growling over its prey in 31:4 conveys a very negative picture of God's "battle against Mount Zion," while the analogy of God as a bird protecting its nest in 31:5 is positive. There are four ways of dealing with the discontinuity between these two images: (a) Clements views 31:4 as God's hostile action against Jerusalem and interprets this figure of speech as "Isaiah's last utterance in Jerusalem, isolated and besieged by Sennacherib's forces, before Hezekiah surrendered."[181] The positive imagery in 31:5 is explained as a later redactional addition in the time of Josiah based on God's eventual deliverance of the city of Jerusalem from Sennacherib in 701 BC. This alleviates Isaiah of making two rather contradictory statements concerning one series of events, but it means that these two verses do not go together as a single unified message. (b) Young understands the two images of God (a destroying lion and a protecting bird) as just two complementary ways God would act toward Judah. He will defeat the wicked people in Judah by permitting an army (the Assyrians) to attack it

---

[180] Wildberger, *Isaiah 28–39*, 210–11, thinks both the "house of the wicked" and the "evildoers" are the Egyptians, but in light of the condemnation of both the helper and the helping nations (31:3b) it makes more sense to follow Oswalt, *Isaiah 1–39*, 572, and conclude that the "house of the wicked" refers to Judah, the nation being helped.

[181] Clements, *Isaiah 1–39*, 256–57, rejects the view that God ever promised to protect Jerusalem in 701 BC.

and destroy nearly all of its fortified cities, yet in the end he will act in mercy by delivering his own righteous remnant within the city of Jerusalem.[182] (c) M. L. Barré interprets both images negatively, contending that the bird would "descend, light on" (based on the use of this root in Syriac) Jerusalem like a predatory bird (31:5a), thus its negative action parallels the lion fighting against Jerusalem in v. 4.[183] (d) Wildberger eliminates the problem of having two radically different pictures of God by interpreting both the image of the lion and the bird positively. In his approach the lion goes down to fight "on Mount Zion" to protect it from other shepherds (kings), rather than fighting "against" Jerusalem.[184]

Elsewhere, God is described as a "lion" (Amos 1:2; 3:8). This comparison pictures God as a lion standing over his captured prey, indicating his defeat of some unidentified animal. The contextual discussion of the perishing of Egypt and Judah in 31:2b–3 suggests that God is standing over one or both of these defeated nations. The story includes a shouting band of shepherds that gathers together to frighten the lion, so that they can take the lion's prey. This rural picture fits the experiences of people in this ancient Near Eastern context, but the "shepherds" are not identified (a king could be described as a shepherd, as in 2 Sam 5:1–2; Ezek 34). O. Kaiser imagines that the Judeans and Egyptians represent the shepherds,[185] but the text may refer specifically to the kings of Assyria and Egypt who wanted to control the people of Judah, the defeated prey that belonged to God. This rather obscure analogy of the lion and its prey is explicitly interpreted (32:4b) as the Divine Warrior, God himself coming down to fight on Zion. He will fight both against those in Jerusalem (the prey in 31:4a) and those who fight against Jerusalem (the shepherds in 31:4a). God's "coming" (*yērēd*, lit. "coming/going down") does not imply that he does not dwell in Jerusalem as Zion theology teaches (Ps 46:6; Mic 3:11). It simply pictures God's coming to do battle against his enemies (cf. his theophany in 29:5–8).

The analogy of God acting like a bird hovering over a nest picks up imagery known from Deut 32:11, where God is compared to an eagle flying over its young in a nest. In Isaiah this hovering is interpreted as the Lord's protecting, shielding, delivering, sparing, and rescuing his people. These concepts are reminiscent of God's great acts of delivering his people from Egyptian control many

---

[182] Young, *Isaiah*, II:377–78. Kissane, *Isaiah*, 342, also finds a contrast between God's present fighting against Zion (31:4) and his later deliverance and restoration (31:5).

[183] M. L. Barré, "Of Lions and Birds: A Note on Isaiah 31.4–5," in *Among the Prophets: Language, Image and Structure in the Prophetic Writings* (ed. P. R. Davies, D. J. A. Clines; Sheffield: JSOT Press, 1993), 55–59.

[184] Wildberger, *Isaiah 28–39*, 219, accepts "upon" since the Hb. preposition עַל can mean both "upon, against." In 29:7 a phrase similar to עַל צָבָא means "to fight against" (cf. Num 31:7; Zech 14:12), but Wildberger argues that עַל is dependent on יָרַד, "he will come down," rather than צבא, "fight."

[185] Kaiser, *Isaiah 13–39*, 316, pinpoints Hezekiah and his allies as the shepherds.

years earlier (Exod 12–13) when God "spared, passed over"[186] the Israelites and defeated the Egyptians. If God delivered the Israelites many years earlier, it is somewhat logical for Isaiah's audience to trust God to deliver them again.

31:6–7 The flow of thought about God's protection of Jerusalem (31:4–5) and defeat of Assyria (31:8–9) is interrupted by a brief parenthetical application to the prophet's readers.[187] What do these promises mean to them and how should they respond to God's grace? The prophet exhorts[188] his readers to repent and return to God.[189] He persuasively calls for a change of heart, for a rejection of the life of rebellion. Interestingly, this act is not presented as a prerequisite of divine deliverance but as a response to God's great deeds of mercy. God took the initiative to demonstrate his love to these sinners who "have deeply revolted" (he'mîqû sārâ). In spite of their apostasy, God will compassionately save his people from their enemies in order to motivate them to freely respond in repentance and thankfulness. The second verb clause, "you have so greatly revolted" (NIV), is actually a third person verb clause, "they had deeply revolted,"[190] but most translations change the verb to second person to agree with the first verb, "return." If the "sons of Israel" are the subject of the second verb, rather than a vocative at the end of the verse, no textual change is required.[191] Verse 6 does not specifically identify why the Israelites should repent. One could assume from the preceding context they need to (a) repent of their apostasy of depending on Egyptian men and horses to save them from the Assyrians, rather than God; and (b) to turn to God who can deliver and protect them. Oswalt suggests that "love prompts a turning back to God,"[192]

---

[186] The infinitive absolute פָּסֹחַ, "sparing," comes from the same root for פֶּסַח, "Passover," when God spared the Hebrew firstborn from death.

[187] Signs of discontinuity within the passage suggest these parenthetical remarks were added when Isaiah put this speech in writing. These signs of a parenthesis are that these verses (a) interrupt the flow of thought; (b) introduce topics (repentance and idols) not discussed elsewhere in this context; (c) repeat ideas from other passages (2:20); (d) use the third person verb ("they have deeply revolted") to show that Isaiah is making a distinction between what he wants his audience to do ("return") and what someone else did earlier when "they revolted"; and (e) draw out an application that is for a future time (the Day of the Lord) rather than the present situation.

[188] The imperative verb שׁוּבוּ, "return/repent," at the beginning of v. 6, functions as an exhortation or admonition (GKC §110a), indicating that the prophet is attempting to persuade his audience to change.

[189] Hayes and Irvine, *Isaiah*, 350, take a political approach to these exhortations and interpret them to be saying that the Hebrews need to reject the pro-Egyptian counselors who were advising the king to make an alliance with Egypt. This would mean that the Israelites would have to return to Jerusalem and submit themselves to the ruling Assyrian king (he views this king as Shalmaneser rather than Sennacherib).

[190] הֶעְמִיקוּ is a *hiphil* perfect, third masculine plural. An apostasy that "they dug deeply" is not a surface problem, but a sinfulness that is ingrained firmly into the theological thinking and practice of the people.

[191] Young, *Isaiah*, II:379, translates the verse: "Return to him against whom the children of Israel have deeply revolted." Wildberger, *Isaiah 28–39*, 216, has a similar translation.

[192] Oswalt, *Isaiah 1–39*, 575, suggests that a response comes from love may be valid, but it comes out of his own experience or NT examples, not from this text.

but there is nothing in this passage that identifies this as the factor that will motivate the people.

Verse 7 surprisingly introduces an eschatological urgency for repentance.[193] Drawing on earlier sermonic teachings in 2:20 and 30:22, Isaiah reminds his audience that when God comes in the splendor of his glory to establish his kingdom on Zion, he will destroy all evil and pride (2:1–22). Then people will see the uselessness of idols and reject these sinful man-made objects. People will recognize the power and holiness of Israel's God and turn to him alone. The implications of this concept also apply to Isaiah's present audience in the midst of the Assyrian crisis. If the full revelation of God's power and glory will bring this kind of response in the future, should not God's gracious display of his power and grace in defeating the Assyrians and protecting his people in Jerusalem bring a similar response at the present time?

31:8–9   The prophet's oracle concludes with a declaration that Assyria will be defeated. Since God will protect Jerusalem (31:3), the failure of the Assyrian army at Jerusalem is required. If God intends to deliver his people, then their enemies must either surrender or be defeated by some stronger power. In this case the sword that will cause the Assyrian troops to flee and their commanders to panic is not the sword of Judah or the Egyptian army. Since human power is not responsible for this act, divine power is the implied reason for Assyria's defeat. This agrees with what is explicitly stated elsewhere (14:24–27; 29:5–8; 30:27–33; 37:37). God is the mighty warrior who will attack and fight this decisive battle for sovereignty over the ancient Near Eastern political world, as well as the spiritual battle for the hearts and minds of the people of Israel and its neighbors.

Who is this God who claims to be able to decide the future by devouring large armies? Can he be trusted when a nation's very existence is on the line? Will he keep his promise to destroy the Assyrian army outside the walls of Jerusalem? Trust is inspired through the contrasting characterization of the combatants in this battle. On the one hand, there are fleeing, panic stricken, terrorized soldiers from Assyria who no longer have a "stronghold, rock" (*sela*ᶜ) to depend on (a symbol of the king of Assyria).[194] On the other hand, there is the mighty sword of God, that dependable Rock (cf. 30:29; Ps 18:3; 31:4; 42:10) that appears as a fierce fiery light[195] when the theophany of God

---

[193] Beuken, *Isaiah II*, 204, does not take this as an eschatological prophecy, but one that relates to the immediate or near future. The contextual use of this idea in earlier literature (2:20) supports an eschatological interpretation.

[194] Blenkinsopp, *Isaiah 1–39*, 426, translates "leaders, captains" in parallelism with "their commanders" later in the verse, while Hays and Irvine, *Isaiah*, 351, think the author is referring to an "Assyrian fortress," possibly Samaria, which the Assyrian forces occupied. Beuken, *Isaiah II*, 206, correctly identifies the "rock" as the king of Assyria, though he does note that the term "rock" and "the great mountain" could also be applied to the Assyrian god Ashur.

[195] The metaphors of God as a light or fire are commonly associated with the theophany appearances of God, but "furnace," תַּנּוּר, is usually a place to bake bread, clay pots, or burn sacrifices

appears in Zion (29:6). Salvation is sure! God is the victor! He is completely trustworthy!

THEOLOGICAL IMPLICATIONS. This short message during Judah's crisis with Assyria repeats many of the themes in chap. 30. This message confirms the central theological principle that it is foolish and sinful to depend on human power to bring deliverance from troubles. Human plans to manipulate a nation's circumstances will inevitably fail, just as an individual's attempt to determine his future without consulting God will end in frustration. In principle, putting trust in many horses, large armies, and fierce soldiers may seem like a reasonable solution in a crisis situation where one is vastly outnumbered, but it misconstrues the nature of a battle as merely a human conflict to see who is stronger. A second principle is that conflicts are not necessarily won by the strongest or fastest, for God is in charge of deciding who will win each battle. So the question is: Who is truly in control of a given situation—some human army, a man-made god, or God himself? God's decisions are not slanted in favor of the biggest player (cf. Gideon's small army in Judg 7; David was a weakling next to Goliath in 1 Sam 17) or the wisest human strategy. At times God favors those who "seek help from the LORD" (31:1b) and he acts against the wicked person that does not trust him. But here one must remember a third theological truth: many times God simply acts out of inexplicable divine grace that fits his eternal plans and his present purposes. No rational explanation is available; but a proper response is appropriate. When God stretches out his hand to carry out his gracious will, people need to humbly bow and acknowledge where their help has come from.

God's wise decisions are sometimes hard to understand, especially when they involve both punishment and protection. One might assume that there would always be clear-cut winners and losers, but frequently in conflict situations both sides have sinned and both sides receive some measure of grace. God may function as a lion that captures his prey (his punishment of Judah), but also as a lion that protects his prey from others (31:4–5). His grace may shield, deliver, and rescue one sinful group in the midst of judgment or bring the fire of his fierce wrath against another sinful group without any hint of grace (31:8–9). Grace is not earned or deserved; yet God richly provides hope for some through acts of divine intervention. Even the Assyrian soldiers who survived God's destruction of their army had the opportunity to respond positively to the experience of seeing the powerful hand of God at work. By grace they had survived to tell the story about God's defeat of the most powerful army in the world. Everyone who knows about the work of God has the opportunity of glorifying his name by telling others about his great deeds.

(Exod 7:28; Lev 2:4; 7:9). God is associated with a fiery furnace in Gen 15:17 that passes through the animals, signifying that God has made an oath to keep his covenant with Abram. Kaiser, *Isaiah 13–39*, 318, identifies God as the fire and the furnace as the hearth where the Assyrian army is burned up.

Those who experience God's grace need to respond appropriately (31:6–7). Three attitudinal and behavioral changes that might represent an acceptable reaction to God's compassion are found in these verses: (a) turning to God in repentance, instead of revolting against his instructions; (b) rejecting all other sources of trust that might take God's place, including idols of gold, alliances with other nations, and trust in horses and soldiers; and (c) trusting in God by seeking his will, following his instructions, and depending on his help. This suggests the principle that God is not concerned with the questions about who deserves his grace (no one does); God is interested in observing how people respond after they have tasted the riches of his grace. The repentant recognize that his grace is greater than their sinful rebellion, so they look to him in trust, knowing that God's wisdom, power, and grace constitute a sure Rock for their faith.

GOD'S EXALTATION OF A RIGHTEOUS KING (32:1–8)

¹See, a king will reign in righteousness
  and rulers will rule with justice.
²Each man will be like a shelter from the wind
  and a refuge from the storm,
like streams of water in the desert
  and the shadow of a great rock in a thirsty land.

³Then the eyes of those who see will no longer be closed,
  and the ears of those who hear will listen.
⁴The mind of the rash will know and understand,
  and the stammering tongue will be fluent and clear.
⁵No longer will the fool be called noble
  nor the scoundrel be highly respected.
⁶For the fool speaks folly,
  his mind is busy with evil:
He practices ungodliness
  and spreads error concerning the LORD;
the hungry he leaves empty
  and from the thirsty he withholds water.
⁷The scoundrel's methods are wicked,
  he makes up evil schemes
to destroy the poor with lies,
  even when the plea of the needy is just.
⁸But the noble man makes noble plans,
  and by noble deeds he stands.

Like the earlier units that begin with a woe oracle, this section (31:1–32:20) contains several messages of hope for the future (cf. 28:5–6,16–17; 29:5–8,17–24; 30:18–26). This new period of divine blessing will include righteous rulers who will protect God's people (32:1–2), the marvelous opening of the eyes of the blind (32:3–5), and the Spirit's gift of fertility to the land, justice among people, and peace for everyone (32:15–19). This future time is contrasted with the present period of complacency in Jerusalem that will lead to mourning, no fertility, and no peace (32:9–14). Such contrasts were intended to cause the heart of the audience to yearn for God's future kingdom of peace and reject the ways of this present hopeless world.

The historical circumstances that surround this sermon are only hinted at in 32:1–14. The author appears to be contrasting (a) a future reign of a righteous ruler, the opening of the eyes of the blind, and the end of foolish talk; with (b) the present situation where foolish men give bad advise, practice ungodliness, and do not care for the poor. This is also a time of complacency, about a year before the nation's destruction (32:10). Since the surrounding chapters discuss the Assyrian attack of Jerusalem in 701 BC, a date approximately one year before that event fits the broad setting of chaps. 30–32. Both the attitude of the people of Judah and the work of preparing Jerusalem to withstand the Assyrian attack in 22:1–14 have some similarities to the situation in this chapter. Hezekiah and his foolish royal wise men still do trust God to deliver them from Assyria; instead, they rest securely in their false hopes and "wicked schemes" (32:7 may refer to their alliance with Egypt).

The vocabulary of this message incorporates wisdom concepts. This relationship is most evident in 32:5–8, which refers to the acts of the fool, scoundrel, and the noble person. Verse 20 is constructed like a wisdom saying (cf. Prov 3:13; 8:34; 28:14) and H. G. M. Williamson even finds proverbial characteristics in 32:1.[196] These associations suggest that this prophetic message purposely addresses the failures of the royal wise men who do not rule righteously. Instead, they act like fools (32:5–8) and give the people a false sense of security (32:9–11).

The king who rules with righteousness (32:1–2) is associated later in the chapter with the pouring out of God's Spirit, the transformation of nature, and the inauguration of a time of peace, security, and prosperity (32:15–20). Sweeney maintains that 32:1 refers to the future righteous king Josiah (640–609 BC), Seitz believes Isaiah is affirming the monarchal rule of Hezekiah, and Motyer connects this king with the messianic figure in chaps. 9 and 11.[197] Childs straddles these positions, observing that the king in 32:1 initially could refer to any righteous ruler, but this king is later connected to changes that will take place in the future when God pours out his Spirit (32:15–20). This later context supports a messianic interpretation for the king in 32:1.[198]

---

[196] H. G. M. Williamson, "The Messianic Texts in Isaiah 1–39," *King and Messiah in Israel and the Ancient Near East: Proceedings of the Oxford Old Testament Seminar* (ed. J. Day; Sheffield: Sheffield Academic Press, 1998), 265, points to this verse's hypothetical form, general reference to kingship, imperfect verbs, and vocabulary, but none of these features is particularly convincing.

[197] Wegner, *An Examination of Kingship and Messianic Expectations in Isaiah 1–35*, 275–301, provides an extensive list of various proposals for interpreting the king in chap. 32 but concludes that this prophecy "was intentionally shaped to engender messianic ideas."

[198] Childs, *Isaiah*, 239, believes that the citation of 29:17 in 32:15 links 32:15–20 with an

Several factors make a messianic identification difficult to confirm from reading 32:1 in isolation: (a) Earlier in chaps. 9 and 11 the messianic figure was not called "king" because God is the King (6:1,5; 24:23; 33:17,22). (b) The Messiah's reign was idealized in a much grander style than in 32:1–2. And (c) princes do not share power with this ruler in chaps. 9 and 11. In spite of these differences, J. J. M. Roberts argues that both the messianic figure and this king in 32:1–2 will rule in righteousness and justice (9:7; 11:4–5), while 1:26 mentions other officials who will function in the future restored city of Jerusalem. Also, the protective characteristics in 32:2 are parallel to images of protection that God will provide when he sets up his kingdom (4:6; 25:4).[199] The time when God opens the eyes of the blind (32:3; 29:18; 35:5; 42:18), pours out his Spirit (11:1), transforms nature (30:23–26), and brings in a new age of security and peace (2:2–4; 9:6; 28:12) are all connected to a future era when God will change the world and the Messiah will reign in Zion. Though the reference to a king in 32:1 is somewhat general and undefined, the progressive revelation of additional contextual factors surrounding the appearance of this righteous king (in 32:15–20) indicates that God's future messianic ruler will be the one who will reign when these conditions exist in Jerusalem.

There are three topical issues discussed in this chapter.[200] The first paragraph announces:

The rule of a righteous king	32:1–2
Opening the eyes of the blind	32:3–4
The folly of the fools will be exposed	32:5–8.

32:1–2 The new paragraph is marked by the opening exclamation "behold; see,"[201] a marker that often announces an astonishing new event in the

---

eschatological messianic age. This editorial shaping of the material in 32:15–20 causes the unclear reference to a king in 32:1 to be understood as messianic.

[199] J. J. M. Roberts, "The Divine King and the Human Community," in *The Quest for the Kingdom of God: Studies in Honor of G. E. Mendenhall* (ed. H. B. Huffmon, F. A. Spina, A. R. W. Green; Winona Lake: Eisenbrauns, 1983), 127–36, concludes that these were the words of Isaiah about the future transformed world spoken of elsewhere (4:3–4; 10:20–23; 29:17–21; 30:18–26; 31:4–9).

[200] Sweeney, *Isaiah 1–39*, 409, divides the material into two paragraphs, vv. 1–2 about the royal savior, and vv. 3–8, a disputation with authorities. Verses 3–8 are then divided into two sections, vv. 3–4 the basic statement and vv. 5–8 fools will no longer dominate. In contrast, Beuken, *Isaiah II*, 209, divides the material into vv. 1–5 and 6–8, with v. 5 separated from vv. 6–8 because vv. 1–5 contain a series of promises.

[201] In most cases הֵן is a shortened form of הִנֵּה, meaning "behold, see," but Irwin, *Isaiah 28–33*, 118–19, proposes that this word should be treated as the conditional particle "if" as in 54:15; Exod 4:1; Lev 25:20. This would result in the translation, "If a king should rule with righteousness." Kaiser, *Isaiah 13–39*, 320, follows GKC §159w, which suggests that הֵן is an Aramaic word ("if, when") that has no connection to the Hb. הִנֵּה, "behold." Beuken, *Isaiah II*, 190, correctly rejects these approaches, for this is a salvation oracle that announces hope, not a conditional "if" promise. Typically, הִנֵּה is used to announce astonishment at something important that is about to happen (1 Sam 12:2; 18:22; 2 Sam 19:9; 1 Kgs 1:18; Jer 23:5).

future (12:2; 13:9; 17:1; 19:1; 21:9; 24:1). In contrast to the present situation in Judah, positive changes will transform the unrighteous leadership (vv. 1–2), the blind and deaf people (3–4), and people's respect for unwise advisors (vv. 5–8). Initially, the text does not reveal who will cause this transformation, but 32:15 attributes this change to the work of God's Spirit.

The unidentified king and his princes serve as a contrast to Judah's present rulers. They will rule "with justice" and they will not boast about their lies and alliances with other nations (28:14–15), reject God's providential power over their lives (29:15–16), or take advantage of people in court (29:20–21). The ideal king's just and righteous rule follows David's example (2 Sam 8:15) and is what God desires (Jer 22:3,15). God's future messianic king is that ruler who will finally establish an everlasting rule of righteousness (9:7; 11:4; 16:5; Ps 72:2; Jer 23:5) by implementing God's justice on earth (5:16; 28:17; 30:18; 33:5). Then each righteous ruler and his wise counselors will metaphorically function to provide shelter from the sun, wind, and storm,[202] plus be like a life-giving source of water in a dry desert (32:2).[203] Beuken notes that these "comparisons are not chosen arbitrarily."[204] These functions mirror other passages where God promises to protect his people from the heat, rain, and storm (4:5–6; 25:4; Ps 27:5). In addition, in 28:2 the Assyrian army was compared to the destructive power of hail, wind, storm, and flood, so the imagery in 32:2 may be an indirect promise of protection from the negative impact of people like the Assyrians. It is not clear if the "rock" (*sela*) is just meant to be a natural part of nature or if it has some metaphorical relationship to the "rock, stronghold" (*sela*) that represents God in 31:9.

32:3–4 Another change involves a reversal of the people's inability to see, hear, understand, and speak. Isaiah 6:9–10; 29:9–12 predict that the nation's eyes will be spiritually blinded and their ears will be deafened. Ahaz's unwillingness to trust God in chap. 7 during the Syro-Ephraimiate War in 743–732 BC and Judah's dependence on Egypt in chaps. 30–31 during the Assyrian attack before 701 BC demonstrate how past leaders of Judah did not listen to God's advice and promises. As a result of this blindness, Judah's priests and prophets did not see clearly or teach what God was saying (28:7–10) because their eyes were sealed (29:10). Judah's rulers made lies and deceitful alliances their refuge (28:14–15; 30:1–2,16; 31:1), lost all intelligence (29:14), and even denied God's sovereignty (29:16). But a

---

[202] Although these functions are not given much emphasis when describing kings in the OT, Wildberger, *Isaiah 28–39*, 237–38, gives examples from ancient Near Eastern texts where kings declared: " I am the shelter of Summer, its sweet shade am I" (the First Dynasty of Isin); "He who leads humans justly gives sweet shade" (Lipit-Ishtar); "my benign shadow is spread over my city" (Hammurabi); or "he is a protecting rampart . . . he is a moist cool shade in summer" (Sesostris III of Egypt).

[203] The Hb. "in the desert," בַּצָּיוֹן, is almost identical to "in Zion," בְּצִיוֹן, and is a word play.

[204] Beuken, *Isaiah II*, 211, points to a fundamental harmony between nature, cosmic order, and a righteous king's moral rule.

miraculous transformation will occur in the future when God removes all hindrances to seeing, hearing, and understanding (cf. 29:18). God's causal connection to this change is not announced in this paragraph (cf. 32:15); instead, one simply learns that the people's eyes will no longer be smeared over or blinded,[205] their ears will pay attention to what is said, and the minds of those who acted irresponsibly will actually have the understanding to know what should be done. The results of this transformation are emphasized, but the means of accomplishing this miraculous change is unstated. As the audience heard promise after promise, the natural questions arise: How will these things happen? Who will do this? What new things will people see and know? The prophet's words are full of hope but very limited in the amount of information provided. His purpose seems to be to contrast the future good times with the present bad time to encourage his audience to yearn for these better days (32:9–14); later, he will reveal the source of this transforming power (32:15–20).

Although commentators have frequently made a connection between the imagery of wisdom literature and the vocabulary of eyes seeing, ears hearing, and the functions of the mind and tongue with,[206] these themes are widely used in Isaiah's preaching. They are fundamental to understanding Isaiah's calling and mission, plus they function as key images that explain God's plan to transform his rebellious people (6:9–10; 29:18; 35:5–6; 42:18; 50:4). Such terminology reflects the prophet's familiarity with the thought world of his royal adversaries as well as his strong opposition to the wise counselors who were foolishly advising Hezekiah to trust in the Egyptians (32:7–8).

32:5–8 The consequences of this new insight (32:3–4) will transform how people honor and respect others. Once people's eyes are open to the truth and they have a new understanding of reality, they will no longer follow or respect the foolish leaders and the scoundrels that paraded around as honorable politicians and noble royal counselors. At some point the people of Judah will see the folly in the fool's advice, recognize his behavior as evil and godless, realize he is not motivated to help people, and know that he misrepresents God's way (32:6).[207] The selfish fool who does not really care about helping others should not be confused with a highly respected person of noble character.

---

[205] The word תִּשְׁעֶינָה comes from the root שָׁעַע, "smear over, blind," not the root שָׁעָה, "see."

[206] R. B. Y. Scott, "Isaiah 1–39," *IB* (Nashville: Abingdon, 1956), 342, concludes, "Isaiah has shown himself able to adapt the method and manner of the wisdom teachers to his prophetic messages."

[207] A person who is called a fool (*nābāl*) can refer to one who (a) does not have the good sense to avoid shameful behavior (Gen 34:7); (b) is stupid enough to get involved with sexual misconduct (Judg 19:23); (c) has the audacity to steal goods dedicated to God (Josh 7:15); (d) is not wise enough to seek God (Ps 14:2); (e) speaks unwise words (1 Sam 25:25); (f) is morally deficient of theological insight; and (g) acts in rebellion against the order God has established for society. M. Saebo, "נָבָל *nābāl* fool," *TLOT*, II, 710–14, also notes that the fool acts just the opposite of the wise, prudent, honorable, and godly person.

The "scoundrel" (*kēlay* 32:7) is one who is cunning, so he uses evil scheming counsel to get his way. In the end, his conniving ways hurt the common people who have no status in society because justice and truth do not guide his path. He speaks false words against the weak and poor people of the land, rather than speaking good words to ensure that they receive justice in the courts. He says and does whatever it takes to manipulate the facts to serve his own selfish goals. Both of these people stand in conflict with the noble person who has high moral standards, gives wise counsel, and exhibits truly honorable motives (32:8). Although the prophet does not accuse any specific person by name, the audience no doubt knew some of the king's royal advisors who fit in each camp. When God fulfilled the prophecies of Isaiah, the outcome would demonstrate that the "wise plans" of some conniving politicians were foolish. Then the people of Judah would have their eyes opened and know whom they should trust.

MOURNING FROM COMPLACENCY: LIFE FROM THE SPIRIT (32:9–20)

> [9]You women who are so complacent,
>   rise up and listen to me;
> you daughters who feel secure,
>   hear what I have to say!
> [10]In little more than a year
>   you who feel secure will tremble;
> the grape harvest will fail,
>   and the harvest of fruit will not come.
> [11]Tremble, you complacent women;
>   shudder, you daughters who feel secure!
> Strip off your clothes,
>   put sackcloth around your waists.
> [12]Beat your breasts for the pleasant fields,
>   for the fruitful vines
> [13]and for the land of my people,
>   a land overgrown with thorns and briers—
> yes, mourn for all houses of merriment
>   and for this city of revelry.
> [14]The fortress will be abandoned,
>   the noisy city deserted;
> citadel and watchtower will become a wasteland forever,
>   the delight of donkeys, a pasture for flocks,
> [15]till the Spirit is poured upon us from on high,
>   and the desert becomes a fertile field,
>   and the fertile field seems like a forest.
> [16]Justice will dwell in the desert
>   and righteousness live in the fertile field.
> [17]The fruit of righteousness will be peace;
>   the effect of righteousness will be quietness and confidenceforever.

¹⁸**My people will live in peaceful dwelling places,**
   in secure homes,
   in undisturbed places of rest.
¹⁹**Though hail flattens the forest**
   and the city is leveled completely,
²⁰**how blessed you will be,**
   sowing your seed by every stream,
   and letting your cattle and donkeys range free.

Blenkinsopp considers 32:15–20 a continuation of 32:1–8 after a lament about Judah's lost harvest that was taken by the Assyrian army in 32:9–14, while Childs hypothesizes that the positive and negative paragraphs in chap. 32 were developed from similar patterns already present in chap. 3.[208] These approaches, which identify historical and theological interrelationships between paragraphs and comparable chapters, are to be preferred over Clement's hypothesis that a later post-exilic redactor inserted later laments after the fall of Jerusalem (32:9–14) in the midst of the nation's idealistic hopes for Josiah's reforms (32:1–8, 15–20).[209] Certainly the women's optimistic complacency about the fate of Jerusalem in 32:9–14 could have developed out of the reckless judgments of the king's foolish advisors. They spoke nonsense and lies about the wonderful benefits of having an alliance with Egypt (it would supposedly save the nation from Assyria: 32:6–7). The destruction of the nation and its agriculture because of war in 32:12–14 is directly related to the Spirit's future restoration of fertility and peace in 32:15,20. From an historical and literary approach, the paragraphs in this chapter fit together.

This paragraph is topically divided into two major sections:

Complacent women of Jerusalem must lament	32:9–14
Call for women to listen	9–10
Call for women to mourn	11–14
God's Spirit will transform their world	32:15–20
The Spirit's work of restoration	15–16
The fruits of righteousness	17–20

Although eschatological markers like "in that day" are not appended to any of these promises, 32:15–20 appears to be connected to divine blessings God will pour out on the earth when he establishes his eternal kingdom through

---

[208] Blenkinsopp, *Isaiah 1–39*, 433, found similarities between the themes in chaps. 32 and 24–27, while Childs, *Isaiah*, 238, 240, finds a connection between the proud women of Jerusalem in 3:16–4:1 and the complacent women in 32:9–14, plus a similar stark contrast between present reality and God's future plans (3:15–20 and 4:2–6).

[209] Clements, *Isaiah 1–39*, 260–61, reconstructs this imaginative thesis out of thin air instead of tying these words to the circumstances in Jerusalem during the Assyrian crisis. Oswalt, *Isaiah 1–39*, 583, rejects this approach, and Childs, *Isaiah*, 237, concludes that "these various redactional schemata are highly unsatisfactory. Not only are they very speculative . . . but the exegetical effort is to shatter the passage's literary integrity by claiming to reconstruct three distinct levels within a process."

a righteous king (32:1–8; 9:1–7). This ideal picture of a wonderful situation in the future (32:15–20) stands in stark contrast to the destruction that Judah experienced during the Assyrian crisis (32:9–14).

32:9–14 The new paragraph is marked by a series of feminine plural imperative verbs[210] that exhort a group of women to lament. The connection with the preceding paragraph is that these women complacently trusted[211] the lies and foolish plans of the fools and scoundrels (32:6–7). These women need to realize that the bright hopes for the future that Isaiah envisioned (32:1–8) are not identical to the optimistic words of the royal wise men. Before the righteous king appears to establish this new world, there will be much distress. These women are victims of deceit and the political spinning of military events that made a bad situation look optimistic. Consequently, these women feel very secure and safe (cf. 3:16–4:1; Amos 6:1) because their complacency was rationally based on the news they heard from the royal court. They accepted the propaganda that they could put their hope in Egypt. They rejected Isaiah's scenario that revealed God's plans for the destruction of the city (28:11–13,18–22; 29:1–4; 30:1–5,12–14; 31:1–3; 32:10,14), for it contradicted the rosy picture painted by the royal advisors in Jerusalem.

The prophet warns these naive women by summoning them to cry out in lamentation and grief, directly addressing them with four imperatives in vv. 9–10. In between the prophet's own tears, he pleads in the first two imperatives for the women to listen carefully to what he has to say (cf. 28:23). He was hoping that they would not ignore his weeping but seriously consider the truthfulness of his words. He had a relevant message that would affect their lives in the coming year.[212] Before their next harvest could be safe and securely stored in Jerusalem, life in Jerusalem would become frightening. The reason the harvest would fail is left unstated, but if the Assyrian army occupied the land of Judah, they would use the harvest to feed themselves and their presence would prevent anyone from planting for the next year.

A second series of unusual imperative forms[213] advises these trusting women and others in the crowd to join the prophet in lamenting (32:11–12) by taking

---

[210] The three imperative verbs in 32:9 (קֹמְנָה, "rise up," שְׁמַעְנָה, "hear," and הַאְזֵנָּה, "give ear") are not ironic. The prophet truly wants these women to wake up and realize what will happen; therefore, they should be classified as admonitions (GKC §110a).

[211] The word translated "complacent" is בֹּטְחוֹת, "trusting ones," which addresses the fundamental issue of their relationship with others. Will they trust God or trust the royal wise men?

[212] The phrase יָמִים עַל־שָׁנָה is lit. "days upon a year," a phrase that is somewhat obscure. Wildberger, *Isaiah 28–39*, 250, translates these words "concerning year and day," which is made more specific by the reference to the coming harvest.

[213] The first imperative (חִרְדוּ, "tremble") is masculine plural, while the second, third and fourth imperatives are either lengthened second masculine singular emphatic imperatives (GKC §48i) or Aramaic forms of the second feminine plural (GKC §48i). The meaning of the words is not in question but the grammar is difficult. The masculine forms are more common when addressing a mixed group. The initial plural form would address them as many people, while the singular forms would indicate the prophet was addressing the whole community as a single group.

off their fancy clothes, putting on sackcloth, beating their breast in agony, and mourning. The reason they should lament is that they will not enjoy the next harvest (32:10); instead, the land of "my people" ('*ammî*) will be overgrown with thorns (5:6; 7:23–25; 10:17; 27:4), the city and fortress on Jerusalem's Ophel hill will be empty, and animals will be wandering around the pasture-land that is now their city (32:13–14; 5:17; 13:19–22; 34:11–14). These are common images of military defeat, which often involved the total destruction of the agricultural economy and fortified urban centers. This means that the life of luxury that these women have enjoyed will end, and the political alliances that were supposed to protect the people of Jerusalem will not protect them. If this is true, the prophet's audience should begin mourning immediately, for they will not enjoy the wonderful days when the righteous king reigns (32:1–8) unless they do something immediately (such as repenting, as in 31:6–7) to stop this disaster from falling on Jerusalem.

32:15–20 The final part of this paragraph indicates that the people will experience trials "until God's Spirit is poured out" (cf. 44:3; 59:21) and transforms their world by reversing the conditions that prevailed in 32:9–14.

32:10 No harvest	32:15 Fertile land
32:10 Falsely complacent and secure	32:18 Secure and undisturbed
32:14 City desolate	32:18 People dwell in homes
32:14 Cattle in the city	32:20 Cattle roam free

The contrast between the lament in 32:9–14 and the offer of hope in the salvation oracle in 32:15–20 illustrates how weak and powerless mankind is when it comes to solving the problems of this world. The peace, prosperity, and security that people long for will not come through their manipulation of military forces or the scheming of royal wise men; it will come from God's marvelous work among his people.

It is difficult to know what Isaiah or his audience understood about the coming of God's Spirit, since the amount of information revealed at this time about the work of the Spirit was somewhat limited. People did know that God's Spirit (lit. "the Spirit from on high," *rûaḥ mimmārôm*) was a powerful force that gave people the ability to make things with their hands (Exod 31:3–5), have extraordinary strength to fight (Judg 14:5–6, 19), lead the nation (Num 11:16–17,25; Num 27:15–23; Deut 34:9; 1 Sam 16:13), and speak the words of God (Num 23:5; 2 Sam 23:2; 1 Chr 28:11–12; Mic 3:8). The Spirit will also have a major role in bringing about the messianic era (Isa 11:1–2). One of the primary changes that the new king (32:1) and the Spirit will introduce will be a period of righteousness and justice (32:16–17; 9:7) that results in peace. This suggests that the spiritual transformation of the hearts and behavior of people is at the center of what God desires to accomplish on earth. This text does not address the relationship between the coming of the righteous king (v. 1) and the Spirit (v. 15), but one must assume that these are complementary forces that will work together (cf. 9:1) to produce this new world order based on righteousness and justice.

32:15–18   No date is provided for the coming of God's Spirit; the date is sometime after the desolation of Jerusalem. The Spirit will be poured out "upon us" (*ʿalênû*), though "us" is not defined specifically. It could refer to mankind in general (cf. Joel 2:28–32), though the reference to "my people" (32:13,18) in both the negative and positive sections argues that the prophet is primarily addressing the future setting of the Hebrew people (cf. 44:3). The act of the Spirit being "poured out"[214] is a gracious gift from God and not something people earn or deserve. The coming of God's Spirit will transform nature and people, an act that implies the removal of God's original curse on the land and human relationships (Gen 3:14–19). The Spirit gives new life, revitalizing the created order back to its original design and purpose. Instead of having a desolate land filled with thorns and briers and no harvests (32:10,12), even the dry desert lands will become green fertile fields or lush forests (repeating 29:17). This idea is used elsewhere to picture their eschatological hope for the future (Hos 2:21–23; Amos 9:13–14), which can be expressed in terminology that indicates a return to the paradise of Eden (41:19; 51:3). Based on this additional progressive revelation, Childs claims, "Whereas it was unclear in 32:1ff. whether the initial oracle was messianic or nonmessianic, the editorial shaping makes it now apparent that vv. 1–8 are to be understood messianically."[215]

Surprisingly, the spiritual change does not describe repentance, though one must assume it will occur (as indicated by the changed behavior in 30:15) sometime between the coming of the Spirit and the initial signs of the presence of righteousness and justice in human relationships. The absence of any mention of repentance only heightens the central importance of the pouring out of the Spirit. This change is totally a work of the Spirit, not brought on by a humanly induced reform (by Hezekiah or Josiah). Once the Spirit comes, his overpowering life-changing power will produce the results of righteousness in the community. Isaiah emphasizes the results of the Spirit's power, not the change process that will happen within the hearts of people. The connections between justice and the desert and between righteousness and the fertile field create an odd metaphor for most Westerners. Together the desert and fertile fields symbolize every place where people dwell. In all these places justice and righteousness will abide because the people in those places will practice justice in their relationships. The use of the verbs "dwell, tabernacle" and "sit, inhabit,

---

[214] The *niphal* passive verb יְעָרֶה demonstrates that when "it will be poured out" on mankind, it will be a gracious work accomplished by someone else for the benefit of mankind.

[215] Childs, *Isaiah*, 241, admits that this passage has a quite different style when it is compared to chaps. 9 and 11, but the themes in vv. 15–18 make it clear that the prophet was dealing with eschatological issues and was not expecting a fulfillment in his own day.

dwell"[216] are employed to describe a situation where a permanent residence is envisioned, not a brief visit.

The fruits of righteous and just living will create a dramatically changed setting among God's people (32:17–18), especially when it is compared to circumstances existing during the Assyrian attack on Judah. Instead of siege and war (29:1–2), the "work, effect"[217] of righteousness will be peace. This idea is consistent with conditions describing the rule of the messianic king (cf. 9:6–7; Ps 72:3–7). This peace is not defined, but one would think that it would include peace with other individuals and nations (cf. 2:3–4) as well as peace with God. Additionally, quietness and calmness will replace fear (cf. 7:2,4; 30:15), and security (or "trust," *betah*) will replace a false, complacent sense of security (as in 32:10–11). These claims demonstrate that people cannot produce peace and security on their own through human efforts or political alliance. Peace and security are the lasting ("forever" in 32:16) results of (a) God's Spirit producing righteousness within people; and (b) righteousness producing peace and security/trust. This peace will be evident (32:18) in all the places where people dwell—pastures, homes, and any other quiet resting place. This might suggest that the fruits of the Spirit (Gal 5:22–23) are an echo of Isaiah's message.[218]

32:19–20   The negative tone of v. 19 is surprising in the midst of a salvation oracle. In order to integrate v. 9 into a paragraph of hope, O. Kaiser maintains that it refers to the destruction of the Assyrians ("the forest," *hayyāʿar*, as in 10:33; 30:31) and the capital city of that nation. Although this gives hope to an Israelite audience, this chapter is not about the destruction of Assyria. Earlier in the immediate context of 32:13–14, the "city" (*ʿîr*) refers to Jerusalem and the "forest" (32:15) describes the land of Israel. Thus the context argues that one should view this verse as a recapitulation of 32:9–15, indicating that the whole land (cities and forests) will be "humbled" (*tišpal*) in God's judgment (cf. 2:11–17).[219] This immediate punishment does not in any way destroy or weaken God's eternal plan for his people.

In proverbial style (32:20), the prophet reiterates God's blessing on the agricultural efforts of his people (30:18–26). First, water, a sign of God's blessing,

---

[216] The verbs שָׁכֵן and יָשַׁב, "dwell, inhabit," indicate that the prophet is not describing a temporary characteristic, but one that remains firmly established in a place. The text does not say the Spirit will dwell in mankind, but if the coming of the Spirit produces righteousness, it is logical to assume that the Spirit must dwell in mankind if righteousness is going to dwell among them.

[217] By using the participle to describe the "working, activity," מַעֲשֵׂה, of righteousness, the prophet is pointing to the active power that righteousness has on people to produce the results described. People do not produce peace, but the Spirit does through the "working of righteousness" in them.

[218] G. K. Beale, "The Old Testament Background of Paul's References to 'the fruit of the Spirit' in Galatians 5:22," *IBR* 15 (2005): 1–38, suggests that Paul used Isa 32 and 57 as his source of information about the transformative changes the Spirit will inaugurate.

[219] Motyer, *The Prophecy of Isaiah*, 261, follows Delitzsch in viewing the destruction of the forest as a sign of Assyria's demise, but then applies the humbling of the city to Jerusalem. The parallelism and use of both terms in 32:9–15 argues against this interpretation.

will be abundantly available everywhere; then the people will freely sow their crops near to these sources of water. Second, there will be such abundance that their animals will freely eat of the abundant food available (cf. 30:23–25 for a similar picture).[220] Although sometimes people tend to think of the eschatological events entirely in spiritual terms, Childs takes a more holistic perspective, concluding that the changes in the kingdom of God will "transform the entire world and that sacred and secular society are held together in an integral unity."[221] This promise of a radical transformation of the cosmos should have caused the prophet's audience to trust God for their future, even though their present circumstances in Jerusalem might appear quite grim.

THEOLOGICAL IMPLICATIONS. Hope is a solid foundation for motivating people to trust God. For the person who has no idea about what might happen in the future and has no idea about who is in charge of the future, life would appear quite hopeless at times. The theological issue that every person must ask is: Does my confidence for today and my hope for tomorrow rest on a sure foundation? Sometimes people appear to be secure and peaceful (the women of Jerusalem in 32:9), but their trust and security are an illusion because they rely on a weak base or a misunderstanding of the facts. That is a lamentable situation that needs to be corrected by shining the light of God's word on the cultural misperception of the day. God's messengers need to present people with a sure hope to give people real security.

The theological principle that Isaiah teaches is that true security and peace are by-products of righteous living, and righteous living is made possible through the gift of God's Spirit and the rule of his just king. Security cannot be gained through human effort or the manipulation of a person's circumstances, but it can be received as a gift because of the Spirit's work in one's life. Although the connections are not clearly drawn out or fully explained, the work of the new king and Spirit will result in protection, opening of people's eyes, a new understanding, the rejection of foolish and wicked ideas (32:2–8), and the renewal of nature (32:15,20). Although these will result in a wonderful and fertile environment on earth, justice and righteousness will be key ingredients that accompany this new era of trust, security, and peace (32:16–18). Past and present readers of Isaiah's words need to ask the fundamental question: Do they want to live complacent, blind lives following the wisdom of this age? And consequently, do they want to risk the chance of being disillusioned by the devastation that will happen in the future. Or do they want to trust God's Spirit and his king to provide them with hope for a peaceful and secure future?

---

[220] On a trip to Egypt some years back, this writer saw work animals staked on barren ground eating a few small handfuls of grass that the owner allotted each animal. When feed is limited, animals are not allowed to walk on the grass, destroying some as they eat freely, nor are they allowed to eat more than what is absolutely necessary. This will not be a problem in the future.

[221] Childs, *Isaiah*, 242, understands Isaiah to be talking about the Spirit's bringing about changes in nature, social relationships, government, and spiritual relationships to God.

(3) Third Woe: Confidence in God's Victory over the Destroyer (33:1–24)

The third woe in this series (30:1; 31:1: 33:1) closes the second group of three woes.[222] All the woes in this section deal with the Assyrian attack on Jerusalem (704–701 BC) and the Hebrews' attempt to survive this military crisis. The first two woes focus on Judah's foolish attempt to solve their problem by making an alliance with Egypt (30:1–7; 31:1–3). Within these oracles there are references to God's plans to defeat the Assyrians in order to save his people (30:27–33; 31:8–9), but in 33:1 the woe oracle itself applies to the destroyer Assyria.

GENRE.   This chapter is made up of several short paragraphs that do not easily fit together into one unified whole. H. Gunkel realized that portions of the first two paragraphs followed the pattern of a communal lament and the third was similar to a "Torah liturgy," so he called the whole chapter a prophetic liturgy.[223] This title seems more like a catchall term, rather than a description of a specific literary genre. Although it sounds a little harsh, Childs states that "his theory remains at best a brilliant piece of speculation."[224] Sweeney makes more specific identifications of various literary genres by finding a woe oracle in 33:1, two petitions to God in 33:2–4, a divine response to the petition in 33:5–6; an announcement of punishment in 33:7–13, an entrance liturgy in 33:14–16, and an announcement of a royal savior in 33:17–24.[225] These designations help connect this material to similar literary writings, but they do not tie the parts together into a unified whole.

In addition to understanding the genre of each paragraph, one must sense how each genre functions to present the prophet's overall message. For example, the announcement of judgment against the enemy in 33:7–13 actually appears to function as a statement of assurance (a frequent part of a lament in Psalms) to create confidence and faith in the heart of the listener in Judah. In light of frequent statements that were intended to encourage the audience to trust God (33:1,3–6,10–13,15–16), 33:1–16 has many of the characteristics of a psalm of confidence, while 33:17–24 is a salvation oracle announcing the coming of their glorious king.

In addition to the traditional form critical analysis, Beuken looks at the role chap. 33 plays in the development of the book of Isaiah. His study of

---

[222] The three woes of the first group begin in 28:1, 29:1, and 29:15. For the structure of this section, see the introduction to chaps. 28–35.

[223] H. Gunkel, "Jesaja 33, eine propheticshe Liturgie: Ein Vortrag," *ZAW* 42 (1924), 177–208, defines a prophetic liturgy as "a poetic composition which is performed by alternating voices," though he does not suggest a specific liturgical setting where this chapter was spoken within the temple worship.

[224] The perspective of Childs, *Isaiah*, 245, is partially based on the conclusion that "there is really no hard evidence for a liturgy."

[225] Sweeney, *Isaiah 1–39*, 426–28, calls the whole chapter a "Prophetic Announcement of a Royal Savior." He interprets the "entrance liturgy" in 32:14–16, not as a challenge to someone's righteousness, but "as a means to assert the righteousness or cultic purity of liturgical participant."

quotations in chap. 33 led him to conclude that this chapter was a "mirror text" that a later writer created to mirror words and phrases from chaps. 1–32 as well as 34–66.[226] Because chap. 33 quotes from all parts of the book, he believes it prefigures the transition to key themes treated in 40–66. It functions in the literary development of the book as a bridge or link between the first half and the second half of the book. Williamson holds that the author of chaps. 40–54 (often called "Deutero-Isaiah") wrote chap. 33, but he does not believe that chap. 33 quotes from chaps. 55–66 (sometimes called "Trito-Isaiah"). Instead, he reverses the order and suggests that the author of chaps. 55–66 quoted from chap. 33.[227] This illustrates the difficulty of proving who copied from whom, for other commentators derive themes and vocabulary in chap. 33 largely from the earlier passages in Isaiah or from Psalms.[228] One could also argue that many of these literary connections are merely incidental and not due to direct literary dependence, or that chaps. 40–66 actually draw on themes from earlier ideas in chap. 33. The exegesis below will attempt to tie chap. 33 primarily to the historical and literary context of its immediate environment in chaps. 28–33. Beuken concludes that "the chapter itself is surprisingly attuned to the core of Isaiah's preaching."[229]

HISTORICAL SETTING. Since chap. 33 is part of the literary unit of woe oracles extending from chaps. 28–33, the first historical option to investigate would be the events around 704–701 BC. This would suggest that the "destroyer" and "arrogant people" with obscure speech, who will be destroyed in 33:1,18–19, are the Assyrians who attacked Judah. They caused distress on "us" (33:2), so the people of Jerusalem are mourning (33:9). The broken treaty in 33:8 must refer to a broken political agreement between Judah and another unidentified nation.

Those who attribute this chapter to someone other than Isaiah connect these prophesies with Judah's conflict with the Babylonian (in 586 BC), the Persians, or the Seleucids in the Greek period,[230] but an historical setting during the Assyrian siege of Jerusalem seems to fit best. Watts maintains, "The most likely

---

[226] W. A. M. Beuken, "Jesaja 33 als Spiegeltext im Jesajabuch," *ETL* 67 (1991), 5–35.

[227] Williamson, *The Book Called Isaiah,* 221–239, argues that "Deutero-Isaiah" wrote chap. 33 and that there is a special connection between chaps. 33 and 54, the concluding chapter of 40–54.

[228] R. Murray, "Prophecy and Cult," *Israel's Prophetic Heritage: Essays in Honor of Peter R. Ackroyd* (ed. R. Coggin, A. Phillips, M. Knibb; Cambridge: Cambridge University Press, 1982), 200–216, finds a strong connection to Pss 15, 24, 46, and Isaiah 24, but his exegesis of chap. 33 seems far off the mark. More acceptable is J. J. M. Roberts, "Isaiah 33: An Isaianic Elaboration of the Zion Tradition," *The Word of the Lord Shall Go Forth* (ed. C. L. Meyers and M. O'Conner; Winona Lake: Eisenbrauns, 1983), 15–25, who finds connections with Ps 15, 24, and 48 and numerous earlier chapters in Isaiah.

[229] Beuken, *Isaiah II*, 247.

[230] Clements, *Isaiah 1–39*, 265, connects these events to the Babylonian conquest of Jerusalem. Kaiser, *Isaiah 13–39*, 342, looks for a Hellenistic date when the Seleucids demanded tribute from Jerusalem, while Wildberger, *Isaiah 28–39*, 271, maintains that the oppressors were the Persians.

identification is Assyria itself."[231] When the Assyrians tried to destroy Jerusalem, it is possible that Hezekiah reached an agreement of peace with Assyria when he paid the tribute that the Assyrian King Sennacherib demanded (2 Kgs 18:14–16). The broken covenant could refer to the Assyrian king changing his demands and requiring unconditional surrender, instead of letting Hezekiah go free after he paid a tribute. If this is the hopeless situation of the people of Jerusalem in chap. 33, Isaiah's message presents great hope if the people will trust in God their great King.

The structure of chap. 33 is complicated, for numerous short sayings are abruptly arranged next to one another without any transitions. The chapter follows the general themes of the psalms of confidence or trust. The chapter can be divided into two paragraphs.

Woe to Assyria, and Jerusalem's Confidence	33:1–16
Woe to Assyria	1
Prayer for God's help	2
Confidence and praise for salvation	3–6
Lament: the land is ruined	7–9
God will judge their enemies	10–13
Instructions on righteous living	14–16
The reign of God in Zion	33:17–24
The King will end this war	17–19
The King will make Jerusalem secure	20–24

WOE TO ASSYRIA, AND JERUSALEM'S CONFIDENCE (33:1–16)

¹Woe to you, O destroyer,
you who have not been destroyed!
Woe to you, O traitor,
you who have not been betrayed!
When you stop destroying,
you will be destroyed;
when you stop betraying,
you will be betrayed.

²O LORD, be gracious to us;
we long for you.
Be our strength every morning,
our salvation in time of distress.
³At the thunder of your voice, the peoples flee;
when you rise up, the nations scatter.
⁴Your plunder, O nations, is harvested as by young locusts;
like a swarm of locusts men pounce on it.

---

[231] Watts, *Isaiah 1–33*, 420–21, suggests that the "Vision has from the beginning viewed the Assyrian role as one of bringing destruction."

⁵The LORD is exalted, for he dwells on high;
    he will fill Zion with justice and righteousness.
⁶He will be the sure foundation for your times,
    a rich store of salvation and wisdom and knowledge;
    the fear of the LORD is the key to this treasure.

⁷Look, their brave men cry aloud in the streets;
    the envoys of peace weep bitterly.
⁸The highways are deserted,
    no travelers are on the roads.
 The treaty is broken,
    its witnesses are despised,
    no one is respected.
⁹The land mourns and wastes away,
    Lebanon is ashamed and withers;
 Sharon is like the Arabah,
    and Bashan and Carmel drop their leaves.

¹⁰"Now will I arise," says the LORD.
    "Now will I be exalted;
    now will I be lifted up.
¹¹You conceive chaff,
    you give birth to straw;
    your breath is a fire that consumes you.
¹²The peoples will be burned as if to lime;
    like cut thornbushes they will be set ablaze."

¹³You who are far away, hear what I have done;
    you who are near, acknowledge my power!
¹⁴The sinners in Zion are terrified;
    trembling grips the godless:
 "Who of us can dwell with the consuming fire?
 Who of us can dwell with everlasting burning?"
¹⁵He who walks righteously
    and speaks what is right,
 who rejects gain from extortion
    and keeps his hand from accepting bribes,
 who stops his ears against plots of murder
    and shuts his eyes against contemplating evil—
¹⁶this is the man who will dwell on the heights,
    whose refuge will be the mountain fortress.
 His bread will be supplied,
    and water will not fail him.

33:1   The group of people that the prophet addresses in this woe oracle is called "the destroyer,"²³² an ambiguous title that could apply to almost any superior nation that attempts to destroy weaker ones. Similar terminology was

---

²³² The active participle שׁוֹדֵד functions as a noun (GKC §116g), while the passive participle שָׁדוּד functions as a verb (GKC §116f,m) since it has a subject "you."

used to describe the foe that was destroying Moab (probably Assyria, in 16:4) and Babylon (probably Assyria, in 21:2), so it makes the most sense to conclude that this woe refers to Assyria. The nation is also described as a "traitor, betrayer, treacherous one" (NIV adds another "woe" in 33:1b that is not in the Hebrew), but in contrast "they did not betray him." This indicates an unjust treatment of some nation, consistent with the idea of breaking a treaty in 33:8. As a result the destroyer will be destroyed, rectifying the present injustice. This will not happen at just any time, but specifically "when you complete, finish"[233] destroying everyone included in God's wise plans (cf. 10:5–6,12; 14:24). This must refer to God's plan to have Assyria bring destruction on Judah and other nations in the ancient Near Eastern world.

It should strike every listener or reader as very odd, if not totally strange and incomprehensible, that God would lead Isaiah to lament the destruction of the nation's powerful enemy. Since there is no indication that the prophet actually shouted this woe oracle over the wall to the Assyrian troops as a curse on them, one must assume that he spoke these words to people in Jerusalem. When the prophet's audience in Jerusalem heard that God would destroy Assyria in this ironic woe oracle, this message functioned as a word of hope and it gave the people in Jerusalem confidence and assurance. It should have motivated his Jerusalem audience to trust God because now they had another announcement that assured them that God would destroy the strong Assyrian army outside their gates.

33:2 Hearing this word of hope for Judah, the prophet prays to God, imploring God to be gracious "to us," the people in Jerusalem. Judah was anxiously waiting in hope for God to act (8:17; 25:9), for God to show his powerful arm[234] of salvation during this time of trouble. The prophet sets the example by openly expressing his dependence on God for "our salvation, deliverance" (*yĕšûʿātēnû*) and strength to endure this present crisis situation. The prophet knew that the only one who could defeat this enemy was God. Maybe some in his audience will follow his example, pray for divine assistance, and put their trust in God.

33:3–4 Now the prophet expresses his confident expectation that God's coming intervention to destroy the destroyer will be marked by the "thunder of your voice." The verse literally says "at the thunderous noise/sound," which Wildberger views as the clashing of swords and the roar of the charging Assyrian troops (17:12; 29:7), but Oswalt draws attention to places where "thunder" is associated with the voice of God (1 Sam 2:10; 7:10; Job 37:4–5; 40:9; Ps 18:13).[235] This creates a better parallelism with the next line that describes

---

[233] NIV has "stop." The Masoretic כַּנְּלֹתְךָ is an infinitive construct from נָלָה, "he obtained, attained," which does not fit well. 1QIsaᵃ changes one letter to ככלתך, from the root כָּלָה, "he ended, completed," which fits the parallelism.

[234] The Hb. זְרֹעָם, "their arm," makes no sense. Since the last line has the parallel "our salvation," NIV and most others assume a scribal error, mixing up נ and ם.

[235] Wildberger, *Isaiah 28–39*, 273, connects the clash of the armies in v. 3 with the taking of booty in v. 4, while Oswalt, *Isaiah 1–39*, 593, relies on v. 10 and the parallelism of the next line.

God's rising up (also in 30:18; 33:10) to cause the enemy soldiers from the nations (the Assyrian army) to flee. As a result of the scattering of the army, people will descend like a massive horde of locusts on the booty that the enemy army will leave behind (33:4).

33:5–6 Verse 5 has themes and grammar (the use of participles in the first line) similar to a hymn of praise. The exaltation of God is also treated in earlier oracles in Isaiah (2:11,17; 12:4), and the future presence of justice and righteousness in Zion is a common prophetic ideal (1:21,27; 5:7; 9:6; 16:5; 28:17; 32:1,16). God will not just encourage people to be righteous, he will also "fill"[236] the place with godly characteristics. These proclamations about who God is and what he will do express the prophet's confidence in God's care to fulfill his plans for his people. Even though at this time the destroyer is destroying and betraying them, the prophet confidently proclaims that God still reigns on high (6:1; 32:15; 40:22); this is no time to give up on God.

The NIV periphrastic reference to God as a "sure foundation" (33:6) misleads the reader to think of the precious cornerstone that would be a sure foundation in 28:16, but the two texts are not saying the same thing. This passage refers to God's bringing "faithfulness, stability, security"[237] (not NIV's "sure foundation") to "your times," that is, the situation of Judah in 701 BC, not some future eschatological situation as in chap. 28. From the human perspective, the chaos of war, the loss of Egyptian help, and the treacherous breaking of a treaty (33:8) made the audience sense that events were hopelessly out of control. From the divine perspective, the prophet could express the faith statement that God would provide a rich abundance of salvation (as requested in 33:2), and knowledge that far surpassed anything their enemies possessed (cf. 10:13; 29:14) plus true wisdom (31:2). The final clause indicates that the audience needed to have an attitude of fear and reverence for God in order to receive these treasured gifts from him. The NIV adds the thought that this is "the key to" (which is not in the Hebrew) his treasure, while other translations change the Hebrew pronoun "his treasure" (God's) to "her treasure" (Judah's).[238] According to the latter interpretation, the fear of the Lord would be considered one of the gifts (along with salvation and wisdom) that God will grant to his people from his treasure house of riches. This verse shows how utterly dependent people are on God's gracious work in their hearts, his illumination for understanding, and his empowerment for service.

---

[236] The prophetic perfect verb מָלֵא (GKC §106n) looks toward that day that the seraphim mentioned in 6:3 when the earth will be full of the glory of God. The glorious work of God on earth before that day gives people a brief glimpse of what the future holds.

[237] The construct noun אֱמוּנַת comes from the verbal root אָמַן and communicates the idea of steadfastness, trustworthiness, or faithfulness that produces security.

[238] Blenkinsopp, *Isaiah 1–39*, 437, translates the final phrase, "her treasure is the fear of Yahweh," which he takes as a summary of the four preceding characteristics. Kissane, *Isaiah*, 362, connects 33:5–6 to God's past gifts to his people in their golden age and understands the fear of the Lord as "treasures that he demanded in payment for His protection."

33:7–9   Although it is exciting and comforting to think about the glories of God's spiritual riches, the historical situation around Isaiah and his audience did not reveal any signs of God's salvation at this time. Sweeney takes vv. 7–9 as an accusation against Judah's enemies, which justifies God's punishment in vv. 10–13, but Beuken characterizes vv. 7–9 as a lament that describes the present disaster Jerusalem faces.[239] Thus the text should be read, not as a rhetorical series of stern attacks on the Assyrians outside the wall, but as a description of the mourning in the city of Jerusalem about the hopeless situation of Isaiah's audience.

The diplomatic envoys that were sent to make peace with the enemy wept with great bitterness while other individuals (NIV "brave men")[240] openly cried out in agony in the streets of Jerusalem. A second observation notices that the roads were empty, an indication that normal commercial and civic activities have ceased. Perhaps people have fled from the area around Jerusalem to escape the Assyrian army, or travel to and from Jerusalem ceased because the gates of the city were closed. One reason people are weeping and discouraged is the broken treaty (33:8b), presumably between Judah and Assyria. Motyer thinks this refers to the Assyrian failure to honor an earlier agreement made with Hezekiah. First, they accepted Hezekiah's tribute that was negotiated as a means of removing the Assyrian threat against them (2 Kgs 18:13–18); then the Assyrian king ignored the agreement and attacked Jerusalem.[241] Such an explanation would account for the utter desperation at this time. Textual alternatives could suggest that "the cities" (NASB) of Judah are despised and ruthlessly destroyed, or that the "witnesses"[242] (NIV) to the covenant are despised and not respected by the enemy. The second choice creates a better parallel and connection with the ideas that the Assyrians broke a treaty agreement.

The mourning of the land (33:9) expresses how the fate of mankind and the land are intimately tied together in Hebrew thinking (as in 24:1–5). Thus when people suffer a military attack, the crops of the field are eaten by troops, fruit

---

[239] Sweeney, *Isaiah 1–39*, 421–23, concludes that "verses 7–9 convey the basis for punishment . . . the prophet's description of the oppression of the unnamed oppressor." Beuken, *Isaiah II*, 251, 260, believes the prophet is "bewailing the fact that the judgment he was forced to announce has now become a reality" on Jerusalem.

[240] The term used here is difficult to translate and the textual evidence varies considerably. 1QIsa^a turns this word into two words אֶרְאָה לָהֶם, "I will see them," similar to the Greek translations. A few Hb. MSS make the word plural to match "messengers" in the next line. These different forms all try to make sense of an unknown word. Blenkinsopp, *Isaiah 1–39*, 438, prefers "Ariel's people," drawing on the similar sounding term used to describe Jerusalem in 29:1. The enigmas of this textual problem and the best translation of this word are still unsolved.

[241] Motyer, *The Prophecy of Isaiah*, 263, presents a very possible political scenario, but others connect this covenant to commercial agreements, or the "everlasting covenant" in 24:5, but neither of these later proposals is very convincing.

[242] The Masoretic text, Targum, and Syriac translations have "cities" (Hb. עָרִים), but 1QIsa^a has "witnesses" (עֵדִים), a simple confusion of ר and ד. Oswalt, *Isaiah 1–39*, 594, also prefers the reading of the Qumran Scroll in this problem passage.

trees are cut for fire wood, farmers abandon their fields and run for cover, and armies cut a deadly swath wherever they move.[243] Four geographic locations are specified: Lebanon, the Sharon plains, Bashan, and the Carmel mountains. These are areas that were renown for their fertility and lush green trees and crops (Deut 32:14; Isa 2:13; 35:2; Ezek 27:6).[244] Now these areas are withered and look more like a desert.

33:10–13 God's promise to act could be seen as an answer to the prayer in 33:2, a response to the lament in 33:7–9, or simply as an explanation of what God will do in the future. These words encourage the audience to have confidence in God's ultimate victory as well as faith in God during their present trial. Since these promises do not use the vocabulary of the prayer in 33:2 or the lament in 33:7–9, it is best to view this as a continuation of the themes of God's exaltation through his defeat of his enemies (expanding 33:3–6). The paragraph announces that:

  (a) God will act now (33:10)
  (b) Judah's human efforts will fail (33:11)
  (c) God will judge the nations (33:12)
  (d) Everyone should acknowledge God's authority (33:13).

33:10 Initially, God's speech is quoted in dramatic fashion. The audience is reminded three times that "now"[245] God will act. The first person verbs loudly proclaim, "Now I will arise; now I will exalt myself,[246] now I will be lifted up." God acts primarily for the purpose of declaring his glory through his acts of power. The motive is not just to help the poor people of Jerusalem who are suffering, for in some sense their suffering is deserved because they were

---

[243] Beuken, *Isaiah II*, 260, oddly disconnects the description in 33:7–9 from a war setting and instead connects this desolation with the moral and physical decline that happens after a disaster. He disassociates this chapter from the Assyrian attack on Judah and gives it a more eschatological orientation comparable to chap. 24. This does not seem like the best approach to interpret this chapter.

[244] Beuken, *Isaiah II*, 263, notices that three of these terms only occur together in chaps. 24, 33, and 40, thus supporting his contention that chap. 33 was a "mirror text" that was composed with chaps. 40–66 in mind. Williamson, *A Book Called Isaiah*, 234–35, properly questions whether this piece of evidence supports this literary conclusion, for the only connection with 40:3 is the word עֲרָבָה, "Arabah, desert." The literary connection between chaps. 24 and 33 is more substantial, though even in this case the common vocabulary may be more dependent on a common topic, not the discussion of the same events (chap. 24 is eschatological while chap. 33 refers to the destruction by the Assyrian army in 701 BC) He also understands the connections between God's exaltation in 33:10 as the fulfillment of 2:6–22, thus marking the end of the first half of the book. These two texts are thematically related, but it is impossible to demonstrate the literary function Beuken claims from this small amount of evidence (in 33:10).

[245] The word "now," עַתָּה, marks an immediate action and is elsewhere used to draw attention to the decisive way God will act (28:22; 29:22 [twice]; 30:8).

[246] NIV translates the second verb as a passive, "I will be lifted up," but the form אֵרוֹמָם appears to be an abbreviated *hithpolel* form (GKC §54c; the unabbreviated form אֶתְרוֹמָם is found in 1QIsaᵃ) that gives a reflexive meaning, suggesting the translation "I will exalt myself" (HCSB).

unwilling to trust God. These themes remind one of God's ultimate purposes at this time in history as well as on the final Day of the Lord (2:11–17). He alone will be exalted; then everything and everyone that is exalted by mankind will be humbled. His actions in modern history also are designed to demonstrate his exalted glory so that people today will exalt him and praise his name.

33:11 The "you" spoken to is unidentified. One could interpret vv. 11–12 together, taking these words as God's declaration that the efforts of Judah's enemies are nothing but chaff that will be burned with fire.[247] On the other hand the idea of giving birth to nothing of value in 33:11 is elsewhere associated with Judah's painful and fruitless efforts to escape Assyrian domination (26:17–18; 35:3; 37:3). The change from second person "you" (v. 11) to third person "peoples, they" (v. 12) also indicates that two different groups are being discussed. Thus in 33:11 the prophet gives the bad news to the people in Jerusalem. The audience was not offered a false perspective of idealized deliverance because of their great worth or their great accomplishments. Judah is unworthy and the royal efforts to survive this crisis will produce chaff (nothing of value) and not bear good fruit. Motyer says, "In the Assyrian crisis the chaff and straw represent people doing their utmost best, thinking their hardest, being their most realistic and practical, applying their collective wisdom to the hard questions of life, but leaving God out."[248]

33:12 The subject is no longer "you," the people of Judah. The efforts of the peoples (*'ammîm*), a likely reference to the Assyrians in this context (as in 33:3), will be completely obliterated. The reference to turning something to lime is associated with the burning of human remains (cf. Amos 2:1), while the burning of dry thorn bushes pictures a hot fire that quickly destroys an object. Both are images of total decimation of Judah's enemies and these pictures should have produced faith and confidence in the hearts of the prophet's audience in Jerusalem.

33:13 The results of God's mighty acts will be that people from "far away" (*rĕhôqîm* implies those in foreign nations) and "near" (*qĕrôbîm*, meaning the people in Judah) will hear and see God in action (33:13). His judgment of Judah and Assyria will be interpreted as divine acts that condemn those who do not follow God's path. This will cause everyone who hears about these events to recognize God's marvelous power at work to accomplish these events (cf. Ps 47:1; 96:1–4; 98:4; 117:1). This must refer to God's miraculous killing of 185,000 Assyrian troops in one night (cf. 37:36).

33:14–16 The final verses in this paragraph are sometimes compared to so-called "entrance liturgies" (Pss 15; 24). Some hypothesize that priests asked people a series of questions as they entered the temple area to make sure they were worthy to enter into the presence of God to worship. It seems more

---

[247] Clements, *Isaiah 1–39*, 267, and many others follow this logic. קַשׁ, "stubble, straw," is a metaphor for something that has no value (40:24; Job 13:25).

[248] Motyer, *The Prophecy of Isaiah*, 265.

practical to see Pss 15 and 24 as having an instructional purpose, rather than being a means of policing large crowds as they come to worship on the Sabbath.[249] Entering the temple for worship is also foreign to the context of chap. 33, so the ideals presented in 33:15 should be interpreted as traditional ideals that would be presented when instructing people in righteous living.

33:14 Having presented to his audience the bad news of v. 11 and the need to acknowledge God's power in v. 13, Isaiah now explains how people in Zion reacted to this news. Fear and trembling strike them because they realize they are sinners who deserve God's wrath. They finally seem to recognize their utter powerlessness before God. Traditionally, the people believed that God dwelt in the temple (31:9) and that his fiery presence there was a guarantee that Jerusalem could never be defeated. They now seem to understand that their "Zion theology" of unconditional divine protection was a false trust, for God's protection would only benefit the righteous nation that serves him. If the people of Judah fell into sin, God would no longer protect them. The issue about who can dwell in the presence of the consuming fire of God's glory testifies to the fact that the audience finally perceives that they are doomed, because as sinners they are not able to stand in the presence of an awesome holy God. The idea of God as a "consuming fire" (*'ēš 'ōkēlâ*) and "everlasting burning" (*môqĕdê 'ôlām*) derive from the revelation of God's presence in a flaming torch (Gen 15:17) and a burning bush (Exod 3:1–6), and in the thunder, lightning, fire, and clouds on Mount Sinai (Exod 19:12; 24:17; Deut 5:23,25). As a consuming fire, God had destroyed Israel's enemies (Deut 9:3), as well as sinners in Israel (Num 16:35; Isa 30:27). His glory is beyond human comprehension and his fiery power is outside the realm of human ability to confront; thus sinful people are doomed before God. People cannot control, oppose, or manipulate the glory and power of a "consuming fire"; all they can do is humbly submit in fear and reverence, confessing their sinful unworthiness to be in the presence of God. The probing questions suggest that some people in Jerusalem were finally beginning to understand what it meant to live in the presence of a holy God. It is possible that some (maybe Hezekiah) were ready to admit their sinfulness and to look to God for help.

33:15 The prophet's answer to the sinners' questions may seem somewhat surprising at first. There is no automatic or absolute protection offered to the holy city of Jerusalem. This is because God conditionally relates to his covenant people based on trust and the fruits of their righteous behavior. There

---

[249] This suggested setting does not make much practical sense. (a) How could any priest prove, while the person was standing at the gates of the temple, that that person had or had not met the standards set down in these texts? If he was suspicious of some sin, he could not call witnesses and decide the matter while others were waiting for their turn to enter. (b) How could the worshipers prove to the priest that they were fit for worship? (c) It would also be impractical and create a long line of worshipers if people had to individually go through a screening process at the gate. Therefore, it makes more sense to interpret these as instructions to help people properly prepare themselves before they go to worship in the temple.

is no direct call for the audience to confess their sins and humble themselves before the almighty power of God. Instead the prophet points to behavioral changes that demonstrate the results of a work of grace in the hearts of transformed people. God is not interested just in pious proclamations or confession at revival meetings; he is interested in seeing how the results of confession and statements of trust actually transform a person's behavior. The existence of outward results proves that a real inward change has taken place in the heart. After all, good trees produce good fruit. God points to six ethical behavior patterns that demonstrate that people truly love God and submit themselves to the goal of honoring God in everything they do. These instructions include two positive and six negative criteria. Although they are not addressed to any specific group of people in Judah, they seem to rebuke the type of sinful behavior the wealthy and powerful leaders of Judah might commit to maintain their power and status.

"Walking righteously"[250] and "speaking uprightly" are positive signs of a transformed life. Walking refers to the way people conduct their lives and is related to the path they follow. The walk characterized by righteous behavior follows the just standards that God has established in his instructions in the law. These sacred instructions organize moral behavior around what is right and acceptable to a holy God. Righteousness involves right actions in social relationships, but also straight talk that is consistent with the truth. These positive criteria are not limited solely to behavior in courts of law, for righteous action should be a characteristic that transforms a person's behavior in every area of life.

The negative statements prohibit behaviors that take advantage of other people and do not follow principles of righteousness. Extortion is the illegal pursuit of undeserved gain (Exod 18:21; 1 Sam 8:3; Isa 56:11) through threats of violence or putting social or political pressure on someone. Bribery is another illegal way of gaining an unfair advantage in commercial or legal situations. Instead of doing what is right and fair, the bribed person will bend the truth or choose to favor the person who offers the bribe (Exod 23:8; Deut 10:17; 16:19). The righteous person refuses to listen or to get involved with plots of oppression and bloodshed against other people. Likewise, righteous people do not contemplate evil plots to see if they want to get involved with this kind of activity. All these positive and negative statements relate to how people choose to treat others. The righteous person will respect others, will want to do what is just, and will not use devious means to take advantage of others. Those who trust God do not need to manipulate circumstances to their advantage through evil talk or bribery, but the ungodly who do not trust God arrogantly put themselves in God's place and attempt to control events to their advantage by works of unrighteousness.

---

[250] הֹלֵךְ and all the other descriptors of righteous people are *qal* active participles indicating "the one who acts in a certain way."

33:16 Isaiah indicates that only righteous people are acceptable to God (33:16), only righteous people will find that God is their refuge on Mount Zion (the "heights" or "mountain fortress"), and only those who exhibit these character traits can expect God to provide their daily needs of food and water. These are the people who will be protected and blessed by God (Ps 15:5; 24:5); these are the people who can expect God to be their refuge.

These reminders of God's expectations should have brought conviction of sin to the sinners in the prophet's audience and should have led some of the powerful people in leadership in Jerusalem to repent of their sins. These behavior patterns should also bring conviction and confession of sins to any believers today who may have allowed themselves to fall into similar ungodly behavior patterns.

THE REIGN OF GOD IN ZION (33:17–24)

> ¹⁷Your eyes will see the king in his beauty
>   and view a land that stretches afar.
> ¹⁸In your thoughts you will ponder the former terror:
>   "Where is that chief officer?
>   Where is the one who took the revenue?
>   Where is the officer in charge of the towers?"
> ¹⁹You will see those arrogant people no more,
>   those people of an obscure speech,
>   with their strange, incomprehensible tongue.
>
> ²⁰Look upon Zion, the city of our festivals;
>   your eyes will see Jerusalem,
>   a peaceful abode, a tent that will not be moved;
>   its stakes will never be pulled up,
>   nor any of its ropes broken.
> ²¹There the LORD will be our Mighty One.
>   It will be like a place of broad rivers and streams.
>   No galley with oars will ride them,
>   no mighty ship will sail them.
> ²²For the LORD is our judge,
>   the LORD is our lawgiver,
>   the LORD is our king;
>   it is he who will save us.
>
> ²³Your rigging hangs loose:
>   The mast is not held secure,
>   the sail is not spread.
>   Then an abundance of spoils will be divided
>   and even the lame will carry off plunder.
> ²⁴No one living in Zion will say, "I am ill";
>   and the sins of those who dwell there will be forgiven.

The chapter concludes with an oracle of salvation announcing the coming of a king. The identity of this royal ruler appears to be announced in 33:22, but some interpret this to refer to the divine king along with another king in 33:17. Hayes and Irvine think Isaiah is referring to God's support of Hezekiah, Childs connects this king with the messianic king mentioned in 32:1, while Wildberger concludes that this king is God himself based on 33:22.[251] It may be best to view this king as a continuing development of what the prophet was saying about God throughout chap. 33 and consider this prophecy to relate to events at the time of the Assyrian crisis rather than an eschatological period.

33:17 The prophet has just finished telling his audience that God is exalted and will fill Zion with justice (33:5), that he will be a source of security, salvation, and wisdom (33:6), and that he will arise and be exalted (33:10). He will bring judgment on Judah and her enemies, but eventually people far and near will recognize his power and glory (33:12–13). At some point he will no longer be hidden; then he will function as the righteous exalted power (the holy king) that will determine the military destiny of both Judah and Assyria. When he arises and is exalted (33:5–6,10), the eyes of the people in Jerusalem will observe him functioning as the Divine Warrior King (33:17). When God acts ("arises" and "exalts himself" in 33:10), they will see with their own eyes his marvelous and beautiful deeds against the Assyrians (33:3–4,12; cf. 37:36). Often God's acts of salvation are expressed as a declaration of God's glory, but the metaphor of "his beauty" (*yāpyô*) may arise as a purposeful ironic contrast with the pomp and splendorous beauty of the defeated Assyrian king (cf. 10:12–14; 37:22–29). Although he may appear to be very glorious, when God comes as the glorious King and destroys the Assyrian army, Sennacherib will not have any power.

Next the prophet contrasts the small amount of territory controlled by the military forces of Judah in 701 BC (only the small city of Jerusalem was not conquered by Sennacherib) and the future situation when Judah's territory will be broad and wide after the divine King comes and defeats their enemies (cf. 33:21). There is no indication that this future situation refers to an idealistic hope that the exiles had about their return to the land after the exile.[252] If it is taken as a prophecy about the land of Israel after the exile, it could be evaluated as a false prophecy, for the post-exilic era was not a time of great strength, prosperity, or expansion.

---

[251] Hayes and Irvine, *Isaiah*, 369, identify 33:17 as references to Hezekiah (see also Calvin, *Commentary on the Prophet Isaiah*, sub. 33:17). Childs, *Isaiah*, 248, and Young, *Isaiah*, II:421, believe this king is the Messiah of 32:1 based on the royal ideology of Pss 45 and 72 and the earthly rule of this king (33:17–19), but Wildberger, *Isaiah 28–39*, 300–301, views the announcement of God as king in 33:22 as a key to identifying the king in v. 17.

[252] Clements, *Isaiah 1–39*, 269, suggests that this was written during Josiah's reform (621 BC) and envisioned the restoration of the Davidic monarchy and the land promised to Abraham (Gen 15:18–21) when the people returned from Babylonian exile. There is little need to go to this approach, for the description fits the time of God's defeat of the Assyrians in 701 BC.

33:18–19   When God comes in power to rule in Zion, Judah will once again be in control of her territory (v. 17), for the Assyrians will leave the land (cf. 37:37). It appears that 33:18–19 contrasts the future situation of freedom from Assyrian military forces with the time when arrogant Assyrians controlled the land. In the future, after God delivers them, the people of Judah will muse, think, or meditate[253] on the "horrors" (*'êmâ*) of war that they endured. They will realize that this period of their history is finished and all their oppressors are gone. The people who have disappeared are (a) the one who counted; (b) the one who weighed; and (c) the one who counted towers. The last individual seems to have a military function involving reconnaissance and directing a battle plan, the second appears to have an economic function of weighting out tribute or booty, but there is no modifying word that helps identify what the first person counted or wrote down (possibly a scribe or one who counted out the soldiers' weekly pay; NIV has "chief officer").[254] All these people were a part of the oppressive rule of Assyria, but the prophet promises that they will soon disappear. The arrogant and strange-talking Assyrians will no longer threaten Jerusalem (33:19; cf. 28:11; 36:11). These promises reinforce the prophet's earlier prophecies about the fall of Assyria (29:5–7; 30:27–33; 31:8–9) and should have caused the people to trust God, for he will deliver them from the oppressive Assyrians.

33:20–24   When God's salvation comes, the people will behold the king (33:17), but they will also see Jerusalem standing as a liberated city, a celebrating city of joyous festivals, a peaceful city, and a secure place to pitch their tents. Consistent with the Zion theology of old (1 Sam 7:10–16; Ps 48:1–14; 132:13–18), the city will stand like an indestructible permanent tent that cannot be destroyed. These promises demonstrate God's unbreakable commitment to Zion's preservation, though at this time God's salvation of Zion came only at the last minute because of the continual unwillingness of the nation to trust God.

The reason Jerusalem will survive the Assyrian crisis will be plain for everyone to see. In contrast[255] to the negative situation in 701 BC in which Jerusalem had no peace and still had Assyrian warriors around it, in the future, the majestic (*'addîr*), all-powerful God of Jerusalem will be there "for us" (*lānû*)—for the people of Zion (33:21). God will powerfully rescue his people from the hands of the superior Assyrian army (37:36).

The logical development and unusual images in 33:21–23 raise many difficult challenges for interpreters. The structure of these verses seems somewhat

---

[253] The root הָגָה is drawn from imagery of the growling of lions or the cooing of birds. Like these meditating animals, people are to "think, reflect, meditate, muse" on God's words (Josh 1:8; Ps 1:2) or on what God has done (Ps 77:13).

[254] Blenkinsopp, *Isaiah 1–39*, 446, suggests that these were the hated officials of a foreign overlord who collected taxes from the Hebrews to pay their yearly tribute.

[255] The introductory כִּי אִם is ignored in NIV, but these particles usually introduce a contrast with an earlier negative situation (GKC §163a), so one should begin v. 21 "instead, but."

disorganized because they appear to discuss the topic of rivers and ships in vv. 21 and 23 (though v. 23 may not refer to ships), but these two verses are interrupted by v. 22. Since there are no rivers near Jerusalem, even the mention of ships seems rather preposterous and inappropriate. Wildberger believes this verse refers to the branches of the Nile River,[256] but the Nile is far removed from Jerusalem. In spite of all the geographical difficulties regarding rivers and ships near Jerusalem, earlier (Ps 46:5) and later (Ezek 47) traditions do mention rivers flowing out of Jerusalem in the future—though it is not always clear if these should be understood literally. Consequently, these images should not be rejected; instead, the idea being conveyed by the imagery, rather than the literal ships, must be the focus of attention. The structure of these verses fits an a,b,a´,b´ poetic pattern with the "a" parts referring to God (21a,22) and the "b" parts referring to images of Jerusalem (21b,23).

The second half of v. 21 appears to describe Jerusalem, the place where God dwells. This is not a description of God in metaphorical language as a large river, the source of life for the Hebrew people (RSV); rather, pictures Jerusalem in comparison to an ideal ancient Near Eastern capital that has a large river flowing by it (like Nineveh, Babylon, or Thebes). The main theological point in this imaginative picture is that in Jerusalem there will be no threat, like the ships that attacked other capitals, for Almighty God will be there to protect his people.

Verse 22 gives the reason (it begins with *kî*, "because," which is omitted in NIV) the people in Jerusalem are safe and secure. God will control what happens to his people for he is their King (6:1–5; 24:23).[257] As king, he fulfills the functions of chief judge who establishes justice and righteousness in the nation and who leads the nation like the judges of old (Judg 2:16). There are two possible ways of understanding the second function: (a) a chief military commander, like the commanders of old (Num 21:18; Deut 33:21; Judg 5:9,14; Prov 8:15); or (b) a "lawgiver" (NIV) who inscribes statutes for his people (10:1; 30:8).[258] Although God is a covenant lawgiver in the Pentateuch, God usually gives the "law" (*tôrâ*) to his people. The *polel* form of this verb (*měḥôqqēnû*) is consistently used of the action of military leaders.[259] Since God is judge, military commander, and king, the audience should have confidence in his promise

---

[256] Wildberger, *Isaiah 28–39*, 307, thinks these verses were added to the text at a much later date and do not fit with the rest of this oracle.

[257] G. V. Smith, "The Concept of God/the gods as King in the Ancient Near East and the Bible," *TrinJ* 3 (1982): 18–38, discusses how the functions of God/the gods, the highest spiritual power in heaven, mirrored many of the functions of the earthly kings, including judge, lawgiver, warrior, ruler, protector, and creator.

[258] מְחֹקְקֵנוּ is a *polel* participle form חָקַק. In the *Qal* verbal form this word means "he inscribed, cut," referring to the process of engraving or writing words on stone (consequently, some translate this nominal participle "lawgiver"). In the *polel* form of this participle, which is found in this verse, this word means "commander."

[259] Watts, *Isaiah 1–33*, 425, translates this participle "our commander."

to save them (as they asked in 33:2) from the terrible situation they faced. God is able to deliver them.

The prophet's message of hope now returns to picture this situation through unusual images, as in v. 21, though the picture is far from being crystal clear. Since the picture is negative in 23a (the two negative particles *bal*), the imagery must either describe the terrible condition of the Assyrian army around Jerusalem or the condition of the people in Jerusalem before God killed the Assyrians (37:36). The second person pronouns in this paragraph often refer to Judah (33:17,18,19,20), though in the context of the whole chapter (33:1,4,11) "you" can refer to Assyria. Since this is a salvation oracle about God's victorious deliverance of Judah, it would be odd for the prophet to refer to Judah's present disarray in 33:23a. It makes more sense to suggest that hope for Isaiah's Hebrew audience would be derived from knowing that the Assyrian army would be in disarray (33:23a). If this is the case, it would explain why it is possible for even the lame to collect the spoils of the defeated Assyrians (33:23b; 37:36).[260]

Beuken interprets the terms in v. 23a as military images instead of shipping symbols. The translation of the words "your rigging," "mast," and "sail" (*ḥăbālāyik*, *nas*, and *tārnām*) are problematic. In all other usages the word translated "sail" in NIV refers to a military "standard, signal, banner,"[261] while the word translated "mast" is a term parallel to "standard, signal, banner" in 30:17 and is translated "flagstaff." Thus it appears that Isaiah is not describing a ship in trouble at sea but the deserted military encampment of the defeated Assyrian army around Jerusalem. The cords that securely held up the banner of the Assyrian army were loose from neglect because the soldiers were either dead or had fled; therefore, the standard did not proudly fly ("spread," *pārśû*) over the encampment of the Assyrian troops. This external sign of the abandonment of Assyria's camp will be a signal to the people of Judah, so everyone will descend on the huge quantity of booty left by the retreating troops. Even the lame will manage to scramble over to the Assyrian encampment to get a few choice objects for themselves (33:23b). None of the inhabitants of Zion will be too sick to plunder the spoils of war (33:24a).[262] Then God will restore his relationship with his people and forgive the rebellious and sinful people of Judah (cf. 1:4; 5:18; 6:7; 30:12–13) who failed to trust God to deliver them from the Assyrians.

Although there is no reference to the people's repenting of their sins in this context, 31:6–7 calls on them to repent, while 30:15 predicts that "in repen-

---

[260] Beuken, *Isaiah II*, 275–76; Kissane, *Isaiah*, 366–67; H. R. Holmyard, "Does Isaiah 33:23 Address Israel of Israel's Enemy?" *BS* 152 (1995): 273–78—all see v. 23a as a reference to the disarray of the Assyrians.

[261] The word נֵס refers to a cloth flag or ensign on a pole that identifies a military unit (5:26; 11:12; 13:2; 18:3; 30:17), though the standard could fly on land or on a ship at sea (Ezek 27:7).

[262] This does not appear to be a reference to the ideal conditions in the future kingdom of God when all sorrow, death, and tears are removed (25:8).

tance and rest is your salvation, in quietness and trust is your strength." Certainly, Hezekiah had a change of heart when he finally went with Sennacherib's letter into the temple to put his trust in God and request God's deliverance (37:14–20). This passage suggests that many people will respond to God when they experience God's great act of deliverance that demonstrates his power and grace. Then they will sanctify God's name and reverence him; then they will know the truth and accept instruction from God (29:22–24).

THEOLOGICAL IMPLICATIONS.   When believers are in trouble and the forces of this world are overpowering them, they need to call on God for deliverance and confidently trust him to act on their behalf. The prophet provides more evidence of God's power to overthrow their enemies in this message in order to increase the people's confidence and trust in God. The audience can gain assurance that God will destroy their enemy (33:1), that the nations gathered around them will be scattered and leave a great deal of booty (33:3–4,23). Their hope is certain because God will rise up and exalt himself (33:5,10). Then everyone will be compelled to acknowledge the power of God (33:13). The audience's present pain is real (33:7–9), but the people of Jerusalem have the hope of dwelling in the glorious presence of God (33:15–16) when their King acts in great power (33:17,22). Their enemies will disappear (33:18–19,23), but Jerusalem will be secured and undefeated because God will be there (33:20–21). These confident prophetic words of hope provide a solid foundation for people to decide to act by faith.

Every messenger of God has the responsibility to proclaim that God's kingly rule extends over the affairs of his own rebellious people and over all the evil powers in this world that oppress them. God has a wonderful and victorious plan, but unfortunately there have been many periods in history when God's chosen people have not been willing to accept or trust God's promises. Sometimes God has to use difficult trials of life to mold and graciously transform the hearts of his stubborn people so that they will learn to trust him and treat him as the King. Since God's promises of an astonishing deliverance came true during the time of Isaiah, those who read Isaiah's words today can confidently know without a doubt that God will fulfill all his future promises and complete the foreordained plan that he has designed for this world.

3. Trusting God to Ruin the Nations and Transform Zion (34:1–35:10)

Chapters 34–35 stand out from the earlier series of "woe oracles" in chaps. 28–33 and are quite different from the narrative stories about the Assyrian attack on Jerusalem in chaps. 36–39. These chapters are also unusual in that they have a large number of common themes and vocabulary that connect them with other chapters in this book. Several commentators have hypothesized that these connections (or quotations) indicate something about the literary function of these chapters. Four issues need to be considered: (a) Are chaps. 34–35 a literary unit, or just two separate chapters? (b) Is chap. 34 connected to the introduction in 13:1–16? (c) Is chap. 35 based on later information in chaps. 40–66? (d) Do chaps. 34–35 function as a conclusion to chaps. 13–33 or an introduction to chaps. 34–66?

First one needs to decide if chaps. 34–35 go together as a unit, or if they should be treated totally separately. Wildberger and O. H. Steck both reject the idea that these chapters form a literary unit[263] but C. R. Matthews and Blenkinsopp believe the two chapters fit together.[264] An analysis of the verbal connections and contrasts within chaps. 34–35 draws them together as a unit:

(a) God's vengeance will save Zion (34:8 and 35:4b).
(b) The jackals will live in the desolate places (34:13), but the jackals will have no place in the fertile land (35:7).
(c) The streams will be polluted (34:9), but the streams will gush with pure water (35:6–7).
(d) No one will pass through the land (34:10), but a highway will be there for many people to walk on (35:8).
(e) The judgment (chap. 34) creates a desert place, while the blessings (chap. 35) will cause the desert to change into a fertile field.

God's destruction of the nations (chap. 34) is a necessary prerequisite to his salvation of his people in Zion (chap. 35). The picture of what God will do to the nations and their land contrasts with the picture of what God will do for his people and their land, bringing the two chapters together. This literary connection implies that they have a common origin and that they function together as a unit.

Another fruitful avenue of inquiry about literary dependence developed from studying the relationship between chaps. 34 and 13. Williamson agrees with J. Vermeylen, who identified a similar structure and strong verbal connections between these two chapters.[265]

(a) preparation for war	13:2–4	34:1
(b) killing of the nations	13:5–9,14–16	34:2–3
(c) cosmic upheaval	13:10–13	34:4–5a
(d) capture of the city	13:17–19	34:5b–8

---

[263] Wildberger, *Isaiah 28–39*, 320, 344, and O. H. Steck, *Bereitete Heimkehr. Jesaja 35 als redaktionelle Brücke zwischen dem Ersten und Zweiten Jesaja* (Stuttgart: Katholisches Biblelwerk, 1985) connect only chap. 35 with the second half of the book (especially chap. 40 and 62:10–12); chaps. 33–34 form the conclusion to the woe oracles in chaps. 28–32.

[264] C. R. Matthews, *Defending Zion: Edom's Desolation and Jacob's Restoration (Isaiah 34–35) in Context,* BZAW (Berlin: de Gruyter, 1995), believes chaps. 34–35 are a diptych that go together. He is critical of Steck's analysis that comes to the opposite conclusion. Blenkinsopp, *Isaiah 1–39,* 450, notices how several of the themes in chap. 34 are reversed in chap. 35, indicating a strong literary connection.

[265] Williamson, *The Book Called Isaiah,* 216–17, and J. Vermeylen, *Du Prophete Isaie a l'Apocalyptique* (Paris: Gabalda).

| (e) land becomes a desert | 13:20 | 34:9–10 |
| (f) wild animals live there | 13:21–22 | 34:11–15 |

These connections suggest that the author made a conscious attempt to connect the beginning of the section in chap. 13 with the end of this literary unit in chap. 34. The universalistic tone in chaps. 13 and 34–35 suggests that these chapters form an eschatological introduction and conclusion to chaps. 13–35.[266] These similarities suggest that there was an intentional theological plan behind the collection of these messages in this book.

The third question relates to the relationship between chaps. 34–35 and chaps. 40–66. The connection is primarily with chap. 35, although a similar judgment against Edom in chap. 63 does suggest a possible connection between chap. 34 and the second half of the book. W. Brownlee divided Isaiah into two parallel volumes based on the space left between chaps. 33 and 34 in the Dead Sea Scrolls.[267] C. C. Torrey and more recently Sweeney conclude that chaps. 34–35 function, not as a conclusion to chaps. 13–35, but as the introduction to the second half of the book of Isaiah.[268] These interpreters usually argue that chaps. 34–35 were actually the writings of a later prophet (called Deutero-Isaiah, the author of chaps. 40–55) because (a) the Hebrews' bitter hostility toward Edom (discussed in chap. 34) arose long after the days of Isaiah when the Edomites abused the people of Jerusalem after the Babylonians destroyed Jerusalem in 586 BC (cf. Obad 10–14; Ezek 35–36; Lam 4:21–22); and (b) the thoughts and phrases in chap. 35 are similar to ideas expressed in Isaiah 40–55.[269] In evaluating the first reason, one can conclude that most of the terms used to describe the Edomite oppression of the Hebrews in Obadiah, Ezek 35–36, and Lam 4 are not found in Isa 34. In addition, chap. 34 probably does not refer to Edom specifically; it just symbolizes all the rebellious nations of the world. Thus, that incident does not help identify the date, author, or function of chaps. 34–35. In evaluating the second reason, Williamson agrees with the evidence Steck marshaled to demonstrate that chap. 35 depends on 40:1–11.[270] But these literary connections are hard to evaluate objectively, for the dependence could hypothetically go either direction. Wildberger noticed

---

[266] Deltizsch, "Isaiah," 66, calls chaps. 34–35 apocalyptic, which give a perfect ideal of the future

[267] W. Brownlee, *The Meaning of the Qumran Scrolls for the Bible* (New York: Oxford University Press, 1964), 247–59, found parallel development of topics in chaps. 1–33 and 34–66, found this structure parallel to the division of Ezekiel, and saw this structure signaled by a space left between chaps. 33 and 34 in the Qumran scrolls. This evidence supported the earlier theory by C. C. Torrey.

[268] C. C. Torrey, *The Second Isaiah: A New Interpretation* (Edinburgh: T & T Clark, 1928), and Sweeney, *Isaiah 1–39*, 435, believe chaps. 34–35 are an introduction to the second half of the book and were written by a later author, though O. H. Steck, *Bereitete Heimkehr,* connects only chap. 35 with the second half of the book (chap. 40 and 62:10–12), and chaps. 33–34 form the conclusion to the woe oracles in chaps. 28–32.

[269] See footnote 9 under "Structure" at the beginning of this section.

[270] Williamson, *The Book Called Isaiah,* 212–15, follows the views of Steck, *Bereitete Heimkehr,* and both also connect chap. 35 to ideas in 62:10–12, verses they attribute to a "Trito-Isaiah."

that many of the proposed verbal connections between chap. 35 and 40–66 are not identical, thus denying dependence, since a true literary connection must demonstrate common thoughts, not the mere reuse of identical terminology. He also observed that many other key themes in chaps. 40–66 were not present in chap. 35.[271] Even when phrases are identical (cf. 35:10 and 51:11), it is hard to develop adequate objective evidence to determine which came first. That is, chap. 35 could depend on chaps. 40–66, or chaps. 40–66 could depend on chap. 35.

Logically speaking, there is no reason the prophet could not choose to insert a message received later in his ministry (received after 40:1–11) into a group of chapters he received much earlier. At times topical (chaps. 13–23) and literary reasons (1:13) motivated the author to place messages out of chronological order. Isaiah may have done this to support the theological conclusions he wanted to draw from chaps. 28–33. But an examination of these chapters shows that these possibilities are unlikely in this case. Chapter 35 is primarily about the transformation of the land and the feeble and unclean people who will return to the land. Isaiah 40:1–11 focuses on the coming of God to his people, not the transformation of the land or God's people. Consequently, the line of dependence proposed by Steck is not especially convincing. It is therefore best to see chaps. 34–35 functioning as a literary conclusion to chaps. 28–33, as well as the conclusion to chaps. 13–33.

In the end, one has to admit that the prophet did not provide sufficient information to objectively date when he spoke the eschatological messages in chaps. 34–35, for these sermons lack the historical hints that are common in chaps. 28–33. Although the emphasis is unique in each chapter, the vocabulary and theology of chaps. 28–33 and 34–35 have much in common. Oswalt and Clements believe chaps. 34–35 function as an eschatological conclusion to woe oracles in chaps. 28–33, just as chaps. 24–27 function as the eschatological conclusion to the oracles against the nations in chaps. 13–23.[272] Chapters 34–35 do not really summarize the issues discussed in chaps. 28–33, but they demonstrate that in a future eschatological era God will repeat similar acts of judgment and deliverance to those found in chaps. 28–33. Once again, God will defeat the nations on the day of his final acts of vengeance in order to protect Zion (chap. 34), just like he will defeat the Assyrians in the days of Isaiah. Then the full blessings of God's covenant promises will be fulfilled on earth (chap. 35).

It is important to recognize the purpose of introducing the theological themes found in chaps. 34–35. The idea that God will destroy the nations (34:1–3) and uphold the people of Zion (34:8; 35:1–10) are fitting promises that would engender trust in God during a period of crisis. If he will accomplish these pur-

---

[271] See footnote 9 above.

[272] Oswalt, *Isaiah 1–39*, 607, and Clements, *Isaiah 1–39*, 271, view chaps. 34–35 as conclusions, though Clements believes chaps. 34–35 were written by a later author.

poses in the future, he may act in a similar manner in dealing with the Assyrian crisis. The encouragement to strengthen the weak because God will come with vengeance to save them (35:3–4) fits the needs of the people who were facing an Assyrian attack. Thus it is not necessary to look for a fitting historical context outside of the present literary context where these chapters are placed. In the end, it is impossible to identify the exact date when the prophet originally spoke these messages.

(1) God's Wrath against the Nations (34:1–17)

¹Come near, you nations, and listen;
 pay attention, you peoples!
Let the earth hear, and all that is in it,
 the world, and all that comes out of it!
²The LORD is angry with all nations;
 his wrath is upon all their armies.
He will totally destroy them,
 he will give them over to slaughter.
³Their slain will be thrown out,
 their dead bodies will send up a stench;
 the mountains will be soaked with their blood.
⁴All the stars of the heavens will be dissolved
 and the sky rolled up like a scroll;
all the starry host will fall
 like withered leaves from the vine,
 like shriveled figs from the fig tree.

⁵My sword has drunk its fill in the heavens;
 see, it descends in judgment on Edom,
 the people I have totally destroyed.
⁶The sword of the LORD is bathed in blood,
 it is covered with fat—
the blood of lambs and goats,
 fat from the kidneys of rams.
For the LORD has a sacrifice in Bozrah
 and a great slaughter in Edom.
⁷And the wild oxen will fall with them,
 the bull calves and the great bulls.
Their land will be drenched with blood,
 and the dust will be soaked with fat.

⁸For the LORD has a day of vengeance,
 a year of retribution, to uphold Zion's cause.
⁹Edom's streams will be turned into pitch,
 her dust into burning sulfur;
 her land will become blazing pitch!
¹⁰It will not be quenched night and day;
 its smoke will rise forever.

From generation to generation it will lie desolate;
   no one will ever pass through it again.
¹¹The desert owl and screech owl will possess it;
   the great owl and the raven will nest there.
God will stretch out over Edom
   the measuring line of chaos
   and the plumb line of desolation.
¹²Her nobles will have nothing there to be called a kingdom,
   all her princes will vanish away.
¹³Thorns will overrun her citadels,
   nettles and brambles her strongholds.
She will become a haunt for jackals,
   a home for owls.
¹⁴Desert creatures will meet with hyenas,
   and wild goats will bleat to each other;
there the night creatures will also repose
   and find for themselves places of rest.
¹⁵The owl will nest there and lay eggs,
   she will hatch them, and care for her young under the shadow of her
      wings;
   there also the falcons will gather,
   each with its mate.

¹⁶Look in the scroll of the LORD and read:

None of these will be missing,
   not one will lack her mate.
For it is his mouth that has given the order,
   and his Spirit will gather them together.
¹⁷He allots their portions;
   his hand distributes them by measure.
They will possess it forever
   and dwell there from generation to generation.

In addition to the main message concerning the day God will establish justice by pouring out his wrath against his enemies (34:1–15), there is a short word of affirmation declaring the authenticity of God's promises in this scroll (34:16–17). Both paragraphs begin with imperative verbs that exhort an audience to action. These imperatives suggest that the primary purpose of this chapter is to instruct listeners about what will happen in the future, so that they will take this information into consideration as they determine how to live in their present circumstances.[273] They need to understand that God will bring judgment against the foreign nations and that his wonderful promises will come true for those who follow the way of holiness. This instruction should

---

[273] Sweeney, *Isaiah 1–39*, 435, 441, and Beuken, *Isaiah II*, 284, properly separates the words of judgment from the overall purpose of the message, which was to instruct an audience about God's future establishment of justice in the world.

lead the audience to trust in God and follow him, for he is sovereignly in control of history and he deeply cares about his people in Zion.

The main paragraph is structured around a series of four divine acts (vv. 2–4, 5–6a, 6b–7, 8–15), each linguistically introduced by "surely, truly" (*kî* is omitted in NIV in 34:2,5 and translated "for" in 34:6b,8).[274] The material can be divided into two main paragraphs:

Learn that God will judge the nations	34:1–15
Judgment on heaven and earth	1–4
The sword against "Edom"	5–7
The devastated land	8–15
Learn that God's plan will happen	34:16–17

These instructions notify the audience that judgment will fall on "Edom" (34:5–7) as well as the nations and the heavens (34:1–4). Most interpreters consider Edom as a representative example of what will happen to all nations, thus the main focus is not on the small nation of Edom.[275] The central theological statement is that God will ultimately uphold his people in Zion by executing his wrathful judgment on all the rebellious nations on the earth (34:1–2,8).

34:1 The introductory "summons to attention" was not intended simply to gather the nations and peoples together for punishment or to call them to come to a meeting of God's court.[276] They should come "in order to listen"[277] (cf. 28:23; 33:13), so that God could instruct and warn all these people about his future plans to destroy his enemies. The call for the whole earth to pay attention is reminiscent of the universalistic judgments announced earlier (13:5,11; 24:1–6). Since Judah was one of the nations of the earth, the invitation to listen to this message also encouraged the prophet's audience to pay close attention to what God has to say. Would this judgment fall on Judah or only on other nations?

34:2–4 The first thing the audience learned is that "truly, assuredly" (*kî*; omitted in NIV) God is angry with the nations on the earth. The basis or

---

[274] J. Muilenburg, "The Literary Character of Isaiah 34," *JBL* I59 (1940): 339–65, observed the key role played by the four ‏כִּי‎ clauses in 34:2,5,6b,8 in introducing the ways God will act. P. D. Miscall, *Isaiah 34–35: A Nightmare/A Dream* (Sheffield: Sheffield Academic Press, 1999), 30, prefers to translate ‏כִּי‎ simply as "yes."

[275] Oswalt, *Isaiah 1–39*, 610, Blenkinsopp, *Isaiah 1–39*, 451, and Seitz, *Isaiah 1–39*, 237, are a few of the commentators who view Edom as a typical representative nation that is treated as the antithesis of Israel. Thus, this chapter is not solely against the small nation of Edom. Less likely is the approach of Kissane, *Isaiah*, 369, who concludes that the oracle originally described the destruction of Assyria because some earlier references to "nations" referred to Assyria (8:9; 17:12; 24:21; 30:28).

[276] Kaiser, *Isaiah 13–39*, 357, indicates that "the poet has in mind the summoning of the people and nations to judgment," while Goldingay, *Isaiah*, 193, suggests that the "nations are summoned to court—but not to a trial."

[277] The infinitive construct ‏לִשְׁמֹעַ‎, "in order to hear," expresses either the purpose for God's summons or the results (GKC §114f). This purpose is repeated later in the verse with the second invitation to "let the earth hear," ‏תִשְׁמַע‎.

rationale for God's anger (*qeṣep*), hot wrath (*hēmâ*), and his decision to totally destroy them (the ban of holy war) is not explained in this verse. It is assumed that the audience (and the reader) is well acquainted with chaps. 13–33, so there is no need to reiterate the sinfulness of mankind. The text focuses on what God will do, not on why God will act in this way. God's actions should not be interpreted as uncontrollable emotional outbursts of inappropriate rage, but as the natural response of a holy God to sin. By these acts he will justly punish wicked people and establish his righteous dominion over the world by removing the ungodly. No intermediary power (an angel, an army, or his righteous people) is assigned to carry out God's will in this context. He himself will directly allow his powerful hand to fall on all nations and "their hosts" (*ṣĕbāʾām*). The "hosts" God opposes could be the "armies" (NIV) of these nations, though Motyer broadens this term to refer to their total population.[278] The slaughter of these nations (34:3) will leave the dead corpses of thousands lying unburied on the ground. The sickening scene pictures death everywhere, the horrible stench of rotting flesh,[279] and blood flowing like water all over the land. This is a ghastly picture of horror from the destruction of millions of people on the earth.

The destructive power of God will also affect the heavens and the hosts that live there (34:4; cf. 13:10; 24:21).[280] The collapse of the heavenly world involves a reversal of God's creative establishment of the heavens. At creation he spread out the heavens like a tent cloth (40:22), but in the future just the opposite will happen when God rolls it up like a scroll.[281] He will reverse the creation by rolling his cloth back up and dimming the bright objects of light in the heavens. Instead of being a vital part of the world, the stars of the sky will fall from the heavens like dead leaves falling from a tree. When the power of God's destructive wrath brings the mighty heavens and its hosts down to the realm of a puny dead leaf falling from a tree, one begins to glimpse the enormity of what God will do. Such comparisons should produce awe and amazement in the hearts of mankind. When people think about the stark reality of the sovereign power of God actively establishing his just rule over all the heavens and the earth, people should be humbled and thoroughly convinced that they do not want to arouse the power of God's wrath or experience the destruction that he will accomplish.

---

[278] Motyer, *The Prophecy of Isaiah*, 270, notes the universal terms used throughout 34:1–4.

[279] The word "and they will rot," וְנָמַקּוּ (v. 4), is written יתבקעו, "they will break open," in 1QIsaᵃ, which is similar to Mic 1:4. The Masoretic text is clearly the more difficult form and therefore original.

[280] These heavenly "hosts" (NIV "stars") could refer to (a) the physical stars and planets that will become dim; (b) the destruction of the pagan gods that were represented by these heavenly hosts; (c) an army of heavenly beings; or possibly (d) all of the above factors are included in one holistic view of the celestial world.

[281] Motyer, *The Prophecy of Isaiah*, 270, connects rolling up the scroll with closing a book. When the book (scroll) is closed, the story is over.

34:5–6a   The second act of God involves the destructive deeds of the sword of the Lord, using the bloody imagery of slaughtering animals. The audience can be assured that "truly, surely" (*kî*; omitted in NIV) God's sword (cf. 27:1; 49:2; 65:12; 66:16) has and will act. The idea of a sword that has "drunk its full"[282] is an image of an instrument of death saturated from killing its victims. After wielding its destructive power in the heavens, this sword will descend to earth on the representative nation of Edom, "my banned people devoted to destruction" (*ḥermî*). The declaration that these are doomed people demonstrates that God controls the destiny of every person, especially those who fall under the wrath of his holy justice. One should understand that in sacrifices the blood and the fat belonged to God and that the prophet uses metaphors familiar to his audience. The gory details may be distasteful to modern readers, but an ancient Near Eastern audience would sense from these words that nothing would stop the sword of God once it begins to slaughter those who opposed God.

34:6b–7   The third act of God drops the sword images and focuses on analogies related to the killing of animals prepared for slaughter or sacrifice (cf. 25:6; 30:32; Jer 46:10; Ezek 39:17). Ideas of confession of sin, substitution, atonement, and forgiveness of sin that are associated with sacrifices in Leviticus are missing from this discussion, for the focus draws an analogy with the slaughter of animals, not the atonement of sins. The specification of Edom and Bozrah (the capital of Edom) is not because the Edomites were especially sinful or violent; they merely represent what God will destroy (cf. 63:1–6). Cities like Bozrah, a very secure Edomite fortification, will not stand. People who act like the Edomites will be destined for slaughter. The oxen, calves, and bulls may simply refer to everything that was living in Edom, though P. Miscall takes these animals as allusions to human leaders in the nation.[283]

34:8–15   The fourth act of God will bring about a time of holy "vengeance" (*nāqām*) to right the wrongs of sinful people on the earth. Vengeance should not be associated with taking better revenge against someone, but with the concept of recompense and the establishment of justice. It will be the time when people will be held accountable for their actions. The times of waiting for people to repent will be past and the just verdicts for sinful behavior will be implemented. Earlier the prophet stated that on the Day of the Lord, God would humble the proud (2:11–17; 13:6–9) so that he alone would be exalted (2:11–12,17), but in this case he will contend[284] against the wicked not only for his own glory, but also on behalf of his people in Zion. The prophet does

---

[282] 1QIsaᵃ has תראה, "will be seen," which Blenkinsopp, *Isaiah 1–39*, 449, accepts as original (the Targum follows this perspective), but the Old Greek follows the Masoretic "be drunk, satiated."

[283] Miscall, *Isaiah 34–35*, 52, and Oswalt, *Isaiah 1–39*, 612, connect these animals to leaders in Edom, but the emphasis is more on the complete and utter slaughter of everything.

[284] There are a variety of ways to translate לְרִיב: "for the cause of" (NASB), "for the controversy" (Oswalt), "for the complaint" (Blenkinsopp); but "to contend," the rendition of Delitzsch, *Old Testament Commentary: Isaiah*, 72, fits the normal meaning of רִיב.

not explain why God needs to fight for Zion or what Zion needs to be repaid for, but O Kaiser's suggestion that "the destruction of Edom, is his revenge for what they have done to Zion (cf. II Kings 24:1; Amos 1:11f.; Ezek 5:12)"[285] interprets this oracle far too locally and misses its universal significance. Many in the prophet's audience would probably agree that nations had taken advantage of God's people down through the centuries and they would have found this promise comforting. Now God will right these wrongs that his people have suffered. This promise would cause all the prophet's audience in Jerusalem to know for certain (*kî*, "truly, surely," introduces 34:8) that God would ensure that justice will be established for the benefit of his abused people. As Wildberger says, "Whoever lays a hand on the holy mountain will have to deal with the issue by interacting with the God of Israel directly."[286]

Chapters 29–33 contain a discussion of God's defeat of the Assyrians who were attacking Jerusalem, but the eschatological nature of these promises in chap. 34 do not include an immediate hope of deliverance from any earthly enemy. They do create a theological principle that God will fight for his people and take vengeance on his enemies, so the people in Judah knew that God's promises in chaps. 29–33 were consistent with what he will do on the Day of the Lord.

God's acts of holy vengeance will have a dramatic effect on the physical earth (34:9–15). The prophet describes what will happen to the land (Edom is not specifically mentioned) in terms reminiscent of what happened to Sodom and Gomorrah (13:19; Gen 19:21–29). Fire, brimstone, pitch, and sulfur from a volcanic eruption will burn up everything on the land (34:9; 30:33). Since humans are helpless before the burning destruction of fire and lava, there will be no way to fight against God's destructive judgment, or to stop what he will do (1:31; 66:24). This devastating burning will leave the land totally useless and uninhabitable forever (34:10). People will no longer live in this kind of place; it will be left to the wild birds (cf. 13:21–22), for it will be uninhabitable (cf. 24:10) and void of any creatures.[287] The final metaphor in 34:11 is rather obscure, but elsewhere cities were measured with a line (2 Kgs 21:13) to demarcate the area where destruction would make the land empty, just like they used a "line" (*qaw*) to measure when a city was built. The analogy for the "stones of emptiness" could draw from the imagery of stones as weights on a scale, stones used for a plumb line, the stones of destiny (the Urim and

---

[285] Kaiser, *Isaiah 13–39*, 358, takes 34:1–4 as having a universal application but limits 34:5–8 specifically to the tiny nation of Edom.

[286] Wildberger, *Isaiah 28–39*, 333, looks at "Zion" not as a location but as a metaphor for the people of God.

[287] At the end of 34:11 the NIV translates תֹּהוּ as "chaos" and בֹהוּ as "desolation," two key words also found in Gen 1:2. The use of these terms suggests the land will go back to its pre-creation status; that is, it will be without form (no structure or organization) and void (empty, without inhabitants). The concept of chaos introduces a Greek idea that is unrelated to Isaiah's intent here.

Thummim), or the stones that marked the borders of various territories. Since the line is a building tool and is used elsewhere in divine judgment passages in the prophets (28:17; Lam 2:8; Amos 7:7–9), the second object is probably a similar building tool, the stone of a plumb line.[288] Both analogies twist the original purpose of these building tools to demonstrate how these instruments will undo what was constructed and leave the land uninhabitable.

If the land is empty and social order has disappeared, the rich and powerful nobles and kings will have nothing to rule over (34:12)[289] and princes will cease to exist. The palaces, fortresses, and strongholds where the kings and nobility used to live will be empty of people. Instead they will be full of thorns and briers (cf. 5:6; 7:23–25; 27:4; 32:13), inhabited by wild animals like jackals and owls (34:13).[290] The exact identity of the animals is problematic, though there is no need to follow Wildberger and connect these unclean creatures (Lev 11) with demonic beings.[291] It is important to recognize that this desolate state will be the fate of all the great civilizations that continue to oppose God (cf. 13:20–22; 24:1–7). No one and nothing will remain; people, places, palaces, and power will not survive the wrath of God.

34:16–17   The second paragraph in the chapter begins with two imperative verbs, just like 34:1. These imperatives exhort a Hebrew audience that has access to God's revelation to search the "scroll of the LORD." If they will read what God has said, they will know that his promises are true. The idea of God having a book is well known from passages that refer to a scroll containing the names and deeds of the righteous (Exod 32:32; Dan 7:10; Mal 3:16), but this appears to be a different scroll. Clements concludes that the scroll about animals inhabiting a city refers to the earlier prophecies about Babylon (13:21–22) or prophecies about the fall of Edom (Jer 49:7–22; Ezek 25:15–25).[292] The

---

[288] Beuken, *Isaiah II*, 301, takes these as instruments used in constructions that are ironically used for purposes of destruction in this context.

[289] The text and translation of 34:12 is problematic and may have suffered the loss of a word (Beuken, *Isaiah II*, 281–82). It appears that the verse had three lines, but all that is left of the first line is the word "nobles," הֲרֶיהָ. The Old Greek fills out the phrase having "its nobles will not exist," but it is impossible to know if they were reading these words in their Hb. text or just trying to make sense out of a difficult verse. Miscall, *Isaiah 34–35*, 74 solves the problem by connecting "her nobles" to the preceding verse (as in RSV). There is no satisfactory answer to these problems.

[290] The root חָצִיר means "grass." It could refer to the place where these animals dwell (the palaces have turned into pastures), but 1QIsa[a] has חָצֵר, "courtyard," which matches the Old Greek (the courtyard of the palaces) and makes more sense.

[291] Wildberger, *Isaiah 28–39*, 315, 335, calls these creatures demons, goblins, goat-demons, and Lilith. Blenkinsopp, *Isaiah 1–39*, 453, suggests that the "goat" is a "goat-demon (satyr), a precursor of Pan" and Lilith was "perhaps originally a minor Assyrian demon (*lilitu*)."

[292] Clements, *Isaiah 1–39*, 274. But this could hardly refer back to later prophecies in Jeremiah and Ezekiel. Seitz, *Isaiah 1–39*, 237, suggests that Isaiah is referring to the book of Noah (Genesis 6:17–22) where each animal went into the ark with its mate, but this is unlikely. Oswalt, *Isaiah 1–39*, 617, maintains that this refers to a heavenly "Book of Destiny" (Mal 3:16; Dan 7;10; Rev 20:12).

repetition of words from v. 15 in v. 16, "each with its mate," argues that this "scroll of the LORD" contains God's promises about the animals mentioned in 34:11–15, thus as O. Kaiser suggests[293] the prophet is referring to his own prophecies that have already appeared in writing. This suggests that 34:16–17 were spoken at some point later in the prophet's career and added here (similar to the final comments about Moab in 16:13) to emphasize the reliability of God's promises. Consequently, the prophet's words from God were considered authoritative, and someone wrote them down so that others could know what God had said (cf. 8:1,16,20; 29:11–12). There is no way of dating this later word in vv. 16–17, for it does not claim that the promises in vv. 11–15 were already fulfilled.

The understanding of v. 16b is complicated by textual difficulties.[294] The prophet communicated his belief that God's past statements are true, that not one of the animals mentioned in 34:14–15 will be missing; each one will have a mate. Why should people believe all this? The proof is assuredly based on the fact that God has "truly, surely" (*kî*; omitted in NIV) commanded "my mouth" (*pî*; not "his mouth," *pô*, as in NIV) to cause this to happen and "his Spirit itself" (*wĕrûḥô hûʾ*) will bring all these things about.

Building on the thought that God originally divided the land among the nations and the Israelite tribes through the casting of lots (Deut 4:19; 32:8; Josh 14:1–2), God himself ironically now casts lots to give each animal a place to live. Though these lands were once the possessions that God gave to the tribes of Israel, after God's devastating judgment these wild animals will possess these lands forever (34:17), just as God said would happen (34:10).

(2) God's Glory Transforming Zion (35:1–10)

> [1]The desert and the parched land will be glad;
> 　the wilderness will rejoice and blossom.
> Like the crocus, [2]it will burst into bloom;
> 　it will rejoice greatly and shout for joy.
> The glory of Lebanon will be given to it,
> 　the splendor of Carmel and Sharon;
> they will see the glory of the LORD,
> 　the splendor of our God.
>
> [3]Strengthen the feeble hands,
> 　steady the knees that give way;

---

[293] Kaiser, *Isaiah 13–39*, 359, says, " the poet anticipates the future, in which it will be possible to read through the book of Isaiah and confirm that everything has been fulfilled which was prophesied." Childs, *Isaiah*, 257, proposes that the prophet is referring to the earlier parallel prophecies in chap. 13.

[294] 1QIsaᵃ omits לֹא פֶקְדוּ, "none will be missing," and has פִיהוּ, "his mouth," rather than פִי, "my mouth." The appearance of הוּא, "he," after "my mouth" is clumsy and some MSS read יהוה, "Yahweh," instead of הוּא. Finally, פָּקַד must have the rather rare meaning of "missing" in this context.

⁴say to those with fearful hearts,
  "Be strong, do not fear;
your God will come,
  he will come with vengeance;
with divine retribution
  he will come to save you."

⁵Then will the eyes of the blind be opened
  and the ears of the deaf unstopped.
⁶Then will the lame leap like a deer,
  and the mute tongue shout for joy.
Water will gush forth in the wilderness
  and streams in the desert.
⁷The burning sand will become a pool,
  the thirsty ground bubbling springs.
In the haunts where jackals once lay,
  grass and reeds and papyrus will grow.

⁸And a highway will be there;
  it will be called the Way of Holiness.
The unclean will not journey on it;
  it will be for those who walk in that Way;
  wicked fools will not go about on it.
⁹No lion will be there,
  nor will any ferocious beast get up on it;
  they will not be found there.
But only the redeemed will walk there,
10   and the ransomed of the LORD will return.
They will enter Zion with singing;
  everlasting joy will crown their heads.
Gladness and joy will overtake them,
  and sorrow and sighing will flee away.

Williamson has discussed the relationship of chap. 35 to 34, and chap. 35 to 40, and extensively evaluated various theories about these relationships.[295] Although these chapters are thematically related, it is best to interpret chaps. 34–35 as the eschatological conclusion to chaps. 28–33, somewhat similar to the eschatological focus of chaps. 24–27, which functions as a conclusion to chaps. 13–23. One should not conclude that these chapters start a new section of the book or that the ideas mentioned here are foreign to the thinking of Isaiah. Several verbal connections between chaps. 34 and 35 draw them together as a unit.[296]

The eschatological message of divine judgment in the previous chapter is contrasted with new promises about God's appearance on earth. He will

---

[295] Williamson, *The Book Called Isaiah*, 212–220, evaluates Steck's theory that chap. 35 functions as a bridge between the two parts of the book and is closely connected to vocabulary in 40:1–11.

[296] This is argued above, at the beginning of 34:1–35:10.

marvelously transform the dry earth into fertile ground (35:1–2,6–7) and the weak and blind into a holy and redeemed people (35:3–4,8–10). This announcement of salvation describes God's final and dramatic transformation of his people and their world. It is not about conditions when the exiles return from Babylon, for exilic conditions were nothing like what is described here.[297] The coming of the glory of the Lord will be the central transformative agent (35:2b,4), thus this salvation oracle seems to deal with some of the same issues considered in 2:1–5; 4:2–6; 29:16–24; 33:1–24).

The prophet's words of encouragement are structured into three paragraphs.

God's transformation of nature	35:1–2
God's transformation of the weak and blind	35:3–6a
God's transformed people will return	35:6b–10

These paragraphs contain many imperative verbs that exhort the audience to change its worldview. The plan of God will be accomplished (35:6b–10) when the transformational power of God's holy presence redeems the earth and mankind.

35:1–2 The introduction to chap. 35 shifts away from the themes of total devastation of the earth, the sword being filled with blood, and the destruction of mankind (the focus of chap. 34), to the opposite themes of an inhabited city, a fertile land, and a joyful life. This paragraph is characterized by imperfect verbs and the repetition of vocabulary of "rejoicing" (*tāgēl*), "blossoming" (*tiprah*), and "splendor" (*hădar*). God's transformation of the dry and dead wilderness was earlier associated with the pouring out of God's Spirit and the establishment of righteousness and peace on the earth (35:15–16; cf. 29:17–19). Later these same deeds will appear as evidence of the "new things" that God will do for his people (43:19–20). Joy and gladness[298] are consistent responses to God's salvific work throughout this book,[299] while the blossom-

---

[297] Beuken, *Isaiah II*, 311, believes the "return to Zion constitutes the main themes of chapter 35," but the "holy highway" (35:8) is not located between any specific locations, and the "return" of the ransomed to Zion (35:10) does not say that they are returning from exile. Blenkinsopp, *Isaiah 1–39*, 456, finds similarities in topics between chaps. 35 and 40–66, but they are not expressed in the same manner. He concludes that the parched wilderness that will be transformed in chap. 35 is not the desert the exiles traveled through to get back to Judah, but the land of Judah itself.

[298] The first verb, "they will be glad," יְשֻׂשׂוּם, has a third masculine plural suffix "them," which does not fit. One might treat this as a jussive, "let them be glad," or conclude that the final ם on this word is a scribal error of dittography, since the next word begins with מ. Because the next verb (וְתָגֵל) is a jussive, one can assume that its parallel in the first line is also a jussive rather than the imperfect as in NIV.

[299] In 9:2 (English 9:3) joy and rejoicing will happen when war ends and the Messiah reigns. In 25:9 joy will come to those who trust God, attend his great banquet, and live in a new era without death or sorrow. Although fertility will be restored and people's blind eyes will be opened, the people will primarily rejoice in the Lord, not in the material blessing of life (29:17–19). The theme is further developed elsewhere (41:16; 42:11; 44:23; 48:20; 49:13; 51:3,11; 52:8–9; 54:1; 55:12; 60:15; 61:3,7,10; 62:5; 64:4; 65:14,18; 66:10–14), and it became a prominent emphasis within the prophet's eschatological scheme.

ing of plants is less pervasive. The prophet was far more concerned with the theological effect of God's work than the botanical, but the two ideas work together rather than against one another. God's work will remove the curse from every part of the earth.

The prophet heightens the dramatic effect of God's transformation by repeatedly emphasizing (35:2) the profuse blossoming[300] of plants and the people's shouts of joy. This transformation will bring the majesty and glory of nature (places like Mount Carmel and the beauty of Lebanon) back to its fullness, but the most significant change that will account for these transformations will be the full revelation of the glory and majesty[301] of God himself. This could simply refer to the glory of God reflected in the glorious changes in nature (41:19–20; 51:3; 60:13), but other similar texts seem to indicate that God himself will appear in splendor in a visible theophany (cf. 4:5; 24:23; 40:5; 52:10; 60:1–2; 66:18). Those who will see God at this time are not identified. While one might guess it is the holy ones (4:2–4) or all flesh (40:5), in this context it is the redeemed (35:9–10).

35:3–6a   A series of imperative verbal clauses interrupts the discussion of the time when God will appear. Surprisingly, these imperatives draw attention to the need for the redeemed to encourage and strengthen those who are weak. The condition of having hands that "sink, drop down" (*rāpâ*) and knees that "stumble, stagger" (*kāšal*) implies that the audience is facing some physical or emotional problem that they are not able to cope with. They need strengthening (mentioned three times in these verses). New strength will come from hearing the encouraging words of God in this salvation oracle. First, the redeemed will assure the weak and anxious that there is no need to fear; and second, they will assure them that God will save them. The exact reason for this fearful and discouraged state is never explained, so one must avoid the temptation of assuming that this describes the condition of exiles in Babylon or the Assyrian crisis in 701 BC. Everything points to an eschatological setting when God will save his people from their enemies and establish justice on the earth.

God's coming is announced in four different clauses at the end of v. 4. First is the announcement of his presence, "behold your God." Then the author turns to explain why God will come and what he will do. The bringing of "vengeance" (*nāqām*) or "recompense" connects these events with those in 34:8 where God's vengeance will defeat the wicked nations on the earth so that[302]

---

[300] The use of the imperfect verb with an infinitive absolute (תִּפְרַח פָּרֹחַ, "blossoming it will blossom") was a common way of making something emphatic (GKC § 113n).

[301] The כָּבוֹד, "glory," is the glorious visible representation of God that is frequently associated with blinding fire, while his הָדָר, "splendor," is associated with the royal majesty of the appearance of a great king (Dan 4:27,33; 5:18). These represent the best that man can do to describe the incomparable magnificence of God's presence (cf. Ps 29:2; 96:8; 145:5).

[302] The use of a *hiphil* jussive verb (וְיֹשַׁעֲכֶם) expresses an intended consequence (GKC § 108d) of God's action, thus giving the translation "so that he can save you."

he can save his people. The weak and fearful can have hope because at this time God will establish his just rule over the wicked and the righteous, bringing a time of joy and peace for the righteous and punishment for the wicked (61:2; 63:4).

Verses 5–6b picture a transformation of the blind and weak. The results of God's transformational presence are introduced with *ʾāz*, "then," in vv. 5 and 6 to emphasize that "then" there will be significant consequences to God's coming. Those who were weak and fearful in vv. 3–4 are probably the same as those who were spiritually blind, deaf, mute, and lame. These are the formerly blind people in Israel (6:9–10) who will one day see and understand God's words (29:18; 32:3–4; 42:18–19) when God establishes his righteous king over his kingdom. There will be no physical or spiritual disabilities then (cf. 33:24). This transformational change will open the hearts that were closed, turn the lame into leapers, and enable the silent to shout for joy.

35:6b–10 The salvation oracle ends with a description of how God will cause his people to return to Zion. "Surely" (*kî*; omitted in 6b in NIV) God's power will transform the desert into a place where there are springs, ponds, and streams with lush vegetation (35:6b–7), reaffirming the changes described in 35:1–2. This is the opposite of what will happen in the nations when God causes their streams to dry up (34:9). Another opposite effect involves the presence of the wild desert animals that will inherit the desolate places of the earth (34:13–14). Since God will bring fertility back to the land, the wild beast will no longer be welcome (35:7).

The content of 35:8–10 is unified around the repeated reference to what will be "there" (*šām*, used three times, drawing a contrast to the parallel in 34:15–16) and what will "not" (*lō*, used five times) be there. A "highway" (*maslul*) is a major graded road, as opposed to a small path, and usually refers to a state-constructed road that supports economic or military operations. Not every use of the highway concept in Isaiah refers to the same road or event. There is the metaphorical highway God uses to come to Jerusalem (40:1–11), which is different from the highway that the Assyrian exiles will use (11:16). The highway in 35:8 is an eschatological highway used by the people of God as they return to Zion to praise God in the distant future (cf. 62:9–12). This highway has the unique name, "Way of Holiness" (*derek haqqôdeš*), a title based on the fact that only holy people will walk on it. The unclean person, the fool, the lion, and the wild beast will not walk on this road, for it will be reserved for God's redeemed people. The unclean are not allowed to enter a holy place, and the fools cannot travel there because they walk in ways that are contrary to the will of God. Neither group is morally or ritually qualified to come before God when he comes in his glory. Those who joyfully enter Zion to fellowship and praise God are the redeemed (*gěʾûlim*) and ransomed (*pědûʾyē*). The term "redeemed" is used when a person delivers a blood relative from some obligation (legal, financial, social), thus those who come to Zion are pictured as the covenant relatives that God has redeemed. "Ransom" comes from the legal practice of making a payment to deliver someone from a debt, obligation, or punishment, though the payment idea is seldom emphasized when referring to God's theological ransoming of his people. Both terms emphasize that the people's status as the redeemed or ransomed is based on an act of divine grace to free them from the bondage of an earlier obligation. This indebtedness is broader than the bondage to a personal sin; it includes all the effects of sin on the world. These acts of God will remove the curse on man and the world[303] and inaugurate the holy kingdom of God. Those who "will return" (*yāšubûn*) to God will experience "everlasting joy," (*śimḥat ʿôlām*), they will be overtaken with gladness, and all sorrow will end (cf. 25:8; 65:19). Certainly, these words would have created hope in those who heard the prophet speak. They can put their trust in a God who will do these things for his people.

Since 35:10 is almost identical to 51:11, many have concluded that the verse was a later addition and that it was given a new meaning different from its original intent in 51:11 (cf. similar ideas also in 62:10–12). Nevertheless, it is nearly impossible to determine which passage was the original and which one was the copy. One can observe that 35:10 does not interrupt the natural flow of thought from 35:9, nor does it appear to be out of place. On the other hand, the coming of God's people singing into Zion in 51:11 did not immediately follow God's redemption of his people in the exodus in 51:9–10. Thus it appears that 34:10 is its original context.

THEOLOGICAL IMPLICATIONS. Chapters 34–35 describe the time when God will settle accounts with mankind on earth and set up his eschatological kingdom. There is no doubt about the theological principle that God will have vengeance on the wicked and violently destroy them and the earth where they live. His judgment is real, it is devastating, and it is final. If one can conceive of a world without divine support and care, that is the world that awaits the nations that will receive God's wrath. It will be the most gruesome, bloody, terrible, and repulsive scene that one can imagine. Death, infertility, and desolation will characterize the planet; everything attractive and beautiful will vanish. The prophet's description of this abominable time was meant to repulse the hearers and motivate them to do everything possible to avoid experiencing these things. It will be a terrible thing to fall into the hands of an angry God.

On the other hand, in chap. 35 God offers an alternative world of fertility, joy, and gladness where he will reveal something of his marvelous glory. The theological principle here is that everyone should be encouraged to experience the salvation of God, no matter how weak or blind they are. God is not only able to remove blindness and strengthen the weak; he will also miraculously open the eyes of many. His kingdom will have abundant water, great fertility,

---

[303] Lev 26:22 and Deut 32:24 refer to God's curse of wild beasts devouring people, while Isa 11:6–8; Hos 2:18; and Ezek 34:25 connect the kingdom of God with the removal of all wild beasts.

and a holy highway for his redeemed people to come to Zion to worship him. Only those who return to God, only the holy, and only the ransomed will experience the joy of that day.

VI. HEZEKIAH'S CHALLENGE TO TRUST GOD (36:1–39:9)
  1. Overcoming Sennacherib's Threats against Hezekiah (36:1–37:38)
    (1) Challenging Hezekiah's Trust for Deliverance (36:1–22)
      The First Challenge: On Whom Can You Depend?
      (36:1–10)
      The Second Challenge: Who Can Deliver You? (36:11–21)
    (2) Cutting Off the Blaspheming Assyrian King (36:22–37:7)
    (3) Sennacherib's Final Warning to Hezekiah (37:8–13)
    (4) God's Promise to Rescue Hezekiah (37:14–35)
      Requesting God's deliverance (37:14–20)
      Promise to Defeat Proud Sennacherib (37:21–29)
      God's Sign of Survival and Promise of Protection
      (37:30–35)
    (5) Assyrians Defeated (37:36–38)
  2. Hezekiah Delivered from Death (38:1–22)
    (1) Hezekiah's Prayer for Healing (38:1–8)
    (2) Hezekiah's Thanksgiving for Healing (38:9–20)
    (3) Concluding Comments (38:21–22)
  3. Trusting Babylon Rather Than God (39:1–8)

VI. HEZEKIAH'S CHALLENGE TO TRUST GOD
(36:1–39:9)

These four chapters contain a theological account of Hezekiah's reign while he was dealing with problems related to Sennacherib's invasion of Judah in 705–701 BC. These chapters are somewhat reminiscent of the narrative report of events when King Ahaz refused to trust God while facing the crisis of the Syro-Ephraimite War in chaps. 7–8.[1] A comparison of the sections exposes several similarities in the way these leaders behaved and also highlights some fundamental differences between these two kings, for in the end Ahaz refused to trust God, while at the last moment Hezekiah did trust God for deliverance from Assyria. The historical events and the dialogues (between the Assyrian general Rabshakeh and the people of Jerusalem, Isaiah and Hezekiah, Hezekiah and God), about whether the king should trust God or some other nation, provide the reader with an historical context for understanding many of

---

[1] P. R. Ackroyd, "The Biblical Interpretation of the Reigns of Ahaz and Hezekiah," in *Studies in the Religious Traditions of the Old Testament* (London: SCM, 1987), 105–20, draws numerous parallels between events in the lives of these two kings.

the preceding chapters (13–35) and particularly God's promises to destroy the Assyrians. The wording of this narrative is so closely related to the literary account of the identical events described in 2 Kgs 18–20[2] that one must assume there is some literary connection between these two narratives. The various attempts to explain this literary interrelationship will be described at the beginning of each section of the text.

The structure of chaps. 36–39 is organized around three main episodes in the life of Hezekiah, each beginning with a temporal formula introducing that time period. "In the fourteenth year of King Hezekiah's reign" (36:1) locates the events described in chaps. 36–37 with phraseology that is similar to what one finds in the book of Kings. This date connects these events to 701 BC when Sennacherib came to Jerusalem to force Hezekiah to surrender the city and his control of the nation. "In those days Hezekiah was ill and was at the point of death" introduces the narrative in 38:1, while "At that time Merodach-baladan . . . had heard of his illness and recovery" introduces the new narrative in 39:1. The temporal introductory formula in 39:1 reveals that chap. 39 chronologically follows the story about Hezekiah's illness recorded in chap. 38. But chaps. 36–39 are not in chronological order, for 38:6 refers to God's future plan to defend Jerusalem from Sennacherib's attack; thus, it is evident that the narrative reports in chaps. 38 and 39 occurred before the events described in chaps. 36–37. Since the Assyrians removed the Babylonian king Merodach-baladan from power in 703 BC,[3] this Babylonian king's trip to Jerusalem to arrange an alliance with Hezekiah must have happened sometime in 703–704 BC. This means that Hezekiah's sickness (chap. 38) happened in the preceding year.

The question that naturally develops from this discovery is: Why were the stories about Hezekiah not arranged in chronological order? What was the author's purpose in changing the order of these events? Are there thematic connections that caused chaps. 36–39 to be placed in their present order or is there some theological reason for structuring the material in this way? It is possible to propose several different answers to these questions.

A. K. Jenkins attempted to remove this chronological problem by suggesting that these texts are actually in their proper historical order. He accomplished this by connecting the fourteenth year of Hezekiah (36:1) to 714 BC[4]

---

[2] 2 Chr 32 also contains an abbreviated account that has some parallels with Isaiah, but these two accounts are not identical stories; therefore, no literary connection needs to be evaluated.

[3] L. D. Levine, "Sennacherib's Southern Front: 704–689 BC," *JCS* 34 (1982): 22–58, discusses Sennacherib's dealings with Merodach-baladan.

[4] J. D. W. Watts, *Isaiah 34–66*, WBC (Waco: Word, 1987), 22, says that, "Hezekiah had surely dealt with Sargon II in 714 BC and declared his loyalty by paying tribute, as 2 Kgs 18:14–16 testify." J. H. Hayes and and S. A. Irvine. *Isaiah, the Eighth-Century Prophet: His Times and Preaching* (Nashville: Abingdon, 1987), 383, believe Merodach-baladan's visit in chap. 39 took place around 713 BC during the reign of Sargon II, but they think Isaiah's tribute (2 Kgs 18:14–16) was paid to Sennacherib.

(rather than 701 BC) based on the idea that Hezekiah became king in the third year of Hoshea (2 Kgs 18:1).[5] Thus his proposal is that the events in chaps. 36–37 originally happened when Sargon II attacked Judah, long before 701 BC.[6] Chapter 38 must fit the same general period since Hezekiah's reign was only twenty-nine years and he lived fifteen years after he was healed of this serious illness. The major problem with this solution is that it wrongly connects a major attack on Jerusalem with the invasion by Sargon II in 712–711 BC,[7] (Sennacherib attacked Jerusalem, not Sargon II), and it assumes that the biblical text has confused these two Assyrian invasions or purposely attributed events to the wrong Assyrian king.

Many scholars have argued that the placement of chap. 39 out of chronological order serves best to prepare the reader for the material to follow. These arguments are examined in more detail in the Introduction (see "The Structure of the Literary Units"). At any rate, we must assume that this inverted chronological order in chaps. 36–39 did serve Isaiah's theological purposes, but it may be that his purposes were less related to creating a bridge to chaps. 40–55 and more related to the prophet's presentation of the figure of Hezekiah. M. A. Sweeney maintains that Hezekiah's exemplary piety in chaps. 36–39 presents him as the fulfillment of the ideal monarch presented in 9:1–6 and "might also fulfill the royal ideal expressed in 11:1–16 and 32:1–20."[8] He classifies Hezekiah as the "ideal Jew" who obeys, trusts, and worships God, the true divine monarch on the throne. He finds in Isa 36–39 a modification of the Hezekiah figure from what was presented in 2 Kgs 18–20. The Isaiah account "tends to remove any sense of wrongdoing or lack of faith on Hezekiah's part."[9] He interprets Hezekiah as a model of piety even in chap. 39 and "considers his role in the book as a model of piety for the Jewish community of the late 6th century."[10] This understanding of Hezekiah seems far too optimistic in light of all the prophet's negative comments about the nation in chaps. 28–32 and Hezekiah's mistakes in chap. 39. It appears that Sweeney himself has exalted

---

[5] This was the date he became coregent with his father, not the sole king of Judah.

[6] A. K. Jenkins, "Hezekiah's Fourteenth Year: A New Interpretation of 2 Kings xviii 13–xix 37," *VT* 26 (1976): 289–94, believes a later redactor reinterpreted all of this material and wrongly associated it with Sennacherib's attack rather than the military campaign of Sargon II.

[7] K. L. Younger, "Recent Study on Sargon II, King of Assyria: Implications for Biblical Studies," in *Mesopotamia and the Bible* (ed. M. W. Chavalas and K. L. Younger; Grand Rapids: Baker, 2002), 313–319, deals with Sargon's campaign in Judah from 712–711 BC.

[8] M. A. Sweeney, *Isaiah 1–39, with an Introduction to Prophetic Literature,* FOTL 16 (Grand Rapids: Eerdmans, 1996), 458–59, seems to idealize the figure of Hezekiah even more than Isaiah.

[9] Sweeney (Ibid., 482) points to the omission of 2 Kgs 18:14–16 where Hezekiah submitted to Sennacherib and paid a large tribute, the modification of 2 Kgs 18:32 in 36:17–18 to soften the suggestion that Hezekiah might mislead the people, and the addition of the pious letter of Hezekiah after his sickness in 38:9–20.

[10] Sweeney, (Ibid., 511) believes "Hezekiah is presented as a model of faith. Despite the fact that his sons will be deported to Babylon, he continues to show faith in YHWH just as he did through the crises of the Assyrian siege and his own illness."

the Hezekiah of chap. 37, failing to balance or integrate this picture with the surrounding negative material.

In contrast to this approach, J. Oswalt suggests that Hezekiah's failures in chap. 39 served the theological purpose of showing "Hezekiah's fallibility," thus demonstrating that Hezekiah was not the Messiah or the answer to all of Judah's problems.[11] This view of Hezekiah is more consistent with the picture throughout 28–32 and 38–39 and shifts the focus of these chapters away from the heroics or piety of the human king Hezekiah, although it is doubtful that anyone actually thought of Hezekiah as the Messiah. God is really the only one who has the power to address Judah's problems. The king and his people must trust him, for he alone is God and Sennacherib is just a proud blasphemer.

In addition, one might suggest that the inverted order of presenting these events demonstrates God's amazing grace in deliverance, for God (a) delivered a city from the grip of a stronger Assyrian army (36–37); (b) delivered a king who had earlier put his trust in other nations (30–31) and failed to trust God; (c) delivered a king from certain death (38); and (d) delivered a king who acted in distrust (39:1–4). The amazing thing is that most of this failure to trust God occurred after God promised to defeat the Assyrians and performed a miraculous sign to assure the king of the truthfulness of his promises (38:5–7). One can be astonished at God's miraculous killing of 185,000 Assyrian troops (37:36), but it is even more shocking to realize that God did this for one who was earlier so faithless despite being richly blessed with a fifteen year extension of his life (38:5–7). This divine benevolence powerfully illustrates how God's grace truly can overcome human depravity. Because of Hezekiah's failures, God takes center stage as the one who should be trusted.

It is hard to read the narrative of Hezekiah's deliverance in chaps. 36–39 without noticing certain parallel trust issues in the life of his father. Through the repetition of similar words, the text of 2 Kings contrasts the life and accomplishments of the father, king Ahaz (2 Kgs 16), with the son, King Hezekiah (2 Kgs 18–20), and some of these contrasts are also present in Isaiah.[12] While Ahaz' life is boldly presented as a life of devotion to pagan gods, dependence on the Assyrian king Tiglath-pileser III during the Syro-Ephraimite War, and an unwillingness to trust God's promises (7:1–12; 2 Kgs 16), the reign of Hez-

---

[11] J. Oswalt, *Isaiah 1–39*, NICOT (Grand Rapids: Eerdmans, 1986), 630, does not ignore Hezekiah's trust in God, but his fallibility causes one to realize that Hezekiah is not the hero of this narrative; God is.

[12] Ackroyd, "The Biblical Interpretation of the Reigns of Ahaz and Hezekiah," 105–20, notes contrast in the presentation of these two men in 2 Kings and 2 Chronicles (and a few in Isaiah) while J. W. Groves, *Actualization and Interpretation in the Old Testament* (Atlanta: Scholar's Press, 1987), 38–46, lists contrasts mainly between Isa 7 and 36–39. Some of these include that both stories have (a) an army attacking Jerusalem; (b) important events happening at the upper pool; (c) the king receiving a "fear not" oracle; (d) a sign is promised; (e) the city of Jerusalem is spared; and (f) promises that the "zeal of the Lord will do this."

ekiah is idealized in 2 Kings as the reign of the greatest religious leader of all kings before or after him (2 Kgs 18:1–5), though he did have to admit a political mistake at one point (2 Kgs 18:13–16). Second Chronicles 29–32 describes Hezekiah's great Temple reforms with glowing terms of praise because he removed the evil influences of his father Ahaz and restored joyful worship back to the temple. But some of Hezekiah's failures, like pride, are noted (2 Chr 32:25,31). In Isaiah both Ahaz and Hezekiah faced similar military circumstances, being overwhelmed by superior forces, and both kings inappropriately made alliances with other nations,[13] but in the end the two kings responded quite differently to the challenge of trusting God. Ahaz rejected God's promises and made an alliance with Tiglath-pileser III of Assyria, but Hezekiah, after some initial failures (30–31,39), finally trusted God and God miraculously delivered him from a huge Assyrian army.

1. Overcoming Sennacherib's Threat against Hezekiah (36:1–37:38)

This account contains two speeches by Rabshakeh (36:4–10, 36:13–20) and a letter (37:10–13). Each is introduced by a "messenger formula" identifying these as the words of the great Assyrian king Sennacherib. These words represent the worldview of one of the combatants in the story who claims to rule the world. On the other side of the battlefield were Isaiah, Hezekiah, and God, whose alternative views of reality are represented in Hezekiah's prayer (37:14–20) and two God speeches proclaimed by Isaiah (37:6–7; 37:22–35), each introduced with a "messenger formula" identifying these as the words of the Lord. Between these speeches are fragmentary references to the historical events taking place (36:1–2; 37:8–9,36–38), introductions that identify the persons speaking (36:4; 37:3,14–15,21), and the reactions of those listening (36:3,11,21–22; 37:1). The overwhelming emphasis on these dialogues and speeches suggests that these chapters are far more interested in the political-theological views of the combatants than in providing an extensive blow-by-blow historical account of what happened on each day of the attack. Chapters 22, 28–31, and 38–39 give some additional historical background concerning the events immediately preceding and following.

HISTORICAL SETTING.   There is no doubt that these two chapters describe Sennacherib's attack on Jerusalem in 701 BC. The general outline of events is verified by similar stories in 2 Kgs 18–19, 2 Chr 32, Sennacherib's own Akkadian account on the Taylor Prism of a war in Judah, the Egyptian Kawa Stela IV concerning the Cushite ruler Tarhaqa, and Babylonian

---

[13] C. R. Seitz, *Zion's Final Destiny: The Development of the Book of Isaiah: A Reassessment of Isaiah 36-39* (Minneapolis: Fortress, 1991), 57, also notices these similarities, which are often ignored because interpreters themselves overemphasize the differences between these two rulers. He also reacts against those who suggest that Hezekiah is being idealized (the presence of chap. 39 undermines this theory).

documents on the reign of Merodach-baladan II.[14] But even with the luxury of multiple sources, scholars cannot agree on what actually happened. These problems arise because of different ways of understanding the historical data as well as alternative approaches to the literary sources. The literature is far too extensive to review all of the alternatives, but some of the key issues are:

1. Tirhakeh, the Cushite king of Egypt, is reported to have engaged in a fight with the Assyrians in 37:9, but he was not king of Egypt until 691/690 BC. In the Taylor Prism, Sennacherib himself refers to a Cushite king coming out to fight him at Eltekah but he does not give his name. There is no question about whether there was conflict between Assyrian and Egyptian troops; the main question relates to the reference to Tirhakeh as king at this time.[15] Based on M. F. L. Macadam's translation of the Kawa Stela IV,[16] J. Bright concluded that Tirhakeh was only nine years old in 701 BC and unable to lead an army; therefore, he proposed the idea that these two kings fought during a second Assyrian campaign against Judah after 688 BC when Tirhakeh was a king.[17] A new reading of the Kawa Stela IV suggests that Tirhakeh was actually 20 years old in 701 BC and able to lead an army as the "crown prince" (Hb. *melek* can mean "king, crown prince") under king Shabataka (702–690 BC).[18] The reference to Tirhakeh as king, then, is a reference to the crown prince who later became king.[19]

2. Hezekiah's payment of tribute to Sennacherib is announced in 2 Kgs 18:14–16 and recorded in Sennacherib's Taylor Prism (with slightly different figures), but was omitted from Isaiah's account. This series of events causes some confusion (Was the tribute promised early in these events as 2 Kgs 18 implies, or later as suggested in the Taylor Prism?) because one would expect that this promise to pay tribute would satisfy Sennacherib's demands; therefore, his later siege of the city of Jerusalem would seem to be unnecessary (or possibly unhistorical). C. R. Seitz and others[20] disconnect 2 Kgs 18:14–16

---

[14] *ANET*, 287–88 and J. A. Brinkman, "Merodach-Baladan II," in *Studies Presented to A. L. Oppenheim, June 7, 1964* (ed. R. D. Briggs and J. A. Brinkman; Chicago: Oriental Institute, 1964), 6–53, indicates Merodach-baladan II was driven from control of Babylon in 703 BC.

[15] *ANET*, 287, indicates he defeated the Egyptians.

[16] M. F. L. Macadam, *Temples of Kawa: The Inscriptions* (Oxford: Oxford University, 1949).

[17] J. Bright, *A History of Israel* (3d ed.; Philadelphia: Westminster, 1981), 300. More recently W. H. Shea, "Sennacherib's Second Palestinian Campaign," *JBL* 104 (1985): 401–18, supports this theory. Most interpreters now reject the idea of a second Assyrian campaign by Sennacherib to explain these facts.

[18] K. A. Kitchen, *Ancient Orient and the Old Testament* (Downers Grove: InterVarsity, 1966), 82–83, corrected Macadam's error of supposing that Tirhakeh was only twenty in the fifth regnal year; instead he was twenty in 701 BC.

[19] J. K. Hoffmeier, "Egypt's Role in the Events of 701 BC in Jerusalem," in *Jerusalem in Bible and Archaeology: The First Temple Period* (ed. A. G. Vaughn and A. E. Killebrew; Leiden: Brill, 2003), 219–34.

[20] C. R. Seitz, "Account A and the Annuals of Sennacherib: A Reassesment," *JSOT* 58 (1993): 50–52. A. K. Jenkins, "Hezekiah's Fourteenth Year: A New Interpretation of 2 Kings xviii 13–xix 37," *VT* 26 (1976): 289–94, and J. Goldberg, "Two Campaigns against Hezekiah," *Bib* 80 (1999):

from the 701 BC events to solve this problem, and instead they associate it with the invasion of Sargon II in 712–711 BC. Thus Sennacherib's attack on Jerusalem in 701 BC makes sense because there was no payment of tribute. On the other hand, O. Kaiser accepts 2 Kgs 18:14–16 and Sennacherib's account as what really happened in 701 BC and rejects any idea of a Hebrew victory because of a miraculous divine deliverance (God's killing of 185,000 Assyrian troops in 37:36 is purely later religious legend).[21] A third approach would connect 2 Kgs 18:14–16 to Hezekiah's defeat in 701 BC, but connect the later defeat of the Assyrians in 37:36 with a second campaign around 690 BC (see above). Although the biblical text does not explain why Sennacherib attacked Jerusalem after he received Hezekiah's tribute, the two are not contradictory, for if one compares what Sennacherib did to other rebellious cities and nations during this same campaign, one finds that those who refused to submit (like Hezekiah)[22] were besieged, captured, spoiled, and removed from power or killed. Thus it is not surprising that Sennacherib was not satisfied with Hezekiah's promise to send tribute, for no other rebellious vassals were given this kind of lenient option.[23] This suggests that it is not historically problematic to accept both Hezekiah's promise to give tribute in 2 Kgs 18:14–16 (which is not mentioned in Isaiah) as well as the narrative about Sennacherib's attack on the city of Jerusalem. Since neither the biblical nor the Assyrian account are pure chronological narratives, the exact timing of Hezekiah's offer to pay tribute remains unknown.

3. Sennacherib's account of his attack on Jerusalem never refers to a loss of 185,000 troops; in fact, the Assyrian account never states that Sennacherib spared the city. R. E. Clements considers the idea that God miraculously spared Jerusalem was a bit of later royal Zion theology redacted into the text in the time of Josiah.[24] This omission is not an historical problem but a literary issue, for Sennacherib's account was intended to declare his glory and royal power, so it would be natural to omit any setbacks from the record (similarly, Isaiah omitted 2 Kgs 18:14–16). Omitting a few facts does not render an account

---

360–90, believe a later redactor reinterpreted all of this material and associated it with Sennacherib's attack rather than Sargon II.

[21] O. Kaiser, *Isaiah 13—39*, OTL. (Philadelphia: Westminster, 1974), 375.

[22] *ANET*, 288. Sennacherib claims that "Hezekiah, the Jew, he did not submit to my yoke." K. L. Younger, "Assyrian Involvement in the Southern Levant," in *Jerusalem in Bible and Archaeology: The First Temple Period* (ed. A. G. Vaughn and A. E. Killebrew; Leiden: Brill, 2003), 235–63, looks at the organized literary structure of Sennacherib's account, the propaganda in it, and some examples of topical instead of chronological reporting.

[23] R. D. Bates, "Assyria and Rebellion in the Annals of Sennacherib: An Analysis of Sennacherib's Treatment of Hezekiah," *NEASB* 44 (1999): 39–61, argues that Sennacherib treated Hezekiah the same way he treated the other rebellious vassals, except he was unsuccessful in defeating Hezekiah. A. R. Millard, "Sennacherib's Attack on Hezekiah," *TynBul* 36 (1985): 61–67, concludes that something unusual happened at the end of these events because Sennacherib does not use the language one would expect to describe his treatment of Hezekiah.

[24] R. E. Clements, *Isaiah and the Deliverance of Jerusalem* (Sheffield: JSOT, 1980), 29.

historically invalid; this is a legitimate option for any author based on his purpose in writing. But there must be some historical reason why Sennacherib's glorification was illustrated on his palace walls by his defeat of Lachish (rather than Jerusalem). Sennacherib's failure to mention that Hezekiah brought out his daughters or that the Assyrian king had mercy on him suggests that something unusual happened that prevented Sennacherib from completing a normal conquest of Jerusalem. Isaiah 37:36 explains these unusual circumstances, and Isaiah's historical value should not be rejected by concluding that it is just some later royal legend.

4. In addition to these historical problems, commentators have had difficulty understanding the literary organization and the progression of action within chaps. 36–37; therefore, it has become difficult to reconstruct the historical setting for each part of the narrative. Many literary critics find three distinct documents within chaps. 36–37 with different (and sometimes contradictory) stories concerning what happened when Sennacherib attacked Jerusalem: (a) source A is identified as an old historical report and is found in 2 Kgs 18:13–17; (b) source B1 is in Isa 36:1–37:9a, 37–38; and (c) source B2 includes 37:9b–36.[25] The two B sources contain two messengers sent from the Assyrian king (36:1–2 and 37:9b), Hezekiah visiting the temple twice (37:1,14), two encouraging messages by Isaiah (37:6–7 and 37:21–35), and what some consider contradictory information.[26] Because of these similarities and differences, B2 is thought to be a late post-exilic retelling of B1 and given little historical value. Consequently, numerous hypothetical reconstructions of these events are proposed, usually discounting the value of the later redactions of this story.

M. A. Sweeney and K. A. D. Smelik maintain that this approach arbitrarily creates conflicting literary sources and ignores the nature of the narrative development of plot, conflict, dramatic tension, and resolution that are a common part of most biblical narratives.[27] The dialogues fit together as a series of "diplomatic disputations" in which the two sides of the conflict attempt to support their own claims for supremacy through diplomatic words that will intimidate their opponent. Either God is the all-powerful ruler who can be trusted by Hezekiah, or Sennacherib is an all-powerful king and he should be trusted. Tension rises at each new stage of the plot as the Assyrians persuasively argue for their supremacy and blaspheme the name of God. Finally, when Hezekiah puts his trust in God (37:14–20), God promises to destroy the blasphemer (37:22–35)

---

[25] B. S. Childs, *Isaiah and the Assyrian Crisis* (London: SCM, 1967), 69–103, discusses this approach in detail.

[26] Some understood the view of God in 36:10 as different from 37:10–12, and a big difference between Isaiah's prophecies in 37:7 and 37:36–38.

[27] K. A. D. Smelik, "Distortion of Old Testament Prophecy: The Purpose of Isaiah xxxvi–xxxvii," *OTS* 24 (1986): 70–93, criticizes Child's reasons for dividing the text into two separate sources and then shows how the narrative naturally progresses as a literary unity with somewhat repetitious arguments in order to persuade the audience to accept a particular point of view. Sweeney, *Isaiah 1–39*, 465–71, traces the plot through seven episodes.

and demonstrate his power by destroying the Assyrians (37:36–38). This provides a much more satisfactory way of dealing with the unity and progressive development of tension within this narrative.

5. The final question asks if Isaiah wrote this narrative himself, or if the text was originally part of another scroll. Did a later editor copy this account from 2 Kings as many have maintained in the past?[28] Such an approach was popularized in the Isaiah commentary by B. Duhm,[29] who argued that:

1. The Kings narrative is a more difficult text, so the smoothed out text in Isaiah must be later (e.g., 2 Kgs 18:14–16 were omitted in Isaiah).
2. Isa 36–39 were added as an appendix to the Isaiah scroll from 18–20, much like Jer 52 was added as an appendix from 2 Kgs 25.
3. The style of the narrative is consistent with what is found elsewhere in 2 Kings, but does not fit the poetic style of Isaiah.
4. The account in 2 Kgs 18:14–16 matches Sennacherib's account so it must be the more historical and trustworthy; Isaiah omits it so it is less historically trustworthy.
5. The book of Isaiah continued to develop after the book of Kings was completed, thus Isaiah's further development was dependent on Kings.

This thesis was not the only hypothesis that attempted to explain the relationship between the account in Kings and Isaiah. Some objected to the idea that the narrative was not an integral part of Isaiah's writings and saw no evidence to support the idea that some later editor added these narratives from an outside source. E. J. Young hypothesized that Isaiah was the original source of this narrative and that Kings and Chronicles copied from him. J. Oswalt's commentary follows him in support of this theory.[30] Recently K. A. D. Smelik produced five arguments to support the priority of the Isaiah account:

1. Kings does not usually contain the personal stories of prophets like Isa 36–39 (there is nothing about the life or sermons of Amos, Hosea, Micah, and Jeremiah), while Isaiah 6–7 does contain another narrative about the prophet, so chaps. 36–37 fit better in Isaiah than in 2 Kings.
2. Chapters 36–39 have poetic compositions, which are normal in prophetic books, but unusual in Kings.

---

[28] Ackroyd, "Isaiah 36–39: Structure and Function," in *Studies in the Religious Traditions of the Old Testament* (London: SCM, 1987), 115, refers to "the common view that 36–39 have simply been extracted from II Kings and added to an already complete book of Isaiah." Sweeney, *Isaiah 1–39*, 482–83, concludes that chaps. 36–39 were drawn from 2 Kgs 18–19 and were "modified to idealize Hezekiah prior to their placement in the book of Isaiah." But later he seems to contradict this when he states that "the narrative seems to have been composed neither for the book of Kings nor for the book of Isaiah; rather, it appears to have been composed independently for some other context." This theory goes back to W. Gesenius, *Der Prophet Jesaja* (Leipzig: Vogel, 1821).

[29] B. Duhm, *Das Buch Jesaia* (Göttingen: Vandenhoeck and Ruprecht, 1892).

[30] E. J. Young, *The Book of Isaiah* (Grand Rapids: Eerdmans, 1969), 2:556–65 and Oswalt, *Isaiah 1–39*, 700, both propose that Isaiah wrote these chapters.

3. The story of Hezekiah's illness in chap. 38 is better composed in the Isaianic account, when it is compared to the story in Kings.

4. Chapters 36–39 serve as a natural editorial bridge to Isaiah 40–55, a function they do not serve in Kings.

5. The inverted order (with chaps. 38–39 coming last, but actually happening before chaps. 36–37) is explainable if the order was first established in the book of Isaiah.[31]

Others have also observed that the longer form of the name Hezekiah appears throughout 2 Kgs 18–19, but the shorter form of his name is used in 18:14–16. They conclude that these verses were actually a later insertion into the book of Kings; thus, originally, Isaiah and Kings agreed.[32] C. R. Seitz' observation that there is a similar structure and vocabulary to the account of the invasion in the time of Ahaz (2 Kgs 16:5–9) and Hezekiah (2 Kgs 18:14–16) implies a common origin in Isaiah (so 2 Kgs 18:14–16 was added to Kings) to demonstrate a comparison between these figures. In this way he removes one of the main reasons for thinking that the 2 Kgs 18–19 has priority over the Isaiah narrative.[33]

This argument for the priority of the Isaiah account is based on an unusual number of parallels evident between the Ahaz and Hezekiah narratives (similar crisis, Isaiah meets both by the same pool, both should not fear, both are given a sign), suggesting that the same author (Isaiah) was trying to contrast one king with the other.[34] These arguments led H. G. M. Williamson to conclude that chaps. 36–39 were written by someone who was very familiar with the Isaiah traditions, though he believes both accounts in Kings and Isaiah were drawn from a common source.[35] A. H. Konkel reaches a similar conclusion after a meticulous comparison of the Old Greek, the *kaige* recension, Qumran scrolls, and the Masoretic text in Kings and Isaiah.[36] H. Wildberger asserts that (a) the source of this material was a third independent text; (b) the material was first borrowed by Kings and

---

[31] Smelik, "Distortion in Old Testament Prophecy," 70–93, also notes that words and themes from the surrounding chapters in Isaiah have influenced the diction in chaps. 36–39, implying that Isaiah wrote this material.

[32] Seitz, *Zion's Final Destiny,* 54–55, refers to the opinions of Norin, Wellhausen, Burney, and Jepsen.

[33] Seitz, *Zion's Final Destiny,* 57, finds similarities in that both have an invasion (16:5; 18:13), contact with the king of Assyria (16:7; 18:14), a capitulation speech (16:7; 18:14), and tribute being paid (16:8; 18:15–16). Seitz also noticed that three times Hezekiah is called king in 2 Kgs 18:14–16, a practice that runs contrary to the usual practice in the rest of the narrative.

[34] Ackroyd, "The Biblical Interpretation of the Reigns of Ahaz and Hezekiah," 105–20, draws numerous parallels between events in the lives of these two kings. E. W. Conrad, *Reading Isaiah* (Minneapolis: Fortress, 1991) 38–46, postulates six connections between chaps. 7 and 36–39, and the study of Groves, *Actualization and Interpretation in the Old Testament,* finds numerous connection outside of chap. 7.

[35] H. G. M. Williamson, *The Book Called Isaiah: Deutero-Isaiah's Role in Composition and Redaction* (Oxford: Clarendon, 1994), 194, 201, thinks the tradition flowed from this independent source to Kings and from there to Isaiah.

[36] A. H. Konkel, "The Sources of the Story of Hezekiah in the Book of Isaiah," *VT* 43 (1993): 462–82.

then put in Isaiah; and (c) the narrative is better transmitted in some parts in Isaiah than in Kings.[37] There is no way to identify this third unknown source, but since it contains Isaianic themes and vocabulary one might guess that this could be the royal record of Hezekiah's reign that Isaiah wrote (2 Chr 32:32).

(1) Challenging Hezekiah's Trust for Deliverance (36:1–22)

The first section of this narrative plot deals with the initial confrontation between Sennacherib's messenger and Hezekiah's representatives. The Isaiah account does not explain why Sennacherib has come to Judah (2 Kgs 18:7 indicates that Hezekiah rebelled) and includes no admission that Hezekiah has done wrong or is willing to pay back tribute to Sennacherib (2 Kgs 18:14–16). The Isaiah account selectively includes only the information that serves its theological purpose. Therefore, it is best to read the Isaiah account as an independent and legitimate theological presentation of these events, rather than constantly reading it thorough the eyes of the account in 2 Kgs 18.

Sennacherib's method of addressing this confrontation is through words of intimidation and persuasive logic that would hopefully undermine the people's "trust" (*bāṭaḥ*) in Egypt, Hezekiah, and God. If Hezekiah can be persuaded to surrender, the Assyrians will have accomplished all their goals without further military losses or effort. In the end Hezekiah's representative and the people on the wall refuse to negotiate with Rabshakeh. This first episode ends with dramatic hopelessness and lamenting (36:22), for Hezekiah has no answer to Sennacherib's challenge.

The structure of the first episode is divided into two incidents that are somewhat repetitive; nevertheless, together they represent the unrelenting effort of the Assyrians to undermine all trust in Hezekiah and God. If the king will just give up his trust in God, Sennacherib will protect the Hebrew people in the future by giving them a wonderful place where they can live in peace and prosperity (36:16–17). Throughout these speeches the Assyrians question God's power to deliver his people, Sennacherib's power is exalted, and Sennacherib offers to provide for the people what God cannot give them. Military tension is created because the people seem to have no choice but to accept Sennacherib's perspective and to surrender. Theological tension is created because this military option is unacceptable, for by surrendering the people would be admitting that their God is unable to save them and is no match for the power of Sennacherib.

THE FIRST CHALLENGE: ON WHOM CAN YOU DEPEND? (36:1-10)

¹In the fourteenth year of King Hezekiah's reign, Sennacherib king of Assyria attacked all the fortified cities of Judah and captured them. ²Then the king of

---

[37] H. Wildberger, *Isaiah 28–39*, CC (Minneapolis: Fortress, 2002), 361–63, examines all the pluses and minuses when comparing Kings and Isaiah but believes both texts were fashioned by their composers to further the different purposes of the authors of each text.

Assyria sent his field commander with a large army from Lachish to King Hezekiah at Jerusalem. When the commander stopped at the aqueduct of the Upper Pool,
on the road to the Washerman's Field, ³Eliakim son of Hilkiah the palace administrator, Shebna the secretary, and Joah son of Asaph the recorder went out to him.
⁴The field commander said to them, "Tell Hezekiah,

> " 'This is what the great king, the king of Assyria, says: On what are you
> basing this confidence of yours? ⁵You say you have strategy and military
> strength—but you speak only empty words. On whom are you depending,
> that you rebel against me? ⁶Look now, you are depending on Egypt, that
> splintered reed of a staff, which pierces a man's hand and wounds him if he
> leans on it! Such is Pharaoh king of Egypt to all who depend on him. ⁷And
> if you say to me, "We are depending on the LORD our God"—isn't he the
> one whose high places and altars Hezekiah removed, saying to Judah and
> Jerusalem, "You must worship before this altar"?
>
> ⁸" 'Come now, make a bargain with my master, the king of Assyria: I will
> give you two thousand horses—if you can put riders on them! ⁹How then
> can you repulse one officer of the least of my master's officials, even though
> you are depending on Egypt for chariots and horsemen? ¹⁰Furthermore,
> have I come to attack and destroy this land without the LORD? The LORD
> himself told me to march against this country and destroy it.' "

The plot begins like most narratives with an introduction that identifies the
time, the place, the people involved, and some initial hints about the disputation in order to orient the reader to the setting of the following speeches. In the
first confrontational dialogue of chap. 36, the Assyrian messenger questions
Hezekiah's sanity in trusting weak Egypt, raises doubts about the wisdom of
trusting in a God who cannot protect his own altars from destruction, and offers
to make an exceptional, gracious deal with the people if they will surrender.
Seven times he asks about the basis for their "trust" (*bāṭaḥ*) in order to undermine their hope and destroy their confidence in God. The structure of this first
encounter is:

The setting of the conflict	36:1–3
Rabshakeh's speech	36:4–10
You have no one to trust	4–7
Make a bargain with me	8–9
God sent me	10

36:1–3 Each sentence in this introduction begins in good narrative style
with a *vav* consecutive verbs. The first verb (*wayĕhî*, "and it came to pass"—
omitted in NIV) is a typical way of introducing a new narrative (cf. 7:1; 37:1;
1 Sam 1:1; 4:1; 7:3; 8:1; 9:1). This is followed by a temporal marker (in the
fourteenth year) to locate these events in the reign of Hezekiah, the king of
Judah. Since Hezekiah became co-regent with his father Ahaz around 726 BC
(2 Kgs 18:1–8) this means that the fourteenth year (712 BC) does not match
the historical facts that Sennacherib attacked Judah in 701 BC. This problem

can be resolved either by concluding that (a) the fourteenth year was the year when Hezekiah became sick (38:1), so that event and Sennacherib's later attack in 701 BC were telescoped into one overall series of events, rather than dating each one individually;[38] (b) the fourteenth year is a scribal error for the twenty-fourth year, a minor scribal confusion of letters;[39] or (c) the fourteenth year begins to count the years from when Hezekiah became the sole king of Judah in 715 BC, it does not count from the date he became co-regent with his father (726 BC), thus the fourteenth year matches 701 BC.[40] The second and third solution could adequately resolve this problem.

The statement that the Assyrian king Sennacherib[41] "went up . . . against" (ʿālâ . . . ʿal NIV "attacked") and captured all the fortified cities of Judah appears to be an introductory summary statement and it generally agrees with Sennacherib's own statement that "I laid siege to 46 of his strong cities, walled forts, and to countless small villages in their vicinity, and conquered them."[42] Having summarized what Sennacherib did to the fortified cities of Judah, the text goes back to discuss in detail Sennacherib's threat to Jerusalem, a process that began near the end of his conquest, but before he had finished conquering Lachish and Libnah (37:2,8).

36:2 While the Assyrian king Sennacherib and most of his army were working on completing the conquest of Lachish, he sent his "field commander" ("Rabshakeh" in HCSB) with a "large army"[43] to Jerusalem to confront King Hezekiah. According to 2 Kgs 18:17, there were three key Assyrian officials, who bore the titles of "Tartan" (Akkadian *turtanu* the supreme commander in 20:1, second in authority under the king), "Rab-saris" the chief officer, and "Rabshakeh" the "chief cupbearer." Like the cupbearer Nehemiah (Neh 2:1), this man seems to be a person the king could trust and a man who had political responsibilities beyond that of merely serving the king wine.[44] Isaiah only

---

[38] F. Delitzsch, *Isaiah*, Commentary on the Old Testament VII (trans. J. Martin; Grand Rapids: Eerdmans, 1969), 369; R. B. Y. Scott, "Isaiah," *IB* (Nashville: Abingdon, 1956), and H. H. Rowley, "Hezekiah's Reform and Rebellion," in *Men of God: Studies in Old Testament History and Prophecy* (Edinburg: Nelson, 1963), 98–99, hold this view.

[39] The confusion between the Hb. "in four and ten" (בְּאַרְבַּע עֶשְׂרֵה) and "in four and twenty" (בְּאַרְבַּע עֶשְׂרִים) involves only the confusion of ה and ם. Oswalt, *Isaiah 1–39*, 631, W. A. M. Beuken, *Isaiah II, Volume 2: Isaiah Chapters 28–39*, HCOT (Leuvan: Peeters, 2000), 346, and R. E. Clements, *Isaiah 1–39*, NCBC (Grand Rapids: Eerdmans, 1980), 280, prefer this view.

[40] Bright, *History of Israel*, 261; Watts, *Isaiah 1–33*, 4–8, and J. A. Motyer, *The Prophecy of Isaiah: An Introduction and Commentary* (Downers Grove, IL: InterVarsity, 1993), 277, prefer this solution.

[41] The vocalization of the name Sennacherib, סַנְחֵרִב, is close to the Akk. *sin-aḥḥē-eriba*, which means something like "May Sin replace the brothers" (Sin is the name of an Mesopotamian god).

[42] *ANET*, 288.

[43] בְּחֵיל כָּבֵד is not the way one usually describes a "large army," for כָּבֵד means "heavy, weighty, honorable, glorious," which may suggest a special elite group of top soldiers.

[44] Wildberger, *Isaiah 28–39*, 389, views Rabshakeh as one having considerable political and military authority.

mentions Rabshakeh, possibly because he was the one who spoke the king's message (possibly from a written text).[45]

The king's messenger and his troops came to a secure spot by an aqueduct connected to the Upper Pool, on the road going by the Washerman's Field. Ironically, this was the same place Isaiah met Ahaz many years earlier (7:3) to challenge him to trust God (7:9) so that God could give him victory over the forces that were opposing him in the Syro-Ephraimite War in 734–732 BC. In chap. 36 Hezekiah will receive the opposite message from an enemy messenger—that he should surrender and not trust God. This spot must have been strategically located on the flat northern side of the city where an army could easily defend itself, not down in the narrow confined area at the bottom of the Kidron Valley by the Gihon Spring.

36:3 While many military people were carefully watching from the wall what the Assyrians were doing (36:11), three official representative from the government of Hezekiah "went out to him" (*wayyēṣē᾿ ᾿ēlāyw*). This could imply that they actually went out of the city to the Assyrian camp, but that would be an extremely dangerous move, and it would be inappropriate to open the city gates while the enemy was close by. Therefore, it is more likely that the king's officials only went out to the wall near the Assyrian camp to listen to what the Assyrian messenger had to say. The Hebrew representatives were not military officials but government officials. Eliakim the son of Hilkiah was the "palace administrator" (lit. "the one over the house"),[46] the man Isaiah earlier prophesied would have a seat of great honor and be in charge of all who entered the king's court (22:20–24). Second was Shebna, "the secretary" (*hassôpēr*) for the king,[47] who has now been demoted from his higher position just as Isaiah predicted (22:15–19). The third person was Joah son of Asaph who was "the recorder, rememberer" (*hammizkîr*), one that H. Wildberger calls the "chancellor."[48]

36:4–7 The first speech (36:4–10) is organized into two sections. The first part of the dispute (36:4–7) includes a series of rhetorical questions about trusting Egypt (36:4–6) and God (36:7), with an Assyrian answer to each question. Some like R. E. Clements doubt the authenticity of these words and claim "this is a free creation by the author of the narrative, but appears to rest on a knowledge of an

---

[45] It is unknown why Rabshakeh was appointed to speak to the Hebrews at Jerusalem. He was not the highest in rank, but perhaps the only one who could speak Hebrew.

[46] This person who was "over the house" (עַל־הַבָּיִת) seems to be in charge of the royal court (22:15; Gen 41:40; 1 Kgs 4:6), but there is no indication that he had the power of a prime minister.

[47] Other passages that mention people in this role include 2 Kgs 12:11; 22:3,8; Jer 36:12,20; 37:15,20.

[48] Wildberger, *Isaiah 28–39*, 389, finds people in this role in 2 Sam 8:16; 20:24; 1 Kgs 4:3; 1 Chr 18:15; 2 Chr 34:8, though he admits that his exact function is not very clear. On p. 390 he surveys various opinions that differ on how closely these officials are understood to mirror those in the Egyptian royal courts. T. N. D. Mettinger, *Solomonic State Officials* (Lund: Gleerup, 1971) ,has a discussion of the role of each of these officials.

authentic collection of Isaiah's prophecies, especially 10:8–9,13–14; 19:1–15; 30:1–5."[49] Others, as Oswalt notes, find this speech "successfully capturing the atmosphere as well as the content" of Rabshakeh's words. Oswalt concludes that "if this is fiction the writer has gone to great trouble to give it air of authenticity, a practice for which there is no evidence in ancient literature."[50]

A written letter sent by Sennacherib is recorded in 37:10–13 and it provides a standard by which one can evaluate the authenticity of the vocabulary, rhetorical argumentation, and logic of Sennacherib's thinking.[51] When comparing it to this first speech, one finds many common elements, such as both deal with avoidance of deception (36:5; 37:10), use rhetorical questions (36:4,5,7; 37:12,13), speak of trusting (36:4,5,6,7; 37:10), and encourage the Hebrews not to follow Judah's God (36:7; 37:10). C. Cohen found numerous Neo-Assyrian elements in Rabshakeh's speech, confirming its essential authenticity.[52] There is no reason the Hebrew secretary and recorder would not be taking notes concerning Rabshakeh's speech so that they could accurately relay Sennacherib's message to Hezekiah; thus, one should probably assume that the text gives a fairly accurate portrayal of what the Assyrian messenger said.

36:4–5 Rabshakeh first announces that his message is to be given to Hezekiah (he does not respect him enough to call him a king), because he was the one who needed to change Judah's political strategy. While ignoring Hezekiah's kingship, Rabshakeh magnifies Sennacherib's royal power by calling him "the great king, the king of Assyria" (a common introductory formula in Assyrian texts).[53] The key issue that baffles and confuses the Assyrian king Sennacherib is the source of the "trust, confidence" (the noun *biṭāḥôn*) in which "you trust" (the verb *bāṭaḥtā*).[54] The Assyrian is dumbfounded that "you speak"[55]

---

[49] According to Clements, *Isaiah 1–39*, 280, "The prophecies attributed to Isaiah do not relate directly to any recorded prophecies from the prophet himself, and we must conclude that they have been composed freely for incorporation into the narratives." This approach denies the authenticity of the speech and proposes that it is just an imaginative creation out of earlier speeches; but 10:9–11 refers to a different time period (that of Tiglath-pileser II), and 30:1–5 refers to Isaiah's warnings, not the words of an Assyrian king.

[50] Oswalt, *Isaiah 1–39*, 633. Kaiser, *Isaiah 13–39*, 379, finds this report full of difficulties, repetitions of questions, contradictions, no ultimatum, and many allusions to other passages in Isaiah; therefore, he questions whether it is authentic and attributes it to a later editor from the Deuteronomistic school.

[51] Wildberger, *Isaiah 28–39*, 380, suggests that "Isaiah's oracle in 37:6f could be completely authentic, at least in terms of its content." He also refers to studies of letters from Nimrud. For example, Letter ND2632 has some similar wording about two diplomats that go to Babylon to persuade the people to support Assyrian interests against the Aramean tribal leader Ukinzer. See H. W. F. Saggs, "The Nimrud Letters, 1952—Part I," *Iraq* 17 (1955): 21–56.

[52] C. Cohen, "Neo-Assyrian Elements in the First Speech of the Biblical Rab-Saqe," *IOS* 9 (1979): 32–48, found parallels between the content and persuasive style when comparing other Assyrian and Babylonian documents.

[53] This is similar to the Prism introduction: "Sennacherib, the great king, the mighty king, the king of everything, the king of Assyria, the king of the four directions of the world."

[54] J. W. Olley, "Trust in the LORD: Hezekiah, Kings, and Isaiah," *TynBul* 50 (1999): 57–77.

[55] The MT has "I say, speak" (אָמַרְתִּי), but 1QIsaᵃ and the parallel passage in 2 Kgs 18:20 have

about having a "strategy, plan" (*ʿēṣeh* also in 8:10; 19:3; 29:15; 330:1) and the military "strength" (*gĕbôrâ* also in 28:6; 30:15; 33:13) to rebel against the Assyrians.[56] These appear to be just words that have nothing to back them up; they are a deception that fails to look honestly at reality. Sennacherib's conquest of 46 fortified cities seems to prove that Hezekiah's strategy backfired and that he did not have enough military strength to withstand the Assyrian army. So the initial question is simply: Why did the Hebrews do this? On whom were they depending?

36:6 Rabshakeh can imagine two possible reasons why the Hebrew were led astray. First, he imagines that they may have "trusted" in Egypt. The Assyrians view this as a hopeless cause, for trusting in Egypt is like leaning for support on a bruised or broken reed, a cane that would not help anyone walk. Instead, such a dependence causes severe injury to the one who relies on it. Of course this agrees with what the prophet Isaiah repeatedly told the people (19:1–18; 20:1–6; 30:1–7; 31:1–3). One assumes that this was spoken before Tirhakah, the Cushite king of Egypt, was defeated (37:9) by the Assyrians.[57] Consequently, Rabshakeh was attempting to remove this as a possible last hope. As J. Oswalt comments, "Sometimes it is only our enemies who see the true folly of our behavior."[58] But in this case it was not only Judah's enemies that understood the stupidity of trusting Egypt; their spiritual prophet Isaiah also warned them not to depend on Egypt but to trust God.

36:7 Rabshakeh hypothesizes ("if," *kî*) that the other possible hope that might have deceived Hezekiah/the Hebrews[59] was a "trust" (the verb *bāṭaḥ*) in

---

"you speak" (אָמַרְתָּ) which makes sense in this context and gives a good parallel with "you say" in 36:7. Beuken, *Isaiah II, Vol 2*, 333 prefers to keep "I say," which fits in this context. All this means is that Rabshakeh was giving his own view, rather than quoting what others said.

[56] J. Goldingay, *Isaiah* NIBC (Peabody: Hendrickson, 2001), 205, takes the phrase, "Why have you rebelled against me?" which refers to their rebellion against the Assyrian king, and twists it to make these "the words of the prophet for whom the 'me' is Yahweh. This accusation opens Isaiah's book in 1:2, though using a different verb . . . rebellion against Assyria *is* rebellion against God." This falsely harmonizes these two different texts. Hezekiah was a man of faith who trusted God when he rebelled against Assyria (that was not an act of rebellion against God); Hezekiah was not faithless like his father Ahaz, who foolishly trusted in the Assyrians to save him in a time of war in 7:1–25 (cf. 2 Kgs 16).

[57] Motyer, *The Prophecy of Isaiah*, 277, concludes that "Rabshakeh had already seen the defeat of *Egypt* at Eltekeh." Although the chronological order of events is difficult in this narrative, it appears that the Egyptian conflict in 37:9 happened later than 36:6. If Egypt was already defeated, it would not still be a source of hope for the Hebrews. Rabshakeh's comment about the broken reed that pierces the hand could be a comment about the useless help Egypt gave Ashdod a few years earlier (20:1–6), for there is no clear incident during these years where Egypt's action actually injured Judah.

[58] Oswalt, *Isaiah 1–39*, 635.

[59] The MT has תֹאמַר, "you (sg.) should say," referring to Hezekiah (which matches the sg. verb in v. 6), while 1QIsaᵃ has the pl. form תאמרו, which matches the Old Greek. Although one might think that Rabshakeh was speaking to the many Hebrews on the wall or the three representatives Hezekiah sent, the verbs in 36:4 directs this message to Hezekiah, and the verb "trust" in vv. 4,5 (twice), the imperative "make a bargain" and "I will give you [sg.]" are all singular. So the

their God. The Assyrian asks the rhetorical question (introduced with *hălō'*),[60] would it not be a foolish waste of time and energy to trust God; has not Hezekiah angered God by destroying many of his altars and requiring people to worship only at Jerusalem (2 Chr 30:14; 31:1)? The Assyrian was playing on the sympathies of people from the countryside whose altars and temples were destroyed during Hezekiah's reform (2 Kgs 18:1–7). Why would they want to follow a heavy-handed king who would ruin their places of worship and require everyone to worship at his altar in Jerusalem?[61] Possibly they needed to rise up against Hezekiah and encourage surrender to the Assyrians.

36:8–9 Rabshakeh concludes his persuasive dispute with additional arguments (introduced with "and now," *wĕʿattâ*) that highlight Judah's weakness. He calls for the people of Jerusalem to "make a bargain"[62] with king Sennacherib, but most agree this is a sarcastic offer,[63] for Hezekiah was not in a strong position to demand anything from the Assyrians, and after defeating so many of the cities of Judah the Assyrians did not need to give up anything. The hypothetical offer to give[64] Hezekiah two thousand horses for his cavalry was not a serious point of negotiation between the parties to resolve their differences, but a rhetorical ploy to show the weakness of Judah and mock her military impotence—she could not even find men to ride that many horses. Rabshakeh arrogantly asks the rhetorical question: How could the weak army of Judah defeat even one of the weakest commanders in Sennacherib's army? It would not have a prayer of a chance, even if they had some help from Egyptian chariots. These defiant words only brought further discouragement and dire hopelessness to the Hebrews who were listening from the wall.

36:10 The final argument (introduced with "and now," *wĕʿattâ*) is theological. Did not God send Sennacherib to do this? Has not God been with him to allow him to destroy this land? He claims that God told him to destroy the land. It was traditional for kings to justify their action by claiming that the gods of a vanquished land had directed them to conquer that territory, thus this statement is not that unusual. Neco claimed he was following God's direction when Josiah interfered with his journey (2 Chr 35:21) and Cyrus stated God directed him to release the Hebrews from exile in Ezra 1:1–3, and in the Cyrus Cylinder he said that Marduk directed him to defeat Babylon.[65] On the one

---

consistent witness is that Sennacherib's message was to Hezekiah. The Qumran and Old Greek readings should not be followed in v. 7.

[60] The sign of the question preceding the negative particle הֲלֹא asks a question "in order to show it to be absolutely true . . . equivalent to *surely it is*" (GKC §150e).

[61] Watts, *Isaiah 34–66*, 28, suggests that Rabshakeh was appealing to those "who may not have been absolutely loyal to the king" (meaning Hezekiah).

[62] The *hithpaʿel* verb from עָרַב means to "exchange a pledge," which would confirm an agreement.

[63] E.g., Beuken, *Isaiah II, Vol 2*, 350.

[64] The verb אֶתְּנָה is a cohortative from נָתַן "he gave." This form can be used to express an "emphatic statement of fixed determination" (GKC §108b).

[65] *ANET*, 314–15. "Marduk, the great lord, a protector of his people/worshipers, beheld with

hand this all seems like pure propaganda, for it is hard to believe that this pre-posterous claim was actually true. But on the other hand, in some sense it did agree with what Isaiah was preaching. Some interpret this claim as a redactor's reapplication of 10:5–6 where Isaiah says that Assyria will be a rod in God's hand.[66] Instead of attributing this to a redactor, it is likely that the Assyrians knew from their intelligence work something about the general content of the sermons of the prophet Isaiah, just as the Babylonians knew about the prophe-cies of Jeremiah (Jer 39:11–40:6), but a specific literary knowledge of 10:5–6 seems questionable.

Significantly, the line of thinking presented in Rabshakeh's speech conflicts with aspects of Isaiah's theology on several points, even though there is some general superficial agreement. Isaiah also thought the Hebrews were deluded with their "covenant with death" (28:15) and their priests and prophets were drunk and without understanding (28:7–8), so he concluded that their alliance with Egypt would bring shame and no help (30:3–5). While Sennacherib saw reliance on Egypt and trust in God as the two pillars of their false confidence, Isaiah viewed these two pillars as mutually exclusive sources of trust.[67] Isaiah rejected military alliances as a solid basis for confidence and demanded that the government officials trust in God alone. Sennacherib also misunderstood the significance of Hezekiah's reform movement when he destroyed pagan al-tars at the high places in Judah. Isaiah would approve of Hezekiah's action and interpret this reform as a very positive move that would have caused God to favor Hezekiah (Sennacherib thought it would bring God's anger). Finally, Isaiah repeatedly promised God's judgment on Judah, but in the same breath he also predicted the deliverance of Jerusalem and the destruction of Assyria (26:16–27:1; 28:18–21; 29:1–7; 30:16–31; 31:8–9) which conflicts with the Assyrian claim that God brought them here to destroy Jerusalem. In a real sense, Sennacherib was putting a challenge to God, for Sennacherib falsely claimed that he was doing God's will by defeating Jerusalem. Later when God acted and destroyed thousands of Assyrian troops, God demonstrated that Sen-nacherib was making false statements. Destroying Jerusalem was not God's will. These contrasting theological differences suggest that this speech was not some creative or imaginative compilation that later editors derived from earlier sermons by Isaiah. These are not Isaiah's teachings; these are the words of a

---

pleasure his (ie Cyrus') good deeds and his upright mind (lit. heart) (and therefore) ordered him to march against his city of Babylon." These kinds of statements are made frequently to justify a kings actions (pp. 277, 283, 286, 289, 293, 301).

[66] Goldingay, *Isaiah*, 206, and Watts, *Isaiah 34–66*, 29, suppose that a later editor was drawing from the prophet's own words in 10:5–6. But would a Hebrew editor totally distort the message of that woe oracle by picking out only one verse from the passage and totally ignoring that this oracle was actually an announcement of God's judgment on a proud Assyrian king?

[67] E. Ben Zvi, "Who Wrote the Speeches of Rabshakeh and When?" *JBL* 109 (1990): 79–92, concludes that these differences imply Isaiah's oracles and Rabshakeh's speeches come from two different authors or traditions.

self-deluded Assyrian king who thinks that God has no power and should not be trusted.

THE SECOND CHALLENGE: WHO CAN DELIVER YOU? (36:11–21)

[11]Then Eliakim, Shebna and Joah said to the field commander, "Please speak to your servants in Aramaic, since we understand it. Don't speak to us in Hebrew in the hearing of the people on the wall." [12]But the commander replied, "Was it only to your master and you that my master sent me to say these things, and not to the men sitting on the wall—who, like you, will have to eat their own filth and drink their own urine?" [13]Then the commander stood and called out in Hebrew, "Hear the words of the great king, the king of Assyria! [14]This is what the king says: Do not let Hezekiah deceive you. He cannot deliver you! [15]Do not let Hezekiah persuade you to trust in the LORD when he says, 'The LORD will surely deliver us; this city will not be given into the hand of the king of Assyria.' [16]"Do not listen to Hezekiah. This is what the king of Assyria says: Make peace with me and come out to me. Then every one of you will eat from his own vine and fig tree and drink water from his own cistern, [17]until I come and take you to a land like your own—a land of grain and new wine, a land of bread and vineyards. [18]"Do not let Hezekiah mislead you when he says, 'The LORD will deliver us.' Has the god of any nation ever delivered his land from the hand of the king of Assyria? [19]Where are the gods of Hamath and Arpad? Where are the gods of Sepharvaim? Have they rescued Samaria from my hand? [20]Who of all the gods of these countries has been able to save his land from me? How then can the LORD deliver Jerusalem from my hand?" [21]But the people remained silent and said nothing in reply, because the king had commanded, "Do not answer him."

The three representatives sent by Hezekiah interrupted the disputational confrontation at this point. They requested that the parties carry out the negotiation of their differences in a more agreeable way using the Aramaic language. Rabshakeh rejected their suggestions and delivered a second speech that attempted to undermine the people's confidence that someone can "deliver" (*nāṣal*) them from the almighty power of the Assyrian army. The second incident can be outlined as:

Request to speak in Aramaic	36:11–12
Rabshakeh's speech	36:13–20
Hezekiah and God cannot deliver you	13–16a
Surrender and live well	16b–17
No god can deliver anyone from Assyria	18–20
No response from Hezekiah's representatives	36:21

36:11–12 When the Hebrew officials realized that Rabshakeh was not at all conciliatory and that his words were apt to discourage anyone who might hear them, they requested that the Assyrian leader speak in Aramaic, the official language of international relations of the day. In their request they humbly referred to themselves as "your servants" and used a polite form of the imperative when they requested this alternative.[68] They may also be trying to test Rabshakeh's flexibility or willingness to negotiate on a small and relatively insignificant point. Although they were commanded by Hezekiah not to answer or negotiate with the enemy, this brief conversation was allowed in an effort to limit the psychological damage to the troops on the wall.

The Assyrian messenger was totally inflexible and unwilling to change his approach (36:12), for one of his main purposes was to inflict psychological damage and division among the Hebrew people remaining in Jerusalem. In another rhetorical question, Rabshakeh asks if his message was intended for everyone to hear or just for "your master" (not mentioning that Hezekiah was king) and a few officials. He wanted to treat Hezekiah as being no more important than the common soldier standing there by the wall. He wanted everyone in Jerusalem who would suffer starvation during the Assyrian siege to make up his own mind about what should be done, not just the king. Everyone will eventually become so hungry that he will stoop to the disgusting extreme of eating and drinking his own excrement just to stay alive, so everyone needs to decide what he will do. The covenant curses even warned that people would eat their own children during severe sieges (Lev 26:29; Deut 28:53–57). The Assyrian's defiant response raises the tension exponentially, for his crude remarks were intended to utterly terrify those who did not fully realize the enormous suffering that they were about to endure if they did not surrender immediately. Instead of softening his tone a little and talking privately in an effort to effect some mutually agreeable compromise, Rabshakeh becomes more belligerent because he realizes that his emotional appeal might turn some of the troops against Hezekiah. Later, when God intervenes (37:36), Rabshakeh will be proven to be a false prophet, for what he expected to happen during the siege of Jerusalem as a result of the strength of the Assyrian grip on Jerusalem never did happen.

36:13–16a Instead of quietly speaking in Aramaic, Rabshakeh loudly called out in Hebrew (called "Judean" *yĕhûdît*), asking all the people to listen very carefully to the words of "the great king, the king of Assyria." Rabshakeh's speech reveals the thinking of his master, King Sennacherib. It is organized into three negative warnings (36:14a,15a,16a), each beginning with the same Hebrew "do not" clause. The first section warns against making the mistake of letting Hezekiah (again he is not called the king) "deceive"[69] you. Deception involves presenting evidence to support the truthfulness of untrue

---

[68] According to Gesenius, the imperative is followed by the particle נָא "sometimes to soften down a command, or to make a request in a more courteous form" (GKC §110d).

[69] The root נָשָׁא may come from two distinct roots: "to lend, to be a creditor," or "to beguile, deceive" (19:13; 37:10). This second meaning is used to describe the snake "deceiving" Eve in the garden in Gen 3:13.

statements. Deception often happens when a trusted person in authority makes a statement that promises an outcome that does not happen. The specific area where Hezekiah would try to use logic, an emotional appeal, theological promises, or other persuasive speech to deceive the people was related to his ability "to deliver" (*nāṣal*) them from Sennacherib's army. In vv. 15 and 18, Rabshakeh warns the Hebrews on the wall that Hezekiah may say he can deliver them, but he will not be able to accomplish it. If he will not be able to do what he says he can do, then what he says is a deceptive lie. Sennacherib's perspective was partially right and partially wrong on this point (a characteristic of most political propaganda). He was right in saying that Hezekiah was not able to deliver Jerusalem. This was pretty obvious to the men who were in Judah's army, for Hezekiah himself did not have the troops to resist the Assyrian conquest of 46 fortified cities in Judah, and there was no tactical plan to defeat the Assyrians in battle at Jerusalem. Nevertheless, Sennacherib was wrong to think that Hezekiah would claim that he had the power to deliver his people from the Assyrians. That would have to be the work of God.

Rabshakeh does not leave the argument there, for he seemed to know that Hezekiah would use religion as his trump card to try to persuade his soldiers to fight and not surrender to the Assyrians. In the second "do not" clause (36:15) Sennacherib warns the people not to trust Hezekiah when he claims, "The LORD will surely deliver us." The Hebrew sentence is constructed using an infinitive absolute from the verb "deliver" (*nāṣal*), followed by the imperfect verb of the same root,[70] lit. "delivering, he will deliver," which is an emphatic way of promising that God will certainly, surely, completely deliver them. Sennacherib may have heard that this was being promised through interviewing captives from other cities of Judah.[71] In fact, this was the message of Isaiah (14:24–27; 26:21–27:1; 29:5–8; 30:27–31; 31:4–5,8–9; 38:6), not Hezekiah. The promise of God was not just that he would deliver the Hebrews, but specifically that the Assyrians would not defeat "this city" (Jerusalem). This promise is consistent with declarations about the inviolability of Zion: because "God is within her, she will not fall" (Ps 46:5; 48:1–3; 76:1–7). Sennacherib's warning ends up questioning the almighty power of God and doubting the promises of God (essentially calling God a liar), for he claims that no one should trust in the promise that God will deliver Jerusalem. This bold harangue against God amounts to blasphemy, for he asserts that God is not really God, he is not really in control

---

[70] When the infinite absolute is placed before a finite verb, they are joined together to express the certainty that an action will take place (GKC §113n).

[71] Seitz, *Isaiah 1–39*, 247, rejects this view and does not believe Rabshakeh got this inside information from his intelligence workers. He believes these themes were "shaped with those concerns in mind by an author from within Isaiah's circles." This seems unlikely, for those associated with Isaiah would not suggest Hezekiah was constantly preaching that people should trust the Lord for Zion's deliverance. Isaiah gave sermon after sermon to try to get Hezekiah to trust God, but it was only at the last minute that Hezekiah finally made that leap of faith and went to the temple to ask God to deliver him from the Assyrians (37:14–20).

of the political affairs of the city of Jerusalem. Sennacherib also questions the whole theological relationship between God and his people. Did God elect them to be his people just to abandon them to the evil Assyrians? Are God's promises concerning Zion without value? But of course there was the practical question that the people in Jerusalem could not avoid: How was God going to deliver Jerusalem from Assyria?

This brief subparagraph concludes with a final warning that the people "should not listen" (*'al tišmě'û*) to the words of Hezekiah (again he is not called the king). Hezekiah will try to reinterpret reality in a slanted way but he should not be trusted; instead, the people need to listen to the wise words of Rabshakeh and act responsibly. The idea that politicians might lie to their constituency to keep themselves in office is not new to the twenty-first century.

36:16b–17 Having admonished the people, now Rabshakeh tells them of Sennacherib's alternative plan that they should follow. The King of Assyria is asking them to make peace (lit. "a blessing") with him. Although the Aramaic Targum translates this word with *šālôm*, "peace," the word *běrākâ*, "blessing" is used in a unique context here. J. D. W. Watts translates it "make a mutually advantageous agreement with me,"[72] while J. Scharbert suggests "agree to a truce and treat the winner as absolute lord."[73] A. Murtonen hypothesizes that the parties give a "mutual blessing" to one another, while others suggest the meaning "surrender, capitulate." [74] The context indicates that Rabshakeh is not offering to treat the rebels as mutual partners (they will be exiled later in v. 17), but as a smooth-talking political propagandist he proposes a way to get the Hebrews out of their present impossible predicament. In order to gain the advantages of this blessing, the Hebrews must come out of the protection of the walled city of Jerusalem; thus, the terms of the offer from Sennacherib require surrender to the Assyrians.

The rewards of this deal are explained in two phases. First, for a while the people can freely go back to their own homes and enjoy an ideal time of prosperity (36:16) comparable to what would be expected in the messianic era (cf. I Kgs 4:25; Mic 4:4; Zech 3:10). At some later time the Assyrians will exile them to a wonderful land very similar to Judah where they can raise their crops and enjoy life (36:17). It would have been foolish for Rabshakeh to lie by failing to mention exile, but he describes the future using positive images of a good life not much different from their present life. This misrepresentation appears much more appealing than staying in Jerusalem and eating their own excrement. In effect, Sennacherib (not God) becomes the only one who can

---

[72] Watts, *Isaiah 33–66*, 19.

[73] J. Sharbert, "ברך *brk* בְּרָכָה *běrākhāh*," *TDOT*, 2:279–308, thinks that the field commander is offering a peace treaty with these words.

[74] A. Murtonen, "The Usage and Meaning of the words *lěbārrek* and *běrākāʰ* in the Old Testament," *VT* 9 (1959): 158–77. *HALAT*, 159, proposes "capitulate," deriving this from the idea that ברך can mean "knee," thus one who kneels in surrender.

"deliver" the people of Judah from their present difficult situation. W. A. M. Beuken suggests that what Sennacherib is promising is to fulfill the promises of God (the giving of peace in a good land) by substituting another land that he will give to them. He is either taking the place of God or serving as the instrument by which God will fulfill these promises.[75] If God cannot fulfill his promises, giving the people peace and a land flowing with milk and honey, grain and vineyards, at least the Hebrews can be assured that Sennacherib will do this.[76] Although the Assyrian offer sounds irresistible and a lot more appealing than starving, one must always count the cost and judge the extent to which later reality will actually match the sales pitch. Maybe Sennacherib is being deceptive in his rosy picture of the future.

36:18–20 The final subparagraph of Rabshakeh's speech tries to seal his rhetorical argument by expressing Sennacherib's concern that the people of Judah not become innocent victims of Hezekiah's religious fanaticism about the power of the God of Israel (36:18). Hezekiah may think that his God will "deliver" (*nāṣal*) the Hebrews, but the people should beware, for this may be a deceitful policy that will "mislead" (*yassît* Deut 13:7; 1 Sam 26:19; 1 Kgs 21:25; Jer 38:22) them and cause an unbelievable disaster. If one logically compares what has happened in the past when the Assyrians came up against other cities that were protected by their gods, one would discover that none of these gods was able to deliver those cities from the power of Assyria (36:19–20). Interestingly, Sennacherib does not give credit for these conquests to the gods of the Assyrians or their large army; instead, all the credit goes to the great "king of Assyria." This choice of words demonstrates that the conflict within the narrative is clearly designed to pit the claims of Sennacherib (not his gods) against the power of the God of Judah.

The text mentions four city-states that the Assyrians conquered. Hamath was a powerful city in northern Syria that the Assyrian king Sargon II conquered in 720 BC. Arphad was about seventy-five miles north of Hamath and the Assyrians defeated it in 740 and 720 BC. The location and the date of the conquest of Sepharvaim are unknown. The Assyrian king Sargon II took Samaria, the capital of the northern nation of Israel, in 722/721 BC (2 Kgs 17:1–5).[77] The emphasis in each of these places is the repeated haunting

---

[75] Beuken, *Isaiah II, Vol 2*, 342, says, "By presenting himself as the bearer of prosperity (vv. 16–17) and YHWH as no more powerful than the gods of the nations (vv. 18–20), Sennacherib lays personal claim to divine characteristics."

[76] P. R. Ackroyd, " An Interpretation of the Babylonian Exile: A Study of II Kings 20 and Isaiah 38–39," in *Studies in the Religious Tradition of the Old Testament* (London: SCM, 1987), 168, says, "Instead of granting of the land to Israel as an act of a God whose promise it is, we have the arrogant claim of the Assyrian that he will take them into a land of promise . . . it is the most blatant parody of the assurances of Deuteronomy that God will give his people the land."

[77] E. Ben Zvi, "Who Wrote the Speeches of Rabshakeh and When?" *JBL* 109 (1990): 79–92, compares the lists of towns in 2 Kgs 17:24–25; 18:34; 19:13 and Isa 10:9–11 and concludes that the similarity between the lists suggests they were all developed from a list of places from which people were deported into Samaria after the Israelites were exiled (2 Kgs 16:6; 18:11). But this is

question: "Where are their gods?" The gods that were supposed to protect these places failed to deliver these people from the hand of Sennacherib. As J. Oswalt points out, apparently the Assyrians "did not perceive Samaria to have worshiped the same God as Jerusalem did. Otherwise, it is impossible to imagine that Rabshakeh would have missed the opportunity to point out the Lord had not been able to save Samaria."[78] The logic of Sennacherib's case claims that if these gods could not deliver those nations in past wars, why should anyone think that the God of Judah would be able to deliver Jerusalem from the Assyrians in this war? In these remarks, Sennacherib has made the serious mistake of equating God with the useless pagan wood and stone gods of these other nations, lifting Sennacherib up above all the gods of the nations, and claiming that God is unable to deliver Jerusalem. These ideas blaspheme the name of the only real, all-powerful God, who controls every aspect of human history. Although many people today would never say these kinds of things about God because it might seem to be a little too irreverent, they too have limited the power of God in their thinking and by their actions they raise questions about his ability to save.

36:21   The first narrative episode ends with a brief note about the response of Hezekiah's three representatives (36:3) and the rest of the people on the wall who were listening to Rabshakeh's ranting speeches. These people were specifically commanded by Hezekiah not to respond to the Assyrians, so they remained silent. They did not hiss, clap, boo, laugh, or mock his misunderstanding of God. They were not given the authority to negotiate terms and they were not to enter into arguments about the veracity of the facts that were presented. Often it is a waste of time to argue with a strong enemy. These matters would not be decided by the one who could shout the loudest, by the one who had the biggest army, or by the one who could intimidate the other with the more gruesome threats. Often threats and intimidation only reveal that a person is proud and acts like a bully, so trying to reason with people who think they are stronger than God is usually a waste of time. They will eventually have to answer to God. Any misguided fool can make bizarre claims and be totally convinced by weak arguments that make sense only to a person who misunderstands reality, but when the theological dust settles, all that really counts is what God has sovereignly decided to do. What God has done in the past does not limit his options in the future, and military weakness will not undermine his plan. However, God's desire to glorify his name does present a sure guide to what he will do in the world. Therefore, it is never wise for anyone to depend on those who try to play God with other people's lives and in the process blas-

---

problematic since the names are not the same in each case (although Hamath and Sepharvaim are common in all of them). A more likely motivation for mentioning these places was that they were known to the Israelites and were examples of recent conquests.

[78] As Oswalt, *Isaiah 1–39*, 641, suggests, the Assyrians probably knew that the people of Israel were not worshiping the same God. Instead they worshiped Baal.

pheme the name of God. Such situations give God an excellent opportunity to demonstrate his sovereignty.

(2) Cutting Off the Blaspheming Assyrian King (36:22–37:7)

²²Then Eliakim son of Hilkiah the palace administrator, Shebna the secretary, and Joah son of Asaph the recorder went to Hezekiah, with their clothes torn, and told him what the field commander had said.

¹When King Hezekiah heard this, he tore his clothes and put on sackcloth and went into the temple of the LORD. ²He sent Eliakim the palace administrator, Shebna the secretary, and the leading priests, all wearing sackcloth, to the prophet Isaiah son of Amoz. ³They told him, "This is what Hezekiah says: This day is a day of distress and rebuke and disgrace, as when children come to the point of birth and there is no strength to deliver them. ⁴It may be that the LORD your God will hear the words of the field commander, whom his master, the king of Assyria, has sent to ridicule the living God, and that he will rebuke him for the words the LORD your God has heard. Therefore pray for the remnant that still survives."

⁵When King Hezekiah's officials came to Isaiah, ⁶Isaiah said to them, "Tell your master, 'This is what the LORD says: Do not be afraid of what you have heard—those words with which the underlings of the king of Assyria have blasphemed me. ⁷Listen! I am going to put a spirit in him so that when he hears a certain report, he will return to his own country, and there I will have him cut down with the sword.'"

The third episode takes place in a different location, new people are involved in this scene, and the conversation about the fall of Jerusalem comes from a different political and theological perspective. This episode reveals how the Hebrews reacted to Rabshakeh's message from Sennacherib. Their mourning, lamenting, and prayer for divine help were appropriate responses for believers in a time of distress and hopelessness. This kind of a crisis situation reveals what a person really believes. If the Hebrews thought that God could not deliver them, then they must either surrender to the stronger Assyrians or find some other nation that is willing to rescue them through military intervention. If they believe that God can deliver his people in Jerusalem as Isaiah has repeatedly promised, then they must trust God to deliver them. Although the initial response by Hezekiah moves in the right direction and Isaiah again promises God's help (37:5–7), the narrative tension mounts as the reader anxiously waits to hear the ultimate outcome of Hezekiah's decision.

The material in this episode is structured around three incidents:

The Hebrews respond with mourning	36:22–37:1
Hezekiah's message to Isaiah	37:2–4
Isaiah's oracle about God's salvation	37:5–7

The repeated themes of "tearing clothes" and putting on "sackcloth" dominate the initial verses. The message and oracle focus on God's "hearing the blasphemous words" of Sennacherib/Rabshkeh and God's response.

36:22–37:1 Once Rabshakeh stopped talking, the three Hebrew officials (36:3) reported to the king. Their initial response to Sennacherib's message was to mourn and tear their clothes (36:22). King Hezekiah had a similar response when he heard these words. In Hebrew culture, tearing one's clothes and putting on sackcloth was frequently associated with mourning and lamenting because someone has just died or is about to die.[79] Earlier Isaiah had condemned the people of Jerusalem for their joyful revelry and senseless eating and drinking (22:2,13) when they should have been weeping, wailing, tearing out their hair, and putting on sackcloth because of the Assyrian threat (22:12). Now the king and his officials realized the dire distress the city was in and they responded more appropriately. In contrast to Ahaz's response of creating an alliance with another nation in a similar time of a national military crisis (2 Kgs 16), Hezekiah went to the temple where God dwelt, but there is no record of what he initially did there.[80] Since God's presence is directly connected to the Holy of Holies in the temple, at least Hezekiah is going to the right place to pray for God's help.[81]

37:2–4 The king sent two of his officials, Eliakim and Shebna, along with some senior priests (lit. "elders of the priest" *ziqnê hākôhănîm*) from the temple to the prophet Isaiah. It is not clear whether the king requested that Isaiah pray before he went to the temple or if after a time of prayer in the temple he decided to make this request of Isaiah. The fact that a priest went with the king's two officials suggests that the message to Isaiah came after the king was already in the temple. This is the first time in this book that Isaiah is actually called a prophet. Since he appeals to "the prophet" Isaiah, he must have had some confidence that Isaiah had told the truth in the past prophecies, would be able to communicate with God again, and might receive another message from God about this situation. Although one might not immediately be surprised by Hezekiah's decision to appeal for help from Isaiah, it probably signals a fairly significant change in Hezekiah's thinking. Up to this point, Isaiah was quite critical of the people who were running the political plans of government in Judah (though he does not specifically condemn the king by name).

---

[79] E.g., Jacob tore his clothes, put on sackcloth, and mourned because he though Joseph was dead (Gen 37:34); A Benjamite man ran from the battle at Shiloh with his clothes torn and dust on his head to tell Eli of his sons' death and the capture of the ark (1 Sam 4:12); David instructed people to tear their clothes, put on sackcloth, and mourn when Abner was killed (2 Sam 3:31); after Absalom's death David tore his clothes, laid down on the ground, and mourned (2 Sam 13:31,37); when Ahab heard the prophecy about his coming death he tore his clothes, put on sackcloth, fasted, and walked around in humility (1 Kgs 21:27–28); when Moab would be defeated the people would weep, shave their heads, put on sackcloth, and wail (Isa 15:2–3).

[80] Kaiser, *Isaiah 13–39*, 383, has the questionable hermeneutical "principle of excluding statements which add a theological content." Therefore, he questions the authenticity of many statements about God and rips the heart out of this very theological narrative.

[81] Oswalt, *Isaiah 1–39*, 643, suggests that Hezekiah "must go to the Lord's house to admit his and his nation's folly in their foolish dependence upon Egypt," but the following instructions to call Isaiah and Isaiah's response do not address these issues.

In 20:5–6 he warns leaders not to depend on Egypt, and in 30:1–7 he argues against those politicians who go down to Egypt to form an alliance so that the Egyptian army might protect them from Assyria (cf. 31:1–3). In a face-to-face confrontation in the royal palace, the prophet rejects Hezekiah's alliance with Merodach-baladan of Babylon (39:1–6) and tells the king that his action will result in God's judgment. In 22:1–14 Isaiah criticizes those who rejoice in the defensive preparations of Jerusalem and in 22:15–19 he condemns Shebna, the high government official who is over the king's house. Isaiah believes the political "treaty with death" that the politicians boasted about was a false hope (28:15–16) and that the nation was suffering from a serious case of blindness, making them unable to understand what God has said (29:9–14). In other words, up to this point Hezekiah had a good record for instituting religious reforms and removing Baalism (2 Chr 29–32), but he was not much better than Ahaz when it came to his leadership on the political front.[82] Consequently, one would assume that Isaiah and Hezekiah were not the best of friends, for there are no examples where Hezekiah actually brought Isaiah into the king's court to ask him whether something he was considering was God's will. Hezekiah probably did not appreciate Isaiah's biting criticism and may have thought of him as a little bit of an impractical religious fanatic who did not understand the difficulty of his political situation. This request for Isaiah's assistance was one of Hezekiah's first major steps in the right direction. It probably points to Hezekiah's desperation as he faced a hopeless situation. His mistake was a common one for many believers; they all too often refuse to consult or trust God initially and then, when things go bad, it is almost too late.

Hezekiah's message to Isaiah describes this Assyrian crisis as "a day of distress, rebuke, and disgrace" (37:3). These words appear to refer to the terrible situation facing Jerusalem because of Sennacherib's threats, similar to the Psalmist's description of times of trouble when he would call out for God's help in his laments (cf. Ps 20:2; 50:15; 77:3; 87:7). J. Oswalt interprets the Assyrians as bringing distress, but "God himself has brought them into contempt"[83] and put them under his reproach. The text in 37:3 is somewhat unclear concerning who brought these problems on Judah, God or Assyria. How one understands this idea is partly dependent on how one understands these three terms and who functions as the subject doing these things. W. A. M. Beuken notes that if this noun, translated "disgrace" in NIV (nĕʾāṣâ), is connected to the meaning of the verb, it could mean "spurn, mock, blaspheme" (if it is derived from the *piel* stem) or the more general idea of "contempt, disgrace" (if it is derived from the *qal* stem). The first usage would describe Sennacherib's blasphemy against God and the Hebrews in Jerusalem, while the second usage normally has God

---

[82] As Blenkinsopp says (*Isaiah 1–39*, 474), "In this respect, therefore, he was no different than Ahaz, who guiltily sought assistance from Assyria."

[83] Oswalt, *Isaiah 1–39*, 645, says, "Not only have his government policies brought Judah into Assyria's contempt . . . they have also brought the country under God's reproach."

as its subject. Beuken prefers the second option, but concludes that this refers to what God should do to Assyria (not what he has done to Judah); he should chastise and reject Assyria.[84] The very next verse refers to God "rebuking" Sennacherib (37:4b), so this approach is hypothetically possible. Nevertheless, 37:4a refers to Sennacherib "ridiculing the living God" and has the imagery of a woman not having the strength to bear a child (cf. 26:17–18). These contextual factors (along with Hezekiah's lamenting in 37:1) suggest that Hezekiah was initially lamenting the disgraceful situation because of Sennacherib's oppression (37:3) and then later suggesting a solution (37:4)—God should hear Sennacherib's contemptuous mocking and rebuke him.

In 37:4 Hezekiah presents some specific suggestions that he wants Isaiah to pray about and hints at the potential results of their prayers. "Perhaps" (*'ûllay*) suggests that Hezekiah is tentative in his request either because (a) he is hesitant to ask Isaiah to pray; (b) he is not sure God will hear and interfere in human history; or (c) he still is not sure what the God's plans are for the Assyrians. The king does have the basic theological understanding that Rabshakeh was sent by Sennacherib "in order to ridicule" (*lĕḥānēp*)[85] the "living God." This terminology is reminiscent of the David and Goliath narrative where David predicted the demise of the giant Goliath because he blasphemed the name of the living God (2 Sam 17:36). Since God came to the rescue of others when their enemies mocked God, Hezekiah had some hope that God might do it again in order to protect his honor and glory. Since God is alive, and not a dead god like the gods the other nations worshiped, he has the ability to hear and act to defend himself. It is interesting that Hezekiah does not blame God for the mess he is in, nor does he mention his own piety, his past reforms, or anything in his own character that might motivate God to act. His silence on these matters could suggest that he knows that he has made some mistakes in not listening to Isaiah and that he realizes that he has failed. He does not claim that he deserves God's help or that God owes his covenant people protection. He is at the end of his rope and as J. Oswalt suggests, "this kind of admission of helplessness is frequently a necessity before divine help can be received."[86] He appears to be spiritually minded enough to know that no one can force God to do anything and no one truly merits or earns any special consideration. The only thing that will turn the tide at this point is that God's justice might cause him to rebuke Sennacherib for his terrible ridicule of God. If God will rebuke the Assyrian's claims and demonstrate to all that Sennacherib was not greater

---

[84] Beuken, *Isaiah II, Vol 2*, 357–58, opts for an approach that basically removes the lamenting aspect from Hezekiah's speech, yet that is the state he is in according to 37:1.

[85] The infinitive construct verb לְחָנֵף was used to reveal the purpose for sending Rabshakeh (GKC §114g). The verbal idea includes "mock, ridicule, blaspheme" (1 Sam 17:26,36; Ps 69:10; 74:10,18,22).

[86] Oswalt, *Isaiah 1–39*, 645–46, notes that sometimes we think "we only need some assistance," since we are not helpless, but "only when we have admitted our bankruptcy are we able to receive what he has for us."

than God, his glory can be reclaimed. It is important to notice that Hezekiah does not tell God what to do to reclaim his glory or when to do it,[87] so his prayer is not a "please save me now" selfish prayer or a bargaining prayer that promises total dedication "if" God will act.

The king's message ends with a request that Isaiah would pray for divine intervention on behalf of the small remnant left in Jerusalem (36:4b), not for himself. Often "the remnant" (*hašš̆ĕrîm*) is a negative term that refers to exiles in a foreign land who remain after the nation has been destroyed, but here it is a positive term that identifies that small group of free people crowded into the city of Jerusalem (cf. 1:9; 4:3; 11:11,16). These are the few people who still have some hope of surviving the Assyrian onslaught.

37:5–7 Apparently, Isaiah provides an immediate response so that the king's messengers could take a word of encouragement back to Hezekiah. There is no indication that the prophet prayed or that he received a new salvation oracle at this time. Isaiah already knew what God would do from previous revelations (14:24–27; 29:5–8; 30:27–33; 31:5–9), though he did not know exactly when God would act. Therefore, he told Hezekiah essentially the same message he told his father Ahaz (7:4). There is no need to fear (*'al tîrā'* cf. 41:10,13,14; 43:1). Sennacherib's words, communicated by his weak "underlings,"[88] were words that mocked God (37:4). Although Sennacherib's threats of starvation and unlimited power over other nations certainly were meant to sound very intimidating, in order to persuade Hezekiah to surrender, these are not the words that concerned God. Defying God's divinity was God's issue and the problem that Hezekiah emphasized (37:4), so Isaiah assures Hezekiah that the Assyrian king had made a major mistake by insulting or "blaspheming" (*gidpû*)[89] God.

What will God do? God's sovereignty over the life of Sennacherib is illustrated by three factors. First, God will put a "spirit in him," which eventually will cause him to return to his own country, where he will die (37:7). Interpreters are not agreed on what this "spirit" is. J. Blenkinsopp compares this to God putting an evil spirit in Saul that would eventually bring about his own destruction (1 Sam 16:14–16,23; 18:10; 19:9–10), while J. Oswalt thinks of this as an "attitude, disposition, or feeling" in the psyche of Sennacherib that

---

[87] God could have decided to reclaim his glory by killing the Assyrian troops *after* Sennacherib had destroyed Jerusalem.

[88] Concerning the use of נַעֲרֵי, "youth, inexperienced, underlings of," instead of עַבְדֵי, "servants of," Watts (*Isaiah 34–66*, 35) points out that *The boys* is deliberately derogatory of the Assyrian commanders," while J. Gray, *I & II Kings: A Commentary* OTL (Philadelphia: Westminster, 1978), 175, translates this term "flunkeys."

[89] The root גדף describes speech that "reviles, stigmatizes, curses, blasphemes" someone. Since speech was thought to have power in the ancient world, speaking against God actually degraded his glory and caused his honor to suffer. The fear of blaspheming the name of God was so great that in Job 1:5,11; 2:5,9 the scribes wrote the euphemism "bless God and die" because they were too fearful to write "curse God and die."

would cause him to worry and become fearful.[90] One approach focuses on the divine source of this spirit while the other emphasizes the divine effects on Sennacherib, but these factors should be united together in order to perceive the total work of God. Second, God will cause the king to hear a rumor and this news will motivate the king to return to his own land of Assyria. This explains how God will bring about this fearful attitude or negative disposition in Sennacherib. Some suggest that this prophetic reference to "hearing" news in 37:7 could be connected to what Sennacherib "heard" in 37:8 and 9 about Tirhakah, the Cushite king, coming out to make war against him.[91] There is an historical problem with seeing this as the rumor that would drive Sennacherib home, for the Akkadian account in the Taylor Prism indicates that Sennacherib did not run home when the Egyptians threatened them; instead, they defeated the Egyptians at Eltekah.[92] In addition, if this were the cause of Sennacherib's fear, there would be no need for a special spirit to be sent from God to cause him to worry. C. Wildberger rejects this approach because he believes "the rumor will not just speak of his retreat but will mention his violent death as well," though in fact, the content of the rumor is never described in Isaiah's prophecy. O. Kaiser assumes that the rumor must have had something to do with political unrest in Assyria or Babylon,[93] but W. A. M. Beuken properly interprets this to refer to a later rumor the king would hear after 185,000 of his troops were killed by God's angel (37:36).[94] Third, God will "cause him to fall by the sword,"[95] a prophetic word whose fulfillment is reported in 37:38. These three promises imply that Jerusalem will not be defeated, hence there is no need to fear. Nevertheless, the prophecy is about God's defeat of Sennacherib; it is not about his salvation of Jerusalem. This is an important lesson for God's people: God's plans and purposes are centered around the establishment of his honor and glory, not theirs.

(3) Sennacherib's Final Warning to Hezekiah (37:8–13)

8When the field commander heard that the king of Assyria had left Lachish, he withdrew and found the king fighting against Libnah.

---

[90] Blenkinsopp, *Isaiah 1–39*, 475, finds God doing the same thing with Ahab's prophets so that they would give a deceptive message leading to Ahab's death (1 Kgs 22:22–23). Oswalt, *Isaiah 1–39*, 647, suggests this refers to God having complete control over the Assyrian king.

[91] Smelik, "Distortion of the Old Testament," 70–93, suggests that "as we notice the triple repetition of 'and he heard' in the following two verses, we will suspect that the fulfillment of the oracle is near."

[92] *ANET*, 287, indicates that Sennacherib soundly defeated the Egyptians.

[93] Kaiser, *Isaiah 13–39*, 378, believes that the Assyrians would not be intimidated by the appearance of an Egyptians army.

[94] Beuken, *Isaiah II, Vol 2*, 358, admits there is no statement in 37:36–38 that the king heard a rumor at this time.

[95] The *hiphil* verb וְהִפַּלְתִּיו is causative, indicating that God is sovereignly acting in history to bring about his will; this was not something that just happened in the normal course of life.

⁹Now Sennacherib received a report that Tirhakah, the Cushite king [of Egypt], was marching out to fight against him. When he heard it, he sent messengers to Hezekiah with this word: ¹⁰"Say to Hezekiah king of Judah: Do not let the god you depend on deceive you when he says, 'Jerusalem will not be handed over to the king of Assyria.' ¹¹Surely you have heard what the kings of Assyria have done to all the countries, destroying them completely. And will you be delivered? ¹²Did the gods of the nations that were destroyed by my forefathers deliver them—the gods of Gozan, Haran, Rezeph and the people of Eden who were in Tel Assar? ¹³Where is the king of Hamath, the king of Arpad, the king of the city of Sepharvaim, or of Hena or Ivvah?"

The next short episode raises the brief possibility of an Egyptian victory over the Assyrians, only to have any fleeting hope of Egyptian deliverance dashed with another defiant threat from Sennacherib. C. R. Seitz interprets the potential of an Egyptian victory over Sennacherib as the possibility of the "squelching of the boasting remarks of Rabshakeh (36:6), but it would be a defeat for Isaiah and Hezekiah."⁹⁶ This is because God did not promise an Egyptian defeat to the Assyrians; he predicted the death of the blasphemous Sennacherib. This episode is structured in two parts:

Assyrian military action	37:8–9a
Sennacherib's threatening letter to Hezekiah	37:9b–13
Do not trust God for deliverance	9b–10
Rationale: No other gods brought deliverance	11–13

The first section describes the Assyrians reacting to what they have "heard" (the root *šāmaʿ* is used three times), while the letter from Sennacherib asks three rhetorical questions. Sennacherib's letter acknowledges that Hezekiah was saying God will deliver Jerusalem, but to prevent any further deception, Sennacherib wants Hezekiah to hear about the inability of all the other gods to bring deliverance to their nations in past military conflicts.

37:8–9a   There is no indication why Rabshakeh left Jerusalem with his troops and went back to meet with King Sennacherib.⁹⁷ Since Hezekiah failed to surrender or negotiate, there was probably no need to waste time in Jerusalem when he could be helping the king defeat other cities in Judah. While Rabshakeh was stationed in Jerusalem, Sennacherib apparently completed the conquest of Lachish and turned his attention to the city of Libnah, a city a few miles to the north.⁹⁸ This was a smaller city than Lachish and its defeat would clear the

---

⁹⁶ Seitz, *Isaiah 1–39*, 249, interprets the problem as blasphemy against God, not the deliverance of Jerusalem. If the Egyptians would have won, that would have contradicted Isaiah's earlier prophecies (chaps. 30–31) and shown that it does pay to make alliances and depend on horses and chariots.

⁹⁷ The NIV "when" is very interpretive. The text just indicates that Rabshakeh returned.

⁹⁸ The location of Libnah is unknown, though Y. Aharoni, *The Land of the Bible*, (Philadelphia: Westminster, 1962), 77, 199, rejects the identification with Tell eṣ-ṣāfi and tentatively suggests it should be located at Tell el-bôrnāt a little farther north.

pathway so that the Assyrian army could safely move up toward Jerusalem. For the Hebrews in Jerusalem and the reader of this text, Rabshakeh's departure from Jerusalem creates a great sense of relief. The threat is over, the gates of the city can be opened and life can go on as normal. The Assyrians did not destroy the city and there is still hope. This relieves some of the tension in the story.

A second source of hope was the possibility of Egyptian help (37:9a). At some point in this campaign Sennacherib[99] received military intelligence that Tirhakah, the Cushite king of Egypt was marching out of Egypt in his direction.[100] Since this event appears in a different chronological order in the biblical and Sennacherib's account, it is difficult to know which text, if any, is following a strictly chronological outline. In addition, it is not clear if this is just a rumor or if this was actually the time when the Egyptians did enter into military conflict with some Assyrian sources. No battle is reported and no victory is described in the biblical account, so the main intention of this verse is to suggest to the reader that there may still be some hope for Judah. Of course, as one soon discovers, basing hope for deliverance in the actions of Rabshakeh or Tirhakeh can be disappointing.

37:9b–10[101]　　The reasons for sending another messenger to Hezekiah could relate to four factors: (a) Having heard[102] from Rabshakeh that Hezekiah did not surrender, the Assyrian king may want to give one final opportunity for Hezekiah to change his mind. (b) Sennacherib may want to demonstrate to Hezekiah that the Egyptian threat will not deter the king from achieving his ultimate goal of defeating Jerusalem.[103] (c) The king's personal letter carries official written notice to Hezekiah; this is not just a warning from Sennacherib's cupbearer. (d) Sennacherib may want to personally push the argument a little stronger than Rabshakeh did by undermining Hezekiah's own confidence in God, not just the confidence of a few troops on the city wall.

---

[99] NIV has "Sennacherib received a report," but the Hb. text merely says "and he heard," וַיִּשְׁמַע. So it is initially unclear whether Rabshakeh or Sennacherib heard this. The "he" who sent messengers to Hezekiah in 37:9b is undoubtedly Sennacherib, so by implication one can assume Sennacherib is also the subject of the verb at the beginning of the sentence.

[100] Consult the "Historical Setting" of this section for a discussion of the historical problems related to the dating of Tirhakeh's kingship.

[101] 37:9b is the place where many critical scholars would begin Account B², which they extend to 37:35. Smelik, "Distortion of the Old Testament," 70–93, makes a strong case against this approach by arguing that this is one unified continuous narrative and that this letter has a unique message and is not a redactional duplicate of earlier speeches by Rabshakeh in chap. 36. Seitz, *Zion's Final Destiny*, 81, follows a similar approach.

[102] Clements, *Isaiah 1–39*, 283, notes that the parallel account in 2 Kgs 19:19 and the LXX both have "and he returned" וַיָּשׁוּב (instead of the Isaiah reading וַיִּשְׁמַע "and he heard") which he considers the more original text. Actually, the Old Greek and 1QIsaᵃ have both verbs. Wildberger, *Isaiah 28–39*, 409, accepts both verbs as original, but translates them "and he *once again* sent."

[103] The Hb. syntax might best support this interpretation. GKC §111d indicates that when two imperfect consecutive verbs appear together (as here) the former functions similar to a temporal clause and is subordinate to the second. This would suggest a translation: "After/when he heard . . . then he sent" which supports the NIV translation.

While Rabshakeh attacked the people's confidence in Hezekiah, lest he deceive them (36:14–15), Sennacherib's letter attacks King[104] Hezekiah's confidence in God, lest God deceive Hezekiah (37:10). Sennacherib expresses the mild prohibition "do not let him deceive you" (*ʾal yaššiʾăkā*), encouraging Hezekiah not to make the foolish mistake of "trusting" (*bôṭēaḥ*) in his God. Somehow news had gotten back to the Assyrians that Hezekiah's resistance was primarily based on what God would do (there is no more talk of trusting Egypt at this point). Is it possible that information about Isaiah's earlier (14:24–27; 29:5–8; 30:27–33; 31:5–9) or latest prophecy (37:6–7) had reached the Assyrians? If so, Sennacherib is denying the veracity of God's promises and questioning his ability to do what he has said. This is a directly blasphemous statement that attributes false or deceptive statements to God. He is boldly contradicting earlier prophecy by claiming that God's statement that "Jerusalem will not be given into the hand of the king of Assyria" is untrue.

37:11–13   The basis for Sennacherib's contradictory claim is drawn from experience, which is somewhat parallel to the earlier argumentation of Rabshakeh (36:18–20). Some small changes in emphasis are evident in the way things are presented by the two Assyrian speakers. In this letter Sennacherib refers to what both he and earlier Assyrian kings have done to emphasize the overwhelming amount of evidence behind his claims. He wanted Hezekiah to remember that Tiglath-pileser III, Shalmanessar V, Sargon II, and he had repeatedly terrorized and decimated cities and countries throughout the ancient Near Eastern world for nearly fifty years. His opinion was not based just on a few minor victories that happened in the last few months; Assyrian dominance was not just a fluke. If these undeniable historical facts are true, then the question that should haunt Hezekiah is: "Will you be delivered?" How can Hezekiah be so blind that he does not realize the inevitable outcome of the Assyrian conquest of Judah? Sennacherib argues that the facts of history do not lie, so Hezekiah should surrender.

Sennacherib knows that the basis for Hezekiah's hope is in the promises of God, so his next step in his persuasive letter is to argue that no other gods delivered these other nations (37:11–12). If this is so, what chance is there that Hezekiah's god can deliver him from the Assyrians? He lists various cities or territories on the east side of the Euphrates River. His point is: Where are these gods and where are their kings? Were these gods and kings able to defend these places? The answer of course is no. These gods did not deliver these cities[105]

---

[104] Surprisingly, this is one of the rare occasions where Hezekiah is called king.

[105] Hamath, Arphad, and Sepharvaim are dealt with in 36:19. Gozan is probably Tell Halaf on the Harbor River. Haran is nearby on the Balik River, Reseph is close to Palmyra near the Euphrates, and Eden is a territory in that region. Little is know about Tell Assar, Hena, or Ivvah, though the people who lived in some of these places were exiled into Samaria by the Assyrians about twenty years earlier (2 Kgs 17:24).

from the Assyrians and these kings are no longer in power. The implications are frightening and all too obvious. Hezekiah must make a life and death decision. Is God truly stronger than these other gods, and is it his plan to deliver Jerusalem from the Assyrians at this time? Although most believers today make daily decisions on much more trivial issues than these, the answer to these two fundamental questions—Is God able? Is it God's will?—must still be answered by all who desire to walk by faith.

(4) God's Promise to Rescue Hezekiah (37:14–35)

The dramatic tension in the story reaches its peak at this point. Some of these events happened weeks after Hezekiah received the letter from Sennacherib, though the exact elapsed time between these events is not reported.[106] It is evident that Hezekiah did not surrender, Sennacherib finished his conquest of Libneh (37:8), and the main army of Sennacherib has now encamped around Jerusalem in order to make preparations to besiege it with ramps, battering rams, and various other methods of attack.[107] God's decisive annihilation of the Assyrian troops (37:36) must have taken place almost immediately after Sennacherib and his army arrived at Jerusalem, for Isaiah prophesied that Sennacherib's army will not "shoot an arrow here . . . or build a siege ramp against it" (37:33).

The king's prayer and Isaiah's answer from God focus on the power of Israel's God, his plans for the nations, and his defeat of the Assyrians. There is no explanation of how God will defeat Sennacherib and the massive Assyrian army or any indication about exactly when it will happen. Prophecies (both in the Old and New Testament) tend to focus the audience's eyes on the God who will do it, rather than on how and when it will happen. Believers need to worry more about trusting God and glorifying his name, rather than trying to figure out the answers to all the how and when questions. God purposely keeps the details of his ways mysterious, for knowing the how and when can have a negative influence on some of the dynamics of trusting God.

---

[106] The fulfillment of this prophecy in 37:36 had to take place shortly after the Assyrian army came to Jerusalem, so there is a gap of time somewhere in the story. 37:9 connects the sending of the letter to the arrival of the Cushite king from Egypt, so there have to be several weeks for the Assyrians to finish defeating Libnah and to move a large army of over 185,000 troops up the narrow valleys of the Judean hill country to Jerusalem. One could hypothesize that (a) Hezekiah delayed some weeks before going to the temple to pray or that he continued to pray about this over a period of several weeks; (b) Isaiah delayed some weeks before giving God's answer to Hezekiah's prayer; or (c) God delayed destroying the Assyrian army for some weeks after Isaiah gave God's answer to Hezekiah. 2 Kgs 19:35 indicates that option (c) is not possible, for it says that the angel of the Lord struck down the Assyrian troops the very night that Isaiah delivered his prophecy to Hezekiah.

[107] The Taylor Prism (*ANET*, 287–88) claims that Sennacherib confined Hezekiah "like a bird in a cage. I surrounded him with earthworks in order to molest those who were leaving his gates," but there is no detailed description of the siege of Jerusalem.

REQUESTING GOD'S DELIVERANCE (37:14–20)

[14]Hezekiah received the letter from the messengers and read it. Then he went up to the temple of the LORD and spread it out before the LORD. [15]And Hezekiah prayed to the LORD: [16]"O LORD Almighty, God of Israel, enthroned between the cherubim, you alone are God over all the kingdoms of the earth. You have made heaven and earth. [17]Give ear, O LORD, and hear; open your eyes, O LORD, and see; listen to all the words Sennacherib has sent to insult the living God.

[18]"It is true, O LORD, that the Assyrian kings have laid waste all these peoples and their lands. [19]They have thrown their gods into the fire and destroyed them, for they were not gods but only wood and stone, fashioned by human hands. [20]Now, O LORD our God, deliver us from his hand, so that all kingdoms on earth may know that you alone, O LORD, are God."

The narrative describes Hezekiah's address to God, then later Isaiah hears an answer from God (37:21–35). Sennacherib and his representatives disappear as active participants from the scene. Now Hezekiah and God speak about them (37:18,23–25,33–35), but they are powerless to affect the will of God. Hezekiah is able to influence the future by his prayers (37:21 "because you have prayed") and Isaiah is able to encourage greater trust in Hezekiah by delivering God's promises (37:21–35). In the final analysis, God did not act to save his people because Jerusalem or Hezekiah deserved to be delivered; God acted based on his plan (37:26), his desire to defend his own reputation (37:35), his decision to cause all the kingdoms on earth to know that he is God (37:20), and his promises to king David (37:35).

The material in this paragraph comprises two parts:

Hezekiah goes to the Temple	37:14–15
Hezekiah's prayer	37:16–20
Invocation	16
First petition and rationale	17–19
Second petition and rationale	20

37:14–15 At some point after Hezekiah received these writings[108] from Sennacherib, he took them into the temple and unrolled the scroll for God to see what was written there. This does not mean that Hezekiah thought that God would not know what was on the scroll unless he saw a physical copy of what Sennacherib wrote. Hezekiah boldly took the scroll as a witness to the blasphemy of Sennacherib. Earlier Hezekiah had asked Isaiah to pray for God to rebuke the one who "ridiculed the living God" (37:4), but now the king takes matters into his own hands and he too intercedes with God. With

---

[108] The Hb. word is plural (הַסְּפָרִים, "the letters, writings") but the later reference to these writings is singular in "and he read it," וַיִּקְרָאֵהוּ, meaning the scroll. 2 Kgs 19:14 has "and he read them" (וַיִּקְרָאֵם) but later has the singular "and he spread it out" (וַיִּפְרְשֵׂהוּ). It would be unlikely that the Assyrian king would send a whole series of scrolls, but there may have been two letters within the same scroll.

this aggressive reaction to Sennacherib's mockery, one finds a clear distinction between the life of Ahaz and Hezekiah, as well as a difference between Hezekiah's earlier fears (37:1) and his present determination. As J. A. Motyer observes, at this point "there is no rending of garments"[109] (contrast 37:1–2); instead, the text presents a man who is determined to let God fight this battle against the one who has attacked and mocked his divine power.

37:16–20 Hezekiah's prayer follows the general structure of a lament in the Psalms,[110] the kind of prayer anyone in trouble could pray. It contains (a) an invocation in 37:16; (b) a petition to hear in 37:17–19, which includes a rationale for this petition in 37:18–19; and (c) a final petition for divine deliverance in 37:20, with an additional rationale at the end. R. E. Clements suggests that "the authors of the Deuteronomic History" added this prayer in the time of Josiah in 621 BC, while P. E. Dion connects this prayer to phrases common in a later writer, "Second Isaiah."[111] C. R. Seitz disagrees with these approaches because the language of the prayer fits the contextual setting of the prayer, includes distinct phrases that are not found in Isaiah 40–55, and has language that later passages borrowed from this initial usage.[112]

37:16 In the invocation, the one praying calls on God, confessing who God is. Six statements identify this God that Hezekiah is calling on to intervene in history. He is (a) "LORD Almighty" (lit. "Yahweh of hosts"), the one who is the military commander of the hosts of heaven in his army (cf. 1Sam 4:4); (b) the "God of Israel" identifies God's connection with all his chosen people, not the Assyrians; (c) "enthroned between the cherubim" refers to God's royal kingly rule from his temple throne above the ark of the covenant (Exod 25:18–22; Ps 99:1); (d) "you alone are God over all the kingdoms of the earth" claims God's sole monotheistic worldwide dominion, which was dramatically illustrated again and again in the prophecies of Isa 13–35; and (e) he is the creator of the heavens and earth, thus he owns the world as his possession and is powerful enough to make or undo what he has made. These descriptive titles are not just a means of identifying God; instead, they are affirmations of trust, assurance, and praise. Hezekiah is not justifying his beliefs to others,

---

[109] Motyer, *The Prophecy of Isaiah*, 281, perceives that Hezekiah is a different man at this point.

[110] Missing from the traditional lament in Psalms is any statement of trust or assurance that God will act and a concluding vow to praise God. Consult C. Westermann, *Praise and Lament in the Psalms* (Atlanta: John Knox, 1981), 52–70, for a survey of the typical lament.

[111] Clements, *Isaiah 1–39*, 284, assigns this material to the redactor he calls DtrG who put several prayers into the mouths of kings. P. E. Dion, "Sennacherib's Expedition to Palestine," *Eglise et Theologie* 20 (1989): 5–25, states that phrases like "you are God, you alone; you have made the heavens and the earth; they are the work of human hands, wood and stone" are characteristic of II Isaiah, the late deuteronomistic writings, and Psalms.

[112] Seitz, *Zion's Final Destiny*, 81–88, argues based on his belief that Isa 36–37 is a unified narrative that fits together in its present form. Others deny this unity by asserting redactional additions within the narrative. The unknown factor that is heavily based on external assumptions is: Who created this unity?

developing an abstract doctrine of theology, or informing God at this point; he is primarily calling out to the only divine king who controls the world because Hezekiah needs this Almighty God to use his power in a very practical way to rectify what Sennacherib has falsely claimed.

As wonderful and as biblical as these affirmations are, there is no sign that these are new beliefs that Hezekiah has just now come to understand. The king in Jerusalem has known these things about God for some time and brought about religious reform in Judah based on these beliefs (2 Chr 29–31); nevertheless, up to this point he has not fully employed these beliefs to guide his military decisions. Instead he tried to make alliances with Egypt (30–31) and Babylon (39:1–8) and failed to trust God completely. Finally, when all other earthly avenues of assistance have disappeared and he is completely broken, he looks to the God who rules the world for help. Hezekiah is not the only believer who has made this initial mistake. Just imagine the agony and misery that he could have avoided if he had acted in faith from the beginning.

37:17–19   The first petition contains five imperative verbs that function as requests[113] for God to listen, hear, and see. Hezekiah wants God to give attention to Sennacherib's words. The rationale for God to act is that these words "insult" (*ḥārap*) or "mock" the living God (cf. 37:4). By this designation or title for God Hezekiah is contrasting his praise of a God who is actively involved in making and ruling nature and history with Sennacherib's blasphemous lowering of God to the level of the powerless gods of other nations who could not defend their own people (cf. 36:18–20; 37:12–13). Hezekiah is not really arguing against those who worshiped idols in the various countries mentioned in Sennacherib's letter (37:12–13), he is arguing against Sennacherib's demotion of a powerful living God to the level of lifeless chunks of carved wood and stone. God does hear and see; he does act to rule creation and human history. It is a blasphemous insult to classify the glorious God who rules the universe as just another useless god who cannot defend his own people.

Hezekiah does recognize the truthfulness of Sennacherib's claim of military superiority over many other ancient Near Eastern city-states (37:18), and his understanding of why this happened is somewhat similar to Sennacherib's reasoning. Both kings would agree that these cities and their gods were destroyed because the gods that were supposed to protect them were not able to defend them. But from this point on the thinking of Sennacherib and Hezekiah part. Sennacherib thought that Judah's God was no different from these other lifeless gods of wood and stone; therefore, Judah's God would not be able to defend Jerusalem (37:11–13). In contrast, Hezekiah knows that the living God who rules the world is totally different from the lifeless gods of the other nations. Consequently, as W. A. M. Beuken suggests, "mighty Assyria is thus robbed of its fear inspiring and superhuman character and is reduced to a quite

---

[113] People cannot command God to do anything, but the imperative verb can be employed when one wants to humbly make requests of him (GKC §110b).

transparent phenomenon."[114] Assyria did not miraculously defeat other divine powers, just lifeless and powerless idols.

How did Hezekiah know about this living God who is totally unique? The text never explains this, but one can assume from hints in this and other texts that he had (a) some knowledge of God's great acts of salvation, God's awesome revelation of his glory at Sinai, and his spoken words from Hebrew religious tradition in the books of Moses (2 Chr 30:1–27 demonstrates his knowledge about Passover); (b) an understanding of how God had dealt with his people to bless and judge them throughout their history (2 Chr 29:6–9; 30:6–9); and (c) a personal faith experience with the living God (2 Chr 29:10; 31:21) as well as personal experience leading his nation in destroying its own useless idols (2 Chr 31:1).

37:20 Based on this firm foundation of information about God and his own personal relationship with God, Hezekiah steps out in a new act of faith and boldly ends his prayer by asking God to demonstrate his power. This conclusion to the prayer includes another petition and another rationale for God's actions. The petition is a simple request (another imperative verb): "would you save us from his hand" (cf. 33:22; 35:4; 38:20). This agrees with what Isaiah has already prophesied would happen (37:6–7) and rejects what Sennacherib has predicted would happen (36:14–15,18,20). Hezekiah does not demand that God must save them or that they deserve to be saved because they are his chosen people or because they worship him. The rationale for "saving us" is related to God's reputation and glory, not to the status of King Hezekiah or the glory of the state of Judah. Hezekiah believes that a totally divine act of salvation that would deliver Jerusalem from the military stranglehold of Sennacherib's huge army would reveal to the entire world God's unique characteristics and glory. W. Zimmerli called the phrase that others would know who God is a "recognition formula;"[115] that is, once God acted others would acknowledge or recognize his divinity and power. This concept plays a vital role in the presentation of the plagues in Egypt: God's powerful action in bringing and ending the plagues caused the Egyptians to acknowledge (Exod 7:3,17; 8:10,19,22; 9:14–16,29–30; 10:2) that their gods were powerless and Israel's God was the divine king who controlled nature and history. Later Solomon prayed that foreigners would come to know God when they came to visit God's temple in Jerusalem (1 Kgs 8:43), and several Psalms ask for God to act so that people would be persuaded to acknowledge his power and glory (Ps 59:13; 109:26–27). Hezekiah's prayer is similar to Elijah's, when the latter called for God to demonstrate his divinity and power by sending fire from heaven so that

---

[114] Beuken, *Isaiah II, Vol 2*, 363. This part of the prayer is destroying the mystique of Sennacherib's invincibility and the Assyrian myth of being all-powerful. It is not really saying very much when one brags about destroying a piece of wood (a so-called pagan god).

[115] W. Zimmerli, *Ezekiel I*, Hermeneia (Philadelphia: Westminster, 1979), 37, thinks this phrase "points to a fact from which this knowledge is to be gained . . . and belongs to the process of proving or demonstrating."

everyone would know that the Lord, not Baal, was God (1 Kgs 18:36). In all these examples, supernatural action proves divinity and divine proof engenders faith in those who come to realize that "you alone, O LORD, are God."[116] This is an explicit monotheistic statement that excludes all other gods from claiming divine status. God's supernatural action would undermine the false and blasphemous claims of Sennacherib and give people all over the world irrefutable proof that the God in Jerusalem was real. This is the kind of unselfish prayer that God honors, for its primary purpose is to bring glory to the name of God.

PROMISE TO DEFEAT PROUD SENNACHERIB (37:21–29)

21Then Isaiah son of Amoz sent a message to Hezekiah: "This is what the LORD, the God of Israel, says: Because you have prayed to me concerning Sennacherib king of Assyria, 22this is the word the LORD has spoken against him:

"The Virgin Daughter of Zion
   despises and mocks you.
The Daughter of Jerusalem
   tosses her head as you flee.
23Who is it you have insulted and blasphemed?
   Against whom have you raised your voice
and lifted your eyes in pride?
   Against the Holy One of Israel!
24By your messengers
   you have heaped insults on the Lord.
And you have said,
   'With my many chariots
I have ascended the heights of the mountains,
   the utmost heights of Lebanon.
I have cut down its tallest cedars,
   the choicest of its pines.
I have reached its remotest heights,
   the finest of its forests.
25I have dug wells in foreign lands
   and drunk the water there.
With the soles of my feet
   I have dried up all the streams of Egypt.'

26"Have you not heard?
   Long ago I ordained it.
In days of old I planned it;
   now I have brought it to pass,

---

[116] The NIV accepts as original the 1QIsaᵃ reading that has אלהים, "God," as the last word of the sentence (which agrees with 2 Kgs 19:19). The MT of 37:20 just has "that you are Yahweh, you alone." Either text makes sense, though the fuller Qumran reading clarifies the statement, indicating that it is probably not original. In other contexts, Isaiah has "I am God, and there is no other" (45:22; 46:9), which is identical in thought and intent as other statements that "I am Yahweh, and there is no other" (45:5,6,18; 46:6,18).

that you have turned fortified cities
    into piles of stone.
²⁷Their people, drained of power,
    are dismayed and put to shame.
They are like plants in the field,
    like tender green shoots,
like grass sprouting on the roof,
    scorched before it grows up.

²⁸"But I know where you stay
    and when you come and go
    and how you rage against me.
²⁹Because you rage against me
    and because your insolence has reached my ears,
I will put my hook in your nose
    and my bit in your mouth,
and I will make you return
    by the way you came.

God's answer to Hezekiah's prayer concerning Sennacherib does not need to prove to the Hebrews that he is God or that the gods of the nations are useless pieces of wood and stone. Hezekiah already knows this. The divine judgment speech by Isaiah against the Assyrian king reveals the divine motivation for destroying this arrogant king who blasphemously claimed to take the place of God. This prophecy confirms that God will frustrate the plans of Sennacherib, who has proudly insulted God.[117]

Isaiah's prophecy of God's plan includes:

God answers Hezekiah's prayer	37:21
Jerusalem will mock Sennacherib	37:22
Reason: Sennacherib has reviled God	37:23–27
Question about reviling God	23a
Quotation proving the king's pride	23b–25
Rebuttal: God is in control	26–27
Verdict: God's plan for Sennacherib's rage	37:28–29

This message contains quotations of what Sennacherib and his messenger have arrogantly claimed in first person style (37:24–25) and a contrasting rebuttal by God in first person style (37:26–29) parallel to an earlier condemnation of an earlier Assyrian king.[118] Initially it may appear surprising that there is very

---

[117] Many critical scholars would assign this answer to prayer to the B² account, which is thought to be a much later interpolation into the text of Isaiah. Seitz, *Zion's Final Destiny*, 88–94, argues convincingly against these interpretative reconstructions by showing that most of these themes are present in earlier chapters in Isaiah and that the internal historical allusions are connected to events around 701 BC (not exclusively with Esarhaddon's later conquest of Egypt).

[118] Chapter 10 refers to an Assyrian king, possibly Tiglath-pileser III. That oracle quotes the king's words in 10:8–11,13–14 and then announces his punishment in 10:12,15–19.

little news about saving Jerusalem (37:22), but since the real issue of Hezekiah's prayer is stopping the arrogant boasts of Sennacherib, who is blaspheming the name of God, it is appropriate that God's main focus is on the punishment of arrogant Sennacherib. Could it be that saving God's reputation is actually more important than saving Jerusalem?

37:21 These verses contain the message Isaiah sent to Hezekiah, probably in a letter, since there seems to be no sign of direct interaction between the two men. Before the message concerning Sennacherib[119] is described in full (37:22–29), Isaiah indicates that the "God of Israel"[120] gave this answer "because"[121] Hezekiah prayed. It would be useless to speculate about what might have happened if Hezekiah had not prayed, but this divine explanation sends a strong message about the importance of prayer in God's eyes. One of the key values in prayer is that it requires the person praying to humbly admit that they cannot successfully control the future and need God's help.

37:22 After assuring the audience that these are the words of God spoken against the king of Assyria, Isaiah announces one initial promise concerning the people in Jerusalem and their future relationship to Sennacherib. Instead of fearing him as they now do because his strong army is presently surrounding Jerusalem (37:5), in the future the personified vulnerable "Virgin Daughter of Zion,"[122] who was being threatened by Assyria, will despise (*bāzâ*) and mock (*lā'ăgâ*) the proud king Sennacherib. Instead of Sennacherib despising and laughing at them, the tables will be reversed. The tossing or wagging of the head is undoubtedly a sign of contempt (cf. Ps 22:7; 109:25; Lam 2:15) toward the enemy as the Assyrians leave the area.[123] Again there is no statement about how or when this will happen. The main focus of the next few verses is on why this will happen.

37:23–25 God will treat Sennacherib this way because God knows about the blasphemous words the Assyrian king has spoken against him. God logically builds the evidence against Sennacherib by asking rhetorical questions

---

[119] Clements, *Isaiah 1–39*, 285, maintains that 37:22–29 "is addressed to Sennacherib (not to Hezekiah)," while 37:30–32 is addressed to Hezekiah. Although there are references to "you" meaning Sennacherib in 37:22–24,26,28–29, there is no indication that this message was sent to Sennacherib. Instead, God is directly addressing the claims of Sennacherib so that Hezekiah can be assured of God's promise to destroy this arrogant king.

[120] "God of Israel" was one of the titles used in Hezekiah's prayer in 37:16, so Isaiah is making a connection with that prayer and assuring Hezekiah that his God has answered.

[121] In 2 Kgs 19:20 the text and syntax is different from this verse. The word אֲשֶׁר does not function as the relative pronoun "who, which" (its most frequent use) but as a causal connector (GKC §158b). Surprisingly, Delitzsch, "Isaiah," 99, translates this as a relative "that which" and prefers the text of Kings and the reading of the LXX.

[122] The implications of personifying the people in Jerusalem as the "Virgin Daughter of Zion" are difficult to understand. Was Isaiah figuratively picturing these people as vulnerable young girls who were about to be raped by the attacking Assyrians? Motyer, *The Prophecy of Isaiah*, 282, takes the idea of "virgin" to refer to the fact that Jerusalem was "untouched by the marauder."

[123] NIV translates אַחֲרֶיךָ, "behind/after you," with the periphrastic clause, "as you flee." Literally the text says, "behind you she shakes a head."

(23a) and then answering the questions (23b–24).[124] The two almost identical questions ask: Whom have you blasphemed?[125] Whom have you defied with a loud voice? These questions interpret the attack of Sennacherib as primarily a theological challenge or battle against God, rather than merely a human military conflict against Judah's army. The spiritual implications of this war are in fact far more fundamental to the outcome of the battle than the military strength of the two armies. Signs of Sennacherib's spiritual defiance of the God of Israel are everywhere. The idea of lifting up a person's voice against someone expresses the concept of rejection or defiance,[126] and in this context it refers to Rabshakeh and Sennacherib's practice of speaking openly to everyone on the wall with a loud defiant voice to belittle God's power (36:13). Lifting up the eyes on high is a sign of pride rather than humility. Although such behavior is deplorable on any occasion, it is especially abhorrent when these words and actions are directed "against the Holy One of Israel."

God's answer to his rhetorical questions (37:23b–25) points the finger of guilt where it belongs. Sennacherib's words, which questioned if God could deliver Jerusalem, primarily aim the brunt of his attack against the power and divinity of Israel's holy divine King who controls history and dwells in unimaginable splendor on his royal throne. Proof that this accusation is true can be found in the insulting remarks that the Assyrian king and his messenger Rabshakeh have spoken. The quotation of their words in 37:24b–25 is in first person style representing what "I" Sennacherib have said, but these words are not an exact quotation of what Rabshakeh said on behalf of Sennacherib in 36:4–10,13–20 or what Sennacherib's letter said in 37:10–13. J. Oswalt recognized that these statements were very similar to arrogant comments kings made in their royal Assyrian annals.[127]

The proud and blasphemous claims of Sennacherib do not relate to his past conquest of many cities, the destruction of their gods, his perspective that it is hopeless to trust God to deliver Jerusalem, or his statement that God was deceiving the people of Jerusalem (all found in chap. 36). M. A. Sweeney suggests, "Sennacherib is portrayed as defying YHWH by claiming that he has the power to reach the heights of heaven and to dig and dry up the waters of the earth."[128] These statements are somewhat reminiscent of the bragging of the king of Babylon in 14:13–14, for both kings claim to be able to ascend up to the

---

[124] This may be an attempt to counter the logical way that Sennacherib asked rhetorical questions and then provided his own answers in his arrogant statements against God in 36:5–7,18–20; 37:11–12.

[125] The response employs the same vocabulary of "mocking," חָרַף, (37:4,17) and "reviling, blaspheming," גָּדַף, (37:6).

[126] Potiphar's wife lied and claimed she screamed (lit., "lifted up her voice") to defy and scare off Joseph's sexual advances (Gen 39:15,18).

[127] Oswalt, *Isaiah 1–39*, 704–5, quotes extensively from Sargon II's letter to the god Ashur, which also uses the first person style of bragging that is present in 37:24–25.

[128] Sweeney, *Isaiah 1–39*, 471, views these words as claims of being the creator of the universe.

heights where the gods live and to control the forces of nature. H. Wildberger views Sennacherib as "praising himself to the point that he claims to have done the impossible."[129] Using some hyperbole, the Assyrian king boasts of climbing high mountains and cutting down trees. But do kings usually walk or do they ride as their servants carry them? Has any great king actually taken an ax and done the hard work of chopping down a large one hundred foot tall cedar tree all by himself? Do powerful kings actually get down in the mud at the bottom of a fifty-foot hole and literally dig the soil to make a well? Has Sennacherib ever been to Egypt and has he ever tried to stop the flow of the mighty Nile River with his foot (hardly a literal truth)? Although Sennacherib may try to take credit for some of the things his army did, these statements include much figurative language and the repetition of traditional royal hyperbolic phraseology. These are boasts that claim the king can do anything he wants and that he has already accomplished superhuman feats. The only answer to the question in 37:23a that a reader could arrive at is that God's reason for judging Sennacherib is valid. He has truly blasphemed the Lord by claiming supernatural attributes and accomplishments.

37:26–27 The second part of God's message rebuts Sennacherib's claims and asserts that God actually controls history, not Sennacherib. The initial rhetorical question is syntactically structured to make it into an obvious statement. "Have you not heard," which begins with a negative question (*hălô*), actually means, "surely you have heard"[130] and you know these things are true. Certainly the king's intelligence gathering process has unearthed the theological claim that the God of Israel controls history with his plans (10:5; 14:24–28; 23:8–9; 30:1). God asserts not only that "I" am the one who shapes[131] events and plans history, but he also asserts that he controls people in order to "accomplish, do" (*ʿāśîtî,* "I do") what he planned earlier. This verse teaches that God shaped certain factors within history long ago, but there is no specific explanation of how Sennacherib's attack on Jerusalem or Hezekiah's prayer fits into or is coordinated with this previously decided plan. This text is limited in what it claims; for example, it does not say that every detail of every person's life is pre-planned, it only states that Sennacherib's victories over his enemies were shaped into God plans years earlier, thus Sennacherib deserves no credit for turning cities into heaps of rubble and bringing great shame on people who wither like the grass (37:27). The truth is that it was God who planned it all and brought it all about. Thus Sennacherib actually received permission and authority to defeat other nations from God. It is hard not to ask the probing question: Why would one who received so much from God blaspheme the very

---

[129] Wildberger, *Isaiah 28–39*, 427, does not view this statement as a "description of actual events; it is to demonstrate the titanic pride of the Assyrian."

[130] The negative particle with the question marker הֲלֹא shows that something is "absolutely true," and the question "is it not" is therefore "equivalent to *surely it is*" (GKC §150e).

[131] The root יָצַר carries the idea of "shaping, forming, molding."

one who gave him his power? Indeed, pride twists the mind; it often ends up destroying the braggart.

37:28–29 God announces the plans he will accomplish concerning the future life of Sennacherib. Everyone hearing Isaiah's prophecy can be assured that this plan will work because God is fully aware of where the Assyrian king sits,[132] when he comes and goes, and what he says that blasphemes the name of God.[133] Divine sovereignty is based on a full knowledge about the life of the people God controls. Divine sovereignty does not turn people into obedient robots, but allows some human freedom to choose to love or hate God, for the Assyrian king proudly chose to "rage against me." Rage is an uncontrollable anger that expresses itself in a strong physical action that goes beyond what is reasonable. God's accusation is that because of Sennacherib's rage and self-confident arrogance, a divine punishment will fall. How this will happen is unclear, for God does not identify any human forces that will force Sennacherib to return home. Using figurative language related to the control of horses or the leading of helpless captives into exile, God describes how his nose hook and mouth bridle will lead Sennacherib back home. Amos 4:2; Ezek 19:4; 38:4; 2 Chr 33:11 and the Assyrian annals[134] refer to literal hooks being set in people's jaws as they were taken captive, but here these instruments seem to be figurative tools God will use to forcibly lead Sennacherib back to his own land. This picture does not present any evidence suggesting that some other king will come and defeat Sennacherib at Jerusalem. In light of 37:22 and 29, one would naturally conclude that Jerusalem will eventually be delivered from Sennacherib's army, but this is not the main point of this oracle.

GOD'S SIGN OF SURVIVAL AND PROMISE OF PROTECTION (37:30–35)

30"This will be the sign for you, O Hezekiah:
"This year you will eat what grows by itself,

> **and the second year what springs from that.**
> **But in the third year sow and reap,**
> **plant vineyards and eat their fruit.**
> **31Once more a remnant of the house of Judah**
> **will take root below and bear fruit above.**

---

[132] Instead of וְשִׁבְתְּךָ, "and your sitting," 1QIsaᵃ has קומכה, "your rising," which in some ways makes more sense, for one rises before one goes in and out, one does not sit before these activities. Nevertheless, this Qumran reading is probably an error caused by a confusion or duplication of the last word of the previous verse קמה, "standing grain."

[133] The four acts of "sitting, going, coming, and raging" are infinitive construct verbs which function as the object of the verb "know"; thus, lit. "I know your sitting, and your going out, and your coming in, and your raging" (GKC §114c).

[134] Wildberger, *Isaiah 13–27*, 333, refers to Assyrian annals where Ashurbanipal mistreated a disobedient vassal Ammuladi by having "a hole bored into his jawbone, had a string pulled through the jaw, attached it to a dog leash, and left him to be watched in the prisoner's cage at the east gate in Nineveh."

³²For out of Jerusalem will come a remnant,
    and out of Mount Zion a band of survivors.
The zeal of the LORD Almighty
    will accomplish this.

³³"Therefore this is what the LORD says concerning the king of Assyria:

"He will not enter this city
    or shoot an arrow here.
He will not come before it with shield
    or build a siege ramp against it.
³⁴By the way that he came he will return;
    he will not enter this city,"
                                        declares the LORD.
³⁵"I will defend this city and save it,
    for my sake and for the sake of David my servant!"'

Two additional divine messages were communicated, probably to Hezekiah, but it is not possible to determine if these were all part of one long oracle
(37:22–35) or if these last two topically (and temporally) related messages
were brought together when the book of Isaiah was written. If these last two
messages were given a few days later than 37:22–29 or at the same time, it
would not materially impact the interpretation of these verses. M. A. Sweeney
suggests that the sign in 37:30–32 "functions as a means of verifying both
the preceding indictment against Sennacherib and the announcement of his
punishment."¹³⁵ This contrasts with J. Blenkinsopp's suggestion that the sign
is "a reassurance that Judah will survive just as the good earth survives devastation."¹³⁶ If the sign relates to things that will happen two or three years
later (37:30–32), it is not a sign of something that the people in Jerusalem
can immediately observe to prove that Isaiah's prophecies are true. Thus it is
similar to the sign Moses received when God told him that after he brought
the people up out of Egypt he would bring them to Mt. Sinai to worship there
(Exod 3:12). In both these cases the signs were not flashy miracles, but were
more like prophetic announcements about the way God would work things out
in the future. Thus J. Goldingay is more on target when he states that this sign
"will be visible only in the future. . . . In the present, Hezekiah has to carry
on living by faith."¹³⁷ If the sign is limited only to 37:30–32, it would be an
invitation to Hezekiah to trust God to provide food for the remnant of people

---

¹³⁵ Sweeney, *Isaiah 1–39*, 475, finds that this sign is integrated into the context of vv. 22–29 by
pointing to God's power to create and control the natural world.

¹³⁶ Blenkinsopp, *Isaiah 1–39*, 477–78, views this sign as "a guarantee of the truth of the prophetic word," though the accompanying promise of the remnant in v. 37a "may have been added
some time in the Second Commonwealth period," rather than by Isaiah at this time.

¹³⁷ Goldingay, *Isaiah*, 212, realizes that the sign is a promise so that God could later point back
to what happened and verify that this was exactly what he promised.

left in Jerusalem after the Assyrian siege has ended. Though the Assyrians will decimate the nation's agriculture, God will provide enough for all to eat.

The second word concerning the king of Assyria (37:33–35), which promises that God will not permit the Assyrian army to enter Jerusalem, envisions a fairly quick fulfillment of God's removal of the Assyrian troops (they will not have time to mount an attack against the city), and predicts the return of Sennacherib to his own country. If 37:30–35 are conceived as two paragraphs within one speech, it is possible that the sign that Isaiah was predicting involved everything mentioned in vv. 30–35, including God's plan to defend Jerusalem (dramatically fulfilled in 37:36).

These messages are structured into two paragraphs:

God's sign concerning a remnant	37:30–32
Instruction on food supply	30
A remnant will survive	31–32a
God will do this	32b
God's judgment of Sennacherib	37:33–35
Sennacherib will not lay siege	33
Sennacherib will go home	34
Divine defense because of David	35

37:30–32 The first message is classified as a sign intended to instruct, assure, and encourage faith, probably addressed to King Hezekiah[138] (37:30a). If this sign was communicated at the same time as 37:22–29 then this information is part of the message given to Hezekiah (37:21). The giving of this sign to Hezekiah would further develop the comparison between the faith of Ahaz (7:10–14) and Hezekiah, but the differences between the signs and the fact that Hezekiah never accepts or rejects this sign weaken the validity of that comparison.

The idea of finding enough food to eat is the focus of 37:30. Although W. A. M. Beuken treats this three-year plan as merely a literary convention, because something similar appears in other texts,[139] it is completely logical for one to

---

[138] The Hb. text never mentions Hezekiah by name in 37:30 (NIV inserts his name); it merely says "this sign is for you" (וְזֶה־לְּךָ הָאוֹת), but the singular "you" is left undefined. Although the "you" in the preceding verses refers to Sennacherib, this information relates to Judah, not the Assyrians.

[139] Beuken, *Isaiah II, Vol 2*, 369, refers to several passages that do not support his case. 2 Sam 13:38 mentions Absalom staying three years in Geshur, but this has nothing to do with the food supply of a nation after a siege. In 2 Sam 24:13 Gad offers David the choice of having three years of famine, but this is not related to a siege. 1 Kgs 10:22 describe the three-year voyage of Solomon's ships, which has no relationship to the Isaiah text. 1 Kgs 22:1 mentions that there was no war between Aram and Israel for three years, but does this text set a literary pattern for understanding Isa 37:31? 2 Kgs 17:5 and 18:10 describe a three-year siege of Samaria, but Isaiah's temporal markers are not related to a long siege. Finally, he lists Isa 20:3, a text that has Isaiah walking around naked for three years. None of his examples support the idea that some kind of standard "literary convention" was being used in 37:30.

expect there to be a literal problem with the food supply in Jerusalem after this war is over. The siege would have cut off the normal flow of goods, the Assyrian army would consume most of the excess food stored in the land, and they would have cut down fruit trees to use the wood for cooking. At this time the people in Jerusalem were so preoccupied with building the defenses of Jerusalem that there was little time to plant seeds in the fields, so one would expect that the inhabitant of Jerusalem would be left with eating only what grew up by itself (37:30a). Things would not improve that much the second year because of a shortness of grain to plant,[140] but by the third year the agricultural economy would basically be back to normal. J. Oswalt follows the suggestion of F. Delitzsch in concluding that this would involve "only about fourteen to fifteen months"[141] that fit into three different calendar years. The point of this promise is that soon life will return to normal, so they are encouraged (imperative verbs) to get back to their normal routine of sowing, planting, and reaping because then they will have enough for all to eat.[142]

The second promise of this sign (37:31–32a) is that a remnant from Jerusalem will survive and take root and prosper. This figuratively compares these people to a healthy plant that is firmly established in the soil and successfully producing fruit. This picks up the theme of the remnant that was mentioned earlier in various contexts in 4:3; 6:13, and 10:21–22, but here it is applied in an entirely new way. This text has nothing to do with a remnant of later (Babylonian) exiles returning to the land of Judah,[143] it describes the survivors who stay in Jerusalem.

The sign oracle ends with a strong word of assurance that God will accomplish what he has promised (37:32b). Hezekiah will not determine what happens and neither will Sennacherib. God will zealously attend to his plan (cf. 9:7), for he is absolutely determined to use his power to control the military situation and use his grace to preserve a remnant of his people.

37:33–35 An introductory phrase announces another word from the Lord, indicating what is about to happen to Sennacherib. Although this is

---

[140] The term שָׂחִיס, "what springs up," is spelled סָחִישׁ in 2 Kgs 19:29, while 1QIsaᵃ has שעיס, so there is some question about the spelling of this rare word.

[141] Oswalt, *Isaiah 1–39*, 665, follows Delitzsch, "Isaiah," 103–4, but he connects these events to 714–712 BC, not to 701 BC.

[142] The spelling of "eat" (וְאָכוֹל) at the end of 37:30 is problematic and different from 2 Kgs 19:29. It is vocalized to match 2 Kgs 19:29, וַאֲכָלוֹ, "and you eat" (a second person plural imperative) in order to match the three preceding imperative forms. Wildberger, *Isaiah 28–39*, 414, suggests that they all should be read as infinitive absolutes, but this does not match the form of the three imperative verbs (sow, reap, plant). There is no clear solution, but the last line seems to read, "In the third year sow, reap, and plant (imperatives), eating their fruit." If the last verb is read as an imperative, it would indicate the certain consequences which are expected (GKC §110i), making the final line something of a promise: "and then you will eat their fruit."

[143] Clements, *Isaiah 1–39*, 286–87, tries to connect the remnant to those who were taken into exile between 598 and 587 BC, but the promise of surviving an enemy attack on Jerusalem, which is discussed in 37:30–35, is entirely different from the fate of the people of Jerusalem in 598 BC.

clearly a new sub-paragraph, it apparently is connected to what the first paragraph says about the siege of Jerusalem. If the sign in v. 30 also includes what is stated in this paragraph, then there would be an immediate verifiable "sign" that all the people in Jerusalem could observe: (a) Sennacherib will not besiege Jerusalem (37:33); (b) Sennacherib will go home; and (c) God will defend Jerusalem.

37:33 This phrase identifies God as the sender of a message about the king of Assyria; thus, it initially looks like the beginning of a new paragraph. Nevertheless, it begins with the word "therefore" (*lākēn*), suggesting a close logical connection with the promise of a sign in 37:30–32. These promises are generally in line with Isaiah's other promises that Jerusalem would not fall and that the Assyrians would not take Jerusalem (14:24–25; 29:1–8; 30:27–33; 31:4–9), but it is difficult to put these interrelated texts in some sort of chronological order or to suggest that one has a literary dependence on another earlier prophecy.[144] One thing is clear; this prophecy came very late when Sennacherib's army was actually encamped at Jerusalem.

The heart of God's message is a resounding "no" to Sennacherib (five times in 37:33–34). Each of the clauses begin with a "not/and not" (*lōʾ* or *wĕlōʾ*) that circumscribes certain prohibited activities as off limits. Because of these constrictions on Sennacherib's activity, God can confidently say at the beginning of v. 33 and then again at the end of v. 34 (repeated for emphasis sake) that, "he will not enter this city," meaning the walled confines of Jerusalem. This promise assures the listeners that in the end Sennacherib's army will not defeat and destroy Jerusalem like he has defeated the 46 other fortified cities of Judah. The second, third, and fourth negative promises (37:33b) describe the limitations God has set on the Assyrian military attack on the city. If arrows, shields, and ramps will not be brought against the city, this implies that God will do something very quickly before the Assyrian army is able to organize and carry out its first attack on the city walls.[145]

37:34 One positive statement describes the action that Sennacherib will be permitted to do. He will return home. The text does not say why he will return home (37:6–7 gives a hint) and there is no mention of God defeating the Assyrian army at this time (30:31 and 31:8 predict this), but it is apparent that Sennacherib will go home without succeeding at Jerusalem (cf. 37:7,29). God will have the last word, not Sennacherib. The king's blasphemous words, that

---

[144] Clements, (Ibid., 287) believes that these verses were written after the fulfillment of the events they describe, but he presents no evidence to support this claim. Beuken, *Isaiah II, Vol 2*, 372, tentatively suggests that v. 35 "may be a later addition given that the David motif has no further role to play in the narrative."

[145] To explain this, Oswalt, *Isaiah 1–39*, 666, suggests that the tradition in Herodotus's history that a plague decimated the Assyrian army on the border of Egypt may be correct, but that approach misses the main point of the story. God does not need a weak Assyrian army at Jerusalem to prevent them from besieging and defeating Jerusalem; in fact, the bigger the Assyrian army the greater the glory that will come to God.

God cannot deliver his people (36:7,15; 37:10) from the hand of the Assyrian army, will be tested and proven false.

37:35   This brief paragraph ends with a description of God's role and purpose in these matters. God himself will "defend, shield" (*gānan* as in 31:5) Jerusalem "in order to save it."[146] Hezekiah had prayed (in 37:20) that God would by gracious and "save us" and that is exactly what God will do. Now Sennacherib and all the people of Jerusalem will see the power of God first hand. Exactly how God will do this is unknown.

The reason God will act is not related to the righteousness of the people in Jerusalem, but it was for his sake[147] and for the sake of David. It is not surprising to hear that God, whose name was reviled, mocked, and blasphemed by Sennacherib, would act on his own behalf in order to protect his glory and honor. God is not obligated in any way to defend any believer who is in trouble (he allowed his son to die on the cross). Yet, at various times in the past (1 Sam 17), he has chosen to vindicate his Holy Name by intervening in history to prove to his own undeserving people—and to many hostile foreign nations throughout the world (Exod 7–14)—that he is the all-powerful Divine King who rules this world. J. Goldingay states that Sennacherib "has behaved as if he himself were God, and in his words he has declared that God is not. It is therefore not surprising that Yahweh acts for my sake."[148]

More surprising is the second reason: "for the sake of David my servant." This phrase is used several times in Kings (1 Kgs 11:12–13,32–34, 36,39; 15:14; 2 Kgs 8:19; 19:34; 20:6) so the idea may have its origin in the literature that frequently focused on the righteous legacy of David. One might think this refers to the covenant with David that a king would reign on his throne forever (2 Sam 7:14–16), but there is nothing in the immediate context to confirm it. In addition J. D. W. Watts observes that there is nothing in the Davidic promise that guarantees God's protection for the city of Jerusalem.[149] Also, later texts refer to God allowing the city of Jerusalem to be defeated when the Babylonian king Nebuchadnezzar attacked the city (2 Kgs 24–25). J. Oswalt presents the possibility that God acted for the sake of the promised future Davidic Messiah (9:6–7; 11:1), but if this is the case why did God later allow the Babylonians to defeat Jerusalem? It seems that there is something different at this time that motivated God to prevent the Assyrians from conquering the city. The reference to "David my servant" may well point to a "Davidic ideal;" an image of an ideal righteous servant king who rules with humility and explicitly trusts in

---

[146] The infinitive construct verb is often used to reveals God's purpose, thus לְהוֹשִׁיעָהּ should be translated "in order to save it" (GKC §116c).

[147] This motivation for action is used a few times in the following chapters (43:25; 48:11; cf. 49:7).

[148] Goldingay, *Isaiah*, 213.

[149] Watts, *Isaiah 34–66*, 46–48, suggests that what happened here may be more dependent on the provocative, sinful arrogance of Sennacherib. He deserved to be judged; therefore, Jerusalem would be saved.

God. At this time Hezekiah followed the ways of David by trusting God (2 Kgs 18:3), so God responded by stating that he will act on behalf of the one who follows these Davidic ideals. This approach would not view this as an eternal promise of divine assistance to every Davidic king. This miraculous act of God would demonstrate to all future kings of Judah that only those who follow the ways of David will receive God's protection.

(5) Assyrians Defeated (37:36–38)

36Then the angel of the LORD went out and put to death a hundred and eighty-five thousand men in the Assyrian camp. When the people got up the next morning—there were all the dead bodies! 37So Sennacherib king of Assyria broke camp and withdrew. He returned to Nineveh and stayed there.

38One day, while he was worshiping in the temple of his god Nisroch, his sons Adrammelech and Sharezer cut him down with the sword, and they escaped to the land of Ararat. And Esarhaddon his son succeeded him as king.

The narrative ends with a dramatic release of tension when God miraculously delivers his people from the Assyrians, fulfilling his earlier promises.[150] The angel of God went out at night (2 Kgs 19:35) to kill the Assyrians (cf. Exod 12:29), and it happened fairly suddenly (29:5 "suddenly, in an instant") and without any human assistance (31:1 "a sword, not of mortals, will devour them"). Although Josephus (Antiquities, 10.19–21) suggests that a plague wiped out the Assyrians,[151] R. E. Clements is correct in insisting that 37:36 does not refer to such a plague.[152] The historical situation requires some dramatic negative event to motivate Sennacherib to walk away from Jerusalem and leave the rebellious King Hezekiah on the throne. The loss of a major segment of an army would cause any king to think twice about continuing a siege, and the dramatic way that this happened certainly should have caused Sennacherib to realize that he was no match for the God that Hezekiah trusted.

Just as Sennacherib earlier sent his messenger (37:9,24) to address Hezekiah and God, now God will send his angelic messenger[153] to deliver God's message to the proud king of Assyria. This was an unusual act of Holy War against

---

[150] One must question Kaiser's rejection (*Isaiah 13–39*, 375) of the view that there was a "miraculous deliverance of the city of Jerusalem in the year 701 BC." He claims that the city "was not conquered then, because Hezekiah submitted in good time."

[151] This tradition must have some historical basis, possibly from experiences at some other battle, for Herodotus (*History*, ii.141) refers to a plague that fell on the Assyrians while they were in Egypt.

[152] Clements, *Isaiah 1–39*, 287, argues this was not a plague. In *Isaiah and the Deliverance of Jerusalem*, 91–94, he claims that Hezekiah merely surrendered to Sennacherib in order to resolve this conflict. This is unlikely, for Sennacherib did not leave other rebellious kings in power if they refused to submit to Assyria. Clements interprets the account of God's angel destroying the Assyrian army as a theological creation of later redactors in the time of Josiah (about 80 years later) who wanted to heighten the story's emphasis on divine sovereignty and God's special care for Jerusalem and the Davidic Dynasty.

[153] The word מַלְאָךְ שַׁם נאשׁ mean either "messenger" or "angel."

God's enemies, for it was more common for God to give Israel's enemies into their hands and then require the Israelites to go in and actually kill their enemies (Josh 6:2–5; 8:1–2; 10:8–11). By killing 185,000 Assyrian troops without any human assistance, God put fear in the hearts of the Assyrians, for they realized that they were not fighting against an enemy that they could defeat. The Assyrians were smart enough and superstitious enough to figure out that this was an act of a divine power. The God of Hezekiah had destroyed a major portion of their army, and there was no way for the few soldiers who were still alive in the morning to fight against him. The terror of seeing thousands of dead comrades and friends must have been overwhelming.

It may be surprising that the angel of God did not kill Sennacherib himself, for he was the main person who was blaspheming God. W. A. M. Beuken suggests that Sennacherib was "obligated to witness the loss of his 'undefeatable' forces and experience the shame of powerlessness."[154] The only sensible thing for Sennacherib to do was to break camp and head for home in Nineveh. By this action Sennacherib admitted his inability to conquer Jerusalem and acknowledged by his action the overwhelming power of the God of Jerusalem. Sennacherib's action fulfilled God's prediction in 37:7 that Sennacherib "will return to his own country," the promise in 37:29 that "I will make him return by the way he came," and the statement in 37:34 that "by the way he came he will return."

37:38   The narrative ends with the announcement that Sennacherib's son killed him while he was worshiping his god in his temple in Nineveh and that Esarhaddon became the next king of Assyria (681 BC). This took place after the death of Hezekiah (688/87 BC).[155] The Assyrian record of Esarhaddon's reign verifies what this account says and also adds some new information. It records that Esarhaddon was the youngest son, but the gods of Assyria chose him to succeed Sennacherib. When he was made the crown prince, his older brothers realized they would not rule so they plotted against Esarhaddon by making false statements against him, so he went into hiding for a time. After his older brothers killed Sennacherib and fought each other for the right to rule, Esarhaddon re-entered the scene, defeated them, and rose to power.[156]

Isaiah's account makes an ironic theological observation. In contrast to Hezekiah, who worshiped a strong and powerful God who delivered him from an almost impossible situation, Sennacherib's god was so weak that it could not deliver him, even though Sennacherib was piously worshiping this god in his temple. This emphasizes the impotence of Sennacherib and his gods. The God

---

[154] Beuken, *Isaiah II, Vol 2*, 373.

[155] How this event relates to the death of Isaiah is unknown, but if Isaiah is still alive, he is very old in 681 BC. It is possible that this was added at a later time to show that Isaiah's prophecy was fulfilled, just as the record of the death of Moses was added to the books of Moses.

[156] *ANET*, 288b, 289, tells the story, but the brothers' names are not included, and there is no reference to Sennacherib worshiping the god Nisroch.

of Jerusalem saved Hezekiah from thousands of hostile Assyrian troops, but the god of Sennacherib could not even save him from his own two sons. Both kings went to the house of their god/God, but one came away with the hope of deliverance while the other ended up dead. As W. A. M. Beuken says, "the king's provocative question: 'Where are the gods of . . . ?' (36:19f.; 37:12f.) now turns back on his own self."[157] This narrative demonstrates that the Holy God of Hezekiah has all power to accomplish his plans.

THEOLOGICAL IMPLICATIONS. The narrative account of God's deliverance of Hezekiah is a testament of the power of God. The uniqueness of the narrative draws the reader to stand in awe of God's grace and power to control the events of history. What was humanly impossible happened because of God's intervention. This kind of narrative implicitly calls the reader to follow the example of Hezekiah—to stand firm against the odds and put complete faith in God's deliverance.

But this narrow reading of the story misses the broader questions that this narrative raises, especially as it is read in the context of chaps. 13–35. Several difficult questions should be probed. First, why was Hezekiah so faithless for so long, depending upon the Egyptians (chaps. 30–31) and Babylonians (chap. 39) until the very last minute? Certainly Hezekiah's great faith is evident in 37:14–20, but his example of faithlessness in other narratives is not one that anyone should follow. Second, was Jerusalem really delivered because of Hezekiah's faith, or would the city have been destroyed if he had not prayed in faith in 37:14–20? Although on the one hand God recognized Hezekiah's prayer of faith as important (37:21), long before his prayer of faith God had made known to the prophet and Hezekiah that God "will deliver you and this city from the hand of the king of Assyria" (38:6), that God would "crush the Assyrians in my land" (14:24), that "your many enemies will become like fine dust, the ruthless hordes like blown chaff, suddenly in an instant" (29:5), that "the voice of the LORD will shatter Assyria" (30:31), and that "Assyria will fall by the sword that is not of man" (31:8). Thus the history of the believer's life is first and foremost determined by the plan and will of God (14:26–27), not by some act of faith that puts God under obligation to act in a certain way. Many godly men and women of great faith have died throughout the centuries, not because they lacked faith, but because it was the sovereign plan of God for them to give their lives at that time.

The story of Hezekiah does provide great encouragement for believers to trust God, but trusting God does not assure anyone that all their prayers will be answered with a miraculous work of divine deliverance. People should have faith in God because he alone is God, he is holy, he is a living God, and he is the creator of the heavens and the earth who rules over all the kingdoms of the earth (37:15). Faith is a commitment to trust the will of God for whatever he

---

[157] Beuken, *Isaiah II, Vol 2*, 375, observes that Hezekiah's God heard his prayer and promised help while Sennacherib's god offered no help to the Assyrian king.

may ask one to experience; it is not a key that will force God's hand to unlock his treasure house. Faith enables people to walk in a way that honors and glorifies God, but in practical terms it daily echoes the profound words of Jesus in the garden, "not what I will, but what you will" (Matt 26:39).

2. Hezekiah Delivered from Death (38:1–22)

The temporal indicator that this story happened "in those days" hides the fact that the events in chap. 38 took place before God rescued the city of Jerusalem from the Assyrians, as 38:6 clearly indicates. Although no biblical author is required to organize his material in chronological order (chaps. 13–23 are not in chronological order), there probably was a good reason why the author put chap. 38 out of chronological order and after chaps. 36–37. One of the main reasons for this may relate to the contrast this arrangement creates between king Sennacherib, who goes home in defeat and is killed (37:38–39), and King Hezekiah, who almost dies but then is delivered by God in chap. 38.[158] One should not extend the meaning of Hezekiah's experience to imply from it through typological exegesis that the community of Israelites will also suffer times of distress in exile (like Hezekiah suffered) but will one day be restored just like Hezekiah.[159] A second reason for putting chap. 38 near chaps. 36–37 is that it draws attention to the importance of David in God's thinking. At the end of God's oracle of hope, which promises that he will defend Jerusalem, God indicates that he will save the city "for my sake and for the sake of my servant David" (37:35). God's motivation for dealing with his people is connected to the way Hezekiah has followed the ways of "David my servant." Hezekiah has acted like the "Davidic ideal," the righteous servant king who rules with humility and explicitly trusts in God. This idea is then connected to God's response, extending the life and reign of Hezekiah in 38:5. It is "the God of your father David" who responds positively to grant the one who follows the ways of David an additional 15 years of rule.[160] A third close connection between these chapters is the announcement of the defeat of the Assyrians in 37:33–37 and 38:6, which proves that

---

[158] Blenkinsopp, *Isaiah 1–39*, 484, noticed this important connection between these chapters.

[159] Ackroyd, "An Interpretation of the Babylonian Exile," 152–71, suggests that since Lamentations and Jeremiah express exile and the return from exile in similar terminology that these themes should be read the same way in chap. 38. Although there may be some general similarities between Hezekiah's personal experience and the exile, there is nothing in this passage to suggest that the author is constructing some sort of parallel pattern. If such were the case, they would be lexically evident in the imagery of chaps. 40–66.

[160] Clements, *Isaiah 1–39*, 289, infers from this reference to David that this story was added to the book of Isaiah much later at a time when people's confidence was shaken. Thus, he hypothesizes that this idea was added when the Babylonians were threatening Jerusalem in the reign of Jehoiakim or Zedekiah (609–587 BC). But if God will protect Jerusalem only when the king loyally follows the ways of David, it would not appear that this story would provide much hope for people during the reign of these ungodly kings (cf. 2 Kgs 24–25).

God has the power to accomplish the things he plans. Fourth, a sign is given both in 37:30–35 and in 38:7,22 to verify God's promise to Hezekiah. Fifth, the Assyrian crisis is resolved when King Hezekiah goes to God in prayer (37:14–20) and God gives an answer of hope through his prophet Isaiah (37:22–35). In a similar manner Hezekiah's health crisis is resolved when Hezekiah goes to God in prayer (38:2) and God sends an answer of hope through his prophet Isaiah (38:4–8). Sixth, the present order allows the later chapters to control the temptation to idealize the piety of Hezekiah based on his faith in 37:14–20[161] by showing that he was fallible, sometimes self-centered, and in need of signs to help him trust in what God said. Chapters 38 and 39 bring Hezekiah back down to earth and fit his characterization into the less than pious way he led the nation in chaps. 22–31 (before 701 BC). Seventh, by first giving a strong example where the sovereignty of God overpowered the forces that brought distress on God's people in chaps. 36–37, the author has enabled the reader to establish a firm foundation for their own trust in the dependability of God so that when the reader finds out about more difficult days ahead (death and exile in chaps. 38–39), the future can be faced with the knowledge that God is still the sovereign ruler over all individuals and nations.[162] Eighth, the author is able to contrast Sennacherib, who went to his temple in Nineveh and was killed by his sons (37:36–38), with Hezekiah, who went to his temple in Jerusalem and was delivered from death by his God (chap. 38).[163] Ninth, God promises in 37:35 that "I will defend this city and deliver it" and then an almost identical phrase occurs again in 38:6, "I will deliver you . . . and I will defend this city."[164] Finally, putting these narratives in this order allows the author to put the good news of God's deliverance of Judah first, and then put the somewhat negative news that Hezekiah will die in fifteen years (38:5) and that his descendents will go into exile (39:7) in a secondary position. This demonstrates to the believer that "trust must be a way of life and not a one-time affair."[165]

Since the text of Isaiah 38 and 2 Kgs 20:1–11 are quite different, commentators have spent a great deal of effort trying to figure out which author borrowed

---

[161] It appears that Sweeney, *Isaiah 1–39*, 455–504, also idealizes the piety of Hezekiah, the exact point that chaps. 38–39 were attempting to undermine.

[162] Goldingay, *Isaiah*, 217, mentions a somewhat similar understanding of this point about the future situations the nation will face. The reader knows from the earlier story that events never run out of control, they are "always within God's purview."

[163] M. L. Barré, *The Lord Has Saved Me: A Study of the Psalm of Hezekiah (Isaiah 38:9–20)* (Washington D. C.: Catholic Biblical Association, 2005), 240, believes these two episodes contrast the destiny of a king who blasphemes God (he will die) and the righteous king who trusts God (he will live).

[164] Barré (Ibid., 241–42) noticed that this wording is also present in 2 Kgs 19:34 and 20:6.

[165] Oswalt, *Isaiah 1–39*, 672–73, finds a logical connection between these chapters, with 38 having both a positive and negative message and 39 having a negative message. Hezekiah could be seduced by this world's values to trust in armies and alliances that have limited value and do not replace trust in God. Thus, these chapters indicate that "salvation is not in Hezekiah."

information from the other, why the two accounts are so different, and what these differences mean. The majority of scholars have argued that the text in the book of Kings was the original source and that the author of the Isaiah text expanded on it by adding Hezekiah's written record about his illness (38:10–20).[166] Since the book of Kings does not have some of the verses in Isaiah and Isaiah does not have all the material in the exact form as it is in Kings, it is hard not to agree with J. A. Motyer and H. Wildberger, who conclude that both the Kings and Isaiah accounts depend on a third account which they each edited in their own unique ways for their own theological purposes.[167]

The structure of this chapter can be divided into three parts:

Hezekiah prays because he is ill	38:1–8
Hezekiah's thanksgiving after his illness	38:9–20
Concluding comments	38:21–22

The flow of the events is somewhat confusing (particularly vv. 21–22), especially if they are compared to a similar series of events described in 2 Kgs 20:1–11 and 2 Chr 32:24–26. An historical inquiry into what "really happened" is nearly impossible, for such a study requires numerous assumptions about what might hypothetically be the more logical order of events, which in the end cannot be substantiated. Therefore, it is best to humbly admit that no one knows exactly how this all happened, but an exact historical reconstruction of events has never been the primary task of an interpreter. Central attention needs to be given to the literary presentation given in the Isaiah text so that its theological significance can be understood.

(1) Hezekiah's Prayer for Healing (38:1–8)

[1]In those days Hezekiah became ill and was at the point of death. The prophet Isaiah son of Amoz went to him and said, "This is what the LORD says: Put your house in order, because you are going to die; you will not recover."
[2]Hezekiah turned his face to the wall and prayed to the LORD, [3]"Remember, O LORD, how I have walked before you faithfully and with wholehearted devotion and have done what is good in your eyes." And Hezekiah wept bitterly.
[4]Then the word of the LORD came to Isaiah: [5]"Go and tell Hezekiah, 'This is what the LORD, the God of your father David, says: I have heard your prayer and seen your tears; I will add fifteen years to your life. [6]And I will deliver you and this city from the hand of the king of Assyria. I will defend this city.

---

[166] Kaiser, *Isaiah 13–39*, 400, or Childs, *Isaiah*, 280–81; Sweeney, *Isaiah 1–39*, 496–502, and Williamson, *The Book Called Isaiah*, 202–11, have an extensive defense of this theory. Seitz, *Zion's Final Destiny*, 149–94, argues that Isaiah's text with the psalm of Hezekiah is more original (it was omitted by the author of 2 Kgs).

[167] Motyer, *The Prophecy of Isaiah*, 285–86, provides a detailed list of some of the minor differences, suggesting that neither author used the other text. Wildberger, *Isaiah 27–39*, 360–68, devises no reason why numerous individual words and incidental phrases would be left out if one of the texts had used the other.

⁷"'This is the LORD's sign to you that the LORD will do what he has promised: ⁸I will make the shadow cast by the sun go back the ten steps it has gone down on the stairway of Ahaz.'" So the sunlight went back the ten steps it had gone down.

The first paragraph presents a narrative account of events that took place some years before Sennacherib attacked Jerusalem in 701 BC (38:6) and before Merodach-baladan's visit in 703 BC, so it is possible to suggest a date for Hezekiah's sickness around 704 BC.¹⁶⁸ At times Isaiah's narrative account is very terse and somewhat incomplete, for he provides no explanation why Hezekiah must die (38:1) and no reason God gave King Hezekiah fifteen more years to live. There is no request for a sign for Hezekiah or negotiation about what the sign should be (as in 2 Kgs 20:8–11), only a promise that God will give a sign. The quick resolution to the narrative tension (in contrast to the extensive development of the unresolved tension in chaps. 36–37) suggests that the primary emphasis of the chapter is on the hymn in 38:10–20, not the brief narrative story of his sickness and healing.

This paragraph is outlined into three main parts:

Hezekiah is about to die	38:1
Hezekiah's prayer	38:2–3
God answers Hezekiah	38:4–8
God will give 15 more years	4–5
God will deliver the city	6
God will give a sign	7–8

38:1 Although some view chap. 38 as a legendary story about a prophetic healing, comparable to legends about Elisha bringing healing to various kings (1 Kgs 17:17–24; 2 Kgs 4:31–37; 5:1–14),¹⁶⁹ this story is presented as another historical crisis in the life of Hezekiah where God graciously intervened on behalf of the king. Hezekiah's illness is not identified in v. 1, though later at least part of the sickness is connected to having a "boil, sore" (šĕḥîn) on his skin, a symptom that might indicate the beginning of leprosy;¹⁷⁰ some even hypothesize the first signs of bubonic plague.¹⁷¹ Whatever the sickness was, it was

---

¹⁶⁸ Hayes and Irvine, *Isaiah*, 383, prefer to date this event by figuring the years based on the time of Hezekiah's co-regency with his father; thus, the fourteenth year after 727 BC would put the Assyrian crisis at 713 BC, the Babylonian visit of Merodach-baladan happened in the reign of Sargon in 714/13 BC, and Hezekiah's sickness was sometime before that.

¹⁶⁹ Clements, *Isaiah 1–39*, 288–89, calls it a royal *Novelle* that justifies the rule of the king by pointing out his piety, while Beuken, *Isaiah II, Vol 2*, 386, claims that a "prophetic legend clearly lies at the foundation of the present chapter."

¹⁷⁰ Wildberger, *Isaiah 28–39*, 445: "One might suspect that a שְׁחִין, a boil, is leprous."

¹⁷¹ M. Barker, "Hezekiah's Boil," *JSOT* 95 (2001): 31–42, suggests that a lump in the groin would be the first sign of bubonic plague. She suggests that there may be some connection to Herodotus's story (*Histories*, 2.141) that the Assyrian forces were destroyed by a bubonic plague. She hypothesizes that Hezekiah was infected when the messenger brought a scroll of Sennacherib's threats (37:14). This theory is undermined by the fact that Hezekiah's sickness happened before Sennacherib attacked Jerusalem.

extremely serious, for he was at the point of death. There is no indication in the Isaiah text why he was struck with such a severe illness, but 2 Chr 32:25 indicates that "Hezekiah's heart was proud and he did not respond to the kindness shown to him; therefore the LORD's wrath was on him." By not mentioning this point, Isaiah has left the reader with a fair bit of ambiguity about the piety of Hezekiah, for famous righteous kings do not die at a young age without some reason and without God's involvement. Isaiah's instruction that Hezekiah needs to put his "house in order" may include more than just the obvious need to make political decisions about who will be the next king to rule over Judah after Hezekiah dies (cf. 1 Kgs 2:1–9). Another aspect of getting spiritual things in order before you die would include getting right with God. This prophetic exhortation surprisingly contains no conditionality to it, for there is no "if," "perhaps," or "might" words connected to Hezekiah's approaching death. Isaiah simply says, "you are dying," and then adds the unnecessary but biting hopeless phrase, "and you will not live."[172]

Another surprising ambiguity is the sudden appearance of Isaiah in the king's court with no indication that Hezekiah ever called the prophet to intercede on his behalf. Did the king not think he was seriously sick or did he assume that he did not need Isaiah to pray for him? Did he refuse to call on Isaiah because Isaiah was quite critical of some of the king's royal policies in dealing with Egypt and the Assyrians (cf. chaps. 22; 28–31)? Without knowing the answers to these questions, it is hard to interpret these events properly and it is all too easy to impose on the story various assumptions that are not true. Consequently, it is best to address what is known from Isaiah's presentation and not try to fill in ambiguous issues with speculative solutions or borrowed hypotheses from Kings.

38:2–3 Oddly, there is no record of the king objecting or questioning Isaiah's announcement that he will die, but it is clear that he does not fully accept the idea that it is now his time to die. J. Oswalt suggests that he was only thirty-nine at this time and without an heir,[173] so one can understand the shock it was to hear Isaiah's prediction. Rather than arguing with the prophet or getting angry with God, the king in grief "turns his face to the wall" away from Isaiah and cries out to God in prayer, a sign that he is totally devastated by this unexpected news and wants to make an appeal to God. He requests that God should "remember" (zĕkār)[174] the past, a method of reasoning that was commonly

---

[172] "You are dying" translates the qal participle מֵת from the root מוּת, while לֹא תִחְיֶה is the imperfect form "you will not live."

[173] Oswalt, Isaiah 1–39, 676, believes that Manasseh was not born until three years later, but it would seem very odd that a king who frequently had many wives would not have any children at age thirty-nine.

[174] The imperative form זְכָר־נָא ("please remember") is a courteous way (with נָא added on) of requesting help, for there is no way for any human person to command or admonish God by telling him what to do.

used in prayers of intercession to seek God's grace.[175] Hezekiah's rationale for mercy is that he has (a) walked "in faithfulness" (*be'ĕmet*) before God; (b) did this with his "whole heart" (*bĕlēb šālēm*); and (c) did what was good in God's eyes. These are all very positive qualities that demonstrate the piety of the king, and H. Wildberger[176] compares them to "declarations of innocence" in various prayers (Ps 26:1–3) or instructions about what people should do to please God (1 Chr 28:9). But the reader is immediately struck by the fact that this prayer is radically different from the humble tone of Hezekiah's prayer in 37:14–20. In this case Hezekiah does not declare his bold and uncompromising faith in God by confessing how great God is or that he is the Creator who rules all the kingdoms of the earth (37:16). He does not repent of any sins (except in 2 Chr 20:26) nor implore God to act in such a way as to proclaim his glory to all the people of the earth (37:20). Why are these two prayers so different? Are they both equally acceptable in the eyes of God? Does Hezekiah actually claim that he deserves better treatment from God because of his good works? Of course one might want to argue with Hezekiah for a while about his perception of the facts, for although he brought about a great revival of worship in Jerusalem (2 Chr 29–31), his political dependence on arms and alliances (chaps. 29–31) were not judged by Isaiah to be acts of faithfulness and whole-hearted devotion.[177] Possibly Hezekiah's bitter weeping (38:2b) eventually caused him to realize his own unworthiness (rather than trumpeting his piety) and his need to trust in God, rather than his own good works. This episode is instructive for believers who are suffering a life-threatening illness. It is evident that good works will not prevent an early death, that all one can do is to confess one's sins and cry out to God for mercy, and that God may sometimes choose to miraculously heal the sick if it is fits into his greater purposes.

38:4–6 Almost immediately (cf. 2 Kgs 20:4–5) God spoke a word of hope for Isaiah to give to Hezekiah. God's answer did not indicate that fifteen years would be added to Hezekiah's life because he was so faithful and had done so many devout works. Isaiah does not present God's response as a merited payback for the king's good deeds; it is simply and completely divine grace. There is no doubt that God does hear prayers and sees the tears of those who weep. A humble response by a sick person is important in his eyes, for this is an

---

[175] Compare the prayer of Moses at the time of the golden calf in Exod 32:13, Samson's prayer for strength to destroy the Philistine temple in Judg 16:28, Hannah's prayer for a child in 1 Sam 1:11, or those who were lamenting the fall of Jerusalem (Lam 5:1).

[176] Wildberger, *Isaiah 28–39*, 446–447, considers Hezekiah's statements as "reasons given to motivate God to act for the benefit of the person who is praying." Wildberger quotes an ancient Near Eastern king from Babylon who also confessed his innocence by saying "I have not sinned, O Lord of the lands; I was not negligent concerning your deity."

[177] Motyer, *The Prophecy of Isaiah*, 291, rightly questions Hezekiah's motivations and believes his view of his own piety was based on "false assumptions" and a "limited awareness" of his own level of integrity. Similarly, Goldingay, *Isaiah*, 218, suggests, "In light of what we know of Hezekiah we may feel some irony in his claims for himself, and it is noticeable that Yahweh's response (vv. 4–6) does not include an explicit acknowledgement that he has spoken truly."

indication of the status of a person's heart. Nevertheless, God does graciously act from time to time in totally undeserving and quite surprising ways that often have nothing to do with a person's past deeds or prayers. Hezekiah never asked to live for fifteen more years or for God to deliver the city of Jerusalem (it was not being attacked by Sennacherib at this time), but God's gracious promises went far beyond Hezekiah's ability to ask or imagine what he needed (cf. Eph 3:20–21). God's plans took into consideration future situations that people were unaware of. God himself connected his gracious action at this point to his faithfulness to David (cf. 37:35), his concern "to deliver" (*nāṣal* as in 36:14,15,18,20) and "defend" (*gānan* as in 37:35) the city of Jerusalem, and his plans to use Hezekiah in the midst of the Assyrian crisis a few years later in 701 BC (about three years after this incident). Of course at this point Hezekiah probably had no idea that in the next few years the Assyrians would defeat all the fortified cities of Judah and surround Jerusalem, but God could foresee the bigger picture and knew that he needed to teach Hezekiah to trust him completely. Looking back on this incident in relationship to events in chaps. 36–37, one might suggest that God was taking Hezekiah through a preliminary trial that challenged him to trust God at this point in order to prepare the king for another big event that would test his faith a few years later when Sennacherib surrounded the city of Jerusalem.

38:7–8 The narrative plot ends with Isaiah offering a promise of a sign for Hezekiah. In the Isaiah narrative the sign comes unexpectedly, with no warning or context to understand why it was provided. In the 2 Kgs 20:7–11 account the sign is requested by Hezekiah to verify that he would indeed be healed quickly and would be able to go to the temple to worship God in three days. Since this information is missing in the Isaiah narrative, it appears that the sign was designed to prove the promises of God in 38:5–6, though much later in the chapter (38:22) one finds that Hezekiah did ask for a sign. The giving of a sign to a king reminds one of the sign that Ahaz refused to accept in 7:1–12, but the situations of the two kings are different, for Hezekiah was never asked to accept or trust in a sign from God in this context (though one assumes he did accept this as a true sign from God). The fact that Hezekiah wants or needs a sign to strengthen his weak faith suggests that the king is not being idealized as that great icon of faith depicted in 37:14–20.[178]

A sign can provide a strong confirmation that God will make something unusual happen, if that sign accomplishes something that is miraculous or unnatural (cf. Judg 6:17,36–40). In this case, God is doing something that is scientifically impossible: stopping the sun's normal movement and putting the solar system in reverse for a while (not just have it stand still as in Josh 10:1–14). The description of what will happen is related to the movement of a shadow on some steps that Ahaz constructed on one side of the king's palace.

---

[178] Childs, *Isaiah*, 282, states, "Those interpretations that see in Isaiah's portrayal of the king a heightened idealization of the character of Hezekiah appear to me to be overly subtle."

There is no indication that this was some sort of "sundial" (RSV) that marked the hours of the day, or that one step represented one hour (implying a 10 hour reversal of the sun). Although it is almost impossible to determine exactly what the original text said because of some minor grammatical and textual difficulties,[179] there is not much disagreement about the general point that the verse is making. M. Barker attributes the backward movement of the shadow to "a 75 per cent eclipse of the sun over Jerusalem in the late afternoon on 6 August 700 BCE, lasting from about half past five until sunset,"[180] but R. E. Clements rightly rejects this interpretation.[181] The date for these events is not in August 700 BC, but sometime late in 704 BC. The verse ends with a confirmation that the sign was accomplished when the sun's movement caused the shadow to turn back ten steps, thus relieving the tension in the story. Unfortunately, more ambiguity is introduced into the story because there is no indication of how Hezekiah responded to the fulfillment of this sign. Some of these ambiguities will be clarified in the poem that follows.

(2) Hezekiah's Thanksgiving for Healing (38:9–20)

[9]A writing of Hezekiah king of Judah after his illness and recovery:

[10]I said, "In the prime of my life
must I go through the gates of death
and be robbed of the rest of my years?"
[11]I said, "I will not again see the LORD,
the LORD, in the land of the living;
no longer will I look on mankind,
or be with those who now dwell in this world.
[12]Like a shepherd's tent my house
has been pulled down and taken from me.
Like a weaver I have rolled up my life,
and he has cut me off from the loom;
day and night you made an end of me.
[13]I waited patiently till dawn,
but like a lion he broke all my bones;
day and night you made an end of me.
[14]I cried like a swift or thrush,
I moaned like a mourning dove.

---

[179] The Qumran, LXX, and Masoretic Hb. traditions do not agree completely (1QIsaᵃ refers to "Ahaz's upper chamber," עלית אהז, LXX refers to "Ahaz's house," the Aramaic Targum has "the stone of the hours" אבן שעיא, while the MT preserves the better reading of "on the steps of Ahaz" בְּמַעֲלוֹת אהז) and the gender of various suffixes do not always match what one would expect (the fem. ending on יָרְדָה "has declined" does not match the masc. noun צֵל "shadow").

[180] Barker, "Hezekiah's Boil," 31–42, derived this data from M. Kudlek and E. H. Mickler, *Solar and Lunar Eclipses in the Ancient Near East* (Neukirchen-Vluyn: Neukirchener Verlag, 1971), 64.

[181] Clements, *Isaiah 1–39*, 291, rejects any association of this event with the eclipse on January 11, 689 BC, concluding, "It would be gratuitous to attempt any association with an eclipse of the sun."

My eyes grew weak as I looked to the heavens.
I am troubled; O Lord, come to my aid!'"

¹⁵But what can I say?
He has spoken to me, and he himself has done this.
I will walk humbly all my years
because of this anguish of my soul.
¹⁶Lord, by such things men live;
and my spirit finds life in them too.
You restored me to health
and let me live.
¹⁷Surely it was for my benefit
that I suffered such anguish.
In your love you kept me
from the pit of destruction;
you have put all my sins
behind your back.
¹⁸For the grave cannot praise you,
death cannot sing your praise;
those who go down to the pit
cannot hope for your faithfulness.
¹⁹The living, the living—they praise you,
as I am doing today;
fathers tell their children
about your faithfulness.

²⁰The LORD will save me,
and we will sing with stringed instruments
all the days of our lives
in the temple of the LORD.

The narrative story of Hezekiah is interrupted with a record of Hezekiah's written reflections about his sickness, written both during and after the sickness (38:9). This poetic record, which is not found in the parallel stories of Hezekiah's life in Kings and Chronicles, recounts Hezekiah's suffering and mental anguish, his call for God to help him, his recovery, and his praise to God. H. Wildberger rejects Duhm's categorization of this piece as a lament because "the one who is praying is caught no longer in some type of distress."[182] J. Oswalt rejects the view that this is a thanksgiving psalm and calls it an individual lament that ends with the typical expectation of deliverance.[183] M. A. Sweeney is probably right to identify the genre as a thanksgiving psalm because of its overall function, but he wisely recognizes that it contains elements of the

---

[182] Wildberger, *Isaiah 28–39*, 452–53, believes this person is looking back and reminiscing on a time of distress in the past and describing what he thought at that time.

[183] Oswalt, *Isaiah 1–39*, 674, makes a very strong statement about the genre, but on p. 681 he recognizes that it is somewhat of an "anomalous form" that "is neither wholly lament nor wholly thanksgiving."

individual lament and the thanksgiving psalm.[184] Although numerous interpreters understand this text typologically, suggesting that it projects a word of
hope to later exiles that God will intervene on their behalf and restore them too,
this typological understanding of the psalm seems to be based more on later
topical parallels with ideas in Jeremiah and the "application" of these words
that later readers might develop, not based on the "meaning" of these words in
the historical content of this thanksgiving psalm.[185]

The structure of the psalm suggests that it can be divided into four subparagraphs, which are preceded by a brief introduction identifying the author:

Narrative introduction	38:9
Lament over approaching death	38:10–13
Petition to God	38:14
Benefits of suffering and restoration	38:15–17a
Thanksgiving for God's salvation	38:17b–20[186]

There is some question about two of these divisions. (a) M. Barré makes 10–14
a unit with two subdivisions in 10–11 and 12–14. He connects v. 13 to 14
because there are two similar similes comparing Hezekiah to a lion (38:13b)
and a bird (38:14). In his view both verses are part of Hezekiah's lament.[187]
Although the natural flow of thought connecting 13 to 14 is enhanced by the
two similes, the outline above is based on the conclusion that v. 14 is not part
of the lament but is actually Hezekiah's petition. In this approach, Hezekiah
expresses his request to God with a crying moan (38:14a). (b) M. Barré also
views 38:20 as a separate coda added at the end of the poem, but few follow
this approach because v. 20 fits in with the general emphasis of giving God
praise in 18 and 19.[188]

---

[184] Sweeney, *Isaiah 1–39*, 492–95, recognizes that this poem does not conform to the ideal
structure that one would expect (based on other examples in Psalms) of either the lament or thanksgiving psalm. The aim of the poem (to praise God after his sickness) in this case determines its
overall role in the passage. Beuken, *Isaiah II, Vol 2*, 389, concludes that this prayer "conforms
to the literary genre of the thanksgiving song of the individual in which elements of lament are
retrospectively incorporated."

[185] Ackroyd, "An Interpretation of the Babylonian Exile," 152–71, emphasized this function of
the text. One must always distinguish "meaning for the author" at that time from "application for
me" at some later date. Ackroyd's approach seems to impose a later possible application that exiles
in Babylon (or the application any other reader in a time of distress might find) with the original
meaning to Hezekiah; thus, he reads into the text ideas that are not there. It would also be wrong
for a person to say that the "meaning" of this text promises that God will heal my friend from
cancer. A later "application" by the exiles or people today should not be confused with the original
"meaning" of the text in that context. Only extrapolated analogical "applications" can project hope
for others in similar situations at a much later date.

[186] J. H. Coetzee, "The 'Song of Hezekiah' (Isaiah 38:9–20): A Doxology of Judgment from
the Exilic Period," *OTE* 2 (1989): 13–26, disagrees with the genre and dating accepted in this commentary, but is one of many authors who argues for a new subparagraph beginning at 38:17b.

[187] Barré, *The Lord Has Saved Me*, 28–31, classifies v. 14 as a part of the lament.

[188] One of the supports for this decision by Barré, (Ibid., 27, 29) is that by omitting v. 20 from

The change of vocabulary and a somewhat confusing mixture of verb forms indicate some progression within the lament. The lament portion uses perfect verbs that describe what happened (38:10a "I said/thought;" 11a "I said/ thought;" 12a "was pulled down;" 13a "I waited") as Hezekiah considers what might happen in the future (imperfect verbs).[189] In the petition in 38:14 the first two verbs are imperfects expressing his determination that "I will chirp . . . I will moan," which are followed by an imperative request for God to help. The third section (38:15–17a) takes place after Hezekiah has heard of God's salvation, so words of hopelessness, death, and agony use perfect verbs ("I suffered anguish" in 38:17a) and words about life and possible benefits employ future verbs ("I will walk humbly" is an imperfect in 38:15). The final part of the poem is characterized with words of praise (38:18,19) and singing (38:20). Although the syntactical shifts are rather frequent and somewhat confusing at times, they are meaningful and should be carefully observed in the process of interpreting the poem.

38:9 The narrative introduction attributes this poem to a written document[190] that Hezekiah authored. The use of the temporal infinitive construct with the preposition *b* most likely indicates that Hezekiah wrote some of the lament portions of the poem "when he was still sick"[191] (NIV has "after") and some of the praise sections later after he recovered.[192]

38:10–13 Initially, Hezekiah records his thoughts about dying. Three concerns haunt his view of the future. He laments what seemed like a premature death (38:10), he voices some regrets about what he will not be able to do in the future because of his death (38:11), and then develops a series of comparative analogies about things being cut short (38:12–13). In some ways this first section sounds a lot like the anguish of Job.

Hezekiah views himself as at mid-life[193] and closer to the prime of his life (NIV), rather than entering retirement and expecting death in the near future.

---

the main body of the poem he is able to find a word count of 60 words in 38:10–14 and a matching word count of 60 words in 38:15–19 (achieved by omitting as intrusive the last line of v. 13).

[189] "I will not see the LORD" or "no longer will I look on mankind" in 38:11.

[190] Delitzsch, "Isaiah," 116, and many since have suggested that the "song which follows might be headed *Mikhtam*," which assumes some confusion between מִכְתָּב, which is in the text here, and the word מִכְתָּם which is a title for Ps 16. Although this requires only a minor textual adjustment from ב to ם, the idea that Hezekiah wrote about his illness should not be easily dismissed, for 1QIsaᵃ agrees with the MT מִכְתָּב.

[191] The infinitive construct has a prefixed preposition and a subject pronoun suffix בַּחֲלֹתוֹ (GKC §114q, 115e). Wildberger, *Isaiah 28–39*, 435, and Childs, *Isaiah*, 279, prefer the translation "when he was ill" instead of "after his illness."

[192] The phrase וַיְחִי מֵחָלְיוֹ (lit. "and he was living from his sickness") points to a time after the danger of dying is past, but it could be as early as the first day after he received the sign when he still had the boil, or some weeks later after all signs of the sickness were gone.

[193] The meaning of דְּמִי in the phrase בִּדְמִי יָמַי is debated. Some identify the root דָּמָה "rest, quiet" (Beuken, *Isaiah II, Vol 2*, 378, 380; Oswalt, *Isaiah 1–39*, 683) and derive the meaning "in the quiet time of my life" (there were no wars or trouble). Wildberger, *Isaiah 28–39*, 438, takes this as "middle," since the middle of the day was the time people would rest from their labors. P. A. H.

If he dies now at middle part of his life, it will seem like he will be "robbed[194] of the rest[195] of my years" that would normally be expected. He is not saying that he fears death; just that it seems unfair and contrary to expectation for one to die at such a young age.[196] This death sentence on him means that he will be like one who is waiting at the gates of a house to go in, for the gates of death (cf. Job 38:17; Ps 107:18)[197] are about to open and he must go in.[198] These words are filled with disappointment and dread. As the king weeps, he is astonished at his approaching inescapable destiny.

His second lament (38:11) starts the same way ("I thought") and expresses his sorrow at being deprived of some of his most prized experiences because of his death. Not seeing God[199] "refers to the king's experience of God's presence in the Temple,"[200] as Ps 27:4 implies. Once he has died, that joyful experience of hearing the trumpets blare, the Levitical choirs sing, the priests pray, and all the other things going on during temple worship on the Sabbath and at the annual festivals will not be possible. He also laments that he will no longer be able to observe and interact with other friends and family in this "world."[201]

Hezekiah's third lament (38:12–13) describes several metaphors of dying. First, the process of dying is compared to someone pulling up and remov-

---

de Boer, "Notes on the Textual Meaning of Isaiah xxxviii 9–20," *OTS* 9 (1951): 170–86, prefers the root דָּמַם, yielding "in the grief/mourning of my days." This matches the interpretation of the Aramaic Targum on Isaiah.

[194] The verb פֻּקַּדְתִּי does not mean to be "robbed," but to "appoint, assign" (Gen 40:4; Num 31:14,48; Neh 7:1). Thus the phrase is lit. "at the gates of Sheol I am appointed/assigned for the rest of my years."

[195] 1QIsaᵃ does not have יֶתֶר but וּמַר "and bitterness" which Barré (*The Lord Has Saved Me*, 58) accepts, thus creating a parallelism between "mourning for my days" in v. 10a and "bitterness for my years" in 10b. Both of these changes in the MT seem unnecessary.

[196] When a similar situation faced Job, his comforters assumed he had committed some great sin and was being punished by God (Job 8:3–6; 11:11–15).

[197] Gen 28:17 mentions the "gates of heaven." Apocryphal books like 3 Macc 5:51 and Psalm of Solomon 16:2 mention the "gates of Hades," as Jesus does in Matt 16:18. Ancient Near Eastern texts like the Descent of Ishtar refer to going through seven gates in the underworld (*ANET*, 107–8).

[198] The verb הָלַךְ "go, walk," used in conjunction with "going in the gates of Sheol," is a common way of talking about death. In Gen 25:32 Jacob says he is "going (הוֹלֵךְ) to die," while Joshua euphemistically announces his approaching death by saying "I am going (הוֹלֵךְ) this day on the path of all the earth" (Jos 23:14).

[199] The shortened Hb. name for God appears twice יָהּ יָהּ, which seems to be a scribal mistake (1QIsaᵃ has the name only once), although Beuken, *Isaiah II, Vol 2*, 378, translates "I shall not see Yahweh, Yahweh in the land of the living," emphasizing how deeply he will miss calling out the name of God.

[200] Coetzee, "The 'Song of Hezekiah'," 13–26.

[201] The word הָדֶל means "cease, cessation," which does not fit well in this context. 1QIsaᵃ agrees with the MT. The Targum refers to the "earth, land," suggesting the idea that metathesis has occurred. The word was probably originally הֶלֶד "world" (cf. that phrase in Ps 49:2) with the ל and ד getting reversed early in transmission. Delitzsch, "Isaiah," 117, keeps the MT and views הָדֶל as a reference to the place where life has ceased, the dwelling of the dead, but this approach creates a poor parallel with the preceding line.

ing the tent of a shepherd. The tent is a temporary dwelling place, just like a person's body, so when someone else has removed, folded up, and taken away the tent, there is no place for "my span of life."[202] He apparently is referring to God's choice to end his life. This is somewhat similar to the second comparative metaphor drawn from the life of the weaver of cloth who ends his work by rolling up his cloth and cutting it off the loom. Here the lamenting king describes both his action and God's. Hezekiah depressingly admits, "I have rolled up"[203] my life; it is over and the divine weaver is wrapping things up. God is the one who will end his life by "cutting off" the cloth from the loom and it is ultimately God who will soon bring his life to an end. It is almost impossible to read between the lines to determine Hezekiah's attitude. He interprets his demise as an act of God, but it is hard to know if he blames God, for he does not accuse God of some wrong. He compares God to a lion who "will break . . . will make an end"[204] of him, revealing God's power and Hezekiah's fear of what God will do to him. Hezekiah admits his weakness before God, but he avoids leveling any moral opinion on God's action. There is great confusion about Hezekiah's state of mind at this time, for there is no agreement on how to translate the first word in v. 13 ("I cry" RSV; "I am racked with pain" NEB; "I waited patiently" NIV; "I thought" HCSB),[205] thus it is unclear if he is calm or very fearful.

38:14 In the midst of this crisis Hezekiah determines to speak to God and request his help in a petition. His weak voice in addressing God is compared to the weak voice of birds.[206] The verbs describe what he will do: "I

---

[202] At the beginning of v. 12 is דּוֹרִי, a word that is often translated "my generation/lifetime." Wildberger, *Isaiah 28–39*, 438, relates this root to Akk. *duru* "ring, city wall," Arabic *dār,* "dwelling," or Aramaic *dōr,* "dwelling place," thus providing a good parallel term for "tent" (NIV "my house"). Oswalt, *Isaiah 1–39*, 679, maintains the usual meaning of דּוֹרִי by connecting it to the span of life of a generation. Barré, *The Lord Has Saved Me*, 80–81, takes the same position based on the usual characteristics of a metaphor, which puts two unlikely concepts together. "My dwelling place" fits the context of tents perfectly, thus destroying the tension that a proper metaphor must contain.

[203] Clements, *Isaiah 1–39*, 292, and Wildberger, *Isaiah 28–39*, 439, both emend the text to "you have rolled up" קִפַּדְתָּ instead of "I have rolled up" to match the second person verb ("you made an end of me") later in the verse. Since first, third, and second person verbs are found in this verse, there is no consistent grammatical pattern that would argue for changing this first person verb to a second person.

[204] One should not translate the verbs with the past tense "broke" or "made an end" as in NIV, for both these verbs are imperfect.

[205] There are two Hb. roots for שָׁוָה, one meaning "to be like," with the possible derived sense *(piel)* "to even out, soothe," and the other "to lie down" (cf. Ps 131:2). But 1QIsaª has שִׁפּוּתִי "I laid bare, I was crushed," the Aramaic Targum has נהימית "I roared." Wildberger, *Isaiah 28–39*, 459, prefers a slight emendation to the root שָׁוַע to give "I cried out" (Ps 18:7; 28:2).

[206] According to the *Qere* tradition of reading the text, the word כְּסוּס "like a horse" is a slight misspelling for כְּסִיס like a swallow," which is obvious from the parallel bird "crane" and the sound that these animals make. Barré, *The Lord Has Saved Me*, 119–21, believes סִיס עָגוּר should be understood as the compound name of one bird (not two birds) based on the appearance of the word *ssʿgr* in the Deir ʿAlla texts and *su–sa–ga–lum* in an Eblite text.

will chirp . . . will moan" to express his desires to speak his petition to God. It almost appears that he is so weak that he cannot address God with a traditional prayer and that he is in such physical and emotional anguish that he can only groan out a few words as he looks toward heaven for help. He does know that God is his only source of hope and he keeps his prayer simple and to the point. "I am oppressed," reveals his urgent need and helplessness. Ironically, he has nowhere else to go except to God his oppressor. His simple request is for God to "be my pledge, surety" ('ārbēnî, "my pledge of safety" HCSB; "my aid" NIV). This legal metaphor pictures God in the role of one who would stand up for a friend or family member in a court setting and guarantees or gives a pledge to support the accused.[207] Hezekiah humbles himself and seeks help from God. Too many times people foolishly wait until they get to the very end of their rope before they will actually cry out to God for help.

38:15–17a The first two lines of v. 15 indicate that the prayer moves to a different time than vv. 10–14, for God has already answered Hezekiah's prayer, is already healing him, and is teaching him new things through this experience. Hezekiah is simply amazed and dumbfounded at what has happened. He does not know exactly what he can or should say now.[208] He certainly cannot continue to say what he said or thought in 38:10 and 11. At that time God said he was going to die (38:1) and now he has had compassion on Hezekiah and has said he would live (38:4–5). Since "he (God) has spoken to me (Hezekiah),"[209] how should Hezekiah respond (cf. Ps 116:12)? One would expect words of praise[210] at this point, but instead he makes various commitments about how his life will change. He "will walk slowly,"[211] which suggests deliberate movement or a less frantic pace of life because "of

---

[207] In Gen 43:9; 44:32 Judah served as a guarantee to his father that Benjamin would return home safely (cf. Job 17:3; Prov 6:1).

[208] The imperfect verb אֲדַבֵּר "can I say" should be understood as a modal verb expressing a subjunctive possibility, particularly in questions (GKC §107m,t).

[209] The MT has וְאָמַר "and he said," but 1QIsaᵃ has ואומר, "and I will say," which agrees with the Aramaic Targum. Barré, *The Lord Has Saved Me*, 143–44, 262, thinks that this would be a nice parallel to the first word "what can I say" so prefers the validity of the Qumran reading over the MT, but this emendation would seem unnecessarily repetitive if he said the same thing twice. Barré's translation which follows the Qumran reading has "since he has taken action against me," but this inappropriately turns a positive statement (NIV "and he himself has done this") into a negative statement, which contradicts the positive tone of 15–20. In these verses God has begun to restore Hezekiah.

[210] Wildberger, *Isaiah 28–39*, 434, 441, rejects the MT אֶדַּדֶּה "I will walk slowly" and prefers אֹדְךָ, "I will praise you." This fits perfectly, but there is no textual support for it. 1QIsaᵃ has the reading אדודה "I will flee, wander" (from נָדַד).

[211] NIV interprets this slow walk as a sign of humility, but that meaning is questionable. "Walking slowly" may refer to changing the speed of busyness involved in the hectic responsibilities of his office and not taking all the pleasures of life for granted, but that is not the same as humility. "Walking slowly" is not pictured as a punishment from God either; it is part of Hezekiah's positive response based on things he has learned.

the anguish (lit. 'bitterness,' *mar*) of my soul." Apparently, he is saying that he will value each day and appreciate the rest of his life because he has had this near death experience.

Uncertainties about Hezekiah's response continue in 38:16 because of difficulty with the Hebrew text.[212] Hezekiah is directly addressing God when he says "O Lord" at the beginning of the verse and then he proclaims, "on account of them, they will live," but it is unclear what the "them" and "they" refer to. Contextually, one might assume that "on account of them" means on account of God's positive words of hope. Thus this may be similar to a general proverbial statement acknowledging that, "people (they) live on account of the things God says." In the second line Hezekiah takes this general principle and applies it to his own situation; that is, "on account of all these (these divine words) my spirit has life." The last line of v. 16 has an imperfect followed by an imperative verb, which some consider unusual. Therefore J. Blenkinsopp emends this line to make both verbs imperative requests of God ("restore me, let me live," similar to HCSB) while H. Wildberger makes them both imperfects that communicate Hezekiah's confidence in God ("you will strengthen me and let me get well") [213] The problem is evident, but neither of these solutions is particularly convincing because they change the Hebrew text. The syntactical use of an imperative after an imperfect, jussive, or cohortative "expresses a consequence that is expected with certainty."[214] Thus these words communicate that "you will cause me to be strong/healthy (not past tense as in NIV) and (the result will be that) you will cause me to live." This is Hezekiah's way of attributing all the glory for his recovery to God's activity and of expressing his confident trust in God to complete the process so that he may live longer.

Hezekiah's final observations about the process he was going through includes his reflections on a few things he now understands more fully (38:17a). First, now he realizes that the bitter experience[215] of facing death had the greater goal of bringing a deeper sense of appreciation for his "well-being, peace" (*šālōm*) after God intervened. This expresses a certain level of acceptance of what has happened and an admission that he has grown through the process. He now has a greater faith in God, an assurance that he will live longer, and a much deeper appreciation for his family and the little things that he would have missed, had he died (38:11).

---

[212] Wildberger, *Isaiah 28–39*, 441, declares, "This text has been a nightmare for exegetes." Barré, *The Lord Has Saved Me*, 154, claims that "no arrangement or redivision of the consonantal MT has yielded good sense, despite many attempts." These comments indicate that all translations are somewhat suspect because the meaning of the words and syntactical relationships between them is unusual or excessively complicated.

[213] Blenkinsopp, *Isaiah 1–39*, 480; Wildberger, *Isaiah 28–39*, 441.

[214] GKC §110i discusses this kind of construction.

[215] 1QIsaᵃ has המעד "very" for the second מָר, "bitter," apparently an attempt to eliminate a problem. Thus the MT should be considered more authentic.

38:17b–20 Now Hezekiah affirms that all the credit goes to God who has "kept back, withheld"[216] him from falling into the pit and dying. Even more importantly, God has forgiven Hezekiah by metaphorically putting all his sins behind his back so they are not seen any more (cf. Ps 103:12; Mic 7:19). This removes some of the earlier ambiguity and suggests that Hezekiah did repent of his sins when he wept by the wall (38:3), which confirms the statements in 2 Chr 32:25 that Hezekiah repented of his pride; therefore, God's full wrath did not come upon him. This repentance of pride may be one of the key things he learned through this near death experience. Unfortunately, many important political and religious leaders are still tempted by pride and some still have not fully understood the practical lesson that Hezekiah had to learn the hard way.

These acts of divine intervention on behalf of Hezekiah cause the king to offer words of praise of God (38:18). These statements should not be seen as the "reason, motivation" (based on the introductory *kî* "because") explaining why God spared Hezekiah.[217] God has already saved Hezekiah from death; there is no need for Hezekiah to give reasons why God delivered him at this point. Instead the asserative use of *kî* "surely, truly"[218] represents a confident man who knows that what God says is 100 percent true.

The negative statement of the argument in v. 18 should be related to its positive counterpart in v. 19. Ps 115:17–18 has a similar contrast between the dead who cannot praise God and the living who can. Together these statements about the dead and the living function as words of thanksgiving that praise God. This reminder is also an encouragement for all readers of this verse to take advantage of their present opportunities and commit themselves to praise while they still can. The author makes a strong contrast between the dead people who do not praise God (cf. 38:11) and "the living, the living" (twice for emphasis)[219] who do praise God. Hezekiah is thanking God for his extended life.

---

[216] The MT has חָשַׁקְתָּ "you have loved, attached," which does not make much sense in the clause, "you have loved my soul from the pit." It is very odd to observe that NIV and HCSB have not only included this root, which is due to a scribal error, in their translations ("in your love/in love") but have also included the correction of this form ("kept, delivered"), instead of choosing one or the other. If a scribal hearing error of replacing the "k" sound of ק for the "k" sound of כ occurred, and שׁ for שׂ, then one might read "you have held back (חָשַׂכְתָּ) my soul from the pit" which is widely accepted in most commentaries. This scribal error must have occurred very early in the process, for the Qumran and Targum texts agree with the MT. Beuken, *Isaiah II, Vol 2*, 401, takes the alternative of keeping the MT and translating it "you have attached yourself to my soul." But then he is required to add a verb "keeping me" in order to make sense of the last clause, "from the pit." This is a more difficult solution that should not be accepted.

[217] Sweeney, *Isaiah 1–39*, 493, interprets this unit as vv. 17–20a. V. 17 gives a statement of God's deliverance, and the reason for deliverance is in vv. 18–19. Kaiser, *Isaiah 13–39*, 406, follows the same interpretation, but Beuken, *Isaiah II, Vol 2*, 402 wisely rejects this approach.

[218] GKC §159ee states that "absolute certainty with which a result is to be expected is frequently emphasized by the insertion of כִּי."

[219] In a similar manner, 38:11 has the word "Yah, Yah," an abbreviated form of the name Yahweh, written twice. Both of these could be due to a scribal mistake of dittography, or their repetition may be to emphasize a point.

The key factors relating to the praise of God are (a) "thanking you" (*tôdekā*); (b) "praising you" (*yĕhallēkā*); and (c) "putting hope" (*yĕśabrû*) in God, which the dead cannot do (38:18). The living can do these things, and Hezekiah did these things (38:19). Although praise was primarily directed to God, two central aspect of praise were (a) to talk about God's acts of faithfulness, his truthfulness to his promises; and (b) to tell other people (especially children in the family) of the wonderful things that God has done. At this point there is no idealization of Hezekiah's wonderful behavior that earned him God's grace; Hezekiah has a very different attitude from his father Ahaz (7:1–12) who did not praise God before his children. Hezekiah also has a different attitude from what he had at the beginning of this episode (38:3), for now he focuses on God's wonderful faithfulness, not the merit of his own deeds. It is a little surprising that Manasseh, Hezekiah's son (2 Kgs 21), did not follow in his father's footsteps and have a heart that followed God. Of course, Hezekiah's welcome reception of the Babylonians (39:1–8), his treaty with the Egyptians (ch 30–31), and several other problems (ch 22,28–29) in the next few years suggest that Hezekiah sometimes forgot about God's faithfulness and did not always trust and praise him for some of the events that came into his life.

Hezekiah ends his words of praise with some confident statements about what will happen in the future (38:20). He begins by affirming what God will do for him, then he describes what he will do for God. The first clause has an infinitive construct form, which normally depends on a verb (or an implied "to be" verb). One could propose the translation "God is at hand to save me" (which unnecessarily emphasizes his closeness), though "the LORD is saving me"[220] would better represent what has happened and is happening to Hezekiah.[221] He commits to be very involved for the rest of his life with others who play and sing in the temple to declare God's glory. This commitment does not limit his worship only to group worship at the temple building and exclude private worship in his palace room. His commitment is primarily to the public worship at the temple so that he can be an example and an encouragement to others as he speaks about God's great acts of faithfulness (38:19). All believers

---

[220] GKC §114o explains that the infinitive construct can function like a gerund in English.

[221] At times the copulative הָיָה, "he was," is implied in Hb. If this verb is assumed here, it would satisfy the grammatical demands of this syntactical construction. The infinitive can show aim, purpose, result, or attendant circumstance, and the addition of "to be" indicates the infinitive construct represents a continuous, or incipient action. The infinitive construct does not have tense. GKC §114h,l suggests the translation "the LORD is ready to save me" (לְהוֹשִׁיעֵנִי) to represent that continuous action, though "the LORD is saving me" GKC §114o seems a simpler representation. The Targum added the word אָמַר "he said" to try to solve this problem. The NIV "the LORD will save me" refers to something in the future, rather than something that is already continuously happening now. Waltke and O'Connor (*IBHS* 11.2.10i) view the ל before the infinitive as an "emphatic lamed" and the verb as an imperative, yielding "YHWH, do save me" but J. Huehnergard, "'Asservative *la* and Hypothetical *lu/law* in Semitics," *JAOS* 103 (1983): 569–93, maintains that this kind of ל is not used with an imperative in Hb. or any of the other Semitic languages.

should have a similar commitment to praise and glorify God even if they have not gone through such a traumatic near death experience.

(3) Concluding Comments (38:21–22)

[21]Isaiah had said, "Prepare a poultice of figs and apply it to the boil, and he will recover."

[22]Hezekiah had asked, "What will be the sign that I will go up to the temple of the LORD?"

The chapter ends with a brief note that describes a medicinal treatment that Isaiah had Hezekiah put on his boil to help with the healing process. There is some uncertainty about when this discussion took place, for in 2 Kgs 20:7 this interaction takes place much earlier in the story, immediately after Isaiah promised that God would allow him to live and before Hezekiah was given a sign. Those who consider the Kings narrative as more historically authentic place these verses between vv. 6 and 7 in the Isaiah account.[222] On the other hand, C. R. Seitz has noticed that (a) both chaps. 37 and 38 follow a similar pattern of having a sign coming after a prayer and a prophetic response from God (37:30–32; 38:20–21); (b) the thanksgiving psalm praises God for saving Hezekiah from death not for healing the boil, so it makes sense for him to be concerned about the healing later after the poem; and (c) the second sign about going up to the temple to worship God (38:22) has nothing to do with the earlier sign in 38:7–8 about the sunlight moving up ten steps.[223] Thus the Isaiah account makes sense in the form that Isaiah tells it.

Isaiah's presentation of the story has Isaiah announcing God's promise that the king will continue to live (38:4–6), giving a sign that he will live (38:7–8), advising the king on how to treat his boil (38:21), and giving the king another sign about going up to the temple (38:22). This is a legitimate way of telling the story. The use of a medicinal patch of figs[224] should not be viewed as an inappropriate after thought and it does not diminish God's miraculous power to heal, any more that Jesus' use of clay diminishes his healing in the New Testament (John 9:1–12). Isaiah predicts that Hezekiah will recover and live, rather than that he has already recovered (2 Kgs 20:7).

The sign that Hezekiah requested is motivated by his desire to go to the temple to worship God and sing his praises. Since his skin disease would make him unclean (Lev 13:18–23) and unable to enter the temple area, he would

---

[222] Watts, *Isaiah 34–66*, 52, places 38:21–22 after 38:8. Clements, *Isaiah 1–39*, 293, suggests that a redactor who brought this story over into Isaiah from the book of Kings omitted these two verses and then a later editor added them at the end of the chapter.

[223] Seitz, *Zion's Final Destiny*, 166–69, focuses on interpreting the Isaiah text by itself and on its own terms rather than trying to determine which narrative is more logical, more consistent, or flows more smoothly.

[224] Wildberger, *Isaiah 28–39*, 451–52, reports the use of figs in the Ugaritic text to heal diseases in horses, in a Mesopotamian text to treat mouth diseases, in an Egyptian text for medicinal purposes, and a similar Arab tradition.

have to wait until the signs of the sickness were past so that the priest could pronounce him clean (Lev 13:6,17,23,28). In Isaiah's account there is no record of what the sign was, if it was a miraculous event, or how many days it was before the king could go to the temple to worship God with the rest of the people and tell everyone his testimony of what God had graciously done for him. This tremendous story of God's deliverance and Hezekiah's commitment to praise God will be tested in a short time (39:1–8).

THEOLOGICAL IMPLICATIONS. Hezekiah came to understand in a startling way that God numbers everyone's days (Job 14:5; 21:21) and sovereignly decides when every person will be born and when they will die. Although Isaiah is silent about the cause of Hezekiah's sickness and Hezekiah only briefly mentions his sins (38:17), there are many people who die because it is simply God's set time for them to die. Since no one knows the details of God's plan for each person's life and death, it is best to focus attention on what the text does tell the interpreter. Isaiah told Hezekiah that he was suppose to be "getting your house in order" (38:1) and praying for divine mercy, rather than worrying about when the end will come. It is evident that Hezekiah's prayer was not answered positively because the king was such a pious individual (38:3); this was a totally undeserved divine act of grace and one that God grants rarely. Although it is not wrong for believers today to ask God for additional years to serve him, believers should not assume that God will frequently grant an additional fifteen years before they face death. God's response of an additional fifteen years was very unusual, but it fit into his plan to defend Jerusalem in the coming years (ch 36–37). In most cases people never know why God answers some prayers positively and others negatively, but the answer always depends on the plan and purposes of God. Believers need not fear death, but should look forward to being with the Lord after death. The positive approach is one that is thankful for each year that God provides here on earth and thankful for the opportunity to spend the afterlife in the presence of the Lord.

Some people react to their approaching death with resignation, while others express despair or bitterness. In light of the common biblical pattern of weeping at the time of death, one can assume that Hezekiah was not in error to weep (38:3) and that it was not wrong for him to want more years of life. Hezekiah's lamenting prayer expresses common emotional feelings as he faced his fast-approaching death. He lamented that he was going to die so young, that he would not be able to worship God any longer in the temple, and that his life was being cut off, but he never blames God of wrong. All he could do was to humbly admit that he was helpless and in need of God's assistance (38:14). Once God surprisingly promised life and recovery, he was reminded of several important principles that most take for granted: (a) God is the source of life; (b) God's promises are true; and (c) God forgives sins (38:17). The only reasonable response to these truths is for people to praise God for his salvation and to share with others how we have experienced his grace (39:19–20). Yes, God does miracles; he heals the sick and controls the solar system. He is the one that deserves all praise—when people are well, when they are sick, and when they die. He has a plan and all of his servants need to accept and follow his plan.

3. Trusting Babylon Rather Than God (39:1–8)

¹At that time Merodach-Baladan son of Baladan king of Babylon sent Hezeki-ah letters and a gift, because he had heard of his illness and recovery. ²Hezekiah received the envoys gladly and showed them what was in his storehouses—the sil-ver, the gold, the spices, the fine oil, his entire armory and everything found among his treasures. There was nothing in his palace or in all his kingdom that Hezekiah did not show them.

³Then Isaiah the prophet went to King Hezekiah and asked, "What did those men say, and where did they come from?"

"From a distant land," Hezekiah replied. "They came to me from Babylon."

⁴The prophet asked, "What did they see in your palace?"

"They saw everything in my palace," Hezekiah said. "There is nothing among my treasures that I did not show them."

⁵Then Isaiah said to Hezekiah, "Hear the word of the LORD Almighty: ⁶The time will surely come when everything in your palace, and all that your fathers have stored up until this day, will be carried off to Babylon. Nothing will be left, says the LORD. ⁷And some of your descendants, your own flesh and blood who will be born to you, will be taken away, and they will become eunuchs in the palace of the king of Babylon."

⁸"The word of the LORD you have spoken is good," Hezekiah replied. For he thought, "There will be peace and security in my lifetime."

The final prose narrative in this section is historically connected to the events in chap. 38 by the phrase "in those days" and by placing it after the Babylonians had heard about Hezekiah's illness and recovery (39:1). Thus chaps. 38–39 are in chronological order, but they both took place before chaps. 36–37.

The reasons for this reversal of the chronological order of events is not stated, but several topical reasons for putting chap. 38 after 36–37 were dis-cussed in the introduction to chap. 38, and the placement of chap. 39 last was addressed in the introduction to chaps. 36–39. These conclusions suggest that chap. 39 has few linguistic connections with 40–55.[225] There it was concluded that chap. 39 does not function as a linguistic bridge to the following chapters. It does not idealize the reign of Hezekiah, plus the prophecy about Judah's ruler going to Babylon does not strengthen a belief in a Zion theology. This chapter does not address the issue of who is the Messiah (Hezekiah or someone else) and does not present Hezekiah as someone who is the opposite of his father Ahaz (both failed by making alliances). There is no additional commentary by Isaiah to explain the implications of Hezekiah's mistake in dealing with the

---

[225] After reading chap. 39, one would not be able to predict that chap. 40 would say what it does.

Babylonians (beyond 39:6–7), so readers are left to make their own connections and draw their own conclusions about these prophecies. Chapter 39 does not end on a positive note like chap. 38, and it views the relationship between the prophet and the king quite differently. Although another "death sentence" somewhat different from 38:1 is predicted for Hezekiah's heirs in chap. 39, one cannot help but be shocked that Hezekiah does not even bother to weep for deliverance (contrast 38:2–3). There is not even a prayer or lament to try to get God to reverse his plans to send the people of Judah to Babylon. Where is this great righteous king that is mentioned in the earlier chapters? What will happen to God's people and the Davidic monarchy if God does not intervene in this downward spiral? Technically, chap. 39 does not address the issue of what will happen to the city of Jerusalem, though one would assume that it will be under foreign control if the king's sons are taken away and everything in the king's treasury is carried away.[226] The doctrine that it was impossible to defeat Jerusalem because God lived on Mt Zion was dealt a serious blow by this prediction about the fate of Hezekiah's children.

The narrative in chap. 39 is an example of Hezekiah's failure to trust God just months after God graciously healed him in chap. 38. Hezekiah left a theological legacy of peace for the time being, but more important was the threat of a much more severe disaster in the future (39:6–7).[227] When great privilege and extraordinary mercy are shown to someone (ch 38), much is required. Hezekiah in some respects is like Moses; both men trusted God and did great things for God, but both failed to live up to God's expectation, and in the end both died under a cloud of great disappointment.

The structure of this narrative can be divided into two segments:

The Babylonians visit Hezekiah	39:1–2
Isaiah condemns Hezekiah	39:3–8
Inquiry about the Babylonians	3–4
God's delayed punishment	5–7
Hezekiah's reaction	8

39:1–2 The final narrative is dated some months after Hezekiah's sickness and recovery. It would take some time for news to travel to Babylon and

---

[226] One should not assume that this chapter was written after captives were exported to Babylon (598 BC) or that it functioned as an apology to explain the painful experience of Judah being conquered by the Babylonians (Clements, *Isaiah 1–39*, 293). Clement considers this narrative is concerned with the deportation of Jehoiachin in 598/597 BC and was written after that event and before the destruction of the temple, since it is not mentioned in this story. Two problems with this are (1) the material is in the Hezekiah material of Kings (as well as Isaiah), and (2) Jehoiachin is never mentioned in this narrative or in the whole book of Isaiah. Blenkinsopp, *Isaiah 1–39*, 488, disagrees with Clement's reasoning for the 597 BC dating (the lack of any reference to the temple) and argues for this date because the fulfillment of these events happened in 2 Kgs 24:10–17 (the deportation of Jehoiachin was a fulfillment of the word of the Lord in earlier prophecy).

[227] Seitz, *Zion's Final Destiny*, 182–91, discusses the implications of his reading of chap. 39 and its impact on how one should read Isaiah. He deals with 39 separately from 36–38.

then additional weeks for an envoy to come to Jerusalem with a letter from the Babylonian king.[228] Since Merodach-baladan II, [229] a prince from the tribe of Bit-Yakin, ruled Babylon from 722–710 BC and then again for a short time from 704–703 BC, this visit must be dated sometime around 704–703 BC, just before Sennacherib chased Merodach-baladan from power.[230] This time period would be just a few years before Sennacherib's attack on Jerusalem in 701 BC, so Hezekiah still had rich treasure in Jerusalem (cf. 2 Kgs 18:14–16).[231] The episode begins with the king of Babylon sending letters[232] and gifts with a Babylonian envoy. The bringing of the letters and gifts are initially related to the news that the Babylonians heard that Hezekiah "was strong" (from the root *ḥāzaq*) after being sick[233] (2 Chr 32:31 connects this visit to the miraculous sign from the sun). The content and the size of the gift from Babylon is not defined, but the gift could be a small innocent present that was merely a token of friendship, or lurking behind the innocent sounding "gift" could be a sizable bribe that would cement a political alliance between these two kings who were both facing strong Assyrian opposition. Isaiah's strong negative reaction to these events (39:5–7) indicates that this visit from a Babylonian ambassador and the gifts that accompanied it had significant political implications.

Hezekiah's response to the visit by the Babylonian envoy (39:2) was to joyfully welcome his guests and show them his riches of silver, gold, and the luxuries in his "treasure house" (*bêt nĕkōtōh*), plus the military weapons he had

---

[228] Blenkinsopp, *Isaiah 1–39*, 487, suggests that this Babylonian envoy did not hear about Hezekiah's sickness until after he arrived in Jerusalem.

[229] J. A. Brinkman, "Merodach-Baladan II," in *Studies Presented to A. L. Oppenheim, June 7, 1964* (ed. R. D. Briggs and J. A. Brinkman; Chicago: Oriental Institute, 1964), 6–53, indicates that his Akk. name was Marduk-apla-iddina. After the death of the Assyrian king Shalmaneser V, Merodach-baladan II ruled Babylon for twelve years. At the end of that time Sargon II defeated Merodach-baladan II, but five years later when Sargon II died around 705 BC he again gained control of Babylon for less than a year before Sennacherib drove him from power. 2 Kgs 20:12 spelled the Babylonian kings name בְּרֹאדַךְ which is "Berodack" but Isa 39:1, 1QIsaᵃ, and Akk. sources all agree that the first letter of his mane is a "m" sound.

[230] Oswalt, *Isaiah 1–39*, 693, dates this chapter in 712/11 BC near the end of his first period in power because he believes Hezekiah died in 697/96; therefore, this event has to be about fifteen years earlier. Childs, *Isaiah*, 285, is surely correct to place these events around 704–703 BC.

[231] In 701 BC he was required to give many of his treasures to Sennacherib to pay tribute he had withheld (2 Kgs 18:14–16), so chap. 39 had to take place before chaps. 36–37.

[232] The introduction says nothing about the envoys that brought the "letters" (סְפָרִים). Some commentators have related this term to the Akk. *šapiru,* "high official"; others change the vocalization to סֹפְרִים "scribes." Apparently the letters were more important than the name of the messenger who brought them. If letters were presented to Hezekiah, it is obvious that a Babylonian envoy brought them, so at this point the messenger is assumed. In 37:9,14 another letter was delivered without identifying the name of the messenger or mentioning his presence. The Old Greek fills in this gap and refers to "letters and ambassadors and gifts."

[233] The word יֶחֱזַק plays off the name of "Hezekiah," relates to his physical recovery, and hints at his political "strength," which would be a reason to send him a letter. Wildberger, *Isaiah 28–39*, 474, records two similar examples where kings sent letters. (a) A prince of Bekhen sent a letter to an Egyptian Pharaoh after the recovery of the sister of the wife of the king. (b) Burnaburiash, king of Karaduniyas scolded a Pharaoh for not sending a letter when he was sick.

in his armory. Again it appears that there is more involved in this visit than just being glad to see an old friend. Hezekiah's actions are viewed as being either (a) an incredibly naïve demonstration of his wealth and power; (b) a calculated political move to establish a treaty with Babylon; or (c) "gestures of courtesy, and nothing of a distinctly 'sinful' nature."[234] Isaiah's later condemnation of Hezekiah's display of his money and military power demonstrates that Hezekiah was sinful, for "human power and glory is exactly what the first half of the book is warning against."[235] Instead of focusing on glorifying God for healing him of his sickness, he was intent on displaying his own earthly glory so that the Babylonians would find him a legitimate partner in their coalition against the Assyrians.[236] It is hard to know how to interpret the final clause concerning showing the Babylonians everything "in all his kingdom" (ûběkol memšaltô). Does this imply that Hezekiah took the Babylonian envoy on a tour of various other cities to show them the agricultural, industrial, and military strength of the whole nation or is this just a rhetorical way of emphasizing that nothing was kept back, that he went overboard in his attempt to impress the Babylonians, answering all their questions?

39:3–4 Since Hezekiah was quite open about showing the Babylonians everything, it is not surprising that the prophet Isaiah heard the exciting news about the king entertaining visitors. There is no indication that God told him to go speak to the king, though the silence of the text does not exclude that as a possibility. At first there is little that indicates that Isaiah was suspicious about the intentions of the visitors.[237] It appears that he did not even know who these foreign visitors were, so why would he be suspicious? Isaiah first asks Hezekiah to identify who the male visitors were and what they said. Hezekiah truthfully told Isaiah that they were from far away in Babylon, but nothing more, suggesting that maybe the king did not want to reveal everything to Isaiah. Instead of insisting that Hezekiah tell him everything they said (part of his first question), Isaiah goes right to the heart of the matter and asks Hezekiah what these men saw while they were in Jerusalem. At this point the prophet may be displaying some suspicion about what might have happened in their private talks, but he does not accuse the king of anything wrong until he has more complete information. Hezekiah's answer to this question would reveal to Isaiah what was truly going on. Hezekiah probably knew he would not be able to hide anything form Isaiah, for God would tell the prophet if the king

---

[234] Beuken, *Isaiah II, Vol 2*, 409, 415, takes the first option; Motyer, *The Prophecy of Isaiah*, 297, views Hezekiah as making a treaty, while Clements, *Isaiah 1–39*, 295, does not see anything sinful about this act of courtesy.

[235] Oswalt, *Isaiah 1–39*, 694, believes Hezekiah was looking for support from Babylon because he knew the Assyrians would be arriving soon.

[236] Wildberger, *Isaiah 28–39*, 474, finds Hezekiah demonstrating "that he too is interested in being a treaty partner."

[237] Blenkinsopp, *Isaiah 1–39*, 488, detects "a note of suspicion and hostility in the two questions put to Hezekiah."

was dishonest. Therefore the king truthfully tells Isaiah that the visitors saw everything in his house (palace) and everything in his storehouses. He admits personal responsibility for this when he says, "there was nothing I did not cause them to see" (39:4b). He does not explain why he did this, makes no excuses for doing it, and says nothing about the implications of his action. But this was unnecessary, for the prophet Isaiah would know that no king would reveal to a foreign nation strategic national security issues unless one was planning on working together on something very important. Since God condemned Judah's foreign alliance with Egypt (chs 30–31) and Ahaz's alliance with Assyria (chs 7–8), there is not much doubt about how Isaiah would respond to this news.

39:5–7 The prophet announced a "word from the LORD Almighty" (39:5). This was not a summary of Isaiah's opinion about the wisdom of a political alliance with Babylon or a laundry list of potential positive or negative consequences that might develop because of this alliance. This was an authoritative promise from God just as powerful and sure as God's earlier promise that he would live and not die (38:4–6). Based on that earlier promise Hezekiah knew that he would survive for fifteen more years, the Assyrians would not defeat Jerusalem, and God would defend the city of Jerusalem. God had also revealed to Hezekiah the key that "in repentance and rest is your salvation, in quietness and trust is your strength" (30:15). Having this knowledge, Hezekiah knew that there really was no need for him to make an alliance with Babylon. Thus one is hard pressed to justify the king's foolish action.

Isaiah announced that "the time will surely come" (yāmîm bāʾîm, lit. "days are coming"), indicating that the fulfillment of this prophecy would happen at some unknown time in the future. God's discipline would directly match the sinful deeds of the king. Hezekiah's pride in his wealth and military resources (cf. 2 Chr 32:25) revealed that he was not fully trusting God to deliver Jerusalem from his enemies. Hezekiah actually believed that he could maintain his independence from Assyrian domination based on his own military strength and the assistance of the Babylonians. God's response to this failure to trust him completely was to remove every material source of human trust. Everything that he and his fathers had stored up in their treasure house would be taken to Babylon. Thus his plan to have the Babylonians save him would backfire in the end, because eventually the Babylonians would take everything he had. A second aspect of God's punishment relates to the exile of some[238] of the royal sons/grandsons of Hezekiah to Babylon to serve as eunuchs in the court of the Babylonian king. This means that these men would have no royal heirs (they will be eunuchs), so the consequences of his action would have some impact on the continuation of the Davidic line. In addition, these Hebrew eunuchs would not be able to work for the greater glory of Judah and her God, but would have

---

[238] The Hb. וּמִבָּנֶיךָ, "and from your sons," uses the preposition מִן "from" in a partitive sense that expresses a separation of some out of a larger group, thus מִן means "some of."

to swear their loyalty to a foreign pagan king.[239] Nothing was said about the continuation of the nation of Judah, its king, or the temple in Jerusalem. This prophecy cast a long black shadow over the reign of Hezekiah and certainly dampened any attempt to idealize this king. He would later learn to trust God more completely (37:14–16), but his legacy would forever be tarnished by this fateful mistake.

39:8 This brief narrative ends with two odd comments from Hezekiah. P. R. Ackroyd outlines three possible ways of interpreting Hezekiah's ambiguous comments: (a) One could understand Hezekiah's response as being a rather smug remark, saying that that he was not really concerned if his descendents faced difficult days in the future; at least there would peace in his own lifetime. (b) Hezekiah's words could be a prayer to God wanting to avoid this disaster ("May there be well-being and security in my lifetime"). (c) Hezekiah could have been affirming that "surely as God earlier promised, there will be peace and security in my days." At this crucial point a commentator's overall interpretation of the Hezekiah persona usually will have a major impact on how one understands what Hezekiah said. M. A. Sweeney, who is strongly committed to the idea that the piety of Hezekiah is being idealized in chaps. 36–39, takes the third approach which views Hezekiah as a person of piety who maintains his faith in God's promise that there will peace and security, in spite of any other more negative news.[240] J. Oswalt, who does not subscribe to the idealization-of-Hezekiah approach, finds Hezekiah's acceptance of God's word as humble thankfulness that judgment will not happen immediately. He interprets Hezekiah's second remark not as a demonstration of faith, but that "the real reason for saying that 'God's word is good' is merely the very human relief that he is not going to be destroyed."[241] C. R. Seitz fits somewhere in between these approaches. He understands Hezekiah's initial response as a positive acceptance of God's judgment, agreeing that what God has decided is right. In a sense, he passes his first test by not rejecting God's will or accusing God of treating him unfairly. On the other hand, the second response is "a realistic appraisal of God's mercy directed to him, similar to the mercy granted to Josiah,"[242] so it is not interpreted negatively. It is impossible to get inside Hezekiah's head or to know his heart at this point, but it is clear that he did not weep because

---

[239] This prophecy was later fulfilled when Israelites were exiled to Babylon in 605, 597, and 586 BC (2 Kgs 24–25), but one could also point to a closer fulfillment when Manasseh spent time in prison in Babylon in 2 Chr 33:11.

[240] Sweeney, *Isaiah 1–39*, 510, says "the king's response indicates his confidence that YHWH will enable Judah to succeed. Hezekiah's statement demonstrates his faith."

[241] Oswalt, *Isaiah 1–39*, 697, notes that his reaction to the future death of others is quite different than his reaction to his own death in 38:3.

[242] Seitz, *Isaiah 1–39*, 263–66, does not believe Isaiah condemned the king or that God negatively judged the king's action, so those factors color his interpretation. Clememts, *Isaiah 1–39*, 296, admits the words "suggest a note of complacency and self-interest, which conflict with the earlier emphasis on his piety," but then he reverses himself and concludes that this probably was not what the author really intended to say.

of this judgment, he did not pray and ask for mercy, and he did not repent or admit any sin—all of which he did earlier in chap. 38. The reference to peace in "my lifetime" shows a certain level of self-interest, and his failure to follow the patterns of chap. 38 demonstrates a lack of concern about the distress that his sinful actions would bring on others. J. Goldingay also notes the significant inconsistency between his pious wish to tell his children of God's faithfulness in 38:19 and his lack of concern about the fate of his children in 39:9.[243]

THEOLOGICAL IMPLICATIONS.   The final Hezekiah narrative illustrates how easy it is for even the greatest of God's people to momentarily slip in their thinking and do things that reveal an underlying trust in human attempts to control the world, rather than trusting in God's sovereign plan to deal with threats and conflict. Numerous theological principles can be developed from these events. First, it is evident from Isaiah's questions to Hezekiah that the king did not come to Isaiah first in order to seek God's wisdom on this matter. Hezekiah's first error in this context was not to ask: What does God want me to do? Second, Hezekiah had a great opportunity to tell the Babylonians about his sickness, his pious prayer, his letter about his experience, God's miraculous sign, and God's healing because his healing was one of the reasons why the Babylonians came. If the focus of attention had been on what God promised to Hezekiah ("I will defend this city" in 38:6), it would have been obvious that there was no need to depend on the Babylonians for help in dealing with the Assyrians. The opportunity for failure came because the king was not focusing on what God had promised and graciously done in the past. Third, there is never an innocent inconsequential compromise with the enemy that does not have some implication on a person's faith relationship with God. The dealings may seem small and momentary, the relationship may seem harmless and unimportant, and the consequence may appear to be for the good of God's people; nevertheless, faith means trusting God alone, so looking to any other source for hope is essentially a denial that one can depend on God. Fourth, it is good to accept God's will (39:8), but it is never too late to cry out to God for mercy and grace. God hears prayers and he knows when people repent of their sins. Therefore it is every believer's privilege and responsibility to intercede for others, especially those of our own family who will be punished for our failures.

---

[243] Goldingay, *Isaiah*, 221, calls this his "spectacular cynicism," a comment that is probably a little too strong.

Bibliography

Achtemeier, E. *The Community and Message of Isaiah 56–66: A Theological Commentary*. Minneapolis: Augsburg, 1982.

Alexander, J. A. *The Prophecies of Isaiah*. Grand Rapids: Zondervan, 1953.

Allis, O. T. *The Unity of Isaiah*. Philadelphia: Presbyterian & Reformed, 1950.

Baltzer, K. *Deutero-Isaiah: a Commentary on Isaiah 40–55*. Minneapolis: Fortress, 2001.

Bartelt, A. H. *The Book around Immanuel: Style and Structure in Isaiah 2–12*. Winona Lake: Eisenbrauns, 1996.

_____. "Isaiah 5 and 9: In– and Interdependence?" Pages 157–63 in *Fortunate the Eyes that See: Essay in Honor of D. N. Freedman*. Edited by A. B. Beck et al. Grand Rapids: Eerdmans, 1995.

Barton, J. *Oracles of God*. New York: Oxford University Press, 1988.

_____. "'The Law and the Prophets': Who are the Prophets?" *OTS* 23 (1984): 1–18.

_____. "Ethics in Isaiah of Jerusalem." *JTS* 32 (1981): 1–18.

Berger, P. "Charisma and Religious Innovation: The Social Location of Israelite Prophecy." *ASR* 28 (1963): 940–950.

Bergey, R. "The Song of Moses (Deuteronomy 32.1–43) and Isaianic Prophecies: A Case of Early Intertextuality?" *JSOT* 28 (2003): 33–54.

Beuken, W. A. M. *Isaiah II: Vol 2: Isaiah Chapters 28–39*. HCOT. Leuven: Peeters, 2000.

_____. "The Manifestation of Yahweh and the Commission of Isaiah: Isaiah 6 Read Against the Background of Isaiah 1." *CTJ* 39 (2004): 72–87.

_____. "The Unity of the Book of Isaiah: Another Attempt at Bridging the Gorge Between Its Two Main Parts." Pages 50–62 in *Reading from Right to Left*. Edited by J. C. Exum and H. G. M. Williamson. JSOTSup 373. Sheffield: Sheffield Academic Press, 2003.

Blank, S. *Prophetic Faith in Isaiah*. New York: Harper, 1958.

Blenkinsopp J. *Prophetic Faith in Israel*. New York: Harper and Row, 1958.

_____. *Isaiah 1–39*. New York: Doubleday, 2000.

_____. *A History of Prophecy in Israel*. 2d ed. Louisville: Westminster/John Knox, 1996.

Boadt, L. "Re-Examining a Preexilic Redaction of Isaiah 1–39." Pages 169–90 in *Imagery and Imagination in Biblical Literature*. Edited by L. Boadt and M. S. Smith. CBQMS 32. Washington, DC: Catholic Biblical Association, 2001.

_____. "The Poetry of Prophetic Persuasion: Preserving the Prophet's Persona." *CBQ* 59 (1997): 1–21.

Bosman, H. J. "Syntactic Cohesion in Isaiah 24–27." Pages 19–50 in *Studies in Isaiah 24–27*. Edited by H. J. Bosman et al.. Berlin: de Gruyter, 2000.

Boutflower, C. *The Book of Isaiah, Chapters I–XXXIX in light of the Monuments*. London: SPCK, 1930.

Brekelmans, C. H. W. "Deuteronomistic Influence in Isaiah 1–12." Pages 167–76 in *The Book of Isaiah*. Edited by J. Vermeylen. Leuven: Peters, 1989.

Brooke, G. J. "Isaiah in the Pesharim and Other Qumran Texts." Pages 609–32 in *Writings and Reading the Scroll of Isaiah*. Edited by C. C. Broyles and C. A. Evans. Leiden: Brill, 1997.

Brownlee, W. H. *The Meaning of the Qumran Scroll for the Bible: With Special Attention to the Book of Isaiah*. New York: Oxford University Press, 1964.

Broyles, C. C. and C. A. Evans, eds. *Writing and Reading the Scroll of Isaiah*. 2 vols. Leiden: Brill, 1997.

Brueggemann, W. *Isaiah 1–39*. WBComp. Louisville: Westminster John Knox, 1998.

Burrows, M. et al. *The Dead Sea Scrolls of St Mark's Monastery, I: The Isaiah Manuscript and the Habakkuk Commentary*. New Haven: American School of Oriental Research, 1950.

Carr, D. "Reaching for Unity in Isaiah." *JSOT* 57 (1993): 61–80.

Carroll, R. P. *When Prophecy Failed: Reactions and Responses to Failure in the Old Testament Prophetic Tradition*. London: SCM, 1979.

_____. "Blindness and the Vision Thing: Blindness and Insight in the Book of Isaiah." Pages 79–93 in *Writing and Reading the Scroll of Isaiah*. Edited by C. C. Boyles and C. A. Evans. Leiden: Brill, 1997.

_____. "Prophecy and Dissonance: A Theoretical Approach to the Prophetic Tradition." *ZAW* 92 (1980): 108–119.

Cheyne, T. K. *The Prophecies of Isaiah*. 3d ed. 2 vols. New York: Whittaker, 1895.

Childs, B. S. *Isaiah*. Louisville: Westminster/John Knox, 2001.

_____. *Isaiah and the Assyrian Crisis*. London: SCM, 1967.

_____. *The Struggle to Understand Isaiah as Christian Scripture*. Grand Rapids: Eerdmans, 2004.

_____. *Introduction to the Old Testament as Scripture*. Philadelphia: Fortress, 1979.

Chilton, B. *The Isaiah Targum: Introduction, Translation, Apparatus and Notes*. Wilmington: Michael Glazier, 1987.

_____. *The Glory of Israel: The Theology and Provenience of the Isaiah Targum*. JSOTSup 23. Sheffield: JSOT Press, 1983.

Chisholm, R. B. "Wordplay in the Eighth-Century Prophets." *BibSac* 144 (1987): 44–52.

Clements, R. E. "A Light to the Nations: A Central Theme of the Book of Isaiah." Pages 57–69 in *Forming Prophetic Literature*. Edited by J. W. Watts and P. R. House. JSOTSup 235. Sheffield: Sheffield Academic Press, 1996.

_____. "The Unity of the Book of Isaiah and its Cosmogenic Language." *CBQ* 55 (1993): 1–17.

_____. "The Prophecies of Isaiah to Hezekiah concerning Sennacherib: 2 Kings 19,21–34/Isa. 37.22–35." Pages 65–78 in *Prophetie und geschichtliche Wirklichkeit im alten Israel*. Edited by R. Liwak and S. Wagner. Stuttgart: Kohlhammer, 1991.

_____. "Patterns in the Prophetic Canon: Healing the Blind and the Lame." Pages 189–200 in *Canon, Theology and Old Testament Interpretation*. Edited by G. Tucker et al. Philadelphia: Fortress, 1988: 189–200.

_____. "The Unity of the Book of Isaiah." *Int* 36 (1982): 117–29.

_____. "The Prophecies of Isaiah and the Fall of Jerusalem in 587 B.C." *VT* 30 (1980): 421–36.

_____. *Isaiah and the Deliverance of Jerusalem: A Study of the Interpretation of Prophecy in the Old Testament*. Sheffield: JSOT, 1980.

_____. *Isaiah 1–39*. NCBC. Grand Rapids: Eerdmans, 1980.

Cogan, M. *Imperialism and Religion: Assyria, Judah and Israel in the Eighth and Seventh Centuries B.C.E.* Missoula, MT: Scholars Press, 1974.

Coggins, R. J. "The Problem of Is. 24–27." *ExpT* 90 (1979): 328–333.

Cole, D. P. "Archaeology and the Messiah Oracles of Isaiah 9 and 11." Pages 53–69 in *Scripture and Other Artifacts*. Edited by M. D. Coogan. Louisville: Westminster/John Knox, 1994.

Conrad, E. W. "Messengers in Isaiah and the Twelve: Implications for Reading Prophetic Books." *JSOT* 91 (2000): 83–97.

_____. *Reading Isaiah*. Minneapolis: Fortress, 1991.

_____. "The Royal Narratives and the Structure of the Book of Isaiah." *JSOT* 41 (1988): 67–81.

Dahood, M. "Textual Problems in Isaiah." *CBQ* 22 (1960): 400.

Darr, K. P. *Isaiah's Vision and the Family of God*. Louisville: Westminster, 1994.

Davies, A. *Double Standards in Isaiah: Re-evaluating Prophetic Ethics & Divine Justice*. Leiden: Brill, 2000.

Davies, G. I. "The Destiny of the Nations in the Book of Isaiah." Pages 93–120 in *The Book of Isaiah: Le Livre D'Isaïe*. Edited by J. Vermeylen. Leuven: Peeters, 1989.

Dearman, J. A. *Property Rights in the Eighth Century Prophets*. SBL Dissertation Series 106. Atlanta: Scholars Press, 1988.

Delitzsch, F. *Isaiah*, Commentary on the Old Testament VII. Trans. J. Martin. Grand Rapids: Eerdmans, 1973.

Dobbs-Allsopp, F. W. *Weep, O Daughter of Zion: A Study of the City-Lament Genre in the Hebrew Bible*. BibOr. 44. Rome: Pontifical Institute, 1993.

Doyle, B. *The Apocalypse of Isaiah Metaphorically Speaking: Study of the Use, Function and Significance of Metaphors in Isaiah 24–27*. Leuven: Peeters, 2000.

Driver, G. R. "Isaiah I–XXXIX: Textual and Linguistic Problems." *JSS* 13 (1968): 36–57.

Dumbrell, W. J. "The Purpose of the Book of Isaiah." *TB* 36 (1985): 111–128.

Eaton, J. "The Origin of the Book of Isaiah." *VT* 9 (1959): 138–57.

Eichrodt, W. *Theology of the Old Testament*. Trans. J. A. Baker. Philadelphia: Westminster, 1961.

_____. "Prophet and Covenant: Observations on the Exegesis of Isaiah." Pages 167–88 in *Proclamation and Presence*. Edited by J. I. Durham and J. R. Porter. London: SCM, 1970.

Engnell, I. *The Call of Isaiah: An Exegetical and Comparative Study*. Uppsala: Lundeqvistska, 1949.

Erlandsson, S. *The Burden of Babylon: A Study of Isaiah 13:3–14:23*. ConBOT 4; Lund: Gleerup, 1970.

Evans, C. A. *To See and Not Perceive: Isaiah 6.9–10 in Early Jewish and Christian Interpretation*. Sheffield: Sheffield Academic Press, 1989.

_____. "On the Unity and Parallel Structure of Isaiah." *VT* 38 (1988): 129–47.

_____. "On Isaiah's Use of Israel's Tradition." *BZ* 30 (1986): 92–98.

Fensham, F. C. "Widow, Orphan, and the Poor in Ancient Near Eastern Legal and Wisdom Literature." *JNES* 21 (1962): 129–39.

Finley, T. J. and G. Payton. "A Discourse Analysis of Isaiah 7—12." *JOTT* 6 (1993): 317–35.

Flint, P. W. "The Isaiah Scrolls from the Judean Desert." Pages 481–90 in *Writing and Reading the Scroll of Isaiah*. Edited by C. C. Broyles and C. A. Evans. Leiden: Brill, 1997.

_____ E. Ulrich, and M. G. Abegg. *Edition of the Cave One Isaiah Scroll*. DJD 37. Oxford: Clarendon, 1999.

Fohrer, G. *Das Buch Jesaja*. 3 vols. Zurich: Zwingli, 1960–67.

Gerstenberger, E. "The Woe-Oracles of the Prophets." *JBL* 81 (1962): 249–63.

Geyer, J. B. "Mythology and Culture in the Oracles Against the Nations." *VT* 36 (1986): 129–145.

Gitay, Y. "Prophetic Criticism—'what are they doing?': The Case of Isaiah—a Methodological Assessment." *JSOT* 96 (2001): 101–27.

_____. *Isaiah and His Audience: The Structure and Meaning of Isaiah 1–12*. Assen: Van Gorcum, 1991.

_____. "Isaiah and the Syro-Ephraimitic War." Pages 217–30 in *The Book of Isaiah*. Edited by J. Vermeylen. Leuven: University of Leuven Press, 1989.

_____. "Isaiah—The Impractical Prophet." *Bible Review* 4 (1988): 10–15.

_____. "Reflections on the Study of the Prophetic Discourse: the Question of Isaiah 1.2–20." *VT* 33 (1983): 207–21.

Goldingay, J. *Isaiah*. NIBC. Peabody: Hendrickson, 2001.

Goshen-Gottstein, M. *The Book of Isaiah* (Hebrew University Bible). Jerusalem: Magnes, 1995.

Gowan, D. E. *When Man Becomes God: Humanism and Hubris in the Old Testament*. Pittsburgh: Pickwith, 1975.

Gray, G. B. *A Critical and Exegetical Commentary on the Book of Isaiah 1–27*. ICC. Edinburgh: T&T Clark, 1912.

Groves, J. W. *Actualization and Interpretation in the Old Testament*. Atlanta: Scholar's Press, 1987.

Hayes, J. H. and S. A. Irvine. *Isaiah, the Eighth-Century Prophet: His Times and Preaching*. Nashville: Abingdon, 1987.

Herbert, A. S. *Isaiah 1–39*. CBC. Cambridge: Cambridge University Press, 1973.

Hogenhaven, J. "The Prophet Isaiah and Judaean Foreign Policy Under Ahaz and Hezekiah." *JNES* 49 (1990): 351–54.

Holladay, W. L. *Isaiah: Scroll of a Prophetic Heritage*. Grand Rapids: Eerdmans, 1978.

Irvine, S. A. *Isaiah, Ahaz, and the Syro-Ephraimitic Crisis*. Atlanta: Scholars Press, 1990.

Jensen, J. *Isaiah 1–39*. Wilmington: Michael Glazier, 1984.

_____. "Weal and Woe in Isaiah." *CBQ* 43 (1981): 167–87.

_____. "The Age of Immanuel." *CBQ* 41 (1979): 220–39.

_____. *The Use of tôrâ by Isaiah: His Debate with the Wisdom Tradition*. Washington: CBA, 1973.

Johnson, D. G. *From Chaos to Restoration: An Integrative Reading of Isaiah 24–27*. Sheffield: JSOT Press, 1988.

Kaiser, O. *Isaiah 13—39*. OTL. Philadelphia: Westminster, 1974.

_____. *Isaiah 1—12: A Commentary*. OTL. 2d ed. Philadelphia: Westminster, 1983.

Kissane, E. J. *The Book of Isaiah*. 2 Vols. Dublin: Browne and Nolan, 1960.

Kitchen, K. A. *The Third Intermediate Period in Egypt (1100 to 650 B.C.)*. Warminster: Aris and Phillips, 1973.

Kooij, A. van der "The Old Greek of Isaiah in Relation to the Qumran Text of Isaiah: Some General Observations." Pages 195–213 in *Septuagint, Scrolls and Cognate Writings*. Edited by G. J. Brooke and B. Linders. Atlanta: Scholars Press, 1992.

_____. "Isaiah in the Septuagint." Pages 513–29 in *Writing and Reading the Scroll of Isaiah: Studies in an Interpretive Tradition*. Vol II. VTSup. Edited by C. C. Broyles and C. A. Evans. Leiden, Brill, 1997.

_____. "The Septuagint of Isaiah: Translation and Interpretation." Pages 127–33 in *The Book of Isaiah: Le Livre D'Isaïe*. Edited by J. Vermeylen. Leuven: Peeters, 1989.

Kutscher, E. Y. *The Language and Linguistic Background of the Isaiah Scroll (1QIs^a)*. Leiden: Brill, 1974.

Laato, A. "Assyrian Propaganda and the Falsification of History in the Royal Inscriptions of Sennacherib." *VT* 45 (1995): 198–226.

Lindblom, J. *A Study on the Immanuel Section in Isaiah, Isa 7,1–9,6*. Lund: Gleerup, 1958.

Lust, J. "The Greek Translator of Isaiah." *Bijdragen* 40 (1979): 2–14.

Macintosh, A. A. *Isaiah xxi: A Palimpsest*. Cambridge: Cambridge University, 1980.

Marshall, R. J. "The Unity of Isaiah 1–12." *LQ* 14 (1962): 21–38.

Mauchline, J. *Isaiah 1–39*. London: SCM, 1962.

McCann, J. C. "The Book of Isaiah—Theses and Hypotheses." *BTB* 33 (2003): 88–94.

Millar, W. R. *Isaiah 24–27 and the Origin of Apocalyptic*. Missoula: Scholars Press, 1976.

Millard, A. "Sennacherib's Attack on Hezekiah." *TB* 36 (1985): 61–77.

Miscall, P. D. *Reading Isaiah: Poetry and Vision*. Louisville: Westminster, 2001.

Motyer, J. A. *The Prophecy of Isaiah*. Leicester: IVP, 1993.

_____. *Isaiah: An Introduction and Commentary*. TOTC. Downers Grove: InterVarsity, 1999.

O'Connell, R. H. *Concentricity and Continuity: The Literary Structure of Isaiah*. Sheffield: Academic Press, 1994.

Orlinsky, H. M. "Studies in the St. Mark's Isaiah Scroll." *JBL* 69 (1950): 149–66.

Oswalt, J. *The Book of Isaiah 1–39*. NICOT. Grand Rapids: Eerdmans, 1986.

_____. "Recent Studies in Old Testament Eschatology and Apocalyptic." *JETS* 24 (1981): 289–302.

Ottley, R. R. *The Book of Isaiah According to the Septuagint*. I. London: Clay and Sons, 1904.

Otzen, B. "Traditions and Structures of Isaiah XXIV–XXVII." *VT* 24 (1974): 196–206.

Pagán, S. "Apocalyptic poetry: Isaiah 24–27." *BT* 43 (1992): 314–325.

Polaski, D. C. *Authorizing an End: The Isaiah Apocalypse & Intertextuality*. Leiden: Brill, 2001.

Porter, A. E. and B. W. R. Pearson. "Isaiah Through Greek Eyes: The Septuagint of Isaiah." Pages 531–46 in *Writing and Reading the Scroll of Isaiah: Studies of an Interpretive Tradition*. Vol. 2. VTSup. Edited by C. C. Broyles and C. A. Evans. Leiden: Brill, 1997.

Rendtorff, R. "The Book of Isaiah: A Complex Unity. Synchronic and Diachronic Reading." *SBL Seminar Papers* 30 (1991): 8–20.

Roberts, J. J. M. "Isaiah in Old Testament Theology." *Int* 36 (1982): 130–43.

Scott, R. B. Y. "Isaiah 1–39." *IB*. Vol V. Nashville: Abingdon, 1956.

_____. "The Literary Structure of Isaiah's Oracles." Pages 175–86 in *Studies in Old Testament Prophesy*. Edited by H. H. Rowley. Edinburgh: T & T Clark, 1950.

Seeligmann, I. L. *The Septuagint Version of Isaiah: A discussion of Its Problems*. Leiden: Brill, 1948.

_____. *The Septuagint Version of Isaiah and Cognate Studies*. Edited by R. Hahnhart and H. Spiechermann. Tübingen: Mohr Siebeck, 2004.

Seitz, C. R. *Isaiah 1—39*. Interpretation. Louisville: Westminster/John Knox, 1993.

_____. *Zion's Final Destiny: The Development of the Book of Isaiah: A Reassessment of Isaiah 36–39*. Minneapolis: Fortress, 1991.

_____. "Isaiah 1—66: Making Sense of the Whole." Pages 105–26 in *Reading and Preaching the Book of Isaiah*. Edited by C. R. Seitz. Philadelphia: Fortress, 1988.

Sheehan, P. "Some Textual Problems in Isaiah." *CBQ* 22 (1960): 47–55.

Sheppard, G. T. "The Anti-Assyrian Redaction and the Canonical Context of Isaiah 1–39." *JBL* 104 (1985): 193–216.

_____. "Isaiah 1–39." Pages 542–70 in *Harper's Bible Commentary*. Edited by J. L. Mays. San Francisco: Harper and Row, 1988.

Skjoldal, N. O. "The Function of Isaiah 24–27." *JETS* 36 (1993): 163–172.

Smith, G. V. *An Introduction to the Hebrew Prophets: The Prophets as Preachers*. Nashville: Broadman and Holman, 1994.

_____. "The Concept of God/the gods as King in the Ancient Near East and the Bible." *TJ* 3 (1982): 18–38.

Sperber, A. *The Bible in Aramaic, Vol III. The Later Prophets According to Targum Jonathan.* Leiden: Brill, 1962.

Stenning, J. F. *The Targum of Isaiah. Edited with a Translation.* Oxford: Clarendon, 1949.

Sweeney, M. A. *Isaiah 1—39, with an Introduction to Prophetic Literature.* FOTL 16. Grand Rapids: Eerdmans, 1996.

_____. "The Book of Isaiah in Recent Research." *CR:BS* 1 (1993): 141–62.

_____. *Isaiah 1–4 and the Post Exilic Understanding of the Isaianic Tradition.* BZAW 171. Berlin: Walter de Gruyter, 1988.

_____. "Textual Citations in Isaiah 24–27: Toward an Understanding of the Redactional Function of Chapters 24–27 in the Book of Isaiah." *JBL* 107 (1988): 39–52.

_____. "Revaluating Isaiah 1–39 in Recent Critical Research." *CR:BS* 4 (1996): 79–114.

Thompson, M. E. W. *Situation and Theology: Old Testament Interpretations of the Syro-Ephraimitic War.* Sheffield: Almond, 1982.

Tucker, G. M. "The Book of Isaiah 1–39." *The New Interpreter's Bible.* Vol VI. Nashville: Abingdon, 2001.

Ulrich, E. "An Index to the Isaiah Manuscripts from the Judean Desert." Pages 477–80 in *Writing and Reading the Scroll of Isaiah: Studies of an Interpretive Tradition.* Vol. 2. VTSup. Edited by C. C. Broyles and C. A. Evans. Leiden: Brill, 1997.

_____ et al. *Qumran Cave 4, X: the Prophets.* DJD 15. Oxford: Clarendon, 1997.

Van Horn, W. W. "The Use of Imagery in Isaiah 1–12." *Theological Educator* 44 (1991): 93–100.

Vermeylen, J. *Du prophète Isaïe l'apocalyptic, Isaïa I–XXXV.* 2 Vols. Paris: Gabalda, 1977–78.

_____. "L'unité du livre d'Isaïe." Pages 11–53 in *The Book of Isaiah: Le Livre D'Isaïe.* Edited by J. Vermeylen. Leuven: University Press, 1989.

Vriezen, T. C. "Essentials of the Theology of Isaiah." Pages 128–46 in *Israel's Prophetic Heritage.* Edited by B. W. Anderson and W. Harrelson. New York: Harper, 1962.

Waard, J. de *A Handbook on Isaiah.* Vol. 1, *Textual Criticism and the Translator.* Winona Lake: Eisenbrauns, 1997.

Watts, J. D. W. *Isaiah 1—33.* WBC 24. Waco: Word, 1985.

_____. *Isaiah 34–66.* WBC 25. Waco: Word, 1987.

Webb, B. G. *The Message of Isaiah.* BST. Downer's Grove: Inter-Varsity, 1996.

_____. "Zion in Transformation: A Literary Approach to Isaiah." Pages 65–84 in *The Bible in Three Dimensions.* Edited by D. J. A. Clines et al. JSOTSup 87. Sheffield: JSOT, 1990.

Wegner, P. D. *An Examination of Kingship and Messianic Expectation in Isaiah 1–35.* Lewistown: Mellon, 1992.

Wildberger, H. *Isaiah 1–12: A Commentary.* CC. Minneapolis: Fortress, 1991.

_____. *Isaiah 13–27.* CC. Minneapolis: Fortress, 1997.

_____. *Isaiah 28–39.* CC. Minneapolis: Fortress, 2002.

Williamson, H. G. M. "The Messianic Texts in Isaiah 1–39." Pages 238–70 in *King and Messiah in Israel and the Ancient Near East: Proceedings of the Oxford Old Testament Seminar.* Edited by J. Day. Sheffield: Sheffield Academic Press, 1998.

Young, E. J. *The Book of Isaiah.* 3 vol. Grand Rapids: Eerdmans, 1965–72.

Selected Subject Index

Person Index

Selected Scripture Index

Proverbs

Ecclesiastes

Song

Jeremiah